THE
INNS OF COURT
OFFICERS TRAINING CORPS
DURING
THE GREAT WAR.

Lieutenant-Colonel F. H. L. Errington, C.B., V.D., commanding the Corps
28th March, 1913, to 1st September, 1916.

THE INNS OF COURT OFFICERS TRAINING CORPS

DURING

THE GREAT WAR.

EDITED BY

LT.-COL. F. H. L. ERRINGTON, C.B., V.D.

"But the sound of War from the Seven Seas
Has filled the Roll of the Devil's Own."
—*J. B. Lloyd, 1900.*

Printed and Published by Printing-Craft, Ltd., 4, Bloomsbury Place, London. W.C. 1.

ADDENDA ET CORRIGENDA.

Substitute.

p. 86.   BARRETT, *Jack Hardy*
Sq/363, 16/3/09; *dis.* 15/3/13; *rcj.* Sq/957, 5/8/14; R. Fus., 15/8/14, R. Lanc. R., secd. W. Af. F.F.; Germ.EA & WA; Capt.; *w.*
57 *Leigham Court Road, Streatham Hill, S.W.* 16.

p. 243.   MACARTHUR, *Don Jessel*
R.A.S.C; Staff Major.
10 *Balham Park Mansions, S.W.* 12.

p. 271. ✠ NOAKES, *Sydney Neville*
Died 30/7/21.

Changed addresses.

p. 104.	BRODIE, *Kenneth*	30 *Matheson Road, W.* 14.
p. 107.	BRUNT, *Frank*	8 *Breams Buildings, W.C.* 2.
p. 136.	CULY, *Leonard Victor*	49 *Crosgrove Road, Walton, Liverpool.*
p. 191.	HARRIS, *Gilbert Stanley*	10 *Launceston Place, W.* 8.
p. 334.	TAPPIN, *Wallace Henry*	36 *Water Lane, South Park, Ilford.*

FOREWORD.

On the 1st August, 1914, the Corps Establishment was one squadron of Cavalry and three Companies of Infantry, in all 424 officers and men. Its actual strength was 268.

On the 22nd September, 1914, its Infantry Establishment was increased to eight Companies of Infantry, making four double companies; and in August, 1915, to six double companies. Its actual strength on the 1st March, 1915, was 1,083; on the 1st January, 1916, 4,008. By the end of the war 13,800 men had passed through its ranks, of whom between 11,000 and 12,000 had received commissions.

The total number of men killed was 2,100, of wounded 5,000. The honours gained were about 2,800, including three Victoria Crosses.

Although no actual record was kept, it is calculated that some 130,000 candidates were interviewed by the Corps Selection Committees, about one in ten being accepted.

Printed and bound in Great Britain by Antony Rowe Ltd, Eastbourne

CONTENTS.

		PAGE.
Foreword		5
Chapter I.	The Corps (August and September, 1914), by Lt.-Col. F. H. L. Errington, C.B., V.D.	11
Chapter II.	,, (Berkhamsted) ,, ,, ,,	16
Chapter III.	,, (1st October to 31st December, 1914) ,, ,,	18
Chapter IV.	,, (1st January to 30th September, 1915) ,, ,,	20
Chapter V.	,, (1st October to 31st December, 1915) ,, ,,	24
Chapter VI.	,, (1st January to 1st September, 1916) ,, ,,	26
Chapter VII.	,, (1st September 1916 to 1st October 1917), by Major A. McLean, M.B.E.	31
Chapter VIII.	,, (1st October 1917 to 27th July 1919) ,,	35
Chapter IX.	The Depôt, by Major J. A. Hay, T.D.	40
Chapter X.	The Squadron, by Lt. H. I. Merriman	44
Chapter XI.	The Company, by Major Sir Frederic Kenyon, K.C.B.	49
Chapter XII.	The Rank and File, by Sergt. E. Deller	58
Chapter XIII.	The Billet (Bedridden), by W. W. Jacobs	61
Chapter XIV.	Conclusions, by Lt.-Col. F. H. L. Errington, C.B., V.D.	63
Appendix I.	Records of Officers	67
Preface to Appendix II.		69
Appendix II.	Records of Rank and File	72
Corps Staff		373
Attached Staff		374
Appendix III.	Hospitals, Nurses. Members of Selection Boards	375

PREFACE.

It is hoped that this history of the Inns of Court O.T.C. during the War may be of interest not only to the men who passed through its ranks, but to a wider circle.

The prominence given to the first two years is not entirely due to egotism on the part of the Editor. The right training of officers is of supreme public importance. Soldiers' battles, such as the first battle of Ypres, may still be incidents of war, but, on the whole, modern war tends more and more to become a fight between officers. Notwithstanding the huge bulk of a modern army, the unit, such as the Battalion, or even the Company, is becoming more and more complete in itself, and the character and brains of the platoon commander on the one side are pitted against the character and brains of the platoon commander on the other side. All will probably agree that the primary object of an officer's training is the building up of his character in the direction of self-control, self-reliance, and action : It is also obvious that methods may differ according to the average age of the men with whom you are dealing, and the time at your disposal. Speaking generally, however, such methods are either positive or negative : they either encourage and seek to develop what is good, or they repress, and try to eradicate what is bad : for the one, discipline, in the sense of strict obedience, is a means; for the other, it is an end. During the first two years the Corps continued the first method, which it had pursued, so far as peace conditions allowed, since its establishment as an Officers' Training Corps in 1909; during the remainder of the War, it had gradually to change into the second method, being that adopted by the Cadet units established in 1916 under the directions of the War Office. The last method may be called the Sandhurst method, and is a familiar one : the first method is less familiar, and is therefore treated here at greater length.

The Editor has been much assisted in the compiling of this work by a committee of ex-members of the Corps. The record of the Corps contained in the Appendices has been very difficult to check, and he will be much obliged by the correction of any errors or omissions.

He takes this opportunity to acknowledge his great indebtedness to Major Sir Frederic Kenyon, K.C.B., for wise counsel, and most loyal co-operation, both in connection with this work, and during the whole period of his command.

The thanks of the Corps are due to its former R.Q.M.S., A. Langridge, who initiated the keeping of the records of the men passing through its ranks—one of the many services he has rendered to the Corps, of whose traditions he has always been the stout upholder, and zealous guardian; also to Mr. H. F. Wallis, an ex-member : without his untiring industry the records could hardly have been completed.

The photographs, other than the frontispiece, are by Mr. Newman, the well known photographer at Berkhamsted.

The book can be obtained on application to 10, Stone Buildings, Lincolns Inn.

FRANCIS H. L. ERRINGTON.

Chapter I.

THE CORPS (AUGUST AND SEPTEMBER, 1914).

On Sunday, the 2nd August, 1914, the Corps, with a strength of 230, left London at 7.55 a.m. for Perham Down, Salisbury Plain, for its annual fourteen days' training, with the rest of the 4th London Infantry Brigade (the Grey Brigade). Colonel F. J. Heyworth, D.S.O. (Scots Guards) commanded the Brigade, and Major General C. C. Monro, C.B., the 2nd (London) Division, of which the Brigade formed part. We had all expected the training to be cancelled, and the camp was full of rumours. In the afternoon, the Brigadier had a look round, and told me he thought it quite possible we should be ordered back to London; but time passed, and nothing happened. About 11.15 p.m. I heard the rush of a motor-cycle up to the Orderly Room, and a few moments later, the adjutant, Captain Rainsford-Hannay, came to my tent with a field message, signed by the Brigade Major, ordering us to be at the station ready to leave for London by 12.30 a.m. At the psychological moment my electric lamp gave out, and I had to dress slowly and impatiently in the dark; but Rainsford-Hannay was everywhere, and thanks to his boundless energy, and the strenuous efforts of all concerned, we were able to leave camp at midnight with kits packed, and to be at the station by 12.15. Then followed the first of many long waits. The men dozed off, mostly on the ground, and we did not entrain till 3.15 a.m., getting to Addison Road at 5.30 a.m. Thence we marched to our Headquarters at Lincoln's Inn, along deserted streets in the beautiful summer morning, and dispersed to search for breakfast, the First Avenue Hotel being the favourite rendezvous.

3rd August.—Expecting the order for the embodiment of the Territorial Force could not be long delayed, we dismissed the men with orders to hold themselves in readiness to rejoin at any moment.

That day we waited anxiously for the rush of recruits the prospect of war should bring in, and were surprised when only six presented themselves. The public evidently required reminding of our existence, and accordingly I wrote a letter to the papers, and the recruiting result was immediate.

4th and 5th August.—Late on the 4th we received the order for the embodiment of the Territorial Force, and during these two days 213 recruits were enlisted. They were handed over to Major Hay, who took charge of all recruits, with Lieutenant A. G. Mathews from the Reserve to help him, and Sergt. C. T. A. Pollock as chief instructor. On the 5th, Kenyon, McLean, Holland, and Gray, who had volunteered for censoring work with the Expeditionary Force, left for Southampton. An urgent appeal for censors had been sent out by the War Office, and the immediate response by these officers had brought me the following letter:—

" WAR OFFICE,
WHITEHALL, S.W.
31st July, 1914.

" MY DEAR COLONEL ERRINGTON,

I should like to thank you and congratulate you on the very prompt manner in which your officers have come forward to volunteer for the duties of Press Censor, if required.

It must be very satisfactory to know your Battalion is so patriotic, and I have written to each individual officer to thank them.

Yours sincerely,
(Signed) E. BETHUNE,
Director General Territorial Forces."

Kenyon was recalled in September, 1914, and McLean returned in March, 1915; both greatly to our advantage. Holland and Gray remained with the Expeditionary Force till the end of the war. Both gained the D.S.O., and Holland finished as Lt.-Colonel, and Gray as Major. Two other of our officers, Captain H. B. Butler and H. W. Malkin, could not be spared by their respective Government Departments, and much against their will were unable to join up.

In the meantime a vital question was exercising my mind affecting the very existence of the Corps. It was by no means clear on our regulations whether we were entitled to survive embodiment at all, and ought not rather to be utilised at once as officers wherever wanted.

This question involved the further practical one of the right to pay and allowances. Fortunately we were in the unique position, so far as Officers' Training Corps were concerned, that we formed part of the Territorial Force, and our men were all sworn in as ordinary privates; perhaps more fortunately still, no copy of our Regulations could be found, and weary officers at the War Office were not inclined to grapple with points of construction. There was no question we formed part of the Territorial Force, and the necessary authority was given us to issue pay and allowances accordingly, " so with a heart at great ease to bed."

THE CORPS (AUGUST AND SEPTEMBER, 1914).

6th August.—Our recruits had brought us well over establishment, and by this time we had a waiting list of 237, of whom 30 per cent. had previous training. Old and tried members of the Corps had flocked to the Orderly Room, clamouring to help; and we placed an old " C " Company man, P. F. Warner (famous in another field) in charge, with P. M. Walters, formerly " E " Company, and H. C. Gutteridge, formerly " C " Company, to assist. J. P. Somers, a well-known Bisley shot, instructed in musketry, until called away to the School of Musketry at Bisley, which was for some time practically run by old Inns of Court men, including Hopkins, Barber (M.C.), Stone, (afterwards killed as a Lt.-Colonel and D.S.O.), and Biddle.

7th, 8th, and 9th August.—We had by this time organised the day's work. Drills were from 10 a.m. to 12.30 and from 2 to 4. The Squadron and Companies carried on in drill and musketry in Lincoln's Inn and the Temple Gardens, the waiting list generally in Gray's Inn. In wet weather, by leave of the Benchers, we were at liberty to use all the Halls, and, in addition, Lincoln's Inn both then, and later, placed at our disposition as many sets of chambers as we required. Not only were these facilities of immense assistance in organisation, but for the first two years all recruits started with some weeks' training at Headquarters, which were used as a recruits' depôt. In touch with these historical surroundings they took a common pride in the old home of the Corps, and so came the first quickening of that mysterious tie, that invincible *esprit de corps*, which binds and always has bound our men so closely together.

10th August.—Our honorary Colonel, Field-Marshal Sir Evelyn Wood, came in unexpectedly, and saw the Squadron and " B " Company in the Temple Gardens. He said a few words to them, and the same day I received the following card from him :—

" UNITED SERVICE CLUB,
PALL MALL, S.W.
August 10th, 1914.

" MY DEAR COLONEL,
I am delighted to hear of the Recruiting. I saw a very good stamp to-day in the Gardens.
Yours sincerely,
(Signed) EVELYN WOOD."

A significant departure from pre-war procedure appeared at this time in the shape of an advertisement in " The Times," and other papers, for 2,000 junior officers for temporary commissions in the Army. I at once went to the War Office to ask why we had not been applied to, and found our existence had been overlooked. I was assured, however, that any names we sent in would have priority.

11th August.—In order to vary the work and improve the training, the Squadron and Companies now went on certain days in the week to Wimbledon or Richmond. Thanks to Mr. Hunt, an American gentleman, who placed his car at our disposal, I was able to keep in touch with everything going on.

12th August.—The Lord Chancellor, Lord Haldane, came down, and saw the Companies and the recruits at Lincoln's Inn, and addressed them. It was very much in my mind to get the Corps out of London as soon as possible, and he was good enough to say he would speak to Lord Kitchener on the subject. I shortly afterwards heard from him that Lord Kitchener had given instructions to the D.M.T. to communicate with us at once, and although some time elapsed before we got away, Lord Haldane's action gave the first push in that direction. I had occasion to consult him on several subsequent occasions, and he invariably gave the Corps his warm support. It was, of course, to his organising ability that the Officers' Training Corps first owed their existence. Lord Reading was also always ready to help.

14th August.—Our first two commissions came along with Corpl. E. S. Atkin and Lce.-Corpl. K. B. Dickson.

15th August.—Dr. McGuire lectured on the general situation in Lincoln's Inn Hall. We were at this time giving intensive training under the Adjutant to men going to the Special Reserve, and they spent all this (Saturday) afternoon and Sunday on map-reading and other subjects.

17th August.—On this day 74 commissions in the Special Reserve came in.

19th August.—Nineteen men were gazetted, mainly to the Special Reserve.

21st August.—I received a message from the War Office asking that, if possible, the Corps should go to the Intercession Service at St. Paul's. We paraded both Corps and Waiting List at 7 p.m. The service commenced at 8 p.m., and lasted for about an hour; the band of the Scots Guards was present, and we were the only formed body of troops. It was an impressive service, and I said a few words to the men before dismissing them at Lincoln's Inn at 9.30 p.m.

23rd August.—Although Sunday, all the men ripe for commissions came to lectures by the Adjutant, on map-reading, and on various subjects dealing with regimental economy.

25th August.—Having regard to the continuous rush of would-be recruits who were swelling our Waiting List, an increase in our establishment was becoming urgently necessary. In the afternoon I saw Sir Francis Lloyd, commanding the London district, who promised to push our application.

26th August.—Having obtained leave to use Regents Park after closing time, we had a useful night exercise there from 8.30 to 10.30 p.m., the Infantry Companies, under O'Brien, assaulting a position held by the Squadron.

THE CORPS (AUGUST AND SEPTEMBER, 1914).

27th August.—The squadron had by this time managed to obtain privately a certain number of horses at Wimbledon, and could do some mounted training. The Waiting List, now 560 strong, formed three Companies: No. 1 under F. P. Lefroy, No. 2 under P. M. Walters, and No. 3 under Sergt. Fraley. The last-named was one of our regular staff-sergeants, who came back to help. Lefroy was a great discovery. He had recently been in the sappers, but having injured himself in some sports, he had been invalided out. With an almost baby face, he was one of the smartest youngsters I have met. Like so many others, he had drifted into our Orderly Room to ask if he could help. Shortly afterwards he joined the Corps, got a commission, and afterwards commanded " D " Co. at Berkhamsted. In 1915 he transferred back to the R.E., and was subsequently killed.

31st August.—I heard from the London District that our camp was sanctioned, and would probably be at Epping. The locality did not sound a favourable one, and, having accidentally learnt that Hatfield Park might be available, I wrote to Lord Salisbury for leave to go there.

1st September.—Lord Salisbury wired his permission to use Hatfield Park.

By this date the Corps had obtained 150 commissions.

3rd September.—Hannay and I were sent for to M.T.3 at the War Office, and were asked if the Corps could supply officers for Kitchener's Army, who, in the dearth of capable N.C.O.'s would be able to carry on without them (a serious innovation !). We promised 100 almost at once. On returning to Lincoln's Inn, we selected 111 men, who, although the conditions of service were altogether vague, at once volunteered for the job. We immediately started giving these men special training by the Adjutant, and this was the beginning of the Special Instruction Class, which continued to play such a prominent part in our system of training.

4th September.—Having heard from Lord Salisbury, that although he was quite willing we should camp in Hatfield Park, it was already very crowded, and that we might find Ashridge Park more suitable, I wrote to Lord Brownlow accordingly.

7th September.—I received a wire suggesting we should look at the proposed site in Ashridge Park, and the Adjutant went down in Hunt's car. He came back with a suggestion by Lord Brownlow, to which he agreed, that a site near the station would be better. Lord Brownlow also wrote that though he was willing to give us every facility for camping in the Park, the water supply was very deficient, and transport would have three miles of hilly road. He recommended a field close to the station, where the Yeomanry had often camped. We adopted the suggestion at once, and applied for authority to move to Berkhamsted.

9th September.—Moore, who had been acting as an A.D.C., came back, and took over the Squadron from Wood Hill. A little later he left us with Robinson for the East Riding Yeomanry, getting command of a squadron at once. He afterwards gained the D.S.O., and Robinson the M.C. Ninety-five commissions in Kitchener's Army came along.

14th September.—At last we received permission to go into camp at Berkhamsted—for six weeks—from the 28th ! We then started clamouring for horses for the Squadron. Squadron Q.M.S. Porter had been down to Berkhamsted, and had discovered an almost derelict brewery, the use of which could be obtained on very reasonable terms.

We were eventually able to stable the whole of the squadron horses, and billet the greater part of the Squadron men there, with the greatest advantage from the point of view of both horsemastership and discipline. General Bethune stood our friend over the horses, and we obtained them early in October.

From this time onward, we received increasingly urgent direct applications from various units for officers. They began with a request from the Post Office Rifles for eight officer instructors for their 2nd Battalion, then one for sixteen officers from the Kensington Battalion of K.1, as the new Army was familiarly called. Then four captains for the Salford Battalion of K.2. The new units of the K.R.R. and the Rifle Brigade asked for five each. Units we had already supplied, like the South Wales Borderers, asked for more; and one of the new Brigades wanted forty.

23rd September.—On this day our Infantry Establishment was increased to eight Companies, and the Squadron to war strength. The new Companies were lettered D. E. F. H. K. A little later we reformed the eight single Companies into four double Companies, numbered 1, 2, 3, and 4.

25th September.—Our advance party proceeded to camp.

28th September.—On this day the Corps moved to Berkhamsted, nominally for a six weeks' camp, really for the period of the war. The new Companies, composed of recruits, were left in London, our previous Headquarters now becoming our depôt, with Major Hay in command.

The Corps marching into Berkhamsted included :—
    Lt.-Col. F. H. L. Errington, V.D., Commanding.
    Major C. W. Mead, T.D., Second-in-Command.
    Capt. J. Rainsford-Hannay, The Queen's Regiment, Adjutant.
    THE SQUADRON :—
        Captain C. Wood Hill.
        Lieutenant W. R. Field.
        Lieutenant W. G. G. Leveson Gower.
        S.S.M. J. T. Morris.
        S.Q.M.S. H. F. Yeatman.

THE CORPS (AUGUST AND SEPTEMBER, 1914).

"A" COMPANY :—
    Captain E. à Court Bèrgne.
    Lieutenant G. O. W. Willink.
    Lieutenant A. E. A. Buller.
    C.S. F. W. J. Jackson.

"B" COMPANY :—
    Captain Sir Frederic Kenyon, K.C.B.
    Lieutenant A. N. Clark.
    C.S. B. Perks.

"C" COMPANY :—
    Captain C. R. Chenevix Trench.
    Lieutenant R. E. Negus.
    Lieutenant C. T. A. Pollock.
    C.S. H. C. Gutteridge.

Major W. Holbourn, Quartermaster.
Captain D. G. Rice-Oxley, M.O.

Although anxious for every reason to get to camp, our enforced sojourn in London had not been without its uses. By the time we left, it was possible to see clearly certain facts on which our future Corps policy would have to be based. In the first place, the casualties in the Army were already very heavy, and having regard to the raising of the new Army, and the increase of the Territorial Force, the demand for officers was certain to become enormous. In the second place, so far from attempting to establish any reserve of men qualified for officers, suitable men, particularly from the universities and public schools, were being allowed, and even encouraged, to join the ranks. The Corps was practically the only training establishment actually functioning; and while, on the one hand, the good material was going to waste, on the other, commissions were being granted through all sorts of agencies, and regardless of any sort of qualification. Again and again we were rung up by the War Office, saying they must have 300, or 400, or 500 officers by the end of the week, and could we not send 100 or so. Our invariable answer was that we would send those we considered sufficiently trained, but no more. It was also apparent that any idea of training an officer after he had received a commission was doomed to failure. An attempt was made in the shape of young officers' companies: it was soon found, however, that they did not really answer the purpose. Plainly, therefore, for some time to come, the Corps would be the only school for training.

From the point of view of material resources, we had many deficiencies. Our equipment was the old Slade-Wallace, so old, that in many cases it had to be held together by string. In the way of rifles, we had a stroke of luck. On the increase of establishment, we received 800 additional rifles, probably by mistake, as their delivery was almost immediately followed by an order to return them. This we resisted, and finally compromised by returning 400. We were then left with 800 rifles and 100 carbines. We had an old Maxim machine gun; no stock of uniforms, practically no transport.

From the moral point of view, however, we were more fortunate. Ever since 1908, and in many ways before that date, we had been training men as officers, and men of the class and age then coming in, mainly 25 to 35; and in this respect we alone had the necessary experience. The Corps had in its ranks an inexhaustible supply of men admirably qualified by character, brains, and physical fitness, to instruct or train. We had, in fact, been preparing for the emergency which had actually arisen, though not knowing whether it would arise in our time or not. Above all, we were a long established unit with high traditions of self-sacrificing duty, and vibrating through and through with *esprit de corps*. The instrument was in essentials there: it only remained to consider the lines on which the training should proceed.

The Sandhurst system of putting boys under the harrow, so as to enable the good seed to be sown in their future regiments was unthinkable when dealing with older men of considerable knowledge of the world, and whose critical faculties were developed; nor was there time for such leisurely training, nor, when they joined their regiments, would the new officers find the old regimental atmosphere, or the time to learn their duties. The period of training was not likely to exceed three or four months, and to spend it on the barrack square would be a crude absurdity. Success could only come from determining the most essential quality in an officer, and concentrating on its development. That quality is undoubtedly *moral*, which in the case of an officer is almost synonymous with character; and our foremost object became to build up character by the strictest discipline, by encouraging keenness, and every civilian qualification that went to support it, and by stimulating in every way *esprit de platoon, esprit de company*, and *esprit de corps*.

In all seasons, in all weathers, at all times of the day and night, our men were over the country; except for musketry, and the minimum amount of close order drill, they were never in camp. They rapidly became hardy and self-reliant: the Infantry always exercising with packs on, could march eight or ten miles, have a long tactical exercise, march the same distance back, and simply regard it as in the day's work. Beyond all, they had the example of their officers: always cheerful and ready to lend a hand, friendly counsellors without familiarity, able every time to do a

THE CORPS (AUGUST AND SEPTEMBER, 1914).

little bit more than the men, setting a magnificent example of discipline and lightning obedience, not only to an order, but to the slightest suggestion from their C.O.

We were equally fortunate in our Squadron and Company Sergeant Majors and Quartermaster-Sergeants—they had mostly long service, and were devoted to the Corps. Imbued with its traditions, they were the heart and soul of its regimental life: socially and by education they were of the same class as the officers, of whom they were the personal friends. They could have taken commissions if they had liked, but being now above the age for active service abroad, they voluntarily remained in the non-commissioned ranks, where they could do invaluable service by instilling into recruits the traditions of the Corps. Resourceful with a wide experience of men and matters, ready to shoulder responsibility, humorous and tactful, but standing no nonsense, and quick to detect any sign of shirking, while able to distinguish between the real and the improveable wrong-un, they could always get the last ounce out of their men. It was mainly due to them that during the whole period of my command, though thousands of men passed through our hands, men of all ages from 18 to 35, coming from all corners of the world, of every possible profession and business, not only was the strictest discipline unquestioned, but any form of obstruction was absolutely unknown. Keenness was and remained the predominant note.

F. H. L. E.

Chapter II.

THE CORPS AT BERKHAMSTED.

The situation of our camp at Berkhamsted was an ideal one, pitched in the field on the north side of the station and sloping gently up to Berkhamsted Place. The Squadron, both men and horses, were in the Brewery. Lord Brownlow placed at our disposal his private waiting-room at the station and also a covered-in shelter, both of which were used for the Quartermaster's office and stores. The proximity of the station did away with all transport difficulties. On the west side we had ample room for expansion, and on the east side another large field, subsequently given the name of " Kitchener's Field," made an admirable drill ground.

The surrounding country was the best imaginable for training, so varied, that during my period of command, although we had a battalion tactical exercise first twice, and then once every week, we never had to repeat the same exercise. To the north lay the big common, later intersected by some 13,000 yards of trenches, then Ashridge Park, undulating and beautifully timbered, placed entirely at our disposal by Lord Brownlow, and so away to the open downland of the Chiltern Hills. To the south, hilly and enclosed land leading to Hawridge and Cholesbury Commons. To the east, farms and enclosures admirably adapted for night operations ; and to the west the private grounds of Rossway and Champneys, always open to us, woods and farms and enclosures to and beyond Tring. We went where we liked, and did what we liked. The big landowner, the small landowner, and the farmer were all equally ready to help. If there was any trouble, Major Mead at once got on his horse, rode over, and smoothed it down.

For the squadron, long treks without touching a road, wide movements, distant reconnaissance; for the infantry, wood-fighting, canal crossings, river crossings, big fights on the open commons or downs, local fighting among the enclosures, every form of open training was available. In the neighbouring villages, Nettleden, Little Gaddesden, Aldbury, Ashley Green, Bovingdon, the awakened villager turned to sleep again with greater security when he realised that the outburst of firing, and the swift rush of feet through the village street, betokened nothing more than a night raid of the Devil's Own.

During the greater part of the week the squadron and companies were left in the hands of their commanders, with an absolutely free hand, bearing in mind only the ultimate object : that a man should leave the Corps with a firm foundation of self-reliance and discipline, and sufficient knowledge of drill, musketry, and map-reading, and some knowledge of the Lewis gun (when that new instrument of war had been invented), and of entrenching. Later we were practically forced to add an exaggerated amount of physical exercise, bayonet fighting, and bombing. On the Friday and Saturday morning there was an hour's Battalion drill; and it is a striking proof of how far keenness, intelligence, and sound company training will supplement practice, that after some 35 years of experience of every kind of drill, I have never seen any regular regiment move with greater steadiness, or with so admirable a combination of precision and promptitude as the Battalion, 2,000 strong, drilling in Kitchener's Field in the spring of 1916. During the first year we had two battalion tactical exercises a week, after that one. In the daytime, it is impossible to reproduce war conditions; but there are certain war essentials which can be practised, and those we thought most necessary for infantry officers were the keeping up of connection, use of ground, continuous flank protection, and real weight in the attack. No intricate schemes, or formal appreciations, or orders, were given out in advance. Some half an hour or so before the start, the commander of each side got the " idea " which he had to carry out. There were no boundaries, no mid-day halt for lunch, the exercise went on until it had reached its limit of usefulness. At the end of the exercise, either in the field, or on arrival back in camp, all the Officers and N.C.O.'s were assembled for a discussion on the operation, and the necessary tactical lessons pointed out. A precisely similar course was adopted with regard to night operations, which took place for the Battalion on Friday nights, and for the Companies on one or two other nights in the week. Great stress was laid on these, not only because of the necessity for movements at night, but also because at night the conditions approximate more closely to the conditions of war : they involve the same nervy atmosphere, the same slowness of movement and absolute boredom, and form the same test of watchfulness and vitality. Our rule was absolute silence in the ranks from start to finish, and this was in itself a useful lesson in discipline. Here again there was no limit of time, and one or two o'clock in the morning was no infrequent hour for the return.

In both the day and night exercises every officer commanded in rotation, and frequently the N.C.O.'s were put in entire charge.

Not only were our training facilities at Berkhamsted of the first order, but our domestic requirements were met in an equally satisfactory manner. Before coming down, I received an offer from Mr. A. J. Ram, K.C., to put up four officers and their horses at Berkhamsted Place, almost in the camp; and some of us billeted with him during the whole period of the war. Our men were made equally welcome everywhere, and we shall never forget the hospitable kindness shown by the people of the town. As soon as we moved into billets, the Rector, Mr. Hart Davies, placed

The Camp, 1914.

Inspection of the Corps by Field-Marshal Sir Evelyn Wood, V.C., G.C.B., G.C.M.G., its Honorary Colonel.

THE CORPS AT BERKHAMSTED.

the Court House at our disposal for an Orderly Room, and by taking over the greater part of Key's Building Yard, we were able to have an Officers' Mess, Sergeants' Mess and feeding accommodation for the men, all practically under one roof. When in camp, our two large marquees were so manipulated as to give sufficient dining and lecturing space. In the summer of 1915, we erected them in the Castle Grounds, which were very kindly put at our disposal by Lord Brownlow, and were used later as our machine-gun school. Out of our savings we were eventually able to put up five Company huts for lectures and recreation, each holding over 400 men; and one open miniature range and two closed ranges were provided. Our messing arrangements were specially successful, from the point of view of both economy and efficiency, the credit being mainly due to our Mess Steward of some 25 years' standing, John Daborn, and his wife. They had to deal with all manner of difficulties, but met them all with unabated cheerfulness and resource. For the first years of the war we received a money payment per man per day in lieu of rations. The rate was gradually reduced to 1s. 5½d., and at that rate we succeeded in feeding at one time 2,400 men; no mean achievement.

Through the kindness of Lady Brownlow, we were able to begin by using for our sick her hospital at Ashridge. Later, with the assistance of the ladies of the town, a V.A.D. hospital was organised, first at Barncroft, and then at the Beeches. Miss M. Blount was commandant up to March, 1917, when she was succeeded by Mrs. Porter, who up to that time had been Matron. Mrs. Porter continued as commandant up to October, 1918, when Mrs. Haygarth Brown took it over until its close in July, 1919. The hospital was run very economically and with great efficiency, and the Corps is greatly indebted to all the ladies concerned who, in addition to arduous duties, ran no small risk to their own families from our not being able to avoid sometimes sending infectious cases. Their names will be found in Appendix III.

The Y.M.C.A. put up a hut for us, which gradually increased in size, and the local secretary was indefatigable in looking after our men, and in assisting in their recreation: boxing and Saturday evening concerts became a great feature there.

Local authorities, school authorities, the clergy did all they could to help us; baths were a difficulty for some time, but the Water Company assisted, and residents placed both baths and sitting-rooms at our men's disposal. Much tried as many billetters must have been by the entry at all times of the night of mud-covered men, complaints were infinitesimal.

Altogether I believe most of our men agree that in spite of inevitable hardships, Berkhamsted gave them the time of their lives. There were no petty jealousies or obstruction—everyone was out to help. The conditions of life and training were for a hard keen man ideal; he could feel himself always growing in efficiency, and consequent ability to serve his country. The Corps had a soul, and was joyously alive.

F. H. L. E.

Chapter III.

THE CORPS (1st OCTOBER TO 31st DECEMBER, 1914).

On the 6th October, the newly-formed "D" Company came down, with O'Brien in command, Lefroy and Isaacs subalterns, and W. R. Briggs colour sergeant.

On the 14th October, the long-awaited "hairies" arrived for the Squadron.

On the 15th October, "E" Company came down with Clark as captain, Geare as subaltern, and P. M. Walters as colour sergeant. Shortly afterwards we obtained nearly 100 recruits from a camp at Epsom that had been formed for public school men, and they became "F" Company. There soon came a further demand for our rifles, having regard to the general shortage, but we managed to compromise on delivery up of 170. The question of equipment remained a burning one; the County of London T.F. Association had first to supply the battalions going abroad, and were themselves greatly handicapped by the War Office taking over several of their sources of supply. They promised us 100 sets of a substitute for the web equipment in a few weeks' time, and these were eventually delivered; but during the first two years we had to manage on very short supplies both of uniform and equipment, greatly to our disadvantage from the point of view of smartness. By the 1st December we had furnished 800 officers, and applications for more were pouring in on all sides. We were congratulated by the War Office on supplying so many officers of a good stamp, and they took over for the D.M.T.'s Department P. F. Warner, who had done us excellent service.

We were able also to help in other directions. At the request of General Sir Edward Hutton, commanding the 21st Division at Aston Clinton, we took over for monthly courses some of his more backward officers, and received his warmest thanks. At our depôt at Lincoln's Inn, in addition to the training of our own recruits, we for two years gave a short training to men, generally sent by the War Office, who had been promised commissions, and had a few weeks to put in before receiving them. They were first known as the Old Brigade under P. F. Warner, and later, as the Unattested Contingent under Major Gregson; they ran into many hundreds, and mostly did well, one getting the V.C. At the instance of the Cavendish Association we also arranged for drills for public schoolboys during the Christmas and Easter holidays, which were largely attended; and at Berkhamsted we were glad to welcome officers from various school O.T.C.'s attached to us during the holidays. Kent, Calvert, and Moorsom from Harrow were our most frequent visitors, also Standfield and Ford from Wellington, and Aston from Tonbridge. Our own system of training was during these months fully developed, and the following letter to the papers sufficiently describes its main features : —

"Sir,

"I have on a previous occasion through your columns urged the necessity of a continuous supply of men to be trained as officers, and with good results to this Corps. Owing, however, to the wastage at the Front, and the recruiting of the New Army, the demand for officers is always increasing. This corps has already supplied some 800 officers, and requires about 100 recruits a week to keep up the proper supply. On the other hand, patriotic impatience to get to the Front has caused a very large number of men, admirably qualified for command, to enlist as privates, to the great detriment, I venture to think, of the country. Many of them no doubt eventually obtain commissions; but the training involved in providing an efficient unit and the training of the individual as an officer are two quite different things, and the country needs officers trained in the quickest and most efficient way. There are also many stray corps or organisations which, though not recognised as Officers' Training Corps, yet offer to men joining them certain facilities for obtaining commissions.

"It is difficult to run a great war on improvised lines, and it is only by co-ordinated and methodical effort that we are likely to gain success. Certain corps have been long designated by the Army Authorities as Officers' Training Corps; it is surely the duty of all men who have the necessary education and aptitude for command, as also of every organisation that is in touch with such men, to see not only that they take their places as officers, but as officers trained on identical lines, and by the recognised and established organisations. The Inns of Court Officers Training Corps consists of Public School and University men, and of men not having these qualifications, but who may be otherwise specially qualified to be officers. We realise the absolute necessity of quick as well as efficient training, and have speeded up our machinery accordingly. A recruit does some fortnight's drills at Headquarters, and is then sent down here, where we have excellent training facilities. As soon as he is ripe for it he is placed in a special instruction class. If, as is almost invariably the case, he is keen, and with a natural aptitude for command, we are generally able to recommend him within two months of his joining; and a commission follows in the regular course. He is by that time a useful officer, well grounded, and able to instruct in drill, musketry, and map-reading, and in the case of the cavalry, with a very fair knowledge of horsemastership. He

THE CORPS (1st OCTOBER TO 31st DECEMBER, 1914).

has also learnt the routine of regimental life; the necessity for strict discipline, the enormous responsibility now attaching to an officer, and the shameful egotism of undertaking it heedlessly and without preparation.

"Our aim is necessarily a limited one, but we work on a system, and, I believe, with good results. Owing, however, to the continuous outflow, we need more and more recruits of the right stamp, both cavalry and infantry. I have little doubt that the publicity of your columns will enable us to get them. All details can be obtained at our Headquarters, 10, Stone Buildings, Lincoln's Inn.—Yours, etc.,

"FRANCIS H. L. ERRINGTON,
Lieutenant-Colonel, Commanding,
Inns of Court Officers Training Corps,
Berkhamsted, December 2nd."

So great was the demand, that the ordinary time available for the individual man rarely exceeded two or three months; we had, however, during this period, a particularly fine stamp of recruit, and though our numbers were in excess of establishment, the keenness and intelligence of the men made everything easy. Still we were not without anxieties; it was obvious that the men of the officer stamp were being encouraged to go into the ranks, and once in, it was almost impossible to get them out owing to the reluctance of Commanding Officers to weaken their units.

We applied frequently, but always in vain, for men who had enlisted in the various Public Schools Battalions. The students at Cardiff were advised to enlist at once, and did so, and there again it was impossible to retrieve them. We were at this time the only working training corps for officers, and although we still had a continuous stream of recruits, it was fairly certain that with our large and increasing output, the question of recruiting would soon assume importance. Still, when Christmas came and brought us 1,000 commissions, we were able to look back at the past few months with pride, and at the future with confidence. Sir Evelyn Wood wrote us a letter of congratulation, saying that if he were Director of Military Training, he would give no direct commissions, but would make all candidates pass through a Training Corps.

We got into billets in November, but had to Mess in camp up to the 7th December, when we moved our Mess into the wood-yard. On Christmas Day we lent our Mess-rooms for a mid-day meal to the New Army, having our own dinner all together in the evening, when Daborn, dressed as Father Christmas, brought in the plum pudding with a guard, and we finished up with a sing-song. Probably the only dissatisfied person in the camp was a man who the evening before, in a moment of exhilaration, had chased a girl out of a teashop and kissed her, as bad luck would have it, just under the eyes of the Adjutant and myself. He was on guard all night.

F. H. L. E.

Chapter IV.

THE CORPS (1st JANUARY TO 30th SEPTEMBER, 1915).

Our four double Companies were now in full swing, " A " and " E " under Bergne formed No. 1, " B " and " H " under Kenyon No. 2, " C " and " F " under Negus No. 3, and " D " under O'Brien No. 4. " K " was the Depôt Company for recruits. The Squadron's demands for horses had also been fairly well satisfied. Mainly Argentines, they picked up wonderfully with good horsemastership. The brewery stables were gradually improved, and two large lofts overhead housed adequately most of the men. They formed of necessity a unit a little apart, and had very properly their own convictions as to the superiority of cavalry over infantry, which was duly reciprocated by the infantry. Their interior economy and discipline, both under Captain Wood-Hill, who commanded them up to September, 1915, and under Captain Field, who commanded them for the rest of the war, were on a very high level. Here again their Sergeant-Majors and Quartermaster-Sergeants were enormously helpful: J. T. Morris, H. T. Witt, H. F. Yeatman, H. Porter, Fisher, Hamilton, Hanworth, and others—and Jim Kerr, the Armourer, an old employé of the Corps, must not be forgotten.

Many of the horses fell victims this winter to pink eye and ringworm, but Farrier-Sergeant J. C. Porter (afterwards Assistant Director of Remounts in France), with Captain Wilson, the Veterinary Officer at Berkhamsted, managed to pull them through. The great advantage for training purposes of cavalry and infantry working together is obvious; we were also fortunate enough to see something of artillery work. Lieut.-Colonel N. C. Coates, who had been wounded at the Marne, and now commanded a Brigade of Field Artillery, brought his guns out on our field-days, umpired for us, and was always ready to give our officers an insight into artillery work. We much missed the Brigade when they left Berkhamsted in the summer.

About the beginning of the year, we found that some of our men upon joining their regiments were being sent to the schools of instruction provided for untrained officers. At an interview, however, with the D.M.T., I ascertained that this had been done in error, and that his instructions were that no men commissioned from the Corps were to be sent to those schools. Similar instructions were re-issued from time to time. On the same occasion a suggestion was made by the D.M.T. that we should take 50 officers for instruction; this suggestion fell through as we were not able to supply messing accommodation, but it was a compliment to our methods of training.

On the 14th March, McLean returned to us from censoring in France. Upon my representations, he had come to the conclusion that his greater sphere of usefulness lay with the Corps. It is difficult to exaggerate the resulting benefit. He became at once Assistant Adjutant, thus setting the Adjutant more free for field duties, and he remained first as Assistant Adjutant, and finally as Adjutant right to the end of the war. It was a position of the first importance to the Corps, not only from the point of view of the masses of work involved, but also having regard to the tact and delicate handling required for meeting the various problems constantly threatening its very existence. In spite of endless work, and continued worries and anxieties of every kind, it is not on record that he ever lost his temper!

For the first year, returns were comparatively light; they increased as the war continued, and we found ourselves in 1916 under five different authorities, but the more personal correspondence that needed individual handling was throughout extremely heavy. The mother who was sure her boy would make a good leader of men as he had been so successful in organising village concerts; the furious father who could not understand why his son had been rejected, and threatened a question in the House; the highly-placed official who confidently recommended the son of a lady friend as a desirable acquisition for the Corps; all these required the courteous answer that turns away wrath. There was an endless volume of correspondence relating to the men leaving day by day for commissions—at this time about 60 a week: letters from Commanding Officers asking for suitable men, and in many cases imploring us to save them from the material unloaded from other quarters. Then arrangements had to be made for Commanding Officers interviewing candidates; all sorts of local matters, and questions affecting the interior economy of the Corps had to be attended to; and during a great part of the war, McLean, except for meals, hardly left the Orderly Room from 8 a.m. to 11 or 12 o'clock at night.

In the Spring of this year the recruiting question began to give us great anxiety. Recruiting was going down all over the country, and we were in a very special position. Up to 1896, the Corps had consisted of members of the Bar and students. Owing to insufficient support, it then opened its ranks to public school and university men. Before the war we confined our recruiting to the greater public schools, but early in the war this particular source ran dry, as boys from these schools received their commission direct on the strength of their training in the School O.T.C.'s. Complaints were made to the War Office that we were excluding various schools, and on applying to the War Office for a definition, I was informed that " a public school " was a " school open to the public!" Finally, however, it was arranged with the D.M.T. that there should be no school test, but that our principle of selection should be the possession by the candidate of such qualifications as we thought necessary for his training as an officer. This ruling was on absolutely sound lines; but it is interesting, in view of future developments, to note that the breaking down of our exclusiveness was due mainly to the action of the War Office. Notwithstanding, however, the widening of our area, recruiting was diminishing; while, at the same time, the demand for our men was constantly on the increase. As a Corps, though largely composed of lawyers, we had always shrunk from self-advertisement. The war had widened our

THE CORPS (1st JANUARY TO 30th SEPTEMBER, 1915).

circle of influence, but we still recruited within rather narrow limits; and there was a general impression about, perhaps founded on our name of the Devil's Own, that only people connected with the Bar were eligible. The question had to be faced whether we should die genteelly of inanition, or advertise and live. Very unwillingly, but greatly influenced by the example of the War Office in advertising for young officers at the beginning of the war, we chose the latter alternative. Having chosen it, we took no half measures.

Under the general direction of Major Hay at the depôt, Ryan collected a number of civilian helpers, and got into touch with the big steamship and railway lines. I wish it were possible to give the names of all, both inside and outside the depôt, who gave us whole-hearted and invaluable assistance. Prominent among them, in addition to the clergy in nearly every parish, and Col. Unsworth, of the Salvation Army, were the High Commissioners and Agents-General for the Dominions, Mr. Cameron McGregor, of the Glen Line; Mr. Hunt, of the Union Castle Line, in fact all the heads of the great shipping and railway lines. Mr. Walter Howard helped on the theatrical side, Mr. W. A. Evans, secretary to the Head Masters' Conference, assisted with the schools, and the late Sir John Boraston gave generous help in all directions; Members of Parliament, too, Sir John Butcher, Sir C. Kinlock Cooke, Sir Ellis Griffiths, Mr. Llewellyn Williams, Mr. A. Biglan, Mr. J. H. Thomas, and, in cases affecting Irishmen, Mr. Redmond. Inside the depôt were A. S. Cooper (afterwards a Brigadier General, C.B., C.M.G.), C. Vincent, R. Montague Scott, G. Ogilvy Jackson, and on the publicity side A. E. Bundy. Gradually a network of voluntary agents for giving information about the Corps to likely applicants spread over Great Britain, and to the Dominions, and friendly countries all over the world. At the same time these agencies were used only for the collection of candidates; their acceptance was entirely in the hands of the Selection Committee at the depôt, to which, as C.O., I had delegated my powers in this respect. For the convenience of candidates, Selection Boards were established in various localities to sift out those who were not likely to be ultimately accepted. The names of the original members of the various Boards will be found in Appendix III., and the Corps owes them, and particularly the London Committee, an immense debt of gratitude for tedious and ungrateful work done with the utmost care and goodwill. The results very quickly showed themselves. The average number of recruits per week for October, November, and December, 1914, was 61. The average for January, February, and March, 1915, sank to 47. For April, May, and June, it rose to 90, and from then onwards, until recruiting was stopped, we had a constant stream. It is calculated that some 130,000 candidates came before our Selection Boards and Committee, of whom one in ten only was accepted.

On the 25th May we lost our Adjutant, Rainsford-Hannay, who, after many applications on his part, got off to France. It was a great piece of luck for us that we were able to keep him so long. He was not only a most able officer, full of energy and initiative, but he understood and sympathised with the territorial spirit. Absolutely free from red tape, he considered it no part of his duty to suppress keenness and enthusiasm; he knew how to direct them into the channel of efficiency, and his influence was accordingly immense. He ran the final Instruction Class, which every man had to go through before leaving, and he was also a lecturer of first-rate ability. Every evening he lectured to the whole Corps for about half an hour on all questions connected with the economy of a regiment, and the duties of an officer on joining. It was mainly owing to his teaching that our men got the reputation of not asking questions, but carrying on at once, when they joined their units.

He was succeeded, at our request, by Captain Iremonger, also of the Queen's Regiment, who had been wounded on the Marne. He, too, quickly identified himself with the Corps.

When we reached our 2,000 commissions, we resolved to celebrate the achievement by asking our Honorary Colonel, Field Marshal Sir Evelyn Wood, to inspect us. In answer, he fixed the 18th June as being the anniversary of Waterloo, and also a day, as he wrote, that he particularly remembered, " for I got a big hole in me that day 60 years ago." (in the assault on Sebastopol). The inspection took place in Kitchener's Field. The day was beautiful, and the field with its gentle slopes made an ideal place for a ceremonial function. The Corps received him in line with a general salute, he then inspected it, and we marched past, first the Infantry in column with the Squadron at the walk, and then the Squadron at the gallop, and the Infantry in close column, finishing up with an advance in review order. The Field Marshal addressed us as follows:—

"Much has happened since 1908, when this historic regiment became an Officers' Training Corps in consequence of a request I made by desire of Colonel Glen and Major Sankey to a sympathetic fellow-barrister in the person of Mr. Haldane, the Secretary of State for War.

"Much more has, however, happened in the ten months from August, 1914, when I looked at some of your squads in the Temple Gardens.

"The fact that the regiment has imparted the rudiments of training to 2,190 men constitutes what is, and I imagine must be an unsurpassable record. It reflects the very greatest credit on Colonel Errington, Major Mead, and the Adjutant. My heart goes out to those men, who, fortunately for themselves, are not as old as I am, and have the honour and satisfaction of preparing you gentlemen to hold commissions and to fight for the country. I am glad to learn that your system of squadron training is mainly devoted to the care of the horse, and to musketry. The first is essential for success in war, for the losses in South Africa, 15 years ago, arising from ignorance were appalling.

"I am an expert in such matters, for a regiment I raised 55 years ago was sent in the last few years to maintain the interests of the Empire in the Southern half of Persia, which is about three times the area of the United Kingdom.

THE CORPS (1ST JANUARY TO 30TH SEPTEMBER, 1915).

"Although 40 years ago I was Commandant of a School of Instruction, yet in order to be up to date I talked over your Synopsis of Instruction with a Major of a Regiment which has helped to make history for 200 years, and he commended warmly your system.

"I took further expert advice from one who is unusually fitted to express an opinion on the subject. Nearly a quarter of a century ago, when commanding at Aldershot, I recommended a sergeant in a Cavalry Regiment, whom I had employed during manœuvres, for a commission. He rose rapidly, and retired some years ago with the rank of colonel and decorations. When he was appointed to command a Battalion of the New Armies and asked me to assist him to find subaltern officers, I referred him to your Colonel, who sent him six, and my friend, the ex-orderly, when allowed to exceed his establishment, asked Colonel Errington for six more. He is thoroughly satisfied with the whole dozen, and says 'There is not one bad one among them.' In reply to my question about the training, he writes 'I do not feel I can make any useful suggestion for its improvement, and heartily wish that every one of my officers new to the Service had had the advantage of the Inns of Court Officers' Corps training. It is an excellent foundation on which a commanding officer can build.'"

We had supplied Sir Evelyn with a horse for the occasion, and he cantered about the field as if the day had been really 60 years ago. He was delightfully unconventional in his inspections. I remember on an occasion before the war, he told the Squadron Commander he wanted to see his men dismount and mount. One with an injured arm had a difficulty in mounting, his saddle slipping over; Sir Evelyn at once went round and held on to the off stirrup till the man was up. It is not an everyday affair to see a Field Marshal helping a trooper to mount!

Our establishment at this time was 1,133, and our strength 1,392; but a threatening cloud now rose over our recruiting horizon. We had made arrangements for meeting the incoming boats at Liverpool, as many of our best recruits came from overseas; this was strongly objected to by Lord Derby, who regarded it as encroaching on the recruiting area of the Lancashire Territorials. Fortunately he was under the misapprehension that we were recruiting for an ordinary Territorial Unit. As soon as he realised our composition and objects, he became our warm supporter. His brother, General Stanley, was commanding the 89th Brigade, and we arranged with Lord Derby to take over and train men selected from the various regiments, and earmark them for the Brigade. The Commanding Officers put forward their selected men, who were then interviewed by Major Hay, and if accepted by him, came on to Berkhamsted, and were dealt with under the above arrangement. We took over on this footing between 200 and 300 men.

The Corps was now, and had been for some time, considerably over establishment, and it was necessary to apply for two more double Companies. We were very fortunate just at this time in having Colonel Adye as chief staff officer in the D.M.T.'s. Department at the War Office. He had stayed near Berkhamsted, and knew our system of training, and our application was granted without demur. Unfortunately, Colonel Adye only remained for about three months, dying, I think, in September, and we had occasion to regret his sympathetic personality and comprehending mind. The two new Companies were numbered five and six. No. 6 for the time being formed the Depôt Company for recruits under Mathews, and only came down to Berkhamsted early in July, 1916. No. 5 Company was placed under the command of Captain O'Brien, and was mainly composed of the Lancashire men we had taken under the arrangement with Lord Derby, and of the men sent over from Ireland by the Dublin Selection Board. This Board was established by us in August under our recruiting scheme. Its formation and successful working in the face of great difficulties was a triumph for Ryan's capacity for organisation, quick decision, and persuasive diplomacy. When he, with two of our best civilian helpers, A. S. Cooper and R. M. Scott, arrived in Dublin, they found it would be comparatively easy to set up an influential Selection Board, but very difficult to obtain the support of all parties, which was our object. The Nationalists and Ulstermen would not easily mingle; Headquarters of the Irish Command were not favourably disposed towards anything new, and the interests of the Dublin University O.T.C. and the Irish Cadet Companies had to be considered. Ryan at once decided that Mr. Redmond's approval was the first essential; having wired for an interview, he motored the many miles to his house, and came back with a promise of his support, which was warmly given. The "Freeman's Journal" published articles pointing out the thoroughly representative character of the Board, and the advantages of joining the Corps; and in a week's time the Board was in full swing with the heartiest support of the public. Nationalist volunteers and Ulster volunteers came over together, trained together, and often insisted on going to the same Irish regiment. The Board carried on its work with the utmost energy and discretion; and while our thanks are due to every member, I may perhaps be allowed particularly to express our gratitude to Mr. Justice Ross, Sir Edward O'Farrel, D. A. Johnson (an old member of the Corps) and R. W. Brown. the Board's most efficient secretary.

The Irish contingent, ably handled by O'Brien in No. 5 Company, had its amusing side. Many men will remember a night on Northchurch Common, when No. 5 Company developed a singularly unanimous and consumptive cough. Individual modes of expression too were sometimes quaint. I always interviewed the Irish candidates for the Corps myself, and remember one of them saying, by way of a polite effort as he left the room, "Well, so long, Colonel; I'll surely be meeting you again hanging round!"

The numbers still continued to rise, and we were now turning out about 80 officers a week. Our relations with the Territorial Force Department at the War Office were always of the happiest, and the Director-General, Sir Edward Bethune, was good enough to come down on several occasions and speak some words of encouragement and advice to the men who were leaving. There had been a constant desire among our officers to get to the Front, a desire I had had to set my face against, since I felt convinced that, as specially chosen and specially trained men, they were doing much better work for the country at Berkhamsted. I am happy to say Sir Edward took the same view, and advised

THE CORPS (1st JANUARY TO 30th SEPTEMBER, 1915).

them accordingly. It was sometimes suggested by people who knew nothing about training that we should take wounded officers in their place. Such a course would have been fatal to our system. A wounded officer means, and was subsequently found to mean, cramped training. It was absolutely necessary for our purpose that the officer should be able to march better, to fight better, to think quicker. and to lecture and instruct better than the men; and every fresh officer was carefully selected from a number of men themselves well above the average, both physically and mentally. Nor was the war experience of a wounded officer a sufficient compensation for his loss of vitality. Trench warfare was in itself a cramping experience, and in its details continually changing.

Our object was to train men for open warfare; specialising came better when they joined their units. It would obviously, however, be of advantage to our officers to have an opportunity of seeing things at the front, and a beginning was made in September, when Kenyon and I, with Colonel Shirley commanding the 2nd Battalion of the Artists, had ten days in France. The 1st Battalion of the Artists very kindly put us up at St. Omer, where we spent five days going over the army machine-gun school, bombing school, and ordinary schools of instruction. We managed also to get a couple of days in the trenches at Aveluy Wood, near Albert, and a day in the Salient. So far as the schools were concerned, we had nothing to learn; certain special features were interesting, but for general purposes they had nothing like our training advantages. In the following year all our officers got the opportunity of 10 days or so experience in the trenches, useful in giving a sense of reality to their instruction.

By the 1st October we had 3,000 Commissions. Several men had lately gone to the Grenadier, Coldstream, and Scots Guards, and I received from Colonel Streatfeild, Col. Drummond Hay and Colonel Strachey letters of warm commendation of our men with an urgent request for more. The letters of thanks and of appreciation we received were really innumerable, and this perhaps represented the high-water mark of the Corps activities as a practically independent unit. Our recruiting system was in full working order. We had some 22,000 voluntary information agencies, 18,500 in the United Kingdom, and 3,500 in the Oversea Dominions and in friendly countries. No political machinery was used; there was no resort to meetings, no Press campaign. The agents brought to the notice of suitable men the needs of the country, and their responsibilities, and the men converted one another. Our Selection Boards were composed partly of old regular officers, and partly of influential civilians. Owing to the want of a definite policy in this respect at the beginning of the war, the original officer class was no longer available; but in fixing the new standard, it would have been difficult to collect a more competent body of men than those who composed our Boards. The recruits did their preliminary training at Lincoln's Inn, and it is impossible to rate too highly the capacity shown by Major Hay, Captain Mathews, Lieutenant Brett, Sergeants Leffman, C. Terrell, Mahaffy, Cusse, C. E. L. Hooper, L. C. Williams, Birks, Bacon, Gregsten, Scholefield, and others, in dealing with the large numbers of recruits who, owing to want of accommodation at Berkhamsted, had to be retained in London for considerably longer than the original time contemplated. Fortunately we were able to add some machine-gun work to their musketry. Brett made the acquaintance of the inventor of the Lewis Gun, who was good enough to let him have a gun, and to allow him to spend two or three days at the manufactory. Recruit drill was also varied by some more advanced work on Wimbledon Common. Still the want of billetting accommodation at Berkhamsted was a great drawback, and really an unnecessary one, as there were plenty of vacant houses, but the authority to take them over was very slow in coming. Our object and methods of training at Berkhamsted remained the same.

The recruits on coming down were taken over by R.S.M. Burns, who had come to us from the Scots Guards in 1913. Immaculate in appearance, with every detail of army life at his fingers' ends, the R.S.M. was also an excellent lecturer, and I believe one of the best speakers at the Army Temperance meetings. He assisted the Adjutant with the Instruction Class, and was in every respect a man of very high standards, and invaluable for our purposes. From him, the recruits passed into their various Companies. The Squadron and Company commanders had a very free hand, and did as much of their work as possible in the open country. Every Infantry man finished up with a month in the Instruction Class under the Adjutant and (at this time) Captain Pollock, and had two or three days' instruction with the Lewis gun under Poyser, an instructor of genius in this line. As soon as a man was passed by the Adjutant he came up to Orders, and was earmarked for a particular unit, or was noted generally as ready for a commission. Every day we had letters from Commanding Officers asking for men, and almost every day we had Commanding Officers down who looked over the men available, and selected those they thought suitable. They then applied to the War Office for the men selected, and their commissions came through as a matter of course. The system was simple, direct, and worked admirably; and the Corps machinery was running with absolute smoothness, every officer and man playing his part.

If one may believe the practically unanimous opinions of Commanding Officers who took officers from us, our men were well grounded, keen, and with plenty of backbone. Undoubtedly we had certain inevitable weaknesses. We had no means of teaching mess manners where they were wanted; on the other hand, the self-restraint, which is at the root of good manners, we could and did teach. A real and a very damaging drawback in the eyes of authority was the impossibility of giving our men a smart appearance. We owed a great deal to the Territorial Force Association and their Secretary, Captain Mansbridge; but in spite of all their efforts they were quite unable to furnish us with proper uniforms or equipment. Many of our men had only one set of uniform, and the cutting and fitting left much to be desired. They were out in all weathers, and at all times, mud, water, brambles, all played havoc with their kits. Personal cleanliness we, of course, could and did insist on, and many a man after getting back at 1 or 2 a.m. from night operations had to sit up another hour or so cleaning up for the C.O.'s parade next morning, but a smart appearance was really beyond us, unless we sacrificed efficiency to outward show.

F. H. L. E.

Chapter V.

THE CORPS (1st OCTOBER TO 31st DECEMBER, 1915).

Hitherto we had been singularly free from any outside interference : we had developed freely, and entirely on our own initiative. Although we had had very little official help, we had also experienced no obstruction. We had filled a gap, and we hoped adequately. The necessity for such training as the Corps was giving could not be questioned, and with the disappearance of the old officer class, it was becoming more and more necessary. Nor was it wasteful to the country. The advantage and economy of such training were put shortly as follows in a memorandum I wrote in connection with the Derby Scheme :—

" A. It may be expected that the men selected for officers will be of the only class now available. It has not had the same advantages, educational and otherwise, as the pre-war class, and therefore requires a more discriminating selection and a longer training. Men can only be successfully broken into habits of discipline, and to a sense of responsibility, before they become officers. After they become officers, they regard any sort of school (except purely technical ones) as irksome and unnecessary. In an O.T.C. a man knows he will not get a commission unless he earns it. Give him a commission straight away, and he has no real stimulus to make himself efficient, beyond the frequently inadequate one of patriotism.

B. The cost of a three months' training in an O.T.C. is as follows :—

	£	s.	d.
Three months' pay at 1/- per day	4	10	0
,, ,, kit allowance at 2d. per day	0	15	0
,, ,, ration allowance at 1/9 per day	7	17	6
	£13	2	6

The cost of a three months' training after commission :—

	£	s.	d.
Three months' pay at 7/6 per day	33	15	0
,, ,, ration allowance at 1/9 per day	7	17	6
	£41	12	6

In addition each officer receives £50 outfit allowance, which is, of course, a great deal more than the cost of providing a private soldier's uniform, and which is entirely lost to the country if the commissioned officer, who is in such cases not tested until he has received his commission, proves to be unsuitable."

The Derby Scheme gave a new stimulus to our recruiting. We were getting towards 2,000 men at Berkhamsted, and for their proper organisation it was very desirable that the Corps establishment should be increased by two more double companies. Our application was, however, turned down, with somewhat serious results in the near future. Elasticity in our numbers was really a necessary condition of our existence, so long, at least, as recruiting was on a voluntary basis. Notwithstanding our widespread organisation, the stream of recruits could never flow quite evenly; and we had to be ready to take advantage of a flood. It was also possible, as indeed happened, that the outflow would be stopped, causing, inevitably, congestion in the ranks. Our establishment of officers per squadron or company was only the usual one, and there came a time, when it was only by almost superhuman efforts they could keep their heads above the surging tide of recruits; an addition to our authorised establishment of two double companies would have made all the difference.

Leveson Gower now left us and became a G.S.O. 3 at Headquarters Central Force; he was subsequently transferred to the Coldstream Guards, and was killed in 1918. When he left us he wrote me that he looked back to his time at Berkhamsted as the very happiest of his life. He had been a long time in the Corps, was an excellent disciplinarian, and a man of all-round knowledge.

Gradually, as we found we could without injury to the training substitute new men from our ranks, I let some others of our officers go. Negus went to a Battalion of the King's Shropshire Light Infantry, which he subsequently commanded, getting the D.S.O., but was severely wounded. Wood-Hill, commanding the Squadron, went to the Northamptonshire Yeomanry, and was succeeded by Field. We lost also an excellent civilian worker at the depôt, A. S. Cooper.

THE CORPS (1ST OCTOBER TO 31ST DECEMBER, 1915).

In November we had an unpleasant shock. A certain number of our men were ready for commissions, and most of them had been chosen by various Commanding Officers. Instead, however, of their commissions coming through, we received for the first time an order from the War Office that they were to be sent up to be interviewed there. They went up accordingly, and were looked over by two officers in one of the long passages. To our surprise ten were rejected, and were declared to be not fit for commissions. The procedure was not satisfactory, as the interviews were necessarily, having regard to the press of business at the War Office, lightning interviews lasting under three minutes, and no attempt could of course be made to gauge the candidate's military knowledge. I went up at once, and pointed out to the D.M.T. that all these men had been selected for the Corps by a Board which included regular officers of long experience and standing, and that while the questions asked, which related mainly to their schools and occupations, were very suitable in regard to their preliminary selection, and had in fact then been gone into, they had no relevance at the end of their training, the obvious result being to waste both their time and ours. I suggested an officer of the department sometimes attending our Selection Board, but it was ultimately arranged that our Adjutant should be present at any such future interviews. There followed, of course, a shower of indignant letters from the parents of the rejected men and from the commanding officers who had selected them. Eventually I think all the men concerned obtained commissions.

Our Adjutant, Captain Iremonger, was now anxious to rejoin his regiment, and I supported his application to the War Office for that purpose: soon afterwards Capt. A. L. Bonham Carter, from the K.R.R.C., reported as our new Adjutant. He very quickly fitted into his place in the Corps, and became a Corps man.

There were considerable changes in the War Office at this time, when Sir W. Robertson and many of his staff came back from France. The D.M.T.'s Department changed its name to S.D. iii. We received an intimation that no commissions at all would for the moment be granted. No explanation, or warning as to future policy was given, and we were faced with a very serious difficulty. Our recruiting had been on an average about 100 a week, which was necessary to replace the outgoing men. The recruiting tap, however, could not be regulated: it was impossible to turn it on or off strictly according to requirements. If a large number of suitable men appeared in one week, they had to be taken, they would not wait. To turn off the tap altogether would have been suicidal. The fact of our having closed recruiting was certain to spread like wildfire, and no amount of explanation that it was purely a temporary measure would have been of the slightest avail. It is very doubtful whether we should ever have been able to catch up again. As officers were wanted as much as ever, I came to the conclusion that the stoppage of commissions was connected with the turnover at the War Office, and would be of very slight duration. As a matter of fact it lasted nearly two months, and acted greatly to our detriment. The Derby Scheme had brought home to a great number of men the country's necessities, and we had a rush of recruits both from home and from abroad. Additional Selection Boards had been established in Edinburgh, Exeter, and Cardiff, all including both military and civil members, and the number of applicants frequently ran to several hundreds a day. Our strength went up by leaps and bounds, creating considerable congestion at Lincoln's Inn, and entailing considerable hardship on the men who had to stay in London as we still lacked authority to take over empty houses at Berkhamsted, and we were short of staff to deal with such numbers, owing to the refusal to raise our establishment.

This Christmas was marked by a most successful entertainment got up by our officers in the shape of a Revue, entitled "Look Level or not a Move." One verse, characterising the different companies may be inserted here:—

"If you go to No. 1, you'll write out papers;
If you go to No. 2, you'll have to walk;
If you go to 3 or 4, you'll do navvies' work galore;
If you go to No. 5, O'B. will talk!"

Later literary efforts included the "Hades Herald" and the "Gehenna Gazette," both edited by Horne, and entertainments were given by the Mummers of Mephistopheles.

F. H. L. E.

Chapter VI.

THE CORPS (1st JANUARY TO 1st SEPTEMBER, 1916).

Several of our officers left us now or later in the year. They had all done such good work, I felt obliged to give way to their desire to get to the front. Isaacs, then commanding No. 4 Company, left in January, being temporarily attached to Headquarters, London District, until he went to France. Attenborough from the Squadron went to the Machine Gun Corps. C. H. Vincent, a most helpful civilian worker at the Depôt, went in May. Trench, commanding No. 3 Company, joined the 2/5th Battalion Sherwood Foresters in April; he was killed in 1918. Willink, then commanding No. 1, went in June to the 2/4th Battalion the Berkshire Regiment; he also was killed in 1918. Pollock, who had run our Instruction Class under the Adjutant, went as an Assistant Instructor to the 2nd Army School in France. It was some time before he was trusted to deliver a lecture. He too was killed in 1918, as also was Edwin Clarke, who had joined the 8th Battalion London Regiment (Post Office Rifles). It would be difficult to find a more brilliant group of young officers than those killed in 1918; they had all been with us before the war, and were typical Corps men, self-sacrificing, enthusiastic, and pre-eminently efficient. O'Brien also left us for France, and finished in command of the 2nd City of London Yeomanry. Johnson of the squadron went to the R.F.A.; and Wakefield, who was killed in 1917, joined the 2/8th London Regiment. A. N. Clark (now commanding the Corps) joined the 24th London.

By the 1st February commissions began to be granted again, and we reached our 4,500. I received a warm letter of congratulation from Sir Evelyn Wood, and a letter about the same time from Mr. Justice Ross saying that General Friend, commanding in Ireland, had spoken to him in the highest terms of the way in which the Irish officers had been trained by us.

We had for some time supplied officers to all branches of the army, and many of both our Squadron and Infantry Companies had gone to the Artillery. We could, however, of course give very little technical training for the latter arm, and in January the War Office gave us the chance of sending some men to an artillery training unit. Very little time was given us, and we were not able to do much selection, but it was of indirect use in drawing attention to our lack of proper clothing and equipment. Immediately after the men arrived I received a letter from the War Office drawing attention to the diversity of uniform, and the lack of suitable breeches. I was able to point out in reply our great difficulties in supply, and after that we were better provided, ultimately securing a corps tailor.

One of the first subjects to engage Sir W. Robertson's attention, when he came back from France, must have been the training of officers. During the first eighteen months of the war, except by the action of Lord French in turning the 1st Battalion of the Artists Rifles into an Officers' Training Corps, nothing had been done towards the preliminary training of the thousands of officers that were required. The School O.T.C.'s provided a certain number of boys with elementary training, and with the invaluable sense of public school discipline, but necessarily with no knowledge of regimental life. The Universities had no undergraduates to fill their O.T.C.'s. The field of training was occupied only by ourselves and the Artists, whose 1st and 2nd Battalions had been established as an O.T.C. in accordance with Lord French's chance intervention. Satisfactory as according to all accounts the quality of their training was, the two Corps could only deal with a limited number in comparison with the thousands required, and the remainder entered practically untrained. They were then hurried from course to course, which, at the best, made the officer a specialist before he had acquired military instincts, or the capacity to command. The task of remedying this state of things was now entrusted mainly to staff officers recently returned from France with a natural bias towards their own old Sandhurst training, and with an equally natural dislike of any exceptions to a uniform plan. No attempt was made during these two months to become practically acquainted with the organisations that had hitherto filled the gap, or to make use of their experience, and on the 12th February, the prevailing silence as to the future was broken in a curiously casual way. I happened to be at the War Office on some small matter, when I was told Colonel X—— would like to see me. I met him on the stairs, and at this staircase interview he informed me it was intended to establish cadet units for training officers all over the country, and asked me whether we would rather train men for cadet units, or embody some cadet companies in the Corps. I, of course, said we should prefer to have some cadet companies, and he agreed to arrange it so. The new scheme at first sight sounded a step in the right direction. We had long pointed out that men ought to receive their training as officers before getting their commissions and not after. On the other hand, I personally distrusted the formation of a number of small Sandhursts for the quick training of men who were no longer boys fresh from school, and so far as the Corps was concerned, it was easy to foresee that our cadet companies, unless forming for all purposes part of the Corps, and under the same command, would drive a wedge in it, as in fact ultimately happened. Our endeavour, therefore, from this time forward was to preserve the unity of the Corps as part of the new organisation.

THE CORPS (1st JANUARY TO 1st SEPTEMBER, 1916).

In the course of this month the Selection Board in Edinburgh had to be dissolved. The military authorities frowned on it, and the Edinburgh University O.T.C. complained of poaching. Scotch feeling was aroused, and acting on a hint from Sir Edward Bethune we thought it best to withdraw. We made preparations, however, to establish a Board at York. The question of our establishment under the new system was now being debated. Our actual numbers were over 4,000, of whom a considerable number were prevented by an epidemic of measles from coming to Berkhamsted; these numbers were abnormal, and the result of the holding up of Commissions. The authority dealing with us suggested an immediate transfer of 2,000 to the ranks of other units. The obvious injustice of such a course being pointed out, various expedients were devised for diminishing the numbers. I put forward a scheme for reducing the numbers by 1,676, mainly by transfers to other O.T.C.'s or cadet schools, and partly by discharges or transfers to the ranks of men under 18, and of men not likely to make good officers. I suggested the increase we had already asked for of our establishment by another two Companies, which would enable us to deal with the remaining 2,300 : two or three of the Companies to be Cadet Companies; Major Sir Frederic Kenyon to be responsible generally for the senior division, and Captain C. T. A. Pollock for the junior, while I exercised general supervision. I pointed out the advantage of training officers on the same lines from start to finish, as against the overlapping which must result from elementary training in one unit and advanced training in another; but such a scheme was not according to plan, and was rejected.

We were in the habit from time to time of sending our record of commissions to the four Inns of Court, and on the 24th February, the Benchers of Lincoln's Inn passed the following resolution, which they were good enough to communicate to us : " That the Benchers of Lincoln's Inn have read with much appreciation the remarkable record which has been presented to them of the work of the Inns of Court O.T.C., and desire to congratulate their fellow Bencher, Colonel Errington, and his fellow officers on the striking success of their efforts, and on the invaluable services which they have rendered to the Army and the State." About this time I heard again from the Regimental Adjutant of the Grenadier Guards that all the men we had sent them were doing excellent work.

We had hitherto been singularly free from official inspections. The only inspection had been of our cooking arrangements, which had been reported on in the highest terms. On the 25th February, however, General Woolley Dod was sent by the Home Forces to inspect the Corps. His report to the Field Marshal Commanding-in-Chief was as follows :—

INSPECTION OF INNS OF COURT OFFICERS TRAINING CORPS.

DATE OF INSPECTION—25TH FEBRUARY, 1916.

The Field Marshal Commanding-in-Chief,
Home Forces.

In spite of there being about nine inches of snow lying, I found out-door work going on.

All the training that I saw was of 1st Class quality, and it was a pleasure to see the keenness and zeal shown by the men.

The only criticism I have to make is that I think that training in bayonet fighting might be given more prominence in the syllabus.

Advantage was taken of the fall of snow to give a very instructive lesson in trench warfare.

By heaping up the snow two lines of opposing trenches were constructed.

The opposing parties " T "ed out from their respective trenches and connected up the " T " heads to make new trenches. When within range, bombing parties were used and casualties practised, the routine of bringing up bombs, replacing casualties, etc., being carried out.

Thus an instructive exercise in trench warfare was carried out in a couple of hours, without breaking any ground, which would have taken about 10 days' work if actual trenches had been made, instead of snow parapets.

I went round the Squadron stables with the Commanding Officer, and the horses were in good hard condition.

A few of them struck me as being more suitable for light draught than for riding.

The administration and discipline of the Corps appeared to be excellent.

(Signed), O.C. WOOLLEY DOD,
Brigadier-General,
Inspector of Infantry.

Horse Guards, S.W.
26th February, 1916.

From this time forward we had continual inspections and staff visits of a different and more limited type, and not, I think, very satisfactory to the inspectors or inspected. The only commonsense way of assessing the merits of a manufacturing business like ours would have been to send someone down for a short period to watch our machinery and output. The looking over of squads in Kitchener's Field, adequate as it may have been in the leisurely preparations of pre-war days, led I believe to somewhat erroneous conclusions. Lack of a sufficient number of trained N.C.O.'s was made a matter of adverse comment, and I was told they could be easily supplied, but we had when the Cadet Companies came into being a disconcerting experience of the type of N.C.O. available. Six were sent down to one of the Cadet Companies, and the next day the regular officer commanding it asked my permission to send the whole

THE CORPS (1ST JANUARY TO 1ST SEPTEMBER, 1916).

lot back as useless, which was done. Unquestionably our own N.C.O.'s had not as a rule the snap or smartness of the pre-war regular. Although we tried to keep a certain number rather longer than the usual period, a man generally became an N.C.O. simply as part of his training, and, of course, went away as soon as he was fit for a commission. If we had been working on the Sandhurst system, the want of experience in the N.C.O.'s might have been a weak point, and it may in any case be asked why we did not try to obtain at least a certain number of permanent N.C.O.'s. The answer, I believe to be a complete one. It might be enough to say that the pre-war N.C.O. no longer existed; but in any case he was not part of our system. Our object was not perfect drill, nor were we dealing with boys, or trying to develop a particular type. Our object was a high standard of character; we were dealing with men, and trying to produce officers according to their individualities. That we all, officers, N.C.O.'s and men, were of the same class was in itself an enormous asset; once place men with lower standards in authority, and corruption and various other evils are simply bound to ensue. Inexperienced in the military sense our N.C.O.'s of course were, but not inexperienced in the wider life, or ignorant of what constitutes true discipline. Above all they had the unfailing advice and guidance of their Regimental and Company-Sergeant-Majors, and in the Squadron, where work was necessarily more concentrated, the close supervision of their officers. The Company-Sergeant-Majors were all men who had declined commissions for the good of the Corps. P.M. Walters was C.S.M. of No. 1, and probably left the deepest impress on every man who came under him. An old and famous 'Varsity blue, he was also a born soldier; to see him deal with his Company was a lesson in the art of training. If he had a weakness, it was for close-order drill; but every detail of military life seemed his peculiar province. He was feared by the slackers, adored by every man of backbone, and a constant source of joy to the C.O. C.S.M. Perks, of No. 2, and C.S.M. Gutteridge, of No. 3 Company, had both had long experience in the Corps: men of the highest standards, and of all-round efficiency, their influence went right through their Companies, giving to each individual man a feeling of support, and a stimulus to action. Nor were the newer men a whit inferior. C.S.M. Briggs fathered No. 4 Company, perhaps with a slightly greater air of autocracy, in the same genial way; C.S.M. Williams, with a touch of sardonic decision, ruled No. 5 Company, an exhilarating though sometimes a little difficult crowd, equally effectively. They were the real backbone of the Corps and the foundation of its stimulating discipline. I can imagine no more wanton or wicked piece of folly from a training point of view than to try to eliminate such men from the Corps, or to substitute for them the ordinary N.C.O.

While, however, such inspections would in the ordinary way have been mere incidents in our training, we soon realised that they were closely connected with the remodelling of our establishment, which gradually developed into a struggle for existence.

From the point of view of rigid adherence to plan, our position was an anomalous one, and from the outset the department concerned, S.D.iii., were inclined to employ rather ruthless cutting-down tactics. On the other hand our object was to carry on as before during the comparatively short period necessary to reduce our strength to the required limit, and then continue on the preparatory and Cadet Companies' system; but above all working on the old lines, and with unity of command. In the meantime, our recruiting was stopped, and I had personally to apply for leave to take any man I desired for special reasons to enlist, but I was told that as soon as our numbers were reduced to the new establishment we should be at liberty to recruit again. An unfortunate step towards reduction was taken about the end of February. We were told to ascertain how many men would be ready to take artillery commissions, and 178 gave in their names. Two officers from the War Office came down to interview them, and rejected the greater number, not only for artillery commissions, but as being fit for commissions at all, and we were ordered to transfer the rejected men as privates to other units. The whole proceeding had taken under five hours, being at the rate of about 1½ minutes per man. The questions asked had, as before, nothing to do with their military requirements, but, as before, referred to their schools, occupation, and in some cases parentage. Rejection for that particular arm on the ground of want of any sort of technical knowledge would have been, of course, quite reasonable, but such rejection worked particularly unfairly, as the men in question were mostly up for infantry commissions, and many had been selected by C.O.'s. They had only offered themselves for artillery as a chance of getting quicker to the front. A storm of protest from their relatives naturally followed. I made strong representations to the authority concerned, and was told the cases might be reconsidered, then that they could not be reconsidered. Mr. Redmond interested himself in one, and his rejection was cancelled, then others. Questions were asked in the House, and eventually the transfers were not insisted on. About the same time we were ordered to transfer 139 men under 18 to the 101st Provisional Battalion without prejudice to their claim to commissioned rank. It proved, however, a mistake to mix up boys of that age with the ordinary private, and eventually they were re-transferred to the Corps. Meanwhile, our commissions reached 5,000, and we now had four Cadet Companies, each of 100 men, added to our establishment. They were all commanded by regular officers attached for that purpose. Major Bromfield commanded No. 1 Cadet Company, Captain Gompertz No. 2, Captain Busfield No. 3, and Captain Loyd No. 4. We gave them some of our best officers—Cave, E. Clarke, Bond, Ledward and Houghton—and did our utmost to make them a success.

Although these incidents and the threatened changes naturally caused some unrest in the Corps, it was surprisingly little, and the normal life flowed steadily on. The Irishmen celebrated St. Patrick's Day by a dinner at the Crown, and on St. David's Day the Welshmen gave us an excellent concert. Boxing became more and more a feature of the Y.M.C.A., and on Easter Monday and again in July we had regimental sports. Various school O.T.C.'s visited us

THE CORPS (1st JANUARY TO 1st SEPTEMBER, 1916).

for fielddays from time to time. In March we had Eton, Harrow, Westminster, Merchant Taylors, and Berkhamsted; and in June, Harrow, St. Paul's, Mill Hill, Highgate, Merchant Taylors, Westminster, Aldenham, and Berkhamsted. We went on our own system of letting an operation work itself out, and the boys acquitted themselves well, the difficulty being to check their propensity to run the whole time. Harrow were our most constant friends, and we sometimes tried them rather high. On one occasion they came on trek and asked for a night show, so we lay out all night and assaulted their bivouac on the common at dawn. A night of alarms between two heavy days was no light test for boys, some on the smaller side, but they stood it manfully. The Berkhamsted school O.T.C. was admirably trained and commanded by Major Parsons, who also took a prominent part in local affairs, and gave us his whole-hearted support in a variety of ways.

By the end of April it looked as if we had arrived at a satisfactory understanding with the War Office. Sir Alfred Goodson, who had interested himself in our recruiting and had already done us excellent service in that direction, now took charge under Major Hay of the recruiting side of the Corps carried on at the depôt. Being myself by nature somewhat tongue-tied, and handicapped in dealing with superior officers by a strong sense of discipline, we arranged that Sir Alfred Goodson should see the War Office authorities on behalf of what may be called our civilian supporters and try to get some definite scheme. He had an interview with Mr. Tennant and representatives of S.D.iii., and arrived at an arrangement on our behalf, which, if adhered to, would have worked well. It was on the following lines: (1) The future establishment of the Corps to be 2,000, including four Cadet Companies; (2) Until the numbers were reduced to 2,000, a fifth Cadet Company of extra strength (say 250) to be allowed; (3) When numbers were down to 2,000, the old right of selection of recruits would revive; (4) No man to be rejected except by me. Unity of command was implied, and our main anxieties appeared to be practically over; but owing to the method, convenient in many ways, of dealing with important matters verbally, it sometimes happened that if a particular officer left the War Office, his successor was not well aware of what had gone before; we had to begin all over again, and from a different point of view. The officer concerned left the War Office soon after the interview, and we found ourselves again on the rocks. Sir Alfred Goodson did his utmost for us, and was then and always indefatigable in our service; but as the establishment of the various Cadet Schools was proceeded with, our somewhat abnormal position stood out more abruptly. The Cadet Schools were mainly commanded by wounded regular officers, and were generally run, so far as my information went, as miniature Sandhursts, their primary objects being to assimilate the new officer to the old in routine, in smartness of appearance, and in knowledge of drill. In the hands of a badly wounded or otherwise handicapped officer, the school would naturally tend to barrack-square methods, very far removed from our views and methods of fostering self-reliance and *moral*. But there was no real dissonance in the ultimate objects to be attained, though the methods might be different, and there was room for all. However, a general system had been established, and unless the engagement was adhered to that we should stand outside it, and retain our individuality as one complete and final training unit, it was evident we should be brought into the same shape. Nor had we long to wait. Discussions as to our new establishment continued, always on the footing of unity of command, and of our retaining our own special place as a training corps. About the middle of June, however, I was sent for to the War Office, and in about ten minutes the whole of the recruiting machinery we had so laboriously built up was scrapped by the shutting down of our depôt, with the result gravely to affect the Corps organisation, and to cut off entirely the supply of overseas men.

Our Adjutant, Captain A. L. Bonham Carter now left us. He had been wounded, but had recovered and was glad of the opportunity of getting back to his regiment, and then to France. Major Sinclair Thomson, from the Suffolk Regiment, took his place. Meanwhile, in accordance with orders, No. 6 Company, which included all the recruits at the depôt, came down under Mathews, with Sergeant Vassila, an excellent staff sergeant, who had been with us many years, as C.S.M.

In July we had a great loss, our medical officer, Captain McManus, leaving us. He was not only most efficient in his work, but had thrown himself into the life of the Corps with the greatest zest and enjoyment. The reason for his going forms an interesting example of medical *esprit de corps*. Two or three of our men returning from a hospital, complained to me of the food and treatment they had received. After hearing their stories, I thought it a matter at least for investigation, and wrote to the Command concerned accordingly. The medical authorities enquired into the question, and I was informed there was nothing in it. This seemed to conclude the matter, but immediately afterwards McManus was ordered to transfer to another unit. I wrote at once to say that he had in no way been concerned in the complaints in question, for which I alone was responsible, and that he was of the greatest use to us. We were informed, however, that his transfer had nothing to do with the matter in question, but was in accordance with his suggested desire to go overseas! All that remained to be said could only be said inwardly, and because I had ventured to touch the sensitive nerve of medical self-appreciation, McManus had, greatly to our detriment, to go.

There soon followed, and in a curiously haphazard fashion, that break in the unity of the Corps which we had tried hard to prevent. The Senior Officer of the Cadet Companies, who was a major in the regular army, asked me casually one day if I had any objection to his applying to be made temporary Lieut.-Colonel in order that he might get the pay and allowance of that rank. I said at first I had none, but on thinking it over told him I could not accept his proposal as it might well interfere with my position as commanding the whole Corps. About a fortnight later, and without any warning, I found this officer gazetted as Lieut.-Colonel while in command of the Inns of

THE CORPS (1st JANUARY TO 1st SEPTEMBER, 1916).

Court Cadet Battalion. I was informed that it would make no difference in the command, but was only a matter of pay and routine. Obviously, however, the four Cadet Companies, being now assumed to form a Cadet Battalion under a Lieut.-Colonel, could only be nominally under my command, and were certain to become more and more (as they did) an independent unit. It is unthinkable that an officer would put up, or persevere in, an application to which his C.O. had objected, and I had to recognise that this appointment, coupled with the closing of our depôt, indicated a re-organisation of the Corps on a footing inconsistent with the methods of training we had hitherto employed. It also made it clear to me that my term of usefulness was coming to an end, and that the rumours that came down from the Cadet Companies that I should soon be leaving were probably well-founded.

On the 1st August the Corps had the great honour and pleasure of a visit from the King. His Majesty, who had expressed a desire to see the Corps at its ordinary work, arrived at 3 p.m., and remained over an hour. He first saw some sword exercise by the Squadron, bayonet fighting, Nos. 2 and 6 Companies at drill, and No. 5 at musketry, all in Kitchener's Field. He then went in McLean's car on to the Common, where the Cadet Companies were practising trench fighting, and No. 1 Company bombing, and thence to the Squadron jumps. From there he walked through Frithsden Beeches, where Nos. 3 and 4 Companies were practising wood fighting. Much to His Majesty's amusement, attack and counter-attack always seemed to culminate where His Majesty happened to be standing. He rejoined his car on the road, and was graciously pleased to express himself well satisfied with what he had seen. The parade state was 2,223, and the only contretemps that occurred is referred to in the following letter from the King's Equerry :—

"BUCKINGHAM PALACE,
2nd August, 1916.

"My dear Colonel Errington,
The King was very glad to have an opportunity yesterday of seeing the Inns of Court Officers Training Corps, and of showing his appreciation of the excellent work being done by this Corps, whose record since the beginning of the war speaks for itself.

His Majesty thought that all your arrangements were well planned and carried out.

I am afraid that on our return journey we took the wrong road into Berkhamsted, and so missed the troops which were lined up along the road. The fact was that those excellent signposts which you had provided to direct us on our arrival had withdrawn, and the chauffeur apparently went straight on when he ought to have turned to the right.

I am sorry that this should have happened, as it would have given the King much pleasure to have seen the men lined up along the road.

Yours sincerely,
(Signed), CLIVE WIGRAM."

On the 15th August, I received a private communication from the Director-General of the Territorial Force, Sir Edward Bethune, that after the work I had done he thought I ought to have a chance of going to France, and offering me the appointment of Base Commandant to one of the Territorial Divisions. He added that he offered me this as he gathered the Chief of the Staff rather wanted to get a man in charge of the O.T.C. who had later experience of the fighting in France. Although we were now directly under the General Staff, and not the Territorial Force, I, of course, took this kindly hint. I was rapidly drifting into an impossible position, having either to accept a cramped form of training in which I thoroughly disbelieved, or to risk the future of the Corps by putting up a fight over what would soon be made to appear to be my personal position. I accepted the offer, and on the 21st was appointed Base Commandant to the 58th Division, then standing by to go overseas. I left Berkhamsted on the 1st September, deeply grieved, indeed, at quitting the old Corps in which I had served for thirty-five years, but proud at having been allowed to share in the days of its greatest achievement, and confident that its fine traditions remained in safe keeping. Not only officers representing pre-war days, Major Mead, Major Hay, Major Sir Frederic Kenyon, Captains McLean, Field, Mathews, Bergne, Geare, Buller, Cave, Clarke, Parkinson, and Merriman, but also magnificent material we had taken since the war, Poyser, Greene, Brett, Foster, Stapylton, Bond, Ledward, Horne, Dane, Foot, West, Bamford, Cow, C. N. Hooper, C. E. L. Hooper, Fisher, Johnston, Brightman, Houghton, Paterson, Teesdale, Haward still remained and formed together a body of men of unsurpassed and unsurpassable efficiency; so long as they, or officers imbued with the same spirit were there, whatever particular form of training the Corps would have to undertake, there was no fear of its falling from its high reputation.

The following appeared in Corps Orders of the 1st September :—" In vacating the command of the Corps for the purpose of taking up an appointment with one of the Divisions proceeding overseas, the Commanding Officer wishes to express his appreciation of the loyal support he has received from all ranks during his period of Command. It has been entirely due to this loyal co-operation that the Corps has been able to establish a war record of unique interest, and to do work second to none in determining the successful issue of this war. The Commanding Officer is very proud to have been in command of the Corps during these strenuous days; he feels sure that under his successor the Corps will remain at the same high level of endeavour and achievement."

F. H. L. E.

Chapter VII.

THE CORPS (1st SEPTEMBER 1916 TO 1st OCTOBER 1917).

The lecture which Colonel Errington gave to the Corps on the eve of his departure will long be remembered by those who were privileged to hear it. Until that afternoon few knew of his impending departure, and most of us heard of it for the first time at this lecture. The news created a great sensation, and everyone realised that the finest chapter in the long history of the Corps was drawing to a conclusion. It was not surprising, therefore, to find all available officers, warrant officers, N.C.O.'s and men present outside the station on the following day to give him a great send-off.

The Adjutant, Major Sinclair Thomson, returned from a visit to the War Office with the information that he had been definitely selected to succeed Colonel Errington. The appointment of an Adjutant therefore became urgent, and later in the month Major Cockburn, of the Suffolk Regiment, was selected for the post.

Some time before Colonel Errington left, the Cadet Companies had been drawn more and more away from the Corps, and the War Office now decided to form them into a separate Battalion, and to reconstitute the Corps on an establishment of four Companies. On September 5th, the new Cadet Battalion, No. 14 (Inns of Court) O.C.B., was formed, and the following Inns of Court Officers posted to it, viz. :—Captains W. T. C. Cave and E. C. K. Clarke, Lieutenants J. C. Ledward, C. G. Houghton, and A. L. Brightman, with Lieutenant H. T. H. Bond as Adjutant. On the same day T. W. Haward received a commission in the Corps and was posted to No. 2 Company in which he had previously served as a sergeant.

The following officers of other regiments had been attached to the Cadet Companies whilst they formed part of the Corps :—

No. 1 CADET COMPANY.

Major W. T. Bromfield	Leic. R.
Capt. M. L. A. Gompertz	108th Inf. Indian Army.
Capt. J. L. Griffiths	Leic. R.
Lieut. G. D. Tanner	R.E.
Capt. D. V. M. Balders	Suff. R.

No. 2 CADET COMPANY.

Major T. B. Harris	Devon R.
Lieut. C. E. S. Beadle	R.W. Surr. R.
Capt. J. A. Busfield	Ches. R.
Lieut. T. S. Wynn	Suff. R.
Capt. C. H. St. J. Smith	Ches. R.
Lieut. A. Fraser	Cam'n Highrs.

No. 3 CADET COMPANY.

Major T. H. H. Bradford-Atkinson	(late Grenadier Gds.)
Capt. G. F. E. Rapson	Wilts R.
Lieut. H. Mantle	E. Kent. R.

No. 4 CADET COMPANY.

Major A. W. K. Loyd	R. Suss. R.
Lieut. C. E. W. Birkett	K.R.R.C.

On September 7th, the commissions granted to members of the Corps reached 5,700.

Colonel Sinclair Thomson was frequently called to the War Office at this time on questions relating to the new establishment of the Corps. It was, at first, proposed to disband the Squadron, but with the aid of friends of the Corps, the Commanding Officer succeeded in keeping it alive although in a much reduced form. The Corps re-opened for infantry recruits on September 14th, and on the following day a Riding School for Infantry Officers was started, much to the amusement of their friends in the Squadron. On the same day (September 15th), the Commanding Officer, who had obtained in our draft establishment provision for a band, appointed a small Committee to organise it. The Private Funds Committee made advances of £280 for the purchase of instruments, and of £20 for preliminary expenses.

THE CORPS (1st SEPTEMBER 1916 TO 1st OCTOBER 1917).

The Commanding Officer was fortunate in finding in C.Q.M.S. Payne, a very capable and experienced bandmaster. With the assistance of Messrs. Hawkes, Payne interviewed a number of C2 and C3 men and made his selection quickly. The men were enlisted, and trained very rapidly, and less than a month later the Band held its opening concert in one of the Company huts.

Forty of the Squadron horses were returned on September 16th to Remounts preparatory to the reduction in establishment.

Our new Adjutant, Major R. Cockburn, Suffolk Regiment, arrived on September 25th and assumed duty as Adjutant.

On September 29th the number of commissions granted to the Corps reached 6,000.

Captain F. M. S. Cassel, K.C.—a former member of the Corps—was appointed Judge Advocate General on October 6th.

On October 12th, 13th and 14th, the Band gave its opening concerts in Kitsbury Huts, the first for the Corps, the second for No. 14 (Inns of Court) O.C.B., and the third for the Residents in Berkhamsted.

About this time it became very cold and windy in Camp. Papers in the Orderly Room were scattered by wind or got covered with dust, and the Staff were much relieved when the Orderly Room was moved on October 16th to its new quarters in Keys Timber Yard, where it remained until demobilisation in July, 1919. During the autumn hostile air raids were frequent, and in order to be available at short notice at night, I obtained a billet near the timber yard. There I slept with a string tied round my arm, the other end of it hanging out of the window down to the ground. Whenever an air raid took place after I had gone to bed, one of the guard awakened me by pulling this string, more or less gently, according to the state of his nerves. On one occasion the sentry mistook the path and fell into the pond, and it became unnecessary for him to pull the string! On another occasion a stray dog became entangled in the string and nearly pulled my arm off. I blessed the supposed sentry, dressed and proceeded to the Orderly Room, only to find that nothing had been heard of an air raid!

On October 24th, Colonel Braine and Colonel Riley visited us to consider the future of the Squadron.

On October 28th, the six Companies were re-organised as " A," " B," " C," and " D " Companies, and on the same day the Inns of Court team finished third out of 20 teams in a military cross-country race at Eltham.

During October two of the Squadron officers, Lieutenants J. E. Johnston and C. S. Johnson, transferred to other units. The Corps moved into billets on November 1st, and on the 7th there was a mounted paper chase for officers, which created much excitement and not a little anxiety in the Officers' Mess.

On November 13th, Poyser, who had done so much good work in the Machine Gun School in the Castle Ground, transferred to the Machine Gun Corps at Grantham. There was a good deal of sickness in the Corps about this time, and the Adjutant, Quartermaster and R.S.M. were all on the sick list together.

At the end of November, P.M. Walters, who had been appointed to a commission in the Corps earlier in the month, was transferred to No. 14 (Inns of Court) O.C.B.

On December 6th the Squadron, consisting of 2 officers, 43 other ranks, with 49 horses, moved to Maresfield Park. The Band played them to the station to the tune of " Nancy Dawson," and the whole of the Infantry turned out and gave them a great send-off.

On December 8th, Captain R. F. C. O'Brien rejoined the Corps after service overseas.

An order was published on December 14th, increasing the rates payable for Class I. billets. This was read in the Corps and in some other units, as applying to Class II. billets. As a result, increased payments were made to the inhabitants of Berkhamsted and a great sensation was caused when six weeks later the mistake was discovered. Steps were then taken to recover the over-payments, but by War Office order this recovery was stopped. The amounts overpaid were disallowed in the various Company Pay and Mess Books, and it was not until early in 1919 that these disallowances were wiped out.

On December 14th, we had a change of Chaplains, the Rev. E. R. Chamney, C.F., relieving the Rev. A. S. Woodward, C.F. The new padre had previously been attached to the Gunners, and managed to bring with him his horse, saddlery, etc.—a very useful addition to our stable.

On December 15th the number of commissions granted reached 7,000.

On December 18th, Major Hay rejoined the Corps from the Depôt in Lincoln's Inn, being relieved by Captain Foster.

From December 21st to 27th, 80% of the Corps had Christmas leave.

On January 5th the Director of Staff Duties at the War Office (General Bird), visited Berkhamsted.

Early in the month the Corps was asked to find men for a new branch of the Machine Gun Corps. The requirements were knowledge of motors, or machine guns, and height under average.

On January 25th the Squadron's new establishment was promulgated (A.C.I. 105 of 1917), and the name changed to " The Mounted Detachment, Inns of Court O.T.C."

With a view to stimulating recruiting, etc., a large number of Press Representatives were invited to Berkhamsted on January 22nd. In the morning they witnessed the Corps at Training (specially arranged). In the afternoon there was a Boxing Tournament, followed by a dinner in the Officers' Mess, and a Band Concert. The whole entertainment was a

The Camp, 1916.

The Squadron led by Captain Field on "Thomas."

THE CORPS (1st SEPTEMBER 1916 TO 1st OCTOBER 1917).

great success, and the Press correspondents thoroughly enjoyed themselves. Late in the afternoon, however, a telegram from the War Office was received stopping all recruiting for the Corps until further order!

On January 29th, 13 attached N.C.O.'s reported for duty. Most of them were useless as instructors, and within a fortnight 10 of them had been returned to their units.

Early in February it was found that Foster could not adequately perform at the same time the duties of O.C. Recruiting Depôt in London and O.i/c Messing at Berkhamsted, and accordingly he was relieved by Lieutenant G. F. T. Horne of his duties as O.i/c Messing.

On February 24th it was notified that the services of Lieutenant-Colonel F. H. L. Errington and Captains McLean and Foster had been brought to the notice of the Secretary of State for War, and the same day Major and Quartermaster W. Holbourn was selected for a reward for Distinguished or Meritorious Service. A few days later a similar notification was made as to the services of R.S.M. A. Burns, of the Scots Guards, C.S.M. B. Perks, and O.R.C/S. Brock.

About this time the Mounted Detachment left Maresfield Park for Tidworth, for attachment to another Reserve Regiment of Cavalry.

On March 10th we played football against the Artists at Queen's Club, and were beaten by 3 goals to 2.

In the early part of the month, Major Mead left Berkhamsted on posting to a Labour Company for service overseas, and Captain Mathews left to take a Siege Artillery Course preparatory to posting to the R.G.A.

About this time we had a large number of men sick with measles or German measles. Training and the provision of drafts to cadet units were considerably interfered with in consequence. Notwithstanding this, on the 13th March a draft of 83 men was sent to join the R.F.C. Training School at Reading.

On March 18th the Band played in London, and on the 19th the Chaplain-General visited us and gave an address in the Parish Church.

On the 20th there was a Field Day on the Common with Harrow, Eton, Berkhamsted, Forest School, and No. 14 (Inns of Court) O.C.B.

On Easter Monday (April 9th) there were Battalion Sports in Kitchener's Field, several of the events being thrown open to No. 14 O.C.B. Late in the afternoon there was a heavy fall of snow, and the wintry weather continued for three more days. However, after one or two postponements the Corps moved into Camp on April 23rd. On the same day the "Hades Herald" was published. About this time Miss Blount, who, as Commandant of the V.A.D., had done so much to make the Beeches Hospital a very successful Corps Hospital, felt the need of a rest and resigned her appointment, and she was succeeded by Mrs. Porter.

On April 26th there was a ceremonial parade of the Corps and No. 14 O.C.B., in Kitchener's Field, for the presentation of medals by Brig.-General J. E. Bush, C.B., Commanding the troops at Halton Park.

Captain R. F. C. O'Brien left Berkhamsted on May 2nd on posting to the Roughriders. On the same day Lieutenant W. W. Allsopp was appointed Quartermaster vice Major Holbourn. The latter had had much trouble with his eyes for some time previously, and on May 29th he resigned his commission.

General Sir F. S. Robb visited the Corps on May 16th, and five days later General Sir William Robertson and Lieutenant-General Sir F. S. Maurice also visited us.

On May 17th the number of commissions was 8,000, and on the same day Lieutenant J. H. Hutcheson (11th A. and S. Hrs.) reported for duty as an attached officer, and a fortnight later Captain Aylwin, M.C., similarly reported.

On May 20th the Band gave a Concert at the Queen's Hall, in London, and on June 8th played in Trafalgar Square.

On May 23rd, Lieutenant J. H. Fisher left the Mounted Detachment at Tidworth for duty with the War Trade Intelligence Department.

On June 1st, Lieutenant A. C. C. Parkinson left for duty under the Colonial Office.

On June 7th notification was received that Captain J. G. Herring-Cooper, Leicester Regiment, had been appointed Adjutant vice Major Cockburn. He reported on the 15th, and the following day was sick and was admitted to the Beeches Hospital, where he found Major Cockburn, and it was not until June 24th that they had sufficiently recovered for the formal handing over to take place.

On June 15th the V.C. was awarded to a former member of the Corps, 2nd Lieutenant John Harrison, M.C., E. Yorks. Regiment. The following appeared in Corps Orders of that date:—

"Honours.

"The King has been graciously pleased to approve of the award of the Victoria Cross to the following officer:

"T/2nd Lieutenant John Harrison, M.C., E. Yorks. Regiment (formerly No. 7203 No. 4 Company and No. 4 Cadet Company). For most conspicuous bravery and self-sacrifice in an attack. Owing to darkness and to smoke from the enemy barrage, and from our own, and to the fact that our objective was in a dark wood, it was impossible to see when our barrage had lifted off the enemy front line. Nevertheless, Second Lieutenant Harrison led his Company against the enemy trench under heavy rifle and machine-gun fire, but was repulsed. Reorganizing his command as best he could in No Man's Land, he again attacked in darkness under terrific fire, but with no success. Then, turning round, this gallant officer, single-handed, made a dash at the machine-gun, hoping to knock out the gun and so save the lives of many of his Company. His self-sacrifice and absolute disregard of danger was an inspiring example to all."

THE CORPS (1st SEPTEMBER 1916 TO 1st OCTOBER 1917).

" He enlisted in the Inns of Court O.T.C. on November 4th, 1915, and was appointed to a commission in the East Yorkshire Regiment on August 4th, 1916. He was granted the Military Cross on April 17th, 1917. All ranks will regret to hear that he is now reported missing (believed killed)."

On June 16th, R.S.M. Johnstone arrived to relieve R.S.M. Burns.

On June 20th, Major General C. G. A. Egerton, C.B., visited the Corps, and on June 26th General Lowther also visited us.

On June 25th, Lieutenant C. N. Hooper left the Corps for duty in East Africa.

On July 2nd, Major Cockburn left us on posting to the M.G.C. at Grantham. When he came to Berkhamsted he was suffering from a badly shattered arm, and he made little or no improvement whilst with us. I never heard him complain, but when he sent for his horse, " Mary," and went for a ride, it was generally a sign that the pain was unbearable. He worked hard for the Corps in many ways, but perhaps his interest in boxing was most generally known —certainly the revival of it was mainly due to his efforts. His departure after an Adjutancy of nine months was greatly regretted by those who knew him best.

On July 5th, R.S.M. Burns left to rejoin the Scots Guards, and on the previous day the following announcement appeared in Corps Orders:—

" Regimental-Sergeant-Major Burns, A.

" R.S.M. Burns is leaving to-morrow to rejoin his unit, the Scots Guards.

" The Commanding Officer takes this opportunity of placing on record his appreciation of the past services R.S.M. Burns has rendered to the Inns of Court O.T.C., and feels that he is expressing the sentiment of all ranks in wishing him every success for the future."

Everyone who served in the Corps whilst Burns was R.S.M., knows what a factor he was in the success of the training which men received in the Corps. How invaluable in the Orderly Room was his extensive knowledge of regulations, orders, etc., is perhaps only known to those whose duties took them there.

On July 17th the construction of the labyrinth in Kitchener's Field was commenced.

On July 29th the Bishop of London visited us and preached at the Parade Service.

On July 31st the number of commissions granted had risen to 8,500.

About this time it was decided that officers attached to the Inns of Court O.T.C. should receive 2s. per day extra duty pay, but officers of the Inns of Court O.T.C. were not to be entitled to this. Unofficially the distinction was supported in several ways, but each in turn was proved to be untenable, but no change was made.

On August 11th, " The Gehenna Gazette " was published and created much amusement. Another change of padres took place on the 15th, the Rev. E. R. Chamney, C.F., being relieved by the Rev. J. J. Griffin, C.F.

A few days later there was much satisfaction in the Officers' Mess over a large number of promotions, some of them dating back—with pay—for several months.

About this time the War Office decided that candidates for commissions in the Infantry should be inspected by Officers from the War Office in the same way as candidates for R.F.A., R.E., and other technical branches. Similar inspections by the War Office had been tried earlier in the war, and had been abandoned, and it was not surprising, therefore, to find that these inspections were soon dropped also.

On August 24th, Brig.-General A. Symonds, C.M.G. (D.D.S.D.) visited the Corps, and on the same day the Corps was attached to the 5th Training Reserve Brigade at St. Albans for supervision of training, discipline and local administration.

On September 17th, General Mackenzie visited us.

On September 29th, Morris and Hawksley were given commissions in the Corps.

On October 1st, Colonel Sinclair Thomson relinquished command of the Corps, and the following announcement appeared in Corps Orders:—

" Command.

" Lieut.-Colonel Sinclair Thomson, on relinquishing command, wishes to take this opportunity of thanking all officers, warrant officers, N.C.O.'s and men for their loyal co-operation and assistance during his period of command.

" He regrets that he, through force of circumstances, is unable personally to thank all those to whom thanks are due, but he knows that they will always continue to uphold all those fine qualities and traditions of which the Corps is justly proud.

" The fact that he has had the honour to command the Inns of Court O.T.C. for over a year, during the period of the war, will ever remain one of the most pleasant memories of his life."

Colonel Sinclair Thomson succeeded to the command at a very difficult time. He was proud of the history of the Corps, keenly alive to its interests, and the Corps had in him a very real friend.

A. McL.

Chapter VIII.

THE CORPS (1st OCTOBER 1917 TO 27th JULY 1919).

A few hours after Colonel Sinclair Thomson left, his successor, Lieutenant Colonel H. L. Stevens, D.S.O., the Welch Regiment, arrived and assumed command. The same evening a cow fell into the labyrinth and was killed. I ought to add that the Court of Inquiry found that it died in an attempt to escape from an aeroplane (believed to be hostile) which flew over Kitchener's Field that night.

On October 22nd, General Sir H. H. Wilson, who had recently been appointed to the Eastern Command, visited the Corps.

On October 24th the Corps moved from Camp into billets.

During November, Major Kenyon left for duty with the Graves Registration and Inquiries Commission. Lieutenant Dane transferred to the M.G. Corps at Grantham, Paterson for duty with the R.F.C., and West for duty at the Ministry of Food.

On November 20th the number of commissions granted reached 9,000.

On November 30th a reorganization of the Training Companies took place.

About this time we were frequently called upon to supply guards for aeroplanes which landed in the neighbourhood, generally on very cold nights.

From December 21st to December 27th, 80% of the Corps went away for Christmas leave.

In the New Year Honours, published on January 1st, 1918, I was promoted to a Brevet Majority.

On January 2nd, General Symons, D.D.S.D., visited us again.

On January 4th, the Rev. H. S. Martin, C.F., relieved the Rev. J. J. Griffin, C.F.

On January 10th, Captain Bergne was appointed O. i/c Messing *vice* Lieutenant G. F. T. Horne, who returned to duty with " B " Company. Captain Aylwin, M.C., took over command of " A " Company, and Lieutenant C. E. L. Hooper became " Bombs " *vice* Aylwin.

On January 11th the Corps ceased to be attached to the 5th Training Reserve Brigade at St. Albans and became attached to the 4th Training Reserve Brigade at Northampton for similar purposes, and on the 15th we received a visit from our new Brigadier, Brigadier-General H. C. de la M. Hill, C.M.G., and his Brigade Major, Major Greenway.

On January 22nd, No. 14 O.C.B. left Berkhamsted for Catterick, and a School of Instruction for Officer Instructors in Cadet Battalions was formed at Berkhamsted, under command of Colonel Williams.

In Army Orders for January the minimum age for enlistment in the Corps was reduced to 18 years 1 month (A.O. 35 of 1918).

For some time past it had become more and more difficult to purchase supplies out of the money allowance in lieu of rations, and early this month it was decided to draw rations in lieu of the money allowance, and the change took place on January 26th.

About this time the Commanding Officer had several inquiries as to the possibility of replacing part of the employed men by members of the W.A.A.C.; and Miss Wilkins—the Area Controller—visited the Corps on January 11th to investigate.

On January 28th, General Pilcher visited the Corps and saw training being carried out.

On February 2nd, the Annual General Meeting of the Corps took place. Nearly everyone forgot it, and a quorum was obtained by searching diligently in the various Company Orderly Rooms, etc. The same day Lieutenant-Colonel Hewlett, D.S.O., S.D.4., visited us.

On February 7th, Captain M. Sayers, D.C.M., reported for duty as an attached officer, and was posted to " D " Company.

On February 14th, the V.C. was awarded to Captain W. N. Stone, a former member of the Corps.

The following announcement appeared in Corps Orders:—

" Honours.

" His Majesty the King has been graciously pleased to approve of the award of the Victoria Cross to:—

" Lieutenant (Acting Captain) Walter Napleton Stone, late Royal Fusiliers.

" Captain Stone enlisted in the Inns of Court O.T.C., on 9th November, 1914, and was posted to " A " Company. At the end of December, 1914, he passed into the Royal Military College, Sandhurst, and was in due course gazetted to the Royal Fusiliers.

" The deed for which this posthumous honour has been awarded is thus described in the ' London Gazette,' of 13th February, 1918:—' For most conspicuous bravery when in command of a Company in an isolated position 1,000 yards in front of the main line, and overlooking the enemy's position. He observed the enemy massing for

THE CORPS (1st OCTOBER 1917 TO 27th JULY 1919).

an attack, and afforded invaluable information to battalion headquarters. He was ordered to withdraw his Company, leaving a rearguard to cover the withdrawal. The attack developing with unexpected speed, Captain Stone sent three platoons back and remained with the rearguard himself. He stood on the parapet with the telephone under a tremendous bombardment, observing the enemy, and continued to send back valuable information until the wire was cut by his orders. The rearguard was eventually surrounded and cut to pieces, and Captain Stone was seen fighting to the last, till he was shot through the head. The extraordinary coolness of this heroic officer and the accuracy of his information enabled dispositions to be made just in time to save the line and avert disaster.'"

On February 15th the O.T.C. Selection Board was formed at Lincoln's Inn, under the Presidency of Sir Alfred Goodson. Captain Foster became the senior military member of the Board, and an officer of the Artists' Rifles became the third member.

The visits of inspecting officers were so numerous about this time that it was considered necessary to prepare different " stunts " to suit the varied tastes of these officers. In one case the letters on trees, gates, etc. (sometimes used for judging distance and similar practices) were whitewashed afresh shortly before one of these inspections. I find that in my diary that night there is a note to the effect that whitewash—to be really effective—should at least be dry before the Inspecting Officer arrives.

About this time there was a shortage of foodstuffs of all kinds, and members of the Corps were encouraged to grow potatoes and vegetables of all kinds. Plots were marked out in the Camp Field and near the Gymnasium, and R.Q.M.S. Langridge was ever ready to assist members with advice or to help them by procuring the necessary implements and seed. Colonel Stevens devoted a great deal of his spare time to the cultivation of a large allotment.

On February 19th, Colonel Earle (S.D.3) visited us.

On February 20th, a Board considered a proposed Field Firing Range for the Corps near Ivinghoe.

On February 21st, Captain Aylwin left the Corps on return to the 3rd Bedfordshire Regiment, and Captain A. R. Wallis took over command of " A " Company.

On March 4th, the number of commissions granted reached 9,500.

On March 6th, the Inns of Court team was third in a Military Cross-Country Race at Epsom Downs, being beaten by the Canadian Machine Gun Regiment first, and the London Rifle Brigade second. The 4th Reserve Regiment of Cavalry was fourth.

For some time past Captain Herring-Cooper had become more and more anxious to return to his regiment, and on March 8th he received instructions to return to the 3rd Leicesters. I was offered a recommendation for the appointment, and though I had refused it on previous occasions, I now felt that I could with, perhaps, some advantage to the Corps, accept the offer, and when Captain Herring-Cooper left I was appointed Adjutant in his place. A few days later Lieutenant T. W. Haward was appointed Assistant-Adjutant.

About the same time R.S.M. Johnstone was discharged to pension, and C.S.M. Vassila appointed acting R.S.M.

On the 19th March the Area Controller, W.A.A.C., again visited us to revise her estimate, and it became obvious that we could not much longer prevent the arrival of the W.A.A.C.'s, even if we wished to do so.

On March 23rd, notification was received that the services of the following had been brought to the notice of the Secretary of State for War, viz. :—Lieutenant Colonel G. A. L. Sinclair Thomson, Major Sir F. G. Kenyon, K.C.B., Captain H. T. H. Bond, C.S.M. A. H. Birks, and Orderly-Room-Sergeant F. C. Arden. Sergeant Arden had succeeded Colour-Sergeant Brock as Orderly-Room Sergeant when the latter left some months previously, and perhaps I may be permitted to record here how much of the efficiency of the Orderly Room was due to these Orderly-Room Sergeants. Colour-Sergeant Brock had an extraordinary good memory and was a very rapid worker, and these qualities were exactly what was required in the early part of the war. Sergeant Arden, on the other hand, relied on carefully kept records and filing systems, which again was exactly what was necessary in the later period of the war.

On March 21st, Lieutenant W. G. G. Leveson-Gower transferred to the Coldstream Guards.

On March 22nd, Harrow School O.T.C. visited us for a battle exercise on the Common.

Sir Arthur Yapp, K.B.E., visited Berkhamsted on March 27th, and gave an address in the Y.M.C.A. Hut.

During the first three or four months of the year, influenza and broncho-pneumonia was very prevalent, and at least six members of the Corps died.

On April 5th, Lieutenant G. F. T. Horne transferred to the 4th D.C.L.I., and Lieutenant P. E. Hawksley to the 3rd Bn. Norfolk Regiment.

On April 8th, Captain P. M. Walters rejoined from No. 14 O.C.B.

On April 10th, General Lynden Bell, D.S.D., visited us. On the same day the Inns of Court team finished first in the Military Cross-Country Race of the Southern Counties C.C.A., the M.G.C. (Cavalry) were 2nd, and the 9th (Reserve) Australian Battalion 3rd.

On April 18th, Lieutenant C. E. L. Hooper became O. i/c Messing vice Captain E. à C. Bergne, who transferred to the Inland Waterways and Docks Section R.E., and a few days later Lieutenant A. J. B. Bamford transferred to the M.G.C., Grantham.

On April 29th, the Corps moved into Camp—for the last time, and the following day saw the new Field Firing Range at Ivinghoe used for the first time. The construction of this range was largely due to the energy of the Musketry Officer, Captain S. Brett.

THE CORPS (1st OCTOBER 1917 TO 27th JULY 1919).

Late in 1917, Captain Buller had been largely instrumental in starting in " D " Company a very successful War Savings Association, and early in 1918 it was reconstituted as a Regimental Association. It rapidly became the most successful association in the Army, and by the end of April it had collected £32,746, the next most successful Association being that of the Household Brigade, O.C.B., which by the same date had collected £17,600. The Association received the thanks and congratulations of Sir Robert Kindersley, K.B.E., Chairman of the War Savings Association.

On May 7th the V.C. was awarded to Lieutenant-Colonel C. Bushell, D.S.O., a former member of the Corps. The following is a copy of the announcement in Corps Orders:—

" Honours.

" His Majesty the King has been pleased to approve of the award of the Victoria Cross to :

" Captain (Temporary Lieutenant-Colonel) Christopher Bushell, D.S.O., Royal West Surrey Regiment.

" Lieutenant-Colonel C. Bushell (formerly No. 544 " A " Company) enlisted in the Inns of Court O.T.C. on February 10th, 1911, and was discharged on May 8th, 1912, on appointment to a commission on the Supplementary List (Special Reserve) of the Queen's (R.W. Surrey) Regiment.

" He was reported wounded on December 12th, 1914, and has been twice mentioned in dispatches (January 4th, 1917, and December 18th, 1917). He was awarded the D.S.O. on January 1st, 1918.

" The deed for which the Victoria Cross was awarded is described in the ' London Gazette ' of May 3rd, as follows :—

" For most conspicuous bravery and devotion to duty when in command of his battalion.

" Lieutenant-Colonel Bushell personally led " C " Company of his battalion, who were co-operating with an Allied Regiment in a counter attack in face of a very heavy machine-gun fire. In the course of this attack he was severely wounded in the head, but he continued to carry on, walking about in front of both English and Allied troops, encouraging and re-organising them. He refused even to have his wounds attended to until he had placed the whole line in a sound position and formed a defensive flank to meet a turning movement by the enemy. He then went to Brigade Headquarters and reported the situation, had his wound dressed, and returned to the firing line, which had come back a short distance. He visited every portion of the line, both English and Allied, in face of terrific machine-gun and rifle fire, exhorting the troops to remain where they were and to kill the enemy.

" In spite of his wounds, the gallant Officer refused to go to the rear, and had eventually to be removed to the dressing station in a fainting condition.

" To the magnificent example of energy, devotion and courage showed by their Commanding Officer, is attributed the fine spirit displayed, and the keen fight put up by his battalion, not only on the day in question, but on each succeeding day of the withdrawal."

Shortly afterwards Colonel Bushell came home on leave. He returned to the Front, and was killed almost immediately afterwards.

On June 15th, Captain A. E. A. Buller left the Corps for service in the East.

On June 21st the Corps took part in another battle exercise with Harrow and Berkhamsted Schools Contingents of the O.T.C.

On June 22nd a very successful Rifle Meeting was held at the Range on the Common. In addition to individual competition, there were battle practice competitions between platoons which was won by Sergeant Scoggins' platoon from " C " Company, and an inter-department shoot won, appropriately enough, by the musketry staff. In one of the earlier rounds there was an exciting struggle between the Orderly Room and the Q.M. Store—and particularly between the Adjutant and the R.Q.M.S.

On June 25th, Netherfield and Holly House were handed over to the Corps, and the Q.M. began to equip them as a W.A.A.C. Hostel.

On June 26th, Major Campbell refereed at a Boxing Tournament in the Castle Ground, and the Brigadier (Brigadier-General H. C. de la M. Hill, C.B., C.M.G.) attended and presented the prizes, and also those won at the Rifle Meeting.

About this time there was a serious epidemic of the so-called " Spanish " Influenza. Fortunately, the Medical Officer, Captain A. F. Flower, R.A.M.C., arranged to house all but the serious cases in marquees in one of the Camp fields, and the difficulties of accommodation were not so great as in the winter.

On July 8th, Captain Chetwynd Stapylton transferred to the Grenadier Guards, and Captain P. M. Walters took over command of " B " Company, and on the following day Captain Wallis handed over " A " Company to Captain C. J. Hardy, M.C.

On July 12th, the number of commissions reached 10,000.

On July 16th, Lieutenant E. W. Greene transferred to the 1st Herts.

On July 19th, Private J. Kerr, an old servant of the Corps, and more especially of the Squadron, died in Hospital from " Spanish " Influenza.

On August 3rd, Captain Geare transferred to the 3rd Rifle Brigade.

On August 14th it was reported that the services of the following had been brought to the notice of the Secretary of State for War, viz. :—Major J. A. Hay, T.D., Captain R. F. C. O'Brien, and Captain Chetwynd Stapylton.

THE CORPS (1st OCTOBER 1917 TO 27th JULY 1919).

About this time the Sergeant-Major of the Army Gymnastic Staff attached to the Corps wrote a pamphlet about the use of the bayonet, and to this the Commanding Officer wrote a preface. The pamphlet, unfortunately, did not meet with favour at the War Office, and a great deal of trouble was taken to recover all issued copies of the pamphlet, and most, if not all, of the copies were recovered and destroyed.

On August 22nd and 23rd we were delighted to have a visit from Lieutenant-Colonel H. W. Smith, D.S.O., a pre-war Adjutant of the Corps, and then in command of one of the Cadet Battalions at Fleet.

On August 23rd, Captain Brett left to join the Guards Machine-Gun Training Centre.

Battalion Sports were held on August 31st.

Captain Walters handed over to me the Treasurership of the War Savings Association on September 3rd.

On September 7th, an "Old Men's" Company ("E") was formed under Captain H. C. Bennett, M.C.

On September 21st news was received with very great regret of the death of Captain A. E. A. Buller, in Palestine, from dysentery.

On October 1st the total amount contributed to the War Savings Association of the Corps was £60,117 5s. 6d., including £10,000 in War Savings Certificates.

On October 12th the long-expected detachment of the Q.M.A.A.C. arrived.

About this time there was a further and serious outbreak of influenza. During the latter part of the month and the early part of November the Corps lost 14 members by death, including one Q.M.A.A.C., and one attached Sergeant.

On October 31st the Corps moved from camp into billets.

On November 5th, Captain Walters resigned his commission.

And on November 11th the Armistice was celebrated by a whole holiday. The Band paraded the High Street in the morning. The Q.M.A.A.C. official took her detachment for a route march, and on the return journey was met by many members of the Corps and attached N.C.O.'s. After a gallant resistance the detachment dissolved and went off with the men to celebrate the occasion, leaving the Administrator and her N.C.O. to return alone to Netherfield. That evening a great bonfire was made in Kitchener's Field, and little remained afterwards of the gallows and bayonet fighting sacks at the labyrinth. The Band broke into Holly House, but withdrew before any serious damage had been done. There was, in fact, very little disciplinary trouble then or afterwards.

After the Armistice, work was much reduced, and to a considerable extent gave way to education, sports and games. There is little in the subsequent history worth recording. There was a great struggle on behalf of many men to get on to the earlier demobilisation drafts, and towards the end some competition to keep off the drafts on the part of those who were quite content to draw pay as long as possible.

In the early months of 1919 the strength was rapidly reduced, and I wanted to stay at Berkhamsted until the Corps had been reduced to cadre. I had, however, suffered from time to time from abdominal trouble ever since September, 1914, and early in 1919 the cause was diagnosed. When the strength got below 50, further reduction became a very slow process, and as it became increasingly dangerous to defer longer an operation for appendicitis, I applied, very reluctantly, to be demobilised. On June 28th I handed over to Lieutenant L. T. Wootton, an attached officer who had been acting as Assistant Adjutant since the demobilisation of Lieutenant T. W. Haward, and on the same day I was demobilised.

The Cadre returned to Stone Buildings, Lincoln's Inn, on July 27th, 1919, when the war services of the Corps came to an end. The demobilisation of the Cadre and the return to his regiment of Colonel Stevens were not finally effected until October 25th, 1919.

The substitution by officers attached to the Corps from other regiments in place of our own officers began in May, 1917. In addition to the two Commanding Officers, their names are as follows:—

Capt. G. A. Angel	R. Fus.
Lieut. E. J. Alpin	E. Surr. R.
Capt. W. E. Aylwin, M.C.	Bedf. R.
Lieut. G. Baker	R. Berks. R.
Lieut. D. N. Barbour	R. Lanc. R.
Capt. B. Barron, M.C.	E. Lancs. R.
Capt. H. C. Bennett	N. Lancs. R.
Lieut. R. A. Buckingham	Middx. R.
Lieut. D. F. Campbell	Sco. Rif.
Lieut. R. J. Carey	19th Lond. R.
Capt. E. M. Cockshutt	E. Lancs. R.
Lieut. N. F. Fabricius	R. Fus.
Lieut. A. Ferrier-Kerr	R. Highrs.
Lieut. C. V. Gavin	W. York. R.
Lieut. P. J. Hall	Hamps. R.
Capt. C. J. Hardy, M.C.	North'n R.

THE CORPS (1st OCTOBER 1917 TO 27th JULY 1919).

2nd Lieut. A. D. Hickman	R. Scots.
2nd Lieut. J. R. Hoyle	E. York. R.
Lieut. J. H. Hutcheson	Arg. & Suth'd Highrs.
Capt. F. H. McClinton	R.I. Rif.
Capt. F. R. Ollerton	W. York. R.
Lieut. A. M. Ranson	K.R. Rif. C.
Lieut. G. A. Robson, M.C.	Rif. Brig.
Capt. M. Sayers, D.C.M.	E. Lancs. R.
2nd Lieut. W. B. Spencer	M.G.C.
Capt. W. L. Spencer-Cox	R.W. Surr. R.
Lieut. E. W. B. Sturrock	Sco. Horse.
2nd Lieut. F. V. Tuthill	Oxf. & Bucks. L.I.
Capt. A. R. Wallis	7th Lond. R.
Capt. T. H. Wilson	R. Scots.
Lieut. V. R. Wilton	Indian Army.
Lieut. L. T. Wootton	York. R.
Lieut. J. L. Wright	E. Surr. R.

A. McL.

Chapter IX.

THE DEPÔT.

The history of the depôt at Lincoln's Inn begins with the transfer of the Corps from London to Berkhamsted, in the month of September, 1914. The chief function of the depôt was the selection of candidates for admission to the Corps, but for a time recruits were clothed and armed there and received the first part of their training, and during this period the establishment at Lincoln's Inn carried on the work of an ordinary regimental depôt. At a later stage the recruits were sent down to Berkhamsted to join the Corps immediately after attestation, and the depôt was then concerned with little else than the business of recruiting. Recruiting involved two problems, namely, first, the attraction of candidates to the depôt, and secondly, the selection of suitable men from those who presented themselves, and, as will be seen hereafter, the tale of the depôt turns mainly on the methods adopted to solve these problems.

At the outbreak of war the Corps used for its Headquarters No. 10, Stone Buildings, Lincoln's Inn, consisting of a Drill Hall with orderly room, armoury and offices. As the war went on, the office work of the depôt increased so greatly that the accommodation at No. 10, Stone Buildings, soon became quite inadequate. The Benchers of Lincoln's Inn very kindly put practically all their vacant chambers at the disposal of the Corps, and at one time the work of the depôt was being carried on not only at the old Headquarters, but also in chambers at No. 7, No. 2, and No. 4, Stone Buildings, and at No. 12, Old Square. The Old Hall also was handed over to the Corps for lectures and other purposes during the period when recruit training was being carried on at Lincoln's Inn. Even the Law Courts were pressed into the service, and when the Central Hall was available it was used in bad weather. The gardens of the Inns were, of course, in constant use as training grounds, and their ancient lawns, the result of centuries of care, were completely ruined.

Before the war, membership of the Corps was open to barristers and bar students, and to university and public school men, and there was power under the rules of the Corps to admit men who did not come within the general qualification, but were considered specially eligible for membership. In the first instance, before it was realised that the war was to involve the whole of the nation's available manhood, the qualification rule was fairly closely adhered to in the selection of candidates, but before long selection came to depend solely on the question whether the candidate appeared to be personally suitable for commissioned rank, and likely to train into an efficient officer.

Under the rules of the Corps, candidates were required to be proposed and seconded by members, and all applications came before a Selection Committee and were decided by ballot. This system was abandoned as impracticable at the very outset, and the responsibility for selection, after the Corps moved to Berkhamsted, was delegated by the C.O. to the officer commanding the depôt, assisted by a committee. For this committee work the Corps was fortunate in obtaining the services of some of its old members and a number of other gentlemen, whose names will be found in Appendix III. To these gentlemen, and the others who worked with them, the Corps is deeply indebted for the care and patience with which they carried out their very laborious and exacting task.

When the system of selection had developed into a routine, the process was as follows:—

Candidates first filled up a form in which a variety of personal particulars were required to be given, and then appeared for an interview before a committee consisting of two or three of the members of the Selection Committee. When recruiting was brisk, it was found necessary at times to have as many as five or six of these committees sitting at the same time. The committee, after conversation with the candidate, formed their opinion as to his suitability and decided there and then whether to accept or reject, and if accepted the candidate was passed on to the O.C. Depôt. Rejection by a committee was treated as final, but acceptance required confirmation by the O.C. Depôt, and if the O.C. Depôt, when the accepted candidate came before him, felt any doubt as to his suitability, he either rejected the candidate or referred the case for further consideration by a larger committee of at least four members, whose decision was final. Occasionally, when there was an extraordinary rush of applicants, as invariably happened at times when conscription was in the air and some fresh development seemed to indicate that its adoption was imminent, it was found necessary to supplement the system described above by a preliminary sifting out of applicants, the obviously unsuitable being rejected at once so as to avoid the delay which would be caused by sending them before a Selection Committee. At one of these times of pressure about 1,200 candidates were dealt with in one single day, with the result that about 100 were finally selected, and of these successful applicants a few had had to pass through the four separate stages of scrutiny mentioned above.

The amount of work accomplished by the Committee of Selection may to some extent be appreciated from the fact that the total number of candidates who came before them must have amounted to some 60,000 or 70,000. The soundness of the committee's judgment is shown by the fact that the number of accepted candidates who were disqualified for commissions owing to misconduct while in training was negligible, and the proportion who failed to obtain commissions owing to want of military aptitude was remarkably small.

THE DEPÔT.

A few words on the principles of selection employed by the committee may be of interest, although perhaps when stated they may seem somewhat obvious. The committees relied mainly on the opinion they formed as to the candidate's personality when he came before them for his interview, and letters of recommendation were looked upon as having a substantial value only in comparatively few cases. A good education was, of course, expected and insisted upon, and sufficient social position to justify the candidate's being trained for a rôle in which he would be called upon to play the part of one in authority from whom both precept and example would be required. Given these conditions, and provided the applicant was within the age limit, the sole question was: " Is the candidate likely to make a good leader?" Proficiency in outdoor sports was looked upon as indicating the possession of the right qualities, and a man who had obtained school or club colours was practically certain of selection. Men who had had colonial experience or had held responsible positions at home or abroad—and many such applied for admission to the Corps—were always favourably considered by the committee, and almost invariably accepted. Every candidate, however, whatever his previous history, was carefully considered, and, if the preliminary conditions as to age and education were satisfied, the committee formed its own judgment as to his character and personality, and if it decided that he was likely to train into an efficient officer, he was accepted.

When compulsory service became the rule, recruiting for the Corps was, of course, carried on under conditions very different from those which had previously obtained, but it would probably be somewhat uninteresting to trace the various stages by which the field of recruiting was gradually narrowed. It will be sufficient to say that eventually the Corps was only able to choose from youths who had not attained sufficient age for service with the colours.

At the outbreak of the war the Inns of Court was the only O.T.C. which formed part of the Territorial Force, and great numbers of men, former members of the Corps and others, flocked to Lincoln's Inn to offer their services. The Corps, however, had only its small peace establishment. The numbers were at once brought up to strength and a waiting list was opened. Men on the waiting list were given such elementary training as was available, and many of them were eventually absorbed into the Corps. The process of absorption was assisted by an increase of the establishment, but in the meantime a large number of those on the list had grown tired of waiting and had enlisted elsewhere, while others had obtained commissions without actually entering the Corps. In these same early days, moreover, other units had been formed with a view to recruiting men of good education and position, and a very great number of men who would have made admirable officers commenced their war service, and in too many cases ended their service, in the ranks. The result was that when the men who joined up in the first enthusiasm for active service had been enlisted in some branch or other of the army, the question how the recruiting for the Corps was to be made to keep pace with its output of officers became a serious one. It was soon recognised that there would be an enormous demand for officers, and at the period now referred to the great call was for officers of infantry and artillery.

Apart from Sandhurst and Woolwich, the only establishments for the training of such officers were the Senior and Junior Officers' Training Corps Contingents at the Universities and Public Schools, the Inns of Court O.T.C., and the Artists' Rifles O.T.C. formed a few months after the commencement of the war out of one of the battalions of the Artists' Corps. The University contingents were almost immediately drained dry, and the school contingents could only turn out a limited number of boys of sufficient age. At the same time there was plenty of the right material in the country, and men anxious to serve and of the proper stamp for commissions were pouring into England from every part of the Dominions. It was found that the real difficulty in the way of recruiting for the Inns of Court was the fact that its very existence, to say nothing of its duties and functions, was practically unknown outside a very limited circle, and the only solution of the difficulty appeared to be to advertise, and to advertise as widely as possible without any regard to considerations of dignity or tradition. It was therefore decided to commence a campaign of advertisement, and Mr. H. K. Ryan, subsequently Captain Ryan, was put in charge of the publicity department. Sentiment had to yield to necessity, and it is practically certain that but for the elaborate system of advertising which was adopted the Corps would have been reduced to a skeleton after the first nine months of the war, and would eventually have reckoned its total number of commissions by hundreds instead of by thousands, to the great detriment of the country. Bills and posters were accordingly printed and displayed at railway stations, hotels, theatres, and other public places, and even on ships, giving particulars of the Corps, and inviting men " desirous of being trained for commissions " to apply at Lincoln's Inn. All the clergy in the country and many in the Colonies were asked to act as representatives of the Corps and to distribute information about the Corps in their parishes. Headmasters of schools were approached and asked to co-operate. Recruiting sergeants were sent to the ports of arrival of passenger liners, and shipping agents at some of the ports of embarkation gave very effective assistance. These measures, particularly the appeal for the assistance of the clergy, were most successful, and a stream of applicants flowed to the depôt.

A further development was then planned, and it was proposed to establish Selection Committees at several centres at a distance from London with a view to dealing with men who were not prepared to spend money and time on what might prove a fruitless journey to London, and to avoid useless expense to applicants, who had no real chance of being selected. There were elements of difficulty about this scheme owing to the possibility of conflict with local interests and activities. A committee was, however, established in Dublin, under the presidency of Mr. Justice Ross, which sent over a large number of young Irishmen. Committees were also set up at Exeter for West of England candidates and at Cardiff for South Wales, both of which proved a success.

This invasion of the provinces led to an important development in connection with the Lancashire Territorial Troops. When the Corps proceeded to make arrangements for recruiting in Liverpool its operations were objected to by the local

THE DEPÔT.

Territorial Force Association as being an encroachment on their recruiting area. The matter was then discussed with Lord Derby, the President of the West Lancs. T.F.A., and an arrangement was speedily arrived at. It was agreed that Lancashire should furnish a supply of recruits for the Corps and that these recruits should be ear-marked for commissions in Lancashire Territorial Battalions after completing their course of training. This arrangement was promptly put into execution and successfully carried on until the full operation of compulsory service rendered it impracticable. A great deal of the success of the Lancashire agreement was due to Major H. R. Parkes, C.B., the Secretary of the West Lancs. T.F.A. Major Parkes arranged for batches of candidates, provisionally approved by himself, to assemble month by month at Liverpool. The O.C. Depôt and another officer of the Corps attended at Liverpool, and, with the assistance of Major Parkes, interviewed the candidates, and decided as to their acceptance or rejection. A further supply of Lancastrians was obtained by transfer from the ranks of one of the Lancashire Brigades then in training at Grantham.

The result of all these activities was a constant and ample flow of recruits to the Corps up to the time of the establishment of the new system of Cadet Battalions, and the reduction in the strength of the Corps.

In December, 1916, Major J. A. Hay, T.D., who had been in command of the depôt from the time when the Corps left London, was succeeded as O.C. Depôt by Captain F. Le Neve Foster, who remained in military charge at Lincoln's Inn until the end of the war.

In the course of Captain Foster's period of duty, the depôt became the office of a Joint Board of Selection for the Artists' Rifles O.T.C. and the Inns of Court. Up to that time these Corps had each carried on their own system of selection and recruiting in friendly rivalry. Compulsory service had, however, completely altered the conditions and opportunities of recruiting, and it was decided by the authorities that one establishment should act as selecting body for both Corps. Some of the members of the old Selection Committee, with the addition of representatives from the Artists, were now officially constituted a Board of Selection for the two Corps, under the presidency of Sir Alfred Goodson. The Board sat at No. 10, Stone Buildings, to interview candidates and decide their fate as before, but for the two Corps and not for the Inns of Court alone. This system remained in force until the end of the war.

As already mentioned, the depôt in the first instance and during a period of about eighteen months had not only to select and enlist the recruits, but had also to see to their being clothed and equipped and to put them through the first stages of recruit training.

When the Corps moved to Berkhamsted, Captain A. G. Mathews was left on the Depôt Staff and was put in charge of the recruit training. Captain Mathews remained at that duty till he was relieved by Captain E. à C. Bergne in the early part of 1916. In the spring of 1915, Mr. Spencer Brett was commissioned in the Corps and added to the training staff of the depôt. To assist these officers a number of N.C.O.'s were supplied from Headquarters at Berkhamsted. The training consisted of the usual recruit course of elementary drill and musketry and physical exercises, with the addition of some instruction in such subjects as elementary tactics and map-reading and occasional lectures.

During the greater part of the year 1915, recruits were sent down in drafts to Berkhamsted as accommodation became available there, and the demand at Berkhamsted, speaking generally, kept pace with the supply at Lincoln's Inn. At the end of 1915, however, an epidemic of measles broke out among the troops at Berkhamsted and no further drafts could be sent there until the Corps was out of quarantine, a matter of some months. In the meantime, recruiting was proceeding at Lincoln's Inn without intermission, and the numbers on the strength at the depôt were daily increasing till at one time they reached almost 2,000. To give adequate training to such numbers with the few instructors available was almost an impossibility, and the energies of Captain Mathews and his staff were very severely taxed. The Gardens of the Inns did not afford sufficient space, and at this time of congestion a large part of the work was done on Hampstead Heath. A disused dancing hall, in the Vale of Health, was rented to provide cover in bad weather, and the Y.M.C.A. gave the Corps very valuable assistance by establishing a marquee on the Heath at which the men could obtain meals and could rest during intervals of drill.

Early in 1916, when the Corps was again free to receive drafts, the congestion at the depôt was relieved and the accumulation gradually absorbed. In June, 1916, orders were received that recruits were to be sent down to Corps Headquarters immediately after enlistment, and training at the depôt came to an end.

In connection with the training it should be mentioned that before the Lewis gun had been introduced into the Army as one of its regular weapons, Captain Brett found an opportunity of learning the gun, and held a series of spare-time classes for instruction in its mechanism and use.

Reference has been made above to the congestion at the depôt in the winter of 1915-16, when men were kept in London for months owing to sickness at Berkhamsted. The men at the depôt received pay and subsistence allowance, but had to find their own board and lodging. One result of this congestion was that a number of men who had not expected to be in London for more than a few weeks found themselves, as weeks grew into months, without any means beyond their pay and allowances and unable to pay their way. To cope with this difficulty the Mess in the Temple was furnished with barrack furniture and made available for housing about thirty men. Arrangements were also made with one of the restaurants in the neighbourhood to supply meals at special prices, and in that way satisfactory provision was made for men who were obliged to live on their military income.

Another branch of the work at the depôt remains to be mentioned. After the absorption of the original waiting list there still remained a number of men who for one reason or another could not become members of the Corps, but were desirous of obtaining some elementary military training, and others from time to time joined the party. The training of

THE DEPÔT.

these men was originally superintended by Captain P. F. Warner, and later on by Major F. R. Gregson, a retired officer of the regular army, and an N.C.O. of the Corps was detailed to act as assistant instructor. This " unattested contingent," as it was called, was further made use of for giving elementary military training to civilians selected for commissions in the Tunnelling Companies R.E., and eventually this became the sole reason for the existence of the unattested contingent. When mining and countermining began to play a large part in the operations at the front, there was a great call, and, for a long time, a constant call for officers with experience in mining and other underground work. No military training or experience was required of them, but it was thought desirable that civilians selected for these commissions should have some little knowledge of military matters before being actually commissioned, and the work of the unattested contingent appeared to meet the requirements of the case. Candidates selected for commissions in the Tunnelling Companies were accordingly sent to Lincoln's Inn for periods of about six weeks, and were there instructed in elementary drill and in such subjects as military law and military etiquette, and given frequent opportunities of drilling and " taking charge " of others. Some hundreds of tunnelling officers received their first military training as members of the unattested contingent. The Flying Corps made use of the unattested contingent for a similar purpose at a time when a number of men were being commissioned without previous military training for service as officers in the Kite Balloon Section.

The depôt had its full share of damage from enemy bombs in the course of the air raids. In October, 1915, bombs were dropped in Lincoln's Inn and in Chancery Lane, just outside Stone Buildings. The bombs which fell in the Inn did a great deal of destruction, notably to the stained glass of the Chapel windows, but did not reach Corps Headquarters. The bomb, however, which fell in the Lane wrecked the interior of No. 10. The main fabric is exceedingly strong and was only superficially damaged, but practically all the windows and window frames on the Chancery Lane side were demolished, parts of the ceilings were brought down, and the interior partitions were broken. Fortunately no one was injured, although there was a small guard on the premises. The next occasion when the enemy got uncomfortably near the depôt was in December, 1917. This time a bomb landed almost immediately in front of the entrance to No. 10. There was again a large amount of superficial damage to the stonework caused by the road metal being hurled in all directions, and again the windows were wrecked, the front door and doorposts were blown in and other damage done to the interior. The men on duty this time also escaped without any casualty.

The depôt was very fortunate in its non-commissioned officers. At the time when recruits were clothed and equipped and commenced their training at Lincoln's Inn, R.Q.M.S. Langridge carried out the whole of the Quartermaster duties, and Staff-Sergeant Vassila (subsequently R.S.M. Vassila) acted as Depôt Sergeant-Major. Later, when only office work was carried on, Staff-Sergeant R. G. Wallis, and subsequently Sergeant C. M. Pembo, acted as Depôt Sergeant-Major. The non-commissioned officers detailed from Berkhamsted to act as assistant instructors to the recruits did extremely good work under circumstances which at times were very difficult and trying.

J. A. H.

Chapter X.

THE SQUADRON.

LINCOLN'S INN.

None of those who played a part in the early war days in London, whatever may have been their subsequent experiences in France, Egypt, Palestine, or elsewhere, will easily forget the indescribable hurry and bustle of the life at the " Devil's Own " Headquarters. Old friends were leaving every day to take up commissions, recruits were pouring in, and many " back numbers " appeared again, eager to play their part in the Great Adventure.

Each morning the Corps paraded on the grass (*real* grass in those early days), North of Lincoln's Inn Hall, under the eagle eye of R.S.M. Burns, whose daily passages of arms over the unfailing regularity of the whole Corps to play the rôle of " right maaarrrkers " will go down to history.

After inspection by Colonel Errington, the Squadron marched off to the Temple Gardens, where they disported themselves in various ways in the somewhat confined space, the routine of troop drill and rifle exercises (we had no swords in those days) being pleasantly varied by lectures on the " noble animal " by J. C. Porter, musketry by Leveson Gower, map-reading by Field, and other kindred subjects, usually held in the open air, on a grassy bank from which could be surreptitiously watched, from the corner of an eye, the antics of the recruits' class (or " waiting-list "), who were being licked into some sort of shape by poor Cotton. All the time, rumours of Camp were bandied about, day after day and week after week, but nothing seemed to come of it. Latterly, the routine was varied by frequent visits to more open country in the shape of Wimbledon Common (Oh! those dismounted attacks under a sweltering August sun!), Richmond Park, and Worcester Park. Occasionally (all too seldom) flashes were given us of the glory to be in the shape of horses—real horses—on which we cut our cavalry teeth (painful process) in a riding school on Wimbledon Common with Waggett (then Farrier-Sergeant) as Master of the Ring, and we also had occasional mounted troop training on the Worcester Park Polo Ground.

During these first weeks the Squadron Commander, Duke Moore, had been away on a staff job, and Wood Hill was running the show, backed up by Field, Leveson Gower, and Robinson, and—for a few days—Cotton. Moore returned for a short time before we left town, and then went, with Robinson, to the E. Riding Yeomanry. J. T. Morris was Squadron Sergeant-Major, and got through a mass of work, as did Yeatman, who was S.Q.M.S. These two saw us safely settled in the country, and then handed over to Witt and Herbert Porter respectively—stalwarts of earlier days. As September wore on, rumours of Camp grew in intensity, and finally the news was officially published that the Corps would proceed to Berkhamsted on September 28th.

BERKHAMSTED.

The day came round and the Corps duly " proceeded," in an atmosphere of suppressed excitement, to the friendly Hertfordshire town, which was to be our home for so long. On detraining, the Infantry made their way into Camp in the field adjoining the Station, and the Squadron, with sturdy independence, headed in the reverse direction and were soon halted in Water Lane, outside a massive pair of gates which screened the entrance yard of the Old Brewery—of blessed and glorious memory. We finally sorted ourselves and inspected our new quarters. They seemed bare enough at first—it was a derelict rabbit-warren of a place—and there was no hint of the comfort and secure isolation of later days, with the home-like " Cosy Corner," " Crow's Nest " and " Parade View." The quarters for " other ranks " consisted of two long lofts (soon christened " A " and " B " Dormitories) over what were to be stables. The officers were, after a few nights, billeted in the town, and the Sergeants were in what was afterwards known as the Old Guard Room. They migrated later to what subsequently became the Armoury, a dark cell-like chamber, entered from the " Covered Yard " (what memories these old names bring back!) from which was also approached the Squadron Office, erstwhile a kitchen. In the Covered Yard stood the wooden hut which became the Pharmacy. Poor old Jim Kerr fathered the Sergeants and saw they were properly turned out. His death in Aylesbury Hospital in 1918 was a real loss to the Squadron. We left him to Berkhamsted when we departed in 1916, and it is said that the change from Squadron to Infantry proved too much for him, and finally broke his honest old heart.

The almost complete lack of horses rather denuded the Squadron gingerbread of its accustomed gilt, but we lived largely on hope in those days and we were not entirely horseless, for had we not Rowena with us? For a fortnight, having no " stables," we were afflicted with a cruel form of sport, viz.: " physical jerks," with the Battalion in the cold grey dawn. How we ground and gnashed our teeth and stifled our Cavalier oaths as we padded round dewy fields or bent our weary frames into unaccustomed angles. In vain, Sister Anne-like, we looked for our horses, who would redeem us from

THE SQUADRON.

this matutinal torture. And then, at last, the great day came—October 14th, 1914—when we filed to the Station, armed with the necessary gear, to await the longed-for " hairies." Finally the trucks sailed slowly in and discipline gave way in heartfelt cheers. Little did those old " plugs," as they were pulled and pushed and heaved from their trucks, realise that some of them were beginning an acquaintance with the Squadron that was to last till the beginning of 1919. With the arrival of the horses, who were followed quickly by others, we began to *live*; before, we had merely *existed*. Our empty spaces in the Brewery were transformed into stables, and before long were filled to overflowing, so that " D " Troop spread out across Water Lane into another building, and " C " Troop had a fresh enclosure made for some of their horses out by the forage store. The men, too, overflowed into the town, and were billeted out at the International Stores and the Progress Hall, over the Co-operative Society.

The life of the Squadron at Berkhamsted is too well remembered by all who lived it to need recapitulation. It will suffice to recall a few incidents and personalities, equine and human. We soon got into our stride and training, and as fast as commissions drained our strength, gaps were filled up. All would-be recruits were " vetted " by a Squadron officer at the depôt in Stone Buildings twice a week, and a party of recruits was formed up in town, who were licked into shape till there were vacancies for a draft at Berkhamsted. The first winter we were dogged by ill-luck in the matter of horse-sickness, nearly every horse falling a victim to pink-eye (brought in by remounts) and ringworm, with an occasional case of strangles or pneumonia thrown in. Training was practically at a standstill, and the Squadron was divided up into parties for temperature-taking, slow exercise, special feeding, and so on. By degrees we began to get up to date—swords, universal saddlery, issue boots, and so on—the whole panoply of war. As regards messing, during the first winter we waded and slithered to our marquee in Camp through a sea of mud and slush, and later we shared a shed in Key's Timber Yard with some of the Infantry, and basked in the sunshine of Mr. and Mrs. Daborn's smiles—always two of the Squadron's staunchest friends. Wood Hill left us in September, 1915, and Field took over the Command, which he kept till the end, steering us with his proverbial tact and bonhomie through the deeps and shallows of our varied career. Many generations now of Squadron men know what they owe to Field in the matter of their early military careers. 'Arry 'Awke is just the old Squadron tradition incarnate.

As training progressed and we had a long day in the field every week, we began to find out the great charm of the country around Berkhamsted, and were fortunate to get fairly regular hunting with the Old Berkeley and the Hertfordshire packs. A Corporal's stripe was the open sesamé to the hunting field—a great incentive. Our drill grounds were limited in number and in size. We tried Ashridge Park, the Common, Haresfoot Park, and (perhaps best of all) a large field adjoining the Chesham Road between Haresfoot and Kingshill. But for field-work the country was admirable, and all who were in the Squadron in those days look back with pleasure to the Thursday schemes—" Whiteland v. Brownland " and so on—and such points on the map as the R of R. GADE, the Pip of POTTEN END, and K of KINGSHILL, and the first M of MARCHMONT HOUSE became burnt into our brain. We blew up every available railway bridge within miles, we burned forage stores at Whipsnade and Markyate, we waylaid valuable convoys on the Watford—Tring Road with resulting horrible massacre, our patrols knew every nook and cranny within a large radius, and we charged with reckless bravery against thickly-manned imaginary trenches on the down-land of the Ivinghoe hills. Other days, too, we had in company with the Infantry, and Public School Field Days on a large scale, when the country side was thickly covered with tireless, racing schoolboys, who stoutly refused to be taken prisoners.

Few feelings are so satisfactory as those of the healthily tired cavalryman after a long day in the field. His saddlery is cleaned, his horse is bedded down, watered, fed and made comfortable for the night, and he goes off for his evening meal (to which he does full justice); he has his last pipe, and rolls himself with contented grunts in his blankets, to fall asleep at once, feeling that after all this is *the* life of lives, and with a heartfelt pity for those who have to spend their days apart from a horse, and the things that appertain thereto. Though the cavalryman's life consists chiefly of toil, the time comes (except for those whose fate is to be on night stable guard) when he can lay aside wisp and feed-tin and turn to other forms of pleasure. The Squadron sing-songs at the " Crown " became a feature of the life, and elsewhere in the town who shall say how many hearts were set a-flutter by clink of spur and jaunty set of cap. There was a trumpeter . . . . but no; we will leave romance discreetly veiled.

When one lives with horses day and night, one gets to know *something* about them and their doings, and those old plugs were good friends to us, whatever we may have thought when the S.S.M. " put us through the hoop " with that deadly thong of his round the Brewery field, what time we appeared from the depôt for the riding test. Ye Gods! was there ever such a crowded five minutes as that! The hairies quickly acquired names—most of them simply *asked* for names. There was the famous quartette which should have been left at the plough, or sent to pull " heavies " out of the Flanders mud—Gossamer (*alias* the Dachshund), Stockings, the Elephant, and Marie Lloyd. Then there was Satan, highly strung and apparently savage, who with gentle humouring became a veritable equine lamb—only breaking out a few days before the Squadron left Berkhamsted in 1916, when in a fit of diabolical humour, he deposited on terra firma an Infantry officer who was proudly caracoling (all against his will) at the head of his admiring Company. And yet there are those who say a horse has no sense of humour! The Dun was another old and hardened sinner, a big golden mulish creature, who resented any handling of his hind legs. Dinky, the little chestnut in " D " Troop, and Mary (" the Hackney ") were with us to the end, as also were the two Peggies, Juliet (who broke the heart of a certain S.Q.M.S.), Delilah, Pinky, Roy, Sonny, Pavlova, Jimcock (whose ugly shape was only equalled by his speed), Baby, Reynolds, Bill, Sambo, Jellicoe, and a few others, who never missed through all the years of war their annual Christmas feast of carrots. Then there was the fat little grey aristocrat Thomas, who carried O.C. Squadron (*alias* Mounted Detachment) through the last years of the war. Others of earlier days we shall not forget are Punch, Black Maria, Margaret, Tealeaves, Bunty, and Tipperary, so called for his sixteen hands; not to mention Susan, and the Knut, lady and gentleman volunteers. We had horses of all shapes, sizes, colours, and denominations thrown at us, and we licked them into shape, taught them to behave, taught them to jump, taught them their drill, taught them the gentle art of patrolling, taught them in fact all or most of the accomplishments that should be in the repertoire of a pukka troop-horse. What a change it must have been to their peace-time avocations. Some have doubtless now returned to these, but with what an added richness of experience and with what (we hope) happy memories of regular and plentiful feeds and personal attention. Now that we too are " Civvies " again, we take off our hats to you, you most lovable " hairies," and when we meet you in your milk-cart or your brewer's dray (*some* of you !) we will stop and have a yarn about those good old far-off days.

We made a host of friends in and around Berkhamsted, and many familiar characters will be remembered—among them Mr. Newman, the ubiquitous and indefatigable photographer; Mr. Bunker, of Northchurch Farm, who helped us in many ways; Mr. Rawle, who ran the Staghounds; Mr. Wingfield, the saddler; Mr. Gubbins, the friendly proprietor of the " Crown," where we had our Squadron Room for lectures and sing-songs; Mr. Blincowe, the helpful Stationmaster; and Mr. Pike, our landlord at the Old Brewery. The hospitality of the inhabitants generally is too well remembered to need any word here. We only hope that they will have as kindly memories of the Squadron as the Squadron has of them.

As the war went on it began to appear that in all probability there would not be a heavy demand for Cavalry and Yeomanry Officer reinforcements, and large numbers of men from the Squadron, who could rub up enough trigonometry to satisfy O.C. Squadron (and, later, " brass hats " from the W.O.), elected the Gunners as a suitable field for the display of their horsemanship. At the beginning of 1916, the Cadet Schools were formed all over the country, and these embryo gunners went off to Exeter and St. John's Wood. For some time it was supposed that we should become a Cavalry Cadet Squadron, but eventually Netheravon and Kildare were selected as the only two, and to these in later times all our men were despatchd, and we formed one of their sources of supply. After the Cavalry slump came a time when Cavalry officers were suddenly needed, and we could not turn them out fast enough. After that again another slump, when the fate of the Squadron hung in the balance, the upshot being that the " wash out " was never sounded, but in the autumn of 1916 the establishment was reduced to three officers, fifty men in training for Commissions, and a staff, and it was decreed that we should be attached for training purposes to one of the Reserve Cavalry Regiments. As our time at Berkhamsted began to draw to a close, and our establishment was in process of reduction, we were not sent any more recruits from the depôt at Stone Buildings, so we had to fill up gaps with would-be gunners from the Infantry, some of whom were overheard to remark that they could do with a bit of a holiday in the Old Brewery. These, we venture to think, lived to regret their outspokenness, and several remembered pressing engagements elsewhere. But many were eventually transferred to the Mounted Detachment (as the Squadron became) and were of our best. Another thing that kept us alive in those days was a decree by the then C.O. (Lieut.-Colonel Sinclair Thomson) that all the Infantry officers should pass through a course of Riding School. We had at that time two Sergeants attached to us for instructional duties from the Vth. Dragoon Guards—Jenkins and Aldridge by name. To their tender mercies the Infantry officers—regardless of rank, height, or weight—were turned over twice a week, and right manfully they went through the ordeal—crossed stirrups and all. Their reward came when, after a long and strenuous course, the day arrived when they lined up mounted in Mill Street for the first of a series of cross-country paper chases. These proved a distinct feature of our last days at Berkhamsted and added a zest to life.

At length the time came for us to leave, and accordingly, on December 6th, 1916, led by the Corps band, we marched away from the Old Brewery, which had been our home for more than two years, and entrained for Maresfield Park, in Sussex. The horses had been sent on by rail with Sergeant Aldridge and a small party. The whole Battalion was at the Station, and many of our good friends the inhabitants of Berkhamsted, not a few of whom (among the young and fair) were observed to dash a tell-tale tear from downcast eye. The Band played selections (" Nancy Dawson " and others) on the platform to keep up our spirits, finishing up with " Auld Lang Syne " as the train steamed away. We felt that we were leaving much behind us in Berkhamsted that we had come to look upon as almost inseparable from our Army life, but the thought that we were going to be attached to the Cavalry gave us a new interest to look forward to. We tramped with brave heart from Euston to London Bridge, and eventually arrived at Uckfield Station, whence we tramped the two miles or so in pitchy darkness to our destination, Maresfield Park.

MARESFIELD PARK.

Here to start with we had a struggle to keep our end up as we were " nobody's child," and we felt the need of a regular S.Q.M.S. and so on to fend for us in the matter of the necessities of life. However, the Colonel and Adjutant of the 13th Reserve Regiment of Cavalry were goodness itself, and we soon found our feet and felt that this was the real thing and that here at last we were in our element. Everyone talked " horse," and the music of many trumpets was pleasant to our ears. Training was seriously interfered with by the long spell of frost, which made anything but Riding School at slow paces almost impossible, there being no covered-in School. However, we had the best of the Instructors at our disposal, of whom we shall not forget S.S.M.I.M. Channer on the Square, S.S.M.R.R. Darby in Riding School (both of the XX. Hussars), and Sergeant Murray (XIV. Hussars) for Musketry. Our staff was

THE SQUADRON.

temporarily reduced to two officers, Merriman and Fisher, and everyone's time was filled up. We were still fed with drafts from Berkhamsted as we needed them, and things were going with a swing, when the re-shuffling of all the Reserve Cavalry Regiments was announced, and we were told that we were to proceed with the 13th R.R.C. to Tidworth, where the then 11th and 13th Reserve Regiments were to be amalgamated into the new 5th R.R.C. Accordingly at midnight, on February 9th—10th, 1917, we marched to Buxted, leading the horses saddled up, and there entrained with the Regiment. After a long and tortuous night journey we arrived in the early morning of February 10th, at Tidworth, which was to prove our home for the next two years.

TIDWORTH.

Detraining at about 9 a.m., we led the horses along the ice-covered road to Aliwal Barracks, where we were met by a Subaltern of the XVIII. Hussars (an old Squadron man), who had been detailed to look after us. After putting the horses into some temporary tin stables at the far end of the barracks, we made them comfortable and then began to turn round and settle in. This was an uncomfortable and laborious process, as the whole place was in a state of flux, a Reserve Regiment of Lancers having vacated our Barracks only the day before, and now two Hussar Reserve Regiments and a whole galaxy of Yeomanry Regiments were being telescoped into one huge Reserve Regiment, and we were somewhere in the middle of the telescope. However, by lying doggo, we more than survived, and things eventually straightened out to our entire satisfaction. We were allotted quarters adjoining "D" Squadron, in Assaye Barrack, which we occupied till the end in 1919. Major Stewart, of the XVIII. Hussars, commanded this Squadron, and as he had bumped into Field in a previous existence, he knew all about us, and proved a good friend to us all along. The horses (they must have thought they were never coming to anchor) were moved in a day or two to other temporary stables near our quarters, and we were allotted two houses in the Married Quarters for our Squadron Office and Storerooms. Here also slept the cook, storeman, and grooms. We were also given a S.Q.M.S. from the Regiment, A. H. Whittingham, of the XXth., and ultimately became a separate accounting unit, which saved a mass of correspondence with Berkhamsted. Later we had as S.Q.M.S., the evergreen veteran of South Africa and Mons, A. O'Connell, of the Xth., who was with us to the end.

At first the weather prevented anything but slow exercise on the roads, but with the advent of Spring, we began to live again and to realise the many advantages of Salisbury Plain as a training ground for Cavalry. Sergeant C. Wash, of the XXth., proved an A1 instructor in equitation. Drafts began to dribble away to the two Cavalry Cadet Squadrons, Netheravon and Kildare. The former, with its genial Commandant, Major Bruce, we soon got to know well, as it was only a few miles away across the Plain. When Sergt. Wash departed to Mesopotamia, Sergeant-Major Darby returned, and remained with us to the end. As time went on many old Squadron men came into the Mess, both hardened veterans from France and elsewhere, and newly-joined subalterns from the Cadet Squadrons, resplendent in the last word in breeches and field boots. We soon found that life at Tidworth was far from undesirable, and when fate, or a too insecure seat in the Riding School, decreed that " owing to the exigencies of the service," dismounted training was more suitable, the unhappy victim, having once tasted the joys of the cavalry life, returned, we fear, with but an ill grace to the foot-slogging treadmill at Berkhamsted. As we were part of a Composite Regiment, which formed a Brigade with the 5th and 6th Reserve Regiments in cases of emergency, we had opportunities of regimental and brigade drill and field work on a comparatively large scale, in addition to the mild excitement of sudden mobilization, brought on by rumours of the German Fleet's appearance in the North Sea, or a bit of extra trouble in " the disthressful counthry." We also took part in inspections by Lord French and Sir William Robertson on Bulford Field. All the time men were leaving with more or less regularity for Netheravon and Kildare, their departure being enlivened by farewell dinners which would have shocked the Food Controller had he been within range, and made his " each particular hair to stand on end." The old Squadron song was revived and brought up to date, and there was plenty of musical talent. Small though our numbers were in these latter days, we ran both a rugger and a soccer team, the former especially distinguishing themselves by defeating, in the Autumn of 1918, the Netheravon Cadet Squadron and the I.C.O.T.C. Infantry at Berkhamsted. We were also freely used for " window-dressing " when inspecting Generals appeared—not always an unmixed blessing. But they were good days, those Tidworth days—just as the earlier ones at Berkhamsted had been. The country grew very familiar to us, and here again we made many friends, though it was among our fellow-men, the fair sex being few and far between. The Regiment were always good to us, from Colonel Pollok-Morris downwards. Captain Storey, of the XX. Hussars, was Musketry Officer, and we had Corporal Mather, of the XVIIIth., as our own instructor. Lieutenants Kyte and Lethbridge-Abell were in charge of Bombing and Anti-Gas Instruction respectively, and there was a danger of our becoming specialists first and cavalryman afterwards. The Squadron (or Mounted Detachment as we then were) retrieved their evil pre-war reputation for indifferent markmanship, and at the last shoot, before demobilisation, obtained what they were told was the highest average in the annals of the local ranges at Bulford.

We had remarkably few casualties among the horses, and those few were usually returned as perfect cures after a few days in the Station Veterinary Hospital, which was in charge of Captain Barry, a big-hearted Irishman with all his countrymen's love and knowledge of a horse. A familiar figure to the last generation at Tidworth was " Bertie," the long-bodied mongrel, who, springing (as is the manner of Camp dogs) from nowhere in particular, attached himself inseparably to us as mascot, " doing his bit " as stable sentry, on all parades (including fire-drill), mounted drills, and field days, when he chased rabbits and field-officers with delightful impartiality. Where is he now, we wonder?

THE SQUADRON.

The German Offensive in March, 1918, came with a crash, and a crop of fresh rumours was freely circulated, the most popular one being that we were to go out to France as an independent Troop (!) to help stem the tide of onrushing Boche. But it was not to be; the tide turned without our assistance, and we were left high and dry, and so continued until the day of Armistice and after. The end came on January 25th, 1919, when the last of our men had been demobilized or sent, in the case of those from overseas, to a repatriation Camp, *via* Berkhamsted. Field was the last to leave the sinking ship. The end had *really* come a few days before, when the old horses, some of whom had been with us since that momentous day in October, 1914, were ridden and led to Marlborough to be put under the hammer. It was an inglorious end, and we only wished that we had a " Squadron Home of Rest for Tired Heroes," where the hairies could have ended their days in well-earned ease. But it was not to be, and they are scattered to the four winds; but they will surely know, with their unfailing intuition, that in the annals of the Old Squadron their name will live for ever.

It is difficult to write of those old Squadron men whom we shall not meet again—and there are all too many. Not a few of their names had become almost household words with us, and we shall always remember their cheery companionship. Good fellows all, they will not be forgotten as the years go on, and we shall often think of them in their different generations—in old pre-war days, in Temple Gardens, in the old Brewery at Berkhamsted, at Maresfield Park, and Tidworth Barracks. During the war, over 1,100 men passed through the Squadron, and of these the proportion of casualties was high, considering the few opportunities the cavalry really had of getting going in the main theatre of war.

At the time of writing (January, 1921) the Corps is being reconstituted on pre-war lines, and the Mounted Detachment, which assumed the chrysalis stage at Tidworth in January, 1919, is now, after two years in a dormant state, bursting forth into the full glories of a Squadron again, under the Command of H. D. P. Francis, a veteran of pre-war days, who brings with him the experiences of the Palestine Campaign (*the* cavalry show of the war), and under whose leadership the old Squadron traditions will be carefully nurtured.

And through the future the memories of the years of war will remain, and all we old sons of the Squadron will often live those days over again, sounding the " Fall In " on the trumpet of memory to summon before us old places and faces (of men and horses) and telling them off, " from the right by sections," on the parade ground of our imagination.

H. I. M.

Chapter XI.

THE COMPANY.

Company training at Berkhamsted was conducted in accordance with the principles laid down in the official manuals, and in the spirit infused into the Corps by its Commanding Officer. The object, always kept steadily in view, was to train men to be officers; and this differentiated the training, not merely in the details of the curriculum, but still more in spirit, from the training of an ordinary battalion. The quality ultimately aimed at was leadership, to be built up on a solid foundation of drill and discipline, with a superstructure of knowledge and practice in command, and with full emphasis on the moral qualities needed in those who have to lead men in the field. The maxim of Napoleon (the truth of which has been so irrefutably established during the war), that the moral is to the material as three to one, lies at the basis of Company training as much as of the major operations of war.

The local conditions of Company training at Berkhamsted were ideal. For drill we had the huge field, measuring about 700 yards by 400, which once had been the playground of Berkhamsted School. What its original local name may have been I do not know; but when we arrived there it was being utilised by the first drafts of " Kitchener's Army," and it was promptly christened " Kitchener's Field," and " Kitchener's Field " it will remain in the memory of all war members of the Inns of Court. In this space the Companies could drill, and the Battalion adopt the most extended order, even when the strength ran into four figures. The neighbouring Castle Grounds, once the abode of the Black Prince, became eventually a convenient and sheltered School of Musketry. For field work, the surrounding country provided a most admirable variety of *terrain*. Berkhamsted Common, stretching for some four miles from Potten End to Norcott Hill, furnished an infinite variety of broken ground, covered with bracken, gorse and heather, to say nothing of space for the practice of field entrenchments. Then there was Ashridge Park, with its long stretches of grass or bracken, and its woods, on the use of which no restrictions were placed by Lord Brownlow. Haresfoot Park was a convenient training ground for night operations, and offered surprising facilities for losing a company on a dark night. Other stretches of open ground were within reach, such as Hawridge, Cholesbury, Aldbury, Ivinghoe, and Hudnall Commons, and, further afield, the down country from Pitstone Hill by Steps Hill to the front of the Chilterns at Ivinghoe Beacon. In addition, especially before much of the grass land was broken up for corn, there was a great variety of enclosed country which was available for part of the year, and the undulating contours of the land gave admirable opportunities both for practice in map-reading and for tactical exercises of every kind. A better district for training troops could not be asked for.

For the first two years of the war, Company officers were given a very free hand in the training of their Companies, the results being tested by frequent Battalion drills and Battalion tactical exercises, both by day and by night. It is not possible, therefore, to give exact programmes of training, since each Company Commander had his own methods and distributed his time in his own way. The ingredients of the composition were, however, the same, though the proportions might vary. The staple subjects were drill (close order and extended order), musketry (theory and practice), field entrenchment, map reading, marching, field work, and night operations. Bombing and gas training were added when the war revealed the necessity for them. Physical training was for the first two years mainly represented by plenty of field work; later, together with bayonet fighting, it became a highly developed and much practised item of regular exercise, further promoted by the encouragement of boxing and cross-country running as recreations. Something may be said on each of the items of training.

(1) DRILL.—That drill is the basis of all military training is a proposition universally accepted, and even in the times of greatest pressure, in the early days of the war, this was recognised as the one fundamental and inevitable necessity. Every man entering the Corps did so as a private, and learnt his recruit, squad and company drill as such. The difficulty in the early days lay in the lack of trained instructors. The mechanical details of drill are best taught by experienced N.C.O.'s, and few were available. The difficulty was met, on the one hand by sending officers and N.C.O.'s for courses of instruction at Chelsea whenever possible, and on the other by the keenness of both instructors and instructed to learn all that could be learnt by study of the training manuals and by assiduous practice; the whole being under the eye of a Regular adjutant.

Of the details of the training of the men as privates there is nothing to say. The essence of the matter is that it should be the same in all cases, and salvation is only to be found in strict adherence to the letter of the manual, and ignoring the latest fads brought back from schools of instruction, unless they are in conformity with the letter of the law. What differentiated the training of the Corps from that of an ordinary infantry battalion appeared at a later stage in the training, when men began to learn to drill others. This was an essential and very vital feature. The object of the Corps was not to produce a well-drilled battalion of privates, but to train officers, and to be drilled in the ranks was only essential because, and so far as, it is the *sine qua non* of learning to drill others. The work of a Company Commander was not complete when (or if) his Company could drill creditably, but only when (or if) each individual could, on leaving

THE COMPANY.

it, make a fair show in drilling at least a platoon or section. Consequently the handling of sections and platoons, and even companies, was not confined to N.C.O.'s, but was entrusted to every man in turn; and though it was impossible to give every man as much practice as was desirable, the training of every man in command was a recognised part of the programme. On wet days it could be usefully supplemented by match drill, and many men voluntarily practised this in their billets or undertook rope drill in their not very frequent hours of leisure.

This training in drill was an important stage in the education of an officer, because it was his first exercise in command. Everyone must feel nervous when first called out to take command of a squad of live men, who, having once been set in motion, will continue to move in the given direction until something is done to stop or divert them; and most of us have experienced an awful sinking of the heart at seeing the group temporarily entrusted to us moving to inevitable catastrophe for want of the command which our mind fails to produce or our lips to form. To some men, who had already held responsibility elsewhere, command came easily; to others, less fortunate in their previous circumstances, it was a plant of slow growth; but to none was this practice unnecessary. Many a man, after leaving Berkhamsted, wrote to say what a satisfaction and source of confidence it had been to him when, on joining a battalion with a commission, he found himself able to acquit himself creditably in charge of a platoon under his new commanding officer.

Of course, if a company or a platoon is used as a chopping block on which beginners try their prentice hand, the drill of the ranks will suffer, and casual visitors will find something to complain of. It is not fair to judge of the drill of a company by its exhibition when under an inexperienced private or lance-corporal; but no one with an intelligent comprehension of the object of an O.T.C. would make the mistake. The corrective of drill under the company officers must be applied frequently; and if the highest polish of drill is not arrived at, the deficiency is more than compensated by the training in command which the men as individuals have received. And the performances of the Corps on ceremonial occasions from time to time proved that in order to produce precision of drill it is not necessary (at any rate when dealing with educated men) to think of nothing else in their training.

(2) MUSKETRY.—The importance of musketry was fully realised at Berkhamsted, but its practice was attended by considerable difficulties. The only range in the neighbourhood was a very small one on the edge of the Common, and that was not available in the earlier part of the war. Rifles out of which anyone could fire with safety were scarce, and ammunition was scarcer still. Indeed, so scanty was the supply of ammunition for the first year or two that it was useless to try to make the range serviceable. The most that could be done was to send the " Instruction Class " once in each course to the Corps' old range at Stanmore, and so to give each man a chance of firing a few rounds in the course of his training.

In the early days, therefore, musketry training was confined to what could be done without firing, and this was carried out very assiduously. The care of arms, the handling of arms, the mechanism of the rifle, the theory of musketry, visual training, judging distance, and fire discipline and control were frequent items in the weekly programme; and it may be claimed that every man obtained a really substantial grounding, and not merely acquired this knowledge for himself but, to some extent, learnt to impart it. The first advance on this programme was made when a miniature range was established: at first, in February, 1915, out of doors, and more effectively when a building containing two covered ranges was erected in July, 1916. From this time forward every man had a fair training in the use of the full-sized rifle with reduced bore; and even when the cult of the bomb was at its height, the prime importance of musketry was never lost sight of.

In the course of 1916, the Castle Grounds were converted into a school of musketry, under a special officer. Lewis guns were obtained early in 1916, and a very thorough course of instruction in mechanism and handling was established. Keen interest was taken in this new development, and the results were very good. Towards the end of 1917, conditions with regard to the supply of ammunition being easier, the range on the Common was put in order, and each Company fired a course of it. A small field-firing range was established in a fold of the Chilterns in 1918, which gave some variety to the instruction; but the distance was too great and the conditions too restricted to enable the Corps to obtain the full advantage of field-firing exercises.

In the earlier part of the war, the musketry training was entirely in the hands of the Company officers; but eventually a small musketry staff was established, which was of great assistance in standardising the course of instruction and in introducing the latest methods from Hythe.

(3) FIELD ENTRENCHMENT.—For this branch of a soldier's training the conditions at Berkhamsted fell short of the ideal. The soil consisted of clay, plentifully besprinkled with flints. Digging was in consequence very strenuous work, and progress slow; and if trenches were left uncared-for for any length of time in the winter, they rapidly deteriorated through the action of frost. Also in wet weather (of which we had an ample share) the trenches quickly filled with water and emptied slowly, the percolation being very bad. Revetting materials were scarce—as indeed they were in France; and the amount of time which could be devoted to this branch of training did not admit of instruction in the more advanced developments of the art, such as elaborate dug-outs, listening posts, machine-gun emplacements, and wiring, except in a very sketchy way.

The men did, however, learn to dig. In quite early days a line of entrenchments was planned on the Common above Northchurch, from the neighbourhood of Hill Farm to that of Norcott Hill, facing north; and a portion of the line was allotted to each Company. A line, not continuous, but covering the whole front, was sketched out; and thereafter each Company was left to develop its portion according to its own taste. One Company, blessed with a subaltern who had

An assault on the Beacon.

The Battalion forming up and marching home.

THE COMPANY.

engineering tastes and knowledge, achieved a dug-out and organised a crater (of which local pits provided a plentiful supply). Another worked steadily for the whole four years at a complete trench-system, with fire-bays, supervision trench, communication trenches, and support line, much too extensive ever to be all in order at the same moment, but enabling recruits to form some idea of the theory of a trench system.

In general, it may be held that, even when trench warfare plays such an important part as it did in 1915, it is waste of time to attempt to teach more than the rudiments at home. Trench life and trench routine cannot be taught under ordinary training conditions, and a week in France or up the Salient taught more than months of playing at it at home could do. What can be taught comprises the principles of trench design and trench siting, the organisation of digging parties, the allotment of tasks, the correct methods of handling pick and shovel, and elementary methods of revetting, drainage, and the like. Further, it is good for every man to have some experience of what a heavy job of digging feels like, and the carrying of tools on the march.

As time went on, some companies deserted their original sites and tried their fortunes elsewhere; and when the Cadet Battalion took up the work as well, a considerable area of the Common near the Rifle Range became highly dangerous for ordinary traffic, especially at night. But no fresh development of training took place worth mentioning.

Incidentally, it may be mentioned that a fine neolithic axehead was turned up outside Haresfoot Park; and quite at the end of the Corps' stay at Berkhamsted, after the Armistice, a large deposit of Roman pottery was brought to light in the neighbourhood of Hill Farm, close to the sphere of operations of the Director of the British Museum, but after his departure.

(4) MAP READING.—Before the war, the use of maps was merely an accessory to Sunday reconnaissance walks or week-ends at Bisley, undertaken by the keener members of the Corps, or to the field operations conducted in the course of the annual camps. It was the same during the early days of the training at Berkhamsted. Field work was an important feature of both Company training and Battalion training; and the use of maps was an essential part of it. Men were required to have maps (the 1-inch uncoloured Ordnance map was the only one generally available), and instruction in the use of them was given incidentally rather than systematically. Owing, however, to the large number of recruits who had little or no previous experience in the use of maps, more methodical training became necessary, and in course of time it became a regular part of the curriculum, to which more and more importance was attached. As time went on, Company examinations in military knowledge were introduced; at first sporadically, then more generally, and in these map-reading took a prominent place; while in 1917 special instruction and examinations in map-reading were made a part of the final course, controlled by the Adjutant, for men who were about to pass from the Corps to a Cadet Battalion.

The following syllabus in use in one Company will indicate the scope of the instruction given. The exact sequence of some of the sections could be varied as convenient.

1. Scales.
2. Variation of compass.
3. Use of protractor.
4. Setting map.
5. Use of squared maps.
6. Conventional signs.
7. Compass: use of prism, setting for night work.
8. Indication of ground features:
    Spot levels, hachures, layers, contours and form-lines.
    V.I. and H.E.
    Salients and re-entrants.
    Convex and concave slopes.
    Visibility of points.
9. Map enlargements.

In special cases instruction was given in such subjects as reconnaissance maps, road traverses, panorama sketching, and the like; but these did not form part of the general course.

It will be seen that the primary object of the course was map-reading, not map-making. The latter, except in its roughest and most elementary form, is skilled work, which few officers will be called upon to undertake; the former is part of the essential training of every officer, the importance of which cannot be too much insisted upon. Every officer must be able (1) to find his way about by the help of the map and compass (including the use of the protractor), (2) to read from a contoured map the tactical features of the ground over which he may have to operate. Inquiries in France as to the kind of knowledge desirable for an officer almost invariably elicited answers including an emphatic reference to map-reading; and the two objectives just named were given a prominent place in the training at Berkhamsted.

The method of instruction was necessarily partly theoretical, in the lecture room, with plentiful use of the blackboard (and, in the case of one Company, of apparatus ingeniously designed by a skilful N.C.O.), and partly practical, in the field. The relative proportion of the two methods differed in different Companies, some devoting more time to lectures and some to practical instruction in the field. The results, as tested by examinations and by practical experience, were emphatically in favour of a preponderance of work in the field. A certain amount of preliminary explanation in the lecture room is essential; but the sooner men can be got into the country in small groups, each with a competent instructor, the sooner will they acquire real

THE COMPANY.

knowledge. Some men do not like to ask questions at a lecture; some do not take the trouble to do so; some, it is to be feared, slumber; some think they understand when they do not, and none can be said to have an assured grasp of the subject until they have practised it for themselves. Working with small groups, it is possible to cross-question each man, and to make each man take his turn in guiding the group across country, in identifying distant localities, in describing a piece of country from the map before it is reached, in taking a bearing from the map with the protractor, in handling a prismatic compass. Indeed, the use of the compass can *only* be really taught in small parties. A whole day, or, at the least, half a day, can be profitably spent in taking a company in small groups of eight or ten men over a considerable stretch of country, part at least of which will be unfamiliar to them. Tactical instruction, distance-judging, and a good deal of physical exercise can be combined with the use of the map and compass; and it was found that the majority of the men took great interest in the work and made marked progress in it. During the last year of the war, when a greater use of lectures was prescribed by higher authority, and a much more restricted time was allowed to practice in the field, the results were much less satisfactory.

During the first eighteen months the map in use, as mentioned above, was the 1-inch uncoloured Ordnance map, of which alone a considerable stock was available. The coloured edition, which is much easier to read quickly, was allowed to go out of print, and only a few fortunate individuals possessed copies of it. When, however, the use of squared maps became general in France, it was necessary to accustom recruits to the use of them, and at the same time to familiarise them with the scales which they would find in use when they went abroad. Accordingly, in 1916, by the kind permission of the Director-General of the Ordnance Survey, a special map of the Berkhamsted area was prepared by the well-known map publishers, Messrs. Sifton, Praed & Co., on the scale of 1 :40,000, and squared according to the system then in use in France* The map was produced by photographic enlargement from the Ordnance sheet, the contours being overprinted in red (with approximate form-lines at 50 ft. V.I.). Owing to the enlargement, the contour-lines were necessarily rather large, and the red colour made them conspicuous. For ordinary use this would be something of a defect, but for instructional purposes it was a clear advantage. Many beginners find the reading of contours a stumbling-block, and on the uncoloured Ordnance sheet care and patience are needed to follow them; but the strongly-printed contours of the Berkhamsted map, taken in conjunction with the very well marked features of this undulating country, made the study of the subject a much easier task.

In the last months of the war instruction was begun in the French system of co-ordinates, the use of which had been prescribed in France for the sake of uniformity among the Allied Armies. Negotiations were in progress with the Ordnance Survey for a map of Berkhamsted on this principle, but the Armistice fortunately averted the necessity for its adoption.

(5) MARCHING.—Marching for marching's sake was not much cultivated at Berkhamsted. Route marches were seldom ordered, except when the weather made any other form of work in the open air impossible. But marching as a means of getting to and from work was a not infrequent form of exercise, both in company training and still more in connection with Battalion field operations. During the first two years, as will be shown below, Battalion field days were frequent, and these involved a considerable amount of marching; when Battalion work was reduced, as it was during the last two years, marching was still done by Companies, though this also was limited by time-tables which restricted the hours available for continuous field work.

Route marches were never of excessive length, though sufficient to allow the Company or Battalion to settle down to the routine. The longest, which was only very occasionally undertaken, since it occupied practically the whole day, was that by Ashridge Park, Ringwood, the Beacon, Ivinghoe, and back by Tring or Aldbury, which amounted to about 17 miles; and any impression that this was a great achievement could be corrected by the Company Commander's reminder that this was about half the distance often covered by troops on manœuvres or active service, and that they had been carrying about half the active service load. Nevertheless, it cannot be said that the Corps at Berkhamsted lacked experience in marching, and they showed themselves well able to cover considerable distances with regularity and in good time.

March discipline was inculcated in lectures and observed in practice. The foundation of steady marching is observance of the regulation 120 paces to the minute (which, with the pace slightly more than the regulation length, as is natural with a Corps of this description, works out at not very much less than four miles an hour, excluding halts, on a good surface). This could be practised in Company work as well as when the whole Battalion was together, and could be applied however short the distance to be covered was. Guides were expected to check their step by reference to the watch at frequent intervals, and not to drop the pace more than was inevitable in ascending the hills, which are neither infrequent nor of very easy gradients round Berkhamsted. When a Company has learnt to keep the regulation rate without distress and as a matter of habit, the foundation of good marching is laid, and the actual distance covered will not trouble it, provided the men are in reasonably good training.

March discipline was also observed in the matter of regulated halts and intervals, and, of course, the formation of the column and adherence to the proper side of the road. In one respect the Corps did not come up to the best standards, and that was in singing, which as a rule was spasmodic and none too good. If men would take the trouble to learn the words of songs, and not merely fragments of choruses, singing on the march would be far more inspiring; and it is

---

*The idea of this map originated with Capt. Gompertz, Indian Army, then a Company Commander in the Inns of Court Cadet Battalion, and author of the series of articles in Blackwood's Magazine, entitled "Fallen Angels," embodying his experiences in that capacity; author also of the "Compendium Protractor," which many officers found useful.

THE COMPANY.

surprising what a large proportion of men can continue to sing contentedly with the beat on the wrong foot, or will attempt to march to rag-time.

A few marches probably linger in the recollections of those who took part in them. Such as a march by Gaddesden Row and Studham, in the course of which a forced march of an hour was prescribed, at a pace which was probably only enjoyed by two particularly long-legged Company Commanders. Or a concentration march by Companies to the ridge near Tring Park, facing Drayton Lodge, at which the outer Company, which had the longest route to cover, arrived, led by a distinguished barrister, heated both in body and in mind, at a pace of not much less than five miles an hour, in a gallant attempt to be punctual at the rendezvous. Or, most of all, a march in deep snow (known to some as " the retreat from Moscow ") by Tring and Ivinghoe and back over the Beacon; when some active spirits spent the luncheon halt in tobogganing down the sides of the Beacon with no seats other than those with which Nature (and the Government tailor) provided them; and when the Commander of the advance guard at one stage sent a message back that the road was blocked by deep drifts of snow, but nevertheless managed to negotiate them. Whatever may have been the feelings at the time of those whose feet or boots were unsound, " *et haec olim meminisse juvat.*"

(6) FIELD WORK.—Field work held a very high place in the philosophy of our first Commanding Officer. His belief, which was shared by many, at any rate, of his officers was that work in the field is of the utmost value in cultivating the intelligence of the men and instilling into them the qualities required in an officer. The orthodox and safe doctrine is, or at least was, that you must not run until you can walk (a doctrine contrary to the experience of every nursery); that training should for a long time be confined to the barrack square, to extended order drill, and to sealed-pattern attack practice; and that anything in the nature of field operations should be reserved for an advanced stage in training. It may be doubted whether this is sound educational theory at any time, and whether a long adherence to totally unreal conditions may not inculcate habits which are not merely useless but dangerous in real action, and take away the elasticity and resourcefulness which are among the most vital qualities in leaders. Certainly in the conditions under which the Corps was working for the first eighteen months or so, early and frequent resort to field work was essential. Officers were being clamoured for on all sides. Practically no machinery for the training of them existed except in the O.T.C.'s, and of these the University contingents were rapidly depleted through the absence of undergraduates. Until the establishment of Cadet Battalions, in 1916, nearly all the training work, outside the public schools, fell upon the Inns of Court and the Artists. The training was necessarily compressed into a few months to meet the urgent need for officers who should at least possess the rudiments of military knowledge, and it was necessary to adopt those methods which were most likely to develop quickly the qualities required in an officer.

In this respect field work has many advantages. It is interesting, and stimulates the fighting instinct. It helps the beginner to realise the nature of military operations. It gives opportunities, which can be widely extended, for individual initiative, whether as scout or messenger or observer or section or platoon leader. It cultivates an eye for ground. It exercises men in the task of leadership. Leadership is the end and aim of the training of an officer, and real progress in the acquisition of it can only come with actual practice. The lance-corporal who has led a handful of men in a patrol or an attack has begun to acquire the sense of responsibility and of power; and most men dated their conscious progress in an officer's qualities from the time when they first commanded a squad in the field.

Field work, consequently, was assiduously practised during the first two years. Normally there were two battalion field days in each week, apart from night operations (which will be dealt with separately). In addition, each Company practised attack and defence, advance and rearguards, wood fighting, reconnaissance and outposts, in such time as was available, and sometimes Company training took the place of a Battalion day. Battalion training is dealt with in an earlier chapter. Here it is only necessary to say that Battalion days were usually supplemented by Company lectures, in which the operations were described and discussed. It is not sufficient to explain the scheme to the Companies in advance, since much of the course of the operations remains obscure until the dispositions and movements of the two sides have been elucidated and compared. This took place at the officers' and N.C.O.'s pow-wow which immediately followed the operations; and it was the business of the Company officers to take the first opportunity of passing on the information so obtained to their men and of rubbing in the morals to be derived from it. Only so can the men get the full value of Battalion operations, and the combination in due proportions of lectures and field work is one of the chief problems of the training of officers.

Company training in field work was not confined to the exercise of the Company as such. It was also a most valuable instrument for practising the men in command. As the N.C.O.'s gained experience, they were given command of sections or platoons or half companies in field exercises, the officers (and sometimes the senior N.C.O.'s) accompanying them to observe, assist, and subsequently criticise. It is of the essence of such methods that the instructors should not interfere too much, but should allow the pupil to use his own initiative, reserving criticism until the operation is concluded. Sometimes, however, intervention is necessary in order to stimulate the pupil into activity, and to prevent the operation from ending in a fiasco, or from being unduly prolonged. It was not possible to give all men much opportunity of handling troops in the field; but that was the ideal, and the benefit derived from it in developing the qualities of command was universally recognised.

The instruction given was strictly in accordance with the principles laid down in the training manuals, which were used as the text-books for all lectures on tactical principles and methods. The training manuals, however, require amplification and illustration, and for this purpose many an officer pinned his faith on " Haking." The war must have

THE COMPANY.

been profitable, in other ways as well as in reputation, to that eminent General. No other handbook was in anything like such demand, or was regarded with such reverent devotion as the Midrash of the inspired text.

There are few parts of the country in a six-mile radius round Berkhamsted which the Inns of Court have not fought over. From Chipperfield to the Beacon, from Gaddesden Row and the Golden Parsonage to Cholesbury and the Danish Camp, all the ground is familiar. All the farms and villages are household words to those who spent their months or years of training there; and Potten End, Little Gaddesden, Nettleden, Hawridge, Haresfoot and Bourne Gutter are the Ypres, Arras, Cambrai and the Somme of their period of tutelage. Never before in England can the armed forces of the Crown have been so free to utilise the whole of a tract of country for the purpose of training; and if fences sometimes got broken, if gates were sometimes left open, if somebody's goat was attacked by one of the many dogs which attached themselves, with touching devotion, to the Corps' operations, if even a local magnate's last shoot on the 28th of February was spoilt, it will not be denied that the country got full value for it on the fields of France and Palestine.

(7) NIGHT OPERATIONS.—It may confidently be asserted that of all experiences connected with the training at Berkhamsted, night operations have left the most indelible memories. The Commanding Officer of the first two years had much faith in their value, and in the importance of familiarising troops with movements at night. Even in peace time they formed a recognised part of week-end programmes at Bisley, and at Berkhamsted they were cultivated with a strenuous energy (not wholly appreciated even by the Regular Adjutant) which earned the respect, but hardly the affection, of all. The programme prescribed one night of Company training and one of Battalion training per week, and no moderate amount of bad weather was allowed to interfere with it. Nor were the operations limited to an hour or two of walking about in the dark. On Company nights, it is true, you might expect to be back in camp on the right side of midnight; but Battalion operations, in the long, dark nights of winter, would begin at 6.30 and last until the small hours of the morning. Hertfordshire is not quite as muddy as Flanders, but the state of uniform and equipment after six or seven hours' wandering over all sorts of country, perhaps ending with a march back along the so-called " broad green track " across the Common, can be imagined by those who have had similar experience; and there was not much spare time to make them respectable before the Battalion parade which followed next (or rather the same) morning.

The elementary training was supposed to be given in the Companies. In them the work was not so far afield, and there was more definite instruction. Plenty of good ground existed in the neighbourhood. There was Kitchener's Field for elementary instruction in sights and sounds by night; for comparing the visibility of extended order, of lines, and of compact masses; for practising getting over fences, and the silent management of equipment. There was Haresfoot Park for practising changes of formation, dispersal and assembly, the ritual of keeping touch between units, and simple patrols or attacks. And there was the Common for movements over broken ground, and for all sorts of attack and outpost schemes. If a deeper shade than mere night was required, there was always Frithsden Beeches, for which some officers were supposed to have a special *penchant*. Compass marches could be practised anywhere—across the Common, through Frithsden Copse, or around Marlin Chapel and the adjoining Farm (where one straying squad was only discovered by its falling into the farmyard pond, thereby breaking the otherwise strictly observed silence).

Battalion operations carried us much further afield. Ashridge Park offered an endless variety of *terrain*, and infinite possibilities of losing oneself, especially when the fern was high. Old Park Lodge, which looked so suitable on the map to serve as G.H.Q. for operations in the northern part of the park, acquired an almost legendary notoriety for its elusiveness on a dark night, when all the valleys and folds in the ground seemed to come in different places from those which daylight revealed. It was no infrequent experience to have an attack on an outpost line timed to come off at 11 p.m.; and when allowance is made for the usual delays, for the collection of scattered forces after the fight, and the march back of several miles, it will be realised that it might often be two, or even three a.m. before camp or billet was reached. And always the last person to leave the rendezvous was the Commanding Officer, to whom every unit must report before marching off.

Apart from the more obvious lessons of night work, these Battalion operations were no small test of endurance. Dinner having been at 5 or 5.30, six or seven hours' exercise in the open air afforded a legitimate excuse for hunger; and it is not surprising that Companies could sometimes be located at night by the odour of chocolate or peppermint which surrounded them, or that cocoa or bovril, which many of our kind hosts most liberally provided, were extremely welcome on the return. It was often very cold, and not infrequently very wet, and in the unbroken silence everyone had plenty of time to think how he was enjoying it. Many will remember a long hour's halt on the Common, about midnight or later, on an exposed spot swept by a keen wind, while an unfortunate Second-in-Command searched for a certain narrow path; and how next day we were told that it was very good for our *moral*; which was perfectly true, but had not struck us so before. But most famous of all was a night, early in the first winter, when, after plunging through inky darkness on the further side of Haresfoot, and miraculously assembling beyond White Hill, the Corps stood in line along the side of a hedge in pouring rain for a mortal hour while the allotted guides, who were to head the advance on compass bearings taken during the day, rectified the errors due to two of them omitting to look at their compasses in the (erroneous) belief that they could find the way without; and to the third having neglected the difference between magnetic and true bearings. It is not surprising that when the attack on Newhouse Farm did come off, the defenders were found so paralysed by cold (or sleep) that nothing but the flashing of electric torches in their faces aroused them to a sense of the presence of their enemy. And the climax (subsequently known as the Retreat from Mons) was the return march, in which the Battalion was led by a confident Company Commander, as we subsequently realised, erroneously, round three sides of a square,

THE COMPANY.

through green lanes of an incredible muddiness and of an apparent length which subsequent reference to the Ordnance map did not confirm, before reaching the sound road four miles from home.

But no one will deny the utility of night training. It is of the first importance to get over the unfamiliarity with night sounds and sights which besets the town-bred man, and acquire some practice in finding one's way in the dark. The terrors of the dark disappear with habituation, and many an officer must have laid the foundations at Berkhamsted for the patrols in No-Man's-Land which formed a necessary part of the routine of France and Flanders.

Nor were the conditions always bad. Brilliant starlight nights gave opportunities for elementary instruction in astronomy, and there is a charm of its own in wandering by night through a great park or common. No doubt the officers had the best of it, being more free to regulate their own movements—the umpires and directors most of all; but there must be many who look back with some regret to the strenuous nights of Berkhamsted.

In the later years the glory of night operations declined. Subsequent Commanding Officers had less enthusiasm for them, and Battalion operations ceased to be. Company Commanders kept them up, but on a more restricted scale, and Old Park Lodge knew us no more. Still the attempt was made to familiarise every recruit with movement by night and the practice of night outposts. The last blow was the introduction of Summer time, for in the Summer months night operations were a mockery unless they began about the hour which passed for being 10 p.m., and that involved too great an intrusion on the hours of rest. So that in 1918 the practice of night work softly and silently faded away, not wholly regretted in less austere moments.

(8) BOMBING was, naturally, a development of the war. When the Colonel and one of his officers made a "Cook's tour" in France, in September, 1915, they visited the Bombing School of the Second Army at Cassel. At that time sixteen patterns of bombs were known, of which three were already obsolete. The supremacy of the Mills bomb was already fairly recognised, but it was little known in the front line trenches, where the "cricket ball" and "T and F" grenades (Nos. 6 and 7) seemed to be the commonest. Shortly afterwards, elementary instruction in bombing was begun at Berkhamsted, and many weird objects of the jam-tin nature were thrown (fortunately without explosives) on a pitch near the Potten End water-tower. Instruction was only systematised, and became a serious part of the training, when the Godstone Bombing School was established, and an officer and some N.C.O.'s went there for the course. Thereafter instruction in the mechanism and use of bombs and rifle-grenades was regularly given, and every man threw or discharged a small number of live bombs and rifle-grenades. The training, however, was regimental, and Company officers, though naturally present, were not responsible for it. In the last year of the war, a good range, replete with modern conveniences, was established on the Common, near Frithsden Beeches, and added materially to the risks of life in Berkhamsted. It may be set down to the credit of the instructors that no casualties occurred.

It may be added that the officer in charge of bombing made an almost complete museum of the various patterns of British bombs. Some French and German patterns were included. This collection is now installed in Lincoln's Inn.

(9) GAS.—Anti-gas instruction was taken into the course during the last two years, and every man was taught the ritual of putting on and wearing gas-helmets. A gas-chamber was established on the Common, and all men were passed through it. This also was extra-Company training, a special officer, with a staff of N.C.O.'s, being in charge of it.

(10) LEWIS GUN instruction has been dealt with under musketry. It was given regimentally, under the officer in charge of musketry, and was a popular and well-taught subject, owing much to the efficiency and enthusiasm of the instructors. The tactical combination of rifles, bombs, rifle-grenades and Lewis guns was taught in the Companies, in accordance with the principles laid down in S.S.143.

(11) PHYSICAL TRAINING AND BAYONET FIGHTING.—This was a comparatively late development, as in the Army generally. In the early part of the war, physical training was given in morning runs and the ample allowance of field work, and bayonet fighting was not practised at all. Systematic instruction came later, through the medium of instructors imported from outside, and in the last year or two it occupied an important place in the programme. It may be questioned whether the physical training was not overdone. Some men needed it; but many of the older men found it very exhausting, while the younger ones, fresh from school, hardly required such things as the "organised games." Nor can it be said that the stereotyped jests of the instructors were always edifying for an Officers' Training Corps. The whole subject belongs rather to the training of the man than of the officer, and consequently it acquired most prominence in the last months, when the training of the men as privates occupied the foreground.

Besides the outdoor work, which formed the main staple of the training, lectures played an important part. During the first year they were given under many difficulties, owing to the lack of accommodation. In Summer they could be given out-of-doors, if the weather was propitious; but when shelter was necessary, the Corps possessed no rooms. Halls attached to the Nonconformist Chapels were used in several cases, and the Corps was at one time much indebted to the Y.M.C.A. for leave to use their hut. Other lectures, including Battalion lectures, were given in the large mess-tents, where the Adjutant instructed us in the tactics of the Byzantine army, the type of underclothing most serviceable in the field, and other useful subjects. It was not until the Corps was able, out of the profits of the canteen, to build a large hut for each Company, that lectures were given under really comfortable conditions. Thereafter they formed a regular, instead of spasmodic, feature in the programme. One or two Company lectures a week were prescribed as an essential part of the curriculum, and Battalion lectures were given (after the Battalion had been reduced to something like the strength of a Battalion, instead of approximating to a Brigade) when the C.O. thought fit.

THE COMPANY.

Programmes of lectures were drawn up, but, like most programmes, they were better on paper than in practice. The orderly sequence would be broken up by the sudden intervention of a C.O.'s lecture; or a wet day would involve spending the greater part of the time in-doors, when the stock of lectures would be drawn on. Companies managed their lectures in their own way, but the following list will give some idea of the staple subjects:

Qualities needed for an officer or soldier (given normally when a new batch of recruits joined the Company).
Discipline.
Sanitation.
Musketry.
March Discipline.
Entrenchment.
Tactical principles.
Advance Guards (also Rear Guards and Flank Guards).
Outposts.
Attack.
Defence.
Trench Warfare.
Map-reading.
Scouting and Reconnaissance.
Night Operations.
Village and Wood Fighting.
Messages.
Wire Entanglements.
Military Law.
Principles of Strategy and Tactics, historically illustrated.
History of the war (especially from Mons to the Marne).

Several of the subjects obviously lent themselves to more than a single lecture, and in addition there were the lectures of the specialists on gas, bombs, etc.

Other indoor work included match drill (very useful as a first stage in training men in command, before they are actually put in charge of sections or platoons), knotting and lashing (occasional), and written examinations, which provided a useful check on the impressions of officers as to the progress of their men, and also demonstrated to the men the gaps in their knowledge. Physical exercise could also be practised to some extent indoors, when the weather made it necessary.

From the summary given in the previous pages, it will have been gathered that a distinction can be drawn between the work of the Corps during the first two years of the war and that of the last two years. This is not wholly due to the change of Commanding Officer in September, 1916. A difference in principle was introduced by the institution of Officer Cadet Battalions, which came into effect that year. Previously it was the duty of the Corps to cover the whole ground between the civilian's entry into the Army and his appointment to a commission in a combatant unit. Subsequently he only received the first part of his training in the Corps, from which he passed to an O.C.B. for the completion of his education. The Army, which at first had no system for the training of the mass of officers required for the greatly expanded Territorial Force and the New Army, had now formulated a course of education. More time was available, and many more instructors; and in the last year of the war it even took in hand the training of instructors. Consequently the pressure on the Corps became less; more stress was laid upon the elementary work, and the Corps was more required to work according to a fixed programme.

Under this system the subjects of instruction remained the same, but the distribution of time among them was altered. Field work was considerably reduced. Battalion field days became rare, and ultimately disappeared altogether, except for an occasional day with some of the public schools. Battalion drills were restricted mainly to ceremonial, simple movements, and arms drill. The hours were more strictly parcelled out to the different subjects, which limited the possibilities of distant excursions into the country. Night operations were reduced both in frequency and in duration, and in Summer became almost impossible through the institution of Summer time. Entrenchment was reduced to a minimum, though a good deal of time was spent in the construction of a few elaborate pattern works, with, it is to be feared, only small profit to those concerned in the manufacture. Marching was less attended to as the opportunities for practising it became less.

On the other hand, Company drill retained its full importance. Musketry, though somewhat curtailed in the matter of theory, became more prominent in the practical matters of position, handling of arms, and firing on the range. Map-reading was taught more systematically and with more uniformity. Bombing and gas-training came in as new and important elements. Field work consisted mainly of Company exercises in advance and reargards, outposts, and attack, including the new formations and tactics introduced in 1918.

In one other respect a difference must also be noted, namely a fuller education in the routine of the internal organisation of both Company and Battalion. It was unquestionably useful to men who were about to become officers in ordinary units to be familiarised with the routine of orderly-room administration. Methods which were quite sufficient for the administration of the Corps in itself did not educate men in the methods required for an ordinary Battalion.

THE COMPANY.

Crime sheets were a novelty to us, with which it was necessary that we should become acquainted; though it is to be feared that Company Commanders never quite came up to the standard expected of them in the production of an adequate supply of criminals.

But with all these changes in the method and details of work, there was, at any rate at first, no change in the underlying principle of the Corps, namely that its duty was to prepare men to be officers. Company Commanders in 1917, as before, still aimed at the training of men in command, and tried to teach them the things which an officer ought to know, and to inspire them with the spirit which an officer ought to have. During the last year, no doubt, increasing stress was laid on the training of men as privates; but it may be hoped that they were never allowed to forget that they were learning to be privates in order that they might learn to be officers.

It would be wrong to conclude this sketch of the principles and methods of Company training at Berkhamsted without reference to one vital element in it, namely the work done by the Company-Sergeant-Majors and Quartermaster-Sergeants. It was not merely that an immense amount of orderly-room work fell upon their shoulders, of which they loyally took the burden, to the relief of the Company Commander; but to them was in great measure due the whole spirit and tone of the Company. A good Sergeant-Major and Quartermaster-Sergeant made a good Company; and no Company Commander can ever forget the debt he owed to the friends and colleagues who served with him in these capacities, and to whom a great part of the credit of the work of the Company is due. The type of Warrant Officer and permanent N.C.O. which the Corps carried on from before the war until its fourth year was an immeasurable source of strength to it and of benefit to the men who served in it.

But it was the Company Officer, and especially the Company Commander, who had the best of everything. High enough in the regimental hierarchy to be in a position of authority and of some independence, yet not so high as to be immersed in regimental organisation and paper work, he enjoyed, more than anyone else, the human side of the training. Company work means companionship, and of that he had the full flavour. Company officers made scores and hundreds of friends among the men who passed through their platoons and companies, and they cherish the hope that these friendships will not be forgotten in after life. It is true that it would require a superhuman memory always to recognise at once, in the mufti of civilian life, men whom one knew for a few months in the not always becoming garb of a private in the days when the Clothing Department was not wholly equal to the demands upon it, and whose expressions have since been changed by the experiences which they have gone through as officers at the Front; but every old officer of the Corps is glad to have recalled to his memory the names of those who served with him at Berkhamsted, and to revive recollections of that time of strenuous preparation for the sterner ordeals which the men who passed through the Corps went away to face, and from which so many of them never returned.

F. G. K.

Chapter XII.

THE RANK AND FILE.

What were the chief thoughts, what are the most enduring recollections, of the 12,000 rank and file of the Inns of Court? Can anyone now write these down and not be sure that he is not merely multiplying himself by 10,000? And had not each one of us, however short his stay at Berkhamsted, many " selves " and many " chief thoughts "?

The writer's stay lasted from 1915 to a few months before the Armistice, when he terminated an inglorious career by being " relegated "—a dustbin sort of word—to the Reserve. He thus served under the three C.O.'s and the three R.S.M.'s, and the Adjutants during the period were, as the newspapers say, both numerous and varied. Perhaps the fact of his not attaining commissioned rank throughout this time gave him some advantages in becoming acquainted with the point of view of the rank and file. Broadly speaking, that point of view falls into three periods coinciding with the tenure of the Commanding Officers. The first, by far the most adventurous and still (to the writer) the most vivid of these periods, merged gradually into the second. The last, in this case, is the least.

The dominating figure, for the rank and file, during the first period was undoubtedly that of the Regimental-Sergeant-Major. The C.O. was, of course, both technically and effectively the Commanding Officer, and his influence pervaded the whole Corps. We scanned his face as attentively as the position of attention allowed, to see if the twinkling eye were on parade, and we knew him as the master of the quiet but terribly effective " tick off," as the student of military history who could damn our feeble tactics by an apt quotation from Napoleon, and as the stern (but fair) judge at " Orders." But his presence was (for us) felt rather than seen, while Burns was everywhere. It was he who from the outset gave us, as raw recruits, a really just idea of our unworthiness to be members of the Corps, and of his great and singular condescension in instructing us. It was he who first expounded to us the great truth that although we might (such pranks Fate played) become lieutenants, or even captains and majors, we should not, we could not, become a real R.S.M. His was the voice which spread desolation all over K.'s field, and his the eye that seemed by a fatality to light on us cowering in the rearest of rear ranks on parade, and that perceived in the darkest corner of Charles Street a chilled hand straying into a great coat pocket. But we were proud of him, and if he was not a member of the Corps in the ordinary way, he was at least one " by adoption and grace." And if he affected to set his own valuation at a high figure, let it be placed on record that a fellow-private solemnly assured another that the R.S.M. was a member of the Army Council! He might have been—certainly he was the best representative of the Regular Army that some of us, especially those to whom he imparted the tricks of the trade, ever met, before, during, or after the war.

It is hard to explain the attitude of the rank and file towards those set over them. " Discipline," in the regular Army sense, doesn't suffice. " Affection " sounds inappropriate, though it largely explains the attitude of the learned No. 1 Company to their C.S.M., as well as the feeling which the tumultuous Irish-Lancastrian No. 5 entertained for O'B. Looking back, one recurs again to the overworked expression *esprit de corps;* we all " belonged," and that is possibly the explanation. Everyone, from C.O. down to the drummer boy, wore the Corps badge, and though perhaps some of us were rather hazy about the functions or the history of the Inns, we were firmly convinced that we were the custodians of a great tradition. The tradition was kept alive up to the end—there was, we knew, a jealous guardian in the Q.M. Store, and another, we suspected, in a more exalted shed, and although we took some of our " attached " folk to our hearts, the presence or absence of our badge was a thing of significance.

The strongest impression of the early days was an extremely pleasant and exhilarating sense of fellowship, a fellowship which, inexplicably perhaps to the Regular Army mind, was compatible with real discipline, and was perhaps the cause of real discipline. We all, from the C.O. down to the newest recruit, " belonged," as the children say. We were all animated by a common purpose, and we all had an intense pride in the Corps; and the things that we had in common were far more potent than the differences, the artificial differences, of rank. A Company officer, his sergeant-major and a lance-corporal could foregather in billets, but this was entirely " without prejudice " to their attitude on parade, and no one watching them there would suspect the relationship. Both on and off parade—and the conduct of troops when not under their officers' eye is the real test of discipline—the right things would be done because we wanted to do them, and we ought to do them; and the wrong things were not done, because " Inns of Court " didn't do such things. There was no need to invoke the penalties of the Army Act or K.R.; we had greater sanctions than these. I do not imply that we were solemn prigs or tame " good boys." There was larking and ragging—of the harmless type—in abundance. Each new lance-jack had to learn that one of the arts of authority is not to be too sensitive to public opinion. Even the great ones were subjected, in the privacy of our tents, to minute and discriminating criticism. There were many versions, more or less humorous, of the proportion which the moral bore to the physical; pointed comments on the value of long route marches in the snow and of our Herculean

THE RANK AND FILE.

"Night Ops," vivid amateur criticisms of our tactical schemes, and parodies of a famous lecture on Discipline. There was plenty of grousing, too, of a good humoured sort, but it was the grousing in which it is the Englishman's privilege to indulge. It was rarely serious and never had the note of real bitterness which came later on.

The training has been dealt with by other hands, but it may be of interest to put on record some impressions from the point of view of the "toad beneath the harrow." To train, in a short time, with miserably insufficient apparatus and few instructors, a vastly swollen Battalion of men to become officers was a formidable task, and the record of the Corps shows how it was accomplished. Our officers and instructors did their share and we did ours, largely by dint of common sense and asking questions. Of the filthiness of gas warfare, I knew (and still know) little. For a long time the material for bombing instructions was limited to cocoa and Swiss-milk tins plugged with earth. It was not until later years that the apparatus for these and kindred "stunts" were doled out by the War Office, and by that time the training was almost entirely the training of private soldiers rather than of officers.

Not that the essentials were neglected. Our drill, for instance, was from beginning to end something to brag about. There was a kind of furious pride in Battalion drill. Violent exertions were required after the dark and strenuous deeds of Friday night, to be ready and clean for the Saturday morning. Then ensued convolutions and evolutions which, as H. used to announce, "recalled the worst excesses of the French Revolution." The Gargantuan Battalion might "drill as a Brigade," or, in extended order, fill K.'s spacious field to overflowing, or wheel itself round and around like a tremendous top, but though we were jig-sawed into patterns that would puzzle a Chelsea course to distraction, everything would come right in the end—how, I don't even now quite understand. By 1918, "C.O.'s Parade" had lost its powers to awe or impress. "The Battalion will drill as a Squad" was the order, and those of us, now "old soldiers" in more than one sense, who looked on from cover on the high ground *suave mari magno turbantibus*, at the endless "sloping" and "presenting," would grant that the show wasn't bad, but our minds would travel back, and we would recall the splendid crashes that our "D.P's.," good for little else, would make at "manual," or, as the revised version had it, at "arms exercise."

Of the practical value of our field work I am not in a position to speak at first hand, though more than one old Corps man has told me how he applied with success on the Menin Road or in the fighting at Arras the lessons he learnt at Potten End and Whelpley Hill. Battalion field days we approached as a continual venture. If you had a motor cycle and a job as an orderly, it was a joyous adventure. But even lacking this, there were all kinds of possibilities. You might, for instance, find yourself suddenly placed in command of a section or a platoon or even of a company. Then you learned, in the bitter school of experience, why things went wrong in a battle, the importance of information ("even negative," as the book says), and of keeping in touch, and how terribly exhausting a ten-mile rearguard action might be to heavily laden men, sustained on bread and cheese, and regretting the Corps cake they had thrown away. Certainly one learned things. I recall T. pointing out suavely, but very effectively, that fire orders lustily given and cheerfully acted on were not likely to produce the maximum of results if the sights were not adjusted, and I remember, too (but must not set it down) how my Company Commander lost entirely his anxious Company. Of course, you might more frequently be a mere "man" (as distinguished from an officer), and your lot might be to tramp round the Beacon in the snow or attack it on a boiling Summer day, and in either case your opinion of the training would be tinged with bias. But here again the Gods might be kind, and there are worse things in life than being "reserves" beside a sunny hedge for hours on end, and realizing with no sense of deprivation that you will probably not share the glory of battle. And if you cared, these excursions gave you heaps of practice in comparing the ground with the map, an art which cannot be taught by lectures, and which nearly vanished when our activities became confined entirely to K.'s field, and men spoke of the Monument and Gaddesden as if they were places over the seas.

Wherever two or more old Corps men—I mean men of the first era—get together, the talk will inevitably turn on "Night Ops," and the questions will stream out. Do you remember? Do you remember the night when we were exhorted to "be statuesque": the night when No. 5 (or was it 3 or 4—No. 1 was too well behaved, and it was always safe to charge 5) the night when X (shall we say) started coughing on Northchurch Common; the night (or nights) when we *couldn't* find the old Park Lodge at Ashridge and swore it must have been moved; the night when an active scout found Sergeant Z not only missing, but engaged in gentle dalliance; the night when you didn't mind being on guard; the nights when the Gods were besought to make the weather impossible, and the nights (too few) when they complied, and triumphant howls went up from the mess sheds? This is the type of question which is asked and answered and capped with another. The terrors of "Night Ops" were instilled into us at the depôt, and by the old hands when we arrived. (The old hands, by the way, "went sick"—or tried to—"in large numbers" on Friday mornings.) Were they really terrible? One man I know, once said he liked them, but as he liked guards too, he was merely regarded as eccentric. For some, the fortunate few who could sleep soundly in a dry ditch on the coldest of cold nights, the hardship was relatively slight. Boredom was, I suppose, their chief characteristic for us of the rank and file—the boredom of forsaking a warm fire and a pipe, to be marched off, we knew not whither, to perform we knew not what (for the "scheme" rarely trickled in an intelligible form, below the Section Commanders). And what aggravated the burden was the fact that we couldn't even grouse! (The coughing fit at Northchurch was, I suspect, the consequence of a suppressed grouse.) We admitted, of course, that it was to the credit of the C.O. that he himself always turned out, though we thought that such devotion to duty was possibly a little too heroic. We knew, too, that he attached high importance to the training, less on account of its instructional than for its moral value. We almost admitted that he might be right. But still . . . . . .

THE RANK AND FILE.

In retrospect we can admit that "Night Ops" *had* an educational value. They comprised all that the books had said of the difficulties of manœuvres in the dark. They taught this and more. How difficult to find at 1 p.m. the "i" of Grim's Ditch (G.26.d.3020); the nocturnal habits of the fauna of Ashridge; the close resemblance of a cigarette-end to a glow-worm; the places where it was inadvisable to lie down—these are some of them. D, whose knowledge of astronomy was aforetime deplorably weak, confessed that it was at Friday Street Farm that the great truth first flashed into his brain that "the stars go round." Many learned the virtues of black peppermints for the first time.

Striking as were the topsy-turvy conditions brought about by the war, in no other regiment could the elements have been more strangely mixed. It goes without saying that the law was well represented, and it is not surprising that a barrister Corporal of several years' standing would find himself saluting a junior recently called (but whom his company deemed as K.C.). There cannot have been many R.Q.M.S. in the Army who amused themselves with turning K.R. into iambics or sergeants who quoted *In Catilinam* to clumsy recruits, but they flourished at Berkhamsted. It was embarrassing, until you got into the way of it, to instruct an eminent mathematician on the meaning of trajectory and observe his puzzled look as you "explained" the drift of the bullet; to initiate a surveyor into the mysteries of the Ordnance map was also a task requiring courage, but it was done, and discipline did not suffer. This galaxy of talent would in normal times have played havoc with the scheme of things; surely never before were official regulations scrutinised with such keenness, or their diction, or their meaning, criticised so acutely. Our meanest logician could show that a regulation was capable of any interpretation you pleased, and that to carry it out, as written, violated the law of contradictions; our mathematical sergeant made hay of the arithmetical explanations set out in manuals. Our accomplishments were not, however, all employed to such purposes. I have known lance-corporals who whiled away wet days of musketry with marvellous card tricks ("and with such tiny hands"). S, his malodorous duties done, seated on a box, would play rag-time in a way that really justified its invention. Our professional singers and actors gave us their best things and received in return admiration never excelled at the Queen's Hall or the West End theatres. I knew but one ventriloquist, and that was enough. He severely compromised the discipline of two platoons before he was discovered, and the number of undeserved reprimands of which he was the cause, made him unpopular. Our Mess Steward, too, was unique. How Mr. and Mrs. Daborn dealt with the needs of the roaring multitude of 1915 was, and remains, a miracle, though perhaps not so much of one as the skill with which they manipulated, in the lean days, the eternal diet of rabbits and dubious sausages, or with which they charmed peppery Brigadiers with subtle advocacy, both verbal and culinary. Many guards must hold their memory dear.

Most of what I have written has been concerned with what I call the first period. The second (or transitory) period, though lacking the sense of adventure of the first, was pleasant in its way. There was a good deal of the momentum of our traditions carried on to it, as we were now, in a sense, the "spoiled darlings" of the War Office. Apparatus was plentiful, our numbers were manageable, and though our field work was much more modest in its scope, we fared abroad over a rather limited area. Our pleasures were organized as thoroughly as our work; our Company sing-songs gave way to arranged concerts and plays, and our Band played us to and from church. The feverish activity in the polishing of leather is perhaps one of the significant symbols of this time. An extremely clipped fashion in hair was another.

Of the last period I do not feel that I want to say much. I was detached most of the time for special work and got somewhat out of touch. The Corps went marching on. The recruits were younger now, and most of the old hands had gone, but on the whole, and in spite of difficulties, the traditions of the Corps persisted. There was still nothing quite like the Devil's Own. With the youngsters came some older men, and it was one of these who slightly irritated us by his complaint of our messing arrangements. He, it was, too, who asked for his batman, and when one (an attached C.S.M.) was indicated, received a liberal education in the vigorous use of the mother tongue as well as an introduction to non-classical Hindustani.

"Berko" has now reverted to its position of a quiet country town—so quiet that one of its most famous residents who took up his abode during our stay, declares that he was lured there under false pretences. Many of the military tailors who supplied convertible tunics, and the other necessaries of dandy subs have vanished. The genial artist who posed many squads and camp parties before the camera, now exhibits studies of bird, and beast, and flower; and the "King's Hipe" is now monopolised by motorists. All the scars in K.'s field have long healed and pheasants strut about where the old "Instrucker" had its great fights in the snow. Only on the Common are the visible remnants of trenches and dug-outs, and these will soon go unless, as a sort of "Grim's Ditch," they remain to puzzle local antiquaries in centuries to come. An old Corps man will come away with mixed feelings from the old scenes, for our "Roll of Honour" is a long one. But it was a great privilege to be a member of the Inns of Court, and to have known such men as we had.

E. D.

Chapter XIII.

THE BILLET.

"Bedridden," originally contributed by Mr. W. W. Jacobs to the "Hades Herald" of August, 1916, and reproduced by his kind permission.

July 12, 1915.—Disquieting rumours to the effect that the epidemic of Billetitis, hitherto confined to the north of King's Road, shows signs of spreading.

July 14.—Report that two Inns of Court men have been seen peeping over my gate.

July 16.—Informed that soldier of agreeable appearance and charming manners requests interview with me. Took a dose of Phospherine and went. Found composite photograph of French, Joffre, and Hindenburg waiting for me in the hall. Smiled (he did, I mean) and gave me the mutilated form of salute reserved for civilians. Introduced himself as Quartermaster-Sergeant Beddem*, and stated that the Inns of Court O.T.C. was going under canvas next week. After which he gulped. Meantime could I take in *a* billet. Questioned as to what day the Corps was going into camp, said that he believed it was Monday, but was not quite sure—might possibly be Tuesday. Swallowed again and coughed a little. Accepted billet and felt completely rewarded by smile. Q.M.S. bade me good-bye, and then with the air of a man suddenly remembering something, asked me whether I could take two. Excused myself and interviewed my C.O. behind the dining-room door. Came back and accepted. Q.M.S. so overjoyed (apparently) that he fell over the scraper. Seemed to jog his memory. He paused, and gazing in absent fashion at the topmost rose on the climber on the porch, asked whether I could take three! Added hopefully that the third was only a boy. Excused myself Heated debate with C.O. Subject: Sheets. Returned with me to explain to the Q.M.S. He smiled. C.O. accepted at once, and, returning smile, expressed regret at size and position of bedrooms available. Q.M.S. went off swinging cane jauntily.

July 17.—Billets arrived. Spoke to them about next Monday and canvas. They seemed surprised. Strange how the military authorities decline to take men into their confidence merely because they are privates. Led them upstairs. They went (for first and last time) on tiptoe.

July 18.—Saw Q.M.S. Beddem in the town. Took shelter in the King's Arms.

Aug. 3.—Went to Cornwall.

Aug. 31.—Returned. Billets received me very hospitably.

Sept. 4.—Private Budd, electrical engineer, dissatisfied with appearance of bell-push in dining-room, altered it.

Sept. 5.—Bells out of order.

Sept. 6.—Private Merited, also an electrical engineer, helped Private Budd to repair bells.

Sept. 7.—Private Budd helped Private Merited to repair bells.

Sept. 8.—Privates Budd and Merited helped each other to repair bells.

Sept. 9.—Sent to local tradesman to put my bells in order.

Sept. 15.—Told that Q.M.S. Beddem wished to see me. Saw C.O. first. She thought he had possibly come to take some of the billets away. Q.M.S. met my approach with a smile that reminded me vaguely of picture-postcards I had seen. Awfully sorry to trouble me, but Private Montease, just back from three weeks' holiday with bronchitis, was sleeping in the wood-shed on three planks and a tin-tack. Beamed at me and waited. Went and bought another bedstead.

Sept. 16.—Private Montease and a cough entered into residence.

Sept. 17, 11.45 p.m.—Maid came to bedroom-door with some cough lozenges which she asked me to take to the new billet. Took them. Private Montease thanked me, but said he didn't mind coughing. Said it was an heirloom; Montease cough, known in highest circles all over Scotland since time of Young Pretender.

Sept. 20.—Private Montease installed in easy-chair in dining-room with touch of bronchitis, looking up trains to Bournemouth.

Sept. 21.—Private Montease in bed all day. Cook anxious "to do her bit" rubbed his chest with home-made embrocation. Believe it is some stuff she rubs chests in hall with. Smells the same anyway.

Sept. 24.—Private Montease, complaining of slight rawness of chest, but otherwise well, returned to duty.

Oct. 5.—Cough worse again. Private Montease thinks that with care it may turn to bronchitis. Borrowed an A.B.C.

Oct. 6.—Private Montease relates uncanny experience. Woke up with feeling of suffocation to find an enormous black-currant and glycerine jujube wedged in his gullet. Never owned such a thing in his life. Seems to be unaware that he always sleeps with his mouth open.

---

*Q.M.S. Redden, of No. 2 Company, for 20 years a member of the Corps.

THE BILLET.

Nov. 14.—Private Bowser, youngest and tallest of my billets, gazetted.

Nov. 15, 10.35 a.m.—Private Bowser in tip-top spirits said good-bye to us all.

10.45.—Told that Q.M.S. Beddem desired to see me. Capitulated. New billet, Private Early, armed to the teeth, turned up in the evening. Said that he was a Yorkshireman. Said that Yorkshire was the finest country in England, and Yorkshiremen the finest men in the world. Stood toying with his bayonet and waiting for contradiction.

Jan. 5, 1916.—Standing in the garden just after lunch was witness to startling phenomenon. Q.M.S. Beddem came towards front-gate with a smile so expansive that gate after first trembling violently on its hinges swung open of its own accord. Q.M.S., with smile (sad), said he was in trouble. Very old member of the Inns of Court, Private Keen, had rejoined, and he wanted a good billet for him. Would cheerfully give up his own bed, but it wasn't long enough. Not to be outdone in hospitality by my own gate, accepted Private Keen. Q.M.S. digging hole in my path with toe of right boot, and for first and only time manifesting signs of nervousness, murmured that two life-long friends of Private Keen's had rejoined with him. Known as the Three Inseparables. Where they were to sleep, unless I——. Fled to house, and locking myself in top-attic, watched Q.M.S. from window. He departed with bent head and swagger-cane reversed.

Jan. 6.—Private Keen arrived, Turned out to be son of an old Chief of mine. Resolved not to visit the sins of the father on the head of a child six feet two high and broad in proportion.

Feb. 6.—Private Keen came home with a temperature.

Feb. 7.—M.O. diagnosed influenza. Was afraid it would spread.

Feb. 8.—Warned the other four billets. They seemed amused. Pointed out that influenza had no terrors for men in No. 2 Company, who were doomed to weekly night ops. under Major Carryon.

Feb. 9.—House strangely and pleasantly quiet. Went to see how Private Keen was progressing, and found the other four billets sitting in a row on his bed practising deep-breathing exercises.

Feb. 16th.—Billets on night ops. until late hour. Spoke in highest terms of Major Carryon's marching powers—also in other terms.

March 3.—Waited up until midnight for Private Merited, who had gone to Slough on his motor-bike.

1.5 a.m.—Awakened by series of explosions from over-worked, or badly-worked, motor-bike. Put head out of window and threw key to Private Merited. He seemed excited. Said he had been chased all the way from Chesham by a pink rat with yellow spots. Advised him to go to bed. Set him an example.

1.10 a.m.—Heard somebody in the pantry.

2.10 a.m.—Heard Private Merited going upstairs to bed.

2.16 a.m.—Heard Private Merited still going upstairs to bed.

2.20-3.15 a.m.—Heard Private Merited *getting to* bed.

April 3, 12.30 a.m.—Town-hooter announced Zeppelins and excited soldier called up my billets from their beds to go and frighten them off. Pleasant to see superiority of billets over the hooter: that only emitted three blasts.

12.50 a.m.—Billets returned with exception of Private Merited, who was retained for sake of his motor-bike.

9 a.m.—On way to bath-room ran into Private Merited, who, looking very glum and sleepy, inquired whether I had a copy of the " Exchange and Mart " in the house.

10 p.m.—Overheard billets discussing whether it was worth while removing boots before going to bed until the Zeppelin scare was over. Joined in discussion.

May 2.—Rumours that the Inns of Court were going under canvas. Discredited them.

May 5.—Rumours grow stronger.

May 6.—Billets depressed. Begin to think perhaps there is something in rumours after all.

May 9.—All doubts removed. Tents begin to spring up with the suddenness of mushrooms in fields below Berkhamsted Place.

May 18, LIBERATION DAY.—Bade a facetious good-bye to my billets; response lacking in bonhomie.

May 19.—House delightfully quiet. Presented caller of unkempt appearance at back-door with remains of pair of military boots, three empty shaving-stick tins, and a couple of partially bald tooth-brushes.

May 21.—In afternoon went round and looked at camp. Came home smiling, and went to favourite seat in garden to smoke. Discovered Private Early lying on it fast asleep. Went to study. Private Merited at table writing long and well-reasoned letter to his tailor. As he said he could never write properly with anybody else in the room, left him and went to bath-room. Door locked. Peevish but familiar voice, with a Scotch accent, asked me what I wanted; also complained of temperature of water.

May 22.—After comparing notes with neighbours, feel deeply grateful to Q.M.S. Beddem for sending me the six best men in the Corps.

July 15.—Feel glad to have been associated, however remotely and humbly, with a Corps, the names of whose members appear on the Roll of Honour of every British regiment.

Chapter XIV.

CONCLUSIONS.

There is no deep mystery about the training of an officer. As in all other professions, his training must have relation to the object in view. To be successful at the Bar, a man requires self-confidence, the art of self-production, a good memory, and quick assimilation. Success, in one branch at least of the medical profession, needs much the same qualities, though, I understand, some knowledge of medicine is almost indispensable. In neither profession is much attention paid during the preliminary training to these necessary attributes, and consequently there are many failures; but in such case, speaking generally, failure only involves the man himself. In the military profession, failure is paid for in the lives of others, and, except in the higher military circles, spurious qualities and attainments crumble at the acid test of war. The object, therefore, of an officer's training must necessarily be to equip him mentally and physically to play his part in the realities of war, and for this purpose it is indispensable to consider the men he will have to command.

Perhaps the most curious feature of the late war was the psychology of the British, and particularly the English soldier. Though drawn from different classes, he maintained his traditional virtues and weaknesses. His furious tenacious courage was beyond all praise, and really saved our share in the war from failure; but he was more formidable in defence than in attack, and required a lot of leading. In no previous war was he so well looked after; he repaid it by his exemplary behaviour, which, located as he mostly was in a friendly country, proved of the greatest possible value to the allied cause.

Of conscious patriotism he showed little trace: his astounding *moral* was founded on the incomprehensibility of his being really beaten. I believe the key to his strength as to his weakness to be the comparatively large amount of individual liberty, implying a developed sense of justice which we have for many centuries enjoyed in this country. Defence or retirement leaves a good deal to the individual, and there he is strong; attack requires intelligent concerted action, and there he is weak. To be beaten means either that the other man has a better case, or that you are being unjustly treated. The British soldier resents, and will not admit defeat, because he can not imagine himself in the wrong, and it seems to him unjust that he should be so treated. Purely as a soldier, he may be inferior to the better educated German, and the more quick-witted Frenchman, but in *moral* he is supreme; and, fortunately for us, the war developed into a struggle in *moral*. Still he is difficult to command in modern war, and will remain so until the general standard of education is considerably raised: he needs both actual leading and much looking after, matters often incompatible with command. While, therefore, the capacity to control, which means character, must always take the foremost place in the training of an officer, the capacity to direct, which means knowledge, has to be exercised under peculiar difficulties, and therefore requires a high development.

Putting aside patriotic prejudice, we have little reason to be satisfied with our share in the late war. Germany, blockaded by sea and fighting on two fronts against armies superior in man power and material, more than held her own for nearly four years, brought Russia to its knees, and finally succumbed in a contest of *moral*. We had the more dependable allies, and during some two years had on the Western Front a large superiority in men and guns. Owing to sea power the whole strategic field was open to us, and frontal attacks in the west were in no way imposed on us as on Germany. Yet we were within almost a few yards of losing the war, and our triumph only came when America threw her gigantic shadow over the arena, and the German *moral* snapped. Given our superiority we ought to have won the war in 1916 or 1917, and certainly should not have nearly lost it in 1918. To blame the politicians is merely to raise a smoke cloud; the men and material were there, clearly the officers were the real cause of failure, and in this connection the regular officer, occupying as he did all the higher posts, cannot escape the greater blame.

There must be something lacking in the training of our regular officers to account for our non-success in civilised warfare. No one can look back to the Crimea, or the South African war as instances of successful leading or command; in both we muddled through after a disproportionate expenditure of men and money. We have done the same again, and with a very narrow margin of safety. The root of the evil is, perhaps, the national distrust of theory. Instead of founding ourselves on sound doctrine, or thinking things out beforehand, we prefer to learn by experience, and in modern war the price is becoming prohibitive. Never again are we likely to be able to use men and money so lavishly, or to proceed so leisurely in learning war first in the field. Excuses will always be made, and it is said that the new officer, and not the regular officer, was at fault. It is sufficient, however, to take the first months of the war, while the regular army was practically alone in the field; a regular army of long-service men, most of whose officers had some war experience, confronted by a much more numerous army, but composed of men of two years' service, and officered by officers of no war experience at all. Apart from the bravery shown by all ranks, there is not much matter for military satisfaction either in the retreat through a friendly and fertile country in summer weather, or the return from the Marne. So far as can be ascertained at present, they leave a general impression of want of grip and concerted action, combined

CONCLUSIONS.

with the over-confidence in ourselves and the under estimation of both the enemy and our allies which have become almost the hall-mark of the British Army.

The best sort of British regular officer is of the salt of the earth, but it is doubtful whether he does not become so in spite of, and not as the result of, his training. He is caught young, and at Sandhurst is licked into shape, in his regiment he is further licked into shape, and from that day he leads the life of his regiment, and not his own; the amount of serious work he does, his amusements, his social relations, even his modes of expression are all in fact governed by his regiment. Within the four corners of that life he can move so easily that he does not realise its limitations, and he becomes a creature of routine in the wider sense without knowing it. The results, too apparent in the late war, are a lack of real discipline, by which I mean self-control when the regimental pressure has ceased; the absence of any public conscience, which was one of the causes of the incredible waste that prevailed; and a certain readiness to stagnate in professionalism rather than learn from without.

It was in ethics he failed, really in ability to rise to the occasion. It must be remembered, however, that modern war, as we waged it, means the survival of the unfittest; and the regular officer was generally placed in positions far above those he would have normally occupied. Of officers who seriously study their profession, whether at the Staff College or elsewhere, there were not enough to go round. The ordinary officer, though he works harder than before the South African War, does not study the theory of his profession, or the teaching and practice of other armies; he makes a good Company officer as regards the care and training of his men, but in more responsible positions he is not on the heights, and his training should be the first matter to be taken into account in any re-organisation of the regular Army. It seems worthy of question whether he should not be taken in older, and whether a University degree in special subjects might not usefully take the place of Sandhurst. Possibly even his exclusively regimental life might be modified. It is dangerous to question the sanctity of the military domestic hearth, and no one doubts the importance of *esprit de corps;* but even *esprit de corps,* supremely important as it is, can only be a means to an end, and it has rather tended to become an idol in itself. No doubt the present system has many advantages, particularly in view of our numerous small wars; it gives us a virile type of officer, well qualified to get the best in bravery out of the class of man who joins the regular Army, and to impose his personality on native troops; it is not a system to be hastily changed, or even amended without a great deal of thinking, and it is only dealt with here because the training of the regular officer re-acts on the Territorial, and new officer : what he is, they inevitably try to become.

So far as the new officer was concerned in the late war, he had little chance of properly qualifying himself for commanding men. During some months men of the normal officer class were encouraged to join the ranks; then as the new armies came into being, men were almost literally swept in as officers through every alley; at last, as it became evident that the old officer class, and even the better educated class had been exhausted, the final and desperate step had to be taken of general promotion from the ranks, in the hope that the good men who had been thrown in might be fished out. Unfortunately, the platoon and even the company commander is human, and is rarely willing to give up his most useful men for the benefit of others. Pulled out of the ranks, the new officer obviously needed training that would free him from its cramping influence; he was sent, however, to a cadet school, where he again paced the equivalent to the barrack yard, learnt the new drill*, and was instructed how to behave at mess. He was then hurried from course to course, and was sent rather bewildered to a regiment to take in his charge the lives of men. He would, in my belief, have been better qualified to do so if he had been given the training in *moral* and initiative which our system provided.

The Territorial officer was in many ways a success : he knew something as a rule of military routine, which in its proper place is an essential factor in making the war machine run smoothly; he generally had the spirit of discipline, and had often done a good deal of military reading; above all he was keen. His weakness lay perhaps in his inequality.

Every regular regiment is of the same pattern, the officers have had the same training, and as to all routine matters can be trusted to do things in the same way; their minimum standard of knowledge is also roughly the same. The Territorial regiment was and remained a more unknown, and therefore in the regular's opinion, a more uncertain quantity; its officers could not be relied on to do the same things as the regular officer, or in the same way. Their keenness was mistaken for empty enthusiasm, the badge of the amateur; and I have heard a regular officer say, and have understood his point of view, that he would rather have under him the worst regular than the best Territorial.

The conclusions to be drawn from the late war are, I think, that it is impossible to force the nation in arms into the framework of our small regular Army. Such an attempt not only leads to huge waste even in matters of pay and allowances (witness the hundred pages of staff jobs in our war Army Lists), but it blights and rules out the spirit of individual enterprise, that is the breath of successful civilian life. The civilian character is bricked in while there is no time to build up over it the sealed pattern military character. Modern war needs the highest qualities of the mind, disciplined self-control, power to think and power to act. It is not enough for the regular officer to train for the regular Army and small wars, he must be prepared to hold his own both in character and knowledge with a wider circle; if he accepts responsibility he must bear criticism, and it is to be hoped that national self-complacency is only a passing phase, and that the preparation of the regular officer for modern war will soon become a matter of real concern.

---

*What importance was attached to the new drill is shown by the fact that in February, 1917, in common with other Commandants of Brigade Schools, I was ordered to attend the School of Instruction at Chelsea Barracks for two days to discuss with the Commandant the exact construction to be placed on the amended "turnings": "to jump or not to jump," that was the question!

CONCLUSIONS.

With regard to the new officer, the circumstances are not likely to recur. It is generally acknowledged that the new armies should have been organised as part of the Territorial force; and, after the lesson we have had, the want of policy that led to wholesale promotion from the ranks is not likely to recur.

The Territorial officer will be the mainstay of the expanded Army, and his training is of supreme importance. At the present moment practically every officer has seen service in the late war. So far as running the domestic show on war lines is concerned, such experience is of the utmost value; but from the point of view of the higher efficiency, it has its dangerous side. The so-called lessons of one war are no guide how to win the next, but only how best to avoid losing it; they are purely negative. The principles of success are well-known, but the method of their application differed widely in the last war from previous wars, and will differ again in the next. The danger of experience is to stereotype previous methods. An officer should know instinctively, and quite decidedly the right thing to do, and have the will to do it, but keep an open mind as to the means; however great an officer's previous experience has been, he is an amateur when a new war begins. Nor did officers have in the late war such a common experience as might have its use in forming a common consciousness; experience in most cases was only an experience in varying details. Such experience is of no value in forming a common body of doctrine, and so long as Territorial officers have no homogeneous training, or common standard of knowledge, the magnificent material in the ranks will be liable to be wasted. Yet there is all the time an instrument at hand framed for the purpose, and of proved value, the Officers' Training Corps.

The simple and logical way to obtain an even standard of training is for every Territorial officer before being commissioned to pass through an O.T.C. For this purpose their number should be increased, if possible, to one in each large command, and the standard of teaching maintained at a high level. The instructors should be chosen not so much because of their experience in the late war, as of their ability to envisage the next. If both can be combined so much the better, but in training officers a pinch of sound theory is worth a peck of practice. Some part of the expense might be met by abolishing the School O.T.C.'s and the University O.T.C.'s as such, while using the University towns as centres for O.T.C. training. They did excellent work during the war, but as part of a general scheme they come at the wrong time, and must fail in uniformity. Public schools teach discipline without any military adjunct; their O.T.C's. cannot reproduce regimental life, they tend to give boys the idea that nothing further is required and they are really an excrescence on school life. The same applies to University O.T.C's. A boy goes to the University to play hard, and in his spare time to read hard; at the most the O.T.C. is another game in fashion or not in fashion, and is really a non-natural side of University life. Soldiering should be part of the serious business of life, and taken up at the same time, and with the same keen and resolute spirit as life's more permanent issues. Nor is it then a disturbing or inharmonious factor. An Officers' Training Corps, carried on in the proper spirit, toughens the character and widens the intelligence. Far from interfering with his career, the man who joins it will find himself a more capable civilian as he becomes a better soldier.

So far as methods of training are concerned, I believed at the time that the methods employed by the Corps during the first two years of the war, though, of course, much improveable in details, were on the right lines, at least as regards men of the age of the ordinary Territorial or new officer. Since I have seen the war at rather closer quarters, I feel no doubt about it. Our theory of training can be gathered from the previous chapters. It may thus be summarised: First, and all the time, to build up *moral* by constant exercises in self-control, and in self-reliance, fostered by strict discipline, not of the repressive type, but founded on *esprit de corps*, and inculcated by N.C.O.'s of the same class as the officers and men. Secondly, by lectures, formal and informal, and, so far as possible, by exercises in the field; to interest men in war, and to give them such a grip of its unchanging general principles that they may contemplate every problem from a common standpoint of theory. The teaching of drill, musketry, map-reading, and the rapid recognition of ground fit in of themselves. Real knowledge of war must be self-taught. The object of training in this respect is to form and stimulate the taste. When a man leaves an O.T.C. morally stronger, and intellectually keener, than when he entered, his training has been a success. This test we, I believe, satisfied. Although two years were allowed to elapse before restarting the Corps, it is now again launched under much the same conditions as heretofore. The Corps has, as these records bear witness, a proud past; that it may have a future useful to the country, and honourable to itself is the fervent wish of all who have had the honour and happiness of serving in its ranks.

F. H. L. E.

Appendix I.
Record of the Officers of the Corps.

ABBREVIATIONS.

✠ = Killed in action or died of wounds.
w = Wounded.
m = Mentioned by the Secretary-of-State for War for Home Services.
M(-) = Mentioned in Dispatches.
F. denotes France, and includes Belgium.

It. denotes Italy.
E. „ Egypt.
M. „ Mesopotamia.
P. „ Palestine.
S. „ Salonika.
G. „ Gallipoli.

Lt.-Col. Francis Henry Launcelot ERRINGTON, C.B., V.D.
Joined 16/2/1880; Sgt. 29/5/86; 2/Lt. ("E." Co.) 17/5/90; Lt. 19/3/92; Capt. 17/5/99; Major 15/1/06; Lt.-Col. commanding 29/3/13 to 1/9/16; Camp Commandant, 58th Division 1/9/16 to January 1917; attached H.Q. 4th Cyclist Brigade (Ipswich), January to April 1917; attached H.Q. 11th Corps (F and It) May 1917 to 6/4/18; S.O.2, 8th Brigade R.A.F. (Independent Force, Lorraine), 6/4/18 to 11/2/19.
C.B. January 1916; m March 1917; M(1) 1918.

Major Charles Walter MEAD, T.D.
Joined (M.I.) 7/1/90; Sgt. 4/2/93; 2/Lt. 8/6/98; Lt. 11/7/99; Capt. 12/9/00; Major 1/4/08; commanded M.I. and then the Squadron 1898 to 1913; attached to Labour Corps (F) 13/3/17 to 20/6/19; commanded 13th Labour Co. Northants Regt. (afterwards 151st Co. Labour Corps).
T.D.

Major James Alexander HAY, T.D.
Joined 9/12/87; Sgt. 14/5/98; C/S. 31/1/00; 2/Lt. ("C" Co.) 6/6/00; Lt. 5/12/00; Capt. 28/2/05; Major 31/3/08. In charge of Depot from September 1914 to 1916; second in command from March 1917 to July 1919. One of the two officers who had the distinction of serving as officers with the Corps for the whole period of the war.
T.D.; m 14/8/18.

Capt. Arthur Guest MATHEWS.
Joined 12/1/00; C/S. 1/2/02; 2/Lt. ("C" Co.) 16/7/04; Lt. 28/2/05; T.F. Reserve 1/9/11; rejoined 4/8/14; Capt. 1/10/14; commanded No. 6 Co. till 1917; attached to R.G.A. February 1917; T/Major June 1917; (F) July 1917 to January 1919.

Major Lancelot Henry ELPHINSTONE
Joined (M.I.) 2/2/00; Sgt. 1/2/05; 2/Lt. 17/7/05; Lt. 1906; Capt. 1910; Major 29/3/13.
A.G. in British Honduras at commencement of War; and retained for whole period; Major in Defence Force.

Major Sir Frederic George KENYON, K.C.B., T.D.
Joined 2/2/00; Sgt. 5/4/05; 2/Lt. ("E" Co.) 7/5/06; Lt. 1/9/09; Capt. ("B" Co.) 27/3/12; Major 1/6/16; Assistant Censor B.E.F. attached to advanced base in France as G.S.O.3 5/8/14 to September 1914; commanded "B" and No. 2 Co. September 1914 to November 1917; attached to Imperial War Graves Commission and T/Lt.-Col. 29/11/17 to end of War.
T.D. 14/3/19; m 23/3/18; 1914 Star.

Major Alan McLEAN, M.B.E., T.D.
Joined 9/2/00; Sgt. 3/3/04; C/S. 8/11/05; 2/Lt. ("A" Co.) 6/12/07; Lt. 22/10/09; Capt. (commanding "A" Co.) 27/7/12; Bt. Major 1/1/18; Assistant Censor, B.E.F., 9/8/14; rejoined Corps and Assistant Adjutant March 1915; Adjt. March 1918 to 27/6/19.
M.B.E. 3/6/19; T.D. 18/8/19; m(2) 24/2/17, 25/3/19; 1914 Sar.

Major Edward Duke MOORE, D.S.O., T.D.
Joined (M.I.) 13/1/00; Sgt. 8/11/05; C/S 1/2/06; 2/Lt. 6/12/07; Lt. (Sqn.) 1/9/09; Capt. 29/3/13; Major 1/6/16; A.D.C. to G.O.C. 2nd London Division 5/8/14; transferred to Yorkshire Yeomanry 8/10/14; T/Major 27/5/15; with 1/1st East Riding Yeomanry to Egypt 1915; a/Lt.-Col. 28/12/17 to 1/2/18; 2nd in command from October 1916; attached to H.Q. 22nd Mounted Brigade E.E.F. as Intelligence Officer 27/7/17 to 26/9/17; Western Desert campaign, and campaign East of Canal; Sinai Desert; and Palestine; appointed 2nd in command of 102nd Machine Gun Bn. (F) May to November 1918.
D.S.O. January 1918; T.D. 14/1/20; M(2) September 1916, January 1918.

Capt. Cyril WOOD-HILL
Joined (M.I.) 23/1/03; Sgt. May 1909; Lt. (Sqn.) 1/9/11; Capt. 21/5/14; commanded Sqn. August 1914 to September 1915; attached to Northants Yeomanry (F) September 1915 to January 1919; seconded to Intelligence Corps December 1917 to September 1918; G.S.O.3 at G.H.Q. September 1918 to January 1919.

Capt. William Robert FIELD
Joined (M.I.) 13/5/03; retired 1/3/06; rejoined 2/11/06; Sgt. 11/1/08; C/S. 1/2/08; 2/Lt. (Sqn.) 1/9/11; Capt. 8/10/14; commanded Sqn. from September 1915 till demobilisation in January 1919. One of the two officers who had the distinction of serving as officers with the Corps throughout the War.

Capt. Henry William HOLLAND, D.S.O., O.B.E., T.D.
Joined ("E" Co.) 17/3/98; Sgt. 1/3/06; C/S. 9/4/07; 2/Lt. ("B" Co.) 18/12/09; Lt. 1/9/11; Capt. 5/8/14; attached to General Staff, B.E.F. 5/8/14; T/Lt.-Col., May 1917; G.S.O.1, G.H.Q., November 1918 to 29/10/19; special appointment War Office, 29/10/19 to 8/1/20.
D.S.O. 1/1/17; O.B.E.; T.D. 1919; Legion of Honour (5th Class); M(4) 22/6/15, 15/6/16, 20/5/18, 20/12/18; 1914 Star.

Capt. Evelyn à Court BERGNE, T.D.
Joined 9/2/00; Sgt. 8/6/06; 2/Lt. ("A" Co.) 18/12/09; Lt. 28/10/11; Capt. 5/8/14; commanded "A" (No. 1) Co. 5/8/14 to 13/2/16, No. 6 Co. 13/2/16 to June 1916 and "A" Co. to January 1918; seconded to R.E. 21/4/18; Marine Co., I.W. and D.R.E. as senior discipline officer and Assistant Adjutant 22/4/18 to January 1919; War Office (M.R.3) in charge of statistical department, January 1919 to November 1919.
T.D. 14/1/20.

Capt. Richard Frederick Charles O'BRIEN
Joined 2/12/07; 2/Lt. ("A" Co.) 6/4/10; Lt. 28/2/12; Capt. 1/10/14; commanded No. 5 Co.; attached to 20th Bn. County of London Regt. (F) June 1916; invalided and rejoined Corps December 1916; commanded "D" Co. and Musketry officer; posted as T/Major to 2nd City of London Yeomanry, March 1917; T/Lt.-Col. commanding 2nd City of London Yeomanry 20/8/17 to 24/2/19.
m(2).

✠ **Lieut. William George Gresham LEVESON GOWER**
Joined (M.I.) 12/1/07; Sgt. 1/1/10; 2/Lt. (Sqn.) 11/9/11; Lt. 21/5/14; attached to H.Q. Southern Command, 1915; 1st Coldstream Guards, 1917. Killed in action at AWOIGNT, near CAMBRAI (F) 9/10/18.

Capt. Harold Beresford BUTLER, C.B.
Joined 2/5/09; Sgt. May 1911; 2/Lt. ("C" Co.) 11/10/11; Lt 27/3/12; Capt. 1/10/14; retained by Home Office, Acting Assistant Secretary; Head of Trading with Enemy Department, 1916; Secretary, Foreign Trade Department of Foreign Office, January 1916; Assistant Secretary, Ministry of Labour, 1917; Member of Government Commissions for Demobilisation and Officers' Resettlement 1917 to 1918.
C.B. for War Services, January 1919.

Lieut. Herbert William MALKIN
Joined 1/4/08; Sgt. 3/4/11; 2/Lt. ("B" Co.) 24/11/11; Lt. 27/7/12; retained by the Foreign Office during the whole War.

Lt.-Col. Albert Nettleton CLARK, M.C.
Joined 21/11/04; Sgt. June 1911; 2/Lt. ("B" Co.) 6/12/11; Lt. 16/4/13; Capt. (No. 2 Co.) 1/10/14; Lt.-Col. commanding the Corps 20/2/20. Transferred to 2/24th Bn. County of London Regt. 23/3/16; 60th Div. (F) 24/6/16; Salonika 3/12/16; Egypt and Palestine 16/6/17; a/Major October 1917; 58th Div. (F) 3/7/18; w 21/9/18.
M.C. 1917; M(2), 21/7/17, 1919.

66

APPENDIX I.—RECORDS OF OFFICERS.

✠ *Capt. Charles Reginald Chenevix* TRENCH
Joined 30/12/09; Sgt. December 1911; 2/Lt. ("C" Co.) 1/4/12; Capt. 1/10/14; commanded No. 3 Co.; attached to 2/5th Sherwood Foresters 1916; a/Major. *Killed in action at* NOREUIL, *near* BULLECOURT (F) 21/3/18.

Major Raymond Ewings NEGUS, D.S.O.
Joined 16/2/10; Cpl. April 1912; 2/Lt. ("C" Co.) 5/6/12; Capt. 1/10/14; transferred to King's Shropshire Light Infantry 15/4/15; Major, July 1915; to France as 2nd in command 26/9/15; T/Lt.-Col. commanding 14/12/15; *w* at Somme 14/7/16; evacuated to England 1/8/16; Chief Instructor, Osborne, August and September 1916; to France 6/9/17; commanded 9th British West Indies Regt. (F) 22/11/17; retired with honorary rank of Lt.-Col. 22/11/18.
D.S.O.; M(2).

✠ *Capt. George Ouvry William* WILLINK, M.C.
Joined 20/11/11; Sgt., May 1912; 2/Lt. ("A" Co.) 16/4/13; Lt. 5/8/14; Capt. 31/7/15; commanded No. 1 Co. 13/2/16 to June 1916; transferred to 2/4th Berkshire Regt. June 1916. *Killed in action near* MARCELEAVE (F) 28/3/18.
M.C.

Capt. James Frederick Martyn ROBINSON, M.C.
Joined (M.I.) 10/3/03; Sgt. 1/1/10; 2/Lt. (Sqn.) 3/5/13; Capt. in 1/1st East Riding of Yorkshire Yeomanry 8/10/14; seconded to 36th Jacob's Horse Indian Cavalry (F) March 1915, 2nd battle of Ypres and on Somme; rejoined East Riding Yeomanry October 1915 (E); Senussi campaign, police work western desert; T/Major October 1916; advance to El Arish; with desert column in 1st and 2nd battles of Gaza, capture of Beersheba, Cathra, and Akir; then to Jaffa and Ludd, and with Yeomanry Division to cut off Jerusalem, 1917; with 102nd Machine Gun Bn. Lincolns and East Riding Regt. (F), July 1918; fighting round Cambrai, and advance of 1st Army till Armistice.
M.C. 27/8/17.

Capt. James Neville GRAY, D.S.O.
Joined 23/11/09; Sgt. May 1913; 2/Lt. ("B" Co.) 15/11/13; Lt. 1/10/14; Capt. 1/6/16; to Censor Staff, B.E.F. 5/8/14; Head Censor, Calais, June 1915; T/Capt. in Army 25/7/15; T/Major in Army 18/11/17; appointed to G.S.(c), G.H.Q., 1/10/18 till 8/8/19.
D.S.O. 1/1/17; M(2) 1/1/16, 10/7/19; 1914 Star.

✠ *Lieut. Ralph Charles Fairbairn* COTTON
Joined (Sqn.) 20/5/08; Sgt. May 1913; Lt. 19/9/14; Hunts. Yeomanry 27/10/14; transferred to 4th Machine Gun Squadron. *Died of wounds received in action near* NOYON (F) 28/3/18.
Croix de Guerre.

Capt. Pelham Francis WARNER, M.B.E.
Joined 4/1/00; retired 1/3/02; rejoined 19/2/08; 2/Lt. 12/8/14; Lt. 1/10/14; T/Capt. 31/7/15; attached to G.S., War Office, 23/1/15 to December 1916; attached to Foreign Office, June 1917; invalided out 21/3/18.
M.B.E. 1919; *m* December 1916.

✠ *Lieut. Francis Percival* LEFROY
Joined 7/9/14; 2/Lt. 26/9/14; Lt. 1/10/14; commanded "D" Co.; transferred to 73rd Field Co., R.E., December 1914. *Killed in action at* HOHENZOLLERN REDOUBT, LOOS (F) 28/4/16.

✠ *Capt. Charles Thomas Anderdon* POLLOCK
Joined 25/11/09; Sgt. July 1911; 2/Lt. ("C" Co.) 26/9/14; Lt. 1/10/14; Capt. 1/6/16; O. i/c Instruction Class under the Adjutant; appointed Instructor at 2nd Army School (F) 1916; attached to 1/4th East Yorkshire Regt. *Killed in action near* VILLERS BRETONNEAU, 31/3/18.

✠ *Capt. Arthur Edward Adderley* BULLER
Joined 14/2/10; Sgt. December 1913; 2/Lt. ("A" Co.) 17/10/14; Lt. 8/6/15; Capt. 1/6/16; commanded No. 3 Co., 1916; attached to 5th Norfolk Regt. 1917. *Died at* LYDDA, PALESTINE, 21/9/18.

Capt. Henry Leslie GEARE
Joined 13/11/05; Sgt. May 1910; C/S. May 1913; 2/Lt. ("C" Co.) 18/10/14; Lt. 8/6/15; Capt. 1/6/16; commanded No. 5 and then "C" Co. from 1/6/16 to 2/8/18; posted to Rifle Brigade 3/8/18 to 25/11/18; to 1st Bn. K.O.Y.L.I (F) 26/11/18; attached to H.Q. 50th Division 9/1/19; Assistant D.A.P.M., Brussels, 25/2/19; D.A.P.M. sub-area of No. 4 area 15/5/19; D.A.P.M., Liege, 25/6/19 to 30/10/19.

✠ *Capt. Edwin Charles Kaye* CLARKE, M.C.
Joined 5/4/11; Sgt. July 1913; 2/Lt. ("C" Co.) 18/10/14; Lt. 8/6/15; Capt. 1/6/16; attached to 8th London Regt. 1917. *Killed in action at* MARRIERE WOOD, *near* PERONNE (F) 31/8/18.
M.C. 1918.

Capt. William Thomas Charles CAVE
Joined 16/3/10; Sgt. 15/8/14; 2/Lt. ("B" Co.) 18/10/14; Lt. (No. 2 Co.) 31/7/15; Capt. 1/6/16; attached to 2/10th London Regt. August 1917; 2/11th London Regt. October 1917; 1/20th London Regt. (F) February 1918; Prisoner of War, March 1918

Capt. Viscount ERLEIGH, M.C.
Joined August 1914; 2/Lt. ("D" Co.) 18/10/14; Lt. 31/7/15; Capt. 1/6/16; commanded No. 4 Co. from December 1914 to January 1916; attached to H.Q. London District, January to October 1916; Staff Capt. March to October 1916; attached to staff of various formations in France from 6/10/16 to February 1917; posted to 1st Bn. Royal Fusiliers February 1917; Staff Capt. 60th Brigade August 1917; a/D.A.A.G. (T/Major), 15th Division July 1918; D.A.A.G, 50th Division, October 1918 to January 1919.
M.C. June 1918; *Croix de Guerre* August 1918.

Lieut. Harold Ian MERRIMAN
Joined (Sqn.) 25/4/12; Sgt. 19/9/14; 2/Lt. 6/12/14; Lt. 23/9/15; served with the Squadron from the beginning to the end of the War.

Capt. Spencer BRETT
Joined 2/12/14; 2/Lt. 20/12/14; Lt. 31/7/15; Capt. 1/6/16; qualified as Bde. Musketry officer at Bisley, passed Lewis Gun Course at Birmingham Small Arms Factory, and instructed in Lewis Gun at Depot; Musketry and Machine Gun officer 1917; transferred to Guards Machine Gun Regiment, August 1918; passed M.G. Course, Grantham, October 1918.

Capt. Harold Thomas Hearne BOND, T.D.
Joined 6/10/14; 2/Lt. ("E" Co.) 9/1/15; Lt. 31/7/15; Capt. 1/6/16; attached to No. 1 Cadet Co. 11/3/16; Adjutant and Quartermaster of No. 14 (Inns of Court) Officer Cadet Battalion 5/9/16 till April 1919.
T.D.; *m*(3) March 1918, March 1919, August 1919.

Capt. Arthur Hampden Ronald Wastell POYSER
Joined 23/9/14; Sgt. 27/10/14; 2/Lt. (No. 1 Co.), 21/1/15; Lt. 31/7/15; Capt. 1/6/16; M.G. officer, Machine Gun Corps, Grantham, October 1916; Bisley, February 1917; M. May 1917 to October 1919; a/Major, 16/2/18.
M(1).

Capt. Jocelyn Charles LEDWARD
Joined August 1914; Sgt. 24/10/14; 2/Lt. (No. 4 Co.) 21/1/15; T/Lt. 31/7/15; Capt. 1/6/16; O. i/c Junior Instruction Class September 1915 to April 1916; attached to "A" Cadet Co. April 1916 to October 1917; Gas Course, Halton (D. Cert.) April 1917; Musketry Course, Hythe (D. Cert.) June 1917; attached to 5th (Res.) Leicesters October 1917 to May 1918; 1/4th Leicesters, 46th Div. (F) May to October 1918; Adjutant September 1918; *w.* near BOHAIN 10/10/18; Certificate for gallant and soldierly conduct on night of 27/18th September 1918 at the capture of PIKE WOOD, near BELLINGLISE.

Capt. Hugh Kroenig RYAN, O.B.E.
Joined 12/2/15; Lt. 22/2/15; T/Capt. 31/7/15; worked at Depot on the organisation of the recruiting, and established the Selection Boards at Dublin, Cardiff, Edinburgh and Exeter; joined Directorate of the Inland Waterways and Docks, War Office in June 1917.
O.B.E.; *m.*

Capt. Fermian LeNeve FOSTER
Joined August 1914; Sgt. 21/5/15; 2/Lt. (No. 3 Co.) 22/2/15; Lt. 31/7/15; Capt. 1/6/16; O.C. Depot December 1916; O.C., O.T.C. Reception Depot, December 1917; attached to Ministry of Labour (Appointments Department), and Assistant District Director, Ministry of Labour, 1/1/19 to May 1919.

Capt. Richard Chetwynd STAPYLTON
Joined 26/9/14; Sgt. 4/12/14; 2/Lt. (No. 2 Co.) 22/2/15; Lt. 31/7/15; Capt. 1/6/16; attached to Grenadier Guards (S.R.) 26/6/18 to 6/2/19 (F).
m 14/8/18.

Lieut. Ralph Ernest ATTENBOROUGH
Joined (Sqn.) 27/5/13; Sgt. 10/10/14; 2/Lt. 7/4/15; Lt. 1/7/17; seconded to M.G.C. 19/1/16; to S. with 77th Co. 5/7/16; a/Capt. i/c 77th Co. 13/4/18; a/Major, O.C. 77th Co. 14/6/18; a/Staff Capt. 77th Inf. Bde. 26/12/18 to 14/2/19; a/Major and O.C., 77th Co. 14/2/19 to 28/3/19; Doiran front, then Bulgaria, Adrianople and Ruschuk.
M(1) 28/11/17.

Capt. Courtney TERRELL
Joined 5/8/14; Sgt. 8/9/14; 2/Lt. (No. 6 Co.) 18/7/15; Lt. 1/6/16; Capt. 23/8/18; seconded in 1916 to the School at Chelsea Barracks as Instructor in Map reading and kindred subjects till February 1919.

Capt. George Francis Troup HORNE
Joined 6/8/14; Sgt. 17/10/14; Lt. 2/14th London Regt. 13/11/14; re-transferred (No. 5 Co. & "B") 21/8/15; Lt. 1/6/16; Capt. 23/8/18; attached to 4th (Res.) D.C.L.I. 6/4/18; Ireland 23/4/18.

APPENDIX I.—RECORDS OF OFFICERS.

Capt. Edward Whitaker GREENE
Joined 16/2/00; Cpl. 9/4/00; retired 1906; rejoined 20/9/14; Sgt. 30/10/14; C.Q.M.S. 3/4/15; 2/Lt. 12/9/15; Lt. 1/6/16; Capt. 31/8/18; commanded No. 4 Co. January to June 1916; attached to Herts. Bn. 23/7/18; then to 5th Bedfords; instructor at Bde. School at Crowborough; commanded Co. of Cadets at Hastings, September to November 1918; attached to 3rd Bedfords 2/12/18 and commanded one of their Companies January to April 1919.

Capt. Arthur Charles Cosmo PARKINSON, O.B.E.
Joined 22/3/09; Sgt. December 1911; 2/Lt. (No. 2 Co.) 12/9/15; Lt. 1/6/16; Capt. 21/9/18; seconded for service with King's African Rifles, East Africa July 1917; T/Capt. D.A.A.G. and T/Major January 1918 to June 1919.
O.B.E.; M(2).

Lieut. Samuel Kenneth WEST
Joined September 1914 from 5th London Regt. (L.R.B.); Sgt. 28/12/14; 2/Lt. (No. 3 Co.) 12/9/15; Lt. 1/6/16; Assistant Director of Finance to Ministry of Food 21/10/17.

Capt. Charles Eric Langton HOOPER
Joined 13/10/14; Sgt. 25/11/14; 2/Lt. (No. 1 Co.) 12/9/15; Lt. 1/6/16; Capt. 21/9/18; Musketry Officer May to September 1917; Bombing Officer October 1917 to November 1918.

Lieut Arthur John Broughton BAMFORD
Joined 9/10/14; Sgt. 21/1/15; 2/Lt. (No. 5 Co.) 12/9/15; Lt. 1/6/16; seconded to M.G.C. March 1918; 38th (Welsh) Bn. M.G.C. (F) July 1918; gassed at GONZEAUCOURT, SOMME 20/9/18.

Lieut. John Pearson FOOT
Joined 13/4/08; retired 12/4/12; rejoined 10/6/15; Sgt. 3/7/15; 2/Lt. (No. 2 Co.) 13/9/15; Lt. 1/6/16; invalided out September 1917.

Lieut. Henry John FISHER
Joined (Sqn.) 9/10/14; Sgt. 12/1/15; S.S.M. 20/9/15; 2/Lt. 15/10/15; Lt. 1/7/17; to War Trade Intelligence Department 23/5/17.

Lieut. Horace FINNEMORE
Joined 3/6/15; Sgt. 22/7/15; 2/Lt. (No. 1 Co.) 15/10/15; T/Capt. and Chemical Adviser to Northern Command August 1916 to May 1917; Anti-gas Department, Ministry of Munitions May 1917; R.E. Anti-gas Department February 1918.

Lieut. Arthur Lindrea BRIGHTMAN
Joined 27/5/15; Sgt. 13/8/15; 2/Lt. 15/10/15; Lt. 1/6/16; to Bucks. Bn. (O. & B.L.I.) (F) 10/9/17; (It) November 1917; w in night attack near ASIAGO 26/6/18; Hospital to 5/4/19.

Lieut. James Edward JOHNSTON
Sgt. in Sussex Yeomanry August 1914; transferred to Corps (Sqn.) 15/6/15; Sgt. 24/7/15; 2/Lt. 14/11/15; transferred to 6th Res. Regiment of Cavalry October 1916; served with 7th Dragoon Guards (F) January 1917 to January 1918; had 4th Troop D. Squadron which was adjudged best turned out troop and best conditioned horses in 5th Cav. Div. containing 612 troops August and September 1917.
M (1) 8/11/18.

Lieut. Noel COW
Joined 15/2/15; Sgt. 28/6/15; 2/Lt. (No. 1 Co.) 10/3/16; Lt. 1/6/16; attached to No. 14 (Inns of Court) Officer Cadet Bn. 19/2/17 to 25/2/17; attached to 4th (Res.) Bn. The Buffs 25/2/18 to 26/8/18; attached to Finance Department, Air Ministry 26/8/18 to 24/1/19.

Capt. William Robert WARD
Rejoined Sqn. 12/4/15; Sgt. 25/6/15; 2/Lt. 16/4/16; T/Capt. 19/5/16; Adjutant Sarhad Levy Corps, Sistan Field Force May 1916; commanded Sarhad Levy Corps July 1917; posted on special duty under Agent to Governor-General in Baluchistan April 1919 to June 1920.

✠ *Lieut. Leonard John* WAKEFIELD
Joined 1/9/15; 2/Lt. (No. 5 Co.) 16/4/16; attached to 2/8th London Regt. 1916.   *Killed in action near* BULLECOURT (F.) 16/6/17.

Lieut. Eric DANE
Joined 23/9/14; Sgt. 4/3/15; 2/Lt. (No. 3 Co.) 16/4/16; Lt. 1/6/16; posted to 39th Bn. M.G.C. (F.) 10/11/17 to end of War.

Lieut. Coningsby Samuel JOHNSON, M.C.
Joined (Sqn.) 26/4/15; Sgt. 9/10/15; 2/Lt. 28/4/16; Lt. 1/6/16; transferred to R.F.A. October 1916; to 2nd Divisional Artillery (F) 30/4/17; 47th Bty., 41st Bde., R.F.A. H.Q., Arras; 3rd battle of Ypres, Cambrai; Retreat and Advance of 1918.
M.C.

Lieut. Cecil Gilbert HOUGHTON
Joined 19/11/14; Sgt. 7/6/15; 2/Lt. (No. 4 Co.) 2/5/16; Lt. 1/7/17; a/Capt. 19/11/17; No. 14 (Inns of Court) Officer Cadet Bn. June 1916 to end of War.

Lieut. Cyril Noel HOOPER
Joined 30/3/08; retired 6/4/10; rejoined 10/11/15; Sgt. 30/3/16; 2/Lt. (No. 3 Co.) 12/5/16; Lt. 1/7/17; attached to King's African Rifles 21/7/17 to 30/7/19; w at battle of Mahiwa (German East Africa) 17/10/17; attached to King's African Rifles H.Q. December 1917; T/Capt. 1/8/18.
M(1).

Lieut. Charles John PATERSON
Joined 8/11/15; Sgt. May 1916; 2/Lt. (No. 5 Co.) 20/7/16; Lt. 20/1/18; R.F.C. School of Military Aeronautics November 1917; passed as bombing pilot June 1918; passed at Midland Area Flying Instructors' School, and returned there as Instructor.

Lieut. Hugh TEESDALE
Joined 17/1/16; 2/Lt. (No. 1 Co.) 6/8/16; Lt. 6/2/18; attached to R.A.F. as Equipment Officer and Liaison Officer December 1917 to July 1919.

Lieut. Tristram Warrington HAWARD
Joined 6/1/16; Sgt. 1/7/16; 2/Lt. (No. 2 Co.) 5/9/16; Lt. 5/3/18; Assistant Adjutant and O.i/c recruits 9/3/18; O.i/c demobilisation December 1918; special report and 100% for drill and topography at Chelsea.
m (2) March 1919, August 1919.

Lieut. Percy Melmoth WALTERS
Joined (E.Co.) 4/11/98; Cpl. 1/4/00; retired 1/10/02; rejoined 29/9/14; C/S (" E " Co.) 1/10/14; C.S.M. (No. 1 Co.) 1/8/15; to Cadet Bn. August 1916 and passed out 1st; 2/Lt. 23/10/16; T/Lt. and Instructor with No. 14 (Inns of Court) Officer Cadet Bn. 27/11/16; a/Capt. 19/11/17; to Catterick with Cadet Bn. 22/1/18; returned to Berkhamsted March 1918.

Lieut. William Lionel MORRIS
Joined 21/6/15; Sgt. 25/3/16; 2/Lt. 29/8/17; Lt. (" D " Co.) 1/3/19 to end of War.

Lieut. Percival Edward HAWKSLEY
Chaplain to 51st Infantry Brigade (F) 10/12/15 to 9/12/17; joined Corps 9/2/17; 2/Lt. 29/8/17; Lt. 1/3/19; attached to 3rd Norfolk Regt. (Felixtowe) 5/4/18; 9th Norfolks (F) 8/10/18; gassed 14/10/18; a/Capt. 4/11/18; attached to Bedfords. 25/3/19; posted to 191 R.O.E. Co. (F) 11/5/19.

Major W. HOLBOURN
Appointed Quartermaster 1/3/12; retired from ill-health 29/5/17. Distinguished service Reward Annuity January 1917.

✠ *Capt. W. W.* ALLSOPP
Appointed Quartermaster 2/5/17; Died 19/11/20.

Capt. L. B. CANE, T.D., R.A.M.C. (T).
Joined 17/4/08; (E) 3/9/14; (G) 1915; India 1916.

Capt. D. G. RICE-OXLEY, M.C, R.A.M.C. (T).
Joined 10/12/04; Capt. i/c the Corps 4/8/14 to 5/7/15; 2/1st London Field Ambulance 6/7/15 to 20/2/16; (F) 21/2/16 to 1/3/19; a/Major 4/1/18; a/Lt.-Col. 29/12/18; Lt.-Col. commanding 1st London Field Ambulance, 1st London Division.
M.C. June 1918; M(1) May 1917.

Preface to Appendix II.

The following Appendix contains the names of all members of the Corps who joined after the formation of the Territorial Force in 1908. At the outbreak of war the total number had only reached 809, of whom nearly all served during the war, and it is for this reason that they are included. Regimental Numbers were granted consecutively throughout the war, and the last number issued was 14,349.

To give some idea of the growth of the Corps: before the end of 1914, 1725 new members had joined; during 1915, 6013 were added to the ranks. During 1916 recruiting was more or less suspended from February to September and consequently this year only gave an increase of 1721. In 1917 we had 2069 recruits, and from the beginning of 1918 to the end of the war, 2012. The greatest recruiting month throughout the whole war was November 1915, when 956 men were attested or transferred to the Corps; and during one day of this month no less than 115 men were brought on the strength of the Corps.

Of these, 11485 were granted commissions; 1065 were transferred to the ranks of other units (this includes, of course, a very large number who were serving in the Corps when the Armistice was signed and who were not eligible for immediate demobilisation); 929 were demobilised direct from the Corps; 341 were discharged as medically unfit.

It has not been possible definitely to ascertain the extent of the casualties suffered by ex-members of the Corps, but at the time of going to press the following figures are known:—

Died whilst serving in the Corps	35
Killed in action, Died of wounds, Killed accidentally or died of disease	2147
Wounded (5 times)	1
,, (4 ,,)	6
,, (3 ,,)	50
,, (twice)	366
,, (once)	2354
Gassed	242

Similarly, the honours gained have been very difficult to check, and as far as they are known at present the figures are as follows:—

Victoria Cross	3
K.B.E.	2
C.B.	3
C.B.E.	3
D.S.O. and one bar	4
D.S.O.	80
O.B.E.	82
M.B.E.	60
D.S.C.	1
M.C. and two bars	4
M.C. and bar	87
M.C.	1062
D.F.C. and bar	1
D.F.C.	36
A.F.C.	16
A.M.	1
D.C.M.	3
M.M.	2
M.S.M.	1
Mentioned in Dispatches (five times)	2
,, (4 times)	15
,, (3 times)	39
,, (twice)	162
,, (once)	841
Mentioned for Service at Home (3 times)	1
,, (twice)	3
,, (once)	31

FOREIGN ORDERS & DECORATIONS:

Legion of Honour	9
Croix de Guerre (French)	48
Médaille d'Honneur	3
Mérite Agricole	1
Croix de Guerre (Belgian)	27
Order of Leopold	4
Order of the Crown (Belgian)	7
Croce di Guerra	13
Italian Silver Medal	13
Italian Bronze Medal	4
Order of Maurice and Lazarus	1
Corona d'Italia	1
S. Stanislaus (Russia)	13
S. Anne ,,	10
S. Vladimir ,,	1
S. George ,,	1
Order of the Nile	3
The Crown of Roumania	3
The Star of Roumania	1
White Eagle of Serbia	5
Cross of Charity (Serbia)	1
Order of the Avis (Portugal)	3
Portuguese War Cross	2
Order of the Rising Sun (Japan)	2
Order of Wen-Ho (China)	1
American Distinguished Service Medal	1
American Flying Medal	1
Greek Military Cross	2
Order of the Redeemer (Greece)	2
Medal for Military Merit ,,	1
Lion and Sun (Persia)	1
White Rose of Finland	1

PREFACE TO APPENDIX II.

Wherever possible the present addresses of ex-members are given in the following pages. In a large number of cases letters have been returned through the Dead Letter Office of the Post Office. Every attempt has been made to trace these through the War Office, Cox & Co. and other agents, and this very often proved successful. When no reply was received through these sources, the address has been omitted altogether. However, if an address is not definitely known to be a wrong one, although we have received no response to letters sent there, it is included in the hope that others may be more successful than we have been. The addresses of the next-of-kin of those who died have not been inserted, but many of these are known and can be obtained, if desired, from Headquarters.

The scheme that has been adopted for the members' Records needs a little explanation.

The first set of letters and figures and a date, with sometimes a rank, indicate the company or companies in which the man served, his Regimental Number, the date he joined and the highest rank he held in the Corps if he gained non-commissioned rank. Next appears the number or name of Cadet Unit to which the man was sent, after these units had been formed in the spring of 1916. The Regiment to which he was commissioned and the date is next (where the name of a Regiment appears with a date afterwards it means in all cases that the man was commissioned to the Regiment with the rank of 2nd Lieutenant on that date. The Regiments shown after the date are those in which the man subsequently served). If a man was transferred from the Corps to another Regiment without obtaining a commission, this is always shown as : *trfr*. Manch. R. etc. Should he have received a commission subsequently in another Regiment, this will be shown in the usual way. The front on which he served is next given, after which comes wounds or other casualties, and lastly, Honours, Mentions in Dispatches, etc.

The following is an example of a man's Record as it will appear in subsequent pages :—

ROBINSON, *John Hugh*
    3/D/Sq/3942, 5/5/15, Cpl.; No. 9 O.C.B., 8/3/16; Arg. & Suth'd. Highrs., 16/6/16, Manch. R., *att.* R.A.F.; F,E,P; Major; *w*(2), *g,p*; *D.S.O., A.F.C.*, M(3).   33 *Milestone Avenue, Wigan. (Now in FMS).*

From this his career can be traced as follows :—Joined the Corps 5/5/15, Regimental Number 3942, served in 3 and " D " Companies and the Squadron, and attained the rank of Corporal in the Corps; went to No. 9 Officer Cadet Battalion on the 8th March 1916 and was commissioned to the Argyll and Sutherland Highlanders on the 16th June 1916. He subsequently served with the Manchester Regiment and was attached to the Royal Air Force. He served overseas in France, Egypt and Palestine and attained the rank of Major. He was wounded twice, gassed and taken prisoner; was awarded the *D.S.O.* and the Air Force Cross and was thrice mentioned in Dispatches. His permanent address in this country is at Wigan and he is now in the Federated Malay States.

The following abbreviations are used throughout : —

✠	*denotes* Killed in action, Died of wounds, Killed, Died.
A.F.C.	Air Force Cross, recipient of
A.M.	Albert Medal, recipient of
att.	attached to
C.B.	Companion of the Order of the Bath
C.B.E.	Commander of the Order of the British Empire
cmd.	commanded
C.M.G.	Companion of the Order of St. Michael and St. George.
cr.	crashed
C/S	Cadet School
D.A.A.G.	Deputy Assistant Adjutant General
D.A.D.O.S.	Deputy Assistant Director of Supplies
D.A.Q.M.G.	Deputy Assistant Quartermaster General
D.C.M.	Distinguished Conduct Medal, recipient of
demob.	demobilised
D.F.C.	Distinguished Flying Cross, recipient of
dis.	discharged
dis. med. unfit	discharged as medically unfit for further service
D.S.C.	Distinguished Service Cross, recipient of
D.S.O.	Companion of the Distinguished Service Order
emp.	employed with
E	Egypt, denotes service in
EA	East Africa, denotes service in
F	France and Flanders, denotes service in
G	Gallipoli, denotes service in
g	gassed
Garr.	Garrison
Germ.EA	German East Africa, denotes service in

PREFACE TO APPENDIX II.

Germ.SWA	German South West Africa, denotes service in
H. Bde. O.C.B.	Household Brigade Officer Cadet Battalion
I	India, denotes service in
Inj	injured
Inst	Instructor
Inv	invalided
It	Italy, denotes service in
K.B.E.	Knight Commander of the Order of the British Empire
K.C.B.	Knight Commander of the Order of the Bath
M	Mesopotamia, denotes service in
M(1), (2)	mentioned in dispatches once, twice etc.
m(1)	mentioned by the Secretary of State for valuable services at home
M. of (Labour etc)	Ministry of (Labour etc.)
M.B.E.	Member of the Order of the British Empire
M.C.	Military Cross, recipient of
M.M.	Military medal, recipient of
M.S.M.	Meritorious Service Medal, recipient of
NR	North Russia, denotes service in
O.B.E.	Officer of the Order of the British Empire
O.C.B.	Officer Cadet Battalion
P	Palestine, denotes service in
p	prisoner of war
R.A.,C/S	Royal Artillery Cadet School
rej	rejoined
R. Mil. Academy	Royal Military Academy, Woolwich
R. Mil. Coll.	Royal Military College, Sandhurst
S	Salonica, Macedonia and the Balkans, denotes service in
SA	South Africa, denotes service in
SR	South Russia, denotes service in
secd.	seconded to
Sig.C/S	Signal Service Cadet School
Sp	Spain, denotes service in
T/1/1/15	transferred to the Corps on the 1st January, 1915.
trfr.	transferred to
Tr. Res. Bn.	Training Reserve Battalion
T.M.Bty.	Trench Mortar Battery
V.C.	Victoria Cross, recipient of
w	wounded once
w(2) etc.	wounded twice etc.
W.O.	War Office
w-p	wounded and taken prisoner

NOTE.—Although every effort has been made to give an accurate record in the following pages, no details are to be quoted or made use of in any way as official.

Appendix II.
Records of Rank and File.

ABBOTT, Anthony John
B/12820, 22/3/18; No. 18 O.C.B., 20/9/18; R. Dub. Fus., 17/3/19; 2/Lieut.
Ovoca, Brangtingham Road, Whalley Range, Manchester.

ABBOTT, Arthur William
D/11536, 21/6/17, L/C.; No. 19 O.C.B., 9/11/17; Hamps. R., 26/3/18, att. R. Suss. R.; NR; Lieut.
64 Redcliffe Square, S.W.10.

✠ ABBOTT, John Gurney
6/A/8707, 4/1/16; No. 13 O.C.B., 4/11/16; Rif. Brig., 28/2/17, att. T.M. Bty.; F; 2/Lieut. Killed in action 21/9/17.

ABBOTT, Maxwell Freer
2/3715, 24/5/15, L/C.; R.G.A., 16/12/15, W.O. Intelligence; F; Capt.; w. 25 Acacia Road, St. John's Wood, N.W.8.

ABBOTT, William John
B/10548, 17/1/17, L/C.; R.F.A., C/S, 22/6/17; R.F.A., 18/11/17; Lieut. 128 Sutton Court, Chiswick, W.4.

✠ ABERCROMBY, John Stevenson
6/1/6961, 22/10/15, L/C.; Midd'x. R., 4/8/16; 2/Lieut.
Died of wounds 29/4/17.

✠ ABERDEEN, Louis Fredcrick
4/2/5002, T/20/7/15; 3rd Lond. R., 14/12/15; 2/Lieut.
Killed in action 10/9/16.

ABRAHAMS, Dudley Cyril
H/1945, 22/10/14; S. Lan. R., 6/3/15, War Office; F; Lieut.; w.
53 Gloucester Gardens, W.2.

✠ ABRAM, Robert
6/1/8473, 20/12/15; No. 8 O.C.B., 4/8/16; Bord. R., 21/11/16; 2/Lieut. (a/Capt.). Killed in action 26/10/17.

✠ ABREY, Charles Gordon
4/4172, 14/6/15; Oxf. & Bucks. L.I., 29/10/15; 2/Lieut.
Killed in action 21/7/16.

✠ ACASON, Hubert
4/1/4591, 5/7/15, L/C.; M.G.C., 25/9/16; F; Lieut.
Died —/4/20.

ACFIELD, Stanley Cable
C/12650, 27/2/18; No. 21 O.C.B., 5/7/18; Hamps. R., 3/3/19; 2/Lieut. 93 Livingstone Road, Southampton.

ACHESON, John
6/4/9272, 3/2/16; R.F.A., C/S, 4/8/16; R.G.A., 1/11/16; Lieut.
The Temple, Keady, Co. Armagh, Ireland.

ACHESON, John George
K/B/2213, 30/11/14; Sea. Highrs., 13/3/15, att. R.A.F.; F,It; Lieut.
c/o. Gellatly, Hankey & Co., Bayenturm 13, Cologne, Germany.

ACHESON-GRAY, Charles Gerald
F/1709, 15/10/14, L/C.; Dorset R., 2/2/15; Lieut.
Chartres Lodge, Lovelace Road, Surbiton, Surrey.

ACKERY, William Melville
F/1816, 16/10/14; E. Surr. R., 17/3/15, R. Dub. Fus., R.F.C., R.A.F.; S,E; Flt. Cmdr.; D.F.C., Croix de Guerre, M(1).
5 Helena Road, Southsea, Hants.

ACKLAND, Cecil Herbert
B/11041, 13/4/17; No. 11 O.C.B., 9/11/17; L'pool R., 30/4/18; 2/Lieut. 15 Wellington Place, Clyde Road, Dublin.

✠ ACKROYD, Thomas Noel
Sq/767, 2/3/14; R. Regt. of Cav., 12/9/14, Bedf. R.; 2/Lieut.
Killed in action 23/4/17.

ACLAND, Edward Fox Dyke
B/692, 7/2/13; Interpreter, 4/9/14, att. Manch. R., R.A.F.; F; Lieut. Thirtover, Cold Ash, Newbury, Berks.

✠ ADAM, Alexander Russell
4/3/4173, 14/6/15; Sea. Highrs., 23/9/15, R.F.C.; Lieut.
Killed in action 3/7/17.

ADAM, David
K/2624, 7/1/15; R.E., 30/1/15; F; Capt.; w(2); M(1).
127 Dartmouth Road, Brondesbury, N.W.2.

✠ ADAM, Walter
K/Sq/2400, 19/12/14, L/C.; R.E. Kent Yeo., 31/3/15, M.G.C.; G,E,F; Capt. Died 3/11/18.

ADAM, William McNicol
K/B/2424, 21/12/14; R.E., 27/3/15; Lieut.
12 Newark Street, Greenock.

ADAMS, Alfred John
C/11760, 30/7/17; Garr. O.C.B., 28/12/17; Lab. Corps, 18/5/18; 2/Lieut. 116 Tenison Road, Cambridge.

ADAMS, Alwyne Kingsley
6/3/6380, 23/9/15; No. 7 O.C.B., 7/4/16; Devon. R., 20/6/16; I,M; Lieut. Royal Grammar School, Henley-on-Thames.

✠ ADAMS, Auriol Charles Andrew
1/3289, 19/4/15; R. Lanc. R., 21/8/15; 2/Lieut.
Killed in action 16-18/8/16.

ADAMS, Bryan
A/13067, 15/5/18, L/C.; demob. 30/1/19.
White House, Fulford, Yorks.

ADAMS, Charles Gofton
6/4/5493, 9/8/15, L/C.; 20th Lond. R., 14/12/15; F; Capt.; w-p; M(2).
Risedale, Bussage, Stroud, Gloucestershire (Now in Hong Kong).

ADAMS, Charles Wilfred
4/6/5153, 29/7/15; R.G.A., 15/10/15; F; Capt.; w.
Haileybury College, Hertford.

ADAMS, Edward Josceline Percy
24, 2/4/08; dis. 26/6/09; 1/4/4104, 7/6/15, Sgt.; R. War. R., 9/9/15; F,It; Lieut.
c/o Rev. J. Adams, 3 Chesterford Gardens, Hampstead.

ADAMS, Edwin Charles
B/13514, 12/7/18; No. 22 O.C.B., 23/8/18; R. War. R., 13/2/19; 2/Lieut. 465 Belchers Lane, Little Bromwich, Birmingham.

ADAMS, Francis Stanley Joseph
6/D/8892, 13/1/16; M.G.C., C/S, 1/1/17; M.G.C., 25/4/17; F; Lieut.; w; M.C. 61 Stonard Road, Palmers Green, N.

ADAMS, Frank Herries
6/8402, 15/12/15; dis. to R. Mil. Academy, 1/6/16.

✠ ADAMS, Frederick Leslie
A/9809, 30/10/16; R.A., C/S, 26/1/17; R.G.A., 22/4/17; 2/Lieut.
Killed in action 15/9/18.

ADAMS, Harold Keith
6/4/7713, 2/11/15; No. 14 O.C.B.; 22nd Lond. R., 24/10/16, 20th, 24th & 9th Lond. R.; F,P, Roumania; Lieut.; w.
Kilsby, nr. Rugby.

ADAMS, Herbert Mayow
D/1487, 29/9/14; Worc. R., 13/3/15, secd. M.G.C.; F,It; Lieut.; M.C., M(1). 50 Bromyard Road, Worcester.

ADAMS, John Hughes
4/2/5020, 22/7/15; R.G.A., 1/12/15; Lieut.
Heatherleigh, Yelverton, S. Devon.

ADAMS, Robert Edgar
D/12101, 5/10/17; No. 15 O.C.B.; Bord. R., 3/2/19; 2/Lieut.
17 Hawarden Avenue, Douglas, Isle of Man.

APPENDIX II.—RECORDS OF RANK AND FILE.

ADAMS, Thomas William George
D/Sq/11173, 1/5/17; No. 2 Cav. C/S, 11/1/18; R. Regt. of Cav., 22/6/18; 2/Lieut.
Wotton, Underwood, Aylesbury.

ADAMSON, Cyril Leonard
6/2/6445, 27/9/15; R.F.C., C/S, 8/10/16; R.F.C., 26/2/17; F; Lieut.; w; A.F.C.
West Ham House, Basingstoke.

ADAMSON, Harold Alan
A/13058, 13/5/18; No. 1 O.C.B., 8/11/18, No. 3 O.C.B.; R.W. Kent R., 20/3/19; 2/Lieut.
49 Broomhill Road, Catford, S.E. 6.

ADAMSON, John Hutton
H/1925, 22/10/14; R.H.A., 1/5/15, emp. M. of Munitions; F; Major; Inv.; M(1).
21 Charterhouse Street, E.C. 1.

ADAMSON, Montague Allan Walters
4/2/4200, 14/6/15; R.W. Fus., 8/10/15, att. Indian Army; E,P; Lieut.
Exminster Vicarage, nr. Exeter (now in F.M.S.)

ADCOCK, Herbert Halford
4/5090, 26/7/15; dis. med. unfit; (joined Art. Rif. 1917); Durh. L.I., 11/9/18; F; Capt.
Wheatley, Oxon.

ADCOCK, Robert Henry
D/12989, 29/4/18, L/C.; demob. 30/5/19. Polesworth, Tanworth.

ADDENBROOKE, Herbert St. Vincent
4/9726, 13/10/16; Sig. C/S, 31/3/17; R.E., 31/7/17; F; Lieut.; M.C.
65 Waterloo Road, Wolverhampton.

✠ ADDERLEY, Charles
A/10072, 1/12/16; No. 14 O.C.B., 30/1/17. Died 23/10/17.

ADDINSELL, Thomas Augustus Arthur
Sq/623, 14/3/12; dis. 1/6/14; Yorks. R. 23/11/14, Bhopal Inf.; F,I; Capt.
c/o. W. J. Richards Esq., Compania Molinera " El Globo," Concepcion, Chile, S. America.

ADDIS, John Henry Lea
6/8276, 10/12/15; R.A., C/S, 9/6/16; R.F.A., 8/9/16; Lieut.

✠ ADENEY, Robert Edward
1/3106, 25/3/15; R.W. Surr. R., 18/6/15, att. R.F.C.; 2/Lieut. Died 11/4/17 as Prisoner of War.

ADKIN, Alexander Fairchild
C/1235, 23/9/14, L/C.; R. War. R., 5/3/15; F; Lieut.
8 Hope Park, Bromley, Kent.

ADLER, Sidney Michael
B/1120, 7/9/14; R. Fus., 5/10/14, att. No. 8 O.C.B Inst.; F; Capt.; w(2); m(1).
38 Hallam Street, Portland Place, W. 1.

ADMANS, Leonard Stephen
D/10025, 27/11/16; No. 14 O.C.B., 6/4/17; Lan. Fus., 31/7/17, att. M.G.C.; F; Lieut.; Inv.
4 Abbey Mansions, Herne Hill, S.E. 24.

AGATE, Robert George
B/10321, 4/1/17, L/C.; No. 14 O.C.B., 5/5/17; Dorset R., 28/8/17, att. Hamps. R.; F; Lieut.
61 Leadale Road, Stamford Hill, N. 16.

AGELASTO, Cyril John
6/2/7065, 29/10/15; R.F.C., 4/8/16; R.A.F.; F; Lieut.
c/o. Messrs. Ralli Bros., Calcutta, India.

AGIUS, Edgar Gordon
K/C/2073, 12/11/14; 3rd Lond. R., 24/1/15; F; Capt.; w.
3 Belsize Grove, Hampstead, N.W. 3. (Now in Paris.)

AGNEW, Albert Thomas
D/E/13818, 12/8/18; No. 22 O.C.B., 20/9/18; Essex R., 5/2/19; 2/Lieut.
35 Errington Road, Colchester.

AGNEW, Robert Vernon
C/10352, 5/1/17; R.A.O.C., 18/4/17; Lieut.
33 Brandling Park, Newcastle-on-Tyne.

✠ AHRENS, Arthur Horace
D/13933, 2/9/18. Died 1/11/18.

AIKMAN, James Alexander Stanley
6/3/5444, T/7/8/15; Essex R., 10/10/15; F; Lieut.; w.
Leeds and County Liberal Club, Quebec Street, Leeds.

✠ AINGER, Thomas Edward
Sq/172, 28/4/08, Sq.S.M.; Berks. Yeo., 23/1/14; G; 2/Lieut. Killed in action 21/8/15.

AIREY, Thomas Mattison
6/5/7323, 9/11/15, L/C.; E. Kent R., 4/8/16; S; Lieut.; w.
11 Station Road, Dovercourt Bay, Essex.

✠ AIRTH, Rennie Alexander
F/1760, 16/10/14; Bedf. R., 2/11/14, att. R.F.C.; Lieut. Killed in action 29/7/17.

AISBITT, Ernest Wheldon Blaxland
C/14284, 11/11/18; trfr. K.R. Rif. C., 25/4/19.
Tyrie, Brockweir, Chepstow.

AITCHISON, Craigie Mason
6/3/6345, 20/9/15; R.A.O.C., 10/11/15, R.G.A.; Lieut.
5 North Charlotte Street, Edinburgh.

AITKEN, John Baird
D/E/13775, 7/8/18; No. 22 O.C.B., 20/9/18; R. Scots., 14/2/19; 2/Lieut.
37 Glebe Road, Kilmarnock, N.B.

AITKEN, John Hogarth
6/3/9339, 4/2/16, L/C.; R. Sco. Fus., 24/1/17; F; Lieut.; Inv
Yeolands, Cessnock Road, Troon, Ayrshire.

AITKEN, John Rennie
D/13830, 14/8/18; demob. 30/5/19.
2 Manse Avenue, Coatbridge, Scotland.

AITKEN, Kenneth Edmonstone
F/2662, 12/1/15; Yorks. L.I., 19/4/15, att. Leic. R.; F; Major; w.
Inglefield, Totland Bay, Isle of Wight. (Now in F.M.S.)

AITKEN, Robert
4/3/4524, 1/7/15; Oxf. & Bucks. L.I., 7/11/15, att. Intelligence Staff; F; Lieut.; w(2).
49 Gordon Mansions, W.C. 1

AITKEN, Robert Menpes
6/3/8151, 6/12/15; trfr. Class W. Res., 6/11/16.
Rough Rew, Dorking, Surrey.

AITKENS, Geoffrey Noel Manning
B/12407, 18/1/18, L/C.; R.A., C/S, 15/3/18; R.G.A., 12/2/19; 2/Lieut.
Windle-Edge, Southborough, Tunbridge Wells.

AKHURST, Edward George
6/2/5546, 12/8/15; Devon. R., 4/8/16, att. Linc. R. and R.A.F; F; Lieut.; w.
Victoria Villa, S. Brent, Devon.

✠ AKRILL-JONES, Edward Trevor
4/3826, 31/5/15; Notts. & Derby. R., 10/9/15, R.F.C.; Lieut.; w. Killed 18/3/18.

✠ AKRILL-JONES, Robert Rowland
6/3/6266, 16/9/15; No. 11 O.C.B., 7/5/16; Yorks. L.I., 4/9/16; 2/Lieut. Killed in action 28/4/17.

ALBRECHT, Edward Castendieck
K/Sq/2442, 28/12/14, Sgt.; dis. to re-enlist in R.E., 20/8/15; R.G.A., 12/12/16, att. R.E. Signals; F; Lieut.; w.
c/o Lond. Joint City & Mid. Bk. Ltd., High Street, Bedford.

ALBRECHT, Henry John Charles
6/3/6545, 30/9/15; trfr. Hamps. R., 21/7/16; M.G.C., 25/3/17; Lieut.; w.
c/o. Messrs. Naumann Gepp & Co., 130 Fenchurch Street, E.C.

ALDEN, Arthur Rhodes
4/5/4776, 12/7/15; 11th Lond. R., 3/12/15; E,P; Capt.; M.B.E.
Eastwyke Farm, Abingdon Road, Oxford.

ALDER, Charles Herbert Lawrence
A/313, 30/6/08; dis. 26/6/10. 9 Lawrence Pountney Hill, E.C.

ALDER, William Dacre
6/3/6191, 13/9/15; S. Lan. R., 9/6/16; Lieut.
2 Northcote House, Heath Street, Hampstead.

ALDERMAN, William John
B/12384, 15/1/18; No. 5 O.C.B., 10/5/18, No. 14 O.C.B.; R. W. Kent R., 3/2/19; 2/Lieut.
The Groves, Birling Road, Snodland, Kent.

ALDERSLEY, Charles Edgar
D/B/Sq/12114, 4/10/17; No. 2 Cav. C/S, 11/4/18, No. 24 O.C.B.; Tank Corps, 22/3/19; 2/Lieut.
Coates Hall, Barnoldswick, Yorks.

ALDERSON, Cecil William
D/12913, 10/4/18; No. 8 O.C.B., 18/10/18; demob.
63 Auckland Road, Ilford, Essex.

ALDERSON, Gerald Graham
Sq/133, 18/4/08; trfr. L.U.O.T.C., 17/4/10; R.A.M.C.; F; Major.
Dudley House, Kenilworth, Warwickshire.

APPENDIX II.—RECORDS OF RANK AND FILE.

ALDINGTON, Hubert Edward
6/9250, 2/2/16; R.E., 7/3/16; F; Major; M(1).
    Canmore, Monmouth Road, Dorchester.

ALDOUS, Alfred Martin
6/3/5494, 9/8/15; E. Sur. R., 3/1/16; E; Lieut.
    25 Ennerdale Road, Kew Gardens.

ALDOUS, Basil Charles
D/10866, 10/3/17, Cpl.; R.E., C/S, 16/9/17; R.E., 14/12/17; F; Lieut.; M(1).   21 Kirkstall Road, Streatham Hill, S.W. 2.

ALDRED, Harold
C/11535, 18/6/17; No. 19 O.C.B., 9/11/17; Notts. & Derby R., 16/6/18; F; 2/Lieut.
    c/o. F. & H. Aldred, Derwent Street, Derby.

ALDRICH, Horace Wilfred
A/10676, 9/2/17; Garr. O.C.B., 23/5/17; Lab. Corps, 14/7/17, Devon R., D. of Corn. L.I.; F; Lieut.   4 New Road, Brighton.

ALDRICH, Leslie
4/2/4487, 28/6/15, L/C.; 25th Lond. R., 27/1/16; Lieut.

ALDRICH-BLAKE, Robert Morison
F/1814, 16/10/14, L/C.; dis. 18/6/15.
    Hill Brow, Goodrich, Ross.

ALDRIDGE, Eustace Farnham
A/Sq/11622, 9/7/17; A.S.C., C/S, 21/1/18; R.A.S.C., 17/3/18; 2/Lieut.   3 Southfield Road, Westbury-on-Trym, nr. Bristol.

ALDRIDGE, William Valentine
6/1/5600, T/14/8/15; No. 14 O.C.B.; N. Lan. R., 20/10/16; F; Lieut.; g.   50 Guildford Avenue, Surbiton.

ALDWORTH, Albert Arthur
C/903, 5/8/14; Leic. R., 12/9/14, G.H.Q.; F; Lt.-Col., D.A.Q.M.G.; M.C.   Kingswood, 130 Stamford Hill, N. 16.

ALDWORTH, Cedric Henry John
C/1139, 14/9/14, L/C.; Hamps. R., 27/2/15; F; Capt.; M.C.
    Ridgeway House, Chingford, E. 4.

✠ ALEXANDER, Alan Mansell
6/6510, 30/9/15; No. 1 O.C.B., 25/2/16; 16th Lond. R., 8/7/16; 2/Lieut.   Killed in action 8/12/17.

ALEXANDER, Arthur Cole
6/3/7787, 24/11/15, L/C.; 8th Lond. R., 4/9/16; F; Capt.; w; M.C.   Salisbury House, Salisbury Road, Southsea.

ALEXANDER, George Douglas
6/3/5823, 26/8/15; Ches. R., 22/1/16; Manch. R., emp. M. of Labour; F; Lieut.; w.
    18 Highbury, West Jesmond, Newcastle-on-Tyne.

ALEXANDER, George Percival
C/A/12039, 27/9/17; R.F.C., C/S, 18/1/17; R.F.C., 6/3/18, R.A.F.; F; 2/Lieut.   The Villa, Oakenholt, Flint, N. Wales.

ALEXANDER, Harold Bernard
C/10140, 7/12/16; trfr. 8th Lond. R., 9/3/17.
    The Rodney, Horncastle, Lincs.

ALEXANDER, James Graham
E/2848, T/30/1/15; R. Innis. Fus., 6/7/15, att. Norf. R.; F,S,P; Capt.; w, Inv.   45 West Street, Boston, Lincs.

ALEXANDER, John
D/10688, 7/2/17; No. 2 Cav. C/S, 13/7/17; R. Regt. of Cav., 14/12/17, att. 16th Lancers; 2/Lieut.
    Milford House, Milford Co. Carlow, Ireland.

ALEXANDER, Russell
B/11379, 30/5/17; A.S.C., C/S, 1/9/17; R.A.S.C., 27/10/17; Lieut.   43 Old Town, Clapham, S.W.

ALEXANDER, Walter Baynes
6/8683, 4/1/16; R.A., C/S, 7/7/16; R.F.A., 13/10/16; Capt.; M.C.   c/o. Rev. G. Duncan, Shipton Rectory, Kidlington, Oxon.

ALEXANDER, William Alfred Drew
B/12692, 6/3/18; R.A., C/S, 26/7/18; R.G.A., 10/4/19; 2/Lieut.
    103 Pembroke Road, Clifton, Bristol.

ALFORD, Richard Cooper
6/1/8433, T/15/12/15, L/C.; No. 5 O.C.B., 14/8/16; North'd Fus., 21/11/16; F; Lieut.; w.   The Hollies, Allison Road, Acton, W.

ALISON, Charles Hugh
D/1417, 29/9/14; Army Pay Dept., 4/11/14; Capt and Paymaster.
    7 Montpelier Terrace, S.W. 7.

ALKEN, Charles Frederick Seffrien
C/13359, 26/6/18; demob. 29/1/19.
    14 Cloudsley Road, Hastings.

ALKER, Francis
4/1/65187, 29/7/15, L/C.; N. Lan. R., 20/12/15, secd. Intelligence Corps and Gen. Staff; F; Major; M.C., M(1).
    Villa Ma Josy, Escalier du Prophète, Marseilles, France.

ALKER, Percy
A/14102, 7/10/18; trfr. 14th Lond. R., 6/12/18.
    Rotherwood, Darley Dale, Matlock.

ALLAM, Frederick William
4/2/4519, T/29/6/15, L/C.; R. War. R., 7/10/15, D. of Corn. L.I., cmd. 12th L'pool. R.; F; Lt.-Col.; w(2); M.C.
    Postlands, Southwater, Horsham, Sussex.

ALLAN, Alexander Robert
6/1/5822, T/26/8/15; Arg. & Suth'd Highrs., 24/1/17; F; Lieut.
    c/o. Messrs. Allan, Whyte & Co., Rutherglen, nr. Glasgow.

ALLAN, Alfred William
D/10450, 10/1/17, L/C.; R.F.C., C/S, 16/4/17; R.F.C., 16/5/17, R.A.F.; F; Flying Officer.
    42 Parkhill Road, Belsize Park, N.W.

ALLAN, Charles Edward
D/E/13819, 12/8/18; No. 22 O.C.B., 22/11/18; R. Berks. R., 15/2/19; 2/Lieut.   14 Carlisle Road, W. Kilburn, N.W. 6.

ALLAN, David Stewart
6/9341, 7/2/16; R.F.C., 12/5/16, R.A.F.; Lieut.
    4 Mornington Road, Liscard, Cheshire.

ALLAN, Frederick Julian
B/12009, 17/9/17; dis. med, unfit, 17/1/18.
    Market Square, St. Neots, Huntingdonshire.

ALLAN, Henry Percival
4/Sq/4265, 17/6/15; R.W. Fus., 31/10/15, Rif. Brig.; E; Lieut.   Linwood, 41 Park Road, Bromley Kent.

ALLAN, Robert
6/1/6265, 16/9/15, L/C.; N. Lan. R., 6/1/16, M.G.C.; Capt.; w; M.C., D.C.M., M(1).   34 Toll Street, Motherwell, Scotland.

ALLAN, William
6/1/8008, 30/11/15; R.F.C., 25/9/16; F; Lieut.
    Larne, Fellows Road, Farnborough, Hants.

ALLAN, William Alexander
6/3/9181, 28/1/16, L/C.; No. 14 O.C.B., 30/10/16; R. Scots., 24/1/17; 2/Lieut.   59 Leamington Terrace, Edinburgh.

ALLANSON, Gerald Vincent
6/3/7166, 3/11/15; trfr. M.G.C., 24/11/16; F; w,g.
    6 King's Avenue, Clapham Park, S.W. 4.

✠ ALLANSON, Wilfred George
6/2/D/7129, 2/11/15, Cpl.; No. 6 O.C.B., 15/2/17; R.F.C., 23/5/17, R.A.F.; F; Lieut.   Killed in action 21/9/18.

ALLDAY, Frank Cuming
D/11109, 23/4/17; A.S.C., C/S, 1/2/18; R.A.S.C., 26/4/18; F; 2/Lieut.   Packwood, St. Bernard's Road, Olton, Warwickshire.

ALLDEN, George
D/11177, 4/5/17; A.S.C., C/S, 1/9/17; R.A.S.C., 27/10/17; 2/Lieut.   Wayside Cottage, Frenshaw, Farnham, Surrey.

ALLDEN, John
C/11430, 2/6/17; A.S.C., C/S, 1/9/17; R.A.S.C., 27/10/17; F; 2/Lieut.   The Rowans, London Road, Guildford, Surrey.

✠ ALLDEN, Joseph Henry
6/5/C/7394, 12/11/15; No. 14 O.C.B.; Oxf. & Bucks. L.I., 22/11/16; 2/Lieut.   Killed in action 28/4/17.

ALLEN, Albert Arthur
B/12750, 13/3/18, L/C.; No. 20 O.C.B., 20/9/18, No. 10 O.C.B.; High. L.I., 16/4/19; 2/Lieut.
    59 Oakfield Road, Highams Park, Walthamstow.

ALLEN, Alfred
A/9823, 1/11/16; R.A., C/S, 23/5/17; R.G.A., 16/9/17; F; Lieut.; M.C.
Exchequer and Audit Department, Victoria Embankment, E.C. 4.

ALLEN, Alfred Henry Charles
D/11575, 2/7/17; No. 1. O.C.B., 5/7/17; Devon. R., 30/10/17, emp. Malacca Vol. Rif.; Lieut.; M.C.
    Castle View, Lismore, Co. Waterford, Ireland.

APPENDIX II.—RECORDS OF RANK AND FILE.

✠ ALLEN, Archibald Stafford
C/406, 28/4/09; R. Fus., 12/9/14; F; Lieut.; M(1).
  Killed in action 3/10/15.

ALLEN, Arthur
4/3753, 27/5/15, Sgt.; Worc. R., 23/12/15, att. T.M. Bty.; F,It; Lieut.; M.C., Italian Bronze Medal for Military Valour, M(1).
  471 Gillott Road, Edgbaston, Birmingham.

ALLEN, Bertie
3897, 31/5/15; dis. same day.

ALLEN, Ernest Cecil
6/2/8713, 5/1/16; No. 8 O.C.B., 4/8/16; Manch. R., 21/11/16, R.E.; Lieut.
  Doriscourt, Whalley Range, Manchester.

ALLEN, Ernest Mortimer
F/1822, 16/10/14; Lt. Hamps. R., 29/10/14, R.W. Surr. R.; F; Major; w(2); M.C. 42, Banbury Road, Oxford. (Now in FMS).

ALLEN, Harold Colin
1648, 9/10/14; Wilts. R., 23/10/14; F; Capt.; w(2).
  Public Schools Club, W. 1.

ALLEN, Herbert Richard
D/A/11861, 16/8/17; Sig. C/S, 1/2/18; R.E., 12/7/18; 2/Lieut.
  88 Clifton Hill, St. John's Wood, N.W.

ALLEN, Hugh Stanley
C/14221, T/26/10/18; trfr. K.R. Rif. C., 25/4/19.
  29 Downs Park West, Bristol.

✠ ALLEN, John Hugh
B/1260, 23/9/14; Worc. R., 20/10/14; G; Lieut.
  Killed in action 13/6/15.

ALLEN, John Kenneth
D/13716, 2/8/18; trfr. K.R. Rif. C., 25/4/19, M.G.C.; Pte.
  Gwynant, Gilbert Road, Hale, Cheshire.

ALLEN, Julian Broome Livingston
B/D/12210, 8/11/17; H. Bde. O.C.B., 20/3/18; Coldstream Gds., 27/8/18; 2/Lieut.

ALLEN, Lemuel Thompson Marsden
D/10003, 24/11/16; No. 14 O.C.B., 6/4/17; R.W. Surr. R., 31/7/17; 2/Lieut.; p.
  56 Cliveden Road, Wimbledon.

ALLEN, Leonard Ewart
6/4/7247, 8/11/15; trfr. Hamps. R., 28/7/16; R.N.A.S.; F; Flt. Sub. Lt.; Inj.
  67 Victoria Road North, Southsea, Hants.

ALLEN, Oliver Wylie
Sq/163, 18/4/08; E. Rid. of Yorks. Yeo., 23/9/14, att. Glouc. R.
  33 Elmfield Road, Bromley, Kent.

ALLEN, Stanley Edward
E/1586, 6/10/14, L/C.; R.A.O.C., 22/1/15; F; Major, D.A.D.O.S.; M(1).
  Denne Hill, nr. Canterbury, Kent.

ALLEN, Vincent George
6/5/7641, 22/11/15; No. 14 O.C.B.; Norf. R., 18/12/16; F; Lieut.; w, Inv.
  Fairfield, Ely Road, Llandaff, S. Wales.

ALLEN, William George
4/1/5021, 22/7/15, Cpl.; Devon. R., 11/12/15; Lieut.
  Lawrenry House, Stubbington Avenue, Portsmouth.

✠ ALLEN, William Henry
B/10320, 4/1/17; M.G.C., C/S, 27/4/17; M.G.C., 26/9/17; 2/Lieut.
  Killed in action 12/4/18.

ALLEN, William Joseph
C/14285, 11/11/18; demob. 30/1/19.
  37 Oakley Road, London.

ALLERTON, Henry Reeve
4/4124, 10/6/15; Suff. R., 24/10/15, att. Essex R.; F; Major; w.
  148 High Street, Lowestoft.

✠ ALLIBAN, William Beaumont
F/2339, 14/12/14; Notts. & Derby. R., 11/3/15; Lieut.; M(1).
  Killed in action 5/5/17.

ALLINGHAM, Eric John
4/6/Sq/4777, 12/7/15, L/C.; R.F.A., 22/10/15; P,F; Lieut.
  Armidale, New South Wales, Australia.

ALLINGHAM, William
4/5/C/4778, 12/7/15, Cpl.; No. 11 O.C.B., 7/5/16; trfr. War. Yeo., 15/11/16.
  c/o. Commercial Bank of Sydney, 18, Birchin Lane, E.C.

ALLPASS, Douglas Harold
A/10950, 30/3/17; No. 14 O.C.B., 5/7/17; Northern Cyc. Bn. 30/10/17, North'd. Fus., att. Durh. L.I.; Lieut.
  27 Selbourne Road, Southgate, N. 14.

ALLPORT, Albert Edward
4/4556, 1/7/15; R.A.S.C., 6/10/15; Germ. E.A.; Capt.
  c/o. Dr. A. E. Griffith, 36 Grove Park, Denmark Hill, S.E.

ALLPORT, Denison Howard
A/11636, 12/7/17; No. 19 O.C.B., 9/11/17; Notts. & Derby. R., 26/3/18, att. Indian Army; I; Lieut.
  Caversham, Townley Road, Dulwich, S.E. 22.

ALLUM, William John
6/5/7858, 26/11/15, L/C.; No. 14 O.C.B.; Suff. R., 24/10/16; Lieut.
  315 Seven Sisters Road, Finsbury Park, N. 4.

ALLWOOD, Ernest Frank
C/A/12063, 1/10/17; R.A., C/S, 2/4/18; R.G.A., 28/10/18; 2/Lieut.
  31 De Montfort Road, Reading.

✠ ALMACK, Alfred Turnour Christopher
K/F/2351, 14/12/14; North'n. R., 3/3/15; 2/Lieut.
  Killed in action 27/9/16.

ALMOND, Arthur James
6/3/8152, 6/12/15, L/C.; No. 14 O.C.B., 28/8/16; Manch. R., 18/12/16, att. Notts. & Derby. R.; F; Lieut.
  16 Kennedy Street, Manchester.

ALPE, Herbert
A/11587, 5/7/17; A.S.C., C/S, 1/11/17; R.A.S.C., 25/1/18; F; 2/Lieut.
  27 Tierney Road, Streatham, S.W. 2.

ALSOP, William
A/10252, 29/12/16; No. 14 O.C.B., 6/4/17; R.W. Surr. R., 31/7/17, emp. M. of Labour; 2/Lieut.
  Belrigge, 1 Uppingham Road, West Derby, Liverpool.

ALTHAM, John
A/13092, 22/5/18; H. Bde. O.C.B., 14/9/18; Gds. M.G.R., 10/3/19; 2/Lieut.
  Reedley Hall, Burnley, Lancs.

ALTHAUS, Frederick Rudolph
C/1035, 24/8/14; Suff. R., 26/8/14, emp. M. of Labour; Capt.; w; M(1).
  2 Strathray Gardens, Eton Avenue, N.W. 3.

ALTMAN, Montague Vincent
C/11467, 11/6/17; A.S.C., C/S, 1/9/17; R.A.S.C., 27/10/17; F,Sp; Lieut.
  44 Pattison Road, Hampstead, N.W. 2.

AMBLER, Eric Frank
B/561, 5/4/11; 22nd Lond. R., 28/8/14, att. R.A.F.; F; Capt.
  70 Iverna Court, Kensington, W. 8.

AMBROSE, Percy Robert
4/1/4355, 21/6/15; Essex R., 24/12/15, att. Herts. R., att. T.M. Bty., att. R.A.F.; F; Lieut.
  Greencroft, Loone, Maidstone, Kent.

AMENT, John Adrian Portielje
4/2/5064, 26/7/15; 18th Lond. R., 19/12/15; Lieut.; F; w.
  Temple Chambers, E.C. 4.

AMEY, Alan Howard
C/12556, 6/2/18; No. 14 O.C.B., 5/7/18; 12th Lond. R., 1/5/19; 2/Lieut.
  1 St. Margarets Street, Canterbury, Kent.

AMEY, Neville Fulcher
6/1/6984, 25/10/15; dis. 11/2/16; R. Mar. Art., —/3/16; F; Lieut.
  99 Heathwood Gardens, Charlton.

AMIES, Ernest Eric Hawkins
4/5/4779, 12/7/15, Sgt.; N. Staff. R., 21/4/16, att. Leic. R.; F; Capt.; Inv.
  Rowley Bank House, Stafford.

AMIS, Henry Glennie
A/1678, 12/10/14; York. R., 13/3/15, secd. R.F.C.; F; Capt.; g,p.
  29 Mincing Lane, E.C. 3.

AMM, Edgar Oxenham
D/11537, 21/6/17; R.F.C., C/S, 2/8/17; R.F.C., 8/9/17, R.A.F.; Lieut.; D.F.C.
  South African Officers' Club, 48 Grosvenor Square, W.

AMOR, Albert Edwin
6/1/6312, T/18/9/15; trfr. H.A.C., 26/5/16.
  82 Gladsmuir Road, Highgate, N.

AMOS, Andrew James Arthur
D/13922, 30/8/18; trfr, K.R. Rif. C., 25/4/19, M.G.C.; Pte.
  St. Paul's House, Deptford, S.E. 8.

AMPS, John Graham
6/3/5495, 9/8/15, L/C.; Essex R., 8/6/16; F; Lieut.; w.
  Khartoum, Magdalen Road, Bexhill-on-Sea.

AMSCHEWITZ, Ivor
4/2/4266, 17/6/15; L'pool. R., 27/11/15; F; Staff Lt.; Inv.
  26 Holmwood Gardens, Church End, Finchley, N. 3.

APPENDIX II.—RECORDS OF RANK AND FILE.

AMSDEN, William Frank
C/978, 5/8/14; 12th Lond. R., 31/10/14; Lieut.; w.
10 Falcon Street, E.C.

ANDERSEN, Reginald Charles
4/3/4015, 7/6/15; R.E., 9/9/15; Lieut.; M.C.
Piccadilly Hotel, W. 1.

ANDERSON, Albert Roland
6/4/5371, 5/8/15; R.A.S.C., 21/10/15; S; Capt.; O.B.E., Order of S. Stanislaus, M(1).
Street House, Street, Co. Westmeath, Ireland.

✠ ANDERSON, Alec David
B/189, 4/5/08; dis. 3/5/09; H. Bde. O.C.B.; Grenadier Gds., 29/5/18; F; 2/Lieut.
Killed in action 6/11/18.

ANDERSON, Alec Marchmont
4/2/4034, 7/6/15, L/C.; Midd'x. R., 21/4/16; F; Lieut.; w.
18 Colville Square, W. 11.

ANDERSON, Charles Scott
A/12509, 31/1/18; R.A.F., C/S, 4/5/18; R.A.F., 13/2/19; EA; 2/Lieut.
Box 6728, Johannesburg, S. Africa.

ANDERSON, Charles Spencer
2/9671, 2/10/16; No. 14 O.C.B., 30/1/17; North'd Fus., 29/5/17; 2/Lieut.; w.
57 Alexandra Road, Swansea.

ANDERSON, Charles William
C/10803, 28/2/17; No. 11 O.C.B., 5/7/17; 16th Lond. R., 30/10/17; Lieut.
Hedge Briers, Radlett, Herts.

ANDERSON, Edward Wright
A/10955, 30/3/17; No. 14 O.C.B., 10/8/17; Oxf. & Bucks. L.I., 27/11/17, K.R. Rif. C., att. P. of War Coy.; F; Lieut.
3D Maida Vale Mansions, W. 9.

✠ ANDERSON, Edwin Frederick Spurrier
F/2822, 1/2/15; N. Staff. R., 31/3/15; Lieut.; w.
Died of wounds 1/11/18.

ANDERSON, George Stafford
4/4201, 14/6/15, Cpl.; Leic. R., 6/10/15; F. Lieut.; Inv.
Hamaden, Old Humberstone, Leicester.

ANDERSON, Gerald Frank
D/11148, 30/4/17; R.F.C., C/S, 1/6/17; R.F.C., 4/7/17, R.A.F.; F; Lieut.; w; D.F.C.
Victory House School, Nelson Road, Sheringham, Norfolk.

ANDERSON, Henry Beveridge
C/14286, 11/11/18; No. 11 O.C.B., 24/1/19; Genl. List, 8/3/19; SA; 2/Lieut.
Fairhaven, Redhouse, S. Africa.

ANDERSON, Henry Norman
2/3213, 12/4/15, L/C.; R.A.S.C., 21/10/15, R. Scots, Intelligence; S,M; Major.
c/o. Buenos Aires Gt. Southern Rly. Co., River Plate House, Finsbury Circus, E.C. 2.

ANDERSON, John Swanzy Wardlaw
K/Sq/2267, 7/12/14, Cpl.; R.A.S.C., 2/3/15; F; Capt.; M(1).
c/o. Messrs. Cocks, Biddulph & Co., 43, Charing Cross, S.W. 1.

ANDERSON, John Varty
6/4/8949, 17/1/16; trfr. 19th Lond. R., 25/4/17.
Bridge End, Hexham, Northumberland.

ANDERSON, Laurence Allfrey Pelham
C/504, 4/11/10; Ind. Med. Serv., 26/7/13; Capt.; p.; M(1).
33 Parkhill Road, Hampstead, N.W.

ANDERSON, Neil Gordon
Sq/952, 5/8/14; R.A.S.C., 8/9/14; F; Capt.; O.B.E., Order of the Crown of Roumania, 3rd Class, M(2).
19 Sussex Place, Regents Park, N.W. 1.

ANDERSON, Norman McCay
9574, 26/4/16, L/C.; R.F.C., C/S, 1/2/17; R.F.C., 12/4/17; R.A.F.; Lieut.; w.
Fotheringham, Stranraer.

ANDERSON, Reginald George de Courcelle
H/1968, 26/10/14; Nat. Res., 1/12/14, att. Rif. Bridg.; F; Capt
4 Blawith Road, Harrow, Middlesex.

ANDERSON, Robert Cecil
6/1/7167, 3/11/15; No. 7 O.C.B., 3/7/16; R. Dub. Fus., 18/12/16, att. Indian Army; F,I; Lieut.
Officers' Mess, 1/22nd Punjabis, Quetta, Baluchistan.

ANDERSON, Robert Duncan
6/3/6434, T/25/9/15, L/C.; 11th Lond. R., 4/6/16; F; Capt.; w(2).
120 Burnt Ash Hill, Lee, S.E. 12.

ANDERSON, Robert Eric
6/Sq/9170, 25/1/16, L/C.; R.A., C/S, 23/6/16; R.F.A., 27/10/16; F; Lieut.
Caledonian Club, St. James' Square, S.W. 2.

ANDERSON, Ronald Stewart
C/14287, 11/11/18; trfr. R. Highrs. 16/4/19.
Pitcorthie, Denton Avenue, Gledhow, Leeds.

ANDERSON, Samuel
6/3/5372, 5/8/15, L/C.; No. 2 O.C.B., 26/2/16; High. L.I., 6/7/16, att. R.F.C.; F; Capt. & Flt. Cmdr.; w; D.F.C.
The Studio, 22 W. Kensington Gardens, W. 14.

ANDERSON, Thomas
4/6/5/4991, 19/7/15; Gord. Highrs., 22/11/15; F, Gold Coast; Lieut.; w.
Springbank, Fordoun, Kincardineshire.

ANDERSON, Victor Vaughan
B/A/12215, 15/11/17; R.F.C., C/S, 15/2/18; R.F.C., 13/3/18, R.A.F.; F; 2/Lieut.
Estancia El Jabali, El Jabali, F.C.C.G.B.A., Argentina.

✠ ANDERSON, Vincent Tollemache
6/5/8153, 6/12/15; No. 14 O.C.B.; M.G.C., 24/10/16; 2/Lieut.
Died of wounds 13/4/18.

ANDERSON, William Charles
6/1/7037, 28/10/15; Lond. Elec. Eng., 30/8/16; Lieut.
6 Perry Rise, Forest Hill, S.E.

ANDERSON, William Montgomery
A/9820, 30/10/16; dis. to R. Mil. Coll., 6/11/16; Sco. Rif., 13/9/17; F; Lieut.; w.

ANDRAS, John Bertram
C/754, 23/1/14; E. Surr. R., 23/7/14; Capt.
Chudleigh, Ewell Road, Surbiton.

ANDRE, Joseph George Wilfred
6/4/7642, 22/11/15; No. 11 O.C.B., 7/5/16; Glouc. R., 4/9/16; Lieut.
8 Newton Road, Westbourne Grove, Bayswater.

ANDREAS, George Ernest
2/3478, 3/5/15; 19th Lond. R., 19/8/15; F,S,P; Capt.; M(1).
Belvoir, 36 Holden Road, Woodside Park, N. 12.

ANDREW, George Hubert
B/12751, 13/3/18, L/C.; R.A., C/S, 26/7/18; R.F.A., 8/4/19; 2/Lieut.
Polkyth, St. Austell, Cornwall.

ANDREW, Melville
6/A/6005, 2/9/15, L/C.; trfr. Class W. Res., 18/1/18.
297 Western Bank, Sheffield.

✠ ANDREWS, Bartram George
6/3/6879, 18/10/15; R.M.L.I., 7/1/16; Capt:; M(1).
Killed in action 21/8/18.

ANDREWS, Cecil Charles
A/11637, 12/7/17; No. 19 O.C.B., 9/11/17; R. Muns. Fus., 26/3/18, att. R. Ir. Regt.; F; 2/Lieut.; w.
238 Nantwich Road, Crewe.

ANDREWS, Francis Ernest
6/4/D/9443, 12/2/16, Cpl.; No. 14 O.C.B., 26/11/16; Notts. and Derby. R., 27/3/17, att. W.O. Intelligence; F,E,P; Capt.; p.
65 Highwood Avenue, N. Finchley, N. 12.

ANDREWS, Frederick Ivan
C/9898, 13/11/16; No. 14 O.C.B., 5/3/17; 3rd Lond. R., 26/6/17, att. M. of Shipping; Lieut.
69 Burnt Ash Road, Lee, S.E. 12.

ANDREWS, Geoffrey Bonython
F/1753, 16/10/14; Linc. R., 11/12/14, York. R.; E,F,NR; Capt.; w.
Wellswood, Northgate, Lincoln.

ANDREWS, Guy Anness Allen
2/3214, 12/4/15; Shrops. L.I., 30/6/15, Rif. Brig., att. R.F.C.; E,P; Lieut.
Avoca, Whetstone, N. 20.

✠ ANDREWS, James William
C/Sq/11431, 4/6/17; Pte.
Died 29/9/17.

ANDREWS, John Spencer Trevor
A/K/2547, 4/1/15; Notts. & Derby. R., 25/6/15, Indian Army; Lieut.

ANDREWS, Laurence Allan
K/D/2077, 13/11/14; Midd'x R., 11/2/15; Lieut.; Inv.
St. Paul's House, 42 Powerscroft Road, Clapton, E. 5.

ANDREWS, Leonard Beckley
6/4/7714, 22/11/15, Sgt.; No. 14 O.C.B.; K.R. Rif. C., 24/10/16, secd. Ind. Div. Sig. Coy.; F,It,E,P; Lieut.; M(1).
65 Highwood Avenue, N. Finchley, N. 12.

76

APPENDIX II.—RECORDS OF RANK AND FILE.

✠ ANDREWS, Leslie Ernest
3/3107, 25/3/15, L/C.; R.W. Surr. R., 30/6/15; F; Major; w.; M.C. and Bar. Killed in action 20/9/17.

ANDREWS, Maurice
A/10723, 12/2/17; No. 14 O.C.B., 5/7/17; Hamps. R., 30/10/17; 2/Lieut. Kenilworth, Sherwood Park Road, Sutton, Surrey.

ANDREWS, Solomon Sydney
1/9662, 29/9/16; No. 14 O.C.B., 27/12/16; trfr. 19th Lond. R., 26/3/17. 158 Newport Road, Cardiff.

ANDRIES, Henri Edouard
D/12116, 15/10/17, Cpl.; No. 2 O.C.B., 20/9/18, No. 11 O.C.B.; demob. c/o. Standard Bank of S. Africa, 10 Clements Lane, E.C.

ANELAY, Thomas
3/6/D/3215, 12/4/15, L/C.; dis. med. unfit, 14/12/18. 46 Bootham, York.

ANGIOR, Geoffrey Matthews
14153, 14/10/18; demob. 30/5/19. Standishgate House, Wigan.

ANN, Louis Douglas
K/B/2139, 19/11/14; R. Suss. R., 2/4/15, Intelligence; G,E,P; Lieut.; w. 27 Carlisle Road, Eastbourne.

ANNAN, Robert
K/E/2465, 28/12/14; R.E., 6/3/15; F; Capt. 82 Gloucester Terrace, Hyde Park, W. 2.

ANNAND, James Burt
B/13595, 24/7/18; demob. 29/1/19. 37 Woodville Road, Ealing, W. 5.

ANNETT, James Bertram
4/2/4061, 7/6/15; North'd. Fus., 11/10/15; F; Lieut.; Inv.; M(1). Stanton Fence, Morpeth, Northumberland.

ANNETTS, Ewart Paul
4/2/4488, 28/6/15; R.W. Kent. R., 9/12/15; Lieut. 2 Banbury Road, Wolvercote, Oxford.

ANSELL, Harold George
9203, 31/1/16; R.A., C/S, 4/8/16; R.G.A., 12/11/16; Lieut. The Briars, Norman Road, Sutton, Surrey.

ANSON, Archibald
A/9824, 1/11/16; A.S.C., C/S, 12/2/17; R.A.S.C., 10/4/17; E,P; Lieut. Hill Brow, Farnborough, Kent.

✠ ANSTEE, Joseph
4/3/4267, 17/6/15; Linc. R., 7/10/15; 2/Lieut. Killed in action 1/7/16.

✠ ANSTEY, Alexander Burgess
6/7976, 29/11/15; R.F.C., 4/8/16; 2/Lieut.; w. Killed 22/2/18.

ANSTIE, John William
2/3570, 10/5/15; dis. 25/8/15.

ANTHONY, Edgar Holden Hollis
C/1330, 26/9/14, L/C.; R.W. Kent R., 10/2/15, Norf. R., emp. M. of Labour; Lieut.; w(2). Lydgate, Park Avenue, Hampstead.

ANTHONY, William Lionel
C/1/8234, 8/12/15; No. 2 O.C.B., 14/8/16; Rif. Brig., 18/12/16; Lieut.; w. 49 Dowanhill Road, Catford, S.E. 6.

ANTON, John Cyril
B/A/12223, 12/11/17; R.F.C., C/S, 15/2/18; R.A.F.; 2/Lieut. 13 Pittville Lawn, Cheltenham.

APPLETON, John Bargate
6/1/9243, 1/2/16, L/C.; E. Ang. Div. Cyc. Coy., 25/9/16, R.A.F.; F,P; Lieut. Mill Cottage, Mill Road, Chelmsford.

APPLETON, John Hoblyn
D/11810, 9/8/17; A.S.C., C/S, 1/2/18; R.A.S.C., 26/4/18; F; 2/Lieut. Glengore, Meads, Eastbourne.

✠ APPLIN, Richard
6/2/6804, 14/10/15; No. 11 O.C.B., 7/5/16; R.F.C., 4/9/16; 2/Lieut. Killed in action 29/4/17.

✠ APTED, Eardley
A/1360, 26/9/14, L/C.; R.W. Surr. R., 10/2/15; Lieut. Killed in action 1/8/17.

✠ ARCHDALE, Charles William
F/1748, 16/10/14, L/C.; Norf. R., 19/11/14; Capt. Killed in action 20/11/17.

ARCHER, Francis Frederic
D/13751, 7/8/18; demob. 23/1/19. 18 Albany Place, Stratford-on-Avon.

ARCHER, Francis William
D/E/13939, 2/9/18; demob. 21/12/18. 14 Cook Street, Liverpool.

✠ ARCHER, Robert William
6583, 4/10/15; dis. med. unfit, 21/4/16. Died —/6/18.

ARCHER, William John Sinclair
B/13627, 26/7/18; demob. 31/3/19. 6 Devonshire Road, Princes Park, Liverpool.

ARCHIBALD, Harry James
D/11104, 23/4/17; No. 14 O.C.B., 10/8/17; Gord. Highrs., 27/11/17; 2/Lieut. 8 Old Road, Huntley, Aberdeenshire.

ARCHIBALD, James
6/4/6313, T/18/9/15; No. 2 O.C.B., 25/2/16; Gord. Highrs., 6/7/16; Capt.; w; M.C. and Bar. 47 West Church Street, Buckie, N.B.

✠ ARCHIBALD, Maxwell Stanfield Eaton
6/3/5785, 23/8/15; R.E., 6/10/15, att. R.A.F.; 2/Lieut.; w; M(1). Died of wounds 12/5/18.

ARCHIBALD, Mungo Tennant
6/2/9500, 15/2/16; No. 14 O.C.B.; 30/10/16; M.G.C., 30/1/17, Tank Corps; F; Capt.; w; M.C. 2 Park Terrace, Ayr, Scotland.

ARDLEY, Ernest Lionel
6/2/5293, 2/8/15, L/C.; K.R. Rif. C., 4/12/15, R.F.C. & R.A.F.; F; Capt.; w(3); M(1). c/o. Cox & Co., 110 St. Martin's Lane, W.C.

AREND, Ralph Waldemar
K/B/2219, 30/11/14, L/C.; R. War. R., 15/3/15, att. M.G.C.; F,NR; Capt.; Order of St. Anne (Russia). 4 Montgomery Drive, Glasgow, W.

ARGENT, William Alfred
D/11862, 16/8/17; A.S.C., C/S, 1/3/18; R.A.S.C., 21/6/18; 2/Lieut. Port Louis, Mauritius.

ARGLES, Claude Arthur Cecil
6/3/8561, 31/12/15, L/C.; North'n. R., 4/8/16, att. Suff. R.; F; Capt.; w; M.C. Dunearn, St. Andrew's Street, Melrose, Johannesburg, S. Africa.

ARGLES, Guy Arthur Eustace
A/362, 15/3/09; dis. 28/6/10; R.A.S.C., 23/8/15; S,It; Cant.; O.B.E., M(1). The White Cottage, Whitchurch, Oxon.

ARGUE, Frederick
F/2765, 25/1/15; Devon. R., 2/6/15, K. Af. Rif., R.E.; Germ. EA,P; Capt. Bailieborough, Co. Cavan, Ireland.

ARGYLE, John Stanley
B/9893, 10/11/16; No. 14 O.C.B., 5/3/17; Leic. R., 26/6/17, Intelligence; F; Lieut. Ferndale, Barwell, Leicestershire.

ARKELL, Edward Norman Gwynn
1/6/7895, 29/11/15, L/C.; No. 14 O.C.B.; Suff. R., 24/10/16, att. M.G.C. and Tank Corps O.C. Bns.; F; Capt. Crinan Cottage, Canford Cliffs, nr. Bournemouth.

ARMITAGE, Edgar
6/2/7342, 10/11/15; North'd. Fus., 4/9/16, emp. M. of Labour; Lieut.; w. 16 Old Buildings, Lincoln's Inn, W.C.2.

ARMITAGE, Reginald Thomas Dickinson
6/1/6142, 9/9/15; R.A., C/S, 29/1/16; R.G.A., 19/6/16; F. Lieut. 35 Sandringham Gardens, Ealing, W. (Now in Buenos Aires.)

ARMOR, Charles Frederick
6/2/5350, 2/8/15; trfr. 5th Lond. R., 10/3/16. Ruthin, N. Wales.

ARMSTRONG, Arthur Claude
6/1/5294, 2/8/15; R.G.A., 8/10/15; 2/Lieut. Ardey Lodge, Paignton, S. Devon.

ARMSTRONG, Bernard Martin
6/1/7324, 9/11/15; R. Scots., 22/11/16; Lieut.; M.C., M(1). Brampton Vicarage, Carlisle.

ARMSTRONG, Clifford Speak
C/9966, 20/11/16; No. 14 O.C.B., 30/1/17; 8th Lond. R., 29/5/17; 2/Lieut.; M.C.

ARMSTRONG, Frank Clayton
6/2/7715, 22/11/15; No. 14 O.C.B.; Devon. R., 24/1/17, M.G.C.; F; Lieut.; w. Bonnington Works, Heavitree, Exeter.

APPENDIX II.—RECORDS OF RANK AND FILE.

ARMSTRONG, Frank Walter
6/8739, 6/1/16; R.A.O.C., 17/9/16; F; Major; M(1).
cia. Suz y Fuerza, Tampico, Mexico.

ARMSTRONG, George Alfred
B/10536, 17/1/17; No. 20 O.C.B., 7/6/17; E. Lan. R., 25/9/17; F; 2/Lieut.; g.
4 Cottingwood Terrace, Morpeth, Northumberland.

ARMSTRONG, James Herbert
A/13997, 7/9/18; demob. 24/1/19.
Rathosey, Coolaney, Co. Sligo, Ireland.

ARMSTRONG, John Henry Nicholas
A/19, 1/4/08; dis. 11/11/10.
127 Biddulph Mansions, Elgin Avenue, W.9.

ARMSTRONG, Robert
B/11660, 16/7/17; No. 14 O.C.B., 7/12/17; Hamps. R., 25/6/18; F; 2/Lieut.
Five Rocks, Chale, Isle of Wight.

ARMSTRONG, Thomas William
B/12675, 4/3/18; No. 22 O.C.B., 7/6/18; demob.
3 Hart Street, Carlisle.

ARNELL, Stuart Burton
C/10971, 2/4/17; No. 14 O.C.B., 10/8/17; Hamps. R., 27/11/17; F; 2/Lieut.
The Cottage, Selsey, Sussex.

✠ ARNHOLZ, Ronald Henry Preuss
B/1324, 26/9/14, Cpl.; Hereford R., 25/3/15, att. E. Kent R., att. Bedf. R.; M,F; Lieut.
Killed in action 23/8/18.

ARNOLD, Arthur Edmund
6/5/5912, D/1/9/15, L/C.; L'pool. R., 20/1/16, M.G.C., Tank Corps; Capt.; w(2); p; M.C.
The Causeway, Deganwy Avenue, Llandudno.

ARNOLD, Clement Broomhall
6/5/5913, D/1/9/15; L'pool. R., 6/12/15, Tank Corps; F; Capt.; w(2), p; D.S.O., M(1).
The Causeway, Deganwy Avenue, Llandudno.

ARNOLD, Dennis William
B/13657, 29/7/18; demob. 31/1/19.
356 London Road, Isleworth, W.

ARNOLD, James Clifford
D/10893, 19/3/17; R.A., C/S, 10/8/17; R.F.A., 6/1/18; F; Lieut.; M(1).
The Lawn, Newmarket.

ARNOLD, John Henry
6/1/5786, 23/8/15, Sgt.; M.G.C., C/S, 1/3/17; M.G.C., 25/6/17; M; Lieut.
23 Ashlake Road, Streatham, S.W.16.

ARNOLD, Lewis George
B/2729, 18/1/15; R. Dub. Fus., 22/4/15; Lieut.
Brooklands, Baildon, Yorks.

ARNOLD, Noel
5/4/4731, 12/7/15; Devon. R., 7/7/16, att. E. Kent R.; I,M; Lieut.
Fairlawn, Chinbrook Road, Grove Park, Kent.

ARNOLD, Norman Ashness
1/9637, 25/9/16; No. 14 O.C.B., 27/12/16; Manch. R., 25/4/17; F; Capt.; w.
32 Haworth Buildings, Cross Street, Manchester.

ARNOLD, Norman Gregory
6/5/5398, 5/8/15, L/C.; No. 7 O.C.B., 7/4/16; R.F.C., 6/7/16, R.A.F.; 2/Lieut.

ARNOLD, Thomas
C/10398, 8/1/17; trfr. 8th Lond. R., 9/3/17.
Everdon, Birchfield Road, Northampton.

✠ ARNOLD, Thomas Wilson
K/2515, 31/12/14; Bedf. R., 7/1/15, Gold Coast R.; W. & E. Africa; Lieut.
Died of wounds 15/9/16.

ARNOLD, Victor Douglas
4/4714, 9/7/15, L/C.; No. 14 O.C.B., 30/1/17; E. Kent. R., 25/4/17, Indian Army; Lieut.
157 Abbey Road, Barrow-in-Furness.

ARNOLD, William Noel
Sq/993, 5/8/14; R.H.A., 6/10/14; F; Capt.; w(3); M.C., M(1).
Coxford Abbey, E. Rudham, Norfolk.

✠ ARNOLD-WALLINGER, Geoffrey Seldon
6/2/8778, 7/1/16, L/C
Died 24/9/16.

✠ ARNOTT, Evan Edward
4/6/5188, 29/7/15; Welsh. R., 4/1/16; 2/Lieut.
Died of wounds 23/9/16.

ARTHUR, Colin Ferguson
6/1/5649, 16/8/15; trfr. R.F.A., 7/7/16; R.G.A., 24/6/17; Lieut.
28 Victoria Road South, Southsea, Hants.

ARTHUR, George James
5/6/5547, 12/8/15; No. 1 O.C.B., 25/2/16; R.W. Fus., 7/7/16, Indian Army; F,P,I; Lieut.
Bryn Eirian, Blaenau, Festiniog, N. Wales.

ARTHUR, Henry Alleyne
B/11380, 30/5/17; No. 14 O.C.B., 7/9/17; Rif. Brig., 17/12/17; 2/Lieut.
Yorkshire, Barbados, British West Indies.

ARTHUR, Percival Charles.
D/13683, 29/7/18; demob. 23/1/19.
8 Montague Road, Ealing, W.13.

ARTUS, Arthur Lancelot
1/3493, 6/5/15; R. Fus., 5/9/15; F; SA; Capt.
c/o Cox & Coy., 16 Charing Cross, S.W.1

ASBURY, Frederick Albert
B/12408, 18/1/18; No. 8 O.C.B., 7/6/18; R. War. R., 6/2/19; 2/Lieut.
91 Allesley Old Road, Coventry.

ASH, Adolphus George Gordon
A/D/11233, 9/5/17, Sgt.; demob. 7/5/19.
33 Dorset Square, N.W.

ASHBEE, Henry Guy Neville
Sq/2/2914, 15/2/15, L/C.; R.A.S.C., 5/7/15, Indian Army; Lieut.
Rose Valley House, Brentwood, Essex.

ASHBY, Cyril Francis
B/10090, 4/12/16, L/C.; R.A., C/S, 27/4/17; R.G.A., 1/9/17, emp. M. of Labour; 2/Lieut.
47 Sandmere Road, Clapham.

✠ ASHBY, Thomas Philip
6/5/7429, 15/11/15; No. 1 O.C.B., 6/9/16; R.F.C., 25/1/17, R. Suss. R.; F; Lieut.
Killed in action 5/9/18.

ASHCROFT, Arthur Lynton
6/5/5234, 31/7/15; L'pool. R., 26/10/15; F; Lieut.; w, Inv.
Woodend, Vyner Road, Bidstone, Cheshire.

✠ ASHCROFT, Edward Stanley
6/5/5235, 31/7/15, L/C.; L'pool. R., 26/10/15; Lieut.; w,p.
Died of wounds 12/5/18.

✠ ASHCROFT, Frederic
6/5/5236, 31/7/15; L'pool. R., 26/10/15; 2/Lieut.
Killed in action 9/4/17.

ASHCROFT, John Marshall
D/11538, 21/6/17; No. 19 O.C.B., 9/11/17; Yeomanry, 30/4/18; 2/Lieut.
Gore House, Altcar, nr. Liverpool.

ASHDOWN, Colin Edmund Thornton
6/4/1/4480, T/26/5/15; No. 14 O.C.B., 26/11/16; E. Kent. R., 28/2/17; F; 2/Lieut.
c/o. F. Rush, Esq., 48 Temple Fortune Lane, Hendon, N.W.

ASHERT, Charles
B/13628, 26/7/18; demob. 21/12/18.
87 Quarry Street, Thornton Colliery, Co. Durham.

ASHLEY, Francis Edgell
6/5/5874, 30/8/15; R.A., C/S, 18/8/16; R.G.A., 10/12/16; F; Lieut.; w; M.C.
Lincoln House, Fairfax Road, Teddington, Mdx.

ASHLEY, Herbert James
6/7430, 15/11/15; No. 1 O.C.B., 6/9/16; R.F.C., 16/3/17, 7th Lond. R.; F; Lieut.; w.
76a High Street, Hampstead, N.W.3.

ASHLEY, Thomas William
4/3676, 20/5/15; Hamps. R., 10/9/15, M.G.C.; F; Lieut.; w, p.
Newlands Cottage, West Hoathley, Sussex.

ASHLIN, Charles Harry Norman
Sq/2002, 2/11/14, Cpl.; E. Rid. Yeo., 20/4/15, Imp. Camel Corps, R.F.C., R.A.F.; F,E,P; Capt.; w(2); M(2).
Yokes Court, nr. Sittingbourne, Kent. (Now in Brazil.)

ASHMEAD-BARTLETT, Percy Arthur Blundell
86, 14/4/08, dis. 13/4/09; Sq/932, 5/8/14; 11th Lond. R., 31/8/14; Major; M.C., M(1).
c/o. W. Burdett-Coutts, Esq., M.P., 1 Stratton Street, W.1.
(Now in Trinidad.)

ASHPITEL, Geoffrey Francis
6/1/9422, 10/2/16; No. 14 O.C.B., 30/10/16; R.W. Surr. R., 24/1/17; F; Capt.; w; M.C. and Bar, M(1).
Melville Hall, Dominica, British West Indies.

APPENDIX II.—RECORDS OF RANK AND FILE.

ASHTON, Leslie Charles
A/10512, 15/1/17; No. 20 O.C.B., 7/6/17; L'pool. R., 25/9/17; F; Lieut.; M.C.
68 Wellhead Lane, Perry Barr, Birmingham.

ASHTON, Peter
Sq/482, 8/4/10; dis. 7/4/14; Sq/B/999, 5/8/14; Hereford R., 23/9/14; G,E,P,F; Major; M.C., M(4).
35 Somers Road, Reigate, Surrey.

ASHWORTH, Bernard J. B.
6/5/7248, 8/11/15; R.G.A., 13/1/16; Capt.
Dawlish House, Kimberley Road, Harrow.

ASHWORTH, John
C/A/D/11725, 23/7/17, L/C.; R.E., C/S, 12/5/18; R.E., 27/9/18; 2/Lieut.
East Bank, Feniscowles, nr. Blackburn.

✠ ASHWORTH, Roger William
4/4008, T/4/6/15; Hamps. R., 20/11/15, att. R.A.F.; Lieut.
Died 26/4/18.

ASHWORTH, William Haughton
B/D/12010, 17/9/17; No. 23 O.C.B., 5/4/18; Durh. L.I., 24/9/18; 2/Lieut.
9 Wroxham Mansions, Canfield Gardens, S. Hampstead, N.W. 6

ASHWORTH, William Percy
4/2897, T/10/2/15; 24th Lond. R., 2/3/15, att. T.M.Bty; 2/Lieut.
26 Alexandra Road, Southport, Lancs.

ASKIN, Robert de Vere Cuming
Sq/568, 5/6/11, L/C.; 20th Hussars, 15/8/14, att. M.G.C.; Capt.; M.C.

✠ ASKWITH, Thomas Nowell
6/8562, 31/12/15; R.A., C/S, 9/6/16; R.F.A., 23/9/16; 2/Lieut.
Killed in action 24/10/17.

ASLIN, Roy Lyall
2/3444, 3/5/15, L/C.; 3rd Lond. R., 17/10/15, R.F.C., R.A.F.; F; Lieut.; w.
Riverdend, Wey Road, Weybridge, Surrey. (Now in Denmark.)

ASPHAR, Charles Herman
C/9929, 15/11/16; M.G.C., C/S, 14/3/17; M.G.C., 26/7/17; F; Lieut.; w.
11 Belsize Park Gardens, Hampstead, N.W. 3.

ASPINAL, Leonard George Horatio
6/4/6600, 4/10/15, L/C.; R.F.C., C/S, 13/3/17; R.F.C., 19/4/17, R.A.F.; F; Lieut.
Eldon Mount, Stephens Road, Tunbridge Wells, Kent. (Now in Burma.)

ASPINALL, Arthur William Payce
6/1/D/6059, 6/9/15, L/C.; dis. Ind. Training Coll., 2/2/17; Indian Army, 27/10/17; Capt.
Fircroft, Wellington College, Berks.

ASPINWALL, Reginald Henry Stableford
5/4/6/4715, 9/7/15; R.F.A., C/S, 21/7/16; R.F.A., 13/10/16; F,It; Capt.
Blair-Atholl, Macclesfield, Cheshire.

✠ ASTON, Herbert Selwyn
A/699, 10/3/13; High. L.I., 6/6/14, M.G.C.; Major; M.C.
Died of wounds 13/7/18.

ASTON, Samuel
C/13391, 24/6/18; trfr. 28th Lond. R., 13/11/18.
Bodlondeb, Grove Road, Wrexham.

ATHERTON, Reginald Robert
6/5/5237, 31/7/15, L/C.; L'pool. R., 6/12/15, M.G.C.; F; Major; g.
Chatteris, Cambridgeshire.

ATKEY, James Frederick Haynes
6/1/5650, 16/8/15, L/C.; R.F.A., 28/12/15; F; Capt.; w.
Cleve Cottage, Ewell, Surrey.

ATKIN, Charles Sydney
Sq/517, 17/11/10, Cpl.; R.A.M.C., 11/8/14; Lieut.
St. Bartholomew's Hospital, E.C.

ATKIN, Edward Douglas
C/13336, 20/6/18, L/C.; trfr. K.R. Rif. C., 7/4/19; Cpl.
71 Park Grove, Princes Avenue, Hull.

ATKIN, Harry Guiselin
4/6/3/4913, 19/7/15, Sgt.; S. Staff. R., 30/11/15, York. R.; F; Lieut.; w; M.C.
15 Sunnyside Road, Ealing, W.

✠ ATKINS, Arthur Charles
4/5/4780, 12/7/15; 3rd Lond. R., 24/12/15; 2/Lieut.
Killed in action 9/9/16.

ATKINS, Frederick Thomas
D/12985, 26/4/18, Sgt.; trfr. K.R. Rif. C., 13/5/19.
88 Chestnut Road, Plumstead, S.E. 18.

ATKINS, Henry Kent
D/13897, 23/8/18; demob. 29/1/19.
Collingtree, 68, Norbury Crescent, Norbury, S.W. 16.

ATKINS, Leslie Cyril
A/12464, 24/1/18; No. 13 O.C.B., 17/6/18; Midd'x. R., 5/2/19; 2/Lieut.
Woodstock, 1 Highbury Grange, N. 5.

ATKINSON, Archie
6/3/7756, 23/11/15, L/C.; Midd'x. R., 25/9/16, att. American Inf.; F; Lieut.; w(2); M.C.
Clinton House, Burlington Gardens, Chiswick, W. 4.

ATKINSON, Arnold Feaver
F/2859, 5/2/15; Rif. Brig., 3/6/15, R.E.; F; Capt.; w.
Hillside, Erdington, Birmingham.

ATKINSON, Arthur Wilton
Sq/529, 16/12/10; dis. 31/3/14, med. unfit.
Heathfield House, Blackheath.

✠ ATKINSON, Bernard Stewart
K/B/2177, 26/11/14; S. Staff. R., 19/2/15; F; Capt.
Killed in action 30/11/17.

ATKINSON, Charles Creswick
6/Sq/6837, 14/10/15; Staff. Yeo., 11/1/16, att. R.E. Sigs.; F; Lieut.; M.C.
Salisbury, Rhodesia, S. Africa.

ATKINSON, David Miles
6/5/5281, T/31/7/15; R.F.A., 10/11/15, Devon. R.; It,F; Lieut.; w; M(1).
c/o Cox & Co., 16 Charing Cross, S.W. 1.

ATKINSON, Edmund Stafford
Sq/528, 16/12/10, Sgt.; Dorset Yeo., 10/10/14, att. R. Regt. of Cav.; E; Capt.
59 Hervey Road, Blackheath, S.E. 3.

ATKINSON, Frank Stuart
A/12522, 1/2/18; No. 16 O.C.B., 7/6/18; trfr. 30th Lond. R., 19/7/18.
East View, Dronfield, nr. Sheffield.

✠ ATKINSON, Fred
6/5/5769, 23/8/15, Sgt.; K.R. Rif. C., 3/2/16; 2/Lieut.; w(2).
Killed in action 23/4/17.

✠ ATKINSON, Geoffrey William
C/1310, 26/9/14, L/C.; Oxf. & Bucks. L.I., 20/2/15; Lieut.; F.
Killed in action 19/7/16.

ATKINSON, Gerald Arthur
B/A/12004, 13/9/17; R.F.C., C/S, 18/1/18; R.A.F., 29/9/18; 2/Lieut.
25 Wilberfore Road, Southsea, Hants.

ATKINSON, Harold James
C/13218, 6/6/18; R.E., C/S, 25/8/18; demob.
East View, Dronfield, nr. Sheffield.

✠ ATKINSON, John Ismay
B/1355, 26/9/14; North'd. Fus., 14/12/14; Lieut.
Killed 29/6/16.

ATKINSON, Joseph Dover
6/5/6036, 3/9/15; Sigs. C/S, 18/3/16; R.E., 6/7/16, R.F.C., R.A.F.; F; Capt.; s.d.; A.F.C.
Rawthey Bank, Sedbergh, Yorkshire. (Now in Denmark.)

✠ ATKINSON, Richard Dermot
6/5/5770, 23/8/15, Sgt.; K.R. Rif. C., 3/2/16; 2/Lieut.
Killed in action 16/7/16.

✠ ATKINSON, Victor Rupert
6/1/9235, 1/2/16; No. 14 O.C.B., 30/10/16; W. Rid. R., 28/2/17; F; 2/Lieut.
Killed in action 23/11/17.

ATKINSON, William Ion
C/9956, 20/11/16; No. 20 O.C.B., 5/5/17; Bord. R., 28/8/17; F,It; 2/Lieut.
Thistleton, 32 Cromwell Road, Wimbledon, S.W.19.

✠ ATKINSON-JOWETT, James
A/1658, 9/10/14; Yorks. L.I., 14/11/14; F; Lieut.; w.
Killed in action 16/9/16.

ATTER, Stanley Ralph
6/2/A/6172, T/11/9/15; Garr. O.C.B., 12/12/16; R.W. Fus., 10/2/17; F,It; 2/Lieut.
49 Northfield Road, Stamford Hill, N. 16.

ATTERIDGE, Brian St. John Harvey
6/2/5578, 12/8/15; R.F.C., C/S, 8/10/16; R.F.C., 26/2/17, R.A.F.; 2/Lieut.; cr, Inv.
3 Randolph Gardens, Maida Vale, N.W. 6.

APPENDIX II.—RECORDS OF RANK AND FILE.

ATTLEE, *Clement Richard*
A/1186, 14/9/14; S. Lan. R., 30/9/14; Major; w; M(1).

ATTRIDGE, *Reginald Thomas*
B/12821, 22/3/18; R.F.C., C/S, 1/7/18; demob. 30/1/19.
5 *Agate Road, W. 6.*

ATTWATER, *Harry Lawrence*
B/62, 8/4/08; dis. 7/4/10; R.A.M.C., Lt., 11/5/15; F; Capt.
48 *Regents Park Road, N.W. 1.*

ATTWOOL, *Thomas Earle*
D/12941, 19/4/18, L/C.; demob. 13/12/18.
15 *Jones Road, Draucondra, Dublin, Ireland.*

AUDEN, *George Bernard*
D/13717, 2/8/18; trfr. K.R. Rif. C., 25/4/19, M.G.C.; Pte.
42 *Lordswood Road, Harborne, Birmingham.*

AULT, *Douglas George*
4/1/5091, 26/7/15; W. Rid. R., 6/6/16; F; Lieut.; Inv.
Kingswood, 89 Redston Road, Hornsey, N. 8.

AULTON, *William Stanley*
4/Sq/4125, 10/6/15; R.A.S.C., 31/8/15, R.F.C., R.A.F.; F; Lieut. *The Woodlands, Holloway, Matlock, Derbyshire.*

AUSTEN, *Alfred Noel*
C/14306, T/30/11/18; demob. 31/1/19.
5 *Heath Gardens, Petersfield, Hants.*

✠ AUSTEN, *Edward John*
K/E/2270, 7/12/14; 3rd Lond. R., 3/4/15; Lieut.; w.
Killed in action 21-23/3/18.

✠ AUSTEN, *William Henry*
6/5/5295, 2/8/15; Midd'x. R., 1/6/16; 2/Lieut.
Killed in action 13/11/16.

AUSTER, *Leslie Whorwood*
D/1423, 29/9/14; R. War. R., 25/9/14; F; Lieut.; w, Inv.
23 *Park Hill, Moseley, Birmingham.*

AUSTERBERRY, *Jack*
6/4/5626, 16/8/15; dis. med. unfit 8/8/16.
The Villas, Stoke-on-Trent.

AUSTIN, *Cyril John*
D/13934, 30/8/18; demob. 29/1/19.
Ravenscourt, 78 Ealing Road, Wembley, Middlesex.

AUSTIN, *Cyril Richard*
A/12474, 29/1/18; No. 11 O.C.B., 7/6/18; Devon. R., 5/2/19; 2/Lieut. 67 *Old Tiverton Road, Exeter.*

AUSTIN, *Edwin*
A/495, 11/5/10; 23rd Lond. R., 23/1/12; Capt.; m(1).
59 *Thurleigh Road, Balham, S.W. 12.*

AUSTIN, *Edwin John*
C/14136, 11/10/18; demob. 25/2/19.
Bryn, Eton Avenue, N. Finchley.

AUSTIN, *Emilius Saunders*
C/11504, 18/6/17, L/C.; No. 14 O.C.B., 9/11/17; 7th Lond. R., 30/4/18, att. 10th Lond. R.; Germ. S.W. and E. Africa, F; Lieut.
c/o. Nat. Bank of S. Africa, Ltd., Newcastle, Natal, S. Africa.

AUSTIN, *Ernest Leslie*
B/12336, 1/1/18; R.F.A., C/S, 15/3/18; R.G.A., 12/2/19; 2/Lieut.
45 *Farrer Road, Crouch End, N. 8.*

AUSTIN, *Frank Hale*
6/5/6037, 3/9/15; R.F.C., 6/7/16, R.A.F.; F,It; Staff Lieut.; w.
Ash Tree House, Audlem, Cheshire.

✠ AUSTIN, *George Frederick*
6/3/5824, 26/8/15, L/C.; Ches. R., 22/1/16; 2/Lieut.; F.
Killed in action 19/7/16.

AUSTIN, *Guy Kingston*
8435, 16/12/15; trfr. Hamps. R., 7/7/16; Inv.; R.A.F., 10/7/18; 2/Lieut. 27 *Inverness Terrace, Hyde Park, W. 2.*

AUSTIN, *John Charles*
C/A/12079, 4/10/17; R.F.A., C/S, 4/2/18; R.G.A., 26/8/18; 2/Lieut. 74 *Sheen Park, Richmond.*

AUSTIN, *William Lloyd*
6/3/7395, 12/11/15; No. 14 O.C.B.; M.G.C., 24/10/16; E; Lieut.; w. 7 *Beam Street, Nantwich.*

AUTY, *Henry James*
B/12844, 25/3/18; No. 1 O.C.B., 6/9/18; Notts. & Derby. R., 16/3/19; 2/Lieut. 143 *Ringinglow Road, Ecclesall, Sheffield.*

AVELINE, *Charles Albert*
2/9790, 26/10/16; No. 14 O.C.B., 30/1/17; Suff. R., 29/5/17, M.G.C.; Lieut.

✠ AVERDIECK, *Godfrey Harold*
4/3/3932, 3/6/15; K.R. Rif. C., 10/8/15; F; 2/Lieut.
Killed in action 11/3/16.

AVERILL, *Arthur Stileman*
Sq/1649, 9/10/14; R.F.A., 12/10/14; Lieut.

AVERILL, *George Ernest*
Sq/1728, 15/10/14; Oxf. Hussars, 18/2/15, att. Oxf. & Bucks. L.I.; 2/Lieut.; w. *Broadway, Worcestershire.*

AVERY, *George W. P.*
Sq/3479, 3/5/15; R.A.S.C., 6/9/15; 2/Lieut.
Craig-y-don, Sevenoaks.

AVON, *Alexander Gordon Vivian*
D/12990, 29/4/18; No. 5 O.C.B., 8/11/18, No. 20 O.C.B.; S. Wales Bord., 17/3/19; 2/Lieut. *Penarth Villa, Penarth, Glamorganshire.*

AXFORD, *Norman*
B/11039, 13/4/17, L/C.; R.G.A., C/S, 26/9/17; R.G.A., 18/2/18; F; 2/Lieut. 3 *Dollis Road, Finchley, N. 3.*

AXTELL, *James William Herbert*
6/4/5579, 12/8/15, Cpl.; R. Lanc. R., 9/6/16; Lieut.; w.
105 *Mayfair Avenue, Ilford, Essex.*

AXTEN, *Albert*
D/13889, 23/8/18; demob. 23/1/19.
Ravenscourt, 78 Ealing Road, Wembley, Middlesex.

AXWORTHY, *Vernon Clifford*
6/2/7491, 15/11/15, L/C.; No. 11 O.C.B., 7/5/16; Devon. R., 4/9/16; Capt.; w.
96 *Lorn Road, Leicester. (Now in Colombo.)*

AYERS-HUNT, *Edward Vickers*
5754, T/21/8/15, L/C.; York. R., 6/7/16; Lieut.
Westbourne House, Marton, Blackpool.

AYLARD, *Robert Frederick Sutherland.*
6/3/7066, 29/10/15; E. Kent. R., 4/8/16; M,I; Lieut.
24 *Sotheby Road, Highbury, N. 5.*

AYLMER, *Christopher*
H/2001, 2/11/14; Wilts. R., 3/1/15, att. Bord. R., War Office; F; Lieut.; Inv. *Bath Club, London, W. 1.*

AYLWARD, *Alfred Richard Leslie*
A/Sq/13083, 20/5/18, L/C.; demob. 21/1/19.
Hall House, Lamington, nr. Alton, Hants.

AYLWARD, *Percy Danford*
A/11248, 14/5/17; No. 16 O.C.B., 5/10/17; Hamps. R., 12/3/18; F; 2/Lieut.; w. *Solicitor, Wilton.*

AYLWARD, *Samuel Edgar Ernest*
C/13408, T/12/6/18; No. 3 O.C.B., 10/2/19; E. Kent R., 31/3/19; 2/Lieut. *Northiam Rectory, E. Sussex.*

AYLWIN, *Claude Beresford Graham*
B/E/13629, 26/7/18; No. 22 O.C.B., 20/9/18; demob.
Well Park House, St. Thomas, Exeter.

AYLWIN, *Robert Henry*
C/4/7788, 24/11/15; No. 14 O.C.B., R.W. Surr. R., 24/10/16, att. E. Lan. R.; S; Lieut.; M(1).
Waitlands, Netherne, Coulsdon, Surrey.

AYNSLEY, *William Cramlington*
6/1/8235, 8/12/15; R.E., C/S, 2/10/16; R.E., 13/3/17; F; Lieut.
46 *Simonside Terrace, Newcastle-on-Tyne.*

✠ AYRE, *Stanley Fawcett*
E/3043, 15/3/15; dis. 7/5/15; R.F.A., 26/5/17; 2/Lieut.
Killed in action 30/11/17.

AYRES, *Charles Frederick*
A/10486, 12/1/17; No. 14 O.C.B., 7/6/17; Tr. Res. Bn., 20/9/17, York. L.I., att. R.E.; F; Lieut.
34, *Burlington Road, Gunnersbury, W. 4.*

AYRES, *Rupert Stanley*
A/11300, 18/5/17, L/C.; A.S.C., C/S, 1/10/17; R.A.S.C., 23/11/17; 2/Lieut. *The Hermitage, Northwood.*

AYRTON, *Bertram Frank*
C/1138, 14/9/14; 7th Lond. R., 28/9/14, R.A.F.; F; Capt.; w.
3 *Erskin Hill, Hendon, N.W.*

APPENDIX II.—RECORDS OF RANK AND FILE.

BABBAGE, Arthur
6/1/6900, 18/10/15; No. 14 O.C.B.; Glouc. R., 18/12/16, Manch. R., Durh. L.I., High. L.I., Worc. R., Midd'x. R.; F; Lieut.; w; M.C.
Binham, Washford, Somerset.

BABBAGE, Herbert Falkiner
C/14288, 11/11/18; No. 11 O.C.B., 24/1/19; Genl. List, 8/3/19; 2/Lieut.
Mayfield, Fansdown Place, Cheltenham.

✠ BABBAGE, John Colston
6/4/6381, 23/9/15, L/C.; Manch. R., 5/5/16; F; 2/Lieut.; w.
Killed in action 18/11/16.

BABER, Frederick Henry
6/2/7716, 22/11/15; R.A., C/S, 4/8/16; R.G.A., 29/12/16; F; Lieut.; w.
Littledale, Radlett, Herts.

BABINGTON, Philip
B/795, 25/5/14; trfr. Hamps. R., 6/8/14; Hamps. R., 31/8/14, R.A.F.; Capt. & Sqd. Ldr.; w; M.C., A.F.C., M(2).

BACK, Adolphus Charles Henry
B/Sq/10847, 7/3/17, L/C.; Cav., C/S, 28/2/18, H. Bde. O.C.B.; Gds. M.G.R., 27/8/18; 2/Lieut.
98 Grove Lane, Denmark Hill, S.E. 5.

✠ BACK, Louis William Alexander
4/2/4202, 14/6/15; L'pool. R., 7/10/15; 2/Lieut.
Killed in action 23/4/17.

BACKHOUSE, Frederick (formerly BACKHAUS)
B/K/2536, 4/1/15, L/C.; W. Rid. R., 22/3/15; Capt.
c/o Leather and Veale, East Parade Chambers, Leeds.

BACKHOUSE, Henry
C/Sq/12306, 14/12/17; Cav., C/S, 11/4/18; R. Regt. of Cav., 18/10/18; 2/Lieut.
Waterside, Balderstone, nr. Blackburn.

BACKLER, John Summers
1/3123, T/24/3/15; R.A.S.C., 1/5/15; E,G,F; Major; M(1).
c/o. Lond. County Westminster & Parrs Bank, Ltd., Southsea, Hants.

BACON, Francis
D/6/1403, 29/9/14, Sgt.; Supernumerary, 29/2/16.
Denham, Bucks.

BACON, Harold
A/B/10076, 1/12/16; trfr. R.G.A., 16/2/17.
Holmesdale, Abbey Park Road, Grimsby.

BACON, Reginald Downey
A/11638, 12/7/17; No. 2 O.C.B., 8/3/18; Rif. Brig., 8/10/18, att. R. Fus.; F; 2/Lieut.
11 Westover Road, Wandsworth Common, S.W. 18.

✠ BADCOCK, Benjamin Morley
A/10930, 28/3/17; No. 11 O.C.B., 5/7/17; Notts. & Derby. R., 30/10/17; F; 2/Lieut.
Killed in action 9/7/18.

BADDELEY, Charles Ronald
6/1/A/9026, 20/1/16; No. 13 O.C.B., 4/11/16; K.R. Rif. C., 28/2/17; F; Capt.; g,w.
23 Parkhill Road, Croydon.

BADDELEY, Harold Grosvenor
3/3082, 22/3/15; Wilts. R., 10/7/15, att. Oxf. & Bucks. L.I., att. T.M.Bty.; F,S; Capt.; w.
139 Bedford Street, Liverpool.

✠ BADDELEY, Kenneth
3/3583, 13/5/15, L/C.; Hamps. R., 7/10/15; 2/Lieut.
Killed in action 15/9/16.

BADGER, Stewart Roberts Magnus
C/14222, 25/10/18; trfr. R. Highrs., 2/5/19; Pte.
7 Bruce Street, Glasgow.

BADGLEY, Clement Christian
6/2/5321, 2/8/15; 11th Lond. R., 29/9/15; E,P; 2/Lieut.; w.
c/o. Col. Badgley, Verecroft, Devizes, Wilts.

BADHAM, George Arthur Cust
6/1/8944, 17/1/16, L/C.; R.A., C/S, 7/8/16; R.G.A., 18/10/16; Lieut.; w; M.C., M(1).
Colgate, Sherwood Park Road, Sutton, Surrey.

BAGENAL, Philip Hope Edward
B/491, 29/4/10; dis. 28/4/14; Sgt., R.A.M.C.; F; w; D.C.M.
Leaside, Hertingfordbury, Hertford.

BAGGALLY, Mervyn Eric Claude
Sq/931, 5/8/14; 11th Huss., 15/8/14; F; Lieut.; M(1).
22 Tedworth Square, Chelsea, S.W. 3.

BAGGULEY, John Ellis
D/13786, 9/8/18; trfr. K.R. Rif. C., 30/5/19; Pte.
19 Marlborough Avenue, Hull.

BAGLEY, John William
C/13378, 24/6/18; trfr. 14th Lond. R., 6/12/18.
Herma, 59 Tennyson Avenue, Bridlington, Yorks.

BAGNALL, Albert Edward
6/5/5914, D/1/9/15; L'pool. R., 6/12/15; F,NR; Lieut.; w(2)
3 Onslow Road, Fairfield, Liverpool.

BAGNALL, Harold Hall
6/3/5373, 5/8/15; York. & Lanc. R., 14/11/15; Lieut.
73 Gardner Road, Prestwich.

BAGOT, Harry E.
Sq/1129, 9/9/14; R.F.A., 28/9/14, R.F.C., R.A.F.; Capt. & Flt. Cmdr.; w.

BAGSHAW, Horace Stanley
K/A/2220, 30/11/14; Manch. R., 3/3/15; Capt.; M.C., M(1).
Holme Lea, Alexandra, Southport.

BAGSHAW, William Browne
K/A/2218, 30/11/14; Manch. R., 3/3/15; F; Brigade Major; w; M.C. and Bar, French Croix de Guerre with gold star, M(1).
Holme Lea, Alexandra Road, Southport.

BAILDON, William Paley
B/74, 13/4/08; dis. 12/4/09.
5 Stone Buildings, Lincoln's Inn, W.C. 2.

BAILEY, Brian Grierson
F/1784, 16/10/14, L/C.; 9th Lond. R., 14/2/15, att. No. 16 O.C.B. Inst.; F; Capt.; w.
5 Berners Street, W. 1.

BAILEY, Edmund Savage
C/1342, 26/9/14; Rif. Brig., 19/10/14, att. Tr. Res. Bn.; F,E; Capt.; w; M(1).
Naval and Military Club, 94 Piccadilly, W. 1.

BAILEY, Francis Robert
6/3/6173, 13/9/15; Indian Army, 1/2/16.
369 Bensham Lane, Thornton Heath.

BAILEY, Frederick William
1/9755, 18/10/16; No. 14 O.C.B., 27/12/16; Suff. R., 25/4/17; F; Capt.; w.
74 Grange Park Road, Leyton, E. 10.

✠ BAILEY, Gerald Hinton
A/2125, T/14/11/14; Durh. L.I., 9/12/14; F; 2/Lieut.
Died of wounds 20/10/15.

BAILEY, Harold Symes
6/2/B/8578, 1/1/16; No. 14 O.C.B., 30/10/16; Denb. Yeo. 24/1/17, att. R.W. Fus.; F; Lieut.
Landsdowne House, Wilburton, Ely, Cambs.

BAILEY, Herbert Jack
4/1/5154, 29/7/15, L/C.; No. 3 O.C.B., 25/2/16; R.F.C., 6/7/16; 2/Lieut.
47 Crompton Street, Derby.

BAILEY, John Arthur
4/6/D/4914, 19/7/15, L/C.; trfr Motor M.G.C., 3/11/16; F,I; Gnr.
2 Chesham Road, Brighton.

✠ BAILEY, Robert Neale Menlen
Sq/106, 18/4/08; dis. 18/4/13; E. Rid. of York. Yeo., 23/9/14; Lieut.; w.
Died of wounds 1/12/17.

BAILEY, William Llewelyn
4/4356, 21/6/15; trfr. R.A.M.C., 9/3/16.
Central Buildings, Matlock, Derby.

BAILEY-HAWKINS, John Bridger
D/10636, 1/2/17; dis. med. unfit, 27/11/17.
Stagenhoe Park, Welwyn, Herts.

BAILLIE, Thomas Hamilton
1/3827, 31/5/15; dis. 10/7/15.

BAILLIE, William Anderson
6/5/7859, 26/11/15, L/C.; No. 14 O.C.B.; Suff. R., 24/10/16; F; Lieut.; w.
The Rookery, Felixstowe.

✠ BAILY, Arthur Alexander Russell
D/10645, 2/2/17, L/C.; R.A., C/S, 10/8/17; R.F.A., 11/2/18; F; 2/Lieut.
Killed in action 4/11/18.

BAILY, Harold Wilson
B/10133, 6/12/16; No. 14 O.C.B., 5/7/17; trfr. 28th Lond. R., 12/10/17; Pte.
c/o. Mrs. Spratley, Aberdeen Tea Rooms, Ham Common, Ham.

APPENDIX II.—RECORDS OF RANK AND FILE.

BAIN, Alfred Manson Rose
4/2/4203, 14/6/15; Shrops. L.I., 4/10/15, R. Scots, att. M.G.C.; F; Major; w; M.C., M(1).
16 Briardale Road, Woodhay, Rock Ferry, Cheshire

✠ BAIN, Andrew Lusk
6/1/8236, 8/12/15, L/C.; Ir. Gds., 30/8/16; Lieut.
Killed in action 4/11/18.

BAIN, Herbert Alexander
3/3828, 31/5/15; K.O. Sco. Bord., 20/8/15; F; Lieut.; Inj.
Deepdene, Snaresbrook, E. 11.

✠ BAINBRIDGE, Carlyle
F/1774, 16/10/14, Cpl; E Kent. R., 27/11/14; F; 2/Lieut.
Killed in action 13/10/15.

✠ BAINBRIDGE, John Stuart
K/C/2392, 17/12/14; Hamps. R., 31/3/15; 2/Lieut.
Killed in action 26/9/17.

✠ BAINBRIGGE, Philip Gillespie
B/11035, 13/4/17; No. 14 O.C.B., 10/8/17; Welch. R., 27/11/17, Lan. Fus.; F; 2/Lieut.
Killed in action 18/9/18.

BAINES, Charles
6/5/7828, 25/11/15; Yorks. L.I., 4/8/16, R.E.; F; Lieut.; g; M.C.
The Winnats, Hathersage, Derby.

BAINES, Francis Talbot
6/Sq/7343, 10/11/15; No. 1 O.C.B., 24/4/16; Norf. Yeo., 28/7/16, Linc. Yeo., 12th Lanc.; F; Lieut.
22 Lansdowne Road, Bedford.

BAINES, Herbert Torry
C/13224, 7/6/18; No. 22 O.C.B., 5/7/18; Oxf. & Bucks. L.I., 11/2/19; 2/Lieut.
58 Cornmarket Street, Oxford.

✠ BAINES, John Hugh
4/1/4062, 7/6/15; Linc. R., 27/10/15; F; 2/Lieut.
Killed in action 3/7/16.

✠ BAINES, Joseph
F/2626, 7/1/15; R. War. R., 2/3/15, Midd'x. R.; F; Capt.
Killed in action 29/7/16.

✠ BAINTON, Herbert Sidney
6/3/6813, 14/10/15, L/C.; Midd'x. R., 4/8/16; 2/Lieut.; w.
Died of wounds 16/2/18.

BAIRD, John
D/13831, 14/8/18; demob. 29/12/18.
Ardgowan, Greenhill, Coatbridge, Scotland.

BAIRD, John Hunter
D/10420, 10/1/17; No. 14 O.C.B., 7/6/17; Midd'x. R., 25/9/17; 2/Lieut.
5 Swinderley Road, Wembley, Middlesex.

BAIRD, Kenneth Alexander
A/12523, 1/2/18; No. 19 O.C.B., 7/6/18; Sea. Highrs., 13/2/19; 2/Lieut.
Durris House, Drumoak, Aberdeenshire.

BAIRD, William Aubrey
C/11505, 18/6/17, L/C.; demob. 10/1/19.
Rufford, Corbar Road, Buxton.

✠ BAIRSTOW, Fred
A/11878, 20/8/17; No. 3 O.C.B., 8/2/18; Ches. R., 30/7/18; 2/Lieut.
Died 3/5/21.

BAKER, Albion Alfred
6/2/5760, T/21/8/15; No. 1 O.C.B., 25/2/16; 25th Lond. R., 8/7/17; Lieut.

BAKER, Arthur Harold
6/2/5296, 2/8/15; Som. L.I., 2/11/15.
48 Lime Grove, New Malden, Surrey.

BAKER, Arthur Henry
B/2785, 26/1/15; R. Berks. R., 29/4/15, Dorset. R., M.G.C.; F; Lieut.
Ashdown, Morgan Road, Reading.

BAKER, Bromley
9985, 22/11/16; No. 14 O.C.B., 5/3/17; Lan. Fus., 26/6/17; F; 2/Lieut.; w.
National Provincial Bank, Wolverhampton.

BAKER, Douglas George
B/11369, 28/5/17; No. 14 O.C.B., 9/11/17; R.W. Surr. R., 30/4/18, att. R.A.S.C, att. T.M. Bty.; F; Lieut.
10 Foxmore Street, S.W. 11.

BAKER, Douglas Glasspool
6/1/7249, 8/11/15, L/C.; Hamps. R., 25/9/16; Lieut.

BAKER, Edward Cecil Arnold
K/A/2122, 16/11/14; Rif. Brig., 27/3/15; F; Lieut.; w.
20 Cottesmore Gardens, Kensington.

BAKER, Francis Dudley
6/6838, 14/10/15; dis. med. unfit, 22/5/16.
The Grove, Tealby, Lincoln.

BAKER, Francis George.
A/10701, 12/2/17; R.F.C., C/S, 13/3/17; R.F.C., 19/4/17, R.A.F.; F; Lieut.; p. Beverley, Leominster, Herefordshire.

BAKER, Francis Ralph.
Sq/1691, 13/10/14; R.F.A., 13/10/14; Lieut.
c/o. S. Gurney, Esq., 6 Albemarle Street, W.

BAKER, Frank.
A/13147, 29/5/18; No. 22 O.C.B., 5/7/18; Education Officer, 8/12/18; F; Capt.
80 Stanfords Avenue, Brighton.

BAKER, Frank Richard.
Sq/171, 28/4/08; dis. 27/4/11. Harlesden Lodge, Harlesden, N.W.

✠ BAKER, Frederick Herbert.
6/4/7196, 4/11/15; M.G.C., 25/9/16; 2/Lieut.
Killed in action 24/3/18.

✠ BAKER, George Edmund Clode.
K/E2455, T/22/12/14; 5th Lond. R., 7/2/15; Lieut.
Killed in action 1/7/16.

BAKER, George Hamilton.
2/3528, 7/5/15; 23rd Lond. R., 3/9/15, att. R.A.F.; F,S,P.; Lieut.
c/o. Baker & Reid, Calgary, Canada.

BAKER, George Hayton.
1/3494, 6/5/15; E. Surr. R., 28/7/15; Lieut.
Embleton, Hook Road, Surbiton.

BAKER, Guy Mervyn.
6/1/8684, 4/1/16; Liverpool R., 25/9/16; F; Lieut.; w.
Bibile Estate, Lunngala, Ceylon.

BAKER, Henry
A/11204, 7/5/17, L/C.; No. 14 O.C.B., 5/10/17; N. Cyc. Bn., 26/2/18; 2/Lieut.
101 St. Leonards Road, East Sheen, S.W.

BAKER, Herbert Charles.
A/10460, 12/1/17; R.A., C/S, 27/4/17; R.G.A., 1/9/17, att. R.A.F.; F,E; 2/Lieut.
40 Barrington Road, Crouch End, N. 8.

BAKER, Hubert John.
B/11381, 30/5/17; trfr. R.F.C., 26/10/17; N.C.O. Inst.
Chamber of London, Guildhall, E.C.2.

BAKER, John Dudley.
4/5/4692, 8/7/15, L/C.; R. Ir. Fus., 20/11/15; Lieut.
58 West Heath Drive, Hampstead.

BAKER, John Herbert.
6/4/9101, 24/1/16, L/C.; R.F.A., C/S, 4/8/16; R.G.A., 12/11/16; F; Capt.
New Inn Chambers, King Street, Gloucester.

BAKER, Joseph Bowman.
1/3620, 17/5/15; R. War. R., 21/8/15; Lieut.; w.
Embleton, Hook Road, Surbiton.

BAKER, Leonard Alfred.
D/9976, 21/11/16; Garr. O.C.B., 26/2/17; Worc. R., 14/4/17, S. Lan. R.; Capt.
87 Vassall Road, Brixton, S.W. 9.

BAKER, Leslie Arthur.
A/10066, 1/12/16; No. 14 O.C.B., 30/1/17; R. Suss. R., 25/4/17; F; Capt.; w.
52 Crowhurst Road, Colchester.

BAKER, Norman.
4/1/4525, 1/7/15; No. 14 O.C.B., 5/5/17; L'pool R., 28/8/17; F; 2/Lieut.; w.
The Bungalow, Derriton Road, Holsworthy, N. Devon.

BAKER, Percy Lytton
6/4/9308, 4/2/16; A.S.C., C/S, 23/10/16; R.A.S.C., 26/11/16; S; Capt.
St. Helier, Knighton Rise, Leicester.

BAKER, Robert
C.D.12028, 24/9/17, L/C.; No. 22 O.C.B., 7/6/18; E. Surrey R., 12/2/19; 2/Lieut.
19 Danecroft Road, Herne Hill, S.E.24.

BAKER, Victor Joseph.
6/4/6795, 13/10/15; dis. med. unfit, 15/7/16.
Speranza, 54 Ulverton Road, Dalkey, Co. Dublin.

BAKER, Walter Raymond.
6/3/6382, 23/9/15; Worc. R., 4/1/16, R.F.C., R.A.F.; F; Lieut.
5 Arlington Villas, Clifton, Bristol.

APPENDIX II.—RECORDS OF RANK AND FILE.

BAKER, *Wilfred.*
A/13998, 13/9/18; *trfr.* K.R. Rif. C., 7/4/19.
9 *Talfourd Road, Peckham, S.E.*15

BAKER *William Henry Benson.*
Sq/134, 18/4/08; *dis.* 17/4/13; *rej.* 1137, 12/9/14, Cpl.; R.F.A., 14/2/15, R.G A.; F; Major; M(2).
*United University Club, Suffolk Street, Pall Mall, S.W.*1.

✠ BALDERSON, *Eric Francis Richard.*
6/4/5462, 9/8/15; R.F.A., 20/11/15; 2/Lieut.
Killed in action 28/3/16.

✠ BALDOCK, *Thomas Agnew.*
F/K/2582, 4/1/15; Rif. Brig., 29/4/15; Lieut.; *w.*
Died of wounds 3/12/17.

✠ BALDWIN, *Allen Aquila.*
6/3/5399, 5/8/15, L/C.; N. Lan. R., 27/12/15; 2/Lient.
Killed in action 26/4/18.

BALDWIN, *Richard Everest.*
A/Sq/14127, T/4/10/18; demob. 11/1/19.
33 *Knatchbull Road, S.E.*5.

BALDWIN, *Robert.*
K/A/2437, 28/12/14; Hamps. R., 13/3/15, att. W. York. R. and York. & Lanc. R.; F; Lieut.
c/o J. Baldwin Esq., Cape of Good Hope Hotel, Oxford.

BALE, *Richard Stuart.*
6/5/C/8589, 3/1/16, Sgt.; demob. 10/1/19
*c/o " The Daily Telegraph," Fleet Street, E.C.*4.

✠ BALE, *Thomas Henry Thriscutt.*
2/3621, 17/5/15; York. R., 20/8/15; Lieut.
Killed in action 24/4/18.

BALFOUR, *The Honourable Harry Robert Chichester.*
Sq/159, 18/4/08; *dis.* 17/4/10; R. Scots, 31/10/14; F; Capt.; *w.*
*Oxford and Cambridge Club, Pall Mall, S.W.*1.

BALFOUR, *John Herbert.*
6/3/9493, 15/2/16, L/C.; No. 14 O.C.B., 27/9/16; Arg. & Suth'd Highrs., 18/12/16; Lieut.
Elmslea, Leven, Fife, Scotland.

BALFOUR, *Robert Frederick.*
B/11382, 30/5/17; A.S.C., C/S, 1/9/17; R.A.S.C., 27/10/17; 2/Lieut.
Elmslea, Leven, Fife, Scotland

BALKWILL, *Reginald Adams.*
B/11411, 1/6/17; A.S.C., C/S, 1/9/17; R.A.S.C., 27/10/17; F; Lieut.
Cintra, Brixham, S. Devon.

✠•BALL, *Benedict Hanby.*
4/3/4447, 28/6/15; Hamps. R., 27/11/15; 2/Lieut.
Killed in action 3/9/16.

BALL, *Francis Dudley.*
6/1/7829, 25/11/15, L/C.; No. 14 O.C.B., 28/8/16; M.G.C., 24/10/16; Lieut.

BALL, *John Metcalfe.*
6/2/5580, 12/8/15, Sgt.; No. 2 O.C.B., 14/8/16; Rif. Brig., 18/12/16, emp. Admiralty, Lieut. 2 *Kenilworth Road, Ealing.*

✠ BALL, *Leslie Shorland.*
3/3584, 13/5/15; R.Ir.Fus., 7/10/15; 2/Lieut.
Killed in action 6/9/16.

BALL, *Robert Walton.*
C/13337, 20/6/18; R.E., C/S, 1/11/18; General List, 8/3/19; 2/Lieut.
c/o Standard Bank of South Africa, 10 Clements's Lane, E.C.

BALL, *William Gerald.*
C/13219, 6/6/18; R.E., C/S, 25/8/18; demob.
Carnfield House, Westcotes Drive, Leicester.

BALLAN, *Lancelot.*
4/1/4330, 21/6/15, L/C.; Manch. R., 18/10/15, R.E.; F; Staff Capt.
c/o Chief Goods Manager, North Eastern Railway Coy., York.

BALLANCE, *Lionel Ernest.*
4/2/5022. 22/7/15; No. 7 O.C.B., 7/4/16; 11th London R., 4/8/16, 9th London R., att. H.A.C., K.R.Rif.C. and T.M. Bty.; F.; Lieut.; *g.* 82 *Lee Road, Blackheath, S.E.*3.

BALLANCE, *Sydney Archibald.*
E/13969, 6/9/18; demob. 11/1/19.
Punchardon Hall, Willian, Herts.

BALLANTINE, *Richard Waverley Head*
6/3/5736, T/21/8/15; R.E., 20/10/15; F,I,Persia; Capt.; *w*; M(1). 70 *Boileau Road, N. Ealing, W.*5.

BALLARD, *Alfred Hunter.*
6/Sq/6322, 20/9/15; *trfr.* Motor M.G.C., 11/8/16; R.A., C/S -/7/18; R.F.A., 18/3/19; F.; 2/Lieut.; *w.*
24 *Woodborough Road, Putney, S.W.*15.

BALLARD, *Frederick George.*
B/12845, 25/3/18; No. 11 O.C.B., 9/8/18, No. 19 O.C.B.; Essex R., 5/3/19; 2/Lieut. 63 *Mayola Road, Clapton, E.* 5.

BALLARD, *James Clark.*
Sq/2986, 1/3/15; R.F.A., 24/4/15, att. R.A.F.; F.; Lieut.; *w.*
Hip-wl. The Avenue, Upper Norwood.

BALSTON, *Thomas.*
Sq/152, 18/4/08; *dis.* 17/4/11; Glouc. R., 28/10/14; F; Major, D.A.A.G.; O.B.E., M.C., M(2).
*Union Club, Trafalgar Square, S.W.*1.

BALY, *Frederick John.*
6/Sq/5748, T/21/8/15, L/C.; R.F.A., 26/11/15; F; Lieut.; M.C., M(1). 154 *Newmarket Road, Norwich.*

BALY, *George Gordon.*
C/11053, 16/4/17; *trfr.* 19th Lond. R., 1/6/17.
Hardingham, Norfolk.

BAMFORTH, *Henry Forbes Ernest.*
E/14158, 14/10/18; demob. 10/1/19.
Glenariff, Second Avenue, Westcliff-on-Sea.

✠ BAMKIN, *Harold Picton.*
B/1067, 2/9/14; Suff. R., 9/9/14; 2/Lieut.
Killed in action 19/7/15.

BANCE, *Frederick Watkins.*
C/D/12040, 27/9/17; No. 24 O.C.B., 26/1/18; Tank Corps, 22/10/18; 2/Lieut. *Essenden, Stanley Road, Newbury, Berks.*

BANCROFT *Harry Francis.*
C/14245, 30/10/18; No. 11 O.C.B., 24/1/19; General List, 8/3/19; 2/Lieut.
13 *Grosvenor Road, Gunnersbury, Chiswick, W.4. (now in Cuba).*

✠ BAND, *Lawrence.*
6/5/5238, 31/7/15, Sgt.; L'pool R., 27/10/15; 2/Lieut.
Killed in action 28/4/17.

✠ BANFIELD, *Cyril Barnet.*
A/11270, 14/5/17; R.F.C., C/S, 1/6/17; R.F.C., 4/7/17; 2/Lieut.
Killed in action 21/3/18.

BANGER, *Ernest John.*
4/3/4557, 1/7/15; 19th Lond. R., 12/11/15, secd. Lab. Corps.; Lieut. *Kent House, East Farleigh, Kent.*

BANISTER, *Arthur Maydwell.*
A/11232, 9/5/17; A.S.C., C/S, 1/10/17; R.A.S.C., 30/11/17; F; Lieut. 15 *Mount Pleasant Road, S.E.*13.

BANISTER, *Frederick Edward Lawford.*
B/11383, 30/5/17, L/C.; Sigs. C/S, 22/9/17; R.E., 1/3/18; F; Lieut. 331 *Kingston Road, Wimbledon, S.W.*19.

BANISTER, *Norman Gaukroyd.*
1/Sq/9642, 26/9/16, L/C.; No. 1 Cav. C/S, 1/9/17; R. Regt. of Cav., 9/5/18; 2/Lieut. *The Nook, Cullingworth, Nr. Bradford.*

BANKS, *Benjamin Edward.*
A/11588, 5/7/17; No. 1 Cav. C/S, 1/9/17, No. 12 O.C.B.; Conn. Rang., 26/2/18, att. R. Ir. Fus.; F; Lieut.
c/o National Bank of South Africa, Ltd., Salisbury, S. Rhodesia, S. Africa.

✠ BANKS, *Edward Francis.*
4/3256, 15/4/15; R. Fus., 28/7/15; 2/Lieut.
Killed in action 28/2/17.

BANKS, *Ernest Guibal le Breton.*
F/1843, 16/10/14; Welch R., 3/1/15; G; 2/Lieut.; *Inv*; M(1).
c/o. Finlay, Fleming & Coy., P.O. Box 181 Rangoon, Burma.

✠ BANKS, *William.*
A/10062, 1/12/16; No. 14 O.C.B., 30/1/17; Durh. L.I., 29/5/17; 2/Lieut.; *p.*
Died of wounds 6/4/18.

✠ BANNATYNE, *Douglas Alexander*
K/2620, 7/1/15; R. Scots, 5/3/15; Lieut.
Killed in action 1/8/18.

✠ BANNEHR, *Harold James Thomas*
4/1/3933, 3/6/15, L/C.; Durh. L.I., 3/10/15; Lieut.
Killed in action 5/11/15.

APPENDIX II.—RECORDS OF RANK AND FILE.

BANNER, Arthur Edward
A/10964, 30/3/17; No. 12 O.C.B., 10/8/17; trfr. 28th Lond. R., 25/2/18; F. 92 Kingswood Road, Goodmayes, Essex.

BANNER, John Wilfred
4/3403, 26/4/15; York. R., 3/5/15; Lieut.
Oakledge, Beech Hill Road, Sheffield.

✠ BANNERMAN, Eric
6/3/9141, 25/1/16, Cpl.; No. 14 O.C.B., 30/10/16; Arg. & Suth'd Highrs., 24/1/17; 2/Lieut. Killed in action 20/11/17.

✠ BANNISTER, Henry William
1/3898, 31/5/15; Linc. R., 27/10/15; 2/Lieut.; w.
Killed in action 14/6/17.

BANNISTER, Herbert Milburn
6/1/8934, 17/1/16, Cpl.; No. 14 O.C.B., 30/10/16; Linc. R., 24/1/17; Lieut.; w. 1 Langside Avenue, Putney, S.W.

BANNISTER, Percy
A/11285, 14/5/17; No. 14 O.C.B., 7/9/17; N. Staff. R., 17/12/17, att. Manch. R.; E; Capt.; M(1).
4 Dover Road, Birkdale, Lancs.

BANTOCK, Julian Richard Granville
A/10951, 30/3/17, L/C.; No. 14 O.C.B., 7/12/17; Cam'n. Highrs., 28/5/18; 2/Lieut.
Ferndale, Elvetham Road, Edgbaston, Birmingham.

✠ BANTOFT, Edward Spencer
E/1504, 1/10/14, Sgt.; 5th Lond. R., 2/4/15; F; Lieut.
Died of wounds 10/9/16.

✠ BANWELL, Leonard Henry
A/10039, 29/11/16; No. 14 O.C.B., 30/1/17; Glouc. R., 29/5/17; 2/Lieut. Killed in action 3/12/17.

BAPTIE, Norman
B/10132, 6/12/16; trfr. 16th Lond. R., 27/4/17, 8th Lond. R.; F; Pte. 35 Abbey Road, Brighton.

BARBER, Arthur Lionel
6/3/6814, 14/10/15, L/C.; Devon. R., 7/7/16; I,M; Lieut.
Kenilworth, Hayesfield Park, Bath.

BARBER, Cecil Blackstone
B/11345, 23/5/17; No. 14 O.C.B., 7/9/17; E. Kent. R., 17/12/17; F; 2/Lieut.; w(2). Gilcroft Estate, Baddegama, Ceylon.

BARBER, Cyril Arthur
6/1/9436, 11/2/16; R.A., C/S, 4/8/16; trfr. R.F.A., 12/1/17; F; Gnr. Chadcote, Harrogate.

BARBER, Cyril Arthur
D/10591, 17/1/17; R.F.C., C/S, 13/3/17; R.F.C., 19/4/17.
9 The Terrace, Plymouth.

BARBER, Cyril Walter
E/1594, 6/10/14, Sgt.; R.G.A., 19/3/15; F; Lieut.
The Cottage, Montana Road, Wimbledon, Surrey.

BARBER, Gordon
6/3/7896, 29/11/15; No. 11 O.C.B., 16/5/16; 9th Lond. R., 4/9/16, att. North'n. R.; E,S; Lieut.
c/o. Mrs. T. T. Hall, Bank House, Kettering, Northants (now in Australia).

BARBER, John Reid
3, 1/4/08; dis. 31/3/10; Staff Sgt., School of Musketry, 11/9/14; T.F. Res., 5/10/15; F; Capt.; M.C.
20 Westbourne Terrace, W. 2.

BARBER, Leonard Cecil
4/9607, 29/8/16; No. 14 O.C.B., 27/12/16; Norf. R., 25/4/17, att. Suff. R. and L'pool. R.; F,It,E; Lieut.
The Glebe House, Hunstanton, Norfolk.

BARBER, Thomas Clive Quinton
4/5/C/4781, 12/7/15; trfr. Class W. Res., 6/4/17.
The Homestead, Thorpe St. Andrew, Norwich.

BARBER, William Montague
D/E/13684, 29/7/18; No. 22 O.C.B., 20/9/18; R. War. R., 5/2/19; 2/Lieut. 31 Frederick Road, Edgbaston, Birmingham.

BARBOUR, Reginald Stanley
6/9273, 3/2/16; R. Ir. Fus., 18/2/16, att. R. Dub. Fus., R.F.C. and R.A.F.; S,E,P; Lieut.; M(1).
Kircubbin, Co. Down, Ireland.

BARCKLEY, Duguid Crichton
6/8916, 14/1/16; Indian Army, 21/4/16; M,I; Lieut.
Calcutta Port Commissioners, Strand Road, Calcutta

BARCLAY, Edgar Norman
4/3/4448, 28/6/15; R. War. R., 4/12/15; F; 2/Lieut.
31 Dennington Park Road, W. Hampstead, N.W.

BARCLAY, Frank Nigel Bruce
B/E/13559, 19/7/18; No. 22 O.C.B., 20/9/18; R. Suss. R., 14/2/19; 2/Lieut. Rietta, Bolesbrook Road, Bexhill-on-Sea.

✠ BARCLAY, George Reinhold
A/184, 1/5/08; dis. 30/4/09; A/824, 4/8/14; Suff. R., 9/9/14, Intelligence Corps; F; Capt. Killed in action 30/10/18.

BARCLAY, Harold Lionel Millar
B/13596, 24/7/18; trfr. 28th Lond. R., 13/11/18; Midd'x. R.; SR; 2/Lieut. 66 Goldhurst Terrace, Hampstead, N.W. 6.

BARCLAY, Herbert Jodrell
Sq/1007, 6/8/14; Pemb. Yeo., 20/11/14, att. Welsh R.; Lieut.
9 Southwood Mansions, Highgate, N.

BARCLAY, John Keith
6/8819, 10/1/16; R.A., C/S, 26/5/16; R.G.A., 30/8/16; F; Lieut.
Inshalloch, Largs, Ayrshire.

BARCLAY, Lindsay
A/10715, 12/2/17; No. 14 O.C.B., 5/7/17; 15th Lond. R., 30/10/17, att. D. of Corn. L.I.; 2/Lieut.
24 Kirkstall Road, Streatham Hill, S.W. 2.

BARCLAY, Thomas
4304, 17/6/15; Welch R., 5/11/15, Army Cyc. Corps; F; Capt.
46 Stanwell Road, Penarth, nr. Cardiff.

✠ BARCLAY-CATFORD, Cyril Herbert
H/1733, 15/10/14; Durh. L.I., 27/10/14, att. R.E.; F; Lieut.; w.
Died of wounds 5/10/16.

BARD, Laurence Percival
C/D/12251, 27/11/17; R.E., C/S, 14/4/18; trfr. K.R. Rif. C., 25/4/19. Hill Field, Harpenden, Herts.

BARDRICK, Harry Gilbert
3411, 29/4/15; Essex R., 16/11/15, Army Cyc. Corps; S; Lieut.; w.
The New Darnel Bay Tobacco Plantations Ltd., Tahad Datu, British North Borneo.

BAREFOOT, Herbert John Leslie
6/3/6079, 6/9/15; R.A.M.C. (Lt.), 15/11/15; E,P; Capt.; M(1).
Langer Ridge, South Hill, Felixstowe, Suffolk.

BARGETON, Stephen Michael
D/11539, 21/6/17, L/C.; No. 14 O.C.B., 5/10/17; Devon. R. 26/2/18; F; 2/Lieut.; w.
81 Hawthorne Road, Willesden Green, N.W. 10.

BARING, Evelyn Bingham
B/765, 16/2/14; trfr. Hamps. R., 6/8/14; Hamps. R., 31/10/14; Lieut.

BARING, John Theodore
1/3495, 6/5/15; Worc. R., 21/8/15, R.E.; F; Lieut.; w.
Marchdyke, Chandlers Ford, Hants. (now in Australia).

✠ BARKER, Cecil Langton Raymond
Sq/609, 26/2/12; Rif. Brig., 12/5/15; F; 2/Lieut.
Killed in action 25/9/15.

BARKER, Geoffrey
Sq/359, 12/3/09; dis. med. unfit, 31/12/09.
65 Westbourne Terrace, W.

BARKER, George William
6/4/8820, 10/1/16; No. 13 O.C.B., 4/11/16; W. Rid. R., 28/2/17; F; Capt.; w(2). 27 Parker's Row, Dockhead, S.E. 1.

BARKER, Harold Ross
A/1289, 23/9/14, Cpl.; York. R., 13/10/14, emp. M. of Food; Capt. Huntercombe Manor House, Henley-on-Thames.

BARKER, Herbert Graham
6/1/8264, 9/12/15, L/C.; No. 5 O.C.B., 14/8/16; Household Bn., 21/11/16, Gren. Gds.; F; Lieut.; w(2); M.C., M(1).
Kolar, Arterberry Road, Wimbledon, Surrey.

BARKER, John
K/2860, 5/2/15; Worc. R., 23/2/15, M.G.C.; F; Lieut.; p; M.C.
Dunsby, Bourne, Lincs.

BARKER, John
4/3404, 26/4/15; L'pool. R., 7/10/15, Lan. Fus.; F; Lieut.
Hill House, Loose, Maidstone, Kent.

APPENDIX II.—RECORDS OF RANK AND FILE.

BARKER, John Bertram
6/3/6238, T/15/9/15; York. Huss., 29/11/15; F; Capt.
10 Algernon Street, Grimsby, Lincs.

BARKER, John James
C/9940, 17/11/16; No. 14 O.C.B., 30/1/17; Dorset. R., 29/5/17, D. of Corn. L.I., Hamps. R.; M, Persia; Lieut.
Woodlands, Todmorden, Yorkshire.

BARKER, Joseph Meek Wilton
6/3/6584, 4/10/15, L/C.; No. 7 O.C.B., 6/4/16; R.W. Fus., 22/6/16, att. S. Wales Bord.; F; Capt.; w; M(1).
The Beeches, Downham Market, Norfolk.

BARKER, Rex
F/1847, 16/10/14; R. Ir. Fus., 31/3/15;
25 Redcliffe Square, Fulham Road, S.W. 10.

BARKER, Robert Denison
A/10041, 29/11/16, L/C.; A.S.C., C/S, 1/9/17; R.A.S.C., 27/10/17; F; 2/Lieut.
Newholme, Pollitt Street, Barnsley, Yorkshire.

BARKER, William Albion
C/11733, 26/7/17; R. Lanc. R., 25/6/18; 2/Lieut.
8 Byron Street, Todmorden, Yorkshire.

BARKER, William James
C/9951, 20/11/16; No. 14 O.C.B., 30/1/17; R.A.O.C., 6/5/17; E; Lieut., Inspector of Ordnance.
Oakwood, Sylvan Avenue, Mill Hill, N.W. 7.

BARKER-BENFIELD, Gustavus Frank William
B/12340, 31/12/17; No. 7 O.C.B., 10/5/18; R. Suss. R., 29/10/18; 2/Lieut.
55 Leinster Square, Bayswater, W.

BARKWORTH, Leslie John
6/2/8299, 11/12/15; A.S.C., C/S, 1/9/17; R.A.S.C., 27/10/17; S,E,P; Lieut.
Highcote, Hale Lane, Mill Hill, N.W. 7.

BARLING, Montague Henry
B/10422, 10/1/17; R.G.A., C/S, 6/6/17; R.G.A., 1/10/17; F; Lieut.
c/o. B. Barling & Sons, 9/11 Park Street, N.W. 1.

BARLOW, Frederick Cecil
4/1/5155, 29/7/15, Cpl.; R.F.C., C/S, 2/8/17; R.F.C., 8/9/17, R.A.F.; 2/Lieut.; cr.
16 Highlands Gardens, Ilford, Essex.

✠ BARLOW, Leslie Charles Jackson
A/11922, 30/8/17; R.F.C., C/S, 30/11/17; R.F.C., 17/12/17, R.A.F.; F; 2/Lieut.
Killed in action 18/6/18.

BARLOW, Reginald Wilfred
6/5/C/7492, 15/11/15, Sgt.; No. 14 O.C.B., 5/3/17; Rif. Brig., 26/6/17; Lieut.

BARNARD, Albert William Stanfield
D/11090, 23/4/17; No. 12 O.C.B., 10/8/17; R. War. R., 27/11/17; 2/Lieut.
31 Whitstable Road, St. Dunstans, Canterbury.

BARNARD, Harold Thomas Benjamin
Sq/2803, 28/1/15, Cpl.; W. Kent Yeo., 26/6/15; E,P,F; Capt.
82 Victoria Street, S.W. 1.

BARNARD, Henry William
F/1877, 16/10/14; R.W. Kent R., 6/11/14; Lieut.
13 King's Bench Walk, Temple, E.C. 4.

BARNARD, John Harington
6/1/6080, 6/9/15, L/C.; K.R. Rif. C., 21/4/16; F; 2/Lieut.; w.
44 Shakespeare Avenue, Bath.

BARNARD, John Marles Sedgwick
D/13923, 30/8/18; demob. 7/1/19.
Monsall Lodge, Prestwich, Lancashire.

BARNEBY, Philip Bartholomew
K/D/2353, 14/12/14; dis. med. unfit, 8/1/15.
Trewyn, Abergavenny.

BARNES, Adam Scott
6/6346, 20/9/15; dis. 27/9/15; R.G.A., 27/9/15, att. R.F.C.; Lieut.; M(1).
25 Northcott Avenue, Wood Green.

BARNES, Algernon Martin
6/4/9102, 24/1/16; R.F.A., C/S, 4/8/16; R.G.A., 3/11/16, emp. M. of Munitions; Lieut.; w.

BARNES, Archie Fairbairn
K/2476, 28/12/14; Glouc. R., 5/3/15, att. Ir Gds.; F; Capt.; Inj., p-w; M.C.
18 Bishopsthorpe Road, Sydenham, S.E. 26.

BARNES, Benjamin
A/1723, 15/10/14; Yorks. L.I., 2/2/15, att. No. 10 O.C.B., Inst; F; Capt.; g; (M(1).
Bank Buildings, Broadstairs.

BARNES, Cecil Bertram
6/3/7574, 18/11/15; No. 14 O.C.B.; K.R. Rif. C., 24/10/16; Lieut.
Sunnyside, Frome, Somerset.

BARNES, Daniel Edward Lloyd
6/8612, 3/1/16; R.A.O.C. (Lt), 9/7/16; F; Capt.
56 Poplar Road, Oxton, Birkenhead.

BARNES, Douglas Molyneux
4/9697, 9/10/16; No. 14 O.C.B., 27/12/16; L'pool. R., 27/3/17; F; Lieut.; w.
Lowton, Newton-le-Willows, Lancashire.

✠ BARNES, Edmund Lyndon
A/444, 10/11/09, dis. 9/11/13; R. Lanc. R., 12/9/14; F; Capt.; M(1).
Killed in action 3/4/16.

BARNES, Edward Edevain Francis
C/12664, 28/2/18; No. 3 O.C.B., 6/9/18; Rif. Brig., 16/3/19; 2/Lieut.

BARNES, Frederick Spencer
D/11811, 9/8/17; No. 14 O.C.B., 4/1/18; R. Fus., 25/6/18; 2/Lieut.
42 Windsor Road, Doncaster.

✠ BARNES, Goodwin Howard Thomas
6/3/8716, 5/1/16; R.N.A.S., 18/8/16, R.A.F.; Capt.
Died 29/10/18.

BARNES, Gordon Albert
6/1/6308, T/18/9/15; W. York. R., 17/6/16; F; Lieut.; w(2); M(1).
Laurel Bank, 30 Great North Road, Highgate, N. 6.

BARNES, Harry Farquharson
6347, 20/9/15; dis. 27/9/15; R.G.A., 27/9/15, att. R.F.C.; Lieut.; M.C. and Bar.
25 Northcott Avenue, Wood Green.

BARNES, Kenneth Ralph
Sq/230, 15/5/08; Midd'x. R., 22/3/09, att. 10th Lond. R., Hamps. R.; 1,M, Siberia; Capt.; M(1).
9 Campden House Chambers, Kensington, W. 8.

BARNES, Lionel Hallyer
4/2/4268, 17/6/15; Mon. R., 9/12/15, Interpreter; Lieut.; Military Order of Avis 5th Class, M(1).
Church Croft, Radlett, Herts.

✠ BARNES, Ralph George
6/3/7539, 17/11/15, L/C.; No. 14 O.C.B., 30/9/16; 8th Lond. R., 22/11/16; 2/Lieut.
Killed in action 30/10/17.

BARNES, Thomas Lucas
6/5/6038, 3/9/15; L'pool. R., 6/6/16, att. R. Ir. Rif.; F,I; Lieut.
59 Wingate Road, Aigburth, Liverpool.

BARNETT, Charles Sherborne
C/10976, 2/4/17, L/C.; No. 14 O.C.B., 5/10/17; Glouc. R., 26/10/18; F; Lieut.; w.
Heightley, King's Road, Cheltenham.

BARNETT, Gerald Isca
A/9803, 30/10/16; No. 14 O.C.B., 7/6/17; W. York. R., 25/9/17; F; 2/Lieut.; w.
56 Crediton Hill, Hampstead, N.W. 6.

BARNETT, Henry Granville
D/9991, 22/11/16; A.S.C., C/S, 1/3/17; R.A.S.C., 27/4/17; Lieut.
150 Sutton Court Road, Chiswick, W. 4.

BARNETT, Henry John Outram
6/3/7757, 23/11/15, L/C.; R.F.C., 6/7/16, R.A.F.; F; Lieut.
19 Copthorne Road, Wolverhampton.

BARNETT, Walter Alfred John
A/10284, 1/1/17, L/C.; No. 21 O.C.B., 5/5/17; R. Lanc. R., 28/8/17, att. Yorks. L.I.; F; Lieut.; w.
58 Harborough Road, Streatham, S.W. 16.

BARNETT, William Lascelles
A/10464, 12/1/17; No. 14 O.C.B., 5/5/17; York. & Lanc. R., 28/8/17; F; Lieut.; g.
56 Crediton Hill, Hampstead, N.W. 6.

BARNSLEY, William Edward
B/12676, 4/3/18, L/C.; No. 4 O.C.B., 6/9/18; Glouc. R., 17/3/19; 2/Lieut.
Sapperton, Cirencester, Gloucestershire.

✠ BARNWELL, George Woodruffe
C/10404, 8/1/17; No. 20 O.C.B., 5/5/17; R. Lanc. R., 28/8/17, att. Yorks. L.I.; 2/Lieut.
Killed in action 13/4/18.

BARON, Herbert
4/4638, 5/7/15; dis. 12/7/15.
19 Gloucester Road, Finsbury Park, N.

BARR, Alaric Cecil
6/8673, 4/1/16; R.A., C/S, 9/6/16; R.G.A., 13/9/16; F; Lieut.
c/o. Miss Bray, 7 St. George's Road, Victoria, S.W. 1.

APPENDIX II.—RECORDS OF RANK AND FILE.

BARR, David Harold
6/2/7575, 18/11/15; No. 14 O.C.B.; R. War. R., 24/10/16, M.G.C., Genl. List (Dental Surgeon); F,It; Lieut.
62 Park Lane, Croydon.

BARR, Lawrence Bend
6/9074, 22/1/16; R.A., C/S, 21/7/16; R.G.A., 26/11/16; F; Lieut.; w.
Sigglesthorne, Hull.

BARR, Robert William
B/11340, 21/5/17; A.S.C., C/S, 1/9/17; R.A.S.C., 27/10/17; F; Lieut.
28 Maryfield Terrace, Dundee.

✠ BARRACLOUGH, William
6/5/5986, 2/9/15, L/C.; W. York R., 7/6/16; F; 2/Lieut.
Killed in action 28/9/16.

BARRATT, Thomas William
K/E/2208, 30/11/14; R.E., 10/3/15; F,It; Capt.; M.C.
Minden, The Drive, Tonbridge, Kent.

BARRENGER, Eric John
A/13109, 24/5/18; No. 5 O.C.B., 8/11/18, No. 20 O.C.B.; R.W. Surr. R., 17/3/19; 2/Lieut.
30 Endymion Terrace, Finsbury Park, N.

BARRENGER, Harold Edgar
4/6/4915, 19/7/15; R.W. Surr. R., 18/12/15; I; Lieut.
30 Endymion Terrace, Finsbury Park, N. 4.

BARRETT, Arthur Leslie
6/9445, T/14/2/16; R.A., C/S, 23/6/16; R.G.A., 11/10/16; F; Lieut.
3 Portland Villas, Victoria Road, Barnstaple.

BARRETT, Bertram Quiller
B/12787, 18/3/18; No. 1 O.C.B., 6/9/18; D. of Corn. L.I., 16/3/19; 2/Lieut.
Creswick, Paget Place, Penarth, S. Wales.

BARRETT, Charles Woodford
B/9865, 6/11/16; trfr. Class W. Res., 8/2/17.
16 Melbourne Street, Leicester.

BARRETT, Ingram Arthur
B/12788, 18/3/18; No. 1 O.C.B., 6/9/18, No. 3 O.C.B.; E. Lan. R., 17/3/19; 2/Lieut.
62 Hitherfield Road, Streatham, S.W. 16.

BARRETT, Jack Hardy
Sq/363, 16/3/08; dis. 15/3/13; rej. Sq/957, 5/8/14; R. Fus., 15/8/14.

✠ BARRETT, Noel Bertram
D/10927, 26/3/17; No. 12 O.C.B., 10/8/17; Essex R., 27/11/17; F; 2/Lieut.
Killed in action 29/4/18.

✠ BARRETT, Reginald James
6/4/5613, 16/8/15; L'pool. R., 4/8/16; Lieut.
Killed in action 21/8/18.

BARRETT, Richard Percival
B/D/13575, 3/7/18.

BARRETT, Sidney Willmott
C/12557, 6/2/18; No. 13 O.C.B., 4/8/18; Essex R., 5/3/19, att. R. Fus.; NR; 2/Lieut.
Toro, Fort Portal, Uganda, British East Africa.

BARRETT, Sydney
B/11686, 19/7/17; A.S.C., C/S, 1/11/17; R.A.S.C., 25/1/18; F; Lieut.
18 Meadway Court, Golders Green, N.W. 11.

BARRETT-LENNARD, Thomas Richard Fynes
B/Sq/D/12935, 23/3/18; No. 5 O.C.B., 4/10/18; R. Suss. R., 17/3/19; 2/Lieut.
43 Eaton Place, Brighton.

BARRITT, Norman
C/D/12263, 30/11/17; No. 9 O.C.B., 10/5/18; N. Lan. R., 5/2/19; 2/Lieut.

BARRON, Charles Howard Washington
B/13578, 22/7/18; trfr. K.R. Rif. C., 7/4/19.
44 Shaftsbury Road, Earlsdon, Coventry.

BARRON, Oswald
A/295, 24/6/08; dis. 23/6/09.
6, West Kensington Mansions, W. 14.

✠ BARROW, Alfred James
E/2963, 25/2/15, L/C.; Lan. Fus., 21/6/15; F; Capt.; w,p; M.C.
Died of wounds 24/6/18.

BARROW, Charles Embleton
K/F/2295, 10/12/14; K.O. Sco. Bord., 27/1/15, emp. Air Ministry; F; Staff Capt.; w.
5 Park Road, Harrogate, Yorkshire.

✠ BARROW, Edmund Sproston Knapp
6/1/6880, 18/10/15; No. 11 O.C.B., 7/5/16; R. War. R., 4/9/16; 2/Lieut.
Killed in action 8/5/17.

BARROW, Howard George
D/10228, 29/12/16; No. 20 O.C.B., 5/5/17; Manch. R., 25/9/17, att. S. Wales Bord., Norf. R., E. Kent R. and Hamps. R.; I,M, Persia; Lieut.
81 Holden Road, Woodside Park, N. 12.

BARROW, John Carus
6/4/6472, 27/9/15; R.A., C/S, 7/12/16; R.F.A., 5/5/17; Lieut.; w.
16 Catherine Road, Crumpsall, Manchester.

BARROWMAN, John
D/11540, 21/6/17; R.E., C/S, 30/9/17; R.E., 9/11/17; F; 2/Lieut.
Staneacre, Hamilton, Scotland. (Now in Australia.)

BARROWS, James Edmund
6/2/5322, 2/8/15; Linc. R., 30/12/15; F; Lieut.; w.
16 Albert Street, Syston, Leicester.

BARRY, Frederick Cecil
4/5/4782, 12/7/15, Sgt.; Dorset R., 1/11/15, Indian Army; I,M,S,SR; Capt.
c/o. Messrs. Grindley & Co., Bombay.

BARRY, John Edward
6/5/7344, 10/11/15; No. 7 O.C.B., 3/7/16; Conn. Rang., 3/11/16, Tank Corps.; F; Capt.; w.
Rathbarry, Ross Carbery, Co. Cork, Ireland.

BARRY, Keith Lewis
C/9973, 20/11/16; No. 14 O.C.B., 30/1/17; Dorset R., 29/5/17; I,E; Lieut.
11 Macquarie Street, Parramatta, New South Wales, Australia.

BARRY, Leo James McCarthy
B/11354, 25/5/17; trfr. 19th Lond. R., 27/7/17.
9 Weatherby Mansions, Earls Court, S.W. 5.

BARRY, Leonard Hayden
1/9744, 16/10/16; No. 14 O.C.B., 27/12/16; E. Surr. R., 25/4/17; F; 2/Lieut.
The Lymes, 35 Woodside, Wimbledon, S.W.

BARRY, Percy Leo
6/2/8867, 12/1/16; Garr. O.C.B., 12/12/16; R. Ir. Fus., 10/2/17, att. R.A.F. and Brit. W.I.R.; S,E, Jamaica; Lieut.
80 Whitworth Road, Glasnevin, Dublin.

✠ BARRY, Shiel Ronald
H/2607, 7/1/15; R. Fus., 29/4/15, 11th Lond. R.; 2/Lieut.
Killed in action 7/10/16.

BARSBY, Frank
1/B/3716, 24/5/15, Sgt.; demob. 23/1/19.
Council School, Bell Lane, Hendon.

BARTHOLOMEW, Frederick William
E/2823, 1/2/15; Bedf. R., 3/6/15, M.G.C.; F; Major; w; M.C.
Moor Cottage, Binfield, Berkshire.

BARTHOLOMEW, James Guy Prendergast
A/10470, 12/1/17; Garr. O.C.B., 23/5/17; Worc. R., 14/7/17, att. R Innis. Fus., R. Lanc. R. and 14th Huss.; Lieut.
52 London Road, St. Leonards-on-Sea.

BARTINDALE, John Lewis
D/12942, 19/4/18; No. 21 O.C.B., 4/10/18; R. War. R., 19/3/19; 2/Lieut.
Melrose, 28 Courtland Avenue, Ilford, Essex.

BARTLEET, Edmund Arthur
6/1/9342, 7/2/16; R.A., C/S, 14/7/16; R.G.A., 18/10/16; F; Lieut.; w; M.C., Croix de Guerre.
Westholme, Hoddesdon, Herts.

BARTLEET, Eustace John
F/1752, 16/10/14; North'd. Fus., 14/11/14, Lab. Corps; F; Capt.; w,g.
Shandon, 98 Middleton Hall Road, King's Norton, Birmingham.

BARTLEET, Frederic Ernest
6/3/5463, 9/8/15; Worc. R., 20/11/15; Lieut.

BARTLEET, Roland Hugh
6/1/6753, 11/10/15; R.A., C/S, 28/9/16; trfr. Tank Corps, 14/8/17; F; L/Cpl.
Westholme, Hoddesdon, Herts.

BARTLETT, Albert Charles
6/4/5825, 26/8/15; No. 14 O.C.B., 27/9/16; Shrops. Yeo., 24/1/17; I, Persia; Lieut.
1 Church Street, Woolwich.

BARTLETT, Charles Brinson
A/14044 23/9/18; demob. 6/1/19.
15 Stapylton Road, Barnet, Herts.

APPENDIX II.—RECORDS OF RANK AND FILE.

BARTLETT, Fred
C/11432, 4/6/17; A.S.C., C/S, 1/9/17; R.A.S.C., 27/10/17; F; 2/Lieut. 116 Plymouth Road, Penarth, Glamorganshire.

BARTLETT, Harry
6/B/7789, 24/11/15; R A., C/S, 7/8/16; R.F.A., 17/11/16; Lieut.; M(1). Draycon House, Ogmore Vale, Glamorganshire.

BARTLETT, Henry Waish
4/3/4526, 1/7/15; 19th Lond. R., 5/11/15; F; Capt.; w; M.C. High Street, Brackley, Northants.

BARTLETT, Norman Edian
Sq/4/3108, 25/3/15; R.F.A., 27/4/15; Major; w; M(1). 56 Victoria Street, Westminster, S.W. 1.

BARTLETT, Percy Ernest
C/10576, 19/1/17, L/C.; No. 14 O.C.B., 16/3/17; Special List, 25/4/17, emp. S. Persian Rifles; Lieut. 70 Woodside Road, Bowes Park, N. 22.

BARTLIFF, John
B/12409, 18/1/18; No. 13 O.C.B., 10/5/18; W. York. R., 3/2/19; 2/Lieut. 10 Sherwood Street, Scarborough.

BARTON, Bertie Bowman
E/1505, 1/10/14; dis. 9/11/14:

BARTON, Charles Thomas Hugh
6/8338, 13/12/15; dis. med. unfit, 12/5/16.

BARTON, George
D/10423, 10/1/17; No. 20 O.C.B., 7/6/17; Midd'x. R., 25/9/17; F,It; Lieut.; w(2). 81 Weston Park, Crouch End. N. 8.

✠ BARTON, Harry
6/2/8277, 10/12/15; No. 14 O.C.B., 30/10/16; 3rd Lond. R., 28/2/17; F; 2/Lieut.; w. Killed in action 22/3/18.

✠ BARTON, James
6/2/8339, 13/12/15; R.A., C/S, 26/10/16; R.G.A., 19/2/17; F; 2/Lieut. Killed in action 17/8/18.

BARTON, John Austin
A/65, 8/4/08; dis. 7/4/11. Torwood, Wimbledon Park, S.W.

BARTON, John Edward Broadbent
4/5690, 16/8/15; Manch. R., 10/11/15, Indian Army; F,It,M; Capt.; M(1). c/o Messrs. Cox & Coy., Hornby Road, Bombay.

BARTON, Joseph Lees
B/11310, 21/5/17; No. 14 O.C.B., 7/9/17; North'd. Fus., 17/12/17; F; Lieut.; w. 36 Canning Street, Liverpool.

BARTON, Michael Kennedy Kingston
4/6/4558, 1/7/15; dis. med. unfit, 22/5/16. 14, Ashburn Place, Courtfield Road, S.W.

BARTON, Robert Childers
6/1/6585, 4/10/15; R. Dub. Fus., 21/4/16.

BARTON, Stanley John
D/10288, 1/1/17; trfr. R.F.A., 16/2/17. Williamstup Farm, Fairford.

BARTON-SMITH, Frank
4/1/5023, 22/7/15; N. Lan. R., 27/12/15; F,S,P; Capt.; M.C. Croxley Green, Herts.

BARTRUM, Eric Reynolds
6/8811, 10/1/16; R.E., C/S, 7/5/16; R.E., 22/7/16; emp. M. of Munitions; Lieut. 10 Argyll Road, Kensington, S.W.

BARWICK, Roy Harold
B/13630, 26/7/18; demob. 6/1/19. Yew Tree Cottage, Old Lodge Lane, Purley, Surrey.

BASAN, Wallace James
4/2/5065, 26/7/15; North'd Fus., 26/11/15; F,E; Capt. Railway Traffic Office, Kantara, Egypt.

BASDEN, Harold Edward Lennox
C/Sq/13261, 11/6/18; demob. 9/1/19. Sandridge, Crowborough, Sussex.

✠ BASFORD, Bromley Alfred
6/1/7576, 18/11/15; Notts. & Derby. R., 4/9/16; 2/Lieut. Killed in action 4/10/17.

BASHER, Oliver Henry
C/14234, 28/10/18; dis. med. unfit, 19/3/19. 23 Havelock Road, Norwich.

BASKCOMB, Gordon Victor
D/13709, 31/7/18; demob. 19/12/18. Bill Office, Bank of England, E.C.

BASKER, Charles Norman
6/5/6985, 25/10/15; No. 11 O.C.B., 7/5/16; R. Lanc. R., 4/9/16; F; Lieut.; w. 5 Watergate, Grantham, Lincolnshire.

BASKETT, George Coppinger Seymour
1/6/5843, 26/8/15; Kent Cyc. Bn., 5/6/15, att. R. W. Kent R.; F; Lieut. 24 Trinity Road, Sheerness, Kent.

BASKETT, Spencer Seymour
6/1/8009, 30/11/15; R.A., C/S, 4/8/16; R.G.A., 3/11/16; F; 2/Lieut.; w; M.C. 24 Trinity Road, Sheerness.

BASS, Raymond John
C/13264, 12/6/18, L/C.; demob. 23/1/19. Tourney Hall, Lydd, Kent.

BASSETT, Herbert Kitchener
A/13084, 20/5/18; No. 1 O.C.B., 8/11/18; Welch R., 16/3/19; 2/Lieut. Rosehill, Terrace Road, Swansea.

BASSETT, Percy John
6/4/5156, 29/7/15, Sgt.; demob. 31/1/19. 28 Richmond Crescent, Barnsbury, N. 1.

BASTABLE, Charles George
1694, 13/10/14.

BASTOW, Herbert
6/2/5496, 9/8/15; R.F.A., 10/12/15; Lieut.

BATCHELOR, Benjamin
E/14082, 30/9/18; R.G.A., C/S, 1/11/18; demob. West Meadow, Caterham, Surrey.

BATCHELOR, Frank
4/3/4527, 1/7/15; R. Highrs., 25/11/15; F; Lieut. 21 Newtown, Cupar, Fife, Scotland.

BATE, Francis Joseph
C/345, 23/2/09; dis. 23/2/13; rej. D/1524, 5/10/14, Sgt.; Manch. R., 31/3/15; F; Capt. 5 Somerset Road, Harrow.

BATE, Geoffrey Fairless
C/1343, 26/9/14; R. Berks. R., 14/12/14; F, Serbia; Capt.; w(3); M(1). The Bungalow, Boyne Hill, Maidenhead, Berks.

BATE, James Richard Trevithick
C/Sq/13202, 5/6/18; trfr. 14th Lond. R., 6/12/18, R.E.; Spr. Upton Villa, Hayle, Cornwall.

BATEMAN, Richard John Sacheverell
K/D/2153, 23/11/14; Essex R., 7/3/15; G,E,P; Capt.; M(1). c/o. Nat. Prov. & Union Bank of England, Ltd., Charing Cross, S.W. 1. (Now in U.S.A.)

BATEMAN, Robert Allan
6/9537, 18/2/16; dis. med. unfit, 11/8/16. 74 Mildred Avenue, Watford.

BATEMAN, William Young
6/Sq/9399, 9/2/16; R.F.A., C/S, 29/9/16; R.F.A., 27/1/17; F,It; Lieut. Prospect House, RossCarbery, Co. Cork, Ireland.

BATES, Arthur Walsgrove
C/D/12042, 27/9/17; No. 23 O.C.B., 7/6/18; Manch. R., 5/2/19; 2/Lieut. Glengarth, Deganwy, N. Wales.

BATES, Francis Osborne
6/5/C/7758, 23/11/15, Sgt.; No. 14 O.C.B., 10/8/17; Notts. and Derby. R., 27/11/17; F; 2/Lieut.; Inv. The Cedars, Chellaston, Derby.

BATES, Reginald Newman
B/11029, 11/4/17; R.A., C/S, 3/9/17, No. 4 O.C.B.; Manch. R., 31/7/18; Lieut. 34 Flanders Mansions, Bedford Park, W. 4. (Now in Ceylon).

BATES, Reginald Walter Melville
6/1/6113, 9/9/15; R.A.S.C., 8/11/15; Germ.EA,P; Capt. c/o. Reuter's Agency, 24 Old Jewry, E.C.

BATES, Ronald James
6/4/9208, 31/1/16; R.A., C/S, 26/10/16; R.G.A., 24/2/17, War Office; Lieut.; w. 20 Redgrave Road, Putney, S.W.

BATES, Sidney Frank
4/6/4916, 19/7/15; Durh. L.I., 9/12/15, R.E.; F; Lieut. Ungava, Barr Common, Walsall, Staffs.

APPENDIX II.—RECORDS OF RANK AND FILE.

BATES, Stacy James
6/8509, 22/12/15; R.F.A., C/S, 9/6/16; R.G.A., 16/9/16; F,It; Capt.
40 Park Road, Southend-on-Sea.

BATES-THOMPSON, Henry
4/5/4783, 12/7/15; R.F.A., 28/9/15; Lieut.
Union Society, Oxford.

BATHGATE, John Linsley
6/2/9400, 9/2/16; No. 8 O.C.B., 4/8/16; Linc. R., 21/11/16, Chinese Lab. Corps; F; Lieut.
c/o. Chartered Bank of India, Australia and China, 38 Bishopsgate, E.C.

BATLEY, William
6/2/D/7790, 24/11/15; R.A.O.C., 16/10/16; M; Lieut.
Municipal Offices, Rordepont, Transvaal. S. Africa.

BATSON, Herbert Mackenzie
B/1003, 5/8/14; Devon. R., 15/8/14, Lab. Corps; Lt.-Col.; O.B.E., M(2).

BATTEN, Cyril Townshend
D/6/7979, 29/11/15, Sgt.; R.G.A., C/S, 18/7/17; R.G.A., 17/12/17; Lieut.; w.
92 Barrowgate Road, Chiswick.

BATTERBURY, Douglas George
6/4/D/8388, 14/12/15; R.F.C., C/S, 16/4/17; R.N.A.S., 20/4/17, R.A.F.; Flt. Sub. Lt.
51 West Mount Road, Eltham, S.E. 9.

BATTING, Herbert Charles
D/10381, 9/1/17; trfr. 16th Lond. R., 9/3/17.
Home Farm, Pattimore, nr. Exeter.

BATTISHILL, George Varian Frederick
A/10300, 1/1/17; No. 20 O.C.B., 5/5/17; R. Lanc. R., 28/8/17; w.

BATTY, Roland Bradshaw
6/4/7431, 15/11/15, L/C.; Manch. R., 4/8/16.
45 South Drive, Chorlton-cum-Hardy, Manchester.

BATTYE, Ben
E/14124, 9/10/18; demob. 23/1/19.
Fisher Green, Honley, Huddersfield.

BATY, John Armstrong
6/4/9264, 3/2/16, Sgt.; No. 14 O.C.B.; North'd Fus., 18/12/16; F; Lieut.; w.
Seal House, Hexham.

✠ BAWDEN, Leslie John
3/3374, 26/4/15; D. of Corn. L.I., 28/7/15; 2/Lieut.
Died of wounds 1/10/16.

BAX, Cyril Ernest Orlando
K/E/2330, 14/12/14; Midd'x. R., 9/3/15; E,S; Capt.
Oakdene, Beckenham, Kent.

BAXTER, Clement Dormer
B/11661, 16/7/17; No. 11 O.C.B., 9/11/17; Yorks. L.I., 30/4/18; 2/Lieut.
28 Hazlett Road, W. Kensington, W.

BAXTER, Herbert James
B/12846, 25/3/18; No. 7 O.C.B., 9/8/18; Rif. Brig., 4/3/19; 2/Lieut.
10 Ashfield Road, Wilton Road, Salisbury.

✠ BAXTER, Leonard Josiah
D/11812, 9/8/17; No. 14 O.C.B., 4/1/18; E. Kent R., 25/6/18; 2/Lieut.
Died of wounds 12/11/18.

✠ BAXTER, Leslie William
6/4/2/4917, 19/7/15, Sgt.; R.A., C/S, 4/8/16; R.F.A., 17/11/16; F; Lieut.
Killed in action 28/5/18.

BAXTER, Thomas Desmond
6/3/8773, 6/1/16, Cpl.; No. 14 O.C.B., 30/10/16; R.N.V.R., 28/2/17; F; Sub. Lt.; w.
12 Hamlet Court Road, Westcliff-on-Sea.

BAXTER, William Cowell
D/11166, 2/5/17, L/C.; No. 14 O.C.B., 5/10/17; E. Lan. R., 26/2/18; 2/Lieut.
70 Lancaster Place, Blackburn, Lancashire.

BAXTER, William Henry
A/11244, 11/5/17; No. 14 O.C.B., 9/11/17; Shrops. L.I., 30/4/18, att. M.G.C.; It; 2/Lieut.
43 Wellington Park, Clifton, Bristol.

BAYLEY, Sidney
6/3/8302, 11/12/15; No. 14 O.C.B.; 19th Lond. R., 18/12/16, emp. M. of Munitions; Lieut.; w.
172 Bedford Hill, Balham.

BAYLIS, Bryan Holbrook
6/1/6240, 16/9/15, L/C.; R.A., C/S, 24/1/16; R.G.A., 19/6/16, att. Bedf. & Herts. R.; F; Lieut.
29 Mincing Lane, E.C.

BAYLIS, Frank Stanley
3/9616, 14/9/16; No. 14 O.C.B., 26/11/16; S. Staff. R., 27/3/17; F; Staff Capt.; w,g(2).
The Leasowes, Barnt Green, nr. Birmingham.

BAYLIS, Frederick George
6/2/6192, 13/9/15, L/C.; No. 5 O.C.B., 14/8/16; Midd'x. R., 21/11/16, Lab. Corps; F; Capt.;
Westcroft, Northwick Road, Evesham, Worcestershire.

BAYLIS, Harold Copper
6/1/5/6610, 4/10/15; trfr. H.A.C., 4/3/16.
286 High Road, Ilford, Essex.

✠ BAYLIS, Joseph Anno Jones
Sq/708, T/10/4/13; S. Lan. R., 19/9/14; Capt.; w.
Killed in action 13/6/17.

✠ BAYLISS, Reginald Blencowe
4/4126, 10/6/15; Manch. R., 11/12/15; F; 2/Lieut.
Died of wounds, 18/11/16.

BAYLY, Charles
6/Sq/9103, 24/1/16; R. 1st Devon. Yeo., 4/8/16; Lieut.
Bank of Australasia, Threadneedle Street, E.C.

BAYLY, Henry Edward
H/2/2015, 2/11/14; dis. med. unfit, 31/3/16.
Bella Vista, Mullingar.

✠ BAYLY, Robert
Sq/240, 22/5/08; dis. 21/5/09.
Died.

BAYLY, William Gordon
K/A/2300, 10/12/14; R. Lanc. R., 30/12/14, att. E. York. R.; F,S; Capt.; M.C., Italian Silver Medal for Military Valour.
c/o. The Chartered Bank, Colombo, Ceylon.

BAYLY-VANDELEUR, Crofton Talbot. See VANDELEUR, C.T.B.

BAYNAM, Nelmes
D/11153, 30/4/17; No. 14 O.C.B., 10/8/17; Hamps. R., 27/11/17; Lieut.
26 Landport Terrace, Southsea.

BAYNE, Thomas Crabtree
B/12847, 25/3/18; No. 11 O.C.B., 9/8/18, No. 19 O.C.B.; Lan. Fus., 5/3/19; 2/Lieut.
9 Hereford Road, Southport, Lancashire.

BAYNES, Edward Stuart Augustus
B/1316, 26/9/14; K.R. Rif. C., 14/11/14; F; Capt.; w(2).
44 Primrose Mansions, Battersea Park, S.W. 11. (Now in New Zealand).

BAYNES, Norman Thomas
6/2/5400, 5/8/15; trfr. 5th Lond. R., 31/1/16.
22 May Place Road, Bexley Heath, Kent.

BAYNES, Stanley Harold
A/B/13946, 4/9/18; No. 24 O.C.B., 15/11/18; Tank Corps, 22/3/19; 2/Lieut.
14 Chatham Road, Walthamstow, E. 17.

BAYNES, William Edward Colston
K/2724, 18/1/15; Cold. Gds., 12/2/15; F; Capt.; w(2); M.C., M(1).
Maadi, Cairo, Egypt.

BAYNES-SMITH, Harry Walter
4/1/4376, 21/6/15; Camb. R., 5/10/15; F; Capt.; w.; M.C. and Bar, M(1).
Contaduria, Ferro Carril Oeste, Buenos Aires, S. America.

BAYNTON, Henry Howard
6/8950, 17/1/16; dis. med. unfit, 26/5/16.
Westmoor, Moor Green, Moseley, Birmingham.

BAZALGETTE, Harry Lautour
A/1361, 26/9/14; R.E., 31/12/14; F; Major; M(1).
West Wing, Fetcham Grove, Leatherhead, Surrey.

BAZELL, John Russell
6/8048, 1/12/15; R.F.A., C/S, 9/6/16; R.F.A., 9/9/16; Lieut.; w.
19 Western Gardens, Ealing Common.

BEACHAM, Tom
B/13478, 8/7/18; demob. 21/12/18.
53 Risca Road, Cross Keys, Monmouthshire.

✠ BEACHCROFT, Cyril Shakespear
206, 6/5/08; Dorset Yeo., 10/10/14, Household Bn;: Capt.; M(1).
Killed in action 12/10/17.

BEADLE, George Walter Baden
B/13410, 1/7/18, L/C.; trfr. K.R. Rif. C., 7/4/19.
31 Verulam Road, St. Albans, Herts.

APPENDIX II.—RECORDS OF RANK AND FILE.

BEADON, Eric
B/1700, 13/10/14; R.A.S.C., 10/11/14, R.F.C.; F; Capt.; M.C., M(1). 17 Cyril Mansions, Battersea Park, S.W.

BEAL, Harold Giveen
3/3829, 31/5/15; 4th Lond. R., secd. R.G.A., and M.G.C.; F,M; Lieut. 37 Ferme Park Road, N. 4.

BEAL, Leslie Wallis
6/3/6754, 11/10/15; R.F.C., 4/8/16, R.A.F.; Lieut.; w(2); M(1). 37 Ferme Park Road, N. 4.

BEALE, Basil Perry
Sq/1219, 14/9/14; R.A.S.C., 28/10/14; Capt.; O.B.E., M.C., M(1). Swanston, Whitchurch, Oxon.

BEALE, Donald Olaf Christopher
H/K/2556, 4/1/15; R. Ir. Rif., 10/4/15; F; Capt.; w(3), Inv. Croft Road, Crowborough, Sussex.

BEALE, Dudley Valentine
F/1870, 16/10/14; R.A.S.C., 21/6/15; F; Lieut. Ersham House, Canterbury.

BEALE, Harold Hubert
6/2/8542, 30/12/15; No. 14 O.C.B., 27/9/16; Hamps. R., 24/1/17, att. R. War. R.; Lieut. Bowness, Stirling Road, Bournemouth.

BEALE, Harold Lansdowne
6/2/8986, 18/1/16, L/C.; No. 14 O.C.B., 28/8/16; Camb. R., 19/12/16; Lieut. Tindon End, nr. Saffron Walden, Essex.

BEALE, Seaman Tristan Tracy
B/A/D/10782, 19/2/17; R.F.A., C/S, 15/3/18; trfr. R.F.A.; Gnr. Finchden Manor, Tenterden, Kent.

BEALE, Wilfred Bennett
4/1/4063, 7/6/15; E. Kent R., 2/9/15, att. Leic. R., R.A.F.; F,I,M,E; Lieut.; w. Humberstone House, Humberstone, Leicester.

BEALES, Rowland
C/11458, 5/6/17; A.S.C., C/S, 1/9/17; R.A.S.C., 27/10/17; F; Capt.; M(1). Barclay's Bank, Ltd., 54 Lombard Street, E.C. 3.

BEAMISH, Leslie Tranter
D/12914, 10/4/18; No. 11 O.C.B., 4/10/18; demob. The Hawthorns, Hampton-in-Arden, nr. Birmingham.

BEAN, Edgar Layton
2/5401, 5/8/15; trfr. R.F.A., 11/2/16. Merton College, Oxford.

BEAN, Percival Frederick
6/9593, 26/6/16; No. 2 Cav. C/S, 1/10/16; 11th R. Regt. of Cav., 20/12/16; 2/Lieut. Pinewood, Burnham, Somerset.

BEAN, R. W.
K/2435, T/19/12/14; R.F.A., 1/3/15; Lieut.

BEARD, Cecil Augustus
4/6/3934, 2/6/15; dis. 3/6/15. The Rocks, Tean, Staffordshire.

BEARD, William Seymour
8/6/8010, 30/11/15; A.S.C., C/S, 24/4/16; R.A.S.C., 28/5/16; S; Lieut.; Order of the White Eagle of Serbia with swords, 5th Class. 40 Bromwich Place, Hove, Sussex.

BEARDER, Harold Ingham
B/11071, 16/4/17, L/C.; R.G.A., C/S, 26/9/17; R.G.A., 4/3/18; F; 2/Lieut. Greenlea, 151 Huddersfield Road, Halifax.

BEARDON, Claud Charles
C/11433, 4/6/17, L/C.; No. 14 O.C.B., 9/11/17; Bedf. R., 30/4/18; F; 2/Lieut. Westcroft, Northwood, nr. Ramsgate.

BEARDON, Percy Fruer
6/4/5288, T/1/8/15; 18th Lond. R., 19/12/15; F; Lieut.; w. 11 Holyoake House, Brentham, Ealing, W. 5.

BEARDSLEY, Harry Howard
K/A/2183, 26/11/14; R. Suss. R., 31/3/15, M.G.C.; F; Lieut. Deeking High Bank, Spalding, Lincs.

BEARE, William Aubrey
D/E/13859, 19/8/18; demob. 10/1/19. 5 Manor Grove, Beckenham, Kent.

BEARN, John Angus
C/10390, 8/1/17; No. 14 O.C.B., 5/5/17; K.R. Rif. C., 28/8/17; Lieut.; p.

BEARY, Matthew Joseph
A/11949, 3/9/17; R.F.A., C/S, 4/2/18; R.H. & R.F.A., 3/10/18, emp. M. of Munitions; 2/Lieut. Toberaheena House, Clonmel, Co. Tipperary, Ireland.

BEATER, Bernard Macpherson
D/10662, 5/2/17; L/C.; No. 14 O.C.B., 5/7/17; Midd'x. R., 30/10/17; 2/Lieut. 7 Cromwell Road, Feltham, Middlesex.

✠ BEATH, William Alexander
B/11341, 21/5/17; No. 14 O.C.B., 7/9/17; Indian Army, 18/12/17; 2/Lieut. Died 7/5/18.

BEATTIE, Arthur Hardwick
6/2/9513, 16/2/16; A.S.C., C/S, 1/9/16; R.A.S.C., 25/10/16, att. Yorks. L.I. and Glouc. R.; F; Lieut. 39 Thorncliffe Road, Oxford.

BEATTIE, Robert Henry Matterson
A/12524, 31/1/18; No. 4 O.C.B., 7/6/18; Yorks. L.I., 4/3/19; 2/Lieut. Newland House, Banbury, Oxon.

✠ BEATTIE, Malcolm Bartlett
6/1/9058, 21/1/16; No. 11 O.C.B., 7/5/16; R. Berks. R., 4/9/16; Lieut. Died of wounds 16/10/17.

✠ BEATTY, David
D/9995, 24/11/16, L/C.; No. 14 O.C.B., 5/3/17; R.N.V.R., 26/6/17; Sub. Lt. Died.

BEATY, William
6/4/5464, 9/8/15; trfr. Dorset. Yeo., 1/5/16. White Hart Hotel, Lewes, Sussex.

✠ BEAUCHAMP, Eric Westgate
C/9917, 15/11/16; No. 14 O.C.B., 30/1/17; Dorset R., 25/4/17, att. Hamps. R.; E,P; 2/Lieut.; w. Died of wounds 23/11/17.

BEAUCLAIR, Charles Alexander
B/11353, 25/5/17, L/C.; R.F.A., C/S, 25/1/18; R.H. & R.F.A., 5/8/18; 2/Lieut. 144a Shooters Hill Road, Blackheath.

BEAUMONT, Ernest
4/Sq/5024, 22/7/15; R.F.A., 21/12/15; M; 2/Lieut. Westcot, Penworthan Road, Purley.

BEAUMONT, Victor
C/14235, 28/10/18; trfr. K.R. Rif. C., 25/4/19, M.G.C.; Pte. 24 Avenue le Notre, Croix (Nord), France.

BEAVAN, Robert William
6/3/8011, 30/11/15; No. 14 O.C.B.; 7th Lond. R., 18/12/16, att. 28th Lond. R.; F; Lieut. c/o. Ward & Mills, 16 Rood Lane, E.C.

BEAVEN, Colin Evelyn
B/C/12366, 4/1/18, L/C.; demob. 29/1/19. St. Aubyns, 127 Church Street, Edmonton, N. 9.

BEAVEN, Cyril Percy
6/Sq/8474, 20/12/15; No. 2 Cav. C/S, 1/10/16; 12th Lanc., 20/12/16, att. Derby. Yeo.; F; Lieut. 9 Collingwood Avenue, Muswell Hill, N. 10.

BEAVEN, Victor
6/4/5614, 16/8/15; trfr. 16th Lond. R., 2/5/16. The Firs, Park Road, Cowes, Isle of Wight.

✠ BEAVER, Felix Victor
F/K/2558, 4/1/15; Midd'x. R., 2/6/15; 2/Lieut. Killed in action 1/7/16.

BECK, Alexander
D/10690, 7/2/17; R.F.C., C/S, 13/3/17; R.F.C., 19/4/17, R.A.F.; F; Flt. Cmdr.; D.F.C. The Green, Ravenstonedale, Westmoreland.

BECK, Edmund
A/11202, 7/5/17; A.S.C., C/S, 1/9/17; R.A.S.C., 27/10/17; 2/Lieut. The Red House, Westwood Park Road, Peterborough.

BECK, Edward Victor
C/Sq/9947, 17/11/16, Cpl.; No. 1 Cav. C/S, 31/7/17; 2nd R. Regt. of Cav., 22/2/18; 2/Lieut. North Thoresby, Lincolnshire.

BECK, George Harold
B/10107, 4/12/16; R.W. Surr. R., 9/3/17, Chinese Lab. Corps; F; Lieut. 22 Ryder Street, St. James, S.W.

BECK, Herbert James
6/2/6158, T/10/9/15; 9th Lond. R., 6/6/16; Lieut.; w.

BECK, Stanley William
9552, 26/2/16; No. 14 O.C.B., 26/11/16; Norf. R., 27/3/17, att. Bedf. R. and T.M.Bty.; F; Lieut. Briggate Old Hall, Worstead, Norwich.

APPENDIX II.—RECORDS OF RANK AND FILE.

BECKETT, *Frank Haseltine*
4/3527, 6/5/15; R. Lanc. R., 7/1/16; 2/Lieut.; *w*.
　　　　　　　　Holly House, Hornby, Lancashire.

BECKWITH, *Harold William*
C/11082, 18/4/17; No. 12 O.C.B., 10/8/17; trfr. 28th Lond. R., 25/2/18; Pte.　　Marnwood, Hestbank, nr. Lancaster.

BECKWORTH, *Cyril*
C/9934, 16/11/16; No. 14 O.C.B., 30/1/17; Dorset R., 29/5/17, *att*. D. of Corn. L.I. *and* Som. L.I.; I; Capt.
　　　　　　96 High Street, Barry, South Wales.

BEDDOE, *Arthur Howard*
D/10399, 8/1/17; No. 20 O.C.B., 7/6/17; Notts. & Derby. R., 25/9/17; F; Lieut.
　　　　Fairholme, North Marsh Road, Gainsborough, Lincs.

BEDDOW, *Besil Josiah*
A/14342, T/6/1/19; demob. 31/1/19.
　　　　　　　　Branksome, Anerley Park, S.E. 20.

✠ BEDDOW, *Cecil Victor*
K/F/2301, 10/12/14, Cpl.; Devon. R., 27/3/15; F; 2/Lieut.
　　　　　　　　　　Killed in action 1/7/16.

BEDWORTH, *Roland Gilbert*
B/12341, 1/1/18; No. 8 O.C.B., 7/6/18; Worc. R., 6/2/19; 2/Lieut.　　44 Thornhill Road, Handsworth, Birmingham.

✠ BEE, *William*
Sq/4/3109, 25/3/15; R.F.A., 22/6/15; Lieut.
　　　　　　　　　　Died of wounds 24/9/17.

✠ BEEBY, *Charles Stuart*
4/3585, 13/5/15; Leic. R., 21/9/15; Lieut.
　　　　　　　　　　Killed in action 27/5/18.

BEER, *Wilfrid*
B/11412, 1/6/17; R.F.C., C/S, 2/8/17; R.F.C., 8/9/17, R.A F.; Lieut.　　　　　1 Lynmouth Road, Reading.

BEERE, *Horace Cecil*
3/3290, 19/4/15; Hamps. R., 22/7/15, *att*. W. Rid. R.; I,M,Afghan; Lieut.　　37 Howard Road, Southampton.

BEESLEY, *Richard Douglas*
6/5/7644, 22/11/15; No. 14 O.C.B.; S. Lan. R., 22/11/16, *att*. R.E. *and* R.A.S.C.; F,M; Lieut.; *w*.
　　　　　　Lyntonholme, Albion Avenue, Blackpool.

BEEVER, *Arthur Cecil*
B/9863, 6/11/16; R.F.C., C/S, 13/3/17; R.F.C., 19/4/17, R.A.F.; 2/Lieut.　　　　Grens Gate, Grenside, Sheffield.

BEEVERS, *Charles*
A/10953, 30/3/17, L/C.; R.G.A., C/S, 10/10/17; R.G.A., 18/3/18; Capt.　Nat. Prov. & Union Bank, Ltd., Folkestone.

BEHARRELL, *George Edward*
D/11553, 25/6/17; Garr. O.C.B., 28/12/17; Lab. Corps, 18/5/18, R.E.; 2/Lieut.　Metcalfe, The Ridgeway, Sutton, Surrey.

BEHN, *John Frederick*
A/11302, 18/5/17; A.S.C., C/S, 1/9/17; R.A.S.C., 27/10/17; F; 2/Lieut.　　Melton House, Moncrieffe Road, Sheffield.

BEHRENS, *Edward Beddington*
1/Sq/3622, 17/5/15; R.F.A., 15/9/15; F; Capt.; *w*.; M.C. *and* Bar, M(1).　　　　21 Hyde Park Square, W.

✠ BEHRENS, *Walter Lewis*
1/Sq/3623, 17/5/15; R.F.A., 15/9/15; F; 2/Lieut.
　　　　　　　　　　Killed in action 9/7/17.

BEIRNSTEIN, *Arthur Emanuel*
K/2318, 10/12/14; N. Staff. R., 31/3/15, secd. M.G.C. *and* Tank Corps; Capt.; *w*(2).

✠ BEIT, *Rupert Owen*
4/3678, 20/5/15; R.E., 24/7/15; F; Capt.
　　　　　　　　　　Died of wounds 29/7/17.

BEITH, *Andrew Edwin*
6/5/7493, 15/11/15; Welch. R., 4/8/16; Lieut.; *w*(2).
　　　　　　　　　　Fairlawn, Pontypridd.

✠ BELAS, *Reginald Charles William*
6/4/6646, 7/10/15; No. 7 O.C.B., 4/11/16; R. Dub. Fus., 28/2/17; 2/Lieut.; *w*.　　　Killed in action 21/3/18.

✠ BELCHER, *George*
6/2/6586, 4/10/15; No. 11 O.C.B., 7/5/16; trfr. 13th Lond. R., 3/11/16; F; Pte.　　　Died of wounds 5/8/17.

BELCHER, *Reginald George Holland*
E/14283, 8/11/18; demob. 23/1/19.
c/o. Standard Bank of S. Africa, 10 Clements Lane, E.C. 4.

BELFORD, *Richard*
6/D/8403, 15/12/15; R.A.O.C., 7/2/17; Lieut.
　　122 St. Catherine's Terrace South, Circular Road, Dublin.

BELL, *Arthur*
6/1/6611, 4/10/15; No. 11 O.C.B., 7/5/16; R.W. Kent. R., 4/9/16, *att*. R.W. Surr. R.; F; Lieut.; *w*.
　　　　　　Magnolia House, Christchurch, Hants.

BELL, *Arthur Edwin*
6/3/8613, 3/1/16; R.F.A., C/S, 4/8/16; R.G.A., 1/11/16; F; Capt.; *Inv*.　　16 Clifton Avenue, Crewe, Cheshire.

BELL, *Arthur Francis*
A/11266, 14/5/17; No. 10 O.C.B., 5/10/17; K.R. Rif. C., 26/2/18; F; 2/Lieut.; *g*.　　15 Queen Street, Cheapside, E.C.

BELL, *Berkeley Craven*
3/3624, 17/5/15; K.O. Sco. Bord., 10/12/15; E,S; Lieut.
　　　　　　　　　　20 Bolton Street, W. 1.

✠ BELL, *Callum Craig Munro*
A/11950, 3/9/17; R.F.C., C/S, 26/11/17; R.F.C., 23/1/18, R.A F.; 2/Lieut.　　　　　　Killed 16/8/18.

✠ BELL, *Harold Stormont*
D/9993, 23/11/16; No. 14 O.C.B., 30/1/17; Worc. R., 29/5/17; F; 2/Lieut.　　　　　　Missing, 2/12/17.

BELL, *Henry Leopold*
6/4/5362, T/3/8/15, L/C.; 3rd Lond. R., 20/12/15, *att*. 5th *and* 16th Lond. R.; F; Lieut.; *w*.　88 Shenley Road, Camberwell, S.E. 5.

BELL, *Herbert Charles Fitzwilliam*
C/14275, 8/11/18; No. 11 O.C.B., 24/1/19; Genl. List, 8/3/19; 2/Lieut.　　Pilgrim's Rest, Transvaal, S. Africa.

BELL, *James Redward*
E/14191, 18/10/18; No. 11 O.C.B., 24/1/19; Genl. List, 8/3/19; 2/Lieut.　　c/o. Geo. Stewart & Coy., Colombo, Ceylon.

✠ BELL, *Kenneth Frederick Hamilton*
K/H/2466, 28/12/14; 1st Lond. R., 9/4/15; 2/Lieut.
　　　　　　　　　　Killed in action 25/9/15.

BELL, *Kenneth Norman*
Sq/641, 9/5/12; R.G.A., 4/8/14; F; Major; M.C.
　　　　　　　　　　All Souls College, Oxford.

BELL, *Leonard Charles*
4/4035, 7/6/15; R. Highrs., 5/9/15, *att*. Wilts. R. *and* Sig. Serv. R.E.; F,Afghan; Capt.; M.C., M(1).　Black Watch, E.D.W. Signals, Peshawar.

BELL, *Leslie William Copeland*
A/13987, 11/9/18; No. 11 O.C.B.; Genl. List, 8/3/19; 2/Lieut.
　　　　　　St. Moritz, Grove Road, Sutton, Surrey.

BELL, *Noel*
C/Sq/12633, 22/2/18; demob. 23/1/19.
　　　　Waterslade Place, Tuam, Co. Galway, Ireland.

BELL, *Oscar Leslie*
D/11152, 30/4/17; No. 14 O.C.B., 10/8/17; Notts. & Derby. R., 27/11/17; F; Lieut.; M.C.
　　　　　　12 Caledon Road, Sherwood, Nottingham.

BELL, *Robert Henry*
6/2/9274, 3/2/16; A.S.C., C/S, 27/10/16; R.A.S.C., 20/12/16; Lieut.　　Hibernian Bank, Ltd., College Green, Dublin.

BELL, *Robert William*
4/Sq/4357, 21/6/15; York. Huss., 26/10/15; Capt.
　　　　　　c/o. Shaw & Coy., James Street, Harrogate.

✠ BELL, *Sydney James*
2/3216; 12/4/15; L'pool. R., 25/8/15; F; 2/Lieut.; *w*.
　　　　　　　　　　Died of wounds 13/10/16.

BELL, *Victor*
6/2/7325, 9/11/15; Bord. R., 4/9/16; Lieut.; *w*(2).
　　　　　　　Kirk Neuk, Lazonby, Cumberland.

BELL, *Walter Loraine*
4/3217, 12/4/15; dis. 7/5/15.

BELL, *William Ernest*
B/12789, 18/3/18, L/C.; No. 21 O.C.B., 4/10/18; R. Ir. Rif., 17/3/19; 2/Lieut.　Ballyness House, Coleraine, Ireland.

APPENDIX II.—RECORDS OF RANK AND FILE.

BELLAMY, Herbert
6/3/5787, 23/8/15; Hereford R., 21/1/16, att. Shrops. L.I.; Lieut.

BELLAMY, Herbert Leslie
6/5/5239, 31/7/15; Lan. Fus., 9/11/15; F; Lieut.; w.
Newlands, Holden Road, Kersal, Manchester.

BELLAMY, James
6/Sq/7286, 8/11/15; No. 2 Cav. C/S, 31/3/16; 3rd County of Lond. Yeo., 6/9/16, att. 19th Lond. R.; Lieut.
S. Peter's Hill, Grantham.

BELLASIS, Brian Maude
A/41, 6/4/08; dis. 5/4/11; Som. L.I., 19/10/15, Glouc. R.; Lieut.; M.C., M(1).
c/o. H. S. King & Coy., 9 Pall Mall, S.W.

BELLINGER, Lancelot William
6/3/6267, 16/9/15; R. Mar. L.I., 19/12/15; Lieut.
26 Trebovir Road, Earl's Court, S.W. 5.

BELLORD, Cuthbert George
B/1047, 31/8/14; Shrops. L.I., 19/9/14, secd. Army Cyc. Corps, att. R.F.C. and R.A.F.; F,S,M; Capt.
St. Margaret's, Tamworth, Staffordshire.

✠ BELLOT, Bryson
Sq/1614, 7/10/14, Cpl.; N. Som. Yeo., 23/2/15, att. T.M. Bty.; F; Capt.
Died 27/3/18.

BELSHAW, Stanley Ainscow
6/3/8951, 17/1/16; No. 5 O.C.B., 14/8/16; W. Rid. R., 21/11/16; F; Lieut.; p.
Christ Church Vicarage, Colne, Lancashire.

BELSHAW, Thomas Sydney
C/651, 1/11/12; 22nd Lond. R., 29/8/14; Capt.; w.; M(1).
70 Iverna Gardens, W. 8.

BEMROSE, Frank Simpson
C/13379, 24/6/18; trfr. 14th Lond. R., 6/12/18.
Abbotsford, Lambert Road, Grimsby.

✠ BEMROSE, Roderick Henry
6/9059, 21/1/16; R.A., C/S, 14/7/16; R.F.A., 3/11/16; Lieut.; M.C.
Died 7/11/18.

BENDALL, Geoffrey Skeat Manley
F/1891, 16/10/14; R.A.S.C., 12/12/14; F; Capt.; M(1).
The Oak House, Rye, Sussex.

BENDALL, Philip Manley
4/1/4528, 1/7/15, L/C.; 19th Lond. R., 10/10/15; F,S,P; Staff Capt.; M.C., Order of the Nile (4th Class).
Jalan Acob Est, Kapar, Selangor, Federated Malay States.

BENHAM, John Cecil
B/13631, 26/7/18; demob. 29/1/19.
8 Waldegrave Road, Upper Norwood, S.E. 19.

BENIANS, Hubert Joseph
K/B/2134, 19/11/14, L/C.; R.E., 31/5/15; F; Capt.; w.; M(1).
High Street, Goudhurst, Kent.

BENJAMIN, Arthur Leslie
E/2810, 29/1/15; R. Fus., 29/4/15; Capt.;

✠ BENJAMIN, Herbert Seymour
K/D/2221, T/28/11/14; Worc. R., 23/3/15; Capt.
Killed in action 9/10/17.

BENJAMIN, Horace Eugene Bernton
6/3/7645, 22/11/15, L/C.; A.S.C., C/S, 28/8/16; R.A.S.C., 2/10/16.
18 Priory Road, Acton Green, Chiswick.

BENN, Sylvester Munro
4/2/5092, 26/7/15; R.A.S.C., 6/11/15. att. R.E.; F,It; Lieut.; M(1).
9 Wayne Street, Worcester, Mass., U.S.A.

✠ BENNER, Walter
6/3/5497, 9/8/15, L/C.; Notts. & Derby. R., 10/1/16; Lieut.; w.
Killed in action 2/9/18.

BENNETT, Arthur Bernard
6/2/5357, T/31/7/15; trfr. R.G.A., 14/7/16.
2 St. Alban's Road, Swansea.

BENNETT, Arthur Gordon
Sq/3529, 10/5/15; City of Lond. Yeo., 28/8/15, M.G.C.; Lieut.
Ravenscliffe, Porthill, Stoke-on-Trent.

BENNETT, Basil Hastings
K/B/2200, 30/11/14; Rif. Brig., 29/1/15, emp. M. of Munitions; Capt.; w(2).
Queen Anne's Mansions, S.W.

BENNETT, Cedric Humphrey
1/3140, 29/3/15; E. Surr. R., 21/6/15, Lab. Corps; F; Lieut.
46 Riggindale Road, Streatham, S.W. 16.

BENNETT, Charles Alan
D/10225, 28/12/16; No. 14 O.C.B., 5/3/17; Rif. Brig., 26/6/17; F; 2/Lieut.; p.
13 Old Square, Lincoln's Inn, W.C. 2.

BENNETT, Cyril Eustace
C/12589, 7/2/18, L/C.; trfr. 14th Lond. R., 6/12/18.
Egremont, 95 Wellmeadow Road, Catford, S.E.

✠ BENNETT, Frederick Barberry
E/1618, 9/10/14, Cpl.; R.F.A., 1/3/15; Major; w.
Died of wounds 22/10/18.

BENNETT, Frederick William
6/2/7898, 29/11/15; No. 14 O.C.B., 28/8/16; Suff. R., 22/11/16 att. T.M. Bty.; F; Capt.; w-p; M(1).
156 Norwich Road, Ipswich.

BENNETT, Geoffrey Neville
B/A/12310, 17/12/17; A.S.C., C/S, 1/8/18; R.A.S.C., 25/10/18; 2/Lieut.
11 The Lees, Malvern.

BENNETT, Guy Whittem
A/1177, 14/9/14, Cpl.; Shrops. L.I., 24/12/14; 2/Lieut.
32 Cowndon Road, Coventry.

BENNETT, Harry Herbert Gladstone
H/2011, 2/11/14; Worc. R., 14/2/15, att. No. 5 O.C.B., Inst.; F; Lieut.
84 Thornton Avenue, Bedford Park, W. 4.

BENNETT, Henry Malcolm
4/1/4592, 5/7/15; 20th Lond. R., 14/7/16, att. Manch. R.; F; Lieut.
Weston House, Deddington, Oxon.

BENNETT, Henry Stanley
6/2/8012, 30/11/15; No. 14 O.C.B., 28/8/16; 22nd Lond. R., 22/11/16, 24th Lond. R.; F; 2/Lieut.; w.
161 Kennington Road, S.E. 11.

BENNETT, John
6/2/9322, 2/2/16; R.A., C/S, 7/7/16; R.G.A., 13/9/16; F; Lieut.
Whelpside, Whitehaven, Cumberland.

BENNETT, John Edwin
6/Sq/5747, T/21/8/15; Fife & Forf. Yeo., 3/11/15, att. R.F.C.; Lieut.; w.
Ashville, Downham Market, Norfolk.

✠ BENNETT, John Francis
6/4/7519, 16/11/15; No. 14 O.C.B., 28/8/16; Hamps. R., 22/11/16; 2/Lieut.
Killed in action 26/8/18.

BENNETT, Kenneth Henry
6/4/6268, 16/9/15; S. Staff. R., 27/7/16, att. N. Staff. R.; M; Lieut.
32 Kensington Square, W. 8.

✠ BENNETT, Leslie Punsfer
4/3/5144, 26/7/15, L/C.; R.W. Surr., 7/12/15; 2/Lieut.
Died of wounds 16/2/17.

BENNETT, Lionel Alexander
B/12410, 18/1/18; R.A.F., C/S, 21/5/18; R.A.F.; 2/Lieut.
Cranleigh, Wallington, Surrey.

BENNETT, Ralph Culver
B/E/13560, 19/7/18; dis. 9/11/18.
Brown's Hotel, Dover Street, W.

BENNETT, Raymond George
D/E/13820, 12/8/18; R.A., C/S, 2/10/18; R.G.A., 11/4/19; 2/Lieut.
46 Corder Road, Ipswich.

✠ BENNETT, Robertis Charles Rudolph Busby
6/1/7897, 29/11/15, L/C.; No. 14 O.C.B.; 20th Lond. R., 18/12/16; Lieut.; w(2); M.C.
Killed in action 24/8/18.

BENNETT, William Ernest
6/5/7717, 22/11/15; No. 14 O.C.B., 28/8/16; Norf. R., 22/11/16; F; 2/Lieut.; w.
104 Mallinson Road, Wandsworth Common, S.W. 11.

BENNETT, William Henry
C/12558, 6/2/18, L/C.; R.F.A., C/S, 17/5/18; R.H. & R.F.A., 10/2/19; 2/Lieut.
28 Aubrey Road, Small Heath, Birmingham.

BENNETT, William Porter
D/1480, 29/9/14; Bord. R., 12/11/14, R.G.A.; F; Capt.; w.
Whelpside, Whitehaven, Cumberland.

BENSON, Harold
Sq/3524, 6/5/15, L/C.; R.F.A., 26/7/15, emp. M. of Labour; F; Lieut.
Melville, Church Stutton, Shropshire.

APPENDIX II.—RECORDS OF RANK AND FILE.

BENSON, *Herbert Walter*
A/13047, 8/5/18; H. Bde. O.C.B., 14/9/18; Oxf. & Bucks. L.I., 17/3/19; 2/Lieut.
St. Michael's Vicarage, Lower Sydenham, S.E. 26.

BENSON, *Thomas Joseph*
A/9815, 30/10/16; R.F.C., C/S, 13/3/17; R.F.C., 19/4/17, R.A.F.; Lieut.
Firwood, Disley, Cheshire.

BENSON, *Wilfrid*
A/12431, 21/1/18; No. 18 O.C.B., 7/6/18; Staff. R., 6/2/19; 2/Lieut.
Bank House, Pontypridd, Glamorganshire.

BENSON-COOPER, *Aubrey*
6/Sq/6383, 23/9/15; No. 1 Cav. C/S, 20/10/16; Notts. & Derby. Yeo., 16/2/17; att. Durh. L.I.; F; Lieut.
Norfolk House, Birchington-on-Sea.

BENSTEAD, *Charles Grey*
6/3/6511, 30/9/15, L/C.; No. 7 O.C.B., 7/4/16; 8th Lond. R., 29/7/16, secd. Tank Corps; F; Capt.; w.; M.C.
Sefton House, Princess Street, Shrewsbury.

BENSUSAN, *Vivian Jack*
C/14167, 16/10/18; No. 11 O.C.B., 6/2/19; R. Suss. R., 8/3/19; 2/Lieut.
c/o F. S. Hampshire & Coy., Ltd., Caixa 10, Santos, Brazil, S. America.

BENT, *Herbert Kenneth Richard*
K/Sq/2287, 8/12/14; R.F.A., 22/6/15, att. R.F.C.; F; Lieut.; w(2); M.C.
Goodworth House, Andover, Hants.

BENTLEY, *Cecil Harold Fletcher*
C/10815, 2/3/17, L/C.; A.S.C., C/S, 1/9/17; R.A.S.C., 27/10/17; F; 2/Lieut.
10 Dale Street, Liverpool.

BENTLEY, *Robert*
A/11226, 7/5/17; No. 14 O.C.B., 7/9/17; North'd. Fus., 17/12/17; 2/Lieut.
Grosvenor Villa, Prestwich, nr. Manchester.

BENTLIFF, *Hubert David*
3/3105, T/25/3/15, L/C.; Essex R., 19/6/15, att. Midd'x. R.; F; Capt.; w.
10 Taviton Street, Gordon Square, W.C. 1.

BENZIES, *Bolton*
A/D/C/14022, 18/9/18; demob. 29/1/19.
44 Keir Street, Pollokshields, Glasgow.

BERESFORD, *Alexander*
6/9417, 10/2/16; A.S.C., C/S, 1/9/16; R.A.S.C., 25/10/16; F; Lieut.
Church Hill, Midhurst.

BERESFORD, *Harold Douglas*
C/12590, 12/2/18; R.A.F., C/S, 3/5/18; R.A.F., 6/9/18; F; 2/Lieut.
9 Maxwell Road, Rathgar, Co. Dublin, Ireland.

BERESFORD, *Salisbury de la Poer*
B/102, 17/4/08; dis. 16/4/13; R.G.A., 7/7/16; Capt.
Kilmore House, Camberley, Surrey.

BERESFORD, *William Martin*
D/12131, 18/10/17, L/C.; dis. 7/3/19.
15 Empress Avenue, Ilford, Essex.

BERGL, *Lewis St. Clair*
4/3291, 19/4/15; Manch. R., 9/9/15, att. Lan. Fus.; E,F; 2/Lieut.; Inv.
St. Katherine's, 86 Teignmouth Road, N.W. 2.

BERGMAN, *William Harris*
A/C/D/12181, 2/11/17; No. 22 O.C.B., 7/6/18; E. York. R, 11/2/19; 2/Lieut.
12 Story Street, Hull.

BERINGTON, *John J.*
B/1071, 2/9/14; R. Mar. Art., 19/9/14; Major.

BERLYN, *Bernard Henry A. F.*
1/3530, 10/5/15; R. Ir. Rif., 2/10/15; 2/Lieut.

BERNARD, *Percy Arthur Ernald*
A/403, 23/4/09; dis. 1/5/11; R.A.S.C., 23/8/15; Lieut.
c/o. Messrs. Strutt & Parker, Broad Street House, E.C.

BERNARD, *Ronald Townsend*
Sq/3292, 19/4/15, Cpl.; trfr. 30th Lond. R., 17/11/16, 8th Lond. R.

BERNARD, *William Cecil*
A/30, 3/4/08, dis. 2/4/10.
1 Hare Court, Temple, E.C. 4.

BERNASCONI, *John Nicholas*
B/13498, 10/7/18; No. 22 O.C.B., 23/8/18; demob. 16/1/19.
18 Prince Alfred Road, Wavertree, Liverpool.

BERNCASTLE, *Herbert Frederick*
A/898, 5/8/14; Bedf. R., 17/4/15; 2/Lieut.
15 Ladbroke Gardens, W.

✠ BERRILL, *Frank Gale*
C/1/9343, 7/2/16; R.F.A., C/S, 21/7/16; R.F.A., 13/10/16; Lieut.
Died 28/9/18.

BERRINGTON, *Adrian*
E/2567, 4/1/15; R.E., 8/5/15; Lieut.

BERRY, *Charles Edgar*
6/5/A/5916, D/1/9/15, Cpl.; demob. 1/2/19.
9 Springfield Street, Warrington.

BERRY, *Edward Hamilton*
6/1/7226, 5/11/15, L/C.; No. 11 O.C.B., 8/5/16; R. War. R., 4/8/16; Capt.
Penshurst, Cobham Park Avenue, S. Croydon.

BERRY, *Henry Arthur Laurence*
4/2/4358, 21/6/15; North'd. Fus., 6/9/15; Lieut.
9 Dornton Road, S. Croydon.

BERRY, *Ralph Noel*
A/13148, 29/5/18; trfr. 14th Lond. R., 6/12/18.
Elm Grove, Edgerton, Huddersfield.

BERRYMAN, *Patrick Edwin*
D/12927, 15/4/18; No. 21 O.C.B., 4/10/18, No. 18 O.C.B.; Notts. and Derby R., 18/3/19; 2/Lieut.
Anstey, Berkhamsted, Herts.

BERTIE, *Louis William Howard*
4/Sq/4204, 14/6/15, L/C.; Intelligence Corps, 4/8/16; Staff Lieut.
The Nook, 110 S. Woodstock Road, Oxford.

BERTIE, *Peregrine Albemarle*
B/Sq/12727, 11/3/18; demob. 31/1/19.
Holbeach, Lincolnshire.

BERTING, *Lewis Joseph Richard*
6/5/C/7899, 29/11/15, L/C.; No. 1 O.C.B., 1/2/17; R.F.C., 12/4/17, R.A.F.; F; 2/Lieut.
Elm Tree House, Chalfont St. Giles, Bucks.

BERTRAM, *Cyril Anthony George*
6/2/B/8514, 29/12/15, L/C.; No. 14 O.C.B., 30/10/16; York and Lanc. R., 24/1/17, att. No. 10 O.C.B., Inst.; F; Lieut.; w.
7 High Street, Streatham, S.W. 16.

BERTRAM, *Ronald Anderson*
A/D/13988, 11/9/18; demob. 30/5/19.
7 Polwarth Crescent, Edinburgh.

✠ BERWICK, *Robert George*
6/3/C/7643, 22/11/15, L/C.; No. 1 O.C.B., 3/2/17; R.F.C., 9/5/17; 2/Lieut.
Killed in action 7/7/17.

BESANT, *Ernest Bryden*
D/13924, 30/8/18; trfr. K.R. Rif. C., 7/4/19.
15 Seething Lane, E.C. 3.

BESLEY, *Ernest Arthur*
C/10375, 8/1/17, Sgt.; R.F.A., C/S, 17/12/17; R.G.A., 19/8/18; S,I; 2/Lieut.
Glen Atholl, Maryland Road, Bowes Park, N. 22.

BESLY, *Lionel William*
B/11328, 21/5/17; R.F.C., C/S, 26/10/17; trfr. R.F.C. as N.C.O. Inst., 13/12/17.
34 Water Lane, E. 15.

BESSANT, *Howard Cormack*
6/2/6977, T/23/10/15; No. 9 O.C.B., 8/3/16; Sea. Highrs., 23/7/16; Lieut.
Tile Kiln, Leverstock Green, Hertford.

BESSANT, *Stanley James*
A/10721, 12/2/17; No. 12 O.C.B., 10/8/17; Hamps. R., 27/11/17, att. Wilts. R.; P; 2/Lieut.; w; M(1).
Rose Bank, Lower Bourne, Farnham, Surrey.

BESSO, *Raphael A.*
Sq/1522, 2/10/14; Linc. Yeo., 22/1/15; F,E,P; Capt.; M(1).
42 Bloom Street, Manchester.

BEST, *Earle*
4/3/4387, 24/6/15; R.E., 6/9/15; F; Capt.; M.C., M(1).
Laburnum House, Hethon-le-Hole, Co. Durham.

BEST, *Isaac James*
D/10906, 23/3/17, L/C.; No. 14 O.C.B., 5/7/17; 16th Lond. R., 30/10/17; P,F; 2/Lieut.
Morwenston, Highfield Lane, Southampton.

BEST, *Maurice George*
10139, 7/12/16; No. 14 O.C.B., 5/3/17; E. Surr. R., 26/6/17, Oxf. & Bucks. L.I.; 2/Lieut.

APPENDIX II.—RECORDS OF RANK AND FILE.

BETHELL, Anthony Patrick Lawrence
A/2038, 9/11/14; Gord. Highrs., 16/12/14; Major; M.C.
342 Morningside Road, Edinburgh.

BETHUNE, George Maximilian
A/10028, 28/11/16; No. 14 O.C.B., 30/1/17; trfr 16th Lond. R., 18/4/17, att. 11th Lond. R.; F; Cpl.; g.
Canje House, St. Andrew's Road, Bedford.

✠ BETHUNE, John
Sq/2873, 8/2/15, Sgt.; R.F.A., 10/9/15; Lieut.
Died of wounds 29/10/17.

BETHUNE, William James
4/2/4205, 14/6/15; Cam'n Highrs., 22/9/15, R.A.F.; F,S,E,P; Lieut.; w(2).
Brae Moray, Abentarff Road, Inverness.

BETT, Alastair Hunter
B/12385, 15/1/18; R.F.A., C/S, 15/3/18; R.G.A., 5/2/19; 2/Lieut.
121 West George Street, Glasgow.

BETTELEY, Charles Ernest Ravenscroft
K/A/2285, 8/12/14, L/C.; Manch. R., 1/4/15; F; Capt.
Cargate Lodge, Cargate Avenue, Aldershot.

BETTELEY, Edward Samuel Charles
A/9807, 30/10/16; R.E., C/S, 10/2/17; R.E., 5/5/17; F; Capt.
Sungate, Surbiton, Surrey.

✠ BETTERIDGE, James Harper
6/2/5982, 2/9/15; Bord. R., 8/7/16, att. 16th Lond. R.; F; 2/Lieut.
Killed in action 14/4/17.

BETTS, Horace Richard
6/4/5983, 2/9/15; E. Surr. R., 23/12/15, att. Camb. R.; F; Capt.; w(2).
1 Cricket Ground Road, Norwich.

BETTS, Hyla Hume
F/1878, 16/10/14; Ches. R., 3/12/14, R.E.; F,It; Lt.-Col.; O.B.E., M(3).
c/o Riegos y Fuerza, 2 Plaza Cataluna, Barcelona, Spain.

BETTS, Reginald
4/1/5008, 22/7/15; E. Ang. Div. Cyc. Coy., 28/9/15, Army Cyc. Corps; Lieut.

BEVAN, John
E/14083, 30/9/18; demob. 29/1/19; (prev. Army Chalpain, 1915-16; E,G.)
186 Hamstead Road, Handsworth, Birmingham.

BEVAN, John Tonkin
6/1/5771, 23/8/15; R.G.A., 6/1/16; F; Capt.
Englefield, Reading, Berkshire.

BEVAN, Roland Stanley
6/9455, 14/2/16; R.F.A., C/S, 9/6/16; R.G.A., 16/9/16; F; Capt.
Junior Constitutional Club, Piccadilly, W.1.

BEVERLEY, George Rutland
6/7759, 23/11/15; R.F.A., C/S, 26/5/16; R.G.A., 30/8/16; F; Capt.
45 Grosvenor Park Road, Walthamstow, E.17.

✠ BEVILLE, Alfred Geoffrey
6/2/6224, 13/9/15, L/C.; No. 7 O.C.B., 6/4/16; 16th Lond. R., 21/6/16; 2/Lieut.
Killed in action 8/4/17.

BEVINS, Edward
6/5/5917, 1/9/15, L/C.; No. 11 O.C.B., 7/5/16; M.G.C., 4/9/16; Lieut.
22 Chermside Road, Aigburth, Liverpool.

BEW, Frank
4/1/4559, 1/7/15; Derby. Yeo., 9/11/15, R.G.A.; Bermuda; Lieut.
c/o Dr. Peterson, 112 East 85th Street, New York City, U.S.A.

BEW, Percy
4/1/4560, 1/7/15; R.F.A., 4/1/16, att. R.A.O.C.; F; Lieut., D.A.D.O.S.
29 Middleton Street, Derby.

✠ BEWLEY, Edward Neville
4/4359, 21/6/15; Notts. & Derby. R., 8/10/15; 2/Lieut.
Killed in action 26/6/17.

BEWLEY, Thomas Kenneth
Sq/783, 27/3/14; R.A.S.C., 9/11/14, emp. Treasury; Lieut.

✠ BEYNON, Ernest John Wilson
2/9694, 6/10/16; No. 14 O.C.B., 30/1/17; York. & Lanc. R., 25/4/17; F; 2/Lieut.
Killed in action 9/10/17.

✠ BEYNON, William Charles
C/6/7345, 10/11/15; No. 11 O.C.B., 7/5/16; R.W. Fus., 4/9/16; 2/Lieut.
Died of wounds 3/5/17.

BEYTS, Cyril Freeman
C/1230, 23/9/14; Suff. R., 5/12/14, M.G.C.; Capt.; M.C., M(1).

BIBBS, Oswald Graham
6/3/6348, 20/9/15; Worc. R., 14/1/16; Lieut.
Vigornia, Sevington Road, Hendon.

BICKER-CAARTEN, Vivian H.
Sq/3625, 17/5/15; Bedf. Yeo., 26/9/15; F; Lieut.; w; M.C.
African Steamship Coy., 23 Billiter Street, E.C.3.

BICKERSTETH, John Burgon
Sq/136, 18/4/08; dis. 17/4/10; R. Drag., 19/9/14; F; Lieut.; M.C. and Bar.
The Precincts, Canterbury, Kent. (Now in Canada.)

BIDDLE, Frederick Arnold
C/212, 8/5/08; dis. 7/5/10; rej. C/963, 5/8/14; C/S. Inst., School of Musketry; Lt. T.F. Res., 10/7/15; F; Capt.
2 Bloomfield Road, Highgate, N.6.

BIDDULPH, Reginald Vivian
E/K/2436, 23/12/14; R. Dub. Fus., 27/2/15, M.G.C.; F; Capt.; w(2).
c/o. The Bank of Montreal, Threadneedle Street, E.C. (now in Canada).

✠ BIDDULPH, Victor Randell George
2/3189, 8/4/15; Rif. Brig., 11/8/15; 2/Lieut.
Killed in action 15/9/16.

BIDELEUX, Claude Emil Ami
E/1/3021, 8/3/15, Sgt.; R.F.A., 20/9/15; F,E,P; Capt.
Quinta Martelli, Florida, F.C.C.A., Argentina, S. America.

BIDGWAY, Arthur Charles
6/3/7791, 24/11/15; No. 14 O.C.B.; Devon. R., 24/10/16, Intelligence; F; Lieut.; w.
37 Mutley Plain, Plymouth, Devonshire.

✠ BIDWELL, Claude Arthur Stephen
K/E/2331, 14/12/14; N. Lan. R., 13/4/15; 2/Lieut.
Killed in action 21/9/15.

✠ BIGG, Walter
6/3/6709, T/8/10/15; Durh. L.I., 6/1/16, att. Worc. R.; F; Lieut.; w.
Killed in action 27/5/18.

BIGGAR, Henry Percival
B/195, 5/5/08; dis. 4/5/13.

BIGGER, Edgar Grimshaw
A/Sq/13074, 17/5/18; demob. 22/1/19.
Riverview, Londonderry.

BIGGER, Theodore Anthony Lennox
4/2/4593, 5/7/15; N. Lan. R., 11/11/15, Indian Army; Major; w.
2 Oliver Grove, S. Norwood, S.W.

✠ BIGGS, Edwin Joseph Melville
K/4/2954, 22/2/15; R. Fus., 10/4/15, emp. M. of Munitions.
Died, 21/11/18.

BIGGS, Herbert Edward
A/9851, 6/11/16; No. 14 O.C.B., 27/12/16; R. Fus., 27/3/17; Lieut.
Rosedene, Canterbury Road, Herne Bay.

BIGGS, Raymond Henry
A/13059, 13/5/18, L/C.; demob. 30/1/19.
The Retreat, Essenden Road, Belvedere, Kent.

BIGGS, William Edward
C/10686, 7/2/17, L/C.; R.G.A., C/S, 31/8/17; R.G.A., 6/1/18; 2/Lieut.

BIGG-WITHER, Arthur Orde
6/5/6156, 9/9/15, L/C.; No. 1 O.C.B., 6/9/16; R.F.C., 25/1/17; Lieut.; w.

BIGLAND, Robert Taylor
6/2/9495, 15/2/16; No. 8 O.C.B., 4/8/16; Ches. R., 21/11/16; F; Capt.
Dee Royd, Heswall, Cheshire.

BIKKER, Andrew Hay
B/13545, 1577/18; No. 22 O.C.B., 23/8/18; L'pool. R., 13/2/19; 2/Lieut.
Gorsby Hayes, Tettershall, Wolverhampton.

BILES, William
B/13479, 8/7/18; No. 22 O.C.B., 23/8/18; R. Suss. R., 13/2/19; 2/Lieut.
Wall Hall, Watford.

BILHAM, David George Rees
6/3/6174, 13/9/15; W. Rid. R., 10/1/16; Capt.; M.C., M(3).

APPENDIX II.—RECORDS OF RANK AND FILE.

BILLETT, *Wesley Frank*
A/Sq/12500, 30/1/18; demob. 3/2/19.
  Montague House, Wylye, Wilts.

BILLINGHAM, *Edgar*
4/2/5066, 26/7/15; trfr. 5th Lond. R., 10/3/16.
  Trinity School, Henley-on-Thames.

BILLINGHAM, *William Frederick*
B/10114, 6/12/16; No. 14 O.C.B., 5/3/17; Dorset R., 26/6/17, Indian Army; E; Lieut.; w.
  St. George's, Holly Lane, Erdington, Birmingham.

BILLINGTON, *Herbert*
D/10929, 26/3/17, L/C.; A.S.C., C/S, 1/9/17; R.A.S.C., 27/10/17; F; 2/Lieut. 26 Earlston Road, Liscard, Cheshire.

BINDER, *Ralph William*
6/2/7432, 15/11/15; No. 11 O.C.B., 7/5/16; R.F.C., 4/9/16.
  6 Hollies Road, S. Ealing, W.

BINGAY, *John Vivian*
A/13075, 17/5/18, L/C.; No. 24 O.C.B., 15/11/18; Tank Corps, 22/3/19; 2/Lieut. 62 New Oxford Street, W.C.1.

BINGLEY, *Ranolph Douglas*
6/Sq/7433, 15/11/15; A.S.C., C/S, 6/3/16; R.A.S.C., 7/5/16; Lieut.
  The Cottage, Bishops Itchington, nr. Leamington, Warwickshire.

BINKS, *Harold Percival*
A/11261, 14/5/17; R.E., C/S, 25/11/17; R.E., 22/2/18; 2/Lieut.
  Ingleton, Holderness Road, Sutton Ingo, Hull.

BINNIE, *William Aikman*
D/13787, 9/8/18, L/C.; demob. 7/3/19.
  54 Polworth Gardens, Edinburgh.

BINNS, *George Marshall Noble*
B/13597, 18/7/18; demob. 11/4/19.
  Hopefield, Cardonagh, Co. Donegal, Ireland.

✠ BINNS, *Raymond Louis*
H/2811, 29/1/15; York. R., 22/4/15; 2/Lieut.
  Killed in action 10/7/16.

BINNS, *Roland Walter*
C/A/11786, 2/8/17, L/C.; demob. 31/1/19.
  c/o. Ross Taylor & Coy., Surabaya, Java.

BION, *Wilfred Ruprecht*
6/1/8685, 4/1/16, Cpl.; No. 14 O.C.B.; M.G.C., 9/12/16, Tank Corps; F; Capt.; D.S.O., Chevalier du Legion d'Honneur, M(1).
  The College, Bishop's Stortford, Hertfordshire.

✠ BIRCH, *Edward Cecil*
6/2/8450, 17/12/15; No. 8 O.C.B., 4/8/16; R.W. Surr. R., 21/11/16, R.A.F.; F; Lieut. Died 26/1/19.

BIRCH, *Henry Priestley*
2148, 19/11/14; dis. 7/5/15.
  Chequers Tree Farm, Witterham, nr. Tenterden.

BIRCH, *Thomas Congreve Wyrley*
F/1815, 16/10/14; S. Lan. R., 24/2/15; F; Capt.; w; M(1).
  37 Prince of Wales Mansions, Battersea Park, S.W. 11.

BIRCH, *William Thomas*
A/10996, 4/4/17; Garr. O.C.B., 23/5/17; Lab. Corps, 14/7/17, att. R.A.F.; Lieut. Orchard Dale, Beaconsfield, Bucks.

✠ BIRCHAL, *Wilfrid Arthur*
Sq/2915, 15/2/15, L/C.; Notts. & Derby. Yeo., 22/4/15; Lieut.
  Killed in action 28/4/17.

BIRCHAM, *William Henry Clarence*
6/1/5739, 20/8/15; Devon. R., 25/11/15; M; Lieut.
  29 College Court Mansions, Hammersmith, W. 6.

✠ BIRD, *Raymond*
2/3250, 12/4/15; Glouc. R., 2/8/15; F; 2/Lieut.
  Killed in action 16/8/16.

BIRD, *Reginald*
6/4/6307, T/17/9/15, L/C.; Devon. R., 18/12/15; M,I; Capt.
  Dolforgan, Exmouth, S. Devon.

BIRD, *Stanley Herman*
C/1140, 14/9/14; Oxf. & Bucks. L.I., 20/10/14, R.F.C., R.A.F.; F,E; Capt.; w. 127 Victoria Street, S.W.1.

✠ BIRD, *William Ryder*
E/1549, 6/10/14; K.R. Rif. C., 14/12/14; F; 2/Lieut.
  Killed 8/10/15.

BIRDWOOD, *Christopher Travers*
6/5/7038, 28/10/15; No. 11 O.C.B., 7/5/16; Devon. R., 4/9/16, secd. Intelligence Corps; F; Lieut.; w.
  19 Corfton Road, Ealing, W. 5.

BIRKETT, *Cuthbert Edwin*
6/3/8237, 8/12/15, L/C.; Mon. R., 4/9/16, att. Tank Corps; F; Lieut.; w; M.C. Bassalleg, nr. Newport, Monmouthshire.

✠ BIRKETT, *Henry*
A/10027, 28/11/16; No. 14 O.C.B., 30/1/17; E. York. R., 25/4/17, R.A.F.; F; 2/Lieut.; w. Killed 24/10/18.

BIRKETT, *John Bertram*
C/1234, 23/9/14, Sgt.; Bedf. R., 24/7/15, R.E.; Lieut.
  Wey Holme, West Byfleet, Surrey.

BIRKETT, *Newton Basil*
D/10481, 12/1/17; R.F.C., C/S, 13/3/17; R.F.C., 19/4/17, R.A.F.; F; Lieut. Bassalleg, nr. Newport, Monmouthshire.

BIRKIN, *Archibald Alexander*
B/11322, 21/5/17; No. 14 O.C.B., 4/1/18, No. 23 O.C.B.; trfr. 28th Lond. R., 17/8/18.
  Hawksworth Manor, Hawksworth, Nottingham.

BIRKINSHAW, *Philip*
A/10043, 29/11/16; No. 14 O.C.B., 5/5/17; Hunts. Cyc. Bn., 28/8/17, att. Cambs. R., Suff. R.; 2/Lieut.
  Bryn Rhosyn, Blackpill, Glamorgan.

BIRKS, *Alfred Harry*
K/6/1/2138, 19/11/14, C.S.M.; dis. med unfit, 19/3/18.
  Enderleigh, Broadlands Road, Highgate, N.

BIRNIE, *Henry George*
K/A/2081, 13/11/14; R.E., 4/2/15; F; Capt.
  United Sua Betong Rubber Estates, Negri Sembilan, F.M.S.

BIRT, *Vernon Shirley*
A/1187, 14/9/14; R.G.A., 18/9/14; F; Major; M.C.
  5 Lloyd's Avenue, Fenchurch Street, E.C. 3.

BIRTILL, *William Walton*
B/C/12677, 4/3/15; R.F.A., C/S, 17/5/18; R.H. & R.F.A., 13/3/19; 2/Lieut. Yataderia Estate, Undugoda, Ceylon.

BIRTLES, *Edgar Gerald*
F/1849, 16/10/14; E. Surr. R., 9/3/15, Intelligence; F; Lieut.; M.C. 3 Church Lane, Merton Park, S.W. 19.

BISCOE, *Thomas Wynne*
3/3830, 31/5/15; trfr. R.W. Surr. R., 13/3/16.
  Norman House, Godalming, Surrey.

BISGROVE, *Leonard Walter*
Sq/B/12371, 8/1/18; No. 2 Cav. C/S, 16/5/18; 1st R. Regt. of Cav., 14/2/19; 2/Lieut.
  9 Woodborough Road, Radstock, Somerset.

✠ BISHOP, *Basil Frederick*
C/1079, 2/9/14; S. Lan. R., 19/9/14; Lt.-Col.; M.C.
  Killed in action 18/9/18.

✠ BISHOP, *Charles Frederick*
6/2/9423, 10/2/16; No. 8 O.C.B., 4/8/16; R. Fus., 21/11/16; F; 2/Lieut.; w. Killed in action 4/4/18.

BISHOP, *Edmund*
D/12982, 25/4/18; No. 22 O.C.B., 7/6/18; Education Officer, 8/12/18; 2/Lieut.
  School House, Speldhurst, Tunbridge Wells, Kent.

BISHOP, *Francis Joseph Lionel*
C/10172, 11/12/16, L/C.; No. 14 O.C.B., 5/3/17, R.F.C., C/S; R.F.C., 31/5/17, R.A.F.; Lieut. Bishop House, Finchley, N. 3.

BISHOP, *George Edward*
B/10554, 19/1/17; No. 14 O.C.B., 5/7/17; Hunts. Cyc. Bn., 30/10/17, Bedf. R.; 2/Lieut.
  53 Buxton Road, Chingford, E. 4.

BISHOP, *Gerald*
H/2028, 7/11/14; North'n. R., 4/2/15; F; Capt.; w.
  17 Park Avenue, Northampton.

BISHOP, *Herbert Francis*
C/10377, 8/1/17; Devon. R., 15/3/17; Capt.
  6 Smithfield, Dublin.

BISHOP, *Kenneth Harley*
6/2/8686, 4/1/16; No. 14 O.C.B., 26/11/16; Bedf. R., 28/2/17; F; Lieut.; g. 17 Park Avenue, Northampton.

APPENDIX II.—RECORDS OF RANK AND FILE.

BISHOP, Lawrence Edward
4/4561, 1/7/15, Cpl.; 7th Lond. R., 15/11/15; F; Capt.; w; M.C.
20 Claverdale Road, Upper Tulse Hill, S.W. 2.

BISHOP, Owen James
A/12475, 29/1/18; R.F.A., C/S, 17/5/18; demob.
Duke of York Hotel, Hanwell, W. 7.

✠ BISHOP, Rowland Bridgeman
E/1542, 6/10/14; North'n. R., 8/10/14; G; Capt.
Killed in action 19/4/17.

BISHOP, Sydney Duvall
A/777, 27/3/14, L/C.; Oxf. & Bucks. L.I., 20/2/15, Yorks. L.I.; Capt.
160 Stapleton Hall Road, Stroud Green, N. 4.

✠ BISHOP, Wilfrid
6/4/7197, 4/11/15; No. 14 O.C.B.; Bord. R., 24/10/16; 2/Lieut.
Died of wounds 6/7/17.

BISS, Frederick Ellis
6/1/6114, 9/9/15; W. Rid. R., 14/6/16, R.A.F.; F; Lieut.; w.
The Old Mill House, Woolavington, Bridgwater.

✠ BISSEKER, John Wallis
6/1/9093, 24/1/16; No. 14 O.C.B.; R. War. R., 18/12/16; F; 2/Lieut.
Killed in action 1/4/17.

BISSETT, Robert
6/3/7021, 27/10/15, L/C.; No. 3 O.C.B., 25/2/16; N. Lan. R., 20/7/16, att. S. Lan. R.; F; Lieut.; w(2).
Bean Road, Fortrose, Rosshire, Scotland.

BISSHOPP, Edward Alfred Fernley
E/H/3022, 9/3/15, L/C.; R.F.A., 20/7/15; Lieut.; w.
Haslemere, St. Edmond's Road, Ipswich.

✠ BISSICKS, Francis
6/8154, 6/12/15; R.F.C., 7/7/16; F; 2/Lieut.
Killed 2/1/17.

BITTLES, Leonard Frederick
K/F/3/2786, 26/1/15; Essex R., 3/6/15; Lieut.; w(3); M.C. M(1).
Sitomagus, Hillboro' Drive, Columbus Estate, Westcliff-on-Sea.

BLABER, Wilfred
2/3257, 15/4/15; 22nd Lond. R., 15/7/15; F; Lieut.; w.
25 Bedford Street, Strand, W.C. 2. (Now in Paris.)

✠ BLACK, Cyril Herbert Charles Packenham
E/1568, 6/10/14; Midd'x. R., 14/12/14; 2/Lieut.
Killed in action 18/8/16.

✠ BLACK, Donald Walter Bryce
A/11004, 4/4/17; R.F.C., C/S, 4/5/17; R.F.C., 14/6/17; 2/Lieut.
Killed 3/1/18.

BLACK, Edward Ealden
A/B/12432, 22/1/18, L/C.; Sigs. C/S, 31/5/18; R.E., 26/10/18; 2/Lieut.
297 Brownhill Road, Catford, S.E. 6.

BLACK, Ladbroke Lionel Day
C/9935, 16/11/16, L/C.; R.G.A., C/S, 28/2/17; R.G.A., 1/7/17; Lieut.
Chiltern House, Wendover, Buckinghamshire.

BLACK, Robert Eric
6/3/6512, 30/9/15; No. 2 O.C.B., 25/2/16; North'd Fus., 5/7/16; F; Lieut.; w, Inv.
213 Park Road, Kingston-on-Thames.

BLACK, Thomas Chalmers
6/4/6500, 28/9/15; No. 14 O.C.B.; Bord. R., 21/11/16, att. R.E.; S; Lieut.
7 Clarendon Road, Putney, S.W.

BLACKALL, Norman
4/5/4784, 12/7/15, Cpl.; Midd'x. R., 23/4/16; Lieut.; w(2).

BLACKBURN, Frank
F/1871, 16/10/14; Intelligence Officer, 3/11/14; F; Lieut.; w.
c/o. A. H. Badger, Esq., Edleston Road, Crewe. (Now in West Africa.)

BLACKBURN, George Darrell
B/A/12411, 17/1/18; trfr 28th Lond. R., 21/6/18.
7 Granby Road, Harrogate.

BLACKBURN, Gideon
B/11413, 1/6/17; No. 14 O.C.B., 7/12/17; W. York. R., 25/6/18; 2/Lieut.

BLACKBURN, Reginald Richardson
1/7646, 22/11/15; No. 14 O.C.B.; R. Marines, 24/10/16; F; Lieut.; p.
Harewood, Trinity Grove, Bridlington.

BLACKER-DOUGLASS, Charles Maxwell Vandeler
B/12822, 22/3/18; H. Bde., O.C.B., 6/9/18; Irish Guards, 12/3/19; 2/Lieut
Bellevue Park, Killiney, Co. Dublin, Ireland.

BLACKETT-ORD, William Edward
6/1/7900, 29/11/15, L/C.; No. 14 O.C.B.; North'd Fus., 18/12/16; F; Lieut.; w.
17 Drayton Gardens, S. Kensington, S.W.

BLACKHALL, James Melville
6/1/5721, 19/8/15; R.A.S.C., 24/1/16; Lieut.
School House, Lunanhead, Forfar, N.B.

BLACKIE, Rowland Compton
4/2/4663, 8/7/15; R. Lanc. R., 27/11/15; F; Lieut.; w.
Redstone Manor, Redhill, Surrey.

BLACKMAN, Richard Diamond
D/1476, 29/9/14, L/C.; R.A.S.C., 11/1/15, R.A.F.; F; Capt.
Poplar House, Kingston Crescent, Portsmouth.

BLACKMORE, Cedric William Platts
A/Sq/2040, 9/11/14; R.F.A., 15/1/15, secd. Nigeria R.; Germ.E.A; Capt.; M.C.
55 Kensington Gardens Square, W. 2.

BLACKMORE, Vivian Charles
D/10014, 27/11/16; No. 14 O.C.B., 5/3/17; Dorset. R., 26/6/17, att. R.F.C.; E; Lieut.
55 Erpingham Road, Putney, S.W. 15.

BLACK-ROBERTS, Emrys Christopher
6/1/6686, 7/10/15; R.F.C., 4/8/16; R.W. Fus.; F; Lieut.
Cleveland House, George Road, Edgbaston, Birmingham.

BLACKSTONE, Ernest Edward
6/9269, 3/2/16; A.S.C., C/S, 15/5/16; R.A.S.C., 18/6/16, att. R.G.A.; F; Capt.
Clare Lodge, Stamford, Lincolnshire.

✠ BLACKWELL, Arthur Gerald
6/2/6901, 18/10/15; No. 2 Cav. C/S, 31/3/16; trfr. War. Yeo., 8/9/16.
Died

✠ BLACKWELL, Basil Bernard
6/2/5615, 16/8/15; E. Kent R., 6/7/16; F; 2/Lieut.
Killed in action 3/9/16.

BLACKWELL, Philip Henry
4/Sq/4360, 21/6/15; R.A.S.C., (Lt) 29/7/15; F; Capt.
Ventura, 75 Addiscombe Road, Croydon, Surrey.

BLACKWELL, Sidney Francis.
4/1/4622, 5/7/15; trfr. R.E., 19/10/16; R.A.F.; F; 2/Lieut.; w.
Chatsworth, Brighton Road, Purley. (Now in West Africa.)

BLACKWOOD, John
B/13515, 12/7/18; No. 22 O.C.B., 23/8/18; R. Sco. Fus., 5/2/19; 2/Lieut.
161 Somerville Road, Small Heath, Birmingham.

BLACKWOOD, Ronald Theodore
6/8987, 18/1/16; R.A., C/S, 7/7/16; R.G.A., 13/9/16, emp. M. of Labour; S; Capt.; Inv.
Oxford and County Club, 33 Holywell, Oxford.

BLACKWOOD, William Thorburn
6/3/9152, 25/1/16; No 14 O.C.B.; R. Scots., 18/12/16; F; Major; M.C.
Southwood, Peebles.

✠ BLADON, Henry James
A/11623, 9/7/17; No. 14 O.C.B., 4/1/18; Welch. R., 25/6/18; 2/Lieut.
Died of wounds 1/9/18.

BLAGDEN, George Chalmers
Sq/434, 29/6/09; dis. 31/7/11; rej. C/13225, 7/6/18; No. 22 O.C.B., 22/11/18; York. & Lanc. R., 15/2/19; 2/Lieut.
10 Wellesley Mansions, W. Kensington, W. 14.

BLAIR, James Hunter
K/B/2088, 16/11/14; Sea. Highrs., 13/3/15, att. R.E. Sigs.; F; Lieut.; w.
Blairquhan, Maybole, Scotland.

BLAIR, John Elliot
D/10926, 26/3/17; R.F.C., C/S, 4/5/17; R.F.C., 14/6/17, R.A.F.; S. Russia; Flt. Cmdr.
5 Radstock Road, Elm Park, Liverpool.

BLAKE, Arthur Alfred
B/12696, 8/3/18; No. 4 O.C.B., 6/9/18, No. 18 O.C.B.; R. Fus., 18/3/19; 2/Lieut.
Woodlands, Broad Walk, Winchmore Hill, N. 21.

✠ BLAKE, Cecil Rodolph
A/828, 4/8/14; K.R. Rif. C., 19/9/14; Capt.
Killed in action 4/4/17.

BLAKE, Claude Stanley
B/2874, 8/2/15; R.A.S.C., 5/7/15; F; Lieut.
Hopelands, Kew Gardens Road, New Gardens.

APPENDIX II.—RECORDS OF RANK AND FILE.

BLAKE, *Clifford Frank Thomas*
A/12533, 4/2/18; No. 20 O.C.B., 7/6/18; Suff. R., 6/2/19; 2/Lieut. *Las Flores, Great Buckland, Meopham, Kent.*

✠ BLAKE, *George Victor*
6/1/8539, 30/12/15; No. 14 O.C.B.; Shrops. L.I., 18/12/16; 2/Lieut. *Killed in action 3/12/17.*

BLAKE, *Henry Albert*
C/13319, 19/6/18; No. 22 O.C.B., 23/8/18; Hamps. R., 13/2/19; 2/Lieut. *26 Upper Derby Road, North End, Portsmouth.*

BLAKE, *John Netterville*
6/1/9338, 7/2/16; No. 14 O.C.B., 30/10/16; L'pool. R., 28/2/17; F; Lieut.; w. *c/o. Bank of Liverpool & Martin's, Ltd., Inspector's Department, 7 Water Street, Liverpool.*

BLAKE, *Roger Derrick Campbell*
Sq/744, 1/12/13; 10th R. Regt. of Cav., 11/9/14, R.A.F.; F; Lieut.; w; D.F.C. *23 Warwick Avenue, Bedford.*

BLAKE, *Thomas Joseph*
6/3/5465, 9/8/15; 3rd Lond. R., 8/12/15, War Office; F; Lieut.; w. *c/o. London and River Plate Bank, 7 Princes Street, E.C.*

BLAKE, *Thomas Richard*
F/2987, 1/3/15; Lan. Fus., 18/8/15; F; Lieut.; w. *Dunkeld, High View Road, Sidcup, Kent.*

BLAKEWAY, *Garnet Conrad*
D/10957, 30/3/17; trfr. R.F.A., 20/7/17, H.A.C.; Sgt. *Thornton House, Exeter.*

BLAMEY, *John*
E/14192, 18/10/18; demob. 10/1/19. *54 High Street, Stroud, Gloucester.*

BLANCH, *Arthur Thomas Henry*
6/5/6574, T/2/10/15; Sigs. C/S, 18/2/16; R.E., 1/7/16, att. R.N.D.; F; Lieut.; M.C., M(1). *Beechcroft, Rodborough, Stroud, Gloucester.*

BLANCHARD, *John Newel*
D/E/13658, 29/7/18; No. 22 O.C.B., 20/9/18; Dorset R., 14/2/19; 2/Lieut. *The Laurels, Parkstone, Dorset.*

BLANCHARD, *Leslie James*
A/D/12537, 5/2/18; Sergt.; trfr. K.R. Rif. C., 13/5/19. *52 Whitehall Road, Thornton Heath, Surrey.*

✠ BLAND, *Alfred Edward*
D/1429, 29/9/14; Manch. R., 18/1/15; Capt. *Killed in action 1/7/16.*

BLAND, *Jack Snell*
D/Sq/12991, 29/4/18, Sgt.; demob. 14/1/19. *63 High Street, Deptford, S.E. 8.*

✠ BLAND, *Thomas Russell*
6/5/6546, 30/9/15; No. 4 O.C.B., 7/3/16; N. Staff. R., 16/7/16, York. & Lanc. R.; F; 2/Lieut. *Killed in action 20/7/17.*

✠ BLANDE, *Arthur Frederick William*
3713, T/14/5/15, Sgt.; Midd'x R., 8/7/15, 8th Lond. R.; Lieut. *Killed in action 20/9/17.*

BLANDY, *Geoffrey Kelvin*
C/826, 4/8/14; E. Surr. R., 15/8/14, R.N.A.S., R.A.F.; S; Capt.; w-p; M(1). *1 Wilton Crescent, S.W. 1.*

BLANEY, *Edward James*
6/4/9275, 3/2/16; No. 7 O.C.B., 11/8/16; R. Ir. Regt., 18/12/16; F; Lieut. *Rosemount, Tobermore, Co. Londonderry, Ireland.*

BLATCHFORD, *Henry Theodore Duncan*
4/6/4732, 12/7/15; R.F.A., C/S, 18/8/16; R.G.A., 9/12/16; F; Lieut.; w. *The Retreat, 6 Spencer Terrace, Lipson Road, Plymouth.*

BLAVER, *John George*
2/3445, 3/5/15; R.F.A., 2/9/15; F; Capt. *3 The Grange, Haverstock Hill, N.W. 3.*

BLAXILL, *Francis Harold*
A/11194, 7/5/17; R.F.C., C/S, 2/8/17; R.F.C., 8/9/17, R.A.F.; 2/Lieut. *1 Temple Road, Hornsey, N.*

✠ BLAXLEY, *Stewart Lenton*
6/3/7647, 22/11/15; No. 14 O.C.B.; R.W. Fus., 22/11/16; F; 2/Lieut. *Killed in action 23/4/17.*

✠ BLEADEN, *Lionel*
E/1540, 6/10/14; R. Fus., 7/11/14; Lieut. *Killed in action 6-9/7/16.*

BLENKINSOP, *John Proctor*
D/10413, 10/1/17, L/C.; Garr. O.C.B., 28/12/17; Lab. Corps, 22/6/18; 2/Lieut. *57 Windsor Terrace, Gosforth, Newcastle-on-Tyne.*

BLENNERHASSETT, *Giles Noble*
6/4/6115, 9/9/15; R. Ir. Fus., 1/6/16, secd. R.A.F.; Lieut.; M.C. *Leoville, Sligo, Ireland.*

BLIGH, *Matthew Murray*
6/5/6039, 3/9/15; trfr. R.G.A., 27/10/16. *109 Mount Pleasant, Liverpool.*

BLIGH, *Neville Melton*
B/12724, 14/3/18; No. 5 O.C.B., 6/9/18; demob. *67 Castle Road, Bedford.*

BLIGHT, *Edward Clare*
Sq/664, 19/11/12; 8th Lond. R., 23/12/13, R.A.F.; F; Capt.; w. *31 Bennetthorpe, Doncaster.*

BLINCOW, *Archibald Brown*
3/D/7760, 23/11/15, R.Q.M.S.; (att. No. 14 O.C.B.); demob. 19/5/19. *11 Greenway, Berkhamsted, Hertfordshire.*

BLISS, *Alfred Howard*
D/11813, 9/8/17; R.F.C., C/S, 26/11/17; R.F.C., 23/1/18, R.A.F.; Flying Officer. *106 Kingsthorpe Grove, Northampton.*

BLISS, *Arthur Edward Drummond*
A/1051, 31/8/14; R. Fus., 5/10/14, Gren. Gds.; Capt.; w; M(1). *21 Holland Park, W.*

BLISS, *Ernest George*
D/12943, 19/4/18; Sigs. C/S, 31/5/18; R.E., 26/10/18; Germ. SWA; 2/Lieut. *c/o South African Police, P.O. Box 164, Durban, Natal, S. Africa.*

BLISS, *Henry Norman*
1/9645, 27/9/16, Sgt.; R.A., C/S, 2/11/17; R.H. & R.F.A., 13/4/18; 2/Lieut. *4 King Street, Cheapside, E.C.*

BLISS, *Methuen*
C/12634, 22/2/18; No. 6 O.C.B., 5/7/18, No. 1 O.C.B.; demob. *113 The Avenue, Highams Park, Chingford.*

BLISS, *Stanley Norman*
C/10148, 8/12/16; Devon. R., 15/3/17; Lieut. *113 The Avenue, Highams Park, Chingford.*

BLOCKSIDGE, *Frank Henry*
4/1/4594, 5/7/15; L/C.; Manch. R., 2/1/16; Lieut. *12 Balmoral Road, Gillingham, Kent.*

✠ BLOFIELD, *Robert Alban*
6/5/6116, 9/9/15, L/C.; Hamps. R., 18/12/15; 2/Lieut. *Died of wounds 20/4/17, as Prisoner of War.*

✠ BLOMFIELD, *Arthur Eustace*
4/Sq/4263, T/16/6/15; R.F.A., 2/10/15; F,It; Lieut. *Died 27/10/17.*

BLOOMFIELD, *Herbert David*
B/11384, 30/5/17, C.Q.M.S.; trfr. K.R. Rif. C., 13/5/19. *Airton, Welbraham Road, Fallowfield, Manchester.*

✠ BLOTT, *Thomas Watkin*
4/1/4785, 12/7/15, Cpl.; North'd. Fus., 1/6/16; F; Capt. *Killed in action 9/4/17.*

BLOUNT, *Cecil*
6/1/5821, 26/8/15; Dorset R., 10/12/15, att. Indian Army; M; Lieut. *c/o. National Provincial and Union Bank, Ltd., Bournemouth.*

BLOW, *Thomas Bertram*
B/12412, 18/1/18; R.E., C/S, 14/4/18; R.E., 15/8/18; 2/Lieut. *6 Blackheath Vale, S.E. 3.*

BLOY, *Clement Richard Johnson Goldworth*
D/13788, 9/8/18; demob. 29/1/19. *Whitchurch, Mannamead, Plymouth.*

BLUCK, *Harold Leonard*
A/10065, 1/12/16, L/C.; R.F.C., C/S, 13/3/17; R.F.C., 19/4/17, R.A.F.; Lieut. *3 Drayton Court Chambers, Argyll Road, W. Ealing, W. 13.*

BLUMER, *Francis*
A/13093, 22/5/18; trfr. 14th Lond. R., 6/12/18. *Rest Harrow, Hightown, nr. Liverpool.*

APPENDIX II.—RECORDS OF RANK AND FILE.

BLUNDELL, Arthur Walmsley
6/5/5240, 31/7/15; trfr. 14th Lond. R., 2/5/16.
Elderslie, Aughton, nr. Ormskirk, Lancashire.

BLUNDELL, Edward Percy
B/10707, 12/2/17; No. 11 O.C.B., 5/7/17; L'pool. R., 30/10/17, att. Rif. Brig.; 2/Lieut.; p.
33 Dacre Hill, Rock Ferry, Cheshire.

✠ BLUNDELL, Jack Benson
B/D/12331, 31/12/17; R.F.C., C/S, 21/5/18; R.A.F., 5/7/18; F; 2/Lieut.
Killed in action 29/9/18.

BLUNT, Hubert Porter
K/F/2272, 7/12/14, L/C.; R. War. R., 13/3/15, R.A.O.C.; F; Major; w; M.B.E.
Craigmoor, Melling Lane, Maghull, nr. Liverpool.

BLUNT, Walter Raymond
4/2/4036, 7/6/15; trfr. R.G.A. 7/7/16; R.G.A., 24/1/17; F; Lieut.
366 Fosse Road North, Leicester.

BLYDE, Geoffrey Alger
C/13291, 17/6/18, L/C.; trfr. 14th Lond. R., 6/12/18.
East Clyffe, Sheffield.

BLYTH, Arthur John
C/12591, 12/2/18; R.E., C/S, 12/5/18; R.E., 27/9/18; 2/Lieut.
c/o. Lond. City and Midland Bank, Threadneedle Street, E.C.

BLYTH, Herbert Cecil
C/12243, 23/11/17; R.F.A., C/S, 15/3/18; R.H. & R.F.A., 29/3/19; 2/Lieut.
44 Fellows Road, Hampstead, N.W. 3.

BLYTHMAN, Laurence
D/10016, 27/11/16; Sigs. C/S, 17/3/17, No. 20 O.C.B.; trfr. 19th Lond. R., Army Pay Corps.
19 Gainsboro' Mansions, Queen's Club Gardens, W. 14.

BOADEN, Harold Evans
C/12227, 16/11/17; No. 18 O.C.B., 7/6/18; D. of Corn. L.I., 3/2/19; 2/Lieut.
18 Marlborough Road, Falmouth, Cornwall.

✠ BOADLE, Frank Chambers
6/5/5918, 1/9/15; trfr. 13th Lond. R., 27/11/15; F; Pte.
Killed in action 1/7/16.

✠ BOAG, Alfred
6/4/6006, 2/9/15; 7th Lond. R., 19/11/15; R.F.C.; 2/Lieut.
Died 29/4/16.

✠ BOARDLEY, Harold Augustus
3/3586, 13/5/15; Shrops. L.I., 10/9/15; M,S,F; Lieut.
Killed in action 26/9/17.

BOARDLEY, Reginald Thomas
6/5/6117, 9/9/15; Linc. R., 24/12/15, att. Lab. Corps; F; Lieut.; w.
90 Park Road, Lowestoft.

BOARDMAN, Francis Joseph
C/14213, 18/10/18; No. 11 O.C.B., 24/1/19; General List, 8/3/19; 2/Lieut.
c/o London Brazilian Bank. Ltd., 7 Tokenhouse Yard, E.C.

BOARDMAN, John Wilberforce
F/1881, 16/10/14; Hamps. R., 27/2/15, 5th Regt. of Cav., 10th Huss., R.E. Sigs.; F; Lieut; g.
Hadley, Woodford Green, Essex.

BOARDMAN, Kingsley Thomas
6/Sq/8102, 2/12/15; No. 2 Cav. C/S, 1/9/16; 5th R. Reg. of Cav., 20/12/16, 10th Huss.; F; Lieut.; w.
Hadley, Woodford Green, Essex.

BOATH, James Cables
E/14174, 16/10/18; No. 22 O.C.B., 22/11/18; Gord. Highrs., 15/2/19; 2/Lieut.
48 Wilton Road, Muswell Hill, N.W.

BOBBY, Frederick Christopher
B/11331, 21/5/17, L/C.; No. 14 O.C.B., 9/11/17; Oxf. & Bucks. L.I., 30/4/18; F; 2/Lieut.; Inv.
The Newlings, White Hill, Hitchin.

BOBBY, Herbert
D/11122, 30/4/17; No. 14 O.C.B., 7/9/17; R.A.O.C., 16/1/18; S; Lieut.; Inv.
St. Ives, 43 Cornwall Gardens, Cliftonville, Margate.

BOBBY, Wilfred
4/1/5157, 29/7/15; Hamps. R., 4/9/16, att. Glouc. R., War Office; F; Lieut.
Woodville, St. Luke's Road, Bournemouth, Hampshire.

BOCK, John Vincent
C/10981, 2/4/17; Garr. O.C.B., 5/10/17; trfr. K.R. Rif. C., 19/11/17.
Bridgwater House, Whitworth Street, Manchester. (Now in Rhodesia.)

BODDY, John George
B/Sq/9889, 10/11/16, L/C.; R.F.A., C/S, 28/12/17; R.H. and R.F.A., 15/8/18; 2/Lieut.
Bolwick Hall Farm, Marsham, Norwich.

BODEN, Ernest John
C/11761, 30/7/17; No. 14 O.C.B., 4/1/18; R. Sco. Fus., 25/6/18; S; 2/Lieut.
15 Fox Street, Greenock, Scotland.

BODGER, John Eric Sturton
4/3/4449, 28/6/15, L/C.; N. Lan. R., 27/12/15; F,S,E,P; Lieut.; M(1).
45 Broadway, Peterborough.

BODILLY, Ralph William Talbot
6/3/7022, 27/10/15; R.F.C., 4/9/16; E;
9 Church Terrace, Blackheath, S.E. 3.

✠ BODVEL-ROBERTS, Harold Owen
C/88, 16/4/08, Sgt.; Inns of Court O.T.C., 1/1/10, 7th Lond. R.; F; Lieut.; M.C., M(1).
Died of wounds 18/11/15.

✠ BODY, Frank Lydford
D/1456, 29/9/14; Bedf. R., 27/11/14; Capt.
Died of wounds 18/6/17.

BODY, Malcolm Maxwell Irving
Sq/3218, 12/4/15, L/C.; R.F.A., 29/6/15; F; Major; w(3); M.C. and Bar.
c/o. Australian Bank, Sydney, Australia.

BODYCOMBE, John
2/9768, 23/10/16; No. 14 O.C.B., 30/1/17; Welch. R., 25/4/17; 2/Lieut.
Bryn Salem, Bony Maen, Swansea.

BOGG, Frank Rowson
B/11332, 21/5/17; No. 5 O.C.B., 5/10/17; R.E., 29/1/18, att. Manch. R.; F; Lieut.
c/o. Pretoria Portland Cement Coy., P.O. Slurry, Marico, Transvaal, S. Africa.

✠ BOGUE, Patrick Yule
6/1/9420, 10/2/16; No. 8 O.C.B., 4/8/16; E. Surr. R., 21/11/16; F; 2/Lieut.
Killed in action 23/7/17.

✠ BOLAM, Reginald Harold
6/3/D/7346, 10/11/15; trfr. R.A.M.C., 13/12/16.
Died 11/11/18.

BOLAND, James Brian
4/1/4064, 7/6/15; R.F.A., 20/9/15; Lieut.

BOLDERO, John Osmund
B/10093, 4/12/16; No. 14 O.C.B., 6/4/17; Dorset R., 31/7/17, att. R.W. Kent. R.; I; Lieut.
Morton Vicarage, nr. Bourne, Lincolnshire.

BOLLARD, Charles William Ellacott
A/10517, 15/1/17; R.F.C., C/S, 13/3/17; R.F.C., 19/4/17, Lab. Corps; 2/Lieut.
8 South Drive, Tewit Park, Harrogate.

BOLTON, Derick
C/12559, 6/2/18; R.F.A., C/S, 17/5/18; R.H. & R.F.A., 12/3/19; 2/Lieut.
Chesham Knoll, Alderley Edge, Cheshire.

BOLTON, Edwin Graham
D/13776, 7/8/18; demob. 5/2/19.
West Plean, Bannockburn, Stirlingshire, Scotland.

BOLTON, Fletcher
6/8130, 3/12/15; R.F.A., C/S, 4/8/16; R.F.A., 24/11/16; F; Capt.; w.
Russell House, Rochdale, Lancashire.

BOLTON, Frederick James
B/Sq/13524, 15/7/18; demob. 24/1/19.
55 Arundel Road, Littlehampton, Sussex.

✠ BOLTON, Geoffrey Charles
4/4127, 10/6/15; Notts. & Derby. R., 10/9/15; 2/Lieut.
Killed in action 1/8/16.

BOLTON, Philip Lea
6/5/6040, 3/9/15, L/C.; N. Lan. R., 2/6/16; Lieut.; w; M.C., M(1).
St. George's Vicarage, Darwen.

✠ BOLTON, Stuart
6/2/5548, 12/8/15; R. Lanc. R., 9/6/16; Lieut.; w.
Killed in action 17/3/18.

BOLTON, Thomas Tertius
E/1508, 1/10/14; trfr. 28th Lond. R., 8/1/15; Manch. R., 22/7/15, Lab. Corps; F; Capt.; w.
The White House, Tower Road, Bournemouth.

APPENDIX II.—RECORDS OF RANK AND FILE.

BOLTON, William Louis
B/Sq/12848, 22/3/18, L/C.; demob. 25/1/19.
Barleyfield, Rose Hill Road, Burnley, Lancashire.

BOND, Douglas George
4/4331, 21/6/15; Essex R., 28/11/15; F; Lieut.
3 Ravenscourt Park Mansions, Ravenscourt Park, W. 6.

BOND, Frederick Morten
6/2/8475, 20/12/15, L/C.; No. 14 O.C.B.; Suff. R., 18/12/16, att. Camb. R.; F; Lieut.
Croylands, Surbiton, Surrey.

BOND, Gladwyn James Trelawny
Sq/2861, 5/2/15, Sgt.; R.F.A., 17/9/15, att. S. Persia Rif.; F,S.Persia; Capt.
5 Manor Gardens, Merton Park, S.W. 19.

BOND, Guy Bateson
4/3677, 20/5/15; R.F.A., 15/9/15; 2/Lieut.; Inv.
34 Kilworth Avenue, Southend-on-Sea.

BOND, Hector
C/14307, T/30/11/18; No. 3 O.C.B., 10/2/19; Devon. R., 19/3/19; 2/Lieut.
1 Woodville Road, Ealing, W. 5.

BOND, Hubert Morten
6/2/8476, 20/12/15, L/C.; No. 14 O.C.B.; Suff. R., 18/12/16; F; Lieut.; w.
Croylands, Surbiton, Surrey.

BOND, John Richard
6/3/7287, 8/11/15; No. 14 O.C.B., 27/9/16; Devon. R., 24/1/17, R.A.F.; F,It; Capt.
Bute Court, Torquay, Devon.

BOND, Leslie William
D/13689, 31/7/18; No. 11 O.C.B., 24/1/19; demob. 9/2/19.
10 Eliot Hill, Blackheath, S.E. 13.

BOND, Percival Arthur William
C/12635, 22/2/18; No. 5 O.C.B., 5/7/18; trfr. 28th Lond. R., 20/9/18.
37 Longfield Road, Bristol.

BOND, Robert Guy
6/1/5699, 19/8/15; R.A.S.C., 8/11/15, att. Bord. R. and E. York. R., M.G.C.; S,F; Lieut.
c/o. Imperial Ottoman Bank, 26 Throgmorton Street, E.C. 2. (Now in Constantinople.)

BOND, Samuel John
6/3/7520, 16/11/15, L/C.; Devon. R., 4/8/16; Lieut.

BOND, Stanley B.
Sq/492, 6/5/10; E. York. Yeo., 22/9/14; Capt.

BOND, Thomas James
A/11639, 12/7/15, L/C.; No. 14 O.C.B., 7/12/17; 3rd Lond. R., 28/5/18; F; 2/Lieut.; w.
Waldron, Woodcote Road, Wallington, Surrey.

BOND, Tom Irving
6/4/5445, T/7/8/15, L/C.; R.F.A., 23/12/15, att. T.M. Bty.; F,It; Capt.; w(3); M.C.
Olney House, Kettering.

BOND, William Niblock
6/2/7637, T/22/11/15; R.A., C/S, 26/10/16; R.G.A., 24/2/17; F; Lieut.; w(2); M.C.; M(1).
Marcus Square, Newry, Co. Down, Ireland.

BONDFIELD, Henry Dale
6/2/5549, 12/8/15; North'n. R., 26/12/15; F; Lieut.
33 Carter Road, Shanghai, China.

BONE, Cedric James
D/11814, 9/8/17, L/C.; No. 3 O.C.B., 8/2/18; R.W. Fus., 30/7/18; 2/Lieut.
Bryn Maelgroyn, Llaurbis, Llandudno

BONE, Charles Belfield
B/197, 5/5/08; dis. 4/5/12; Devon. R., 7/10/14; Capt.
Innerdown Close, Budleigh Salterton.

✠ BONE, John Hugh
6/4/5984, 2/9/15; E. Surr. R., 23/12/15; F; 2/Lieut.
Killed in action 22/7/16.

BONE, Reginald Arthur
A/Sq/K/2439, 28/12/14; R.W. Kent R., 7/3/15, Imp. Camel Corps, R.F.C.; E,G,P; Lieut.
3 Hartfield Road, Eastbourne.

BONESS, Walter Leslie
A/10671, 9/2/17; R.F.C., C/S, 16/4/17; R.F.C., 16/5/17, R.A.F.; F,It; Lieut.
4 Rondu Road, Cricklewood, N.W. 2.

BONFIELD, Hedley John
D/10942, 27/3/17; No. 11 O.C.B., 5/7/17; R. War. R., 30/10/17, att. Norf. R. and T.M. Bty.; F; 2/Lieut.; w, Inv.
37 Coleshill Street West, Atherstone, Warwickshire.

BONHAM, Walter Landowne
4/3997, 3/6/15; R.F.A., 5/11/15.
11 Montpelier Crescent, Brighton.

BONNER, Arthur Octavius
4/5093, 26/7/15; dis. med. unfit, 8/8/16.
8 Park Grove, Hull.

BONNER, Cecil Arthur James
D/2609, 7/1/15; Lan. Fus., 22/4/15, emp. M. of Labour; Capt.; w; M(1).
3 Woodbine Street, Leamington.

BONNER, Edward Marshall
4/4305, 17/6/15; Notts. & Derby R., 8/11/15, att. N. Lan. R., M.G.C.; F; Lieut.; w.
The Firs, Heanor, Nottinghamshire.

✠ BONNEY, James Patterson
6/3/Sq/7901, 29/11/15; R.F.A., C/S, 29/9/16; R.G.A., 24/12/16; 2/Lieut.
Killed in action 3/10/17.

✠ BONSER, Winfield Joyce
B/1110, 7/9/14; Rif. Brig., 29/9/14; Capt.
Killed in action 25/9/15.

BONSEY, Edwin Kenneth
6/2/9266, 3/2/16; R.A., C/S, 26/10/16; R.G.A., 19/2/17; 2/Lieut.
Died of wounds 2/7/18.

BOOKER, Robert Eric Erskine
D/11576, 2/7/17; No. 14 O.C.B., 9/11/17; E. Kent. R., 30/4/18; F; 2/Lieut.
35 Corfton Road, Ealing, W. 5.

BOOKLESS, John Thomas
6/1/8049, 1/12/15, L/C.; No. 14 O.C.B., 26/11/16; Cam'n. Highrs., 27/3/17; F; Lieut.; Inv; M.C.
The Rigg, Inverness.

BOOTH, Alfred
4/5/4875, 15/7/15; 17th Lond. R., 17/4/16, emp. M. of Munitions; F; Lieut.; w; M.C., M(1).
26 Victoria Road, New Brighton.

BOOTH, Charles Victor
B/553, 24/2/11; Suff. R., 12/9/14, R.A.F.; F; Capt.
17 Victoria Street, Westminster, S.W. 1.

BOOTH, Francis Lawrence
3/9620, 18/9/16; A.S.C., C/S, 27/10/16; R.A.S.C., 20/12/16; F,It; Capt.; M(1).
Villa Matilde, 308 Calle Garibaldi, Temperley F.C.S., Argentina, S. America.

BOOTH, George
6/2/7718, 22/11/15; No. 2 O.C.B., 14/8/16; Glouc. R., 18/12/16, R. Suss. R.; F,P; Capt.; w, Inj.
19 Church Hill, Aldershot, Hampshire. (Now in S. America.)

BOOTH, Gerald Bousfield
C/1141, 14/9/14; Midd'x. R., 27/11/14, att. R.F.C. and R.A.F.; F; Lieut.; f, Inj.
The Red House, Palace Road, East Molesey.

BOOTH, Henry
4/6/5/4876, 15/7/15; No. 4 O.C.B., 7/3/16; W. Rid. R., 13/7/16; F; Lieut.; w.
17 Norman Drive, Eccleshill, Bradford, Yorkshire.

BOOTH, Henry
C/14168, 16/10/18; demob. 11/1/19.
61 Leathwaite Road, S.W. 11.

BOOTH, John Castlemaine
4/Sq/4249, 14/6/15, L/C.; R.G.A., 31/12/15; Major.
Penrhyn, Wellington Road, Maldon, Surrey.

BOOTH, John Lionel
Sq/725, 25/7/13; R.E., 19/12/13; Major.
Hoe Place, Woking.

BOOTH, Oswald
A/10740, 16/2/17; No. 11 O.C.B., 5/7/17; Essex R., 30/10/17; F; 2/Lieut.; w.
Thornley House, Thornley Lane, Reddish, nr. Stockport, Lancs.

BOOTH, Raymond George
C/14223, 25/10/18; trfr. K.R. Rif. C., 7/4/19.
41 Woodstock Road, Golder's Green, N.W. 4.

BOOTH, Thomas John
B/11015, 11/4/17, L/C.; No. 14 O.C.B., 10/8/17; 6th Lond. R., 27/11/17, att. 15th Lond. R.; F; Lieut.; M.C.
2 Eversleigh Gardens, Loughton, Essex.

✠ BOOTHBY, Ernest Brooke
C/1635, 9/10/14; Rif. Brig., 30/12/14; 2/Lieut.
Killed in action 10/7/16.

BOOTHBY, Leslie Herbert
C/A/12041, 27/9/17; R.F.C., C/S, 18/1/18; R. Marines, 15/11/18; Lieut.
19 Regents Park Terrace, N.W.

APPENDIX II.—RECORDS OF RANK AND FILE.

BORASTON, John Herbert
C/Sq/1231, 23/9/14; R.F.A., 30/1/15, att. G.H.Q.; F; Lt.-Col.; C.B., O.B.E., Chevalier du Legion d'Honneur, M(4).
4 Gower Street, Bedford Square, W.C. 1.

BORMAN, Frederick Ernest
4/3679, 20/5/15; Oxf. & Bucks. L.I., 28/10/15; F; Lieut.; w.
King's Weir Cottage, Broxbourne, Hertfordshire.

BORMAN, Rupert Lionel Dalbiac
B/10549, 17/1/17; A.S.C., C/S, 1/8/17; R.A.S.C., 29/9/17; F; 2/Lieut.
Doric Lodge, Woodbridge, Suffolk.

✠ BOROUGH, Alaric Charles Henry
E/2695, 14/1/15; R. Innis. Fus., 22/5/15, Welsh Gds.; Lieut.
Killed in action 1/12/17.

✠ BORRER, John Maximilian
A/1379, 26/9/14; R. Suss. R., 21/10/14; 2/Lieut.
Died 9/9/17.

BORRETT, Walter Keith
6/2/7980, 29/11/15; No. 8 O.C.B., 4/8/16; M.G.C., 28/10/16, Tank Corps, emp. M. of Shipping; F; Lieut.; w.
3 Molesworth Cottages, Stoke Devonport, Devon.

BORTHWICK, John Telfer
6/2/8779, 7/1/16; R.F.A., C/S, 7/7/16; R.G.A., 11/10/16, secd. R.F.C., R.A.F.; Lieut.
62 Princes Road, Teddington.

BORTHWICK, The Honble. William
A/1362, 26/9/14, Sgt.; R.H.A., C/S, 24/1/16; K.R. Rif. C., 4/8/16; F; Capt.; w(2).
43 Putney Hill, S.W. 15.

BOST, George William
1/3754, 27/5/15; R.E., 24/8/15; F; Capt.; M.C., M(1).
Strathie, Bishopston, Renfrewshire.

BOSTOCK, Eric Lever
6/5/5921, 1/9/15, L/C.; M.G.C., 25/9/16, Tank Corps; F; Lieut.; w-p.
Plas Euryn, Colwyn Bay, N. Wales.

✠ BOSTOCK, Eric Norman
6/5/C/8155, 6/12/15; No. 14 O.C.B., 26/11/16; North'n. R., 27/3/17; F; 2/Lieut.; M.C.
Missing 27/5/18.

BOSTOCK, Eustace George
6/Sq/7603, 19/11/15; No. 2 Cav. C/S, 31/3/16; 2nd Cty. of Lond. Yeo., 19/8/16; Lieut.
4 Colville Mansions, Powis Terrace, Bayswater.

BOSTOCK, Francis Edward
K/D/2472, 28/12/14; Dorset. R., 2/6/15, Midd'x. R.; F,E,S; Lieut.
44 Kensington Mansions, S.W. 5.

BOSTOCK, Harold King
6/5/5922, 1/9/15, Cpl.; R.E., 1/5/16; F; Capt.
Plas Euryn, Colwyn Bay, N. Wales.

BOSTOCK, Neville Frederick
E/1583, 6/10/14; North'n R., 13/11/14, R.G.A.; F; Capt.
Springfield, Northampton.

BOSTON, Arthur Skakerley
6/5/5241, 31/7/15, L/C.; L'pool. R., 1/6/16, R.A.O.C.; F,S; Lieut.; w.
Halton Grange, nr. Runcorn, Cheshire.

BOSUSTOW, Gordon William
H/2645, 11/1/15; Durh. L.I., 6/5/15; Lieut.
3 Station Road, Houghton-le-Spring.

✠ BOSWELL, Claude Oliver
4/6/3938, 3/6/15; dis. 3/6/15; E. Lan. R., 17/12/15; Lieut.
Killed in action 9/10/17.

BOSWELL, Ralph William
6/3/6384, 23/9/15; No. 11 O.C.B., 7/5/16; trfr. 14th Lond. R., 16/10/16.
49 Highfield Road, Dartford.

BOSWELL, Reginald Douglas
A/D/13019, 2/5/18; H.Bde. O.C.B., 14/9/18; trfr. Rif. Brig., 7/2/19. Heniker Lane House, Sutton Valance, nr. Maidstone.

BOSWORTH, Francis Edwin
B/12748, 12/3/18, L/C.; No. 4 O.C.B., 6/9/18; R. Ir. Regt., 17/3/19; 2/Lieut.
33 Northfield Road, King's Norton, Birmingham.

BOSWORTH, Frank Victor
4/6/2/4951, 19/7/15; R.F.A., 14/12/15; M; Capt.; M(1).
Lidlington, Ampthill, Bedfordshire.

✠ BOSWORTHICK, William Howard
A/D/11879, 20/8/17; No. 3 O.C.B., 8/2/18; Devon. R., 30/7/18; 2/Lieut.
Killed in action 7/11/18.

BOTHAM, George William
C/10171, 11/12/16; No. 14 O.C.B., 5/3/17; Lan. Fus., 26/6/17; F; Lieut.; w(2), g. 40 Mayfield Road, Whalley Range, Manchester.

BOTHWELL, John Randolph
4/5/4693, 8/7/15; No. 11 O.C.B., 7/5/16; M.G.C., 4/9/16; F; Lieut.; w(2); M.C., M(1).
13 Tyrwhitt Road, Brockley, S.E. 4.

BOTT, Alan John
Sq/3220, 12/4/15; L/C.; R.G.A., 22/7/15, R.A.F.; P,S; w-p, (escaped to Salonica); Capt.; M.C. and Bar, M(1).
2A Artillery Mansions, Victoria Street, Westminster, S.W. 1.

BOTTERILL, William Ronald
B/1262, 23/9/14; 4th Lond. R., 23/9/14, R.F.A.; E,G,F; Capt.; w; M.C.
Junior Army and Navy Club, Whitehall, S.W. 1.

BOTTING, Reginald John Henry
D/13743, 2/8/18; trfr. K.R. Rif. C., 13/5/19.
66 St. George's Road, Brighton.

✠ BOTTING, William Rolph
6/4/D/9027, 20/1/16; No. 13 O.C.B., 4/11/16; R. Suss. R., 28/2/17; 2/Lieut.
Killed in action 25/9/17.

BOTTOMLEY, Arthur Leslie
B/12193, 6/11/17, L/C.; No. 12 O.C.B., 10/5/18; W. Rid. R., 3/2/19; 2/Lieut.
Platts Terrace, Ripponden, Halifax, Yorkshire.

BOTTOMLEY, Clifford Hodgson
6/Sq/5891, 30/8/15; No. 1 Cav. C/S, 24/4/16; Oxf. Huss. Yeo. 28/7/16; F; Lieut.
Beckfield, Beckwithshaw, Harrogate.

BOTTON, Claude Wilfrid
4/5094, 26/7/15, L/C.; R.W. Surr. R., 22/11/15; Lieut.; w.
c/o. A. Quicke, Esq., 94 Grayshot Road, Lavender Hill, S.W. 11.

BOTTON, Oswald Victor
4/5095, 26/7/15, Cpl.; R.W. Surr. R., 22/11/15; Lieut.
c/o. A. Quicke, Esq., 94 Grayshot Road, Lavender Hill, S.W. 11.

✠ BOUCHER, Albert Adolphe
4/1/3936, 3/6/15; Shrops. L.I., 10/9/15, att. T.M. Bty.; 2/Lieut.
Died of wounds 16/10/16.

✠ BOUGHEY, John Fletcher
6/4/5466, 9/8/15; No. 4 O.C.B., 7/3/16; trfr. E. Kent R., 16/6/16
Missing 4/10/17.

BOULGER, Edmund Francis
6/1/7023, 27/10/15; Garr. O.C.B., 19/2/17; Worc. R., 14/4/17; Lieut.
4 Kent Terrace, Dalkey, Co. Dublin, Ireland.

✠ BOULTER, Sidney Frederick
6/5/6881, 18/10/15; 10th Lond. R., 4/9/16, 25th Lond. R.; F; 2/Lieut.
Killed in action 18/2/17.

✠ BOULTON, Clifford John
4/4206, 14/6/15; Welch R., 5/11/15; Capt.; M.C.
Killed in action 30/8/18.

✠ BOULTON, Nicholson Stuart
D/11089, 23/4/17; R.F.C., C/S, 1/6/17; R.F.C., 4/7/17; F; 2/Lieut.
Killed in action 29/9/18.

BOULTON, Walter Llewellyn
B/D/13411, 1/7/18; demob. 23/1/18.
Walsall Wood Vicarage, Walsall.

BOUMPHREY, Harold Briscoe
6/5/5915, 1/9/15; L'pool. R., 1/6/16; F; Lieut.; w.
The Briars, Willaston, Birkenhead.

BOURJEAURD, Philip Ambrose Ernest
D/10963, 30/3/17; No. 14 O.C.B., 5/7/17; Suff. R., 30/10/17; 2/Lieut.
22 Davies Street, Berkeley Square, W. 1.

BOURKE, Bryan Longley
6/1/9563, 18/3/16; No. 8 O.C.B., 4/8/16; K.R. Rif. C., 21/11/16; F; Lieut.; Inv. w.
Monycrower, Maidenhead.

BOURKE, Geoffrey John
D/13718, 2/8/18; trfr. K.R. Rif. C., 7/4/19.
Monycrower, Maidenhead.

✠ BOURKE, James Gay Shute
6/2/7651, 22/11/15, Sgt.; No. 14 O.C.B.; L'pool. R., 24/1/17, att. R. War. R., F; 2/Lieut.
Killed in action 15/4/18.

BOURKE, Richard Vandeleur
C/11805, 4/8/17; trfr. R.A.S.C., 14/12/17; Pte.
Thornfields, Lisnagry, Co. Limerick.

APPENDIX II.—RECORDS OF RANK AND FILE.

BOURN, John Archibald
D/13690, 31/7/18; trfr. D. of Corn. L.I., 10/5/19.
130 Weston Park, Hornsey, N. 8.

BOURNE, John Fourdrinier
B/647, 4/7/12; North'n. R., 1/9/14, att. Welsh Gds.; F; Capt.; Inv, w; M.C., M(1).
10 Cole Park Road, Twickenham.

BOURNE, William
6/4/9209, 31/1/16, L/C.; R.F.C., C/S, 16/11/16; R.F.C., 16/3/17, R.A.F.; Lieut.
South View, Freshfield Road, Brighton.

BOURNEFIELD, Arthur William
A/1281, 23/9/14; R. Suss. R., 14/12/14, Army Cyc. Corps.; Lieut.
17 Crescent Wood Road, Sydenham, S.E.

✠ BOURNER, Rowland Moody Nicholson
2/9674, 2/10/16; M.G.C., C/S, 14/3/17; M.G.C., 26/7/17; F; 2/Lieut.; w.
Died of wounds 28/3/18.

BOUSFIELD, Albert Greenhill
A/13169, 31/5/18; No. 22 O.C.B., 5/7/18; Essex R., 5/2/19; 2/Lieut.
Kedington, Hoddesdon, Hertfordshire.

BOUSFIELD, Edward Alexander Robert
6/3/7902, 29/11/15; R.A., C/S, 15/9/16; R.G.A., 10/12/16; F; Lieut.
49 Fontenoy Road, Bedford Hill, Balham, S.W. 12.

BOUSFIELD, John Southwell
E/1539, 6/10/14; E. Lan. R., 14/12/14; F; Lieut.; g.
The Malm, Rickmansworth.

BOUSFIELD, Stanley Philip Angus
E/2824, 1/2/15; Sea. Highrs., 2/6/15, R.A.F.; Lieut.

BOUSTEAD, Philip Malré Nelson
4/2/4595, 5/7/15; Hamps. R., 29/11/15; F; Lieut.; w(2), g; M.C., M(1).
74 Goldsmith Avenue, Acton, W. 3. (Now in Belgian Congo.)

BOUTROY, Henry Edward A. A.
4/1/4529, 1/7/15; D. of Corn. L.I., 15/11/15, M.G.C.; Lieut.
42 Linden Gardens, Kensington, W. 2.

BOWDEN, Ernest
6/4/9024, 20/1/16, Sgt.; No. 14 O.C.B., 30/10/16; Lan. Fus., 24/1/17; F; Lieut.; w.
79 Hare Hill Road, Littleboro', Lancashire.

BOWDEN, John Henry
4/3/5052, 22/7/15; Arg. & Suth'd. Highrs., 5/11/15, att. Div Sig. Coy.; I; Lieut.
St. Paul's Vicarage, Kipling Street, Bermondsey, S.E. 1. (Now in India.)

BOWDEN, John Stewart
B/11312, 21/5/17, L/C.; No. 14 O.C.B., 7/9/17; Yorks. L.I., 17/12/17; 2/Lieut.
Clifton House, Hay, Herefordshire.

BOWDEN, Spencer Albert
4/3/4388, 24/6/15, C.S.M.; No. 14 O.C.B., 26/11/16; Suff. R., 28/2/17, Indian Army; F; Lieut.; w.
Oakroyd, Newlay Wood, Horsforth, nr. Leeds.

✠ BOWDEN, Sydney
D/13752, 7/8/18.
Died 5/11/18.

✠ BOWELL, Archibald Gordon Edward
K/2787, 26/1/15; Leic. R., 25/1/15; 2/Lieut.
Killed in action 15/7/16.

BOWELL, Charles William
B/12413, 18/1/18, L/C.; No. 22 O.C.B., 7/6/18; R. Suss. R., 13/2/19; 2/Lieut.

BOWEN, Alfred Edward
6/8816, 10/1/16; R.F.C., 2/6/16, R.A.F.; Capt.

BOWEN, Charles
B/13458, 5/7/18; No. 11 O.C.B., 6/2/19; General List, 8/3/19; 2/Lieut.
Armley, Greatbatch Avenue, Stoke-on-Trent.

BOWEN, Harold Claude Bingham
4/3717, 24/5/15; R. War. R., 5/9/15, att. Yorks. L.I.; F; Lieut.; w(2).
c/o. Messrs. Cox & Coy., "A" Branch, 16 Charing Cross, S.W. 1. (Now in British West Africa.)

BOWEN, George Malcolm
4/5189, 29/7/15, L/C.; Devon R., 8/6/16; M; Lieut.
Fernleigh, Woodsetton, nr. Dudley.

BOWEN, Norman Edgar
6/4/6815, 14/10/15; R.A.S.C., 24/1/16; Lieut.; Inv.
c/o. Mrs. Helsby, Edgecliffe, Newquay, Cornwall.

BOWEN, Richard Basil Montague
D/12962, 22/4/18; trfr. K.R. Rif. C., 12/6/19.

BOWEN, Richard William
1/3899, 31/5/15, Sgt.; Yorks. L.I., 12/12/15; Lieut.; w(2).
Audley House, Oakamoor, Stoke-on-Trent.

✠ BOWER, Charles Francis
4/3/4389, 24/6/15; Notts. & Derby. R., 25/10/15; F; Capt.
Killed in action 13/9/17.

BOWERING, John
B/706, 9/4/13; 19th Lond. R., 3/10/14, Intelligence Corps; F; Capt.; M(1).
c/o. Lloyds Bank, Ltd., Oxbridge, Somerset.

BOWES, Charles
D/10207, 18/12/16; R.E., C/S, 24/3/17; R.E., 15/6/17; F; Lieut.
Yewhurst, Woodside Grange Road, Woodside Park, N. 12

✠ BOWES, Ellis Arthur
B/10108, 4/12/16; No. 21 O.C.B., 5/5/17; Leic. R., 28/8/17; 2/Lieut.
Killed in action 12/3/18.

BOWLBY, Russell Frank
D/1424, 29/9/14; 3rd Lond. R., 23/4/15, att. 1st and 30th Lond. R.; F; Capt.; Inv. 5 Cleveland Gardens, Lancaster Gate, W. 2.

BOWLER, Ernest Matthew John
B/10767, 19/2/17; No. 14 O.C.B., 10/8/17; R. Fus., 27/11/17; F; 2/Lieut.
61 Elderton Road, Westcliff-on-Sea.

✠ BOWLER, Joseph Buxton
6/5/6578, T/2/10/15; trfr. 14th Lond. R., 2/5/16; p;
Killed in action 30/4/18.

✠ BOWLES, Bernard Geoffrey
A/1625, 9/10/14; E. Kent R., 10/2/15; F; 2/Lieut.
Killed in action 3/9/16.

✠ BOWLES, Geoffrey Charles
4/1/3935, 3/6/15, L/C.; R. Naval Div., 11/2/16.
Killed in action 25/4/17.

BOWLES, George
B/9877, 8/11/16; A.S.C., C/S, 1/9/17; R.A.S.C., 30/11/17; F; Lieut.
125 Gresham Road, Staines.

✠ BOWLES, Wilfrid Spencer
4/1/4530, 1/7/15, L/C.; Essex R., 11/11/15, M.G.C.; 2/Lieut.
Killed in action 10/7/16.

✠ BOWMAN, Arthur William
Sq/3680, 20/5/15; trfr. 16th Lond. R., 2/5/16; w-p.
Died of wounds 12/4/18, as Prisoner of War.

BOWMAN, Joseph Hood
B/1109, 7/9/14, L/C.; Durh. L.I., 27/11/14; NR; Capt.; Order of St. Anne (3rd Class) with crossed swords.
Wyvestow, Cambridge Road, Colchester.

BOWMAN-BURNS, Victor Lindemann William Allan
6/3/5772, 23/8/15; R.F.A., 27/12/15, R.A.F.; Lieut.
53 Great King Street, Edinburgh.

BOWN, Wilfred Leslie
6/1/7830, 25/11/15; No. 14 O.C.B., 28/8/16; M.G.C., 28/12/16; F,M; Lieut.
213 Clive Road, W. Dulwich, S.E.

BOWRING, Harvey
2/9773, 24/10/16; R.A., C/S, 11/1/17; R.G.A., 8/4/17, emp. M. of Shipping; F; Lieut.
The Pines, Woodham Road, Woking.

BOWYER, Charles Henry Edward
D/11815, 9/8/17; No. 3 O.C.B., 8/2/18; R. Suss. R., 30/7/18; 2/Lieut.
North Street, Midhurst, Sussex.

BOWYER, Herbert James
A/11923, 30/8/17; No. 14 O.C.B., 7/12/17; Midd'x. R., 28/5/18, att. L'pool. R.; F; Lieut.; w.
St. Ives, Mackenzie Street, Slough, Bucks.

✠ BOX, George Roland Holyoake
C/10380, 8/1/17; R.F.C., C/S, 13/3/17; R.F.C., 19/4/17, R.A.F.; F; Lieut.; D.F.C.
Killed 25/8/18.

BOYCE, Maurice Rant
6/3/8780, 7/1/16; R.E., C/S, 18/11/16; R.E., 10/2/17; F; Lieut.
Bramfield Vicarage, Halesworth, Suffolk.

✠ BOYD, Alexander Charles
K/H/2250, 7/12/14; R. Suss. R., 31/3/15; 2/Lieut.
Killed in action 4/6/16.

APPENDIX II.—RECORDS OF RANK AND FILE.

BOYD, Alexander Kenneth
E/1562, 6/10/14; R.W. Surr. R., 13/11/14; G; Capt.; w.
1 London Wall Buildings, E.C. 2.

BOYD, Lionel Cecil
6/3/9276, 3/2/16; No. 7 O.C.B., 11/8/16; R. Muns. Fus., 18/12/16; Lieut.; w; M(1). Rose Hall, Templesgue, Co. Dublin, Ireland.

BOYD, Martin à Beckett
6/2/7650, 22/11/15; E. Kent R., 4/9/16, att. R.F.C. and R.A.F.; F; Lieut.
c/o. British Australasian, 51 High Holborn, W.C. (Now in Australia.)

BOYER, Thomas Johnson
C/9919, 15/11/16, Sgt.; H. Bde. O.C.B., 6/3/17; Sco. Gds., 29/5/17, R.A.F.; 2/Lieut. The Garth, Westfield, Peterborough.

BOYES, Cecil Edward Cubitt
C/13376, 22/6/18; trfr. 28th Lond. R., 18/10/18.
Gorse Cottage, Haslemere, Surrey.

BOYLE, John Caird Carson
B/11414, 1/6/17; No. 10 O.C.B., 5/10/17; R. Innis. Fus., 26/2/18; 2/Lieut. The Manse, Lisbellow, Co. Fermanagh, Ireland.

BOYLE, Joseph Harold
A/13953, 6/9/18; trfr. Class W. Res., 19/11/18.
13 Latham Road, Twickenham.

BOYLE, Thomas Mulholland
6/4/9277, 3/2/16; No. 7 O.C.B., 11/8/16; R. Ir. Rif., 18/12/16; F; Lieut. 9 Landscape Terrace, Crumlen Road, Belfast.

BOYLE, William Edmund
4/3/5096, 26/7/15; R. Ir. Fus., 20/11/15, att. M.G.C., emp. M. of Labour; F; Lieut.; g.
Broken Hill Station, Northern Rhodesia Police, Northern Rhodesia.

BOYLES, Ernest Edward
D/10912, 26/3/17; R.A., C/S, 10/8/17; R.F.A., 6/1/18; F; Lieut.; w. 84 St. Stephen's Road, Hounslow.

BOYLETT, William Alfred
A/11640, 12/7/17; No. 14 O.C.B., 7/12/17; Midd'x. R., 28/5/18; R.A.F.; 2/Lieut. 46 Brondesbury Road, N.W. 6.

BOYS, Hugh Christopher
6/4/5025, 22/7/15; R.A.S.C., 16/8/15; Capt.; M(1).
Miljord-on-Sea, Lymington, Hampshire.

BOYSE, Vivian Henry
C/11734, 26/7/15; No. 14 O.C.B., 4/1/18; 10th Lond. R., 25/6/18, att. 19th Lond. R.; F; 2/Lieut.; w.
4 Tirlemont Road, Croydon.

BOYT, William Lunn
2/9682, 2/10/16; M.G.C., C/S, 1/2/17; M.G.C., 27/5/17; F,M,I; Staff Capt.; M(1).
c/o. Lond. Cty. West. & Parr's Bank Ltd., 79 High Street, Sidcup, Kent.

BOYTON, Albert Edward
A/14045, 23/9/18; No. 11 O.C.B., 24/1/19; General List, 8/3/19; 2/Lieut.
c/o. British South Africa Coy., 2, London Wall Buildings, E.C.

BRABY, Frederick Cyrus
3/3376, 26/4/15, L/C.; Lan. Fus., 8/7/15, Intelligence; F; Capt.; w(2); M.C., M(1). Slynfolde, Sutton, Surrey.

✠ BRACEY, Victor Charles Edelsten
6/8436, 16/12/15; No. 1 O.C.B., 6/9/16; R.F.C., 16/3/17; 2/Lieut.
Killed 23/9/17.

BRACKEN, Herbert Charles Edwin
6/A/8156, 6/12/15, L/C.; No. 14 O.C.B., 5/7/17; Som. L.I., 30/10/17, R. Fus.; F,NR; Lieut.
5, Carfrae Terrace, Plymouth.

BRADBEER, Benjamin Frank John
6/1/8157, 6/12/15; No. 14 O.C.B., 30/10/16; M.G.C., 30/1/17, Tank Corps; F; Capt.; M.C., M(1).
15 North Parade, Lowestoft, Suffolk.

BRADBEER, Ernest Gustave
A/11589, 5/7/17; No. 14 O.C.B., 9/11/17; Devon. R., 30/4/18, att. Glouc. R.; F; 2/Lieut. Bristol Royal Infirmary, Bristol.

BRADBURY, George Hartley
D/10231, 29/12/16; No. 14 O.C.B., 5/5/17; York. & Lanc. R., 28/8/17; F; Lieut.; w. Tweedside, Milton Road, Lowestoft.

BRADBURY, Raymond Gordon
A/11590, 5/7/17; R.F.C., C/S, 23/10/17; R.F.C., 12/12/17, R.A.F.; 2/Lieut.
Abu-Klea, Pinewold Road, Branksome Park, Bournemouth.

BRADEN, Ronald Eric Noel
E/2812, 29/1/15; R.F.A., 16/8/15; Lieut.
Rosedene, South Woodford, Essex.

BRADEN, William Eric
D/12871, 3/4/18, L/C.; No. 5 O.C.B., 8/11/18, Nos. 20 & 12; Oxf. & Bucks. L.I., 16/3/19; 2/Lieut.
Denehurst, Bois Avenue, Chesham Bois, Bucks.

BRADFIELD, Edmund Louis
4/1/4105, 7/6/15; L'pool. R., 7/10/15, emp. M. of Munitions; Lieut.; w.

BRADFIELD, William Henry
4/9706, 9/10/16; R.F.A., C/S, 20/4/17; R.F.A., 21/9/17; F; Lieut. Guy's Hospital, S.E. 1.

BRADFORD, Christopher Hobart
C/10603, 22/1/17; No. 20 O.C.B., 7/6/17; K.R. Rif. C., 25/9/17; F; 2/Lieut. Flakefield House, Carluke, Lanarkshire.

BRADFORD, Claude Farrant
6/3/6962, 22/10/15, L/C.; No. 11 O.C.B., 7/5/16; Som. L.I., 4/9/16, Glouc. R.; S,E; Lieut.; w.
Alma House, Rugeley, Staffordshire.

BRADFORD, Edouard Jules Gaston
H/2592, 4/1/15; R.G.A., 15/5/15; F; Capt.; g; M(1).
The University, Sheffield.

BRADFORD, Stanley Victor
6/5/7090, 1/11/15, L/C.; No. 11 O.C.B., 7/5/16; North'd. Fus., 4/9/16; F; Capt.; w(3); M.C.
Spring House, New Upperton Road, Eastbourne.

BRADFORD, William Isaac
4/6/2/4918, 19/7/15, L/C.; No. 1 O.C.B., 25/2/16; Midd'x. R., 7/7/16; F; Lieut.; w. 51 Deodar Road, Putney, S.W.

BRADGATE, Lionel
D/1448, 29/9/14; Bedf. R., 14/11/14; Lieut.

BRADLEY, Claude
4/3808, 27/5/15; Shrops. L.I., 20/11/15, Intelligence; E,S; Lieut.
14 Clarence Road, Kew Gardens, Surrey. (Now in Uganda.)

BRADLEY, George Ernest
A./14064, 27/9/18; demob. 10/1/19. Diglis, Worcester.

BRADLEY, George Herbert
B/12697, 8/3/18, L/C.; H. Bde. O.C.B., 9/8/18; trfr. 5th Lond. R., 11/2/19. The Vines, Runcorn, Cheshire.

BRADLEY, Horace Alexander
4/4639, 5/7/15; R.A.S.C., 27/11/15, att. Norf. R.; F; Lieut.; M.C., M(1). East Bradenham, Thetford, Norfolk.

✠ BRADLEY, Horace Walter
6/4/5467, 9/8/15; R.W. Fus., 8/6/16; 2/Lieut.
Killed in action 10/2/17.

BRADLEY, Hubert Frederick
C/Sq/10624, 26/1/17, L/C.; No. 1 Cav. C/S, 31/7/17; R. Regt. of Cav., 22/2/18; 2/Lieut. Gwels, Rhodesia.

BRADLEY, John Francis
6/5/8238, 8/12/15; No. 7 O.C.B., 11/8/16; trfr. R.G.A., 12/1/17; F. Farrangalway, Kinsale, Co. Cork, Ireland.

BRADLEY, Micah Gedling
E/1563, 6/10/14; Rif. Brig., 30/11/14, Midd'x. R., Lab. Corps; Major. Public Schools Club, 19 Berkeley Street, W.

BRADLEY, Michael Lewis Spencer
B/11037, 13/4/17; R.G.A., C/S, 26/9/17; R.G.A., 18/2/18; F; Lieut. The College, Chester.

✠ BRADLEY, Richard
6/5/6572, 1/10/15; R. Lanc. R., 22/1/16; Lieut.
Killed in action 31/7/17.

BRADLEY, William
6/5/7577, 18/11/15; Intelligence Corps, 19/7/16; F; Staff Lieut.; Inv The County School, Whitby, Yorkshire.

BRADSHAW, Alan Darcy
B/12698, 8/3/18; H. Bde. O.C.B., 9/8/18; trfr. 14th Lond. R., 4/1/19. Broadshade, Paignton, Devon.

✠ BRADSHAW, Ernest Edwin
K/E/2394, 17/12/14, L/C.; R.F.A., 26/4/15; F; Lieut.; w(3).
Killed in action 30/9/17.

BRADSHAW, George Lowes Birch
B/12319, 28/12/17, L/C.; No. 22 O.C.B., 7/6/18; R. Scots., 11/2/19; 2/Lieut. 13 Morningside Park, Edinburgh.

APPENDIX II.—RECORDS OF RANK AND FILE.

BRADSHAW, Herbert Randolph
4/5/4786, 12/7/15, L/C.; Yorks. L.I., 12/12/15, emp. M. of Food; F; Lieut.; w.
Lincoln Hall Hotel, Upper Bedford Place, W.C. 1.

BRADSHAW, John Russell
D/12920, 12/4/18; No. 5 O.C.B., 8/11/18, No. 20 O.C.B.; R. Muns. Fus., 17/3/19; 2/Lieut.
National Bank House, Wicklow, Ireland.

BRADSHAW, Stanley Goodwin
B/716, 27/5/13; E. Lan. R., 19/9/14; F; Capt.; M.B.E.
2 Vanbrugh Park, Blackheath, S.E. 3.

BRADSHAW, William Thomas Liggins
B/13480, 8/7/18; No. 22 O.C.B., 23/8/18; R. War. R., 13/2/19; 2/Lieut.
Kroonstad, Orange Free State, South Africa.

✠ BRADSTREET, Lionel Arthur
K/D/2163, 23/11/14; Midd'x. R., 7/5/15; F; 2/Lieut.
Killed in action 1/6/16.

BRADY, James Joseph
6/8999, 19/1/16; dis.
13 Longford Terrace, Monckstown, Co. Dublin.

BRAGG, George Sydney
C/11434, 4/6/17; R.F.C., C/S, 2/8/17; R.F.C., 8/9/17, R.A.F.; F; Lieut.
The Beeches, Keswick, Cumberland.

BRAGG, Roland
6/1/7649, 22/11/15; No. 14 O.C.B.; R. Marines, 24/10/16, att. T.M. Bty.; F; Lieut.
Ash Dene, Church Hill Road, Solihull, nr. Birmingham.

BRAIME, Lewis
B/D/13579, 22/7/18; trfr. 6th R. Regt. of Cav., 11/6/19, 4th Drag. Gds.
Westcourt House, Burbage, Marlborough, Wiltshire.

BRAIN, Edward Robert
4/1/4333, 21/6/15; North'd. Fus., 20/9/15; F; Lieut.; w.
19 Turney Road, Dulwich, S.E. 21.

BRAIN, John Atkins
6/9501, 15/2/16; No. 3 O.C.B., 25/2/16; R. Berks. R., 21/7/16; F; Lieut.; w.
Rostrevie, 60 Elmhurst Road, Reading.

BRAINE, Henry Edward
4/2/4361, 21/6/15; Manch. R., 18/10/15; Lieut.; w.
Mount Avenue, Hutton, Essex.

✠ BRAINE, William Thomas Coker
6/4/8340, 13/12/15, Sgt.; W. Rid. R., 22/6/16; Germ.WA,F; 2/Lieut.
Killed in action 9/10/16.

✠ BRAITHWAITE, James Leslie
Sq/K/2674, 12/1/15, Sgt.; R.F.A., 21/5/15; F; 2/Lieut.
Killed in action 22/7/16.

BRAITHWAITE, John Passmore
4/6/1/7378, 11/11/15; No. 14 O.C.B.; R.N.V.R., 21/11/16, R.A. Chap. D., att. E. York. R.; F; Capt.; M(1).
54 Queen Street, Horncastle, Lincolnshire.

BRAITHWAITE, Thomas Augustus
C/12595, 13/2/18; trfr. 14th Lond. R., 16/12/18, Gord. Highrs.
26 Myddleton Road, Bowes Park, N. 22.

BRAKSPEAR, Harold William Lethbridge
2048, 9/11/14; 16th Lond. R., 26/2/15; F,S,P; Lieut.
14 Cowley Street, Westminster, S.W. 1.

BRAMWELL, Cedric Charles
2/3219, 12/4/15; York. R., 20/8/15; F; Lieut.; w; m.
Dayton House, 17 Elms Road, Clapham, S.W. 4.

✠ BRAMWELL, Norman
C/10578, 19/1/17; No. 20 O.C.B., 7/6/17; Lan. Fus., 25/9/17; F; 2/Lieut.
Killed in action 30/3/18.

BRANCH, Geoffrey Roger
C/11477, 14/6/17; Garr. O.C.B., 5/10/17; R.W. Fus., 15/12/17, att. Ches. R.; F,E; Capt.
59 Kingston Road, Staines.

BRAND, Thomas Norman
6/Sq/8744, 6/1/16; No. 2 Cav. C/S, 5/1/17; R. Reg. of Cav., 30/4/17, att. City of Lond. Yeo.; Lieut.
Bungalow, Ballyholm, Bangor, Co. Down, Ireland.

BRANDER, Alexander George
C/12668, 1/3/18; No. 18 O.C.B., 9/8/18; Gord. Highrs., 6/3/19; 2/Lieut.
1 Virginia Place, Glasgow.

BRANDON, Cyril James
6/5/5740, 20/8/15; Cpl.; trfr. R.G.A., 19/7/16.

✠ BRANDON, Edgar
C/A/D/12043, 27/9/17; R.F.C., C/S, 12/4/18; R.A.F., 12/7/18; F; Lieut.
Killed in action 8-11/8/18.

BRANDON, Gerald
B/A/12311, 17/12/17; No. 22 O.C.B., 7/6/18; R. Fus., 11/2/19; 2/Lieut.
c/o. Mrs. R. Brandon, 11 Burlington Road, Gunnersbury, W.

BRANNON, Allan Cuthbert
6/8303, 11/12/15; A.S.C., C/S, 17/4/16; R.A.S.C., 28/5/16, Tank Corps; Germ.SWA,F; Capt.; w.
Winton Lodge, Stockbridge, Hampshire.

BRANSOM, Walter Henry
D/12093, 8/10/17; dis. med. unfit, 29/1/18.
4 Park Road, Colliers' Wood, Merton, S.W. 19.

BRANSTON, Reginald
A/B/12165, 29/10/17, Sgt.; No. 22 O.C.B., 7/6/18; Suff. R., 12/2/19; 2/Lieut. 122 Gough Road, Edgbaston, Birmingham.

BRASHAW, Arthur Clement
A/11281, 14/5/17; No. 10 O.C.B., 5/10/17; Shrops. L.I., 26/2/18; F; Lieut.; w.
Wortley Vicarage, Sheffield.

BRASS, William Homrigh
6/4/7521, 16/11/15, L/C.; No. 11 O.C.B., 7/5/16; 20th Lond. R., 4/9/16; F; Lieut.; M(1).
Craighall, 262 Willesden Lane, N.W. 2.

BRASSEY, Eustace Charles
A/1302, 26/9/14, Cpl.; 22nd Lond. R., 13/3/15; F,S,P; Capt.; w(2); M.C.
43 Avonmore Road, W. Kensington, W. 14.

BRASSEY, John Eric
D/12898, 8/4/18; R.F.A., C/S, 26/7/18; R.H. & R.F.A., 5/4/19; 2/Lieut.
Curzon Park, Chester.

BRATTON, Allen Basil
Sq/662, 19/11/12, L/C.; Drag. Gds., 14/8/14, N. Lan. R.; F; Capt.; w; D.S.O., M.C., M(1).
32 Westbourne Park Road, W. 2.

✠ BRAY, Aubrey Mellish
K/2788, 26/1/15; R. Berks. R., 25/1/15; Lieut.; M.C.
Died of wounds 8/8/18.

BRAY, Charles
C/13265, 12/6/18; No. 22 O.C.B., 5/7/18; Devon. R., 12/2/19; 2/Lieut.
6 Crown Office Row, Temple, E.C. 4.

BRAY, Frederic Horace Arthur
6/4/7091, 1/11/15; dis. to re-enlist in R.A.M.C., 27/2/16; Sgt.
455 New Cross Road, S.E. 14.

BRAY, Gerald
C/10357, 5/1/17, L/C.; R.G.A., C/S, 15/8/17; R.G.A., 31/12/17; F; Lieut.
566 Caledonian Road, N. 7.

BRAY, Reginald Davies
6/1/9332, 7/2/16, L/C.; No. 13 O.C.B., 4/11/16; Welch. R., 28/2/17; P,E,F; Lieut.; w.
Gadlys, South Road, Porthcawl, S. Wales.

BRAY, Sydney Arthur
F/1797, 16/10/14, L/C.; Essex R., 9/2/15, att. Bedf. R.; G; Capt.
Kotree, Arkwright Road, Sanderstead, Surrey.

BRAYBROOKE, Patrick Philip William
1/3681, 20/5/15; dis. to re-enlist in R. Fus., 13/9/15, R.A.M.C.; F; g.
48 Maple Road, Surbiton, Surrey.

BREACH, William Thomas
Sq/5826, 26/8/15; R.A.S.C., 9/10/15, R.F.C., R.A.F.; G,E,F; Flt. Cmdr.; A.F.C.
c/o. Standard Bank of S. Africa, Bulawayo, Southern Rhodesia, S. Africa.

BREAKELL, James
B/10670, 9/2/17; No. 14 O.C.B., 10/8/17; Manch. R., 27/11/17, att. R. Berks. R.; F; Lieut.; w(2).
106 Gainsborough Avenue, The Coppice, Oldham, Lancashire.

BREAREY, Robert Arthur Victor
2/3755, 27/5/15; E. Surr. R., 2/9/15, att. R.A.F.; F; Lieut.
Springfield, Braddan, Douglas, Isle of Man.

BRECKELL, Harold Stretton
6/5/5919, 1/9/15; L'pool. R., 23/4/16; Lieut.
12 Alexandra Road, Waterloo, Liverpool.

APPENDIX II.—RECORDS OF RANK AND FILE.

BREEN, William Ernest
6/1/8477, 20/12/15; No. 14 O.C.B., 30/10/16; M.G.C., 30/1/17, Tank Corps; Lieut.; w.

BREETHING, William Joseph
4/1/4908, T/17/7/15, Cpl.; York. R., 9/12/15, Indian Army; F,I,P; Capt.
c/o T. Cook & Son, Rangoon, Burma.

BREMNER, Norman Graeme
Sq./764, 16/2/14, L/C.; Cam'n Highrs., 23/1/15; Lieut.
129 Roseberry Road, Muswell Hill, N.

BREN, Robert
B/13481, 8/7/18; demob. 19/2/19.
13 Crystal Palace Park Road, Sydenham, S.E. 26.

BRENAN, Ernest Vivian
6/5/5985, 2/9/15; Herts. R., 4/6/16, secd. W. African Frontier Force; Germ.E&WA; Lieut.
Apapa, Leighton Court Drive, Leigh-on-Sea.

BRENAN, John Fitzgerald
Sq./538, 27/1/11; dis. 16/10/11; Lab. Corps; Capt.
58 St. George's Road, S.W.

✠ BRENNAN, Jeremiah
6/Sq/6647, 7/10/15; Lanc. Huss., 1/12/15; Lieut.
Killed 18/8/18.

BRETT, Edward Bryan
6/1/5875, 30/8/15; R.A.S.C., 27/11/15; Germ.EA; Lieut.; Inv.
Floradale, Flushing, nr. Falmouth, Cornwall.

BREW, Frank Lawrence
A/11208, 7/5/17; No. 12 O.C.B., 10/8/17; Essex R., 27/11/17; F; 2/Lieut.
Augley Farm, Cranbrook, Kent.

BREWER, Francis George
B/Sq/A/10327, 4/1/17, L/C.; R.F.A., C/S, 25/1/18; R.G.A., 22/7/18; 2/Lieut
4 New Quebec Street, Portland Square, W.1.

BREWER, Joseph
Sq/618, 29/2/12; R.A.M.C., 15/8/14 (Lt).
Hatfield, County Gates, Poole Road, Bournemouth.

✠ BREWER, Morris Pascoe
6/5/8449, 17/12/15; dis. med unfit, 27/11/17.   Died 1918.

BREWIN, Sidney
4/6/5/4952, 19/7/15; North'd Fus., 6/7/16, att. Durh. L.I.; F; Lieut.; w(2); M.C. and two Bars.
50 Trafalgar Square, Scarborough.

BREWIS, Leslie Marr
B/1323, 26/9/14; R.W. Kent R., 29/10/14; Lieut.
Sandringham Hotel, Cromwell Road, S. Kensington.

BREWSTER, Gordon David
A/831, 4/8/14; Bedf. R., 19/9/14, R.F.C., R.A.F.; F; Capt.; w(3); M.C., M(1).   3 King's Bench Walk, E.C.

BREWSTER, Henry Sturgeon
6/4/5542, T/9/8/15; K.R. Rif. C., 7/10/15, secd. R.F.C.; F; Lieut.; w.
33 St. Germains Road, Forest Hill, S.E. 23. (Now in Spain.)

✠ BREWSTER, Hugh Percival
K/A/2379, 17/12/14; N. Staff. R., 31/3/15, M.G.C.; 2/Lieut.
Killed in action 9/9/16.

BREWSTER, James Arnold
B/554, 17/3/11, Cpl.; R. Fus., 15/8/14; F; Capt.; w.
Alderden Manor, Sandhurst, Kent.

BREWSTER, Josiah
4/4269, 17/6/15; Norf. R., 7/9/15; F; Lieut.
Akasoa, Hoveton-St. John, Wroxham, Norfolk.

✠ BRIAN, Arthur Gerald
F/K/2677, 12/1/15, Sgt.; D. of Corn. L.I., 20/8/15; Lieut.
Died of wounds 16/10/17.

BRIAN, Frederick Reginald Hugh
4/3/5190, 29/7/15, Sgt.; R.A., C/S, 26/10/16; R.G.A., 5/1/17; F; Lieut.; w.   Holmbury, Berkhamsted, Hertfordshire.

BRIANCE, Bernard Arthur
6/2/5455, 7/8/15; North'd. Fus., 6/7/16, Leic. R.; Lieut.
158 Walm Lane, Cricklewood, N.W.

BRIANT, Alfred Arthur
C/B/12632, 20/2/18; No. 8 O.C.B., 20/9/18; demob.
Shalbourne Mills, Hungerford, Berkshire.

BRIANT, Bruce Edgar Dutton
6/3/7340, 10/11/15; M.G.C., 25/9/16; F.M; Lieut.
12 Compton Road, Brighton.

BRICKDALE, Matthew Fortescue
A/1363, 26/9/14; 8th Lond. R., 7/9/14; Capt.; w.
79 Cromwell Gardens, S.W. 7.

BRIDE, Thomas Joseph
D/A/11816, 9/8/17; A.S.C., C/S, 1/2/18; R.A.S.C., 26/4/18; F; Lieut.
c/o Sir C. R. McGrigor, Bart & Coy., 39 Panton Street, S.W. 1.

BRIDGE, Wallace John
6/2/8917, 14/1/16; No. 5 O.C.B., 14/8/16; R.W. Fus., 21/11/16, Som. L.I.; I; Lieut.
Fernhill, Kirribilli Road, Sydney, Australia.

BRIDGER, Arthur Edward
5/6/7347, 10/11/15; Dorset R., 4/9/16, R.A.S.C.; M,Persia; Capt.   Greywell, Basingstoke, Hampshire.

BRIDGWATER, Arthur John
6/4/7648, 22/11/15, Cpl.; M.G.C.. 25/9/16, R.E.; Lieut.
3 Carlton Road, Sidcup, Kent.

BRIDGWATER, Derrick Lawley
C/11435, 4/6/17, L/C.; No. 14 O.C.B., 4/1/18; R. War. R., 25/6/18; F; 2/Lieut.   Bank House, Dudley, Worcestershire.

BRIER, Albert
6/4/9138, 25/1/16, L/C.; No. 14 O.C.B., 30/10/16; R.A.O.C., 10/12/16; F,E; Lieut.
19 Alexander Road, Ulverston, Lancashire.

✠ BRIERLEY, George Raworth
6/1/7007, 26/10/15; Yorks. L.I., 4/9/16; 2/Lieut.
Died of wounds 9/5/17.

BRIERLEY, Henry Osborne
A/10268, 1/1/17; R.A., C/S, 27/4/17; R.G.A., 1/9/17; F; Lieut.
53 Lavington Road, W. Ealing, W.

BRIERLEY, James
1/9751, 18/10/16; No. 14 O.C.B., 27/12/16; Manch. R., 25/4/17; F; Lieut.; w.   Del Rey House, Cheltenham, Gloucestershire.

BRIGGS, Alan Geoffrey
A/11591, 5/7/17; No. 14 O.C.B., 7/12/17; Arg. & Suth'd. Highrs., 28/5/18; S; 2/Lieut.
Westfield, Kibworth Harcourt, Leicestershire.

BRIGGS, Cyril Ferdinand
6/4/5446, T/7/8/15, L/C.; R.W. Surr. R., 14/11/15, R.A.F.; Lieut.   Villa Monceau, Leighton Buzzard.

✠ BRIGGS, Eric Mackie
6/5/5651, 16/8/15; No. 6 O.C.B., 17/4/16; Lan. Fus., 4/9/16; 2/Lieut.
Killed in action 3/5/17.

BRIGGS, George Grant
2/3682, 20/5/15; E. Surr. R., 2/9/15, att. R.W. Surr. R.; F; Lieut.; Inv.
The Haven, Queen's Road, Weybridge.

BRIGGS, Thomas Arthur
A/10742, 16/2/17; R.F.C., C/S, 16/4/17; R.F.C., 16/5/17.
Bank House, Baildon Green, Shipley, Yorkshire.

BRIGGS, Thomas Fielden
6/1/8952, 17/1/16; R.F.A., C/S, 18/8/16; R.F.A., 24/11/16; F; Lieut.; w.
39 Queen's Road, Wimbledon, S.W. 19.

BRIGGS, Waldo Raven
B/D/769, 2/3/14, C.S.M.; Courts Martial Officer, 16/10/16; F; Staff Capt.; O.B.E., M(2).   2 Garden Court, Temple, E.C. 4.

BRIGHT, John Arthington
K/C/2246, T/4/12/14; R.E. Kent Yeo., 8/2/15, E. Kent R.; Lieut.
5 Hampstead Hill Gardens, Hampstead.

BRIGHT, Leslie Leonard
C/759, 23/1/14; Suff. R., 9/9/14, att. Egyptian Army; Lieut.; w; Order of the Nile 4th Class, M(3).
Westlands, Two-Mile-Ash, Horsham.

BRIGSTOCKE, Charles Reginald
A/217, 11/5/08; dis. 10/5/13.
The Admiralty, Whitehall, S.W. 1.

BRIMELOW, Edward Horrocks
4/5/4640, 5/7/15; No. 1 O.C.B., 25/2/16; 16th Lond. R., 8/7/16, att. Indian Army; F,I; Capt.; w.
Scottsdale, St. Alban's, Hertfordshire.

APPENDIX II.—RECORDS OF RANK AND FILE.

BRIMMELL, Charles Ernest Sydney
6/1/9050, 20/1/16; No. 13 O.C.B., 4/11/16; Worc. R., 28/2/17, War Office; F; Lieut.; w. 17 Stoke Terrace, Devonport.

BRINDLEY, Charles Ernest Bloom
K/A/2113, 16/11/14; Notts. & Derby. R., 20/2/15; F; Capt.; w. 24 Moor Oaks Road, Sheffield.

BRIN-DU-CHATLET, Arthur Leon
6/1/8304, 11/12/15; R.E., 24/6/16. 14 Kendall Avenue, Sanderstead.

✠ BRINSLEY-RICHARDS, Roland Herbert Wyndham
4/3/4016, 7/6/15; W. Rid. R., 10/9/15; F; 2/Lieut. Killed in action 30/7/16.

BRISCOE, Eustace
D/Sq/13659, 29/7/18; demob. 8/1/19. 83 Alexandra Park Road, Muswell Hill, N. 10.

✠ BRISCOE, Henry Whitby
6/5/7792, 24/11/15; No. 7 O.C.B., 11/8/16; R. Ir. Rif., 14/12/16; 2/Lieut. Died 15/4/17.

BRISCOE, John Paul
Sq/3258, 15/4/15; R.A.S.C., 5/7/15; Capt. Greenwood, Kidbrooke Grove, Blackheath, S.E. 3.

BRISLEY, Frank de Bock
4/4174, 14/6/15; North'd. Fus., 23/12/15, Indian Army; F,I,M,S; Lieut. Lurganbrae, Shankill, Co. Dublin, Ireland.

BRISTOW, Claude Robert Alfred
E/1/3009, T/5/2/15, L/C.; R.G.A., 6/8/15; 2/Lieut.

BRITTAIN, John Vincent
C/12613, 18/2/18, L/C.; R.E., C/S, 16/6/18; demob. Bideford, Wolstanton, Stoke-on-Trent.

✠ BRITTEN, Charles Wells
K/Sq/2245, 5/12/14; R.F.A., 5/12/14; Major; w(2); M(1). Killed in action 26/4/17.

BRITTON, Arthur
6/2/7578, 18/11/15; No. 14 O.C.B.; R. Lanc. R., 24/10/16; F; 2/Lieut.; w; M.C. and Bar. 28 Deepdene Road, Denmark Hill, S.E. 5.

BRITTON, Arthur Leonard Morgan
C/12264, 30/11/17, L/C.; R.F.A., C/S, 15/3/18; R.G.A., 3/2/19; 2/Lieut. The Laurels, Westbury-on-Fryn, Bristol.

BRITTON, Harold Wallace
4/4207, 14/6/15; Manch. R., 11/12/15; F; Lieut. One Ash, Cleveland Road, Higher Crumpsall, Manchester.

BRITTON, William Arthur
E/14070, 27/9/18; demob. 10/1/19. Moult Tors, Salcombe, S. Devon.

✠ BROAD, Alfred Evans
K/E/2296, 10/12/14; Dorset R., 8/2/15; Lieut.; M.C., M(1). Died of wounds 2/3/16.

BROADBENT, Gerald
C/Sq/13203, 5/6/18; No. 11 O.C.B., 6/2/19; General List, 8/3/19; 2/Lieut. c/o. T. W. & J. Walker, 38 Basinghall Street, E.C. 3.

BROADBENT, John
A/13989, 11/9/18; demob. 23/1/19. 56 Holdenhurst Avenue, N. Finchley, N. 12.

BROADHURST, Paul
B/10790, 26/2/17; No. 14 O.C.B., 5/7/17; L'pool. R., 30/10/17; 2/Lieut. 13 Belmont, Bath, Somerset.

BROADLEY, Charles Edward Matthew
C/10, 1/4/08; dis. 31/3/11. Ecclesiastical Commission, Millbank, S.W.

BROADLEY, Reginald Spencer
C/14289, 11/11/18; trfr. K.R. Rif. C., 7/4/19. The Dell, 142 Kingsbury Road, Erdington, Birmingham.

BROADMEAD, Harold Hamilton
B/1107, 7/9/14; Som. L.I., 9/10/14; I; Staff Capt., D.A.A. and Q.M.G.; M(1). Enmore Castle, Bridgwater, Somerset.

BROCK, Arthur Gordon
F/2683, 14/1/15; E. Kent R., 24/3/15; F; Lieut.; M.C. Quarry Bank, Belper, Derby.

BROCK, Raymond Sidney
A/11592, 5/7/17; No. 19 O.C.B., 9/11/17; E. Kent R., 26/3/18, att. R.A.F.; 2/Lieut. 21 Harbord Road, Waterloo, Liverpool.

✠ BROCKBANK, Herbert
6/4/6849, T/16/10/15; North'd. Fus., 4/9/16; 2/Lieut. Killed in action 28/4/17.

BROCKBANK, Sydney Rushton
6/5/5892, 30/8/15; No. 1 O.C.B., 25/2/16; Manch. R., 8/7/16; Lieut.

BROCKELBANK, Colin Turner Seymour
6/1/8984, 18/1/16; R.F.A., C/S, 18/8/16; R.G.A., 2/12/16; F; Lieut. Elm Lodge, The Glebe, Blackheath, S.E. 3.

BROCKHURST, George Norman
6/3/7250, 8/11/15; R.F.C., 7/8/16, R.A.F.; F; Lieut.; w-p. c/o. Singleton, Benda & Coy., 27 London Wall, E.C. 2.

BROCKLEBANK, Frank Reginald
3/3375, 26/4/15; Cold. Gds., 7/7/15, emp. Gds. M.G.R.; Lieut.

✠ BROCKMAN, Albert John
6/2/5700, 19/8/15; R. Lanc. R., 31/12/15; F; 2/Lieut. Killed in action 8/8/16.

BROCKMAN, William Dominic
B/871, 4/8/14; 8th Lond. R., 31/10/14; Rif. Brig., M.G.C.; Lieut.; w.

BROCKMAN, William James
E/2717, 18/1/15; Lan. Fus., 23/4/15, att. T.M. Bty.; F; Capt.; w(2); D.S.O., M(1). Meadhill, Meadfoot Road, Torquay.

BROCKWELL, Samuel Gardiner
4/Sq/4128, 10/6/15, Cpl.; Cav. C/S, 20/3/16; N. Ir. Horse, 27/7/16; Lieut.; w-p. 12 Hamilton House, Bishopsgate Street, E.C. 2.

✠ BRODBELT, Arthur Dell
4/1/4175, 14/6/15; R.G.A., 16/9/15; F; Lieut. Died of wounds 18/4/18.

BRODIE, Kenneth
4/3147, 31/3/15, Cpl.; Dorset R., 2/6/15, att. Bedf. R.; F; Lieut.; w(2). 47 Belsize Avenue, N.W. 3.

BRODIE, Thomson
6/3/9182, 28/1/16, Cpl.; No. 14 O.C.B., 30/10/16; High. L.I., 24/1/17; P,F; Lieut. 9 Windsor Terrace West, Kelvinside, Glasgow.

✠ BRODRICK, Eric William
H/1909, 16/10/14; York. R., 13/3/15; 2/Lieut. Died of wounds 22-23/7/16, as Prisoner of War.

BROERS, Alec William
A/12433, 22/1/18; demob. 31/1/19. 52 Ramsbury Road, St. Alban's, Hertfordshire.

BROMLEY, Charles Edward
C/10388, 8/1/17; No. 21 O.C.B., 5/5/17; E. Lan. R., 28/8/17; Lieut. 81 Holmleigh Road, Stamford Hill, N. 16.

BROMLEY, George Patteshall
C/13392, 24/6/18; demob. 27/12/18. Birches Green Farm, Erdington, Birmingham.

BROMMAGE, Joseph Charles
6/1/7092, 1/11/15; No. 8 O.C.B., 4/8/16; R.W. Fus., 21/11/16; 2/Lieut.; w. 141 Wood Road, Pontypridd, S. Wales.

BROMWICH, Charles Thomas
A/14056, 25/9/18; demob. 29/1/19. 44 Sydenham Road, Croydon.

BROMWICH, Frank Curtis
4/5/4830, 13/7/15, L/C.; R.A.S.C., 6/11/15; F; Lieut. 44 Sydenham Road, S. Croydon, Surrey.

BROOK, Charles Herbert
C/13226, 7/6/18; No. 22 O.C.B., 5/7/18; Ches. R., 12/2/19; 2/Lieut. 52 Rusholm Road, Putney Hill, S.W. 15.

BROOK, Derrick Beale
6/3/6513, 30/9/15; R.W. Kent R., 27/12/15; F; Lieut.; w; M.C. Dachurst, Hildenborough, Kent.

BROOKE, Edmund Joseph
B/12863, 26/3/18; trfr. 28th Lond. R., 2/9/18. 80 Gracechurch Street, E.C.

APPENDIX II.—RECORDS OF RANK AND FILE.

BROOKE, Justin
C/11478, 14/6/17; No. 14 O.C.B., 9/11/17; Dorset R., 30/4/18; 2/Lieut. 52 Tavistock Square, W.C.1.

✠ BROOKE, Thomas Wickham
F/1798, 16/10/14; 6th Lond. R., 25/3/15; Capt.; w; M.C. Died of wounds 30/11/17.

BROOKE, Walter Robert
F/1927, 22/10/14; R. Fus., 10/2/15; F; Lieut.; w(2). 15 Bayswater Terrace, Hyde Park, W.

BROOKE-LITTLE, Raymond. See LITTLE R. B.

✠ BROOKER, Leonard Pagden
6/5/8239, 8/12/15; No. 14 O.C.B., 28/8/16; Dorset R., 22/11/16; F; 2/Lieut. Died 13/5/19.

BROOK-GREAVES, Richard Brook
6/2/A/5323, 2/8/15, L/C.; demob. 7/2/19. Rock House, Ecclesfield, nr Sheffield.

BROOKS, Bernard Clifford
H/1887, 16/10/14; R.A.S.C., 8/12/14, Welch R.; F; Capt.; Inv. 48 Parkhill Road, Hampstead, N.W.3.

BROOKS, Eric Sydney Clifford
E/2699, T/9/1/15, L/C.; 12th Lond. R., 11/4/15, Sco. Rif., att. R.A.F.; F; Lieut. 29 Queensgate Terrace, S.W.7.

BROOKS, Harley George
B/12790, 18/3/18; trfr. 28th Lond. R., 26/7/18. 173 Sloane Street, W.

BROOKS, Henry James
F/1792, 16/10/14, Sgt.; Manch. R., 10/12/14; F,It; Major; D.S.O., M.C., Croce di Guerra (Italy), M(2). Odiham, Hampshire.

BROOKS, Hubert
2/9681, 2/10/16; A.S.C., C/S, 26/3/17; R.A.S.C., 21/5/17; E,P,S; Capt. 7 Cresswell Terrace, Sunderland.

BROOKS, John Bernard
6/5/7410, 12/11/15, L/C.; No. 14 O.C.B.; R. Lanc. R., 24/10/16; Lieut.; w. 5 Rossett Road, Great Crosby, Liverpool.

✠ BROOKS, Leonard William
4/6/4953, 19/7/15; Hamps. R., 7/6/16, att. R.F.C.; 2/Lieut. Killed in action 6/7/17.

BROOKS, Walter Samuel
C/11762, 30/7/17; R.F.C., C/S, 23/10/17; R.F.C., 12/12/17, R.A.F.; 2/Lieut. Hutton Grammar School, nr. Preston, Lancashire.

BROOM, James Aleson
6/Sq/D/9104, 24/1/16; trfr. R.G.A., 8/12/16. The Manse, Leuckars, Fifeshire, Scotland.

BROOM, John Russell
C/11763, 30/7/17; R.E., C/S, 7/10/17; R.E., 11/1/18; F; Lieut. Box 3, Brakpan, Transvaal, South Africa.

BROTCHIE, George Herbert Bedford
F/1738, 15/10/14, Sgt.; 12th Lond. R., 25/3/15, R.A.S.C.; F; Capt. The Neuk, Walton-on-Thames.

BROTHERS, Ernest Lynwood
C/12560, 6/2/18, L/C., No. 5 O.C.B., 6/9/18; Midd'x. R., 17/3/19; 2/Lieut. 3 Bruton Street, Bond Street, W.

BROUGH, George Darroll
6/2/7652, 22/11/15; No. 14 O.C.B.; K.R. Rif. C., 24/10/16; F; Lieut.; w. Milton Grange, Arundel Road, Eastbourne.

BROUGHTON, Brian Evelyn Delves
1/6/8745, 6/1/16; R.F.C., 7/8/16, 3rd Lond. R. Doddington, Nantwich, Cheshire.

BROUGHTON, Frederick Albert
C/14257, 1/11/18; trfr. K.R. Rif. C., 7/4/19. 59 Null Hill Lane, Derby.

✠ BROWELL, Henry Herbert
A/1, 1/4/08, dis. 31/3/10.

BROWETT, Joseph Garnett Seymour
B/10875, 15/3/17; No. 14 O.C.B., 5/7/17; R. War. R., 30/10/17; F; 2/Lieut. The Corner House, Solihull, Warwickshire.

✠ BROWN, Angus Graham
6/3/8614, 3/1/16; No. 14 O.C.B., 27/9/16; 20th Lond. R., 18/12/16; Capt. Killed in action 1/9/18.

BROWN, Anthony
Sq/127, 18/4/08; dis. 17/4/11; rej. Sq/711, 6/5/13; 1st Drag. Gds., 16/9/14; F,I,Afghanistan; Lieut.; M.C. 29 Southend Road, Beckenham, Kent.

BROWN, Arthur Cuthbert
C/14236, 28/10/18; demob. 31/1/19. 23 Holmbury View, Upper Clapton, E.5.

✠ BROWN, Arthur Horace Mortimer
4/1/4362, 21/6/15; Manch. R., 18/10/15; F; 2/Lieut. Killed in action 10/7/16.

BROWN, Austin Charles
Sq/125, 18/4/08; dis. 17/4/10; R.F.A., 7/7/16; F; Lieut.; w. Tegwan, Manor Park Road, Chistlehurst, Kent.

BROWN, Benjamin Vernon
D/10848, 7/3/17; R.F.C., C/S, 4/5/17; R.F.C., 14/6/17, R.A.F.; Lieut.; cr. 181 Walmersley Road, Bury, Lancashire.

BROWN, Brian Hougton
D/11183, 3/5/17; Sigs. C/S, 25/8/17; R.E., 22/2/18; F; 2/Lieut.; g. 32 The Avenue, Bedford Park, W.4.

BROWN, Cecil Eastland
6/Sq/5788, 23/8/15; No. 1 Cav. C/S, 24/4/16; Suff. Yeo., 28/7/16, att. S. Wales Bord.; Lieut. Crabbe Hall, Burnham Market, King's Lynn.

BROWN, Charles
D/E/13753, 7/8/18; No. 22 O.C.B., 20/9/18; Manch. R., 14/2/19; 2/Lieut. 1 Chatsworth Road, Chorlton-cum-Hardy, Manchester.

BROWN, Charles Carnegie
Sq/169, 22/4/08; dis. 31/12/09.

BROWN, Clive Lewis
6/3/7242, 7/11/15; Notts. & Derby. R., 15/4/16; Lieut.; w. 7 Musters Road, West Bridgford, Nottinghamshire.

BROWN, Cuthbert Chalmers
K/2889, 9/2/15; R.E., 25/2/15; Lieut.; M(1). 11 Little College Street, Westminster.

BROWN, Donald Houghton
F/1782, 16/10/14; Dorset R., 7/3/15, att. T.M. Bty.; M; Lieut. 66 Inverness Terrace, Hyde Park, W.2.

BROWN, Douglas
Sq/6/6948, 21/10/15, Cpl.; No. 2 Cav. C/S, 31/3/16; Cty. of Lond. Yeo., 19/8/16, Midd'x. Huss., att. R. Fus. and T.M. Bty.; F; Capt.; w(2); M.C. 16 Aldrington Road, Streatham Park, S.W.16.

BROWN, Edgar Peter
C/11506, 18/6/17; No. 19 O.C.B., 9/11/17; R. Highrs., 26/3/18; F; Lieut. The Retreat, Perth Road, Dundee.

BROWN, Edward
6/5/6323, 20/9/15; trfr. Lond. Elec. Eng., 12/5/16; R.E.; F; Lieut.; m. 36 Fitzgeorge Avenue, Kensington, W.14.

BROWN, Eric Edward
Sq/6/7831, 25/11/15; No. 2 Cav. C/S, 1/9/16; 13th R. Regt. of Cav., 20/12/16; Lieut. Doncaster, Hill Lane, Southampton.

BROWN, Ernest John Neville
6/2/D/6058, 6/9/15, L/C.; No. 1 O.C.B., 1/2/17; R.F.C., 12/4/17, R.A.F.; Lieut. Leacroft, Leeside Crescent, Golders Green.

BROWN, Frank Macdonald
D/B/12132, 18/10/17; trfr. 14th Lond. R., 17/12/18, Gord. Highrs. Clydesdale, Crewe, Cheshire.

BROWN, Frederick Norman
6/3/6269, 16/9/15; R.F.A., 14/12/15; F; Capt. Stafford House, Nottingham Road, Melton Mowbray.

✠ BROWN, Geoffrey Hubert
6/1/7761, 23/11/15; No. 8 O.C.B., 4/8/16; Welch. R., 21/11/16; Lieut.; w. Killed in action 23/10/18.

BROWN, Geoffrey William Stephenson
A/1636, 9/10/14; dis. med. unfit, 7/1/16. Sunnyside, Bickley, Kent.

BROWN, George MacCurrach
C/13220, 6/6/18; R.E., C/S, 25/8/18; demob. Forgandenny, Perthshire, Scotland. (Now in Singapore.)

BROWN, Gerald Few
2/3221, 12/4/15; 1st Cty. of Lond. Yeo., 10/8/15, Tank Corps; Capt. Brokes Lodge, Reigate.

105

APPENDIX II.—RECORDS OF RANK AND FILE.

BROWN, *Gerald Hastings*
A/D/13954, 6/9/18; demob. 30/5/19.
       Clydesdale, Crewe, Cheshire.

BROWN, *Harcourt Glyn*
H/2008, 2/11/14; 12th Lond. R., 27/2/15, R.A.S.C., R.G.A.; F; Lieut.; w.
   Villette, Tuddenham Road, Ipswich. (Now in F.M.S.).

BROWN, *Harold Kingsley*
A/11017, 11/4/17; No. 14 O.C.B., 10/8/17; R. Scots., 27/11/17; F; 2/Lieut.   *65 Braid Road, Edinburgh.*

✠ BROWN, *Harry Cliff*
5/1/6936, 20/10/15; No. 7 O.C.B., 3/7/16; R. Marines, 24/10/16; F; 2/Lieut.   *Killed in action 17/2/17.*

BROWN, *Henry Wilfrid*
6/1/9049, 20/1/16, L/C.; No. 14 O.C.B., 26/11/16; R.W. Surr. R., 28/2/17; I,M; Capt.   *Cottingham, Cintra Avenue, Reading.*

✠ BROWN, *Horace Leslie*
B/10322, 4/1/17; No. 14 O.C.B., 7/6/17; E. Kent R., 25/9/17; 2/Lieut.   *Died of wounds 11/3/18.*

BROWN, *Ian Alexander*
C/12265, 30/11/17, L/C.; No. 10 O.C.B., 10/5/18; R. Scots., 3/2/19; 2/Lieut.
    36 Carless Avenue, Harborne, Birmingham.

BROWN, *James*
6/3/8615, 3/1/16; R.F.A., C/S, 4/8/16; R.G.A., 12/11/16; F; Capt.; M.C., M(2).
    H.M. Borstal Institution, Feltham, Middlesex.

BROWN, *James Alexander Melville*
C/12636, 22/1/18; No. 22 O.C.B., 7/6/18, No. 11 O.C.B.; General List, 8/3/19; 2/Lieut.
    231 Edgecombe Avenue, New York City, U.S.A.

✠ BROWN, *James Cavet*
1/9756, 18/10/16; No. 14 O.C.B., 27/12/16; Arg. & Suth'd. Highrs., 27/3/17; F; 2/Lieut. *Wounded and Missing, 24/3/18.*

BROWN, *James Cross*
D/1451, 29/9/14; R.A.S.C., 9/11/14; E,P; Lt.-Col.; D.S.O., M(4)
       87 Cannon Street, E.C. 4.

BROWN, *James Leonard*
C/11764, 30/7/17, L/C.; R.F.C., C/S, 30/10/17; R.F.C., 17/12/17, R.A.F.; F; Flt. Cmdr.   *Wick Court, nr. Bristol.*

BROWN, *James MacLeod.* See MacLEOD-BROWN, J.

BROWN, *James Tawse*
D/12103, 11/10/17; M.G.C., C/S, 25/1/18; Tank Corps, 8/10/18; 2/Lieut.   *34 Thomson Street, Dundee.*

BROWN, *John Duncan*
D/12102, 11/10/17; Garr. O.C.B., 8/3/18; Lab. Corps, 4/9/18; 2/Lieut.
   c/o. Crown Agents for the Colonies, 4 Millbank, S.W. 1.

✠ BROWN, *John Edward*
6/8451, 17/12/15; R.F.A., C/S, 9/6/16; R.F.A., 8/9/16; Capt.
       Killed in action 14/9/18.

BROWN, *John Redvers*
B/12802, 20/3/18; No. 2 O.C.B., 20/9/18; North'd. Fus., 14/2/19; 2/Lieut.   *The Hollies, Guilsborough, Northampton.*

BROWN, *John Robert*
B/E/13561, 19/7/17; No. 22 O.C.B., 20/9/18; North'n. R., 17/3/19; 2/Lieut.   *The Rectory, Portsoy, Banffshire, N.B.*

BROWN, *John Spencer*
C/9797, 27/10/16; trfr. Leic. Yeo., 2/2/17.
      Northfields, Belgrave, Leicester.

BROWN, *Leonard Theodore*
K/6/D/2845, 1/2/15; trfr. 8th Lond. R., 26/2/17, 12th Lond. R., R. Fus., att. Intelligence Corps; F; Pte.
      39 Herne Hill Road, S.E. 24.

BROWN, *Leslie Ewart*
4/4531, 1/7/15, L/C.; North'd. Fus., 23/4/16; F; Lieut.
    Tregarthen House, Wimborne, Dorset.

BROWN, *Montagu Wilhelm*
A/1378, 26/9/14; R.E., 16/11/14; F,It; Lt.-Col.; O.B.E., Italian Orders of Maurice and Lazarus and Croce di Guerra, M(4).
Cordoba Central Railway Coy., Buenos Aires, South America.

BROWN, *Reginald Frederick*
B/9902, 13/11/16; No. 14 O.C.B., 6/4/17; R. Suss. R., 31/7/17, att. R.W. Surr. R.; F; Lieut.; Inv.
    Ivanhoe, 8 Lancaster Villas, Brighton.

BROWN, *Richard Charles*
6/8265, 9/12/15; R.F.A., C/S, 26/5/16; R.G.A., 30/8/16, emp. M. of Labour; Lieut.   *34, Holyoake Walk, Ealing.*

BROWN, *Richard Hamilton*
6/8501, 21/12/15; No. 9 O.C.B., 8/3/16; High. Div. Cyc. Coy., 3/8/16, att. Essex Yeo. and 16th Lond. R.; F; Lieut.
    18 Wilson Street, Hillhead, Glasgow.

BROWN, *Robert Charles*
B/10977, 2/4/17, L/C.; R.F.A., C/S, 17/12/17; R.H. & R.F.A., 3/6/18; F; 2/Lieut.
    Mount Pleasant, Upton, Macclesfield.

BROWN, *Stanley*
1/A/9633, 25/9/16; R.A.O.C., 2/1/17; F; Lieut.
    Fairholm, Freta Road, Bexley Heath, Kent.

BROWN, *Sydney Clifford*
B/A/D/11975, 10/9/17; R.E., C/S, 14/4/18; R.E., 15/8/18; 2/Lieut.   *Heather Bank, Albany Walk, Ilkley, Yorkshire.*

BROWN, *Sydney Temple*
C/D/12080, 4/10/17; No. 8 O.C.B., 7/6/18; Notts. & Derby. R., 5/2/19; 2/Lieut.   *Old School House, Breaston, Derby.*

✠ BROWN, *Sylvester Samuel*
6/4/5876, 30/8/15; 9th Lond. R., 22/9/15, att. M.G.C.; Lieut.; M.C. and Bar.   *Killed in action 25/4/18.*

✠ BROWN, *Theodore Anthony*
Sq/583, 20/11/11; Drag. Gds., 15/8/14, E. Kent. R.; F; Capt.; M.C.   *Killed in action 15/4/17.*

BROWN, *Thomas Gilbert*
4/3/4416, 24/6/15, Sgt.; W. Rid. R., 26/10/15; F; Capt.; w; M.C.   *West View, Clitheroe, Lancashire.*

BROWN, *Thomas Hugh Maldwyn*
C/11479, 14/6/17; R.F.C., C/S, 2/8/17; R.F.C., 8/9/17, R.A.F., att. R.N.A.S.; Submarine Patrol; Flt. Cmdr.; cr.
  7 Short Bridge Street, Newtown, Montgomeryshire.

BROWN, *Victor Cumberledge*
4/3/4450, 28/6/15; dis. med unfit, 22/5/16.
      17 Westbourne Square, W. 2.

BROWN, *Walter Hafford*
C/11687, 19/7/17; demob. 29/1/19.
      39 St. Peter's Road, Leicester.

✠ BROWN, *Walter Ravenhill*
6/4/D/8852, 11/1/16, L/C.; No. 14 O.C.B., 30/10/16; W. York. R., 24/1/17; Lieut.; M.C.   *Killed in action 21/11/17.*

BROWN, *William*
B/9895, 10/11/16; No. 14 O.C.B., 6/4/17; Lan. Fus., 31/7/17; F; Lieut. *64 Grosvenor Road, Handsworth, Birmingham.*

BROWN, *William Ernest*
F/3/2890, 9/2/15; S. Wales Bord., 1/6/15, Welch. R.; F; Lt.-Col.; w; D.S.O., M.C. and Bar, M(2).
    Brantwood, Dee Banks, Chester.

BROWN, *William Henry*
3/3339, 22/4/15; R.E., 7/7/15; E,S; Lieut.; M.C.
    Glaslyn, Western Road, Sutton, Surrey.

BROWN, *Alexander*
4/3626, 17/5/15; S. Lan. R., 30/9/15, R. Dub. Fus., Ches. R.; E,F; Capt.; w.   *99 Victoria Street, Grimsby.*

BROWNE, *Arthur Wentworth*
6/2/5324, 2/8/15; dis. med. unfit, 22/5/16.
   1 Portland Court, Great Portland Street, W.

BROWNE, *Bernard Walter*
B/13459, 5/7/18; demob. 23/1/19.
      3 St. Leonard's Place, Exeter.

BROWNE, *Edgar Dennis*
D/10880, 16/3/17; trfr. R.F.A., 23/6/17.
    29 Claremont Road, Forest Gate, Essex.

BROWNE, *Francis George*
6/5/7251, 8/11/15; R.A., C/S, 14/7/16; R.G.A., 4/10/16; Lieut.
    29 Claremont Road, Forest Gate, E. 7.

BROWNE, *George Hall*
B/11976, 10/9/17; R.E., C/S, 4/11/17; R.E., 22/2/18; F; 2/Lieut.; M.C.
  3350 Echeverria, Belgrano, Buenos Aires, Argentina.

APPENDIX II.—RECORDS OF RANK AND FILE.

✠ BROWNE, Herbert Maxwell
K/C/2189, 26/11/14; Essex R., 12/1/15; 2/Lieut.
Killed in action 26/3/17.

BROWNE, Hubert Warner
4/6/4992, 19/7/15; 11th Lond. R., 25/1/16; relinquished commission 11/5/16; enlisted in R.E. and M.G.C.; F; L/Cpl.; Inv.
c/o. Weigall & Crowther, 459 Chancery Lane, Melbourne, Australia.

BROWNE, Hugh Gillespie
Sq/119, 18/4/08; dis. 31/12/09.
Bornhill, Hagesland, Bromley, Kent.

BROWNE, James Stark
4/3/3937, 3/6/15; R.N.A.S., 19/7/15, R.A.F.; G,E; Capt.; A.F.C., M(1).
c/o. London County Westminster & Parrs Bank, Ltd., 217 Strand, W.C.2.

BROWNE, Leonard
A/B/D/12180, 1/11/17; No. 9 O.C.B., 10/5/18; Bord. R., 5/2/19; 2/Lieut. 8 Hensingham Road, Whitehaven, Cumberland.

BROWNE, Percy Edward
C/12307, 14/12/17; R.E., C/S, 14/4/18; R.E., 15/8/18; 2/Lieut.
Flat 3, 12 Holland Road, Hove, Sussex.

✠ BROWNE, Peter
6/5/8240, 8/12/15; No. 7 O.C.B., 11/8/16; Conn. Rang., 18/12/16; 2/Lieut. Killed in action 1/10/18.

BROWNE, Reginald Douglas Heygate
E/14002, 13/9/18; demob. 10/1/19.
The Shrubbery, Barnham, Bognor.

BROWNE, Richard Danton
4/5/4733, 12/7/15; North'd. Fus., 2/10/15, K. Af. Rif.; F,It,EA; Lieut.; w. Union Castle Line, 3 Fenchurch Street, E.C. 2.

BROWNE, Robert Steele
D/11817, 9/8/17; No. 14 O.C.B., 7/12/17; Arg. & Suth'd. Highrs., 28/5/18; F; 2/Lieut. Ard Calin, Sligo, Ireland.

BROWNE, Travers Stewart
C/12596, 13/2/18; R.E., C/S, 12/5/18; R.E., 27/9/18; F; 2/Lieut.; w. 89 Lexington Avenue, New York City, U.S.A.

BROWNE, Walter Marshall
B/13412, 1/7/15; demob. 23/1/19. Bramcote, Nottinghamshire.

✠ BROWNE, William Denis
B/1102, 7/9/14; R. Naval Bde., 14/9/14; 2/Lieut.
Killed 7/6/15.

BROWNELL, Reginald Samuel
B/D/12021, 20/9/17; No. 20 O.C.B., 5/4/18; M.G.C., 8/10/18; 2/Lieut. 7 Botanic Road, Glasnevin, Dublin. (Now in Egypt.)

BROWNING, Charles Robert
4/1/4510, 28/6/15; R.W. Surr. R.; 3/10/15; F; Lieut.; w.
Boxgrove, 17 Park Lane, Wallington, Surrey.

BROWNING, Robert Campbell
C/13278, 14/6/18; No. 22 O.C.B., 23/8/18; R. Suss. R., 13/2/19; 2/Lieut. Wineham Hall, Enfield, Sussex.

BROWNING, Robert Gann
6/2/5616, 16/8/15, Sgt.; No. 11 O.C.B., 7/5/16; North'd. Fus., 4/8/16; F; Capt.; w(2). 64 Drayton Park, Highbury, N. 5.

BROWNLIE, William Crichton
4/3/4412, 24/6/15; Gord. Highrs., 3/12/15; F; Staff Capt.; M.C., M(2). Ivy Cottage, Fauldhouse, Linlithgowshire.

✠ BROWNRIGG, Thomas
3/3151, 1/4/15; Midd'x. R., 21/6/15, R.A.F.; F; Lieut.
Drowned 21/8/18.

BRUCE, Harold Eric Warren
A/12538, 5/2/18; L/C.; No. 2 O.C.B., 7/6/18; Arg. & Suth'd. Highrs., 6/2/19; 2/Lieut. 25 Calais Street, Camberwell, S.E. 5.

BRUCE, Hugh Edward Brice
A/14095, 4/10/18; No. 11 O.C.B., 24/1/19; General List, 8/3/19; 2/Lieut.
c/o. National Bank of South Africa, London Wall, E.C. 2.

BRUCE, John Purvis
6/5/5363, 4/8/15, Cpl.; Manch. R., 2/12/15; F; Lieut.; w.
56 Oxford Street, Manchester.

BRUCE, Walter
6/5/5242, 31/7/15; L'pool. R., 13/12/15, R.F.C., R.A.F.; F; Flt. Cmdr.; w; A.F.C. 13 Montpellier Crescent, New Brighton.

BRUCE-AUSTIN, Francis Preston
Sq/3412, 29/4/15; R.F.A., 8/10/15, R.A.F.; Lieut.
9 Hartington Mansions, Eastbourne.

BRUCE-MAJOR, Lancelot
6/4/5617, 16/8/15; R.A.S.C., 6/11/15, Manch. R.; Lieut.
5 Bessborough Street, S.W.

✠ BRUDENELL-BRUCE, James Ernest John
C/1142, 14/9/14; North'n. Yeo., 9/12/14; F; Lieut.
Died of wounds 11/4/17.

BRUFORD, Edward Jeffries
C/14246, 30/10/18; trfr. K.R. Rif. C., 7/4/19.
Nerrols, Taunton, Somerset.

BRUNDRETT, Walter
B/12414, 18/1/18; R.E., C/S, 21/7/18; demob.
Lacton Hall, Willesborough, Kent.

BRUNDRIT, Daniel Fernley
6/3/8616, 3/1/16; No. 14 O.C.B., 30/10/16; M.G.C., 30/1/17, Tank Corps; 2/Lieut.; w-p. Fir Grove, Frodsham, Cheshire

BRUNNER, George Kenehn
B/259, 25/5/08; dis. 24/5/09.

BRUNT, Frank
4/3809, 27/5/15; Durh. L.I., 10/1/16; F; Capt.; w(2).
18 Abbey Road, Oxford.

✠ BRUNT, Henry John Francis
K/B/2225, 3/12/14, Cpl.; R.W. Fus., 13/3/15; Lieut.
Killed in action 25/9/15.

BRUNTON, Albert Howard
4/3/4065, 7/6/15; R.G.A., 10/9/15; Lieut.
30 Westbourne Terrace, Hyde Park, W. 2.

BRUNTON, George Delta
Sq/3587, 13/5/15, L/C.; R.F.A., 2/9/15; F; Lieut.; w.
Craiglearan, Moniaive, Dumfrieshire.

BRUNTON, William Alexander
5920, 1/9/15; trfr. R.G.A., 28/7/16.
Sandycroft, Blundellsands.

BRUORTON, Harry Russell
6/4/8821, 10/1/16; dis. to re-enlist in K.R. Rif. C., 19/5/16; F; Pte. Mazunga, Messina, Northern Transvaal, South Africa.

BRUTEY, Clarence Robert
6/1/9056, 21/1/16; No. 8 O.C.B., 4/8/16; Yorks. L.I., 18/12/16; Lieut. Carmel View, Wadebridge, Cornwall.

BRYAN, Augustus Hugh
A/D/11969, 6/9/17; R.E., C/S, 13/3/18; R.E., 12/7/18; 2/Lieut.
6 Cliveden Place, Eaton Square, S.W. 1.

BRYAN, John Maurice
3/Sq/3293, 19/4/15, L/C.; No. 1 Cav. C/S, 24/4/16; Norf. Yeo., 28/7/16, Norf. R.; E,P,F; Capt.
Guyhirne, Ampthill, Bedfordshire.

BRYANT, Arthur Gilbert
Sq/1227, 16/9/14, L/C.; R.A.S.C., 13/4/15, Tank Corps; E,F; Major; M.C., M(1). Chelwood, St. John's, Tunbridge Wells.

BRYANT, Eric John
A/C/12501, 29/1/18; No. 14 O.C.B., 7/6/18; Arg. & Suth'd. Highrs., 5/2/19; 2/Lieut.
Sydney Cottage, 19 Wolseley Road, Wealdstone.

BRYANT, Frank Venning
6/5/8013, 30/11/15; R.F.C., 25/9/16, R.A.F.; Lieut.
22 Diamond Avenue, Plymouth.

BRYANT, Frederick George
4/5/4877, 15/7/15, L/C.; R.E., 20/10/15; F; Lieut.; M.C.
Lynwood, 143 Preston Road, Brighton.

BRYANT, Gerard King
B/11688, 19/7/17; trfr. 28th Lond. R., 24/9/17.
c/o. Bryant & Coy., Newcastle-on-Tyne.

BRYANT, John
6/2/6902, 18/10/15; R.A.S.C., 24/1/16; Lieut.
5 High Street, Broadstairs.

APPENDIX II.—RECORDS OF RANK AND FILE.

BRYANT, John Wilkin
4/2/5097, 26/7/15; Suff. R., 25/9/16, R. Berks. R., Lab. Corps; F; Capt.
11 Victoria Road, Wrexham, N. Wales. (Now in Canada.)

BRYANT, William Harold
6/2/8014, 30/11/15, Cpl.; Mon. R., 22/11/16, att. Shrops. L.I. and R. War. R.; F; Lieut.; w.
3 Rochester Road, Newport, Monmouthshire.

BRYCE, Walter Colin
6/5/5745, T/21/8/15; R.F.A., C/S, 31/3/16; R.F.A., 12/8/16; Lieut.
11 Pilkington Road, Southport, Lancashire.

BRYDEN, Frank
D/10872, 14/3/17; No. 14 O.C.B., 10/8/17; S. Staff. R., 27/11/17, att. Notts. & Derby. R.; F; Lieut.
1 Crown Court, Chancery Lane, W.C.2.

BRYDON, Walter Dalgliesh
D/11854, 13/8/17; A.S.C., C/S, 12/11/17; R.A.S.C., 6/1/18; F,S.Russia; 2/Lieut.
6 Mitre Court, Milk Street, E.C.

BRYERS, George
4/1/6/5191, 29/7/15; N. Lan. R., 6/1/16; F; Lieut.
Lucerne, St. Andrews Road South, St. Annes-on-Sea, Lancs.

BRYSON, John
D/13691, 31/7/18, L/C.; demob. 3/3/19.
24 West Woodstock Street, Kilmarnock, N.B.

BUCHAN, John Marsh
B/11385, 30/5/17; A.S.C., C/S, 1/11/17; R.A.S.C., 25/1/18; F; 2/Lieut.
1 Ferndale, Teignmouth, Devon.

BUCHANAN, George William Carter
A/10289, 1/1/17; R.G.A., C/S, 25/4/17; R.G.A., 19/8/17; 2/Lieut.
Worcester Lodge, 23 Langroyd Road, Upper Tooting.

BUCHANAN, Harold George
4/3259, 15/4/15; Devon R., 4/9/16, att. R. Berks. R.; F,It; Lieut.
Colne House, Brantham, nr. Manningtree, Essex.

BUCHANAN, Ronald Gray
Sq/229, 15/5/08; dis. 14/5/12; E. African Rif., 21/12/14, Cold. Gds.; EA,F; Capt.; Inv.
c/o. C. J. Hambro & Son, 70 Old Broad Street, E.C.

✠ BUCK, Charles
4/4037, 7/6/15; R. War. R., 17/10/15, R. Berks. R.; Capt.
Killed in action, 15/5/18.

BUCK, Charles Frederick
E/1604, 6/10/14, Sgt.; Bedf. R., 24/7/15; E,P; Capt.; w.
93 Finchley Road, N.W.8.

BUCK, Harry
C/13198, 4/6/18; R.E., C/S, 25/8/18; demob.
Jellygron, Caerleon, Newport, Monmouthshire.

BUCK, Hugh Decimus
D/10436, 10/1/17, L/C.; No. 14 O.C.B., 7/6/17; Hunts. Cyc. Bn., 25/9/17, Household Bn., secd. M.G.C.; F; Lieut.
141 Park Lane, Wallington, Surrey.

BUCK, Wilfred James
D/2576, 4/1/15; R. War. R., 3/4/15, secd. M.G.C.; F,S,P; Lieut.; w.
The Crofts, Horbury, nr. Wakefield.

BUCKBARROW, Harold
6/1/8305, 11/12/15; No. 2 O.C.B., 14/8/16; M.G.C., 30/11/16, Tank Corps; Lieut.

BUCKELL, Francis Richard Molineux
C/14195, 21/10/18; trfr. K.R. Rif. C., 7/4/19.
Stonecroft, Maldon, Essex.

BUCKHAM, Sydney Ernest
B/12823, 22/3/18, Sgt.; trfr. K.R. Rif. C., 13/5/19; C.S.M.
10 Creighton Road, Brondesbury Park, N.W.6.

BUCKINGHAM, Thomas Herbert
6/2/9080, 24/1/16; No. 14 O.C.B., 26/11/16; E. Kent R., 28/2/17, att. R. War. R. and R. Suss. R.; F; Lieut.; w.
Laudkey, Barnstaple, Devon.

BUCKLAND, Charles John
4/6/5/4839, 15/7/15; R.G.A., 10/8/15; F; Capt.; Inv.
112 St. James Street, Brighton.

BUCKLAND, Sidney Lawrence
6/2/7434, 15/11/15, L/C.; No. 11 O.C.B., 7/5/16; Welch. R., 4/9/16; F; Lieut.
Sunninghill, Sketty Avenue, Swansea

BUCKLE, Noel
B/12803, 20/3/18; No. 20 O.C.B., 20/9/18, No. 11 O.C.B.; demob.
58 Campden Hill Court, Kensington, W.

BUCKLE, Robert Harold
4/3/4413, 24/6/15; Durh. L.I., 21/12/15; 2/Lieut.
28a Nevern Place, S.W.5.

BUCKLEY, The Honble. Bryan Burton
A/1068, 2/9/14; 12th Lond. R., 21/10/14; Lieut.
7 Melbury Road, W.14.

BUCKLEY, Francis
1/3531, 10/5/15, L/C.; North'd. Fus., 6/7/15; F; Capt.; w; M(1).
Tunstead, Greenfield, Yorkshire.

BUCKLEY, James Reginald
A/10067, 1/12/16; R.A., C/S, 20/4/17; R.G.A., 31/7/17; Lieut.
39 Plymouth Road, Penarth.

BUCKLEY, John George Ernest
B/11033, 13/4/17; No. 12 O.C.B., 10/8/17; Leic. R., 27/11/17; 2/Lieut.
St. Andrews, Kimberley Road, Leicester.

BUCKLEY, Richard Charles
6/2/9268, 3/2/16; R.A., C/S, 15/9/16; R.G.A., 26/11/16; F; Lieut.; g.
76 Aldborough Road, Seven Kings, Essex.

BUCKMASTER, Henry Stephen Guy
Sq/386, 24/3/09; dis. 30/11/10; Oxf. & Bucks. L.I., 21/9/14; F,Siberia; Major; O.B.E.; Inv.
3 New Square, Lincoln's Inn, W.C.2.

BUCKNALL, Silvio Paul Bernini de Moyse
K/Sq/2207, 30/11/14; Hamps. Yeo., 17/3/15, att. 6th Drag., R. Fus.; Lieut.
Hawthorne Dene, Bonchurch, Isle of Wight.

BUCKNER, Cedric Stanley
B/11336, 21/5/17; No. 11 O.C.B., 9/11/17; Indian Army, 26/3/18.
Taunton School, Taunton.

BUCKNILL, Alfred Townsend
B/1263, 23/9/14; Surr. Yeo., 4/11/14; F,E; Major, D.A.A.G.; O.B.E.
2 Paper Buildings, Temple, E.C.4.

BUCKTON, Percy
A/11292, 16/5/17; No. 19 O.C.B., 9/11/17; R. Fus., 30/4/18; F; 2/Lieut.
5 Ashwood Villas, Headingley, Leeds.

BUCKWORTH, John Francis
D/12899, 8/4/18; No. 11 O.C.B., 4/10/18; demob.
Thorney, nr. Peterborough.

BUDDERY, Harold Martins
4/4489, 28/6/15, Sgt.; W. York. R., 4/6/16; F; Lieut.
57 Southtown, Great Yarmouth.

BUDDS, Arthur Bernard
A/13110, 24/5/18; No. 5 O.C.B., 8/11/18, No. 20 O.C.B.; Yorks. L.I., 17/3/19; 2/Lieut.
140 Nottingham Street, Sheffield.

BUDGE, John Stuart
C/13349, 26/6/18; demob. 29/1/19.
112 High Street, Boston, Lincolnshire.

BUDGEN, John Percy
6/5/7795, 24/11/15; No. 14 O.C.B., 28/8/16; M.G.C., 28/12/16; F; Lieut.
Rosemead, Croham Road, South Croydon.

BUFFEY, William
B/12367, 4/1/18; R.F.A., C/S, 15/3/18; R.G.A., 12/2/19; 2/Lieut.
54 Wearside Road, Lewisham, S.E.

BUGBIRD, Alfred William Cyril
A/12456, 23/1/18, L/C.; No. 5 O.C.B., 8/11/18, No. 20 O.C.B.; L'pool. R., 17/3/19; 2/Lieut.
21 Gloucester Street, S.W.1.

BUGDEN, Gerald Tomlin
B/12849, 25/3/18; No. 18 O.C.B., 20/9/18; E. Kent R., 18/3/19; 2/Lieut.
23 Alexandra Road, S. Margate.

BUGG, Edmund Preston
D/10924, 26/3/17; No. 11 O.C.B., 5/7/17; Essex R., 30/10/17; F; 2/Lieut.; w.
3 Park View Gardens, Grays, Essex.

✠ BUGLER, Leonard Hallett
B/10704, 12/2/17; No. 11 O.C.B., 5/7/17; Glouc. R., 30/10/17; F; 2/Lieut.; w.
Died of wounds 2/4/18.

BUISSERET, Edmund Joseph
6/2/6385, 23/9/15; R.F.A., C/S, 31/3/16; R.G.A., 2/8/16, att. R.E.; F,It; Lieut.; g; French Croix de Guerre, M(1).
St. Joseph's, Totland Bay, Isle of Wight.

BUISSERET, Louis Joseph Victor
C/D/12308, 14/12/17; No. 3 O.C.B., 10/5/18; trfr. 28th Lond. R., 25/8/18; F; Pte.; Inv.
St. Joseph's, Totland Bay, Isle of Wight.

APPENDIX II.—RECORDS OF RANK AND FILE.

BULEY, Douglas MacPherson
6/2/6007, 2/9/15; 3rd Lond. R., 24/12/15; F; Lieut.; w.
17 Spencer Road, S. Croydon, Surrey.

BULFORD, Lewin
6/1/6386, 23/9/15; S. Lan. R., 9/6/16; F; Lieut.
Rosemary Lodge, Cranes Park, Surbiton, Surrey.

BULKELEY, Thomas D'Oyly (Junr.)
6/1/6270, 16/9/15; dis. med. unfit, 31/12/15.
5 Heathcote Road, St. Margarets-on-Thames.

BULKLEY-BYNG, David George
K/2375, 17/12/14; E. Surr. R., 31/3/15; F; Lieut.
80 Hamlet Gardens, Ravenscourt Park, W.6.

BULL, Arthur Gilbert
6/7860, 26/11/15; R.F.A., C/S, 26/5/16; R.G.A., 18/8/16; Capt.

BULL, Arthur Herbert
A/10509, 15/1/17; No. 14 O.C.B., 7/6/17; Notts. & Derby. R., 25/9/17, 25th Lond. R.; F,It,I,Persia; Lieut.; M(1).
Redclyffe, Halton Park, Wellingborough, Northamptonshire.

BULL, Edward George
C/12637, 22/2/18, L/C.; No. 11 O.C.B., 9/8/18; General List, 8/3/19; 2/Lieut.
c/o. Rawes & Coy., Ruada Nona, Alfandega, Oporto, Portugal.

BULL, Frederick James
B/10570, 15/1/17; R.F.C., C/S, 13/3/17; R.F.C., 19/4/17, R.A.F.; Lieut.
50 Florence Road, Wimbledon, S.W.19.

BULL, Henry Cecil H.
B/1074, 2/9/14; Yorks. L.I., 19/9/14, 21st Lond. R.; Lieut.; w; M.C.

BULL, Kenneth Burkitt
B/12824, 22/3/18; No. 6 O.C.B., 6/9/18; R. Berks. R., 16/3/19; 2/Lieut.
27 School Lane, Kettering.

✠ BULL, Percival John
6/1/6501, 28/9/15; R. Fus., 28/1/16; 2/Lieut.; w.
Killed in action 7/10/16.

BULL, Philip Cecil
C/1061, 31/8/14; Suff. R., 19/9/14; F; Major; D.S.O., M(3).
27 Launceston Place, Kensington, W.8.

BULL, Walter Richard John
D/10258, 29/12/16; trfr. R.G.A., 14/2/17; R.G.A., 8/2/19; F; 2/Lieut.
3 Templars Avenue, Golders Green, N.W.

✠ BULL, Wilfred Herbert
B/888, 5/8/14; Bedf. R., 12/9/14; Capt.; w.
Killed in action 3/5/17.

BULL, William George
C/12597, 13/2/18; No. 19 O.C.B., 5/7/18; trfr. 28th Lond. R., 7/10/18.
34 Mount Road, Hendon.

BULLARD, Cecil Austin
6/1/5550, 12/8/15; trfr. 14th Lond. R., 2/5/16; F,S,P,E; Pte.
54 Vesta Road, Brockley, S.E.4.

BULLEN, Brian William
B/13546, 17/7/18; No. 11 O.C.B., 24/1/19; General List, 8/3/19; 2/Lieut.
Welgemoed, P.O. Belville, nr. Capetown, Cape Province, South Africa.

BULLEN, Frederick John
6/8619, 3/1/16; R.F.A., C/S, 26/5/16; R.G.A., 30/8/16; Lieut.
48 Norland Square, Holland Park, W.

✠ BULLER, Richard Francis Montagu
A/412, 5/5/09; Midd'x. R., 9/11/11; Capt.; w.
Killed in action 24/8/18.

BULLER, William John
D/12992, 29/4/18; No. 16 O.C.B., 18/10/18; R. Ir. Rif., 17/3/19; 2/Lieut.
Loughbuckland, Co. Down, Ireland.

BULLMORE, Francis Edward
6/1/5827, 26/8/15; No. 1 Cav. C/S, 2/8/16; Oxf. Huss., 27/11/16; Lieut.
Tennyson Avenue, King's Lynn.

BULLOCK, Charles
4/3/4270, 17/6/15; Shrops. L.I., 10/9/15; M.G.C.; Lieut.

BULLOCK, Dennis Argent
Sq/763, 16/2/14; Devon. R., 11/11/14, att. O.C.B. Inst.; Capt.; w.
19 The Grove, The Boltons, S.W.

BULLOCK, Ernest James
6/5/8101, 2/12/15; No. 8 O.C.B., 4/8/16; Yorks. L.I., 24/10/16; F; Capt.; M(1).
The Cathedral, Manchester.

✠ BULLOCK, Gervas Frederic
4/6/2/4993, 19/7/15, L/C.; S. Wales Bord., 4/1/16; F; 2/Lieut.
Killed in action 31/7/17.

BULLOCK, Reginald Norton
6/1/6060, 3/9/15; S. Staff. R., 24/1/16, att. R.F.C., R.A.F.; F; Lieut; w.
Wynberg, Alexandra Road, Wednesbury, South Staffordshire.

BULLOUGH, Thomas Guy
A/13127, 27/5/18; No. 1 O.C.B., 8/11/18; Arg. & Suth'd. Highrs., 16/3/19; 2/Lieut.
Fasnacloick, Argyll, Scotland.

✠ BULMER, Frank Stedman
2/3260, 15/4/15; 20th Lond. R., 30/7/15; F; 2/Lieut.
Killed in action 1/10/16.

✠ BUNDEY, Albert Arthur
6/4/7719, 22/11/15, L/C.; No. 14 O.C.B.; M.G.C., 24/10/16; 2/Lieut.
Killed in action 21/3/18.

BUNDY, Alfred Edward
1/3616, 13/5/15; Midd'x. R., 20/9/15, R. Lanc. R., Tank Corps, R.A.O.C.; F,S; Major.
29 Shakespeare Road, Hanwell, W.7.

BUNKER, Leslie John Daniel
C/13393, 24/6/18, L/C.; trfr. K.R. Rif. C., 25/4/19.
83 Church Road, Hove.

BUNNING, Hugh Wickliffe
C/D/12228, 16/11/17; R.A.F., C/S, 21/5/18; trfr. R.A.F.
Yosemite, Walsoken, Norfolk.

BUNT, Charles Lionel
E/2825, 1/2/15; D. of Corn. L.I., 6/4/15; F; Lieut.
The Sycamores, Penzance, Cornwall.

BURDEKIN, Harold Benjamin
B/Sq/12786, 16/3/18; demob. 22/1/19.
Causton Way, Bilton, nr. Rugby.

BURDEN, Albert Edward John
B/10326, 4/1/17; No. 14 O.C.B., 7/6/17; R.W. Kent R., 25/9/17; F,It; Lieut.; w; M.C.
11 Bina Gardens, Kensington, S.W.5.

✠ BURDICK, Frederick William
4905, T/16/7/15; Lond. Div. Cyc. Coy., 10/12/15, 20th Lond., R.A.F.; F; Capt.; M.C.
Killed in action 29/8/18.

BURDICK, John Howard
6/7024, 27/10/15; R.A., C/S, 15/9/16; R.G.A., 29/11/16; Lieut.
Shandon, North Road, Cardiff.

BURFORD, Edgar Henry
C/12289, 7/12/17, L/C.; R.E., C/S, 14/4/18; R.E., 27/9/18; 2/Lieut.
167 Walm Lane, Cricklewood, N.W.2.

BURGE, Charles Stafford
6/3/8617, 3/1/16; R.F.A., C/S, 8/12/16; R.G.A., 18/3/17; F; Lieut.; w.
Iddesleigh, Kingston Hill, Surrey.

BURGE, John Charles Thornton
6/8618, 3/1/16; dis. to re-enlist in R.E., 1/5/16; Sgt.; R.N.V.R., -/4/18; F; Sub. Lt.
Moorlands Road, West Moors, Dorset.

BURGER, George Samuel Hans
C/D/11641, 12/7/17; No. 3 O.C.B., 8/2/18; Lan. Fus., 30/7/18, att. Yorks. L.I., Intelligence; F; 2/Lieut.
9 Vincent Avenue, Chorlton-cum-Hardy, Manchester.

✠ BURGES, Walter Travers
6/4/9344, 7/2/16, L/C.; Glouc. R., 22/6/16; Germ.SWA,F; 2/Lieut.
Killed in action 8/5/17.

BURGES, William John Clere Hart
A/14062, 25/9/18; trfr 14th Lond. R., 6/12/18; Sgt.
5 Phireas Pelt Road, Well Hall, S.E.9.

✠ BURGESS, Edward Patrick
6/3/A/7168, 3/11/15, L/C.
Died 3/10/18.

✠ BURGESS, Eric Archibald
6/5/6061, 6/9/15; R. Fus., 24/10/16; 2/Lieut.
Killed in action 17/2/17.

BURGESS, Frank
C/11067, 16/4/17; No. 12 O.C.B., 10/8/17; North'd. Fus., 27/11/17, Durh. L.I.; F; 2/Lieut.; w,p.
Westholme, Lower Peover, Knutsford, Cheshire.

APPENDIX II.—RECORDS OF RANK AND FILE.

BURGESS, George
6/8856, 11/1/16; R.F.A., C/S, 4/8/16; R.F.A., 24/11/16; Lieut.
Westholme, Lower Peover, nr. Knutsford, Cheshire.

BURGESS, Joseph White
4/6/7720, 22/11/15; No. 14 O.C.B.; 19th Lond. R., 18/12/16, att. Lan. Fus.; F; Lieut.; Inv. 131 Bellemoor Road, Southampton.

BURGHES, John McLeod
6/1/6587, 4/10/15; R.A., C/S, 24/1/16; R.G.A., 2/7/16, emp. M. of Shipping; Capt.; w.

BURGIN, Edward Leslie
D/11557, 28/6/17, L/C.; Intelligence Corps, 28/11/17; lt; Staff Lieut.; Italian Croce di Guerra, M(1).
3 Grays Inn Place, W.C. 1.

BURGIN, Harold Charles
C/75, 13/4/08; 11th Lond. R., 12/4/10, 3rd and 9th Lond. R.; F; Capt.; w; M(1). 3 Grays Inn Place, W.C. 1.

BURGIS, Frederic
B/11689, 19/7/17; No. 14 O.C.B., 9/11/17; Shrops. L.I., 30/4/18; 2/Lieut. 31 Budge Row, E.C. 4.

BURGOYNE-JOHNSON, George Harold
K/B/2326, 14/12/14; Durh. L.I., 9/4/15, ott. R.A.F.; M; Lieut.
Brockley, Saltburn-by-the-Sea, Yorkshire.

BURHENNE, John Benjamin
D/10234, 29/12/16; trfr. 16th Lond. R., 2/3/17, 6th Lond. R.; F; Pte.; g. 123 Cumberland Road, Plaistow, E.13.

BURKE, Edward Joseph Augustine
6/8078, 1/12/15; R.F.C., C/S, 8/10/16; R.F.C., 3/4/17, R.A.F.; Flt. Cmdr.
5 Alexandra Terrace, Bray, Co. Wicklow, Ireland.

✠ BURKE, Ernest Henry Harwell
B/13431, 3/7/18. Died 2/11/18.

✠ BURKE, Sydney Slaven
6/2/9029, 20/1/16; No. 14 O.C.B., 27/9/16; 18th Lond. R., 24/1/17; 2/Lieut. Killed in action 22/12/17.

BURKITT, Eric Hammond Beaumont
6/5/7411, 12/11/15, L/C.; No. 11 O.C.B., 7/5/16; Manch. R., 4/9/16, att. R.F.C., R.A.F.; F; Lieut.
35 Kensington Avenue, Victoria Park, Manchester.

BURLES, Sydney Harold
B/10366, 5/1/17; trfr. R.G.A., 3/8/17.
29 Murillo Road, Lee.

BURLINGHAM, Geoffrey
4/2608, 7/1/15; R. Sco. Fus., 8/2/15, Gord. Highrs., att. T.M. Bty.; F; Lieut.; w. Morley's Hotel, Trafalgar Square, W.C. 2.

BURLS, Harold Edwin Grant
C/21, 1/4/08; dis. 31/3/13. Thornlea, Shortlands, Kent.

BURLTON, Edward Richard Jenks
Sq/374, 23/3/09; dis. 22/3/13; rej. Sq/846, 4/8/14, L/C.; R.A.S.C., 5/12/14, R.F.A.; S,F; Major; Inv.; M.C., French Croix de Guerre.
Sunnyside, Hoop Lane, Golders Green, N.W. 4.

BURLTON, Francis Arthur
Sq/1225, 16/9/14, Cpl.; Herts. Yeo., 15/3/15, att. M.G.C.; E,P,F; Lieut.; w.
c/o. Elders & Fyffes, Ltd., 1 Pearl Buildings, Portsmouth.

BURMINGHAM, Arthur Frederick
C/13363, 21/6/18; trfr. 14th Lond. R., 6/12/18, Gord. Highrs.; Sgt.
48 Kingsholm Road, Gloucester.

BURN, James Herbert
C/B/13292, 17/6/18; R.E., C/S, 1/11/18; demob.
57 Julian Avenue, South Shields, Co. Durham.

BURNAND, Guy Matthey
Sq/747, 1/12/13; Lan. Fus., 7/11/14; Lieut.; w.
12c Oxford and Cambridge Mansions, N.W. 1.

BURNE, Arthur Henry
6/5/6796, 13/10/15; R.A., C/S, 6/10/16; R.G.A., 12/11/16; F; Lieut. 26 Perham Road, W. Kensington, W. 14.

BURNELL, Norman Ryan Scott
B/12200, 9/11/17, L/C.; R.F.A., C/S, 3/5/18; R.H. & R.F.A., 11/3/19; 2/Lieut.
85 Portsmouth Road, Woolstan, Southampton.

BURNELL, Reginald George
6/5/7130, 2/11/15; No. 11 O.C.B., 7/5/16; Hunts. Cyc. Bn. 4/9/16, Indian Army; I; Major
c/o. Messrs. King, King & Coy., Bombay, India.

BURNES, Percival Gordon
4/5/4662, T/7/7/15, Sgt.; R.A., C/S, 24/1/16; R.F.C., 27/8/16.
Uplands, Grosvenor Road, Westcliff-on-Sea.

✠ BURNET, Stanley
6/3/5374, 5/8/15; Bedf. R., 9/12/15, secd. R.F.C.; Lieut.
Died 31/5/18.

BURNETT, Alan Hodgson
C/12651, 27/2/18; Sigs. C/S, 14/6/18; demob.
Glenthorne, Thorne Road, Doncaster.

✠ BURNETT, Ian Alastair Kendall
Sq/731, 11/11/13; R. Regt. of Cav., 8/9/14, E. Lan. R.; Capt.; w(2). Killed in action 31/5/17.

BURNETT, Mervyn Eady Haliburton
B/12398, 15/1/18; No. 6 O.C.B., 10/5/18; Gord. Highrs., 3/2/19; 2/Lieut. 22 Polmini Road, Aberdeen.

BURNETT, Reginald Penrith
C/13293, 17/6/18; trfr. K.R. Rif. C., 25/4/19.
The Vicarage, Rounds Green, Nelbury, Worcestershire.

BURNETT-HURST, Alexander Robert
C/380, 24/3/09; dis. 24/3/11.

BURNEY, Edward
C/475, 16/3/10; dis. 25/4/12.

BURNHAM, Stanley John
C/13294, 17/6/18; trfr. 28th Lond. R., 13/11/18.
Westwood, Leavesden Road, Watford, Hertfordshire.

BURNS, Angus George
4/2/4363, 21/6/15; Manch. R., 10/1/16; Lieut.
Students' Club, St. Thomas' Hospital.

BURNS, Francis Joseph
6/5/C/9000, 19/1/16; No. 14 O.C.B., 26/11/16; Shrops. L.I., 28/2/17, M.G.C.; F; Lieut.; w.
45 Church Crescent, Church End, Finchley, N. 3.

BURNS, Harold Bertram
B/10969, 2/4/17, L/C.; A.S.C., C/S, 1/9/17; R.A.S.C., 27/10/17; F; 2/Lieut.
Elmhurst, 13 Derby Road, Withington, Manchester.

BURNS, James Percival
6/5/6339, T/16/9/15; No. 7 O.C.B., 7/4/16; N. Lan. R., 17/7/16, att. R. Lanc. R.; F; Lieut.; w.
34 Reads Avenue, Blackpool.

✠ BURNS, Walter Bell
4/3718, 24/5/15; Shrops. L.I., 5/9/15, att. Glouc. R.; Lieut.
Killed in action 9/10/17.

BURNS, William Robert Wheatley
B/10778, 19/2/17; R.F.C., C/S, 4/5/17; R.F.C., 14/6/17, R.A.F.; F; Lieut. Kent House, Portland Square, Carlisle.

BURNSIDE, George Frederick Carl
4/6/5/4954, 19/7/15, L/C.; Devon R., 4/12/15; 2/Lieut.
c/o. Capt. G. H. Burnside, c/o. Cox & Coy., 16 Charing Cross, S.W. 1.

BURR, Alan Edgar Lucius
D/A/10224, 20/12/16; No. 14 O.C.B., 5/3/17; R. Suss. R., 26/6/17; F; Lieut. 5 Walpole Terrace, Brighton.

BURR, Robert Page
B/D/13632, 26/7/18; No. 11 O.C.B., 24/1/19; demob. 6/2/19.
Lawrence, Long Island, New York, U.S.A.

BURRA, Septimus Henry
C/452, 15/12/09; dis. 18/1/13; rej. Sq/4/3222, 12/4/15; R.F.A., 5/5/15; F; Capt.; Inv.; M(1).
Lower Voakes, Thakeham, Sussex.

BURRAGE, David Alexander
6/4/5468, 9/8/15; Midd'x. R., 2/1/16; F; Lieut.; M.B.E.
49 Queen Street, Bryanston Square, W. 1.

BURRELL, Ellis Morgan
E/1513, 1/10/14; R.W. Fus., 9/11/14; F; Capt.
9 Winchester Avenue, Brondesbury, N.W.

BURRELL, Herbert Emil
E/1548, 6/10/14; S. Staff. R., 14/12/14, R.F.C., R.A.F.; G,E,F; Capt.; Inv.
c/o. Barclays Bank, Ltd., Foreign Branch, 168 Fenchurch Street, E.C.

110

APPENDIX II.—RECORDS OF RANK AND FILE.

✠ BURRELL, *Raymond Francis Topham*
B/1303, 26/9/14; R.W. Kent R., 29/10/14; F; 2/Lieut.
Killed in action 26/9/15.

BURRELL, *Robert Eric*
E/1518, 1/10/14; R.W. Fus., 14/12/14, Army Cyc. Corps; F; Capt.; *Inv.*   9, *Winchester Avenue, Brondesbury, N.W.* 6.

BURRELL, *Thomas Lewis*
1/3831, 31/5/15; R.G.A., 27/8/15; F,It; Lieut.; M.C.
377 *Queen's Road, S.E.* 14.

BURRIDGE, *Arthur Charles*
Sq/196, 5/5/08; *dis.* 31/12/09.   *Elmington, Bexley, Kent.*

BURRIDGE, *Percy Arundel*
B/1197, 14/9/14; N. Staff. R., 9/10/14; Lieut.
Elmington, Bexley, Kent.

✠ BURROUGHES, *Stephen*
6/Sq/5618, 16/8/15, L/C.; K.R. Rif. C., 24/4/18; 2/Lieut.
Killed in action 4/11/18.

✠ BURROWS, *Arthur Cecil*
C/938, 5/8/14; Manch. R., 5/10/14, Ches. R.; 2/Lieut.; *w.*
Died of wounds 5/6/16.

BURROWS, *Brian Bolton*
C/D/12266, 30/11/17, L/C.; *demob.* 31/1/19.
65 *Hagley Road, Edgbaston, Birmingham.*

BURROWS, *John Herbert*
6/2/7977, 29/11/15; No. 14 O.C.B., 28/8/16; L'pool. R., 22/11/16; F; Lieut.   6 *Bertram Road, Liverpool.*

BURROWS, *John Stanley*
A/12502, 30/1/18; No. 23 O.C.B., 7/6/18; L'pool. R., 5/2/19; 2/Lieut.   16 *Walmer Road, Waterloo, Liverpool.*

✠ BURROWS, *Leonard Righton*
H/1973, 26/10/14, L/C.; North'd. Fus., 3/12/14; F; 2/Lieut.
Killed in action 2/10/15.

BURROWS, *Lionel Beeley*
6/2/5498, 9/8/15; Linc. R., 14/11/15, Indian Army; SA,I,E,P; Capt.   23 *Vernon Road, Harrogate.*

BURSTOW, *Maxwell John*
C/D/12044, 27/9/17, L/C.; R.F.A., C/S, 15/3/18; R.G.A., 8/2/19; 2/Lieut.   52 *St. George's Road, S.W.* 1.

BURT, *George Arthur*
4/6/3/4955, 19/7/15; North'd. Fus., 20/12/15, R.A.F.; F; Lieut.;
w.   27 *Deauville Court, Clapham, S.W.*

BURT, *Ivor Stanley Day*
B/12749, 13/3/18; No. 1 O.C.B., 6/9/18; Glouc. R., 16/3/19; 2/Lieut.   *Castle Commercial Hotel, Maesbeg, S. Wales.*

BURT, *Reginald Edward*
4/3757, 27/5/15, Cpl.; Notts. & Derby. R., 17/9/15; F; Capt.; M.B.E.   145 *Wimbledon Park Road, Southfields, S.W.* 18.

BURTENSHAW, *Henry George*
C/14169, 16/10/18; *demob.*   71 *Bell Street, Reigate, Surrey.*

BURTON, *Charles Ernest*
4/4208, 14/6/15, Cpl.; Mon. R., 3/12/15, *att.* R.W. Fus.; F,P; Capt.   5 *St. Michael's Avenue, Northampton.*

BURTON, *Herbert Frank*
C/12561, 6/2/18; R.E., C/S, 16/6/18; *trfr.* 14th Lond. R., 6/12/18; *demob.* -/7/19.
Drayton Lodge, Gravelly Hill, Birmingham.

BURTON, *John Henry*
C/13227, 7/6/18; *trfr.* 14th Lond. R., 6/12/18, Gord. Highrs.
12 *Ashburton Road, Southsea, Hampshire.*

BURTON, *Percy Merceron*
Sq/110, 18/4/08; *dis.* 17/4/09.

BURTON, *William*
E/14159, 14/10/18; R.G.A., C/S, 1/11/18; *demob.*
165 *Osbaldeston Road, Clapton Common, N.* 16.

BURTON, *William Edward Alan*
A/10992, 4/4/17; No. 12 O.C.B., 10/8/17; *trfr.* Class W. Res., 16/2/18.   *Brockton, Frodsham, Cheshire.*

BURTSAL, *Henry Nelson*
6/3/7832, 25/11/15; R.F.A., C/S, 4/8/16; R.F.A., 24/11/16; F; Lieut.; M(1).   *Red Oaks, Theydon Bois, Essex.*

BURT-SMITH, *Basil*
E/1498, 1/10/14; 6th Lond. R., 15/11/14, Oxf. & Bucks. L.I.; Lieut.; *w*(2); M.C. *and Bar,* M(1).
Crossways, Arden Road, Finchley.

BURY, *Ernest*
B/13495, 9/7/18; *trfr.* 14th Lond. R., 13/11/18.
The Parsonage, Reigate, Surrey.

BUSER, *Charles Frederick*
D/1486, 29/9/14, Cpl.; R. Ir. Rif., 28/4/15, M.G.C., Indian Army; F,M,E,P; Capt.; *w.*   12 *Versailles Road, Anerley, S.E.*

BUSH, *Sydney Lee*
6/3/6882, 18/10/15; Devon R., 10/6/16; I,M; Lieut.; M(1).
Brantwood, Southstoke, Bath.

BUSH, *Victor Kingham*
6/1/8341, 13/12/15; No. 14 O.C.B., 27/9/16; Bord. R., 18/12/16; F; Staff Capt.
c/o. Standard Bank of S. Africa, Adderley Street, Cape Town, S. Africa.

BUSHE, *William Francis*
2/3446, 3/5/15, L/C.; N. Staff. R., 3/9/15, R. Highrs.; S,F; Lieut.; M.C., M(1).
Knowsley, Queen's Park Road, Trinidad, B.W. Indies.

✠ V.C. BUSHELL, *Christopher*
A/544, 10/2/11; R.W. Surr. R., 8/5/12; Lt.-Col.; *w*(2); V.C., D.S.O., M(1).   *Killed in action* 8/8/18.

BUSHELL, *Hugh Sidney*
D/1439, 29/9/14; 24th Lond. R., 4/11/14, *att.* Rif. Brig. *and* R.A.F.; F,It; Capt.; *w.*   *Ravensholt, Harrow-on-the-Hill.*

BUSHELL, *John Eric Eden*
B/10329, 4/1/17; R.A., C/S, 27/4/17; R.F.C., 26/9/17, R.A.F.; Lieut.   85 *Ashworth Mansions, W.* 9.

BUSHER, *Walter Paul Kevin*
6/5/7348, 10/11/15; No. 7 O.C.B., 3/7/16; R. Ir. Regt., 21/11/16, R.A.F.; F; Lieut.
Box 621, *Pontuville, Tucare Co., California, U.S.A.*

BUSSY, *George Thomas Moir*
1/3439, T/1/5/15, L/C.; Arg. & Suth'd. Highrs., 10/7/15; 2/Lieut.

BUSTARD, *Thomas Stokes*
2/3124, 29/3/15; R.A.S.C., 14/6/15, Som. L.I., R.A.F.; F; Capt.
32 *Priory Road, Bedford Park, W.* 4.

BUSWELL, *Arthur Philip*
4/6/5/4919, 19/7/15, L/C.; S. Staff. R., 8/11/15; Lieut.
32 *Clarendon Road, Manchester.*

✠ BUSZARD, *Stanley George*
4/6/Sq/4787, 12/7/15, L/C.; No. 1 Cav. C/S, 24/4/16; Norf. Yeo., 28/7/16; E,P; Lieut.   *Killed in action* 8/12/17.

✠ BUTCHER, *Frederick William*
6/5/6726, 11/10/15; *trfr.* 5th Lond. R., 1/11/16, *att.* R. Ir. Rif.; F; Pte.   *Killed in action* 9/8/17.

BUTCHER, *Hugh John*
A/14096, 4/10/18; *demob.* 31/1/19.
31 *Malvern Road, Southsea, Hampshire.*

BUTCHER, *Laurence George*
6/2/7252, 8/11/15; E. Kent. R., 4/9/16, *att.* Midd'x. R.; Lieut.
24 *Addington Square, Margate, Kent.*

✠ BUTCHER, *Percival Drew Pitts*
6/3/7039, 28/10/15, L/C.; R.E., 16/6/16; Capt.
Died 3-4/11/18.

BUTCHER, *Percy George*
1/3532, 10/5/15; Devon. R., 21/8/15; F; Lieut.
Soham, Cambridgeshire. (*Now in Nigeria.*)

BUTCHER, *Richard Charles*
6/2/8206, 7/12/15, L/C.; R.A., C/S, 7/8/16; R.G.A., 24/11/16; F; Capt.; M(1).   *The Homestead, Epsom, Surrey.*

BUTE, *Marquess of*
6/9028, 20/1/16; No. 6 O.C.B., 17/4/16; Welch R., 4/9/16; Colonel, R.G.A.   *St. John's Lodge, Regents Park, N.W.*

BUTEMENT, *John Charles Innes*
B/9885, 8/11/16, L/C.; M.G.C., C/S, 1/2/17; M.G.C., 27/5/17, Tank Corps; F; Lieut.
c/o. Dr. Butement, 127 *West End Lane, West Hampstead.*

APPENDIX II.—RECORDS OF RANK AND FILE.

BUTLER, Alec William
1/1646, 9/10/14; R. Suss. R., 25/11/14, secd. M.G.C.; G,E,P;
Capt.   12a York Mansions, Battersea Park, S.W. 11.

BUTLER, Alfred Trego
1/3832, 31/5/15; Worc. R., 21/8/15; F; Lieut.; p; M.C.
40 Redcliffe Square, S.W. 10.

✠ BUTLER, Charles Reginald
6/3/8508, T/23/12/15, L/C.; No. 14 O.C.B.; 19th Lond. R.,
24/10/16; F; Lieut.; g.   Died 28/11/18.

BUTLER, Charles Theophilus
6/4/7978, 29/11/15, Sgt.; Dorset R., 30/6/16, att. Som. L.I. and
Indian Army; F,I; Lieut.; w.
c/o. National Provincial & Union Bank Ltd., Portsea, Portsmouth, Hants.

BUTLER, Charles Travers
Sq/669, 26/11/12; Dorset Yeo., 10/10/14; G,E,P; Capt.; w.
Hobart, Tasmania.

BUTLER, Eaton Garner
4/3/5098, 26/7/15, L/C.; Linc. R., 14/11/15; F; Lieut.
South View, Sea View Road, Skegness, Lincolnshire.

BUTLER, Frank William
D/11125, 30/4/17, Cpl.; R.A., C/S, 15/12/17; R.G.A., 1/7/18; F;
2/Lieut.   Stamford, Victoria Road, Mill Hill, N.W. 7.

✠ BUTLER, Frederick Charles
D/11577, 2/7/17; R.F.C., C/S, 23/10/17; R.F.C., 12/12/17,
R.A.F.; Lieut.; M.B.E.   Killed 25/4/18.

BUTLER, Geoffrey Lawrence
B/10758, 21/2/17, L/C.; No. 14 O.C.B., 5/7/17; Herts. R.,
30/10/17, att. Bedf. R.; E,F; Lieut.; w.
The Knoll, Eliot Hill, Blackheath, S.E. 13.

BUTLER, Harold Talbot
6/1/6271, 16/9/15; dis. med. unfit, 8/8/16.
7 Church Road, Cardiff.

✠ BUTLER, John Goodwin
6/2/5652, 16/8/15; W. Rid. R., 22/7/16; 2/Lieut.
Died of wounds 29/3/17.

BUTLER, John Walter
6/2/9401, 9/2/16, L/C.; No. 14 O.C.B., 27/9/16; R. Highrs.,
18/12/16, att. Bord. R.; F,I,E; Lieut.; Inv.
6 Villiers Road, Rathgar, Dublin.

BUTLER, Robert Mudie
4/1/5026, 22/7/15; R.A.S.C., 9/10/15; Capt.; M(l).
161 Gleneldon Road, Streatham.

BUTLER, Roland Harry
6/3/7522, 16/11/15; Shrops. L.I., 4/9/16, att. Rif. Brig.; S;
2/Lieut.   51 Cosmeston Street, Cardiff.

BUTLER, Theobald Blake
A/Sq/11218, 7/5/17; A.S.C., C/S, 1/11/17; R.A.S.C., 25/1/18;
2/Lieut.   7 Earls Terrace, Kensington, W. 8.

BUTLER, Walter William
B/11690, 19/7/17; No. 14 O.C.B., 4/1/18; Norf. R., 25/6/18; F;
2/Lieut.   Ravenswood, Sandon Road, Edgbaston, Birmingham.

BUTLER-KEARNEY, George
6/8909, 13/1/16; No. 2 Cav. C/S, 31/3/16; trfr. City of Lond.
Yeo., 24/10/16.   Three Castles, Kilkenny, Ireland.

✠ BUTT, Francis Wilfred
6/4/6648, 7/10/15; R.F.C.. C/S, 4/5/17; R.F.C., 14/6/17, R.A.F.;
F; Lieut.   Killed 26/5/18.

BUTT, Leslie Maurice
3/3152, 1/4/15; E. York. R., 28/7/15; Lieut.
Langport House, Eastfield Park, Weston-super-Mare.

✠ BUTT, Lewis John Dalgleish
4/3413, 29/4/15; Rif. Brig., 21/10/15; 2/Lieut.
Killed in action 4/7/16.

BUTT, Robert Arthur
F/3/2651, 11/1/15, L/C.; Notts & Derby. R., 5/5/15, emp. M. of
Munitions; Capt.; w.   1, Eastfield Park, Weston-super-Mare.

BUTTERWORTH, Edmund Numa Man
6/6446, 27/9/15; York. & Lanc. R., 20/10/15; Capt.
Oak Bank, Park Road, St. Annes-on-Sea, Lancashire.

BUTTERWORTH, Lionel Milner
B/13660, 29/7/18; trfr. 28th Lond. R., 13/11/18.
Leahurst, St. Margaret's Road, Dunham Massey, Cheshire.

BUTTERWORTH, P.
C/Sq/13654, T/27/7/18; demob. 24/1/19.
Lyndhurst, Hooley Range, Heaton Moor, Stockport.

BUTTERWORTH, Victor
B/9811, 30/10/16; R.F.C., C/S, 13/3/17; R.F.C., 19/4/17.
134 Liverpool Road, Great Crosby, Liverpool.

BUTTLE, Edward Alfred
D/1472, 29/9/14; E. Surr. R., 24/11/14; F; Capt.; Inv.
Kingsley, Chipstead, Surrey.

BUTTLE, John Frederick
4/A/9716, 11/10/16, L/C.; dis. med. unfit, 19/4/17.
3 Upper Grove, South Norwood, S.E. 25.

BUTTLER, Frank Leslie
1/9738, 16/10/16; No. 14 O.C.B., 27/12/16; R. War. R., 25/4/17;
F; Lieut.   Bridge View, Haslocks Green, Shirley, nr. Birmingham.

BUTTOLPH, William Golding
4/Sq/4250, 14/6/15; Herts. Yeo., 11/11/15; Lieut.
Ivy Deane, 491 Wherstead Road, Ipswich.

BUTTON, Charles Howard
A/13142, T/23/5/18; No. 1 O.C.B., 8/11/18; Notts. & Derby. R.,
16/4/19; 2/Lieut.   144 Harlaxton Drive, The Park, Nottingham.

BUXTON, Eric Cunliffe
4/6/4815, 12/7/15; R.A.S.C., 26/7/15; Capt.
51 Holland Park Avenue, W. 11.

BUXTON, Percy Edward
A/10702, 13/5/17, Cpl.; No. 14 O.C.B., 10/8/17; 7th Lond. R.,
27/11/17, att. R.W. Kent R. and R.A.F.; 1; Lieut.
Illawarra, Totland Bay, Isle of Wight.

BYLES, Cecil Maurice Barnard
B/539, 27/1/11, Sgt.; 13th Lond. R., 19/2/15, K.R. Rif. C.,
Lab. Corps.; F; Lieut.   3 Princes Gardens, S.W.

✠ BYNG, Leonard Gustav
Sq/A/2080, 13/11/14, L/C.; R.W. Kent R., 14/4/15, Gren. Gds.;
Lieut.; M.C.   Died of wounds 24/8/18.

✠ BYRNE, Edmund James Widdrington
A/834, 4/8/14; Durh. L.I., 12/9/14, S. Wales Bord.; Capt.
Killed in action 29/4/16.

✠ BYRNE, Edward Aloysius
6/2/8278, 10/12/15; No. 2 O.C.B., 14/8/16; R. Dub. Fus.,
18/12/16; F; 2/Lieut.   Killed in action 24/4/17.

BYRNE, Gerald
C/Sq/12298, 29/11/17; No. 7 O.C.B., 10/5/18; trfr. 28th Lond. R.,
30/8/18.   96 Mount Haig, Kingstown, Co. Dublin.

BYRNE, James Thomas
6/9236, 1/2/16; trfr. R.F.A., 28/3/16.

BYRNE, John Francis Taafe
C/9933, 15/11/16; No. 14 O.C.B., 30/1/17; R. War. R., 29/5/17,
att. Som. L.I.; F,It; Lieut.; w.   1 Kerrsland Street, Hillhead, Glasgow.

BYRNE, Laurence Austin
B/9894, 10/11/16; R.W. Surr. R., 9/3/17, att. R.A.S.C. and R.E.;
Lieut.   6 Thorncliffe Road, Clapham Park, S.W. 2.

BYRNE, Lucius Widdrington
C/193, 4/5/08; dis. 3/5/09; R.N.V.R., -/1/15; Lt. Cmdr.
7 New Square, Lincoln's Inn, W.C. 2.

BYRNE, Terence Charles
D/12944, 19/4/18; No. 21 O.C.B., 4/10/18; R. War. R., 17/3/19;
2/Lieut.   Brunswick House, Olton, nr. Birmingham.

BYRNE, Thomas Joseph
C/11765, 30/7/17; No. 14 O.C.B., 4/1/18; R. Dub. Fus., 25/6/18;
2/Lieut.   13 Rathgar Avenue, Dublin.

BYRON, Charles
B/1325, 26/9/14, L/C.; R. Dub. Fus., 10/3/15, att. R.F.C.,
R.A.F.; E,S,F; Flt. Cmdr.   13 Angles Road, Streatham, S.W. 16.

APPENDIX II.—RECORDS OF RANK AND FILE.

CABRETT, Harold Gordon
6/4/8342, 13/12/15; dis. to R. Mil. Academy, 28/11/16.
c/o —. Herschhorn Esq., 4 Monahan Avenue, Purley, Surrey.

CADDICK, Sydney David
D/E/13925, 30/8/18; No. 22 O.C.B., 22/11/18; Hamps R., 15/2/19; 2/Lieut.
93 Avenue Road, Southampton.

CADE, Cecil Ewart
C/11735, 26/7/17; No. 14 O.C.B., 7/12/17; Midd'x. R., 28/5/18; F; Lieut.; p.
Bay Tree Cottage, Old Southgate, N. 14.

✠ CADE, Arthur Gordon
C/389, 29/3/09; 11th Lond. R., 12/5/10, Midd'x. R., cmd. Wilts. R.; F; Lt.-Col.; w(2); D.S.O., M.C. and Bar, M(3).
Killed in action 26/4/18.

CADMAN, Alfred Parkes
B/C/12674, 2/3/18; trfr. R.A.F., 21/5/18; E.
69 Idsworth Road, Firth Park, Sheffield.

CADMAN, Peter Alfred
3/Sq/9627, 21/9/16, L/C.; No. 1 Cav. C/S, 1/9/17; R. Regt. of Cav., 9/5/18; 2/Lieut.
Willersley, Filey Road, Scarborough.

✠ CAHILL, Alfred Gilbert
6/3/5602, 15/8/15, Sgt.; 3rd Lond. R., 3/12/15; 2/Lieut.
Killed in action 3/10/16.

CAHUSAC, Edmund Barry
6/4/5158, 29/7/15; S. Staff. R., 20/12/15, att. R.F.C.; Lieut.; p; M.C.
171 Castellain Mansions, Maida Vale, W. 9.

CAIN, James Mylchreest
6/3/D/5499, 9/8/15, L/C.; No. 14 O.C.B., 30/10/16; Linc. R., 24/1/17; 2/Lieut.; w.
The Parade, Castletown, Isle of Man.

CAIRD, Andrew Hector
B/D/12399, 15/1/18; trfr. R.A.F., 20/4/18.
Newlands, 90 New Park Road, Clapham Park, S.W.

✠ CAIRD, James Robert
B/695, 7/2/13; K.O. Sco. Bord., 15/8/14; F; Capt.
Killed in action 23/4/15.

CAIRNS, Alfred Charles
D/10641, 1/2/17; No. 14 O.C.B., 5/7/17; Gord. Highrs., 30/10/17; F; 2/Lieut.; w(2).
Torlundie, Colinton, Midlothian.

✠ CAIRNS, Herbert
6/2/7523, 16/11/15, L/C.; K.R. Rif. C., 25/9/16; 2/Lieut.; w.
Killed in action 4/10/17.

CAIRNS, William
6/4/8953, 17/1/16, R.F.A., C/S, 4/8/16; R.G.A., 12/11/16; F; Lieut.; w; M(1).
31 Nassington Road, Hampstead, N.W. 3.

CALDER, David Robert
A/11880, 20/8/17; No. 14 O.C.B., 7/12/17; R. Highrs., 28/5/18; 2/Lieut.
Marguerite Villa, 399 Clepington Road, Dundee.

✠ CALDER, John
F/2661, 12/1/15; R. Berks. R., 27/2/15.

CALDER, John Alexander
A/14009, 16/9/18; demob. 13/12/18.
8 Ambrose Avenue, Golders Green, N.W. 4.

✠ CALDER, John Kellish
6/1/5819. 26/8/15; No. 9 O.C.B., 8/3/16; Sea. Highrs., 23/7/16; Lieut.
Killed in action 22/3/18.

✠ CALDERON, George
B/819, 4/8/14; Interpreter, 4/9/14, R. Horse Gds., R. War. R., O. & B.L.I., York. L.I., att. K.O. Sco. Bord.; F,G; Lieut.; w.
Killed in action 4/6/15.

CALDERWOOD, John Lindow
F/1846, 16/10/14; L'pool. R., 20/10/14; S,F; Capt.; M(1).
Beech House, Egremont, Cumberland.

CALDWELL, Stanley
K/E/2277, 7/12/14; S. Staff. R., 31/3/15, att. No. 4 O.C.B. Inst.; F; Lieut.; w, Inv; M.C., M(1).
263 Woodstock Road, Oxford.

✠ CALEY, Vernon Christopher Russell
F/1778, 16/10/14; R. War. R., 27/2/15; Capt.; M.C.
Killed in action 22/8/17.

✠ CALKIN, Brian Penry Bernard
1/3833, 31/5/15; R W. Surr. R., 20/8/15; F; Lieut.; g(2).
Killed in action 10/7/18.

CALLAGHAN, Patrick Joseph
4/3/3900, 31/5/15, L/C.; dis. 30/7/15.

CALLAGHAN, Richard Marcus
6/5/C/9561, 4/3/16; No. 7 O.C.B., 4/11/16; R. Innis. Fus., 28/2/17, R.A.S.C.; F,Turkey; Lieut.; Inv.
Belfast Banking Coy. Ltd., Limavady, Ireland.

✠ CALLARD, William Kingsley
4/6/4958, 19/7/15; Leic. R., 21/11/15; F; 2/Lieut.
Killed in action 1/7/16.

✠ CALLENDER, Gerald Claude
6/1/6649, 7/10/15; R. Scots., 1/6/16; Lieut.; w.
Killed in action 26/4/18.

CALLIS, Arthur Edward
6/2/9478, 14/2/16; No. 14 O.C.B., 26/11/16; Shrops. L.I., 27/3/17; 2/Lieut.
Salford Rectory, Chipping Rectory, Oxon.

CALROW, Richard
A/11228, 7/5/17; R.F.C., C/S, 2/8/17; R.F.C., 8/9/17, R.A.F.; Lieut.
10 School Brow, Bury, Lancashire.

CALTHROP, Claude David Usticke
A/1651, 9/10/14; Bord. R., 14/11/14; 2/Lieut.
Auliss, Cedar Road, Sutton.

CALVER, Harry Thomas
C/13295, 17/6/18, L/C.; demob. 29/1/19.
198 Heythorp Street, Southfields, S.W. 18.

✠ CALVERT, Eric Ruegg
6/2/9397, 9/2/16; No. 8 O.C.B., 4/8/16; R. Suss. R., 21/11/16; 2/Lieut.
Killed in action 8/8/17.

CALVERT, Ernest Thomas
6/D/6755, 11/10/15, Cpl.; No. 14 O.C.B., 6/4/17; R.W. Surr. R., 31/7/17; F; Lieut.; w.
Baden House, Camden Square, N.W.1.

CALVOCORESSI, George
4/3/5068, 26/7/15; Interpreter, 3/5/16; Lieut.
c/o. Chartered Bank of India, Australia and China, 38 Bishopsgate, E.C.

CAMERON, Donald James
B/13499, 10/7/18; trfr. 28th Lond. R., 13/11/18.
113 Warwick Road, Earls Court, S.W. 5.

CAMERON, Ernest William
A/C/D/12510, 31/1/18; R.A.F., C/S, 4/5/18; demob. 30/5/19.
48 Darnley Road, E. 9.

CAMERON, Frank
6/2/7580, 18/11/15; No. 9 O.C.B., 8/3/16; Arg. & Suth'd. Highrs., 23/7/16; Lieut.; p.

CAMERON, Robert Charles
B/Sq/12759, 15/3/18; No. 2 Cav. C/S, 26/6/18; demob. 22/1/19.
Balnakyle, Munlochy, Ross-shire, N.B.

CAMERON, Stuart Evan
B/737, 11/11/13; Arg. & Suth'd. Highrs., 12/9/14, War Office; Lieut.; w.

✠ CAMM, Bertram Cunliffe
1/3615, 13/5/15; York. R., 28/7/15; Capt.; w; M.C.
Killed 7/1/18.

CAMM, Frederick Jackson
1/3294, 19/4/15; Essex R., 13/7/15; E,P; Capt.; w; M.C. and Bar.
50 Leinster Square, Hyde Park, W. 2.

CAMMACK, Francis John
B/13432, 3/7/18; demob. 30/1/19.
132 Prescot Road, St. Helens, Lancashire.

CAMMACK, William Henry
A/13972, 9/9/18; trfr. K.R. Rif. C., 7/4/19.
24 Lodge Lane, Derby.

CAMP, Jack Ralph
A/14097, 4/10/18; No. 11 O.C.B., 24/1/19; General List, 8/3/19; 2/Lieut.
132 Claremont Road, Forest Gate.

CAMPBELL, Albert Graham
B/12728, 11/3/18, Sgt.; trfr. K.R. Rif. C., 13/5/19.
75 Park Lee Road, Blackburn, Lancashire.

CAMPBELL, Alexander
B/13931, 28/8/18, Sgt.; demob. 29/1/19.
236 Tollcross Road, Glasgow.

APPENDIX II.—RECORDS OF RANK AND FILE.

CAMPBELL, *Algernon John*
K/B/2454, 28/12/14; R. Bucks. Huss., 19/3/15; 2/Lieut.; w.

CAMPBELL, *Archibald*
Sq/3377, 26/4/15, L/C.; R.G.A., 15/8/15; Lieut.; M(1).
90 *Spit Road, Mosmin, Sydney, New South Wales, Australia.*

CAMPBELL, *Archibald Kenneth*
6/5/6118, 9/9/15; No. 9 O.C.B., 8/3/16; Sco. Rif., 6/7/16; Capt.; w.

CAMPBELL, *Bernard*
6/5/7793, 24/11/15, L/C.; No. 14 O.C.B.; Norf. R., 24/10/16; F; Lieut.; w(2). 3 *East Holm, Golders Green, N.W. 4.*

CAMPBELL, *Charles Graham*
B/C/12216, 15/11/17; trfr. 28th Lond. R., 8/4/18.
88 *Norbury Crescent, Norbury.*

CAMPBELL, *Charles Moulson*
4/1/4532, 1/7/15; R. Glasgow Yeo., 2/10/15, att. R. Ir. Fus. and L'pool. R.; S; Capt.
Rose Cottage, Threshfield, nr. Skipton, Yorkshire.

CAMPBELL, *Colin Decie*
Sq/307, 29/6/08; dis. 29/6/10; rej. Sq/872, 4/8/14; R.N.V.R., 15/8/14; North and Irish Seas; Lieut. Cmdr.; M.(1).
Belsize, Harrow-on-the-Hill.

CAMPBELL, *Douglas Harry*
4/6/1/4596, 5/7/15; Manch. R., 6/1/16; Lieut.
1 *Elgin Court, Maida Vale, W. 9.*

CAMPBELL, *Duncan*
4/3/3939, 3/6/15; Sco. Rif., 7/1/16; Lieut.
3 *Wellshot Drive, Cambuslang, nr. Glasgow.*

CAMPBELL, *Edmund Colin Murray*
6/Sq/6062, 6/9/15; R.F.A., C/S, 31/3/16; R.F.A., 5/8/16; Capt.
24 *Lincoln's Inn Fields, W.C. 2.*

CAMPBELL, *George Ernest*
6/Sq/8954, 17/1/16; No. 1 Cav. C/S, 12/10/16; trfr. County of Lond. Yeo., 10/4/17. *The Abbey, Carlisle.*

CAMPBELL, *George Osmond Lorne*
K/2666, 5/8/14, 10/3/15, att. Tank Corps; F; Capt.; M.C., M(4). *Glenaliel, Tarbert, Loch Fyne, Argyll.*

CAMPBELL, *Henry James*
1/3002, 4/3/15, L/C.; Worc. R., 18/12/15; F; Lieut.; w.
c/o. *Messrs. Clarke, Sons & Press, 28 Broad Street, Bristol.*

CAMPBELL, *Harry Armstrong*
D/11541, 21/6/17; R.E., C/S, 11/11/17; R.E., 21/12/17; F; 2/Lieut. *Clanholme, Houghton-le-Spring, Co. Durham.*

CAMPBELL, *Ian Edward FitzGerald*
6/9345, 7/2/16; dis. to R. Mil. Coll., 29/4/16; D. of Corn. L.I., 27/10/16; Lieut.; w. 21 *Hyde Park Gate, Kensington, S.W.*

CAMPBELL, *James Alexander*
6/2/6903, 18/10/15; R. Suss. R., 25/9/16, att. American Division; F; Capt. *Laneham, Retford, Nottinghamshire.*

CAMPBELL, *James Warren*
D/12884, 5/4/18; No. 16 O.C.B., 18/10/18; Essex R., 17/3/19; 2/Lieut. *The Lindens, Cliff Parade, Leigh-on-Sea.*

CAMPBELL, *John*
4911, 17/7/15; dis. med. unfit, 8/8/16.

CAMPBELL, *John Dermot*
B/10521, 15/1/17; dis. to R. Mil. Academy, 1/3/17; R.G.A., 6/6/18; E,P; 2/Lieut. *Coolgreany, Fortwilliam Park, Belfast.*

CAMPBELL, *John Young*
6/9539, 18/2/16; R.F.A., C/S, 26/5/16; R.G.A., 30/8/16; P; Lieut.; M(1).
United Free Church Manse, Peterailter, Aberdeenshire.

CAMPBELL, *Kenneth Charles*
F/2706, 18/1/15; Bord. R., 12/5/15; R.F.C.; 2/Lieut.

CAMPBELL, *Reginald Theodore Ollson*
B/11386, 30/5/17; No. 2 Cav. C/S, 16/7/17, No. 7 O.C.B.; North'd. Fus., 29/1/18; Germ.E. & W.Africa; 2/Lieut.

✠ CAMPBELL, *Ronald Walker Francis*
A/527, 16/12/10, L/C.; R. Fus., 12/9/14; Capt.
Died of wounds 11/8/16.

✠ CAMPBELL, *Walter Stanley*
6/2/6193, 13/9/15; 1st Lond. R., 20/12/15; 2/Lieut.; M.C.
Killed in action 7/10/16.

CAMPBELL, *William Gordon*
6/2/B/9071, 21/1/16, L/C.; No. 14 O.C.B., 26/11/16; Suss. Yeo., 28/2/17, att. R. Suss. R.; Lieut.

CAMPBELL, *William Lawson Walford*
6/1/6650, 7/10/15, L/C.; R. Highrs., 21/6/16; F; Lieut.
Edina, Berkhamsted, Hertfordshire.

✠ CAMPBELL, *William Watson*
4/5/4734, 12/7/15; Manch. R., 6/1/16; 2/Lieut.
Killed in action 9/1/17.

CAMPBELL-BAYARD, *Dudley*
6/4/7093, 1/11/15; trfr. R.G.A., 8/12/16.
1 *Alcester Road, Wallington, Surrey.*

CAMPION, *Gilbert Francis Montriore*
Sq/160, 18/4/08; dis. 28/2/10; rej. Sq/821, 4/8/14; R.A.S.C., 27/8/14; Capt. 39 *Cromwell Road, S.W.*

✠ CAMPION, *Ralph René*
3/3067, 18/3/15; R. Marine Art., 28/5/15, R.G.A.; Lieut.
Killed in action 17/2/17.

CANDY, *Leonard Adams*
B/13534, 17/7/18, L/C.; R.A.F., C/S, 16/10/18; demob. 27/3/19.
Kilmersdon, Bath, Somerset.

CANE, *Arthur Skelding*
C/90, 16/4/08; R.A.M.C., 1/8/09; M,S; Major D.A.D.M.S.; p; D.S.O., O.B.E., M(3).
c/o. *Messrs. Holt & Co., 3 Whitehall Place, S.W. 1.*

CANE, *Edmund*
A/38, 3/4/08; dis. 2/4/09.

CANE, *Leonard Buckell*
C/101, 17/4/08; R.A.M.C., 1/11/08. See under Appendix 1.
Minster Precincts, Peterborough.

CANE, *Maurice Hereward*
C/469, 24/2/10; dis. 22/2/14; Lieut. R.A.M.C., 17/5/15; G,E,P; Capt. *Homewood, Peterston-super-Ely, Glamorganshire.*

CANNELL, *Walter Percy*
4/2/4306, 17/6/15; Bedf. R., 16/11/15; F; Lieut.; w(2).
Shrublands, Horsford, Nr. Norwich.

CANNEY, *Charles Campbell*
B/71, 10/4/08; dis. 10/4/09.

CANNEY, *Joseph Robson*
6/1/5697, 19/8/15, L/C.; R.A., C/S, 24/1/16; R.G.A., 6/7/16; F; Lieut. w.
Hawthorn Villa, Moor Lane, Cleadon, Sunderland.

CANNING, *Cyril Augustine*
D/4144, 10/6/15; trfr. R.E. Sigs., 28/2/17.
56 *Sandringham Road, Cardiff.*

✠ CANNON, *Richard*
F/1804, 16/10/14; Wilts. R., 17/3/15; M; Lieut.
Killed in action 5/4/16.

✠ CANNON, *Sidney Leslie*
3/3378, 26/4/15; Shrops. L.I., 8/7/15; R.A.F.; F,S,E; Lieut.; w.
Died 14/9/18.

CANT, *Thomas Hilton*
4/1/4441, 26/6/15; N. Lan. R., 2/11/15, Lab. Corps; Lieut.
115 *Liverpool Road, Great Crosby, Liverpool.*

CANTRELL-HUBBERSTY, *Edward de Burgh*
C/10189, 13/12/16; No. 14 O.C.B., 6/4/17; Lan. Fus., 31/7/17; F; Lieut. 1 *St. Martins, Leicester.*

CAPENER, *Norman Leslie*
D/11136, 30/4/17; No. 14 O.C.B., 10/8/17; R.M.L.I., 27/11/17, R.N.V.R.; Surgeon Sub. Lt.
Oatlawn, Holly Park, Crouch Hill, N. 4.

CAPITER, *Frederick Milner*
6/2/7349, 10/11/15; R.F.C., 16/6/16; Inv. from R.F.C., -/8/16; Paymaster Lieut. R.N.R. *Clieveden, Brighowgate, Grimsby.*

CAPRON, *Henry Murray*
A/14333, 30/12/18; demob. 2/2/19.
33 *Cunnington Street, Acton Green, W.*

CARBINES, *John Coopan*
6/5/7128, 2/11/15; No. 11 O.C.B., 7/5/16; L'pool. R., 4/9/16; F; Lieut.; w(2).
c/o *F. E. Spedding Esq., Piarere, via Tirau, Auckland, New Zealand.*

APPENDIX II.—RECORDS OF RANK AND FILE.

CARDELL, *Ivor Southwell*
6/2/8981, 18/1/16; R.A., C/S, 7/8/16; R.G.A., 18/10/16, att. R.A.O.C.; F; Lieut.; g.   5 Whitchurch Road, Cardiff.

CARDEN, *Percy Theodore*
B/203, 6/5/08; dis. 5/5/10.

CARDEW, *George Harold*
H/1976, 26/10/14, L/C.; Hamps. R., 23/12/14, R.E. Sigs.; S,E,SR; Lieut.; M(1).
    9 Stafford House, Maida Hill West, Paddington, W.2.

CARELESS, *Richard Sidney*
C/11459, 5/6/17; A.S.C., C/S, 1/9/17; R.A.S.C., 27/10/17; F; 2/Lieut.   31 Newton Road, Bayswater, W.2.

CAREW-RYDER, *Richard*
Sq/3617, 13/5/15; R.F.A., 12/7/15, R.A.S.C.; F; Lieut.
    Kingswear, South Devon.

CAREW-ROBINSON, *Courtenay Denis*
A/614, 29/12/12; dis. 28/2/16.   27 Ashley Gardens, S.W.1.

✠ CAREY, *Allan Stewart*
6/1/6241, 16/9/15, L/C.; R.F.C., 6/7/16; 2/Lieut.
    Killed 27/5/17.

CAREY, *Clifford Howes*
B/12342, 1/1/18, Cpl.; R.F.A., C/S, 19/8/18; R.H. & R.F.A., 8/4/19; 2/Lieut.
    Whitley Lodge, Beulah Road, Thornton Heath, Surrey.

CAREY, *Nigel Edward*
B/628, 29/3/12, Cpl.; Rif. Brig., 12/9/14; F; Lieut.
    5 Verulam Buildings, Grays Inn, W.C.1.

CAREY, *Stephen William*
6/2/5893, 30/8/15; Midd'x. R., 12/1/16; Lieut.; w.
    Normanhurst, 52 Corringham Road, N.W.4.

CARISS, *Karl Godfrey*
B/11662, 16/7/17, L/C.; No. 17 O.C.B., 10/5/18; trfr. 28th Lond. R., 1/9/18.
    6 Alcester Road, Kings Heath, Birmingham.

✠ CARLILE, *John Arthur*
4/2/5067, 26/7/15; Notts. & Derby. R., 1/6/16, Leic. R.; F; Staff Capt.; w; M(1)   Died -/12/19.

CARLISLE, *Charles Valentine*
Sq/742, 11/11/13; 16th Lancers, 15/8/14; F; Lieut.; w.
    46 Bedford Square, W.C.1.

✠ CARLISLE, *Frederick Albert*
6/2/6547, 30/9/15; No. 14 O.C.B.; 3rd Lond. R., 22/11/16, 4th Lond. R.; 2/Lieut.; w.   Killed in action 15/9/17.

CARLISLE, *John Craig*
6/3/7824, 24/11/15, L/C.; No. 14 O.C.B.; M.G.C., 25/9/16; F; Lieut.; Inv.   18 Redston Road, Hornsey, N.8.

CARLISLE, *Malcolm Richard*
6/5/5601, 14/8/15, L/C.; Manch. R., 2/1/16; F; Lieut.; w.
    50 Mabfield Road, Fallowfield, Manchester.

CARLISLE, *Philip Edmund*
6/Sq/6272, 16/9/15, L/C.; No. 2 Cav. C/S, 31/3/16; Ches. Yeo., 19/8/16, att. Manch. R.; F; Lieut.; w.
    Brookside, Alderley Edge, Cheshire.

CARLISLE, *Robert*
4/3719, 24/5/15, L/C.; R.G.A., 25/10/15; F; Lieut.
    Room 54, Supreme Court Pay Office, Law Courts, W.C.2.

✠ CARLYON, *Lionel George*
K/2691, 14/1/15; Sco. Rif., 5/1/15; F; 2/Lieut.
    Killed in action 3/5/17.

CARMAN, *John Stanley*
6/5/5987, 2/9/15; Derby. Yeo., 2/12/15; S; Lieut.
    2 Hangar Lane, Ealing Common, W.5.

✠ CARMAN, *Leslie Guy*
K/E/2468, 28/12/14; E. Kent. R., 2/6/15; 2/Lieut.; M(1).
    Killed in action 4/10/16.

CARMICHAEL, *Claude Hamilton Ross*
2/B/9767, 23/10/16, L/C.; R.F.C., C/S, 13/3/17; R.F.C., 19/4/17.
    116, Princes Road, Liverpool.

CARMICHAEL, *George*
C/11787, 2/8/17; No. 14 O.C.B., 7/12/17; Arg. & Suth'd. Highrs., 25/6/18; 2/Lieut.
    Teluk Buloh Estate, Utan Melentang P.O., Lower Perak, Federated Malay States.

CARMICHAEL, *Gilbert*
A/10071, 1/12/16; No. 14 O.C.B., 6/4/17; R. Fus., 31/7/17; F; Lieut.   Screel, 19 Avington Grove, Penge, S.E.20.

CARMICHAEL, *William Maurice*
Sq/3010, 8/3/15; R.E., 12/6/15; Capt.
    51 Earls Court Square, S. Kensington, S.W.

✠ CARNE, *John Reeves*
6/2/7094, 1/11/15; No. 14 O.C.B.; R. Suss. R., 24/10/16; 2/Lieut.
    Died of wounds 25/7/17.

CARNE, *John Thomas*
6/3/6986, 25/10/15, L/C.; No. 7 O.C.B., 7/4/16; Hamps. R., 4/8/16, King's African Rifles; F,EA.; Lieut.; w.
    43 Sydenham Road, Sydenham, S.E. (Now in W. Africa).

✠ CARNEGIE, *Theodore Arthur*
6/1/9210, 31/1/16, L/C.; K.R. Rif. C., 25/9/16; Lieut.
    Killed in action 16/8/17.

CARNLEY, *William Birch*
6/1/9456, 14/2/16; R.A.O.C., 7/7/16, R.F.C., R.A.F.; Capt.
    13 Old Cavendish Street, W.1.

CAROE, *Valdemar B.*
F/2627, 7/1/15; Conn. Rang., 10/4/15, Lab. Corps; Capt.; w.
    Bessemer House, Denmark Hill, S.E.

CAROLIN, *Patrick Silvester*
A/14033, 20/9/18; trfr. Class W. Res., 14/12/18.
    Dunree, Buncrana, Co. Donegal, Ireland.

CAROLIN, *William Hugo*
D/13719, 25/7/18; demob. 29/1/19.
    Dunrea House, Buncrana, Co. Donegal, Ireland.

✠ CARPENTER, *Cedric Theodore Arundel*
H/1915, 16/10/14, L/C.; Ches. R., 14/5/15, att. Shrops. L.I.; E,P,F; Lieut.   Died of wounds, 6/11/18.

CARPENTER, *Daniel*
6/Sq/6056, 4/9/15; Surr. Yeo., 28/1/16; Lieut.
    19 Ross Road, South Norwood, S.E.

CARPENTER, *Edward James Burfield*
4/6/1/D/4038, 7/6/15, Sgt.; R.F.C., C/S, 23/10/17; R.F C., 12/12/17; 2/Lieut.   42 Farnham Farm, Nr. Blandford.

✠ CARPENTER, *Ronald Percy Victor*, B.A.
6/3/7903, 29/11/15, L/C.; M G.C., 25/9/16, F; Lieut.
    Killed in action 6/9/18.

CARPENTER, *Thomas Bernard Boyd*
4/4145, 10/6/15; R.G.A., 11/10/15; M,I; Lieut.
    1m Portman Mansions, Baker Street, W.1.

✠ CARPENTER-TURNER, *Eric Walter*
6/3/5426, 5/8/15; Hamps. R., 28/11/15; F; Lieut.
    Died of wounds 9/8/16.

CARPMAEL, *Ernest Vincent*
E/14084, 30/9/18; No. 22 O.C.B., 22/11/18; K.R. Rif. C., 19/2/19; 2/Lieut.
    c/o. HongKong & Shanghai Bank Ltd., 9 Gracechurch Street, E.C.

CARR, *Arthur Neville*
D/13806, 9/8/18; demob. 29/1/19.
    The Woodlands, Milverton, Leamington Spa.

CARR, *Arthur Strettell Comyns*
B/13548, 19/7/18; demob. 25/1/19.
    1 Temple Gardens, Temple, E.C.4.

✠ CARR, *Charles Alexander Emsley Lascelles*
4/3261, 15/4/15; trfr. 5th Lond. R., 6/3/16.
    Killed in action 20/9/17.

CARR, *Ernest Heron*
C/9964, 20/11/16; M.G.C., C/S, 1/2/17; M.G.C., 27/5/17, Tank Corps; Lieut.   Rustington, The Bridle Road, Purley.

CARR, *Newton Hazelrigg*
1/3627, 17/5/15; E. Surr. R., 10/9/15, M.G.C.; Lieut.; Inv.
    Lynton, S. Augustine's Avenue, S. Croydon.

CARR, *Norman*
6/1/5500, 9/8/15; E. Surr. R., 1/6/16, M.G.C.; F; Lieut.
    Xophil, Herbert Road, Hornchurch, Essex.

CARR, *Walter Gordon*
6/Sq/9105, 24/1/16; No. 2 Cav. C/S, 10/9/16; dis. med. unfit, 26/10/16.
    c/o. Mrs. Leigh, 12 Dennington Park Road, W. Hampstead.

APPENDIX II.—RECORDS OF RANK AND FILE.

CARRALL, Christopher Emanuel
3/3834, 31/5/15; E. Surr. R., 10/9/15; F; Staff Capt.; w.
19 Folkestone Road, Walthamstow, E.17.

CARRALL, Eric Fawcus
E/1537, 6/10/14, L/C.; Devon. R., 9/12/14. Indian Army; I,M; Capt.
26 Crescent Road, Kingston Hill, Surrey. (Now in HongKong.)

CARRICK, David Robertson
6/9234, 1/2/16; R.A., C/S, 31/5/16; R.G.A., 18/8/16; Lieut.

✠ CARRICK, Richard Hamilton
6/2/5402, 5/8/15; Devon. R., 27/1/16; 2/Lieut.
Killed in action 2/4/17.

CARRIGAN, Henry Charles
3/3295, 19/4/15, Cpl.; dis. to R. Mil. Coll., 19/1/16; Suff. R., 16/8/16; Lieut.
Bramble Hill, Heswall, Cheshire.

CARRITT, Reginald Graham
D/1427, 29/9/14; 1st Lond. R., 14/2/15; Lieut.

CARROLL, Cola Ernest
3940, 3/6/15; R.G.A., 1/11/15, att. R.A.F.; F; Lieut.; w,p.
17 Slade Street, Hythe.

CARROLL, Edmond John
C/12238, 19/11/17, Sgt.; R.A., C/S, 2/10/18; R.G.A., 10/3/19; 2/Lieut.
16 Campden Hill Gardens, W.8.

✠ CARROTHERS, John Samuel
6/5/8406, 15/12/15; No. 7 O.C.B., 11/8/16; R. Innis. Fus., 18/12/16; 2/Lieut.
Killed in action 16/8/17.

CARR-SAUNDERS, Alexander Morris
Sq/619, 29/2/12; dis. 2/8/12.

CARRUTHERS, Percy George
6/3/6447, 27/9/15, L/C.; Midd'x. R., 1/6/16; F; Lieut.; p.
65 Wymering Mansions, Maida Vale, W.9.

CARRUTHERS, Whitfield William
B/10986, 2/4/17; No. 12 O.C.B., 10/8/17; 1st Lond. R., 27/11/17; Lieut.; w.

CARRUTHERS, William Frederick
6/2/5677, 16/7/15; 7th Lond. R., 15/11/15; Lieut.; w(2).
Stansted, Essex.

CARRUTHERS, William Stephen
D/2719, 18/1/15; 18th Lond. R., 3/6/15; F; Capt.; w.
Gaskmore, Reigate, Surrey.

CARRYER, Nigel Rupert
4/3/4390, 24/6/15; R. Marine Art., 30/8/15.
78 Gwendolen Road, Leicester.

CARSON, Joseph Baldwin
Sq/2597, 6/1/15, L/C.; R.H.A., 24/3/15; Capt.; M.C., M(1).
4 Vicarage Gardens, Kensington, W.

✠ CARTE, Alan Simpson
6/3/5844, 26/8/15; 12th Lond. R., 30/12/15; F; 2/Lieut.
Died of wounds 9/6/17.

CARTE, Geoffrey Williams
Sq/338, 17/12/08; dis. 25/3/11; Surgeon, Royal Navy.
17 Cavendish Road, St. John's Wood, N.W.

CARTER, Albert
6/1/6316, 18/9/15; Devon. R., 7/7/16, secd. M.G.G.; Lieut.

CARTER, Albert Reginald Whitworth
C/10612, 25/1/17, Sgt.; R.A., C/S, 29/6/17; R.G.A., 1/4/18; Lieut.
60 Pollards Hill North, Norbury, S.W.16.

✠ CARTER, Archibald Wren
4/3/3942, 3/6/15; Midd'x. R., 30/11/15; 2/Lieut.
Killed in action 13/5/17.

✠ CARTER, Bernard Robert Hadow
C/10853, 9/3/17; R.F.C., C/S, 4/5/17; R.F.C., 14/6/17; 2/Lieut.
Killed 7/11/17.

CARTER, Cecil Arthur
4/1/4597, 5/7/15; Rif. Brig., 11/12/15; Lieut.; w.
51 Mildred Avenue, Watford, Hertfordshire.

CARTER, Dudley Horace
A/10717, 12/2/17; No. 14 O.C.B., 7/6/17; 7th Lond. R., 25/9/17, att. Norf. R.; P,E; Staff Capt.
12 Elm Bank Mansions, Barnes, S.W.13.

CARTER, Edward Philip
B/908, 5/8/14; R. Berks. R., 12/9/14; F,NR; Major, D.A.A.G.; w; O.B.E., M(1).
6 Parkside Gardens, Wimbledon Common.

CARTER, Ernest Albert
B/E/13562, 19/7/18, L/C.; No. 22 O.C.B., 22/11/18; R. War. R., 15/2/19; 2/Lieut.
1 High Street, St. Albans, Hertfordshire.

CARTER, Frank Rix
A/11642, 12/7/17; A.S.C., C/S, 12/11/17; R.A.S.C., 6/1/18; F; 2/Lieut.; M(1).
12 Broadlands Road, Highgate, N.6.

CARTER, Frederick Maslin Beilby
A/20, 1/4/08; dis. 31/3/10; Capt. T.F. Res., 25/11/15.
Common Room, Lincoln's Inn, W.C.2.

CARTER, George Edward
E/C/1605, 6/10/14; Midd'x. R., 23/11/14; F,S; Staff Capt.; Medaille d'Honneur.
Royal Auto Club, Pall Mall, S.W.

✠ CARTER, Gerald Mark
K/H/2129, 19/11/14; dis. to R. Mil. Coll., 28/12/14; R. War. R., 16/6/15, R.F.C., R.A.F.; F; Flt. Cmdr.
Died 17/1/20.

CARTER, Guy Ashton
D/13841, 16/8/18; demob. 15/3/19.
Princes Court, 48 Princes Square, Hyde Park, W.2.

CARTER, Hubert G.
4/2/3941, 3/6/15, Sgt.; Gren. Gds., 17/11/15; Lieut.; w.
34 Albert Bridge Road, S.W.

CARTER, John Frederick Heathcote
6/3/8515, 29/12/15; No. 14 O.C.B., 28/8/16; Shrops. L.I., 22/11/16; Lieut.
Broad Street House, E.C.2.

CARTER, Joseph
6/5/6342, 19/9/15; Lan. Fus., 17/1/16; E,P,F; Lieut.
Compania de Mercantil de Ultramar, Barranquilla, Rep. de Colombia.

CARTER, Lawrence Herbert
2/B/9774, 24/10/16, L/C.; Garr. O.C.B., 8/3/18; Lab. Corps, 4/9/18, att. R.A.S.C.; 2/Lieut.
46 Manor Heath Road, Halifax, Yorkshire.

✠ CARTER, Malcolm Russell
E/1566, 6/10/14, Cpl.; E. Surr. R., 10/2/15; Capt.
Killed in action 23/3/18.

CARTER, Maurice Bonham
Sq/416, 14/5/09; dis. 29/10/12.
5 Hyde Park Square, W.2.

CARTER, Morland
B/E/13633, 26/7/18; No. 22 O.C.B., 20/9/18; R.A.S.C., 31/10/18; 2/Lieut.
509 Beacon Street, Boston, U.S.A.

CARTER, Oliver Eric
C/10797, 26/2/17; R.F.C., C/S, 16/4/17; R.F.C., 16/5/17, R.A.F.; F; Capt.
Dulce Domum, Shenley, Hertfordshire.

CARTER, Robert Charles Heathcote
6/3/8516, 29/12/15; No. 14 O.C.B., 28/8/16; Shrops. L.I., 22/11/16; Capt.
c/o Treasury Solicitor (Law Courts Branch), Royal Courts of Justice, Strand, W.C.2.

CARTER, Ronald Norman
2/3190, 8/4/15; Dorset R., 28/7/15, att. R.F.C.; F; Lieut.; p.
61 Carey Street, Lincoln's Inn, W.C.2.

CARTER, Vivian John
D/10012, 27/11/16, Sgt.; A.S.C., C/S, 1/9/17; R.A.S.C., 30/11/17; F; 2/Lieut.; Inv.
Greenhayes, Upper Woodcote, Purley.

CARTER, William Bede
A/11907, 27/8/17; No 14 O.C.B., 7/12/17; Arg. & Suth'd. Highrs., 28/5/18; 2/Lieut.
Kimbolton, Huntingdon.

CARTER-BRAINE, Eric
6/3/8620, 3/1/15, L/C.; R.A., C/S, 28/9/16; R.G.A., 10/2/17; F; Lieut.; M.C.
55 Wimpole Street, W.1.

CARTER-SMITH, James
4/Sq/5053, 22/7/15; E. Rid. Yeo.
10 Pearson Avenue, The Park, Hull.

CARTMAN, Thomas
6/5/5361, 4/8/15; Manch. R., 15/1/16; F; Capt.; w(2); M.C.
109 Bury and Bolton Road, Radcliffe.

CARTMELL, Alec
A/10962, 30/3/17; R.A., C/S, 7/9/17, No. 18 O.C.B.; 1st Lond. R., 29/5/18; 2/Lieut.
9 Victoria Road, St. Annes-on-the-Sea.

116

APPENDIX II.—RECORDS OF RANK AND FILE.

CARTMEL-ROBINSON, Harold Francis
C/10802, 28/2/17, Sgt.; R.A., C/S, 7/6/17; R.F.A., 4/11/17; F;
Capt.   Fort Jameson, Northern Rhodesia, South Africa.

CARTON, Ronald Lewis
4/4307, 17/6/15, Sgt.; D. of Corn. L.I., 23/4/16; S; Lieut.; Inv.
          The Times (Editorial Department), E.C. 4.

✠ CARTTER, Arthur Edward
6/2/6651, 7/10/15; No. 7 O.C.B., 7/4/16; 3rd Lond. R., 17/7/16;
F; Lieut.   Died 4/4/19.

CARTWRIGHT, George Hamilton Grahame Montagu
Sq/686, 24/1/13; 5th Lond. R., 27/3/14, att. Cold. Gds. and Gds.
M.G.R.; F; Major; w; M(1).   264 St. James Court, S.W. 1.

CARTWRIGHT, Harold James
D/11163, 2/5/17; No. 14 O.C.B., 7/9/17; R Berks. R., 17/12/17,
att. Hamps. R. and R. Fus.; F; Lieut.
                      Newlyn, Downs Road, Luton, Bedfordshire.

CARTWRIGHT, Thomas Henry
6/5/7657, 22/11/15, L/C.; No. 14 O.C.B.; L'pool. R., 24/10/16,
Indian Army; F,I; Lieut.
          Holt Lea, Lyndhurst Road, Wallasey, Cheshire. (Now in India.)

CARUS-WILSON, Charles Denny
Sq/148, 18/4/08; C. of Lond. Yeo., 12/6/12; Capt.; w; M.C.
          c/o. Messrs. Sage & Co., Valparaiso, Chile, S. America.

CARUS-WILSON, Eric
Sq/1004, 6/8/14; R.E., 2/9/14; F; Capt.; M.C., M(1).
              5 St. Petersburgh Place, Bayswater, W. 2.

CARUS-WILSON, Frederick Maynard
Sq/484, 8/4/10, Sgt.; R.F.A., 9/8/14.   Millfield, Keston, Kent.

CARUTH, Richard Alexander Youle
C/Sq/14164, 14/10/18; No. 11 O.C.B., 31/1/19; General List,
8/3/19; 2/Lieut.   Drunard, Ballymena, Co. Antrim, Ireland.

CARVER, Edmund Tucker
Sq/675, 10/12/12; dis. 23/12/13; rej. A/857, 4/8/14; R.A.S.C.,
31/8/14; G,F; Major; M(1).   York Lodge, Walton-on-Thames.

CASEBOURNE, Oswald James
C/10179, 13/12/16; trfr. 19th Lond. R., 1/6/17.

CASEMORE, William Archibald
A/13076, 17/5/18; No. 5 O.C.B., 8/11/18, Nos. 12 & 20 O.C.Bs.;
E. Kent R., 16/3/19; 2/Lieut.   Corran, Biddenden, Kent.

CASEY, William Francis
D/13754, 7/8/18; demob. 10/1/19.   6 Emperor's Gate, S.W. 7.

CASH, Rowland Walker
A/1170, 14/9/14, L/C.; Notts. & Derby. R., 7/10/14, secd.
R.F.C.; F,P; Capt.; w.   10 Clifford Street, W. 1.

CASH, Thomas James
C/13228, 7/6/18; trfr. 14th Lond. R., 6/12/18.
                         58 Dunsmure Road, Stamford Hill, N. 16.

CASPELL, Alfred John
C/Sq/11736, 26/7/17; No. 2 Cav. C/S, 11/1/18; R. Regt. of Cav.,
22/6/18; 2/Lieut.   Felderland House, Sandwich, Kent.

✠ CASS, Hugh Launcelot
A/456, 3/1/10; Res. of Officers, 16/1/13, S. Wales Bord.; G;
2/Lieut.   Killed in action 19/6/15.

CASS, Thomas Stafford
3/3296, 19/4/15; E. Surr. R., 4/8/16, Oxf. & Bucks. L.I.; S;
Lieut.   10 Avonmore Road, W. Kensington, W. 14.

CASSELS, Oliver Chance
A/11203, 7/5/17; R.F.C., C/S, 2/8/17; R.F.C., 8/9/17, R.A.F.;
F; Lieut.; D.F.C.   La Cumbre, Ottery St. Mary, Devonshire.

CASSIDY, Cecil Ralph
A/11234, 9/5/17; trfr. 28th Lond. R., 26/10/17.
                            Normandy, Hayes Road, Bromley, Kent.

CASSWELL, Frank Slade
A/13163, 30/5/18; No. 22 O.C.B., 5/7/18; Som. L.I., 5/2/19;
2/Lieut.   Midsomer Norton, Somerset.

CASTELLAIN, Ernest Frederic
Sq/467, 23/2/10, Cpl.; 5th Lancers, 15/8/14; F; Lieut.; M(1).
     c/o Messrs. Frederick Huth & Coy., 12 Tokenhouse Yard, E.C. 2.

CASTELLO, Daniel
H/1948, 22/10/14; Herts. R., 25/3/15.
                                  5 Drapers Gardens, E.C. 2.

CASTELLS, Francis Theodore
2/3588, 13/5/17; York. & Lanc. R., 12/10/15; 2/Lieut.; Inv.
                Chartered Accountant, Cawnpore, India.

CASTLE, Arthur Thomas Clowes
A/10743, 16/2/17; trfr. 19th Lond. R., 15/6/17.
                                   Froxmer Court, Nr. Worcester.

CASTLE, Ernest Reginald Martin
H/1970, 26/10/14, L/C.; R.A.S.C., 1/3/15; Capt.

CASTLE, Harry Frederick Lincoln
B/10706, 12/2/17, L/C.; No. 14 O.C.B., 10/8/17; R. Suss. R.,
27/11/17; F; Lieut.; Inv.
              Seafield, Hatherley Road, Winchester, Hampshire.

CASTLE, Norman Percival
6/3/8621, 3/1/16, L/C.; No. 14 O.C.B., 30/10/16; M.G.C.,
30/1/17, Tank Corps; F; Lieut.   7 Davenant Road, Oxford.

CASWELL, Frederick Walter
1/3683, 20/5/15; North'd. Fus., 4/1/16, secd. M.G.C.; F; Lieut.;
w-p.   60 Gladsmuir Road, Highgate, N.

CATCHPOLE, Cyril Bolton
4/5/4840, 15/7/15; R. Fus., 24/12/15, M.G.C.; F; Capt.
                              Milestone House, Staplehurst, Kent.

CATCHPOLE, Joseph
6/8015, 30/11/15; dis. med. unfit, 19/5/16.

CATCHPOLE, Victor William
B/9874, 7/11/16; No. 14 O.C.B., 30/1/17; R. Fus., 29/5/17, West.
and Cumb. Yeo.; F; Lieut.; g.
                              Milestone House, Staplehurst, Kent.

✠ CATFORD, Cyril Herbert Barclay. See Barclay-Catford C. H.

CATHERALL, Cyril
4/3/4490, 28/6/15; Durh. L.I., 17/12/15, Linc. R., Lab. Corps;
F; Capt.   Brooklands, Hipperholme, Halifax, Yorkshire.

CATHERALL, George Henry Frederick
D/10451, 10/1/17; R.N.V.R., 13/4/17, att. R.N.A.S., R.A.F.;
Eastern Mediterranean; Capt.   49 Cecile Park, Hornsey, N.

CATLING, Cecil Thurgood
2/3338, 22/4/15; 18th Lond. R., 19/7/15; 2/Lieut.
                          6 Baldwin Crescent, Camberwell, S.E. 5.

CATLOW, Hubert Ernest
6/5/8016, 30/11/15; No. 14 O.C.B., 30/10/16; Leic. R., 28/2/17;
F; Lieut.   Abertawe, 35 Ewington Road, Leicester.

✠ CATON, Frederick William
2/3153, 1/4/15; S. Staff. R., 21/6/15, R.E.; 2/Lieut.
                                       Killed in action 23/6/16.

CATON, Stanley Orr
4/9721, 12/10/16; No. 14 O.C.B., 6/4/17; R. Fus., 31/7/17; F;
Capt.; g   16 Monument Station Buildings, E.C. 4.

CATON, William Cooper
2/3752, 26/5/15; R.A., C/S, 29/1/16; trfr. R.F.A., 8/3/16; F,S,P;
Gnr.   6 Waterloo Street, Hove, Sussex.

CATON-THOMPSON, Arthur
F/1755, 16/10/14; Bord. R., 26/3/15; 2/Lieut.; M(1).

CATTELL, Arthur Skeeles
2007, 2/11/14, L/C.; Midd'x. R., 4/2/15, Indian Army; I,M;
Capt.   Hadleydene, Hadley Wood, Middlesex.

CATTLE, Frank Barr
D/13918, 26/7/18; dis. med. unfit, 23/2/19.
                                 2 Caple Road, Harlesden, N.W. 10.

CATTLEY, Patrick Oswald
C/D/12267, 30/11/17; No. 20 O.C.B., 10/5/18; Interpreter,
31/10/18; 2/Lieut.   43 Oxford Gardens, N. Kensington, W. 10.

CATTLIN, Frederick Percival
4/3758, 27/5/15, L/C.; Shrops. L.I., 10/9/15, att. W. India R.;
Germ.EA,E,P; Capt.   83 Westbourne Grove, Bayswater, W. 2.

CATTON, John Edward
6/4/6580, 2/10/15; Essex R., 8/6/16, Intelligence; Lieut.
                        Paddockhurst, Quilten Road, Felixstowe, Suffolk.

APPENDIX II.—RECORDS OF RANK AND FILE.

✠ CAUDWELL, Thord
6/2/9347, 7/2/16; No. 14 O.C.B., 27/9/16; 16th Lond. R., 18/12/16; F; Capt.   Killed in action 30/11/17.

CAULFEILD-STOKER, Talbot
D/3026, 11/3/15; R.F.A., 28/5/15; Lieut.
  Pinewood, Highland Road, Bromley, Kent.

CAUSTON, Ernest Neville
167, 19/4/08; dis. 18/4/12.   300 Heron Street, Toronto, Canada.

CAUSTON, Richard Harold
B/300, 26/6/08; dis. 25/6/09; R. Berks. R., 30/1/15; Capt.; w.
  9 Eastcheap, E.C.

CAUTY, Douglas Butler
6/5/5923, 1/9/15; trfr L'pool. R., 21/4/16.

CAVALIER, Cyril Gordon
6/1/6273, 16/9/15; Army Chaplain, 12/1/16, att. 15th and 13th Lond. R.; F,S,P; Capt.; Chevalier of the Crown of Roumania.
  The Vicarage, Fulham, S.W. 6.

CAVALIER, Francis Bernard
Sq/2988, 1/3/15, L/C.; Bedf. Yeo., 4/6/15; F; Lieut.
  Grimwade House, Caulfield, Melbourne, Victoria, Australia.

CAVANAGH, Frederick Horace
6/1/6652, 7/10/15, L/C.; No. 7 O.C.B., 3/7/16; trfr. M.G.C., 29/12/16.   5 Haigh Terrace, Kingstown.

CAVE, Edward Charles
A/896, 5/8/14; Som. L.I., 5/10/14; Lieut.; w.

CAVE, Guy
B/541, 27/1/11; R. Fus., 15/8/14, att. R. War. R.; F; Capt.; g
  Services Club, 19 Stratford Place, W.

CAVE, Laurence Charles Henry
6/4/9189, 28/1/16; No. 5 O.C.B., 14/8/16; R.F.C., 21/11/16, R.A.F.; Lieut.   Kitcham Park, Petersfield, Hampshire.

CAVE, Maurice Raphael John
6/Sq/6274, 16/9/15, L/C.; Worc. Yeo., 18/12/15, M.G.C.; Lieut.
  Beechfield, Bromley, Kent.

CAVELL, William Hill
C/13279, 14/6/18, L/C.; demob. 7/2/19.
  5 Milton Place, Gravesend, Kent.

CAWDRY, Frederic George Victor
D/Sq/10449, 10/1/17; No. 1 Cav. C/S, 31/7/17; R. Regt. of Cav., 22/2/18; 2/Lieut.   Portland House, Halifax, Yorkshire.

CAWSTON, George Stevenson
6/5/5877, 30/8/15; Notts. & Derby. R., 17/1/16; Lieut.
  Home Crest, 5 Vale Avenue, Tunbridge Wells.

CAWTHORNE, Alfred Stuart Bloomfield
Sq/1131, 9/9/14; Norf. Yeo., 29/1/15, Midd'x. Yeo.; E,P,S; Lieut.   121 Victoria Street, Westminster, S.W. 1.

CAZALET, Ronald de Bode
F/1817, 16/10/14; Hamps. R., 29/10/14; Capt.; M.C., M(1).

CECIL, Lawrence Henry
6/3/7904, 29/11/15, Sgt.; K.R. Rif. C., 4/8/16, att. T.M. Bty.; Capt.; w(2); M.C., M(1).
  c/o. London & Provincial Bank Ltd., 841 Fulham Road, S.W.

CHADWICK, Edgar Ignatius
4/5/4788, 12/7/15; R.E., 28/8/15, Midd'x. R.; S; Lieut.; M(1).
  c/o. Capital and Counties Bank Ltd., Evesham, Worcestershire.

CHADWICK, John
A/B/12166, 29/10/17, L/C.; A.S.C., C/S, 4/3/18; R.A.S.C., 28/4/18; F; 2/Lieut.   Holmleigh, Northfields, Dewsbury.

✠ CHADWICK, John Collinge
6/3/7169, 3/11/15; No. 7 O.C.B., 6/4/16; W. York. R., 17/7/16; F; 2/Lieut.   Killed in action 25/3/17.

CHAFFER, Richard
6/5/7396, 12/11/15; No. 11 O.C.B., 7/5/16; S. Lan. R., 4/9/16; F; Capt.; M.C.   Brougham House, Ulton, Warwickshire.

CHALCRAFT, Henry William Terrell
D/10010, 24/11/16; No. 14 O.C.B., 6/4/17; R. Lanc. R., 31/7/17.
  62 Bishopsgate, E.C. 2.

✠ CHALLONER, Alan Crawhall
B/913, 5/8/14; D. of Corn. L.I., 1/9/14; F; 2/Lieut.
  Killed in action 30/7/15.

CHALLONER, Charles Stuart
K/4/C/2198, 26/11/14; R.F.C., C/S, 4/5/17; R.F.C., 14/6/17, R.A.F.; Lieut.; cr.   47 Selhurst Road, South Norwood, S.E. 25.

CHALMERS, Edward Arthur
6/8500, 20/12/15; dis. med. unfit, 14/8/16.
  c/o. Mrs. Fox, 40 Eardley Crescent, Earls Court, S.W.

CHAMBERLAIN, Geoffrey Lister
C/11480, 14/6/17, L/C.; R.A., C/S, 15/12/17; R.G.A., 13/5/18.
  37 Birch Grove, Acton, S.W.

CHAMBERLAIN, Neville Grahame
Sq/751, 23/1/14; R.G.A., 10/10/14; F; Capt.; M(1).
  Bowness, St. Martin's Avenue, Epsom.

CHAMBERLAIN, Robert Warren
6/4/7640, 22/11/15; 4th Lond. R., 4/9/16, att. R.A.S.C.; F,E,P; Lieut.; w.   457 London Road, Thornton Heath, Surrey.

CHAMBERS, Alan Spence
3/6/7981, 29/11/15, L/C.; Ches. R., 8/7/16, Gren. Gds.; Capt.; M.C.   80 Bidston Road, Birkenhead.

CHAMBERS, Alec John
6/Sq/2/5695, 19/8/15; R.F.C., C/S, 8/10/16; R.F.C., 26/2/17, R.A.F.; Lieut.; cr.   Aberfeldy, Dunstable, Bedfordshire.

CHAMBERS, Bertram Francis
Sq/1834, 16/10/14; R.A.S.C., 8/2/15, att. R.F.C.; F; Capt.
  Bishop's Hostel, Lincoln.

CHAMBERS, Douglas Brian
6/3/9244, 1/2/16; No. 2 O.C.B., 14/8/16; Life Gds., 18/12/16; Lieut.   Arlington, Barnstaple, Devonshire.

CHAMBERS, Hugh Cecil Warren
6/3/8622, 3/1/16; No. 8 O.C.B., 4/8/16; Essex R., 21/11/16, att. Linc. R.; F; Lieut.; w.   60 Creffield Road, Colchester.

✠ CHAMBERS, James Edward
1/3759, 27/5/15; R.F.A., 4/11/15; 2/Lieut.
  Died of wounds 1/10/16.

CHAMBERS, John Addenbrooke
B/12343, 1/1/17; No. 8 O.C.B., 10/5/18; R. War. R., 12/11/18, att. Lan. Fus.; F; 2/Lieut.
  The Croft, Chantry Road, Moseley, Birmingham.

CHAMBERS, John Laurence
C/11465, 8/6/17; No. 14 O.C.B., 7/12/17; R. Innis. Fus., 25/6/18; 2/Lieut.   Brookwood, Fintone, Co. Tyrone, Ireland.

CHAMBERS, Kenneth William
C/A/12045, 27/9/17; A.S.C., C/S, 4/3/18; R.A.S.C., 12/5/18; F,It, the Balkans; 2/Lieut.
  21 Broadway, Withington, Manchester.

CHAMBERS, Norman Fitzroy
6/3/5325, 2/8/15; trfr. R.G.A., 25/9/16; S; Inv.
  The Rectory, Poynings, Sussex.

CHAMBERS, Percy Charles
B/12760, 15/3/18, L/C.; Gds. O.C.B., 9/8/18; Scots Gds., 4/3/19; 2/Lieut.   68 Hazeldene Road, Grove Park, Chiswick, W. 4.

CHAMBERS, Reginald
K/H/2519, 31/12/14; R.N.A.S., 31/5/15, R.A.F.; North Sea; Capt.   Fubourne, Cambridge.

CHAMBERS, William Edward
D/A/12974, 24/4/18; R.A.F., C/S, 23/10/18; demob.
  1401 North Sixteenth Street, Philadelphia, U.S.A.

CHAMPION, Kenneth Graham
4/Sq/4562, 1/7/15, L/C.; R.A.S.C., 27/11/15; F; Lieut.
  41a High Street, St. Johns Wood, N.W. 8.

CHAMPION, Raymond Everard
C/13186, 3/6/18, L/C.; No. 11 O.C.B., 24/1/19; General List, 8/3/19; 2/Lieut.   P.O. Box 345, Bloemfontein, South Africa.

✠ CHAMPION, Roland Laughton
6/1/7062, 27/10/15; No. 11 O.C.B., 16/5/16; 20th Lond. R., 4/9/16; F; 2/Lieut.   Killed in action 17/3/17.

CHAMPION, Thomas Cheyney
C/Sq/10389, 8/1/17, L/C.; R.A., C/S, 22/6/17; trfr. R.F.A., 27/9/17.   Elmgrove House, Lancing, Sussex.

CHAMPNESS, Norman Creswick
E/1608, 6/10/14, L/C.; Dorset R., 21/2/15; M; Capt.; w.
  c/o. Messrs. Sedgwick Collins & Coy. Ltd., 7 Gracechurch Street, E.C. 3.

APPENDIX II.—RECORDS OF RANK AND FILE.

CHAMPNEYS, *Edward Geoffrey Stanley*
6/Sq/9142, 25/1/16; R.F.A., C/S, 18/8/16; R.F.A., 12/1/17; F; Lieut.; *M.C.*   *Otterpool Manor, Sellindge, Hythe.*

✠ CHANCE, *Eric Godwin*
C/11056, 16/4/17; R.F.C., C/S, 1/6/17; R.F.C., 4/7/17; It; 2/Lieut.   *Killed in action 19/1/18.*

✠ CHANCELLOR, *Geoffrey Ellis*
4/3628, 17/5/15, Sgt.; R. W. Surr. R., 28/7/15, att. R.F.C.; 2/Lieut.   *Killed in action 9/7/16.*

CHANCELLOR, *George Walter*
4/5/4664, 8/7/15, L/C.; No. 14 O.C.B.; 8th Lond. R., 24/10/16, att. R. Fus.; F; Lieut.; w; *M.C.*
Athol Lodge, 21 Miskin Road, Dartford.

CHANCELLOR, *Henry Edward*
D/10262, 29/12/16; No. 21 O.C.B., 5/5/17; R. Lanc. R., 28/8/17 att. S. Lan. R.; F; Lieut.; w.   *The Locks, Ryders Green, West Bromwich.*

CHANDLER, *Cecil John Golding*
K/B/2061, 12/11/14; R.A.O.C., 8/2/15; E; Major, D.A.D.O.S.; O.B.E.   *34 Bath Road, Bedford Park, W. 4.*

CHANDLER, *Clement Leslie*
B/12761, 15/3/18.

CHANDLER, *Frederick Joseph*
10637, 1/2/17; R.A., C/S, 26/7/17; R.G.A., 17/12/17; Lieut.; M.B.E., m(1).   *69 Crouch Hall Road, Crouch End, N. 8.*

CHANDLER, *Jack*
6/5/5243, 31/7/15, L/C.; Manch. R., 6/1/16, emp. R.E.; Lieut.; p.   *286 Waterloo Street, Oldham, Lancashire.*

✠ CHANDLER, *John*
4/4271, 17/6/15; 19th Lond. R., 1/11/15; 2/Lieut.; *M.C.*
Killed in action 2/10/16.

CHANDLER, *John Thomas*
B/10096, 4/12/16; R.G.A., C/S, 22/6/17; R.G.A., 25/11/17; F; 2/Lieut.; M(1).   *34 Boulevard, Halifax, Yorkshire.*

CHANDLER, *Sidney John*
B/13460, 5/7/18; No. 22 O.C.B., 23/8/18, No. 11 O.C.B.; General List, 8/3/19; 2/Lieut.
c/o. Oriental Club, Hanover Square, W. 1.

CHANDLER, *Walter Hugh*
2/3447, 3/5/15; Notts. & Derby. R., 23/8/15; F; Lieut.; w.
17 Craven Avenue, Ealing. W. 5.

CHANNING, *Edgar Norman*
B/10669, 9/2/17; No. 12 O.C.B., 10/8/17; N. Staff. R., 27/11/17; F; 2/Lieut.; w.
36 Upper Grosvenor Road, Handsworth Wood, Birmingham.

CHANTER, *Francis*
6/Sq/8231, 8/12/15; No. 1 Cav. C/S, 2/8/16; Dorset Yeo., 27/11/16; P; Lieut.; w; M(1).
27 The Quadrant, Highbury, N. 5.

CHAPLIN, *Edward James Morgan*
A/42, 6/4/08; dis. 5/4/09.   *15 Addison Gardens, W. 14.*

✠ CHAPLIN, *George Douglas*
A/11593, 5/7/17; A.S.C., C/S, 1/11/17; R.A.S.C., 25/1/18; F; 2/Lieut.   *Died in South Africa 27/6/20.*

CHAPLIN, *Roland Henry*
D/11855, 13/8/17; R.E., C/S, 4/11/17; R.E., 1/2/18; F; 2/Lieut.
130 London Road, Kingston-on-Thames, Surrey.

CHAPMAN, *Allan*
2/3589, 13/5/15, Cpl.; E. Surr. R., 16/11/15, R.F.C., R.A.F.; Lieut.; *Inj.*   *Gillwell Park, Chingford, Essex.*

CHAPMAN, *Allan Simpson*
6/1/5722, 19/8/15, L/C.; No. 11 O.C.B., 7/5/16; Lan. Fus., 4/9/16; 2/Lieut.; w.   *School House, Grassington, Skipton.*

CHAPMAN, *Cecil*
6/5/8161, 6/12/15; R.F.A., C/S, 4/8/16; R.F.A., 24/11/16; F; Lieut.; g.   *291 Iffley Road, Oxford.*

✠ CHAPMAN, *Douglas Collier*
6/4/8792, 3/1/16, L/C.; R.E., C/S, 18/11/16; R.E., 10/2/17; Lieut.   *Killed in action 20/10/18.*

CHAPMAN, *Ernest John*
C/13364, 21/6/18; dis. med. unfit, 23/12/18.
34 Lower Hastings Street, Leicester.

CHAPMAN, *Guy Patterson*
A/1188, 14/9/14, Cpl.; R. Fus., 27/11/14; F; Capt.; O.B.E., M.C., M(2).   *35 Nevern Place, S.W. 5.*

CHAPMAN, *Henry*
K/A/2131, 19/11/14; S. Staff. R., 31/3/15; F; 2/Lieut.
1 Knowe Terrace, Lambhill, Glasgow.

CHAPMAN, *Henry Robert George Tydd*
3/3340, 22/4/15; Shrops. L.I., 8/7/15, 10th Lond. R.; F; Capt.; w. *M.C.*   *Hawthornden, Englefield Green, Surrey.*

CHAPMAN, *Horace Stanley*
C/A/13296, 17/6/18, L/C.; No. 5 O.C.B., 8/11/18, 20 O.C.B.; Midd'x. R., 17/3/19; 2/Lieut.   *16 Crewys Road, S.E. 15.*

CHAPMAN, *Robert Stannard*
A/10260, 29/12/16; No. 21 O.C.B., 5/5/17; Midd'x. R., 25/9/17; I; Lieut.   *29 Old Nelson Street, Lowestoft.*

CHAPMAN, *Roland Bristow*
6/4/6349, 20/9/15, L/C.; Notts. & Derby. R., 1/6/16, Leic. R.; 2/Lieut.; w.
c/o. Lewis Byron & Coy., Solicitors and Notaries, Gardiner Street, Durban, South Africa.

CHAPMAN, *Vivian Rougier*
3/3154, 1/4/15; R.G.A., 8/9/15, att. R.F.C.; F; Lieut.
5 Woodborough Road, Putney, S.W. 15.

CHAPMAN, *Walter William*
A/10384, 8/1/17; trfr. 15th Lond. R., 9/3/17.
9 Row 117, South Quay, Great Yarmouth.

CHAPMAN, *Wilfrid Astley*
6/3/6548, 30/9/15; Notts. & Derby. R., 1/6/16, Leic. R.; Lieut.
c/o. Lewis Byron & Coy., Solicitors and Notaries, Gardiner Street, Durban, South Africa.

✠ CHAPMAN, *William Ronald Cecil*
C/11507, 18/6/17; Household Bde. Q.C.B., 5/10/17; trfr. 13th Lond. R., 29/4/18.   *Died 24/6/19.*

CHAPMAN, *William Ross*
A/12784, 29/1/18, L/C.; No. 4 O.C.B., 7/6/18; North'd. Fus., 3/3/19; 2/Lieut.
9 Moorfield, High West Jesmond, Newcastle-on-Tyne.

CHAPPELL, *Roy Williamson*
6/9030, 20/1/16; R.F.C., 16/6/16; R.A.F.; F; Capt.; w; M.C., M(1).   *14 Addiscombe Grove, East Croydon.*

CHAPPLE, *John Howard*
5/5326, 2/8/15; Worc. R., 4/1/16, Lab. Corps; Capt.
Waveney, Haywards Heath.

CHARD, *Alexander Richard*
Sq/750, 23/1/14; 5th Drag. Gds., 15/8/14; Capt.
21 Roland Gardens, S. Kensington, S.W.

CHARITY, *Frederick William*
4/3/B/4451, 28/6/15, Sgt.; trfr. R.F.C., 13/12/17.
8 Hermitage Road, Richmond, Surrey.

✠ CHARLES, *Albert*
4/3760, 27/5/15, L/C.; Notts. & Derby. R., 17/9/15; 2/Lieut.
Killed in action 1/7/16.

CHARLES, *James*
4/3/4209, 14/6/15; N. Staff. R., 7/10/15; F; Capt.; w.
Breeze Hill, Bury, Lancashire.

CHARLES, *Reginald Pendrill St. John*
D/10607, 22/1/17; R.A., C/S, 26/7/17; R.G.A., 6/1/18; F; 2/Lieut.   *28 Esplanade, Porthcawl, Glamorganshire.*

CHARLES, *Samuel Davenport*
Sq/510, 4/11/10, L/C.; Linc. Yeo., 28/11/14; F; Capt.; w; M.C.
13 West Hill, Highgate, N. 6.

CHARLES, *William Thomas*
6/1/7131, 2/11/15, L/C.; Mon. R., 4/8/16; F; Lieut.; M(1).
Glanhafren, Lisvane Road, Llanishen, Nr. Cardiff.

CHARLES-EDWARDS, *Llewelyn*   See EDWARDS, L. C.

CHARLESWORTH, *Edward Fitzgerald*
A/1364, 26/9/14, L/C.; R.W. Surr. R., 18/2/15, secd. M.G.C.; I; Capt.   *Littlegrange, Whyteleafe, Surrey.*

CHARLTON, *Douglas Vincent*
6/Sq/6317, 19/9/15; No. 1 Cav. C/S, 24/4/16; Fife & Forfar Yeo., 28/7/16, att. High. L.I., M.G.C.; F; Lieut.
38 Howgate Road, East Sheen, S.W. 14.

APPENDIX II.—RECORDS OF RANK AND FILE.

CHARLTON, *Foster Ferrier*
6/8746, 6/1/16; No. 9 O.C.B., 8/3/16; Gord. Highrs., 23/7/16, att. Cam'n. Highrs.; Capt.; *w*.
  Riverside, Castle Street, Salisbury.

CHARLTON, *Nicolas Poyntz*
B/13525, 15/7/18; trfr. K.R. Rif. C., 26/6/19, R.A.O.C.; L/C.
  Chilwell Hall, Nottinghamshire.

CHARLTON, *Samuel Ernest*
A/11594, 5/7/17; A.S.C., C/S, 1/11/17; R.A.S.C., 25/1/18; F; 2/Lieut. *42 Trafalgar Road, Birkdale, Southport.*

✠ CHARLTON, *William Godfrey*
6/4/5192, 29/7/15; Durh. L.I., 20/1/16; Lieut.
  Killed in action 26/8/18.

CHART, *Roland*
C/10836, 5/3/17, L/C.; No. 11 O.C.B., 5/7/17; E. Surr. R., 30/10/17; F; Lieut.; *w*(2).
  West Cot, 4 Clarendon Grove, Mitcham, Surrey.

CHARTER, *Sydney Herbert*
Sq/3487, 4/5/15; trfr. R.F.A., 29/10/15.
  25 Beauval Road, Dulwich, S.E.

CHASE, *Allan St. John Centlivres*
B/Sq/13661, 29/7/18; dis. med unfit, 5/2/19.
  c/o. Messrs. W. A. Longman, 18 Belmont, Bath.

CHASE, *Geoffrey Herbert*
6/2/6653, 7/10/15; No. 11 O.C.B., 7/5/16; North'n. R., 4/9/16; F; Lieut. *150 Philip Lane, N. 15.*

✠ CHASE, *Harold Charles*
6/5/7855, 26/11/15; No 14 O.C.B.; Linc. R., 24/10/16; F; 2/Lieut. Killed in action 8/6/17.

CHASE, *Henry Nuttall Centlivres*
1/3223, 12/4/15; N. Lan. R., 24/1/16; F,S,P; 2/Lieut.
  Uitenhage, Cape Province, South Africa.

CHASE, *Philip Hugh*
E/1601, 6/10/14, Sgt.; Midd'x. R., 27/11/14; 2/Lieut.; M(1).
  Died of wounds 1/7/16.

CHATER, *Frank*
B/E/13563, 19/7/18; No. 22 O.C.B., 20/9/18; Dorset R., 5/2/19; 2/Lieut. *Broadstone, Dorset.*

CHATFIELD, *Arthur William Freeston*
D/12900, 8/4/18, L/C.; No. 8 O.C.B., 20/9/18; R.W. Surr. R., 16/3/19; 2/Lieut. *47 Botley Road, Oxford.*

CHATFIELD, *Hugh Stanton*
C/22, 1/4/08; dis. 31/3/10.

CHAUNCY-BRYANT, *Thomas Algernon Read*
6/2/7905. 29/11/15; A.S.C., C/S, 29/5/16; R.A.S.C., 3/7/16; 2/Lieut. *Riverside, Grove Park Road, Chiswick, W. 4.*

CHAVASSE, *Geoffrey Dickson*
6/5/6805, 14/10/15, L/C.; No. 14 O.C.B., 30/10/16; L'pool. R., 24/1/17, att. R.A.F.; F; Lieut.; *Inv*.
  128 West Princes Street, Helensburgh.

CHEESMAN, *Alban Cecil*
B/10087, 4/12/16, L/C.; No 14 O.C.B., 6/4/17; Dorset R., 31/7/17, att. R.A.F.; Lieut. *57 Empress Avenue, Ilford, Essex.*

CHEETHAM, *Cyril Stewart*
D/Sq/12938, 17/4/18; No. 2 Cav. C/S, 7/11/18; demob.
  c/o. Asiatic Petroleum Coy. Ltd., Shanghai, China.

CHEETHAM, *Ralph Hyde*
6/3/8600, 3/1/16; No. 5 O.C.B., 14/8/16; Yorks. L.I., 18/12/16, S. Staff. R.; I; Capt. *6 Irton Road, Southport, Lancashire.*

✠ CHEETHAM, *William*
6/5/8325, 10/12/15, Sgt.; No. 14 O.C.B., 28/8/16; N. Lan. R., 22/11/16, R.E.; F; Lieut.; *Inv*. Died -/2/20.

CHERRY, *Cyril William*
6/5/7132, 2/11/15; C.Q.M.S.; demob. 23/4/19.

CHESHIRE, *Harold Theodore*
4/2/4598, 5/7/15; R. War. R., 24/11/15; F; Lieut.; *g*.
  Rayleigh, Warwick Avenue, Coventry.

CHESNEY, *George Lawrence*
K/A/2241, 3/12/14; R. Lanc. R., 23/12/14; Lieut.; *w*.

CHESTER, *Bernard Fry*
6/4/5159, 29/7/15; Bord. R., 7/1/16; Afghan.; Capt.
  c/o. W. M. Douët, Esq., 138 Dalmeny Avenue, Norbury, S.W. 16.

CHESTER, *Stephen Radcliffe*
B/12678, 4/3/18, L/C.; demob. 10/1/19.
  77 Montpelier Rise, Golders Green, N.W. 4.

✠ CHESTERS, *John Richard*
4/3191, 8/4/15, Sgt.; E. Surr. R., 2/9/15; F; Lieut.
  Killed in action 15/9/16.

CHESTERTON, *Ernest Charles*
4/1/4364, 21/6/15, L/C.; R.A.S.C., 16/10/15, R.N.A.S., R.A.F.; F; Lieut.; *w*. *30a George Street, Hanover Square, W. 1.*

CHESTERTON, *George Laval*
A/9836, 3/11/16; No. 14 O.C.B., 27/12/16; R.F.C., 16/3/17, R.A.F.; 2/Lieut.
  77 Englewood Road, Clapham Common, S.W. 12.

CHETTLE, *Henry Francis*
54, 7/4/08; dis. 6/4/12; R.A.S.C., -/9/14; F; Major; O.B.E., *m*(1). *United University Club, Pall Mall East, S.W. 1.*

CHETTLE, *Norman*
A/14343, 6/1/19; demob. 29/1/19. *The Manor Farm, Reading.*

CHETTOE, *Cyril Stapley*
2/3083, 22/3/15; E. Surr. R., 8/7/15; F; Lieut.; *w*.
  9 Highland Road, Bromley, Kent.

CHETWYND-STAPYLTON, *William Eric*
B/1101, 7/9/14; 8th Lond. R., 31/10/14; Capt.
  Larchwood, Weybridge, Surrey.

CHEVASSUT, *Frederick George*
6/8868, 12/1/16; R.F.A., C/S, 9/6/16; R.F.A., 5/9/16; Lieut.; *w*.

CHEW, *Thomas Leslie*
B/1306, 26/9/14, L/C.; R.F.A., 5/6/15; M,I; Lieut.
  29 Platts Lane, Hampstead, N.W. 3.

CHEYNE, *George Basil Watson*
B/9899, 13/11/16; R.W. Surr. R., 9/3/17; F; 2/Lieut.
  Beechgrove, 55 Sydenham Hill, S.E. 26.

CHEYNEY, *Reginald Southouse*
4/1/4068, 7/6/15, L/C.; R. War. R., 3/9/15; Lieut.; *w*.
  92 High Street, Whitechapel.

✠ CHIBNALL, *Ronald Stanley*
B/1196, 14/9/14, Cpl.; Suff. R., 12/12/14; F; Lieut.
  Killed in action 31/7/17.

CHICK, *Lionel Talbot*
4/3720, 24/5/15; trfr. E. Kent R., 24/3/16.
  61 Argyle Road, Ealing, W.

CHIDSON, *Lowthian Hume*
C/917, 5/8/14; E. Surr. R., 15/8/14, secd. M.G.C.; F,S; Major; M.B.E., M(3) *13 Eardley Road, S.W. 16.*

✠ CHILD, *Philip Herbert*
B/11436, 4/6/17; No. 10 O.C.B., 5/10/17; R. War. R., 26/2/18; F; 2/Lieut. Killed in action 23/8/18.

CHILDE-PEMBERTON, *Roland Ivo Lacon*
4/5054, 22/7/15, L/C.; 18th Huss., 11/12/15; Lieut.
  12 Portman Street, Portman Square, W.

CHILDERS, *William Leslie Eardley*
B/383, 24/3/09; dis. 27/4/10; Scots. Gds., 16/12/15, Cold. Gds., R.E.; Lieut.; *w*.

CHILTON, *Geoffrey*
6/5/8537, 30/12/15; 16th Lond. R., 6/6/16, Intelligence; F; Lieut.; *Inv*. *Heath View, Clapham Common, S.W. 4.*

CHILVERS, *Percy Monkman*
B/12723, 12/3/18; No. 20 O.C.B., 20/9/18; demob.
  53 Caledon Road, Sherwood, Nottingham.

✠ CHILVERS, *Reginald Cuthbert*
A/2024, 5/11/14; Norf. R., 26/3/15; 2/Lieut.
  Killed in action 19/4/17.

CHINNECK, *George Edwin*
B/10089, 4/12/16, L/C.; No. 20 O.C.B., 5/5/17; N. Lan. R., 28/8/17; F; Lieut.; *w*. *37 Silverdale, Sydenham, S.E. 26.*

✠ CHINNERY, *Reginald Charles*
6/5/6242, 16/9/15; L'pool. R., 6/6/16; 2/Lieut.
  Killed in action 31/7/17.

CHOLERTON, *Joseph Roberts*
2/3496, 6/5/15; Notts. & Derby. R., 3/8/15, Lab. Corps; Capt.; *w*; *M.C.* *Penny Long Lane, Derby.*

APPENDIX II.—RECORDS OF RANK AND FILE.

✠ CHOLMELEY, Hugh Valentine
4/2/4641, 5/7/15; Gren. Gds., 15/9/15, att. M.G.C.; F; 2/Lieut.
Killed in action 7/4/16.

CHOLMONDELEY, Hugh Grenville
6/1/5678, 16/8/15; K.R. Rif. C., 1/6/16; F; Lieut.; w.
Eckington Manor, Pershore, Worcestershire.

CHORLEY, Leslie William
B/12729, 11/3/18; No. 16 O.C.B., 23/8/18; R. Fus., 6/3/19; 2/Lieut.
Hibernia, 24 Wellmeadow Road, Lewisham, S.E. 13.

CHOWN, John Stanley
A/201, 6/5/08; dis. 5/5/10; joined 8th Lond. R., L/Cpl.; 8th Lond. R., 1/3/17, att. K.R. Rif. C.; F; Lieut.; p; M.C.
6 Bond Court, Walbrook, E.C.

CHOWNE, Cecil Tilson
Sq/3011, 8/3/15; W. Som. Yeo., 3/6/15, Gren. Gds.; E,P; Lieut.
14 Coleherne Court, S.W. 5.

CHOWNE, William Maurice
A/10931, 28/3/17; R.F.C., C/S, 4/5/17; R.F.C., 14/6/17, R.A.F.; F; Lieut.
The White House, Mackney, Wallingford, Berkshire.

CHRISTALL, Francis James
D/10817, 2/3/17; No. 11 O.C.B., 5/7/17; 1st Lond. R., 30/10/17, att. 19th Lond. R.; F; Lieut.
West Croft, Brambledon Road, Wallington, Surrey.

CHRISTIAN, Richard Edward Edmonds
3/3533, 10/5/15, Cpl.; R.W. Surr. R., 28/7/15; Lieut.

CHRISTIE, Alfred Ernest
2/9779, 24/10/16; No. 14 O.C.B., 5/3/17; trfr. R.F.A., 16/5/17, M.G.C., Tank Corps; Sgt.
Ikona, 45 Observatory Road, East Sheen, S.W. 14.

✠ CHRISTIE, Harold Reginald Monro
D/2460, 28/12/14, L/C.; Sco. Rif., 18/4/15; 2/Lieut.
Killed in action 16/7/16.

CHRISTIE, Ivor Crawley Luxmoor
6/8918, 14/1/16; R.A., C/S, 4/8/16; R.G.A., 3/12/16; F; Lieut.
Salmon Arm, British Colombia, Canada.

CHRISTIE, Percy James
A/11239, 11/5/17, Sgt.; demob. 7/4/19.
Ingleside, 41 Warpole Road, Wimbledon, S.W.

CHRISTIE, Ralph Lindsay
6/4/9194, 29/1/16; No. 8 O.C.B., 4/8/16; York. R., 21/11/16; Lieut.; w; M(1).
Durie, Leven, Fifeshire.

CHRISTIE, William Marshall
6/3/6727, 11/10/15, L/C.; No. 9 O.C.B., 8/3/16; R. Scots., 23/7/16; F; Lieut.; w.
9 Ravelston Park, Edinburgh.

CHRISTMAS, Herbert Russell
4/1/4623, 5/7/15; York. R., 10/1/16; F; Lieut.
Columbia Cottage, Porchester, Nr. Fareham, Hampshire.

CHRISTOPHER, Charles de Aquilar Mordaunt
Sq/537, 13/1/11; dis. med. unfit. 5/6/13.

✠ CHRISTY, Thomas Hills
6/Sq/7379, 11/11/15; No. 1 Cav. C/S, 6/12/16; Essex Yeo., 16/4/17, att. Essex R.; F; 2/Lieut.
Killed in action 12/4/18.

CHRYSTAL, George William
A/442, 8/11/09; dis. 30/10/11.
99 St. George's Square, S.W.

✠ CHRYSTAL, Ian Campbell
6/7721, 22/11/15; No. 9 O.C.B., 8/3/16; Sea. Highrs., 6/7/16; F; 2/Lieut.
Killed in action 1/5/17.

CHUBB, Clovis Michael
3/3297, 19/4/15; dis. med. unfit, 30/10/15.
The Orchard, Fordingbridge, Hampshire.

CHUBB, Philip Bernard
C/14214, 23/10/18; demob.
6 Southwood Lane, Highgate, N. 6.

CHUBB, Stanford Frank
B/11342, 21/5/17; No. 14 O.C.B., 5/10/17; Devon. R., 26/2/18; 2/Lieut.
Granville Lodge, Olveston, Gloucestershire. (Now in China.)

CHURCH, Frank
6/3/7861, 26/11/15, L/C.; No. 14 O.C.B.; K.R. Rif. C., 24/10/16; F,NR; Capt.; w; M(1).
The Cedars, Bassingbourn, Cambridgeshire.

CHURCH, Frederick John Allan
6/5/7288, 8/11/15; E. Lan. R., 4/8/16, att. Lan. Fus.; Lieut.
49 Bath Road, Swindon.

✠ CHURCH, Harold
C/1317, 26/9/14; Oxf. & Bucks. L.I., 31/10/14; Capt.
Killed in action 19/7/16.

CHURCHER, Archibald Edward
6/5/8801, 10/1/16; R.F.A., C/S, 4/8/16; R.G.A., 12/11/16; Capt.; w(3).
Walsingham, Golders Green Road, N.W. 4.

CHURCHILL, Arthur Charles
6/5/8079, 1/12/15; No. 14 O.C.B.; Yorks. L.I., 24/10/16; Lieut.; w.
Corsham, Wiltshire.

CHURCHILL, Ernest Frank
K/E/2327, 14/12/14; R.E., 19/3/15; F; Major; M.C., M(2).
12 Station Road, Reading.

CHURCHLEY, Reginald Ernest
6/5871, 28/8/15, L/C.; R.F.A., C/S, 4/8/16; R.G.A., 3/11/16; F; Capt.
54 Wightman Road, Harringay, N. 4.

CHUTE, Lawrence Vere
1/3155, 1/4/15; E. Surr. R., 8/7/15, att. Durh. L.I., R. Lanc. R.; I,M; Capt.; M.C.
Bulhams Covert, Wissett, Halesworth, Suffolk.

CHUTE, Trevor Victor
6/9278, 3/2/16; R.F.A., C/S, 26/5/16; R.G.A., 13/9/16; Lieut.
3 Belleville Avenue, Rathgar Road, Dublin.

CLAGUE, John Thorpe
6/5/6119, 9/9/15; 1st Lond. R., 20/12/15; F; Lieut.; w.
Northfield, High Street, Sidcup, Kent.

CLAMP, Ernest Edward
6/5/6904, 18/10/15, L/C.; trfr. Army Pay Corps, 4/1/17.
93 Pepys Road, St. Catherine's Park, S.E.

CLAPHAM, Wilfrid Verso
3/8623, 3/1/16; R.F.A., C/S, 29/9/16; R.G.A., 19/12/16; Lieut.
3 Kingston Square, Hull.

CLAPP, John Henry
6/Sq/7906, 29/11/15; No. 2 Cav. C/S, 1/9/16; Bedf. Yeo., 27/1/17, Indian Army; I,E,P; Lieut.
Ashley Rectory, Kingsomborne, Hampshire.

✠ CLAPP, William Gilbert Elphinstone
4/Sq/3910, 31/5/15, L/C.; Norf. Yeo., 20/9/15, att. Norf. R.; F; 2/Lieut.
Died of wounds 29/4/17.

CLAPPEN, Herbert John
6/1/7253, 8/11/15, Sgt.; Ches. R., 4/8/16; F; Lieut.; w.
Elm Grove, Circencester, Gloucestershire.

CLAPPEN, Stanley Graham
6/1/6375, 20/9/15, L/C.; 16th Lond. R., 15/4/16, Indian Army; F,I,Persia; Capt.
Elm Grove, Circencester, Gloucestershire.

CLAPPEN, Victor Allan
6/5/6687, 7/10/15; No. 7 O.C.B., 6/4/16; R.W. Fus., 17/7/16, att. 2nd Lond. R.; F; Lieut.; w(2).
27 Parkwood Road, Boscombe, Bournemouth.

CLARENCE, Charles Dudley Beverley
D/Sq/C/13742, 2/8/18; No. 11 O.C.B., 31/1/19; General List, 8/3/19; 2/Lieut.
c/o. National Bank of South Africa Ltd., London Wall, E.C. 2.

CLARK, Alan Edwin Nelham
E/1516, 1/10/14; R.F.A., 13/7/15; Lieut.
85 Leigham Court Road, Streatham.

CLARK, Alexander Nielson
6/5/8103, 2/12/15; No. 8 O.C.B., 4/8/16; Yorks. L.I., 21/11/16; F; 2/Lieut.; w.
35 Mercers Road, Tufnell Park, N.

✠ CLARK, Alfred Matthew
6/4/5878, 30/8/15; R. Lanc. R., 31/12/15; Lieut.
Killed in action 20/11/17.

CLARK, Donald Aubrey Vaughan. See VAUGHAN-CLARK, D. A.

CLARK, Edmund Arthur
6/4/6949, 21/10/15; No. 14 O.C.B., 27/9/16; L'pool. R., 24/1/17, att. Midd'x. R., secd. M.G.C.; F; Lieut.
Foxfield, Broughton-in-Furness.

CLARK, Edward
B/13433, 3/7/18; demob. 14/2/19.
35 Maple Street, Woodlands Road, Middlesborough.

APPENDIX II.—RECORDS OF RANK AND FILE.

CLARK, Ernest Reginald
D/11818, 9/8/17, Sgt.; demob. 22/1/19.
212 Bond Street, Macclesfield.

✠ CLARK, Frank Nelham
E/1/6/1502, 1/10/14, L/C.; R.F.C., 25/9/16; 2/Lieut.
Killed 29/4/17.

CLARK, Frederick Hugh
A/13043, 7/5/18; R.E., C/S, 23/8/18; demob.
c/o. H. D'Adhemar, Esq., 19 Buckingham Street, W.C. 2.

CLARK, George Herbert
A/11643, 12/7/17; No. 19 O.C.B., 9/11/17; E. Kent. R., 26/3/18; 2/Lieut.
71 Court Lane, S.E. 21.

CLARK, George William James
4/2/4210, 14/6/15; R.E., 23/12/15; F; Lieut.
Silver Birches, Longdene Road, Haslemere, Surrey.

CLARK, Godfrey Henry Jocelyn
6/2/9457, 14/2/16; Intelligence Corps, 3/8/16; F; Lieut.
Batchelor's Club, Hamilton Place, W.

CLARK, Harold Bennett
4/4272, 17/6/15; 12th Lond. R., 27/11/15, secd. M.G.C.; Lieut.
44 Hillfield Park, Muswell Hill.

CLARK, Henry
6/2/7654, 22/11/15; R. Fus., 25/9/16; F; Capt.; g; M.C. and Bar.
15 Fife Street, Dufftown, Banffshire, Scotland. (Now in British West Indies.)

CLARK, Henry Birch
A/10293, 1/1/17, L/C.; No. 20 O.C.B., 7/6/17; W. Rid. R., 25/9/17, York & Lanc. R.; It; 2/Lieut.
4 Ewelme Road, Forest Hill, S.E. 23.

CLARK, Herbert Milburn
6/9060, 21/1/16; R.A., C/S, 21/7/16; R.F.A., 10/11/16; F; Lieut.; w.
Rosedale, Gosforth, Newcastle-on-Tyne.

CLARK, John Cosmo
H/2936, 18/2/15; Midd'x. R., 24/4/15; F; Capt.; w(3); M.C.
44 Rusthill Avenue, Bedford Park, W. 4.

CLARK, John Henry
6/1/8610, 3/1/16, L/C.; No. 14 O.C.B., 26/11/16; Worc. R., 27/3/17; F; Lieut.; w.
Battledene, Campden, Gloucestershire.

✠ CLARK, John Mactaggart
H/1994, 29/10/14, L/C.; R.W. Surr. R., 8/2/15, att. Durh. L.I.; F; Capt.; w; M(1).
Died 18/11/18.

CLARK, Leslie Ebenezer
6/3/5789, 23/8/15, L/C.; K.R. Rif. C., 1/6/16; Lieut.; w.
207 Evering Road, Upper Clapton, E. 5.

✠ CLARK, Lyonel Latimer
2/3125, 29/3/15; R.H.A., 7/8/15, secd. R.F.C.; F; 2/Lieut.
Killed in action 2/8/16.

CLARK, Malcolm
Sq/1090, 4/9/14, L/C.; R.A.S.C., 16/11/14; Lieut.
The Elms, Watford, Hertfordshire.

✠ CLARK, Norman Harry
6/Sq/7862, 26/11/15, L/C.; No. 2 Cav. C/S, 1/9/16; Bedf. Yeo., 10/1/17; F; 2/Lieut.
Died of wounds 25/11/17.

CLARK, Robert Leslie
B/13413, 1/7/18, L/C.; demob. 24/1/19.
25 Bracken Road, Darlington.

CLARK, Robert Thomson
6/8993, 18/1/16; No. 9 O.C.B., 8/3/16; R. Highrs., 6/7/16; F; Lieut.
Editorial Staff, Glasgow Herald, Glasgow.

CLARK, Stanley Ward
B/11387, 30/5/17, L/C.; No. 14 O.C.B., 4/1/18; Norf. R., 25/6/18; F; 2/Lieut.; w.
6 Lisson Grove, Hale, Nr. Manchester.

CLARK, Walter
A/12511, 31/1/18; R.E., C/S, 12/5/18; R.E., 27/9/18; 2/Lieut.
Wallington, 11 Lodge Road, Hendon, N.W. 4.

CLARK, Walter Henry
H/2964, 25/2/15, L/C.; Dorset R., 2/6/15, secd. M.G.C.; F; Lieut.; w.
Lorraine, 10 Manor Road, Twickenham.

✠ CLARK, William M.
6/5/5924, 1/9/15, L/C.; Manch. R., 4/8/16; 2/Lieut.
Killed in action 27/3/17.

CLARK, William Ernest
6/3/5501, 9/8/15; R.F.A., 3/11/15; Lieut.
42 Alfred Street, Ripley, Derby.

CLARK, William Graham
C/10169, 11/12/16, L/C.; trfr. Class W. Res., 12/3/18.
Heather Cottage, Port Erin, Isle of Man.

CLARK, William James
6/5/5701, 19/8/15; R. Ir. Fus., 4/8/16, att. T.M. Bty., Indian Army; F,It,E; Lieut.; w.
Westminster House, 7 Millbank, S.W. 1.

CLARK, William Smith
E/1494, 1/10/14; dis. med. unfit, 1/12/14.
Lamb Building, Temple, E.C. 4.

CLARKE, Albert Edward
4/6/2/4956, 19/7/15, L/C.; Hamps. R., 7/6/16; Lieut.

CLARKE, Alexander Hyde
A/11595, 5/7/17; No. 8 O.C.B., 8/3/18; Shrops. L.I., 10/9/18; F; 2/Lieut.
Marionville, Old Catton, Norwich.

CLARKE, Bernard Allatt
B/11415, 1/6/17; No. 14 O.C.B., 5/10/17; Yorks. L.I., 26/2/18; 2/Lieut.
St. James Cottage, Heckmondwike, Yorkshire.

CLARKE, Cecil Alexander
3/3629, 17/5/15, L/C.; 4th Lond. R., 5/8/15; F,NR; Capt.; w; M.C., M(2).
11 Barnfield Road, Ealing, W. 5.

✠ CLARKE, Charles St. Aubyn
6/2/5427, 5/8/15; M.G.C., C/S, 25/10/16; M.G.C., 24/2/17, Indian Army; 2/Lieut.
Killed in action 30/7/18.

CLARKE, Cyril
D/10684, 7/2/17; R.F.C., C/S, 16/4/17; R.F.C., 16/5/17.
19 Blencathra Street, Keswick, Cumberland.

CLARKE, Donovan Ralph
6/2/6387, 23/9/15; dis. to re-enlist in R.F.C., 6/8/16.
Holmleigh, Woodland Park, Colwyn Bay.

CLARKE, Frank Bromwich
A/D/13970, 6/9/18; demob. 30/5/19. 6 Swan Street, Warwick.

CLARKE, Frank James
A/9839, 3/11/16; R.F.A., C/S, 9/3/17; R.F.A., 3/9/17; F; Lieut.
Westmead, Thornton Hough, Nr. Birkenhead.

CLARKE, Frederick Arthur Stanley
C/449, 19/11/09; 10th Lond. R., 16/11/12, att. 25th Lond. R.; G,E,P,I; Major; D.S.O., M(1).
Lieut., Essex Regt., c/o. Cox & Coy., 16 Charing Cross, S.W. 1.

CLARKE, Geoffrey Read Garnett. See GARNETT-CLARKE, G. R.

CLARKE, George Ernest
C/10835, 5/3/17; No. 14 O.C.B., 5/7/17; Som. L.I., 30/10/17; F; 2/Lieut.; w.
18 The Boulevard, Weston-super-Mare.

CLARKE, Harold Watson
6/2/6194, 13/9/15; R. Muns. Fus., 4/9/16, att. R. Innis. Fus.; F; Lieut.; w(2).
The Strand, Athlone, Ireland.

CLARKE, Henry Laurence
B/Sq/12320, 28/12/17; No. 1 Cav. C/S, 16/5/18; R. Regt. of Cav., 14/2/19; 2/Lieut.
Penco, St. Mary's Road, Surbiton, Surrey.

CLARKE, Horace Joseph
6883, 18/10/15; R.A., C/S, 24/1/16; North'd. Fus., 4/8/16; Capt.; w.

CLARKE, Hubert Victor
4/3298, 19/4/15; R.E., 9/7/15; Lieut.

CLARKE, Humphrey Tredway
6/2/8306, 11/12/15; Shrops. L.I., 4/9/16; Capt.; w(3).
c/o. Miss Bourdillon, King's Home for Nurses, 6 Lower Clapton Road, E. 5.

CLARKE, James Blasdale
C/14290, 11/11/18; trfr. K.R. Rif. C., 25/4/19, M.G.C.; Cpl.
Shirley, Penshurst Road, Ramsgate.

CLARKE, John Arthur
6/1/6816, 14/10/15; E. Kent R., 4/9/16, Indian Army; Lieut.
Shirley, Penshurst Road, Ramsgate.

APPENDIX II.—RECORDS OF RANK AND FILE.

CLARKE, John Henry Williamson
4/5/4563, 1/7/15; R.N.V.R., 8/12/15.
22 Palace Road, Streatham Hill, S.W.

CLARKE, Lawrence Joyce
B/413, 5/5/09; 22nd Lond. R., 3/3/11, secd. R.E. Sigs.; F; Capt.; M.C., M(1).
Wayste Court, Abingdon, Berkshire.

CLARKE, Lionel William
E/14053, 23/9/18; demob. 10/1/19.
5 Ladbroke Square, W. 11.

CLARKE, Marshall Neville
6/4/A/9279, 3/2/16, L/C.; demob. 22/1/19.
Graiguenoe Park, Thurles, Ireland.

CLARKE, Neville Anderson
6/5/8241, 8/12/15; No. 8 O.C.B., 4/8/16; Yorks. L.I., 21/11/16; Lieut.
The Bank, Walkden, Lancashire.

CLARKE, Orme Bigland
K/2804, 28/1/15; R.F.A., 13/3/15; F,E,P; Lt.-Col.; M(2).
106 Eaton Square, S.W. 1.

CLARKE, Philip Harwood
K/Sq/2422, 21/12/14; R.F.A., 1/1/15, R.A.F.; F; Lieut.
36 Westwood Road, Southampton. (Now in Chile.)

CLARKE, Reginald Harry
6/3/7653, 22/11/15, L/C.; M.G.C., C/S, 30/9/16; M.G.C., 23/11/16, Tank Corps; F; Lieut.; Inj.
397 Marshall Street, Jeppestown, Johannesburg, S. Africa.

CLARKE, Thomas
D/10884, 19/3/17; No. 14 O.C.B., 10/8/17; Hunts. Cyc. Bn., 27/11/17; Bedf. R.; Lieut.
c/o. The Daily Mail, Carmelite House, E.C. 4.

CLARKE, William Edward
4/5/4816, 12/7/15; Devon. R., 16/12/15; Lieut.
6 Holyrood Terrace, Theltoe, Plymouth.

CLARKE-SMITH, Douglas Alexander
6/2657, 12/1/15; R.G.A., 5/8/15; Lieut.

CLARKE-WILLIAMS, Alfred Ronald
Sq/1296, 24/9/14; R.F.A., 1/12/14, R.H.A.; F; Lieut.; w; M(2).
Hillside, West Hill, Sydenham, S.E. 26.

CLARKSON, Edward Stanley
6/1/8535, 30/12/15, L/C.; No. 14 O.C.B., 28/8/16; K.R. Rif. C., 18/12/16, secd. R.F.C.; Lieut.
4 Turners Road, Hendon, N.W. 4.

CLARKSON, Herbert
C/9965, 20/11/16; No. 14 O.C.B., 30/1/17; 8th Lond. R., 29/5/17; Lieut.
Smedley Lodge, Cheetham, Manchester.

CLATWORTHY, Raymond F.
H/2561, 4/1/15; R.A.O.C., 23/3/15; F; Capt.
10 Westbourne Terrace, Saltash.

☦ CLAXTON, Eric Abley
A/10051, 29/11/16; No. 14 O.C.B., 30/1/17; K.R. Rif. C., 25/4/17; 2/Lieut.
Died of wounds 31/7/17.

CLAY, Arthur Bryan
B/10889, 19/3/17, L/C.; R.F.C., C/S, 26/11/17; R.F.C., 23/1/18, R.A.F.; 2/Lieut.
Netherfield, Lightcliffe, Nr. Halifax, Yorkshire.

CLAY, Norman Cyril
D/10428, 10/1/17, L/C.; No. 20 O.C.B., 7/6/17; Midd'x. R., 25/9/17, Indian Army; Persia; Lieut.
c/o. Messrs. Grindlay & Coy., Bombay, India.

CLAY, Robert Angus
K/B/2511, 31/12/14, Cpl.; Arg. & Suth'd. Highrs., 31/3/15, att. R. Dub. Fus., K. Af. Rif.; G,S,Germ.EA; Lieut.; w.
St. Martins, Hooton, Cheshire. (Now in British East Africa.)

CLAY, Robert Hugh
4/3287, 16/4/15; Linc. R., 22/4/15; Capt.; w; M.C., Italian Silver Medal for Military Valour.

CLAY, Wilfrid Albert
4/3835, 31/5/15; N. Cyc. Bn., 14/10/15, M.G.C.; F; Lieut.
5 Haldane Terrace, Newcastle-on-Tyne.

CLAYTON, Arthur James Balfour
Sq/625, 14/3/12; 6th Drag. Gds., 15/8/14, secd. Lab. Corps; Lieut.
6 Palace Gardens Mansions, Hyde Park, W. 2.

CLAYTON, Cyril Fletcher
A/D/13052, 10/5/18; trfr. R. Suss. R., 7/5/19.
Ocean Chambers, West Street, Brighton

CLAYTON, Daniel Preece
4/4438, 26/6/15; S. Wales Bord., 21/8/15, att. Yorks. L.I.; F,NR; Lieut.; g.
158 Liverpool Road, Birkdale, Southport, Lancashire.

CLAYTON, Frank
Sq/317, 30/6/08; dis. 29/6/10.

CLAYTON, Frederick Ernest
6/3/7198, 4/11/15; Manch. R., 4/9/16; 2/Lieut.
Avalon, Cross Green, Formby, Lancashire.

CLAYTON, Gerard Charles Henry
A/13045, 8/5/18; demob. 29/1/19.
53 Calton Road, Dulwich Village, S.E. 21.

CLAYTON, Rex Spencer
6/3/6448, 27/9/15; R.F.A., C/S, 14/4/16; R.G.A., 2/8/16; F; Lieut.
17 Mansfield Road, Luton, Bedfordshire.

CLAYTON, Robert Cecil
Sq/622, 14/3/12; R.F.A., 7/10/14.
6 Palace Gardens Mansions, Hyde Park, W. 2.

CLAYTON, Sidney Francis
E/2805, 28/1/15; Hamps. R., 2/6/15; Lieut.
291 Wellington Road, Rushden, Northamptonshire.

CLAYTON, Wilfrid
A/10272, 1/1/17.

CLAYTON, William Robert
2/9792, 26/10/16; No. 14 O.C.B., 27/12/16; Ches. R., 25/4/17; F; Lieut.; w.
Wranglands, Freshfield, Liverpool.

CLAYTON-SMITH, Guy Vernon Heukensfeldt
D/10638, 1/2/17, L/C.; No. 14 O.C.B., 10/8/17; Yorks. L.I., 27/11/17; 2/Lieut.
Ropergate, Pontefract, Yorkshire.

CLEAN, Reginald John Nevill
B/10535, 17/1/17; R.G.A., C/S, 25/4/17; R.G.A., 19/8/17; F; Lieut.
The Acacia, Alma Road, Windsor.

CLEAN, Rupert Lionel James
6/2/9083, 21/1/16; No. 13 O.C.B., 4/11/16; R. Suss. R., 28/2/17, att. R.E.; F; Lieut.; p.
53 Thingwall Park, Fishponds, Bristol.

CLEAR, William Lawrence
6/1/8717, 5/1/16; No. 8 O.C.B., 4/8/16; R. Dub. Fus., 21/11/16, M.G.C.; F; Capt.; Inv.
38 St. Alphonsus Road, Drumcondra, Dublin.

CLEAVER, Kenneth Crunden
H/2005, 2/11/14; dis. to Armoured Car Aeroplane Support, 5/3/15; R.F.C., 20/2/16, R.A.F.; Lieut.

CLEAVER, William Bath
6/1/8563, 31/12/15; M.G.C., C/S, 1/1/17; M.G.C., 25/4/17; F; Lieut.; g,w.
5 Gibbs Road, Newport, Monmouthshire.

☦ CLEEVE-EDWARDS, Cecil
A/11596, 5/7/17; R.E., C/S, 7/10/17; R.E., 11/1/18; 2/Lieut.
Killed in action 16/10/18.

CLEGG, Edward Cyril
A/2937, 18/2/15; Wilts. R., 18/6/15, att. R.F.C.; F; Lieut.; w(2); M.C., M(1).
3 Royal Terrace East, Kingstown, Co. Dublin

CLEGG, Ernest Arthur
6/D/7631, 20/11/15, L/C.; No. 6 O.C.B., 15/2/17; R.F.C., 9/5/17, R.A.F.; Lieut.
Belmont, Highbury New Park, N.

CLEGG, George Thornley
C/12029, 24/9/17, L/C.; No. 21 O.C.B., 10/5/18; R. Highrs., 3/2/19; 2/Lieut.
Holly Bank, Croxteth Road, Liverpool.

CLEGG, Gilbert Samuel
F/1848, 16/10/14, Cpl.; R.A.O.C., 23/3/15; M; Capt.
19 Copers Cope Road, Beckenham, Kent.

CLEGG, Thomas Harry
K/E/2415, 21/12/14; Manch. R., 7/4/15, War Office; F; Lieut.; M.B.E., M.C.
39 Heath Gardens, Twickenham, Middlesex.

CLELAND, James William
A/68, 10/4/08; 19th Lond. R., 15/11/09.
32 Doughty Street, W.C. 1.

CLEMENT, Frank
1/3630, 17/5/15; 18th Lond. R., 10/8/15, att. R. Sco. Fus.; F; Lieut.
90 Elms Road, Clapham Common, S.W. 4.

APPENDIX II.—RECORDS OF RANK AND FILE.

✠ CLEMENT, William Honeycott
4/6/1/4920. 19/7/15; L/C.; 18th Lond. R., 9/5/16, att. 11th Lond. R.; F,S,E,P; Capt.; M(1). Died 27/6/19.

CLEMENTS, Herbert William
F/2671, 12/1/15; R.N.V.R., 9/4/15, York. & Lanc. R., Sco. Rif.; Major; M(1). 19 Old Buildings, Lincoln's Inn, W.C. 2.

CLEMENTS, Jack Francis
D/10424, 10/1/17; R.F.C., C/S, 16/4/17; R.F.C., 14/6/17; resigned and rej. Corps, C/A/12064, 1/10/17; trfr. 14th Lond. R., 16/2/18. Dalkeith, 12 Wilton Grove, Wimbledon, S.W. 19.

CLEMENTS, Jules
C/10176, 11/12/16; No. 5 O.C.B., 8/2/17; demob.

CLEMENTS, Sydney Charles
B/12850, 25/3/18; No. 11 O.C.B., 9/8/18; trfr. Class W. Res., 5/12/18. Squirrel Farm, Battle, Sussex.

CLEMOW, John Maakwell
6/6514, 30/9/15; R.A., C/S, 24/1/16; R.F.A., 16/6/16; Lieut. Highfield House, Walton-on-Thames.

✠ CLERK, Cecil Alexander
6/4/5551, 12/8/15, L/C.; R.N. Div., 11/2/16. Died of wounds 4/2/18.

CLERK, Donald Ewart
1/3146, 30/3/15, L/C.; R.E., 22/10/15; F; Capt.; M(1). 115 Balshagray Avenue, Jordanhill, Glasgow, W.

CLEUGH, Dennis Walter
C/9928, 15/11/16; No. 14 O.C.B., 30/1/17; K.R. Rif. C., 25/4/17; F; Capt.; w. Garden Lodge, Garden Road, St. John's Wood, N.W. 8.

CLEVELAND-STEVENS, Edward Carnegie
A/1270, 23/9/14; R.A.O.C., 6/10/14, R.E.; E,F; Capt.; M(1). Winchet Hall, Goudhurst, Kent.

CLEWS, Percy Barford
6/Sq/7639, 22/11/15; No. 1 Cav. C/S, 24/4/16; Sherwood Rang. Yeo., 1/8/16, R.F.C., R.A.F.; P,S; Lieut.; cr. Fairlight, Thickleburgh Hill, Herne Bay.

CLIFF, Eric Francis
C/K/1312, 26/9/14, C.Q.M.S.; R.G.A., 24/11/15; P; Capt. Redland, Tenyson Road, Harpenden, Hertfordshire.

CLIFFORD, Frederick
6/3/8624, 3/1/16, L/C.; No. 14 O.C.B., 27/9/16; L'pool. R., 18/12/16; Lieut. 33 Dumbarton Road, Brixton Hill.

✠ CLIFFORD, Herbert James
D/1418, 29/9/14; K. R. Rif. C., 28/11/14; Capt. Killed in action 20/9/17.

CLIFFORD, William Cecil
4/2/4491, 28/6/15; R.W. Kent R., 27/1/16; F; Capt.; w; M.C. 85 Bank Street, Maidstone, Kent.

CLIFTON, Frederick William
K/F/2398, 17/12/14; Linc. R., 20/2/15, secd. No. 19 O.C.B. Inst.; F; Capt.; g; M.C. c/o. Reiss & Coy., Shanghai, China.

CLIFTON, Hubert Beverley
D/12104, 11/10/17; Household Bde. O.C.B., 8/2/18; Oxf. & Bucks. L.I., 30/7/18; att. Notts. & Derby. R.; 2/Lieut. 23 Camberley Road, Norwich.

CLILVERD, Graham Barry
3/4/6/Sq/4176, 14/6/15; R.F.A., 1/11/15, secd. R.E.; F; Capt. 142 Holborn Bars, E.C. 1.

CLINTON-ABBOTT, James Cecil Nethervil
6/5/5925, 1/9/15; L'pool. R., 21/4/16; F; Capt.; w; Order of the Rising Sun (Japan). 31 Pleasant Street, New Brighton, Cheshire.

CLIXBY, Charles Geoffrey
D/13926, 30/8/18; trfr. K.R. Rif. C., 7/4/19. c/o. Messrs. Aspinwall & Coy. Ltd., Cochin, S. India.

CLODE, Cecil William
6/4/5581, 16/8/15; R.A.S.C., 24/1/16; Germ.EA; Lieut. 6 The Mount, Caversham, Oxfordshire. (Now in S. India.)

CLODE, Harold John
6/9453, 10/2/16; A.S.C., C/S, 15/5/16; R.A.S.C., 18/6/16; Lieut.

✠ CLODE-BAKER, George Edmund   See BAKER, G. E. C.

CLOSE, Charles Victor
4/3810, 27/5/15; R.E., 5/10/15; E,P; Capt.; M(2). P.O. Box 258, Haifa, Palestine.

CLOSE, Hubert John
C/10161, 11/12/16; No. 14 O.C.B., 5/5/17; N. Lan. R., 28/8/17; F; 2/Lieut. 18 Sneath Avenue, Golders Green, N.W. 4.

CLOSE, James
6/4/7494, 15/11/15; Mon. R., 4/8/16, att. Glouc. R.; F; Lieut.; Inv. Ilston, Oakland Road, Abergavenny.

CLOTWORTHY, William Wiffen Robert
B/12337, 1/1/18; No. 20 O.C.B., 10/5/18; Devon. R., 3/2/19; 2/Lieut. Aberlone, Tavistock, Devonshire.

✠ CLOUDSLEY, Hugh
A/57, 7/4/08; dis. 6/4/12; rej. A/1123, 7/9/14, Cpl.; R.W. Surr. R., 14/11/14; Lieut. Killed in action 1/7/16.

CLOUDESLEY, John Leslie
Sq/1297, 24/9/14, L/C.; R.A.O.C., 20/3/16; Lieut.; Croix de Guerre, M(1). Three Gables, Reigate, Surrey.

CLOUDESLEY, Oswald
K/Sq/2319, 11/12/14; R.F.A., 27/2/15; F; Capt.; Inj.; M.C., M(1). Brightlands, Reigate, Surrey.

CLOUGH, Arthur Robert
C/547, 15/2/11; dis. 6/7/14.

CLOUGH, Ernest
6/5/6473, 27/9/15, Cpl.; W. York R., 4/8/16; F; Lieut.; g,w; M.C. Sycamore Terrace, Haswell, Nr. Sunderland.

CLOUGH, George Alwyn
B/12699, 8/3/18, Cpl.; demob. 24/1/19. 32 Grosvenor Avenue, Jesmond, Newcastle-on-Tyne.

CLOUGHLEY, John Henry
1/3299, 19/4/15; Shrops. L.I., 10/9/15, W. York. R.; F; Lieut.; Inv. 124 Barlow Moor Road, Chorlton-cum-Hardy, Manchester.

CLOVER, John Manning
6/3/7722, 22/11/15; No. 14 O.C.B., 26/11/16; Essex R., 27/3/17; P; Lieut.; M.C. The Hall, Dedham, Essex.

CLOW, Arthur Lachlan
H/Sq/1936, 22/10/14; Oxf. Huss., 11/2/15, att. R.F.C.; Lieut. Turnford Hall, Broxbourne, Hertfordshire.

CLOWES, Ivo Charles Danyers
A/10084, 1/12/16; R.E., 23/4/17; F; Capt. 3 Ruvigny Gardens, Putney, S.W. 15. (Now in Paris.)

CLOWES, Reginald
D/10683, 7/2/17; No. 14 O.C.B., 5/7/17; 19th Lond. R., 30/10/17; E,P; Lieut. New Buckenham, Norfolk.

CLOWES, Richard Norman
C/A/11766, 30/7/17; demob. 31/1/19. Oakhill House, Surbiton, Surrey.

CLUNIES-ROSS, Wilfred
A/E/13986, 6/9/18; R.G.A., C/S, 19/11/18; demob. High Garth, Balcombe, Sussex.

CLUTTERBUCK, George William
6/Sq/7540, 17/11/15, L/C.; R.F.A., C/S, 4/8/16; R.F.A., 1/12/16; F; Lieut.; g. 35 Paget Road, N. 16.

COAD, Samuel
6/8467, 20/12/15; R.F.A., C/S, 9/6/16; R.F.A., 10/11/16; F,It; Lieut.; M.C. Pengelley, Callington, Cornwall.

COANE, Roger Patrick
B/C/12380, 14/1/18; No. 7 O.C.B., 5/7/18; trfr. 28th Lond. R., 11/11/18. 20 Westend Park, Londonderry, Ireland.

COAST, James Percy Chatterton
4/3/4066, 7/6/15, L/C.; R.W. Surr., 5/9/15, att. R. War. R.; F; Capt.; Inv. Petros, Queens Road, Beckenham.

✠ COATES, Alan David
K/B/2171, 26/11/14; 4th Lond. R., 29/1/15; F; Lieut. Killed in action 27-28/4/15.

COATES, Arthur Vivian
E/1652, 9/10/14, L/C.; Essex R., 30/11/14; G,P; Capt. Virginia House, Buckhurst Hill.

COATES, Christopher Oliver
6/5/5280, 31/7/15; Manch. R., 11/12/15, att. R.N. Devon Huss.; E,P,F; Capt. Greenend, 287 Marshalls Cross Road, St. Helens, Lancs.

APPENDIX II.—RECORDS OF RANK AND FILE.

COATES, Donald
6/7834, 25/11/15; R.F.C., 2/6/16, R.A.F.; F; Lieut.
      Stanmore, Middlesex.

COATES, Douglas George
C/9948, 17/11/16; R.W. Surr. R., 9/3/17.
      19 Holmdene Avenue, Herne Hill, S.E. 24.

COATES, Frank Piesse
6/4/8822, 10/1/16; No. 14 O.C.B., 27/9/16; Rif. Brig., 18/12/16; F; Capt.; g,w.
      High Carrs, Elstree, Hertfordshire.

COATES, Kenneth
B/12402, 17/1/18; No. 21 O.C.B., 7/6/18; trfr. 14th Lond. R., 18/12/18.

COATES, Maurice
B/11691, 19/7/17; No. 14 O.C.B., 7/12/17; Norf. R., 28/5/18, att. Bedf. R.; F; 2/Lieut.; w.
      York House, Brayton Road, Selby, Yorkshire.

COATES, Philip Adrian
6/3/6728, 11/10/15; No. 1 O.C.B., 25/2/16; Essex R., 7/7/16, att. Oxf. & Bucks. L.I.; F; Lieut.; w.
      Virginia House, Buckhurst Hill, Essex.

COATS-BUSH, William
6/2/8207, 7/12/15; No. 13 O.C.B., 4/11/16; Rif. Brig., 25/4/17; 2/Lieut.
      11 Vincent Mansions, Westminster, S.W. 1.

COBB, Arthur Kennedy
C/13248, 10/6/18; trfr. 28th Lond. R., 13/11/18.
      59 Upper Clapton Road, E. 5.

COBB, Charles Graham
6/4/6449, 27/9/15, L/C.; demob. 15/3/19.
      10 Croxted Road, West Dulwich, S.E. 21.

COBB, Frederick
C/648, 9/7/12; dis. to Postal Censorship, 25/1/15.
      c/o. H. F. Bosman, Esq., 45 Rue d'Ulm, Paris.

✠ COBB, John Preston
6/2/7326, 9/11/15; dis. to R. Mil. Coll., 29/8/16; W. Rid. R., 1/5/17, R.F.C.; 2/Lieut.
      Killed in action 11/10/17.

✠ COBB, Kenneth Rhodes
C/1311, 26/9/14, Cpl.; K.R. Rif. C., 10/12/14; G; Capt.
      Killed in action 1/7/15.

COBB, Stanley
4/2938, 18/2/15; Midd'x. R., 26/3/15, S. Staff. R.; F; Capt.
      39 Lime Street, E.C. 3.

COBBOLD, Alfred Michael Gordon
B/12866, 27/3/18; R.E., C/S, 14/4/18; R.E., 1/11/18; 2/Lieut.
      Bramford House, Nr. Ipswich, Suffolk.

COBLEY, Augustus Otto Fresenius
4/4273, 17/6/15; R.E., 6/11/15; F; Lieut.; w; M.C., M(1).
      Burnham House, 2 Rothesay Road, Luton, Bedfordshire.

COBLEY, George Hugh
C/13280, 14/6/18, L/C.; demob. 23/1/19.
      c/o. Mrs. Kay, Claigmar, Long Lane, Finchley.

✠ COBURN, Charles
A/9808, 30/10/16; No. 14 O.C.B., 27/12/16; K.R. Rif. C., 25/4/17; 2/Lieut.
      Killed in action 31/7/17.

COBURN, Francis
A/K/2562, 4/1/15; K.R. Rif. C., 15/5/15, Oxf. & Bucks. L.I.; I,Afghan.; Major, D.A.Q.M.G.
      39 Pembridge Villas, W. 2.

COCHRAN, Peter
F/2587, 4/1/15; R.E., 1/6/15; E,F; Major; w; M.C., Croix de Guerre (Belge), M(1).
      4 Hecklegirth, Annan, Scotland.

COCHRANE, Arthur
B/13482, 8/7/18; demob. 21/12/18.
      Peak House, New Mills, Nr. Stockport.

COCHRANE, Ernest Alexander
6/5/8080, 1/12/15; R. Ir. Rif., 25/4/17; Lieut.; w.
      Ravenna, Cregagh Road, Belfast, Ireland.

COCHRANE, John Athol
C/12563, 6/2/18; No. 10 O.C.B., 5/7/18; Sea. Highrs., 3/3/19; 2/Lieut.
      Green Knowe, Boreham Wood, Hertfordshire.

COCHRANE, Walter Bevan
6/Sq/6498, 27/9/15, L/C.; R.F.C., 2/6/16, R.A.F.; F; Lieut.; Inj.
      c/o. T. R. Cochrane, Esq., National Bank of South Africa Ltd., 18 St. Swithin's Lane, E.C. (Now in N.W. Australia.)

COCHRANE, William Gibson
K/A/2493, 31/12/14; R. Scots., 10/2/15; F,S,Russia; Capt.; w; M.C.
      3 Queen's Terrace, Aberdeen, Scotland.

COCKBURN, Alexander Grant
A/11947, 31/8/17; No. 14 O.C.B., 7/12/17; High. L.I., 28/5/18; F; 2/Lieut.
      Fidra, Forteath Avenue, Elgin, Scotland.

COCKBURN, Ernest Henry
B/1072, 2/9/14; R.Fus., 16/9/14, R.A.F.; F; Major, D.A.Q.M.G.; Inv.
      29 Collingham Road, S.W. 5.

✠ COCKBURN, Henry Howard
6/5/8081, 1/12/15; No. 7 O.C.B., 11/8/16; R. Ir. Rif., 18/12/16; att. R. Innis. Fus.; 2/Lieut.
      Killed in action 1/4/17.

COCKBURN, John Jenkinson
6/1/6588, 4/10/15, Sgt.; A.S.C., C/S, 1/9/16; R.A.S.C., 25/10/16; F; Lieut.; M(1).
      La Corbiere, Coggeshall Road, Braintree, Essex.

COCKBURN, Noel Christy Everist
3/2/9605, 28/8/16; No. 14 O.C.B., 26/11/16; Bedf. R., 28/2/17; F; Lieut.; w.
      c/o. H.M.'s Legation, Mexico City.

COCKBURN, Reginald Stapylton
A/983, 5/8/14; K.R. Rif. C., 12/9/14; F; Major; M.C., M(1).
      29 Collingham Road, S.W. 5.

COCKER, Clarence Stewart
6/5/5221, 30/7/15; Manch. R., 21/12/15, N. Lan. R.; F; Lieut.
      Thornlea, Ramsey, Isle of Man.

COCKER, Norman Arnold
6/5/5222, 30/7/15; Manch. R., 21/12/15, att. N. Lan. R. and Notts. & Derby R.; E; Lieut.
      20 Beardwood Road, Hill Lane, Blackley, Manchester.

COCKLE, Harold Pudens
C/11788, 2/8/17; No. 14 O.C.B., 7/12/17; Noth'n. R., 28/5/18; F; 2/Lieut.
      102 Baker Street, Semilong, Northampton.

COCKRILL, Kenneth Arthur
4/6/1/4957, 19/7/15; R. Fus., 24/12/15, R.E., emp. M. of Labour; F; Lieut.
      64 Springfield Road, Gorleston, Great Yarmouth.

COCKSHUT, Eric Sutherland
F/1863, 16/10/14; Midd'x. R., 27/11/14, Tank Corps; Capt.; M.C.
      Meadside, Golders Green, N.W. 4.

CODLING, Geoffrey Barnard
F/3/2739, 21/1/15; E. Kent R., 4/9/16, att. Shrops. L.I., R.A.F.; S,E; Lieut.; Inj.
      8 Brookside, Cambridge.

COE, Frederick Augustus
C/926, 5/8/14, L/C.; S. Wales Bord., 20/9/14, Welch R.; F,S; Capt.
      Junior Carlton Club, Pall Mall, S.W. 1.

COE, Harold David
6/5/6170, 11/9/15, Cpl.; R.E., C/S, 18/2/16; R.E., 1/7/16, Sigs.; F; Lieut.; w.
      Parton Lane, Churchdown, Nr. Gloucester.

COE, Harry Leslie Baldwin
D/10871, 14/3/17; No. 11 O.C.B., 5/7/17; Midd'x. R., 30/10/17, att. Lab. Corps; E,P; Lieut.; Inv.
      95 Cumberland Road, Hanwell, W. 7. (Now in Egypt.)

COFFEY, Edward
6/8719, 5/1/16; trfr. 101st Prov. Bn., 21/7/16.
      38 Lower New Street, Killarney, Co. Kerry, Ireland.

COFFIN, Bertram Gilbert
4/3811, 27/5/15; 12th Lond. R., 21/10/15, secd. Intelligence, att. R.F.C.; F; Lieut.; w.
      17 Bedford Row, W.C. 1.

COGDELL, Herbert
4/5/4713, 9/7/15, Sgt.; R.N.R., 20/10/16; Atlantic and North Sea; Eng. Lieut.
      Gwaenyscor, Poulton-le-Fylde, Lancashire. (Now in Canada.)

COGGINS, Harold
6/1/7541, 17/11/15; 10th Lond. R., 22/11/16, 20th Lond. R., R.A.F.; Lieut.
      The Hall, Rounds, Wellingborough.

COGGINS, John Theodore
A/13053, 10/5/18, L/C.; demob. 22/1/19.
      Farnborough, Hampshire.

COGHLAN, Michael Robert
6/3/6515, 30/9/15; No. 11 O.C.B., 7/5/16; 9th Lond. R., 4/9/16; F; Capt.
      Wootton, New Milton, Hampshire.

APPENDIX II.—RECORDS OF RANK AND FILE.

COHEN, Donald Henry
1/3156, 1/4/15; Notts. & Derby. R., 14/6/15; F; Staff Capt.; w.
68 Hamilton Terrace, N.W. 8.

COHEN, Eustace Gresley
K/2526, 31/12/14; R.E., 24/4/15; F; Capt.; M(2).
Perth Club, Perth, Western Australia.

☩ COHEN, George Hubert
Sq/298, 24/6/08; dis. 23/6/09; L'pool. R., 19/9/14; F; Lieut.
Killed in action 16/5/15.

COHEN, Harold George
6/2/8543, 30/12/15, Cpl.; No. 14 O.C.B., 30/10/16; Intelligence Corps, 20/1/17; F; Lieut.; M(1).
104 Greencroft Gardens, N.W. 6.

COHEN, Leslie Winston
4/5/4705, 9/7/15; No. 3 O.C.B., 25/2/16; trfr. 13th Lond. R., 20/6/16.
Keith House, Porchester Gate, W.

COHEN, Lewis George
1/3414, 29/4/15, L/C.; S. Staff. R., 28/7/15; Worc. R.; 2/Lieut.
171 Gloucester Terrace, Hyde Park, W. 2.

COHEN, Stuart Samuel
6/1/7327, 9/11/15, L/C.; No. 11 O.C.B., 7/5/16; R.E., 9/8/16; 2/Lieut.
171 Gloucester Terrace, Hyde Park, W. 2.

COKER, Henry William
6/5/5244, 31/7/15, Sgt.; A.S.C., C/S, 8/5/16; R.A.S.C., 11/6/16; F; Lieut.
20 Castle Street, Liverpool.

COLBECK, Henry Oliver
D/12885, 5/4/18; trfr. Tank Corps, 11/11/18.
Lyndhurst Road, Benton, Northumberland.

COLCHESTER, Maurice Travers
H/2044, 9/11/14; R.N.V.R., 9/1/15, Indian Army; G,F; Major; w, Inv.
2 Park Hill Road, Croydon. (Now in Burma.)

COLDBECK, George Henry
A/10055, 29/11/16; No. 14 O.C.B., 6/4/17; N. Lan. R., 31/7/17; 2/Lieut.
52 West Side, Wandsworth Common, S.W.

COLDHAM, Cecil Brown
6/1/5762, 21/8/15; N. Lan. R., 6/1/16; Lieut.

COLDHAM, Guy Glemsford
K/4/3/3110, 25/3/15, L/C.; dis. med unfit, 1/10/15; enlisted R.G.A., 24/7/16; Pte.
Ormond Lodge, Weston Road, Bath.

☩ COLDICOTT, Hubert Eric
6/1/2/6917, 15/10/15, L/C.; No. 14 O.C.B.; 15th Lond. R., 24/10/16; F; 2/Lieut.
Killed in action 21/5/17.

COLDREY, Ronald Shearsmith
D/11092, 23/4/17; R.F.C., C/S, 1/6/17; R.F.C., 4/7/17; 2/Lieut.; Inj.
The Laurels, Brighton Road, Purley, Surrey.

COLDRIDGE, Harry Wilton
6/3/5403, 5/8/15; R.A.S.C., 4/12/15; F; Lieut.
c/o A. Gifford, Esq., Silverlands, Epsom, Surrey.

COLE, Alexander Caxton
A/13947, 4/9/18; demob. 13/12/18.
Great Ouseburn, York.

COLE, Arthur Bertram
6/4/7762, 23/11/15; A.S.C., C/S, 27/10/16; R.A.S.C., 20/12/16; F,It; Capt.
Ullswater Crescent, Radipole, Weymouth.

COLE, Arthur Paget
6/5/8594, 3/1/16; No. 14 O.C.B., 30/10/16; 9th Lond. R., 24/1/17; Lieut.; w.
Penn Cottage, Queen's Road, Uxbridge.

☩ COLE, Charles Henry
6/2/6107, 6/9/15; 11th Lond. R., 10/1/16; 2/Lieut.
Killed in action 14/10/16.

☩ COLE, Cyril Charles
4/3/4013, 7/6/15; Essex R., 21/8/15, R.A.F.; 2/Lieut.
Died 14/11/18.

COLE, Edward Hamilton
A/12465, 24/1/18; No. 22 O.C.B., 7/6/18; Education Officer, 8/12/18; Capt.
Assistant Commissioner, Mafeteng, Basutoland, South Africa.

COLE, Edward Harold
D/10653, 2/2/17, Cpl.; A.S.C., C/S, 1/2/18; R.A.S.C., 26/4/18; Siberia; Capt.
148 East Dulwich Grove, S.E. 22.

COLE, Edward Howard
4/6/SQ/4789, 12/7/15; R.F.A., 25/10/15; I,M,P,F; Lieut.
Royal Exchange Assurance, P.O. Box 357, Calcutta, India.

COLE, Harry James
6/5/6794, 13/10/15, L/C.; No. 11 O.C.B., 7/5/16; Manch. R., 4/9/16, att. K. Af. Rif.; F,EA; Capt.; w; M(1).
Penn Cottage, Queen's Road, Uxbridge. (Now in Nyassaland.)

COLE, John Marriott
4/3721, 24/5/15, Sgt.; K.R. Rif. C., 14/9/15; Lieut.
67 Abingdon Villas, Kensington, W. 8.

COLE, Ronald Frank
D/10452, 11/1/17; R.F.C., C/S, 13/3/17; R.F.C., 19/4/17.
23 Richmond Gardens, W. 12.

COLE, Walter Philip
4/5/4841, 15/7/15; R.W. Surr. R., 8/1/16, R. Dub. Fus., Lan. Fus.; E,S,P,F; Capt.
5 Marine Parade, Appledore, Devon. (Now in India.)

COLEBROOK, Edward Hilder
C/10825, 2/3/17; No. 11 O.C.B., 5/7/17; E. Surr. R., 30/10/17; F; Lieut.; w(2); M.C.
Holly Mount, Austen Road, Guildford.

☩ COLEBROOK, Leslie Charles
4/1/4332, 21/6/15; Hamps. R., 4/12/15; 2/Lieut.
Killed in action 1/2/17.

COLEMAN, Geoffrey John
6/2/5456, 7/8/15; 8th Lond. R., 25/9/16; 2/Lieut.; w.
147 Dunstans Road, East Dulwich.

COLEMAN, George Drury
C/855, 4/8/14; Norf. R., 15/8/14, Lab. Corps; Capt.
307 High Holborn, W.C.

COLEMAN, Henry Oswald
6/4/7170, 3/11/15, L/C.; R. Lanc. R., 4/8/16, Intelligence; F; Lieut.; Inv.
Moville, Berkhamsted, Hertfordshire.

COLEMAN, James Patrick
B/11663, 16/7/17; R.F.C., C/S, 23/10/17; R.F.C., 12/12/17, R.A.F.; 2/Lieut.
95 Townshend Avenue, Keyham, Devonport.

COLEMAN, William Edward Beaumont
A/12139, 22/10/17; trfr. 28th Lond. R., 27/3/18.
4 The Close, Pollard's Hill West, Norbury.

COLERIDGE, The Honble. Geoffrey Duke
K/E/2228, 3/12/14, Sgt.; Devon. R., 21/5/15; Capt.
5 Barnfield Crescent, Exeter.

COLERIDGE, Paul Humphrey
K/C/2308, 10/12/14, Sgt.; Notts. & Derby. R., 19/7/15; F; Capt.; w; M.C.
Little Heath Farm, Chobham, Surrey.

COLERIDGE, Wilfred Duke
B/1098, 7/9/14; 7th Lond. R., 28/9/14; Capt.
11 Roland Gardens, S.W. 7.

COLES, Albert
6/1/6175, 13/9/15; R.E., 23/2/16; F; Capt.; w(2), g; M.C., M(1).
Bloomfield House, Peasedown St. John, Bath.

COLES, Ernest James
A/2732, 18/1/15, L/C.; R.A.O.C., 8/4/15; Lt.-Col.; M(1).
Burntwood, Dorking, Surrey.

COLES, Reginald William
6/1/6225, 13/9/15; E. Ang. Div. Cyc. Coy., 22/12/15, att. R.W. Kent. Yeo., Linc. Yeo. and Hamps. R.; M,I,E; Lieut.; Inv.
Bloomfield House, Peasedown St. John, Bath.

☩ COLES, Sidney Harcourt
C/447, 15/11/09; R. Fus., 20/1/11, Midd'x. R.; F; Lieut.
Killed in action 12/10/14.

COLIN, Alfred
B/D/12344, 1/1/18; demob. 29/1/19.
41 Alleyn Park, West Dulwich, S.E. 21.

COLLARD, Frank Allen
6/4/8893, 13/1/16; No. 8 O.C.B., 4/8/16; K.R. Rif. C., 21/11/16, R.E.; Lieut.
27 Glenluce Road, Blackheath, S.E. 3.

COLLEDGE, George
4/3722, 24/5/15, L/C.; Lovats Scouts, 25/1/16, att. R.F.C.; F; Lieut :; p.
53 Holbein House, Sloan Square, S.W. 1.

COLLEN, Arthur Roland
K/2092, 16/11/14; R.G.A., 16/11/14, R. Marines; Capt.
9 Baskerville Road, Wandsworth Common.

APPENDIX II.—RECORDS OF RANK AND FILE.

✠ COLLEN, Norman Owen
4/1/5027, 22/7/15; E. York. R., 24/12/15; 2/Lieut.
Killed in action 25/9/16.

COLLER, Raymond Geoffrey
B/11075, 30/3/17; R.F.A., C/S, 27/7/17; R.F.A., 21/12/17; 2/Lieut.
Judge's Walk, Norwich.

COLLETT, Austin Etheridge
4/1/4177, 14/6/15; R.A.S.C., 8/10/15; S,It,NR; Major.
6 Girdlers Road, W. Kensington, W. 14.

COLLETT, Ronald Leslie
3/3111, 25/3/15, Sgt.; Midd'x. R., 26/7/15, R.A.M.C.; F; Capt.
c/o. The Institute of Chemistry, 30 Russell Square, W.C. 1.

✠ COLLEY, Harold
F/2955, 22/2/15; W. York. R., 2/4/15; 2/Lieut.
Killed in action 1/7/16.

COLLEY, Walter Douglas
H/2003, 2/11/14; Manch. R., 17/3/15, M.G.C.; F; Capt.; w.
c/o. B. Colley & Sons Ltd., 135 Portland Road, Kensington, W. 11.

COLLIER, Charles Saint John
Sq/620, 29/2/12; dis. 8/10/13.
Twyford Mansions, Marylebone, W.

COLLIER, Frank Batten
6/2/5988, 2/9/15; trfr. R.F.A., 21/7/16; R.F.A., 14/10/17; F; 2/Lieut
22 Craven Hill Gardens, Hyde Park, W. 2.

✠ COLLIER, Frederick
6/5/5279, 31/7/15, Sgt.; Manch. R., 6/12/15; 2/Lieut.
Died of wounds 11/5/17.

COLLIER, James Henry
E/1541, 6/10/14; North'n. R., 8/10/14, secd. War Office; Major.
33 West Avenue, Hendon, N.W. 4.

COLLIER, John Cates Rashleigh
D/12901, 8/4/18, L/C.; trfr. R.A.F., 16/10/18.
19 Queen's Gardens, Ealing. (Now in S. America.)

COLLING, Robert John
D/13883, 21/8/18; demob. 25/1/19.
Waterwitch House, Newmarket, Cambridgeshire.

COLLINGE, Cyril Ernest
6/3/7723, 22/11/15; No. 14 O.C.B., 28/8/16; 8th Lond. R., 22/11/16, Rif. Brig.; F; Lieut.; w.
c/o. Messrs. J. Travers & Sons, Ltd., 12 Battery Road, Singapore, Straits Settlements.

✠ COLLINGS, Frank Reginald
6/2/6388, 23/9/15; No. 2 O.C.B., 14/8/16; North'd. Fus., 18/12/16; 2/Lieut.; w(2).
Killed in action 3/12/17.

COLLINGS, Wilfred Jesse
6/5/7412, 12/11/15; L'pool. R., 4/8/16; 2/Lieut.
26 Hartington Road, Sefton Park, Liverpool.

COLLINGWOOD, William Edward
A/12525, 1/2/18; No. 4 O.C.B., 7/6/18; Bord. R., 14/3/19; 2/Lieut.
17 Anerley Park, Anerley, S.E.

COLLINS, Adrian John France
6/1/8266, 9/12/15; R.F.A., C/S, 4/8/16; R.G.A., 1/11/16; Lieut.
Strathmore, Camborne Terrace, Richmond, Surrey.

COLLINS, Arthur Edgar Gerard
Sq/3300, 19/4/15; R.E., 22/7/15; Lieut.; M.C.
21 Collingtree Road, Sydenham, S.E.

COLLINS, Arthur Oscar
2/3173, 6/4/15; 10th Lond. R., 21/7/15; w.
Avondale, Dean Road, Willesden Green.

COLLINS, Brian Merrick
B/D/12201, 9/11/17, L/C.; trfr. Lab. Corps, 4/6/18.
7 Gracechurch Street, E.C.

COLLINS, Charles
4/3/4452, 28/6/15; Linc. R., 3/9/15, att. K. Af. Rif.; F,Germ.EA.; Capt.; w(2); M.C., M(1).
Box 595, Bulawayo, Rhodesia, South Africa.

COLLINS, Cornelius Kershaw
D/10626, 29/1/17, L/C.; No. 14 O.C.B., 5/7/17; R. Highrs., 30/10/17; Lieut.
74 Neville Road, Forest Gate, Essex.

COLLINS, Edward Stephen
D/10805, 28/2/17, L/C.; R.A., C/S, 10/8/17; R.G.A., 28/1/18; 2/Lieut.
c/o. H.M. Inspector of Taxes, Market Hill, Barnsley, Yorkshire.

COLLINS, Edwin Kingsley
6/Sq/8404, 15/12/15; No. 1 Cav. C/S, 12/10/16; 4th Drag., 16/2/17, Essex Yeo., Essex R.; F; Lieut.
Chalbury, Witchampton, Wimborne.

COLLINS, Ellis Taylor
6/1/6612, 4/10/15; R.F.C., 6/7/16, R.A.F.; Lieut.
22 Hornsey Lane Gardens, Highgate.

✠ COLLINS, Ernest Stanley
6/5/8743, 6/1/16; No. 8 O.C.B., 4/8/16; Worc. R., 24/10/16; 2/Lieut.
Killed in action 31/7/17.

COLLINS, Francis Richard
6/4/9160, 26/1/16; No. 2 O.C.B., 14/8/16; Dorset R., 28/2/17; P,I,E; Lieut.
1 St. Hiliary Villa, Doubletrees, Par Station, Cornwall.

COLLINS, Frederick
6/7755, 23/11/15; dis. med. unfit, 8/8/16; W. York. R., 11/3/17, emp. M. of Munitions; Lieut.
27 Norfolk House Road, Streatham, S.W. 16.

COLLINS, Frederick Charles
6/5/6081, 6/9/15; R. Ir. Fus., 4/9/16, Worc. R., Indian Army; M; Lieut.
Rathverde, Knock, Belfast, Ireland.

COLLINS, Geoffrey Abdy
D/1426, 29/9/14; Rif. Brig., 2/11/14, att. R.W. Surr. R.; F; Capt.
The Park, Beckenham, Kent.

COLLINS, George Ferdinand
Sq/3084, 22/3/15, L/C.; R.A.S.C., 28/8/15; F,It; Capt.
54 Great Tower Street, E.C. 3.

COLLINS, Harold Wynne
6/2/7724, 22/11/15; R.F.A., C/S, 1/9/16; R.G.A., 10/12/16; F; Major; M.C., M(1).
20 Argyle Street, Pembroke Dock, S. Wales.

COLLINS, Henry Aikeroyde
B/1332, 26/9/14; Midd'x. R., 3/10/14, emp. R.E.; Capt.
25 Vincent Square, S.W.

COLLINS, Henry Akerman Desmond
C/46, 7/4/08; 11th Lond. R., 1/12/08; Capt.
26 Overton Road, S.W.

COLLINS, John Lissant
E/1603, 6/10/14; Lan. Fus., 10/10/14; G,E; Capt.
West Hill, Rochdale, Lancashire.

COLLINS, Owen Hyman
F/1820, 16/10/14; R. Berks. R., 23/11/14, att. Durh. L.I.; Capt.
The Chestnuts, Wooburn, Buckinghamshire.

✠ COLLINS, Philip
B/954, 5/8/14; Rif. Brig., 9/9/14; F; Capt.
Killed in action 30/7/15.

COLLINS, Reginald Sedley
6/4/5828, 26/8/15; R.F.A., C/S, 21/3/16; R.G.A., 2/8/16; F; Capt.
18B Breakspeare Road, Brockley, S.E. 4.

COLLINS, Rupert Edwart
4/3/5028, 22/7/15, L/C.; R.E., 21/9/15; Capt.; M(1).
2 Lucien Road, Tooting, S.W.

COLLINS, Stephen John
C/12282, 4/12/17; R.F.A., C/S, 15/3/18; R.F.A., 17/10/18; 2/Lieut.
74 Neville Road, Forest Gate, E. 7.

COLLINS, Thomas Chandler
6/2/7656, 22/11/15; No. 14 O.C.B.; K.R. Rif. C., 24/10/16; Lieut.
Fernlea, Ladbroke Road, Epsom.

COLLINS, Victor Hubert
6/2/8279, 10/12/15; No. 8 O.C.B., 4/8/16; R.W. Kent R., 21/11/16; F; Lieut.; Inv.
Ninnings Bungalow, Chalfont St. Peter, Bucks.

COLLINSON, James West
K/2432, 21/12/14; War Office, 8/1/15.

COLLINSON-JONES, Horace Norman Spenser
4/1/4211, 14/6/15; Essex R., 8/10/15, secd. M.G.C.; Lieut.
103 Shrewsbury Road, New Southgate, N. 11.

COLLIS, Eric William
4/2/5140, 26/7/15; Manch. R., 7/12/15, R.A.F.; F; Lieut.; w, cr.
Rectory, Biddenden, Kent.

COLLIS, John Stuart
C/Sq/D/13266, 12/6/18; Household Bde. O.C.B., 4/10/18; Ir. Gds., 9/3/19; 2/Lieut.
Killmore, Killiney, Co. Dublin, Ireland.

APPENDIX II.—RECORDS OF RANK AND FILE.

COLLISON, Harold Randolph
C/12564, 6/2/18; No. 16 O.C.B., 5/7/18; Ches. R., 4/3/19; 2/Lieut. Tulketh Mount, Ashton-on-Ribble, Preston, Lancashire.

COLLISON-MORLEY, Egbert Yea
6/1/8267, 9/12/15; No. 2 O.C.B., 14/8/16; E. Kent R., 18/12/16; Lieut. 3 Scarsdale Villas, Kensington.

✠ COLLIS-SANDES, Maurice James
A/535, 13/1/11; R. Fus., 12/9/14; Capt.; M(1). Killed in action 17/2/17.

COLLISSON, Evelyn Ernest Arnold
A/705, 9/4/13; dis. 1/6/14. The Homestead, Hillcrest Road, Sydenham.

COLLMANN, Charles Frederick
Sq/3379, 26/4/15, S.Q.M.S.; dis. 25/2/16.

✠ COLLOT, Thomas Alexander
K/2172, 26/11/14; Dorset R., 18/12/14, R. Berks.; F; 2/Lieut. Killed in action 1/7/16.

COLLYMORE, Eric Claude
A/11881, 20/8/17; R.F.C., C/S, 26/11/17; R.F.C., 6/3/18, R.A.F.; Lieut. c/o. Colonial Bank Ltd., 51 Threadneedle Street, E.C.

✠ COLLYMORE, Hubert Aubrey
F/1713, 15/10/14, Sgt.; Bedf. R., 13/11/14, att. M.G.C.; Lieut. Killed in action 17/4/18.

COLMAN, Arthur Thomas
2/3491, 6/5/15; trfr. R.A.M.C., 2/6/16. Holmesdale, Burgess Hill, Sussex.

COLMAN, Dudley Maple
2058, 12/11/14; R.F.A., 15/1/15; F; Capt. Wick Hall Hove, Sussex.

COLMAN, Eric Fraser
4/3/4492, 28/6/15; S. Staff. R., 2/10/15, R.A.F.; F; Capt. 50 Sidney Road, Staines.

COLMAN, Esca Houghton
D/2610, 7/1/15; R.F.C., 14/5/15, R.A.F.; E,S; Capt.; w; M(1). c/o. London & River Plate Bank Ltd., Calle Reconquista, Buenos Aires.

COLQUHOUN, Edgar Edmund
D/1484, 29/9/14, Cpl.; Bedf. R., 9/2/15; Lieut.; M.B.E., M(1). 16 Westbourne Terrace, W.

COLQUHOUN, James
6/5/5245, 31/7/15, L/C.; L'pool. R., 13/12/15, M.G.C.; F; Major; M(1). 13 Merton Grove, Bootle, Liverpool.

COLQUHOUN, James Allen Noel Grant. See GRANT-COLQUHOUN, J. A. N.

COLQUHOUN, Victor Alexander
4/2/4837, 19/7/15, L/C.; R.F.A., 19/12/15; F; Capt.; w(2); O.B.E., M(1). 687 Mulvey Avenue, Winnipeg, Canada.

COLTMAN, Frank Thomas
4/5/4665, 8/7/15, L/C.; Camb. R., 29/10/15, att. North'd. Fus.; F; Lieut.; w. c/o. Messrs. Spencer & Coy., 26 Halford Street, Leicester.

COLTMAN, Frederic Joseph
13, 1/4/08; dis. 31/3/10. Redlands, Grove Avenue, Finchley.

COLTMAN, Thomas Lister
C/13229, 7/6/18; dis. med. unfit, 19/9/18. Burbush, Burley, Ringwood, Hampshire.

COLTON, William Douglas
A/D/13069, 15/5/18; demob. 23/10/19. c/o. Standard Bank of South Africa, 10 Clements Lane, E.C. (Now in South Africa.)

COLTSON, Sydney
6/D/8470, 20/12/15; R.F.C., C/S, 8/10/16; dis. med. unfit, 3/9/17; R.N.V.R.; Lieut. 15 Baker Street, Portman Square, W.1.

COLVIN, Albert Osmond
6/2/5894, 30/8/15; 3rd Lond. R., 30/12/15, 12th Lond. R., War Office; Lieut.; w; M.C., M(2). 17 Ashford Avenue, Hornsey, N.

COLWELL, Arthur Ernest
C/11737, 26/7/17; No. 14 O.C.B., 7/12/17; Midd'x. R., 28/5/18; F; 2/Lieut. 14 Wallingford Avenue, N. Kensington, W.6.

COMBE, Ronald Edmond
E/1653, 9/10/14; R. War. R., 5/3/15, att. Lan. Fus.; F; Capt.; w; M.C. Heathercot, St. Olaves, West Great Yarmouth, Norfolk. (Now in India.)

COMBER, Bernard Forstall
E/A/13948, 22/8/18; No. 22 O.C.B., 22/11/18; R.W. Fus., 15/2/19; 2/Lieut. 19 Lower Leeson Street, Dublin, Ireland.

COMBER, William George
C/533, 13/1/11; 11th Lond. R., 9/5/14; Capt. 23 Clarendon Court, Maida Vale, W.9.

COMLEY, Rowland Henry
6/5/8158, 6/12/15; No. 8 O.C.B., 4/8/16; North'd. Fus., 21/11/16; F; Lieut.; w-p. 97 Trowbridge Road, Bradford-on-Avon, Wiltshire.

COMPSTON, Gerald Edmonds
B/13535, 17/7/18, L/C.; demob. 25/1/19. 3 Mincing Lane, E.C.3.

COMPTON, Albert Sidney
4/3761, 27/5/15, Cpl.; 12th Lond. R., 21/10/15; F; Lieut. 46 Newick Road, Clapton, E.5.

COND, James Herbert
C/12290, 7/12/17, L/C.; No. 8 O.C.B., 10/5/18; Tank Corps, 12/11/18; 2/Lieut. The Grange, Little Sutton, Four Oaks, Birmingham.

CONERNEY, Cyril Jack G.
6/5/8720, 5/1/16; No. 7 O.C.B., 11/8/16; R. Dub. Fus., 18/12/16, att. R. Ir. Regt.; Lieut. 1 Templemore Avenue, Rathgar, Dublin, Ireland.

✠ CONLAN, Arthur Underhill
3/3380, 26/4/15; 18th Lond. R., 28/7/15; 2/Lieut. Killed in action 22/5/16.

CONLIN, Thomas William
B/A/12381, 14/1/18; R.F.A., C/S, 17/5/18; R.F.A., 18/2/19; 2/Lieut. Townview, Omagh, Co. Tyrone, Ireland.

CONNELL, Alan Bourke
D/11558, 28/6/17; dis. med. unfit, 2/10/17. Luncies Farm, Pitsea, Essex.

CONNELL, Barry Bourke
K/B/2161, 23/11/14; R.E., 1/3/15; Lieut.

CONNELL, Joseph
C/11508, 18/6/17; dis. 19/9/17 to join Royal Aircraft Factory. c/o. Messrs. Wilkinson & Gaviller, 34 Tower Street, E.C.

CONNELL, Richard Francis
6/3/8687, 4/1/16; No. 5 O.C.B., 14/8/16; K.R. Rif. C., 21/11/16, R.A.F.; F; Lieut.; w. 89 Balfour Road, Ilford, Essex.

CONNELL, William Jocelyn
C/14170, 10/10/18; trfr. K.R. Rif. C., 25/4/19, R.A.O.C. Harbour View, Kilbeggan, Co. Westmeath, Ireland.

CONNOLLY, Albert Edward
C/10813, 2/3/17; R.F.C., C/S, 16/4/17; R.F.C., 22/5/17, R.A.F.; Lieut. 77 Lower Beechwood Avenue, Ranelagh, Dublin.

CONNOLLY, Francis Clayton
C/13297, 17/6/18; demob. 10/1/19. 77 Lower Beechwood Avenue, Ranelagh, Dublin.

CONNOLLY, Reginald Charles Herbert
C/D/12030, 24/9/17; No. 11 O.C.B., 5/4/18; Wilts. R., 24/9/18; 2/Lieut. Exton Rectory, Bishops Waltham, Hampshire.

CONOLEY, Cornelius Walter
D/11129, 30/4/17; No. 12 O.C.B., 10/8/17; 2nd Lond. R., 27/11/17; 2/Lieut. Craig-y-don, Orsett Road, Grays, Essex.

CONOLEY, Thomas Gamage
A/14076, 30/9/18; trfr. K.R. Rif. C., 6/7/19. Westcliff Towers, Priory Road, Bournemouth.

CONOLLY, Arthur Egbert Hugh
C/66, 9/4/08; dis. 8/4/10; rej. B/11308, 17/5/17, Sgt.; demob. 11/4/19.

CONSIDINE, Harold William Howe
6/3/A/6987, 25/10/15, Sgt.; No. 14 O.C.B., 30/1/17; K.R. Rif. C., 25/4/17; 2/Lieut.; p. 33 Gordon Place, Kensington, W.8.

CONSTABLE, Douglas La Costa
6/4/8955, 17/1/16; No. 5 O.C.B., 14/8/16; Norf. R., 18/12/16; 2/Lieut. 111 Lauderdale Mansions, Maida Vale, W.9.

APPENDIX II.—RECORDS OF RANK AND FILE.

✠ CONSTABLE, Douglas Oliphant
H/2/5/2826, 1/2/15, Sgt.; Gren. Gds., 17/11/15; F; Lieut.
    Killed in action 25/9/16.

CONSTABLE, Hugh Lowenberg
1/3085, 22/3/15, Cpl.; York. R., 11/6/15, emp. R.E.; Lieut.
    14 Redcliffe Road, S.W.

CONSTABLE, Sydney John
A/10467, 12/1/17; No. 14 O.C.B., 5/7/17; 20th Lond. R., 30/10/17; 2/Lieut.; p. 94 Goldhurst Terrace, Crouch End, N.

CONSTABLE, William George
D/1442, 29/9/14, Sgt.; Notts. & Derby. R., 5/5/15, Lan. Fus.; F; Major; Inj; M(1). 11 Vicarage Avenue, Derby.

✠ CONSTANT, Martin
B/323, 30/6/08; dis. 29/6/09; rej. Sq/832, 4/8/14; dis. med. unfit, 8/9/14.

CONWAY, Edward John
6/Sq/9135, 25/1/16; trfr. R.A.S.C., 9/6/16.
    Glen Lyon, Alexandra Park, Andover.

CONWAY, James Maurice
D/E/13867, 21/8/18; No. 22 O.C.B., 22/11/18; L'pool. R., 15/2/19; 2/Lieut. 40 Ravensdale Mansions, Crouch End, N.8.

COODE, Bernard Henry
Sq/878, 5/8/14; R. Regt. of Cav., 9/9/14, Army Cyc. Corps; F; Lieut. Ormonde House, North Gate, Regents Park, N.W. 8.

COOK, Albert Ewart William
4/D/9701, 9/10/16; No. 14 O.C.B., 27/12/16; Ches. R., 25/4/17; Lieut.; w.
    Norwell, Cambridge Road, King's Heath, Birmingham.

COOK, Bruce Lionel
4/3684, 20/5/15; Essex R., 11/9/15, R.A.S.C.; Lieut.
    School House, Chingford.

✠ COOK, Cecil Haddon
6/4/9086, 24/1/16; No. 2 O.C.B., 14/8/16; Manch. R., 18/12/16; F; 2/Lieut. Killed in action 22/10/17.

COOK, Christopher Randall
C/14224, 25/10/18; trfr. K.R. Rif. C., 7/4/19.
    St. Mary's, Branksome Road, Southend-on-Sea.

COOK, Eustace Walter
D/13720, 2/8/18; demob. 23/1/19. 21 Ethelbert Road, Margate.

COOK, Francis Ainsley
B/12762, 15/3/18; No. 14 O.C.B., 23/8/18; North'd. Fus., 6/3/19; 2/Lieut. 26 Grosvenor Place, Jesmond, Newcastle-on-Tyne.

COOK, Francis John
4/1/4334, 21/6/15, L/C.; Manch. R., 18/10/15; Lieut.; w(2).
    70 Grandison Road, Battersea Rise.

COOK, Frederick William
B/11692, 19/7/17; Garr. O.C.B., 28/12/17; Lab. Corps, 18/5/18; F; 2/Lieut. Old Bank House, Sale, Cheshire.

COOK, Herbert
A/11199, 7/5/17; No. 12 O.C.B., 10/8/17; North'd. Fus., 27/11/17; 2/Lieut. The Avenue, Coxhoe, Co. Durham.

COOK, Horatio William
A/13054, 10/5/18, Sgt.; Special List, 15/1/19; NR; 2/Lieut.; p.
    British Empire Club, 12 St. James Square, S.W.

COOK, John Cecil
C/12652, 27/2/18; No. 6 O.C.B., 5/7/18; Sea. Highrs., 3/3/19; 2/Lieut 46a Brook Mews, Grosvenor Square, W. 1.

COOK, Joseph William
4/1/4251, 14/6/15; N. Staff. R., 13/1/16; Capt.
    23 Petherton Road, Highbury New Park, N.

COOK, Malcolm Archibald
6/9201, 28/1/16, L/C.; No. 14 O.C.B., 27/9/16; 22nd Lond. R., 18/12/16, att. Lan. Fus. and 24th Lond. R.; F; Major; M(1).
    Lower Fox Hangers, Devizes, Wiltshire.

COOK, Russell Henry
B/10550, 17/1/17; No. 11 O.C.B., 5/7/17; Indian Army, 30/10/17; I, Persia; Capt.
    233 Norwich Road, Ipswich, Suffolk. (Now in India.)

COOK, Sidney Courtney
6/3/8307, 11/12/15, L/C.; No. 14 O.C.B.; M.G.C., 24/10/16; Lieut.; M.C. 58 Fillebrook Road, Leytonstone, E. 11.

COOK, Warren Percy
A/10984, 2/4/17; R.G.A., C/S, 31/8/17; R.G.A., 6/1/18; 2/Lieut.
    Woodcroft, Stoke Bishop, Bristol.

COOKE, Alan Kenneth Donovan
B/12345, 1/1/18; No. 8 O.C.B., 10/5/18; trfr. 28th Lond. R., 9/9/18. Carroll House, Berkswell, Nr. Birmingham.

✠ COOKE, Cecil Pybus
A/9848, 3/11/16; No. 14 O.C.B., 27/12/16; Shrops. L.I., 25/4/17; 2/Lieut. Killed in action 22/8/17.

COOKE, Cyril Hands
E/2721, 18/1/15, L/C.; R. Berks. R., 22/4/15; F; Capt.; M.C., M(2). Rest Harrow, Newton, Newbury, Berkshire.

COOKE, Eric Masters
D/10008, 24/11/16; R.F.C., C/S, 13/3/17; R.F.C., 19/4/17.
    Grange Cottage, Overton, Nr. Wakefield.

COOKE, Geoffrey Cotton
Sq/3126, 29/3/15; R.F.A., Kent Yeo.; Lieut.
    22 Priory Road, Bedford Park, W. 4.

COOKE, Harry Geoffrey
C/10795, 26/2/17; No. 12 O.C.B., 10/8/17; 3rd Lond. R., 27/11/17; 2/Lieut. The Hall, Rockland, St. Mary, Norwich.

COOKE, Harry Riblon
4/5610, 16/8/15, L/C.; R.W. Surr. R., 6/11/15; Capt.; w; M.C.
    Radnor, 21 Aika Road, Westcliffe.

COOKE, Hubert Croft.
A/10698, 14/2/17; R F.C., C/S, 13/3/17; R.F.C., 19/4/17, R.A.F.; Lieut. Cage House, Tonbridge, Kent.

COOKE, John
6/7725, 22/11/15, L/C.; No. 14 O.C.B.; M.G.C., 24/10/16; F; 2/Lieut. 2 Lidyard Road, Upper Holloway, N. 19.

COOKE, Leonard
6/2/9470, 14/2/16; No. 14 O.C.B., 26/11/16; R.W. Surr. R., 27/3/17; Lieut. Fishpond Drive, The Park, Nottingham.

COOKE, Oswald Hayward
B/1207, 14/9/14, L/C.; Yorks. L.I., 18/12/14; F; Capt.; w(4); M.C. and Bar, M(1). Crossfield House, Winsford, Cheshire.

COOKE, Reginald Bertram
A/400, 5/4/09; dis. 5/4/13. 11 Grays Inn Square, W.C. 1

COOKE, Reginald Harold
D/10248, 29/12/16; No. 14 O.C.B., 7/6/17; R.W. Surr. R., 25/9/17; I; Lieut.; Inv.
    80 Selwyn Avenue, Richmond, Surrey.

COOKE, Richard Lindsay
6/4/8919, 14/1/16; No. 13 O.C.B., 4/11/16; Bedf. R., 28/2/17, Indian Army; Lieut. Shirley, Luton, Bedfordshire.

COOKSON, George Craven
2/6/7907, 29/11/15; No. 14 O.C.B., 28/8/16; W. York. R., 22/11/16; F; Lieut.; w(2).
    Fairburn, Ferrybridge S.O., Yorkshire.

COOLING, John Herbert
A/K/2560, 4/1/15; R. Suss. R., 31/3/15, att. American Army; F; Staff Capt.; M(1). 4 Frognal, Hampstead, N.W. 3.

COOMBES, Alfred Leslie
6/Sq/6171, 12/9/15; R.F.A., 26/11/15; F; Lieut.
    Inglewood, Longcroft Avenue, Harpenden, Hertfordshire.

COONEY, Ralph Carson
4/4274, 17/6/15, L/C.; R. Sco. Fus., 30/11/15, Tank Corps; Capt.; w. Lakeview, Enniskillen, Co. Fermanagh, Ireland.

COOPER, Alexander David
6/Sq/7133, 2/11/15, L/C.; A.S.C., C/S, 1/9/16; R.A.S.C., 25/10/16; Lieut. 17 Chilworth Street, Hyde Park, W. 2.

COOPER, Alfred William Howden
H/2692, 14/1/15; Cam'n. Highrs., 23/4/15; F; Lieut.; w.
    Free High Church, Inverness, Scotland.

COOPER, Arthur Cyril
6/2/5763, 21/8/15; 19th Lond. R., 7/7/16, secd. R.F.C.; Lieut.; w. 164 Pool Road, Leicester.

COOPER, Arthur Herbert
B/2916, 15/2/15; Ches. R., 24/5/15; F; Capt.; w; M.C
    12 Walpole Gardens, Twickenham. (Now in Paris.)

COOPER, Aubrey Benson. See BENSON-COOPER, A.

APPENDIX II.—RECORDS OF RANK AND FILE.

COOPER, Austin Eric Sissen
C/D/12295, 10/12/17; No. 3 O.C.B., 10/5/18; trfr. 28th Lond. R., 8/9/18.
29 Eccleston Street, S.W 1.

COOPER, Bernard
6/3/6918, 19/10/15; No. 11 O.C.B., 7/5/16; Yorks. L.I., 4/9/16; Lieut.; w.
Eton House, Woodlands, Beverley.

✠ COOPER, Cecil Davey
6/Sq/9246, 2/2/16; No. 2 Cav. C/S, 10/9/16; R. Regt. of Cav., 20/12/16, att. Wilts. R.; F; 2/Lieut.
Died of wounds 29/1/18.

COOPER, Charles Alfred
6/3/8159, 6/12/15; No. 14 O.C.B., 28/8/16; Notts. & Derby. R., 7/12/16; Lieut.; w.
The Manor House, Linton, Nr. Burton-on-Trent.

COOPER, Donald Ernest
4/3/4414, 24/6/15, Sgt.; R.E., 13/9/15; F; Lieut.; w; M.C., M(1).
Greenwood, Dinas Powis, S. Wales.

COOPER, Edgar Clement
C/13365, 21/6/18; trfr. 14th Lond. R., 6/12/18.
Connington, 15 Clifton Avenue, Church End, Finchley, N. 3.

COOPER, Ernest Frederick
6/3/6416, 23/9/15; No. 4 O.C.B., 7/3/16; N. Lan. R., 15/7/16; 2/Lieut.
Elton Lodge, Hornchurch, Essex.

COOPER, Francis D'Arcy
Sq/3301, 19/4/15; R.F.A., 9/7/15; F; Capt.; w.
Waverley, Reigate, Surrey.

✠ COOPER, Geoffrey Rowsell
2/6/4/5160, 29/7/15; R. Mil. Coll., 22/11/15; R. Berks R., 19/7/16; 2/Lieut
Died 8/11/16.

COOPER, George Alister
6/5/5246, 31/7/15, L/C.; L'pool. R., 20/1/16, R.E.; Major; O.B.E.
1 Alton Terrace, Broughty Ferry, Dundee.

COOPER, George Conroy
C/1687, 12/10/14, L/C.; dis. to R. Mil. Coll., 13/5/15; Rif. Brig., 20/10/15; Capt.; w,p
Canford Cliffs, Dorset.

COOPER, George Lionel John
6/4/6654, 7/10/15, Cpl.; No. 11 O.C.B., 7/5/16; Linc. R., 4/9/16; Lieut.
150 Stapleton Hall Road, Stroud Green.

COOPER, Gerald Percy
D/1420, 29/9/14; E. Surr. R., 17/3/15; F,It; Capt.
Suwanee, Gordon Road, Shoreham-by-Sea, Sussex.

COOPER, James Askey
3/9604, 28/8/16; R.A., C/S, 26/10/16; R.G.A., 5/1/17; Lieut.; w.
Forest House, Shepshed, Loughborough, Leicester.

COOPER, Joseph Charles Stanley
A/D/11948, 31/8/17; R.F.A., C/S, 15/3/18; R.F.A., 4/11/18; 2/Lieut.
Fulbrooks, Bridport.

COOPER, Lancelot Head
B/802, 9/6/14; R.W. Kent R., 15/8/14, Hamps. R.; Capt.
Redroofs, Henley-on-Thames.

COOPER, Lanée Harries
6/1/5755, 21/8/15, L/C.; R.F.A., C/S, 17/3/16; R.F.A., 13/7/16; Lieut.
Hasland, Bath Road, Slough.

COOPER, Leslie Gordon
6/4/7328, 9/11/15; Sea. Highrs., 4/9/16, Indian Army; F,I; Lieut.; w.
c/o. Messrs. King, King & Coy., P.O. Box 110, Bombay, India.

✠ COOPER, Nowell Edwin
4/3/4834, 13/7/15, L/C.; Hunts. Cyc. Bn., 26/1/16; Lieut.
Died of wounds 16/10/18.

COOPER, Percy Morris
A/10042, 29/11/16; No. 14 O.C.B., 30/1/17; Manch. R., 25/4/17; Lieut.
149 Withington Road, Whalley Range, Manchester.

COOPER, Percy Perrin
B/13634, 26/7/18; trfr. K.R. Rif. C., 7/4/19.
Tudor House, High Street, Harrow-on-the-Hill.

✠ COOPER, Thomas Gill
6/5/5926, 1/9/15, L/C.; L'pool. R., 23/4/16, M.G.C.; 2/Lieut.
Died 25/3/18.

COOPER, William Claude
K/A/2413, 21/12/14, L/C.; Manch. R., 7/4/15; F; Capt.; w; M(1).
59 Beaconsfield Road, New Southgate, N. 11.

COOPER, William Luther
4/5/5193, 29/7/15; R.A., C/S, 24/1/16; R.F.A., 23/6/16; F; Capt.; w; M.C., Portuguese War Cross, M(1).
Talane, Sydney Buildings, Bath.

COOPER-READE, John Bacon. See READE, J. B.

COOPER-WILLIS, Guy
C/1318, 26/9/14, L/C.; 20th Lond. R., 13/11/14; Staff Capt.; M.C.
132 Sloane Street, S.W.1.

COOPS, Frank Cecil
6/5/5247, 31/7/15, Sgt.; L'pool. R., 13/12/15, R.F.C., R.A.F.; Lieut.; p.
The Limes, Dudley Road, Whalley Range, Manchester.

COOTE, Arthur Bernard
C/13298, 17/6/18; No. 22 O.C.B., 23/8/18; Bedf. & Herts. R., 13/2/19; 2/Lieut.
16 Lancaster Gate Terrace, W. 2.

COOTE, John
D/1457, 29/9/14; R.N.V.R., 18/10/14; M(1).
The Manor House, Marston Magna, Somerset.

✠ COOTE, Richard Markham
C/562, 5/4/11; R. Berks. R., 19/9/14; F; Capt.
Killed in action 13/10/15.

COPE, Charles Cooper
6/1/9237, 1/2/16; Camb. R., 23/6/16; Lieut.

COPE, Geoffrey Silverwood
B/739, 11/11/13; dis. 4/8/14, Med. Unfit.
24 Collingham Gardens, S.W.

COPE, Herbert Ernest
C/11789, 2/8/17; No. 2 O.C.B., 4/1/18; N. Cyc. Bn., 12/11/18; F; 2/Lieut.
5 Hollingdourne Road, Herne Hill, S.E. 24.

COPE, Reginald
4/4178, 14/6/15; 5th Lond. R., 14/9/15; F; Capt.; w; Croix de Guerre, M(2).
c/o. Messrs. Arthur Rutter, Sons & Coy., 30 Abbeygate, Bury St. Edmunds.

✠ COPE, Walter Gordon
K/A/2486, 28/12/14; York. R., 25/3/15, R.F.C., R.A.F.; F; Capt.
Killed 6/9/18.

COPELAND, William Brian
C/1665, 10/10/14; N. Staff. R., 18/12/14; F; Capt.; w(2); M(1).
4 Bolton Gardens, S.W. 5.

COPLAND, Henry Townsend
A/13111, 24/5/18; No. 22 O.C.B., 5/7/18; R.W. Kent R., 4/2/19; 2/Lieut.
Banks Terrace, Sheerness.

COPP, Alexander Foreman
C/1624, 9/10/14; E. Surr. R., 9/3/15; F,It; Capt.; w; M.C.
Uplands, Leatherhead, Surrey.

COPPOCK, Arthur Leslie
K/B/2324, 14/12/14; Welch. R., 31/3/15, att. Mon. R.; F; Capt.
124 Colum Road, Cardiff.

COPPOCK, Thomas Lewis
K/Sq/2332, 14/12/14; R.F.A., 9/6/15; F; Capt.; w.
Culle San Martin 333, Buenos Aires, Argentina.

✠ CORBISHLEY, Wilfrid James
K/H/2226, 3/12/14; Lond. Div. Cyc. Coy., 18/3/15; R.A.F.; Capt.; w.

CORIN, Thomas
6/5/8160, 6/12/15; No. 8 O.C.B., 4/8/16; Yorks. L.I., 21/11/16, att. York. R. and Indian Army; F,I; Capt.
557 Alexandra Park Road, N. 22.

CORKETT, Cecil Mansfield
6/2/6589, 4/10/15; No. 11 O.C.B., 7/5/16; Lan. Fus., 4/9/16; F; Lieut.; w(2).
Brampton, Ontario, Canada.

CORLETT, Cyril Norman
4/6/5/4900, 15/7/15; North'd. Fus., 1/6/16, att. High. L.I. and York. R.; F,NR; Lieut.; w,p.
11 Woodbourne Road, Douglas, Isle of Man.

CORLETT, Robert Frederick
4/6/5/4901, 15/7/15, L/C.; R.F.A., C/S, 24/1/16; Yorks. L.I., 9/6/16; F; Lieut.; w-p.
Earle Terrace, Douglas, Isle of Man.

CORLEY, Francis Stanley
B/11693, 19/7/17; No. 14 O.C.B., 9/11/17; Bedf. R., 30/4/18, att. North'n. R.; F; 2/Lieut.
19 Broomfield Lane, Palmers Green, N. 13.

APPENDIX II.—RECORDS OF RANK AND FILE.

CORMACK, David
6/3/9333, 7/2/16; R.F.A., C/S, 4/8/16; R.F.A., 10/11/16; Lieut.
Royal Bank House, Lockerbie.

CORMACK, George Edwin
D/13868, 21/8/18, Sgt.; trfr. K.R. Rif. C., 23/5/19.
5 Glenisla Gardens, Grange, Edinburgh.

CORNELIUS, Cecil
A/2021, 5/11/14, L/C.; North'd. Fus., 20/5/15; F; Capt.
Stock Exchange, London, E.C.

CORNELL, Harold Henry
B/12209, 8/11/17, L/C.; R.E., C/S, 14/4/18; R.E., 15/8/18; 2/Lieut.
P.O. Box 34, Molteno, South Africa.

CORNER, Percy Vernon
6/4/5088, 22/7/15; dis. med unfit, 1/9/16.
46 Grosvenor Road, Westminster, S.W.1.

CORNES, Reginald William
D/Sq/11819, 9/8/17; Shrops. L.I., 30/7/18, att. T.M. Bty.; F; 2/Lieut.
Westfields, Underdale Road, Shrewsbury.

CORNEY, Wulstan Joseph
B/470, 24/2/10; dis. 22/12/11.

CORNISH, Fred
6/Sq/8503, 22/12/15; No. 1 O.C.B., 6/9/16; R.F.C., 3/4/17, R.A.F.; Lieut.
Tortoise House, Sible Hedingham, Halstead, Essex.

CORNISH, Leo Kenneth
C/14137, 11/10/18; demob. 29/1/19.
Warren Lodge, Edmonton, E.9.

CORNISH, Vivian Christopher Montague
E/1577, 6/10/14; R. Fus., 10/2/15; F; Lieut.; w.
2 Cambridge Court, Twickenham.

CORRALL, William Harford
B/C/12221, 13/11/17; trfr. 28th Lond. R., 8/4/18; F; w.
45 Fulham Road, Sparkhill, Birmingham.

CORRIE, Alfred John
B/12386, 15/1/18, L/C.; R. Marines, 10/4/18; 2/Lieut.
North High Street, Musselburgh, Scotland.

CORRIE, Owen Cecil Kirkpatrick
Sq/879, 5/8/14, L/C.; N. Som. Yeo., 7/1/15, R.F.A.; F,P; Capt.; M.C., M(2).
Law Courts, Jerusalem.

CORSAN, Reginald Arthur
B/572, 7/11/11; R.F.A., 27/4/12; F,It; Major; w(2); D.S.O., M.C., M(3).
Hollisdene, Southville Road, Thames Ditton.

✠ **CORSCADEN, James Noel**
D/11117, 27/4/17; No. 10 O.C.B., 5/10/17; R. Innis. Fus., 26/2/18; F; 2/Lieut.
Killed in action 17/10/18

CORSER, Harold Desmond
C/10369, 5/1/17; No. 11 O.C.B., 5/7/17; Indian Army, 30/10/17; M; Lieut.; w.
c/o. Dr. Hackett, St. Peter's Vicarage, Belsize Park Gardens, Hampstead. (Now in India.)

CORT, James Constantine
B/10960, 30/3/17; trfr. Class W. Res., 10/8/18.
Breighhurst Bleach Works, Bolton, Lancashire.

CORT-COX, Raymond Robert
B/12387, 15/1/18, L/C.; No. 16 O.C.B., 23/8/18; R. Berks. R., 6/3/19; 2/Lieut.
Netherleigh, Warwick Road, Stratford-on-Avon.

CORY, Reginald Frank
A/Sq/C/12539, 5/2/18; No. 1 O.C.B., 9/8/18; demob.
116 Headstone Road, Harrow.

CORYN, Frederick Sidney
A/11597, 5/7/17; No. 19 O.C.B., 9/11/17; Wilts. R., 26/3/18; F; 2/Lieut.
c/o. F. J. Horne, Esq., Rutland Court Hotel, 63 Lancaster Gate, W.2.

COSGROVE, Norman Reseigh
F/2939, 18/2/15, L/C.; Shrops. L.I., 21/6/15; F,S; Lieut.; w(2); M(1).
Hillside, Colney Hatch Lane, Muswell Hill, N.10.

COSTELLO, Ernest James
6/8437, 16/12/15; dis. med. unfit, 16/6/16.

COSTELLO, Ralph Edgar
B/1647, 9/10/14; W. Rid. R., 28/11/14, North'n. R., R.W. Surr. R.; E,P; Lieut.; w(2).
Callington, Stanthorpe Road, Streatham, S.W.16.

COSWAY, Charles Henry
6/4/9530, 12/2/16; No 14 O.C.B., 26/11/16; Devon. R., 27/3/17; 2/Lieut.
Lyme Villa, Tiverton, Devonshire.

COTCHING, Alfred
2/9652, 28/9/16; No. 14 O.C.B., 30/1/17; E. Kent R., 29/5/17; M.I; Lieut.
68 Sandford Road, Bromley, Kent.

COTCHING, Edward Glenister
6/2/7495, 15/11/15; No. 14 O.C.B., 28/8/16; E. Kent R., 22/11/16; F; Lieut.; w; M.C.
Wootton Lodge, Ashleigh Road, Horsham, Sussex.

COTES, Herbert Victor Merton
E/14014, 13/9/18; R.G.A., C/S, 1/11/18; demob.
1 Yelverton Road, Bournemouth, Hampshire.

COTON, Charles Owen
4/3762, 27/5/15; Shrops. L.I., 10/9/15, R. Ir. Rif.; E,S; Lieut.; w.
Gipsy Lodge, Bexley Heath, Kent. (Now in Bombay.)

COTTAM, Joseph
C/13350, 26/6/18; trfr. 14th Lond R., 6/12/18.
Estcourt, Chamber Road, Oldham, Lancashire.

COTTAM, Joseph Stanley
6/2/7794, 24/11/15; A.S.C., C/S, 1/9/16; R.A.S.C., 25/10/16; I; Lieut.; Inv; M(1).
6 Hangleton Road, Hangleton, West Hove, Sussex.

COTTERELL, James Ronald
6/2/6389, 23/9/15; No. 7 O.C.B., 7/4/16; S. Staff. R., 17/7/16; F; Lieut.
Roseleigh, Buchanan Road, Walsall, Cheshire.

✠ **COTTERELL, Robert Victor**
6/2/6390, 23/9/15; No. 7 O.C.B., 7/4/16; S. Staff. R., 17/7/16; 2/Lieut.
Killed in action 23/4/17.

COTTLE, Sidney George
D/10443, 10/1/17; No. 14 O.C.B., 7/6/17; Manch. R., 25/9/17; 2/Lieut.

COTTON, Arthur
6/3/8162, 6/12/15, L/C.; No. 14 O.C.B., 16/11/16; R.W. Fus., 28/12/17; F; Lieut.; M(1).
Duke Street, Ruabon, N. Wales.

COTTON-COOKE, Geoffrey. See COOKE, G. C.

COUCHER, Alfred Edwin Reneson
4/3/3943, 3/6/15; R.G.A., 29/9/15; F; Major; Inv; M(1).
Cumnor, 51 Butler Road, Harrow.

COUCHMAN, Henry Theodore
4/6/5/4959, 19/7/15; R.F.A., 10/11/15; Capt.
Frogmoor House, Rickmansworth, Hertfordshire.

COUGHTRIE, Oliver
6/5/5428, 5/8/15, Sgt.; K.R. Rif. C., 17/11/15; Capt.
Selbourne, Edgar Road, Sanderstead, Surrey.

COULDREY, Herbert Mill
6/2/7227, 5/11/15, L/C.; R.E., 8/7/16; S; Lieut.
Sunniva, Paignton, S. Devon.

COULSON, Arthur Tranmer
D/Sq/10916, 26/3/17, L/C.; No. 2 Cav. C/S, 11/1/18; R. Regt. of Cav., 22/6/18; 2/Lieut.
Watton Abbey, Beverley, East Yorkshire.

COULSON, Frederick
6/3/6195, 13/9/15; R. War. R., 7/1/16; F; Lieut.; w(2).
21 Selby Road, Anerley, S.E.20.

COULSON, John Norman
A/C/13140, 28/5/18; trfr. 28th Lond. R., 16/11/18.
103 High Street, Wapping.

COULSON, Raymond Arthur
H/2940, 18/2/15; R. Suss. R., 22/4/15, Indian Army; I; Capt.
68 Corringham Road, Golders Green, N.W.4.

COULTER, James Reginald
B/13663, 29/7/18; No. 11 O.C.B., 24/1/19; General List, 8/3/19; 2/Lieut.
c/o. Standard Bank of South Africa Ltd., 10 Clements Lane, E.C.

✠ **COULTHWAITE, James**
6/2/9031, 20/1/16; No. 14 O.C.B., 30/10/16; Bord. R., 28/2/17; 2/Lieut.
Killed in action 5/8/17.

COUNSEL, James Milne Vincent
B/11355, 25/5/17; Lab. Corps, 1/8/17; F; Major; Order of Wen-Ho (China).
c/o. Agent-General for Tasmania, Australia House, Strand, W.C.2.

APPENDIX II.—RECORDS OF RANK AND FILE.

COUNSELL, Harold Herbert
6/5702, 19/8/15, L/C.; R. Lanc. R., 7/1/16, att. R.E. Sigs.; F,E; Lieut.
    Fairlea, Aspley Road, Bedford.

COUNSELL, Thomas Lawrence
3/3836, 31/5/15; R.G.A., 8/10/15; Asst. Paymaster, R.N.R., 25/5/17.
    Holly House, Brackenbury Road, Preston, Lancashire. (Now in Demerara.)

COURT, Alfred Walter Philip
3/6/5879, 30/8/15; 19th Lond. R., 12/1/16; F,E; Lieut.
    34-40 Ludgate Hill, E.C. 4.

COURT, Cecil Hales
C/617, 29/2/12; 19th Lond. R., 3/10/14; Capt.
    43 Marlborough Hill, N.W. 8.

COURT, Gerald Frankcombe
C/1344, 26/9/14; Essex R., 3/4/15, R.A.F.; F; Flt. Cmdr.
    Riverside, Taplow, Buckinghamshire.

COURTENAY, Henry Drury
4/6/Sq/4817, 12/7/15; Bucks. Huss., 15/11/15, att. 10th and 20th Huss.; F; Lieut.
    District Inspector's Office, R.I.C., Co. Galway, Ireland.

COURTENAY-MACKNESS, Reginald James Eustace
A/13037, 6/5/18; trfr. K.R. Rif. C., 7/4/19.
    Kiaora, 9 Geraldine Road, Wandsworth Common, S.W.

COURTIER, Reginald Frederick
6/2/6884, 18/10/15; No. 14 O.C.B.; Hamps. R., 22/11/16; Lieut.; p.
    17 Greville Road, Southampton.

COUTTS, William Fisher
6/4/6756, 11/10/15; No. 9 O.C.B., 14/4/16; R. Scots, 4/8/16, High. L.I.; Lieut.
    Grahamville, Bearsden, Nr. Glasgow.

COUVELAS, George
C/14112, 9/10/18; demob. 20/3/19.
    Lingmel, Heswall, Cheshire.

COVENTRY, Ernest Arthur
2/9690, 4/10/16; No. 14 O.C.B., 26/11/16; Ches. R., 27/3/17, att. Lab. Corps; Lieut.; w.
    Green Gable, Middle Road, Harrow.

COVERLEY, John Basil Sanderson
6/4/6729, 11/10/15; Garr. O.C.B., 12/12/16; Yorks. L.I., 10/2/17, att. Durh. L.I.; Lieut.
    19 Harvard Road, Chiswick, W. 4.

COVINGTON, Crescens Kingsley
6/4/9161, 26/1/16, Sgt.; No. 14 O.C.B.; Notts. & Derby. R., 24/10/16, Intelligence; F; Lieut.; w; M.C., Croix de Guerre.
    North House, Putney Heath, S.W.

COW, Charles Stuart
A/11437, 4/6/17; A.S.C., C/S, 1/9/17; R.A.S.C., 27/10/17; F; 2/Lieut.
    30 Prentis Road, Streatham.

COWAN, Eric Rea
6/Sq/6474, 27/9/15; No. 1 Cav. C/S, 24/4/16; Lovat's Scouts, 28/7/16; Lieut.
    South African Union, Edinburgh.

COWAN, William Lindsay
B/12825, 22/3/18; R.A.F., C/S, 1/7/18; R.A.F., -/12/18; 2/Lieut
    Hallguards, Ecclefechan, Dumfrieshire, Scotland.

COWARD, Alfred George Robert
2/3262, 15/4/15, L/C.; R.E., 22/7/15; G,E,F; Lieut.; w(2).
    9 The Retreat, Southsea, Portsmouth, Hampshire.

COWARD, Edwin Gordon Whitaker
4/Sq/9613, 13/9/16; R.A., C/S, 12/1/17; R.F.A., 19/5/17, att. R.F.C.; Lieut.; w; M(1).
    c/o. Commercial Bank of Sydney, 18 Birchin Lane, E.C

COWBURN, George Herbert Percy
B/13434, 3/7/18; No. 22 O.C.B., 23/8/18; R.W. Kent R., 3/2/19; 2/Lieut.
    101 Priory Road, Hastings.

COWBURN, Thomas Arnold
6/Sq/6275, 16/9/15; R.A.S.C., 27/11/15; SWA,F; Lieut.; w.
    c/o. National Bank of South Africa, Sea Point, C.P., South Africa.

COWELL, Clarence Berkeley
A/11598, 5/7/17; Garr. O.C.B., 28/12/17; Durh. L.I., 18/5/18; F; 2/Lieut.
    56 Percy Terrace, Sunderland.

COWELL, Cyril Henry George
D/11145, 30/4/17, L/C.; M.G.C., C/S, 10/8/17; Tank Corps, 30/1/18, North'n R.; 2/Lieut.

COWELL, Norman
6/8560, 31/12/15; R.F.A., C/S, 26/5/16; R.G.A., 30/8/16; F; Capt.; M.C., Croix de Guerre (French and Belgian), Chevalier de l'Ordre de Leopold, M(1).
    22 Burnt Ash Lane, Bromley, Kent.

COWELL, Robert Edward
6/2/5583, 12/8/15; North'd. Fus., 4/6/16; F; 2/Lieut.
    Reseleigh, Hawarden Avenue, Douglas, Isle of Man.

COWEN, Hugh Francis Durbin
4/2/4415, 24/6/15; R.A.S.C., 4/12/15; E; Lieut.
    Dunurlin, New Malden, Surrey.

COWIE, James Robert
B/12338, 1/1/18; No. 5 O.C.B., 10/5/18, No. 14 O.C.B.; Midd'x. R., 3/2/19; 2/Lieut.
    38 Argyle Square, St. Pancras, W.C. 1.

COWIE, William George. Attested as RAYNE, W. G.
6/3/7033, 27/10/15; No. 1 O.C.B., 25/2/16; R.F.C., 27/8/16.
    5 Bettoney Vere, Bray, Berkshire.

COWLES, Denis Evelyn
6/4/9211, 31/1/16; No. 14 O.C.B.; R. War. R., 24/10/16, Welch. R.; F; Lieut.; Inv.
    The Square, Tollesbury, Essex.

COWPE, Thomas Alexander
B/11022, 11/4/17; No. 14 O.C.B., 10/8/17; Ches. R., 27/11/17, att. R.F.C.; 2/Lieut.
    Pendlehurst, Burnley, Lancashire.

COWPER, Joseph Archibald McDougall
6/3/5845, 26/8/15; Midd'x. R., 1/6/16, att. R. Fus.; F; Lieut.; w; M(1).
    70 Coniston Road, Muswell Hill, N. 10.

COWPER, William Haslett
6/1/6176, 13/9/15; No. 7 O.C.B., 3/7/16; R. Ir. Regt., 3/11/16; F; Lieut.; w.
    Rathfriland, Co. Down, Ireland.

✠ COWPER-COLES, Sherard William
Sq/2941, 18/2/15; R.A.S.C., 5/7/15, R.A.F.; F; Capt.
    Killed in action 14/10/18.

✠ COWTAN, Francis Scott
Sq/581, 13/11/11, Sgt.; Wilts. Yeo., 14/4/15; Capt.
    Killed in action 24-25/4/17.

COX, Alan Herbert
D/13710, 14/7/18; demob. 29/1/19.
    Syren Cot, Fairfield Road, Croydon.

✠ COX, Arthur George
6/8747, 6/1/16; R.F.C., C/S; R.F.C., 17/7/16; 2/Lieut.
    Killed in action 15/12/17.

COX, Arthur James
6/2/6108, 6/9/15, L/C.; No. 7 O.C.B., 7/4/16; Hamps. R., 17/7/16, secd. Indian Army; I; Lieut.
    24 Friar Lane, Leicester.

COX, Dudley Fisher
6/3/6243, 16/9/15; R.F.C., 7/8/16, R.A.F.; F,E; Capt.; M(1).
    2 Bank Mansions, Golders Green, N.W. 4.

✠ COX, Harold
6/2/7243, 7/11/15; No. 11 O.C.B., 7/5/16; 9th Lond. R., 4/9/16, att. M.G.C.; F; Lieut.
    Died of wounds 16/4/18

COX, Henry
C/D/12256, 26/11/17; No. 16 O.C.B., 7/6/18; trfr. 14th Lond. R., 1/12/18.

COX, Herbert Alexander
4/3/3946, 3/6/15; Hamps. R., 24/10/15; E,P; Lieut.; w-p.
    16 Hampstead Hill Gardens, N.W. 3.

COX, Herbert John Kendall
D/10437, 10/1/17, C/S, 29/6/17; R.F.A., 2/12/17; 2/Lieut.
    The Bungalow, Tadworth, Surrey.

COX, John Cecil
1/3837, 31/5/15, Cpl.; R.G.A., 28/10/15; F; Lieut.
    Rosslyn House, Twickenham Park, East Twickenham, Middlesex.

COX, Leonard Charles
6/5/8588, 3/1/16; No. 8 O.C.B., 4/8/16; Worc. R., 21/11/16; F; Lieut.; w.
    12 Vine Street, Evesham.

COX, Leonard Donovan
B/11694, 19/7/17; No. 11 O.C.B., 9/11/17; R. War. R., 28/5/18; F; Lieut.
    The Poplars, Henley-in-Arden.

COX, Reginald Charles Harry
C/11011, 2/4/17, L/C.; R.G.A., C/S, 31/8/17; R.G.A., 6/1/18; F; Lieut.; Inv.
    26 Chapel Street, Liverpool.

APPENDIX II.—RECORDS OF RANK AND FILE.

COX, Richard Allen
E/14003, 13/9/18; No. 22 O.C.B., 22/11/18, No. 11 O.C.B.; General List, 8/3/19; 2/Lieut.
P.O. Box 102, Salisbury, Southern Rhodesia, South Africa.

COX, R. M.
1749, 15/10/14; S. Wales Bord., 20/10/14; Capt.; M.C., M(1).

COX, William Frederick
1/3723, 24/5/15; Notts. & Derby R., 21/8/15, M.G.C.; Capt.
85 Forest Road, Nottingham.

COX, William Mitchell
5/6/7726, 22/11/15; trfr. R.W. Kent R., 10/11/16.
59 Chalk Hill, Bushey, Hertfordshire.

COYLE, James Patrick
6/1/9238, 1/2/16; 21st Lond. R., 23/6/16; F,S,E,P,Germ.SWA; Capt.; M.C., M(1).
P.O. Box 1058, Johannesburg, South Africa.

COYNE, Patrick Stirling
6/4/6120, 9/9/15, Sgt.; North'd. Fus., 22/6/16, Lab. Corps; Lieut.; w(2).

COYSH, Harold Arthur
6/1/7095, 1/11/15, L/C.; R.F.A., C/S, 4/8/16; R.G.A., 3/11/16, att. R.A.F.; F; Major; D.F.C.
373 High Road, Chiswick, W. 4.

CRACKNALL, Hartley Christopher Herbert
3/3838, 31/5/15; Dorset R., 4/11/15; P; Capt.
12 Gay Street, Bath.

CRAFER, Charles Cleveland
A/Sq/12477, 29/1/18, Cpl.; No. 1 Cav. C/S, 16/5/18; R. Regt. of Cav., 14/2/19; 2/Lieut.
Lodge Farm, Gisleham, Lowestoft, Suffolk.

✠ CRAGGS, John James
6/4/9265, 3/2/16, L/C.; No. 8 O.C.B., 4/8/16; K.R. Rif. C., 21/11/16; 2/Lieut.
Killed in action 17/2/17.

CRAIG, Alexander
C/12638, 22/2/18; No. 9 O.C.B., 5/7/18; Sco. Rif., 2/3/19; 2/Lieut.
11 Sea View Terrace, St. Abbs, Berwickshire, Scotland.

✠ CRAIG, Archibald
6/5/5327, 2/8/15, Sgt.; No. 9 O.C.B., 6/3/16; Gord. Highrs., 6/7/16, att. T.M. Bty.; Capt.; M.C.
Killed in action 23/3/18.

CRAIG, Harold Stewart
4/2/4445, 26/6/15; dis. 10/8/15; rej. 6/2/8748, 6/1/16; dis. to re-enlist in M.G.C., 17/7/16.

CRAIG, Harward
B/1322, 26/9/14, L/C.; L'pool. R., 8/1/15; Capt.
163 Strand, W.C. 2.

CRAIG, John Pickstone
B/10355, 5/1/17; R.G.A., C/S, 22/6/17; trfr. R.G.A., 22/6/17.
14 Oakley Street, S.W.

CRAIG, Malcolm Chisholm
A/14297, 5/11/18; No. 9 O.C.B., 5/11/18; trfr. K.R. Rif. C., 25/4/19.

CRAIG, Robert Henry Alfred
4/5/4666, 8/7/15, L/C.; Worc. R., 22/12/15, att. Lab. Corps; F; Lieut.
Mayfield, Crewkerne, Somerset.

CRAIGIE, Alex
6/8749, 6/1/16; trfr. Div. Amm. Col., 10/4/16; R.F.A., 3/6/17; F; Lieut.
Finglan, Co. Dublin, Ireland.

CRAIGIE, Kenneth Robert
6/4/9106, 24/1/16; No. 14 O.C.B., 30/10/16; Arg. & Suth'd. Highrs., 24/1/17; F; Lieut.; w.
New Lindsay P.O., Alberta, Canada.

CRAIGIE, Robert Pollock
A/B/D/12154, 25/10/17; No. 9 O.C.B., 10/5/18; Sco. Rif., 5/2/19; 2/Lieut.
125 Forth Street, Pollokshields, Glasgow.

CRAMER-ROBERTS Claud Hamilton Lewis
D/12945, 19/4/18; No. 5 O.C.B., 8/11/18, No. 20 O.C.B.; Welch. R., 17/3/19; 2/Lieut.
Gwynfryn, Abergele, N. Wales. (Now in U.S.A.)

CRAMPIN, Ronald William
6/2/7542, 17/11/15, L/C.; No. 14 O.C.B.; R. Berks. R., 24/10/16, Indian Army; F,I; Capt.; w.
13 Bradbourne Street, S.W. 6.

CRAMPTON, Percy
4/3/4067, 7/6/15; N. Lan. R., 15/9/15; F; Lieut.; w; M.C.
14 Grange Street, Leigh, Lancashire.

CRANFIELD, Arthur Leslie
4/1/4660, 6/7/15; Essex R., 15/11/15; Capt.; m.
3 Noel House, The Park, Ealing.

CRANFORD, Arthur Cyril
6/2/7329, 9/11/15, Cpl.; M.G.C., 25/9/16; F; Lieut.; w.
Victoria Road, Dartmouth, S. Devon. (Now in North Brazil.)

CRASTER, Albert Kenneth Greaves
H/Sq/683, 24/1/13; E. Surr. R., 8/4/15; F; Capt.; O.B.E., m.
Kintyre, Sutton, Surrey.

✠ CRAVEN, Asa
6/4/1/5552, 12/8/15; No. 9 O.C.B., 8/3/16; R. Highrs. 6/7/16; 2/Lieut.
Killed in action 19/10/16.

CRAVEN, Edward
1/3619, 15/5/15; R.W. Surr. R., 28/7/15; Lieut.; Inv.
St. Kitts, Canford Cliffs, Bournemouth.

CRAVEN, John
6/2/7581, 18/11/15, Cpl.; Garr. O.C.B., 15/1/17; Manch. R., 10/3/17.
59 Solon New Road, Clapham, S.W. 4.

✠ CRAVEN, Richard
4/4303, 17/6/15; trfr. 7th Lond. R., 4/8/16; F; Pte.
Killed in action 15/9/17.

CRAWFORD, Donald Frank
B/10771, 19/2/17, L/C.; No. 12 O.C.B., 10/8/17; 4th Lond. R., 27/11/17; 2/Lieut.; w.

CRAWFORD, George Douglas
C/14247, 30/10/18; trfr. K.R. Rif. C., 7/4/19.
Isemonger Farm, Tenterden, Kent.

CRAWFORD, John Douglas Hamilton
Sq/2827, 1/2/15, Sgt.; N. Som. Yeo., 25/6/15, att. 4th Drag. Gds.; F; Lieut.
8 Greenway, Berkhamsted, Hertfordshire. (Now in China.)

CRAWFORD, John Noel
6/7655, 22/11/15; No. 9 O.C.B., 8/3/16; Arg. & Suth'd. Highrs., 6/7/16, att. K. Af. Rif.; F,EA; Lieut.
8 Church Row, Hampstead, N.W. 3. (Now in British West Indies.)

CRAWFORD, Reginald Trevor
6/7199, 4/11/15; dis. med. unfit, 8/8/16.
Glencairn, Coulsdon, Surrey.

CRAWFURTH-SMITH, Malcolm Douglas
C/Sq/11738, 26/7/17; trfr. R.F.A., 18/3/18.
5 Stafford Mansions, Battersea Park, S.W.

✠ CRAWLEY-BOEVEY, Thomas Russell
A/2654, 11/1/15; R. Suss. R., 29/4/15, Glou. R.; Capt.
Died of wounds 30/8/16.

CRAWSHAW, Charles Felix Harbord
4/6/3/4878, 15/7/15; R. Lanc. R., 29/6/16; F,S; Lieut.; w(2).
Cottenham, Cambridge.

CRAWSHAW, Thomas Clarke
C/10830, 5/3/17; No. 11 O.C.B., 5/7/18; E. Lan. R., 30/10/17, att. Lan. Fus.; F; Lieut.; w.
Plantation House, Ramsbottom, Nr. Manchester.

CREASEY, George May
E/1606, 6/10/14, L/C.; Norf. R., 17/11/14; G,E,F; Capt.; w.
Beltoft, Sidcup, Kent.

CREASY, Frank Hay
K/2240, 3/12/14, L/C.; Wilts. Yeo., 15/4/15, R.F.C., R.A.F.; F; Capt.
c/o. Colombo Commercial Coy. Ltd., Colombo, Ceylon.

CREASY, Alfred Harrold
6/1/7008, 26/10/15; R. Lanc. R., 25/9/16, Essex R.; F; Lieut.; w.
17 Ramsey Drive, Westcliff-on-Sea.

CREASY, Harry Markby
Sq/634, 25/4/12; dis. 18/1/13.
The Paddock, Windlesham, Surrey.

✠ CREASY, Harry William Hay
A/1001, 5/8/14; Devon R., 19/9/14, Essex R.; Capt.; M.C.
Killed in action 13/6/16.

APPENDIX II.—RECORDS OF RANK AND FILE.

✠ CREE, Arthur Thomas Crawford
C/964, 5/8/14, L/C.; Durh. L.I., 27/11/14; F; Lieut.
Killed in action 12/5/15.

✠ CREE, Charles Edward Victor
D/1446, 29/9/14, Cpl.; Notts. & Derby. R., 4/3/15; F; Lieut.
Killed in action 20/7/16.

CREE, John Francis George
C/1237, 23/9/14, L/C.; Bedf. R., 6/12/14, Welch. R.;
F,S,S.Russia; Lieut.; w. 13 Grays Inn Square, W.C.1.

CREEDY, Cecil Douglas
C/11076, 18/4/17; R.E., 15/7/17; Lieut.

CREGEEN, Geoffrey Hugh Stowell
6/3/6391, 23/9/15; R.F.C., 7/8/16, R.A.F.; F; Lieut.; w.
14 Westbourne Villas, Hove, Sussex.

CREIGHTON, Harold
B/2689, 14/1/15; R.F.A., 19/8/15; F; Lieut.
32 Esplanade, Fowey, Cornwall.

CREMER, Frederick
A/13022, 3/5/18; trfr. 14th Lond. R., 6/12/18.
Preston Lea, Faversham, Kent.

CREMONINI, Henry James
B/13483, 8/7/18; No. 22 O.C.B., 23/8/18; Shrops. L.I., 13/2/19;
2/Lieut. The Bank, Bridgnorth.

✠ CREMONINI, James Henry
D/10651, 2/2/17; R.F.C., C/S, 16/4/17; R.F.C., 16/5/17; 2/Lieut.
Killed in action 18/10/17.

CRESSWELL, Francis James
3/9609, 5/9/16; R.A.O.C., 7/2/17; Lieut.
70 Gayton Road, Harrow.

CRESSWELL, Frederick Winder
B/12415, 18/1/18; No. 13 O.C.B., 10/5/18; Leic. R., 3/2/19;
2/Lieut. 1 Ennersdale Road, Hither Green, S.E. 13.

CRESSWELL, Harold
6/3/6885, 18/10/15; No. 7 O.C.B., 7/4/16; R.F.C., 4/8/16; F;
2/Lieut.; w. St. Helens, Elsecar, Barnsley, Yorkshire.

CREW, Andrew Seddon
6/5/9133, 25/1/16; No. 8 O.C.B., 4/8/16; M.G.C., 24/10/16; F;
Capt.; w. 120 Nelson Road, Hornsey, N.

CREW, Dennis
D/10860, 12/3/17; No 14 O.C.B., 5/7/17; Hunts. Cyc. Bn.,
30/10/17, att. T.M. Bty.; F; Lieut.
Reculver, Lansdowne Road, Luton, Bedfordshire.

CREW, Douglas John Arthur
A/12536, 4/2/18; No. 11 O.C.B., 7/6/18; General List, 8/3/19;
2/Lieut. P.O. Box 3986, Santiago, Chile, South America.

CREW, George Duncan
D/12117, 15/10/17, Cpl.; No. 5 O.C.B., 6/9/18; General List,
8/3/19; 2/Lieut.
c/o. Mrs. J. W. Rogers, 5 Ensworth Road, Mossley Hill,
Liverpool.

CRICHTON, Andrew Gavin Maitland Makgill
See MAITLAND-MAKGILL-CRICHTON, A. G.

CRICHTON, Douglas
B/13461, 5/7/18; trfr. K.R. Rif. C., 25/4/19.
59 Belsize Park, Hampstead, N.W. 3.

CRICHTON, George
2/4/4014, 7/6/15; Arg. & Suth'd. Highrs., 7/10/15, att. Sea.
Highrs.; F; Lieut.; w(2).
Flat 2, 30 Roland Gardens, S. Kensington.

CRICHTON-STUART, John. See Bute, Marquess of

CRICK, Frederick Edward
6/1/7982, 29/11/15; No. 8 O.C.B., 4/8/16; M.G.C., 23/11/16,
Tank Corps; F; Capt. 70 Cleveland Road, West Ealing, W.

CRICK, Harold Ewart
6/4/3/4842, 15/7/15; W. York. R., 9/12/15; Lieut.
1 Wellington House, St. Johns Wood.

✠ CRICK, William Edward
6/5/7863, 26/11/15, Cpl.; Yorks. L.I., 4/9/16; 2/Lieut.
Died of wounds 9/4/17.

✠ CRIGHTON, Harold Reginald
D/10499, 15/1/17, L/C.; No. 14 O.C.B., 7/6/17; L'pool. R.,
25/9/17; 2/Lieut. Killed in action 10/4/18.

CRIPPS, Alfred Edward
6/1/6314, 18/9/15; K.R. Rif. C., 15/1/16, R.A.F.; F; Capt.; w.
Hilda Lodge, Eaton Terrace, St. John's Wood, N.W. 8. (Now
in U.S.A.)

CRIPPS, Frank Eustace
C/1743, 15/10/14, Sgt.; R.A.S.C., 26/7/15; S,F; Lieut.; Inv;
M(1). Lavender Cottage, Great Bookham, Surrey.

CRISP, Fred
6/8718, 5/1/16; R.F.C., 26/5/16; Lieut.

CRITCHLEY, Edward Oswald
K/Sq/2813, 29/1/15; dis. 9/7/15.
Mendip, Queens Road, Cheltenham.

CRITCHLEY, Harry Fordham
K/2483, 28/12/14; Herts. Yeo., 18/3/15, Lab. Corps; E.F; Capt.
c/o. W. A. Fordham, Esq., Ashwell Bury, Baldock, Hertfordshire.

✠ CRITTENDEN, Frederick
6/1/7496, 15/11/15; R.F.A., C/S, 31/3/16; R.G.A., 2/8/16;
2/Lieut. Died 7/9/17.

CROAL, David Thomson
D/10215, 18/12/16; No. 9 O.C.B., 7/4/17; Cam'n. Highrs.,
31/7/17; 2/Lieut.; w. Fordoun, Trinity, Edinburgh.

✠ CROCKER, Francis George
F/1807, 16/10/14; E. York. R., 11/12/14; 2/Lieut.
Killed in action 14/7/16.

CROCKER, William Reginald
C/13281, 14/6/18, L/C.; No. 11 O.C.B., 14/2/19; General List,
8/3/19; 2/Lieut. 63 Berlin Road, Catford, S.E.

CROCKETT, John
F/2703, 18/1/15; R. Ir. Rif., 21/5/15; F; Lieut.; w.
13 Yarrell Mansions, Queens Club Gardens, W. Kensington.

CROFT, Arthur
2/3436, 1/5/15; Lan. Fus., 18/8/15, emp. M. of Munitions; F,EA;
Lieut.; w. 13 St. Austin's Drive, Carlton, Nr. Nottingham.

CROFT, Christopher
K/B/2429, 21/12/14; R.E., 23/8/15; F; Capt.
The Elms, Dallington, Northampton.

CROFT, Desmond Warwick
A/672, 10/12/12; S. Wales Bord., 12/9/14; F; Major; w(2);
D.S.O., M.C., M(3). Egmont, Winchester.

CROFT, George Herbert
E/14020, 13/9/18; demob. 13/12/18.
Pasture House, Northallerton, Yorkshire.

CROFT, Gilbert Colin
E/1572, 6/10/14; Som. L.I., Yorks. Huss. Yeo., Cold. Gds.; Lieut.
St. Margaretsbury, Ware, Hertfordshire.

CROFT, Norman Thirmbeck
6/1/6109, 6/9/15; 11th Lond. R., 25/1/16, att. R.F.C. and R.A.F.;
F; Lieut. Woodmansterne, Caterham Valley, Surrey.

CROFT, Philip Reginald
Sq/466, 23/2/10; dis. 29/10/12; R.F.A., 21/9/14; E,F,P; Capt.
The Manor House, St. Margarets, Ware, Hertfordshire.

CROFT, William James
4/6/2/4921, 19/7/15; R. War. R., 27/11/15; Lieut.
22 Durnsford Avenue, Wimbledon.

CROFTON, William Gerald
D/Sq/10026, 27/11/16; No. 1 Cav. C/S, 31/7/17; R. Regt. of Cav.,
22/2/18; 2/Lieut.
c/o. Messrs. O'Keiff & Lynch, 30 Molesworth Street, Dublin.

CROFTS, Herbert Jarrett
C/10400, 8/1/17; R.F.C., C/S, 13/3/17; R.F.C., 19/4/17, R.A.F.;
F; Lieut. Hendidley, Newtown, Mont, N. Wales.

CROMBIE, Francis Bernard
C/13282, 14/6/18; No. 11 O.C.B., 24/1/19; General List, 8/3/19;
2/Lieut. 181 Nelson Road, Gillingham, Kent.

CROMPTON, John
B/12804, 20/3/18; No. 4 O.C.B., 6/9/18, No. 18 O.C.B.;
W. Rid. R., 17/3/19; 2/Lieut.
647 Chorley Old Road, Bolton, Lancashire.

CROMPTON, William Arthur
B/13500, 10/7/18; No. 22 O.C.B., 23/8/18; Manch. R., 13/2/19;
2/Lieut.
141 St. Andrew's Road South, St. Annes-on-Sea, Lancashire.

APPENDIX II.—RECORDS OF RANK AND FILE.

CRONE, John
6/5/5815, 10/8/15; N. Lan. R., 27/12/15, att. Leic. R.; F;
Lieut.; w,g.   Wyndhurst, St. Annes-on-Sea, Lancashire.

CRONIN, Ronald Herbert
B/11313, 21/5/17; Sigs. C/S, 14/12/17; R.E., 24/5/18; F;
2/Lieut.; Inv.   14 Salisbury Road, Moseley, Birmingham.

CROOK, Hargreaves
C/10197, 15/12/16; No. 20 O.C.B., 7/6/17; R. Lanc. R., 25/9/17;
Lieut.   Ribblehurst, Fairhaven, Nr. Lytham, Lancashire.

CROOK, Herbert Clifford
A/13990, 11/9/18; trfr. Class W. Res., 19/11/18.
                      Ferndale, Alexandra Crescent, Bromley, Kent.

✠ CROOKE, Elliott Hampden
C/910, 5/8/14; Glouc. R., 12/9/14; Capt.
                                       Killed in action 3/7/16.

CROOM-JOHNSON, Stafford
6/4/8956, 17/1/16; R.F.A., C/S, 4/8/16; R.G.A., 9/12/16; F;
Lieut.; Inv.   7 Carelon Mansions, Clifton, Bristol.

CROPPER, James Winstanley
Sq/226, 13/5/08; West. & Cumb. Yeo., 2/9/08; F; Major.
                      Ellergreen, Kendal, Westmoreland.

CROSBIE, Riginald Pierce
K/C/2244, 30/11/14; R. Berks. R., 31/3/15; Lieut.

✠ CROSLAND, John Herbert
4/5/4718, 9/7/15, Cpl.; Garr. O.C.B., 12/12/16; R.W. Fus.,
10/2/17, K. Af. Rif.; EA; Lieut.   Died 13/4/19.

CROSLAND-TAYLOR, Winthrop James. See TAYLOR, W. J. C.

CROSOER, Edward Tong
A/11644, 12/7/17; Garr. O.C.B., 28/12/17; Lab. Corps, 22/6/18;
2/Lieut.   Bank House, Faversham, Kent.

✠ CROSS, Robert Singlehurst
D/10192, 14/12/16; No. 14 O.C.B., 5/3/17; L'pool. R., 26/6/17;
F; Lieut.   Died 2/1/20.

CROSS, Stanley Arthur
6/7867, 26/11/15; A.S.C., C/S., 27/10/16; R.A.S.C., 20/12/16;
F; Lieut.   Heath View, London Road, Leigh-on-Sea.

CROSS, Stanley Herbert
6/1/7983, 29/11/15, Sgt.; 5th Lond. R., 29/7/16, secd. R.E.; F;
Capt.; M.C.   38 Fenchurch Street, E.C. 3.

✠ CROSS, Wilfrid
4/4533, 1/7/15; Leic. R., 20/12/15; 2/Lieut.
                                       Killed in action 22/7/16.

CROSS-BUCHANAN, Eustace
6/3/5553, 12/8/15, L/C.; Midd'x. R., 24/11/15, att. Worc. R.;
Lieut.; M(1).

CROSSE, Colin Stanley
6/4/6276, 16/9/15; dis. med. unfit, 22/5/16.
                      92 Gloucester Terrace, W. 2.

CROSSE, William Wickham Reeder
B/12388, 15/1/18; Household Bde., O.C.B., 8/4/18; Welch Gds.,
24/9/18; 2/Lieut.   Petrockston Rectory, Dolton, Devonshire.

CROSSKILL, Cyril Riches
6/4/9137, 25/1/16; No. 14 O.C.B., 30/10/16; Norf. R., 24/1/17,
att. Bord. R.; F; Lieut.; w.
                      Highbury Lodge, Thorpe Road, Norwich.

CROSSLAND, Cecil Robert
6/4/7067, 29/10/15, Cpl.; No. 14 O.C.B., 4/6/17; 8th Lond. R.,
31/7/17, att. 6th and 17th Lond. R.; F; Lieut.; w; M.C.
                      3 Elsinore Road, Forest Hill, S.E.

CROSSLAND, Francis
A/13112, 24/5/18; No. 1 O.C.B., 8/11/18; R. Berks. R., 16/3/19;
2/Lieut.   75 Vineyard, Abingdon, Berkshire.

CROSSLEY, Eli
D/11174, 2/5/17; A.S.C., C/S, 1/9/17; R.A.S.C., 27/10/17; F;
Lieut.   Cliff Villas, Todmorden, Yorkshire.

CROSSLEY, Robert Thomas
D/13890, 23/8/18; trfr. K.R. Rif. C., 7/4/19.
                      197 High Street, Kensington, W.

CROSSMAN, Henry Hardwick
B/13516, 12/7/18; trfr. 28th Lond. R., 13/11/18.
                      Ham Farm, Yatton, Somerset.

CROSTHWAITE, Vivian Forsyth
C/13366, 21/6/18; trfr. 14th Lond. R., 6/12/18.
                      Uplands, West Derby, Liverpool.

✠ CROUCH, Augustus Barton
attached 13/10/15; Linc. R., 4/8/16; 2/Lieut.; M(1).
                                       Killed in action 27/4/17.

CROUCH, Charles Howard Percy
4/6/3944, 3/6/15; dis. 3/6/15.

✠ CROUCH, Foster Brooke
6/2/5554, 12/8/15; D. of Corn. L.I., 4/8/16; Lieut.
                                       Killed in action 23/3/18.

✠ CROUCHER, Cecil
6/5/5880, 30/8/15; Notts. & Derby. R., 17/1/16; 2/Lieut.
                                       Died 26/2/17.

CROW, Gerald Henry
4/3/4843, 15/7/15; R. War. R., 8/6/16, emp. M. of Labour; Lieut.
                      The Firs, Monkhams Avenue, Woodford Green.

CROWDY, Arthur Alan Gordon
C/12669, 1/3/18; trfr. Rif. Brig., 20/5/18.

CROWE, Herbert Lee
B/11664, 16/7/17; A.S.C., C/S, 1/11/17; R.A.S.C., 25/1/18; P;
2/Lieut.   10 Milton Road, Eastbourne.

CROWE, Stanley Leeson
3/3157, 1/4/15; Leic. R., 10/7/15; F; 2/Lieut.; w,Inj.
99 Evington Road, Highfields, Leicester. (Now in Australia).

CROWEST, Walter Henry Newman
4/6/5/4879, 15/7/15; dis. 14/1/16.
                      19 Hepbridge Avenue, Streatham Common.

CROWHURST, Harold
E/3/3045, 15/3/15, L/C.; R. Berks. R., 21/6/15, att. Devon R.;
F; Capt.; w; M(1).
Westward Ho! Western Elms Avenue, Reading. (Now in F.M.S.)

CROWTHER, James Aubrey Thornton
6/D/9380, 8/2/16; trfr. R.W. Surr. R., 9/3/17, North'n. R.; Cpl.
                      Littlemoor House, Mirfield, Yorkshire.

CROWTHER, Neville John Vaux
B/10103, 4/12/16; R.G.A., C/S, 6/6/17; R.G.A., 1/10/17; F;
Lieut.; w.   Wincobank Vicarage, Sheffield.

CROWTHER, Robert
A/12473, 28/1/18; No. 19 O.C.B., 7/6/18; York. & Lanc. R.,
5/2/19; 2/Lieut.

CRUICKSHANK, Douglas John
C/D/12081, 4/10/17; No. 21 O.C.B., 5/4/18; Gord. Highrs.,
24/9/18, att. Arg. & Suth'd. Highrs.; F; 2/Lieut.
c/o. National Bank of South Africa Ltd., Grey Street Branch, Durban, South Africa.

CRUICKSHANK, Robert Scott
D/1416, 29/9/14; R.A.S.C., 11/11/14; Major; O.B.E., M(3).
                      Lenham, Horsell, Woking, Surrey.

CRUMP, Bertram Eversley
A/11924, 30/8/17; A.S.C., C/S, 1/10/17; R.A.S.C., 31/12/17; F;
2/Lieut. The Wyche, Thornhill Road, Streetley, Staffordshire.

CRUMP, Clarence Aylward
4/5/4735, 12/7/15, L/C.; 19th Lond. R., 6/11/15; F; Lieut.; w;
M.C.   Selbourne, Springfield Road, Wallington, Surrey.

CRYER, James Bruce
6/2/8280, 10/12/15; No. 8 O.C.B., 4/8/16; R.W. Kent R.,
21/11/16, att. Hamps. R.; F; Lieut.; w; M.C.
                      St. Benet's Vicarage, Mile End Road, E. 1.

CUDEMORE, Charles William
2/2072, 12/11/14, Cpl.; Shrops. L.I., 21/6/15, R.A.F.; F; Capt.;
M.C., D.F.C.
                      The Châlet, Loughton, Essex. (Now in British Columbia.)

CUDEMORE, John Richardson
6/2/5469, 9/8/15; 5th Lond. R., 4/8/16, R.A.F.; F; Lieut.; w.
                      The Châlet, Loughton, Essex.

CUFFE-ADAMS, Edward Arthur
1/3590, 13/5/15; Midd'x. R., 21/8/15, M.G.C.; F; Lieut.; w(2)
                      140 Thornbury Road, Osterley Park, Middlesex.

CULE, Ivor Morgan
6/2/6177, 13/9/15; Welch. R., 22/1/16; F; Lieut.
                      Brynglas, Ystradd, Rhondda, S. Wales.

APPENDIX II.—RECORDS OF RANK AND FILE.

CULL, Alma Claude Burlton
A/2020, 5/11/14; 20th Lond. R., 19/3/15, Rif. Brig.; M,I; Capt.
The Moorings, Lee-on-the-Solent.

✠ CULL, Arthur Tulloch
K/E/2178, 26/11/14; Sea. Highrs., 20/3/15, R.F.C.; F; Capt.
Killed in action 11/5/17.

CULL, Sydney James
6/2/8688, 4/1/16, L/C.; No. 14 O.C.B., 30/10/16; N. Cyc. Bn., 24/1/17, att. North'd. Fus.; F; Lieut.
Pendower, Beacon Hill, Camborne, Cornwall.

CULLEN, Eric Graham
A/13983, 2/9/18; demob. 30/1/19.
71 Brighton Road, Rathgar, Dublin.

CULLEN, Thomas Joseph
C/A/12031, 24/9/17, L/C.; Garr. O.C.B., 8/3/18; Lab. Corps, 4/9/18; 2/Lieut. 36 Buckingham Palace Mansions, S.W.1.

CULLEN, William
6/4/5461, 9/8/15, Sgt.; R.A.S.C., 27/11/15; F; Lieut.; Inv.
39 Baring Road, Addiscombe, East Croydon.

CULLEY, Arthur
C/10796, 26/2/17; No. 11 O.C.B., 5/7/17; Indian Army, 30/10/17; I; Capt.; M(1). Holt, Norfolk.

CULLIMORE, William
B/615, 29/2/12; dis. 28/8/14. 218 Strand, W.C.2.

CULLINGFORD, Maxwell
B/12700, 8/3/18, L/C.; trfr. K.R. Rif. C., 13/5/19.
Riley Works, Riley Street, Chelsea, S.W.10.

CULROSS, Colin Campbell
D/11820, 9/8/17; No. 14 O.C.B., 4/1/18; R. Highrs., 25/6/18, att. Cold. Gds.; F; 2/Lieut.; g,w. 10 Studley Road, Harrogate.

CULVER, Cyril John
A/12434, 22/1/18; No. 20 O.C.B., 7/6/18; Devon. R., 6/2/19; 2/Lieut. 31 Windermere Road, Muswell Hill, N.10.

CULVERWELL, Geoffrey James Northcott
6/4/7497, 15/11/15; dis. to R. Mil. Coll., 29/8/16; R. Berks. R, 1/5/17, secd. M.G.C.;

CULVERWELL, Wilfrid Lovedere
6/3/7864, 26/11/15; No. 1 O.C.B., 6/9/16; R.F.C., 10/11/16, R.A.F.; F; Lieut.
181 Chepstow Road, Newport, Monmouthshire.

CULY, Leonard Victor
6/5/5927, 1/9/15; L'pool. R., 4/8/16, M.G.C.; F; Lieut.; p.
23 Egerton Road, Wavertree, Liverpool

CUMBERLAND, James Albert
6/2/8082, 1/12/15; No. 14 O.C.B., 27/9/16; Worc. R., 24/1/17; F; Lieut.; Inv. 13 Birkland Avenue, Nottingham.

CUMMING, Alfred Robert
6/4/6757, 11/10/15; No. 9 O.C.B., 14/4/16; High. L.I., 4/8/16, R. Scots.; F; Capt.; w; M(1).
55 Edgemont Gardens, Langside, Glasgow.

CUMMING, George
4/4534, 1/7/15; Sea. Highrs., 13/10/15, secd. R.E. Sigs.; F; Capt.; p. 12 Pentland Terrace, Edinburgh. (Now in Ceylon.)

CUMMING, Reginald Holmes
6/4/9196, 31/1/16; No. 14 O.C.B., 26/11/16; Devon. R., 28/2/17; F; Lieut.; w. 17 Kingsley Road, Plymouth.

CUMMING, Robert Francis William
A/11272, 14/5/17; No. 14 O.C.B., 7/9/17; Sea. Highrs., 17/12/17; F; 2/Lieut.; p. Eastbury Manor, Hallow, Worcestershire.

CUMMINGS, Henry Reginald
6/1/8308, 11/12/15; trfr. Class W. Res., 20/10/16.
4 Morland Close, North End, Hampstead, N.W.3.

CUMMINS, Bertram William
4/6/4922, 19/7/15; No. 11 O.C.B., 7/5/16; Dorset R., 4/9/16, att. Bedf. R.; F; Lieut.; w.
4 Waddon Park Avenue, Croydon.

CUMMINS, David Patrick
6/2/8750, 6/1/16; No. 7 O.C.B., 11/8/16; M.G.C., 28/12/16; F; Lieut.; w. Lowergate, Cashel, Co. Tipperary, Ireland.

CUNINGHAM, Robert Fairrie
C/11739, 26/7/17; No. 14 O.C.B., 4/1/18; demob. 23/1/19.
Lockwood, Hawthorne Grove, Wilmslow, Nr. Manchester.

CUNINGHAME, Robert Dick Smith
4/2/5069, 26/7/15; Scots. Gds., 2/10/15; F; Capt.; w(3); M(1)
Gruline, Isle of Mull, Oban, Scotland.

CUNLIFFE, John Robert Ellis
Sq/866, 4/8/14; R.F.A., 27/8/14; Lieut.
34 The Grove, The Boltons, S.W.10.

CUNLIFFE, John Thompson
6/2/5328, 2/8/15; Glouc. R., 4/1/16, Leic. R., D. of Corn. L.I., att. S. Wales Bord.; F; Lieut.
13 Somerset Road, Bolton, Lancashire.

CUNLIFFE, Kenneth Vivian
B/12003, 11/9/17; R.E., C/S, 4/11/17; R.E., 1/2/18; I; 2/Lieut.
Evedine, Donos Street, Besca, Johannesburg, South Africa

CUNLIFFE, Thomas
K/F/2497, 31/12/14; Manch. R., 31/3/15, R.F.A.; F,S; Lieut.
Colyton, Totteridge, N.20.

CUNLIFFE, William Thompson
6/D/8625, 3/1/16; trfr. Army Pay Corps, 7/12/16.
Meadowcroft Farm, Turton, Nr. Bolton, Lancashire.

✠ CUNNINGHAM, Douglas Murray
B/10757, 21/2/17; No. 11 O.C.B., 5/7/17; R. Highrs., 27/11/17; 2/Lieut. Died of wounds 11/6/18.

CUNNINGHAM, Philip
4/6/5/4960, 19/7/15, Sgt.; Midd'x. R., 23/4/16; F; Capt.; w.
13 Widcombe Crescent, Bath

✠ CUNNINGHAM, Robert Cocks
B/1331, 26/9/14; R. Highrs., 14/11/14; F; Capt.; M.C.
Killed in action 3/9/16.

CUNNINGHAM, Stephen John
6/5/C/7909, 29/11/15; dis. med. unfit, 27/7/17.
13 Widcombe Crescent, Bath.

CUNNINGHAM, Thomas Gurnall
C/5/6/7908, 29/11/15; trfr. R.G.A., 2/2/17.
13 Widcombe Crescent Bath.

CUNNINGHAM-JONES, Robert
C/14276, 8/11/18; dis. to re-enlist in R. Highrs., 11/4/19.
Moylgrove Vicarage, Cardigan, S. Wales.

CUNNINGHAM-REID, DUNCAN F. See REID, D.F.C.

CUNNINGTON, William Alfred
C/39, 6/4/08; dis. 5/4/10.
13 The Chase, Clapham Common, S.W.

CURNOW, William Iggulden
6/4/9473, 14/2/16; No. 13 O.C.B., 4/11/16; Durh. L.I., 28/2/17; Lieut.; w(2). New Theatre, Mountain Ash.

CURRY, Alan Austin
6/3/5869, 28/8/15; R.A.S.C., 4/12/15, R.F.A.; S,E; Lieut.
15 Langham Avenue, Sefton Park, Liverpool.

CURRY, William Clive
2/3415, 29/4/15; R.W. Kent R., 18/8/15, M.G.C.; F; Lieut.; M.C. 45 Stradella Road, Herne Hill, S.E.

CURSITER, Stanley
6/8791, 7/1/16; No. 9 O.C.B., 8/3/16; Sco. Rif., 23/7/16, att. R.E.; F; Capt.; O.B.E., M(2). 28 Queen Street, Edinburgh.

✠ CURTIS, Arthur John Powles. See POWLES-CURTIS, A. J.

CURTIS, Cecil Montagu Drury
B/746, 1/12/13; S. Wales Bord., 12/9/14; F; Staff Capt.; w(2); O.B.E., M(1). Hampton Court Palace, Middlesex.

CURTIS, Claude Stanley
A/10488, 12/1/17; A.S.C., C/S, 1/9/17; R.A.S.C., 30/11/17; F; Lieut. 19 Cromer Gardens, Ilford.

CURTIS, Edward Victor
6/5/7543, 17/11/15; No. 7 O.C.B., 3/7/16; R. Innis. Fus., 3/11/16; F; Lieut.; w. 18 Upper Fitzwilliam Street, Dublin

CURTIS, Geoffrey Edgar
C/D/12065, 1/10/17; R.F.A., C/S, 15/3/18; R.F.A., 17/10/18; 2/Lieut. Pytchley Vicarage, Nr. Kettering, Northamptonshire.

CURTIS, James Walter
6/Sq/7910, 29/11/15, L/C.; R.A., C/S, 26/9/16; R.G.A., 24/2/17; Lieut. Milton, Ernest, Bedfordshire.

APPENDIX II.—RECORDS OF RANK AND FILE.

CURTIS, John Stanley
4/2/3945, 3/6/15; R.F.A., 11/8/15; F; Capt.; g.
c/o. 10 Harringay Park, Crouch End, N. 8. (Now in Canada.)

CURTIS, Stanley James
6/3/6196, 13/9/15; North'd. Fus., 2/1/16, att. M.G.C.; F; Lieut.;
w. 259 Oxford Road, Reading.

CURWEN, Allan Henry
C/14308, 30/11/18; demob. 22/12/18.
Workington Hall, Workington, Cumberland.

CURWEN, Brian Murray
B/1623, 9/10/14, Sgt.; Rif. Brig., 18/2/15; Capt.
1 Upper Terrace, Hampstead, N.W. 3.

✠ CURWEN, Cecil Neil
B/1654, 9/10/14, Sgt.; K.R. Rif. C., 23/2/15; Lieut.
Killed in action 15/9/16.

CURWEN, Geoffrey Edward
F/1818, 16/10/14, Sgt.; Manch. R., 10/2/15; F,S; Lieut.
2 Lyndhurst Road, Hampstead, N.W. 3.

CUSSE, Clement Archibald
H/6/1913, 16/10/14, Sgt.; Devon. R., 21/4/16; M,I; Major,
D.A.Q.M.G.; M(1). 6 New Court, Carey Street, W.C. 2.

CUSSEN, Edward Joseph
6/5/C/8405, 15/12/15; No. 7 O.C.B., 11/8/16; trfr. M.G.C.,
3/11/16; R. Muns. Fus., 22/8/17; P,F; Lieut.
Glengarriff, Charleville, Co. Cork, Ireland.

CUSSONS, Benjamin Joseph
6/2/8083, 1/12/15; No. 14 O.C.B., 30/10/16; W. York. R.,
4/10/17; F; Lieut.; w. High Cross, Appleby, Westmoreland.

CUTCLIFFE, Ernest Francis
Sq/302, 29/6/08; dis. 28/6/09; R.F.A., 14/1/16; F; Capt.
Longfield, Coulsdon, Surrey.

CUTHBERT, Alexander
6/8544, 30/12/15; No. 9 O.C.B., 8/3/16; Gord. Highrs., 23/7/16,
att. 14th Lond. R.; F,S; Lieut.; w.
11 Alexandra Place, St. Andrews, Fifeshire, Scotland. (Now in Dutch East Indies.)

CUTHBERT, Eric Tom
A/13094, 22/5/18; No. 1 O.C.B., 8/11/18, No. 3 O.C.B.; E. Lan.
R., 18/3/19; 2/Lieut.
Tattershall, Dukes Avenue, Church End, Finchley, N. 3.

CUTHBERT, Frank Gray
C/10465, 12/1/17; R.G.A., C/S, 15/8/17; R.G.A., 4/3/18; It;
Lieut. 67 Greenvale Road, Eltham, S.E. 9.

CUTHBERT, George Victor
6/5/7865, 26/11/15, L/C.; No. 14 O.C.B., 28/8/16; Norf. R.,
18/12/16; Lieut. 38 Lammus Park Road, Ealing.

CUTLACK, Cyril
C/26, 2/4/08; dis. 1/4/11.

CUTLER, Seymour Bernard Egerton
B/1057, 31/8/14; W. York. R., 12/9/14, att. Lab. Corps; F;
Capt.; Inv.
Junior Army and Navy Club, Horse Guards Avenue, S.W. 1.

CUTLER, Thomas Basil Everard
A/D/14103, 7/10/18; trfr. K.R. Rif. C., 23/5/19.
Scopwick Vicarage, Lincoln.

CUTTS, Ernest Joshua
C/9968, 20/11/16; No. 14 O.C.B., 30/1/17; Dorset R., 29/5/17,
att. R.A.F.; I,E; Lieut.
Westfield House, Blackwell, Alfreton, Derbyshire.

DABELL, Charles
A/13164, 30/5/18; R.E., C/S, 7/8/18; R.E., 16/2/19; 2/Lieut.
c/o G. W. Dabell Esq., 115 Victoria Street, S.W. 1.

DADE, Reginald Travers
F/2965, 25/2/15; R. Dub. Fus., 22/4/15, Indian Army; F,I,M;
Capt.; M(1).
19 St. John's Terrace, Lewes, Sussex. (Now in India.)

DADE, Sylvester Travers
6/4/6988, 25/10/15; R.F.A., C/S, 8/12/16; R.F.A., 13/4/17,
R.G.A.; F; Lieut. 19 St. John's Terrace, Lewes, Sussex.

DADSWELL, Cyril Fairthorne
D/9996, 24/11/16; R.W. Surr. R., 9/3/17; S; Capt.; M(1).
121 Abington Avenue, Northampton.

DAHL, William
6/1/9330, 7/2/16; R.F.A., C/S, 4/8/16; R.F.A., 15/12/16; F;
Capt.; w. 38 Hawarden Avenue, Liverpool.

DAIMPRÉ, Louis Francois Wolfe
A/D/Sq/11920, 23/8/17; No. 2 Cav. C/S, 26/6/18; demob.,
29/1/19. Colebrooke Vicarage, Copleston, N. Devon.

DAIN, Arthur Edward
B/A/11665, 16/7/17; trfr. 28th Lond. R., 25/2/18; F; L/Cpl.; w.
Rose Glen, Jordan Road, Sutton Coldfield.

✠ DAINTITH, James
B/9872, 6/11/16, Cpl.; R.E., C/S, 25/2/17; R.E., 18/5/17; F;
2/Lieut. Killed in action 13/8/17.

DAISH, William Herbert
6/5/7413, 12/11/15; L'pool. R., 4/9/16, R.A.F.; F; Lieut.; w.
Glenridding, Ormskirk, Lancashire.

DAKERS, Norman James
6/3/D/6475, 27/9/15; No. 6 O.C.B., 15/2/17; R.F.C., 3/4/17,
R.A.F.; F; Lieut. Whitnash, Church End, Finchley, N. 3.

D'ALBUQUERQUE, Nino Peter
Sq/919, 5/8/14; trfr. West. Drag., 12/9/14, Cpl.; Shrops. L.I.,
26/2/15; F; Lieut.; w. 14 Malmains Way, Beckenham.

DALE, Algernon Barclay
C/Sq/14, 1/4/08; Midd'x. Yeo., 28/6/13; E,P,S,It; Capt.
28 Elm Park Gardens, S.W. 10.

DALE, Edgar Thornley
A/179, 30/4/08; dis. 29/4/12.
12 King's Bench Walk, Temple, E.C. 4.

✠ DALE, Robert Jacob Norris
B/458, 19/1/10; dis. 25/6/12; Manch R., 18/6/15, R.F.C.; Lieut.
Killed in action 31/1/18.

DALE-LACE, Lance E. C.
Sq/1093, 5/9/14; 11th Huss., 9/9/14, 2nd Drag.; Lieut.; M.C.
14 Sherwood Place, Onslow Gardens, S.W.

DALGETY, Giles Hill
6/2/7254, 9/11/15; No. 9 O.C.B., 8/3/16; R. Scots, 3/8/16;
Lieut.; w-p. 3a Devon Road, Bedford.

✠ DALLAS, George Barnes
6/7911, 29/11/15, Cpl.; dis. to R. Mil. Coll., 28/8/16; Som. L.I.,
1/5/17, att. M.G.C.; Lieut. Killed in action 1/9/19.

DALLAS, Hugh Waldron
C/933, 5/8/14; Norf. R., 12/9/14, Indian Army; M; Capt.
46 Arkwright Road, Hampstead, N.W. 3.

DALRYMPLE, Hugh Gordon
B/13435, 3/7/18; demob. 24/1/19.
59 Queens Road, Tunbridge Wells.

DALTON, Gordon Lewis
C/10799, 28/2/17, L/C.; R.E., 9/6/17; Lieut.
21 Norman Road, Canterbury, Kent.

DALTON, Hugh
K/2522, 31/12/14; R.A.S.C., 4/5/15, R.G.A.; F,It; Lieut.;
Medaglio Al Valore (Italy). 107 Albert Bridge Road, S.W. 11.

✠ D'ALTON, James George
6/Sq/8751, 6/1/16; R.F.A., C/S, 24/11/16; R.F.A., 1/4/17;
2/Lieut. Killed in action 27/10/17.

DALTON, Paul
D/2541, 4/1/15; Rif. Brig., 6/4/15; F; Capt.; w; M.C.
Balaglas, Maney Hill Road, Sutton Coldfield.

✠ D'ALTON, Thomas Joseph
6/5/9001, 19/1/16, L/C.; No 2 O.C.B., 14/8/16; R. Ir. Regt.,
18/12/16; 2/Lieut. Died of wounds 9/6/17.

✠ DALY, Cyril Francis St. Felix
6/4/9078, 24/1/16; No. 5 O.C.B., 14/8/16; R.W. Surr. R.,
21/11/16; 2/Lieut.; w. Killed in action 14/10/17.

DALY, Hubert Dean
6/9002, 19/1/16; R.F.A., C/S, 9/6/16; R.F.A. 9/9/16; F; Lieut.
Donacarney House, Drogheda, Ireland.

DALY, John Stephen
6/2/6758, 11/10/15; No. 7 O.C.B., 3/7/16; trfr. 18th Lond. R.,
12/1/17. Liffey Bank, Island Bridge, Dublin.

DALY, McCarthy
4/5/4667, 8/7/15, L/C.; R. Lanc. R., 4/12/15, att. L'pool. R.;
Lieut.; p. Craven Hotel, 1 Chilworth Street, W. 2.

APPENDIX II.—RECORDS OF RANK AND FILE.

DALZELL, John
B/10540, 17/1/17; trfr. 16th Lond. R., 25/5/17.
  13 Macaulay, Bath.

DALZIEL, Gordon Noel Colman
A/2898, 11/2/15; 24th Lond. R., 12/5/15; Capt.; w(2), p; M(1)
  Chase House, Kingswood, Surrey.

DAMANT, Hugh Atherstone
B/13531, 15/7/18, L/C.; No. 11 O.C.B., 24/1/19; General List, 8/3/19; 2/Lieut.
  P.O. Box 46, Johannesburg, Transvaal, South Africa.

DAMPIER, Arthur Digby
A/678, 24/1/13; R. Fus., 15/8/14, att. Bedf. R., Ches. R. and Manch. R.; F; Capt.; w.
  The Haven, Berkhamsted, Herts (Now in France.)

DAMPIER, Colin Raymond
A/1269, 23/9/14; R.A.S.C., 20/11/14, Lab. Corps; F; Capt.
c/o. Messrs. Cox & Co., R.A. Dept., 16 Charing Cross, S.W.1.

DAMPIER, Dennis Francis Ludwell
A/680, 24/1/13; dis. 2/7/13; joined K.R. Rif. C.; F; Pte.
  The Haven, Berkhamsted, Herts.

DAMPIER, Kenneth Alan Hew
H/1998, 2/11/14; Essex R., 28/3/15; F; Capt.
  The Haven, Berkhamsted, Herts.

DANCER, William Hector Trenberth
C/11461, 5/6/17; R.F.C., C/S, 2/8/17; R.F.C., 8/9/17, Lan. Fus.; F; Lieut.
  The Hayes, Cardiff.

DANCKWERTS, Harold Otto
Sq/728, 11/11/13, L/C.; E. Rid. of York. Yeo., 23/9/14, secd. M.G.C.; Capt.; m.
  6 New Square, Lincoln's Inn, W.C.2.

DANCY, Wilfrid
6/4/5619, 16/8/15, Sgt.; R.F.A., C/S, 17/3/16; R.G.A., 6/7/16, att. R.A.F.; F; Capt.; w(2); M(1).
  75 Beaconsfield Villas, Brighton.

DANE, Alan
4/3192, 8/4/15, L/C.; R.A.S.C., 15/11/15; Lieut.
  Daneholme, Rickmansworth, Hertfordshire.

DANGER, Charles Instone
D/10242, 29/12/16; No. 14 O.C.B., 5/5/17; L'pool. R., 28/8/17; F; Lieut.; M.C.
  60 Rice Lane, Egremont, Cheshire.

DANIEL, Francis Leslie
B/Sq/10131, 6/12/16; No. 21 O.C.B., 5/2/17; Indian Army, 29/8/17; 2/Lieut.
  99 Lexham Gardens, Earls Court, S.W.

DANIEL, Hector Robert
B/12701, 8/3/18; No. 4 O.C.B., 6/9/18, No. 18 O.C.B.; R. Fus., 18/3/19; 2/Lieut.
  50 Tunnel Avenue, East Greenwich, S.E. 10.

DANIEL, Jasper Gordon
6/8281, 10/12/15; Welch R., 15/4/16; 2/Lieut.
  5 Worcester Place, Swansea.

DANIEL, John
6/8468, 20/12/15; R.F.A., C/S, 14/7/16; R.F.A., 27/10/16; F; Capt.; Croix de Guerre (Belgium).
  8 Carrick Dhu Road, St. Ives, Cornwall.

DANIELL, Frederick Stanley
D/10455, 11/1/17, L/C.; R.A., C/S, 27/4/17; R.G.A., 1/9/17; F; Lieut.
  2 Inglis Road, Colchester.

DANIELL, John Gordon
A/11245, 14/5/17; No. 14 O.C.B., 9/11/17; Bedf. R., 30/4/18; F; 2/Lieut.
  70 High Street, Wandsworth, S.W. 18.

DANIELS, Ernest Cantrell
Sq/2979, 25/2/15; R.E., 8/4/15; F; Capt.; M.C., M(2).
  Gaika House, Queque, Southern Rhodesia, South Africa.

DANIELS, Martin Lester
6/1/7437, 15/11/15, L/C.; R. Berks. R., 25/9/16, emp. M. of Munitions; F; Lieut.; w.
  114 Old Hall Street, Liverpool.

DANIELS, Reginald Wilfred
A/10471, 12/1/17; Household Bde. O.C.B., 16/4/17; Cold. Gds., 31/7/17, emp. Gds. M.G.R.; F; Lieut.; w; M.C., M(1).
  80 High Street, Borough, S.E

DANIELS, Thomas Goldsworthy
A/D/12457, 23/1/18; R.F.C., C/S, 21/5/18; R.A.F., 9/3/19; 2/Lieut.
  69 Derby Lane, Stoneycroft, Liverpool.

DANKS, Reginald George
4/3/3947, 3/6/15; R.W. Surr. R., 10/9/15, emp. M. of Munitions and Air Ministry; Capt.; w; M.C.
  52 Tregon Road, Clapham.

DANN, Leslie Herbert
6/4/6502, 28/9/15; Devon. R., 4/8/16; F; 2/Lieut.
  Lyndhurst, Queen's Road, Wisbech, Cambridgeshire

DANVERS, Ernest James
D/13755, 7/8/18; demob. 25/1/19.
  17 Priory Avenue, Hornsey, N. 8.

DANVERS, Gerald Rochfort Ellis. See ELLIS-DANVERS, G. R.

DARBISHIRE, Charles Stephen
6/4/8946, 17/1/16, Sgt.; R.E., 9/1/17; F; Capt.
  Plas-y-Eifl, Trevor, Chwilog.

DARBY, Frank Norval Sims
6/1/6963, 22/10/15; No. 9 O.C.B., 8/3/16; R. Scots, 23/7/16, M.G.C., R.E.; F; Lieut.; w.
  Cameron House, Beccles, Suffolk.

D'ARCY, Percy Edwin
D/Sq/10020, 27/11/16, L/C.; No. 14 O.C.B., 5/5/17; 8th Lond. R., 28/8/17, secd. M.G.C.; F; Lieut.
  15 Buckingham Street, Strand, W.C.

DARE, Alfred Julius
A/B/12182, 2/11/17; R.E., C/S, 13/1/18; R.E., 26/4/18; F; 2/Lieut.
  Charminster Vicarage, Dorchester.

DARE, Mark
6/Sq/6111, 28/8/15; West. & Cumb. Yeo., 20/12/15, att. R.A.F.; F; Lieut.
  Manor House, Poling, Arundel, Sussex.

✠ DARRICOTTE, Gilbert Haley
C/10569, 19/1/17; No. 14 O.C.B., 6/4/17; Hunts. Cyc. Bn., 31/7/17, att. Essex R.; F; 2/Lieut.
  Killed in action 6/9/18.

DART, Frederick Harold
4/2/3263, 15/4/15, Cpl.; R.E., 29/11/15; F; Lieut.
  14 Exeter Road, Southsea.

DARVILL, George William Francis
C/10378, 8/1/17; R.F.C., C/S, 13/3/17; R.F.C., 19/4/17, R.A.F.; Lieut.; D.F.C.
  Court House, East Meon, Petersfield.

BASHFIELD, Leonard Charles
C/11481, 14/6/17, L/C.; No. 14 O.C.B., 5/10/17; Linc. R., 26/2/18; 2/Lieut.
  3 Olivor Mansions, Gondar Gardens, West Hampstead, N.W. 6.

✠ DAVENPORT, Cyril Francis
K/C/2303, 10/12/14; Hamps. R., 31/3/15; F; 2/Lieut.
  Killed 2/8/16.

DAVENPORT, Edward Vivian Tinham
2/9672, 2/10/16; No. 14 O.C.B., 30/1/17; trfr. R.F.A., 20/4/17.
  29 Evelyn Mansions, Carlisle Place, Victoria, S.W. 1.

DAVENPORT, Guy Crosley
2/2035, 9/11/14, Sgt.; 7th Lond. R., 8/7/16; F; Lieut.; w(2).
  6 Queen's Park, Ballygunge, Calcutta, India.

DAVENPORT, Terence Hope
C/Sq/12588, 7/2/18; No. 16 O.C.B., 5/7/18; trfr. 28th Lond. R., 12/9/18, K.R. Rif. C.; Pte.
  Sycamore Hill, Macclesfield.

DAVEY, Alfred
E/1/2918, 15/2/15; Midd'x. R., 27/7/15, att. Wilts. R.; M; Lieut.
  42 Redbourne Avenue, Church End, Finchley, N. 3

DAVEY, Edwin Clissold
6/1/6886, 18/10/15; No. 11 O.C.B., 7/5/16; Midd'x. R., 4/9/16, Lab. Corps; F; Lieut.
  42 Redbourne Avenue, Church End, Finchley, N. 3.

DAVEY, Victor George
1/3534, 10/5/15; N. Staff. R., 28/7/15, M.G.C., emp. M. of Labour; F; Lieut
  High Road, Loughton, Essex.

✠ DAVEY, William Aubrey Carthew
C/10980, 2/4/17; No. 14 O.C.B., 10/8/17; Ches. R., 27/11/17; 2/Lieut.; w.
  Killed in action 21/8/18.

DAVID, Allen Trevor
6/3/6112, 9/9/15; R.F.A., 26/11/15, att. T.M. Bty.; F; Lieut.
  61 Kimberley Road, Cardiff.

DAVID, Leonard Cunliffe
D/13722, 2/8/18; trfr. K.R. Rif. C., 7/4/19.
  10 Doddington Grove, Kennington Park, S.E. 17.

DAVID, Thomas Edward
C/11509, 18/6/17; R.F.C., C/S, 2/8/17; R.F.C., 8/9/17, R.A.F.; F; Lieut.
  2 Goring Road, Llanelly, Carmarthen.

DAVID-DEVIS, Willie Ernest
F/B/334, 3/12/08; dis. 2/12/08. Capt., 13th Lond. R., att. R A.O.C.
  11 Chepstow Villas, Bayswater.

APPENDIX II.—RECORDS OF RANK AND FILE.

DAVIDS, Maurice
4/3/4564, 1/7/15, Sgt.; Worc. R., 23/12/15, Intelligence Corps; F,It; Capt.; w; O.B.E., M(2).
Bell House, Bierley Lane, Dudley Hill, Bradford.

✠ DAVIDSON, Andrew Pearson
B/3080, 20/3/15, L/C.; Gord. Highrs., 21/6/15; 2/Lieut.
Killed in action 5/9/16.

DAVIDSON, James Richardson
6/2/7330, 9/11/15; No. 9 O.C.B., 8/3/16; Arg. & Suth'd. Highrs., 23/7/16; F; Capt. *6 Wingrove Road, Newcastle-on-Tyne.*

DAVIDSON, Ranald Victor
4/5607, 16/8/15, Cpl.; Manch. R., 10/11/15; F,It; Capt.; Croce di Guerra (Italy).
Ennismore Lodge, Guildford, Surrey. (Now in Singapore.)

DAVIE, John Sidney
6/5/5928, 1/9/15, L/C.; dis. to re-enlist in Canadian L.I., 5/4/16.

DAVIE, Russell
4/5/4668, 8/7/15; Norf. R., 7/10/15; F; Lieut.; w.
Belhaven, Cranleigh, Surrey.

✠ DAVIES, Albert Gordon
6/3/7868, 26/11/15, L/C.; No. 14 O.C.B., 28/8/16; R.W. Fus., 22/11/16; 2/Lieut. *Died of wounds 1/8/17.*

DAVIES, Alfred Crossley
D/11010, 5/4/17, L/C.; No. 14 O.C.B., 7/12/17; Suff. R., 28/5/18; F; Lieut. *St Aubins, Brockley View, Forest Hill, S.E. 23.*

✠ DAVIES, Arthur Peter
D/11559, 28/6/17; R.F.C., C/S, 23/10/17; R.F.C., 12/12/17; 2/Lieut. *Killed 22/3/18.*

DAVIES, Arthur Thomas
C/10585, 22/1/17; Household Bde. O.C.B., 7/6/17; Cold. Gds., 25/9/17, att. Gds. M.G.R.; F; Lieut.
Upland, Carmarthen, South Wales.

DAVIES, Arthur Vaughan
6/5/8781, 7/1/16, Sgt.; No. 14 O.C.B.; North'd. Fus., 24/10/16, Notts. & Derby. R., Essex R.; Capt.; w.
Hadley, Droitwich.

DAVIES, Cadivor
C/14113, 9/10/18; demob. 30/1/19.
St. Aubins, Brockley View, Forest Hill, S.E. 23.

DAVIES, Daniel
6/2/9310, 4/2/16; No. 14 O.C.B., 26/11/16; R. Lanc. R., 27/3/17; F; Lieut. *Pant Llanddewibrefi, Cardiganshire.*

DAVIES, David Glyndwr
6/5/7498, 15/11/15; R.W. Fus., 4/8/16, att. 2nd Lond. R.; Lieut.; w. *Oak Villa, Cynmer, Porth, Glamorganshire.*

DAVIES, David Josy Picton
3/3685, 20/5/15; North'd. Fus., 25/8/15, att. Sco. Rif.; E,P,F; Lieut.
c/o D. V. Byford Esq., Colomendy, Ruthin, North Wales.

DAVIES, Douglas Joseph
6/5/8752, 6/1/16; No. 7 O.C.B., 4/11/16; R. Dub. Fus., 28/2/17; F; Lieut.; M.C.
24 Rathgar Avenue, Rathgar, Dublin. (Now in F.M.S.)

DAVIES, Edward Francis Gwynne
K/F/2736, 18/1/15, L/C.; Devon. R., 2/6/15; Capt.; w(2); M.C., M(1).

DAVIES, Elwyn Thomas
6/5/7833, 25/11/15; R.E., C/S, 21/8/16; R.E., 3/11/16; F; Capt.; M.C. and Bar, M(2). *Bryn Rhos, Tredergar, Monmouthshire.*

DAVIES, Eric
Sq/596, 11/1/12, Cpl.; Sherwood Rangers Yeo., 8/8/14, att R.F.C.; E,G,S,P; Capt.; w(2).
Jesmond, Blackheath Park, S.E. 3.

DAVIES, Eric Edgar
F/1802, 16/10/14, Cpl.; Dorset R., 5/3/15; Lieut.; w; M(1).
c/o Messrs. Duncan Fox & Co., 29 Great St. Helens, E.C.

✠ DAVIES, Ernest Frank
1/3671, 17/5/15; D. of Corn. L.I., 21/8/15; 2/Lieut.
Killed in action 24/8/16.

DAVIES, Evan Walis Puw
6/5/7499, 15/11/15; Welch R., 22/7/16; Lieut.
Oak Villa, Cynmer, Porth, Glamorganshire.

DAVIES, George Edward Albert
A/10693, 14/2/17; No. 14 O.C.B., 5/7/17; 7th Lond. R., 10/10/17, att. 11th Lond. R. and Midd'x. R.; E,P; Lieut.; Inv.
Braeside, Teesdale Road, Leytonstone, E. 11.

✠ DAVIES, George Henry Douglas
4/5/Sq/4880, 15/7/15; trfr. Shrop. Yeo., 7/11/15; F; Pte.
Killed in action -/7/16.

DAVIES, Glyn Idris
D/10417, 10/1/17; R.G.A., C/S, 16/5/17; R.G.A., 17/9/17; F; Lieut.; w; M.C. *13 Winchester Avenue, Cardiff.*

DAVIES, Godfray William Herbert
B/D/12206, 8/11/17, L/C.; Household Bde. O.C.B., 5/7/18; Cold. Gds., 2/3/19; 2/Lieut.
c/o. National Bank of Egypt, London, E.C

DAVIES, Harold Arthur
D/10559, 19/1/17, L/C.; No. 14 O.C.B., 5/7/17; Welch R., 30/10/17; 2/Lieut. *88 Roath Court Road, Cardiff.*

DAVIES, Harry Gordon
B/13414, 1/7/18; demob. 23/1/19.
The Elms, Seymour Grove, Manchester.

DAVIES, Hubert Benson
6/3/5846, 26/8/15; Mon. R., 7/9/15, Indian Army; F,Afghan; Capt.; M.C.
57th Wildes Rifles F.F., c/o. King, King & Co., Bombay, India.

✠ DAVIES, Idris Gwyndwr
6/2/8017, 30/11/15; R.F.A., C/S, 4/8/16; dis. med. unfit, 7/1/17.
Died 3/2/19.

DAVIES, Jack Wallis
4/6/2/4844, 15/7/15; E. Kent R., 23/9/15; M; Lieut.; w.
Common Room, Grays Inn, W.C. 2.

DAVIES, John Hayton
C/Sq/13345, 25/6/18; demob. 10/1/19.
Cowell House, Llanelly, South Wales. (Now in South America.)

✠ DAVIES, John Howard
6/5/7545, 17/11/15; R.W. Fus., 4/8/16; 2/Lieut.
Killed in action 4/7/17.

DAVIES, John Lee
4/2/5099, 26/7/15; dis. med. unfit, 21/4/16.

DAVIES, John Lloyd
6/5/5929, 1/9/15; L'pool. R., 20/1/16; Lieut.
30 Alderson Road, Sefton Park, Liverpool.

DAVIES, John Trevor
4/2/4259, 10/6/15; Welch R., 5/9/15, Indian Army; I,P,E; Lieut. *12 Bernard Street, Uplands, Swansea.*

✠ DAVIES, Joseph Charles Gladstone
4/1/4535, 1/7/15; R.F.A., 16/11/15; Lieut. *Drowned 6/1/18.*

DAVIES, Leonard
D/10446, 10/1/17; dis. med unfit, 26/9/17.
58 Waterloo Road, Wolverhampton.

✠ DAVIES, Leslie
B/574, 13/11/11; 15th Lond. R., 10/5/13; Capt.
Killed in action 15/9/16.

DAVIES, Lionel Edward
6/4/7796, 24/11/15; No. 14 O.C.B.; Ches. R., 24/10/16; F; Capt.; Inv; M.C. *13 Lipson Avenue, Plymouth.*

DAVIES, Llewellyn Guy
B/12689, 5/3/18; No. 20 O.C.B., 20/9/18; R.W. Fus., 17/3/19; 2/Lieut. *The Rectory, Glan Conway, North Wales.*

DAVIES, Owen Henry
6/9346, 7/2/16; dis. med unfit, 24/3/16.
13 Church Road, Forest Hill, S.E. 23.

DAVIES, Percy Oswald
F/1813, 16/10/14; R. Dub. Fus., 6/3/15, att. R.F.C.; Lieut.
Glanmor, Fields Park, Newport, Monmouthshire.

DAVIES, Philip Oswald
6/5/7546, 17/11/15; R.W. Fus., 8/7/16, att. N. Lan. R.; F; Lieut.; w(2); M.C. *Maesywern, Pontardawe, Glamorganshire.*

DAVIES, Philip Theodore
B/311, 30/6/08; dis. 29/6/10. *1 Grange Road, Ealing, W.*

DAVIES, Reginald Carter
2/3120, 25/3/15; Notts. & Derby. R., 21/7/15; F; Lieut.; w(2); M.C., M(1). *33 Clyfford Crescent, Newport, Monmouthshire.*

APPENDIX II.—RECORDS OF RANK AND FILE.

✠ DAVIES, Rhys Beynon
3/3480, 3/5/15; North'd. Fus., 5/8/15, att. R.F.C.; F; Lieut.;
w. Killed in action 1/5/17.

DAVIES, Robert William Home
6/8753, 6/1/16; R.F.A., C/S, 26/5/16; R.F.A., 9/9/16, att. T.M.
Bty.; F; Capt. Dean Rectory, Overton, Hampshire.

DAVIES, Ronald Brynmor
4/3/4326, 21/6/15, L/C.; K.R. Rif. C., 2/10/15, E. Lan. R.;
Lieut. The Laurels, 3 Peckham Road, S.E.

DAVIES, Thomas Henry Ronald
6/8343, 13/12/15; R.F.A., C/S, 5/8/16; R.F.A., 24/11/16; 2/Lieut.
University College Hospital, W.C.

DAVIES, Thomas Morris
B/E/13635, 26/7/18, L/C.; No. 22 O.C.B., 20/9/18; Glouc. R.,
5/2/19; 2/Lieut. The Grove. Nr. Tintern, Monmouthshire

DAVIES, Thomas Robert
4/9702, 9/10/16; R.G.A., C/S, 28/2/17; R.G.A., 1/7/17; Lieut.
163 Evering Road, Stoke Newington, N. 16.

DAVIES, Tom
6/1/7912, 29/11/15; R.F.C., C/S, 8/10/16; dis. med. unfit, 17/8/17.
The Great House, Dorstone, Herefordshire.

DAVIES, Tom Abraham
6/8051, 1/12/15; dis. med. unfit, 9/6/16.
The Gables, Sketty Road, Swansea.

DAVIES, William Evan
B/13636, 26/7/18; demob. 21/12/18.
62 Collenna Road, Tonyrefail, Glamorganshire.

DAVIES, William Frederick
4/6/5/4845, 15/7/15; S. Wales Bord., 16/12/15; F; Lieut.; w.
Brook House, Saughall Road, Chester.

✠ DAVIES, William John
6/4/8626, 3/1/16; R.F.A., C/S, 4/8/16; R.G.A., 12/11/16;
Lieut.; w. Died of wounds 14/10/18.

DAVIES, William Mydrim
6/2/8052, 1/12/15; No. 8 O.C.B., 4/8/16; trfr. R.G.A., 8/12/16.
2 Dunraven Street, Treorely, Glamorganshire.

DAVIS, Alistair Jeffreys
D/13927, 30/8/18; dis. med unfit, 14/1/19.
138 Leadenhall Street, E.C.

DAVIS, Anthony Frank
6/1/6244, 16/9/15, L/C.; Essex R., 15/4/16, Suss. Yeo., Nigeria
R.; F,WA; Capt.; M(1)
P.O. Box 75, Salisbury, Southern Rhodesia, South Africa.

✠ DAVIS, Arthur George
6/4/7096, 1/11/15; No. 11 O.C.B., 7/5/16; 9th Lond. R., 4/9/16,
11th Lond. R.; 2/Lieut. Killed in action 16/8/17.

✠ DAVIS, Bernard Samuel
6/2/7228, 5/11/15; Bord. R., 4/8/16; 2/Lieut.; M(1).
Killed in action 9/4/17.

DAVIS, Bertie Warren
6/4/8309, 11/12/15; trfr. Berks. Yeo., 30/6/16.
The Warren, Milford Haven.

DAVIS, Cecil Kenneth
B/1247, 23/9/14; E. Surr. R., 14/11/14, Indian Army; Capt.

✠ DAVIS, Felix Arthur
A/23, 1/4/08; dis. 31/3/10.

✠ DAVIS, Francis Edward
6/5/6868, 18/10/15; No. 14 O.C.B.; Yorks. L.I., 21/11/16;
2/Lieut. Killed in action 9/10/17.

DAVIS, Gordon Charles
6/5/2/7500, 15/11/15, Cpl.; N. Lan. R., 25/9/16; F; Lieut.
Constitutional Club, Southend-on-Sea.

✠ DAVIS, Guy Clifton
D/1399, 29/9/14; North'd. Fus., 4/2/15; Lieut. Died 11/5/18.

✠ DAVIS, Harold Pashley
B/D/11977, 10/9/17; No. 4 O.C.B., 15/6/18; trfr. Devon. R.,
19/6/18, att. Som. L.I.; F; L/Cpl. Killed in action 22/8/18.

DAVIS, Harold Shirley
6/2/7763, 23/11/15; Notts. & Derby. R., 4/9/16, emp. M. of
Labour; Lieut. Oakholme, Avenue Road, Duffield.

DAVIS, Harry Heyworth-
4/6/4923, 19/7/15; R.E., 26/12/15, att. R.F.C.; F; Lieut.
The Hard, Hythe, Hampshire.

✠ DAVIS, Henry Christopher
4/3724, 24/5/15; K.R. Rif. C., 2/10/15; 2/Lieut.
Killed in action 2/7/16.

DAVIS, Howard John Vaisey
K/Sq/2416, 21/12/14; R.A.S.C., 2/3/15; F; Capt.; M.C., M(1).
Lechlade, Gloucestershire.

✠ DAVIS, John Charles Reginald
C/489, 25/4/10; Essex R., 15/8/14; F; Lieut.
Killed in action 13/5/15.

DAVIS, John Duvall
C/11767, 30/7/17; No. 14 O.C.B., 4/1/18; Suff. R., 25/6/18; F;
2/Lieut.; Inv. 70 Orford Street, Ipswich.

DAVIS, John Francis
C/9923, 15/11/16; No. 14 O.C.B., 30/1/17; Worc. R., 29/5/17;
2/Lieut. Claremont, Ramsey, Huntingdonshire.

DAVIS, John Frederick
F/3/2754, 21/1/15; Glouc. R., 29/4/15; Capt.
Mayfield, Mortimer Crescent, Kilburn, N.W. 6.

DAVIS, John Harvard
D/10560, 19/1/17; R.A., C/S, 20/4/17; R.G.A., 31/7/17; F;
Lieut. 38 Plymouth Road, Penarth.

DAVIS, Kenneth Edgar Ross
D/C/12963, 22/4/18; demob. 29/1/19.
6 Alfred Street, Bath.

DAVIS, Lionel Howard
A/12155, 25/10/17; Sigs. C/S, 14/12/17; R.E., 9/8/18; Lieut.
Norfolk Lodge, Sunmead Road, Sunbury-on-Thames

DAVIS, Nathaniel Johnson
Sq/3046, 15/3/15; R.A.S.C., 29/6/15; Lieut.
44 Regent Street, Clifton, Bristol.

DAVIS, Oswald Vernon
6/4/5881, 30/8/15; 9th Lond. R., 22/9/15; Germ.WA,F; Capt.;
w. P.O. Box 28, Durban, Natal, South Africa.

DAVIS, Rushworth Kennard
A/13095, 22/5/18; demob. 10/1/19.
School House, Woodbridge, Suffolk.

DAVIS, Sydney Douglas
C/10151, 8/12/16; Devon. R., 15/3/17; Lieut.
Foygate, Orerton Road, Sutton, Surrey.

✠ DAVIS, William Stanley
1/3497, 6/5/15, L/C.; Bedf. R., 18/8/15; Lieut.
Killed in action 22/3/18

DAVISON, Clement
A/Sq/10046, 29/11/16; Cav. C/S, 1/9/17, No. 14 O.C.B.; trfr.
28th Lond. R., 17/9/18, 4th Drag. Gds.; Pte.
18 Moss Grove, Prenton, Birkenhead.

DAVISON, Henry Asquith
D/11821, 9/8/17; A.S.C., C/S, 12/11/17; R.A.S.C., 6/1/18; F;
2/Lieut.
c/o W. H. Davison Esq., Derwent Avenue, Sefton Park,
Liverpool.

DAVISON, Lionel
C/B/D/11783, 30/7/17; Household Bde. O.C.B., 8/3/18; Welch
Gds., 27/8/18; 2/Lieut. Sports Club, St. James Square, S.W. 1.

✠ DAVISON, Rashell Montague Rashell
4/2/4493, 28/6/15, L/C.; N. Staff. R., 7/10/15, att. Leic. R.; F;
Capt.; w-p. Died of wounds 27/1/19.

DAVY, Herbert
C/14225, 25/10/18; No. 11 O.C.B., 24/1/19; General List, 8/3/19;
2/Lieut. Porthfellin, Park Drive, Grimsby, Lincolnshire.

DAVY, William Kenneth
6/1/D/6613, 4/10/15; No. 14 O.C.B., 5/3/17; Midd'x. R., 26/6/17,
att. L'pool. R.; F; Lieut.; w-p.
Twyneham, 91 Argyle Road, Ealing, W.

DAW, Alfred Thomas
4/6/Sq/4846, 15/7/15; No. 2 Cav. C/S, 31/3/16; Bedf. Yeo.,
19/8/16, R.A.F.; F; Lieut.; w.
Hockerill, Brewood, Staffordshire.

140

APPENDIX II.—RECORDS OF RANK AND FILE.

DAW, Charles Bennett
4/2/4212, 14/6/15; Sea. Highrs., 9/10/15; S; Lieut.; Inv.
                            27 Palace Gate, Kensington. W. 8

DAW, Fabyan Bennett
6/4/6031, 3/9/15, Cpl.; R.F.A., C/S, 31/3/16; R.G.A., 11/8/16; Lieut.
                            The Grange, Ealing, W.

✠ DAW, Reginald Samuel
A/1953, 26/10/14, Cpl.; K.R. Rif. C., 10/12/14; Capt.; M(1).
                            Died of wounds 25/9/16.

DAWE, Basil
B/10528, 17/1/17; R.F.C., C/S, 13/3/17; R.F.C., 19/4/17, R.A.F.; Lieut.
                            Menston Vicarage, Nr. Leeds.

DAWE, George Hunt
4/2/5070, 26/7/15; Norf. R., 4/11/15; 2/Lieut.
                          15 Battlefield Avenue, Langside, Glasgow.

DAWE, Henry Stuart
A/Sq/14128, 4/10/18; demob. 11/1/19.
                            Millbrook, West Coker, Yeovil

✠ DAWES, Oswald Stephen Bernard
6/1/6476, 27/9/15; No. 7 O.C.B., 7/4/16; N. Staff. R., 4/8/16, York. & Lanc. R.; F; 2/Lieut.   Killed in action 8/5/17.

DAWES-SIMPSON, Ernest (or Thomas Ernest William). (See SIMPSON, T. E. W. D.).

DAWKES, Robert Bolton
6/1/6590, 4/10/15; Dorset R., 6/7/16, Durh. L.I., Indian Army; I,M,S,S.Russia; Capt.
          37 South Eaton Place, Eaton Square, S.W. (Now in India.)

DAWSON, Arthur Kenneth
B/10116, 6/12/16, Sgt.; R.E., C/S, 30/9/17; R.E., 9/11/17; F; 2/Lieut.; w.   Holme House, West Auckland, Co. Durham.

DAWSON, Arthur Leopold
4/Sq/4669, 8/7/15; R.F.A., 12/10/15; F; Capt.
                c/o Butterfield and Swire, Yokohama, Japan.

DAWSON, Edward Clifton
B/13594, 19/7/18; demob. 23/1/19.   93 Green Hill, Derby.

DAWSON, Frank
B/12321, 28/12/17; No. 16 O.C.B., 7/6/18; Manch. R., 6/2/19; 2/Lieut.   43 Park Road South, Birkenhead.

DAWSON, Frank Bateson
6/4/6843, 15/10/15; No. 11 O.C.B., 7/5/16; North'd. Fus., 4/9/16, R. War. R.; F; Lieut.; w.
                    Gildholme, Oldfield Road, Altrincham.

✠ DAWSON, Frederick William
6/4/6790, 13/10/15; S. Lan. R., 15/6/16; 2/Lieut.
                            Killed in action 8/9/16.

DAWSON, George Aspinal
6/1/7984, 29/11/15; No. 14 O.C.B., 28/8/16; R. Lanc. R., 18/12/16, att. N. Lan. R.; E,F; Capt.; w; M.C.
                 20 Huntley Road, Fairfield, Liverpool.

DAWSON, Harold Willie
6/1/5582, 16/8/15; R.W. Surr. R., 6/6/16; Capt.
                        Southleigh, Dorking, Surrey.

DAWSON, Henry
D/11578, 2/7/17; No. 19 O.C.B., 9/11/17; W. Rid. R., 30/4/18; 2/Lieut.   Sunnybank, Egerton, Huddersfield.

DAWSON, Herbert Forbes
A/D/13007, 1/5/18; R.A.F., 21/10/18; demob. 3/3/19.
                        St. Patricks, Raynes Park, S.W.

DAWSON, Joseph Arnold
D/10007, 24/11/16; Garr. O.C.B., 23/4/17; Lab. Corps, 16/6/17; 2/Lieut.
      c/o John Dawson Esq., Alston, Cumberland. (Now in Shanghai.)

DAWSON, Leonard Goodhugh
C/1621, 9/10/14; E. Surr. R., 9/3/15; Lieut.
            c/o M. P. Cross, Coomkeote, Francis Road, Windsor.

DAWSON, Louis Henry
C/1143, 14/9/14, L/C.; Midd'x. R., 26/11/14; F; Lt.-Col.
                 10a Lunham Road, Upper Norwood, S.E. 19.

✠ DAWSON, Norman Curry
6/5/5248, 31/7/15; L'pool. R., 27/12/15; Lieut.
                          Killed in action 28/3/18.

DAWSON, William Bell
K/B/2440, 28/12/14; R. Sco. Fus., 31/3/15, secd. R.E.; F; Major; w; M.B.E., M.C., M(1), m.
                        26 Queen Square, Glasgow.

✠ DAWSON, William Healey
6/4/8854, 8/1/16; No. 14 O.C.B., 30/10/16; W. York. R., 28/12/17; F; 2/Lieut.; w.   Killed in action 20/7/18.

DAWSON-JONES, Richard
1/3158, 1/4/15; S. Wales Bord., 9/8/15, att. R.E. Sigs.; Lieut.

DAY, David
6/Sq/6161, 11/9/15; West. & Cumb. Yeo., 21/1/16.
                         Heathbrow, Hampstead, N.W.

DAY, Eric Cornwallis
B/965, 5/8/14; Shrops. L.I., 19/9/14; F,S; Capt.; M.C. and Bar, M(2).   33 Bramham Gardens, S.W. 5.

DAY, Francis Charles
D/13902, 26/8/18; trfr. D. of Corn. L.I., 10/5/19.
  Etchingham Lodge, Etchingham Park Road, Church End, Finchley, N. 3.

DAY, Frank Ford
A/9814, 30/10/16; R.A.O.C., 18/4/17; Capt.
                      103 Sutton Court, Chiswick, W. 4.

✠ DAY, George Samuel
6/2/5502, 9/8/15; 12th Lond. R., 4/8/16, att. R.F.C., R.A.F.; F; Lieut.   Killed in action 1/10/18.

DAY, Leonard
A/11001, 4/4/17; No. 14 O.C.B., 10/8/17; Herts. R., 27/11/17; F; Lieut.; g.   45 Wellington Street, Hertford.

DAY, Leslie Robert William
D/13721, 2/8/18; demob. 23/1/19.
                      77 Shuttlewood Road, Bolsover.

✠ DAY, Percy Oliver James
4/3/4453, 28/6/15, L/C.; K.R. Rif. C., 4/1/16; 2/Lieut.
                         Killed in action 19/7/16.

✠ DAY, Samuel Albert
4/3/4522, 30/6/15; W. York. R., 5/9/15; 2/Lieut.
                        Killed in action 10/11/16.

DAY, Travers Frank
B/10122, 6/12/16; No. 14 O.C.B., 5/5/17; York. R., 28/8/17; It,F; Lieut.; w.   210 Cricklewood Lane, N.W. 2.

DAYER-SMITH, Norman
A/10105, 4/12/16; No. 14 O.C.B., 30/1/17; Ches. R., 28/8/17, att Midd'x. R. and Essex R.; E,P; Lieut.; w.
                112 Melrose Avenue, Cricklewood, N.W. 2.

DEACON, Maurice George
6/Sq/8208, 7/12/15, L/C.; R.F.A., C/S, 23/6/16; R.F.A., 23/9/16; F; Capt.   Constitutional Club, Northumberland Avenue, W.C. 1.

DEAKIN, Edward Cair
F/2625, 7/1/15; D. of Lanc. Own Yeo., 11/3/15; E,P; Lieut.
                      Dimple Hall, Egerton, Bolton.

DEAKIN, George Vyvyan
A/Sq/11243, 11/5/17; R.N.A.S., 19/9/17.
             Blawith, Grange-over-Sands, Lancashire.

DEAKIN, Ralph
4/6/4961, 19/7/15; 20th Lond. R., 28/11/15, Intelligence Corps; F; Capt.; O.B.E., M(3).
      The Times, Foreign Dept., Printing House Square, E.C. 4.

DEAN, Alfred William
A/10259, 29/12/16; A.S.C., C/S, 1/6/17; R.A.S.C., 28/7/17; F; 2/Lieut.; M(1).   Barrow Lodge, Baxter Avenue, Southend.

DEAN, Arthur Edis
D/E/13685, 29/7/18; No. 22 O.C.B., 20/9/18; Education Officer, 24/11/18; Capt.   Rosebarn, Loose, Nr. Maidstone.

DEAN, Arthur Wellesley Stewart
A/10444, 10/1/17; Household Bde. O.C.B., 5/5/17; 2nd Life Gds., 31/7/17, Gds. M.G.R.; F; 2/Lieut.
                 Dowsby Hall, Bourne, Lincolnshire.

DEAN, Charles Oswald
2/3498, 6/5/15; N. Lan. R., 15/9/15; F; Capt.; M(1).
                    Pendlehurst, Ulverston, Lancashire.

DEAN, Claude Walter
1/4/5029, 22/7/15, Cpl.; R.F.A., C/S, 4/8/16; R.F.A., 1/12/16; F; Lieut.; w.   Mowshurst, Edenbridge, Kent.

APPENDIX II.—RECORDS OF RANK AND FILE.

✠ DEAN, Cyril Charles Stephen
B/79, 13/4/08; dis. 12/4/12. Died 1916.

DEAN, Josiah
Sq/6/8627, 3/1/16; R.F.A., C/S, 5/8/16; R.F.A., 24/11/16; F; Capt.; w(3); M.C. 36 St. Helens Road, Ormskirk, Lancashire.

DEAN, Reginald Charles William
6/4/D/9200, 31/1/16; No. 14 O.C.B., 30/10/16; Oxf. & Bucks. L.I., 28/12/17; F; Capt. Clifton Lodge, Swanage, Dorset.

DEAN, Sidney Harry
6/3/5757, 21/8/15, Sgt.; Lond. Div. Cyc. Coy., 13/7/16; F; Lieut.; w. Burncroft, Albion Street, Shaldon, Teignmouth, S. Devon.

DEANE, Bernard Frederic
6/4/7604, 19/11/15; R. Suss. R., 4/8/16, R.A.F.; F,It; Lieut.; w. 16 Station Road, Winchmore Hill, N. 21.

DEANE, Harry Cuthbert
Sq/1299, 24/9/14; R.G.A., 6/10/14, R.F.A.; Lieut. Heatherlea, The Vale, Hampstead, N.W.

DEANS, Cecil Charles
B/43, 6/4/08; dis. 5/4/12; rej. 6/2/8465, 20/12/15, Sgt.; K.R. Rif. C., 4/8/16; F; Lieut.; Inv. Land Registry, Lincoln's Inn Fields, W.C. 2.

DEAR, Frank Henry
K/E/2403, 21/12/14, L/C; R. Suss. R., 19/6/15, R.F.C., R.A.F.; E,Germ.EA; Lieut.; M.C. 42 The Avenue, Beckhenham, Kent.

DEARLOVE, Hubert Joseph Stanley
6/1/7009, 26/10/15; No. 7 O.C.B., 7/4/16; S Lan. R., 20/7/16, att. Lan. Fus.; F; Lieut.; w. 32 Oakfield Street, Cardiff. (Now in France.)

DEARNALEY, Roy
A/14046, 23/9/18; trfr. K.R. Rif. C., 7/4/19. Mossgiel, White Knowle Road, Buxton.

DEASON, Thomas George
Sq/771, 2/3/14; Sherwood Rangers Yeo., 14/9/14, att. R.F.C.; F; Capt.; p. 33 Queen's Gate Terrace, S.W. 7.

D'EATH, Claude Hanby
B/10522, 15/1/17, L/C; No. 14 O.C.B., 7/6/17; W. York. R., 25/9/17; F; 2/Lieut.; w. 72 Southwood Road, Ramsgate.

✠ DE'ATH, Ralph Eric
B/10842, 7/3/17. Died 11/1/18.

DE BEER, Harold Wynberg
E/14107, 7/10/18; demob. 10/1/19. 54 Norshead Mansions, Maida Vale, W, 9.

DEBENHAM, William Frederick Southwell
4/3763, 27/5/15, Sgt., R.A., C/S, 24/1/16; R.G.A., 19/6/16; Lieut.; w. 88 Merton Road, Wimbledon.

DEBNAM, Percy Gerald Carter
4/3/4353, 19/6/15, Sgt.; K.R. Rif. C., 21/4/16; S,F; Lieut.; w. Avenue House, Chelmsford, Essex.

DE BOISSIÈRE, George Valton
6/4/4565, 1/7/15, L/C; R.F.C., C/S, 13/3/17; R.F.C., 19/4/17, R.A.F.; Lieut. 20 Hogarth Road, Earls Court, S.W.

DEBY, Reginald Bedford
D/9975, 21/11/16; No. 14 O.C.B., 30/1/17; Notts. & Derby. R, 29/5/17; 2/Lieut. 27 Meadow Bank Avenue, Sheffield.

DE CASTRO, Lionel Stanley
4/4694, 8/7/15, L/C; R.F.A., 28/10/15, emp. R.E.; F; Lieut. Holland House, 33 Torrington Square, W.C.

✠ DE CAUX, William
B/694, 7/2/13, L/C.; Norf. R., 6/12/14; Capt. Killed in action 15/9/16.

DEEDES, John Gordon
Sq/610, 29/2/12; R.E., 19/2/14; Capt.; M.B.E., M(2). 19 Foxley Road, Stockwell, S.W.

DE FONBLANQUE, John Berkeley
1/9634, 25/9/16; Garr. O.C.B., 24/4/17; Worc. R., 16/6/17; Lieut. 5 Grays Inn Square, W.C. 1.

DE FONTENAY, Réné
B/C/11980, 10/9/17; No. 11 O.C.B., 24/1/19; General List, 8/3/19; 2/Lieut. Beau Bassin, Mauritius.

DEFRIEZ, Lancelot Ernest Robert
D/12946, 19/4/18; trfr. 14th Lond. R., 6/12/18; Cpl. 43 Norfolk Road, Seven Kings, Ilford, Essex.

DE GROOT, Walter Lawrence
6/1/6032, 3/9/15; W. York. R., 7/7/16; F; Lieut.; w. Avondale, Highfield Road, Golders Green.

DEHN, Curt Gustav
6/D/9600, 17/7/16; No. 13 O.C.B., 4/11/16; Wilts. R., 28/2/17; 1; Lieut. 85 London Wall, E.C.

DEIGHTON, Kenneth Eric
Sq/1294, 24/9/14, L/C.; R.A.S.C., 9/2/15; Lieut. 65 Porchester Terrace, Hyde Park, W.

DE JANASZ, George Kazimir Arthur
Sq/2180, 26/11/14; dis. med. unfit, 24/12/14. Kilmorna, Kerry, Ireland.

DE JONGH, Alfred Alexander
B/741, 11/11/13; Suff. R., 1/9/14, M.G.C.; F,It; Capt.; w. 129 Widmore Road, Bromley, Kent.

DE JONGH, Vernon Henry Price
K/E/2605, 7/1/15; Manch. R., 31/3/15; S; Lieut.; Inv. Bloomfield House, Widmore Road, Bromley, Kent.

DE JONQUET, Adolph Frederick
1/3448, 3/5/15; Yorks. L.I., 31/7/15; F; Lieut,; w.

DEKIN, George
4/3/4494, 28/6/15, L/C.; R. Fus., 5/2/16; F; Lt.-Col.; g; M.C. M(2). Brendon, Regent Road South, Hanley, Staffordshire.

DELABERE, James Alan Henry
6/3/A/9429, 11/2/16; dis. Med. unfit, 20/12/16. Woolsery Rectory, Morchard Bishop, North Devonshire.

DE LAESSOE, Harold Henry
K/2279, 7/12/14; Rif. Brig., 23/2/15; F; Major; D.S.O., M.C., M(2). c/o Messrs. Henry S. King & Co., 9 Pall Mall, S.W. 1.

DELAMERE, William Percival
6/2/8869, 12/1/16, L/C.; R.F.C., C/S, 28/12/16; R.F.C., 4/4/17, R.A.F.; F; Lieut.; w. Rathgowan, Mullingar, Ireland.

DELANY, Arthur Sebastian
B/2753, 21/1/15, Cpl.; R. Dub. Fus., 22/4/15; F; Capt.; g; M(1). Junior Army and Navy Club, Horseguards Avenue, S.W. 1 (Now in Egypt).

DELANY, William James Charles Bennett
D/12105, 11/10/17; Tanks O.C.B., 18/1/18; Tank Corps, 22/10/18; 2/Lieut. Ayton House, Finsbury Park, N. 4.

DE LA PENHA, Alfred Eugene
C/Sq/818, 4/8/14; S. Lan. R., 18/9/14, Lab. Corps; F,Balkans; Capt.; Inv. United University Club, Suffolk Street, Strand, W.C. 2.

DE LAUBENQUE, Jean Joseph
6/1/7200, 4/11/15; R.A., C/S, 26/10/16; R.F.A., 11/3/17; F; Lieut. 99 Corringham Road, Golders Green, N.W. 4.

DE LAVISON, Adrian Max
6/3/Sq/6392, 23/9/15; 7th Lond. R., 3/12/15, R.F.C., R.A.F.; Lieut.; w. 131 Cromwell Road, S.W.

DE LAVISON, Serge
C/11517, 18/6/17, L/C.; No. 14 O.C.B., 7/12/17; High. L.I., 28/5/18; 2/Lieut.

D'ELBOUX, Raymond Herbert
6/2/5470, 9/8/15; E. Kent R., 19/11/15, att. N. Lan. R.; F; Lieut.; M.C. Westend Lodge, Medstead, Hampshire.

✠ DE LISLE-SMITH, Frank
6/7913, 29/11/15; R.A., C/S, 24/1/16; R.F.A., 23/6/16; 2/Lieut. Died 31/10/18.

DELL, John Edward Flowers
C/11438, 4/6/17; R.F.C., C/S, 2/8/17; R.F.C., 8/9/17, R.A.F.; 2/Lieut. Weppons, New Shoreham, Sussex.

DELLER, Edwin
6/5/C/7134, 2/11/15, Sgt.; trfr. Class W. Res., 25/7/18. University of London, South Kensington, S.W. 7.

DELMA-HARRINGTON, Bernard Hubert Walter
6/4/5620, 16/8/15.

DE MELLO, Frank John
4/3/3948, 3/6/15; R.A.S.C., 16/10/15, att. H.A.C.; F; Capt. c/o Strangers Club, Buenos Aires, South America.

APPENDIX II.—RECORDS OF RANK AND FILE.

DE MORGAN, *Richard Coghill*
6/3/8957, 17/1/16; R.A., C/S, 7/7/16; R.G.A., 4/10/16; F,It; Lieut.; M(1).   10 *Harley Gardens, The Boltons, S.W.*

DE MOYSE-BUCKNALL, *Silvio Paul Bernini.* See BUCKNALL, S. P. B.

DEMPSTER, *John Cumming*
D/13928, 20/8/18; *demob.* 1/2/19.
   52 *Union Street, Larkhall, Scotland.*

DEMUTH, *Walter Edgar*
6/3/8517, 29/12/15, L/C.; No. 8 O.C.B., 4/8/16, M.G.C., C/S; M.G.C., 23/11/16, Tank Corps; F; Capt.; M.C., M(1).
   c/o *Allen & Gledhill, 22a Raffles Place, Singapore.*

DENING, *Samuel John Claude*
6/3/7255, 8/11/15; No. 11 O.C.B., 7/5/16; Devon. R., 4/9/16, Indian Army; P,F,I; Capt.; *w.*
   c/o *Messrs. Cox & Co., Bankers, Hornby Road, Bombay.*

DENISON, *Frederick*
D/E/13821, 12/8/18; No. 22 O.C.B., 20/9/18; W. York. R., 5/2/19; 2/Lieut.   61 *Bradford Road, Shipley, Yorkshire.*

DENNIS, *Arthur Donald*
C/11439, 4/6/17; No. 19 O.C.B., 9/11/17; R.W. Fus., 26/3/18; 2/Lieut.   *Heswall Villa, Ffynnongroen, Chester, North Wales.*

DENNIS, *Ernest Arthur*
6/2/8054, 1/12/15, L/C.; No. 14 O.C.B., 30/10/16; Linc. R., 24/1/17, att. R.A.F.; F; Capt.; *w.*
   School House, Eastchurch, Isle of Sheppey, Kent.

DENNIS, *Ernest Edward*
6/1/7436, 15/11/15, Sgt.; No. 14 O.C.B., 28/8/16; R. Berks. R., 18/12/16, att. Bedf. R.; 2/Lieut.; *p.*   *Park House, Hitchin.*

DENNIS, *Patrick Gill Dyke.* See DYKE-DENNIS, P. G.

DENNIS, *Richard Henry*
D/11542, 21/6/17; R.F.C., C/S, 2/8/17; R.F.C., 8/9/17, R.A.F.; F,M; Lieut.   6 *Clarenden Gardens, Cranbrook, Ilford, Essex.*

✠ DENNIS, *Richard Thomas*
C/11060, 16/4/17; No. 14 O.C.B., 10/8/17; R. Ir. Rif., 27/11/17, att. North'd. Fus.; F; 2/Lieut.; *w-p.*   Died 19/12/18.

✠ DENNISTON, *Jack Evelyn*
C/1144, 14/9/14; R. Highrs., 2/11/14; 2/Lieut.; *w.*
   Died of wounds 20/9/16.

DENNY, *Charles Edward*
K/D/2491, 26/12/14; R.G.A., 28/7/15; Lieut.

DENNY, *Edward Maynard Coningsby*
C/974, 5/8/14; *dis.* 15/8/14; D. of Corn. L.I., 14/4/15, Midd'x. R.; F; Capt.; *w*(2); M.C. and Bar, M(1).
   34 *Cartwright Gardens, Tavistock Square, W.C.1.*

DENNY, *John Anthony*
A/901, 5/8/14; Gren. Gds., 15/8/14, att. Scots. Gds.; F; Lieut.; *w.*   19 *Upper Berkeley Street, W.1.*

DENNY, *Robert Edward*
4/6/2/4881, 15/7/15, L/C.; R.A., C/S, 24/1/16; R.F.A., 16/6/16, emp. Min. of Labour; 2/Lieut.; *w.*

DENNYS, *Cyril George*
6/8628, 3/1/16; R.A., C/S, 26/5/16; R.G.A., 30/8/16; F; Lieut.; M.C.   19 *Castletown Road, W.14.*

DENROCHE-SMITH, *Lewis Paget*
6/5/9061, 21/1/16; No. 14 O.C.B., 30/10/16; R. Highrs., 28/2/17; F; Lieut.; *w.*   *Balhany, Meigle, Perth, Scotland.*

DENSHAM, *Alfred Russell*
6/3/7435, 15/11/15, L/C.; No. 8 O.C.B., 4/8/16; K.R. Rif. C., 21/11/16; 2/Lieut.
   c/o *H. Densham & Son, Ltd.; Redcross Street, Tannery, Bristol.*

DENSHAM, *Lionel Upton*
C/14258, 1/11/18; *demob.* 23/1/19.
   St. Helen's Cottage, Byfleet, Surrey.

DENSHAM, *Philip Heyward*
B/Sq/13750, 7/8/18; *demob.* 24/1/19.
   Landour, The Shrubbery, Weston-super-Mare.

DENT, *Edmund William*
6/2/7135, 2/11/15; M.G.C., 25/9/16; F; Lieut.
   c/o *Lloyd's Bank Ltd., Weymouth.*

✠ DENTON, *Brian Maurice*
D/1392, 29/9/14; Som. L.I., 27/11/14; Lieut.
   Killed in action 19/8/16.

DENTON, *George Moss*
6/5/5503, 9/8/15; R.E., C/S, 5/8/16; R.E., 21/10/16; F; Lieut.; *w*; M.C.   *Council Offices, Whitefield, Lancashire.*

DENTON, *Joshua*
C/11482, 14/6/17; A.S.C., C/S, 1/10/17; R.A.S.C., 30/11/17; F; 2/Lieut.   *Christ Church Square, Macclesfield, Cheshire.*

DENTON-CARDEW, *Alfred Roger*
D/10222, 20/12/16; A.S.C., C/S, 1/5/17; R.A.S.C., 28/7/17; 2/Lieut.   6 *Camborne Terrace, Richmond, Surrey.*

DENTON-THOMPSON, *Bernard James*
F/1938, 22/10/14; Glouc. R., 4/11/14, Manch. R.; F; Capt.; *w*(2); M.C., M(1).   *Bishop's Court, Isle of Man.*

DENYER, *Jack Stanley*
8301, 11/12/15; *trfr.* Essex R., 1/5/17; R.E., 25/11/17; Lieut.
   110 *St. Helens Road, Hastings.*

DE PARAVICINI, *Percy Gerald*
A/1172, 14/9/14; K.R. Rif. C., 23/11/14; F; Capt.; *w.*
Riverside, Datchet, Buckinghamshire. (Now in Hong Kong.)

DE POIX, *Hugh Tyrell*
E/1595, 6/10/14; R.G.A., 26/3/15, emp. Admiralty; Lieut.
   2 *Pembroke Studios, Pembroke Gardens, W.*

DE PONTHIEU, *Louis A.M.R. de Vismes*
Sq/3159, 1/4/15; R.A.S.C., 6/9/15; Lieut.
   1 *Warrington Crescent, Maida Vale, W.9.*

DERBYSHIRE, *John George*
A/14319, 30/12/18; No. 11 O.C.B., 24/1/19; General List, 8/3/19; 2/Lieut.
   50 *Didsbury Terrace, Ackers Street, Charlton, Manchester.*

✠ DE RITTER, *Victor Frank*
1/3764, 27/5/15; Som. L.I., 21/8/15; 2/Lieut.
   Died of wounds 9/8/16.

✠ DERRICK, *Alan James*
6/5/6817, 14/10/15; No. 7 O.C.B., 6/4/16; North'd. Fus., 17/7/16; F; 2/Lieut.   Killed in action 15/11/16.

DERRY, *Cyril*
4/3/5100, 26/7/15; R.A.S.C., 29/11/15, att. R.E. Sigs.; F; Lieut.; M(1).   *Garthowen, The Broadway, Letchworth, Hertfordshire.*

DERRY, *Oscar Arthur*
A/1066, 2/9/14; Dorset R., 27/11/14; Lieut.; *w.*
   62 *Redington Road, Hampstead, N.W.*

DE SAULLES, *Norman Philip*
3/3370, 24/4/15, L/C.; 12th Lond. R.; 15/6/15; Lieut.; M(1).

DES COUX-STEVENS, *Richard Carnegie.* See STEVENS, R. C. des C.

DE SELINCOURT, *Leslie*
C/497, 26/5/10; *dis.* 2/2/12; Hamps. R., 3/11/14, Conn. Rang., Oxf. & Bucks. L.I.; M; Staff Capt.; *w.*
   24 *Whitehall Court, S.W.1.*

DESMARES, *Francis Arthur*
6/8131, 3/12/15; R.F.A., C/S, 9/6/16; R.F.A., 9/9/16, att. R.E. Sigs.; F,M; Lieut.; *w*(4); M.C.
   New York Villa, Longueville, Jersey, Channel Islands.

D'ESTE, *Henri Gayton*
6/2/6450, 27/9/15; No. 3 O.C.B., 25/2/16; R. War. R., 19/7/16, att. Manch. R.; F,It,E; Lieut.
   70 *Stanmore Road, Edgbaston, Birmingham.*

DE STEIN, *Edward*
A/864, 4/8/14; K.R. Rif. C., 2/10/14, M.G.C.; F; Major.
   9 *Palace Gate, W.8.*

DETMOLD, *Frederick Guy*
C/439, 2/11/09; *dis.* 1/11/13; *rej.* 5/8/14; *dis. med. unfit,* 5/9/14; R.G.A., 16/10/14, R.F.C.; F; Capt.
   100 *Redcliffe Gardens, S.W.10.* (Now in South Africa.)

✠ DEVAS, *Bertrand Ward*
Sq/150, 18/4/08; *dis.* 17/4/09; *rej.* K/2224, 2/12/14; Suff. R., 7/12/14; Lieut.   Killed in action 13/11/16.

DEVENISH-MEARES, *Frederick*
A/56, 7/4/08; *dis.* 6/4/13; D. of Corn. L.I.; Lieut.
   Meares Court, Mullingar, Ireland.

DEVEREUX, *John Lionel Francis*
B/11358, 28/5/17; No. 14 O.C.B., 7/9/17; R. Suss. R., 17/12/17, M.G.C.; Lieut.   *Selby House, Haverfordwest, Somerset*

APPENDIX II.—RECORDS OF RANK AND FILE.

DEVEREUX, Vere Eugene
3/3591, 13/5/15; R.G.A., 7/8/15; F; Lieut.
                Melrose, Park Drive, Swansea.

DEVEREUX, William Thomas
B/12695, 6/3/18; No. 5 O.C.B., 6/9/18, No. 11 O.C.B.; General List, 8/3/19; 2/Lieut.   573 High Road, Tottenham, N.

DE VESIAN, Norman Ellis
C/690, 7/2/13; Midd'x. R., 25/8/14; M; Lieut.
            6 Gayton Crescent, Hampstead, N.W. 3.

DE VINE, Henry
6/2/9280, 3/2/16; No. 7 O.C.B., 4/11/16; R. Ir. Rif., 28/2/17; Lieut.; w.
    Wilson Hospital, Muttyfarnham, Co. Westmeath, Ireland.

DE VISMES-DE PONTHIEU, Louis A. M. R. See
    DE PONTHIEU, L. A. M. R. de V.

DEVONSHIRE, Ernest Warrick
B/11666, 16/7/17; Garr. O.C.B., 8/3/18; Lab. Corps, 4/9/18, att. S. Lan. R.; 2/Lieut.   Monganna, 94 Waverley Road, Southsea.

✠ DEW, Albert William John
6/4/6842, 15/10/15; North'd. Fus., 15/6/16; 2/Lieut.
                            Killed in action 10/4/17.

DEWAR, David
A/13096, 22/5/18; trfr. 14th Lond. R., 6/12/18.
              Harden Villa, Eskbank, Midlothian

✠ DEWAR, James Evan
6/3/8053, 1/12/15, L/C.; 5th Lond. R., 7/7/16; 2/Lieut.
                            Killed in action 8/10/16.

DEWAR, Peter
4/4213, 14/6/15; R.M.L.I., 30/8/15; S,F; Lieut.; w.
                  1 Colinette Road, Putney, S.W. 15.

DEWDNEY, Edward Robert
A/13113, 24/5/18, L/C.; demob. 24/1/19.
               Hill Crest Road, Newhaven, Sussex.

DE WESSELOW, Roger Christopher Vaughan
D/10219, 20/12/16; Household Bde. O.C.B., 6/3/17; Cold. Gds., 26/6/17; F; Lieut.   Down Lodge, Epsom.

DEWEY, Herbert Burford
6/4/8678, 4/1/16; No. 2 O.C.B., 14/8/16; York. R., 18/12/16, att. T.M. Bty.; F; Capt.; Inv.
              The Red House, Saffron Walden.

DEWEY, Thomas Lewis
C/D/14226, 25/10/18; trfr. K.R. Rif. C., 13/5/19.
           Rectory, Moretonhampstead, Devonshire.

DEWHIRST, Percy Moffat
A/B/C/D/12152, 24/10/17; No. 8 O.C.B., 10/5/18; trfr. 28th Lond. R., 7/10/18.
           Hawthorn Terrace, New Earswick, Yorkshire.

DEWHURST, Robert Cyril
K/B/2160, 23/11/14; Rif. Brig., 27/1/15; F; Capt.; w; M.C.
            Eaton Banks, Tarporley, Cheshire.

DEXTER, John Eric
C/959, 5/8/14; R. Fus., 12/9/14; Lieut.; w.
           Grosvenor House, North Finchley, N.

DIBB, Christopher Ernest
4/3951, 3/6/15; dis. 14/6/15.

DIBBEN, Percy Roland Radford
1/3572, 10/5/15, L/C.; R.A.S.C., 4/12/15; F; Capt.
           Overdale, New Barnet, Hertfordshire.

DIBBEN, Ralph Harry
6/1/9438, 12/2/16; R.A., C/S, 26/10/16; R.F.A., 11/3/17; Lieut.
           4 Levendale Road, Forest Hill, S.E.

DIBBLE, Sidney James
6/2/8233, 4/12/15; No. 14 O.C.B.; Glouc. R., 24/10/16, emp. M. of Shipping; Lieut.; w.

DIBDIN, Lewis George
B/82, 13/4/08; R.W. Surr. R., 5/7/08; I,M; Major, D.A.A.G.
           Nobles, Dormansland, Surrey.

DICK, Henry Pfeil
C/1229, 23/9/14; R.G.A., 9/10/14; F; Capt.; w; M(2).
           41 Lee Road, Blackheath, S.E. 3.

DICK, John Fernley
3/3176, 6/4/15; 4th Lond. R., 28/7/15; 2/Lieut.

DICK, Robert
6/3/8738, 6/1/16, Cpl.; No. 14 O.C.B., 30/10/16; Sco. Rif., 24/1/17; F; Lieut.
    Woodside House, Ibrox Holm, Ibrox, Glasgow.

✠ DICKASON, Reginald Percy
6/5/7630, 20/11/15; No. 8 O.C.B., 4/8/16; Midd'x. R., 21/11/16; 2/Lieut.   Killed in action 14/2/17.

DICKE, Fred Eugene
3/9621, 19/9/16; trfr. Midd'x. R., 13/10/16.
         33 Christchurch Road, Streatham Hill.

DICKENS, Charles
A/2589, 4/1/15; Lan. Fus., 11/3/15; 2/Lieut.

DICKENS, George Bertram
D/9980, 22/11/16, Sgt.; R.E., C/S, 1/7/17; R.E., 21/9/17; F; 2/Lieut.   79 Eastfield Road, Peterborough.

DICKIE, David Harper
4/4439, 26/6/15, L/C.; Bord. R., 15/9/15; I; Capt.
     71 Cromwell Road, Queens Park, Glasgow.

DICKIE, Frederick John
A/11275, 14/5/17; Lab. Corps, 16/11/17; F; Lieut.
    c/o Messrs. Dodwell & Co., Hong Kong, China.

DICKIN, Eric Sutton
6/9197, 31/1/16; Dental Surgeon, 29/10/16; F; Capt.
          Pen Villa, Yeovil, Somerset.

DICKINSON, Arthur Percival
K/C/H/Sq/1699, 13/10/14; R.A.S.C., 21/1/15; F; Lieut.; Inv.
        111 Ritherdon Road, Balham, S.W. 17.

DICKINSON, Charles John
C/1326, 26/9/14; R.W. Kent R., 10/2/15, R.F.C., R.A.F.; F; Capt.   Gayles, West Wickham, Kent.

DICKINSON, Claude William Cromack
6/1/Sq/7136, 2/11/15, L/C.; Garr. O.C.B., 15/1/17; R.W. Fus., 10/3/17, att. R. Muns. Fus.; Lieut.   15 Temple Road, Windsor.

DICKINSON, Henry Baron Humphrey
Sq/141, 18/4/08; dis. 17/4/12.
     Sherwell, Dartmouth Place, Blackheath, S.E. 10.

✠ DICKINSON, John Archibald
6/1/6143, 9/9/15, L/C.; R.W. Surr. R., 19/1/16; Lieut.; w.
                     Killed in action 13/4/18.

DICKINSON, Ralph Percy Ferdinand
C/1730, 15/10/14; R.F.A., 9/7/15; F; Lieut.; Inv.
          11 Kenilworth Court, Putney, S.W. 15.

DICKINSON, Rupert Patrick
4/2/4129, 10/6/15; R.A.S.C., 11/10/15; M,Persia; Major; Inv; M(3).   c/o Lloyds Bank, 16 St. James Street, S.W. 1.

✠ DICKINSON, Thomas Arthur
4/3/5071, 26/7/15; S. Staff. R., 8/11/15; F; 2/Lieut.
                        Killed in action 1/7/16.

DICKINSON, Vincent Neville
C/11768, 30/7/17; R.F.C., C/S, 23/10/17; R.F.C., 12/12/17, R.A.F.; 2/Lieut.
    Whiletall Road, Rhos-on-Lees, Colwyn Bay.

DICKINSON, Wilfred
D/10885, 19/3/17; No. 14 O.C.B., 10/8/17; Hunts. Cyc. Bn., 27/11/17, att. Bedf. R.; 2/Lieut.
     92 Cemetery Road, Southport, Lancashire.

DICKINSON, William
1/6/7835, 25/11/15; R.E., C/S, 5/8/16; R.E., 20/10/16; F; Lieut.; M.C.
   101 Heathfield Road, Birmingham. (Now in Singapore).

DICKS, Albert Edward
B/12702, 8/3/18; R.E., C/S, 16/6/18; demob.
     4 Brookwood Terrace, Warwick Road, Banbury.

DICKSON, Archibald Annan
6/1/6144, 9/9/15, L/C.; Notts. & Derby. R., 9/1/16; F; Capt.; w(2).   The Cottage, Winton Place, Worthing.

DICKSON, David Law
D/12872, 3/4/18; No. 11 O.C.B., 4/10/18; demob., 21/1/19.
              Victoria House, Tayport, Fife.

APPENDIX II.—RECORDS OF RANK AND FILE.

DICKSON, Joseph William Edmund
C/1666, 10/10/14; Sea. Highrs., 13/1/15; F,M,P; Capt.; w(3); M.C.   Claughton House, Gaistang, Lancashire.

DICKSON, Kenneth Bruce
Sq/530, 16/12/10, L/C.; R.A.M.C., 13/8/14, att. Cold. Gds.; F,P; Lt.-Col.; w.   14 Hertford Street, Mayfair, W.1.

DICKSON, Percy Livingstone
6/5/7040, 28/10/15; trfr. 7th Lond. R., 23/6/16, L/C.; Lab. Corps, 7/11/17, E. Lan. R.; F; Capt.; w.
Western House, The Park, Nottingham.

DICKSON, Robert
E/14108, 7/10/18; demob. 11/1/19.
22 Camperdown Road, Aberdeen.

DICKSON, Walter John Ryles
6/3/5471, 9/8/15; Midd'x. R., 12/1/16; Lieut.
15 Wingrove Road, Newcastle.

DIERICX, Walter Martin
A/13973, 9/9/18; demob. 29/1/19.
67 Alwington Terrace, Gosforth, Newcastle-on-Tyne.

DIESPECKER, James Edward Lance
F/3047, 15/3/15, L/C.; R.F.A., 11/8/15, R.G.A.; E,F; Capt.; g(2).
c/o A. S. Clemow Esq., 15 Empress Street, Kensington, Johannesburg. South Africa.

DIGBY-JOHNSON, Eric. See JOHNSON, E. D.

DILKS, Arthur Charles
4/3416, 29/4/15, L/C.; 20th Lond. R., 8/7/15, Indian Army; Lieut.   68 Hargave Park, Highgate, N.

DILLEY, Arthur
2/9677, 28/9/16; No. 14 O.C.B., 5/5/17; K.R. Rif. C., 28/8/17; Lieut.
New Oxford and Cambridge Club, Stratton Street, W.1.

DILLON, Samuel
6/2/8754, 6/1/16; No. 8 O.C.B., 4/8/16; Shrop. L.I., 21/11/16; 2/Lieut.   3 Fair Hill, Cork.

✠ DIMENT, Harry Stanley
6/4/5161, 29/7/15; R.F.C., C/S, 28/12/16; R.F.C., 3/4/17; 2/Lieut.   Killed in action 23/5/17.

DIMERY, Gerald Christopher
B/13532, 15/7/18, L/C.; demob. 3/2/19.
Shadwell Lane, Moortown, Leeds.

DIMOND, Frederick Martyn
4/3949, 3/6/15; R.A.S.C., 5/7/15; Capt.

DIMOND, John Martyn
4/3950, 3/6/15; R.A.S.C., 5/7/15; Lieut.

DIMOND, Reginald John
C/12653, 27/2/18; No. 1 O.C.B., 9/8/18; trfr. 14th Lond. R, 20/12/18, Army Pay Corps; F; Cpl.
154 Samuel Street, Woolwich, S.E. 18.

DINES, Edward Watson
4/1/3998, 3/6/15, L/C.; W. Rid. R., 6/6/15; F; Lieut.
Palmhurst, Capworth Street, Leyton, Essex.

DINGWALL, Alexander
6/3/9095, 24/1/16; R.F.A., C/S, 4/8/16; R.G.A., 1/11/16; F; Capt.   6 Carlton Gardens, Crookston, Cardonald, Glasgow.

✠ DIPPLE, Thomas Denis
6/3/7582, 18/11/15; No. 14 O.C.B., 30/10/16; Oxf. & Bucks. L.I., 28/2/17; F; Lieut.; w.   Died 30/11/18.

DISNEY, Sydney Cecil William
C/697, 10/3/13, Cpl.; Linc. R., 18/8/14; F; Major; w, Inv; M.C., M(2).   The Rectory, Skegness, Lincolnshire.

DISS, Horace Cecil
6/5/5472, 9/8/15; 8th Lond. R., 21/4/16; F; Capt.; w; m.
Abbey Road, Barrow-in-Furness.

✠ DITCHFIELD, Samuel Eric
A/9840, 3/11/16; No. 14 O.C.B., 27/12/16; K.O. Sco. Bord., 25/4/17; F; 2/Lieut.   Killed in action 31/7/17.

DITTMER, Arthur Robert
2/3571, 10/5/15; Hamps. R., 14/8/15, 5th Lond. R.
The Red House, Ferndown, Dorset.

✠ DIXON, Cecil Hargreave
B/2665, 12/1/15; R.A.S.C., 22/3/15, R.F.C.; F; Lieut.
Killed in action 28/11/17.

DIXON, Charles Edward Trevelyan. See MURRAY-DIXON, C. E. T.

DIXON, Charles Guy
6/4/6658, 7/10/15; No. 11 O.C.B., 7/5/16; D. of Corn. L.I., 4/9/16; Lieut.; w.   31 Mount View Road, Stroud Green. N.

DIXON, Cuthbert
6/1/9458, 14/2/16; R.E., C/S, 5/8/16; R.E., 21/10/16; F; Lieut.; w.   2 Sandygate Park, Sheffield.

DIXON, Henry
C/222, 12/5/08; dis. 11/5/10.   27 Welbeck Street, W.1.

DIXON, Henry Jacques
6/7524, 16/11/15; Intelligence Corps, 12/1/16, R.A.F.; Lieut.; Inj.
1 Queen Victoria Street, E.C.

✠ DIXON, Henry Oliver
6/5/8577, 1/1/16; R.F.A., C/S, 23/6/16; R.G.A., 27/9/16; 2/Lieut.   Killed in action 6/9/17.

DIXON, Hubert John
6/3/6121, 9/9/15, L/C.; No. 11 O.C.B., 7/5/16; R. War. R., 4/9/16; F; Capt.; M.C., M(1).   Elmhurst, Olton, Warwickshire.

DIXON, James Ernest
4/4706, 9/7/15, L/C.; N. Lan. R., 9/12/15; Lieut.
Woodside, Parva Lane, Great Harwood, Lancashire.

✠ DIXON, James Galloway
6/5/5249, 31/7/15, Sgt.; L'pool. R., 6/12/15; 2/Lieut.
Killed in action 12/10/16.

DIXON, John Moore
Sq/598, 22/1/12; dis. 1/6/14.   Greenfield, Watlington, Oxon.

DIXON, Myles
6/3/8708, 5/1/16; R.E., C/S, 21/10/16; R.E., 13/1/17; F; Lieut.; M.C.   24 Heathfield Road, Wavertree, Liverpool.

DIXON, Philip Burton Bainbrigge
6/2/9062, 21/1/16; dis. med unfit, 8/8/16.

DIXON, Reginald Francis
6/5/6759, 11/10/15; R.G.A., 29/12/15; F; Major; M.C.
Allandale, 49 Layton Avenue, Mansfield, Nottinghamshire.

DIXON, Reginald Samuel
4/3/4536, 1/7/15; R.A.S.C., 20/11/15, att. R.F.C.; F; Lieut.; w.
13 Granville Road, Stroud Green, N. 4.

DIXON, Richard
B/12851, 25/3/18; No. 18 O.C.B., 20/9/18; E. Kent R., 18/3/19; 2/Lieut.   The Red House, Salvington, Worthing.

DIXON, Richard Walter
6/Sq/7985, 29/11/15; R.F.A., C/S, 4/8/16; R.G.A., 26/11/16; F; Capt.; M.C.   37 Winsham Grove, Clapham Common, S.W. 11.

DIXON, Thomas Frank
6/2/5813, 26/8/15; E. Ang. Div. Cyc. Coy., 1/11/15, att. R. Sco. Fus.; E,P,F; Capt.; Inv.
Greenside, Village Road, Church End, Finchley, N. 3.

✠ DIXON, William Alexander
4/1/4495, 28/6/15; R. Ir. Fus., 7/10/15; 2/Lieut.
Killed in action 16/8/17.

✠ DIXSON, Thomas Storie
4/3725, 24/5/15; Cold. Gds., 31/8/15; Lieut.
Killed 8/12/16.

✠ DOBBIE, Robert Stewart
B/A/11375, 28/5/17; trfr. R.A.F., 18/1/18; Sgt.; w.
Died of wounds 27/7/18.

DOBINSON, Percy Leonard
4/2/4642, 5/7/15; Durh. L.I., 21/12/15; F; Lieut.; w(2).
157 St. Andrew's Road South, St. Annes-on-the-Sea, Lancashire.

DOBLE, Arthur James Stanley
6/4/9376, 8/2/16; No. 1 O.C.B., 6/9/16; R.F.C., 25/1/17, R.A.F.; F; Lieut.; w.
Trelassick, Ladock, Grampound Road, Cornwall.

DOBNER, Charles Leslie
6/4/6324, 20/9/15; Worc. R., 4/9/16; F,It; Lieut.; M(1).
Faith Villa, King Edward Street, Slough.

DOBSON, Alban Tabor Austin
6/1/8531, 29/12/15, L/C.; No. 14 O.C.B.; Hamps. R., 24/10/16; Lieut.   4 Auriol Mansions, Barons Court, W.

145

APPENDIX II.—RECORDS OF RANK AND FILE.

DOBSON, Alexander Maurice
4/1/3952, 3/6/15; L'pool. R., 7/10/15, M.G.C.; Lieut.

DOBSON, Alfred
C/13283, 15/6/18; R.E., C/S, 18/10/18; demob.
9 Joffre Avenue, Briggs Field, Glasshoughton, Castleford, Yorkshire.

DOBSON, Donald Norman
A/1940, 22/10/14; R.A.O.C., 8/2/15; E; Staff Capt.
P.O. Box 388, Jerusalem.

DOBSON, George Francis Clement
D/E/13664, 29/7/18; R.G.A., C/S, 2/10/18; R.G.A., 11/4/19; 2/Lieut. 6 St. Matthews Drive, St. Leonards-on-Sea.

DOBSON, Laurence Parkinson
C/D/12032, 24/9/17; No. 19 O.C.B., 5/4/18; W. York. R., 24/9/18; 2/Lieut. Moorfield House, West Garforth, Leeds.

DOBSON, Reginald Crawshaw
6/5/8629, 3/1/16; R.F.A., C/S, 23/6/16; R.G.A., 27/9/16; F; Major; M.C. 6 Vernon Street, Leeds.

DOBSON, Reginald Wheeler
6/5250, 31/7/15; R.F.A., 2/9/15; F; Lieut.; M.C.
Dorincourt, Talbot Road, Oxton, Birkenhead.

DOBSON, Robert
B/11388, 30/5/17; No. 14 O.C.B., 7/9/17; W. Rid. R., 17/12/17, att. Lan. Fus.; 2/Lieut. 4 Roydstone Road, Bradford.

DOBSON, William Greswell
D/12993, 29/4/18; No. 22 O.C.B., 7/6/18; Lan. Fus., 11/2/19; 2/Lieut. 178 Oakwood Court, Kensington, W. 14.

DOCTON, Horace Martin
A/13143, 23/5/18; No. 1 O.C.B., 8/11/18; R. Lanc. R., 16/3/19; 2/Lieut. 15 Fern Bank, Lancaster.

DODD, Aaron
A/E/13963, 6/9/18; demob. 10/1/19.
Speedwell Inn, Staveley, Chesterfield.

DODD, Arthur Hughes
D/10200, 15/12/16; R.E., 9/1/17; Lieut.
The Bungalow, Alwen Waterworks, Cerrigydrindion, N. Wales.

DODD, Arthur Vernon
6/3/6451, 27/9/15; No. 14 O.C.B.; D. of Corn. L.I., 7/11/16; F,M; Lieut. 4 Ventnor Villas, Hove, Sussex.

DODD, Edwin Ashley
Sq/534, 13/1/11, Cpl.; Bedf. Yeo., 18/10/14, R. Horse Gds.; F; Lieut. Tudor Cottage, Ightman, Kent.

DODD, Ernest Leigh
C/1746, 15/10/14, L/C.; Manch. R., 10/2/15; F; Major; M.C.
Ravenscroft, Longton, Nr. Preston, Lancashire.

DODD, Henry Jaques
6/7914, 29/11/15; dis. med. unfit, 14/3/16.
16 Livingston Avenue, Sefton Park, Liverpool.

DODD, Maurice
2/3449, 3/5/15; L'pool. R., 6/8/15, R.A.F.; F; Lieut.
10 Bank Parade, Preston, Lancashire.

DODD, Ronald Fielding
6/1/7137, 2/11/15; M.G.C., 25/9/16; F; Lieut.
The Cottage, Castletown, Isle of Man.

DODD, Walter James
D/12902, 8/4/18; R.F.A., C/S, 17/5/18; F; demob.
57 Disraeli Road, Forest Gate, E. 7.

DODDS, John Henry
A/10264, 29/12/16; No. 20 O.C.B., 5/5/17; L'pool. R., 28/8/17, N. Lan. R.; 2/Lieut. 12 Arno Road, Birkenhead.

✠ DODDS, Robert William Lee
A/1081, 2/9/14, Sgt.; North'd. Fus., 19/9/14; F; Lieut.
Killed in action 25/9/15.

DODGE, Sidney Christopher
6/6905, 18/10/15, L/C.; R.F.A., C/S, 21/7/16; R.G.A., 1/11/16; F; Lieut.; Inj. 1B East Dulwich Road, S.E. 22.

✠ DODSON, Herbert Leigh Midleton
4/1/5030, 22/7/15; R.A.S.C., 25/10/15, att. R.A.F.; F; Lieut.
Killed in action 25/8/18.

DODSON, Stanley
C/12274, 3/12/17, L/C.; demob. 23/1/19.
105 Darenth Road, Stamford Hill, N. 16.

DODSWORTH, Robert Dickinson
B/10756, 21/2/17; M.G.C., C/S, 13/7/17; M.G.C., 26/1/18; F; 2/Lieut.; w.
Kenwyn Lodge, Western Road, Fortis Green, N. 2.

DODWELL, George Melville
6/9212, 31/1/16; R.F.A., C/S, 9/6/16; R.F.A., 9/9/16; F; Capt.; w, Inv.
c/o Messrs. Dodwell & Co., Ltd., 24 St. Mary Axe., E.C. 3.
(Now in Hong Kong.)

DODWELL, John Eric
B/12368, 4/1/18; R.F.A., C/S, 24/5/18; R.F.A., 18/3/19; 2/Lieut. 102 West Street, Grimsbury, Banbury, Oxon.

✠ DOE, Alfred Bramhill
6/1/6277, 16/9/15; No. 9 O.C.B., 8/3/16; R. Highrs., 3/9/16, att. R.E.; F; 2/Lieut. Killed in action 23/4/17.

DOHERTY, Francis Cecil
6/2/6818, 14/10/15, Sgt.; Essex R., 8/6/16, emp. M. of Munitions; Lieut. 101 Worple Road, Wimbledon.

DOHERTY, Gregory
6/1/Sq/9281, 3/2/16; R.A., C/S, 12/10/16; R.F.A., 1/7/17; F; Lieut.; w.
Ulster Bank Ltd., Castlerea, Co. Roscommon, Ireland.

DOHERTY, John William
6/4/8815, 10/1/16; R.F.A., C/S, 4/8/16; R.F.A., 10/11/16; Lieut.
73 Taunton Road, Lee, S.E.

DOHERTY, Rodney Whittard
Sq/2899, 11/2/15; Norf. Yeo., 3/4/15, secd. M.G.C., Tank Corps; F; Capt.; M(l).
Estancia El Cardo, Loa Cordos, F.C.C.A., Argentina.

DOLEMAN, Alfred Hamilton
6/2/8344, 13/12/15; R.A., C/S, 26/10/16, M.G.C., C/S; N. Lan. R., 26/6/17; 2/Lieut. 3 Graham Road, W. Kirby.

✠ DOLLEY, Reginald Charles Francis
6/2/8310, 11/12/15, Sgt.; No. 14 O.C.B., 30/10/16; Notts. and Derby. R., 24/1/17; 2/Lieut. Killed in action 30/6/17.

DOLLMAN, John Guy
4/3726, 24/5/15; 19th Lond. R., 1/11/15; Capt.
Hove House, Bedford Park.

DOLMAN, Frederick William
4/3/6/4179, 14/6/15; R.N.A.S., 2/9/16, R.A.F.; Grand Fleet; Lieut.; cr.
The Cottage, 7 Ranulf Road, West Hampstead, N.W. 2.

✠ DOLPHIN, William Heathcote
B/296, 25/6/08; dis. 31/12/09; R.F.A., 8/2/15; F,G; Lieut.
Died 11/4/21.

DOLTON, Walter William
B/13549, 19/7/18; demob. 7/1/19.
Gordon House, 109 Blackheath Park, S.E. 3.

✠ DOMEGAN, Christopher Patrick
6/5/8084, 1/12/15; No. 7 O.C.B., 4/11/16; R. Ir. Fus., 28/2/17, R.A.F.; F; Lieut. Drowned 10/10/18.

DOMMETT, John
6/D/7538, 17/11/15; dis. med. unfit, 9/3/17; R.N. Res.; F; Lieut.; Inj. Innisbury, Banbury, Oxon.

DONALD, William Ellis
A/11599, 5/7/17; No. 5 O.C.B., 7/9/17; R.E., 29/1/18; Lieut.
c/o Anderson, 32 Grafton Square, Glasgow.

DONALDSON, Eric
Sq/104, 18/4/08; dis. 17/4/09; R.A.M.C., 11/7/14; S,It; Capt.
2 Melbury Road, Kensington, W. 14.

DONALDSON, William Ainsworth
D/B/12133, 18/10/17; No. 9 O.C.B., 10/5/18; Scottish Horse, 6/2/19; 2/Lieut. 362 Maxwell Road, Pollokshields, Glasgow.

DONGRAY, Frederick Baden
B/12805, 20/3/18; trfr. K.R. Rif. C., 13/5/19; demob. 4/6/19.
Woodville, Upper Walthamstow Road, Walthamstow, E. 17.

DONNE, Duncan James
E/14148, 11/10/18; demob. 11/10/18. Jesmond, Hendon, N.W.

DONNELL, Murray
4/5031, 22/7/15; R.F.A., 12/8/15; Lieut.

DONNELLAN, Cuthbert
D/13851, 8/8/18; trfr. K.R. Rif. C., 7/4/19.
Mount Royal, Londonderry, Ireland.

APPENDIX II.—RECORDS OF RANK AND FILE.

DONNELLAN, John Nolan
6/5/8407, 15/12/15; No. 7 O.C.B., 11/8/16; R. Innis. Fus., 18/12/16; F; Lieut.; w.
Mount Royal, Londonderry, Ireland.

✠ DORAN, Edward Sheridan
6/9063, 21/1/16; R.F.A., C/S, 23/6/16; R.F.A., 5/8/16; 2/Lieut.
Killed in action 1/11/16.

✠ DORE, Alfred Clarence
B/1307, 26/9/14; York & Lanc. R., 18/12/14, M.G.C.; 2/Lieut.
Killed in action 1/7/16.

DORÉ, Frank Russell
B/1085, 2/9/14; North'd. Fus., 19/9/14; Capt.; M(1).
Stormont, Potters Bar, Middlesex.

DORÉ, Roy Holdsworth
B/1075, 2/9/14; Welch R., 12/9/14; 2/Lieut.
Stormont, Potters Bar, Middlesex.

DORÉE, Sydney George
4/6/5/4882, 15/7/15, L/C.; Yorks. L.I., 15/10/15; Lieut.
5 Granville Road, Stroud Green, N. 1.

DORMER, Ernest John
4/2/4214, 14/6/15; Indian Army, 18/11/16; Capt.
Radnage, Wallingford, Buckinghamshire.

DORRINGTON, Edwin Walter
A/D/13006, 1/5/18; demob. 29/1/19.
179 Grove Road, Sparkhill, Birmingham.

DOUBLEDAY, Hugh Methuen
A/12512, 31/1/18; No. 13 O.C.B., 7/6/18; Camb. R., 20/2/19; 2/Lieut.
1 Cumberland Gardens, St. Leonards-on-Sea.

DOUBLET, Reginald Francis Mark
A/13114, 24/5/18; No. 1 O.C.B., 8/11/18, No. 3 O.C.B.; Essex R., 20/3/19; 2/Lieut.
Rushton, Hillside Crescent, Leigh, Essex. (Now in Brazil.)

✠ DOUCET, Gerald Danby
6/4/9245, 2/2/16; North'd. Fus., 18/12/16; F; 2/Lieut.
Killed in action 26/10/17.

DOUGHERTY, John Gerald
C/13199, 4/6/18; No. 22 O.C.B., 23/8/18; R. Dub. Fus., 13/2/19; 2/Lieut.
41 Le Baggot Street, Dublin.

DOUGLAS, Cuthbert Sholto
D/13692, 31/7/18; No. 11 O.C.B., 23/1/19; General List, 8/3/19; 2/Lieut.
c/o Standard Bank of South Africa, 10 Clements Lane, E.C.

DOUGLAS, David Charles
D/13790, 9/8/18; demob. 27/12/18.
45 Central Hill Norwood, S.E. 19.

DOUGLAS, Edgar Wellesley
A/10728, 12/2/17; No. 20 O.C.B., 7/6/17; Welch R., 25/9/17; F; Lieut.
19 Kennington Terrace, Kennington Park, S.E. 11.

DOUGLAS, Edward James
6/8242, 8/12/15; No. 9 O.C.B., 8/3/16; Arg. & Suth'd Highrs., 6/7/16, att. Wilts. R.; I,M; Capt.
38 Hopefield Avenue, Belfast, Ireland.

DOUGLAS, Francis Fraser Shepherd
Sq/2828, 1/2/15; R.A.S.C., 13/4/15; G,F; Lieut.; w.
Hedgefield, Inverness.

DOUGLAS, Frederick Scott
C/A/D/11769, 30/7/17; Garr. O.C.B., 8/3/18; W. York. R., 4/9/18; 2/Lieut.
c/o Anglo Egyptian Bank Ltd., Cairo, Egypt.

✠ DOUGLAS, George Archibald Percy
C/621, 14/3/12; 10th Lond. R., 11/11/13, Essex R.; G; Capt.
Died of wounds 30/11/15.

DOUGLAS, Harry Guy Stuart
6/3/7171, 3/11/15; No. 9 O.C.B., 8/3/16; Sco. Rif., 3/8/16; F; Staff Capt.; w.
19 Ravensbourne Gardens, West Ealing. W. 13.

DOUGLAS, Percy Gordon
Sq/2919, 15/2/15; R.E., 16/4/15; G,S; Lt.-Col.; M.C., Médaille d'Honneur, M(3).
c/o Lond. County & Westminster's Bank, Charing Cross Branch, S.W. 1.

DOUGLAS, Robert Broadfoot Crawford
B/11378, 28/5/17; Lab. Corp, 10/7/17; Lieut.
121 Alexandra Terrace, Greenhead, Glasgow.

DOUGLAS, Vincent Lionel
6/2/8408, 15/12/15; A.S.C., C/S, 23/10/16; R.A.S.C., 26/11/16; Lieut.
Thornthwaite, Avenue Road, Torquay.

DOUGLAS-MENZIES, Norman Edward
6/9585, 3/6/16; R.F.A., C/S, 4/8/16; R.F.A., 10/11/16; F; Capt.; w; M(1).
Newtonairds, Dumfries, N.B.

DOUGLASS, Albert Cecil
6/5/5251, 31/7/15; L'pool. R., 13/12/15; F; Lieut.; w.
8 Sandringham Drive, Wallasey, Cheshire.

DOUGLAS, Lucius James Hugo
A/9906, 13/11/16; dis. 16/5/18.
The Agricultural College, Wye, Kent.

DOULTON, James Duncan
6/Sq/7025, 27/10/15; Life Gds., 22/3/16.
25 Adelaide Road, Surbiton.

✠ DOUTHWAITE, Robert Christopher Morris
2/3255, 16/4/15, L/C.; R.F.A., 8/10/15, York & Lanc. R.; F,It; Capt.
Died 19/6/19.

✠ DOVE, Edward Maddison
4/1/5162, 29/7/15; E. Surr. R., 29/12/15; Lieut.; M.C.
Killed in action 23/3/18.

DOVER, Reginald Harry
B/13662, 29/7/18; trfr. K.R. Rif. C., 7/4/19.
8 Statham Grove, Clissold Park, N.

✠ DOVER, William
6/1/7638, 20/11/15, L/C.; No. 14 O.C.B., 28/8/16; Norf. R., 22/11/16; Lieut.
Killed in action 28/4/17.

DOVETON, Edwin Herbert
C/11510, 18/6/17, L/C.; No. 14 O.C.B., 9/11/17; 7th Lond. R., 30/4/18; Lieut.
Domodder B, via Benoni, Transvaal, South Africa.

DOVEY, Edward Thomas
A/Sq/14264, 29/10/18; demob. 28/1/19.
Sherrards Green, Malvern.

DOW, George Greig
E/14073, 27/9/18; demob. 11/1/19.
Huntly, Aberdeenshire.

DOW, Harold Victor
6/3/8328, 11/12/15; trfr. L'pool. R., 7/7/16.
Baroda, Elton Avenue, Blundellsands.

DOWDALL, Herbert
B/9859, 6/11/16, Sgt.; R.E., C/S, 16/6/17; R.E., 7/9/17; F; Lieut.; M.C.
Estate Office, Adlingfleet, Goole, Yorkshire.

DOWDESWELL, Gerald Austin
A/11600, 5/7/17; No. 11 O.C.B., 9/11/17; R.W. Surr. R., 30/4/18, att. York. R.; I; Lieut.
Caixa 486, Rio de Janciro, Brazil.

DOWDING, Edgar James
A/E/13962, 6/9/18; No. 22 O.C.B., 22/11/18; Som. L.I., 15/2/19; 2/Lieut.
14 Baker Street, Weston-super-Mare.

DOWELL, William Bertram
A/10403, 8/1/17, L/C.; R.E., C/S, 16/6/17; R.E. 7/9/17; F; Lieut.
78 Goodwin Terrace, Carlisle.

DOWER, Eric Leslie Gandar
Sq/3127, 29/3/15; R.N.A.S., 9/10/15, att. R.F.C.; Flt. Sub. Lieut.
Royal Aero Club, 3 Clifford Street, W. 1.

DOWLAND-RYAN, Frank Michael
A/Sq/14031, 18/9/18; demob. 12/2/19; F,M; Army Chaplain; w; M.C.
St. Cuthberts Vicarage, Thetford.

DOWNE, Rupert Noel
2/3128, 29/3/15; dis. to re-enlist in R.F.C., 20/1/16, Tank Corps; F; Gnr.
3 Bolingbroke Road, West Kensington, W. 14.

✠ DOWNEND, John Middleton
6/3/5847, 26/8/15, L/C.; North'd. Fus., 23/4/16; Capt.
Killed in action 24/11/17.

DOWNER, George Collins
4/6/Sq/4847, 15/7/15; R.F.A., 8/1/16; F; Lieut.
South View, Heathfield Tower, Sussex.

DOWNES, Edward Arthur
6/Sq/5790, 23/8/15; Shrop. Yeo., 22/12/15, att. Shrop. L.I.; P,E,F; Capt.
Calverhall, Nr. Whitchurch, Salop.

DOWNES, Geoffrey Richmond
4/1/5101, 26/7/15; trfr. 5th Lond. R., 24/3/16.

APPENDIX II.—RECORDS OF RANK AND FILE.

DOWNES, *Maurice Hall*
B/12730, 11/3/18; No. 2 O.C.B., 20/9/18; K.R. Rif. C., 17/3/19; 2/Lieut.   21 Friern Park, North Finchley, N. 12.

DOWNES, *William Robert Hugh*
6/8823, 10/1/16; R.F.A., C/S, 9/6/16; R.F.A., 13/10/16; F,It; Lieut.   Sudbrooke, Lincoln.

DOWNHAM, *Francis Cyril Yorke*
C/11740, 26/7/17; No. 23 O.C.B., 4/1/18; trfr. York. R., 18/7/18.

✠ DOWNIE-LESLIE, *Edwin Victor*
6/8959, 17/1/16; No. 9 O.C.B., 8/3/16; Sea. Highrs., 23/7/16; 2/Lieut.   Killed in action 8/4/17.

DOWNING, *Francis John Andrews*
2/9786, 25/10/16; No. 14 O.C.B., 30/1/17; Glouc. R., 29/5/17; F; Lieut.; w.   South Bank, The Shrubbery, Weston-super-Mare.

✠ DOWNING, *Herbert George*
6/3/6197, 13/9/15, L/C.; No. 11 O.C.B., 7/5/16; R.F.C., 4/9/16; 2/Lieut.; M.C.   Killed in action 6/11/17.

DOWNING, *Lionel Edward Lowder*
C/14196, 21/10/18; demob. 22/1/19.
c/o E. C. Downing Esq., Consulate Chambers, Bute Docks, Cardiff, South Wales.

DOWNING, *Richard Ewart*
A/10061, 1/12/16; trfr. 19th Lond. R., 6/4/17.
    Horwood, Bideford, North Devon.

DOWNS, *Henry Summer*
6/1/7727, 22/11/15; No. 8 O.C.B., 4/8/16; York. R., 21/11/16, War Office; 2/Lieut.

DOWNTON, *Lionel Arthur*
5346, 2/8/15; Lieut., R.A.S.C.   57 Yale Court, West Hampstead.

DOWSETT, *Arthur Oldfield*
D/12928, 15/4/18; No. 21 O.C.B., 4/10/18; Midd'x. R., 17/3/19; 2/Lieut.   58 The Parade, Leamington Spa.

DOWSON, *Cyril James*
6/2/7350, 10/11/15; Essex R., 4/9/16, att. Rif. Brig., R.A.M.C. and R.F.C.; F; Lieut.; w.
    160 Prospect Road, Woodford Green, Essex.

DOWSON, *Evelyn Cecil Reginald*
6/2/6417, 23/9/15; trfr. 7th Lond. R., 18/8/16, R. Dub. Fus., Conn. Rang.; F; w.   17 Argyle Street, Bath.

DOWSON, *William Bertram*
6/5/7127, 2/11/15, L/C.; No. 11 O.C.B., 10/5/16; L'pool. R., 4/9/16; F; Capt.; w, p; M(1).
    Bankfield House, Sefton Road, Litherland, N. Liverpool.

✠ DOWSWELL, *Charles Victor*
6/5/6063, 6/9/15; No. 7 O.C.B., 7/4/16; 9th Lond. R., 17/7/16; 2/Lieut.   Killed in action 8/10/16.

DOWTY, *George Drage*
4/2/4215, 14/6/15; Midd'x. R., 22/8/15; F; Lieut.; p.
    3 Crescent Mansions, Elgin Crescent, W. 11.

DOYLE, *Cecil Walter*
C/A/D/12299, 11/12/17; trfr. 28th Lond. R., 17/5/18.
    Kingsclere, 70 Dovercourt Road, East Dulwich, S.E. 22.

DOYLE, *George Ralph*
6/6350, 20/9/15; R.A.O.C., 13/10/15; F,E; Lieut.
    13 Jesmond Road, Clevedon.

DOYLE, *John Edgcumbe*
Sq/2862, 5/2/15; R.A.S.C., 24/5/15, R.F.C., R.A.F.; F; Flt. Cmdr.; w; D.F.C.   2 Mount Radford Crescent, Exeter.

DOYLE, *John Joseph*
6/1/9282, 3/2/16; No. 8 O.C.B., 4/8/16, M.G.C., C/S.; M.G.C., 23/11/16, Tank Corps; F; Capt.; Inj.
    Ruthnew, Co. Wicklow, Ireland.

DOYLE, *William*
B/12826, 22/3/18; R.E., C/S, 23/8/18; demob.
    545 Oldham Road, Newton Heath, Manchester.

DRABBLE, *Alec William*
4/3/4454, 28/6/15, L/C.; Durh. L.I., 21/12/15.

DRABBLE, *Frederick*
A/B/13097, 22/5/18; demob. 23/1/19.
    Hillcot, Matlock, Derbyshire.

DRADER, *Harry Cecil Frank*
2/3765, 27/5/15; North'd. Fus., 5/8/15, secd. Tank Corps; F; Major; M.C., M(2). The Ryelands, Colney Hatch Lane, N. 11.

DRAFFEN, *Charles Henry*
H/2/1944, 22/10/14.

DRAKE, *Herbert*
4/1/4599, 5/7/15; Manch. R., 15/1/16; Lieut.
    57 St. Michael's Road, Headingley, Leeds.

DRAKE, *Percy Charles*
6/2/8209, 7/12/15; L/C.; No. 14 O.C.B.; Devon R., 18/12/16, Indian Army; I,P,E; Lieut.; Inv.
    24 Panmuir Road, Wimbledon, S.W. 19.

DRAKE, *Roger Garnett Clayton*
4/5/4790, 12/7/15; Som. L.I., 4/11/15; F; Lieut.; p; M.C.
    9 Powderham Crescent, Exeter.

DRAKE, *Wilfred James*
6/5/7041, 28/10/15, L/C.; Dorset R., 4/8/16, Som. L.I.; F; Lieut.   Lindell, Teignmouth, Devonshire.

DRAKE, *William Cecil Pickard*
6/3/6591, 4/10/15; trfr. R.G.A., 7/7/16; R.G.A., 24/6/17; Lieut.
    99 Gower Street, W.

✠ DRAPE, *Norman*
6/4/Sq/6477, 27/9/15, Cpl.; R.A., C/S, 26/10/16; R.G.A., 5/1/17; 2/Lieut.   Died of wounds 15/7/17.

DRAPER, *George Alison Donald*
D/12921, 12/4/18; No. 5 O.C.B., 8/11/18, No. 20 O.C.B.; R.W. Surr. R., 16/3/19; 2/Lieut.   Bingham, Stoke Road, Guildford.

DRAPER, *Roland Dudley Herbert*
6/5/7728, 22/11/15; No. 14 O.C.B.; Yorks. L.I., 21/11/16; Lieut.; w.   Ditchley, Stoke Road, Guildford.

DREHER, *William Gothard*
B/11695, 19/7/17; General List, 4/12/17, att. M.G.C.; It; Lieut.
    Poggio Mirasole, Malnate (varese), Italy.

DREW, *Daniel Edward*
6/4/6278, 16/9/15; No. 14 O.C.B., 26/11/16, M.G.C., C/S; M.G.C., 25/4/17; F,NR; Lieut.; g.
    Barcie Croft, Burnage, Manchester.

✠ DREW, *Frederick James*
2/9730, 16/10/16, L/C.; R.G.A., C/S, 14/3/17; R.G.A., 23/6/17; 2/Lieut.   Killed in action 29/3/18.

DREW, *Harold Harman*
C/12614, 18/2/18; R.E., C/S, 12/5/18; R.E., 27/9/18; 2/Lieut.
    8 Hughenden Road, Clifton, Bristol.

DREW, *Peter Shaw*
6/5/6325, 20/9/15; W. York. R., 4/6/16, R.E.; F,S; Capt.
    8 Cumberland Terrace, Annan, Dumfrieshire.

✠ DREWETT, *Herbert Ben*
6/5/7836, 25/11/15; No. 14 O.C.B.; E. York. R., 24/10/16; 2/Lieut.   Killed in action 30/10/17.

DREWETT, *John William*
A/10741, 16/2/17; No. 11 O.C.B., 5/7/17; Surr. Yeo., 30/10/17, att. R.W. Surr. R.; F; Lieut.; w.
    Courtlands, Effingham Road, Surbiton, Surrey.

DREWITT, *Francis Drayton*
C/461, 17/2/10; dis. 2/2/12; Worc. R., 1/4/15; M,SR,Persia; Capt.; w(2); M.C.   75 Old Broad Street, E.C.

DREWSEN, *Joseph Bernard Ray*
6/5/9337, 7/2/16, L/C.; No. 14 O.C.B., 27/9/16; Lan. Huss. Yeo., 18/12/16, att. L'pool. R.; F; Lieut.
    Darley, West Derby, Liverpool.

DRISCOLL, *Brian O'Neil*
6/1/7915, 29/11/15; R.F.A., C/S, 31/3/16; R.F.A., 5/8/16; 2/Lieut.

✠ DRISCOLL, *Dermoth O'Neil*
D/2829, 1/2/15; Midd'x. R., 8/7/15, secd. R.F.C.; Lieut.
    Died 13/8/18.

✠ DRIVER, *Bernard Henry*
4/3839, 31/5/15; R.W. Surr. R., 20/8/15; F; Major; w; M C., M(1).   Killed in action 4/10/17.

DRIVER, *Graham John*
D/11114, 27/4/17; trfr. R.F.A., 8/6/17.

APPENDIX II.—RECORDS OF RANK AND FILE.

DRIVER, *Harold Samuel*
D/11168, 2/5/17; No. 14 O.C.B., 5/10/17; R. Scots, 26/2/18; F;
Lieut.; w; M.C., M(1). 56 *Eversleigh Road, East Ham.*

DRIVER, *John Haworth*
6/2/8345, 13/12/15; No. 14 O.C.B., 30/10/16; N. Lan. R., 28/2/17;
F; Lieut.; w(2).
Woodlands, Hawkesworth Avenue, Guiseley, Nr. Leeds.

✠ DRIVER, *Percy Scott*
4/3/4180, 14/6/15, Sgt.; R.A.S.C., 4/12/15, R.F.C.; 2/Lieut.
Killed in action 26/3/18.

DRIVER, *Reginald Charles William*
D/10654, 5/2/17; trfr. 16th Lond. R., 9/3/17.
Woodmancote Manor, Nr. Cirencester, Gloucestershire.

DRONSFIELD, *William Brideoake*
B/Sq/10993, 4/4/17; No. 14 O.C.B., 10/8/17; D. of Lan. Yeo., 27/11/17; F; Lieut.
Blackden Manor, Nr. Holmes Chapel, Cheshire.

DROUET, *Adrian Gustave Edward*
6/4/7397, 12/11/15; trfr. Worc. Yeo., 10/11/16, M.G.C.; P.
Ajon House, Speedwell Road, Edgbaston, Birmingham.

DRUCQUER, *Maurice Walford*
C/9798, 27/10/16; M.G.C., C/S, 1/2/17; Manch. R., 26/6/17; F;
Lieut.; Inv. *Eastwood, Wardle Road, Sale, Manchester.*

DRUMMOND, *Andrew Malcolm*
F/2726, 18/1/15; Gord. Highrs., 10/4/15, R. Highrs.; Capt.

DRUMMOND, *Douglas Henry Balcarres*
6/4/7042, 28/10/15, L/C.; 7th Lond. R., 14/7/16; F; Lieut.
c/o Cox & Co., Charing Cross, S.W. 1.

DRUMMOND, *George Campbell*
6/3/8346, 13/12/15; No. 14 O.C.B.; Suff. R., 24/10/16; F; Lieut.;
w. 30 *Dover Road, Birkdale, Lancashire.*

DRUMMOND, *James Ekstrand*
6/3/6351, 20/9/15; No. 9 O.C.B., 8/3/16; R. Highrs., 6/7/16;
Lieut.; w(2); M.C. 58 *The Avenue, Brondesbury Park.*

DRUMMOND, *James Montagu Frank*
E/2852, 4/2/15, L/C.; High. L.I., 4/6/15, att. R. Sco. Fus.; P,F;
Capt. *Department of Botany, University of Glasgow.*

DRUMMOND, *Kenneth Piggott*
C/10791, 26/2/17, L/C.; R.A., C/S, 3/9/17; R.F.A., 9/2/18; F;
2/Lieut. 14 *Dover Road, Birkdale, Liverpool.*

DRYDEN, *John Samuel*
6/5/8782, 7/1/16; No. 7 O.C.B., 11/8/16; Conn. Rang., 18/12/16,
att. R.E.; F; Lieut.; Inv.
36 *Kidderminster Road, Croydon, Surrey.*

DRYDEN, *William Henry*
C/14151, 5/10/18; demob. 20/3/19.
Millers House, Newcastle, Galway, Ireland.

DUBOIS, *Aubrey Cyril*
6/3/7785, 24/11/15; trfr. R. Suss. R., 7/7/16.
Holmbury, 33 Headstone Road, Harrow-on-the-Hill.

DUBOIS, *Edgar Arthur Chester*
6/3/5447, 7/8/15; 19th Lond. R., 12/11/15, att. R.A.F., Essex R.,
and Ches. R., 22nd Lond. R.; F,S,E; Lieut.; w.
Holmbury, 33 Headstone Road, Harrow-on-the-Hill. (Now in S. India.)

DUBUISSON, *David William*
D/Sq/9710, 10/10/16; R.F.A., C/S, 22/6/17; R.F.A., 12/1/18;
F; 2/Lieut. *Coombe Field, Godalming. (Now in Southern Rhodesia.)*

DUBUISSON, *James Melmoth*
A/1039, 26/8/14; R.W. Surr. R., 12/9/14; F; Capt.; w(3).
Cheriton, Dartford Road, Sevenoaks.

DUCK, *Frederick Stanley*
6/3/6516, 30/9/15; Mon. R., 4/9/16; F; Lieut.; Inv.
Hereford Road, Abergavenny, Monmouthshire.

DUCKER, *Herbert Charles*
D/13756, 7/8/18; demob. 29/1/19.
Menavawr, Lower Green Road, Esher, Surrey.

DUCKER, *Philip Walley*
A/11238, 11/5/17; No. 14 O.C.B., 5/10/17; Ches. R., 26/2/18,
emp. M. of Labour; 2/Lieut. 15a *North Audley Street, W.* 1

DUCKET, *Alexander Armstone*
D/1386, 29/9/14; R.E., 30/1/15; 2/Lieut.
25 *Apsley Road, Clifton, Bristol.*

DUCKWORTH, *Cyril*
A/Sq/14125, 4/10/18; demob. 20/1/19.
Rocklands, Church Lane, Marple, Cheshire

DUCKWORTH, *Geoffrey*
C/14248, 30/10/18; demob. 23/1/19.
Saltaire, Southport, Lancashire.

✠ DUCKWORTH, *William Henry*
2/3224, 12/4/15; Lan. Fus., 10/7/15; F; 2/Lieut.
Died of wounds 19/4/16.

DUDENEY, *Charles Harold*
A/2707, 18/1/15; R. Suss. R., 22/4/15, att. K.R. Rif. C.; F;
Capt.; g. *Brooklands, Newport Pagnell, Buckinghamshire.*

DUDENEY, *Eric Alvan*
6/Sq/8335, 11/12/15, Cpl.; No. 1 Cav. C/S, 24/4/16; E. Kent
Yeo., 28/7/16, att. E. Kent R.; F; Lieut.; w; M.C.
74 *St. James Square, Brighton.*

DUDLEY, *Edmund*
A/13098, 22/5/18; demob. 10/1/19.
Hill Crest, Mount Pleasant, Newcastle, Staffordshire.

DUDLEY, *Harold Benjamin*
6/2/6614, 4/10/15, L/C.; Garr. O.C.B., 12/12/16; Bedf. R.,
10/2/17, Midd'x. R.; Siberia; Lieut.
Highcroft, Coleshill, Warwickshire.

✠ DUDLEY, *Leonard Thomas*
4/1/5072, 26/7/15; R. Fus., 20/1/16; Lieut.; M.C.
Died of wounds 8/10/18.

DUDSON, *Hubert Scrivener*
A/B/12156, 25/10/17; R.F.C., C/S, 16/2/18; R.F.C., 13/3/18,
R.A.F.; F; 2/Lieut. *Northern Hey, Alsager, Cheshire.*

✠ DUERDEN, *Henry*
A/10480, 12/1/17; R.F.C., C/S, 1/6/17; R.F.C., 4/7/17; 2/Lieut.
Killed 27/7/17.

DUFF, *Charles St. Lawrence*
6/3/9283, 3/2/16, Sgt.; trfr. 28th Lond. R., 28/11/17; F,It;
Interpreter. *Erne View, Enniskillen, Ireland.*

DUFF, *Francis Edward*
B/10968, 30/3/17, L/C.; No. 14 O.C.B., 10/8/17; R. Dub. Fus.,
27/11/17, att. Linc. R.; F; Lieut.; w.
84 *Rathgar Road, Dublin.*

DUFF, *Malcolm*
4/2652, 11/1/15; Bord. R., 6/3/15; G,E,F; Capt.
59 *Sloane Street, S.W.*

✠ DUFF, *William Peter*
3/3086, 22/3/15; Notts. & Derby. R., 11/6/15; 2/Lieut.; M.C.
Killed in action 23/4/17.

DUFFIELD, *Edgar William*
6/9336, 7/2/16; R.F.A., C/S, 7/7/16; R.F.A., 13/10/16; Lieut.

DUFFIELD, *Edgar Willoughby*
H/2966, 25/2/15; Hamps. R., 15/5/15; G,E,P; Staff Major;
O.B.E., M(3). *Minia, Upper Egypt.*

DUFFIELD, *Henry William*
F/1758, 16/10/14, Cpl.; D. of Corn. L.I., 12/1/15, M.G.C.; F;
Lieut.; w.
c/o P. B. Fearon Esq., Wortham Manor, Diss, Norfolk.

DUFFIELD, *Roland Leslie*
D/13723, 2/8/18; demob. 22/2/19.
Tenby Villa, Green Street, Smethwick, Staffordshire.

✠ DUFFUS, *Gordon Charles*
2/3686, 20/5/15; R.F.A., 22/8/15; 2/Lieut.
Killed in action 16/1/17.

DUFFY, *Michael Louis*
F/1928, 22/10/14, L/C.; R.E., 8/2/15, War Office; F; Major;
w; O.B.E. 7 *Strathview Gardens, Bearsden, Dumbartonshire.*

DUFOSEE, *Geoffrey Robert*
C/Sq/13320, 19/6/18; demob. 28/2/19.
Church Farm, Longbridge Deverill, Warminster, Wiltshire.

DUFOSEE, *Harold Arthur*
A/Sq/12435, 22/1/18, L/C.; No 2 Cav. C/S, 27/6/18; 5th R
Regt. of Cav., 15/2/19; 2/Lieut.
Church Farm, Longbridge Deverill, Warminster, Wiltshire.

APPENDIX II.—RECORDS OF RANK AND FILE.

DUGGAN, *Cecil Evans*
C/10582, 19/1/17; No. 14 O.C.B., 16/3/17; S. Persian Rifles, 25/4/17; S.Persia; Lieut.; *w.*
    c/o Messrs. Cox & Co., 16 Charing Cross, S.W.1.

DUGGAN, *Eric Oswyn*
K/C/2063, 12/11/14; 22nd Lond. R., 17/3/15, Tank Corps; F; Capt.; *w.*   11 Belsize Park Gardens, Hampstead, N.W.

DUGGAN, *Joseph Patrick*
6/1/8755, 6/1/16; No. 8 O.C.B., 4/8/16; M.G.C., 23/11/16, Tank Corps; Lieut.; *w.*   35 Prussia Street, Dublin, Ireland.

DUGMORE, *Arthur Radcliffe*
K/F/2338, 14/12/14; Yorks. L.I., 15/3/15; F; Major; *g.*
    Royal Societies Club, St. James Street, S.W.1.

DUGMORE, *Henry Hare*
6/2/6393, 23/9/15, Cpl.; E. Lan. R., 21/4/16; 2/Lieut.; *M.C.*

✠ DUGUID, *Alexander Ritchie*
4/3911, 31/5/15; E. York. R., 18/11/15; 2/Lieut.
    Killed in action 3/5/17.

DUGUID, *George Douglas*
B/A/11667, 16/7/17; R.F.A., C/S, 4/2/18; R.G.A., 19/8/18; 2/Lieut.   South View, Kirkby, Lonsdale.

DUKE, *Edgar William Francis*
6/3/5473, 9/8/15; N. Lan. R., 2/11/15; Capt.

DULCKEN, *Harold Edward*
4/3302, 19/4/15, Sgt.; 9th Lond. R., 22/9/15, secd M.G.C.; F; Lieut.; *w.*
    c/o E. G. Dulcken Esq., Economic Fencing Co. Ltd., Billiter House, Billiter Street, E.C. (Now in India.)

DULLEY, *Hubert William*
C/11790, 2/8/17; A.S.C., C/S, 12/11/17; R.A.S.C., 6/1/18; F; Lieut.   The Gables, Knighton Park Road, Leicester.

DUMBLE, *Thomas Murdock*
3/3592, 13/5/15; Bord. R., 7/10/15.
    Chestnut Hill, Keswick, Cumberland.

DUMMETT, *George Herbert*
6/1/8534, 30/12/15, L/C.; No. 14 O.C.B.; M.G.C., 24/10/16, R. Marines, att. Admiralty; F; Capt.; *w.*
    Norleigh, Prentis Road, Streatham, S.W.

DUNAND, *Ernest Lennox*
D/1473, 29/9/14, Cpl.; Manch. R., 7/6/15; 2/Lieut.; *w.*
    5 St. Simon's Avenue, Putney, S.W.15.

DUNBAR, *Alexander Joshua*
B/13637, 26/7/18; demob. 4/3/19.   29 Eltham Road, Lee, S.E.

DUNBAR, Sir *Archibald Edward*
C/657, 1/11/12; W. York. R., 31/1/15; F; Major; *M.C.*, M(2).
    Duffres House, Elgin.

DUNBAR-SUTHERLAND, *Cyril Francis*
4/3/4511, 28/6/15; Bord. R., 27/10/15, Indian Army; Lieut.

DUNCALF, *Edwin Allen*
6/5/5882, 30/8/15; 12th Lond. R., 27/11/15; F; Lieut.; *w.*
    20 Chiswick Lane, W.4.

DUNCAN, *Douglas Alexander*
B/10136, 6/12/16; No. 14 O.C.B., 5/5/17; R. Lanc. R., 28/8/17, att. S. Lan. R.; F; Lieut.; w(2); *M.C.*
    The Vicarage, Bassenthwaite Lake, Cumberland.

DUNCAN, *Ernest Bolton*
6/2/8715, 5/1/16, L/C.; No. 14 O.C.B., 27/9/16; 3rd Lond. R., 18/12/16, att. R.W. Surr. R.; Capt.
    43a Spencer Park, Wandsworth Common, S.W.18.

DUNCAN, *Francis Brand*
2/9788, 25/10/16; M.G.C., C/S, 1/3/17; M.G.C., 26/6/17, Tank Corps; F; Lieut.
    Auburn, Cambridge Avenue, Great Crosby, Liverpool.

DUNCAN, *Francis Thomas*
6/Sq/7583, 18/11/15, L/C.; No. 2 Cav. C/S, 1/9/16; Surr. Yeo., 10/1/17; S; Lieut.   The Retreat, Llandaff, South Wales.

DUNCAN, *Harold*
1/Sq/9649, 27/9/16; R.A., C/S, 2/2/17; R.F.A., 16/6/17; F; Capt.; M(1).   Weetwood, Menston-in-Wharfedale.

DUNCAN, *Harold Handasyde*
Sq/997, 5/8/14, Cpl.; Norf. Yeo., 29/1/15, secd. R.E. Sigs.; F,It; Capt.   87 Victoria Street, S.W.1.

DUNCAN, *John Alfred Alexander*
4/2/4069, 7/6/15; York. R., 10/9/15; 2/Lieut.
    53 Bridge Street, Middlesbrough.

DUNCAN, *John Ronald Scarlett*
K/C/2166, 23/11/14, Cpl.; Essex R., 16/4/15; Lieut.
    c/o Clydesdale Bank Ltd., Lombard Street, E.C.

DUNCAN, *John William*
B/11318, 21/5/17; A.S.C., C/S, 1/9/17; R.A.S.C., 27/10/17; 2/Lieut.   Larct, Llandaff, Glamorganshire.

✠ DUNCAN, *Kenneth*
6/4/7501, 15/11/15, L/C.; Devon R., 4/9/16; F; 2/Lieut.
    Killed in action 9/5/17.

DUNCAN, *Leslie*
Sq/707, 9/4/13; dis. 1/12/13.
    384 Stanstead Road, Catford Bridge, S.E.

DUNCAN, *Norman*
Sq/1221, 14/9/14, Cpl.; Dorset Yeo., 13/2/15, att. S. Lan. R.; F; Lieut.; *w*; *M.C.*   6 King's Bench Walk, Temple, E.C.4.

DUNCAN, *Peter Colin*
K/E/2368, 17/12/14; R.W. Surr. R., 18/2/15; G,E,P,F; Capt.; *w*; *M.C.*, M(1).   48 Park Lane, Croydon.

DUNCAN, *Richard Edward Bert*
6/5/5287, 2/8/15, L/C.; trfr. 5th Lond. R., 17/3/16.

DUNCAN, *Thomas Graeme*
C/11468, 11/6/17, L/C.; No. 14 O.C.B., 4/1/18; Dorset R., 25/6/18, att. Indian Army; P; 2/Lieut.
    Rondebosch, Capetown, South Africa.

✠ DUNCANSON, *Ian Fergusson*
6/3/7097, 1/11/15; No. 9 O.C.B., 8/3/16; Arg. & Suth'd. Highrs., 23/7/16; 2/Lieut.   Killed in action 12/10/17.

DUNCOMBE, *Harold Edwin*
4/5/4670, 8/7/15, Sgt.; demob. 5/2/19.
    Dunain, Springfield Park, W.3.

DUNDAS, *Duncan James*
6/1/7138, 2/11/15; dis. med. unfit, 19/6/16; rej. C/11770, 30/7/17; trfr. Army Pay Corps, 13/2/18, Tank Corps.
    20 Ormond Road, Wantage, Berkshire.

DUNDAS, *George*
B/13517, 12/7/18; demob. 7/2/19.   Elmbank, Kirriemuir, N.B.

✠ DUNDAS, *James Robert Duncan*
D/11863, 16/8/17; R.F.C., C/S, 30/11/17.   Died 1/2/18.

✠ DUNLOP, *James Wilkie*
2/3129, 29/3/15, Cpl.; R. Highrs., 3/6/15, R. Ir. Regt.; Lieut.
    Died 5/3/17.

DUNLOP, *William Philip*
C/A/D/12066, 1/10/17; R.F.A., C/S, 5/4/18; R.G.A., 8/2/19; 2/Lieut.   123 Clarence Street, Sydney, Australia.

✠ DUNN, *John*
6/4/6245, 16/9/15; Sco. Rif., 27/1/16; 2/Lieut.
    Killed in action 21/6/17.

DUNN, *John Gordon*
D/10244, 29/12/16; No. 20 O.C.B., 5/5/17; Manch. R., 28/8/17; Lieut.   230 Burton Road, West Didsbury, Manchester.

DUNN, *Robert Fyffe*
A/2863, 5/2/15; Notts. & Derby R., 20/6/15, M.G.C.; F,S,P; Lieut.
•   Western, 21 Longton Road, Blackpool. (Now in East Africa.)

DUNN, *Robert Laverick*
6/Sq/6517, 30/9/15; No. 2 Cav. C/S, 1/9/16; Dorset Yeo., 27/1/17; P; Lieut.
•   Plantation Providence, East Bank, Demerara River, British Guiana.

DUNN, *Wilfred Herbert*
A/12476, 29/1/18; No. 19 O.C.B., 7/6/18; Suff. R., 5/2/19; 2/Lieut.   14 Birchington Road, Crouch End, N.8.

DUNN, *William Thomas*
C/14197, 21/10/18; demob. 29/1/19.
    West Ashford, Barnstaple, North Devon.

DUNN-YARKER, *John Henry*
6/1/8721, 5/1/16; No. 8 O.C.B., 4/8/16; North'd. Fus., 21/11/16; F,It; Lieut.; Medaglio Al Valore Militare, M(2).
    83 Cornwall Gardens, S.W.7.

APPENDIX II.—RECORDS OF RANK AND FILE.

DUNSTAN, Arthur Reginald Brabyen
6/4/7658, 22/11/15; No. 14 O.C.B., 28/8/16; Mon. R., 22/11/16, att. Shrop. L.I. and Ches. R.; F; Lieut.
9 Uplands Crescent, Swansea.

DUNSTAN, Wallace
6/1/7837, 25/11/15, L/C.; No. 11 O.C.B., 7/5/16; Devon. R., 4/9/16; E,P; Lieut.
Montpellier, 40 Queen's Road, Portsmouth.

DUNSTER, John Eugene de Mohun
F/1779, 16/10/14; Devon. R., 10/2/15, att. Som. L.I.; F; Capt.; w.
The Laurels, Golden Manor, Hanwell, Middlesex.

DUNTON, Albert William
6/1/8268, 9/12/15, Cpl.; No. 14 O.C.B.; M.G.C., 24/10/16; F,M; Capt.; M.C.
Sepham, Halstead, Nr. Sevenoaks.

DUNTON, Victor Frederick Shapleigh
6/1/7605, 19/11/15; R.F.C., 4/8/16, R.A.F.; F; Capt.
Fairfax House, Conway Road, Paignton, South Devon.

✠ DUPREY, Seymour Gordon
E/1587, 6/10/14; R.N. Res., 4/11/14; Asst. Paymaster.
Killed in action 8/8/15.

DURANT, Victor Edmund Bruce
A/9855, 6/11/16; No. 14 O.C.B., 27/12/16; High. L.I., 27/3/17, K. Af. Rif.; Germ.EA; Lieut.
105 Bedford Hill, Balham, S.W. 12.

DURHAM, George Patrick
6/3/6326, 20/9/15; No. 14 O.C.B., 27/9/16; Manch. R., 18/12/16; F,It; Lieut.; w; M.C.
Lapford, Coombe Lane, Kingston Hill, Surrey.

DURLACHER, Bertram Ronald
A/847, 4/8/14; Bord. R., 5/9/14; Capt.; M.C., M(1).

✠ DURNO-STEELE, Frederick Arthur   See STAHLSCHMIDT, F. A. D.

DURRANT, George
6/3/5492, 9/8/15, Sgt.; No. 14 O.C.B., 30/9/16; trfr. 2nd Lond. R., 19/1/17.
Hortus House, Carlton Colville, Lowestoft.

✠ DURRANT, Trevor
6/5/7659, 22/11/15; R.F.C., 4/8/16, R.A.F.; F; Capt.
Killed in action 16/5/18.

DURTNELL, Harry Watson
C/990, 5/8/14; Welch R., 12/9/14, R.F.C.; F,S; Lieut.; w.
Belmore, Otford Road, Sevenoaks, Kent.

✠ DURTNELL, Richard Neville
4/3631, 17/5/15, Sgt.; Suff. R., 8/10/15; F; 2/Lieut.; M(1).
Killed in action 28/4/17.

DUTTON, Francis Bridger
Sq/135, 18/4/08; dis. 17/4/12; R.N., -/12/17; North Sea; Surgeon Lieut.
Dormer Cottage, Old Avenue, W. Byfleet, Surrey.

DUTTON, James Wilkinson
C/10409, 8/1/17, Sgt.; demob. 23/1/19.
Lombinha, Sudden, Rochdale, Lancashire.

DUTTON, Richard Broadhurst
B/Sq/12763, 15/3/18; demob. 23/1/19.
Cleeve, Stamford Road, Bowdon, Cheshire.

DUUS, Harold McIntosh
K/2/2345, 14/12/14; S. Staff. R., 24/12/14, R.A.S.C.; Lieut.

DUVALL, Francis
C/12598, 13/2/18; Household Bde. O.C.B., 5/7/18; Midd'x. R., 3/3/19; 2/Lieut. *26 Woodhouse Terrace, North Finchley, N. 12.*

DWELLEY, William Edwin
1/9650, 27/9/16; No. 14 O.C.B., 27/12/16; North'd. Fus., 27/3/17, R.W. Fus., Indian Army; F,E; Lieut.
5 Crawley Road, Leyton, E. 10.

DWERRYHOUSE, William Rosser
6/6343, 18/9/15; Derby. Yeo., 1/10/15, R.A.S.C.; Lieut.
Bronygarn, Sketty, Glamorgan.

DYAS, George Eldridge
Sq/516, 16/11/10; dis. 22/12/11.

DYE, Horace Harvey
6/2/7525, 16/11/15, L/C.; Oxf. & Bucks. L.I., 4/9/16; F,It; Lieut. *10 Lawrie Park Crescent, Sydenham. (Now in China).*

DYER, Alfred
A/10035, 29/11/16; R.F.C., C/S, 13/3/17; R.F.C., 19/4/17; 2/Lieut. *33 Evans Square, Newington, Hull.*

DYKE, Adolph Henry Mabille
C/14183, 18/10/18; No. 11 O.C.B., 14/2/19; General List, 8/3/19; 2/Lieut. *24 Sardinia Terrace, Hilhead, Glasgow.*

DYKE, Ashley Francis Hart
C/D/13221, 6/6/18; demob. 31/1/19.
Great Nast Hyde, Hatfield, Hertfordshire.

DYKE, George
4/3687, 20/5/15; R.E., 2/11/15; F; Capt.; w.
12 Lockyer Road, Mannamead, Plymouth.

DYKE, Harold George
4/2/4308, 17/6/15; R.E., 6/9/15; Lieut.

DYKE, Harold Rodney
6/2/6760, 11/10/15; No. 2 Cav. C/S, 1/9/16; Bucks. Huss. Yeo., 18/1/17, att. D. of Lanc. Yeo.; Lieut.
155 Goddard Avenue, Swindon.

DYKE, Louis Meredith
6/2/6178, 13/9/15, Sgt.; No. 14 O.C.B.; Mon. R., 24/10/16, att. Ches. R.; F; Lieut.; g. *21 Plymouth Road, Penarth.*

DYKE-DENNIS, Patrick Gill
B/12011, 17/9/17; Household Bde. O.C.B., 7/12/17; Welch Gds., 28/5/18; 2/Lieut. *New Hall, Ruabon, North Wales.*

DYNE, John Bradley
A/13149, 29/5/18; No. 22 O.C.B., 5/7/18; R. Fus., 11/2/19; 2/Lieut. *5 New Square, Lincoln's Inn, W.C. 2.*

DYNES, Robert Stanley James
6/8824, 10/1/16; No. 1 O.C.B., 6/9/16; R.F.C., 16/3/17; 2/Lieut *Wharncliffe, Greenhithe, Kent.*

✠ DYSON, Gamm
D/11171, 2/5/17; trfr. 28th Lond. R., 14/9/17; F; Pte.
Killed in action 30/12/17.

DYSON, William Dixon
B/D/12222, 13/11/17; No. 4 O.C.B., 10/5/18; Bord. R., 3/2/19; 2/Lieut.

EADEN, John
6/Sq/8210, 7/12/15; R.F.A., C/S, 31/3/16; R.F.A., 5/8/16; Lieut. *Baitley Grange, Baitley, Southampton.*

EADY, Kenneth Wilfred
6/1/7606, 19/11/15; 20th Lond. R., 4/9/16, R.A.S.C.; F; Lieut. *Rose Cottage, North Row, Warminster, Wiltshire.*

EAGAR, Geoffrey Edward
Sq/2989, 1/3/15; R.A.S.C., 12/5/15; Capt.

EAGLES, Leslie Edmund
4/3/4039, 7/6/15; Essex R., 7/10/15, att. Hamps. R.; F; Lieut. *368 Commercial Road, E. 1.*

✠ EALES, Francis Daw Sherbrooke
6/3/8018, 30/11/15, L/C.; No. 14 O.C.B., 27/9/16; Leic. R., 18/12/16; 2/Lieut. *Killed in action 3/5/17.*

EAMES, Gerald
6/2/6160, 11/9/15; 11th Lond. R., 14/1/16.
55 Craven Avenue, Ealing.

EAMES, Maurice
C/13380, 24/6/18; trfr. 14th Lond. R., 6/12/18, Gord. Highrs.; Pte. *2 West Park, Mottingham, S.E. 9.*

EARL, Arthur Munro
B/13598, 24/7/18; dis. med. unfit. 8/4/19.
2 Pickwick Road, Dulwich Village, S.E. 21.

✠ EARLE, Ernest Clifford
4/5608, 16/8/15, Sgt.; R.F.A., 26/12/15; Lieut.; w(3).
Killed in action 27/5/18.

EARLE, Henry Arthur
6/4/9023, 20/1/16; A.S.C., C/S, 3/7/16; R.A.S.C., 6/8/16; 2/Lieut.

EARLE, John
6/2/6615, 4/10/15, L/C.; trfr. R.G.A., 10/11/16, R.E.; F; Sgt. *22 Lytton Avenue, Letchworth, Hertfordshire.*

EARLE, William Geoffrey
D/11157, 3/5/17; No. 14 O.C.B., 7/9/17; Yorks. L.I., 17/12/17; Lieut.

EASON, Cecil Bert
6/3/6549, 30/9/15; No. 11 O.C.B., 7/5/16; E. York. R., 4/9/16, att. K. Af. Rif.; Germ.EA; Lieut.
Valetta, Granville Road, Chester.

APPENDIX II.—RECORDS OF RANK AND FILE.

EASON, *Ernest William*
D/13745, 2/8/18; demob. 31/1/19.
83 *High Street, Hoddesdon, Hertfordshire.*

✠ EASSON, *David*
4/1/4567, 1/7/15; 19th Lond. R., 12/11/15; F; Lieut.; w.
Killed in action 21/3/18.

EASSON, *David*
C/12599, 13/2/18; demob. 29/1/19.
Penlan Fach, Tonna, Nr. Neath.

EAST, *Harold Alan*
C/10589, 22/1/17; A.S.C., C/S, 1/11/17; R.A.S.C., 25/1/18; Lieut.
284 *Kew Road, Kew.*

EAST, *John Charles*
C/13351, 26/6/18; trfr. 14th Lond. R., 6/12/18, Gord. Highrs.; Pte.
58 *Barclay Road, Leytonstone, E. 11.*

EAST, *Nigel Charles*
A/10057, 30/11/16; No. 14 O.C.B., 30/1/17; Rif. Brig., 29/5/17; Lieut.; w.

EASTER, *George Ernest*
B/D/13665, 29/7/18; demob. 19/1/19.
12 *Algernon Road, Hendon, N.W. 4.*

EASTERBROOK, *William George Nickels*
D/10905, 23/3/17, Cpl.; R.E., C/S, 16/9/17; R.E., 14/12/17; Lieut.
London House, Hadleigh, Suffolk.

EASTERFIELD, *Walter Bilson*
4/6/3/4883, 15/7/15; Notts. & Derby. R., 15/11/15, att. M.G.C.; F; Lieut.; w; M.C.
20 *London Road, Newark-on-Trent.*

EASTON, *Harold Kingsley*
C/14138, 11/10/18; No. 11 O.C.B., 24/1/19; demob. 4/2/19.
Ormidale, 52 Maxwell Drive, Pollokshields, Glasgow.

EASTON, *James William*
6/8756, 6/1/16; R.F.A., C/S, 26/5/16; R.G.A., 30/8/16, Intelligence Corps; F; Capt.
Murston Rectory, Sittingbourne, Kent.

EASTWOOD, *Charles Seymour*
B/630, 29/3/12; 21st Lond. R., 29/8/14; F; Capt.; M.C.
West Stoke House, Chichester.

EASTWOOD, *Christopher William*
B/10546, 17/1/17; trfr. 19th Lond. R., 25/5/17.
Glengarth, Billinge Avenue, Blackburn.

EASTWOOD, *Eric Wolfenden*
D/13693, 31/7/18; demob. 31/3/19.
26 *Portland Crescent, Plymouth Grove, Manchester.*

EASTWOOD, *John Patrick Basil*
Sq/1018, 7/8/14; R.F.A., 1/10/14; F; Capt.; M(1).
West Stoke House, Chichester, Sussex. (Now in China)

EASTWOOD, *Victor Arthur*
C/D/12275, 3/12/17; No. 6 O.C.B., 10/5/18; trfr. 28th Lond. R., 9/9/18.
Homeside, Wylde Green, Nr. Birmingham.

EATON, *Godfrey Lewis Trevor*
6/5/6122, 9/9/15; S. Staff. R., 6/7/16, att. Manch. R.; F,It; Lieut.; M.C.
85 (F.4) *Ladbroke Grove, Notting Hill, W. 11.*

EATON, *Oscar Alfred Mortimer*
6/5/9003, 19/1/16; No. 14 O.C.B., 30/10/16; 23rd Lond. R., 28/2/17, 16th Lond. R.; F; Capt.; M.C.
3 *Belgrave Terrace, Rathmines, Co. Dublin.*

EATON, *Sydney Edmund*
6/5/5989, 2/9/15, Sgt.; No. 3 O.C.B., 25/2/16; Manch. R., 3/8/16, N. Lan. R., secd. Lab. Corps; F; Capt.; Inj.
90 *Wellington Road, Oldham.*

✠ EATON-JONES, *Stafford Thomas*
6/5/5252, 31/7/15, L/C.; L'pool. R., 21/4/16; 2/Lieut.
Killed in action 28/10/16.

EBEL, *Clement*
B/11389, 30/5/17; A.S.C., C/S, 1/9/17; R.A.S.C., 27/10/17; Lieut.
The Laurels, Benhill Avenue, Sutton, Surrey.

EBERHARDIE, *Roberts Edward*
A/10527, 12/1/17, L/C.; Indian Army, 2/6/17.

✠ EBERLI, *John Friederich*
6/2/5504, 9/8/15, L/C.; R. Ir. Regt., 21/4/16, att. T.M. Bty.; 2/Lieut.
Died of wounds 16/8/17.

ECCLES, *Charles Edward Stuart Sherratt*
1/6/4/5163, 29/7/15; K.R. Rif. C., 15/1/16, att. T.M. Bty.; F; Lieut.; w,p.
Stentwood, Dunkeswell Abbey, Honiton, Devon.

ECCLES, *Clifford William*
6/Sq/6711, 9/10/15; R.A., C/S, 26/10/16; R.G.A., 17/3/17; F; Lieut.; w.
41 *Mount Pleasant Road, Exeter.*

ECCLES, *Ronald Edward Anstie*
6/1/7043, 28/10/15; trfr. H.A.C., 26/5/16; L/C.
124 *Harley Street, W. 1.*

✠ ECCLES, *Walter*
6/5/5223, 30/7/15; N. Lan. R., 8/1/16; 2/Lieut.
Killed in action 30/5/16.

ECHLIN, *Richard Fleming Warren*
4/4695, 8/7/15, Sgt.; Gren. Gds., 28/9/15; Capt.

ECKSTEIN, *Bernard Friedrich*
C/1145, 14/9/14; E. Surr. R., 15/8/14, att. R.A.F.; F; Capt.; Inv.
Oldlands Hall, Uckfield, Sussex.

EDDISON, *Colin Rucker*
D/1414, 29/9/14; R.A.S.C., 11/11/14; S; Capt.
51 *Eaton Terrace, S.W.*

EDDY, *Richard Bulford*
4/2/4566, 1/7/15; R.F.A., 7/10/15, R.G.A.; F; Capt.; w; Croix de Guerre (Belge), M(1).
Morro Vellio, Raposas E.F.C.B., Minas, Brazil.

EDELSTEN, *Miles*
K/2211, 30/11/14; R.A.S.C., 1/1/15; Capt.
Conservative Club, St. James, S.W. 1.

EDEY, *Reginald Muirhead*
6/2/7547, 17/11/15; A.S.C., C/S, 17/4/16; R.A.S.C., 21/5/16; Lieut.
Westnor, Bromley, Kent.

EDGAR, *Basil*
6/2/5555, 12/8/15; 20th Lond. R., 28/11/15, att. K.R. Rif. C.; F; Lieut.; w.
Moyenville, Aldwick Road, Beddington, Surrey.

EDGAR, *John Black*
4/2/4181, 14/6/15, L/C.; R. Sco. Fus., 20/10/15; F; Capt.
Auchencrost, Ballantrae, Ayrshire.

EDGAR, *Samuel Westey*
4/4568, 1/7/15; 10th Lond. R., 1/11/15; 2/Lieut.

EDGAR, *Stanley Clarence*
4/3766, 27/5/15, Sgt.; E. Surr. R., 29/8/15; Lieut.
The Oaks, Ashstead, Surrey.

✠ EDGAR, *Surrey*
6/4/8689, 4/1/16, L/C.; 7th Lond. R., 23/6/16; 2/Lieut.
Killed in action 7/10/16.

EDGAR, *Thomas Hunter*
4/3/6/5194, 29/7/15, L/C.; R. Fus., 20/1/16, M.G.C.; F; Lieut.; w.
52 *Queens Road, Reading Berkshire.*

EDGE, *Bernard Broughton*
Sq/3193, 8/4/15, L/C.; dis. to R. Mil. Academy, 29/10/15; R.F.A., 10/5/16; F,It; Lieut.; w.
Marlborough Lodge, Harrow.

✠ EDGE, *Frank Goodair*
6/5/7660, 22/11/15, Cpl.; No. 14 O.C.B., 28/8/16; N. Lan. R., 22/11/16; 2/Lieut.
Died of wounds 10/8/17.

EDGE, *Thomas Frederick Jenkinson*
A/12722, 24/1/18, L/C.; No. 13 O.C.B., 20/2/19; trfr. K.R. Rif. C., 25/4/19.

EDGELL, *Arthur Rolls*
C/1009, 6/8/14; S. Staff. R., 19/9/14, E. Lan. R.; G,F; Major; w.
Southdene, Dunstable, Bedfordshire.

EDGLEY, *Eric William John*
4/3490, 4/5/15; N. Lan. R., 2/9/15, att. L'pool. R.; F; Lieut.; Inv.
Pavings, Kings Langley, Hertfordshire.

✠ EDIS, *Walter Owen*
Sq/2920, 15/2/15, L/C.; Bedf. Yeo., 28/8/15; Lieut.
Killed in action 29/3/18.

EDLIN, *George Frederick Glenny*
C/14259, 1/11/18; No. 11 O.C.B., 24/1/19; General List, 8/3/19; 2/Lieut.
Rosedale, Abergavenny, Monmouthshire.

EDMED, *Wilfred*
6/5/7827, 25/11/15; No. 14 O.C.B., 28/8/16; 25th Lond. R., 22/11/16; F; Lieut.
Cambria, Orpington, Kent.

APPENDIX II.—RECORDS OF RANK AND FILE.

✠ EDMETT, *Arthur William*
4/3/4417, 24/6/15; R.W. Kent R., 28/12/15; F; Lieut.; w(2).
Died of wounds 16/3/18.

EDMISTON, *Hugh Fleming*
D/Sq/A/10632, 1/2/17; R.F.A., C/S, 4/2/18; demob.

EDMISTON, *Robert Drysdale*
6/2/6550, 30/9/15; Mon. R., 8/1/16; Capt.
282 High Street, Berkhamsted, Hertfordshire.

EDMONDS, *Frederick John*
C/9967, 20/11/16; No. 14 O.C.B., 30/1/17; 8th Lond. R., 25/4/17; F; Lieut.; w, Inj.
4 Queen's Road, Salisbury.

EDMONDS, *Hubert*
2/9684, 2/10/16; R.A., C/S, 29/12/16; R.G.A., 27/3/17, emp. M. of Munitions; F,E; Lieut.; g.
46 Wickham Road, Brockley, S.E. 4.

EDMONDSON, *Thomas Richard Verley*
A/13955, 6/9/18; demob. 24/1/19.
22 Albany Road, Victoria Park, Manchester.

EDMUNDS, *Howard*
6/1/7797, 24/11/15; R.F.A., C/S, 4/8/16; R.G.A., 1/11/16, War Office; F; Lieut.; w.
25 Church Road, Burry Port, Carmarthenshire.

EDMUNDS, *John Lansdell*
6/9514, 16/2/16; Linc. R., 18/2/16, att. York. R., and E. Lan. R.; M,I; Lieut.
c/o A. Edmunds Esq., Sussex House, Soham, Cambridgeshire. (Now in Argentina).

✠ EDWARDES, *Henry Arthur*
6/D/8910, 13/1/16; No. 1 O.C.B., 16/11/16; R.F.C., 16/3/17; 2/Lieut.
Killed 16/2/18.

✠ EDWARDS, *Arthur*
6/4/6712, 9/10/15, L/C.; E. Kent R., 25/9/16; 2/Lieut.
Killed in action 16/6/17.

EDWARDS, *Augustus Charles*
A/11220, 7/5/17; No. 14 O.C.B., 7/9/17; Hereford R., 17/12/17, att. Yorks. L.I.; 2/Lieut.
Cae Glas, White Cross Road, Hereford.

EDWARDS, *Christopher Frederick*
A/13115, 24/5/18; R.E., C/S, 23/8/18; demob.
Biskra, Bushey Heath.

EDWARDS, *Coryndon Stanley*
6/2/6730, 11/10/15; R.F.C., 7/7/16, R.A.F.; E; Lieut.
97 Holland Road, Harlesden, N.W.

EDWARDS, *Douglas Alfred*
Sq/3130, 29/3/15; dis. 23/4/15.

EDWARDS, *Edwin Maurice*
4/5/4848, 15/7/15, L/C.; D. of Corn. L.I., 1/6/16; 2/Lieut.
Broadwindsor, Dorset.

EDWARDS, *Eric Norman*
6/4/9157, 26/1/16; M.G.C., C/S, 1/3/17; M.G.C., 26/6/17, Tank Corps; F; Capt.; M.C.
Osmont, Grove Park, Wanstead, Essex.

EDWARDS, *Ernest William*
B/3038, 11/3/15; R.W. Surr. R., 18/6/15, att. R.F.C. and R.A.F.; E; Lieut.; w.
c/o Anglo-Egyptian Oilfields Ltd., Burghada, Suez, Egypt.

EDWARDS, *Frederick*
6/4/5831, 26/8/15; W. York. R., 7/7/16; Lieut.
10 St. Hilda's Terrace, Whitby.

EDWARDS, *George Chenis*
D/10445, 10/1/17; trfr. 16th Lond. R., 26/2/17.
Cheniston, Egham, Surrey.

EDWARDS, *Gordon*
D/12118, 15/10/17; R.E., C/S, 25/1/18; Tank Corps, 8/10/18; Lieut.
179 Norbury Crescent, Norbury, S.W. 16.

EDWARDS, *Harold*
C/10346, 5/1/17; trfr. R.G.A., 16/2/17; R.G.A.; F; 2/Lieut.; w.
73 Newmarket Road, Norwich.

EDWARDS, *Henry Chivers*
B/12416, 18/1/18; No. 5 O.C.B., 7/6/18, No. 14 O.C.B.; Suff. R., 5/2/19; 2/Lieut.
Cantilupe Farm, Haslingfield, Cambridge.

EDWARDS, *Henry James*
F/3102, 24/3/15; 17th Lond. R., 6/5/15; Lieut.; w.
Trevale, Queen's Avenue, Woodford Green, Essex.

EDWARDS, *Henry Ouseley*
E/14060, 25/9/18; No. 22 O.C.B., 22/11/18; R. Berks. R., 5/2/19; 2/Lieut.
The Vicarage, Edenbridge.

EDWARDS, *Henry Threlkeld*
B/10473, 12/1/17; A.S.C., C/S, 14/5/17; R.A.S.C., 28/6/17; Lieut.
44 Outram Road, Addiscombe, Croydon.

EDWARDS, *Herbert Alfred*
B/12764, 15/3/18; No. 4 O.C.B., 6/9/18, No. 18 O.C.B.; demob.
10 Scarsdale Villas, Kensington, W. 8.

EDWARDS, *Herbert James*
6/2/5653, 16/8/15; No. 1 O.C.B., 6/9/16; R.F.C., 25/1/17, R.A.F.; F; Capt.
Thornton, St. Arnaud, Victoria, Australia.

EDWARDS, *James Trevor Rhys*
4/5/4736, 12/7/15; S. Wales Bord., 20/11/15; Lieut.; w.
Plasgwyn, Rhymney, Monmouthshire.

EDWARDS, *John*
C/D/A/12082, 4/10/17, L/C.; No. 21 O.C.B., 10/5/18; R. Highrs., 2/2/19; 2/Lieut.
Bessborough, Bennetts Hill, Oxton, Birkenhead.

EDWARDS, *John Verney*
6/2/6110, 28/8/15; No. 7 O.C.B., 6/4/16; R.W. Fus., 3/8/16; F,NR; Lieut.; g.
10 College Hill, Llanelly, South Wales.

EDWARDS, *Joseph Stephen*
6/2/5830, 26/8/15; trfr. 13th Lond. R., 2/5/16.
49 Manchester Street, W.

EDWARDS, *Leslie Kirk*
C/14220, 23/10/18; trfr. K.R. Rif. C., 25/4/19, M.G.C.
Honeywood, Carshalton, Surrey.

EDWARDS, *Llewelyn Charles-*
6/2/8050, 1/12/15, Cpl.; No. 14 O.C.B., 27/9/16; Denbigh. Yeo., 24/1/17; F; Lieut.
20 Rhiw Road, Colwyn Bay, North Wales.

✠ EDWARDS, *Osborne Montague*
6/4/8347, 13/12/15; M.G.C., C/S, 28/8/16; M.G.C., 28/12/16; F; Lieut.
Killed in action 23/8/18.

EDWARDS, *Pryce*
6/2/9202, 31/1/16; No. 14 O.C.B., 30/10/16; R.M.L.I., 28/2/17; F; Lieut.; g.
Lond. Joint City & Midland Bank Ltd., Newcastle, Emlyn, Wales.

EDWARDS, *Richard David*
6/9402, 9/2/16; R.F.A., C/S, 5/8/16; R.F.A., 15/12/16; Lieut.
Penrice Villa, Morriston, Swansea.

EDWARDS, *Richard Owen*
A/D/11925, 30/8/17; demob. 14/1/19.
519 Royal Liver Buildings, Liverpool.

EDWARDS, *Roderick Willoughby Gore-*
B/12806, 20/3/18; No. 8 O.C.B., 20/9/18.

✠ EDWARDS, *Roy*
4/5/9705, 9/10/16; No. 14 O.C.B., 30/1/17; Rif. Brig., 25/4/17; 2/Lieut.; w.
Died of wounds 30/11/17.

✠ EDWARDS, *Spencer Ernest*
4/2/4624, 5/7/15; E. Kent R., 23/9/15; 2/Lieut. Died 9/3/17.

EDWARDS, *Stanley*
D/12119, 15/10/17; dis. med. unfit, 29/4/18.
109 Hurlingham Road, S.W. 6.

EDWARDS, *Thomas Gilbert*
C/12226, 16/11/17, L/C.; No. 18 O.C.B., 9/8/18; demob. 6/2/19.
12 Portsea Place, Connaught Square, W. 2.

EDWARDS, *Thomas Maddock*
2/1/3593, 13/5/15, Sgt.; R.F.A., C/S, 17/3/16; R.F.A., 14/7/16; Lieut.; w; M.C.

EDWARDS, *William Tregelles*
6/3/7438, 15/11/15; R.F.C., 25/9/16, R.A.F.; Lieut.
54 Richmond Road, Cardiff.

EDWICKER, *Albert Clarence*
B/13484, 8/7/18, L/C.; demob. 3/2/19.
6 Beauchamp Road, Lavender Hill, S.W. 11.

EDYE, *Henry George Morley*
6/2/D/6601, 4/10/15; dis. med. unfit, 27/7/17.
Tante Villa, Wembdon, Bridgwater, Somerset.

APPENDIX II.—RECORDS OF RANK AND FILE.

EELES, *Henry Swanston*
6/4/6887, 18/10/15, Sgt.; R.F.A., C/S, 21/7/16; R.F.A., 27/10/16; F; Capt.; M.C.   *Greencroft Park, Lanchester, Co. Durham.*

EGAN, *Alexander Joseph*
B/35, 3/4/08; dis. 3/4/08.   *3 Burgess Hill, N.W. 2.*

EGAN, *Alfred Gillham*
C/14291, 11/11/18; demob. 5/3/19.
    Box 3204, Johannesburg, South Africa.

EGGETT, *Donald Rolls*
A/D/14130, 8/10/18; No. 13 O.C.B., 10/2/19; trfr. K.R. Rif. C., 30/5/19.

EHRHARDT, *William Charles Leslie*
4/3953, 3/6/15; R.F.A., 2/10/15; F; Lieut.
    190 Hamstead Road, Handsworth, Birmingham.

✠ EKIN, *Leslie Montrose*
A/1365, 26/9/14; York. & Lanc. R., 18/12/14; 2/Lieut.; M.C.
    Killed in action 1/7/16.

ELDER, *Robert*
C/13204, 5/6/18; R.E., C/S, 25/8/18; demob.
    10 Carlton Terrace, Kelvinside.

ELDRIDGE, *Edwin Harold*
6/1/8099, 2/12/15; No. 11 O.C.B., 7/5/16; Worc. R., 24/10/16, R.A.F.; F; Lieut.   *59 Arundel Road, Littlehampton, Sussex.*

ELDRIDGE, *Percival*
4/1/B/4791, 12/7/15, L/C.; demob. 13/2/19.
    1 Hope Villas, Kings Road, Berkhamsted, Hertfordshire.

ELDRIDGE, *Reginald Alfred*
C/11791, 2/8/17; R.F.C., C/S, 23/10/17; R.F.C., 12/12/17, R.A.F.; 2/Lieut.   *18 York Road, New Southgate, N. 11.*

ELGOOD, *Vivian Arthnox Alsager*
B/654, 1/11/12; 19th Lond. R., 2/10/14; F,S,P; Capt.; w; M.C.
    218 Strand, W.C. 2.

ELIOTT-WOOD, *Derek Arthur William*
C/D/13406, 29/6/18; demob. 30/1/19.
    13 Montagu Street, Portman Square, W. 1.

ELL, *Donald Phillips*
4/1/B/4643, 5/7/15; demob. 29/1/19.
    1 Chudleigh Road, Twickenham, Middlesex.

ELLAM, *Reginald Charles Holme*
4/5/4707, 9/7/15, Cpl.; L'pool. R., 3/1/16; Lieut.; w; M.C.
    72 Park Road North, Birkenhead.

ELLERBECK, *Ernest Alfred Victor*
6/Sq/6906, 18/10/15; York. Huss., 18/1/16, att. R.F.C.; F; Lieut.; p.   *37 Chester Terrace, Regents Park, N.W. 1.*

ELLERY, *Charles Allen*
A/10271, 1/1/17; R.A., C/S, 27/4/17; R.G.A., 1/9/17; F; Lieut.; w.   *The Nook, Windsor, Berkshire.*

ELLICE-CLARK, *Stuart Tulk*
6/967, 5/8/14, Cpl.; Suff. R., 24/11/14, att. Tank Corps; F; Capt.; w.
    c/o Messrs. Barrett & Elers, Wallis Road, Hackney Wick, E. 9.

✠ ELLICOTT, *Frederick Arthur John*
B/1725, 15/10/14, L/C.; K.O. Sco. Bord., 27/1/15; 2/Lieut.
    Killed in action 8/7/16.

ELLIOT, *John Gilbert*
D/11134, 30/4/17; R.A., C/S, 2/11/17; R.G.A., 13/5/18; F; 2/Lieut.   *Woodcroft, 1 Tapton House Road, Sheffield.*

ELLIOT, *Leslie*
4/6/5195, 29/7/15, Cpl.; dis. 10/8/17.
    Royal Geographical Society, Lowther Lodge, Kensington Gore, S.W. 7.

ELLIOTT, *Angus George Corser*
B/1356, 26/9/14; Glouc. R., 13/11/14; Capt.

ELLIOTT, *Arthur Frank*
6/2/6806, 14/10/15; No. 11 O.C.B., 7/5/16; R.F.C., 4/9/16, R.A.F.; F; Lieut.   *Glendale, King Charles Road, Surbiton, Surrey.*

ELLIOTT, *Bernard*
6/2/8409, 15/12/15; R.F.C., 7/7/16, R.A.F.; Capt.
    12 The Carfax, Horsham, Sussex.

✠ ELLIOTT, *Clarence William*
D/10210, 18/12/16; No. 14 O.C.B., 6/4/17; R.W. Surr. R., 31/7/17; F; 2/Lieut.   *Killed in action 14/4/18.*

ELLIOTT, *Edgar Lionel*
Sq/131, 18/4/08; dis. 28/2/10; R.N.; Mediterranean; Surgeon
    Stokenchurch, Buckinghamshire.

✠ ELLIOTT, *Eric Cuthbert John*
D/1471, 19/9/14, L/C.; Essex R., 8/4/15, R.F.C.; Lieut.
    Killed in action 22/11/17.

ELLIOTT, *Ernest*
4/5/4792, 12/7/15, L/C.; Linc. R., 19/10/15; F; Capt.; w; M(2).
    17 Orchard Road, Stevenage, Hertfordshire.

ELLIOTT, *Frank Tomes*
6/2/6179, 13/9/15; K.R. Rif. C., 6/7/16, att. K. Af. Rif. and Hamps. R.; Germ.EA; Lieut.   *Crofton Road, Orpington, Kent.*

✠ ELLIOTT, *Hugh William*
6/2/7139, 2/11/15; R.F.C., C/S, 6/9/16; R.F.C., 5/2/17, R.A.F.; F; Lieut.; M(1).   *Killed 22/6/18.*

ELLIOTT, *Lawrence Rory*
4/1/6/5196, 29/7/15; R. Dub. Fus., 2/1/16; Lieut.; w.
    Tremona, Knockdene Park, Belfast.

ELLIOTT, *L. Furner.* See Furner-Elliott, L.

ELLIOTT, *Myles Layman Farr*
A/1176, 14/9/14; Glouc. R., 18/11/14; G,M; Capt.; M.B.E.
    1 Garden Court, Temple, E.C. 4.

ELLIOTT, *Percy*
H/2009, 2/11/14; Sea. Highrs., 3/3/15; F,M,P; Capt.; w(2); M.C.   *P.O. Box 5455, Johannesburg, South Africa.*

ELLIOTT, *Thomas Renton*
Sq/260, 26/5/08; dis. 25/5/10; R.A.M.C., -/10/14; F; Col.; D.S.O., C.B.E., M(2).   *8 Cheyne Walk, Chelsea, S.W. 3.*

ELLIOTT, *William Jannion*
C/14215, 23/10/18; trfr. K.R. Rif. C., 7/4/19.
    The Manor House, Dowles, Bewdley.

ELLIOTT-LAWSON, *John Hubert.* See SCHMITZ, J. H.

ELLIS, *Alan Edward*
C/1240, 23/9/14; 12th Lond. R., 31/10/14; F; Capt.
    99 Church Road, Norwood, S.E. 19.

ELLIS, *Alexander Reginald Hale*
6/4/9183, 28/1/16; trfr. 16th Lond. R., 8/9/16.

ELLIS, *Angus Wynn*
3/9624, 20/9/16; M.G.C., C/S, 1/3/17; Tank Corps, 27/8/17; F; Capt.   *49 Lexham Gardens, Kensington, W.*

ELLIS, *Arthur Isaac*
D/11543, 21/6/17; No. 14 O.C.B., 4/1/18; R. Fus., 25/6/18; F; Capt.   *79 South Hill Park, Hampstead, N.W. 3.*

ELLIS, *Charles George Howson*
6/5/5220, 30/7/15; W. Rid. R., 28/7/16; F; Capt.; D.S.O., M.C M(1).   *39 Harrington Street, Pear Tree, Derby.*

ELLIS, *Conway Trevor*
E/1511, 1/10/14, Sgt.; R.W. Fus., 11/5/15; F; Capt.; M.C.
    59/60 Cornhill, E.C. 3.

ELLIS, *Cuthbert Ryton*
6/8933, 17/1/16; R.E., 12/8/16; Lieut.
    The Willows, Westhouses, Nr. Alfreton.

ELLIS, *Donald Wilson*
C/1309, 26/9/14, L/C.; E. Surr. R., 26/2/15, Scots Gds.; F,It; Major; w; Croce di Guerra.   *17 Ampton Road, Edgbaston, Birmingham.*

✠ ELLIS, *Edward Vezian*
K/B/2297, 10/12/14; R.N.V.R., 9/1/15; w; M.C.
    Died of wounds 19/2/17.

ELLIS, *Ernest Archibald*
B/A/D/11978, 10/9/17; trfr. R.G.A., 6/5/18.

ELLIS, *Frank*
C/11741, 26/7/17; R.E., C/S, 23/11/17; Som. L.I., 25/6/18; F; 2/Lieut.   *Treglow, Empire Road, Torquay.*

ELLIS, *Geoffrey Hender Stuart*
A/11951, 3/9/17; R.E., C/S, 10/2/18; R.E., 31/5/18; 2/Lieut.
    70 Madeley Road, Ealing, W. 5.

ELLIS, *Henry Carl Noel*
A/10292, 1/1/17; No. 14 O.C.B., 6/4/17; W. Rid. R., 31/7/17; F; 2/Lieut.   *14 Melville Road, Barnes, S.W. 13.*

APPENDIX II.—RECORDS OF RANK AND FILE.

ELLIS, *Henry Carthew*
C/1633, 9/10/14; Ches. R., 14/12/14, *att.* 23rd Lond. R. and Indian Army; G,M,P,I; Capt.
c/o Arthur Ellis, Esq., Solicitor, Burslem, Stoke-on-Trent. (Now in India).

ELLIS, *Henry Lee*
C/1345, 26/9/14; Notts. & Derby. R., 18/12/14, York. R., Lab. Corps; 2/Lieut.; *w.*
Speldhurst, Epsom.

ELLIS, *Henry Richard*
2/9771, 23/10/16, Cpl.; M.G.C., C/S, 10/4/17; Tank Corps, 27/7/17; F; Lieut.; *w.*
15 Woodbury Park Road, Ealing, W.13.

ELLIS, *Hugh Sidney*
2/3594, 13/5/15; Leic. R., 20/8/15; 2/Lieut.

ELLIS, *Jack Gilbey*
B/12731, 11/3/18; R.F.A., C/S, 2/8/18; R.G.A., 8/4/19; 2/Lieut.
7 Park Village West, Regents Park, N.W.1.

ELLIS, *Lionel Frederic*
6/1/9490, 15/2/16; Welch Gds., 12/7/16; F; Capt.; *w*; D.S.O., M.C., M(3).
Millon Cottage, The Vale, Hampstead, N.W.

ELLIS, *Lovell Strange Eaton*
A/11952, 3/9/17; R.E., C/S, 10/2/18; R.E., 15/8/18; 2/Lieut.
70 Madeley Road, Ealing, W.5.

ELLIS, *Nelson*
4/3/4455, 28/6/15; Bord. R., 24/12/15; F; Lieut.; *w.*
155 Finchley Road, N.W.

ELLIS, *Neville Sherrard*
A/13068, 15/5/18; demob. 30/1/19.
Dene Thorpe, Salisbury Road, Carshalton.

ELLIS, *Percy Haughton*
6/2/5883, 30/8/15; Midd'x. R., 16/1/16; Lieut.; *w.*

ELLIS, *Reginald Percy*
K/F/2571, 4/1/15, L/C.; Durh. L.I., 6/5/15, M.G.C.; F,E; Major.
44 Surrey Square, Walworth, S.E.17.

ELLIS, *William Jamieson*
6/1/6616, 4/10/15; Devon. R., 22/7/16; Lieut.

ELLIS-DANVERS, *Gerald Rochfort*
C/9945, 17/11/16; R.W. Surr. R., 9/3/17, Lab. Corps; Lieut.
10 Little College Street, Westminster, S.W.1.

ELLISON, *Edward*
6/1/5818, 26/8/15; 25th Lond. R., 8/7/16.
Shirley, Glen Road, Leigh-on-Sea.

ELLISON, *John*
C/550, 24/2/11; dis. 4/8/14.
23 Glebe Place, Chelsea, S.W.

✠ ELLISON, *Theodore Sarleton*
C/979, 5/8/14; Welch. R., 12/9/14; 2/Lieut.
Killed in action 14/3/16.

ELLISON, *Thomas Frederick*
D/1388, 29/9/14, Sgt.; R.G.A., 4/11/14; F; Capt.
Strathairley, Gravesend, Kent.

ELLISTON, *William Rowley*
A/92, 16/4/08; dis.; Suff. R.; F; Major. *The Ridge, Ipswich.*

ELMER, *Leslie Arthur*
6/5/7351, 10/11/15; R.F.A., C/S, 31/3/16; R.G.A., 11/8/16; F; Capt.; *w.*
Sunnyside, Elmswell, Bury St. Edmunds, Suffolk. (Now in South Africa.)

ELMER, *Thomas Horner*
B/11324, 21/5/17, L/C.; *trfr.* Class W. Res., 4/1/18.
13 Woodbine Terrace, Headingley, Leeds.

ELPHICK, *Alick*
B/11337, 21/5/17, L/C.; R.G.A, C/S, 27/12/17; R.G.A., 24/6/18; 2/Lieut.
46 Glengarry Road, East Dulwich, S.E.22.

✠ ELPHICK, *Kevin*
K/2419, 21/12/14; R. Ir. Rif., 26/6/15; 2/Lieut.
Died of wounds 28/9/16.

ELPHICKE, *Frank Hemming*
1/3481, 3/5/15; E. Surr. R., 27/9/15.

ELPHINSTON, *John William Robert*
6/8019, 30/11/15; R.F.C., 12/3/16.
Glack, Deal, Kent.

ELSBURY, *Arthur*
6/5/6223, 13/9/15; 7th Lond. R., 23/6/16, *att.* Tank Corps; Germ.SWA,F; Lieut.; *w*; M.C.
Shepstone Hall, Smith Street, Durban, South Africa.

ELSE, *Michael Jack*
D/13724, 2/8/18; No. 11 O.C.B., 23/1/19; General List, 8/3/19; 2/Lieut.

ELTOFT, *George Jackson*
6/3/Sq/8499, 11/12/15; No. 2 Cav. C/S, 1/1/17; North'n. Yeo., 7/7/17; Capt.
Sunnyside, St. Anne's Road East, St. Anne's-on-the-Sea, Lancashire.

ELTOFT, *William Holland*
B/Sq/10097, 4/12/6; No. 2 Cav. C/S, 11/1/18; R. Regt. of Cav., 22/6/18; 2/Lieut.
Sunnyside, St. Anne's Road East, St. Anne's-on-the-Sea, Lancashire.

ELTRINGHAM, *Alan*
6/Sq/8348, 13/12/15; No. 1 Cav. C/S, 2/8/16; County of Lond. Yeo., 27/11/16, *att.* 20th and 18th Lond. R.; F; Lieut.; *p.*
Springfield Grange, Great Missenden, Buckinghamshire.

✠ ELVEY, *Charles Leslie*
6/1/8104, 2/12/15; No. 14 O.C.B., 28/8/16; Suff. R., 18/12/16; 2/Lieut.
Killed in action 9/4/17.

✠ ELVIDGE, *Jabez Gordon*
C/10353, 5/1/17; No. 21 O.C.B., 5/5/17; W. York. R., 28/8/17; 2/Lieut.
Killed in action 17/11/17.

EMDEN, *Alfred Brotherston*
A/673, 10/12/12; dis. 4/8/14; R.N.V.R. as Seaman; Grand Fleet
St. Edmund Hall, Oxford.

EMDEN, *Cecil Stuart*
A/674, 10/12/12; R.W. Kent R., 3/9/14, R.A.F.; F; Capt.; *w*(3); D.F.C.
Elmfield Lodge, Bromley, Kent.

EMERY, *Henry William*
1/3417, 29/4/15; Linc. R., 8/7/15; Lieut.

EMERY, *Stephen Egbert*
C/10401, 8/1/17, Sgt.; No. 22 O.C.B., 22/11/18; Wilts. R., 15/2/19; 2/Lieut.
The Rest, Audley Road, Chippenham.

EMMERSON, *Charles Macklin Woolf*
6/5/7729, 22/11/15; No. 14 O.C.B., Norf. R., 22/11/16; Lieut.
Gwalecliffe Rectory, Nr. Whitstable, Kent.

EMMETT, *William Thomas Jonathan*
6/3/Sq/6057, 1/9/15; M.G.C., C/S, 25/10/16; M.G.C., 24/2/17; Lieut.; *w.*

EMSELL, *Basil Samuel Vincent*
Sq/784, 28/3/14; Drag. Gds., 15/8/14; F; Lieut.; *w.*
c/o Messrs. Holt, Bankers, 3 Whitehall Place, S.W.1. (Now in France.)

ENFIELD, *Ernest Arthur*
Sq/2095, 16/11/14, Cpl.; R.A.S.C., 24/3/15; Capt.
6 Pilgrim's Lane, N.W.3.

ENGELBACH, *John Alfred*
6/2/D/6478, 27/9/15; M.G.C., C/S, 1/1/17; Army Cyc. Corps, 26/4/17; Lieut.
10 Neville Court, St. John's Wood, N.W.

ENGLAND, *Conrad Charles*
A/12478, 29/1/18; No. 14 O.C.B., 7/6/18; demob. 31/1/19.
Sparrow Wycke, Purleigh, Essex.

ENGLAND, *Jack*
A/10469, 12/1/17; No. 14 O.C.B., 5/5/17; R.W. Fus., 28/8/17; P,F; Lieut.; *w*; M.C.
22 Dock Road, Penarth.

ENGLAND, *John Croom*
B/11333, 21/5/17, L/C.; R.A., C/S, 15/12/17; R.G.A., 24/6/18; F; 2/Lieut.
122 Poole Road, Bournemouth.

ENGLAND, *John Edward*
D/13686, 29/7/18; demob. 21/12/18.
12 St. Joseph's Road, Handsworth, Sheffield.

ENGLAND, *John Reginald*
F/1756, 16/10/14; Glouc. R., 13/3/15; 2/Lieut.

ENGLAND, *John Russell*
B/343, 4/2/09; dis. 3/2/13; S. Wales Bord., 18/9/14; F,S; Capt.; *Inv, w*; M.C.
Fairleigh Lodge, Hinton Charterhouse, Bath.

APPENDIX II.—RECORDS OF RANK AND FILE.

ENGLAND, Robin
6/2/8055, 1/12/15; No. 14 O.C.B., 30/10/16; Devon. R., 28/2/17; F,lt; Lieut. 25 Brookdale Terrace, Teignmouth.

ENGLEBURTT, John Francis
F/2789, 26/1/15; Midd'x. R., 24/4/15, att. R.W. Kent R.; F; Capt.; w(2), Inv.; M.C., M(1).
12 Hillside Gardens South, Wallington, Surrey.

ENGLISH, Cecil Rowe
D/1411, 29/9/14; K.R. Rif. C., 28/11/14, emp. M. of Munitions; Lieut.; w.

ENGLISH, Henry Bazeley Christopher
D/E/13725, 2/8/18; No. 22 O.C.B., 26/9/18; Som. L.I., 5/2/19; 2/Lieut. Ardwick, Crieff, Perth.

ENNALS, William Hedley
A/C/13170, 31/5/18; trfr. 14th Lond. R., 6/12/18; F; M(1).
14 Mellish Road, Walsall, Cheshire.

ENNION, Sidney Terence Evelyn Pook
C/13249, 10/6/18, L/C.; trfr. 14th Lond. R., 6/12/18, Gord. Highrs.; Pte.
Harlech, Bury Road, Newmarket, Cambridgeshire.

ENOCH, Henry Ainsley
6/1/7256, 8/11/15; M.G.C., C/S, 30/9/16; M.G.C., 23/11/16, Tank Corps; F; Lieut. Casterbridge, Bernard Street, Swansea.

ENSOM, Alfred Lambert
4/3/4569, 1/7/15; Berks. Yeo., 20/10/15; 2/Lieut.
34 Wilmington Avenue, Chiswick, W.4.

ENTWISLE, Ralph
6/1/8825, 10/1/16; R.A., C/S, 15/9/16; R.G.A., 10/12/16; F,I; Lieut.; g. Hollins House, Putney, S.W.

✠ ENTWISTLE, Charles Egerton
6/5/6279, 16/9/15, Sgt.; Manch. R., 6/1/16; Lieut.
Died of wounds 22/3/18.

ENTWISTLE, Clarence Howard
C/12615, 18/2/18; No. 17 O.C.B., 5/7/18; dis. med. unfit, 5/2/19.
181a Seabank Road, New Brighton, Cheshire.

ENTWISTLE, Joseph
K/E/2471, 28/12/14; R.E., 12/5/15; G,E,F; Major; M.C., M(1).
6 Milner Road, Ansdell, Lytham, Lancashire.

ENTWISTLE, Joseph
6/5/5451, 7/8/15, Sgt.; Lan. Fus., 22/12/15, att. R. War. R.; F; Lieut.; Inv; M(1).
Riversdale, Hawthorn Grove, Wilmslow, Cheshire.

EPTON, Robert
C/13205, 5/6/18; No. 22 O.C.B., 26/9/18; trfr. Class W. Res., 15/10/18. 2 Bank Street, Lincoln.

EREAUT, Edgar James
H/1888, 16/10/14; R.A.S.C., 3/5/15; Lieut.
16 Clanricarde Gardens, Bayswater, W.2.

✠ ERLEBACH, Arthur Woodland
6/1/4/5164, 29/7/15; R.F.C., 13/8/16; 2/Lieut.
Killed in action 5/7/17.

✠ ERWOOD, Cecil Victor
4/3840, 31/5/15, Sgt.; K.R. Rif. C., 17/11/15; 2/Lieut.
Killed in action 17/2/17.

ESCOMBE, Robert Douglas
A/1680, 12/10/14; R.E., 3/2/15, R.A.S.C.; F,E; Lieut.; Inv.
South Park, Sevenoaks, Kent

ESSE, Frank Adolphus
2/3450, 3/5/15; Manch. R., 18/8/15, Indian Army; F,I; Capt.; w. c/o Alliance Bank of Simla, Dehra Doon U.P., India.

✠ ESSEX, Robert Charles
6/4/5694, 17/8/15; R.F.A., 26/11/15; Lieut.; w.
Died of wounds 14/5/18.

ESSEX, William
6/5/8870, 12/1/16; No. 8 O.C.B., 4/8/16; R. Suss. R., 18/12/16; F; Lieut. Cedar House, Milton, Cambridgeshire.

ESTRIDGE, Delmé Graham
A/B/12458, 23/1/18; No. 1 O.C.B., 9/8/18; Som. L.I., 4/3/19; 2/Lieut. 146 King Edwards Road, Swansea, South Wales.

✠ ETHEREDGE, Eckley Oxtoby
6/4/8452, 17/12/15; R.F.A., C/S, 4/8/16; R.F.A., 9/12/16; 2/Lieut. Killed in action 12/7/17.

✠ ETHERINGTON, Herbert Field
Sq/342, 3/2/09; dis. 18/1/11; rej. Sq/1021, 7/8/14; R. Regt. of Cav., 9/9/14, Drag. Gds.; F; 2/Lieut.
Died of wounds 8/1/16.

EUSTACE, William Rowland George
6/4/9174, 27/1/16; R.A., C/S, 7/7/16; R.G.A., 13/9/16; F; Major. 19 Malvern Road, Southsea, Hampshire.

EVANS, Albert Edward
A/B/D/12157, 25/10/17; No. 8 O.C.B., 10/5/18; Tank Corps, 12/11/18; 2/Lieut. Yorke House, Creswell, Nottinghamshire.

✠ EVANS, Albert Illtyd
6/2/7440, 15/11/15; R.A., C/S, 29/9/16; R.F.A., 27/1/17; 2/Lieut. Killed in action 17/8/17.

EVANS, Alec Tilsley
B/12765, 15/3/18; No. 20 O.C.B., 20/9/18; demob.
Newlands, Teynham, Nr. Sittingbourne, Kent.

EVANS, Alfred John
Sq/890, 5/8/14; Intelligence Corps, 7/8/14, R.F.C., R.A.F.; F,P; Major; Captured by Turks -/7/16, escaped -/6/17; M.C. and Bar, M(1). The Ramblers, Rodmersham Green, Sittingbourne.

EVANS, Arthur William
6/8211, 7/12/15; R.F.A., C/S, 26/5/16; R.G.A., 30/8/16; Lieut.
2a Gordon Mansions, Belsize Lane, Hampstead.

EVANS, Arthur William
D/10429, 10/1/17; No. 20 O.C.B., 7/6/17; L'pool. R., 25/9/17, att. Hamps. R.; 2/Lieut.
57 Stirling Road, Edgbaston, Birmingham.

EVANS, Bertram George
D/13694, 31/7/18; trfr. K.R. Rif. C., 25/4/19, R.A.O.C.; Pte.
Rosslyn, Crescent Road, Kingston Hill, Surrey.

EVANS, David Beynon
6/7987, 29/11/15; Sigs. C/S, 25/3/16; R.E., 28/7/16; Lieut.
18 Morlais Street, Roath, Cardiff.

EVANS, David Leslie Colwyn
4/3194, 8/4/15; dis. 2/8/15.

EVANS, Douglas Scott
B/11390, 30/5/17; A.S.C., C/S, 1/11/17; R.A.S.C., 25/1/18; E,P; Lieut.; Inv; M(1). 3 Down View, Bude, North Cornwall.

EVANS, Dudley
C/10997, 4/4/17, L/C.; No. 14 O.C.B., 7/9/17; Yorks. L.I., 17/12/17; F; 2/Lieut.; w. 14 Stratford Place, W.1.

✠ EVANS, Edward Herbert Sandford
E/2790, 26/1/15; Lan. Fus., 1/5/15; F; Capt.
Killed in action 22/7/16.

EVANS, Edward St. John Stanley
B/13536, 17/7/18; trfr. K.R. Rif. C., 7/4/19, att. R.A.O.C.
Vrondeg Hall, Bronwylfa, Wrexham, North Wales.

EVANS, Edward Trevor
D/10661, 5/2/17; R.F.C., C/S, 13/3/17; R.F.C., 19/4/17, R.A.F.; F,It; Lieut. 18 Dudley Road, New Brighton, Cheshire

EVANS, Ernest
6/8518, 29/12/15; R.A.S.C., 2/5/16; Lieut.

✠ EVANS, Ernest
C/10164, 11/12/16; R.A., C/S, 27/4/17; R.G.A., 1/9/17; 2/Lieut.
Died of wounds 21/9/18.

EVANS, Ernest Gordon Briscoe
C/D/14123, 9/10/18; trfr. K.R. Rif. C., 13/5/19.
9 Kirkstall Road, Streatham Hill, S.W.2.

EVANS, Evan Lloyd Estlin
C/13343, 17/6/18; trfr. 14th Lond. R., 6/12/18, Gord. Highrs.
The Parsonage, Dukinfield, Cheshire.

EVANS, Francis Alfred
D/12873, 3/4/18; No. 8 O.C.B., 18/10/18; demob.
The Manor Cottage, Woodborough, Wiltshire.

EVANS, Frank Hopkinson
B/E/13564, 18/7/18; No. 22 O.C.B., 20/9/18; Manch. R., 14/2/19; 2/Lieut. 1315 Walnut Street, Philadephia, U.S.A.

EVANS, Frederick William
H/1966, 26/10/14, Sgt.; Lan. Fus., 24/2/15; Capt.; M.C.
1 Tanfield Court, Temple, E.C.4.

APPENDIX II.—RECORDS OF RANK AND FILE.

EVANS, *Griffith Wilton*
A/11882, 20/8/17; R.F.A., C/S, 4/2/18; R.G.A., 19/8/18; 2/Lieut. *Enmore House, Durand Gardens, S.W. 9.*

EVANS, *Guy Ernest James*
6/5/5297, 2/8/15, L/C.; R.W. Fus., 6/7/16, att. Ches. R.; F,E; Lieut.; w. *Werna, Tregavon, Cardiganshire.*

EVANS, *Guy Hubert*
B/10541, 17/1/17, L/C.; R.A., C/S, 29/6/17; R.G.A., 2/12/17; Lieut. *Eason House, Broadstairs.*

EVANS, *Harold Llewellyn*
6/8478, 20/12/15; R.F.A., C/S, 26/5/16; R.G.A., 30/8/16; Lieut. *21 Kerry Road, Newtown, North Wales.*

EVANS, *Harold Vaughan*
6/4/7380, 11/11/15; E. York. R., 4/8/16; F; Lieut.; *Inv.*
541a Aulaby Road, Hull.

EVANS, *Henry Francis Owen*
4/5/4737, 12/7/15, L/C.; Manch. R., 30/11/15, R.A.S.C.; F; Staff Capt.; w; M(1). *315 Cowley Road, Oxford.*

EVANS, *Henry Franklin*
4/1/4537, 1/7/15; R.W. Kent R., 1/11/15; Lieut.
6 Rosehill Terrace, Swansea.

EVANS, *Henry Worthington Dorsett*
6/2/8722, 5/1/16; No. 8 O.C.B., 4/8/16; Shrop. L.I., 21/11/16; F; Lieut.; *p.*
Penymaes, Llansantffraid, Monmouthshire. (Now in F.M.S.)

EVANS, *Herbert Clyde*
A/1189, 14/9/14; R.N.V.R.; M(1). *50 Charlwood Street, S.W.*

EVANS, *Herbert Farmer*
2/3688, 20/5/15; R.H.A., 26/9/15, att. R.A.F.; F; Lieut.; *p.*
Fairview, Nantwich Road, Crewe.

✠ EVANS, *Horace Thomas Royston*
6/1/5703, 19/8/15; No. 11 O.C.B., 7/5/16; R. War. R., 4/9/16; 2/Lieut. *Killed in action 8-9/5/17.*

EVANS, *Hugh Price*
6/2/9559, 1/3/16; dis. to re-enlist, 1/12/16.

EVANS, *Isaac*
10216, 19/12/16; No. 20 O.C.B., 7/6/17; Shrop. Yeo., 25/9/17; Lieut. *19 Hampden Road, Oswestry.*

EVANS, *John Harry Fisher*
6/1/7916, 29/11/15; R.F.A., C/S, 23/6/16; R.G.A., 27/9/16; F; Lieut.; g, w; M.C. *Glasfryn, Pencoed Road, Burry Port.*

EVANS, *John Henry*
6/3/6198, 13/9/15; No. 7 O.C.B., 6/4/16; R. Lanc. R., 16/7/16, att. Lan. Fus.; F; Major; w, g; M.C. and Bar, M(1).
Broadfield, Gomshall, Nr. Guildford.

EVANS, *John Victor*
6/4/8757, 6/1/16; No. 14 O.C.B., 27/9/16; Mon. R., 18/12/16, att. R.W. Fus.; E,P,F; Lieut.; *Inv.*
Albion House, Cilfynydd, Pontypridd, South Wales.

EVANS, *Leonard Valentine*
6/3/6551, 30/9/15; trfr. M.G.C., 16/10/16.
The Mount, Fields Park, Newport, Monmouthshire.

EVANS, *Leslie Francis*
D/13869, 21/8/18; trfr. K.R. Rif. C., 7/4/19.
26 North Crescent, St. Anne's-on-the-Sea, Lancashire.

EVANS, *Leslie Wynn.* See WYNN-EVANS, L.

EVANS, *Lewis Noel Vincent*
E/1620, 9/10/14; R.W. Fus., 14/12/14; F; Major; w.
Arthog, Beeches Avenue, Carshalton, Surrey.

EVANS, *Myrddin*
6/2/7661, 22/11/15; No. 8 O.C.B., 4/8/16; Welch. R., 18/12/16; F; Lieut.; M.C.
12 Brook Street, Ystrad, Rhondda, Glamorganshire.

✠ EVANS, *Norman Harden*
C/726, 11/11/13; R.W. Kent R., 18/10/14; Lieut.
Died of wounds 19/4/17.

EVANS, *Owen Gwynne*
D/12947, 19/4/18; No. 16 O.C.B., 18/10/18; Linc. R., 17/3/19; 2/Lieut. *Austinfriars, Stamford, Lincolnshire.*

EVANS, *Percy Daniel*
6/4/7439, 15/11/15; No. 11 O.C.B., 7/5/16; Northd. Fus., 4/9/16, att. Chinese Lab. Corps; F; Capt.
The Grange, Brimscombe, Nr. Stroud, Gloucestershire.

EVANS, *Randle James*
B/D/A/12006, 13/9/17; R.F.C., C/S, 12/4/18; R.A.F., 19/7/18; F; 2/Lieut.; w.
Coftar House, Penn Road, Penn, Wolverhampton.

EVANS, *Reginald Compton*
6/4/7548, 17/11/15, Sgt.; No. 11 O.C.B., 7/5/16; Devon. R., 4/9/16, att. R. Berks. R.; F; Capt.; w.
Hameline, Seabroke Road, Gloucester.

EVANS, *Rowland Henry*
B/10553, 17/1/17; No. 14 O.C.B., 7/9/17; R. Berks. R., 17/12/17.
5 St. John's Road, Mainder, Newport, Monmouthshire.

EVANS, *Seiriol John Arthur*
C/13206, 5/6/18; demob. 23/1/17.
Gentleshaw, Rugeley, Staffordshire.

EVANS, *Sidney Archibald*
6/3/8105, 2/12/15; R.A., C/S, 7/8/16; R.G.A., 18/10/16; F; Lieut.; M(1).
1 Brunswick Street, Merthyr Tydfil, South Wales.

EVANS, *Stanley Johnston*
A/10713, 12/2/17; R.F.A., C/S, 22/6/17; R.F.A., 18/11/17; Lieut.
30 Chichele Road, Cricklewood, N.W.

✠ EVANS, *Stewart Nicholson*
H/2/3023, 9/3/15, L/C.; Suff. R., 7/7/15, R.F.C.; Lieut.
Killed 9/7/17.

EVANS, *Ulick Richardson*
E/1557, 6/10/14; E. Surr. R., 14/10/14, secd. R.E. Sigs.; E; Lieut. *9 Merton Street, Cambridge.*

EVANS, *Wilfrid Evan*
4/3767, 27/5/15, Sgt.; R.F.A., C/S, 31/3/16; R.F.A., 11/8/16; F; Capt.; w.
c/o Barclay's Bank Ltd., 109 Fenchurch Street, E.C.

EVANS, *William Arthur Avenel*
A/25, 2/4/08; dis. 24/11/10.

EVANS, *William Ewart*
6/3/8243, 8/12/15, Sgt.; No. 14 O.C.B.; M.G.C., 24/10/16; Capt. *Lismoyle, Bryngwyn Road, Newport, Monmouthshire.*

EVANS, *William Howel*
6/1/7986, 29/11/15, L/C.; R.A., C/S, 14/9/16; R.F.A., 22/1/17; F; Lieut.; g.
Maesderwen, Vicarage Road, Morriston, Glamorgan.

EVANS-JACKSON, *James Noel*
A/1366, 26/9/14; K.R. Rif. C., 27/11/14; Capt.; w; M.C. and Two Bars.

EVENS, *Hubert Cragg*
4/7662, 22/11/15; R.A.S.C., 28/1/16.

EVERARD, *Cyril Edwin*
4/4335, 21/6/15; Essex R., 10/10/15, R.A.F.; E,F; Lieut.
25 Philip Road, Ipswich.

EVERARD, *Louis Edward Cameron*
4/4017, 7/6/15; Cold. Gds., 31/8/15; Capt.; w(2); M.C., M(1).
Hill Brow, Richmond Park Avenue, Bournemouth. (Now in Burma.)

EVEREST, *Henry Bertram*
E/1672, 12/10/14, L/C.; R. War. R., 10/2/15, att. 9th Lond. R and Hamps. R., R.A.F.; M; Capt.; w.
24 Madeira Road, Streatham, S.W. 16.

EVERETT, *Edgar Stephen*
6/3/6452, 27/9/15; No. 14 O.C.B.; Midd'x. R., 21/11/16; F; Lieut.; w. *Stone Pine, Nether Street, Finchley, N. 3.*

EVERILL, *Guy Raymond*
Sq/2942, 18/2/15, L/C.; R.F.A., 8/6/15, emp. M. of Munitions; Lieut.; w. *79 Corringham Road, Golders Green, N.W.*

EVERILL, *Kenneth Alfred Nevins*
6/Sq/5429, 5/8/15; R.A., C/S, 24/1/16; R.F.A., 23/6/16; F; Lieut. *9 St. Albans Villas, Highgate Road, Highgate, N.W. 5.*

EVERITT, *Charles Ernest*
6/1/7663, 22/11/15; No. 14 O.C.B., 28/8/16; W. Rid. R., 22/11/16; F; Lieut.; w(2).
The Elms, Broomhall Park, Sheffield.

✠ EVERITT, *John Wilson*
6/1/9032, 20/1/16; No. 13 O.C.B., 4/11/16; K.R. Rif. C., 28/2/17; F; 2/Lieut.; *Inv.*, w.
Died as Prisoner of War 12/4/18.

APPENDIX II.—RECORDS OF RANK AND FILE.

EVERS, Alfred Noel
4/5/4738, 12/7/15, Sgt.; Yorks. L.I., 7/10/15; F; Lieut.; w.
Clareville. Kenilworth Avenue, Harrogate.

✠ EVERS, Leslie Montague
D/10247, 29/12/16; No. 20 O.C.B., 5/5/17; York. R., 28/8/17; 2/Lieut. Killed in action 30/3/18.

EVERY-CLAYTON, Reginald Arthur Eric
D/E/13829, 7/8/18; No. 22 O.C.B., 20/9/18; Worc. R., 14/2/19; 2/Lieut. Hanley Swan, Worcester.

EVETT, John Howard
A/10474, 12/1/17; No. 14 O.C.B., 7/6/17; York & Lanc. R., 25/9/17, att. York. R.; I,S; Lieut.
9a Lunham Road. Upper Norwood, S.E. 19.

✠ EVILL, Chetwode Percy
Sq/154, 18/4/08; dis. 17/4/10; Indian Army; EA; Capt.; M.C., M(2). Died 17/7/18.

EWART, Christopher Bell
Sq/521, 18/11/10; dis. 30/4/12. The Copse, Limpsfield, Surrey.

EWART, George
B/Sq/10562, 19/1/17; No. 1 Cav. C/S, 31/7/17; R. Regt. of Cav., 22/2/18; 2/Lieut.
33 Cholmondeley Park, Highgate, N. 6.

EWART, Herbert James
6/4/5829, 26/8/15; North'd. Fus., 23/4/16, att. Lan. Fus.; F; Lieut.; Inv. Rockall House, Long Buckley, Rugby.

EWBANK, George
6/3/8995, 19/1/16; R.F.A., C/S, 23/6/16; R.G.A., 27/9/16, emp. M. of Munitions; Lieut. Langford Vicarage, Biggleswade.

EWEN, Hector Paul McDonnell
B/12766, 15/3/18; No. 2 O.C.B., 20/9/18; demob. 7/4/19.
80 Aldborough Road, Seven Kings, Essex.

EWERS, Leslie Frank
3/3595, 13/5/15; Bord. R., 15/9/15, att. M.G.C., Indian Army; M,I; Lieut.
c/o F. Ewers Esq., Southwell, Nottinghamshire. (Now in India).

✠ EWING, Harold Gordon
6/5/5930, 1/9/15, L/C.; L'pool. R., 23/4/16; 2/Lieut.
Killed in action 9/4/17.

EYDEN, Maurice Victor
6/2/6394, 23/9/15; North'n. R., 25/9/16; F; Lieut.; w-g.
Denaby, St. Matthews Parade, Northampton.

EYRE, Humphrey Walter
B/724, 18/7/13; 22nd Lond. R., 29/8/14; F; Capt.; w(2).
42 Lancaster Gate, W. 2.

EYRE, William Joseph
B/9882, 8/11/16, L/C.; R.E., C/S, 24/3/17; R.E., 15/6/17; F; Lieut.; M.C. Heath Bank, Longstone, Derbyshire.

✠ EZRA, David
3/3381, 26/4/15; R.A., C/S, 24/1/16; R.G.A., 6/7/16; Lieut.
Killed in action 6/8/18.

FABB, Percy John
6/2/7441, 15/11/15; No. 8 O.C.B., 4/8/16; R.W. Kent R., 21/11/16, emp. M. of Munitions; Lieut.; w.

FABER, Geoffrey Cust
C/1923, 22/10/14; R.F.A., 4/11/14, 8th Lond. R.; F; Capt.; w.
Weyhill, Andover.

FABLING, John Roy
D/12874, 3/4/18; No. 22 O.C.B., 7/6/18; R. Fus., 11/2/19; 2/Lieut. 33 Comeragh Road, W. 14.

FÂCHE, Gordon Lancaster Mountford
A/981, 5/8/14; Suff. R., 30/9/14; F; Major; w; M.C. and Bar.
13 John Street, Bedford Row, W.C. 1.

FAGAN, James Courtenay
4/1/5102, 26/7/15, L/C.; R. Berks. R., 15/4/16; 2/Lieut.
41 Chepstow Villas, Kensington Park Road.

FAGG, Frank Roberts
D/12912. 9/4/18, L/C.; No. 21 O.C.B., 4/10/18, No. 18 O.C.B.; R.W. Kent R., 18/3/19; 2/Lieut.
55 Mount Pleasant Road, Lewisham, S.E.

FAGNANI, Henry Hutchinson
F/1775, 16/10/14, Sgt.; R. Suss. R., 1/12/14, Indian Army; M,P,I; Lt.-Col.; M(1). 8 Vale Court, Maida Vale, W. 9.

FAICHEN, James Aitchison
F/1775, 16/10/14, Sgt.; R. Suss. R., 1/12/14, Indian Army; M,P,I; Lt.-Col.; M(1). 8 Vale Court, Maida Vale, W. 9.

FAICHEN, James Aitchison
6/4/C/9018, 20/1/16, Sgt.; M.G.C., C/S, 1/1/17; Army Cyc. Corps, 12/4/17; Lieut. Grangeville, Sunderland.

FAILES, Collingwood Christopher
6/Sq/7607, 19/11/15; R.F.A., C/S, 4/8/16; R.F.A., 10/11/16; F; Lieut.; M(1). Castle Rising, Nr. Kings Lynn.

FAIR, Arthur
B/1118, 7/9/14; Suff. R., 28/11/14; E,P; Capt.; M.C.
11 Mount Street, Wellington, New Zealand.

FAIRBAIRN, Clive Prell
4/1/4739, 12/7/15, L/C.; Scots Gds., 2/10/15; Lieut.
c/o Dalgety & Coy., 45 Bishopsgate, E.C.

FAIRBARNS, Brian Wellesley
A/12540, 5/2/18; No. 11 O.C.B., 7/6/18; E. Kent R., 5/2/19; 2/Lieut. 13 Flodden Road, S.E. 5.

FAIRCLOUGH, Laurence
6/4/6199, 13/9/15; Kent Cyc. Bn., 26/1/16, M.G.C.; F; Lieut.
8 Eliot Park, Lewisham, S.E. 13.

FAIRFIELD, Ronald Anthony
4/3689, 20/5/15; 19th Lond. R., 6/11/15, att. Hamps. R. and Glouc. R.; Lieut. 70 Melrose Avenue, Cricklewood, N.W. 2.

FAIRHURST, John
6/5/6041, 3/9/15; L'pool. R., 6/6/16; F; Lieut.; Inv.
21 Church Street, Pemberton, Wigan.

FAIRLEIGH, Donovan H. E.
3/4/6/4728, 10/7/15; R.F.A., 7/10/15, Derby. Yeo.

✠ FAIRLIE, Edward
B/861, 4/8/14; K.R. Rif. C., 9/9/14; Major; w.
Killed in action 30/3/18.

FAIRLIE, Gerald Roylance Chichester
B/10524, 15/1/17, Cpl.; No. 14 O.C.B., 7/6/17; R. Scots., 25/9/17; F; Lieut.; w.
3 St. Julian's Farm Road, West Norwood, S.E. 27.

FAIRLIE, Hugh Ogilvie
B/13501, 10/7/18, L/C.; No. 11 O.C.B., 24/1/19; demob.
3 St. Julian's Farm Road, West Norwood, S.E. 27. (Now in California.)

FAIRLIE, John Evelyn
A/10933, 28/3/17; No. 14 O.C.B., 10/8/17; R. Lanc. R., 27/11/17, att. Indian Army; S; 2/Lieut.
14 Carmalt Gardens, Putney, S.W. 15.

FAIRS, John Joseph
4/2/4113, 8/6/15; E. Surr. R., 10/9/15, M.G.C.; F,S,P; Lieut.; M(2). 10 Cumberland Road, Kew, Surrey.

FAIRWEATHER, John Christopher
A/13141, 28/5/18; No. 24 O.C.B., 18/10/18; Tank Corp., 21/3/19; 2/Lieut. Merdon, Chaulesford, Hampshire.

FAITHFULL, Malcolm Ernest
6/1/6552, 30/9/15; No. 1 O.C.B., 6/9/16; R.F.C., 25/1/17 R.A.F.; Lieut.; M(1).
c/o F. Faithfull Esq., 105 High Street, Winchester.

FALCKE, Joseph
Sq/3535, 10/5/15; R.F.A., 26/7/15; F; Major; M(1).
34 Alexander Street, Berea, Johannesburg, South Africa.

FALCONAR, George Magnus Gurney
C/10852, 9/3/17; A.S.C., C/S, 30/6/17; R.A.S.C., 29/9/17; 2/Lieut.

FALCONER, Harry
4/2/5103, 26/7/15; Manch. R., 4/11/15; Lieut.; w(2); M.C.
Falkland. Park Drive, Grimsby.

FALCONER, John Philip Egerton
K/6/D/2921, 15/2/15, Sgt.; demob. 24/3/19.
Solicitor's Department, General Post Office, E.C

✠ FALCY, Humphrey Ned
6/3/5832, 26/8/15; North'd. Fus., 1/6/16; F; 2/Lieut.; M.C.
Killed in action 21/11/16.

FALLOWFIELD-COOPER, Harold Walter
6/3/6655, 7/10/15; No. 11 O.C.B., 7/5/16; Lan. Fus., 4/9/16; 2/Lieut.; w. 196 St. James Road, East Croydon

APPENDIX II.—RECORDS OF RANK AND FILE.

FALLOWFIELD-COOPER, Vernon Maitland
6/3/6656, 7/10/15; R.F.C., 6/7/16, Dorset R.; M,F; Lieut.
    c/o Messrs. Cox & Coy., Charing Cross, S.W. 1.

FALLOWS, Thomas Harold
A/12462, 24/1/18; R.E., C/S, 23/8/18; demob.
    Prospect House, Harwood, Nr. Bolton, Lancashire.

FANE, Frederick Luther
D/1433, 29/9/14; W. Rid. R., 29/10/14, att. Midd'x. R.; F; Capt.; M.C.
    Priors, Nr. Brentwood, Essex.

FANNER, William Rogers
A/874, 4/8/14; Lan. Fus., 7/11/14; F; Major; w; M.C., M(1).
    42 Cavendish Road, Clapham, S.W. 12. (Now in Egypt.)

FANSHAWE, Cecil Marmaduke
B/9870, 6/11/16; trfr. R.G.A., 14/2/17; F; g.
    30 Saxe Coburg Street, Leicester.

✠ FARDELL, Hubert George Henry
C/971, 5/8/14; E. Surr. R., 15/8/14; F; Lieut.
    Killed in action 23/4/15.

FARFAN, Joseph Harry Luis
4/1/4496, 28/6/15; R.A.S.C., 9/10/15, Lab. Corps; Lieut.; w.

FARFAN, Joseph Raymond Anderson
B/12005, 13/9/17; R.F.C., C/S, 26/11/17; R.F.C., 23/1/18, R.A.F.; 2/Lieut.
    Hopeville, Sydenham Avenue, St. Anne's, Port of Spain, Trinidad, British West Indies.

FARGHER, Philip Nelson
6/5/5931, 1/9/15; No. 11 O.C.B., 7/5/16; L'pool. R., 4/9/16; Lieut.
    Lindores, Blundellsands.

FARLEY, Edward Mary
6/5/6937, 20/10/15; dis. med. unfit, 8/8/16.
    Ardmore, Blackrock, Co. Dublin, Ireland.

FARLEY, Fred Arthur
D/11139, 30/4/17; No. 14 O.C.B., 10/8/17; Indian Army, 27/11/17; Capt.
    38 Queens Road, Leytonstone, E. 11.

✠ FARMAR, Cyril Herbert Berkeley
A/398, 5/4/09; 10th Lond. R., 11/11/13; Capt.; w.
    Killed in action 19/4/17.

FARMER, Albert Henry
D/9978, 22/11/16; Special List, 15/1/17; Capt.

✠ FARMER, Arthur William
6/2/7526, 16/11/15; Bord. R., 4/9/16; 2/Lieut.
    Killed in action 7/6/17.

FARMER, Brian
B/13599, 24/7/18; trfr. K.R. Rif. C., 25/4/19, att. R.A.O.C.
    Chieveley, May Place Road, Bexley Heath.

FARMER, Edward Francis
D/10691, 7/2/17, L/C.; No. 14 O.C.B., 5/7/17; Leic. R., 30/10/17; F; Lieut.; w.
    Ivanhoe House, Ashby-de-la-Zouche.

FARMER, Ernest Harold
4/5/4708, 9/7/15; N. Lan. R., 6/12/15; Lieut.; w(2).
    The Heath, Shackerstone, Atherstone, Leicestershire.

FARMER, Roland Ernest
6/5/6919, 19/10/15; 25th Lond. R., 4/8/16, att. R.A.F.; F; Lieut.
    20 Clarendon Road, Lewisham, S.E. 13.

FARMER, Sydney Morley
6/7664, 22/11/15; dis. med. unfit, 15/3/16.
    95 Merton Road, Bootle.

FARNELL-WATSON, Francis Baxter Crawford
C/D/12077, 1/10/17; No. 8 O.C.B., 5/4/18; trfr. 28th Lond. R., 23/8/18.
    15 Alumdale Road, Bournemouth.

FARNSWORTH, Charles
6/4/8329, 11/12/15, L/C.; A.S.C., C/S, 1/9/16; R.A.S.C., 25/10/16; I; Lieut.
    3 Cambridge Road, Crosby, Liverpool.

FARNSWORTH, John
1/3341, 22/4/15; W. York. R., 7/8/15; F; Capt.; w.
    96 Kimberley Road, Leicester.

FARNWORTH, William
6/5/8410, 15/12/15, L/C.; No. 11 O.C.B., 7/5/16; L'pool. R., 4/9/16; 2/Lieut.
    The Anchorage, Markland Hill Lane, Bolton.

FARQUHAR, Nathaniel Gordon
6/2/1/5704, 19/8/15; Cpl.; K.R. Rif. C., 21/4/16; F; Lieut.; M.C., M(1).
    c/o R. Williams & Coy., Friars House, London, E.C. (Now in Belgian Congo.)

FARQUHARSON, John Langwell
6/1/6657, 7/10/15; Devon R., 4/8/16; F; Capt.; Inv.
    Hazelhurst, Hulse Road, Southampton.

FARQUHARSON-ROBERTS, Kenneth Farquharson
E/1535, 6/10/14, Cpl.; R.A.O.C., 22/1/15; F,I; Major, D.A.D.O.S.; O.B.E., M(2).
    c/o Dr. A. Campbell, 2 Spencer Road, Southsea, Hampshire.

FARQUHARSON-ROBERTS, Murray
2/3195, 8/4/15; R.A.S.C., 26/7/15, att. R.F.C.; F,S; Lieut.; Inv.
    5 Grand Parade, Eastbourne.

FARR, Guy Liddell
A/11926, 30/8/17; No. 8 O.C.B., 5/7/18, No. 11 O.C.B.; General List, 8/3/19; 2/Lieut.
    c/o Paterson, Simons & Coy. Ltd., Singapore.

✠ FARR, Percival Walter Kaye
6/7869, 26/11/15.   Died 19/12/15.

FARR, Reginald Frank Kaye
6/Sq/5375, 5/8/15; R.A.S.C., 9/10/15; F; Lieut.
    c/o Sir C. R. McGrigor Bart. Ltd., 39 Panton Street, Haymarket, S.W. 1. (Now in Canada.)

FARRANT, Dover Pearce
1/3225, 12/4/15; R. Fus., 28/7/15, att. R.F.C.; Lieut.

FARRANT, Percival Curphey Callister
6/5/6453, 27/9/15; S. Lan. R., 1/6/16; F; Lieut.; Inv.
    Church Cottage, Grappenhall, Cheshire.

✠ FARRANT, Percy
6/Sq/7172, 3/11/15.   Died 30/6/16.

FARRANT, Roydon Arundel
4/3/4456, 28/6/15; trfr. 14th Lond. R., 2/5/16.
    Bursfield, Clarendon Road, Woodford.

FARRAR, John Edmund
B/12791, 18/3/18; No. 3 O.C.B., 6/9/18; R.W. Surr. R., 17/3/19; 2/Lieut.
    65 Queens Road, Tunbridge Wells.

FARRAR, Walter Frederick
3/6/7730, 22/11/15; No. 8 O.C.B., 4/8/16; M.G.C., 23/11/16, Tank Corps; F; Capt.; M.C.
    c/o British Controlled Oilfields Ltd., Santa Lucia, Williamsville, Trinidad, B.W.I.

FARRELLY, Victor
6/3/6602, 4/10/15; Garr. O.C.B., 19/2/17; R. Ir. Fus., 14/4/17, R. Ir. Regt., B.W.I. Regt., Oxf. & Bucks. L.I.; E; Lieut.
    Whitefield Works, Govan, Glasgow (Now in Egypt.)

FARRER, Arthur Gilbert Dacre
B/E/13565, 19/7/18; No. 22 O.C.B., 20/9/18; York. R., 14/2/19; 2/Lieut.
    The Hollins, Luddenden, Yorkshire.

✠ FARRER, Richard Bracken
D/1430, 29/9/14; Leic. R., 11/3/15; Lieut.; w.
    Killed in action 8/6/17.

FARRER, Sidney James
A/1902, 16/10/14; Suss. R., 31/3/15; F; Capt.; M(1).
    Ingleborough, Clapham, Lancaster.

FARRINGTON, Frederick William
B/10897, 21/3/17; R.A., C/S, 7/6/17; R.F.A., 4/11/17; F; 2/Lieut.
    56 West Park, Eltham, S.E.

✠ FARRINGTON, William Bowker
6/2/B/9381, 8/2/16, L/C.; No. 14 O.C.B., 26/11/16; Manch. R., 28/2/17; 2/Lieut.
    Killed in action 25/3/18.

✠ FARROW, Clifford Willis
C/10194, 14/12/16; No. 14 O.C.B., 6/4/17; Dorset R., 31/7/17; 2/Lieut.
    Died of wounds 9/4/18.

✠ FARROW, Eric Tom
K/D/2136, 19/11/14, L/C.; Midd'x. R., 10/2/15, R.F.C.; 2/Lieut.
    Killed 7/2/17.

FARROW, Leslie Ralph
4/2/4216, 14/6/15; trfr. 14th Lond. R., 5/5/16.

FARROW, William Thomas
K/B/2737, -/1/15; Midd'x. R., 20/3/15; F; Lieut.
    Barwan, Upper Terrace Road, Bournemouth.

APPENDIX II.—RECORDS OF RANK AND FILE.

FASSNIDGE, William
C/11792, 2/8/17; R.E., C/S, 23/11/17; L'pool. R., 25/6/18; 2/Lieut.
47 Tennyson Road, Southampton.

✠ FAULDER, Harold
3/3303, 19/4/15; York. & Lanc. R., 18/6/15; Capt.; M.C.
Killed in action 26/4/18.

FAULKNER, Ralph Cartwright
C/13381, 24/6/18; trfr. 14th Lond. R., 6/12/18.
28 Springwell Avenue, Harlesden, N.W. 10.

FAULKNER, Stafford Henry Douglas
4/1/6/5165, 29/7/15; N. Lan. R., 9/12/15; Capt.
29 Holland Road, Loughborough Road, Brixton.

FAULL, Arthur Norman
2/3226, 12/4/15; North'd. Fus., 3/7/15; F; Lieut.; w.
Bank House, 141 High Street, Bromley, Kent.

FAULL, John Langdon
4/1/4644, 5/7/15; Linc. R., 22/12/15, att. W. York. R.; F; Lieut.; w.
c/o Barclay's Bank, 43 Borough High Street, Southwark, S.E.

FAURE, John Pieter
C/11793, 2/8/17, L/C.; Tank Corps, 8/10/18.
c/o Hales, Caird & Coy., 11 Great St. Helens, E.C.

FAUX, Arthur Vernon
6/5/6518, 30/9/15; Manch. R., 1/6/16, att. R.W. Surr. R.; F; Lieut.; w.
37 Balfour Road, Southport, Lancashire.

FAUX, William James Christopher
6/5/6519, 30/9/15, L/C.; Manch. R., 1/6/16, emp. M. of Labour; F; Capt.; w.
Studley, 9 Cumberland Road, Southport, Lancashire.

FAWCETT, Frank Nelson
4/3536, 10/5/15; Yorks. L.I., 15/10/15; F,E,P; Lieut.; w.
213 Albany Road, Cardiff.

FAWCETT, Howard
A/393, 31/3/09; dis. 7/8/10.

FAWCUS, Charles Gordon
D/2669, 12/1/15, L/C.; Midd'x. R., 22/4/15; F; Capt.; w.
P.O. Box 158, Salmon Arm, British Columbia, Canada.

FAZAN, Eric Moon
B/12752, 13/3/18; No. 2 O.C.B., 20/9/18; K.R. Rif. C., 18/3/19; 2/Lieut.
44 Bloomsbury Street, Bedford Street, W.C. 1.

FEARNSIDE, George Alan
6/5/8606, 3/1/16; R.A., C/S, 7/8/16; R.F.A., 3/12/16; F; Lieut.; w.
26 Basinghall Street, Leeds.

FEARNSIDE-SPEED, Digby Geoffrey William Worsley
C/1236, 23/9/14; 7th Lond. R., 28/9/14; F; Capt.; w.
119 Piccadilly, W. 1.

✠ FEARNSIDE-SPEED, Ronald Nelson de Diesken
K/E/2357, 14/12/14; 7th Lond. R., 12/3/15; Lieut.
Killed in action 25/9/15.

FEATHERSTON, George Alfred
C/14237, 28/10/18; demob. 29/1/19.
Broxholme, Cottingham, Nr. Hull.

✠ FEAVEARYEAR, Albert George
C/10620, 25/1/17; No. 20 O.C.B., 7/6/17; 7th Lond. R., 25/9/17; 2/Lieut.
Killed in action 5/9/18.

FEENY, Alfred Grosvenor
B/10324, 4/1/17, L/C.; R.F.A., C/S, 22/6/17; R.F.A., 18/11/17; F; 2/Lieut.
Dripshill House, Hanley Castle, Worcester.

FEGGETTER, James Young
C/12616, 18/2/18; No. 12 O.C.B., 5/7/18; North'd. Fus., 4/3/19; 2/Lieut.
9 Dilston Terrace, Gosforth, Newcastle-on-Tyne.

FEILD, Armistead Littlejohn
C/523, 18/11/10; dis. 29/10/12; rej. C/996, 5/8/14; Essex R., 7/8/14, att. Worc. R., M.G.C.; F,It; Major; M.C., Croce di Guerra.
c/o Messrs. Shaw, Wallace & Coy., Calcutta.

FELL, Charles Arthur
4/6/5/4884, 15/7/15; R.F.A., C/S, 17/3/16; R.F.A., 13/7/16; F; Lieut.; w,p.
47 Durham Road, East Finchley, N. 2.

FELL, Donald Edwin
6/5/6964, 22/10/15; No. 11 O.C.B., 7/5/16; M.G.C., 4/9/16; F; Lieut.; w.
Glen Royd, Beaumont Park, Huddersfield. (Now in California).

FELLOWES, Ernest
4/1/4740, 12/7/15; N. Lan. R., 5/9/15, emp. M. of Munitions; EA; Lieut.; M(1).
c/o Standard Bank of South Africa Ltd., Gwelo, South Africa.

FELLS, Herbert William
6/1/7010, 26/10/15; M.G.C., 4/8/16; F; Lieut.; w(2); M.C.
c/o Barclay's Bank Ltd., Saffron Walden, Essex.

FENDER, Percy George Herbert
B/1201, 14/9/14; R. Fus., 7/10/14, att. R.F.C.; Lieut.
85 Philbeach Gardens, S.W. 5.

FENN, Edward Percy
6/1/6280, 16/9/15; dis. med. unfit, 7/4/16.
83 Beauval Road, Dulwich.

FENN, Thomas Frederick
6/1/7838, 25/11/15; 20th Lond. R., 4/9/16, att. R.E.; F; Capt.; w; M.C., M(1).
693 Finchley Road, Childs Hill, N.W. 2.

FENNELL, John
6/5/7352, 10/11/15; R. Dub. Fus., 4/9/16, M.G.C.; F; Lieut.; W. Johnstown, Waterford.

FENNER, James Lionel
D/12883, 4/4/18; Household Bde. O.C.B., 10/5/18; Scots Gds., 3/2/19; 2/Lieut.
Lynn, Blenheim Road, Bickley, Kent.

FENNER, Raymond Henry George
6/4/7173, 3/11/15; R.F.C., C/S, 28/12/16; R.F.C., 26/2/17, R.A.F.; Lieut.
7 Glebe Road, West Tarring, Worthing.

✠ FENTON, Alan Hughes
6/3/6520, 30/9/15, L/C.; R.F.C., 2/6/16; 2/Lieut.
Missing believed killed 4/3/17.

FENTON, Harold
6/2/5430, 5/8/15; S. Lan. R., 9/12/15, R.A.F.; F; Lieut.; w.
42 Newry Park, Chester.

FENTUM, Charles Alfred
A/13150, 29/5/18; trfr. 14th Lond. R., 6/12/18.
Norville, 11 Addiscombe Road, Croydon.

FENWICK, Fairfax Edmund
D/10911, 26/3/17; dis. med. unfit, 2/5/18.
11 Uxbridge Road, Kingston-on-Thames.

FEORE, Cecil Alphonsus
6/5/8282, 10/12/15; No. 14 O.C.B., 28/8/16; Suff. R., 18/12/16, Essex R.; F; Lieut.
Norfolk House, 64 King's Road, Willesden Green, N.W. 10.

FEORE, Emmanuel Archibald
1/3451, 3/5/15; 9th Lond. R., 22/9/15, secd. M.G.C.; E,P,F; Lieut.
Norfolk House, 64 King's Road, Willesden Green, N.W. 10.

FEREMAN, Albert Edward
4/1/4600, 5/7/15; Midd'x. R., 16/12/15, R.F.C.; F; Lieut.; p.
Watchfield Parsonage, Watchfield, Shrivenham, Berkshire.

FERGUSON, Douglas
A/B/13949, 4/9/18; No. 24 O.C.B., 15/11/18; Tank Corps, 22/3/19; 2/Lieut.
1 Rosemount Terrace, East Somerville Place, Dundee.

FERGUSON, Francis Forbes Mackay
2/9679, 2/10/16; R.A., C/S, 12/1/17; R.F.A., 19/5/17; Lieut.
7 Hunton Hill, Erdington, Birmingham.

FERGUSON, George Coutts
A/11209, 7/5/17; R.E., C/S, 25/11/17; R.E., 22/2/18; 2/Lieut.
1 Fairfield Road, Crouch End, N. 8.

FERGUSON, Harold McLeod
Sq/3499, 1/5/15; R.F.A., 15/7/15, att. R.F.C.; Lieut.
3 Hogarth Road, Earls Court, S.W.

FERGUSON, Henry Corry
4/6/Sq/4924, 19/7/15, L/C.; R.A., C/S, 24/1/16; R.F.A., 16/6/16; F; Lieut.; w. St. Peter's Vicarage, Tunbridge Wells.

✠ FERGUSON, James Duncan
F/1837, 16/10/14, Sgt.; Essex R., 27/11/14; Lieut.; w.; M(1).
Died of wounds 27/10/16.

FERGUSON, John Hill
6/1/8283, 10/12/15; No. 14 O.C.B., 28/8/16; 7th Lond. R., 22/11/16, att. R. Fus.; F; 2/Lieut.; w.
Carlyle Club, 211 Piccadilly, W.

FERGUSON, Ronald
2/9631, 25/9/16, Cpl.; No. 14 O.C.B., 30/1/17; W. Rid. R., 25/4/17; F,It; Lieut.
Stock Exchange, E.C. 2.

APPENDIX II.—RECORDS OF RANK AND FILE.

FERGUSSON, Donald
4/6/C/3768, 27/5/15, Sgt.; R.A.O.C., 10/11/16; F; Lieut.
26 Morland Road, East Croydon, Surrey.

FERGUSSON, James Thomson
D/E/13825, 13/8/18; R.G.A., C/S, 2/10/18; R.G.A., 11/4/19; 2/Lieut.
Hudson Square, Montrose, Forfarshire, N.B.

FERGUSSON, John Herbert
4/5/4741, 12/7/15; S. Wales Bord., 20/11/15, emp. M. of Labour; Lieut.

✠ FERGUSSON, Norman Stuart
6/5698, 19/8/15.
Died 21/10/15.

FERGUSSON, Thomas Graeme
6/2/7201, 4/11/15; No. 7 O.C.B., 7/4/16; 13th Lond. R., 17/7/16.
26 Belsize Crescent, Hampstead, N.W.3.

FERNIE, Robert Samuel
6/4/7398, 12/11/15; No. 9 O.C.B., 8/3/16; Cam'n. Highrs., 6/7/16; F; Capt.
Dunedin, Stanwell Road, Penarth, South Wales.

FERNIHOUGH, Sidney
6/2/8479, 20/12/15; trfr. 16th Lond. R., 8/9/16.

FERNS, George Hubert
6/5/5751, 31/7/15, L/C.; R. Lanc. R., 27/12/15, emp. Tank Corps; F; Capt.; g.
Holford, The Lane, Bebington, Cheshire.

FERNYHOUGH, John
1/9638, 25/9/16; No. 14 O.C.B., 26/11/16; W. York. R., 27/3/17; F; 2/Lieut.; w(4); M.C.
30 Kingston Road, Didsbury, Manchester.

FERRERS, Hugh Norman
K/E/2349, 14/12/14; dis. 12/2/15.
Kualalumpur, Federated Malay States.

FERRIER, Reginald Willoughby
C/13321, 19/6/18; demob. 22/1/19.
77 Lancaster Road, Plashet Park, Forest Gate, E.7.

FERRIER, William
A/C/12190, 3/11/17; No. 10 O.C.B., 10/5/18; R. Highrs., 3/2/19; 2/Lieut.
69 Southesk Street, Brechin, Forfarshire.

✠ FERRIMAN, Frederick Samuel
6/1/5761, 21/8/15; Oxf. & Bucks. L.I., 1/6/16, R.F.C.; 2/Lieut.
Killed in action 7/6/17.

✠ FERRIS, Alfred William
6/1/6159, 11/9/15; 3rd Lond. R., 8/12/15; 2/Lieut.
Died of wounds 5/3/17.

FERRIS, William Hamilton
4/6/5/4925, 19/7/15; Dorset R., 7/6/16; I,E,P; Lieut.; M(1).
Burwood, 15 Sydenham Avenue, Sydenham, S.E.

FETHERSTONHAUGH, Lewis Holmes
A/Sq/13116, 24/5/18, L/C.; dis. med. unfit, 14/12/18; R.A.S.C., 2/1/15; F.
Grouse Lodge, Moate, Co. Westmeath, Ireland.

FETTES, James Dollery
6/5/8163, 6/12/15; R.E., C/S, 2/7/16; R.E., 15/9/16; F; Major; M.C.
Municipal Offices, Penang, Straits Settlements.

FEWINGS, Norman Cadle Trask
C/D/12067, 1/10/17; No. 18 O.C.B., 7/6/18; Dorset R., 5/2/19; 2/Lieut.
Ferndale, Bream, Gloucestershire.

FFINCH, Matthew Maule
B/12767, 15/3/18; R.A.F., 25/2/19; 2/Lieut.
Ifield Rectory, Gravesend, Kent.

FFOLLIOTT, Charles Henry
6/5/6797, 13/10/15; R. Innis. Fus., 4/8/16, secd. M.G.C.; F; Lieut.; g, w.
Headfort Place, Kills, Co. Meath, Ireland.

FICKLING, Frank Patrick Lawrence
A/13023, 3/5/18; trfr. 14th Lond. R., 6/12/18.
45 Norbury Crescent, Norbury, S.W.16.

FIDDES, Henry William
D/12915, 10/4/18; No. 22 O.C.B., 7/6/18; demob. 29/1/19.
Common Room, Lincoln's Inn, W.C.2.

FIELD, Albert Eric
6/Sq/7229, 5/11/15; trfr. R.E. Sigs., 12/5/16.
12 The Broadway, Woking, Surrey.

FIELD, Charles Austin
4/2/4019, 7/6/15, Sgt.; 2nd Lond. R., 4/8/16; F; Lieut.; p.
2 Carver Road, Herne Hill, S.E.24.

FIELD, Charles Geoffrey
6/5/7665, 22/11/15; No. 14 O.C.B., 28/8/16; L'pool. R., 18/12/16; F; 2/Lieut.; w.
Kennans House, Crown Court, Cheapside, E.C.2.

FIELD, Edward Percy Fairne
C/9942, 17/11/16; R.A., C/S, 30/3/17; R.F.A., 12/8/17; 2/Lieut.
Hazelwood, Dunton Green, Sevenoaks.

FIELD, Guy Cromwell
F/1896, 16/10/14; R. War. R., 16/12/14; F; Capt.; p.
Courtlands, Edgbaston, Birmingham.

FIELD, Harold Hayward
D/11864, 16/8/17; No. 3 O.C.B., 8/2/18; 21st Lond. R., 30/7/18; F; 2/Lieut.
77 Knatchbell Road, Camberwell, S.E.5.

✠ FIELD, Oliver
K/E/2489, 29/12/14; Durh. L.I., 27/4/15; 2/Lieut.
Killed in action 18/7/15.

✠ FIELD, Robert Alistair
K/E/2084, 13/11/14, L/C.; W. York. R., 6/3/15; Capt.; M.C., M(2).
Killed in action 2/4/17.

✠ FIELD, Roy Hammersley
D/11186, 4/5/17; trfr. 28th Lond. R., 14/9/17; F; Pte.
Died of wounds 29/6/18.

FIELD, Walter Harold
6/2/5298, 2/8/15; trfr. 25th Lond. R., 21/7/16.
122 Gough Road, Edgbaston, Birmingham.

✠ FIELDEN, Gilbert Sutcliffe
4/1/4538, 1/7/15; R. Lanc. R., 4/12/15; 2/Lieut.
Died 18/7/17.

✠ FIELDING, Gerald Trueman
6/9284, 3/2/16; R.A., C/S, 13/10/16; R.F.A., 29/4/17; F; 2/Lieut.
Killed in action 17/4/18.

FIELDING, Henry
6/5/9554, 28/2/16; No. 8 O.C.B., 4/8/16; R. Dub. Fus., 18/12/16; F; Lieut.; p.
Ulster Bank Ltd., Wexford.

FIELDING, John Felix
4/2967, 25/2/15; Suff. R., 25/4/15, att. R.F.C.; Lieut.
9 Claremont Gardens, Surbiton.

FILLERY, Thomas Carey
C/10193, 14/12/16; No. 14 O.C.B., 5/3/17; E. Kent R., 26/6/17; Lieut.; p.
Hawkhurst Lodge, Loose, Nr. Maidstone.

FILMER, John Russell
4/3/4497, 28/6/15; R.F.A., 30/10/15, R.A.F.; F; Lieut.; g.
Elmslie House, Sittingbourne, Kent.

FIMISTER, George Cadenhead
E/14004, 13/9/18; No. 22 O.C.B., 22/11/18; Gord. Highrs., 15/2/19; 2/Lieut.
Oporto British Club, Rua da Virtudes, Oporto.

FINCH, Colin Hales
D/10432, 10/1/17; No. 20 O.C.B., 7/6/17; Indian Army, 15/10/17.
9 Heyworth Street, Derby.

FINCH, Edmund Charles Trimmer
A/9833, 1/11/16; No. 14 O.C.B., 27/12/16; 8th Lond. R., 25/4/17, emp. M. of Labour; F; Lieut.
6 Semley Road, Brighton.

FINCH, Ernest Victor
B/2623, 7/1/15; Lan. Fus., 22/4/15; F; Capt.; w(2); M.C.
73 Oakwood Court, Kensington, W.14. (Now in Straits Settlements.)

FINCH, Fred James
A/D/11258, 14/5/17, Sgt.; dis. med. unfit, 16/5/19.
Eldra, Landscore Road, Teignmouth, Devon.

FINCH, George Fladgate
B/666, 19/11/12; Rif. Brig., 11/9/14; F; Capt.; w; M(2).
144 Inverness Terrace, W.2.

FINCH, George Frederick
6/1/7289, 8/11/15, L/C.; Glouc. R., 4/8/16, att. M.G.C.; F; Lieut.; Inv.
7 Crouch Hall Road, Crouch End, N.8.

FINCH, James Bass
6/Sq/7764, 23/11/15; No. 1 O.C.B., 6/9/16; R.F.C., 25/1/17, R.A.F.; F; Flt. Cmdr.; w.
1 St. John's Road, Golders Green, N.W.11.

FINCH, Sidney Hugh Powell
6/4/Sq/8826, 10/1/16; R.F.A., C/S, 12/1/17; trfr. R.F.A., 9/7/17.
9 Crockerton Road, Wandsworth Common, S.W.

APPENDIX II.—RECORDS OF RANK AND FILE.

FINCHAM, Francis James Michael
C/14114, 9/10/18; demob. 19/12/18.
St. Winifred's, Orpington, Kent.

FINCHAM, Herbert Cyril
B/12841, 23/3/18; No. 20 O.C.B., 20/9/18; E. Kent R., 17/3/19; 2/Lieut.
St. Winifred's, Orpington, Kent.

FINDING, Hugh Lambert
A/9826, 1/11/16; No. 14 O.C.B., 27/12/16; Camb. R., 27/3/17; Lieut.
74 Foulser Road, Upper Tooting.

✠ FINDLAY, Arthur Bertram
E/1496, 1/10/14, L/C.; K.R. Rif. C., 7/12/14; Lieut.
Killed in action 30/7/15.

✠ FINDLAY, Cyril Olney
A/9806, 30/10/16; No. 14 O.C.B., 27/12/16; Som. L.I., 25/4/17; 2/Lieut.
Died of wounds 17/10/17.

FINDLAY, Joseph Duncan
D/13687, 29/7/18; demob. 21/12/18.
10 Wigan Lane, Wigan.

FINDLAY-SMITH, Gordon Wynne
B/1267, 23/9/14; National Reserve, 27/10/14.
64 Shooters Hill Road, S.E. 3.

FINLAN, Reginald Patrick
D/12983, 25/4/18; No. 18 O.C.B., 20/9/18; E. Lan. R., 17/3/19; 2/Lieut.
83 South Circular Road, Kilmainham, Dublin.

✠ FINLAY, Edward Norman Alison
C/681, 24/1/13; Rif. Brig., 1/7/15; 2/Lieut.
Killed in action 4/7/16.

FINLAY, Harry William
4/5/4742, 12/7/15; 13th Lond. R., 15/12/15; F; Capt.; M.B.E.
Torwood, Nairn.

FINLAY, Thomas Victor William
C/13322, 19/6/18; demob. 29/1/19.
Drumadd House, Armagh.

FINLAYSON, Raymond Alfred
A/2783, 6/2/15; Sea. Highrs., 24/4/15; F; Lieut.; w.
72 Eaton Park Road, Palmers Green, N. 13.

FINN, Norman
A/11196, 7/5/17; No. 14 O.C.B., 10/8/17; R. Suss. R., 27/11/17; It; 2/Lieut.; Croce di Guerra.
9 Elmwood Avenue, Palmers Green, N. 13.

FINN, Wilfrid William
C/13284, 14/6/18; demob. 24/1/19.
32 Railway Terrace, Fitzwilliam, Nr. Wakefield, Yorkshire.

FINNEY, Harold John Stuart
4/4645, 5/7/15; dis. Med. unfit, 22/5/16.
11 Lockett Street, Birches Head, Hanley, N. Staffordshire.

FIRMAN, William Edward Harley
C/10837, 5/3/17; No. 14 O.C.B., 5/7/17; Som. L.I., 30/10/17; 2/Lieut.
14 Burnaby Gardens, Gunnersbury, W. 4.

FIRTH, Eric Harold
6/5/8056, 1/12/15; Yorks. L.I., 4/9/16; F; Lieut.; Inv.
19 The Broadway, Worthing, Sussex.

FIRTH, Fred Cunningham
F/Sq/2751, 21/1/15, L/C.; Lan. Huss., 16/9/15; Lieut.
Kenmure, Blundellsands, Liverpool.

FIRTH, Samuel Dearden
6/2/9348, 7/2/16; R.F.A., C/S, 27/10/16; R.G.A., 19/12/16; Lieut.

FISH, Bernard Weston
H/2006, 2/11/14; N. Lan. R., 9/1/15; F; Capt.; w; M.C.
Conservative Club, St. James Street, S.W. 1.

FISH, Ernest Gordon
6/Sq/8203, 7/12/15; Berks. Yeo., 21/1/16, att. M.G.C.; Lieut.
3 Corfton Road, Ealing, W. 5. (Now in Uganda).

✠ FISH, Jack
1/3596, 13/5/15; Som. L.I., 21/8/15, Worc. R.; 2/Lieut.
Killed in action 22/7/16.

✠ FISHER, Arthur James
6/6980, 23/10/15; R.F.C., 2/6/16; 2/Lieut.
Killed in action 25/10/16.

FISHER, Ernest Arthur
D/2588, 4/1/15; R.G.A., 16/4/15; Lieut.

FISHER, Fred Metcalfe
B/10719, 12/2/17, L/C.; A.S.C., C/S, 1/9/17; R.A.S.C., 27/10/17; 2/Lieut.
Holby Dene, Beeston, Nottinghamshire.

✠ FISHER, George William
6/3/9311, 4/2/16, Cpl.; No. 14 O.C.B., 26/11/16; Suff. R., 28/2/17; 2/Lieut.
Killed in action 18/11/17.

✠ FISHER, Harold
6/1/7290, 8/11/15; R.E., 14/4/16; Lieut.; w(2).
Died of wounds 14/4/18.

FISHER, James McIntosh
D/12886, 5/4/18; No. 22 O.C.B., 7/6/18; R. Scots., 12/2/19; 2/Lieut.
39 Scotland Street, Edinburgh.

✠ FISHER, John Wilfred
A/1037, 26/8/14; Notts. & Derby. R., 5/9/14; F; Capt.; w(3); D.S.O.. M(1).
Died of wounds 8/7/16.

FISHER, Laurence Coulthard Sealy
C/12237, 19/11/17; R.E., C/S, 10/3/18; trfr. 14th Lond. R., 6/12/18, Gord. Highrs.; Pte.
45 High Street, Fareham, Hampshire. (Now in Assam.)

FISHER, Lionel Robert D'Arcy
H/2043, 9/11/14; Herts. R., 6/3/15; Lieut.; w; M.C., M(1).
Egremont House, Sudbury, Middlesex.

FISHER, Maurice
A/13024, 3/5/18, L/C.; demob. 23/1/19.
Greycourt, Idle, Bradford, Yorkshire.

FISHER, Murray Montague
2/3171, 3/4/15; R.G.A., 21/4/15; F; Major.
c/o National Provincial Bank Ltd., Newark, Notts.

✠ FISHER, Norman Hill
4/2/4833, 10/7/15; N. Lan. R., 8/1/16; F; Lieut.
Died of wounds 16/4/17.

FISHER, Percy
F/2956, 22/2/15; North'd. Fus., 12/5/15, Indian Army; F,I; Major.
Roseberry, Watford, Hertfordshire.

✠ FISHER, Percy Harold
D/2782, 25/1/15; R. Suss. R., 29/4/15, att. M.G.C.; 2/Lieut.
Died of wounds 4/7/16.

FISHER, Robert
6/3/9312, 4/2/16; No. 14 O.C.B., 26/11/16; Suff. R., 27/3/17, att. K. Af. Rif.; F,Germ.EA; Lieut.; w(2).
Tower House, Aldeburgh-on-Sea.

FISHER, Ronald Aylmer
B/804, 13/7/14; dis. 22/10/14.

FISHER, Stanley Howe
K/C/2195, 26/11/14, L/C.; R.E., 27/2/15; F; Major; w; M.C., M(5).
Elmsthorpe, 37 Barrington Road, S.W. 9.

FISHER, Walter Donald
6/7731, 22/11/15; R.F.A., C/S, 9/6/16; R.F.A., 8/9/16; Lieut.
Westfield, Evesham.

✠ FISHER, Wilfrid Frederick
4/3342, 22/4/15; R. Suss. R., 10/7/15; 2/Lieut.; w.
Killed in action 24/7/17.

FISHER, William Philips
6/3/9313, 4/2/16, L/C.; No. 14 O.C.B., 26/11/16; Suff. R., 28/2/17, att. K. Af. Rif.; F,Germ.EA; Lieut.
c/o National Bank of South Africa Ltd., Circus Place, London Wall. E.C. 3.

FISHER, William Thomas
6/5/7584, 18/11/15; R.F.A., C/S, 31/3/16; R.F.A., 6/7/16; F; Lieut.
Woodford, Garth Drive, Mossley Hill, Liverpool.

FISHER-BROWN, Marcus Arthur
1/3150, 31/3/15; R.F.A., 15/7/15; R.A.F.; F; Lieut.
The Rectory, Folkton, Scarborough.

FISHWICK, John Frankland
6/3/8519, 29/12/15, L/C.; No. 14 O.C.B., 28/8/16; R. Suss. R., 22/11/16; F; Lieut.
The Grange, Eastbourne.

FISHWICK, Victor Charles
6/2/8057, 1/12/15; No. 8 O.C.B., 4/8/16; Bedf. R., 21/11/16 R.E.; F; Lieut.; w.
S.E. Agricultural College, Wye, Kent.

FISK, Victor Grantham
5/6/7917, 29/11/15; No. 14 O.C.B., 22/11/16; Lieut.
42 Bell Road, Hounslow.

APPENDIX II.—RECORDS OF RANK AND FILE.

FISKE, *Cyril Ernest*
4/3/Sq/4838, 14/7/15; R.A., C/S, 29/1/16; R.F.A., 6/7/16; F;
Capt.; Croix de Guerre with Palm.
9 *Wharton Street, Bungay, Suffolk.*

FISON, *Alexander Key*
A/1278, 23/9/14; Essex R., 27/11/14; Capt.; w(3); M.C.,
Legion of Honour (5th Class), Croix de Guerre.
147 *Dartmouth Road, Cricklewood, N.W. 2.*

FISON, *Francis Geoffrey*
K/D/2462, 28/12/14, Cpl.; K.R. Rif. C., 8/4/15; F; Capt.;
w, p; M.C., M(1).
Boarzell, Hurst Green, Sussex.

FITCH, Sir *Cecil Edwin*
F/2681, 14/1/15; Glouc. R., 24/3/15, Worc. R., R.W. Fus.; F;
Lt.-Col.; K.B.E., M(1).
1 *Garden Court, Temple, E.C. 4.*

☩ FITCH, *Douglas*
4/4743, 12/7/15; R.F.A., C/S, 31/3/16; R.F.A., 11/8/16; F;
2/Lieut.
Killed in action 16/10/17.

FITCH, *Horace Francis*
B/11371, 28/5/17; No. 10 O.C.B., 5/10/17; 8th Lond. R., 26/2/18,
att. 22nd Lond. R.; F; Lieut.
455 *New Cross Road, S.E. 14.*

FITCH, *Richard Sherman*
D/B/13807, 9/8/18; No. 24 O.C.B., 13/11/18; Tank Corps,
22/3/19; 2/Lieut.
25 *Holland Villas Road, Kensington, W.*

FITTON, *John Hall*
B/11320, 21/5/17; No. 14 O.C.B., 5/10/17; York. & Lanc. R.,
26/2/18, att. Yorks. L.I.; F; 2/Lieut.
Halliwell, Tower Road, Darlington.

FITZ-GERALD, *Eric Yarnold*
Sq/1957, 26/10/14; Herts. Yeo., 18/3/15, R.F.C., R.A.F.; E,S,F;
Lieut.
University College, Gower Street, W.C. 1.

FITZGERALD, *Gerald Milnes*
Sq/140, 18/4/08; 3rd Cty. of Lond. Yeo., 23/2/12, M.G.C.;
E,G,S,P,F; Capt.; w.
King's Farm, Little Shelford, Cambridgeshire.

☩ FITZGERALD, *Gerald Thomas*
A/868, 4/8/14; Durh. L.I., 12/9/14; F; Capt.; w.
Killed in action 3/12/15.

FITZGERALD, *John Herbert Wilson*
D/10287, 1/1/17; No. 14 O.C.B., 7/6/17; Dental Surgeon,
31/7/17; Capt.
42 *High Street, Ventnor, Isle of Wight.*

FITZGERALD, *Walter James*
6/2/7442, 15/11/15; trfr. 14th Lond. R., 2/5/16.

☩ FITZGERALD, *William Herbert Leslie Vesey-*
F/2718, 18/1/15; L/C.; Devon. R., 2/6/15; 2/Lieut.
Killed in action 14/8/16.

FITZ-PATRICK, *John*
D/1458, 29/9/14; Manch. R., 7/1/15; Capt.; w.

FITZPATRICK, *William Henry Mulleneux*
B/C/D/12217, 15/11/17, Sgt.; demob. 9/5/19.
Midland Adelphi Hotel, Liverpool.

FITZPATRICK-ROBERTSON, *Antony Mario*
6/4/9213, 31/1/16; No. 7 O.C.B., 11/8/16; Conn. Rang., 18/12/16,
att. R. Dub. Fus.; Lieut.; w.

☩ FLANAGAN, *Joseph Samuel*
4/2/4444, 26/6/15; 20th Lond. R., 28/11/15; F; Lieut.
Killed in action 23/8/18.

FLAVELL, *Thomas*
C/12654, 27/2/18; R.F.A., C/S, 17/5/18; R.G.A., 3/4/19;
2/Lieut.
68 *Hill Street, Hinckley, Leicestershire.*

☩ FLEETWOOD, *Cyril Percy*
4/5061, 24/7/15, L/C.; 9th Lond. R., 5/10/15; 2/Lieut.; p.
Died of wounds 12/7/16.

FLEMING, *David Gibson*
4/2/3264, 15/4/15; Suff. R., 8/7/15, Essex R., Gord. Highrs.;
E,F; Major; w; M.C.
Fontenailles, Cornillé, Maine et Loire, France.

FLEMING, *Edward Lowe*
6/5/6145, 9/9/15; Bord. R., 26/1/16; F; Lieut.; p.
Barco Bank, Penrith, Cumberland.

FLEMING, *Edward Willis.* See WILLIS-FLEMING, E.

FLEMING, *James*
B/D/12211, 12/11/17; R.F.A., C/S, 15/3/18; R.G.A., 2/9/18;
2/Lieut. 16 *Alexandra Crescent, Hyde Park Road, Leeds.*

FLEMING, *William Charles Hogan*
A/11027, 11/4/17; No. 14 O.C.B., 5/10/17; Ches. R., 26/2/18;
2/Lieut. 139 *Woodwarde Road, East Dulwich, S.E. 22.*

☩ FLEMMING, *Douglas Sidney*
C/1308, 26/9/14, L/C.; R. Lanc. R., 28/1/15; 2/Lieut.
Died of wounds 1/6/17.

FLENLEY, *Denis*
D/A/11822, 9/8/17; R.F.A., C/S, 4/2/18; R.G.A., 26/8/18;
2/Lieut. 164 *Anfield Road, Liverpool.*

FLETCHER, *Herbert Reginald*
B/10923, 26/3/17, L/C.; R.F.A., C/S, 28/12/17; R.G.A., 17/6/18;
F; 2/Lieut. 10 *Mayfield Avenue, Victoria Park, Cardiff.*

FLETCHER, *Ian Archibald*
A/407, 28/4/09; dis. 27/3/10.
Caledonian Club, S.W.

FLETCHER, *John Allan*
A/13117, 24/5/18; No. 1 O.C.B., 8/11/18, No. 3 O.C.B.; Leic
R., 18/2/19; 2/Lieut.
5 *Albion Terrace, Hartlepool.*

☩ FLETCHER, *John Holland Ballett*
Sq/115, 18/4/08; 7th Lond. R., 25/11/10; F; Lieut.
Died of wounds 13/5/15.

FLETCHER, *John Leslie*
C/9952, 20/11/16; No. 14 O.C.B., 30/1/17; Dorset R., 29/5/17,
att. Som. L.I. and R.A.F.; I,P; Lieut.
17 *Reservoir Road, Brockley, S.E.4.*

FLETCHER, *John Sidney*
C/D/12068, 1/10/17; R.F.A., C/S, 15/3/18; R.G.A., 3/2/19;
2/Lieut.
c/o Messrs. *Carment & Coy., 2 Hill Street, Edinburgh. (Now in F.M.S.)*

FLETCHER, *Lyle Clark*
C/14198, 21/10/18; trfr. K.R. Rif. C., 7/4/19.
88 *Prenton Road, East Birkenhead.*

FLETCHER, *Maurice Purcell*
D/Sq/13003, 30/4/18; No. 2 Cav. C.S., 7/11/18; demob. 13/1/19.
c/o Miss *Purcell, Astoria, West Drive, Cleveleys, Lancashire.*

FLETCHER, *Nigil Henry Nevil*
6/4/D/6920, 19/10/15, Sgt.; R.N.A.S., 30/7/17; It,S,SR; Lieut.
Lower Ravenhurst, Harborne, Birmingham. (Now in Burma.)

FLETCHER, *Reginald Gordon*
D/12875, 3/4/18, Sgt.; demob. 5/7/19.
102 *Grosvenor Avenue, Carshalton, Surrey.*

FLETCHER, *Tom Walter*
A/E/13151, 29/5/18; No. 22 O.C.B., 22/11/18; L'pool. R.,
15/2/19; 2/Lieut.
33 *Green Leys Road, Liverpool.*

FLETCHER, *Victor Robert*
C/501, 1/11/10, L/C.; 21st Lond. R., 23/9/14; F; Capt.
Norwood Lodge, Caterham Valley.

FLETCHER, *Walter Archibald*
6/3/7331, 9/11/15; Notts. & Derby. R., 4/9/16; F; Capt.; w.
Oxenhope, Carew Road, Wallington, Surrey.

☩ FLETT, *Arthur David*
6/9090, 24/1/16; No. 9 O.C.B., 8/3/16; R. Scots, 3/8/16; Lieut.
Killed in action 9/4/17.

FLIGHT, *Walter Claude*
K/Sq/2595, 24/12/14; R.A.S.C., 1/3/15; Capt.

☩ FLINDT, *Leighton Harold Richard Edward*
2/4070, 7/6/15; N. Staff. R., 7/10/15, att. Leic. R.; 2/Lieut.
Died of wounds 4/10/16.

FLINN, *Frank Bishop*
C/D/14265, 6/11/18; trfr. Gord. Highrs., 29/5/19.
Mynthurst, Speen, Nr. Princes Risborough.

FLINN, *Sydney Torbet*
6/5/6042, 3/9/15, L/C.; No. 11 O.C.B., 7/5/16; Ches. R.,
24/10/16; F; Lieut.; g; M(1).
Briar Bush, Street Lane, Roundhay, Leeds.

FLINT, *Eric Charles M.*
Sq/1006, 6/8/14; Suff. Yeo., 12/9/14, secd. M.G.C.; G,E,P;
Major; D.S.O., M(1).
Grafton House West, Sandgate, Kent.

FLINT, *Francis Carey*
4/3769, 27/5/15, Cpl.; Notts. & Derby. R., 17/9/15; F; Lieut.; w.
Merridale, Stoneygate, Leicester.

APPENDIX II.—RECORDS OF RANK AND FILE.

FLINT, Frederick Nelson LaFargue
6/2/5556, 12/8/15; Linc. R., 22/1/16; F; Lieut.; w.
The High House, Orford, Suffolk.

FLINT, Harold Cecil
6/4/8349, 13/12/15; No. 14 O.C.B.; Notts. & Derby. R., 22/11/16; F; Lieut.; w(2). Merridale, Stoneygate, Leicester.

✠ FLINT, Wilfred Ernest
4/4825, 13/7/15, L/C.; Notts. & Derby. R., 17/9/15; F; 2/Lieut.
Killed in action 1/7/16.

FLINT, William Fielder
B/13416, 1/7/18; demob. 5/2/19.
11 Serle Street, Lincoln's Inn, W.C. 2.

FLOOD, Frederic Charles
6/5/5282, 31/7/15; N. Lan. R., 4/9/16; F; Lieut.; g.
49 Kings Court Road, Streatham, S.W. 16.

FLOOD, John Ernest William
C/11055, 16/4/17; R.G.A., C/S, 31/8/17; R.G.A., 6/1/18; F; Lieut.; w. Colonial Office, Downing Street, S.W. 1

FLOOD, Stanley John
6/2/6888, 18/10/15; N. Lan. R., 25/9/16; F; Capt.; w.
19 Kevenming Road, Shanghai, China.

FLOWER, Clement Bamborough
6/5/6454, 27/9/15, L/C.; Rif. Brig., 6/7/16; Lieut.
5 Yacht Lane, Royal Cornwall Yacht Club, Falmouth.

FLOWER, Leonard Robert
D/12105, 11/10/17; Tank Corps C/S, 25/1/18; Tank Corps 8/10/18; 2/Lieut.
Rua dos Queimados 20, Villa Nova de Gaya, Portugal.

FLOWER, Walter Maurice
D/Sq/11823, 9/8/17; No. 1 Cav. C/S, 28/2/18; R. Regt. of Cav., 28/8/18; 2/Lieut. Chilmark Salisbury.

✠ FLOWERS, Humphrey French
2/3579, 10/5/15; R.F.A., 5/8/15; R.A.F.; F; Capt. & Flt. Cmdr.
Killed in action 14/10/18.

FLUX, William Charles
B/11979, 10/9/17, L/C.; Tank Corps C/S, 18/1/18; Tank Corps, 8/10/18; 2/Lieut.

✠ FLYNN, John Hoskins
6/5/7140, 2/11/15; No. 11 O.C.B., 16/5/16; R.F.C., 4/9/16; 2/Lieut. Killed in action 30/9/17.

FOÀ, Aubrey Henriques
Sq/559, 5/4/11; dis. 8/10/13; 5th Lancers, 15/9/15, M.G C.; F,E,P; Lieut.
Holywell Park, Wrotham, Kent. (Now in India.)

FOAKES, Harry Charles
B/11305, 21/5/17; No. 24 O.C.B., 10/11/17; Tank Corps, 27/3/18; F; 2/Lieut. c/o Great Central Railway, London, N.W. 1

FOARD, Francis Cyril
6/6455, 27/9/15; dis. 13/10/15.

FOCKE, Eberhard
Sq/569, 5/6/11; dis. 30/10/11.

FOERS, Hardwicke Kenyon
6/5/8595, 3/1/16; R.A., C/S, 13/10/16; R.F.A., 2/2/17; F; Lieut.; w. Edenfield, Moorgate Grove, Rotherham.

FOGDEN, Clifford Albert Edward
6/1/9162, 26/1/16; R.F.A., C/S, 4/8/16; R.G.A., 1/11/16; F; Capt. 146 Knights Hill, West Norwood, S.E. 27.

FOLEY, Frank Edward
6/4/8960, 17/1/16, L/C.; No. 14 O.C.B., 27/9/16; Herts. R, 24/1/17, att. N. Staff. R., Intelligence Corps; F; Capt.; w; M(1).
Brendon House, Bernham-on-Sea, Somerset. (Now in Germany.)

FOLEY, Timothy Vincent
B/13600, 24/7/18; trfr. K.R. Rif. C., 7/4/19.
27 Hanover Road, Willesden, N.W. 10.

FOLKARD, Harold
C/10144, 8/12/16; Garr. O.C.B., 23/4/17; dis. med. unfit, 20/8/17.
Copford Green, Nr. Colchester.

FOOKS, Sidney Frank
4/5/4849, 15/7/15; 12th Lond. R., 15/11/15; Lieut.; M.C.
49 Meadow Road, Salisbury.

FOORD, Herbert Quallett
D/1405, 29/9/14; R.W. Kent. R., 10/2/15, att. R.W. Surr. R.; F; Capt. Denham House, Bromley, Kent.

✠ FOORD-KELSEY, William Beverley
Sq/228, 15/5/08; dis. 14/5/09; R.F.A.; Lieut.
Killed in action 24/9/18.

FOOT, Howard Owen
4/2/4570, 1/7/15, Cpl.; R. Lanc. R., 27/11/15, att. Indian Army; Lieut.; w.

FOOT, Robert William
B/69, 10/4/08; dis. 9/4/13; Calcutta Light Horse, -/11/13; I,F; Major; O.B.E., M.C., M(2).
14a Chester House, Eccleston Place, S.W. 1

FOOTE, John Dick
C/12565, 6/2/18; No. 9 O.C.B., 5/7/18; R. Sco. Fus., 2/3/19; 2/Lieut. 17 Craigmillar Road, Langside, Glasgow.

FOOTMAN, David John
F/1788, 16/10/14; R. Berks. R., 13/10/15; F; Capt.; w; M.C., Croix de Guerre, M(1). Lambourn, Berkshire. (Now in Egypt.)

✠ FORAN, Edward Cornelius
6/5/6907, 18/10/15, L/C.; R. Muns. Fus., 4/8/16; 2/Lieut.
Killed in action 28/12/17

✠ FORBES, Alexander Bruce
A/11645, 12/7/17; No. 19 O.C.B., 9/11/17; Arg. & Suth'd. Highrs., 26/3/18; 2/Lieut. Died of wounds 29/10/18.

FORBES, Arthur Harold
4/5/6/5141, 26/7/15, Sgt.; R.A.S.C., 10/4/16; S; Staff Capt.; Inv.; M(1). 2 Pump Court, Temple, E.C. 4.

✠ FORBES, Arthur John
6/1/6064, 6/9/15, L/C.; Lovats Scouts, 12/12/15; Lieut.
Killed in action 21/10/17.

FORBES, Charles Edward
6/Sq/8106, 2/12/15; dis. med. unfit, 8/8/16.
Woodhead, Kinloss Forres, N.B.

FORBES, James Alexander
B/9867, 6/11/16; No. 14 O.C.B., 6/4/17; R. Lanc. R., 31/7/17, S. Lan. R.; F; Lieut.; w. 2 Church Crescent, Muswell Hill, N. 10.

FORBES, Lester Harry
A/11968, 5/9/17; R.F.C., C/S, 26/11/17; R.F.C., 23/1/18, R.A.F.; Lieut.
c/o Miss D. Forbes, Ladies Imperial Club, Dover Street, W.

FORBES, Robert Sain
Sq/1949, 24/10/14, Sgt.; R.A.S.C., 1/7/15; Capt.; M(1).
71 Brodrick Road, Wandsworth Common, S.W.

FORBES, Ronald Bethune
6/2/8758, 6/1/16; No. 14 O.C.B., 28/8/16; W. York. R., 22/11/16; F; Capt.; w; M.C.
c/o Union Bank of Australia, Collins Street, Melbourne, Victoria, Australia.

FORBES, Sydney Frederick
6/2/7257, 8/11/15, Cpl.; 7th Lond. R., 23/6/16; Capt.
c/o F. Polse Esq., 45 St. James Road, Wandsworth Common.

FORBES, William
Sq/164, 18/4/08; dis. 17/4/10.

FORD, Charles Bell
K/2524, 31/12/14; R. Fus., 5/1/15, Indian Army; Capt.; w.

FORD, Ernest Arthur
6/3/5460, 7/8/15; 19th Lond. R., 2/11/15; F; Lieut.; w, g.
79 St. Gabriels Road, Cricklewood, N.W. 2.

FORD, Frank Gilbert
A/12436, 22/1/18; No. 15 O.C.B., 7/6/18; Hamps. R., 4/2/19; 2/Lieut. 33 Cowley Road, South Hackney, E. 9.

FORD, Harry Spry
6/3/7044, 28/10/15, L/C.; A.S.C., C/S, 17/4/16; R.A.S.C., 21/5/16; Lieut.; M.B.E.
4c Montague Manssions, Portman Square, W.

✠ FORD, Kenneth George Haslam
A/719, 23/6/13; dis. 31/3/14; Ches. R., -/9/14; Lieut.
Died of wounds 1/12/15

FORD, Percy George
A/12513, 31/1/18; Sigs. C/S, 14/6/18; R.E., 4/2/19; 2/Lieut.
28 Latchmere Road, Kingston-on-Thames.

164

APPENDIX II.—RECORDS OF RANK AND FILE.

✠ FORD, *Percy Hadley*
6/5/C/9535, 18/2/16; No. 14 O.C.B., 30/10/16; Bedf. R., 28/2/17; Lieut. Died 2/12/20.

FORD, *Richard Hugh*
D/13903, 26/8/18; trfr. K.R. Rif. C., 25/4/19, R.A.O.C.; L/C.
Wigginton House, Tamworth, Staffordshire.

✠ FORD, *Robert Englefield*
4/1/5009, 22/7/15; N. Lan. R., 27/12/15; Capt.; w
Died of wounds 3/4/17.

FORD, *Ronald Mylne*
C/1146, 14/9/14; S. Wales Bord., 8/10/15; F; Lieut.; w; Croix de Guerre. 1 Broadlands Road, Highgate, N.

FORD, *Thomas Alfred*
A/10032, 29/11/16; R.F.C., C/S, 4/5/17; R.F.C., 14/6/17, R.A.F.; F; Lieut.; w.
11 Appleton Gate, Newark, Nottinghamshire.

FORD, *Thomas Francis*
D/A/12975, 24/4/18; No. 24 O.C.B., 15/11/18, No. 11 O.C.B.; General List, 8/3/19; 2/Lieut.
1124 Fillmore Street, Sanfrancisco.

FORD, *William*
D/12976, 24/4/18; demob. 23/1/19. Allanford, Clydebank.

FORD, *Wolfram Onslow*
Sq/2031, 9/11/14; Oxf. & Bucks. L.I., 9/11/14; Lieut.; w.
New Orchard, Wendover, Buckinghamshire.

FORDE, *Theophilus James Elliott*
6/Sq/9107, 24/1/16; No. 2 Cav. C/S, 5/1/17; R. Regt. of Cav., 30/4/17; Lieut. The Rectory, Dundrum, Co. Down.

FORDHAM, *Edward King*
3/3304, 19/4/15, Cpl.; R.A.S.C., 15/9/15; F; Lieut.
Elbrook House, Ashwell, Baldock, Hertfordshire.

✠ FORDHAM, *Reginald Frederick*
4/2/4040, 7/6/15; Essex R., 10/10/15; Capt.
Killed in action 5/11/17.

FORDYCE, *John Frederick Dingwall*
6/3/6713, 9/10/15; dis. to Indian Training Coll., 19/4/16; Indian Army, 23/7/17; Lieut. 18 Brunswick Road, Kingston Hill.

FORGET, *Charles Anthony*
6/Sq/9349, 7/2/16; A.S.C., C/S, 27/10/16; R.A.S.C., 20/12/16; Germ EA,E,F; Lieut.
c/o Sres Romero, Hinds, Sarmiento 459, Buenos Aires, Argentina.

FORREST, *Herbert Leonard*
6/Sq/C/6340, 19/9/15; No. 14 O.C.B., 30/10/16; Lovats Scouts, 28/2/17, att. K.O. Sco. Bord.; F; 2/Lieut.
20 Adamson Road, Swiss Cottage.

FORREST, *John*
A/10945, 29/3/17; No. 11 O.C.B., 5/7/17; S. Staff. R., 30/10/17, att. M.G.C.; Lieut. 20 Lilley Road, Fairfield, Liverpool.

FORREST, *Neville Blair*
C/13187, 3/6/18; No. 11 O.C.B., 24/1/19; demob. 4/2/19.
c/o Mrs. Bassett, Crowhurst, Sussex. (Now in Japan.)

FORROW, *Arthur Ernest*
A/13044, 7/5/18; No. 5 O.C.B., 8/11/18, Nos. 20 & 12 O.C.B.; Midd'x. R., 16/3/19; 2/Lieut.
Hildercroft, 100 Fox Lane, Palmers Green, N. 13.

FORSAYETH, *Richard Martin*
2/3334, 21/4/15; 18th Lond. R., 15/9/15; 2/Lieut.

FORSDYKE, *Edgar John*
Sq/233, 18/5/08; dis. 17/5/10; R.F.A., -/9/14; F,S,P; Capt.; Inv.
British Museum, W.C. 1.

FORSELL, *Alfred Norman*
6/Sq/8827, 10/1/16; R.A., C/S, 7/8/16; R.F.A., 3/12/16; 2/Lieut.
Thurnby, Leicester.

FORSELL, *Francis Meadows*
6/3/Sq/7141, 2/11/15; R.A., C/S, 7/8/16; R.F.A., 3/12/16; F; Capt.; M.C. Thurnby, Leicester.

FORSELL, *Thomas Edgar*
B/12768, 15/3/18; No. 1 O.C.B., 6/9/18; demob.
Thurnby, Leicester.

FORSHAW, *Cyril Henry*
6/5/5224, 30/7/15; N. Lan. R., 8/1/16; F; Lieut.; w.
Park Edge, Holden Road, Kersal, Manchester.

FORSHAW, *Harold Lionel*
B/10764, 19/2/17; R.F.C., C/S, 16/4/17; trfr. 10th L'pool. R., 8/6/17. 2 Drummond Road, Hoylake, Cheshire.

FORSHAW, *John Henry*
4/6/5/4962, 19/7/15; R.E., 25/11/15; F; Capt.; w; M.C.
Merridale, Burscough Road, Ormskirk, Lancashire.

FORSTER, *Francis*
A/9804, 30/10/16; R.A.O.C., 14/2/17; Capt.

FORSTER, *Harold John*
C/12600, 13/2/18; No. 23 O.C.B., 5/7/18; Midd'x. R., 3/3/19; 2/Lieut. 162 Coombe Lane, Wimbledon, S.W. 19.

FORSTER, *John Frederic*
6/3/6395, 23/9/15; Bord. R., 7/6/16, R.A.F.; F; Lieut.; w.
14 Lawn Terrace, Silloth, Cumberland.

FORSTER, *John Newton*
6/4/5621, 16/8/15; dis. med. unfit, 31/3/16.
Chidlock Hill, Bridport, Dorset.

FORSTER, *Richard Helden*
B/629, 29/3/12; dis. med. unfit, 4/9/14; Midd'x. R., 6/11/14, att. York. R.; F,NR; Major; M.C., Order of St. Anne (2nd Class, Russia). 32 South Croxted Road, Dulwich, S.E. 21.

FORSTER, *Robert Burke*
6/3/9285, 3/2/16; trfr. M.G.C., 6/12/16.
Elva Villa, Lisdoonvarnee, Co. Clare, Ireland.

FORSYTH, *Graham*
B/11079, 18/4/17, L/C.; R.A., C/S, 7/9/17; R.F.A., 1/3/18; F; Lieut. 10 Esslemont Road, Edinburgh.

✠ FORSYTH, *William Matthew*
4/1/5032, 22/7/15; No. 14 O.C.B.; Midd'x. R., 24/10/16; 2/Lieut. Died of wounds 20/4/17.

FORT, *Harold Mellor*
6/5/7918, 29/11/15; No. 14 O.C.B., 28/8/16; Manch. R., 22/11/16, att. R. Suss. R., secd., R.E.; F; Lieut.
305 Park Road, Oldham.

FORTESCUE, *Albert Edward Muspratt*
D/1463, 29/9/14; dis. 9/2/15. 34 & 35 High Holborn, W.C.

FORTESCUE, *George Alan*
B/1305, 26/9/14; Essex R., 19/2/15; Capt.

FORTH, *Charles Ogilvie*
6/8058, 1/12/15; Lovats Scouts, 17/4/16, Indian Army; Capt.

FORTUNE, *Clifford Dudley*
B/13472, 5/7/18; trfr. 14th Lond. R., 6/12/18.
73 Westover Road, Wandsworth Common, S.W. 18.

FORWELL, *William Lynn*
C/13230, 7/6/18; R.E., C/S, 1/11/18; demob. 27/1/19.
Inglemere, 85 Pitkirro Road, Dundee, N.B.

FORWOOD, *Ian Brittain*
6/5/5253, 31/7/15; L'pool. R., 6/12/15, M.G.C.; Capt.

FORWOOD, *Leslie Langton*
A/1069, 2/9/14; Oxf. & Bucks. L.I., 5/10/14, Dorset R.; Capt.

FORWOOD, *Stanley Muspratt*
B/11073, 16/4/17, L/C.; R.G.A., C/S, 10/10/17; R.G.A., 18/3/18; F; 2/Lieut. 45 Roxburgh Park, Harrow-on-the-Hill.

FORWOOD, *Stephen Langton*
6/8564, 31/12/15; R.A., C/S, 26/5/16; R.G.A., 30/8/16; F; Capt.; w. Bendrose Grange, Amersham, Buckinghamshire.

FOSTER, *Alan*
D/13695, 31/7/18; trfr. K.R. Rif. C., 7/4/19, R.A.O.C.; It; Cpl
48 Blackburn Road, Padiham, Burnley.

FOSTER, *Alfred Leslie*
4/1/4365, 21/6/15; R.A.S.C., 6/11/15; Lieut.
Rye House, Woodsetton, Nr. Dudley.

FOSTER, *Charles Gilbert*
6/5/C/9515, 16/2/16; No. 7 O.C.B., 4/11/16; R. Innis. Fus., 28/2/17; F; Lieut.; w.
4 Mall View Terrace, The Mall, Armagh, Ireland.

FOSTER, *Ernest George*
6/2/5353, 31/7/15; Mon. R., 8/7/16; F; Lieut.
152 Dukes Avenue, Muswell Hill, N.

APPENDIX II.—RECORDS OF RANK AND FILE.

FOSTER, Geoffrey La Trobe
6/3/8630, 3/1/16; No. 8 O.C.B., 4/8/16; R. Fus., 21/11/16; F;
Lieut.; w. Glendower, St. Margaret's Bay, Dover.

FOSTER, Gerald
6/D/8350, 13/12/15, L/C.; No. 14 O.C.B., 27/12/16; Dorset R.,
25/4/17, att. Hamps. R.; Lieut.
186 Amyard Park Road, St. Margarets-on-Thames.

FOSTER, Gerald William Victor
6/5/7174, 3/11/15; 20th Lond. R., 4/8/16, att Manch. R.; F;
Lieut. Nordrach-on-Dee, Banchory, Scotland.

FOSTER, Herbert Douglas
D/10205, 18/12/16; No. 14 O.C.B., 5/5/17; York. R., 28/8/17;
F,It; Capt.; w. 24 Grand Drive, Raynes Park, S.W.19.

FOSTER, Hugh P. R.
A/909, 5/8/14, L/C.; D. of Corn. L.I., 25/2/15; S,M,SR; Capt.
69 Ennismure Gardens, S.W.7.

FOSTER, Maurice Kirshaw
F/1862, 16/10/14; dis. 14/11/14.
14 Iverna Court, Kensington, W.8.

FOSTER, Norman Fiennes
4/3/4071, 7/6/15; R.E., 19/10/15; F,NR; Lieut.
Ourden, Uplands Park Avenue, Loughton, Essex.

FOSTER, Reginald Duncan
B/1199, 14/9/14; Dorset R., 20/10/14, R.G.A.; F; Lieut.; w.
8 Northcourt Road, Worthing, Sussex.

FOSTER, Robert Tonge
K/2212, 30/11/14; E. Rid. of York. Yeo., 23/2/15, L'pool. R.;
Lieut. 21 Holbeck Hill, Scarborough.

FOSTER, William Stevens
C/13250, 10/6/18; No. 22 O.C.B., 5/7/18; Oxf. & Bucks. L.I.,
11/2/19; 2/Lieut. 14 Abbey Park Terrace, Northampton.

FOUCAR, Emile Charles Victor
K/A/2069, 12/11/14; 12th Lond. R., 24/7/15, att. W. Som. Yeo.;
F; Capt.; M.C. 77 Elgin Crescent, W.11.

FOULDS, Henry Stanley
A/13085, 20/5/18; demob. 25/1/19.
The Burlington, Sheringham, Norfolk.

FOULDS, William Alfred
F/2968, 25/2/15; Manch. R., 22/6/15; Lieut.
c/o Mrs. Leyland, Newburgh, Nr. Wigan.

FOULKES-JONES, John Arthur Stephens
4/Sq/4146, 10/6/15, L/C.; Mont. Yeo., 5/10/15, att. R.W. Fus.;
E,P,F; Lieut.; w(2). 32 Dean Road, Cricklewood, N.W.

FOULKES-JONES, John William
6/2/8212, 7/12/15, L/C.; R.A., C/S, 7/8/16; R.G.A., 8/11/16;
Capt. Stanley Villa, Lewis Road, Sutton, Surrey.

FOULSTON, Samuel
6/8545, 30/12/15; R.A., C/S, 26/5/16; R.G.A., 18/8/16; F;
Lieut.; Inj. Catwick, Nr. Hull.

FOUNTAIN, George Cecil Newland
D/13726, 2/8/18; trfr. K.R. Rif. C., 30/5/19.
42 Griffith Street, Rushden, Northamptonshire.

FOURDRINIER, Norman Douglas
B/177, 29/4/08, Sgt.; dis. 28/4/13; Midd'x. R., 15/8/14; F;
Capt.; w. Broad Street, Pershore, Worcestershire.

FOWKES, Arthur Fred Reeve
C/11457, 5/6/17; A.S.C., C/S, 1/9/17; R.A.S.C., 27/10/17; E;
2/Lieut. The Oaks, Pevensey, Sussex.

✠ FOWLER, Charles Jefford
K/E/2446, 28/12/14, L/C.; R. Fus., 25/3/15; 2/Lieut.
Died of wounds 1/6/16.

✠ FOWLER, Edward Wareham
E/1607, 6/10/14, L/C.; R. War. R., 28/1/15; Lieut.
Killed in action 15/7/16.

FOWLER, Ralph Howard
K/2479, 28/12/14; R. Marines, 18/1/15; G; Capt.; w; O.B.E.
Trinity College, Cambridge.

FOWLER, Raymond Hugh Vaughan
6/D/7045, 28/10/15, Cpl.; R.N.A.S., 27/3/17, R.A.F.; F;
Lieut. Earls Colne, Essex.

FOWLER, Reginald Curteis
A/13152, 29/5/18; No. 1 O.C.B., 8/11/18; Oxf. & Bucks. L.I.,
17/3/19; 2/Lieut. Bodicote Vicarage, Banbury.

FOWLER-DIXON, Edwin Dagnall
C/9939, 17/11/16; R.W. Surr. R., 9/3/17, Lab. Corps; F; Capt.
406 Camden Road, N.7.

FOWLES, George
Sq/2875, 8/2/15, Farr. Sgt.; A.S.C., C/S, 27/10/16; R.A.S.C.,
20/12/16, Glouc. R., Lan. Fus., R.E.; F; Lieut.
The Hall, Stanford-in-the-Vale, Faringdon, Berkshire.

FOX, Claude Ernest Montague
B/D/13638, 26/7/18; A.S.C., C/S, 14/10/18, No. 11 O.C.B.;
General List, 8/3/19; 2/Lieut.
5 Grey Street, Newcastle-on-Tyne.

FOX, Eric John
A/12541, 5/2/18, L/C.; No. 3 O.C.B., 9/8/18; Rif. Brig., 5/3/19;
2/Lieut. Northfield, Cecil Road, Sutton, Surrey.

FOX, Eric Smart
E/2784, 25/1/15; Lond. Div. Cyc. Coy., 18/3/15, att. R.A.S.C.;
F; Lieut.; w. 2 Lansdowne Road, Leicester.

FOX, George William
F/3048, 15/3/15; Hamps. R., 15/5/15; Capt.; w(2); M.C., M(1)
Annandale, Kints River, Cape Province, South Africa.

FOX, James Toplis
6/5/C/6521, 30/9/15; trfr. R.G.A., 12/1/17.
Oakmede, Belts Hill, High Barnet.

FOX, John
4/6/4926, 19/7/15; Manch. R., 19/12/15; E,F; Capt.; w(2); M.C.
17 High Street, Rochdale.

FOX, Noel Bassett
6/Sq/8603, 3/1/16; No. 1 Cav. C/S, 6/12/16; 1st Lancers,
16/4/17, M.G.C.; 2/Lieut. Syston, Leicestershire.

FOX, Reginald James
B/10777, 19/2/17; No. 11 O.C.B., 5/7/17; Indian Army, 30/10/17.
The Rectory, Temple Combe, Somerset.

FOX, Russell Toplis
6/3/5376, 5/8/15; Essex R., 3/9/15; F; Lieut.
Oakmede, Bells Hill, High Barnet.

FOX, Stanley
6/3/6571, 30/9/15; dis. 21/4/16.
Eidleweiss, Saville Street, Jersey.

FOX, Thomas Vernon
Sq/165, 18/4/08; dis. 18/4/09.

✠ FOX, Victor William Darwin
D/1493, 29/9/14; Irish Gds., 10/10/14; F; Lieut.
Killed in action 18/5/15.

FOX, William Edward
6/5/7230, 5/11/15, L/C.; North'd. Fus., 6/7/16, Tank Corps;
2/Lieut. 7 Wells Buildings, Well Street, Oxford Street, W.

FOX, William Harold
6/1/5679, 16/8/15, Cpl.; K.R. Rif. C., 10/1/16, Lab. Corps;
Capt.; w(2); M.C. 18 Bridge Street, Stratford-on-Avon.

FOX, William Kenneth
B/11391, 30/5/17, L/C.; No. 14 O.C.B., 7/9/17; Leic. R.,
17/12/17; Lieut.

FOX, William Reginald Leslie
C/12617, 18/2/18; trfr. 28th Lond. R., 30/10/18.
65 Fallows Road, Sparkbrook, Birmingham.

✠ FOXALL, Thomas William
D/10561, 19/1/17; No. 11 O.C.B., 5/7/17; Welch Fus., 25/11/17,
att. L'pool. R.; F; 2/Lieut. Killed in action 2/10/18.

FOX-ANDREWS, Norman Roy
F/1777, 16/10/14; D. of Corn. L.I., 17/10/14, M.G.C.; Lieut.
Elmsleigh, Oldfield Park, Bath.

✠ FOY, William Archibald
F/2922, 15/2/15; R. Suss. R., 19/6/15; G,E,P; Lieut.; w; M.C.
Killed in action 6/11/17.

FOYSTER, Eric Ross
4/1/5197, 29/7/15; R.A., C/S, 29/1/16; Hamps. R., 14/7/16;
I,Arabia; Lieut.
National Provincial and Union Bank, Eastgate, Exeter.

FOYSTER, Guy
6/1/5723, 19/8/15, L/C.; Devon. R., 4/8/16; I,M; Lieut.
Glenbrook, Middle Deal Road, Deal, Kent. (Now in Nyassaland)

APPENDIX II.—RECORDS OF RANK AND FILE.

☦ FOYSTER, *Philip Tillard*
Sq/543, 10/2/11; dis. 24/11/13; R.E., 24/10/14; Capt.
Died of wounds 11/12/16.

FRAMPTON, *Hugh Albert*
D/A/12115, 12/10/17; R.F.C., C/S, 18/1/18; demob. 28/1/19.
c/o A. Aspinall Esq., W. India Contingent Centre, 15 Seething Lane, E.C.

FRANCE, *George*
6/8059, 1/12/15; No. 9 O.C.B., 8/3/16; Arg. & Suth'd. Highrs., 6/7/16; S; Lieut.; Inv. 145 West George Street, Glasgow.

☦ FRANCE, *John Galbraith*
6/8060, 1/12/15; No. 9 O.C.B., 8/3/16; Sco. Rif., 23/7/16; 2/Lieut. Killed in action 12/4/17.

FRANCE, *Norman*
C/10586, 22/1/17; trfr. 13th Lond. R., 26/2/17.
4 Carr Mount, Bury Road, Rawtenstall, Lancashire.

FRANCE, *Selwyn*
D/12960, 19/4/18; No. 22 O.C.B., 7/6/18, No. 11 O.C.B.; General List, 8/3/19; 2/Lieut. 565 West 190th Street, New York, U.S.A.

FRANCE, *Walter Frederick*
A/13956, 6/9/18; No. 11 O.C.B., 26/2/19; General List, 8/3/19; 2/Lieut. Northgate Hall, Warham, Weles, Norfolk.

FRANCIS, *Cecil William Robert*
E/Sq/2780, 23/1/15, Cpl.; R.A.S.C., 5/7/15, Worc. R.; F; Capt.
Sauston House, Cromwell Road, Maidstone, Kent.

FRANCIS, *Clement Alexander*
D/10435, 10/1/17, L/C.; R.F.A., C/S, 22/6/17; R.F.A., 17/11/17; P; Lieut. Corinda, Frinton, Essex.

FRANCIS, *Edward Geoffrey*
A/9825, 1/11/16; No. 14 O.C.B., 27/12/16; Camb. R., 25/4/17; F; Capt.; w. 23 Lonsdale Road, Harborne, Birmingham.

FRANCIS, *Frederick Thomas*
B/11696, 19/7/17; No. 14 O.C.B., 4/1/18; Essex R., 25/6/18, att. Indian Army, R. Ir. Fus. and E. Surr. R.; E; 2/Lieut.
The Grange, Howbury, Erith, Kent.

FRANCIS, *Harold Cobb*
4/3/5104, 26/7/15; E. Surr. R., 3/1/17, att. M.G.C., Sco. Rif. and Indian Army; I; Capt.
76 Cheriton Road, Folkestone, Kent.

FRANCIS, *Hugh Arthur*
6/8164, 6/12/15; No. 1 O.C.B., 6/9/16; R.F.C., 25/1/17, R.A.F.; F; Lieut.; A.F.C., M(1). Homeleigh, Uxbridge, Middlesex.

FRANCIS, *Hugh Douglas Peregrine*
Sq/143, 18/4/08; dis. 17/4/10; rej. Sq/841, 4/8/14; E. Rid. of York. Yeo., 23/9/14, att. M.G.C.; E,P,F; Capt.; M.C., M(1).
19 Great Winchester Street, E.C. 2.

FRANCIS, *John Edmund*
6/4/7406, 13/11/15; Devon. R., 4/8/16; I,E; Lieut.
41 Woodhouse Grove, Manor Park, Essex.

FRANCIS, *Kenneth*
D/1402, 29/9/14; K.R. Rif. C., 7/12/14, att. S. Notts. Huss.; F; Capt. Elkstone House, Thornton Road, Clapham Park, S.W.12.

FRANCIS, *Leslie Howard*
6/5/6869, 18/10/15; A.S.C., C/S, 3/4/16; R.A.S.C., 21/5/16; Lieut. Casanette, Titehurst Road, Reading.

FRANCIS, *Marcus*
C/13231, 7/6/18, L/C.; demob. 29/1/19.
558 Leek Road, Stoke-on-Trent.

FRANCIS, *Reginald Grant*
6/4/6246, 16/9/15, L/C.; D. of Corn. L.I., 8/6/16; I; Lieut.
Groombridge, Sussex.

FRANCIS, *Thomas Burney*
4/2/4182, 14/6/15, Sgt.; No. 14 O.C.B., 28/8/16; 15th Lond. R, 24/10/16, att. M.G.C.; F,It; Lieut.; Inv.
c/o T. E. Francis Esq., c/o Barclay's Bank Ltd., 170 Fenchurch Street, E.C.

FRANCIS, *Wilfrid*
C/12566, 6/2/18; No. 17 O.C.B., 9/8/18; demob. 19/1/19.
578 Leek Road, Stoke-on-Trent.

FRANCIS, *William John*
D/13791, 9/8/18; trfr. K.R. Rif. C., 7/4/19.
99 Cheapside, E.C. 2.

FRANK, *Charles Mitchell*
6/1/6855, 16/10/15; Glouc. R., 4/8/16, secd. M.G.C.; M,I; Lieut.; w. 20 High Street, Lewes, Sussex.

FRANKLAND, *Albert Ernest*
A/11909, 27/8/17; No. 14 O.C.B., 7/12/17; Lan. Fus., 28/5/18; F; 2/Lieut.; w. 28 Coronation Drive, Great Crosby, Nr. Liverpool.

☦ FRANKLAND, *John Cecil*
6/3/6180, 13/9/15; N. Lan. R., 9/1/16; F; 2/Lieut.
Killed in action 10/1/17.

FRANKLIN, *Albert George*
6/D/9732, 16/10/16; R.F.C., C/S, 13/3/17; R.F.C., 19/4/17, R.A.F., Glouc. R.; Lieut.
Faringdon, Langton Grove, Charlton Kings, Gloucestershire.

FRANKLIN, *Frederick Leaf*
6/4/7549, 17/11/15; North'n. R., 21/11/16; 2/Lieut.; w.
166 Ancona Road, Plumstead, S.E.

FRANKLIN, *James Howard*
4/2/4018, 7/6/15; R. Fus., 20/9/15, R.A.O.C.; F; Major; w; M(1). Osborne House, Steyning, Sussex.

FRANKLIN, *John Veasey*
B/13436, 3/7/18; dis. med. unfit, 23/2/19.
Melton, 107 Church Road, Richmond, Surrey.

FRANKLIN, *Leslie Trevor*
6/5/6008, 2/9/15; Leic. R., 4/9/16, att. R. Highrs.; F; Lieut.; Inv. 40 Evington Drive, Leicester.

FRANKLIN, *Walter Temple*
A/11927, 30/8/17; A.S.C., C/S, 12/11/17; R.A.S.C., 6/1/18; F; 2/Lieut. Sheafdale, St. Albans, Hertfordshire.

FRANKLYN, *Francis Edward Hazelwood*
6/6146, 9/9/15; R.F.A., 27/9/15; F; Lieut.
Canberra, 30 Alleyn Road, West Dulwich, S.E. 21.

FRANKS, *Neville Coleman*
A/10722, 12/2/17; R.A., C/S, 29/6/17; trfr. R.G.A., 6/8/17.
Sarnia, The Grove, Coulsdon, Surrey.

FRANZINI, *Victor Lodovico*
6/3/9403, 9/2/16; No. 14 O.C.B., 26/11/16; E. York. R., 27/3/17, M.G.C.; F,P; Lieut. 88 North End Road, West Kensington, W.

☦ FRASER, *Arthur Cecil*
C/11483, 14/6/17; R.F.C., C/S, 2/8/17; R.F.C., 8/9/17; 2/Lieut. Killed in action 22/1/18.

FRASER, *Claud Lovat*
K/1734, 15/10/14; Durh. L.I., 23/10/14; F; Capt.; g; M(1).
The Red House, Buntingford, Hertfordshire.

FRASER, *Donald Beeton*
C/11440, 4/6/17; A.S.C., C/S, 1/9/17; R.A.S.C., 27/10/17; F; 2/Lieut.
National Provincial & Union Bank, Ltd., 59/60 High Street, Exeter.

FRASER, *Douglas Cecil Hector*
6/4/6247, 16/9/15; Bord. R., 14/7/16; Lieut.; w.
Elmfield, Crowstone Road, Westcliffe-on-Sea.

FRASER, *Ian Jasper*
D/13862, 19/8/18; trfr. R.A.O.C., 28/6/19.
12 Buchanan Street, Glasgow.

☦ FRASER, *James Lesley*
A/2900, 11/2/15; Sea. Highrs., 2/6/15; M; Lieut.; w(2).
Died 31/3/19.

FRASER, *James McCardle*
A/11928, 30/8/17; R.E., C/S, 11/11/17; R.E., 21/12/17; F; 2/Lieut. 169 Berkeley Street, Glasgow.

FRASER, *Neil Duncan*
A/14035, 20/9/18; demob. 30/1/19.
The Grove, Woodchurch Road, Birkenhead.

FRATER, *John Wilberforce*
B/C/12679, 4/3/18; R.F.A., C/S, 17/5/18; R.F.A., 10/2/19; 2/Lieut. Bilton Barns, Lesbury S.O.

FRAYLING, *Gerard Dunstan Warren*
C/14199, 21/10/18; dis. med. unfit, 23/4/19.

FRAZER, *Kenneth Alexander*
6/1/6922, 19/10/15; No. 14 O.C.B.; R.W. Surr. R., 24/10/16; F; Lieut.; w. 121 East Dulwich Grove, S.E. 22.

APPENDIX II.—RECORDS OF RANK AND FILE.

FRAZER, Kenneth Gerard
6/D/9602, 7/8/16; No. 14 O.C.B., 30/10/16; K.R. Rif. C., 24/1/17; F; Capt.
Upton Lodge, 15 Devonshire Place, Eastbourne.

FRECKER, Frederick James
6/8232, 8/12/15; dis. med. unfit, 29/7/16.
Inishowen, Upper Teddington Road, Hampton Wick.

✠ FREEAR, Eric Charles
6/2/9064, 21/1/16; No. 5 O.C.B., 14/8/16; Bedf. R., 21/11/16; 2/Lieut.
Killed in action 13/4/17.

FREELAND, Cecil George Scott
1/3632, 17/5/15; R.W. Surr. R., 10/9/15; F; 2/Lieut.; Inv.
Dreenagh House, Smarden, Nr. Headcorn.

FREELAND, Frank Hughes
A/Sq/B/12514, 31/1/18; demob. 31/1/19.
High View, Warwick Road, Redhill.

FREELING, Francis Frederick
A/13171, 31/5/18; R.E., C/S, 11/10/18; demob.
Wellesley House, Wellington Square, Cheltenham.

FREEMAN, Albert Edward
D/11102, 23/4/17; No. 12 O.C.B., 10/8/17; 7th Lond. R., 27/11/17; Lieut.
c/o A. Crumplin Esq., 52 Brocklebank Road, Earlsfield, S.W. 18.

FREEMAN, Alexander Claud
A/11646, 12/7/17; Garr. O.C.B., 28/12/17; Lab. Corps, 18/5/18, att. R. Ir. Rif.; 2/Lieut.; Inv.
Gadebridge Park, Hemel Hempsted, Hertfordshire.

FREEMAN, Anthony
A/1014, 6/8/14.
24a Bryanston Square, W.

FREEMAN, Arthur Frederick Ashwell
C/840, 4/8/14; Hamps. R., 10/11/14, M.G.C.; I,M; Lieut.
Belair, Albion Road, Sutton, Surrey.

FREEMAN, Edmund
6/8213, 7/12/15; R.F.A., C/S, 23/6/16; R.F.A., 24/11/16; Lieut.; w.
9 Lensden Place, Golden Lane, E.C. 2.

FREEMAN, Edward Rollo
A/12479, 29/1/18; No. 20 O.C.B., 7/6/18; R.W. Fus., 6/2/19; 2/Lieut.
Gallt-y-beren, Pwllheli, North Wales.

FREEMAN, Jesse Alfred
4/3770, 27/5/15, L/C.; 1st Lond. R., 15/11/15; F,E; Capt; w(2).
Betham House, Greenford, Middlesex.

FREEMAN, John
C/199, 5/5/08; dis. 1/5/11.
30 Devonshire Place, W. 1.

✠ FREEMAN, John Roland
6/4/6123, 9/9/15; North'd. Fus., 1/6/16; 2/Lieut.; M(1).
Died of wounds 12/2/17.

FREEMAN, Lawrence Austin
1/3452, 3/5/15; trfr. R.A.M.C., 18/2/16.
2 Woodview Terrace, Gravesend.

FREER, Ronald Branston
A/D/13025, 3/5/18; demob. 23/10/19.
St. Mark's Vicarage, Spencer Park, S.W. 18. (Now in India.)

FREESTON, Charles Garner
6/3/5377, 5/8/15; R.F.A., 3/11/15; Lieut.; w.
25 Huskisson Street, Liverpool.

FREETH, John Cedric
C/10209, 18/12/16; trfr. R. Regt. of Cav., 27/3/17.
Dudgrove, Fairford, Gloucestershire.

FRENCH, Cyril Aldom
A/12480, 29/1/18; No. 18 O.C.B., 7/6/18; R.W. Surr. R., 8/2/19; 2/Lieut.
12 Elmbourne Road, Upper Tooting, S.W. 17.

FRENCH, Cyril Alfred
C/D/12046, 27/9/17; R.F.A., C/S, 15/3/18; R.G.A., 12/2/19; 2/Lieut.
Nethersole, Manor Court Road, Nuneaton.

FRENCH, Louis Richard
D/1437, 29/9/14; R.A.S.C., 21/10/14; Lieut.

FRENCH, Nicholas
Sq/748, 1/12/13; dis. 29/6/14.
c/o 47 Threadneedle Street, E.C.

FRENCH, Percy Albert
D/11544, 21/6/17, L/C.; No. 2 O.C.B., 5/4/18; Oxf. & Bucks. L.I., 12/11/18, att. R. War. R.; 2/Lieut.
9 St. Andrews Hill, Cambridge.

FRERE, John Geoffrey
Sq/987, 5/8/14; Norf. Yeo., 27/10/14, M.G.C., att. Norf. R.; Capt.
51 Tergunter Road, S.W. 10.

FRERE, Philip Beaumont
C/825, 4/8/14; E. Surr. R., 12/9/14, K.R. Rif. C., War Office Intelligence; F; Capt.; g; M.C., M(2).
11 The Charterhouse, E.C. 1.

FRESHWATER, Charles Hervé
6/2/5329, 2/8/15; E. Surr. R., 24/12/15, K.R. Rif. C., att. R. Fus.; F; Capt.; w;
42 Beatrice Avenue, Norbury, S.W. 16.

FRICKER, Bernard Osborne
D/13757, 7/8/18; demob. 31/1/19.
99 St. Leonards Road, East Sheen, S.W. 14.

FRICKER, William Shapland
B/11697, 19/7/17; No. 11 O.C.B., 9/11/17; Norf. R., 30/4/18; F; 2/Lieut.
21 Denton Road, Canton, Cardiff.

FRIEDBERGER, Henry Charles Bryham
C/793, 8/5/14; R. Fus., 14/8/14; Lieut.

FRIEDLANDER, Jonas Rudolph
A/12481, 29/1/18; R.F.A., C/S, 17/5/18; demob.
Bryn-Helen, 15 Woodborough Road, Putney, S.W. 15.

FRIEL, Benjamin Herbert
6/1/9350, 7/2/16; No. 2 O.C.B., 14/8/16; R. Dub. Fus., 29/5/17; Lieut.

FRIEND, Harry
D/13727, 2/8/18; trfr. K.R. Rif. C., 7/4/19.
152 Folkestone Road, Dover.

FRIEND, Maurice
6/8165, 6/12/15; Lothian & Bord. Horse, 5/5/16; F; Lieut.
41 St. Andrews Road, N.W. 4.

FRIEND, Walter Maples
6/1/6124, 9/9/15; dis. med. unfit, 22/5/16.
Kimberley House, Bourne, Lincolnshire.

FRIPP, George Christie
4/3/4114, 8/6/15; Manch. R., 29/9/15; F; Lieut.; w; M.C.
Bank Chambers, Queen Street, Oldham.

FRIPP, Thomas Morley
F/2750, 21/1/15; R.W. Surr. R., 29/5/15, secd. Indian Army; Lieut.

FRITH, John Arthur
B/E/13587, 19/7/18; No. 22 O.C.B., 20/9/18; Devon. R., 5/2/19; 2/Lieut.
13 South Summerlands, Exeter, Devonshire.

FRITH, Philip Francis Oliver
2/9780, 25/10/16; R.F.C., C/S, 13/3/17; R.F.C., 19/4/17, R.A.F.; Lieut.
Dialstone, Rossett, Denbighshire.

FROGLEY, Harold George
A/Sq/13070, 15/5/18; demob. 11/1/19.
Sparsholt, Wantage, Berkshire.

✠ FROMANT, Herbert Dudley Sands
6/1/8462, 18/12/15; No. 13 O.C.B., 4/11/16; North'd. Fus., 28/2/17; 2/Lieut.
Killed in action 29/4/17

FROOM, Charles
4/3771, 27/5/15; R.A.S.C., 31/8/15; Capt.
44 North Side Clapham Common.

FROST, Basil Claude
C/13323, 19/6/18, L/C.; No. 11 O.C.B., 24/1/19; General List, 8/3/19; 2/Lieut.
The Cedars, Rondebosch, Capetown, South Africa.

FROST, Cyril Charles James
4/1/4571, 1/7/15; North'd. Fus., 4/10/15, att. Arg. & Suth'd Highrs., Indian Army; F,I; Capt.
c/o Alliance Bank of Simla Ltd., Hornby Road, Bombay.

FROST, Harold Hayles
6/1/5691, 17/8/15; No. 11 O.C.B., 16/5/16; Suff. R., 4/9/16; F; Lieut.
The Poplars, Woodlands Road, Redhill, Surrey.

FROST, John Charles Harris
B/Sq/10568, 19/1/17; trfr. Class W. Res., 13/6/17.
Hinxworth Manor, Baldock, Hertfordshire.

FROST, John George
E/14116, 9/10/18; R.G.A., C/S, 1/11/18; R.G.A., 20/4/19; 2/Lieut.
36 Northenden Road, Sale, Cheshire.

APPENDIX II.—RECORDS OF RANK AND FILE.

FROST, Joseph Entwisle
6/D/7732, 22/11/15, L/C.; R.F.C., C/S, 13/3/17; R.F.C., 19/4/17, R.A.F.; F; Lieut.; w.
Riversdale, Prestwich Park, Prestwich, Nr. Manchester.

FROST, Stanley Charles
K/F/3/2259, 7/12/14, Sgt.; R.G.A., 17/5/15; F; Lieut.; M(1).
17 Charleville Circus, Sydenham, S.E. 26.

FROWEN, John Harold
6/3/6456, 27/9/15; dis. to R. Mil. Academy, 8/11/15; R.G.A., 26/8/16; F; Lieut.
48 Lichfield Street, Burton-on-Trent. (Now in India.)

✠ FRY, Alfred Harold
B/599, 22/1/12, Sgt.; 22nd Lond. R., 6/3/15; F; 2/Lieut.
Died of wounds 30/10/16.

FRY, Dudley Athelstan Beresford
6/4/D/8961, 17/1/16; No. 14 O.C.B., 26/11/16; R. Fus., 27/3/17; 2/Lieut.; p.
8 Torrington Place, W.C.

FRY, Eric Arthur Lawrence
C/12647, 25/2/18, Cpl.; demob. 1/5/19.
31 Grosvenor Road, Rathgar, Dublin.

FRY, Eric Charlton
A/14131, 8/10/18; demob. 29/1/19.
Arden, 5 The Park, North End, Hampstead, N.W. 3.

FRY, John George
D/10239, 29/12/16, Sgt.; R.A., C/S, 27/4/17; R.G.A., 1/9/17; F; 2/Lieut.
23 Alexandra Road, Reading.

FRY, Thomas George
4/5/4850, 15/7/15; Mon. R., 9/12/15, att. Lan. Fus.; F; Lieut.
11 Charnwood Road, Loughborough, Leicestershire.

FRYER, Charles Henry Barr
D/11034, 13/4/17, Sgt.; R.A., C/S, 15/12/17; R.G.A., 1/7/18; F; 2/Lieut.
21 Mincing Lane, E.C. 3.

✠ FRYER, Christopher John Gwynne
6/5/C/9502, 15/2/16; No. 14 O.C.B., 30/10/16; Herts. R., 24/1/17; Lieut.; w; M.C. and Bar. Killed in action 4/11/18.

FRYER, John Harwood
C/10542, 17/1/17; No. 20 O.C.B., 7/6/17; S. Lan. R., 25/9/17, att. N. Lan. R., R. Lanc. F. and R.A.F.; F; Lieut.; w.
Stonwall House, Blackburn Road, Bolton, Lancashire.

FRYER, Roderick George
A/1367, 26/9/14; Worc. R., 27/11/14, M.G.C.; Lieut.

FRYER, Walter Frank
E/13992, 11/9/18; No. 22 O.C.B., 22/11/18; Wilts. R., 15/2/19; 2/Lieut.
10 Julius Road, Bishopston, Bristol.

FULLARD, Philip Fletcher
6/5/5884, 30/8/15; R.F.C., 4/8/16, R.A.F.; F; Major; D.S.O., M.C. and Bar, A.F.C., Croix de Guerre, American Flying Medal, M(1).
R.A.F. Club, Bruton Street, W. 1.

FULLER, Albert
B/10115, 6/12/16; No. 14 O.C.B., 5/5/17; Hunts. Cyc. Bn., 28/8/17; Lieut.

FULLER, Alfred Walter Francis
H/1910, 16/10/14, L/C.; Oxf. & Bucks. L.I., 17/3/15, att. Tank Corps; F,S; Capt.
The Lodge, 7 Sydenham Hill, S.E. 26.

FULLER, Arthur Loraine Claude
Sq/703, 9/4/13; Drag. Gds., 15/8/14, att. R.F.C.; Lieut.
10 Hill Street, Mayfair, W.

FULLER, Charles Hutson
6/2/7733, 22/11/15; No. 8 O.C.B., 4/8/16; Midd'x. R., 21/11/16, att. R. Fus.; F,NR; Capt.; w(2); M.C., M(1).
39 Chapel Road, Worthing.

✠ FULLER, Dunstan Milloy
4/1/5010, 22/7/15; R. Fus., 30/12/15; Capt.; w; M.C.
Killed in action 10/8/17.

FULLER, Evered Gerald
4/3955, 3/6/15; E. Ang. Div. Cyc. Coy., 1/9/15; 2/Lieut.
10a Ashworth Mansions, Maida Vale, W. 9.

FULLER, Harold George
C/13232, 7/6/18; No. 22 O.C.B., 5/7/18; R. Suss. R., 5/2/19; 2/Lieut.
Church Norton, Chichester, Sussex.

FULLER, William Ernest Randolph
C/12620, 18/2/18; No. 15 O.C.B., 5/7/18; North'd. Fus., 3/3/19; 2/Lieut.
19 Olympia Hill, Morpeth, Northumberland.

FULLHAM, Ernest Beltram
4/1/4625, 5/7/15, L/C.; Worc. R., 23/12/15.
70 Greystoke Avenue, Newcastle-on-Tyne.

✠ FULLIN, John Francis
6/5/6761, 11/10/15; R. Muns. Fus., 4/8/16; F; 2/Lieut.; M.C.
Killed in action 22/3/18.

FULLJAMES, Reginald Edgar Gilbert
6/3/6433, 24/9/15; R.F.C., 6/7/16, R.A.F.; F; Capt. & Flt. Cmdr.; M.C.
St. Briavel, Queens Grove, Southsea, Hampshire.

FULLJAMES, Ronald Monckton
1/3633, 17/5/15; Durh. L.I., 27/7/15; F; Capt.; w; M.C. and Bar.
4 Eastern Road, Brockley, S.E. 4.

FULLWOOD, Charles
6/2/5286, 2/8/15; dis. med unfit, 26/6/16.
1 Merrick Square, Brough, S.E. 1.

FULTON, John
D/12120, 15/10/17; No. 9 O.C.B., 10/5/18; High. L.I., 5/2/19; 2/Lieut.
Broxwood, Bridge of Weir, Renfrewshire.

FULTON, Robert Andrew
6/4/5557, 12/8/15; W. Rid. R., 6/6/16; F; Lieut.
32 Queen Anne's Grove, Bush Hill Park, N.

FURLEY, Guy Mainwaring
F/2646, 11/1/15, L/C.; R.W. Fus., 9/7/15; E; Lieut.
c/o Mrs. Peele, Bryn Meirion, Llangollen

FURLONG, Peter Claude
6/5/9286, 3/2/16; R.F.A., C/S, 4/8/16; R.F.A., 10/11/16; F; Lieut.; M.C.
68 Fitzwilliam Square, Dublin.

FURMEDGE, Cecil George
C/11742, 26/7/17; No. 14 O.C.B., 7/12/17; D. of Corn. L.I., 28/5/18; S; 2/Lieut.
c/o Lloyds Bank Ltd., Brockenhurst C. & C. Branch, Hampshire.

FURNER, Arthur Stanley
6/5/6870, 18/10/15; Glouc. R., 4/9/16, att. R.E. Sigs.; I,M; Lieut.; M(1).
12 Normandy Avenue, High Barnet.

FURNER-ELLIOT, Leonard
6/2/7502, 15/11/15; No. 11 O.C.B., 7/5/16; Manch. R., 4/9/16, att. R.A.F.; F,I,It,E; Lieut.
Isis Court, Grove Park, Chiswick.

FURNISS, Edward Favell
6/2/5540, 10/8/15; York. & Lanc. R., 26/10/15, att. M.G.C.; F; Capt.; w-g.
37 Elmore Road, Moorleahs, Sheffield.

✠ FURNISS, James
6/5/C/9404, 9/2/16; No. 7 O.C.B., 4/11/16; R. Ir. Rif., 28/2/17; 2/Lieut.
Killed in action 31/7/17.

FYFE, Alfred Maule Paxton
B/13666, 29/7/18; trfr. Class W. Res., 19/11/18.
10 Bay View Crescent, Swansea.

FYFE, Robert George
6/5/7414, 12/11/15, L/C.; No. 14 O.C.B.; Manch. R., 24/10/16, R.A.F.; F,S; Capt.; M.B.E., M(1).
55 Cavendish Road, Clapham Park, S.W. 4

✠ FYSON, George Dumills
K/D/2147, 19/11/14, Cpl.; Glouc. R., 17/3/15; P; 2/Lieut.
Killed in action 20/4/16.

✠ GABB, Stanley Frederic
2/6/6617, 4/10/15; No. 11 O.C.B., 7/5/16; M.G.C., 4/9/16; 2/Lieut.
Died of wounds 8/12/16.

GABY, Victor Francis
4/3/4336, 21/6/15, Sgt.; Dorset R., 25/9/16; Lieut.
28 Fonncrean Road, Ipswich.

GADBAN, Victor John
2/3227, 12/4/15, Sgt.; No. 6 O.C.B., 17/4/16; R.W. Kent R., 6/7/16, Lab. Corps; F; Capt.; w; O.B.E.
Rosebank, Alton, Hampshire.

GADE, Felix William
6/4/8865, 12/1/16, L/C.; No. 8 O.C.B., 4/8/16; R. Fus., 24/10/16; F; Capt.; p; M.C.
46 Pembroke Square, Kensington, W. 8.

✠ GADSDEN, Crawford Cunningham
4/4590, 3/7/15; R.W. Surr. R., 25/11/15, att. R.F.C.; Lieut.
Died of wounds 16/10/17.

169

APPENDIX II.—RECORDS OF RANK AND FILE.

GAFFNEY, *Eugene*
B/Sq/A/12375, 11/1/18; No. 19 O.C.B., 7/6/18; *trfr.* 28th Lond. R., 4/9/18. 104 *St. Mary's Villas, South Areular Road, Dublin.*

GAGE-BROWN, *Charles Lewis*
Sq/502, 2/11/10; *dis.* 29/10/12; *rej.* Sq/1135, 10/9/14; Interpreter, 24/9/14; F; Lieut.; *p.*
c/o Lloyds Bank Ltd., 33 Belgrave Road, S.W. 1.

GAIN, *Cecil Harry Goodenough*
C/14211, 21/10/18; No. 11 O.C.B., 24/1/19; General List, 8/3/19; 2/Lieut. (*Now in South Africa.*)

GAINE, *Herbert Hornby*
H/1965, 26/10/14, Sgt.; Devon. R., 24/3/15; It,F; Capt.; *Inv.*
10 *Queen's Elm Square, Church Street, Chelsea, S.W.*

GAINES, *Edward John*
2/3672, 17/5/15; R.A.S.C., 16/10/15; F,E; Lieut.
91 *Bridge Road, Battersea Park, S.W.*

GAINS, *Stanley George*
6/1/9004, 19/1/16; R.F.A., C/S, 4/8/16; R.G.A., 1/11/16; 2/Lieut. 99 *Highbury Quadrant, N.*

✠ GAIR, *Henry Burgh*
C/9961, 20/11/16; No. 14 O.C.B., 30/1/17, No. 11 O.C.B.; Dorset R., 30/10/17; 2/Lieut. *Died of wounds* 15/5/18.

GALBRAITH, *David Dudley*
Sq/2969, 25/2/15; R.A.S.C., 25/5/15; F; Capt.; *Inv*; M(1).
115 *Mountview Road, Stroud Green, N. 4.*

GALBRAITH, *Hugh*
6/1/8214, 7/12/15; No. 7 O.G.B., 4/11/16; R. Dub. Fus., 28/2/17; F,E; Lieut.; *w*; M.C., M(1).
Calaroga, Castle Avenue, Clontay, Dublin.

GALBRAITH, *Robert Forbes*
6/3/7098, 1/11/15; No. 14 O.C.B.; M.G.C., 24/10/16; F; Lieut.; *p*; M.C. 44 *Longton Grove, Upper Sydenham, S.E. 26.*

GALE, *Anthony Richard*
K/B/2060, 12/11/14; R.A.O.C., 22/1/15; F; Major.
2 *Clifton Road, Winchester, Hampshire.*

GALE, *Lionel Ernest Bradley*
B/11317, 21/5/17; Garr. O C.B., 28/12/17; Hamps. R., 18/5/18; F; Lieut. *The Chute, Parkstone, Dorset.*

GALL, *Edgar Wauchope*
E/14039, 20/9/18; R.G.A., C/S, 8/11/18; *demob.*
12 *College Road, Exeter.*

GALLAGHER, *Christopher Francis*
B/12703, 8/3/18; No. 2 O.C.B., 20/9/18; R. Dub. Fus., 17/3/19; 2/Lieut. 2 *Bellgrove Villas, Clontarf, Dublin.*

GALLEYMORE, *George Reginald*
6/1/9482, 16/2/16, L/C.; R.A.O.C., 11/12/16; F; Capt.
253 *Buxton Road, Macclesfield.*

GALLIE, *Aubrey Edwin*
4/3/4042, 7/6/15; S. Wales Bord., 30/9/15; F; Capt.; *g*; M.C.
25 *Carlton Terrace, Swansea.*

GALLOWAY, *Norman Horace*
E/2629, 7/1/15; L/C.; 8th Lond. R., 6/7/15, *secd.* M.G.C.; F; Lieut. 51 *Second Avenue, Selby Park, Birmingham.*

GALPIN, *Douglas George*
6/3/7870, 26/11/15; No. 14 O.C.B., 28/8/16; Linc. R., 21/11/16; Germ.SWA, F; 2/Lieut.; *w.*
Flaatjesfontein, Dwaal Station, Cape Province, South Africa.

GALVIN, *Daniel Joseph*
6/2/9405, 9/2/16; No. 5 O.C.B., 14/8/16; R. Dub. Fus., 21/11/16; Lieut.; *w.* *Victoria Road, Cork.*

GAMBELL, *Herbert Beresford*
4/9704, 9/10/16; R.G.A., C/S, 14/3/17; R.G.A., 1/10/17; Lieut.
75 *Morris Road, Southampton.*

GAMBLE, *Arnold Massey*
D/Sq/11806, 6/8/17; No. 1 Cav. C/S, 28/2/18; R. Regt. of Cav., 28/8/18; 2/Lieut. *Gainston Manor, Retford, Nottinghamshire.*

GAMBLE, *Edward Goodnow*
C/A/12276, 3/12/17; R.F.C., C/S, 15/2/18; R.A.F.; 2/Lieut.
Royal Colonial Institute, Northumberland Avenue, W.C. 2.

✠ GAMBLE, *Frank Burfield*
4/2/4041, 7/6/15; Notts. & Derby R., 17/9/15; F; 2/Lieut.
Killed in action 1/7/16.

✠ GAMBLE, *Hugh Valentine*
4/3/3957, 3/6/15, L/C.; Sea. Highrs., 14/9/15; Lieut.
Killed in action 3/5/17.

GAMBLE, *Laurence Harry*
6/4/9163, 26/1/16; No. 1 O.C.B., 6/9/16; R.F.C., 25/1/17, R.A.F.; 2/Lieut. *Ratonagh, Colwyn Bay, North Wales.*

GAME, *George Geoffry*
6/4/6479, 27/9/15; R.F.A., 21/12/15; F; Lieut.; M.C., M(1).
Barn House, Broadway, Worcestershire.

✠ GAMESON, *George Henry Molyneux*
6/1/8937, 13/1/16; No. 8 O.C.B., 4/8/16; North'd. Fus., 21/11/16; 2/Lieut. *Died of wounds* 14/3/17.

GAMMAN, *Albert Osborne*
H/2559, 4/1/15; Hamps. R., 31/3/15; F; Capt.; *w*(2); M.C., M(1). *Woodstock, 40 Wickham Avenue, Bexhill-on-Sea, Sussex.*

GAMMON, *Horace William*
6/3/5378, 5/8/15, L/C.; R.F.C., 6/7/16, R.A.F.; F; Lieut.; *w.*
R.R.2, Chilliwack, British Columbia, Canada.

GAMSBY, *Alden Leslie*
D/Sq/C/12891, 9/4/18, Sgt.; No. 11 O.C.B., 31/1/19; General List, 8/3/19; 2/Lieut. *Sunapec, New Hampshire, U.S.A.*

GANDER, *Harry*
D/11824, 9/8/17; No. 14 O.C.B., 4/1/18; 7th Lond. R., 25/6/18; Lieut. *Norton House, Shipston-on-Stour, Worcestershire.*

GANDY, *Cyril*
6/4/9451, 14/2/16; No. 14 O.C.B., 26/11/16; Notts. & Derby. R., 27/3/17; 2/Lieut. 20 *Swinburne Street, Derby.*

GANN, *Claude George*
6/2/6281, 16/9/15; Midd'x. R., 1/6/16, *att.* R. Fus.; F; Capt.; *g.*
Torquay, St. James Avenue, Sutton, Surrey.

✠ GANNON, *John Howard*
6/5/7291, 8/11/15; No. 11 O.C.B., 7/5/16; R.W. Fus., 4/9/16; 2/Lieut. *Killed* 9/10/17.

GANNON, *Peter*
C/12639, 22/2/18; No. 22 O.C.B., 7/6/18; Education Officer, 8/12/18, *att.* R. War. R.; Capt.; *m.*
R.A. Club, Pall Mall, S.W. 1.

✠ GANSON, *Andrew*
4/5/4744, 12/7/15; No. 9 O.C.B., 8/3/16; High. L.I., 6/7/16; 2/Lieut. *Killed in action* 14/12/16.

✠ GANT, *Robert Wilfred*
6/3/7503, 15/11/15; R.N.A.S., 24/10/16; R.A.F.; Lieut.
Died 3/8/18.

GAPP, *Leonard Paterson*
K/2957, 22/2/15; Welch. R., 1/3/15, M.G.C.; Lieut.; M(1).

GARBUTT, *Walter Francis Drummond*
6/6054, 4/9/15; Lovats Scouts, 24/9/15, *secd.* M.G.C.; Lieut.; *w.*

GARCIA, *Arnold Russell*
4/4745, 12/7/15; *dis.* 22/7/15.

✠ GARD, *Frederick*
2/3634, 17/5/15; D. of Corn. L.I., 21/8/15; Lieut.
Killed in action 28/6/18.

GARDENER, *Guy William Carr*
B/12769, 15/3/18; R.F.A., C/S, 17/5/18; R.F.A., 10/2/19; 2/Lieut.

GARDINER, *Doane*
K/B/2292, 10/12/14, L/C.; 3rd Lond. R., 7/4/15, *secd.* M.G.C.; Lieut.; *w*; M(2). 65 *Upper Gloucester Place, N.W.*

GARDINER, *Eric Gordon*
C/1346, 26/9/14; Lan. Fus., 5/4/15; F; Major; M.C., M(1).
10 *Sergeants Inn, E.C. 4.*

GARDINER, *Ernest Murrell*
6/5/5932, 1/9/15; L'pool. R., 1/6/16, R.A.F.; F; Capt.; *w*; M.C. 9 *Tithebarn Street, Liverpool.*

GARDINER, *Hubert*
C/182, 30/4/08; *dis.* 29/4/11; R.F.A., 17/5/15; F; 2/Lieut.
12 *Lauriston Road, S.W. 19.*

✠ GARDINER, *James Totton*
D/11865, 16/8/17; No. 3 O.C.B., 8/2/18; R. Ir. Rif., 30/7/18; 2/Lieut.; *p.* *Died of wounds* 1/11/18.

170

APPENDIX II.—RECORDS OF RANK AND FILE.

GARDINER, Thomas Arthur Mansfield
1/3500, 6/5/15; Midd'x. R., 10/7/15, att. R.A.F.; F; Lieut.
Uxbridge, Middlesex.

✠ GARDINER, William Edward Mansfield
1/3501, 6/5/15; 5th Lond. R., 5/8/15; 2/Lieut.
Killed in action 20/7/16.

✠ GARDNER, Alfred Ernest
6/4/6480, 27/9/15; Yorks. L.I., 9/6/16; 2/Lieut.
Killed in action 13/1/17.

GARDNER, Edward Norman
A/10077, 1/12/16; R.F.A., C/S, 4/4/17; R.F.A., 3/9/17; Lieut.
8 Walton Park, Liverpool.

GARDNER, Harold Douglas
D/13842, 16/8/18; trfr. K.R. Rif. C., 7/4/19.
44 Bethune Road, Stoke Newington, N. 16.

GARDNER, Harold Francis John
B/12403, 17/1/18; No. 19 O.C.B., 10/5/18; Lan. Fus., 16/2/19; 2/Lieut.
The Bintan Estates Ltd., c/o Barker & Coy. Ltd., Singapore, Straits Settlements.

GARDNER, Harold Rolfe
6/3/5379, 5/8/15; Bedf. R., 22/11/15, R.A.F.; E,M; Capt.; w.
22 Selbourne Road, Ilford.

GARDNER, Harry Leonard
4/6/5/4927, 19/7/15; L'pool. R., 6/6/16, R.A.F.; F; Lieut.; w(2).
7 The Square, Fairfield, Manchester.

GARDNER, Herbert Patrick Legge
6/1/5764, 21/8/15; Norf. R., 20/11/15, R.A.F.; F; Capt.
108 Hatfield Road, Ipswich, Suffolk.

GARDNER, John Henry
4/2/4183, 14/6/15; Durh. L.I., 12/11/15; F; Lieut.; w.
204 Evering Road, Upper Clapton.

GARDNER, Ralph Graham
C/12567, 6/2/18; No. 15 O.C.B., 5/7/18; Suff. R., 3/3/19; 2/Lieut.
Tillingham Vicarage, Southminster, Essex.

✠ GARDNER, Thomas
B/780, 27/3/14; 20th Lond. R., 31/8/14; Lieut.
Killed in action 22/7/16.

GARDNER, Thomas Alfred Arthur
B/Sq/10120, 6/12/15; No. 20 O.C.B., 5/2/17; Dorset R., 28/8/17, R.W. Kent R., Hamps. R.; I,M,Persia; Lieut.
Fairlawn, 32 Priory Avenue, Hoe Street, Walthamstow.

GARDNER, Walter Paterson
6/8166, 6/12/15; dis. med. unfit, 31/5/16.
Cairnhope, Walton Park, Liverpool.

GARLAND, Ewart James
6/9351, 7/2/16; R.F.C., 17/3/16, R.A.F.; Capt.; M(1).
14 Regent Street, W.

✠ GARLAND, George Arthur
4/2/4184, 14/6/15; Durh. L.I., 12/11/15; F; 2/Lieut.
Killed in action 16/9/16.

GARLAND, James Francis
A/101513, 15/1/17; R.F.A., C/S, 29/6/17, Garr. O.C.B.; demob.
170 Telford Avenue, Streatham Hill, S.W.2.

GARLICK, Gerald
2/6200, 13/9/15; No. 1 O.C.B., 25/2/16; 16th Lond. R., 8/7/16; 2/Lieut.
39 Tufnell Park Road, N.

GARLICK, Harold Ross
6/5/C/8922, 14/1/16; No. 14 O.C.B., 26/11/16; Manch. R, 27/3/17; F; Lieut.; g.
22 Northenden Road, Gatley, Cheshire.

✠ GARLICK, Vivian
6/2/7353, 10/11/15, L/C.; No. 11 O.C.B., 7/5/16; Oxf. & Bucks. L.I., 4/9/16; Lieut.; w.
Killed in action 15/6/18.

GARNER, Clifford
B/11981, 10/9/17, L/C.; R.E., C/S, 24/2/18; R.E., 5/4/18; 2/Lieut.
Clifford House, Pontefract, Yorkshire.

✠ GARNER, Frank Leslie
6/5/7415, 12/11/15, L/C.; R.F.C., 25/9/16; 2/Lieut.
Killed in action 20/12/16.

GARNER, John Douglas
6/2/6082, 6/9/15, L/C.; Dorset R., 7/6/16; M; Lieut.
5 Alexandra Road, Crosby, Liverpool.

GARNER, Leonard
B/A/12346, 1/1/18; trfr. 14th Lond. R., 6/12/18.
Caerleon, Moughland Lane, Runcorn, Cheshire.

GARNETT, Philip Raymond Tennant
A/Sq/14263, 29/10/18; demob. 9/1/19.
Greenholme, Burley in Wharfdale, Yorkshire.

GARNETT-CLARKE, Geoffrey Read
K/2373, 17/12/14; R.G.A., 1/1/15, R.F.A.; F; Capt.; w; M.C
Comision Local, F.C.Sud, Calle Coryallo 564, Buenos Aires, Argentina.

GARNHAM, Archibald Scott
4/5166, 29/7/15; No. 11 O.C.B., 7/5/16; Hamps. R., 4/9/16; F; Capt.
Aulderney, 1 St. Edwards Road, Gosport, Hampshire.

GARNHAM, Reginald Rance
6/3/6935, 20/10/15; R.F.A., C/S, 4/8/16; R.F.A., 1/12/16; F; Lieut.; Inv.
Chislon House, Lowther Hill, Forest Hill, S.E. 23.

GARRARD, Ernest Edward
C/12649, 25/2/18; R.E., 19/6/18; F; Capt.
54 Grange Drive, Winchmore Hill, N. 21.

✠ GARRARD, Frederic George
6/1/8167, 6/12/15; dis. to R. Mil. Coll., 29/8/16; Gord. Highrs., 5/7/17; 2/Lieut.
Died of wounds 22/5/18.

GARRARD, Norton Rochfort
A/1190, 14/9/14; N. Staff. R., 6/11/14; F; Capt.
Southfield, Kenilworth, Warwickshire.

GARRATT, Arthur Poynder
B/757, 23/1/13; W. Rid. R., 27/11/14, M.G.C.; Lieut.; w(2). M(1).
16 Hardy Road, Blackheath, S.E. 3.

GARRETT, Alfred Henry
E/1556, 6/10/14, Cpl.; R.E., 18/6/15; F; Lieut.; M(1).
2 Kenilworth Avenue, Wimbledon, S.W. 19.

✠ GARRETT, Hyde Tregellas
6/4/8168, 6/12/15; No. 11 O.C.B., 7/5/16; R.F.C., 4/9/16; 2/Lieut.
Killed in action 20/5/17.

GARRETT, Laurence Hugh
D/10944, 27/3/17, L/C.; Garr. O.C.B., 28/12/17; Essex R., 18/5/18; Lieut.
28 Old Town, Clapham, S.W. 4.

GARRETT, Ronald Thornbury
A/337, 10/12/08, Cpl.; dis. 9/12/08; R.A.S.C., 31/8/14, att. K.R. Rif. C. and Bedf. R.; F.
5 Fenchurch Avenue, E.C. 3.

GARRETT, William Leigh
D/11560, 28/6/17; Garr. O.C.B., 28/12/17; Lab. Corps, 18/5/18, att. R.W. Kent R.; 2/Lieut.
39 Eastwood Road, Goodmayes, Essex.

GARRETT-PEGGE, Wilfrid George
6/9503, 15/2/16; A.S.C., C/S, 27/3/16; R.A.S.C., 1/5/16; F; Lieut.
Cheshaw Bois Manor, Chesham, Buckinghamshire

✠ GARROD, Thomas Martin
Sq/608, 13/2/12; dis. 2/5/14; N. Lan. R., -/8/14; F; Lieut.
Died of wounds 10/5/15.

GARROW, William
4/3/4457, 28/6/15, L/C.; No. 9 O.C.B., 8/3/16; Cam'n. Highrs., 23/7/16; F; Lieut.; g(2), w,p.
Hong Kong and Shanghai Bank, 9 Gracechurch Street, E.C.

GARSIA, Marston de la Paz
B/1664, 10/10/14; Som. L.I., 20/2/15; F; Lieut.
2 Queen Alexandra Mansions, Judd Street, King's Cross, W.C. 1

GARSIA, Willoughby de la Paz
B/1663, 10/10/14; dis. med. unfit, 7/1/15.

✠ GARSIDE, Frank Gerald
4/4147, 10/6/15, L/C.; 9th Lond. R., 28/10/15; Lieut.; w; M(1).
Killed in action 27/8/18.

GARSIDE, Maurice William
B/11698, 19/7/17; No. 11 O.C.B., 9/11/17; Norf. R., 26/3/18; F; 2/Lieut.
28 Warley Grove, Halifax, Yorkshire.

✠ GARSIDE, Thomas Oughtilridge
1/3502, 6/5/15; R. Berks. R., 6/8/15; F; 2/Lieut.; w.
Killed in action 5/4/17.

GARTON, Thomas Bowley
A/10726, 12/2/17; No. 1 Cav. C/S, 5/7/17, No. 12 O.C.B.; Notts. and Derby. R., 27/11/17; F; 2/Lieut.; M.C.
Baxter Gate, Loughborough.

APPENDIX II.—RECORDS OF RANK AND FILE.

GARTON, Wilfrid Cecil
A/14057, 25/9/18; demob. 13/12/18.
39 Wilton Crescent, Wimbledon, S.W. 19.

GARTSIDE, John Travis
2/9669, 2/10/16; R.F.C., C/S, 8/3/17; R.F.C., 6/6/17, R.A.F.; F; Lieut.; Inj.
Highlands House, Royton, Lancashire.

GARWOOD, Claud Risdon
C/11441, 4/6/17, L/C.; R.F.A., C/S, 28/1/18; R.F.A., 23/9/18; 2/Lieut.
19 Florence Park, Redlands, Bristol.

✠ GARWOOD, Gerald Dennis
6/5/8565, 31/12/15, L/C.; R. War. R., 4/9/16; 2/Lieut.
Killed in action 13/11/16.

GASCOYNE, George
4/3/4458, 28/6/15; R.F.A., 11/10/15; F; Lieut.; w.
93 Bath Road, Worcester.

GASCOYNE, Walter Hubert Noel
6/5/6909, 18/10/15; dis. to re-enlist in R. Marine Art., 24/10/16; F; Gnr.; w.
Court Lodge, Westwell, Ashford, Kent.

GASKELL, Humphrey
D/Sq/11091, 23/4/17; No. 1 Cav. C/S, 28/2/18; R. Regt. of Cav., 28/8/18, 13th Huss.; 2/Lieut.
61 Parkfield Road, Sefton Park, Liverpool.

GASKELL, Harold Penn
2/3503, 6/5/15; Ches. R., 21/8/15; 2/Lieut.
8 Pennard Mansions, Goldhawk Road, W. 12.

GASKELL, Leonard
B/12827, 22/3/18; No. 20 O.C.B., 20/9/18; trfr. 28th Lond. R., 12/11/18.
28 Genesta Road, Westcliff-on-Sea.

GASKELL, William Lace
6/3/5/5491, 4/8/15; dis. med. unfit, 8/8/16.
1 Coronation Street, Openshaw, Manchester.

✠ GASKELL, Wallace William Penn
B/555, 17/3/11, Sgt.; 24th Lond. R., 26/2/15; F; 2/Lieut.
Killed in action 25-26/5/15.

GASS, Andrew James
6/5/5654, 16/8/15; No. 11 O.C.B., 7/5/16; Suff. R., 24/9/16, att. Midd'x. R.; F; Lieut.
133 Englefield Road, Canonbury, N. 1.

GASS, Frenwick Temperley
6/5/7504, 15/11/15, L/C.; No. 14 O.C.B.; Oxf. & Bucks. L.I., 24/10/16; F,Persia,I; Capt.
2/113th Infantry, c/o Messrs. Cox & Coy., Ltd., Bombay.

✠ GASTER, Ernest
3/3597, 13/5/15; North'd. Fus., 5/8/15; F; Lieut.; w.
Died of wounds 23/10/18.

GATENBY, Edward Vivian
C/12670, 1/3/18; trfr. 14th Lond. R., 6/12/18.
48 Wrentham Avenue, N.W. 10.

✠ GATES, Eric Chasemore
B/213, 8/5/08; dis. 7/5/11; Joined 13th Lond. R., -/8/14; 13th Lond. R.; F; Capt.
Killed in action 15/3/15.

GATES, Eric Chris
6/2/6989, 25/10/15; No. 14 O.C.B., 28/8/16; Shrop. Yeo., 21/11/16, att. Shrop. L.I.; Lieut.; w.
48 The Drive, Golders Green.

GATHERCOLE, Arnold
4/3956, 3/6/15; Bedf. R., 13/7/15, att. R. Suss. R.; F; Lieut.
Cavendish Club, 119 Piccadilly, W. 1.

GAUDIE, Andrew Dow
6/3/9382, 8/2/16; R.A., C/S, 28/9/16; R.F.A., 12/2/17; 2/Lieut.
10 Craighall Gardens, Edinburgh.

GAUDIE, Eric Dyson
B/13475, 5/7/18; dis. med. unfit, 1/11/18.
Beech Bank, Ulverston, Lancashire.

GAUNTLETT, William Wallace
4/Sq/9720, 12/10/16; trfr. Class W. Res., 15/3/17.
Buttermere Manor, Hungerford, Berkshire.

GAUSDEN, Sidney Harold Edwin
4/6/4851, 15/7/15, L/C.; Worc. R., 9/11/15; 2/Lieut.
London County and Westminster Bank Ltd., Tunbridge Wells.

GAWTHORNE, Arthur Richardson
6/4/5655, 16/8/15; R.G.A., 6/10/15; F; Lieut.
4 Park Road, Radlett, Hertfordshire.

GAWTHORNE, Leslie Everard
D/10877, 16/3/17; R.F.C., C/S, 4/5/17; R.F.C., 14/6/17, R.A.F.; F; Lieut.; w.
23 Woolwich Road, Belvedere, Kent.

GAY, Bernard Clement
6/7871, 26/11/15; No. 1 O.C.B., 6/9/16; R.F.C., 5/2/17, R.A.F.; F; Capt.; w.
80 Wilton Avenue, Southampton, Hampshire.

✠ GAY, Edgar Percy
6/4/6352, 20/9/15; D. of Corn. L.I., 1/6/16; 2/Lieut.; M(1).
Died of wounds 6/1/17.

GAY, Gerald
A/9805, 30/10/16, L/C.; M.G.C., C/S, 1/3/17; M.G.C., 25/6/17; F; Lieut.; p.
62 Princes Avenue, Alexandra Park, N. 22.

GAYFORD, Douglas Byron
2/3525, 6/5/15, L/C.; R.W. Surr. R., 28/7/15, att. R.F.C.; 2/Lieut.; w-p.

GEAKE, James Stanley
6/5/7666, 22/11/15; R.F.A., C/S, 4/8/16; R.G.A., 1/11/16; F; Lieut.; Inv.
70 Stroud Road, Gloucester.

GEAKE, John Douglas
A/11625, 9/7/17; No. 14 O.C.B., 9/11/17; Glouc. R., 30/4/18; F; 2/Lieut.; w.
5 Gladwell Road, Crouch End, N. 8.

GEAKE, Thomas Henry
A/11621, 6/7/17; No. 11 O.C.B., 9/11/17; R.N.V.R., 30/4/18, att. R. Fus.; F,NR; Sub. Lieut.
Castella, Kingswear, South Devon.

GEARY, Edward Francis
4/5/4601, 5/7/15, L/C.; 18th Lond. R., 19/12/15; F; 2/Lieut.; Inv.
31 Sneyd Road, Cricklewood, N.W. 2.

GEARY, Herbert Mashiter
6/2/8631, 3/1/16; No. 14 O.C.B.; R. Suss. R., 21/11/16; F,NR; Capt.; w.
7 Ashbourne Road, West Southbourne, Bournemouth.

GEARY, Percival Leonard
6/1/7381, 11/11/15; No. 11 O.C.B., 7/5/16; Som. L.I., 4/9/16, att. N. Som. Yeo.; F; Lieut.; w.
c/o Messrs. Wilson, Sons & Coy., Ltd., Las Palmas, Grand Canary.

GREAVES, William Lyon
A/12167, 29/10/17; trfr. 30th Lond. R., 5/4/18.
31 Norfolk Square, W. 2.

✠ GEDDES, David Scott
A/10256, 29/12/16; No. 14 O.C.B., 6/4/17; Manch. R., 31/7/17; 2/Lieut.
Killed in action 26/10/17.

GEE, Charles Baker
A/14077, 30/9/18, L/C.; demob. 7/4/19.
60 Hamilton Road, Oxford.

GEE, John Percy
D/11144, 30/4/17; No. 12 O.C.B., 10/8/17; 5th Lond. R., 27/11/17; F; 2/Lieut.; w; M.C.
301 Mare Street, Hackney, E. 8.

GEE, Raymond Edward
4/3/4459, 28/6/15; S. Staff. R., 8/10/15, att. R.E. Sigs.; F; Capt.
American Tobacco Coy., Sundholmsvej 65, Kobenhavn, Denmark.

GEE, Thomas
6/7988, 29/11/15; dis. med. unfit, 20/9/16.
Bank House, Deangate, Bolton.

GEERING, John Philip
6/4/6353, 20/9/15; No. 1 Cav. C/S, 2/8/16; Hamps. Yeo., 27/11/16, att. Hamps. R.; F,It; Lieut.
Laurel Dene, Ashford, Kent.

✠ GEESON, Leslie Frederic
D/10648, 2/2/17; R.F.C., C/S, 13/3/17; R.F.C., 19/4/17; 2/Lieut.
Killed 15/6/17.

GEHRKE, Arthur Richard
F/1785, 16/10/14; R. Dub. Fus., 3/3/15; E,S,NR; Lieut.; w(2); D.S.O., M(1).
176 Willesden Lane, Brondesbury, N.W. 6. (Now in Mexico.)

GELL, John Herbert Morlett
4/1/4602, 5/7/15; 19th Lond. R., 12/11/15; F; Lieut.
22 Castle Street, Liverpool.

APPENDIX II.—RECORDS OF RANK AND FILE.

GELLETLIE, Frederick Cecil
C/13314, 18/6/18; demob. 29/1/19.
Main Street, Wicklow, Co. Wicklow, Ireland.

✠ GEMMELL, Cecil Woodburn
6/9065, 21/1/16; No. 9 O.C.B., 8/3/16; Sco. Rif., 3/7/16; Lieut.
Killed in action 24/4/17.

GEMMELL, George
6/3/5724, 19/8/15; Norf. R., 23/11/15, secd. Indian Army; Lieut
9 Kings Street, Kings Lynn.

GEMMELL, John
6/7765, 23/11/15; No. 9 O.C.B., 8/3/16; Sea. Highrs., 6/7/16; F;
Lieut.; w. Oxenwood House, Kilwinning, Ayrshire.

GENNINGS, Arthur Greenway
6/3/7142, 2/11/15; E. Surr. R., 4/8/16; Lieut.
7 Alleyn Road, West Dulwich, S.E. 21.

GENTLE, Joseph Alfred Hector Roberts
D/12903, 8/4/18; No. 5 O.C.B., 8/11/18, No. 20 O.C.B.; Rif.
Brig., 17/3/19; 2/Lieut.
21 Owenite Street, Abbey Wood, S.E. 2.

GENTRY, Jack Sidney Bates
A/12482, 29/1/18; No. 18 O.C.B., 7/6/18; S. Staff. R., 5/2/19;
2/Lieut. 23 St. Swithins Road, Bournemouth, Hampshire.

GENTRY, Victor Percival
C/13324, 19/6/18; trfr. 14th Lond. R., 6/12/18, R.A.S.C.; L/C.
Villette, 114 Standen Road, Southfields, S.W. 18

GEOGHEGAN, Geoffrey
6/8061, 1/12/15; R.E., C/S, 16/4/16; R.E., 1/7/16; M,P; Lieut.
17 Westland Row, Dublin, Ireland.

GEORGE, Alexander
4/6/5/4852, 15/7/15; 12th Lond. R., 24/12/15, secd. Indian Army;
Lieut. Caenantmelyn, Hay, Hereford.

✠ GEORGE, Edgar James
4/3772, 27/5/15; trfr. 14th Lond. R., 17/3/16; F; Pte.
Killed in action 7/9/16

GEORGE, Owen James Burgess
A/10030, 28/11/16; R.W. Surr. R., 9/3/17; Lieut.; w.
The School House, Evershot, Dorset.

GEORGE, William Hubert
6/2/7443, 15/11/15; trfr. 15th Lond. R., 2/5/16
Henllan, Rhoscrowther, Pembroke.

GERAGHTY, James Gerard
6/3/9287, 3/2/16; No. 14 O.C.B., 30/1/17; R. Muns. Fus., 29/5/17,
att. York. R., Durh. L.I. and R.A.S.C.; I; Lieut.
Ballymore, Co. Galway, Ireland.

GERAHTY, Charles Cyril
A/344, 15/2/09; E. Lan. R., 12/4/10, Nigeria R.; F,WA; Capt.;
Inj. President District Court, Larnaca, Cyprus.

GERAHTY, James Echlin
A/405, 28/4/08; dis. med. unfit, 28/6/10.

GERARD, George Vincent
D/11856, 13/8/17; No. 14 O.C.B., 7/12/17; E. Kent R., 28/5/18;
F; 2/Lieut.; M.C.
c/o Union Bank of Australia, 71 Cornhill, E.C. 3.

GERARD, Robert John Leslie
A/1690, 12/10/14, Sgt.; Gord. Highrs., 25/3/15, att. R.F.C.,
R.A.F.; F,E; Capt.; Inv.
Allamore, Braemar, Aberdeenshire.

✠ GERMAIN, Harry Gordon
4/2/4391, 24/6/15; North'd. Fus., 20/9/15; F; 2/Lieut.
Killed in action 12/7/16.

✠ GERMAN, Ivon Hector
C/1147, 14/9/14; Hamps. R., 27/11/14; G,F; Capt.; w; M.C.
Died 1/12/18.

GERMAN, John William
6/2/7919, 29/11/15, L/C.; No. 14 O.C.B., 28/8/16; 3rd Lond. R.,
22/11/16; Lieut. 115 West Side, Clapham Common, S.W. 4.

GERSON, Frank Joseph
A/1194, 14/9/14; S. Staff. R., 13/11/14, North'd. Fus.; Lieut.
St. Prex, Thyra Grove, North Finchley, N. 12.

GETHING, James Frederic Edwards
A/12437, 22/1/18; No. 4 O.C.B., 7/6/18; Midd'x. R., 6/3/19;
2/Lieut. 64 Westbourne Park Road, W. 2.

✠ GETHING, Stanley
6/5/5538, 9/8/15; R.F.A., 19/12/15; resigned and joined 28th
Lond. R.; F; Pte. Killed in action 30/10/17.

GIBB, James Skirving
4/2/4512, 28/6/15; R. Sco. Fus., 7/10/15; Lieut.; w.

✠ GIBB, William Ian
6/5/6083, 6/9/15; No. 1 O.C.B., 25/2/16; 11th Lond. R., 9/8/16;
2/Lieut. Killed in action 14/4/17.

GIBB, William Oliphant Plenderheath
F/2766, 25/1/15; R. Scots, 5/5/15; Lieut.; w.
9 Finchley Road, N.W. 8.

GIBBIN, Owen
6/4/8828, 10/1/16; No. 8 O.C.B., 4/8/16; R.W. Fus., 21/11/16;
F; Capt.; w. Penrallt, Logion S.O., Carmarthenshire.

GIBBINS, Norman Martin
E/1/2853, 4/2/15; R. Dub. Fus., 20/4/15; Lieut.; w.
21 Little Welbeck Street, W. 1.

GIBBON, Alexander Robert Turing
D/Sq/11857, 13/8/17; No. 2 Cav. C/S, 11/4/18; R. Regt. of Cav.,
18/10/18; 2/Lieut.
c/o Messrs. Leichman & Coy., Colombo, Ceylon.

GIBBON, Bruce Scott
4/3382, 26/4/15; Sco. Rif., 3/5/15, M.G.C.; F; Capt.
c/o Messrs. Markwood Ltd., Colombo, Ceylon.

GIBBON, Douglas Stewart
K/2525, 31/12/14; Hamps. R., 31/3/15, R.W. Fus.; F,S; Capt.;
w(2); M.C. 85 Gracechurch Street, E.C.

GIBBON, Wilfrid St. Martin
H/1995, 29/10/14; Welch. R., 15/11/14; Lieut.
The Vicarage, Glasbury-on-Wye.

GIBBONS, Gilbert
6/3/6181, 13/9/15; 22nd Lond. R., 7/1/16, att. R.F.C.; Lieut.

GIBBONS, Joseph Hornsby
C/13207, 5/6/18; R.E., C/S, 25/8/18, No. 11 O.C.B.; General
List, 8/3/19; 2/Lieut. 74 Thurlow Park Road, Dulwich, S.E. 21.

GIBBONS, William Kenrick
Sq/268, 3/6/08; dis. 3/6/11; rej. Sq/814, 3/8/14; E. Lan. R.,
25/10/14; F,S; Capt.; Inv. Pine Grove House, Weybridge.

GIBBS, Arthur Hamilton
Sq/591, 27/11/11; dis. 25/6/12; R.F.A.; Capt.; M.C.

GIBBS, George Montagu
C/Sq/14227, 25/10/18; demob. 14/1/19.
Montagu House, Retford, Nottinghamshire.

✠ GIBBS, Ivan Richard
B/762, 13/2/14; Glouc. R., 19/9/14; Capt.
Killed in action 25/9/15.

GIBBS, Percival Raymond
6/4/6327, 20/9/15; Mon. R., 8/1/16; Lieut.
Newport Conservative Association, Tredegar Hall Buildings,
Stow Hill, Newport, Monmouthshire.

GIBBS, Robert Albert
A/11262, 14/5/17; No. 10 O.C.B., 5/10/17; Leic. R., 26/2/18; F;
Lieut.; w. 104 High Street, Oxford.

GIBBS, Robert John Lidgett
D/11018, 11/4/17; dis. med. unfit, 3/12/17.
50 Plymouth Road, Penarth, Glamorganshire.

GIBBS, William Reginald
B/13537, 17/7/18; demob. 31/1/19.
9 New Quebec Street, Portman Square, W. 1.

GIBSON, Arnold Mackenzie
1/9639, 26/9/16; R.G.A., C/S, 28/2/17; R.G.A., 26/5/17; F,It;
Lieut.; Croce di Guerra. Repton, Nr. Derby.

GIBSON, Arthur Harvey
6/Sq/9066, 21/1/16; R.F.A., C/S, 4/8/16; R.F.A., 9/12/16; F;
Lieut.; w(2), g. Highbury, Wolstanton, Staffordshire.

GIBSON, Douglas Graham
6/9185, 28/1/16; No. 9 O.C.B., 8/3/16; Sco. Rif., 6/7/16;
Germ.WA,F; Lieut.
P.O. Box 18, Standerton, Transvaal, South Africa.

GIBSON, Edward Milner
A/10956, 30/3/17; No. 12 O.C.B., 10/8/17; Ches. R., 27/11/17;
F; Lieut.; w-p. Dinder, Bramhall, Cheshire.

APPENDIX II.—RECORDS OF RANK AND FILE.

GIBSON, John Coggin
6/2/7143, 2/11/15, L/C.; No. 14 O.C.B.; Worc. R., 24/10/16, att. War Office; F; Lieut.; w. 70 Wellesley Road, Ilford.

GIBSON, Robert
6/4/7505, 15/11/15; No. 14 O.C.B., 28/8/16; R. Suss. R., 22/11/16; S; 2/Lieut. 112 Beaconsfield Villas, Brighton.

GIBSON, Roland Lilburne
C/10153, 8/12/16; No. 14 O.C.B., 6/4/17; Dorset R., 31/7/17; Lieut. 20 Branksomwood Road, Bournemouth.

GIBSON, Thomas Arnold
6/5/7087, 30/10/15, L/C.; D. of Corn. L.I., 8/6/16; F; Lieut.; Inv. Westcroft House, Butter Hill, Carshalton.

GIBSON, Thomas Richard
6/2/6644, 5/10/15; York. R., 25/9/16, att. T.M. Bty.; F; Lieut.; w; M.C. 16 Rugby Terrace, West Hartlepool.

GIDDINS, Frederick Vivian Chaffey
B/Sq/11982, 10/9/17; No. 1 Cav. C/S, 16/5/18; R. Regt. of Cav., 14/2/19; 2/Lieut. Crowood Park, Ramsbury, Wiltshire.

GIFFARD, Campbell Walter
Sq/122, 18/4/08, Sgt.; 4th Huss., 15/8/14, secd. M.G.C.; F,M,I; Capt. 48 Brook Street, W.

GIFFARD, Charles Henry
B/12389, 15/1/18; No. 11 O.C.B., 10/5/18; R.W. Surr. R., 5/2/19; 2/Lieut. Bulkeley House, Englefield Green, Surrey.

GIFFARD, Edgar Osbert
C/11047, 16/4/17, L/C.; No. 14 O.C.B., 7/12/17; Denbigh Yeo., 28/6/18; 2/Lieut. Chaplains House, Morden College, Blackheath, S.E. 3.

GIFFARD, George Godfrey
K/D/2475, 28/12/14; Manch. R., 7/4/15, K. Af. Rif.; F,EA; Lieut. c/o B.E.A. Corporation, Mombasa, British East Africa.

GIFFARD, John Stephen
K/D/2370, 17/12/14; R. Fus., 17/3/15, Manch. R., R.A.F.; F; Capt.; Croix de Guerre (Belgian), M(1). Chaplains House, Morden College, Blackheath, S.E. 3.

GIFFIN, William Charles Disraeli
6/5/8085, 1/12/15; No. 7 O.C.B., 11/8/16; R. Ir. Regt., 18/12/16; F; Lieut.; w; D.S.O., M.C., M(1). 58 Belgrave Square, Rathmines, Dublin.

GIFFORD, Hubert Stuart
A/12515, 31/1/18; No. 11 O.C.B., 14/2/19; General List, 8/3/19; 2/Lieut. 47 Westbourne Gardens, Glasgow. (Now in F.M.S.)

GIFFORD, Rupert Cyril D'Arcy
A/11026, 11/4/17; R.F.C., C/S, 2/8/17; R.F.C., 8/9/17, R.A.F.; F; Lieut. Moor Street, Brierley Hill, Staffordshire.

GIGGS, Alfred George
C/10155, 8/12/16, L/C.; No. 14 O.C.B., 5/3/17; R.N.V.R., 26/6/17; F; Sub. Lieut. 8 Colchester Villas, Stanley Road, Croydon.

GILBANKS, George William
D/12964, 22/4/18; demob. 21/12/18. Rawcroft, Penrith, Cumberland.

GILBART, Marcus Mervyn
A/13081, 18/5/18; dis. med. unfit, 29/6/18. 37 Twyford Avenue, West Acton, W. 3.

GILBERT, Ernest Henry Stuart
C/10174, 11/12/16, L/C.; M.G.C., C/S, 4/4/17; M.G.C., 26/8/17; Lieut. Ashbourne Lodge, Honor Oak Road, Forest Hill, S.E. 23.

GILBERT, Ernest William
B/13437, 3/7/18; demob. 23/1/19. Alverstone House, Shanklin, Isle of Wight.

GILBERT, Geoffrey Augustine Benjamine
6/1/6457, 27/9/15; Suff. Yeo., 25/9/16, att. Suff. R. and Bedf. R.; F; Lieut.; w. St. Margarets, Uxbridge Road, Slough, Buckinghamshire.

GILBERT, George Septimus
D/10307, 29/12/16; No. 1 Cav. C/S, 5/7/17; R. Regt. of Cav., 22/2/18, att. Bedf. Yeo; 2/Lieut. Inversnaid, Park Crescent, Wellingford, Hampshire.

GILBERT, Gilbert Garnet
6/3/6522, 30/9/15; No 8 O.C.B., 4/8/16; Dorset R., 21/11/16; 2/Lieut.

GILBERT, Harold John
D/1409, 29/9/14; R.A.O.C., 22/2/15, R.A.F.; Lieut. Whittenbury, 21 Sutton Court Road, Chiswick, W. 4.

✠ GILBERT, Joseph Plumptre
6/2/8710, 5/1/16; No. 14 O.C.B., 28/8/16; Hamps. R., 22/11/16; 2/Lieut. Killed in action 11/4/17.

GILBERT, William
A/12438, 22/1/18, Cpl.; demob. 25/1/19. Carlton House, Rathgar Avenue, Ealing, W. 13

✠ GILBERTSON, Graham Sydney
6/1/D/6481, 27/9/15; No. 14 O.C.B., 27/12/16; Bedf. R., 25/4/17; F; 2/Lieut.; w. Killed in action 28/11/17.

GILBEY, Alban James
6/D/9612, 11/9/16, L/C.; Gds. O.C.B., 6/3/17; Gren. Gds., 26/6/17; F; Lieut.; w. The Lea, Denham, Buckinghamshire.

GILBY, Walter George
4/5/4774, 12/7/15; trfr. 5th Lond. R., 24/3/16; F; Pte.; w. 4 Chichester Street, St. Georges Square, S.W. 1.

GILDEA, John Rudolph
A/11601, 5/7/17, Sgt.; No. 8 O.C.B., 18/10/18; General List, 8/3/19; 2/Lieut. Fort Terrace, Malacca, Straits Settlements.

GILES, Arthur Clifford
F/1795, 16/10/14, L/C.; dis. to R. Mil. Coll., 28/12/14; R. War. R., 16/6/15; F; Lieut. 29 Broadwater Down, Tunbridge Wells, Kent.

GILES, Claude Harold
A/13172, 31/5/18; No. 22 O.C.B., 5/7/18; R.W. Kent. R., 11/2/19; 2/Lieut. The Priory, Malvern.

GILES, Leslie William
F/2819, 29/1/15; dis. to R. Mil. Coll., 13/5/15; Oxf. & Bucks L.I., 24/11/15; F,NR; Lieut.; M.C. and Bar, M(1). 29 Broadwater Down, Tunbridge Wells, Kent.

GILES, Maurice Graham
6/5/9504, 15/2/16; A.S.C., C/S, 1/9/16; R.A.S.C., 25/10/16; I; Lieut. c/o Bank of Adelaide, 11 Leadenhall Street, E.C. 3.

GILES, Oliver Pemberton
2/9678, 2/10/16, Cpl.; R.A., C/S, 12/1/17; R.F.A., 5/6/17; F; Lieut.; M(1). c/o Lond. Joint City and Mid. Bank Ltd., Bennets Hill, Birmingham.

GILFILLAN, William Wallace
6/3/7258, 8/11/15; No. 9 O.C.B., 8/3/16; High. L.I., 23/7/16; F; Lieut.; w. c/o Mrs. Niner, 41 Montgomerie Street, North Kelvinside, Glasgow.

GILL, Claude Arundal
F/2870, 6/2/15; Durh. L.I., 3/6/15, secd. M.G.C.; Lieut.; w. Husthwaite, Easingwold, Yorkshire.

GILL, Colin Unwin
2/2644, 11/1/15; R.G.A., 15/6/15, att. R.E.; F; Capt.; M(1). Sewhurst Farm, Abinger Bottom, Dorking, Surrey. (Now in Italy.)

GILL, Dudley Arthur
D/13898, 23/8/18; trfr. K.R. Rif. C., 25/4/19, M.G.C.; Pte. Fairfield Lodge, Blandford, Dorset.

GILL, Dudley Marius Claxton
F/2701, 18/1/15; R Fus., 25/3/15; F; Lieut.; M(1). 164 Finchley Road, Hampstead, N.W. 3.

GILL, Ernest Woollaston
4/3/4835, 15/7/15; R.E., 2/10/15; Lieut. Bursledon, Dawlish, South Devon.

GILL, Leo Bernard
A/D/11921, 24/8/17; Tank Corps O.C.B., 1/3/18; Tank Corps, 3/3/19; 2/Lieut.

GILL, Sanderson Henry Briggs
6/3/8389, 14/12/15, L/C.; No. 14 O.C.B.; W. York. R., 24/10/16; F; Lieut. 6 St. John's North, Wakefield.

GILL, Stanley
A/10295, 1/1/17; R.W. Surr. R., 9/3/17, Lab. Corps; F; Capt. 4 St. Nicholas Buildings, Newcastle-on-Tyne.

✠ GILL, William Gerald Oliver
E/1584, 6/10/14, Sgt.; Essex R., 18/3/15; 2/Lieut. Killed in action 27/3/17.

APPENDIX II.—RECORDS OF RANK AND FILE.

GILL, William Harold
1/3537, 10/5/15; Leic. R., 28/7/15; Lieut.; w.
4 Brecon Road, Abergavenny.

✠ GILLARD, Frederick
D/10006, 24/11/16; No. 20 O.C.B., 5/5/17; R. Lanc. R., 28/8/17; York. L.I.; 2/Lieut. Killed in action 24/8/18.

✠ GILLESPIE, Alexander Douglas
Sq/768, 2/3/14; trfr. Sea. Highrs., 4/9/14; F; 2/Lieut.
Killed in action 26/9/15.

GILLESPIE, Allan Lawson
D/10882, 16/3/17; No. 12 O.C.B., 10/8/17; Bord. R., 27/11/17; 2/Lieut. Bonnyside House, Bonnybridge, Scotland.

GILLESPIE, Harold
B/11416, 1/6/17; No. 11 O.C.B., 9/11/17; trfr. 28th Lond. R., 5/4/18.

GILLESPIE, James Knox
K/2256, 7/12/14; dis. to R. Mil. Coll., 26/12/14; R.A.S.C., 12/5/15; Lieut. 4 Riverview Mansions, East Twickenham.

GILLESPIE, Patrick
6/5/C/7823, 24/11/15; No. 7 O.C.B., 3/7/16; trfr. 5th Lond. R., 28/9/17. West Port, Ballyshannon, Co. Donegal.

GILLETT, Frederick Edward
6/7444, 15/11/15; dis. to R. Mil. Coll., 27/4/16; 5th Drag. Gds., 1/5/17; F; Lieut. 41 Stockwell Park Road, S.W. 9.

GILLETT, Harold Dickin
A/14344, 6/1/19; trfr. K.R. Rif. C., 7/4/19.
Highfield, Milton Avenue, Gerrards Cross, Buckinghamshire.

GILLETT, Robert Doyle
6/2/5895, 30/8/15; trfr. R.F.A., 27/3/16; F; Bdr.; g.
Shalimar Estate, Kuala Selangor, Selangor, F.M.S.

GILLETT, Thomas Harold
C/2032, 9/11/14; R. War. R., 27/2/15; F; Capt.; M.C.
Newton House, Faversham, Kent.

GILLIBRAND, Clement
B/12322, 28/12/17; No. 1 O.C.B., 10/5/18; Rif. Brig., 29/10/18; 2/Lieut. 15 Heaton Street, Heaton Park, Manchester.

GILLIES, George Turnbull
6/1/7292, 8/11/15; No. 9 O.C.B., 8/3/16; Sea. Highrs., 23/7/16; F; Lieut.; w(2); M(1). 3 Hurst Road, Bexley, Kent.

GILLIES, Robert Alexander
A/12468, 25/1/18; No. 8 O.C.B., 7/6/18; Arg. & Suth'd. Highrs., 6/2/19; 2/Lieut. 289 Croxted Road, Dulwich, S.E.

GILLILAND, Robert
A/13091, 20/5/18; R.F.A., C/S, 26/7/18; R.G.A., 8/4/19; 2/Lieut.

GILLING, Frederick Cuthbert
6/3/7382, 11/11/15; No 14 O.C.B., 30/10/16; R. Lanc. R., 28/2/17, att. Manch. R.; F; Lieut.; w.
The Elms, Hadley Green, Barnet.

✠ GILLMAN, Bernard Tuite
D/A/12094, 8/10/17; R.F.C., C/S, 18/1/18; R.F.C., 11/2/18; F; 2/Lieut. Killed in action 24/9/18.

✠ GILMOUR, Archibald Kelke
B/1050, 31/8/14; K.O. Sco. Bord., 19/9/14; F; Capt.; w.
Killed in action 15/8/16.

✠ GILMOUR, Robert Wallace
6/5/8872, 12/1/16; No. 2 O.C.B., 14/8/16; R. Innis. Fus., 18/12/16; F; 2/Lieut.; w. Killed in action 29/3/18.

GILMOUR, Wallace Duff
F/1838, 16/10/14; R.A.S.C., 7/1/15; S Staff. R.; F; Lieut.
59 Gresham Street, E.C.

✠ GILPIN, Albert John
4/1/5033, 22/7/15, Cpl.; K.R. Rif. C., 20/1/16; F; 2/Lieut.
Killed in action 17/9/16.

GILSENAN, Terence Dermot Cole
6/1/6182, 13/9/15; W. York. R., 7/6/16; F; Lieut.; w; M.C., Croix de Guerre (French) with Palm.
2 Ravenscroft Avenue, Golders Green, N.W. 4.

✠ GILSON, Alex Ivan
6/1/8107, 2/12/15; R.F.C., 4/9/16; 2/Lieut.
Killed in action 17/3/17.

GILSON, Charles Stanley
A/10490, 12/1/17; R.F.C., C/S, 13/3/17; R.F.C., 19/4/17, Lab. Corps; F; Lieut. 54 Auckland Road, Ilford, Essex

GIMSON, Albert Yeomans
Sq/2723, 18/1/15; Norf. Yeo., 7/6/15; G,E,P; Capt.; w.
Rothesay, Victoria Road, Leicester.

GIMSON, Allen
6/2/8453, 17/12/15, Cpl.; 7th Lond. R., 4/8/16, att. 2nd Lond. R.; F; Capt.; w. 16 Woodridings Avenue, Hatch End, Middlesex.

GIMSON, Allynne Farmer
K/F/2360, 14/12/14; R.F.A., 12/1/15; F; Capt.; w(3); M.C., M(1). White House, Clarendon Road, Leicester.

GIMSON, Franklin Charles
A/13086, 20/5/18; No. 11 O.C.B., 24/1/19; General List, 8/3/19; 2/Lieut. The Secretariat, Colombo, Ceylon.

GINN, George
6/8323, 11/12/15; dis. 11/12/15.

GIRAUDEAU, Reginald Henry
C/11463, 6/6/17; dis to re-enlist in S. African Forces, 30/8/17.
c/o Major Oakes, Beechcroft, Hook Road, Surbiton.

GIRLING, Geoffrey Nottidge
C/Sq/12568, 6/2/18, L/C.; No. 1 Cav. C/S, 16/5/18; Suff. Yeo., 14/2/19; 2/Lieut. White House, Frostenden, Wangford, Suffolk

GISPERT, Arthur Joseph Modesto
6/2/6396, 23/9/15; Garr. O.C.B., 23/5/17; Lab. Corps, 14/7/17; Lieut. 12 Church Road, Forest Hill, S.E. 23.

GITTINGS, Daniel Carter
B/D/13639, 26/7/18; No. 11 O.C.B., 24/1/19; demob. 6/2/19
613 St. Paul Street, Baltimore, Maryland, U.S.A.

✠ GJERS, Laurence
1/2791, 26/1/15; Sea. Highrs., 2/6/15; Capt.
Killed in action 4/10/17.

GLADDEN, Roberts Baden
C/14139, 11/10/18; trfr. K.R. Rif. C., 21/6/19.
The Hall, Sutton, Stalham, Norfolk.

GLADSTONE, Holt Lindsay
6/4/7506, 15/11/15, L/C.; Bord. R., 4/8/16; Lieut.
1 Woodland Road, Rock Ferry, Cheshire.

GLANCY, Bernard Patrick
4/1/4626, 5/7/15; R. Dub. Fus., 16/12/15; Lieut.; w(2).

✠ GLANCY, Hugh
B/11668, 16/7/17; No. 11 O.C.B., 9/11/17; R. Muns. Fus., 26/3/18, M.G.C.; 2/Lieut. Killed in action 30/9/18.

GLANVILLE, Arthur Evanson
6/1/9516, 16/2/16; No. 7 O.C.B., 11/8/16; R. Dub. Fus., 18/12/16, att. North'd. Fus.; F; Lieut.; w-g, p.
Ben Inagh, Blackrock, Dublin.

GLANVILLE, Ivan Cecil Abbott
6/4/8351, 13/12/15; M.G.C., C/S, 31/10/16; M.G.C., 9/12/16; F; Capt.; w(2); M.C. and Bar.
42B Wickham Road, Brockley, S.E. 4.

GLANVILLE, Richard
3/3690, 20/5/15; Divl. Cyc. Coy., 1/9/15, att. Suff. Yeo.; Lieut.
Devonia, 63 Alexandra Road, Hornsey, N. 8.

GLANVILLE, William Henry
B/12732, 11/3/18; No. 20 O.C.B., 20/9/18; demob.
10 Sylvia Gardens, Wembley, Middlesex.

GLASGOW, William Ewart
B/9879, 8/11/16; No. 14 O.C.B., 30/1/17; W. York. R., 29/5/17; Lieut. 24 Third Avenue, Acton, W. 3.

GLASSBOROW, Reginald Walter Charles
F/1853, 16/10/14, L/C.; Sea. Highrs., 2/6/15, att. R.A.F.; M,E; Lieut. 4 Glenshiel Road, Eltham, S.E. 9. (Now in Ceylon.)

GLEADOWE, Reginald Morier Yorke
Sq/702, 9/4/13; dis. med. unfit, 4/8/14; R. Marines; Capt.; Order of St. Anne (Russia), Order of the Rising Sun (Japan).
National Gallery, W.C.

GLEAVE, Edward Thornton
F/2815, 29/1/15; R.A.S.C., 13/3/15; F; Capt.
Lloyd's Bank, Oxford. (Now in Cairo.)

APPENDIX II.—RECORDS OF RANK AND FILE.

GLEDHILL, Arthur Davey
6/Sq/5791, 23/8/15, L/C.; No. 1 Cav. C/S, 24/4/16; Suff. Yeo., 28/7/16, R.A.F.; S,P; Lieut.; w.
Walden, Myddelton, Ilkley, Yorkshire.

GLEDHILL, Herbert
D/11545, 21/6/17, L/C.; No. 14 O.C.B., 4/1/18; W. Rid. R., 25/6/18; F; Capt.
9 Windsor Road, Penarth, South Wales.

GLEN, Archibald
6/8675, 4/1/16; R.F.A., C/S, 26/5/16; R.G.A., 18/8/16, att. R.F.C.; F; Lieut.; w(2).
245 Abbey Road, Barrow-in-Furness.

✠ GLEN, David
6/1/7175, 3/11/15, L/C.; No. 14 O.C.B., 27/9/16; Suff. R., 18/12/16; 2/Lieut.
Died of wounds 24/4/17.

GLEN, John Mackenzie
B/72, 10/4/08; dis. 10/4/10; rej. A/1205, 14/9/14, Sgt.; Bedf. R., 24/7/15; Lieut.

GLENCROSS, George Alexander
6/5/5254, 31/7/15; L'pool. R., 13/12/15; F; Lieut.; w.
Knockrea, Maud Road, Liscard, Cheshire.

GLENISTER, Harold William
C/11484, 14/6/17, L/C.; R.A., C/S, 15/12/17; R.G.A., 20/5/18; P,E; 2/Lieut.
Melrose, Carew Road, Eastbourne.

GLENNY, Edward Bernard
6/5/7667, 22/11/15; No. 8 O.C.B., 4/8/16; R. Suss. R., 21/11/16; F; Capt.; M(1).
St. David's, Aldersbrook Road, South Wanstead.

GLIDDON, Donald Gilbert
4/1/4661, 6/7/15; North'd. Fus., 7/10/15; 2/Lieut.; w.

GLIDDON, Kenneth Yorke
A/11253, 14/5/17; R.F.C., C/S, 1/6/17; R.F.C., 4/7/17, R.A.F.; Lieut.

GLOSSOP, Antony Charles
E/14193, 18/10/18; demob. 23/1/19.
5 High Street, Arundell, Sussex.

GLOSTER, Ernest
B/10967, 30/3/17; No. 16 O.C.B., 5/10/17; Suff. R., 12/3/18, att. Camb. R.; F; Lieut.; w.
Parkdale, Streetsbrook Road, Solihull, Nr. Birmingham.

GLOSTER, Joseph
B/13462, 5/7/18; demob. 22/1/19.
Sylwood, Ashleigh Road, Solihull, Warwickshire.

GLOVER, Alfred Kendall
6/4/7068, 29/10/15; Devon. R., 4/9/16, att. R. Berks. R.; F,It; Capt.; w(2).
30 Telford Avenue, Streatham Hill, S.W. 2.

GLOVER, Cedric Howard
E/1645, 9/10/14; Midd'x. R., 27/1/15, secd. Intelligence Corps; F; Capt.; M(1).
35 Albert Road, Regents Park, N.W. 8.

GLOVER, Edward John
D/11825, 9/8/17, L/C.; No. 14 O.C.B., 4/1/18; E. Kent. R., 25/6/18; Lieut.
Acton College, Acton.

GLYN, John Paul
4/Sq/4498, 28/6/15; N. Ir. Horse, 8/1/16, R. Horse Gds.; F; Lieut.
25 Dulverton Mansions, Grays Inn Road, W.C. 1.

GLYN-JONES, Hildreth
F/1840, 16/10/14; Midd'x. R., 2/2/15, att. Norf. R., M.G.C.; G,F; Lieut.; Inv.
26 Old Park Villas, Palmers Green, N. 13.

GOALBY, Ernest
B/12807, 20/3/18; No. 20 O.C.B., 20/9/18; R. War. R., 17/3/19; 2/Lieut.
White House, Longford, Nr. Coventry, Warwickshire.

✠ GODBER, Hugh Gerald
C/1742, 15/10/14; North'd. Fus., 5/12/14; Capt.
Killed in action 11-18/7/16.

GODDARD, Edgar Douglas
6/1/8352, 13/12/15; No. 13 O.C.B., 4/11/16; Midd'x. R., 28/2/17; F; Lieut.
93 Meadvale Road, Ealing, W. 5.

GODDARD, Horace Rowland
Sq/114, 18/4/08; dis. 31/12/09.

GODDARD, Noel Leybourn
E/D/1573, 6/10/14, Sgt.; supernumerary 22/5/15 — demob. 23/7/19.
24 Paragon Grove, Surbiton, Surrey.

GODDARD, Richard Henry
E/2767, 25/1/15; Midd'x. R., 3/6/15, M.G.C.; F; Capt.; w(2).
3 Curzon Street, Slough, Buckinghamshire.

GODDARD, Robert Percy
3/3305, 19/4/15; 9th Lond. R., 18/9/15, att. Midd'x. R.; F; Capt.
Plumptre Place, Nottingham

GODFREY, George Edgar
A/D/13165, 30/5/18, Sgt.; trfr. K.R. Rif. C., 23/5/19; NR; Sgt.
52 York Road, Southend-on-Sea.

GODFREY, George Leslie
6/5/7668, 22/11/15; No. 8 O.C.B., 4/8/16; R.N.V.R., 21/11/16; F; Lieut.; w.
Crofton, Groes Road, Grassendale, Liverpool.

GODFREY, Ivor Samuel
A/13008, 1/5/18; trfr. 14th Lond. R., 6/12/18, Gord. Highrs.; Pte.
Whitefield House, Whitefield, Heaton Norris, Stockport.

GODFREY, Jack Henry
4/2/4185, 14/6/15; Worc. R., 11/10/15; F; Lieut.; w, g.
The Chantry, Fladbury, Worcestershire.

GODFREY, John Aubrey
6/5/C/8108, 2/12/15; No. 13 O.C.B., 4/11/16; North'd. Fus., 28/2/17; F; Lieut.
30 Connaught Road, Roath, Cardiff, South Wales.

GODSELL, James Stanley Paul
H/1698, 13/10/14; Glouc. R., 6/12/14; Lieut.; M.B.E.
c/o Messrs. Longmores, 24 Castle Street, Hertford.

GODSELL, Thomas Kempthorne
D/10804, 28/2/17; No. 2 R.G.A. C/S, 18/7/17; R.G.A., 21/1/18; Lieut.
The Grey House, Rodborough Common, Nr. Stroud, Gloucestershire.

GODWARD, Edgar Osmar
C/12553, 6/2/18; No. 19 O.C.B., 5/7/18; R. Fus., 3/3/19; 2/Lieut.
63 Ardoch Road, Catford, S.E. 6.

GOETZSCHE, Eric Christian
D/13888, 23/8/18; No. 11 O.C.B., 24/1/19; General List, 8/3/19; 2/Lieut.

GOFFE, Cecil Sidney
A/10491, 12/1/17; No. 14 O.C.B., 7/6/17; Manch. R., 25/9/17, att. York. R.; I,Siberia; Lieut.
198a Station Road, Westcliff-on-Sea.

✠ GOFFEY, John Graham
6/1/6125, 9/9/15, L/C.; K.R. Rif. C., 1/6/16; 2/Lieut.
Killed in action 3/9/16.

GOING, Joseph Arthur
6/Sq/6762, 11/10/15, L/C.; R.F.A., C/S, 4/8/16; R.F.A., 27/10/16; Lieut; w-p.
78 Gordon Avenue, Southampton.

GOLBORNE, Leon Gerard
4/3538, 10/5/15; trfr. Fife & Forfar Yeo., 9/3/16.

GOLBY, Maurice Edward
6/2/5558, 12/8/15, L/C.; R. Fus., 27/1/16, R.W. Surr. R.; 2/Lieut.
148 Albert Palace Mansions, Battersea Park.

GOLD, Alec Henry
A/1025, 24/8/14; R. Berks. R., 12/9/14; Lieut.
31 Gloucester Square, W. 2.

GOLD, Eric Norman
C/13325, 19/6/18; trfr. 14th Lond. R., 6/12/18, Gord. Highrs.; Cpl.
c/o Wellman, Smith & Owen Engineering Corporation, King's House, Kingsway, W.C. 2.

GOLD, Patrick Hugh
B/1029, 24/8/14; R. Berks. R., 12/9/14; Lieut.; w.
31 Gloucester Square, W. 2.

✠ GOLD, Percy
6/3/7445, 15/11/15; Scots Gds., 12/2/16; F; 2/Lieut.
Killed in action 19/7/16.

✠ GOLDBERG, Frederick William
4/3/4186, 14/6/15; R.W. Surr. R., 20/11/15, att. R. Dub. Fus.; 2/Lieut.
Killed in action 3/10/16.

✠ GOLDBERG, Herbert Walter
K/B/2411, 21/12/14, L/C.; R.W. Surr. R., 31/3/15; 2/Lieut.
Died of wounds 31/7/15.

APPENDIX II.—RECORDS OF RANK AND FILE.

GOLDEN, Dennis Thorold
B/D/12347, 1/1/18; R.F.C., C/S, 21/5/18; trfr. R.A.F., 21/5/18.
2 Riverview, Belvedere, Kent.

GOLDEN, Harold Arthur
3/3383, 26/4/15, L/C.; R.E., 13/10/15, att. Indian Army; P,E,I;
Lieut. 190 College Road, Norwich.

GOLDEN, Harry Norman
6/1/7231, 5/11/15; M.G.C., 25/9/16; F; Lieut.; w; M.C.
41 Blenheim Avenue, Highfield, Southampton.

GOLDIE, Donald Stewart McLeod
6/3/A/8020, 30/11/15, Sgt.; demob. 22/1/19.
7 Warwick Mansions, 10 Warwick Court, W.C.

GOLDIE, Noel Barré
K/B/2135, 19/11/14; R.G.A., 15/1/15; F; Capt.; M(1).
5 Harrington Street, Liverpool.

GOLDING, Hugh
6/5/7669, 22/11/15; No. 8 O.C.B., 4/8/16; R. Suss. R., 21/11/16;
F; Lieut.; Inv. 15 Pretoria Road, Cambridge.

GOLDINGHAM, Dick Dalrymple
B/849, 4/8/14; Midd'x. R., 15/8/14, att. Norf. R.; F.I; Major;
Inv; M(1).
Templecombe, Great Missenden, Buckinghamshire.

GOLDMAN, Joseph Wolfe
A/2910, 10/2/15; Dorset R., 3/6/15, M.G.C.; F; Lieut.; w-g.
12 Park Rise, Finchley Road, Golders Green.

GOLDRING, Horace
6/3/7259, 8/11/15, L/C.; E. Kent. R., 4/9/16; I; Capt.
Grasmere, Onslow Crescent, Woking.

GOLDRING, Stephen Spencer
C/13352, 26/6/18; trfr. 14th Lond. R., 6/12/18.
Beaford Rectory, North Devonshire.

GOLDWATER, Harry Gerald
A/10054, 29/11/16, L/C.; R.G.A., C/S, 9/5/17; R.G.A., 2/9/17;
F; Lieut. Vryburg, Bechuanaland, South Africa.

GOLLANCZ, Victor
4/5/4793, 12/7/15, L/C.; North'd. Fus., 3/10/15, Manch. R.;
Lieut. 73 Ladbroke Road, W. 11.

GOMME, Geoffrey James Lyon
E/1637, 9/10/14; Ches. R., 23/2/15, R.G.A.; F; Capt.
19 Melcombe Court, N.W. 1. (Now in Japan.)

COMPERTZ, Richard Humfrey Lytton
C/12612, 16/2/18; R.A.F., C/S, 21/5/18; trfr. 28th Lond. R.,
13/11/18. 4 Richmond Villas, Ilfracombe.

GOOD, Cecil Albert
K/F/2328, 14/12/14; Dorset R., 27/2/15; Lieut.

GOOD, John
B/Sq/11348, 23/5/17, Cpl.; No. 2 Cav. C/S, 11/4/18; R. Regt. of
Cav., 18/10/18; 2/Lieut. Barry's Hall, Timoleague, Co. Cork.

GOOD, Ronald D'Oyly
6/2/9352, 7/2/16; No. 14 O.C.B., 26/11/16; Dorset R., 28/2/17,
att. Linc. R.; F; Lieut.
48 High West Street, Dorchester, Dorset.

GOOD, Stuart Duncan
D/10149, 8/12/16; No. 20 O.C.B., 5/5/17; R.F.C., 28/8/17,
R.A.F.; 2/Lieut. Edgegate, Osborne Road, Buncliffe, Sheffield.

GOOD, Thomas Geoffrey
A/D/14326, 30/12/18; trfr. R. Regt. of Cav., 11/6/19.
Rose Garth, Driffield, East Yorkshire.

GOODACRE, Kenneth Roy
C/D/12244, 23/11/17; R.F.C., C/S, 5/4/18; trfr. R.A.F., 5/4/18.
Belmont, East Finchley, N. 2.

GOODAIR, William Edward
D/10414, 10/1/17; trfr. R.G.A., 14/2/17.
2 Sloane Gate Mansions, S.W. 1.

GOODALE, Henry John
K/2140, 19/11/14; 20th Lond. R., 6/7/15; F; Lieut.
9 Essex Street, Strand, W.C.

GOODALL, Alexander Gerald
6/Sq/7069, 29/10/15; R.F.A., C/S, 4/8/16; R.F.A., 1/12/16; F;
Lieut.; g, w. 64 Park Road, Dulwich, S.E. 21.

✠ GOODALL, Arthur
6/1/6960, 22/10/15; 12th Lond. R., 4/8/16; 2/Lieut.; w(3).
Died of wounds 20/2/18.

GOODALL, Ernest Victor
B/10672, 9/2/17; R.A., C/S, 11/5/17; R.G.A., 1/9/17; F; Lieut.
Hendra, Chaldon, Caterham.

✠ GOODALL, Harold Armitage
6/8546, 30/12/15; R.F.A., C/S, 23/6/16; R.F.A., 13/10/16;
2/Lieut.; w. Killed in action 22/3/18.

GOODCHILD, George Frederick
A/308, 29/6/08; dis. 28/6/12; University of London O.T.C.;
Lieut. 34 West Hill Road, Wandsworth, S.W. 18.

GOODCHILD, Hugh Napier
4/4115, 8/6/15; Norf. R., 7/9/15; 2/Lieut.
The Chestnuts, Unthank Road, Eaton, Norwich.

GOODCHILD, Norman James Hicks
C/11469, 11/6/17, L/C.; No. 14 O.C.B., 5/10/17; 21st Lond. R.,
26/2/18; 2/Lieut. Hepworth Hall, Halstead, Essex.

GOODE, George Herbert
2/3384, 28/4/15; Leic. R., 28/7/15, Army Cyc. Corps; M; Lieut.;
M(1). 51 Cambridge Road, Seven Kings, Essex.

GOODE, Josiah Arthur
C/D/12069, 1/10/17; No 2 O.C.B., 7/6/18; Midd'x. R., 5/2/19;
2/Lieut. 1 Hillside Crescent, St. James Lane, Muswell Hill, N. 10.

GOODE, Raymond Sheffield
6/3/8412, 15/12/15; No. 8 O.C.B., 4/8/16; R.W. Fus., 21/11/16;
F; Lieut. 312 Hagley Road, Edgbaston, Birmingham.

✠ GOODES, George Leonard
F/2923, 15/2/15; 4th Lond. R., 5/5/15; F; Capt.; w; M.C. and
Bar. Killed in action 6/10/16.

GOODEY, Arthur Nelson
C/10356, 5/1/17; No. 20 O.C.B., 5/5/17; Norf. R., 28/8/17; P;
2/Lieut. St. Mary's School, Ware, Hertfordshire.

GOODEY, Edward George
B/13601, 24/7/18; demob. 29/1/19.
9 Sunnyside, Stansted, Essex.

GOODGER, Herbert William
6/1/6618, 4/10/15; trfr. R.F.A., 16/6/16; R.G.A.; F; Lieut.
16 Macoma Terrace, Plumstead, S.E. 18.

GOODHEW, Rudolph Victor Felix
6/5/7393, 11/11/15, L/C.; R. Fus., 4/8/16; Capt.
600 Wandsworth Road, Clapham, S.W.

GOODING, Anthony Trevor
6/Sq/5559, 12/8/15, L/C.; R.F.A., 16/12/15; F; Capt.; w; M.C.,
Star of Roumania, M(2).
London & Brazilian Bank, B. Mitre 402, Buenos Aires, South
America.

GOODINGE, Wallinger
E/1534, 6/10/14; 9th Lond. R., 6/2/15, emp. M. of Munitions;
F; Lieut.; w. 17 Devonshire Place, W. 1.

GOODMAN, Alfred
A/9913, 14/11/16; A.S.C., C/S, 12/2/17; R.A.S.C., 24/3/17,
att. R.G.A.; F; Lieut. Red Lodge, Reigate, Surrey.

✠ GOODMAN, Gilbert Anthony
F/1751, 16/10/14, L/C.; N. Lan. R., 24/12/14, att. R.A.F.; It;
2/Lieut.; w. Killed in action 28/10/18.

GOODMAN, Montague
A/9834, 2/11/16, L/C.; A.S.C., C/S, 12/2/17; R.A.S.C., 24/3/17;
Lieut.; w. Merleswood, Woodford Green, Essex.

GOODMAN, Peter Vincent
C/D/12083, 4/10/17; No. 7 O.C.B., 10/5/18; R. Dub. Fus.,
29/10/18; 2/Lieut. New Street, Carrickmacross.

GOODMAN, William Arthur Harold
6/4/6162, 11/9/15; No. 14 O.C.B., 30/10/16; Hunts. Cyc. Bn.,
28/2/17, att. Oxf. & Bucks. L.I.; F; Lieut.
Laburnum Grange, Boughton, Chester.

GOODRICH, Edmund Richard
6/Sq/6643, 5/10/15, L/C.; R.F.A., C/S, 7/7/16; R.F.A., 8/9/16;
F; Capt.; M(1).
Branscombe, Mayfield Avenue, Woodford Green, Essex.

GOODWIN, Frederick Claude
C/11470, 11/6/17; No. 16 O.C.B., 5/10/17; Sco. Horse, 12/3/18;
2/Lieut. South Side, Friern Barnet, N. 11.

APPENDIX II.—RECORDS OF RANK AND FILE.

GOODWIN, George Frederick
D/12095, 8/10/17, Cpl.; demob. 23/1/19.
Barclay's Bank Ltd., Stafford.

GOODWIN, George Frederick Storer
3/3635, 17/5/15; Glouc. R., 16/11/15, att. R. Ir. Regt.; Lieut.

GOODWIN, Harold Ralph Otway
B/Sq/12022, 20/9/17; No. 2 Cav. C/S, 11/4/18; R. Regt. of Cav., 18/10/18; F; Lieut.
The Manor Farm, Herringswell, Mildenhall, Suffolk.

GOODWIN, Laurence Frank
6/6846, 16/10/15, Sgt.; No. 14 O.C.B., 28/8/16; North'n. R., 24/10/16, R.F.C., R.A.F.; F; Lieut.; M.C.
89 Osborne Road, Forest Hill, E.7.

GOODWIN, Philip John Laughton
C/12655, 27/2/18; trfr. R.A.F., 21/5/18.
120 Hillfield Avenue, Hornsey, N.8.

GOODWIN, Vernon Knott
6/1/6921, 19/10/15; A.S.C., C/S, 13/11/16; R.A.S.C., 3/12/16, att. R.A.F.; S; Lieut.; Inv.
Heath House, Hyde Heath, Amersham.

GOODWORTH, Reginald Frederick
1/3435, 1/5/15; 9th Lond. R., 22/9/15; F; Lieut.; g. w.
3 Meteor Road, Westcliff-on-Sea.

GOODWYN, Charles Colin
F/1852, 16/10/14, L/C.; Oxf. & Bucks. L.I., 22/12/14, R.E.; F; Capt.
The Gables, Boxmoor, Hertfordshire.

GOODWYN, Lawrence John
B/341, 2/2/09; Oxf. & Bucks. L.I., 15/8/14, att. Yorks. L.I.; F; Capt.; w(2).
The Gables, Boxmoor, Hertfordshire.

GOODWYN, Julius Norton
D/12940, 16/4/18, L/C.; trfr. K.R. Rif. C., 13/5/19.

GOODYER, Leonard Boyce
4/2/4072, 7/6/15; R.W. Surr. R., 3/10/15, att. R.F.C., R.A.F.; F; Lieut.
64 Birdhurst Road, South Croydon, Surrey.

GOOLDEN, Reginald Ollivant
D/10227, 29/12/16; No. 21 O.C.B., 5/5/17; Worc. R., 30/10/17; 2/Lieut.; w.
Ravenoak, Cheadle Hulme, Cheshire.

GOOSE, Thomas Halley
6/B/5474, 9/8/15, C.Q.M.S.; No. 4 O.C.B., 10/5/18; Suff. R., 4/2/19; 2/Lieut.
1 Burwash Road, Plumstead, S.E.18.

GORDON, Alan
F/1732, 15/10/14; Bord. R., 27/11/14, Tank Corps; F; Capt.
Fairholme, Langley Avenue, Surbiton.

GORDON, Alban Godwin
6/8783, 7/1/16; A.S.C., C/S, 29/5/16; R.A.S.C., 3/7/16; F; Capt.; M(2).
439 Oxford Street, W.1.

GORDON, Francis
A/9843, 3/11/16, L/C.; R.A., C/S, 7/6/17; Dental Surgeon, 19/9/17; Capt.
33 Canal, Salisbury.

GORDON, James Miller
1921, 22/10/14; R. Sco. Fus., 13/11/14, Nigeria R.; Lieut.
Fernbank, Harrow-on-the-Hill.

✠ GORDON, James Richard
2/3177, 6/4/15; Arg. & Suth'd. Highrs., 17/4/15; Asst. Paymaster, R.N.R.
Died 18/2/18

✠ GORDON, John Cameron
6/1/9328, 7/2/16; No. 13 O.C.B., 4/11/16; R. Berks., 28/2/17; 2/Lieut.
Killed in action 21/3/18.

GORDON, Laurence Victor
A/12542, 5/2/18; R.E., C/S, 12/5/18; R.E., 27/9/18; 2/Lieut.
270 Elgin Avenue, Maida Vale, W.9.

GORDON, Michael
Sq/602, 22/1/12; dis. 28/2/14.

GORDON, William Macdonald
6/2/8723, 5/1/16; No. 7 O.C.B., 11/8/16; R. Innis. Fus., 18/12/16; Lieut.
1 Alexandra Terrace, Londonderry, Ireland.

✠ GORE-BROWNE, Harold Thomas Thirlwall
3/3636, 17/5/15; K.R. Rif. C., 2/9/15; F; 2/Lieut.
Died of wounds 23/8/16.

GORMAN, John Karney
E/3024, 9/3/15; Bord. R., 5/4/15, R.F.A., R.G.A.; E,P; Major; w;M.C.
Adjutant, R.I.C., Depôt, Phœnix Park, Dublin.

GORNALL, Gerald Francis
B/12725, 14/3/18; No. 5 O.C.B., 6/9/18.

✠ GORRIE, John William
4/5/4746, 12/7/15; Worc. R., 29/9/15; F; 2/Lieut.
Killed in action 19/7/16.

GOSLING, Arthur Starr
A/10724, 12/2/17, L/C.; R.E., 10/9/17; Lieut.

GOSLING, Cuthbert Laurence
K/2864, 5/2/15; dis. 5/2/15.

GOSLING, Fred Hampton
H/1967, 26/10/14; Notts. & Derby. R., 15/1/15; Capt.; w; M.C.

GOSLING, Gerald Francis
A/10858, 9/3/17; trfr. 16th Lond. R., 3/8/17; E,P,F; Pte.
Rushmere, Leighton Buzzard, Bedfordshire.

GOSS, Leslie George
6/3/7070, 29/10/15; trfr R.G.A., 7/7/16;
18 Tarboy, Aylesbury.

GOSSE, Philip George Wilkes
C/11464, 7/6/17, Cpl.; demob. 29/1/19.
4 Cadogan Road, Surbiton, Surrey.

GOSSELL, Kenneth Otto Theodore
Sq/209, 7/5/08; 1st County of Lond. Yeo., 13/6/13; E,G,S,P; Capt.; M.C.
5 Eton Avenue, N.W.3.

GOSSIP, Oliver Howden
4/1/4460, 28/6/15; Cam'n. Highrs., 5/11/15, att. 14th Lond. R., R.F.C.; F,S,E,P; Lieut.
54 High Street, Inverness.

GOTELEE, Campbell St. John
6/5/8873, 12/1/16; No. 8 O.C.B., 4/8/16; E. Surr. R., 21/11/16; F; Capt.
Runfold House, Nr. Farnham, Surrey.

GOTELEE, Guy Stanley
C/A/12070, 1/10/17, L/C.; R.F.A., C/S, 15/3/18; R.G.A., 8/2/19; 2/Lieut.
St. Crantock, Crichton Road, Carshalton, Surrey.

✠ GOTT, Albert Ernest
4/1/4366, 21/6/15; R. War. R., 6/11/15; 2/Lieut.
Killed in action 18/11/16.

✠ GOULD, Ernest William
B/10208, 18/12/16; No. 21 O.C.B., 5/5/17; S. Lan. R., 28/8/17, att. Som. L.I.; E; 2/Lieut.
Killed in action 10/4/18.

GOULD, Frederic Victor
B/10119, 6/12/16, L/C.; No. 21 O.C.B., 5/5/17; S. Lan. R., 28/8/17, att. Som. L.I.; P,F; Lieut.
Maisonette, Ashford, Middlesex.

GOULD, Granville Loris
H/3/3068, 18/3/15, L/C.; R.W. Kent R., 7/10/15, att. R.A.F.; E,P; Lieut.; w(2).
23 Manor Road, Folkestone.

GOULD, Joseph
C/10809, 28/2/17; R.F.C., C/S, 16/4/17; R.F.C., 20/6/17, Lab Corps; 2/Lieut.
50 Albert Road, Levenshulme, Manchester.

GOULD, Norman Carruthers
6/3/8520, 29/12/15; No. 14 O.C.B., 30/10/16; Shrop. L.I., 28/2/17; F; 2/Lieut.
Upway, Porlock, Somerset.

GOULD, Walter Charles
6/2/8169, 6/12/15; No. 8 O.C.B., 4/8/16; Dorset R., 21/11/16; F; Lieut.
Church Street, Yetminster, Sherborne, Dorset.

GOULDESBROUGH, Arthur Evelyn
6/2/D/5896, 30/8/15; No. 14 O.C.B., 30/1/17; Sea. Highrs., 25/4/17; Lieut.

GOULDING, Llewellyn John Boydell
6/A/Sq/7766, 23/11/15; No. 14 O.C.B., 30/10/16; Hamps. R., 28/2/17, att. Essex R.; F; Lieut.
186 Adelaide Road, South Hampstead, N.W.3.

GOULSTONE, Frederick Thomas
C/12618, 18/2/18, L/C.; demob. 23/1/19.
Hill House Farm, Box, Wiltshire.

GOULT, Garfield Gustavus George
A/D/11883, 20/8/17; No. 3 O.C.B., 8/2/18; Suff. R., 30/7/18; 2/Lieut.
17 Tollgate Lane, Bury St. Edmunds.

GOURLAY, Eric Thornbrough
C/11062, 16/4/17, L/C.; Household Bde. O.C.B., 8/3/18; Scots Gds., 24/9/18; 2/Lieut.
Luffness Mill house, Aberlady, East Lothian.

APPENDIX II.—RECORDS OF RANK AND FILE.

GOURLAY, William Balfour
C/99, 17/4/08; dis. 15/4/09; rej. C/433, 18/6/09; dis. 17/6/13;
R.A.M.C.; E,F,NR; Capt.; M.C.
c/o K. M. Gourlay Esq., 23 St. Andrews Square, Edinburgh.
(Now in U.S.A.)

GOURLEY, Rupert Platt
B/13667, 29/7/18, L/C.; demob. 29/1/19.
48 Grosvenor Street, Liscard, Wallasey, Cheshire.

GOVER, Charles Cecil
4/5/4671, 8/7/15; R.E., 5/9/15; Capt.; w.

GOVER, Henry
6/1/6084, 6/9/15, L/C.; R.W. Kent R., 6/6/16, att. 24th Lond.
R.; F; Capt.; M(1). 5 Monument Street, E.C. 3

GOW, Ronald
B/13589, 22/7/18; demob. 29/1/19.
Oakleigh, Portland Road, Bowden, Cheshire.

GOWAR, Lancelot John
6/3/6418, 23/9/15; R.F.C., C/S, 8/10/16; R.F.C., 26/2/17;
2/Lieut. Killed 1/5/17.

GOWING, Sidney Albert
6/5/C/8510, 21/12/15, Sgt.; demob. 22/1/19.
91 Woodgrange Avenue, North Finchley, N.

GOWLAND, Thomas Stockton
D/12904, 8/4/18; demob. 24/1/19.
Hutton Mount, Ripon, Yorkshire.

GOWLETT, William Robert
C/A/12084, 4/10/17; R.F.C., C/S, 18/1/18; R.F.C., 6/3/18,
R.A.F.; 2/Lieut. Great Canfield Hall, Dunmow, Essex.

GOWRING, Humphrey John
B/13580, 22/7/18; trfr. 28th Lond. R., 13/11/18.
49 High West Street, Dorchester, Dorset.

GRACE, Cleveland Raphael
Sq/1301, 25/9/14; Lovats Scouts, 24/2/15; Lieut.

GRACE, Cyril Stuart
C/13262, 10/6/18; No. 11 O.C.B., 24/1/19; General List, 8/3/19;
2/Lieut. Highwoods, Kingswood, Epsom.

GRACE, Frank William
B/13511, 11/7/18; trfr. 28th Lond. R., 6/9/18.
Kingslea, Kendall Avenue South, Sanderstead, Surrey

GRACIE, Archibald Leslie
6/1/8566, 31/12/15; No. 8 O.C.B., 4/8/16; K.R. Rif. C., 21/11/16,
att. 9th Lond. R.; F; Capt.; M.C.
c/o Cox & Coy., 38 Lombard Street, E.C. 3.

GRAHAM, Alexander Mitchell
6/8711, 5/1/16; No. 9 O.C.B., 8/3/16; Arg. & Suth'd. Highrs.,
23/7/16; 2/Lieut.
c/o J. A. Graham Esq., 104 Commercial Street, Dundee.

GRAHAM, Charles Gorden
6/3/5833, 26/8/15; Worc. R., 26/1/16; F; Capt.; M.C., M(1).
Penquite, Teignmouth, South Devonshire. (Now in Ceylon.)

GRAHAM, Charles James
6/5/6354, 20/9/15; 4th Lond R., 4/6/16; F; Major; D.S.O.,
M.C. and Bar, M(1). 25 Clanricarde Gardens, Hyde Park, W. 2.

GRAHAM, Edward Arnold
B/11699, 19/7/17, L/C.; No. 14 O.C.B., 9/11/17; R. War. R.,
30/4/18, R.A.F.; SR; Lieut.
Crofton Vicarage, Barnt Green, Birmingham.

GRAHAM, Evelyn Ronald Brodrick
C/10989, 3/4/17, L/C.; No. 14 O.C.B., 7/12/17; 22nd Lond. R.,
28/5/18, att. 10th Lond. R., Indian Army; E,P; Lieut.
222 Strand. W.C. 2.

GRAHAM, Gerald
B/2630, 7/1/15; R.F.C., 17/3/15, R.N.V.R.; F,E; Lieut.; w.
The Red House, Kilverstone, Thetford.

GRAHAM, Harold Howe
B/9886, 9/11/16; No. 14 O.C.B., 30/1/17; Rif. Brig., 25/4/17;
2/Lieut.; Inj. Fernside, Theydon Bois, Essex.

GRAHAM, Hugh Nelson
C/12592, 12/2/18, L/C.; dis. med. unfit, 19/9/18.
Little Rock, Rostrevor, Co. Down, Ireland. (Now in U.S.A.)

✠ GRAHAM, John Wilfred
B/730, 11/11/13; High. L.I., 15/8/14, att. Cam'n. Highrs.; F;
Lieut. Killed in action 21/12/14.

✠ GRAHAM, Lachlan Seymour
6/3/9370, 9/2/16; No. 14 O.C.B., 27/9/16; High. L.I., 18/12/16;
F; 2/Lieut. Died of wounds 29/8/17.

GRAHAM, Norman
6/3/7585, 18/11/15; Bord. R., 4/9/16, att. R. Innis. Fus.; F;
Lieut.; p. Richmond House, Howard Place, Carlisle.

GRAHAM, Peter
A/10273, 1/1/17; No. 20 O.C.B., 5/5/17; Arg. & Suth'd. Highrs.,
28/8/17; F; Lieut.; w.
Craigmore, Stoughton Drive North, Leicester.

GRAHAM, Robert
A/14334, 30/12/18; demob. 11/1/19. Braehill, Ruthwell, N.B

GRAHAM, Robert Charles
4/1/5198, 29/7/15; trfr. 16th Lond. R., 18/4/17, K.R. Rif. C.,
M.G.C.; F; Pte. 45 Grange Avenue, Scarborough.

GRAHAM, Sidney Hamilton
6/Sq/8632, 3/1/16; R.F.A., C/S, 21/7/16; R.F.A., 30/9/16; F;
Lieut.; w. The Mount, Normacot, Stoke-on-Trent.

GRAHAM, Thomas
6/5/6807, 14/10/15; No. 11 O.C.B., 7/5/16; Essex R., 4/9/16,
Rif. Brig.; F; Capt.; w. Church Hill, Beckenham.

GRAHAM, Thomas Leslie
K/B/2449, 28/12/14; Sea. Highrs., 3/3/15; Lieut.; M.C.
Ardwick, Walton-on-Thames.

✠ GRAHAM-KING, Reginald See KING R. G.

GRAMMER, Douglas
6/3/6226, 13/9/15; R. War. R., 8/6/16; F; Lieut.; g,w.
Bank House, South Farnborough, Hampshire.

GRANDISON, Andrew Cameron
B/11392, 30/5/17; A.S.C., C/S, 1/9/17; R.A.S.C., 27/10/17;
Lieut. 2 Bevon's Terrace, Southampton.

✠ GRANGE, James Burness
6/1/9415, 16/2/16; No. 8 O.C.B., 4/8/16; W. York. R., 21/11/16;
2/Lieut. Killed in action 20/4/18.

GRANT, Cyril Thomas
1/2985, 27/2/15; Hamps. R., 12/10/15; Lieut.
9 Durban Road, Beckenham, Kent.

GRANT, Frank Mortimer
6/9205, 26/1/16; trfr. R.F.A., 4/5/16; R.F.A., 1/10/17; F;
Capt.; M.C. 152 Seaview Road, Wallasey, Cheshire.

GRANT, Gerald Charles Lancelot
D/12121, 15/10/17; trfr. K.R. Rif. C., 13/5/19; L/C.
Prospect House, Upton, Didcot.

GRANT, Herbert MacDonald
C/14238, 28/10/18; demob. 16/1/19.
423 Itailia, Lomas, Argentina.

✠ GRANT, John Anderton
6/4/6009, 2/9/15, Sgt.; No. 14 O.C.B., 27/12/16; R. Suss. R.,
27/3/17; F; 2/Lieut.; w. Killed in action 14/5/18.

GRANT, John Michael Hay
D/E/13893, 23/8/18; R.A., C/S, 2/10/18; demob.
Newlands, Seaford, Sussex.

GRANT, William
6/7734, 22/11/15; No. 9 O.C.B., 8/3/16; Gord. Highrs., 23/7/16,
att. Rif. Brig.; I; Lieut.
c/o Messrs. Grindlay & Coy., Bankers, Bombay.

GRANT-COLQUHOUN, James Allen Noel
B/10874, 15/3/17; R.F.A., C/S, 21/9/17; R.F.A., 25/2/18,
R.G.A.; F,It,E,I; Lieut.; w.
4 Caxton Grove, Vanse Road, Durban, South Africa.

✠ GRANTHAM, Edward Rodney Hasluck
6/1/8927, 14/1/16; No. 5 O.C.B., 14/8/16; North'd. Fus.,
21/11/16; 2/Lieut. Died of wounds 31/3/17.

GRANTHAM-HILL, Clermont
Sq/670, 26/11/12, L/C.; 3rd Huss., 15/8/14; F; Lieut.; w.
46 Lexham Gardens, W. 8.

GRAPES, Leslie Onslow
C/11794, 2/8/17, Sgt.; demob. 6/1/19.
Thorncliffe, East Lane, Wembley, Middlesex.

APPENDIX II.—RECORDS OF RANK AND FILE.

GRATION, Donald Walter
A/11201, 7/5/17, L/C.; R.A., C/S, 7/6/18; R.G.A., 13/2/19; 2/Lieut.   Estate Duty Office, Somerset House, W.C.2.

GRAVES-SMITH, Norman Henry
2/3453, 3/5/15; Glouc. R., 3/8/15; F; Lieut.; w.
   Aldreth, Stonehouse, Gloucestershire.

GRAY, Alfred Leslie
6/1/6820, 14/10/15, L/C.; Notts. & Derby. R., 4/8/16, Indian Army; F,I; Lieut.; w.
   The Datcha, Bushey Hall Road, Watford.

GRAY, Audley
F/1890, 16/10/14; Oxf. & Bucks. L.I., 24/11/14, Army Cyc Corps.   Eastfield, Whitchurch-on-Thames.

GRAY, Charles Dowie
D/11128, 30/4/17; No. 14 O.C.B., 10/8/17; dis. med. unfit, 27/2/18.   50 Grange Mount, Claughton, Birkenhead.

GRAY, Colin William McLachlan
6/1/9053, 21/1/16; No. 1 O.C.B., 6/9/16; R.F.C., 25/1/17, R.A.F.; Lieut.; w.   39 Gainsborough Road, Crewe, Cheshire.

GRAY, George Gladwin
4/5/1/4539, 1/7/15, L/C.; M.G.C., 4/8/16; F; Lieut.
   Ashland House, Tennyson Avenue, Bridlington, Yorkshire.

GRAY, Harry
6/9251, 2/2/16; dis. to re-enlist in R.A.O.C., 27/5/16, Staff Sgt.; R.A.O.C., 6/5/18; F; Lieut.; Inv.
   The Priory, Beaufort Road, Kingston-on-Thames.

GRAY, Joseph Leslie
C/1711, 15/10/14, L/C.; K.O. Sco. Bord., 8/4/15; G,E,P,F; Lieut.   Murrayville, Flower Lane, Mill Hill, N.W.7.

✠ GRAY, Maurice
Sq/685, 24/1/13; 2nd Drag. Gds., 15/8/14; Capt.
   Killed in action 8/8/18.

GRAY, Maurice Charles Harrison
C/13398, 28/6/18, L/C.; trfr. 14th Lond. R., 6/12/18.
   The Rectory, Ingatestone, Essex.

GRAY, Percy
6/5/6793, 13/10/15, Sgt.; L'pool. R., 4/9/16; F; Lieut.
   12 St. Albans Road, Bootle, Lancashire.

GRAY, Reginald
6/4/8829, 10/1/16; No. 14 O.C.B., 26/11/16; North'd. Fus., 28/2/17; F; 2/Lieut.; w.
   5 Mount Pleasant, Coniscliffe Road, Darlington.

GRAY, Richard Forsyth
6/4/5522, 16/8/15; R.A.S.C., 15/11/15; It; Major.
   28 Frognal, Hampstead, N.W.3.

GRAY, Richard William
D/10201, 15/12/16; Garr. O.C.B., 23/5/17; Lab. Corps., 14/7/17; 2/Lieut.   Evanstowe, Avondale Road, South Croydon.

GRAY, Wilfrid Henry
K/E/2423, 21/12/14; R.E., 11/4/15; F; Capt.; Inv.
   c/o Hybart, Broadland & Coy. Ltd., 6 Suffolk Street, Pall Mall, S.W.1.

GRAY, William
6/3/8567, 31/12/15, L/C.; No. 14 O.C.B., 27/9/16, No. 2 O.C.B.; Interpreter, 24/1/17; Shrops. L.I., att. 15th Lancers and S. Persia Rif.; Persia; Capt.; M(2).
   c/o Yangtsze Insurance Assn., The Bund, Shanghai, China.

✠ GRAY, William Leslie
A/11280, 14/5/17; No. 14 O.C.B., 9/11/17; Suff. R., 30/4/18; F; 2/Lieut.   Died of wounds 28/9/18.

GRAYSTON, George Arthur
4/3/3958, 3/6/15; Cold. Gds., 17/8/15; F; Capt.; M.C.
   Lichfield Street, Tamworth.

GRAZEBROOK, Christopher John
A/10418, 10/1/17; No. 14 O.C.B., 7/6/17; Worc. R., 25/9/17, M.G.C.; F; 2/Lieut.; w,Inv.
   The Dene, Pedmore, Nr. Stourbridge.

GREAR, Arthur Thomas Lantsbery
D/2849, 30/1/15, Cpl.; Herts. R., 11/6/15, Glouc. R.; F,It; Lieut.; w(2).   20 Avondale Road, Southport.

GREAR, Ernest John Lantsbery
K/D/2499, 31/12/14, L/C.; Midd'x. R., 3/6/15, M.G.C.; F,It; Lieut.; w.   50 Amhurst Park, London, N.16.

GREATHED, Archer Jack
A/14078, 30/9/18; demob. 29/1/19.
   Stubbins, Waltham Abbey, Essex.

GREATOREX, Heyrick Anthony
6/5/7670, 22/11/15, Cpl.; Norf. R., 25/9/16; F; Lieut.; w.
   Witton, Norwich.

GREAVES, Arthur Reginald
C/10614, 25/1/17; No. 14 O.C.B., 5/7/17; Notts. & Derby. R., 30/10/17; F; Lieut.; g.
   The Cottage, Wirksworth, Derbyshire.

GREAVES, Walter Fernie
6/1/9143, 25/1/16; No. 14 O.C.B., 30/10/16; York. & Lanc. R., 24/1/17; F; Lieut.; w.
   Wickersley House, Nr. Rotherham, Yorkshire.

GREEN, Alfred George
6/3/6576, 2/10/15; 11th Lond. R., 20/12/15, Army Cyc. Corps; Lieut.

GREEN, Archibald Hewlett
6/3/7586, 18/11/15; No. 11 O.C.B., 7/5/16; Manch. R., 4/9/16; F; Lieut.; w.
   St. Margaret's Vicarage, Altrincham, Cheshire. (Now in Singapore.)

GREEN, Arthur
B/11417, 1/6/17; trfr. 28th Lond. R., 24/9/17, Intelligence Corps; F; Pte.   24 Woodlands Avenue, Church End, Finchley, N.3.

✠ GREEN, Arthur Vivian
6/2/8724, 5/1/16; No. 7 O.C.B., 11/8/16; R. Dub. Fus., 18/12/16; 2/Lieut.   Killed in action 17/8/17.

GREEN, Brian Michael
A/1368, 26/9/14; S. Lan. R., 26/3/15, att. Devon. R.; F; Lieut.
   26 Upper Hamilton Terrace, N.W.8.

✠ GREEN, Charles James
C/11077, 18/4/17; No. 12 O.C.B., 10/8/17; R. Suss. R., 27/11/17; Capt.   Killed in action 16/4/18.

GREEN, Charles James Salkeld
B/8, 1/4/08, Sgt.; 7th Lond. R., 8/7/10, att. 22nd and 19th Lond. R.; F; Lt.-Col.; D.S.O., M.C., Croix de Guerre (Belge), M(4).
   61 Glenmore Road, N.W.3.

GREEN, Cyril Arnold Howell
D/12994, 29/4/18; No. 16 O.C.B., 18/10/18; K.R. Rif. C., 17/3/19; 2/Lieut.
   c/o W. A. Green Esq., Petersburg, Transvaal, South Africa.

GREEN, Digby
6/3/9232, 25/1/16; R.F.A., C/S, 4/8/16; R.G.A., 1/11/16; F; Lieut.; M.C.
   Harlgate House, Howden, East Yorkshire. (Now in Nairobi.)

✠ GREEN, Ernest Michael
K/B/2237, 3/12/14, Sgt.; Hamps. R., 31/3/15; F; Capt.; w.
   Killed in action 3/9/16.

GREEN, Frederick Mason
B/211, 8/5/08; 23rd Lond. R., 8/7/10.

GREEN, George
6/1/7507, 15/11/15; Manch. R., 4/8/16, att. N. Lan. R.; F; Capt.; w.   13 Wendover Road, Bromley, Kent.

GREEN, George Ewin
B/2635, 7/1/15; R.A.S.C., 5/7/15, M.G.C.; Lieut.; M(2).
   103 Revelstoke Road, Wimbledon Park, S.W.18.

GREEN, George Morgan Devereux
6/4/9371, 8/2/16; R.A., C/S, 26/1/17; trfr. R.G.A., 26/1/17.
   7 Bridge Street, Haverfordwest, South Wales.

✠ GREEN, Gilbert Pitcher
6/5/7260, 8/11/15, Cpl.; Ches. R., 4/8/16; 2/Lieut.
   Died of wounds 25/10/16.

✠ GREEN, Henry Edwin
B/221, 12/5/08; 22nd Lond. R., 28/6/11; Capt.
   Died of wounds 13/10/16.

GREEN, Herbert Williams
6/2/8790, 7/1/16, Cpl.; No. 14 O.C.B., 30/10/16; R. Suss. R., 24/1/17.
   c/o L. P. Newman Esq., Oakeynoe Road, Eastbourne.

✠ GREEN, Horace Salkeld
B/33, 3/4/08; 7th Lond. R., 20/10/10; F; Major; M(1).
   Killed in action 20/9/17.

APPENDIX II.—RECORDS OF RANK AND FILE.

GREEN, Hugh Henderson
4/3691, 20/5/15; R. Fus., 10/9/15; Lieut.; w.
3 Alwyn Place, Canonbury, N. 1.

GREEN, James Noel Scott
4/3774, 27/5/15; R.H.A., 19/11/15; F; Lieut.; w,g; M.C.
21 The Fosse, Central, Leicester.

GREEN, Leslie Douglas
6/1/6976, 23/10/15; M.G.C., 25/9/16; Lieut.
64 Avondale Avenue, Woodside Park, N. 12.

GREEN, Michael Arthur
B/1252, 23/9/14; Glouc. R., 15/8/14; Major; M.C., M(2).
26 Upper Hamilton Terrace, N.W. 8.

✠ GREEN, Philip Louis Samuel
K/H/2513, 31/12/14; W. York. R., 22/4/15; 2/Lieut.
Killed in action 18/9/16.

GREEN, Reginald Leslie
6/3/7826, 25/11/15; No. 8 O.C.B., 4/8/16; K.R. Rif. C., 21/11/16; 2/Lieut.

✠ GREEN, St. John
A/10282, 1/1/17; No. 21 O.C.B., 5/5/17; R. Innis. Fus., 28/8/17; 2/Lieut.
Killed in action 6/12/17.

GREEN, Thomas Lewis Lionel
F/3/3049, 15/3/15; R.F.A., 8/5/15, att. R.F.C.; F; Lieut.; Inv.
8 Bishopsgate, E.C. 2.

GREEN, Walter
6/5/8894, 13/1/16, L/C.; No. 5 O.C.B., 14/8/16; Household Bn., 15/11/16, W. Rid. R.; F; Capt.; w(2); M.C.
3 St. Dunstans Gardens, Acton, W. 3.

GREEN, William Edward
B/10961, 30/3/17; R.F.C., C/S, 1/6/17; R.F.C., 4/7/17, R.A.F.; Lieut.; D.F.C.
1 George Street, Huntingdon.

GREEN, William Gordon
B/10339, 4/1/17, Cpl.; R.G.A., C/S, 9/5/17; R.G.A., 2/9/17; F; Lieut. Home Glen, Haydon Park Road, Wimbledon, S.W. 19.

GREEN, William Harry Topliss
6/5/8607, 3/1/16; R.A. C/S, 7/8/16; R.F.A., 17/11/16; F; Lieut.; w; M.C., M(1).
13a Orchard Street, W. 1.

GREEN, William Henry
6/5/6413, 23/9/15; L'pool. R., 19/12/15, secd. Lab. Corps.
32 Hollybank Road, Birkenhead.

GREEN, William Herbert
6/5/8871, 12/1/16; No. 7 O.C.B., 11/8/16; R. Muns. Fus., 18/12/16, att. R. Ir. Rif.; F; Lieut.
Glasfryn, Netherton, Dudley, Worcestershire. (Now in West Africa.)

GREENBERG, Bernard Morris. See GREENHILL, B. M.

GREENE, Felix John Wilkinson
6/2/6688, 7/10/15; Glouc. R., 21/4/16; F; Lieut.; w; Croix de Guerre (French).
107 Earls Court Road, W. 8.

✠ GREENER, Francis Pemberton
B/371, 22/3/09, Sgt.; E. Surr. R., 15/8/14; F; 2/Lieut.
Killed in action 15/2/15.

GREENER, Hugh Martin
6/5/5255, 31/7/15, Sgt.; No. 9 O.C.B., 6/3/16; North'd. Fus., 6/7/16; F; Capt.; M.C.
123 Wallgate, Wigan, Lancashire.

GREENFIELD, John Richard Frederick
B/12792, 18/3/18; No. 4 O.C.B., 6/9/18; R.W. Kent. R., 16/3/19; 2/Lieut.
The Common, Chistlehurst.

GREENFIELD, Sidney Richard
6/4/6415, 23/9/15; No. 11 O.C.B., 16/5/16; North'd. Fus., 4/9/16; F; Lieut.; w; M.C.
22 Marlow Road, Leicester.

✠ GREENFIELD, Thomas Bevil
Sq/3112, 25/3/15; R.E., 16/6/15; G; 2/Lieut.
Killed in action 19/9/15.

GREENHALGH, Cecil
A/9802, 30/10/16; No. 14 O.C.B., 27/12/16; E; York. R., 27/3/17; F; Lieut.; w.
Elmhurst, Runcorn, Cheshire.

GREENHALGH, Nathaniel
B/12404, 17/1/18; R.E., C/S, 14/4/18; R.E., 15/8/18; 2/Lieut.
c/o West India Centre, Seething Lane, E.C.

GREENHILL, Albert Edward
4/6/5/4928, 19/7/15, Sgt.; Bord. R., 20/1/16; F,S; Major; M.C., M(3).
132a Shooters Hill Road, Blackheath. (Now in Constantinople.)

GREENHILL, Bernard Morris
6/Sq/5848, 26/8/15; Bucks. Huss., 12/12/15, R. Horse Gds.; F; Lieut.; w-p.
Cleveland House, St. James Square, S.W. 1.

GREENHOW, Edward Relph
6/8411, 15/12/15; R.F.C., C/S, 8/10/16; R.F.C., 26/2/17, R.A.F.; 2/Lieut.

GREENHOW, Richard York Woollett
4/1/4187, 14/6/15; Ches. R., 9/6/16; F; Capt.; Inj.
High House, Langrove, Nr. Ross, Herefordshire.

GREENLAND, Albert Edward
1/6/6950, 21/10/15, Cpl.; No. 7 O.C.B., 7/4/16; 8th Lond. R., 21/6/16, secd. Chinese Lab. Corps; F; Lieut.
41 Sandon Road, Edgbaston, Nr. Birmingham.

GREENLAND, George Donald
F/1805, 16/10/14, Cpl.; Norf. R., 2/11/14; Lieut.; M.C.
Attleborough, Norfolk.

✠ GREENLAND, Walter Edward
6/2/6397, 23/9/15; No. 14 O.C.B.; R. Marines, 24/10/16.
Killed in action 31/5/17.

GREENLEES, William
C/D/12283, 4/12/17; No. 10 O.C.B., 10/5/18; R. Scots, 3/2/19; 2/Lieut.
Davaar, Uddingston, Lanarkshire.

GREENLEES, Samuel
K/B/2470, 28/12/14; Hamps. R., 6/3/15.
8 Wilton Place, S.W. 1.

GREENSLADE, William Henry Walter
Sq/3539, 10/5/15; R.F.A., 21/8/15; Lieut.
21 Graham Road, Weston-super-Mare.

GREENSTED, Leslie
C/12569, 6/2/18, Sgt.; demob. 29/1/19.
8 William Street, Herne Bay.

GREENWELL, Ronald Eyre
F/Sq/1803, 16/10/14, Sgt.; trfr. R.G.A., 26/9/16; Lab. Corps, 16/9/17; F; Capt.
Upper Warren House, Brean, Burnham-on-Sea, Somerset.

GREENWOOD, Francis Dene
4/1/5199, 29/7/15, Sgt.; Berks. R., 15/4/16; F; Capt.
Orchard Cottage, Maidenhead, Berkshire.

GREENWOOD, Harry Ryley
6/4/8062, 1/12/15; No. 14 O.C.B., 28/8/16; Linc. R., 18/12/16, Notts. & Derby R.; F; Lieut.; w-g.
Park House, Easton, Stanford.

✠ GREENWOOD, Herbert
6/5/6923, 19/10/15; M.G.C., 4/8/16; F; 2/Lieut.
Died of wounds 8/6/17.

GREENWOOD, Herbert Arthur
D/Sq/12995, 29/4/18; demob. 7/1/19. 2 High Street, Sheffield.

GREENWOOD, Jack Kenneth
D/12905, 8/4/18; No. 16 O.C.B., 18/10/18; E. Surr. R., 17/3/19; 2/Lieut.
34 Prideaux Road, Eastbourne.

GREENWOOD, James Paradise
6/4/D/9326, 5/2/16; No. 14 O.C.B., 30/10/16; Shrop. Yeo., 25/1/17, att. Welch R.; F; Lieut.
42 Springfield Road, Crawley, Sussex.

GREENWOOD, Kenneth
Sq/3131, 29/3/15, L/C.; Linc. Yeo., 8/7/15; Gds. M.G.R.; Lieut.
Shoreham, Kent.

GREER, Frederick John
A/14349, 2/11/18; demob. 10/1/19.
1 Woodleigh Terrace, Londonderry.

GREER, Stewart Peddie
6/1/6938, 20/10/15; No. 7 O.C.B., 3/7/16; M.G.C., 24/10/16; F; Lieut.; w-p.
1 Woodleigh Terrace, Londonderry.

✠ GREEVES, John
6/4/9573, 25/4/16, L/C.; No. 14 O.C.B., 26/11/16; N. Staff. R., 28/2/17; 2/Lieut.
Killed in action 1/7/17.

GREGG, Basil E. P.
K/A/2078, 13/11/14, L/C.; York. R., 17/2/15, emp. Admiralty

APPENDIX II.—RECORDS OF RANK AND FILE.

GREGG, J.
2/3820, 28/5/15; E. Surr. R., 10/9/15, emp. M. of Munitions; Lieut. 14 Blenheim Gardens, Brixton Hill, S.E

GREGORY, Alan Alfred
A/13026, 3/5/18; trfr. 14th Lond. R., 6/12/18.
Thornhurst, Acrefield Road, Prenton, Birkenhead

GREGORY, Edmund Douglas
K/B/2231, 3/12/14, L/C.; R.F.A., 13/3/15; F; Capt.
The White House, Bickley, Kent.

GREGORY, Harry Welbourn
B/D/12194, 6/11/17, L/C.; A.S.C., C/S, 31/8/18; R.A.S.C., 22/11/18; NR; 2/Lieut. 11 French Street, Derby.

GREGORY, Henry James Maurice
6/2/8480, 20/12/15; R.F.A., C/S, 18/8/16; R.F.A., 10/2/17; F; Capt. c/o Thomson & Gregory, 17-19 Cockspur Street, S.W.1.

GREGORY, Leslie Heber
A/13027, 3/5/18; trfr. 14th Lond. R., 6/12/18.
Thornhurst, Acrefield Road, Prenton, Birkenhead.

GREGORY, Thomas Campbell
5/6/6509, 30/9/15; S. Notts. Huss., 3/1/16; F; Lieut.
The Brewery House, Gateacre, Nr. Liverpool.

GREGORY, Walter Edward
6/2/7587, 18/11/15, Cpl.; 7th Lond. R., 4/9/16; F; Lieut.; g.
17 St. George's Road, Beckenham, Kent.

GREGORY, Walter Henry
D/E/13792, 9/8/18, L/C.; No. 22 O.C.B., 22/11/18; demob. 18/1/19. 28 Milestone Road, Upper Norwood, S.E.19.

GREGSON, Edward Cecil
C/11442, 4/6/17, L/C.; R.A., C/S, 8/2/18; R.F.A., 5/8/18; 2/Lieut. 5 Chelford Road, Whalley Range, Manchester.

✠ GREGSON, Herbert
6/5/6965, 22/10/15; No. 11 O.C.B., 7/5/16; M.G.C., 4/9/16; 2/Lieut. Killed in action 30/11/17.

GREGSON, Philip
2/9680, 2/10/16, Cpl.; R.G.A., C/S, 16/2/17; R.G.A., 3/5/17; F; Lieut.; M(1). The Beeches, Loughton, Essex.

GREGSTEN, Ernest Bernard
C/6/659, 19/11/12, Sgt.; North. Cyc. Bn., 4/9/16, att. Manch R.; F; Lieut.; w. 13 Creswick Walk, Hendon, N.W.4.

GREGSTEN, John Alan
A/10995, 4/4/17, L/C.; No. 14 O.C.B., 10/8/17; North. Cyc. Bn., 27/11/17, M.G.C.; F; 2/Lieut.
13 Creswick Walk, Golders Green, N.W.11.

GREIG, Douglas James
6/3/5404, 5/8/15; Bedf. R., 22/11/15; Lieut.
21 High Street, Cardiff.

GREIG, Ian Borthwick
C/921, 5/8/14; D. of Corn. L.I., 9/9/14; Capt.; M.C., M(1).

GREIG, James Edwin
B/12733, 11/3/18; Household Bde. O.C.B., 9/8/18; Scots. Gds., 5/3/19; 2/Lieut.
c/o O. Laatvester Esq., 5 Upper Wimpole Street, W.1

GREIG, Thomas Andrew
D/11046, 16/4/17; No. 9 O.C.B., 10/8/17; Durh. L.I., 17/12/17, R.A.F.; F; 2/Lieut.; Inj. 8 Maxwell Street, Edinburgh.

GRELLET, Reginald Charles
F/1886, 16/10/14, Cpl.; York. R., 6/12/14; Lt.-Col.; w(2); D.S.O., M(3). Oxford Lodge, Hitchin.

GRELLIER, Cecil
C/355, 9/3/09; dis. 8/3/13; rej. E/1509, 1/10/14; Hamps. R., 27/11/14; G,S; Capt.; w; M.C., Serbian Order of the White Eagle. St. Martins Croft, Epsom, Surrey.

GRELLIER, Ernest Franz Waldemar
C/445, 11/11/09; R.A.M.C., 19/8/13; F,M,I; Capt.; Inv.
36 Lincoln's Inn Fields, W.C.2. (Now in India.)

✠ GRELLIER, Gordon Harley
C/354, 9/3/09; dis. 29/3/10; R.G.A.; 2/Lieut.
Killed in action 31/10/18.

GRENON, Neville Ernscliffe
B/13602, 24/7/18; demob. 29/1/19.
Keswick, St. Andrews Road, Malvern, Worcestershire.

GRESHAM, Frank Howard
D/10657, 5/2/17, Cpl.; R.A., C/S, 16/11/17; R.G.A., 20/5/18; F; 2/Lieut. La Estancia, Marine Drive, Bridlington, East Yorkshire.

GRESSON, Roland Arbuthnot Regnell
C/14309, 30/11/18; No. 3 O.C.B., 10/2/19; R. Dub. Fus., 18/3/19; 2/Lieut. Thornton, Dunlavin, Co. Wicklow, Ireland

GREY, Egerton Charles
A/867, 4/8/14; R. Fus., 5/10/14; 2/Lieut.; w.

✠ GREY, Norman
6/5/5897, 30/8/15; N. Lan R., 9/1/16; Lieut.
Killed in action 26/10/17.

✠ GRIBBEN, James Grenfell
6/1/5741, 20/8/15; S. Staff. R., 10/1/16; 2/Lieut.; w.
Killed in action 12/6/17.

✠ GRIBBLE, Charles Ethelbert
6/4/6065, 6/9/15; Leic. R., 1/6/16; Capt.; M.C.
Died of wounds 15/10/18.

✠ GRIBBLE, Charles Herbert
K/E/2421, 21/12/14; E. Kent. R., 19/3/15; Lieut.
Killed in action 30/11/17.

GRIBBLE, Charles William
6/1/8690, 4/1/16; No. 14 O.C.B., 30/10/16; R. Lanc. R., 24/1/17; 2/Lieut. Bungalow, Aberavon, Port Talbot, South Wales.

GRIBBLE, David Curle
B/11334, 21/5/17; No. 14 O.C.B., 7/9/17; Lan. Fus., 17/12/17; 2/Lieut.; w. 9 Montague Street, Russell Square, W.C.1.

GRIBBLE, Reginald Henry
6/Sq/7202, 4/11/15; R.F.A., C/S, 18/8/16; R.F.A., 9/12/16; F,M; Capt.; p. Mansfield, Overton Road, Sutton, Surrey.

✠ GRICE, Harold George
6/3/5431, 5/8/15; R. Scots, 12/11/15; Lieut.
Died of wounds 27/3/18.

GRICE, John Hubert
6/2/6458, 27/9/15; S. Staff. R., 29/12/15; F; Capt.; w; M.C.
7 Luxborough House, Northumberland Street, Baker Street, W.

GRIEVE, Angus MacLeod
A/616, 29/2/12; R. Highrs., 15/8/14, att. Gord. Highrs.; F,M; Capt. Queens Crescent, Edinburgh.

GRIEVE, Daniel Bryson
E/14175, 16/10/18; demob. 11/1/19.
Craighall Crescent, 34 Albert Street, Dundee.

GRIEVE, James Henry
K/F/2276, 7/12/14; R.A.O.C., 8/2/15; G,E,F,It; Lt.-Col.; w; M.C., M(2). c/o Lond. Cty. West. & Parr's Bank, Chichester, Sussex.

GRIEVE, William Weir
6/8540, 30/12/15; No. 9 O.C.B., 8/3/16; Arg. & Suth'd. Highrs., 6/7/16; F; Lieut. 58 Queen Street, Edinburgh.

GRIFFIN, Gordon William
6/Sq/9526, 16/2/16; No. 1 Cav. C/S, 16/10/16; Surr. Yeo., 16/2/17; Germ.SWA & EA; Lieut. 17 Lancaster Road, Brighton.

GRIFFIN, Stanley Augustus James
B/11360, 28/5/17, L/C.; No. 14 O.C.B., 7/12/17; Devon. R., 28/5/18; F; 2/Lieut. 12 York Street, Plymouth.

GRIFFIN, Thomas Archer
4/6/3/4963, 19/7/15; R.G.A., 1/12/15; F; Lieut.; w.
20 Weatheroak Road, Sparkhill, Birmingham.

GRIFFIN, Tom
2/3087, 22/3/15; Lan. Fus., 26/8/15; F; Lieut.; Inv.
13 Church Road, Urmston, Manchester.

GRIFFITH, Charles Croft
6/8725, 5/1/16; A.S.C., C/S, 17/4/16; R.A.S.C., 21/5/16; Lieut.
25 Balls Road, Birkenhead.

GRIFFITH, Cyril Cobham
C/691, 7/2/13; Hamps. R., 1/9/14; G,S; Capt.; w; M.C., Greek Military Cross, M(1). Springfield Cottage, Cuckfield, Sussex.

GRIFFITH, Frank Llewelyn
6/2/9459, 14/2/16; R.F.A., C/S, 4/8/16; R.F.A., 9/12/16; F; Lieut.; w. Bryn, Carnarvon.

APPENDIX II.—RECORDS OF RANK AND FILE.

GRIFFITH, Geoffrey Comber
H/2016, 2/11/14, L/C.; Sea. Highrs., 9/2/15; Lieut.

GRIFFITH, Gronwy Robert
C/314, 30/6/08; dis. 29/6/09.

GRIFFITH, Harold Kinder
Sq/331, 27/11/08; 9th Lond. R., 29/3/09; F; Capt.
Roydon, Asheldon Road, Torquay.

GRIFFITH, Richard Owen
6/1/7839, 25/11/15, L/C.; R.A., C/S, 26/10/16; R.G.A., 5/1/17; F; Lieut.
Bronwen House, Penrhyndendraeth, North Wales.

GRIFFITH, Richard Thomas
D/9977, 21/11/16; Devon. R., 15/3/17; 2/Lieut.
Ddol Helyg Farm, Cwmygle, Carnarvon.

GRIFFITH, Stanley Vincent
B/11717, 19/7/17; No. 11 O.C.B., 9/11/17; D. of Corn. L.I., 30/4/18; F; Lieut.; w. g.
Parc-an-Cairn, Porthleven, Cornwall. (Now in South America)

✠ GRIFFITH, Walter Stanley Currie
A/59, 8/4/08; dis. 7/4/09; Lein. R.; G; 2/Lieut.
Killed in action 10/8/15.

✠ GRIFFITH, William Henry
6/2/8284, 10/12/15; No. 8 O.C.B., 4/8/16; R.W. Fus., 21/11/16; 2/Lieut.; M.C.
Died of wounds 5/7/17.

✠ GRIFFITH, William Key
6/1/6924, 19/10/15; No. 11 O.C.B., 7/5/16; 9th Lond. R., 4/9/16, 12th Lond. R.; F; 2/Lieut.; w.
Killed in action 26/9/17.

GRIFFITH-JONES, John Stanley
K/C/2029, 9/11/14; S. Wales Bord., 9/4/15; F,It; Capt.
Drews, Beaconsfield, Buckinghamshire

GRIFFITHS, Arthur Brynmor
4/1/4572, 1/7/15; R.F.A., 19/12/15; Capt.; M(1).

✠ GRIFFITHS, Arthur Ivor
6/1/7446, 15/11/15; Welch R., 25/9/16, Suff. R.; 2/Lieut.
Killed in action 3/8/17.

✠ GRIFFITHS, David George
6/Sq/6010, 2/9/15, Cpl.; R.A., C/S, 24/1/16; R.F.A., 16/6/16; Lieut.; w.
Died of wounds 15/12/18.

GRIFFITHS, David John
A/10278, 1/1/17; R.A.O.C., 22/4/17; Lieut.
28 Penallt Road, Llanelly, Carmarthenshire.

GRIFFITHS, Evan Cyril
6/5/8109, 2/12/15; No. 14 O.C.B.; M.G.C., 24/10/16; F; Lieut.; M(1).
Clynder House, Morriston, Glamorganshire.

✠ GRIFFITHS, George Richards
6/2/5810, 21/8/15, Sgt.; K.R. Rif. C., 21/4/16; Lieut.
Died of wounds 15/9/16.

GRIFFITHS, Griffith Walter Harding
D/13758, 7/8/18; demob. 22/1/19.
Walnut Tree Hotel, Rhosddu, Wrexham.

GRIFFITHS, Henry John Martin Saunders
4/3773, 27/5/15; S. Wales Bord., 2/9/15, att. R. Fus.; F; Lieut
37 Coleshill Road, Teddington.

✠ GRIFFITHS, John Enos
D/10659, 5/2/17; No. 11 O.C.B., 5/7/17; Glouc. R., 30/10/17; F; 2/Lieut.
Killed in action 23/4/18.

GRIFFITHS, Oscar Elwy
6/5/6043, 3/9/15; dis. med. unfit, 31/12/15.
The School House, Wrenbury, Nr. Nantwich, Cheshire

GRIFFITHS, Robert Stanley
4/1/5034, 22/7/15; trfr. R.G.A., 7/7/16; R.G.A., 24/6/18; F; Lieut.
9 Mona Terrace, Victoria Road, Wrexham. (Now in Brazil.)

GRIFFITHS, Robert Stanley
C/11743, 26/7/17; R.F.C., C/S, 23/10/17; R.F.C., 12/12/17, R.A.F.; 2/Lieut.
Craig-y-derw, Ynysmudw, Pontardawe, South Wales.

✠ GRIFFITHS, William George
6/1/8939, 17/1/16; No 13 O.C.B., 4/11/16; R.W. Fus., 28/2/17; P; 2/Lieut.
Killed in action 9/3/18.

GRIGG, Donald Richardson
B/12828, 22/3/18; R.A., C/S, 26/7/18; R.G.A., 8/4/19; 2/Lieut.
21 Derwent Villas, Whetstone, N. 20.

GRIGG, Gilbert Hutton
4/Sq/4823, 12/7/15; N. Ir. Horse, 26/8/15; Lieut.
c/o Bank of New Zealand, 1 Queen Victoria Street, E.C.

GRIGG, John Hutton
4/Sq/4822, 12/7/15, Cpl.; N. Ir. Horse, 26/8/15; Lieut.
c/o Bank of New Zealand, 1 Queen Victoria Street, E.C.

GRIGG, Raymond
6/2/5680, 16/8/15; Yorks. L.I., 2/1/16; F; Lieut.; p.
5 Neale Street, Roker, Sunderland.

GRIGGS, Harold Alfred
D/10901, 21/3/17; R.A., C/S, 10/8/17; R.F.A., 6/1/18; F; Lieut.
29 Lushington Road, Eastbourne. (Now in India.)

GRIGGS, William Joshua
6/5/9531, 11/2/16; R.A., C/S, 4/8/16; R.G.A., 26/11/16, emp. M. of Munitions; F; Capt.; g; M.C. and Bar, M(2).
Riverview, 51 Catford Hill, S.E. 6.

GRILLS, Ernest Robert
4/5/5035, 22/7/15; Durh. L.I., 17/12/15, Devon. R.; Lieut.
122 Butler Road, Harrow, Middlesex.

GRIMBLE, Eric George Norton
3/2059, 12/11/14; Herts. R., 6/3/15, secd. R.A.F.; F; Capt.
1 Princes Buildings, Chater Road, Hong Kong, China.

GRIME, Lindsay
D/10681, 6/2/17; R.F.C., C/S, 13/3/17; R.F.C., 19/4/17, R.A.F.; Lieut.
Bankfield, Clitheroe, Lancashire.

GRIMMER, Wilfred Ernest
B/13603, 24/8/18; No. 11 O.C.B., 24/1/19; General List, 8/3/19; 2/Lieut.

GRIMSHAW, Job
C/10622, 26/1/17; No. 14 O.C.B., 5/7/17; W. York. R., 30/10/17; F; Lieut.; g.
Brook House Farm, Halsall, Ormskirk, Lancashire.

GRIMSLEY, Frederick George Hawks
C/1727, 15/10/14; Leic. R., 13/3/15, att. M.G.C.; F; Major; M(1).
Hope Villas, Kings Road, Berkhamsted, Hertfordshire.

GRIMSTON, Robert Villiers
6/4/8830, 10/1/16; R.A., C/S, 14/7/16; R.G.A., 4/10/16; S,P; Lieut.
Darrowfield, St. Albans, Hertfordshire.

GRIMWADE, Charles Donovan
6/4/8962, 17/1/16; R.A., C/S, 24/11/16; R.G.A., 8/4/17; P,E; Lieut.
Fairlands, Trent Vale, Stoke-on-Trent.

✠ GRIMWADE, Edward Ernest
K/E/2269, 7/12/14; Lan. Fus., 13/3/15; 2/Lieut.
Killed in action 17/9/16.

GRIMWADE, Edward Norman
B/11043, 13/4/17, Sgt.; demob. 29/1/19.
The Bungalow, St. James Road, Sutton, Surrey.

GRIMWADE, Frederick Clive
C/499, 16/6/10; 4th Lond. R., 4/7/13; F; Major; w.
64 York Mansions, Battersea Park, S.W. 11.

GRINLEY, Walter Gerald
4/Sq/6/4964, 19/7/15; L/C.; R.A., C/S, 24/1/16; R.F.A., 15/1/16; F; Lieut.; Croix de Guerre (French).
The Cottage, Mayfield Road, Sutton, Surrey. (Now in India.)

GRIPPER, Cedric Basil
D/13793, 9/8/18; trfr. K.R. Rif. C., 25/4/19.
Hartham House, Hertford, Hertfordshire.

✠ GRIPPER, Edward Cutbush
6/5/7989, 29/11/15; Yorks. L.I., 4/8/16; Capt.; w.
Died of wounds 5/12/17

GRIPPER, Henry Ernest
6/3/5405, 5/8/15; R.W. Kent. R., 20/1/16; I,M; 2/Lieut.
Beechwood, Bromley Park, Bromley, Kent.

GRIPPER, Hubert Jasper
C/1246, 23/9/14; Herts. R., 12/1/15, att. Bedf. R.; F; Lieut.
Beechwood, Bromley Park, Bromley, Kent.

GRITTON, Frank Esmond
6/4/5705, 19/8/15; 21st Lond. R., 25/12/15, att. R.F.C.; Lieut.
148 Ramsden Road, Balham, S.W. 12

APPENDIX II.—RECORDS OF RANK AND FILE.

GROGAN, John Reginald
D/10863, 12/3/17; R.A., C/S, 10/8/17, No. 1 Cav. C/S; R. Regt. of Cav., 14/2/19; 2/Lieut.
Moyle, Carlon, Ireland.

✠ GROGAN, Richard Lawrence Remy
4/3178, 6/4/15, L/C.; R.E., 22/7/15; G,F; 2/Lieut.
Killed in action 30/1/17.

GROOM, Cyril Octavius
6/B/6908, 18/10/15, L/C.; No. 14 O.C.B., 5/5/17; Linc. R., 28/8/17, Indian Army; F,I; Lieut.; w.
Sulehay House, Wisbech, Cambridgeshire. (Now in India.)

GROOM, Harold Lester Robert Joseph
C/1682, 12/10/14, L/C.; R. War. R., 5/3/15; F,It; Capt.; w(2); D.S.O., M.C. and Bar, M(1).
36 Airedale Avenue, Chiswick, W. 4.

GROOM, Henry Theodore
A/9908, 13/11/16; R.W. Surr. R., 9/3/17, Lab. Corps; F; Lieut.
75 Brigstock Road, Thornton Heath.

GROOM, Philip Lewis
3/6282, 16/9/15; No. 1 O.C.B., 25/2/16; dis. to re-enlist in K.R. Rif. C., 6/8/16.

GROOM, William Howard Montague
6/4/8353, 13/12/15, Sgt.; R.F.C., C/S, 13/3/17; R.F.C., 19/4/17, R.A.F.; F; Capt.; M(1).
Gratwicke Cottage, Gratwicke Road, Worthing.

✠ GROSART, William David
4/5/4965, 19/7/15; Manch. R., 21/12/15, N. Lan. R.; 2/Lieut.
Died of wounds 15/4/17.

GROSCH, Harry
6/4/9314, 4/2/16, L/C.; Suff. R., 22/6/16; SWA,F; Capt.; Inj.
81 Huron Road, Balham, S.W. 17.

GROSE, James Frederick
6/3/7011, 26/10/15, L/C.; No. 11 O.C.B., 7/5/16; R.F.C., 4/9/16, R. War. R.; F; Lieut.
Thurlestone, King's Bridge, South Devon.

GROSE, Nicholas Alfred
6/3/7383, 11/11/15, L/C.; Devon. R., 7/7/16, att. Bord. R.; I,M; Lieut.
West View, Newton Abbot, South Devon.

GROSE, Philip
D/10213, 18/12/16; No. 14 O.C.B., 5/5/17; N. Lan. R., 28/8/17; 2/Lieut.
20 Sydenham Park, S.E. 26.

✠ GROSS, Geoffrey Yates
B/441, 5/11/09; R.W. Kent. R., 15/8/14; Capt.
Killed in action 9/4/16.

GROSS, William Stovell
C/947, 5/8/14; dis. 5/9/14.

GROSSMAN, Edward
K/B/2094, 16/11/14, L/C.; 12th Lond. R., 20/3/15; Lieut.; w.
53 Portland Court, Great Portland Street, W. 1.

✠ GROSSMAN, Victor David
6/1/6482, 27/9/15, L/C.; North'd. Fus., 1/6/16; 2/Lieut.
Killed in action 17/9/16.

✠ GROUND, Edward George
C/348, 24/2/09; dis. 23/2/13; 11th Lond. R.; Lieut.
Killed in action 15/8/15.

GROUNDWATER, James McGrigor
A/10479, 12/1/17; No. 14 O.C.B., 5/5/17; Essex R., 17/12/17; 2/Lieut.
National Bank of India, 26 Bishopsgate, E.C.

GROUNDWATER, Stanley Thompson
3/3343, 22/4/15, L/C.; R.F.A., 28/9/15, Indian Army; F; Capt; Inv.
14 Meteor Road, Westcliff-on-Sea.

✠ GROVE, Ernest Richard
C/10621, 25/1/17; No. 20 O.C.B., 7/6/17; L'pool. R., 25/9/17; 2/Lieut.
Killed in action 10/2/18

GROVE, George Frederick
F/1845, 16/10/14; Glouc. R., 22/12/14, att. North'd. Fus.; F,E; Lieut.
Ferne House, 22 Mill Road, Salisbury, Wiltshire

GROVES, Keith Grimale
A/839, 4/8/14; 17th Lond. R., 14/10/14; F,S,P; Capt.; M(1).
1 Essex Court, Temple, E.C. 4

✠ GROVES, Leonard Alloway
K/A/2425, 21/12/14; R. Suss. R., 31/3/15; F; Lieut.
Killed in action 3/9/16.

GROVES, Wilfred William
6/K/H/2216, 30/11/14, L/C.; R.G.A., 25/1/16; S,E,F; Capt.
1 Watling Street, Radlett, Hertfordshire.

GRUBB, Maurice Edward
D/13794, 9/8/18; demob. 7/4/19.
77 Wellington Road, Bush Hill Park, Enfield.

GRUBB, Sydney Percival
B/10318, 4/1/17; No. 20 O.C.B., 7/6/17; Devon. R., 25/9/17, att. M.G.C.; F,It; 2/Lieut.
5 Newland Road, Banbury, Oxon.

GRUBB, William Henry
C/12291, 7/12/17, Sgt.; demob. 3/2/19.
50 Robertson Road, Eastville, Bristol

GRUMBAR, Julian Charles
D/E/13860, 19/8/18; No. 22 O.C.B., 22/11/18; E. Kent. R.; 2/Lieut.; M.B.E., Chevalier de l'Ordre de Leopold.
58 Kensington Court, W. 8.

✠ GRUNDTVIG, Humphrey Halgrim
E/1547, 6/10/14; R. Berks. R., 27/11/14, Leic. R.; F; Lieut.; M.C.
Died of wounds 22/3/18.

GRUNDY, Frank Douglas
6/1/6085, 6/8/15; K.R. Rif. C., 1/6/16, Lab. Corps; F; Lieut.; w.
c/o Messrs. Izod & Grundy, 11 Arundell Street, Strand, W.C.

GRUNDY, Harold
D/10017, 27/11/16; A.S.C., C/S, 26/2/17; R.A.S.C., 4/4/17; F; Lieut.
223 Hornby Road, Blackpool.

GUDGIN, Leslie Hubert
4/2/4555, 1/7/15; E. Surr. R., 20/7/15, Tank Corps; F; Capt.
38 Oakfield Road, Croydon.

GUERRIER, Hugh Trevor
B/13438, 3/7/18; No. 22 O.C.B., 23/8/18; Midd'x. R., 13/2/19; 2/Lieut.
c/o National Bank of South Africa, Circus Place, E.C. 2.

GUEST, Harold Edward Raphael
6/1/6619, 4/10/15; dis. 15/4/16.

GUEST, John
6/3/7447, 15/11/15; No. 8 O.C.B., 4/8/16; Manch. R., 21/11/16, emp. M. of Labour; 2/Lieut.; p.
Ingleside, Orrell Road, Orrell, Nr. Wigan.

GUEST, Leslie Bate
E/1535, 6/10/14; R. War. R., 21/2/15; F,It; Lieut.; Italian Bronze Medal for Valour.
Highcroft, Etchingham Park, East Finchley, N. 3.

GUEST, Peter Healey
6/3/9327, 4/2/16; R.A.O.C., 26/12/16; Capt.
Ingleside, Orrell Road, Orrell, Nr. Wigan.

GUILFOYLE, Denis Paul
6/8021, 30/11/15; dis. med. unfit, 27/8/16.
Murray Street, Perth, Western Australia.

GUIMARAENS, Herbert Edward
F/1897, 16/10/14, Sgt.; N. Lan. R., 1/4/15, Lab. Corps; F; Capt.; w.
Badminton Club, 100 Piccadilly, W. 1.

GUINNESS, Alan Henry
C/895, 5/8/14; Suff. R., 19/9/14; Capt.; w.

GUINNESS, William Andrews
4/3841, 31/5/15; 22nd Lond. R., 16/11/15, secd. Lab. Corps, att. 29th Lond. R. and R. Fus.; F; Lieut.; w.
7 Belmont Road, Wallington, Surrey.

GUITON, Philip Andrew
Sq/790, 8/5/14; Interpreter, 16/10/14, R.G.A.; Lieut.; w.
Lancaster Lodge, Bolingbroke Grove, Wandsworth Common, S.W. 11.

GULLAND, Alan Hepburn
Sq/353, 9/3/09; R.F.A.; F,M; Major; w.
c/o Messrs. Cox & Coy., 16 Charing Cross, S.W. 1.

GULLIVER, Reginald
D/13759, 7/8/18; demob. 10/1/19.
32 Fambridge Road, Maldon, Essex.

GULLY, Arthur Hutton
4/2638, 11/1/15; R.A.S.C., 13/5/15; Lieut.
Theydon Hall, Theydon Bois, Essex.

APPENDIX II.—RECORDS OF RANK AND FILE.

GULSON, Edgar Alfred
6/8460, 18/12/15; R.F.C., 24/5/16, R.A.F.; F; Lieut.; g.
c/o Nat. Prov. & Union Bank of England Ltd., 15 Bishopsgate, E.C.

GUMBY, Leonard
A/10060, 1/12/16, L/C.; No. 14 O.C.B., 5/3/17; W. Rid. R., 26/6/17; 2/Lieut.; M.C. 53 Saville Mount, Halifax.

GUMMER, Henry Edward
D/12970, 23/4/18, L/C.; R.A.F., C/S, 4/11/18; demob. 27/3/19.
4 De Burgh Terrace, Phœnix Park, Dublin.

GUNDRY, Wilfrid George Cuthbert
A/1179, 14/9/14; Rif. Brig., 30/11/14, att. R. Fus.; G,F; Capt.
North Lodge, Enfield, Middlesex.

GUNION, Arthur Hume
B/2746, 21/1/15; Midd'x. R., 3/6/15; It; Lieut.
2 Elton Gardens, Darlington, Co. Durham.

GUNN, George Livingston
B/11418, 1/6/17; No. 10 O.C.B., 5/10/17; R.W. Surr. R., 26/2/18; F; Lieut.; w.
Edenhurst, Llanishen, Nr. Cardiff.

GUNN, Kenneth Geoffrey Hugo Raleigh
K/D/2450, 28/12/14, L/C.; Lond. Div. Cyc. Coy., 18/3/15, att R.A.F.; F,E; Capt.; w; M(1). Wilgers Farm, Horley, Surrey.

GUNNER, Raymond Woodroffe
6/9055, 20/1/16; R.F.C., 17/3/16; resigned and rej. A/11278, 14/5/17; R.F.C., C/S, 2/8/17; R.F.C., 8/9/17, R.A.F.; Lieut.
15 Stanhope Road, Highgate.

✠ GUNNERY, Cedric Leopold
5/2/6731, 11/10/15; R.F.C., 4/8/16; 2/Lieut.
Killed in action 22/5/17.

GUNTER, William Ewart
6/1/8521, 29/12/15; No. 14 O.C.B., 30/10/16; R. War. R., 24/1/17; Lieut.; w(2). Morland, Wellington, Shropshire.

GUNYON, Joseph William Henry
4/3959, 3/6/15, Cpl.; R.F.A., 3/11/15; F,It; Lieut.
7 Ickburgh Road, Clapton, E. 5.

GURNEY, Frederick George
4/3418, 29/4/15; 19th Lond. R., 19/8/15; F; Major; M.C., M(1).
20 Lewisham Road, Dartmouth Park, N.W. 5.

GURNEY, John Arthur
A/10458, 12/1/17; R.F.C., C/S, 16/4/17; R.F.C., 16/5/17, R.A.F.; resigned and rej. C/D/14179, 11/10/18; demob. 14/5/19.
3 Salisbury Road, New Brighton, Wallasey.

GURNEY, Joseph Thomas
D/A/11138, 30/4/17; demob. 20/3/19.
21 Dovedale Road, New Brighton, Cheshire.

GUTHRIE, Charles Clement
A/11896, 23/8/17; R.F.A., C/S, 4/2/18; R.G.A., 3/9/18; 2/Lieut.
The Roscote, Heswell, Cheshire.

GUTHRIE, Donald Stewart
K/F/2579, 4/1/15; R. Highrs., 30/3/15; att. Cam'n. Highrs.; F; Capt.; w. c/o F. J. Yarrow Esq., 18 Abbey Road, N.W.

GUTHRIE, Michael
6/4/6732, 11/10/15, L/C.; No. 14 O.C.B., 28/8/16; North'd. Fus., 21/11/16; F; Lieut.; M.C.
Tremayne, Claude Avenue, Middlesborough.

GUTTERIDGE, Harold Cooke
C/49, 7/4/08; rej. C/1023, 10/8/14, C.S.M.; R.A.O.C., 25/4/16; S; Capt.; M(1). 2 Pump Court, Temple, E.C. 4.

GUTTMANN, Leo Frank
Sq/289, 22/6/08; dis. 21/6/09. 18 Aberdare Gardens, N.W. 6.

GUY, Henwood
K/H/2/4/2254, 7/12/14; R.G.A., 6/4/15; F,EA; Lieut.
Treherne, Bodmin, Cornwall.

GUY, James Stephens
A/11231, 9/5/17; No. 16 O.C.B., 5/10/17; D. of Corn. L.I., 12/3/18; Lieut. Bank House, Bude, Cornwall.

GUYATT, Thomas
6/3/7176, 3/11/15, L/C.; Worc. R., 4/9/16, M.G.C.; F,It; Lieut.; p. 29 Strafford Road, Barnet, Hertfordshire.

GUYMER, Charles Stanley
6/5/8354, 13/12/15; A.S.C., C/S, 13/10/16; R.A.S.C., 23/2/17, att. Devon. R.; 2/Lieut. 110 London Road, Redhill, Surrey.

GWATHMEY, William Riddle
6/4/5849, 26/8/15; R.F.A., C/S, 31/3/16; R.F.A., 21/8/16; F,NR; Capt.; w(4).
1720 West End, Nashville, Tenn., U.S.A. (Now in British West Indies.)

GWILYM, Edward Glynn
6/4/6966, 22/10/15; trfr. R.E., 27/11/16; R.E., 23/2/18; 2/Lieut.
Bron-y-Garth, Glais, Glamorganshire.

GWYN, Cyril H.
6/8355, 13/12/15; R.E., 1/5/16; Capt.; M(1).

GWYNN, Denis Rolleston
6/4/9553, 26/2/16; No. 7 O.C.B., 3/7/16; R. Muns. Fus., 3/11/16, att. R. Innis. Fus.; F; Lieut. Author's Club, S.W.1.

✠ GWYTHER, Guy Llewellyn
K/F/2512, 31/12/14; Leic. R., 19/3/15; M; 2/Lieut.
Killed in action 6/1/16.

GWYTHER, Reginald Duncan
K/A/2120, 16/11/14; R.E., 30/1/15; F; Capt.; M.C., M(1).
Hallcroft, Dufton, Westmoreland. (Now in F.M.S.)

GWYTHER-JONES, Frank
6/1/6283, 16/9/15; No. 1 O.C.B., 6/9/16; R.F.C., 16/3/17, R.A.F.; F; Capt. Lyndhurst, Matlock, Derbyshire.

GYE, Hugh Montague
6/Sq/9325, 5/2/16, L/C.; No. 1 Cav. C/S, 12/10/16; R. Regt. of Lancers, 16/2/17, att. Linc. Yeo. and 12th Lancers; P,F; Lieut.
90 Plymouth Road, Penarth, Glamorganshire.

GYE, Norman
K/D/2482, 28/12/14; Yorks. L.I., 22/4/15; F; Lieut.
167 West Road, Westcliff-on-Sea, Essex.

HACKETT, George
2/3825, 29/5/15; E. Ang. Div. Cyc. Coy., 7/9/15, Army Cyc. Corps; Lieut.

HACKETT, George Osbourn Francis Marius
A/13099, 22/5/18; No. 1 O.C.B., 8/11/18, No. 3 O.C.B.; R.W Kent. R., 20/3/19; 2/Lieut.
82 Rue Charles Laffitte, Neuilly s/Seine, France

HADDOCK, Harry
6/2/8726, 5/1/16; No. 7 O.C.B., 11/8/16; R. Dub. Fus., 18/12/16; F; Lieut. Allerton, Belgrave Road, Monketown, Co. Dublin.

HADDON, Roy Thomas
6/5/8923, 14/1/16; R.A., C/S, 7/8/16; trfr. R.F.A., 9/10/16; R.F.A., 2/12/17; F; 2/Lieut.; w.
11 Hooley Range, Heaton Moor, Nr. Stockport.

HADDON, Sidney Joseph Jewson
C/D/12284, 4/12/17; demob. 29/1/19.
15 Galpin Road, Thornton Heath, Surrey.

HADEN, Henry Frank
C/13315, 18/6/18; R.E., C/S, 18/10/18; demob.
St. Lukes Road, Pontnenynydd, Nr. Pontypool, Monmouthshire.

HADFIELD, William Helm
D/10831, 5/3/17; No. 14 O.C.B., 5/7/17; Glouc. R., 30/10/17, Leic. R.; F; Lieut. Delaval, Davenport Crescent, Stockport.

✠ HADLER, Lionel Horace
B/13473, 5/7/18, trfr. K.R. Rif. C., 25/4/19, M.G.C.
Died 30/11/19.

✠ HADRILL, Arthur William
B/844, 4/8/14; Linc. R., 28/11/14, att. R. Muns. Fus.; Lieut.
Killed in action 12/8/15.

HAGART, Richard Bein
D/C/12122, 15/10/17; Sigs. C/S, 14/12/17; R.E., 24/5/18; 2/Lieut.
c/o D. B. Nevin Esq., Gwydir Chambers, 104 High Holborn, W.C.1.

HAGEMEYER, John Gerald
B/D/13640, 26/7/18; demob. 23/1/19.
72 Carlton Hill, St. Johns Wood, N.W. 8.

HAGEN, Walter
H/A/3012, 8/3/15, L/C.; Essex R., 3/6/15, Lab. Corps; Capt.; w; M(2). 60 Cherry Orchard Road, Croydon.

APPENDIX II.—RECORDS OF RANK AND FILE.

HAGGARD, Amyand James Rider
E/1593, 6/10/14; 5th Lond. R., 11/10/14, R.W. Surr. R.; F;
Capt.; w, g, Corner Cottage, Cobham, Surrey.

HAGGARD, Andrew
B/1655, 9/10/14; K.R. Rif. C., 7/12/14; F; 2/Lieut.; Inv.
c/o Barcloy's Bank Ltd., 19 Fleet Street, E.C.

HAGGARD, Daniel Amyand
H/1934, 22/10/14, Sgt.; Sea. Highrs., 9/2/15, R.E.; F; Capt.
c/o Barcloy's Bank Ltd., 54 Lombard Street, E.C. 3. (Now in Brazil.)

HAGGAS, William Rockby
E/2768, 25/1/15; N. Lan. R., 21/5/15, att. R.F.C.; Lieut.; w.
Oakworth Manor, Keighley.

HAGON, Charles Stanley
3/4461, 28/6/15; R.G.A., 27/10/15; F; Capt.; Inv; M(1).
17 Holland Park Gardens, W.

HAGUE, Edwin Leslie
A/14063, 21/9/18; demob. 6/3/19.
53 Caty Road, Birmingham.

HAGUE, Thomas Henry
K/E/2337, 14/12/14; R.F.A., 23/4/15; Major; m.
17 Hogarth Road, Earls Court

HAIGH, Fred
B/12770, 15/3/18, L/C.; Household Bde. O.C.B., 9/8/18; Scots Gds., 5/3/19; 2/Lieut. 27 Ashgrove, Bradford, Yorkshire.

HAIGH, Joseph Herbert
D/13668, 29/7/18; demob. 21/12/18.
26 Carlton Street, Featherstone, Pontefract, Yorkshire.

HAIGHT, Ingersoll Ernest
6/8440, 16/12/15; R.E., 27/5/16; 2/Lieut.

HAIGH-WOOD, Maurice
Sq/1347, 26/9/14; dis. to R. Mil. Coll., 31/12/14; Manch. R., 12/5/15; F,It; Staff Lieut.; Inv.
9 Clarence Gate Gardens, N.W. 1.

HAILEY, Victor
4/4521, 30/6/15; R.F.A., 20/7/15; F; Major; w(3); M(1).
Delamere, Great Wymondley, Stevenage, Hertfordshire.

HAILSTONE, Hugh Walter
A/51, 7/4/08; dis. 6/4/11.

HAINE, Mervyn Joseph
4/6/3/4853, 15/7/15; E. Surr. R., 27/10/15, att. Leic. R., secd M.G.C.; F; Lieut.; Inv. 49 Montpelier Vale, Blackheath.

HAINES, Alfred Farmer
6/D/8691, 4/1/16; M.G.C., C/S, 1/1/17; M.G.C., 26/4/17, Tank Corps; F; Lieut.; w. Knight's Hill, Stoke Prior, Bromsgrove.

HAINES, Eric Ross
6/4/6499, 27/9/15, L/C.; R.F.C., 25/9/16, R.A.F.; Lieut.
100 Newbridge Hill, Bath.

HAINES, Geoffrey Colton
C/D/12300, 11/12/17; No. 2 O.C.B., 10/5/18; E. Surr. R 4/2/19; 2/Lieut. 14 Gwendwr Road, West Kensington, W. 14.

✠ HAINES, Godfrey Alfred Victor
K/H/2551, 4/1/15, L/C.; Notts. & Derby. R., 29/4/15; Lieut.
Died of wounds 22/4/17.

✠ HAINES, Stephen Gilbert
4/6/7920, 29/11/15; R.A., C/S, 26/10/16; R.F.A., 20/2/17; 2/Lieut. Died of wounds 4/5/17.

HAIR, Gilbert
A/12721, 24/1/18; No. 2 R.G.A., C/S, 19/4/18; R.G.A. 21/10/18; 2/Lieut. Pembroke College, Oxford.

HAKE, George Reginald
B/9869, 6/11/16, L/C.; No. 14 O.C.B., 5/3/17; R.N.A.S., 23/5/17 R.A.F.; F; Lieut.; M(1).
6 Thornhill Park, Sunderland. (Now in India.)

HALDANE, Fred Alexander
6/5/8413, 15/12/15; No. 7 O.C.B., 11/8/16; R. Muns. Fus., 18/12/16, secd. M.G.C.; Lieut.
Benburl, Co. Tyrone, Ireland.

HALE, Francis Arthur
B/13485, 8/7/18; demob. 21/12/18.
2 Belmont Villas, Warm Turn, Aberbeeg, Monmouthshire.

HALE, Norman Wyatt
C/10829, 2/3/17; R.F.A., C/S, 22/6/17; R.F.A., 18/2/18; 2/Lieut. 11 The Avenue, Colchester.

✠ HALE, William John Douglas
4/2/3999, 3/6/15; R.W. Fus., 10/9/15; Capt.; w.
Killed in action 28/4/17.

HALES, Eric Gordon
6/1/7244, 8/11/15, L/C.; R. Berks. R., 21/11/16; Lieut.; w.
Sandeman Road, Quetta, Baluchistan.

HALES, Geoffrey Trafford
C/11771, 30/7/17; Garr. O.C.B., 30/11/17; Worc. R., 27/3/18; 2/Lieut. 1 Oppidans Road, N.W. 3.

HALES, John Baseley
C/1148, 14/9/14, Sgt.; Oxf. & Bucks. L.I., 20/2/15; F,It; Capt.; M.C., M(2). The Close, Norwich.

HALES, Sidney James
B/Sq/12202, 9/11/17; No. 1 Cav. C/S, 16/5/18; trfr. 28th Lond R., 6/9/18. Rougham, Suffolk.

HALEY, John Stanley
F/1855, 16/10/14; dis. 19/2/15.

HALFHIDE, Frederick William
4/Sq/4148, 10/6/15, L/C.; No. 2 Cav. C/S, 31/3/16; Linc. Yeo., 19/8/16; 2/Lieut. 105 Glenseleton Road, Streatham, S.W. 16.

HALFORD, George
6/8022, 30/11/15; dis. to re-enlist in Australian Army, 25/7/16; Aust. F.A., 25/3/17; F; Lieut.; M(1).
14 Cranbourne Road, Bradford, Yorkshire.

HALFORD, John Alfred
E/2924, 15/2/15; E. Surr. R., 21/6/15; F; Capt.; w.
6 St. Georges Road, Golder's Green, N.W. 11.

HALKETT, Alan Templeton
C/Sq/11795, 2/8/17, L/C.; No. 2 Cav. C/S, 11/1/18; R. Regt. of Cav., 22/6/18; 2/Lieut.
c/o Messrs. Grindlay & Coy., Parliament Street, S.W. 1. (Now in India.)

HALKYARD, Alfred
6/5/7293, 8/11/15; No. 11 O.C.B., 16/5/16; Leic. R., 4/9/16; F; Lieut.; p; M.C. Portland Towers, Stoneygate, Leicester.

✠ HALL, Alan Ryder
4/3775, 27/5/15; North'd. Fus., 12/8/15, att. Notts. & Derby. R.; F; Lieut.; M(1). Killed in action 30/5/18.

HALL, Albert Avondale
A/10484, 12/1/17; No. 2 R.G.A., C/S, 6/6/17; R.G.A., 1/10/17; F; Lieut.; w. 13 Rosebery Avenue, South Shields.

HALL, Arthur Anderson
B/11343, 23/5/17; A.S.C., C/S, 1/9/17; R.A.S.C., 27/10/17; F; 2/Lieut. Solicitor, Malton, Yorkshire.

✠ HALL, Arthur James Melville
4/3/3960, 3/6/15; 20th Lond. R., 27/8/15; F; 2/Lieut.
Killed in action 15/9/16

HALL, Aubrey George
3/3693, 20/5/15, Sgt.; R.E., 3/9/15; Lieut.
17 Richmond Bridge Mansions, East Twickenham.

HALL, Barrington Evelyn Basil
B/Sq/C/13550, 18/7/18; No. 11 O.C.B., 31/1/19; General List, 8/3/19; 2/Lieut. Middleburg, Virginia, U.S.A.

HALL, Bernard Peace
6/8601, 3/1/16; R.F.A., C/S, 26/5/16; R.G.A., 30/8/16; Major; M(1). 4 Bucklersbury, E.C. 4.

HALL, Charles Cameron
A/12439, 22/1/18, L/C.; No. 16 O.C.B., 23/8/18; L'pool. R., 5/3/19; 2/Lieut.
19 Wormald Street, Almondbury, Huddersfield, Yorkshire.

HALL, Charles Harold William
B/12771, 15/3/18; No 14 O.C.B., 23/8/18; Suff. R., 6/3/19; 2/Lieut. Guilden Monden, Nr. Royston, Hertfordshire.

HALL, Charles Wimette Durham
4/5/6/4854, 15/7/15; trfr. R.G.A., 26/9/16; F; Gnr.
Central Police Station, Klang, Federated Malay States.

HALL, Daniel George Edward
B/11669, 16/7/17, L/C.; demob. 6/1/19.
University College, University of Rangoon, Burma.

APPENDIX II.—RECORDS OF RANK AND FILE.

HALL, *Edward Gwyn*
C/D/11796, 2/8/17; No. 14 O.C.B., 4/1/18; S. Staff. R., 25/6/18; F; Lieut. 392 Princes Road, Stoke-on-Trent.

HALL, *Edward Ransden*
D/13795, 9/8/18; trfr. K.R. Rif. C., 25/4/19.
32 Greenhead Road, Huddersfield

HALL, *Ernest William*
K/B/2162, 23/11/14; R.G.A., 21/12/14; F; Major.
79 Canfield Gardens, West Hampstead, N.W. 6.

HALL, *Frank Harvey*
A/10503, 15/1/17; R.G.A., C/S, 25/4/17; R.G.A., 19/8/17; F; Lieut.; w. 33 Cornhill, E.C. 3.

✠ HALL, *George Dorrington*
6/5/6011, 2/9/15, L/C.; No. 14 O.C.B., 28/8/16; Devon. R., 22/11/16; P,F; Lieut.; w. Died of wounds 16/9/18.

✠ HALL, *George Elliott*
A/9817, 30/10/16; R.A., C/S, 1/2/17; R.G.A., 4/8/17; 2/Lieut.
Killed in action 29/5/18

HALL, *Gilbert*
6/1/6066, 6/9/15; 11th Lond. R., 20/6/16, att. 5th Lond. R., R.A.F.; F; Lieut.; w; M(1).
c/o Post Office, Vernon, British Columbia, Canada.

HALL, *Henry Douglas Philpott*
3/4729, 10/7/15; R.W. Kent. R., 17/9/15; F; Lieut.; w.
Stella Dale, 26 Marmora Road, Honor Oak, S.E. 22.

✠ HALL, *Henry Leonard*
6/5/8481, 20/12/15; R.F.A., C/S, 4/8/16; R.G.A., 12/11/16; Lieut.; w. Killed in action 27/10/18.

HALL, *Henry Sydney Hofman*
C/985, 5/8/14; R. Fus., 12/9/14; Capt.; w; D.S.O., M(2).
Ardmore, Upper Cumberland Walk, Tunbridge Wells

HALL, *Herbert Stanley*
C/14154, 14/10/18; demob. 25/1/19.
230 York Road, Kings Cross. N. 7.

HALL, *Horace Edward*
6/2/7840, 25/11/15, L/C.; No. 14 O.C.B., 28/8/16; Manch. R., 18/12/16; Lieut. Blackthorn House, Bacup, Lancashire.

✠ HALL, *Hugh Wilfred*
6/4/9431, 11/2/16, Sgt.; 3rd Lond. R., 23/6/16; Germ.SWA,F; 2/Lieut.; w. Killed in action 15/5/17.

HALL, *James*
C/11078, 18/4/17; R.A., C/S, 7/9/17; R.F.A., 6/4/18; F; 2/Lieut. Holmer Grange, Hereford.

✠ HALL., *James Muir*
6/Sq/8311, 11/12/15; R.F.A., C/S, 4/8/16; R.F.A., 1/12/16; 2/Lieut. Died of wounds 23/4/17.

HALL, *James Robert Baden*
13728, 2/8/18, L/C.; demob. 30/5/19.
144 Hainault Road, Leytonstone, E. 11.

HALL, *John Foljambe*
B/285, 20/6/08; dis. 19/6/09.

✠ HALL, *John Gilbert*
6/1/9374, 8/2/16; No. 14 O.C.B., 30/10/16; W. York. R., 24/1/17; F; 2/Lieut. Killed in action 3/5/17.

HALL, *John Leslie*
A/D/13038, 6/5/18; trfr. R.A.O.C., 7/6/19.
West End Farm. Offley. Hitchin. Hertfordshire.

HALL, *John Maxwell*
B/13476, 5/7/18; No. 11 O.C.B., 6/2/19; General List, 8/3/19; 2/Lieut. Jesselton, British North Borneo.

HALL, *Philip James*
B/2554, 4/1/15; Hamps. R., 3/6/15; F; Lieut.; w.
Pishill Vicarage, Henley-on-Thames.

HALL, *Raymond Eglington*
A/13128, 27/5/18; trfr. 14th Lond. R., 6/12/18.
Pennare, Victoria Avenue, Surbiton.

HALL, *Ridley Martin*
A/9828, 1/11/16; No. 14 O.C.B., 27/12/16; North'd. Fus., 27/3/17; F,I; Lieut.; w.
55 St. Margaret's Road, Wanstead Park, E. 12. (Now in India.)

HALL, *Romilly Furneaux*
D/10824, 2/3/17; No. 11 O.C.B.; Indian Army, 30/10/17; 2/Lieut. 34 Royal York Crescent, Clifton, Bristol.

HALL, *Ronald Acott*
H/2/4/6/2537, 4/1/15; R.G.A., 11/8/15; F; Capt.
Southmead, Abbots Langley, Hertfordshire.

HALL, *Stanley Alfred*
6/3/6163, 11/9/15; Midd'x. R., 20/1/16; Lieut.
8/11 Queen Square, Bloomsbury. W.C. 1.

HALL, *Thomas Edward*
6/2/7026, 27/10/15; No. 11 O.C.B., 7/5/16; Hamps. R., 4/9/16. emp. M. of Labour; F; Lieut.; w.
43 Muschamp Road, Dulwich, S.E

HALL, *Wilfrid John*
C/1348, 26/9/14, L/C.; Bedf. R., 10/2/15, M.G.C.; F; Major; M.C.
36 Baskerville Road, Wandsworth Common, S.W. 18. (Now in India.)

HALL, *William Donald de Putron*
4/3/4730, 10/7/15; R.W. Kent. R., 6/7/16; F; Lieut.; w; M.C, M(1). Stella Dale, 26 Marmora Road, Honor Oak, S.E. 22.

HALL, *William George*
A/12440, 22/1/18; No. 1 O.C.B., 8/11/18, No. 3 O.C.B.; Dorset R., 18/3/19; 2/Lieut. Lodway, Pill, Nr. Bristol.

✠ HALL, *William Holden*
6/9353, 7/2/16; R.F.A., C/S, 23/6/16; R.F.A., 30/9/16; F; 2/Lieut. Killed in action 26/9/17.

HALLAM, *George Henry*
D/11108, 23/4/17; R.A., C/S, 10/8/17; R.F.A., 6/1/18; F; Lieut.; w. 123 Widdenham Road, Holloway, N. 7.

HALLAM, *Guy Griffith*
C/11511, 18/6/17; No. 14 O.C.B., 5/10/17; 9th Lond. R, 26/2/18; 2/Lieut. Hillview, Stanley Park Road, Wallington.

HALLATT, *William Edward*
6/1/9548, 22/2/16, L/C.; No. 14 O.C.B., 28/8/16; L'pool. R., 24/10/16; Lieut.

HALL-DARE, *Robert Westley*
A/Sq/13077, 17/5/18; trfr. K.R. Rif. C., 30/6/19.
Newtown Curry, Co. Wexford, Ireland

HALLETT, *Denys Bouhier Imbert*
C/28, 3/4/08; dis. 2/4/09; R.A.M.C., 10/6/15; F; Major.
56 Eltham Road, Lee, S.E. 12.

HALLETT, *Ernest Montague*
6/2/5898, 30/8/15, L/C.; K.R. Rif. C., 1/6/16, Lab. Corps; Capt.; w. 15 Craven Street, Strand, W.C. 2.

HALLETT, *George David*
B/D/12207, 8/11/17; A.S.C., C/S, 4/3/18; R.A.S.C., 28/4/18; F; 2/Lieut. Shamley Green, Guildford, Surrey.

HALLETT, *Henry Gerard*
3/3160, 1/4/15, L/C.; R. Fus., 8/7/15; F; Capt.
45 Warwick Gardens, Kensington, W. 14

HALLETT, *Hugh Imbert Periam*
C/219, 11/5/08; 24th Lond. R., 3/9/14, secd. R.E. Sigs.; F; Capt.; M.C., M(1). 3 Elm Court, Temple, E.C. 4.

✠ HALLEY-JONES, *Percival*. See JONES, P. H.

HALLIDAY, *Arthur Horace Basil*
D/12972, 23/4/18; No. 11 O.C.B.; demob. 21/1/19.
5 York Road, Rathmines, Dublin, Ireland.

HALLIDAY, *Ian Andrew*
D/12929, 15/4/18; No. 5 O.C.B., 8/11/18, Nos. 20 & 12; High. L.I., 16/3/19; 2/Lieut.
Bellhaven, Castlehill Road, Kilmalcolm, Renfrewshire, Scotland

HALLIDAY, *Matthew Alfred Corrie*
Sq/1217, 14/9/14; Bedf. Yeo., 7/11/14, att. M.G.C.; Lieut.
31 Talbot Road, W. 2.

HALLINAN, *Charles Stewart*
6/Sq/7232, 5/11/15; R.F.A., C/S, 17/3/16; R.F.A., 17/7/16, att. R.F.C.; 2/Lieut. 63 Cathedral Road, Cardiff.

HALLIWELL, *Leonard Openshaw*
D/6/8633, 3/1/16, L/C.; M.G.C., C/S, 1/1/17; N. Lan. R., 26/6/17, att. R.A.F.; F; Lieut.
Wave Crest, 49 East Beach, Lytham.

APPENDIX II.—RECORDS OF RANK AND FILE.

HALL-PATCH, Edmund Leo
Sq/3410, 17/4/15; R.F.A., 9/6/15; Capt.
21 Pond Place, Onslow Square, S.W. 3.

HALLSMITH, Guthrie W.
6/5/8086, 1/12/15; No. 14 O.C.B., 28/8/16; Suff. R., 18/12/16; F; Lieut.; w(2), p; D.S.O., M(1).
35 Avondale Avenue, North Finchley, N. 12.

HALSALL, Daniel
5/6/7449, 15/11/15; trfr. M.G.C., 18/10/16.
31 Portland Street, Southport.

☩ HALSALL, Donald Court
B/10121, 6/12/16, L/C.; No. 14 O.C.B., 6/4/17; Lan. Fus., 31/7/17; F; 2/Lieut.
Killed in action 9/10/17.

HALSALL, Robert
6/5/7448, 15/11/15; trfr R.G.A., 6/10/16.
19 Chester Road, Southport, Lancashire.

HAMBLIN, Edward Charles Clifford
C/1304, 26/9/14; dis. med. unfit, 14/10/14.

HAMBLIN, Leslie Reginald
Sq/3540, 10/5/15, L/C.; R.G.A., 15/8/15; 2/Lieut.

HAMBLY, John Jennings
6/1/3637, 17/5/15, L/C; dis. med. unfit, 22/5/16.
c/o Nat. Prov. & Union Bank Ltd., Mayfair.

☩ HAMER, Samuel
6/4/6355, 20/9/15; North'd. Fus., 23/4/16; Capt.; w.
Killed in action 14/4/17.

HAMILL, Robert Hugh
6/2/6553, 30/9/15; dis. med. unfit, 14/8/16.
20 Cambridge Mansions, Battersea Park.

☩ HAMILL, William
6/1/6248, 16/9/15; Manch. R., 9/1/16; Lieut.
Killed in action 16/8/17.

HAMILTON, Allister McNicoll
6/3/6318, 18/9/15; 11th Lond. R., 6/1/16; E,P; Lieut.; w.
The Nursery, Knowsley, Prescot.

☩ HAMILTON, Andrew Douglas
6/3/7626, 19/11/15; R.F.A., C/S, 4/8/16; R.F.A., 27/10/16; F; Lieut.; w.
Died 26/4/19.

HAMILTON, Arthur Douglas Bruce
D/13744, 2/8/18; demob. 30/1/19.
2 Burlington Gardens, Chiswick, W. 4.

HAMILTON, Bryant Charles
6/Sq/6659, 7/10/15, L/C.; Cav. C/S, 20/3/16; N. Ir. Horse, 27/7/16; Lieut.; F.
Bank of Adelaide, Adelaide, South Australia.

HAMILTON, Charles Daniel
6/8285, 10/12/15; trfr. Dorset Yeo., 14/4/16.
Glencoe House, Dromore, Co. Down.

HAMILTON, Cyril Julien
6/8634, 3/1/16; R.F.A., C/S, 26/5/16; R.G.A., 30/8/16; F; Lieut.
Hollyholm, Huke Road, Southampton.

HAMILTON, David
Sq/1659, 9/10/14, S.S.M.; R.A.O.C., 19/11/16; F; Capt.; M.C. Revelstoke, 79 St. Gabriel's Road, Cricklewood, N.W. 2.

HAMILTON, David Lionel
A/Sq/13028, 3/5/18, L/C.; demob. 23/1/19.
The College, Lismore, Co. Waterford.

HAMILTON, Eustace Arthur Douglas
B/11393, 30/5/17; Garr. O.C.B., 5/10/17; Lab. Corps, 15/12/17; 2/Lieut.
Wharncliffe House, Lancaster.

HAMILTON, George Cecil Hans
A/472, 14/3/10; Manch. R., 30/12/13; Lieut.; w.

☩ HAMILTON, Guy Stanley Gerald
K/F/3/2383, 17/12/14, Sgt.; R.W. Surr. R., 22/4/15; F; Lieut.; w.
Killed in action 1/8/17.

HAMILTON, Henry Francis Trayton
C/10391, 8/1/17; No. 14 O.C.B., 5/5/17; Norf. R., 28/8/17, att. Suff. R.; F; Lieut.; p.
27 West Parade, Norwich.

☩ HAMILTON, James
6/4/5990, 2/9/15; Bord. R., 26/1/16; F; 2/Lieut.
Killed in action 5/11/16.

HAMILTON, James Henry Peyton
A/D/11897, 23/8/17; Garr. O.C.B., 8/3/18; Essex R., 4/9/18; F,E; Lieut.
40 High Road, Ilford, Essex.

HAMILTON, John
A/11602, 5/7/17; R.F.C., C/S, 30/11/17; trfr. R.A.F., 30/11/17.
124 Venner Road, Sydenham, S.E. 26.

HAMILTON, John
A/13153, 29/5/18; No. 22 O.C.B., 5/7/18; E. Surr. R., 12/2/19; 2/Lieut.
14 Park Mansions, Battersea Park, S.W. 11.

HAMILTON, John Montgomery
Sq/2821, 30/1/15, Cpl.; R.A.S.C., 25/5/15; Lieut.

HAMILTON, Josceline Paul
6/1/8448, 17/12/15; No. 5 O.C.B., 14/8/16; dis. med. unfit, 28/11/16.

HAMILTON, Patrick Swinglehurst
E/1585, 6/10/14; Bord. R., 20/11/14; Capt.
62 Chester Terrace, S.W. 1.

HAMILTON, Robert Claude Victor
6/5/C/8895, 13/1/16; No. 7 O.C.B., 4/11/16; R. Ir. Regt., 28/2/17; S,P; Lieut.
10 Proby Square, Blackrock, Dublin, Ireland.

HAMILTON, Samuel
6/3/9375, 8/2/16; R.F.A., C/S, 4/8/16; R.G.A., 24/11/16; M; Lieut.
40 Keir Street, Pollokshields, Glasgow.

HAMILTON, William John
2/9630, 25/9/16; Garr. O.C.B., 23/5/17; Suff. R., 14/7/17, York. Drag.; Lieut.
Marchmont Cottage, Hemel Hempsted.

HAMILTON, William Norman
6/1/6126, 9/9/15, L/C.; North'd. Fus., 4/2/16, R.A.F.; F; Lieut.; w-p.
c/o Alexander Jubb & Taylor, 124 Vincent Street, Glasgow. (Now in India.)

☩ HAMILTON, William Robert
6/3/8963, 17/1/16; Cold. Gds., 23/8/16, att. Gds. M.G.R.; 2/Lieut.
Killed in action 12/10/17.

HAMILTON-JONES, Leslie Morris
A/14034, 20/9/18; demob. 29/1/19.
Glenderg, Seymour Park, Mannamead, Plymouth.

☩ HAMLETT, George Froude
6/5/7671, 22/11/15; No. 8 O.C.B., 4/8/16; Bord. R., 18/12/16; 2/Lieut.
Killed in action 13/8/17.

HAMLETT, Ronald Williams
1/9754, 18/10/16; No. 14 O.C.B., 27/12/16; Ches. R., 25/4/17; F; Lieut.; Inv.
Summer Hill, Winsford, Cheshire.

HAMLEY, Cecil Francis Osbertus
2/3088, 22/3/15; Hamps. R., 22/8/15; Major; M(2).

HAMLIN, James Alfred
D/12887, 5/4/18; R.F.A., C/S, 26/7/18; R.G.A., 8/4/19; 2/Lieut.
Childrens Hospital, Paddington Green, W. 2.

HAMLYN, Ralph Furneaux
6/Sq/7450, 15/11/15; Devon. Yeo., 1/7/16, 11th Lond. R., att. R.F.C.; Capt.; w.
2 Riding Cottages, Clifton, Bristol. (Now in South Africa.)

HAMMERSLEY, Eric Victor
D/10663, 5/2/17; No. 11 O.C.B., 5/7/17; Worc. R., 30/10/17; F; 2/Lieut.; g.
4 Earls Road, Trentham.

HAMMERSLEY, Godfrey
C/12619, 18/2/18, L/C.; demob. 23/1/19.
Red Earth, Leek, Staffordshire.

HAMMERTON, Philip Moy
6/4/4696, 8/7/15; 1st Lond. R., 8/12/15; 2/Lieut.
c/o National Provincial Bank, Portsea.

HAMMOND, Charles Clifford
1/3385, 26/4/15; R.W. Surr. R., 10/7/15; F,It; Lieut.; w(2).
Brookleigh, 36 Lancaster Road, West Norwood, S.E. 27.

HAMMOND, Edgar
C/Sq/9914, 14/11/16; R.F.A., C/S, 17/12/17; R.F.A., 3/6/18; F; 2/Lieut.
45 Brookhouse Hill, Fulwood, Sheffield.

☩ HAMMOND, Leonard
C/1113, 7/9/14; W. Rid. R., 19/9/14; F; Capt.
Killed in action 5/7/16.

APPENDIX II.—RECORDS OF RANK AND FILE.

HAMMOND, Martin
B/1256, 23/9/14; Lan. Fus., 20/10/14, E. Kent. R.; F; Staff Capt.; M(1).
Knockholt, Kent.

✠ HAMMOND, Paul
C/1114, 7/9/14; E. Lan. R., 19/9/14; F; Major; M(1).
Died of wounds 25/2/16.

HAMPSHIRE, Claude Dennis
4/1/4513, 28/6/15; R. Berks. R., 22/11/15, Hamps. R., R. Fus.; F ╻ Capt.; w(2); M.C.
34 Russell Street, Reading.

HAMPSHIRE, John Pollit
H/K/1737, 15/10/14; R. Innis. Fus., 29/1/15, M.G.C.; Lieut.; w.
Redcourt, Pyrford, Surrey.

HAMPSHIRE, Thomas Henry
B/10563, 19/1/17; R.F.C., C/S, 13/3/17; R.F.C., 19/4/17, R.A.F.; F; Lieut.
Park Cottage, Holmfirth, Nr. Huddersfield, Yorkshire.

✠ HAMPSON, Harold Norman
6/3/7636, 18/11/15; S. Lan. R., 20/6/16. R.F.C.; 2/Lieut.
Died of wounds 8/4/17.

HAMPSON, Hector Benton
K/B/2310, 10/12/14; R. Dub. Fus., 27/2/15, secd. M.G.C.; F,It; Lieut.
Wykefield, Ambleside, Westmorland.

HAMPSON, John Nicholl
B/215, 9/5/08; Kent. Cyc. Bn., 30/9/08; Capt.
Commonwood, Thurnham, Kent.

HAMPSON, Robert Ernest Victor
6/3/9228, 31/1/16; R.E., 28/7/16, emp. M. of Munitions; Lieut.; w.
140 Duke Street, Southport.

HAMSON, Joseph Robert Lucas
C/10347, 5/1/17; R.F.C., C/S, 13/3/17; R.F.C., 19/4/17; 2/Lieut.
6 Shrigley Road, Bollington, Nr. Macclesfield.

HANAN, John Dart
B/10496, 15/1/17; A.S.C., C/S, 1/5/17; R.A.S.C., 28/6/17; F; Lieut.; w.
28 Shalstone Road, East Sheen, S.W. 14.

✠ HANBURY, Herbert Wood
1/3113, 25/3/15; Midd'x. R., 4/6/15; Capt.
Killed in action 15/11/16.

HANBY, Evlyn John Jolliffe Halsted
D/10223, 20/12/16; No. 14 O.C.B.; 7th Lond. R., 28/8/17; Lieut.
c/o Messrs. Cox & Coy., 16 Charing Cross, S.W. 1.

✠ HANBY, Francis James
K/D/2448, 28/12/14, L/C.; R. Suss. R., 31/3/15; 2/Lieut.
Killed in action 30/6/16.

HANBY, Thomas
D/13808, 9/8/18; demob. 30/1/19.
Manor View, Altofts, Normanton, Yorkshire.

HANCOCK, Alexander Edwin
6/2/8692, 4/1/16; No. 8 O.C.B., 4/8/16; K.R. Rif. C., 21/11/16; Lieut.

HANCOCK, Charles Victor
6/1/7294, 8/11/15; S. Lan. R., 4/9/16, secd. M.G.C.; Lieut.; w.
48 Westbourne Park, Penarth.

HANCOCK, Frank
6/3/6201, 13/9/15, L/C.; Essex R., 1/6/16; F; Capt.; M.B.E., M(1).
School House, Shenley, Hertfordshire.

HANCOCK, Gerald Rattenbury
4/4275, 17/6/15; Devon. R., 12/12/15, att. E. Kent. R.; M,I; Capt.
Tors View, Callington, Cornwall.

HANCOCK, John
6/3/8438, 16/12/15, Sgt.; R.F.C., 25/9/16, att. York. R. and M.G.C.; I; Lieut.
Ashdene, Lower Landywood, Nr. Walsall, Staffordshire.

HANDCOCK, Gustavus McMahon Forbes
C/11443, 4/6/17, L/C.; R.A., C/S, 15/12/17; R.G.A., 26/8/18; 2/Lieut.
Gra-Machree, Pagoda Avenue, Richmond.

HANDCOCK, Russell
6/5/C/8439, 16/12/15; No. 14 O.C.B., 30/10/16; North'd. Fus., 28/8/17; F; 2/Lieut.
Orchard Vale, Corbridge-on-Tyne, Northumberland.

HANDFORD, Leonard Francis
4/3842, 31/5/15; trfr. 13th Lond. R., 5/5/16; 13th Lond. R., 28/3/17, R.F.C., R.A.F.; F; Lieut.; w; M.C.
20 Crediton Road, Kensal Rise, N.W. 10.

HANDLEY, Ernest William
C/11080, 18/4/17, L/C.; No. 10 O.C.B., 5/10/17; K.R. Rif. C., 26/2/18, R.A.F.; 2/Lieut.
55 Percy Road, Shepherd's Bush, W. 12.

HANDSCOMBE, Harold Tom
6/5/C/8170, 6/12/15; No. 14 O.C.B., 30/10/16; R.W. Surr. R., 28/2/17, att. Midd'x. R.; Lieut.

HANFORTH, Thomas Frederick
B/12808, 20/3/18; No. 20 O.C.B., 20/9/18; York. & Lanc. R., 17/3/19; 2/Lieut.
45 Clarendon Road, Fulwood Park, Sheffield.

HANITSCH, Philip Hugh Vernon
4/3386, 26/4/15; Dorset R., 8/7/16, att. Hunt. Cyc. Bn.; F; Capt.
99 Woodstock Road, Oxford.

HANKINSON, George Herbert
A/11290, 16/5/17, Sgt.; No. 3 O.C.B., 8/3/18; York. & Lanc. R., 27/8/18; 2/Lieut.
2 Morecumbe Bank, Grange-over-Sands, Lancashire.

HANKINSON, George Stanley
D/10457, 11/1/17; R.F.C., C/S, 16/4/17; R.F.C., 16/5/17, R.A.F.; Lieut.
Tullamore, King's Co., Ireland.

HANKINSON, Harold Frederick
3/7451, 15/11/15; dis. med. unfit, 31/5/16.
11 Pulborough Road, Southfields, S.W. 18.

HANMAN, John Leo Stanley
B/10112, 4/12/16; R.F.C., C/S, 13/3/17; R.F.C., 19/4/17, R.A.F.; Lieut.; M.C.
c/o Holt's Bank, Whitehall, S.W. 1.

HANNAFORD, Charles Arthur
6/4/6952, 21/10/15, Cpl.; D. of Corn. L.I., 25/9/16; Capt.
Monasty House, Canterbury.

HANNAFORD, John
4/1/6/5200, 29/7/15; Suff. R., 3/12/15, War Office; F; Lieut.; w.
78 Fillebrook Road, Leytonstone, E. 11.

HANNAFORD, William Mortimore
4/1/4831, 10/7/15; R.A.S.C., 9/10/15; P; Capt.
25 North Street, Exeter, Devonshire.

HANNAN, Neil
Sq/1835, 16/10/14, L/C.; N. Som. Yeo., 18/2/15, 2nd & 3rd Drag. Gds.; F; Capt.
Riverstoun, Killucan, Co. Westmeath, Ireland.

HANNAY, William
Sq/3344, 22/4/15; R.F.A., 15/9/15; E,S; Lieut.; M(1).
54 Withens Lane, Wallasey, Cheshire.

✠ HANNON, Thomas James
6/4/9199, 31/1/16; No. 14 O.C.B., 26/11/16; Shrop. L.I., 28/2/17; 2/Lieut.; w.
Died of wounds 1/12/17.

✠ HANSEN, William George
6/5/5706, 19/8/15; L'pool. R., 17/1/16; 2/Lieut.
Killed in action 25/9/16.

HANSON, William Brooks
D/13669, 29/7/18; demob. 21/12/18.
21 Sunnyside Terrace, Coatbridge, Scotland.

✠ HANSON, William Edward
6/4/9555, 28/2/16; No. 13 O.C.B., 4/11/16; North'd. Fus., 28/2/17; 2/Lieut.
Killed in action 28/4/17.

HANTON, Michael Joseph
6/5/6554, 30/9/15; dis. 22/9/16.
42 John Street, Wexford, Ireland.

HANWORTH, Frederick Arthur
4/Sq/4217, 14/6/15, S.Q.M.S.; A.S.C., C/S, 27/10/16; R.A.S.C., 20/12/16; Lieut.
Oulton Broad, Lowestoft, Suffolk.

HANWORTH, William Charles
D/2585, 4/1/15; R. War. R., 3/4/15; F; Capt.; M.C.
Ponders, Margaretting, Nr. Ingatestone, Essex.

HARBORNE, Ralph Samuel
6/4/6660, 7/10/15; dis. to re-enlist in R.E., 4/4/16; F; Pnr.; g.
Close Cottage, Tetbury, Gloucestershire.

HARBOTT, Leonard Gabriel
6/4/7508, 15/11/15; E. Ang. Div. Cyc. Coy., 28/8/16, Army Cyc. Corps; Lieut.
120 Southchurch Road, Southend-on-Sea.

HARBRON, Frank
6/5/6127, 9/9/15, L/C.; Manch. R., 1/6/16; F; Lieut.; w-p.
159 Lytham Road, South Shore, Blackpool.

APPENDIX II.—RECORDS OF RANK AND FILE.

HARDEN, *Guy Baldwin*
4/3196, 8/4/15; R.E., 15/7/15; Lieut.; M.C.

HARDEN, *Malcolm de Haviland*
6/1/5330, 2/8/15; 19th Lond. R., 6/11/15; Lieut.
36 *Duke Street, St. James Street, S.W.*

HARDEN, *William Wallace*
A/11929, 30/8/17; R.F.A., C/S, 7/2/18; R.F.A., 10/10/18; 2/Lieut.
5 *Manor Gardens, Merton Park, S.W. 19.*

✠ HARDEY-MASON, *Harold Victor*
6/3/8547, 3/1/16, Cpl.; No. 14 O.C.B., 30/10/16; E. Kent. R., 24/1/17; F; 2/Lieut.
Killed in action 3/5/17.

HARDIE, *Frederick Russell*
Sq/740, 11/11/13; 3rd Huss., 14/8/14, secd. R.F.C., R.A.F.; F; Capt.; w.
c/o Messrs. Balfour, Williamson & Coy., 43 Exchange Place, New York City, U.S.A.

✠ HARDIE, *John*
D/10917, 26/3/17; R.F.C., C/S, 4/5/17; R.F.C., 14/6/17; 2/Lieut.
Killed 7/2/18.

HARDING, *Arthur Gibson*
6/2/8063, 1/12/15; Welch. R., 18/12/16; Lieut.; w.
Rodborough, The Grove, Uplands, Swansea.

HARDING, *Arthur Merlyn*
A/12168, 29/10/17; Sigs. C/S, 14/12/17; R.E., 24/5/18; 2/Lieut
c/o H. B. Beaumont, 8 *Waterloo Place, S.W. 1.*

✠ HARDING, *Clive Scotland*
C/1149, 14/9/14; E. Surr. R., 20/10/14, att. Hamps. R.; E,G; Lieut.
Killed in action 6/8/15.

HARDING, *George Richardson*
F/1770, 16/10/14, L/C.; R.E., 6/12/14; F; Lt.-Col.; D.S.O., M(2).
30 *St. James Square, S.W. 1.*

HARDING, *Herbert*
6/3/6202, 13/9/15, L/C.; R.A., C/S, 24/1/16; Devon. R., 8/6/16, att. T. M. Bty.; M; Capt.; M(1).
The Patent Office, 25 *Southampton Buildings, Chancery Lane, W.C. 2.*

HARDING, *Leonard Charles William*
4/4276, 17/6/15; Devon. R., 24/10/16; Lieut.; w; M.C.
Bovey, Beer, Devonshire.

✠ HARDING, *Reginald J. W*
6/2/9383, 8/2/16; No. 8 O.C.B., 4/8/16; R.W. Surr. R., 21/11/16; 2/Lieut.; w; M.C. and Bar.
Killed in action 27/3/18.

HARDING, *Robert*
3/4/4499, 28/6/15; R.G.A., 15/10/15; Lieut.
19 *Gladstone Street, Hartlepool.*

HARDING, *Ronald Albert*
2/3598, 13/5/15; R.E., 16/10/15; F; Lieut.; g,w; M.C., M(2).
Borough Surveyor's Office, High Wycombe, Buckinghamshire.

HARDING, *Thomas Roland*
6/2/8132, 3/12/15; No. 5 O.C.B., 14/8/16; M.G.C., 30/11/16, Tank Corps; F; Lieut.; w.
24 *The Avenue, Roundhay, Leeds.*

HARDING, *William Shrewsbury*
4/5/5105, 26/7/15; R.A.S.C., 12/9/15; F; Lieut.; w.
Charford Manor, Downton, Salisbury, Wiltshire.

✠ HARDMAN, *Adrian Thomas*
B/1702, 13/10/14, Cpl.; R. Fus., 17/2/15; F; Lieut.
Died of wounds 30/3/16.

HARDMAN, *Harold*
A/10708, 12/2/17; R.G.A., C/S, 6/6/17; R.G.A., 1/10/17; 2/Lieut.
Fernlea, 67B Upper Tulse Hill, S.W. 2.

HARDWICKE, *Cedric Webster*
4/1/5106, 26/7/15; R.A.S.C., 27/11/15, North'd. Fus.; F; Lieut
The Lye, Stourbridge, Worcester

HARDWICKE, *Herbert Junius Allen*
A/11190, 7/5/17; trfr. R.F.C., 13/12/17.
c/o *Barclay's Bank, Crowborough, Sussex.*

✠ HARDWICK-TERRY, *Leonard Alfred.* See TERRY, L. A. H.

HARDY, *Alan*
A/2865, 5/2/15; Notts. & Derby. R., 20/6/15, att. Yorks. L.I.; F; Capt.; w(2).
Underfell, Barbon, Nr. Kirkby Lonsdale, Westmorland.

HARDY, *Alfred Cecil*
B/13576, 19/7/18; demob. 25/1/19.
San Remo, Cromer, Norfolk.

HARDY, *Arthur Yorke*
B/12023, 20/9/17, L/C.; R.A., C/S, 7/2/18; R.G.A., 26/8/18; 2/Lieut.
8 *Mosella Road, Wandsworth Common, S.W.*

HARDY, *Charles Edwin*
B/13604, 24/7/18; demob. 29/1/19.
Winston-on-Tees, Darlington, Co. Durham.

HARDY, *Christopher Charles*
6/3/5773, 23/8/15; R.F.A., 26/11/15; Lieut.; w(2).
20 *Clevedon Mansions, Highgate Road, N.W.*

HARDY, *Cyril Jack*
B/10126, 6/12/16; No. 20 O.C.B., 7/6/17; S. Wales Bord., 25/9/17; F; Lieut.; M.C.
Bryn-Glas, St. David's Road, Pengam, Via Cardiff.

HARDY, *Frank Walter*
4/5/4794, 12/7/15; dis. med. unfit, 22/5/16.

HARDY, *Herbert Alfred*
B/C/12680, 4/3/18; H. Bde. O.C.B., 5/7/18; Leic. R., 10/6/19; 2/Lieut.
Abb-Kettleby, Heathside Park Road, Woking, Surrey.

HARDY, *John Durrofield*
C/1244, 23/9/14; dis. med. unfit, 9/10/14.

HARDY, *John Gardiner*
D/13004, 30/4/18; No. 22 O.C.B., 7/6/18; Rif. Brig., 12/2/19; 2/Lieut.
25 *West 45th Street, New York, U.S.A.*

HARDY, *Wilfrid*
C/10788, 23/2/17; R.F.C., C/S, 16/4/17; R.F.C., 22/5/17, R.A.F.; Lieut.
Seatown Place, Dundalk, Co. Louth, Ireland.

HARDY, *William Henry Clement*
A/656, 1/11/12; R. Suss. R., 19/9/14; Capt.; w(2); M.C.
15 *Old Square, Lincoln's Inn, W.C. 2.*

HARE, *Alan Millington*
3/3365, 22/4/15; trfr. 13th Lond. R., 2/5/16.
The Cottage, Southwold, Sussex.

HARE, *Geoffrey William Mortimer*
6/5/5292, 2/8/15; 7th Lond. R., 14/12/15; Lieut.
Kirk Ireton Rectory, Derby.

HARE, *Victor Frederick*
6/D/7841, 25/11/15; trfr. R.E., 20/11/16; F; Cpl.
Mayfield, Fishery Road, Boxmoor, Hertfordshire

HARFORD, *Charles Edward Pretorius*
A/13942, 2/9/18; demob. 15/3/19.
Regents Park Barracks, N.W. 1

HARGREAVES, *Frederick Bertram Fielden*
6/1/6523, 30/9/15; S. Lan. R., 23/12/15; F; Capt.; p; M(1).
Clifton Chambers, Wood Street, St. Annes-on-the-Sea.

HARGREAVES, *John Arthur*
6/1/8023, 30/11/15, L/C.; L'pool. R., 24/10/16; F; Lieut.; w.
Parkside, Neston, Chester.

HARKE, *Wilfred Vaughan*
K/A/6/1213, 14/9/14, Sgt.; R.A., C/S, 26/10/16; R.G.A., 3/5/17; F; Lieut.
Rooks Nest, Chatsworth Road, Croydon.

HARKES, *Alexander*
B/13641, 26/7/18; demob. 28/2/19.
205 *Langside Road, Queens Park, Glasgow.*

HARLAND, *Charles*
6/4/8133, 3/12/15; No. 8 O.C.B., 4/8/16; R.W. Fus., 24/10/16; Lieut.
39 *Plymouth Road, Penarth.*

HARLAND, *Edward*
6/3/6661, 7/10/15; North'd. Fus., 1/6/16; F; Lieut.; w(2).
165 *Falsgrave Road, Scarborough.*

HARLAND, *Robert Main*
A/11898, 23/8/17; R.E., C/S, 30/9/17; R.E., 9/11/17; Lieut.; p

HARLING, *William*
B/10539, 17/1/17; R.G.A., C/S, 6/6/17; R.G.A., 1/10/17; Lieut.
389 *Lytham Road, South Shore, Blackpool.*

✠ HARMAN, *Brian Relton*
6/2/8635, 3/1/16; No. 8 O.C.B., 4/8/16; E. Kent. R., 21/11/16, Indian Army; Lieut.; w.
Died 4/11/19

APPENDIX II.—RECORDS OF RANK AND FILE.

✠ HARMAN, John Augustus
B/590, 27/11/11; dis. 2/5/14; R.N.A.S.; Lieut.
Killed 18/11/17.

HARMAN, Lewis
A/Sq/13100, 22/5/18, L/C.; demob. 16/1/19.
Carlyle Club, 211 Piccadilly, W.

✠ HARMON, Wilfred Baldwin
6/4/5201, 29/7/15; K.R. Rif. C., 1/6/16; 2/Lieut.
Killed in action 1/8/17.

✠ HARMS, William
6/1/6249, 16/9/15; North'd. Fus., 1/6/16, att. R.F.C.; 2/Lieut
Killed in action 4/3/17.

HARPER, Alan Randolph
C/13188, 3/6/18; demob. 30/1/19.
30 Upper Montague Street, Montague Square, W.1.

HARPER, Alfred Noble
E/1499, 1/10/14, L/C.; R.A.S.C., 26/11/14; Capt.

HARPER, Alfred Trevor
6/2/6689, 7/10/15; No. 11 O.C.B., 7/5/16; R.W. Fus., 4/9/16, att. 4th Lond. R., R.F.C., R.A.F.; F; Lieut.
109 Plymouth Road, Penarth.

✠ HARPER, Charles Croke
4/2/4337, 21/6/15; Oxf. & Bucks. L.I., 7/10/15; 2/Lieut.
Killed in action 3/5/17.

HARPER, Harold John Cardnell
K/H/2510, 31/12/14; Welch R., 9/4/15; Lieut.; w.

HARPER, Kenneth Brand
Sq/624, 14/3/12; dis. 29/10/12.
25 Rosary Gardens, South Kensington, S.W.7.

HARPER, Leslie Clifford
C/14200, 21/10/18; demob. 19/12/18.
6 St. Ann Street, King's Lynn, Norfolk.

HARPER, Robert William
1/3727, 24/5/15; R.F.A., 1/12/15; F; Lieut.
45 Tressillian Road, Brockley, S.E.4.

HARRADINE, Robert
B/11314, 21/5/17, L/C.; R.A., C/S, 15/12/17; R.G.A., 30/6/18; 2/Lieut.
3 Woodthorpe Road, Putney, S.W.15.

HARRAL, Leonard
A/10816, 2/3/17; R.G.A., C/S, 6/6/17; R.G.A., 1/10/17; F; Lieut.
Thorpe Heys, Dovedale Road, Leicester.

HARRAP, Robert Evan
6/3/7672, 22/11/15; No. 8 O.C.B., 4/8/16, M.G.C., C/S; M.G.C., 28/10/16, Tank Corps; F; Lieut.
61 Warminster Road, South Norwood, S.E.25.

HARRIES, Bertram Genge Gibson
E/1500, 1/10/14; R.A.O.C., 22/1/15; Capt.; M.C., M(1).

✠ HARRIES, James Francis
4/3/5107, 26/7/15; E. Surr. R., 3/1/16; I; Lieut.
Died 30/6/18

HARRILD, William Leonard
D/1474, 29/9/14; 12th Lond. R., 30/3/15, att. N. Staff. R.; F; Capt.; w.
Sherlies, Orpington, Kent.

HARRILL, Frederick Pilkington
C/12305, 13/12/17; No. 24 O.C.B., 10/8/18, No. 11 O.C.B.; General List, 8/3/19; 2/Lieut.
52 Russell Road, Wimbledon, S.W.19.

HARRINGTON, Bernard Hubert Walter. See DELMA, B. or DELMA-HARRINGTON, B. H. W

HARRIS, Arnold Frank Stapleton
B/K/2098, 16/11/14; R.G.A., 2/3/15; F; Major.
12 Lincoln's Inn Fields, W.C.2

HARRIS, Arthur Douglas Vigers
H/2000, 2/11/14, L/C.; Oxf. & Bucks. L.I., 12/1/15.

✠ HARRIS, Arthur Stanley
6/2/8390, 14/12/15; L'pool. R., 18/12/16; 2/Lieut.
Killed in action 31/7/17.

✠ HARRIS, Cecil Alfred
4/5/4795, 12/7/15; R.W. Surr. R., 20/12/15; 2/Lieut.
Died of wounds 3/11/16

HARRIS, Cecil Mann
4/6/2/4929, 19/7/15; R. Ir. Fus., 9/12/15; Lieut.; w, w-p.
22 Carlton Road, Putney, S.W.15. (Now in F.M.S.).

HARRIS, Cecil Vivian
A/11254, 14/5/17; trfr. R.F.C., 26/10/17, R.A.F.; Sgt.
Rectory Drive, Hawarden, Nr. Chester.

HARRIS, David Sutherland Fraser
4/2/6/Sq/4149, 10/6/15; No. 1 Cav. C/S, 31/7/17; R. Regt. of Cav., 22/2/18; 2/Lieut.
11 Belsize Park Gardens, N.W.

HARRIS, Eric Whitehead
4/Sq/5073, 26/7/15; R.A.S.C., 9/10/15; F,It; Capt.; M(1).
Shelsley Lodge, Western Place, Worthing, Sussex.

HARRIS, Eric Freer
B/11327, 21/5/17; No. 11 O.C.B., 9/11/17; Worc. R., 26/3/18; 2/Lieut.
Hillfields, Pedmore, Nr. Stourbridge.

HARRIS, Eric William
1/3843, 31/5/15; W. Rid. R., 20/8/15; F; Lieut.; w(2); M.C.
56 Clifton Gardens, Maida Vale, W.9.

HARRIS, Ernest Reginald
C/10630, 30/1/17; R.F.C., C/S, 1/6/17; R.F.C., 4/7/17, R.A.F.; Lieut.
Wesley House, Skipton.

HARRIS, Frank Boulton
C/10682, 7/2/17, L/C.; R.E., C/S, 7/10/17; R.E., 11/1/18; 2/Lieut
80 Church Street, Woking.

HARRIS, Gilbert Stanley
6/2/8356, 13/12/15; No. 2 O.C.B., 14/8/16; N. Lan. R., 18/12/16; F; Lieut.; M(1).
10 Collingham Place, S.W.5.

HARRIS, Harold Arthur
6/5/5380, 5/8/15; 12th Lond. R., 8/6/16, att. 9th Lond. R.; Lieut.
1 Kingston Hill, Kingston-on-Thames.

HARRIS, Harold Cecil Dunstan
6/3/5432, 5/8/15, L/C.; Mon. R., 9/12/15, att. R.A.F.; E,F; Lieut.
26 Rhymney Terrace, Cathays, Cardiff.

✠ HARRIS, Henry James Lawrence
K/F/2578, 4/1/15; Hamps. R., 31/3/15; Lieut.
Killed in action 6/11/16.

HARRIS, John Edwin
D/10655, 5/2/17; No. 20 O.C.B., 7/6/17; W. Rid. R., 25/9/17, York. & Lanc. R., att. Indian Army; F; 2/Lieut.; g.
Victoria Cottage, Staplehurst, Kent

HARRIS, Morgan Rhys Howel
4/1/4367, 21/6/15; R.F.A., 1/12/15; Capt.; M.C. and Bar.
Dynevor Avenue, Neath, South Wales.

HARRIS, Percy
4/2/4446, 26/6/15; N. Mid. Div. Cyc. Coy., 17/9/15, secd. R.E.; F,E; Staff Lieut.; M(1).
35 Lovelace Gardens, Surbiton, Surrey.

HARRIS, Philip
B/12705, 8/3/18; No. 16 O.C.B., 23/8/18; Devon. R., 6/3/19; 2/Lieut.
117 London Road, Twickenham, Middlesex.

✠ HARRIS, Reginald Arthur
6/4/9098, 24/1/16; No. 8 O.C.B., 4/8/16; W. York. R., 21/11/16; F; 2/Lieut.
Killed in action 9/10/17.

✠ HARRIS, Ronald Arthur
6/5/6856, 16/10/15; R.F.C., 4/8/16, R.A.F.; Lieut.
Missing believed drowned 21/11/17.

HARRIS, Stanley
D/Sq/12107, 11/10/17; No. 1 Cav. C/S, 16/5/18; trfr. 28th Lond. R., 15/10/18.
Knocklong, Co. Limerick.

HARRIS, Stuart James
6/3/Sq/7332, 9/11/15, Sgt.; R.A., C/S, 24/11/16; R.F.A, 24/3/17; F; Lieut.; w.
7 Princes Street, E.C.3.

HARRIS, Sydney Bosworth
A/14104, 7/10/18; demob. 29/1/19.
87 Abington Avenue, Northampton

HARRIS, Thomas Noel Cleatler
H/1893, 16/10/14; Oxf. & Bucks. L.I., 12/1/15; Capt.; M.C., M(1).

HARRIS, William Eastwood
1/4/4108, 7/6/15; North'd. Fus., 17/9/15, emp. M. of Munitions; F; Capt.; w(2).
50 Springfield Road, St. Johns Wood, N.W.

APPENDIX II.—RECORDS OF RANK AND FILE.

HARRIS, William Leslie Freer
A/11291, 16/5/17; No. 11 O.C.B., 9/11/17; Worc. R., 26/3/18; F; Lieut.; g.   Hillfields. Pedmore, Stourbridge.

HARRISON, Albert
3/9737, 16/10/16, Sgt.; demob. 10/1/19.
Breakspear Road, Harefield, Uxbridge, Middlesex.

HARRISON, Alfred Ernest
6/4/8357, 13/12/15; Norf. R., 18/12/16; F; Capt.; w.
10 Jefferies Road, Ipswich, Suffolk.

HARRISON, Alfred Percy
C/1052, 31/8/14; W. Rid. R., 19/9/14; Capt.; w; M.C.

HARRISON, Charles
D/10405, 8/1/17, L/C.; No. 14 O.C.B., 7/6/17; L'pool. R., 25/9/17; 2/Lieut.   Stanley House, Ormskirk.

HARRISON, Charles Gordon
A/14036, 20/9/18; No. 11 O.C.B., 24/1/19; General List, 8/3/19; 2/Lieut.   Seascape, Carry Crescent, Torquay.

HARRISON, Christopher Bennett
6/5/5256, 31/7/15, L/C.; L'pool. R., 7/10/15; Lieut.; w.
The Coombs, Moor Park. Great Crosby, Lancashire.

HARRISON, Edmund Louis
C/787, 8/5/14; Wilts. R., 1/9/14, Indian Army; G,M,S; Capt.; w.   59 Belsize Avenue, Hampstead, N.W.3. (Now in India).

✠ HARRISON, Edward
6/1/6891, 18/10/15; R.A., C/S, 29/1/16; R.G.A., 19/6/16; 2/Lieut.   Killed in action 28/4/17.

HARRISON, Francis Henry
C/10158, 11/12/16, L/C.; No. 14 O.C.B., 6/4/17; Lanc. R., 31/7/17; Lieut.   Newstead, Caterham Valley, Surrey.

HARRISON, Frank Fox
A/D/11910, 27/8/17; No. 14 O.C.B., 4/1/18; S. Staff. R., 25/6/18; F; 2/Lieut.; g.
Elgin House, 51 Lower Hall Lane, Walsall, Staffordshire.

HARRISON, Frank Hamilton
6/5/C/8358, 13/12/15; No. 14 O.C.B., 26/11/16; Sco. Rif., 27/3/17; S; Lieut.; w.   Croft House, Helensburgh, N.B.

HARRISON, George
6/5/5257, 31/7/15, L/C.; L'pool. R., 27/12/15, M.G.C.; F,E,P; Major; w; M.C. and Bar, M(1).
46 Haworden Avenue, Wallasey, Cheshire.

HARRISON, Harold Ernest
A/14058, 25/9/18; demob. 30/1/19.
20 Pearson Avenue, Beverley Road, Hull, East Yorkshire.

HARRISON, Ivan Robert Sinclair
A/10495, 12/1/17; No. 14 O.C.B., 7/6/17; W. York. R., 25/9/17; F; Lieut.; M.C.   10 Church Walk, Peterborough.

HARRISON, John
6/A/Sq/7767, 23/11/15; A.S.C., C/S, 27/10/16; trfr. 14th Lond. R., 19/1/17.   Newbiggin House. Dacre, Penrith, Cumberland.

✠ V.C. HARRISON, John
6/4/7203, 4/11/15; E. York. R., 4/8/16; 2/Lieut.; Victoria Cross, M.C.   Killed in action 3/5/17.

✠ HARRISON, John German
6/9252, 2/2/16; R.A., C/S, 14/9/16; R.F.A., 22/1/17; F; Capt.   Killed in action 9/4/18.

✠ HARRISON, Percy Pool
4/5/4747, 12/7/15; Notts. & Derby. R., 14/10/15; F; Capt.
Died of wounds 20/10/17.

✠ HARRISON, Ronald
6/4/3/4855, 15/7/15, L/C.; 11th Lond. R., 4/6/16; 2/Lieut.
Killed in action 18/9/16.

HARRISON, Swainston
C/387, 24/3/09; dis. 24/3/09.   Died -/4/17.

HARRISON, Thomas Dalkin
D/2728, 18/1/15; Hamps. R., 16/4/15; Lieut.
Kneighton, Oriental Road, Woking.

✠ HARRISON, Thomas Walter
2/3454, 3/5/15; Linc. R., 14/8/15; Lieut.
Drowned (R.M.S. Leinster) 10/10/18.

✠ HARRISON, Wilfred Ernest
2/4/3265, 15/4/15; Suff. R., 8/7/15; Capt.; w; M.C.
Died of wounds 10/4/18.

HARRISON, William
14335, 30/12/18; No. 11 O.C.B., 24/1/19; General List, 8/3/19; 2/Lieut.   96 Haverstock Hill, N.W.3.

HARRISON, William Bromley
6/Sq/7204, 4/11/15; A.S.C., C/S, 27/10/16; R.A.S.C., 20/12/16, 3rd R. Regt. of Cav., att. 7th Huss.; Lieut.
Horton House, Cumberland Street, Macclesfield, Cheshire.

HARRISON, William Norman
B/1042, 26/8/14; R. Innis. Fus., 7/11/14; Lieut.

HARRISON, William Stanley
A/13009, 1/5/18; R.F.A., C/S, 26/7/18; R.F.A., 5/4/19; 2/Lieut.
34 Hamilton Road, Ealing, W.5.

HARRISON-BARKER, F. R.   See BARKER, Rex

HARRISS, Edward
D/E/13735, 2/8/18; No. 22 O.C.B., 20/9/18; trfr. 29th Lond. R., 18/11/18.   185 Tottenham Court Road, W.

HARROD, Alfred
K/E/2377, 17/12/14; R. War. R., 2/3/15; F,It; Capt.; M.C., Croce di Guerra, M(1).
Junior Naval & Military Club, 96 Piccadilly, W.1.

HARROP, Frederick Hardy
6/3/8775, 7/1/16; No. 8 O.C.B., 4/8/16, M.G.C., C/S; M.G.C., 23/11/16, Tank Corps; F; Lieut.
Heaton Lodge, Heaton Mersey, Manchester.

HARRY, Gwilym Osbert Moor
4/3901, 31/5/15; Manch. R., 12/9/15; E,F; Capt.; w.
R.R. 2, Rigaud, P.Q., Canada.

HART, Charles Alfred Percival
D/B/13688, 29/7/18; trfr. K.R. Rif. C., 7/4/19.
115 Ware Road, Hertford, Hertfordshire.

HART, Charles Vernon
4/1/5036, 22/7/15; Hamps. R., 8/7/16; Lieut.; w; M.C.
3 Park Row, Hornsea, East Yorkshire.

✠ HART, Clarence Herbert
D/1464, 29/9/14, Sgt.; Bedf. R., 13/3/15; F; Capt.
Killed in action 23/10/18.

✠ HART, Conway John
1/3844, 31/5/15, L/C.; Notts. & Derby. R., 18/10/15; Lieut.; w.
Killed in action 10/10/16.

✠ HART, Francis Henry
6/5/5284, 31/7/15, Sgt.; Manch. R., 21/12/15; Lieut.; w.
Died 4/7/18.

HART, Frank Oliver
C/13299, 17/6/18; No. 22 O.C.B., 23/8/18; R. Fus., 13/2/19; 2/Lieut.   33 Bedford Row, W.C.1.

HART, George
C/13353, 26/6/18; trfr. 14th Lond. R., 6/12/18, Gord. Highrs.; Pte.
Canes, Harlow, Essex.

HART, Henry Lowe
6/6250, 16/9/15; N. Staff. R., 27/9/15; F; Capt.
12 Fernley Road, Sparkhill, Birmingham.

HART, Herbert Thomas
B/13502, 10/7/18; No. 22 O.C.B., 23/8/18; E. Surr. R., 13/2/19; 2/Lieut.   7 Monkwell Street, E.C.2.

HART, James Arthur
F/3013, 8/3/15; North'n. R., 3/6/15; 2/Lieut.; w.

HART, Leslie St. Clair
C/Sq/11772, 30/7/17; No. 2 Cav. C/S, 11/1/18; R. Regt. of Cav., 22/6/18; 2/Lieut.   252 Rye Lane, Peckham Rye, S.E.

✠ HART, Neil Lancefield
3/3161, 1/4/15, Sgt.; Notts. & Derby. R., 27/9/15, M.G.C.; 2/Lieut.   Killed in action 31/7/17.

HART, Oswald
A/10498, 15/1/17; No. 14 O.C.B., 7/6/17; S. Wales Bord., 25/9/17; F; Lieut.; M.C.
c/o Barclay's Bank Ltd., Tring, Hertfordshire.

✠ HART, Philip Ewing
K/B/2176, 26/11/14; R.G.A., 10/12/14, R.E.; F; Capt.; w; M.C.   Died 10/8/20.

HART, Vernon Anwyl
6/4/9108, 24/1/16; No. 8 O.C.B., 4/8/16; Manch. R., 24/1/17; F; Lieut.   Heytesbury House, Heytesbury, Wiltshire.

APPENDIX II.—RECORDS OF RANK AND FILE.

HART, *Vivian David*
 4/5/4748, 12/7/15; York. & Lanc. R., 18/10/15; F; Lieut.
  10 *Marlborough Place, St. John's Wood, N.W.* 8.

HART, *Wilfrid Daglish*
 6/4/5202, 29/7/15; dis. 13/8/15.

HART, *William*
 A/10501, 15/1/17, L/C.; No. 4 O.C.B., 10/12/17; Sco. Rif., 29/5/18; 2/Lieut.
  St. Ronan's, 160 Lordship Road, Stoke Newington, N. 16.

HART, *William Philip Woollard*
 B/11038, 13/4/17; No. 2 R.G.A., C/S, 26/9/17; R.G.A., 18/2/18; 2/Lieut.
  County Buildings, Dumfries.

HARTCUP, *Geoffrey Hamilton William*
 4/3/3961, 3/6/15, L/C.; R.G.A., 8/10/15; F; Major; *M.C.,* M(1).
  27 *Bedford Row, W.C.* 1.

HART-DAVIES, *Reginald Guy de Vere*
 6/C/7842, 25/11/15; Garr. O.C.B., 12/12/16; Suff. R., 10/2/17, att. Durh. L.I.; F; 2/Lieut.
  The Rectory, Chigwell Row, Essex.

HART-DYKE, *Ashley Francis.* See DYKE, A. F. H.

✠ HARTIGAN, *Patrick Francis*
 6/Sq/9354, 7/2/16, L/C.; R. Regt. of Cav., 20/12/16, 19th Huss., Bedf. Yeo.; F; Lieut.; *w.* Died 18/3/21.

✠ HARTLEY, *Bernard Harold*
 A/2846, 1/2/15; Lan. Fus., 4/6/15; F; Lieut.
  Killed in action 4/11/16

HARTLEY, *James Clifford Heap*
 6/5/D/7416, 12/11/15; No. 14 O.C.B., 27/12/16; N. Lan. R., 25/4/17, att. R.A.F.; F; Lieut.
  53 *Albert Road, Colne, Lancashire.*

HARTLEY, *Kenneth Baron*
 D/10212, 18/12/16; No. 14 O.C.B., 5/3/17; 7th Lond. R., 26/6/17; F; Capt.; *w.* 81 *Shaftesbury Avenue, W.* 1.

HARTLEY, *Ralph Radcliffe*
 4/6/5/4930, 19/7/15, L/C.; S. Lan. R., 9/6/16; F,I,S; Capt.; M(1). 54 *Neston Street, Higher Openshaw, Manchester.*

HARTLEY, *Reginald*
 6/1/7099, 1/11/15; R.A., C/S, 4/8/16; R.G.A., 3/11/16; F; Capt.; *w*; Croix de Guerre (French).
  Junior Constitutional Club, Piccadilly, W. 1.

HARTLEY, *William Henry*
 6/4/D/9079, 24/1/16; No. 14 O.C.B., 30/10/16; W. York. R., 24/1/17; F; Lieut.; *w-g*; *M.C.*
  Dunleary, Street Lane, Roundhay, Leeds.

HARTNETT, *Daniel Vincent*
 C/14266, 6/11/18; trfr. K.R. Rif. C., 7/4/19.
  c/o *The Collector, Customs and Excise, Custom House, Liverpool.*

HARTOP, *Albert Clarence*
 B/12852, 25/3/18; R.F.A., C/S, 26/7/18; R.F.A., 5/4/19; 2/Lieut. *Park House, Lutterworth Road, Blaby, Nr. Leicester.*

HARTOPP, *Edward Liddell*
 D/1391, 29/9/14; Suff. R., 10/11/14, Worc. R.; Lieut.
  30 *Essex Street, Strand, W.C.* 2.

HARTOPP, *Reginald Liddell*
 K/2405, 21/12/14; Suff. R., 30/12/14; Lieut.; *w.*

✠ HARVARD, *Lionel De Jersey*
 4/5/4749, 12/7/15; Gren. Gds., 28/9/15; Capt.; *w.*
  Killed in action 30/3/18.

HARVEY, *Alfred Laird*
 6/1/8414, 15/12/15; R.E., C/S, 13/1/17; R.E., 30/4/17; F; Lieut.; *w*(2); *M.C.* 1 *Talbot Road, Highgate, N.* 6.

HARVEY, *Bernard Shaw*
 4/Sq/5037, 22/7/15, Cpl.; N. Ir. Horse, 8/1/16, Oxf. Huss.; F; Lieut. c/o *Nat. Prov. & Union Bank Ltd., 15 Bishopsgate, E.C.*

HARVEY, *Charles Edward*
 6/Sq/6507, 30/9/15; S. Nott. Hus., 8/1/16, att. Notts. & Derby. R.; F; Lieut. *Illington, Thetford, Norfolk.*

HARVEY, *Edward Murray*
 6/2/9452, 14/2/16, L/C.; Ir. Gds., 20/8/16; Lieut.; *w*(3); *M.C.* and Bar. 11 *Dean Street, W.* 1.

HARVEY, *Ernest*
 6/4/6483, 27/9/15; E. Surr. R., 8/7/16; Lieut.
  7 *York Road, Great Yarmouth, Norfolk.*

HARVEY, *Frank Cecil*
 3/3541, 10/5/15; S. Staff. R., 28/7/15; F; Lieut.; *w.*
  Ellerslie, Pollards Hill South, Norbury, S.W. 16.

HARVEY, *George Henry*
 4/1/4252, 14/6/15, L/C.; R.A.S.C., 4/11/15.

HARVEY, *George Leonard Hunton*
 C/13267, 12/6/18; No. 22 O.C.B., 23/8/18; York. R., 13/2/19; 2/Lieut. *Gawthorpe Vicarage, Chickenley Heath, Dewsbury.*

HARVEY, *John Steinitz*
 K/A/2484, 28/12/14; Dub. Fus., 11/4/15, R.F.C.; E,S,F; Capt.
  22 *Stanhope Road, Highgate, N.* 6. (Now in *Australia*).

HARVEY, *Keppel Baylis*
 A/11884, 20/8/17, L/C.; R.F.A., C/S, 15/3/18; General List, 8/3/19; 2/Lieut.
  Box 132, *Pretoria, Transvaal, South Africa.*

✠ HARVEY, *Leslie*
 B/385, 24/3/09; Midd'x. R., 29/8/14; 2/Lieut.
  Killed in action 25/4/15.

HARVEY, *Patrick Roger*
 B/12829, 22/3/18; No. 8 O.C.B., 20/9/18; demob.
  8 *Palm Hill, Oxton, Birkenhead.*

HARVEY, *Percy Redcliffe*
 4/4277, 17/6/15; Devon. R., 27/11/15; S; Capt.
  22 *Mount Gold Road, Plymouth, South Devonshire.*

HARVEY, *Reginald Norman*
 D/11170, 2/5/17; R.F.C., C/S, 1/6/17; R.F.C., 4/7/17, Som. L.I.; F; Lieut.
  Kia Ora, Peverell Park Road, Plymouth. (Now in Straits Settlements).

HARVEY, *Richard Perry Calvert*
 6/3/5381, 5/8/15, L/C.; Devon. R., 29/10/15; F; Capt.; *w*; M.C., M(1). 17 *Victoria Street, S.W.* 1.

HARVEY, *Roy Warren*
 4/2/4309, 17/6/15, L/C.; Dorset R., 20/11/15, R.A.F.; F; Lieut. *Hillsborough, Beechen Cliff, Bath.*

HARVEY, *Sydney Thomas*
 B/2830, 1/2/15; Sgt.; K.R. Rif. C., 17/11/15; F; Capt.; *w*(2); *M.C.*
  c/o *Mrs. E. L. Harvey, Lond. Cty. West. & Parrs Bank, Sutton, Surrey.*

HARVEY-SAMUEL, *Frederick Keith*
 K/H/2146, 19/11/14; Herts. R., 25/3/15.
  19 *Devonshire Place, W.* 1.

HARVEY-SAMUEL, *Guy*
 H/2634, 7/1/15; Midd'x. R., 29/4/15; F; Lieut.; M(1).
  19 *Devonshire Place, W.* 1

HARWOOD, *Maurice Wells*
 6/1/6889, 18/10/15; R. War. R., 21/11/16; F,It; Lieut.; M(1).
  Eckington, Uphill Road, Mill Hill, N.W. 7.

HASELER, *Hubert Leslie*
 C/13326, 19/6/18, L/C.; demob. 18/2/19.
  Stapleton Rectory, Dorrington, Shrewsbury.

HASELDEN, *Reginald Berti*
 K/2487, 28/12/14; Lan. Fus., 22/4/15; F,WA,EA; Capt.
  306 *Earls Court Road, S.W* 5

HASELGROVE, *Reginald Howard*
 6/4/5355, 3/8/15, Sgt.; R.G.A., 8/10/15; Lieut.

HASELL, *Roy Eric Edgar*
 A/D/12526, 1/2/18; R.F.C., C/S, 21/5/18; R.A.F., 5/7/18; 2/Lieut.

HASERICK, *Harold William*
 1/3179, 6/4/15; Essex R., 23/7/15; E,F; Capt.
  8 *Currer Street, Bradford. (Now in U.S.A)*

HASKINS, *Adrian William*
 6/4/8813, 10/1/16; R.F.A., C/S, 4/8/16; R.F.A., 10/11/16; Major.

HASKINS, *Frederick Cyril*
 E/1644, 9/10/14; Yorks. L.I., 27/11/14, Lab. Corps; F; Major.
  Kenmore, Thrale Road, Streatham Park, S.W. 16.

APPENDIX II.—RECORDS OF RANK AND FILE.

HASLAM, Bernard Francis
B/12809, 20/3/18, L/C.; demob. 23/1/19.
Tresco, Windsor Road, Worthing, Sussex.

HASLAM, Ralph Alexander McEwen
A/384, 24/3/09; dis. 24/3/09.

HASLAM, Reginald
6/4/9097, 24/1/16, L/C.; A.S.C., C/S, 13/11/16; R.A.S.C., 3/12/16; Germ.EA; Lieut.; Inv.
Minster Lodge, Ormskirk, Lancashire.

HASLAM, Victor Kingdon
K/B/2417, 21/12/14; R.G.A., 27/2/15; F; Lieut.
Woodbury, Sutton, Surrey.

HASLAM, William Leslie Culloden
6/1/6319, 18/9/15; K.R. Rif. C., 15/1/16; Lieut.

HASLETT, Douglas
A/10267, 29/12/16; M.G.C., C/S, 4/4/17; M.G.C., 27/10/17; F; 2/Lieut.
25 Overstrand Mansions, Battersea Park, S.W. 11

HASLETT, Sidney
6/2/8286, 10/12/15, Cpl.; 11th Lond. R., 22/11/16; R. Fus., 15th Lond. R.; F; Lieut.
7 Philpot Lane, E.C.

HASLETT, Thomas Mitchell
6/Sq/9140, 25/1/16; R.F.A., C/S, 18/8/16; R.F.A., 9/12/16; Lieut.; w.
3 College Park, E. Belfast.

HASLEWOOD, Guy Harrop
6/2/8215, 7/12/15; No. 14 O.C.B., 30/10/16; Worc. R., 28/2/17; Lieut.; w.
Field House, Bridgnorth.

HASLOCH, John
6/4/4931, 19/7/15; R.A., C/S, 24/1/16; R.G.A., 19/6/16; F; Lieut.; w.
Fairmile, Cobham, Surrey.

HASSAN, Arthur
A/10998, 4/4/17; A.S.C., C/S, 1/9/17; R.A.S.C., 27/10/17; F; 2/Lieut.
Catmose Road, Oakham, Rutland.

HASSAN, Eric Victor
A/Sq/13106, 16/5/18; trfr. 28th Lond. R., 24/8/18.
25 Arundel Road, Eastbourne.

HASSELL, Frederick Percy
6/3/8636, 3/1/16; Ches. R., 25/9/16; F; Capt.; M(1).
Duncan, British Columbia, Canada.

HASSETT, Patrick Francis
10750, 20/1/17; R.F.C., C/S, 13/3/17; R.F.C., 19/4/17, R.A F.; Lieut.
Doolick Ennis, Co. Clare, Ireland.

HASTIE, William Oliver
A/11953, 3/9/17; R.E., C/S, 4/11/17; R.E., 1/2/18; 2/Lieut.
Wyver Belper, Derbyshire.

HASTINGS, Alexander Hannay
D/11147, 30/4/17, Sgt.; Household Bde. O.C.B., 5/10/17; Cold. Gds., 26/3/18; 2/Lieut.

HASTINGS, Basil
A/C/12543, 5/2/18; No. 23 O.C.B., 5/7/18; General List, 8/3/19; 2/Lieut.
c/o The Peninsular Engineering Coy., Ltd., Alfonso XII,24, Madrid, Spain.

✠ HASTINGS, Herbert Richard
6/1/7100, 1/11/15, Sgt.; No. 1 O.C.B., 28/12/16; R.F.C., 4/4/17; Major; A.F.C.
Killed 6/8/19.

HASTINGS, René Francis
A/13118, 24/5/18; R.E., C/S, 11/10/18; demob.
Ashburton, Grove Park, Denmark Hill, S.E. 5.

✠ HATCH, Reginald William
K/C/2108, 16/11/14; Hamps. R., 31/3/15, Rif. Brig.; Lieut.
Killed in action 3/9/16.

✠ HATCHER, Reginald Gordon
1/4166, 10/6/15; R. Lanc. R., 9/6/16; Lieut.
Died of wounds 20/9/17.

HATTERSLEY, John Alfred
C/11444, 4/6/17; M.G.C., C/S, 31/8/17; Tank Corps, 27/3/18; F; 2/Lieut.
Trinity House, Blackwall, London.

HATTON, George Cuthbert
6/5/9488, 15/2/16, L/C.; R.A., C/S, 5/9/16; R.G.A., 3/12/16; Lieut.
3 Vernon Chambers, Southampton Row, W.C. 1.

HAUGHAN, John Holliday
6/3/6398, 23/9/15; Bord. R., 14/6/16, R.A.F.; F; Lieut.; w.
The Grey House, Silloth, Cumberland.

HAUGHTON, George Bertram
B/11040, 13/4/17, trfr. R. Ir. Fus., 10/10/17; North'd. Fus., 19/5/18, att. Lab. Corps; F; 2/Lieut.
32 Highfield Road, Dublin.

HAUSSER, Eric Cheyne Greenwood
6/2/7205, 4/11/15, L/C.; M.G.C., C/S, 30/9/16; M.G.C., 28/10/16, Tank Corps; F; Capt.
Public Schools Club, 61 Curzon Street, Mayfair.

HAVERCROFT, Arthur
E/B/14180, 16/10/18; demob. 1/5/19.
201 North Boulevard, Hull.

HAVERS, Henry Leslie
B/94, 16/4/08; R.F.A., 6/7/10; I; Major.
Little Hale, South Molton, Devonshire.

HAW, Laurence Walter
B/12842, 23/3/18; No. 2 Cav. C/S. 16/4/18, No. 11 O.C.B.; General List, 8/3/19; 2/Lieut.
c/o Standard Bank of South Africa, 10 Clements Lane, E.C.

HAWARD, Cecil Percy
A/891, 5/8/14; Midd'x. R., 5/10/14; F,S; Capt.
17 Ashborne Avenue, Finchley Road, N.W. 4.

HAWES, Edward James
6/2/5475, 9/8/15; R.A., C/S, 13/1/16; R.F.A., 19/1/16; Lieut.; M.C.

✠ HAWKE, Albert Edward Mountain Aysh
4/3/4392, 24/6/15, L/C.; K.R. Rif. C., 1/6/16; 2/Lieut.
Died of wounds 11/9/16.

HAWKEN, Thomas Harvey
2/3504, 6/5/15; R.F.A., 15/9/15; Lieut.; w.
Pentyne, Padstow, Cornwall.

✠ HAWKEN, William Victor Joseph
6/1/6311, 18/9/15; Notts. & Derby. R., 9/1/16; Lieut.
Killed in action 26/4/16.

HAWKER, Manley Livingston
D/1465, 29/9/14; Army Pay Corps, 17/10/14; F; Capt.
9 Thurloe Square, S.W. 7.

HAWKES, Harold Spencer
D/10453, 11/1/17; No. 20 O.C.B., 7/6/17; 9th Lond. R., 25/9/17; F; Lieut.; w.
25 Milton Street, Nottingham.

HAWKINGS, Reginald John
A/12516, 31/1/18; No. 5 O.C.B., 7/6/18, No. 14 O.C.B.; R. Fus., 5/2/19; 2/Lieut.
146 Sutherland Avenue, W. 9

HAWKINS, Charles Lawrence Marcus
D/12096, 8/10/17; No 20 O.C.B., 10/5/18; Dorset R., 2/2/19; 2/Lieut.
11 Lowther Road, Bournemouth. (Now in Ceylon).

HAWKINS, George Cæsar
4/Sq/4368, 21/6/15; R.A.S.C., 9/10/15; Lieut.; M(1).
Allanvale, Mashaba P.O., Victoria, Southern Rhodesia.

✠ HAWKINS, Herbert Edwin
A/788, 8/5/14; Essex R., 12/9/14; F; Capt.
Killed in action 1/7/16.

HAWKINS, Horace Joseph Forester
K/D/Sq/2132, 19/11/14; R.A.S.C., 3/5/15; F,P; Lieut.; w.
51 Boundary Road, St. Johns Wood, N.W. 8.

HAWKINS, J. B. B. See BAILEY-HAWKINS, J. B.

HAWKINS, Villiers Frederick Cæsar
Sq/365, 17/3/09; dis. 3/4/11. 19 York House, Kensington, W. 8.

HAWKINS, Walter Cyril
C/10844, 7/3/17; No. 14 O.C.B., 5/7/17; Hunt. Cyc. Bn., 30/10/17; 2/Lieut.
16 Wheathouse Road, Huddersfield.

HAWKINS, William George
6/1/6524, 30/9/15, Sgt.; R.E., C/S, 4/6/16; R.E., 30/9/16; Lieut.; w.
St. Merryn, Padstow, Cornwall.

HAWKINS, Willoughby Ralph
D/11178, 4/5/17; No. 16 O.C.B., 5/10/17; S. Wales Bord., 12/3/18; 2/Lieut.
5 Fitzalan Place, Cardiff.

HAWLEY, Bertram
A/10602, 22/1/17; No. 11 O.C.B., 5/7/17; E. Lan. R., 30/10/17; F; Lieut.
13 Portland Road, Gorse Hill, Stretford, Lancashire.

APPENDIX II.—RECORDS OF RANK AND FILE.

HAWLEY, James Miller
D/10434, 10/1/17; No. 20 O.C.B., 7/6/17; Notts. & Derby. R, 17/12/17.
Park View, Scarborough Avenue, Skegness.

HAWLEY, Michael Charles
D/E/13879, 21/8/18; No. 22 O.C.B., 22/11/18; Linc. R., 15/2/19; 2/Lieut.
Tumby Lawn, Mareham le Fen, Boston, Lincolnshire.

HAWLEY, Percy
6/2/8024, 30/11/15; No. 8 O.C.B., 4/8/16; trfr. R.G.A., 8/12/16.
Bishopston, Glamorgan.

HAWORTH, Edwin
D/11826, 9/8/17; No. 14 O.C.B., 7/12/17; trfr. Class W. Res., 20/4/18.
44 Rhyddings Street, Oswaldtwistle, Lancashire.

HAWORTH, Frank Abraham
D/E/13711, 31/7/18; No. 22 O.C.B., 20/9/18; Ches. R., 5/2/19; 2/Lieut.
Sandy Ford, Holmes Chapel, Cheshire.

HAWTHORN, Frank Frederic Flint
D/Sq/12916, 10/4/18, L/C.; No. 1 Cav. C/S, 3/9/18; R. Regt. of Cav., 12/3/19; 2/Lieut.
Roycroft Lodge, Uttoxeter.

HAWTHORNE, Guy David de Livier
A/11911, 27/8/17; No. 14 O.C.B., 7/12/17; 7th Lond. R., 25/6/18, att. 1st Lond. R.; F; Lieut.
c/o Eastern Telegraph Coy. Ltd., Electra House, Finsbury Pavement, E.C. (Now in Egypt).

HAWTIN, Alfred Powell Rawlins
C/11744, 26/7/17; A.S.C., C/S, 12/11/17; R.A.S.C., 6/1/18; F; 2/Lieut.
24 Abington Avenue, Northampton.

HAWTREY, Rupert John Craven Wilmot
H/1905, 16/10/14, Cpl.; Worc. R., 14/2/15; Capt.
8 Sackville Street, W 1.

HAY, Alexander Cyril
2047, 9/11/14; N. Lan. R., 7/12/14; F; Capt.; w.
Messrs. Naylor, Benson & Coy. Ltd., 20 Abchurch Lane, E.C. 4.

✠ HAY, Donald Yalden
A/1369, 26/9/14; R.W. Kent R., 12/11/14, R.F.C.; F; Lieut.
Killed in action 11/8/17.

HAYDEN, Denis Gerard
6/5/C/8727, 5/1/16; No. 7 O.C.B., 11/8/16; trfr. R.G.A., 2/2/17.
2 Rostrevor Terrace, Clontarf, Dublin.

HAYDN-MORRIS, Harold
6/4/6020, 2/9/15; dis. med. unfit, 19/2/16; lt.
Isthmian Club, 4 Down Street, Piccadilly, W.

✠ HAYDON, Nathaniel Maurice
A/14065, 27/9/18.
Died 1/11/18.

HAYES, Daniel Joseph
B/11352, 25/5/17; No. 11 O.C.B., 9/11/17; R. Muns. Fus., 30/4/18; 2/Lieut.
National Bank Ltd., Great Britain Street, Dublin.

HAYES, Ernest Charles
6/2/8931, 15/1/16, Sgt.; 16th Lond. R., 18/12/16; Lieut.
7 Lothair Road South, Harringay, N.

HAYES, Reginald
D/12973, 20/4/18; No. 18 O.C.B., 30/2/19; trfr. 5th Lond. R., 7/3/19.
8 Alma Grove, Basford Park, Stoke-on-Trent.

HAYFORD, Norman M.
C/1059, 31/8/14, Cpl.; 22nd Lond. R., 18/10/14; F,S,P,E; Capt.; w; M.C.
Inanda, 65 Alleyn Park, Dulwich.

HAYGARTH, John Eric
A/10949, 30/3/17; No. 11 O.C.B., 5/7/17; North. Cyc. Bn., 30/10/17, North'd. Fus.; Lieut.
Hanover House, Sheffield.

HAYLOR, Leslie Jack Hutton
C/11797, 2/8/17, L/C.; R.E., C/S, 30/11/17; R.E., 3/5/18; 2/Lieut.
98 Blenheim Gardens, Cricklewood, N.W.

✠ HAYNES, John Lorenzo Patrick
6/3/6419, 23/9/15; N. Lan. R., 25/1/16, att. R.F.C.; Lieut.
Missing believed killed 11/3/18

HAYNES, Norman Pilkington
6/8312, 11/12/15; R.E., C/S, 20/3/16; R.E., 2/6/16; Lieut.
The Cottage, Clifton, Nottingham.

HAYTHORNTHWAITE, Edwin
A/D/12483, 29/1/18; R.F.C., C/S, 21/5/18; trfr. R.A.F., 21/5/18.
13 Kingswood Avenue, Brondesbury, N.W.

HAYWARD, Edgar
B/10475, 12/1/17; No. 20 O.C.B., 7/6/17; Midd'x. R., 25/9/17.
91 Fore Street, E.C. 2.

✠ HAYWARD, Edmund John
F/K/2456, 28/12/14; R. Fus., 20/2/15; 2/Lieut.
Killed in action 12/11/15.

HAYWARD, Jesse Jack George Norman
A/14132, 8/10/13; demob. 29/1/19.
19 Combe Park, Weston, Bath.

HAYWARD, John Hartley
6/4/D/9581, 12/5/16; R.F.C., 13/8/16, R.A.F.; Lieut.; w.

HAYWARD, Percy Shackel
B/13439, 3/7/18; No. 22 O.C.B., 23/8/18; Lein. R., 13/2/19; 2/Lieut.
Brookdale, Clonmel, Co. Tipperary.

HAYWARD, Ronald Charles Crofton
6/8110, 2/12/15; dis. med. unfit, 31/5/16.
North Lodge, Mendham, Harleston, Norfolk.

HAYWARD, Stanley George
6/5505, 9/8/15; dis. med. unfit, 8/8/16.
9 Rutland Terrace, Stamford, Lincolnshire.

HAYWARD, William
A/D/14023, 18/9/18; demob. 3/2/19.
121 Annandale Road, East Greenwich, S.E. 10.

HAYWARD, William Hansell
6/7673, 22/11/15; R.E., 24/12/15; F; Lieut.; w.
8 Bream's Buildings, Chancery Lane, W.C. 2.

HAYWOOD, Arthur Eric
D/13870, 21/8/18; trfr. K.R. Rif. C., 7/4/19.
8 Carson Road, West Dulwich, S.E. 21.

HAZARD, Robert Valentine
K/F/2553, 4/1/15; Norf. R., 31/3/15; Lieut.; w.
Caltofts, Harleston, Norfolk.

HAZELL, Conrad Ormond
B/C/12192, 5/11/17, L/C.; R.F.A., C/S, 17/5/18; R.F.A., 13/3/19; 2/Lieut.
c/o West India Committee, 15 Seething Lane, E.C.

HAZELL, Spencer Taylor
6/4/5506, 9/8/15; trfr. Dorset Yeo., 14/4/16.
12 Moat Croft Road, Eastbourne.

HAZELWOOD, Andrew Cecil Hazelwood
B/11718, 19/7/17, Sgt.; R.E., C/S, 14/4/18; R.E., 15/8/18; 2/Lieut.
21 Court Farm Gardens, Epsom, Surrey.

HAZLEY, Harold Edward
C/11512, 18/6/17; A.S.C., C/S, 1/9/17; R.A.S.C., 27/10/17; Lieut.
7 Beechwood Grove, Shipley, Yorkshire.

HEAD, Alfred Howard
B/12332, 31/12/17; No. 18 O.C.B., 7/6/18; trfr. Gord. Highrs., 19/12/18.
c/o Sir W. S. Hamilton Bart., Woodgates, Southwater, Sussex.

HEAD, Bertram
6/3/5756, 21/8/15, L/C.; North'd. Fus., 1/10/15, att. R.F.C., R.A.F.; Lieut.; w(2); M.C.
125 Second Avenue, Little Ilford, Essex.

HEAD, Eric Edward
6/D/8728, 5/1/16; trfr. 16th Lond. R., 26/2/17.
Merton, Ladymount, Dublin.

HEAD, Gilbert Alan Worwell
D/Sq/B/A/11561, 28/6/17, L/C.; R.F.A., C/S, 26/7/18; demob.
c/o J. Head & Coy., Box 207, Port Elizabeth, South Africa.

HEAD, Peter Charles Aislabie
6/1/6990, 25/10/15; R.F.A., C/S, 31/3/16; R.F.A., 11/8/16; F; Capt.; w; M.C.
c/o Messrs. Cox & Coy., 16 Charing Cross, S.W. 1.

HEAD, Wilfred Oscar Rees
6/5/7027, 27/10/15; No. 11 O.C.B., 7/5/16; Devon. R., 4/9/16, att. Tank Corps; F; Lieut.; w.
49 Heber Road, Cricklewood, N.W. 2.

HEAD, William
B/12830, 22/3/18; No. 23 O.C.B., 9/8/18; North'd. Fus., 5/3/19; 2/Lieut.
131 Capel Road, Forest Gate, Essex.

HEADING, Bertram Somerset
6/2/5433, 5/8/15; 2nd Lond. R., 26/11/15; F; Lieut.; w.
Bingham, 36 Ashburton Avenue, Addiscombe, Surrey.

APPENDIX II.—RECORDS OF RANK AND FILE.

HEAL, Edgar Charles
6/1/6157, 9/9/15; R.E., 3/11/15, emp. M. of Munitions; Lieut.
St. Edmunds, Coleford, Bath.

HEALE, Sydney Herbert Croker
C/10633, 1/2/17; Garr. O.C.B., 23/5/17; Lab. Corps, 14/7/17; Lieut.
Whitley, Reading.

HEALE, William Vernon
1/6/7768, 23/11/15, L/C.; R. Berks. R., 24/10/16; F; 2/Lieut.; p.
61 Popes Avenue, Strawberry Hill, Twickenham.

HEALEY, Lancelot Reginald
13144, 23/5/18; No. 5 O.C.B., 8/11/18, No. 20 O.C.B.; York. R., 17/3/19; 2/Lieut.
242 Sheffield Road, Tinsley, Sheffield.

✠ HEALEY, Philip
K/D/2089, 16/11/14, L/C.; Manch. R., 20/2/15, att. N. Lan. R.; 2/Lieut.
Killed in action 25/9/15.

✠ HEALY, Dermot Joseph
6/3/9288, 3/2/16; No. 7 O.C.B., 11/8/16; R. Muns. Fus., 18/12/16, att. T.M. Bty.; 2/Lieut.
Killed in action 5/8/17.

HEALY, Joseph Patrick
A/10970, 2/4/17, L/C.; R.A., C/S, 2/11/17; R.G.A., 22/7/18; 2/Lieut.
6 Lawn View Terrace, Dawlish, South Devonshire.

HEALY, William
A/14029, 12/9/18; demob. 20/1/19.
43 Kenilworth Square, Rathgar, Dublin.

HEAP, Albert William
4/3/3962, 3/6/15; N. Lan. R., 11/11/15; F; Lieut.
45 Derby Street, Prescot, Lancashire.

HEARN, John Frederick
C/11798, 2/8/17, Sgt.; demob. 5/3/19.
5 Frankfurt Road, Herne Hill, S.E. 24.

HEARN, Lancelot Alfred
F/3089, 22/3/15, L/C.; R.F.A., 8/3/15; Lieut.; w.

✠ HEARN, Robert Cecil
K/D/2498, 31/12/14; 20th Lond. R., 7/7/15; F,S,P; Capt.; M.C.
Killed in action 30/4/18.

HEARSON, William Hugh
6/3/7674, 22/11/15; No. 14 O.C.B., 30/10/16; E. Kent. R., 24/1/17, att. R.W. Surr. R.; F; Lieut.
Lynton, Sevenoaks, Kent.

HEATH, Clifford Stanley
E/14015, 16/9/18; No. 22 O.C.B., 22/11/18; Midd'x. R., 15/2/19; 2/Lieut.
98 Derwent Road, Palmers Green, N. 13.

HEATH, Douglas Frank
6/2/5457, 7/8/15, L/C.; Manch. R., 4/8/16, att. M.G.C.; F,M,E,I,P; Lieut.; w.
98 Derwent Road, Palmers Green, N. 13. (Now in India.)

HEATH, Rupert Colling
4/3776, 27/5/15, Cpl.; York. & Lanc. R., 21/8/15, att. Rif. Brig., M.G.C., Linc. Yeo. and Shrop L.I.; F,E,P; Lieut.
c/o Wm. Heath Esq., c/o Nat. Prov. & Union Bk. Ltd.; Lincoln's Inn Branch, W.C. 2. (Now in New Zealand.)

HEATH, William Stanley
B/Sq/13581, 22/7/18; demob. 29/1/19.
Hockley Heath, Nr. Birmingham.

HEATH-BROWN, Reginald Job
F/2888, 4/2/15; 6th Lond. R., 3/6/15; F; Lieut.; p.
Little Acre, Tilford, Surrey.

HEATHCOTE, George Malcolm
A/12527, 1/2/18, L/C.; H. Bde. O.C.B., 7/6/18; Cold Gds., 5/2/19; 2/Lieut.
Beechwood, Bartley, Southampton.

HEATHCOTE, James Shirley
Sq/155, 18/4/08; dis. 17/4/09.

HEATHER, George Reginald
6/1/5406, 5/8/15; trfr. H.A.C., 29/3/16; F; demob
49 Sisters Avenue, Clapham Common, S.W.

HEATHER, Thomas William
4/1/4218, 14/6/15; Midd'x. R., 24/10/15; F; Staff Capt.; M.C. and Bar, M(1).
Kolar, 214 Hagden Lane, Watford, Hertfordshire.

HEATH-WHITE, Claude
C/10583, 22/1/17; trfr. 16th Lond. R., 1/6/17.
39 Wilton Grove, Wimbledon, S.W. 19.

HEATON, Arthur Douglas
Sq/2/3211, 10/4/15; Midd'x. R., 8/7/15, 8th Lond. R., Indian Army; F,I,M; Capt.; M.C.
Dunorlan, Pembury Road, Tunbridge. (Now in India.)

HEATON, John
3/F/K/2577, 4/1/15, L/C.; Lanc. Yeo., 16/6/15, N. Lan. R., R. Lanc. R., Manch. R.; F; Lieut.; w.
The Whins, Lostock, Nr. Bolton.

HEATON, Wallace James
2/9685, 2/10/16; Chaplain, 28/4/17; S,SR; Capt.; Order of S. Stanislaus, M(1).
Dunorlan, Pembury Road, Tunbridge.

HEAVER, Stanley Hall Homewood
6/1/6871, 18/10/15; Ches. R., 4/8/16, R.A.F.; F; Lieut.; w.
c/o Junior Army & Navy Club, Horse Guards Avenue, W.

HEBDITCH, Gerald Aubrey
C/14249, 30/10/18; trfr. K.R. Rif. C., 7/4/19.
29 Kidderminster Road, Croydon.

HEBER-TREVOR, Charles Reginald. See TREVOR, C. R. H.

✠ HECHT, Marcus Francis
D/1468, 29/9/14, Sgt.; K.R. Rif. C., 25/5/15; F; Major.
Killed in action 3/9/16.

HEDGE, Cecil Randolph
6/3/8776, 7/1/16; A.S.C., C/S, 14/8/16; R.A.S.C., 22/9/16; F; Lieut.
Ingle-Nook, Cimla Road, Neath, South Wales.

HEDGES, William
C/14184, 18/10/18; demob. 13/12/18.
78 Longley Road, Harrow.

HEELIS, John
A/11885, 20/8/17; No. 14 O.C.B., 7/12/17; Lan. Fus., 28/5/18, att. N. Cyc. Bn.; F; 2/Lieut.; g. w.
Crosthwaite Vicarage, Kendal, Westmorland.

HEGARTY, Hugh Aloysius
1/3728, 24/5/15; Midd'x. R., 21/8/15, att. R. E. Sigs.; F; Lieut.; M.C.
16 Strathearn Road, Wimbledon, S.W. 19.

HEGLEY, Henry Robert
C/10610, 22/1/17; A.S.C., C/S, 30/6/17; R.A.S.C., 25/8/17; Lieut.

HEIGHWAY, George Henry
C/9955, 20/11/16, Cpl.; A.S.C., C/S, 1/9/17; R.A.S.C., 30/11/17; F; Lieut
38 Grosvenor Road, Manningham, Bradford.

HEILBRUN, Leslie Bernard Oscar
A/11648, 12/7/17; No. 14 O.C.B., 9/11/17; Hamps. R., 30/4/18; F; Lieut.; w.
321 Green Lanes, Finsbury Park, N. 4.

HELE, George Clive
4/1/4329, 19/6/15; D. of Corn. L.I., 10/9/15; Lieut.
The Crossways, Boxmoor, Hertfordshire.

✠ HELLIAR, Leonard Jeffery
Sq/3486, 4/5/15; R.F.A., 16/7/15, att. T.M. Bty.; F; 2/Lieut.; w.
Killed in action 14/5/17.

HELM, Alexander Knox
B/10753, 21/2/17; R.F.A., C/S, 22/6/17; R.F.A., 17/11/17; E,P; Lieut.; w.
Hoddesdon Bury, Hoddesdon, Hertfordshire. (Now in Constantinople).

HELM, Herbert Paul Dundas
D/9324, 5/2/16; R.E., C/S, 7/5/16, A.S.C., C/S; R.A.S.C., 2/10/16; F; Lieut
6 Laverockbank Terrace, Edinburgh, Scotland.

✠ HELSDON, Harold Leofric
2/3228, 12/4/15; Dorset R., 28/7/15, att. R. War. R.; 2/Lieut.
Killed in action 26/11/16.

HEMELRYK, Charles Joseph
Sq/936, 5/8/14; dis. med. unfit, 14/9/14.

HEMINGTON, Arthur John
A/11259, 14/5/17; No. 14 O.C.B., 9/11/17; Linc. Yeo., 30/4/18, att. Linc. R.; F; Lieut.
Spring Hill, Bulwell, Nottingham.

HEMMANT, George
D/6/3/6620, 4/10/15; No. 14 O.C.B., 26/11/16; R. Lanc. R., 27/3/17; F; Lieut.; g, w.
54 Whitehall Road, Thornton Heath, Surrey.

HEMMING, Frank
D/10246, 29/12/16, L/C.; R.A., C/S, 27/4/17; R.G.A., 1/9/17; Lieut.
57 Cemetery Road, Porth, Glamorganshire.

APPENDIX II.—RECORDS OF RANK AND FILE.

HEMMINGS, Henry
D/11827, 9/8/17; No. 14 O.C.B., 7/12/17; Oxf. & Bucks. L.I., 28/5/18, att. Notts. & Derby. R.; F; 2/Lieut.
255 Abington Avenue, Northampton.

HEMMINGS, William George
D/11828, 9/8/17; No. 14 O.C.B., 4/1/18; Essex R., 25/6/18; F; 2/Lieut.
Kingsley, Friern Lane, New Southgate, N.11.

HEMMOND, Aglen
4/3/5/4020, 7/6/15, L/C.; R.F.A., 13/9/15; Lieut.
Holford, Bridgwater, Somerset.

HEMMONS, Alfred
6/5/7245, 8/11/15, L/C.; M.G.C., 25/9/16; F; Lieut.; w.
36 Huskisson Street, Liverpool.

HEMMONS, John Aubrey Hubert
A/Sq/D/9827, 1/11/16; R.E., 30/4/18; 2/Lieut.
30 Woodstock Road, Redland, Bristol.

HEMPSON, Leonard Amis
2650, 11/1/15, L/C.; R.G.A., 5/5/15; F; Major; M(1).
West Hill, Copstock, Ipswich.

HEMSLEY, Frederick William Coultas
A/10226, 28/12/16; trfr. R.F.A., 20/4/17.
30 Bellevue Crescent, Ayr, Scotland.

✠ HEMSTED, John
4/Sq/4750, 12/7/15; R.F.A., 23/9/15; 2/Lieut.; M(1).
Killed in action 16/4/17.

HENCHY, Albert Francis
4/3/5108, 26/7/15, L/C.; R. Dub. Fus., 4/12/15; F; Lieut.; w.
c/o Sir C. R. McGrigor Bart & Coy. Ltd., 39 Panton Street, Haymarket, S.W.1.

HENDERSON, Alan Keith
Sq/468, 23/2/10; dis. 2/8/12; R. Wilt. Yeo., 7/2/15, secd. Intelligence Corps; F; Capt.; O.B.E., M(2).
Commons Corner, Burleigh, Gloucestershire.

HENDERSON, Cecil Henry
6/Sq/7012, 26/10/15, Cpl.; No. 1 Cav. C/S, 20/10/16; Sherwood Rang. Yeo., 16/2/17, att. Notts. & Derby. R., Indian Army; F; Major.
7 Argyll Mansions, Cricklewood.

✠ HENDERSON, David
F/1791, 16/10/14; Midd'x. R., 17/2/15; F; Capt.
Killed in action 15/9/16.

HENDERSON, David Sim
B/13518, 12/7/18; No. 11 O.C.B., 24/1/19; General List, 8/3/19; 2/Lieut.
4 Comely Bank Place, Edinburgh.

✠ HENDERSON, Edward Francis
6/2/6484, 27/9/15; E. Kent. R., 4/8/16; Lieut.
Killed in action 27/3/18.

HENDERSON, Harry Stuart
6/5/7609, 19/11/15; No. 9 O.C.B., 8/3/16; Arg. & Suth'd. Highrs., 6/7/16, att. R. Sco. Fus., W. Rid. R. and Ches. R.; I,M; Staff Capt.
Hampton-in-Arden, Warwickshire.

✠ HENDERSON, Jacob Johnson
6/Sq/6525, 30/9/15; No. 1 Cav. C/S, 24/4/16; Suff. Yeo., 28/7/16; Lieut.
Died of wounds 17/10/18.

HENDERSON, James Bruce Seton
A/11626, 9/7/17; R.E., C/S, 11/11/17; R.E., 21/12/17; F; Lieut.
c/o Crown Agents for the Colonies, 4 Millbank, S.W.1.

HENDERSON, James Herbert
4/1/4106, 7/6/15; Mon. R., 19/9/15, secd. R. Berks. R.; Major.

HENDERSON, John
A/11930, 30/8/17; R.E., C/S, 11/11/17; R.E. 21/12/17; Lieut.; w.
Clifton, Ashbourne, Derbyshire.

HENDERSON, John Gilbert
4/Sq/4500, 28/6/15; Worc. Huss., 28/10/15, secd. M.G.C.; Lieut.
12 Avenue Malesherbes, Maisons Lafille, S.et O., France.

HENDERSON, Maurice James
D/11554, 25/6/17; No. 14 O.C.B., 4/1/18; Arg. & Suth'd. Highrs., 25/6/18; 2/Lieut.
c/o Messrs. Matheson & Coy. Ltd., 3 Lombard Street, E.C.

✠ HENDERSON, Noel Charles
A/1273, 23/9/15; dis. to R. Mil. Coll., 23/10/14; R. Highrs., 17/2/15; F; 2/Lieut.
Died of wounds 9/10/15 as Prisoner of War.

HENDERSON, Ronald Bruce
1/3132, 29/3/15, Sgt.; R.A.S.C., 27/11/15, att. R.G.A.; S; Lieut.
59/60 Old Bailey, E.C.4

HENDERSON, Samuel John
6/5/8244, 8/12/15; No. 7 O.C.B., 11/8/16; R. Innis. Fus., 18/12/16; F; Lieut.; w.
Gortamney, Tobermore, Co. Londonderry.

✠ HENDERSON, Thomas
6/5/7550, 17/11/15; M.G.C., C/S, 3/7/16; M.G.C., 23/11/16, Tank Corps; 2/Lieut.
Killed in action 23/11/17.

HENDERSON, Walter Brooks Drayton
A/B/D/12158, 25/10/17; R.F.A., C/S, 7/2/18; R.F.A., 4/11/18; 2/Lieut
Brown's Town, St. Ann's, Jamaica, British West Indies.

HENDERSON, Walter Edward Bonhote
6/4/9566, 29/3/16, L/C.; R.G.A., C/S, 28/2/17; R.G.A., 1/7/17; Lieut.
120 Barons Court Road, W.14.

HENDRIE, Alford
D/A/12977, 24/4/18; R.A.F., C/S, 16/10/18; R.A.F.; 2/Lieut.
139 Union Avenue, Ashbourne, Penn., U.S.A.

✠ HENERY, Hewett Walter Lewis
K/F/2532, 31/12/14, Sgt.; K.O. Sco. Bord., 8/4/15; Lieut.
Killed in action 19/4/17.

✠ HENLEY, Frederick
6/3/5507, 9/8/15; R. Fus., 28/12/15; F; 2/Lieut.
Killed in action 27/10/16.

✠ HENLEY, Frederick Louis
4/4796, 12/7/15; Notts. & Derby. R., 16/7/15; 2/Lieut.
Killed in action 1/10/16.

HENLEY, Percy
C/A/D/10780, 19/2/17, Cpl.; dis. med. unfit, 3/6/19.
Lane Farm, Totternhoe, Dunstable, Bedfordshire.

HENNELL, Sidney Thorn
D/2769, 25/1/15; Welch. R., 15/6/15, Leic. R.; F; Lieut.; Inj.
16 Earlsfield Road, Wandsworth, S.W.18.

HENNESSEY, Hendry Ernest
A/13974, 9/9/18; demob. 30/1/19.
35 St. Leonard's Road, East Sheen, S.W.14.

HENNESSY, Patrick
C/10789, 23/2/17; No. 14 O.C.B., 7/6/17; R. Innis. Fus., 25/9/17, att. Hamps. R.; F; Lieut.; g, p.
Carrigwhane, Co. Cork, Ireland.

HENNING, Charles Edward
A/11198, 25/4/17; No. 12 O.C.B., 10/8/17; 18th Lond. R., 27/11/17; F; 2/Lieut.; p.
61 Park Avenue, Sydney Parade, Dublin.

HENRI, William Ainsworth
K/E/2182, 26/11/14; North'd. Fus., 20/12/14; F,It; Capt.; M.C.
63 Cheapside, E.C.2.

HENRIQUES, Wilfrid Quixano
A/1370, 26/9/14; R.W. Surr. R., 27/11/14, M.G.C.; F,S; Major; M(3).
1 St. Andrews Road, Claughton, Birkenhead.

✠ HENRY, George Cecil
A/10255, 29/12/16; No. 14 O.C.B., 6/4/17; Suff. R., 31/7/17; 2/Lieut.
Died of wounds 9/12/17.

HENRY, James Griffiths
C/582, 13/11/11; dis. 6/10/14.

HENRY, Leonard William
6/8831, 10/1/16; dis. med. unfit, 23/6/16.
Herga, Harrow-on-the-Hill.

HENRY, Rowland Edward
D/10266, 19/12/16; No. 21 O.C.B., 5/5/17, H. Bde. O.C.B., 14/9/18; Guards M.G.R., 12/3/19; 2/Lieut.
Overseas Club, General Buildings, Aldwych. (Now in Trinidad).

HENSHAW, Hugh Victor
C/Sq/13233, 7/6/18; demob. 24/1/19.
Postling Court, Postling, Nr. Hythe, Kent.

HENSHAW, John
C/13234, 7/6/18, L/C.; demob. 24/1/19.
Wylfa, Beechfield Road, Davenport, Stockport.

✠ HENSHILWOOD, Alexander Russell
6/5/5331, 2/8/15; L'pool. R., 7/1/16; F; Lieut.
Died of wounds 27/9/16.

APPENDIX II.—RECORDS OF RANK AND FILE.

HENSLOW, *Thomas Geoffrey Wall*
4/6/2/4994, 19/7/15; Arg. & Suth'd. Highrs., 7/10/15; 2/Lieut.

✠ HENSMAN, *Henry John*
B/10531, 17/1/17; No. 20 O.C.B., 7/6/17; Herts. R., 25/9/17; 2/Lieut.; M.C.
                                  Killed in action 18/9/18.

HENVILLE, *Douglas*
4/3/3963, 3/6/15, L/C.; Hamps. R., 24/10/15, emp. M. of Munitions; E,P; Lieut.; w.
                    40 Lowgate, Hull, Yorkshire.

HENWOOD, *William Ellis*
C/D/13251, 10/6/18, L/C.; demob. 30/5/19.
           The Grammar School, Bromyard, Nr. Worcester.

HENZELL, *George Oswin*
6/5/6690, 7/10/15; No. 11 O.C.B., 7/5/16; North'd. Fus., 4/9/16; F; Lieut.; w; M.C.
             70 Gracechurch Street, E.C. 3.

HENZELL, *Hugh Peregrine*
6/Sq/6733, 11/10/15, L/C.; North'd. Fus., 28/1/16, Tank Corps; F; Capt.; Inv.
       30 Elmfield Gardens, Gosforth, Northumberland.

HEPBURN, *Wallace*
3/9614, 14/9/16; No. 14 O.C.B., 26/11/16; Dorset R., 28/2/17; 2/Lieut.
              2 Lyndale, Childs Hill, N.W. 2.

HEPHERD, *James*
6/5/5933, 1/9/15; L'pool. R., 6/12/15, M.G.C., att. R.A.V.C.; F; Lieut.
     Clifton Villa, Stamford Road, Mossley, Nr. Manchester.

HEPPEL, *John Benedict*
4/6/5/4966, 19/7/15; Hereford R., 18/12/15, R.A.F.; Lieut.
      Lorets, Mornington Road, Woodford Wells, Essex.

HEPPER, *Douglas*
C/Sq/13268, 12/6/18; demob. 24/1/19.
                  Marshwood, Washford, Somerset

✠ HEPWORTH, *Frederick Joseph*
6/3/8087, 1/12/15, L/C.; R. Muns. Fus., 25/9/16, Lan. Fus.; 2/Lieut.
                       Killed in action 20/5/17.

HEPWORTH, *Reuben Stanley*
6/1/6459, 27/9/15; W. York. R., 7/6/16.
                      66 Ongar Road, Brentwood.

HEPWORTH, *Sidney Robert*
B/11700, 19/7/17; No. 11 O.C.B., 9/11/17; Hamps. R., 30/4/18; F; Lieut.
             Marsh-Gibbon, Bicester, Oxfordshire.

HEPWORTH, *William Adolphus*
6/4/7509, 15/11/15, A.S.C., C/S, 17/4/16; R.A.S.C., 21/5/16; F; Lieut.
     Low-wood, 12 Kings Avenue, Clapham Park, S.W. 4.

✠ HERBERT, *Alfred James Anthony*
4/5/4709, 9/7/15; Lond. Div. Cyc. Coy., 21/11/15; F; Lieut.
                         Died of wounds 17/9/17.

✠ HERBERT, *Johnstone Erskine Galway*
H/1930, 22/10/14; York. R., 13/3/15; F; Capt.
                           Killed in action 23/4/17.

✠ HERBERT, *Reginald Strickson*
4/5/5109, 26/7/15; 11th Lond. R., 24/12/15; Lieut.
                           Killed in action 21/5/17.

HERMANNI, *Gerald*
6/1/8759, 6/1/16; Intelligence Corps, 31/8/16; F; Staff Lieut.; M(1).
      5 Mount Tallant Terrace, Harold's Cross, Dublin.

HERMELIN, *Alexander*
C/10410, 8/1/17; No. 14 O.C.B., 7/6/17; S. Wales Bord., 25/9/17; Lieut.

HERON, *Oscar Aloysius Patrick*
D/11866, 16/8/17; R.F.C., C/S, 30/10/17; R.F.C., 12/12/17, R.A.F.; Lieut.; w; D.F.C.
                 Banbrook, Armagh City, Ireland.

HERON-MAXWELL, *John Edward Blors*
C/13409, 12/6/18; demob. 31/1/19.
                Author's Club, St. James Street, S.W.

HERRICK, *Francis Sudlow*
C/14201, 21/10/18; demob. 30/1/19.
         70 Sutton Court, Grove Park, Chiswick, W. 4.

✠ HERRING, *Homer Reginald*
2/3441, 2/5/15; Durh. L.I., 23/7/15; F; Capt.
                         Killed in action 23/4/17.

✠ HERVEY, *Gerald Arthur*
4/3729, 24/5/15; R.G.A., 28/7/15; F; Lieut.
                          Killed in action 8/8/17.

HERVEY, *Harold Eustice*
C/198, 5/5/08; dis. 4/6/11; R.F.C., 14/6/16, R.A.F.; M.C.
        Haslemere, Ravenscroft Road, High Barnet.

HESELDEN, *Frank*
D/E/13894, 23/8/18; No. 22 O.C.B., 22/11/18; W. Rid. R., 15/2/19; 2/Lieut.
           20 Walkley Terrace, Heckmondwike.

HESELTINE, *William Robert Newson*
D/11176, 4/5/17; No. 16 O.C.B., 5/10/17; R. War. R., 12/3/18; F; Lieut.
        4 Alexandra Road, Edgbaston, Birmingham.

HESKETH, *John Hinnell*
A/13046, 8/5/18; R.E., C/S, 23/8/18; demob.

HESKETH, *Tom Hilton*
6/3/7013, 26/10/15; R.E., C/S, 2/9/16; R.E., 18/11/16, R.A.F.; S,E; Lieut.
          Orrell House, Stretford, Lancashire.

HESLOP, *William*
6/5/7101, 1/11/15; trfr. 15th Lond. R., 21/7/16.
        The Red House, Wantage, Berkshire.

HESSION, *Colin Joseph*
A/11931, 30/8/17; Lab. Corps, 22/10/18; 2/Lieut.
          4 St. Johns Road, Golders Green, N.W.

HETHERINGTON, *Francis Herbert*
K/H/2363, 15/12/14; Sea. Highrs., 9/2/15, R.E.; F,NR; Major; w; M.C., Order of S. Stanislaus 3rd Class, M(1).
   Eastbrooke House, Alton, Hampshire. (Now in Canada.)

HETHERINGTON, *Herbert*
C/D/12047, 27/9/17; Indian Army, 8/10/18, Manch. R.; 2/Lieut.
  5 Belgrave Terrace, Burnage Lane, Levenshulme, Manchester.

HETHERINGTON, *John Ralton*
Sq/988, 5/8/14; R. Fus., 6/11/14.
                   236 North Hill, Highgate, N. 6.

HETHERINGTON, *Thomas Liddell*
B/11719, 19/7/17; trfr. R.F.C., 13/12/17, R.A.F.; Sgt.
              Bathgate House, West Hartlepool.

HEVIN-JONES, E.   See JONES, E. H.

HEWART, *Hugh Vaughan*
C/A/12245, 23/11/17; dis. med. unfit, 3/4/18.
           26 Kensington Park Gardens, W. 11.

HEWETSON, *Edward St. George*
F/2727, 18/1/15; R. Berks. R., 3/6/15; Capt.
                   58 Onslow Gardens, S.W. 7.

HEWETSON, *Harry Raynor*
1/9736, 16/10/16; R.A., C/S, 8/6/17; R.F.A., 3/11/17; F; Lieut.
                   26 Princes Street, Southport.

HEWETT, *Arthur Edmund*
D/13884, 21/8/18; trfr. K.R. Rif. C., 25/4/19.
     Waiwera, Newtown, Bishops Waltham, Hampshire.

HEWETT, *Harry William*
6/5/5382, 5/8/15; E. Kent. R., 27/1/16, R.W. Surr. R., R.A.F.; F; Lieut.; Inv.
      Constitution Hill, Chatham, Kent. (Now in F.M.S.)

✠ HEWETT, *Howard Dudley*
4/3/4278, 17/6/15; E. Kent. R., 7/10/15, R.A.F.; F; Lieut.
                        Died of wounds 27/10/18.

HEWETT, *James Henry*
D/13885, 21/8/18; trfr. K.R. Rif. C., 25/4/19.
     Waiwera, Newtown, Bishops Waltham, Hampshire.

HEWITT, *Cecil James*
C/485, 11/4/10; dis. 9/3/11; rej. A/1192, 14/9/14; S. Wales Bord., 10/10/14; Gren. Gds., emp. Gds. M.G.R.; Lieut.; w(2).
          Royal Automobile Club, Pall Mall, S.W. 1.

HEWITT, *George Graily*
E/1661, 10/10/14; 9th Lond. R., 12/2/15, War Office; Lieut.
        Junior Constitutional Club, Piccadilly, W.

HEWITT, *James Herbert*
B/11028, 11/4/17; R.F.C., C/S, 2/8/17; R.F.C., 8/9/17, R.A.F.; F; Lieut.
                4 Abbeville Road, Clapham, S.W. 4.

HEWITT, *Walter Albert*
B/C/13367, 21/6/18; trfr. K.R. Rif. C., 7/4/19.
             28 Thornton Hill, Wimbledon, S.W. 19.

APPENDIX II.—RECORDS OF RANK AND FILE.

HEWLAND, Arthur Douglas
4/3014, 8/3/15; E. York. R., 30/6/15; Lieut.
The Avenue, Broadhinton Road, Clapham, S.W.4.

HEWLETT, Henry Martyn
A/10056, 29/11/16; R.E., 25/3/17; F; Lieut.
Lampetts, Manor, Fyfield, Essex.

HEWLETT, John James
4/3/4540, 1/7/15; E. Surr. R., 8/6/16; F,It; Lieut.; w.
201 Queens Road, Peckham, S.E.

HEXTALL, Henry Cecil
A/2720, 18/1/15, L/C.; R.A.S.C., 14/6/15; Capt.

✠ HEYWOOD, Herbert
B/782, 27/3/14; Midd'x. R., 15/8/14, att. M.G.C.; Capt.; w(2).
Died of wounds 22/8/17.

HEYWOOD, Richard Percival
6/5/5258, 31/7/15, L/C.; L'pool. R., 6/12/15; F; Major; w(2); M.C. and Two Bars, M(1).
Lyndale, St. Anthonys Road, Blundellsands.

✠ HEYWORTH, Wilfrid Alexander
6/5/5259, 31/7/15; L'pool. R., 24/10/15; 2/Lieut.
Killed in action 23/5/16.

HIBBERT, Horace Reginald
B/11048, 16/4/17; A.S.C., C/S, 1/8/17; R.A.S.C., 29/9/17; F; 2/Lieut.
40 Trinity Square, E.C.3.

✠ HIBBS, Richard John Walmsley
6/2/9392, 8/2/16; No. 8 O.C.B., 4/8/16; Manch. R., 21/11/16; Lieut.; w.
Killed in action 8/10/18.

HICHENS, Eric Boyle
4/6/5/4967, 19/7/15; dis. med. unfit, 7/4/16.
College Farm, Chevington, Bury St. Edmunds.

HICKES, Arthur Gould Remington
6/9587, 15/6/16; dis. med unfit, 18/8/16.
4 Milestone Road, Upper Norwood, S.E.19.

HICKMAN, Alan
F/3/2605, 7/1/15; dis. med. unfit, 31/3/16; R.A.S.C., 4/12/16; F; Lieut.; Inv.
Castle Grove House, Chobham, Surrey.

HICKMAN, Jack
C/D/12285, 4/12/17, L/C.; demob. 4/3/19.
Virginia, 4 Wilson Road, Reading, Berkshire.

✠ HICKMAN, John George
Sq/6/3/7798, 24/11/15; R.A., C/S, 9/11/16; R.F.A., 11/3/17; 2/Lieut.
Killed in action 4/10/17.

HICKS, Allen Sydney
4/3/4073, 7/6/15; Devon. R., 10/9/15; F; Capt.; w(2).
Elmcroft, Nr. Laird, Plymouth.

✠ HICKS, Basil Perrin
A/973, 5/8/14; R. Berks. R., 19/9/14; F; Lieut.
Killed in action 25/9/15.

HICKS, Charles Mervyn Hedge
6/8359, 14/12/15; R.F.A., C/S, 23/6/16; R.F.A., 13/10/16; F; Lieut.
Glencairne, Hanger Hill, Ealing, W.5.

✠ HICKS, Eric Raymond
6/4/5203, 29/7/15; R.F.A., 26/11/15; F,E,P; Lieut.; M.C.
Died 25/12/18.

HICKS, Frederick Murray
Sq/204, 6/5/08; Hamps. R., 17/9/14; Capt.; w.

HICKS, Gilbert
D/11088, 23/4/17, L/C.; No. 14 O.C.B., 10/8/17; N. Cyc. Bn., 27/11/17, att. Glouc. R.; F; Lieut.
Lyndon House, Barnard Castle.

HICKS, Harry Edmund
4/3/3964, 3/6/15; R.G.A., 8/10/15; S; Lieut.
2 Osterley Park Road, Southall, Middlesex.

HICKS, Henry Arthur Hugh Gerard
D/11167, 2/5/17, L/C.; No. 10 O.C.B., 5/10/17; Sea. Highrs., 26/2/18, att. Arg. & Suth'd. Highrs.; F; Lieut.
131 Cromwell Road, South Kensington, S.W.7.

HICKS, Richard Thomas Brindley
6/5/6991, 25/10/15, L/C.; R.E., 11/6/16; F; Lieut.
c/o Mrs. Brindley-Hicks, 13 Stanley Crescent, Notting Hill Gate, W.11.

HICKS-BEACH, William Guy
Sq/712, 6/5/13; dis. 15/1/14.
23 Hyde Park Place, W.2

HICKSON, Charles William
A/D/13119, 24/5/18; demob. 7/5/19.
West House, Grampound Road, Cornwall.

HICKSON, Harold Stephen
H/K/1831, 16/10/14, L/C.; R.A.O.C., 23/3/15; Lieut.
5 Thyra Grove, North Finchley, N.12.

HICKSON, James Arthur Durham
C/Sq/13655, 27/7/18; demob. 9/1/19.
20 Ellerdale Road, N.W.3.

HIDDEN, Hugh Rensburg
C/D/13316, 18/6/18, Sgt.; demob. 30/5/19.
Sandon, Queens Road, Windsor.

HIDDINGH, John
D/Sq/12965, 22/4/18; No. 11 O.C.B., 6/2/19; General List, 8/3/19; 2/Lieut.
c/o Standard Bank of South Africa, 10 Clements Lane, E.C. (Now in France.)

✠ HIELD, John Hamer
D/3050, 15/3/15, Sgt.; Rif. Brig., 4/6/15; F; Capt.; w.
Killed in action 3/9/16.

HIGDON, Robert Stanley
B/12372, 8/1/18; No. 3 O.C.B., 10/5/18; R.W. Kent R., 29/10/18; 2/Lieut.
2 Marlborough Road, Lee, S.E.13.

HIGGINS, Frank Wilfrid
6/3/7453, 15/11/15, L/C.; R.F.C., C/S, 8/10/16; R.F.C., 26/2/17, R.A.F.; lt; Lieut.
12 Egerton Street, Chester.

HIGGINS, Gordon Lea
C/471, 7/3/10; Midd'x. R., 26/8/14; Lieut.

HIGGINS, Sydney James
Sq/200, 6/5/08; R.A.M.C., 12/2/11; Major.

HIGGINSON, Henry Reginald
C/12665, 28/2/18; No. 3 O.C.B., 6/9/18; Scottish Horse, 17/3/19; 2/Lieut.
The Hollies, Knockin, Oswestry, Salop.

HIGGINSON, Reginald Wilfred
6/2/6555, 30/9/15; R. Lanc. R., 9/6/16; F; Lieut.
Trevor, Ruabon, North Wales. (Now in Gold Coast Colony.)

✠ HIGGINSON, William Clifton Vernon
C/9946, 17/11/16, L/C.; R.F.C., C/S, 13/3/17; R.F.C., 19/4/17; 2/Lieut.
Killed in action 20/11/17.

HIGGS, Clyde
4/3/4043, 7/6/15; R.E., 9/9/15; F; Major; M.C., M(1).
Clynor Cottage, Little Aston Road, Aldridge, Staffordshire.

HIGGS, Leslie Greenwood
C/Sq/9930, 15/11/16, L/C.; No. 1 Cav. C/S, 31/7/17; R. Regt. of Cav., 22/2/18, 18th Huss.; 2/Lieut.
Fairholme, Atkins Road, Clapham Park, S.W.12.

HIGHAM, Joseph
D/12906, 8/4/18; R.E., C/S, 23/8/18, No. 11 O.C.B.; General List, 8/3/19; 2/Lieut.
45 Chapel Street, Hyde, Nr. Manchester.

HIGHAM, Ronald Harry
B/1070, 2/9/14; R.W. Fus., 12/9/14, W.O. Intelligence; F; Capt.; w(2).
9 Gloucester Place, Portman Square, W.1.

HIGHMORE, Geoffrey William
6/4/9099, 24/1/16; No. 8 O.C.B., 4/8/16; W. York. R., 21/11/16; F; Lieut.; w.
c/o Messrs. Crompton & Co. Ltd., Chelmsford, Essex.

HIGHTON, Ross Digby Charles
H/2051, 9/11/14; R.W. Surr. R., 15/1/15, att. R. Innis. Fus.; G,E,F; Capt.; p.
c/o Mercantile Bank of India Ltd., Gracechurch Street, E.C. (Now in India).

HIGLETT, Allen Shepard
4/Sq/4219, 14/6/15; R.F.A., 20/9/15; F; Capt.; w.
Dunford, Guildford, Surrey.

HIGMAN, Bernard Drake
1/3387, 26/4/15; 25th Lond. R., 15/12/15, R.A.F.; F; Lieut.
Oak Lodge, St. Austell, Cornwall.

✠ HIGSON, William Marsh
6/5/8431, 15/12/15; No. 8 O.C.B., 4/8/16; R. Lanc. R., 21/11/16; F; 2/Lieut.
Died of wounds 9/4/17.

APPENDIX II.—RECORDS OF RANK AND FILE.

HILDITCH, Arthur Neville
6/2/9070, 20/1/16; R.A., C/S, 7/8/16; R.G.A., 18/10/16; F; Capt.
c/o A. R. Mowbray & Coy. Ltd., 28 Margaret Street, Oxford Circus, W. 1.

HILDRED, Colin Gerard Ernest
A/13975, 9/9/18; trfr. K.R. Rif. C., 7/4/19.
11 Dorset Gardens, Brighton.

HILL, Albert Edward
4/6/5/4968, 19/7/15; No. 7 O.C.B., 7/4/16; 17th Lond. R., 21/7/16; Lieut.
50 Silver Crescent, Gunnersbury, W. 4.

✠ HILL, Alfred Saunders
6/1/9517, 16/2/16; R.A., C/S, 4/8/16; R.G.A., 1/11/16; F; 2/Lieut.
Killed in action 20/11/17.

✠ HILL, Arthur Moberly
Sq/3090, 22/3/15, L/C.; N. Som. Yeo., 23/6/15, att. Som. L.I.; F; 2/Lieut.
Killed in action 9/4/17.

HILL, Arthur Percy
6/5/6044, 3/9/15; No. 1 O.C.B., 25/2/16; Manch. R., 8/7/16; F; 2/Lieut.; w.
4 Market Street, Altrincham.

HILL, Cyril James
B/12831, 22/3/18; R.E., C/S, 23/8/18; demob.
93 Stondon Park, Honor Oak Park, S.E. 23. (Now in Holland.)

HILL, Cyril Robert Stanton
4/3266, 15/4/15; Dorset R., 24/9/15; Lieut.; w.

HILL, Eben Erskine
B/12333, 31/12/17; R.A., C/S, 15/3/18; R.G.A., 4/11/18; 2/Lieut.
6 Austin Friars, E.C. 2.

HILL, Edgar Russell
6/4/7102, 1/11/15; Devon R., 7/7/16, att. North'n. R.; E; Lieut.
202 Green Lanes, Finsbury Park, N. 4.

HILL, Edward Copeman
6/3/5753, 21/8/15; York Huss., 25/10/15, att. W. York. R.; F; Lieut.; w.
Prospect House, Blyborough, Kirton-Lindsey, Lincolnshire.

HILL, Ernest Saphir
K/F/3/2293, 10/12/14; 3rd Lond. R., 20/4/15, Essex R.; G,E,P; Lieut.
35 Narbonne Avenue, Clapham, S.W. 4.

HILL, Frank Wilson. Also see WILSON-HILL, F. W.
6/2/6460, 27/9/15; R.F.A., C/S, 14/4/16; R.F.A., 12/8/16; E,S; Lieut.; w.
71/2 King William Street, E.C. 4.

HILL, Fred
6/5/8387, 14/12/15; L'pool. R., 4/9/16; F; Major; w; M.C., M(1).
Shipton Gorge, Bridport, Dorset.

HILL, Frederick
6/9396, 9/2/16; R.F.A., C/S, 9/6/16; R.F.A., 8/9/16; F; Lieut; w.
13 Hamilton Street, Greenock, Scotland.

HILL, Frederick William Charles
6/3/7452, 15/11/15, L/C.; E. Surr. R., 4/8/16, att. R. Berks. R.; S; Capt.; M(1).
School House, Tadworth, Surrey.

HILL, George Edward
6/4/8832, 10/1/16; No. 8 O.C.B., 4/8/16; R.F.C., 13/1/17.
35 Bassett Road, Notting Hill, W. 10.

HILL, George Francis Gordon
1/9646, 27/9/16; R.W. Surr. R., 9/3/17, att. Lab. Corps; F; Capt.
The Lodge, Thornton-le-dale, Pickering, Yorkshire.

HILL, Harold
B/12734, 11/3/18; R.F.A., C/S, 17/5/18; R.F.A., 10/2/19; 2/Lieut.
Wood View, 129 Windsor Road, Penarth, Glamorgan, South Wales.

HILL, Harold Stretton
6/5/6925, 19/10/15; No. 11 O.C.B., 7/5/16; 4th Lond. R., 4/9/16, att. S. Lan. R., R.A.F.; F; Lieut.
Warkworth, 40 Greenhill Road, Moseley, Birmingham. (Now in Straits Settlements).

HILL, Henry Britton
K/3091, 22/3/15; dis. 22/3/15.

HILL, Henry Ellis
6/7990, 29/11/15; R.E., 16/12/15; F,M,I; Capt.; w; M.C., M(1).
c/o Messrs. Reckitt & Sons, Ltd., Dansom Lane, Hull.

HILL, John Gray
A/58, 8/4/08; dis. 7/4/09.

✠ HILL, John Rowland
4/5/4818, 12/7/15; Yorks. L.I., 1/1/16; F; 2/Lieut.
Killed in action 5/8/16.

HILL, John Taylor
6/3/5850, 26/8/15; Worc. R., 13/1/16, R. Suss. R.; F; Lieut.; w.
Cawney Hill House, Dudley, Worcestershire.

HILL, Joseph
C/Sq/13235, 7/6/18; demob. 11/3/19.
Ellwood House, Crowell, Wallingford.

HILL, Leslie Gordon Baron
6/2/6485, 27/9/15; 22nd Lond. R., 4/8/16; F,S,P; Lieut.; w.
18 Beatrice Avenue, Norbury, S.W. 16.

HILL, Martin Spencer
4/5/6/4912, 17/7/15; dis. to re-enlist in R.A.M.C., 8/6/16; Sgt.
Osborne House, Loughton, Essex.

HILL, Octavius Vernon
A/11230, 9/5/17, L/C.; trfr. 28th Lond. R., 22/10/17.
131 Ladbroke Road, W. 11.

✠ HILL, Reginald Percy
4/9711, 10/10/16; R.A., C/S, 20/2/17; R.F.A., 9/6/17; 2/Lieut.
Died of wounds 25/8/18.

HILL, Reginald Reis
6/1/6691, 7/10/15; trfr. R.G.A., 7/7/16; R.A.F.; F; 2/Lieut.; w.
199 Camp Street, Georgetown, Demerara, British Guiana, South America.

HILL, Ronald
A/Sq/2866, 5/2/15; R.A.S.C., 10/6/15; F; Capt.
Meads Cottage, Esher, Surrey.

HILL, Stanley Harding
6/2/6183, 13/9/15; R. Fus., 3/1/16; F; Capt.; g.
30 Windsor Road, Forest Gate, Essex.

HILL, Walter Samuel
6/3/9253, 2/2/16; R.A., C/S, 12/10/16; R.G.A., 19/12/16; Lieut
10 Quay Road, Bridlington, East Yorkshire.

HILL, Wilfred Neave. See NEAVE-HILL, W.

✠ HILL, William Alfred
6/4/6763, 11/10/15; D. of Corn. L.I., 6/7/16, att. T.M. Bty.; Capt.
Killed in action 23/3/18.

HILL, William John
4/1/4107, 7/6/15, L/C.; D. of Corn. L.I., 1/6/16, att. E. Surr. R.; F; Lieut.; w(2).
Brightside, Rodney Terrace, Cheltenham.

HILLARY, Ernest
4/5/4856, 15/7/15; R.F.C., 4/8/16, R.A.F.; Lieut.
The Peak, Basingstoke.

HILLARY, Norman
6/5/8171, 6/12/15; R.A., C/S, 23/6/16; R.G.A., 26/9/16; F; Capt.; w; M.C., M(2).
The Peak, Basingstoke.

HILL-CLARKE, Ernest Charles
A/10304, 1/1/17; No. 14 O.C.B., 5/3/17, R.F.C., C/S; R.F.C., 13/7/17, R.A.F.; 2/Lieut.
Rosslyn, Priory Road, Hampton-on-Thames.

HILLER, Charles Thomson
1/3845, 31/5/15, L/C.; R.A.S.C., 15/9/15; G,EA,F; Lieut.
19 Downside Crescent, Hampstead, N.W. 3.

HILLIARD, Horace
4/9713, 10/10/16, L/C.; R.A., C/S, 2/2/17; R.F.A., 2/6/17; F; Lieut.
Dinmore, Tudor Road, Sutton Coldfield, Warwickshire.

HILLIER, Arthur James
C/12601, 13/2/18, L/C.; R.A.F., C/S, 21/5/18; demob. 5/3/19.
90 Canonbury Road, Highbury, N. 1.

HILLIER, Frank Norton
Sq/2831, 1/2/15, Sgt.; R.F.A., 28/4/15; Capt.; w; M.C., M(1).

HILLIER, Walter Walker
B/10099, 4/12/16; R.F.C., C/S, 13/3/17; R.F.C., 19/4/17; 2/Lieut.
197 High Street, Rochester.

HILLIER, William John Frederick
6/2/6890, 18/10/15; North'd. Fus., 6/7/16.
1 Mostyn Gardens, Willesden, N.W. 10.

APPENDIX II.—RECORDS OF RANK AND FILE.

✠ HILLS, *Arthur Hyde*
4/3/3965, 3/6/15; Hamps. R., 29/9/15; 2/Lieut.
Killed in action 19/4/17.

HILLS, *Charles Robe*
D/E/13777, 7/8/18; No. 22 O.C.B., 20/9/18; R.W. Surr. R., 5/2/19; 2/Lieut. Fair View, Alexandra Road, Epsom.

HILLS, *Francis Eric*
4/3306, 19/4/15; R.G.A., 6/8/15, R.A.F.; Lieut.; *p*.
5 Warltersville Road, Crouch Hill.

HILLS, *Leslie Conway*
D/10914, 26/3/17; R. Marines, 19/8/17; Lieut.
64 Kingsfield Road, Watford.

HILLYARD, *Vandeleur Osborne*
4/4541, 1/7/15; North'd. Fus., 2/1/16, secd. R.F.C.; Lieut.

HILMAN, *Robert John*
4/2/5110, 26/7/15, L/C.; R.W. Surr. R., 15/6/16; Lieut.
The Glen, Norbury W., Streatham, S.W.

HILPERN, *Wilfred Thomas Henry*
Sq/797, 25/5/14; 5th Drag. Gds., 15/8/14, E. Lan. R.; F; Lieut.; *p*. Sutton Valence School, Kent.

HILTON, *Alan Howard*
A/11603, 5/7/17; No. 13 O.C.B., 9/11/17; R.E., 30/4/18; F; Lieut. 92 Hollin Lane, Middleton, Manchester.

HILTON, *Charles Lacy*
B/12793, 18/3/18; No. 20 O.C.B., 20/9/18; Midd'x. R., 15/3/19; 2/Lieut. 12 Tavistock Road, Westbourne Park, W. 11.

✠ HILTON, *George*
6/5/5260, 31/7/15; R. Lanc. R., 31/12/15; 2/Lieut.
Killed in action 8/8/16.

HILTON, *Sydney Rayner*
3580, 6/5/15, L/C.; North'n. R., 6/7/15; Lieut.
Ruthby, Leicester.

HILTON-HESKETH, Tom. See HILTON, T. H.

HINCHLIFFE, *Elliot John*
A/11032, 13/4/17; No. 12 O.C.B., 10/8/17; Bedf. R., 27/11/17; F; Lieut.; *w*.
c/o H.M. Inspector of Taxes, Market Hill, Barnsley, Yorkshire.

HIND, *Fred Malcolm Jonas*
A/10692, 14/2/17; R.F.C., C/S, 3/3/17, H. Bde. O.C.B.; Indian Army, 27/11/17; M,I; Lieut.; *Inv*.
Oak Dene, Oakenshaw, Nr. Bradford.

HIND, *George Edward Lockhart*
B/13670, 29/7/18; demob. 20/3/19.
Fern House, Victoria Road, Brimscombe, Nr. Stroud, Gloucestershire

HIND, *John Arthur Lewis*
C/14267, 6/11/18; demob. 22/4/19.
The Hawthornes, Southey Street, Nottingham.

✠ HIND, *Reginald Charles*
6/3/8798, 10/1/16; R.A., C/S, 4/8/16; R.F.A., 10/11/16; 2/Lieut.
Killed in action 6/2/18.

HINDE, *John Egerton Berthon*
Sq/1675, 12/10/14; R.F.A., 10/10/14; F; Lieut.; *w*.
Hauslope, Stony Stratford, Buckinghamshire.

HINDLE, *Alfred*
B/13522, 12/7/18; demob. 23/1/19.
154 Richmond Hill, Accrington, Lancashire.

HINDLEY, *Harold Brailsford*
6/5/6764, 11/10/15; No. 11 O.C.B., 7/5/16; M.G.C., 4/9/16; Lieut. 5 Crane's Park, Surbiton, Surrey.

HINDLEY, *John Ivy*
4/2/4501, 28/6/15, L/C.; W. York. R., 3/12/15; Capt.; M(1).
Croft Villa, Great Horton, Bradford.

HINE, *Algernon George*
E/1579, 6/10/14, Cpl.; 12th Lond. R., 11/4/15; F,S; Staff Lieut.; *w*; M(1). Whitegates, Horsell, Woking.

HINE, *Ernest Daryll*
Sq/147, 18/4/08; dis. 17/4/09; 24th Lond. R., 7/6/15; F,S,E; Capt. 88 Nightingale Lane, S.W. 12.

✠ HINE, *Godfrey Valentine Brooke*
A/322, 22/7/08; dis. 21/7/12; 25th Lond. R., 26/10/14, Ir. Gds.; F; Lieut. Killed in action 6/10/15.

HINE, *James Burnett*
6/5/6808, 14/10/15, L/C.; R.F.C., 7/8/16, R.A.F.; F; Lieut.; *p*.
c/o Standard Bank of South Africa, 10 Clements Lane, E.C.

HINE, *Joseph Walter*
2/Sq/9791, 26/10/16, Sgt.; No. 1 Cav. C/S, 1/12/17; R. Regt. of Cav., 9/5/18; 2/Lieut. Nithsdale, The Cliffs, Westcliff-on-Sea.

HINE, *Rudolph Frank*
K/B/2323, 14/12/14; R. Berks. R., 9/3/15; Lieut.

HINE, *William Arthur*
B/10323, 4/1/17; R.F.C., C/S, 16/4/17; R.F.C., 16/5/17, Devon. R.; F; Lieut. Massingham House, 46 Haverstock Hill, N.W. 3.

HINES, *Norman Leslie*
6/4/7261, 8/11/15, L/C.; 7th Lond. R., 10/6/16; F,Germ.SWA; Lieut.; *w*. 1 Claverley Grove, Church End, Finchley, N. 3.

HINGSTON, *Harold Cuddeford*
K/E/2342, 14/12/14; 1st Lond. R., 3/4/15; F; Capt.
43 Chatsworth Road, Croydon.

HINKLEY, *Arthur Stanley*
4/4220, 14/6/15; R.E., 4/1/16; F; Major.
17 Lassa Road, Eltham, S.E. 9.

✠ HINKLEY, *Seigfried Thomas*
3/3345, 22/4/15; E. Kent. R., 21/8/15; F; 2/Lieut.
Killed in action 3/7/16.

HINMAN, *George Ernest*
1/9656, 29/9/16; R.A., C/S, 23/3/17; R.G.A., 1/7/17; Lieut.
Fyvie, Eastcote, Middlesex.

HINTON, *Cecil Henry*
B/10763, 19/2/17; Garr. O.C.B., 23/5/17; dis. med. unfit, 13/9/17.
58 Belsize Avenue, Hampstead, N.W. 3.

HINTON, *Eric Edmund*
2/3638, 17/5/15; R.F.A., 12/10/15; F; 2/Lieut.
Elm House, Berkhamsted, Hertfordshire.

HINTON, *Wilfred Samuel*
C/14268, 6/11/18; demob. 27/12/18.
22 Eastwood Road, Goodmayes, Essex.

HINTON, *William James*
B/10312, 4/1/17; No. 20 O.C.B., 7/6/17; trfr. 28th Lond. R., 10/9/17. 18 Crescent Road, Crouch End, N. 8.

HIPWELL, *Lewis William*
C/727, 11/11/13; R.W. Surr. R., 15/8/14, att. T.M. Bty.; F; Major; M(1). Olney, Buckinghamshire.

HIPWELL, *Thomas Collier*
Sq/2596, 26/12/14; R.F.A., 6/1/15; F; Lieut.; *w*(2); M.C., M(1)
27 The Embankment, Bedford.

HIRD, *John Stalker*
C/10394, 8/1/17, L/C.; R.A., C/S, 27/4/17; R.G.A., 1/9/17; F; Lieut. Walton Mount, Ambleside.

✠ HIRST, *Harold Hugh*
A/2070, 12/11/14; Manch. R., 1/3/15; EA,F; Lieut.
Died 29/2/19.

HIRST, *John Clifford*
C/13317, 18/6/18; trfr. 14th Lond. R., 6/12/18.
Fieldhead, Cleckheaton, Yorkshire.

✠ HIRST, *Stanley Ewart*
3/6/4/Sq/4077, 7/6/15; R.A., C/S, 29/12/16; R.G.A., 3/5/17; 2/Lieut. Killed in action 24/10/17.

✠ HISLOP, *Frederick Laurence*
6/8833, 10/1/16; No. 9 O.C.B., 8/3/16; Arg. & Suth'd. Highrs., 27/7/16; F; 2/Lieut. Killed in action 23/4/17.

✠ HISLOP, *Robert Wilson*
H/2/2642, 11/1/15; Sea. Highrs., 18/4/15; 2/Lieut.
Killed in action 4/7/17.

HISLOP, *William*
C/13368, 21/6/18, L/C.; demob. 18/2/19.
16 Third Avenue, Kings Park, Cathcart, Glasgow.

HITCHCOCK, *Lawrence Hiron*
6/2/6692, 7/10/15; Suff. R., 13/7/16, att. Lab. Corps; F; Capt.; M.B.E. Snitterfield, Stow Upland, Stowmarket, Suffolk.

APPENDIX II.—RECORDS OF RANK AND FILE.

HITCHINGS, Edward Harry Clare
D/10211, 18/12/16; R.W. Surr. R., 9/3/17, R.E.; It; Staff Capt.; M(1).
39 Belsize Avenue, N.W. 3.

✠ HITCHINGS, Francis Noel Wells
4/2601, 7/1/15; R.W. Surr. R., 21/5/15; Lieut.
Killed 3/12/18.

HOADE, John Robert
H/1744, 15/10/14; Midd'x. R., 18/2/15, E. Kent R., Indian Army; E,F; Capt.; w.
Oakley Lodge, Addlestone, Surrey.

✠ HOADE, Reginald William
H/1745, 15/10/14, Cpl.; Midd'x. R., 2/2/15; F; 2/Lieut.
Killed in action 15/7/16.

✠ HOARD, Henry Herbert Hoare
6/1/8269, 9/12/15, Cpl.; No. 14 O.C.B., 5/3/17; North'd. Fus., 26/6/17; 2/Lieut.
Killed in action 9/9/17.

HOARE, Bertram Trevelyan
6/9164, 26/1/16; trfr. 16th Lond. R., 4/5/16.
Knowle House, Knowle, Bristol.

✠ HOARE, Eric Sutherland
6/3/6662, 7/10/15; R.F.A., C/S, 31/3/16; R.F.A., 14/8/16; F; 2/Lieut.
Died of wounds 11/11/16.

HOARE, John George
2/3846, 31/5/15; Leic. R., 10/9/15, Indian Army; SR; Capt.
26 Nithdale Road, S.E. 18.

HOARE, Samuel
6/8415, 15/12/15; No. 9 O.C.B., 8/3/16; Cam'n. Highrs., 23/7/16, att. Sco. Rif. and Devon. R.; S; Lieut.
Granard, Inverness, Scotland.

✠ HOARE, Walter John Gerald
Sq/364, 16/3/09; dis. 5/7/11; R. Fus.; Capt.; D.S.O., M(1).
Killed in action 25/10/16.

HOBBS, Charles Rienzi Hurle
D/10888, 19/3/17, L/C.; R.G.A., C/S, 15/8/17; R.G.A., 31/12/17; F; Lieut.
5 Essex Court, Temple, E.C. 4.

HOBBS, Francis Benjamin
2/9787, 25/10/16; No. 14 O.C.B., 27/12/16; trfr. 14th Lond. R., 1/6/17, M.G.C., R.A.O.C.; F; Pte.; w.
Lloyds Bank Ltd., Seaton, Devonshire.

HOBBS, Frank
Sq/8964, 17/1/16; No. 1 Cav. C/S, 20/10/16; R.W. Kent Yeo., 16/2/17, att. R.W. Kent R.; F; 2/Lieut.
Evegate Manor, Smeeth, Kent.

HOBBS, Frank Freeman
B/10359, 5/1/17; Sig. C/S, 12/5/17; R.E., 30/9/17; F; Lieut.
46 Sutton Court, Chiswick, W. 4.

HOBBS, Harry Watts
1/3542, 10/5/15; York. R., 28/7/15, M.G.C.; Lieut.
Union of Lond. & Smith's Bank, Princes Street, E.C.

HOBBS, Reginald Clonsilla Edward
C/Sq/11063, 16/4/17; No. 2 Cav. C/S, 29/9/17; R. Regt. of Cav., 5/4/18; 2/Lieut.
Great Bowden House, Market Harborough, Leicestershire.

HOBBS, Thomas
E/14040, 20/9/18; No. 22 O.C.B., 22/11/18; R. War. R., 19/2/19; 2/Lieut.
Heskyn, High Road, New Southgate, N. 11.

HOBBY, Harold Spurgeon
4/3692, 20/5/15, Cpl.; York. R., 5/9/15, att. R.A.F.; F; Lieut.; w(3); M.C.
Fairholme, Park Lane, Macclesfield.

HOBHOUSE, Arthur Laurence
Sq/139, 18/4/08; dis. 17/4/10.
15 Bruton Street, W. 1.

HOBHOUSE, Reginald Oliver
C/1233, 23/9/14; Som. L.I., 27/11/14, secd. R.F.A.; Lieut.; w.

HOBOURN, Percy Leonard
3/3455, 3/5/15, L/C.; Leic. R., 10/9/15, M.G.C.; F; Major; M.C.
1 Barrs Hill Terrace, Coventry.

HOBSON, Alec
D/12961, 19/4/18; No. 11 O.C.B., 4/10/18; R.W. Surr. R., 17/3/19; 2/Lieut.
Ruckcroft, Armathwaite, Carlisle.

HOBSON, Francis William Eland
C/11485, 14/6/17; Garr. O.C.B., 5/10/17; Lab. Corps, 5/12/17; 2/Lieut.
53 Belsize Park Gardens, Hampstead, N.W. 3.

HOBSON, Henry Arthur
B/10772, 19/2/17; No. 14 O.C.B., 5/7/17; Suff. R., 30/10/17; F; 2/Lieut.; w.
British Agency, Tangier, Morocco.

✠ HOBSON, John Collinson
B/1031, 24/8/14; R. Scots, 2/9/14, M.G.C.; F; Lieut.
Killed in action 31/7/17.

HOBSON, Joseph Reginald
B/3003, 4/3/15, Cpl.; R.E., 28/8/15; E,F; Capt.; M.C., M(1).
Box 365, Salisbury, Southern Rhodesia, South Africa.

HOBSON, Montagu
6/8025, 30/11/15; R.A.S.C., 13/2/16; Lieut.

HOBSON, Oscar Rudolf
A/13029, 3/5/18; R.A., C/S, 26/7/18; R.G.A., 8/4/19; 2/Lieut.
47 Frognal, Hampstead, N.W. 3.

HOCKEN, Garth Warlow
4/6/1/4969, 19/7/15; K.R. Rif. C., 17/11/15; F; Lieut.; Inv.
Shirley, Berkhamsted, Hertfordshire.

✠ HOCKEN, Stephen Lotan
4/6/1/4970, 19/7/15; K.R. Rif. C., 17/11/15; F; 2/Lieut.
Killed in action 3/9/16.

HOCKING, Arthur Vivian
K/H/2117, 16/11/14; dis. 12/3/15.
4 Paper Buildings, Temple, E.C. 4.

HOCKING, William Thomas Hambly
6/2/8287, 10/12/15; R.F.C., 18/6/16, R.A.F.; F,It; Lieut.
61 Dorset Road, Ealing, W. 5.

✠ HODDING, Henry Ellis
K/F/2315, 10/12/14; Notts. & Derby. R., 17/3/15; F; Lieut.; M.C.
Died of wounds 8/11/18.

HODGE, Archibald
4/2/4044, 7/6/15; R.A.S.C., 13/9/15; F; Capt.
Solicitor, Hoole Park, Chester.

HODGE, Charles Hellyer
6/1/8507, 24/12/15; No. 8 O.C.B., 4/8/16, M.G.C., C/S; M.G.C., 23/11/16, Tank Corps; F; Capt.
32 Burlington Avenue, Kew Gardens, Surrey.

HODGE, Donald Grant
6/9033, 20/1/16; No. 9 O.C.B., 8/3/16; R. Highrs., 4/8/16, att. Gord. Highrs.; F; Capt.
Albany Club, Grahamstown, South Africa.

HODGE, Francis Percy
4/3847, 31/5/15; R.F.A., 3/11/15; F; Lieut.; w; M.C.
47 Culverden Road, Balham, S.W.

HODGE, Henry St. John Blissard
C/D/12085, 4/10/17; No. 8 O.C.B., 10/5/18; R. Highrs., 12/11/18; 2/Lieut.
38 West Gate, Chichester, Sussex.

HODGE, James Philip
B/701, 15/3/13; Army Pay Dept., 30/9/14; F,S,E; Lt.-Col.
5 Paper Buildings, Temple, E.C. 4.

✠ HODGE, Wilfred
A/11229, 10/5/17; R.F.C., C/S, 2/8/17; R.F.C., 8/9/17, R.A.F.; 2/Lieut.
Died 24/4/18.

HODGE, William Harry Lea
B/10466, 12/1/17; No. 14 O.C.B., 7/6/17; Welch R., 25/9/17, att. Hamps. R., M.G.C.; I; Lieut.
27 Lynmouth Road, Fortis Green Road, N. 2.

HODGES, Cecil Stuart
C/10566, 19/1/17; Lab. Corps, 19/6/17; F; Lieut.
Vernon House, Lucknow Avenue, Nottingham.

✠ HODGES, Daniel Alfred
6/3/7375, 11/11/15; No. 8 O.C.B., 4/8/16; R.W. Kent R., 21/11/16; 2/Lieut.
Killed in action 5/5/17.

HODGES, Graham
B/D/12225, 13/11/17; Tank Corps, C/S, 22/2/18; Tank Corps, 3/3/19; 2/Lieut.
37/8 Friday Street, Cannon Street, E.C. (Now in Canada).

HODGES, Herbert Roland
6/5/8134, 3/12/15; No. 8 O.C.B., 4/8/16; Dorset R., 21/11/16, att. Tank Corps; F; Lieut.
5 Cheverton Road, Hornsey Rise, N.

HODGES, Hugh Hilton
4/3966, 3/6/15, L/C.; Devon. R., 7/7/16; Lieut.
New Zealand Golf Club, West Byfleet.

APPENDIX II.—RECORDS OF RANK AND FILE.

HODGES, John D.
A/1117, 7/9/14; R.W. Surr. R., 27/11/14; Lieut.

HODGKINSON, Arthur
B/12735, 11/3/18, L/C.; demob. 10/1/19.
Ronkswood, Knebworth, Hertfordshire.

HODGKINSON, Robert
4/6/5/4971, 19/7/15; N. Lan. R., 27/12/15, R.E.; Capt.
55 Danvers Street, Chelsea, S.W. 3.

HODGSON, Albert Arthur
4/2/4075, 7/6/15; Notts. & Derby. R., 17/9/15, secd. Lab. Corps; F; Lieut.
High Holme Villa, South Lincolnshire.

HODGSON, Anthony
6/2/9052, 21/1/16; No. 14 O.C.B., 30/10/16; Bord. R., 24/1/17; F; Capt.; M.C.
43 Frithville Gardens, Shepherds Bush, W. 12.

HODGSON, Claude Beresford Vernon
A/K/2546, 2/1/15; Manch. R., 3/3/15, att. R.A.F.; F; Lieut.; w.
Steep Down, Steyning, Sussex.

✠ HODGSON, Frederick James
6/5/5934, 1/9/15, Cpl.; L'pool. R., 27/12/15, K. Af. Rif.; F,EA; Lieut.; w.
Died 5/5/18.

HODGSON, Horace Edwards
D/13832, 14/8/18; dis. med. unfit, 23/2/19.
The Hollins, Triangle, Halifax, Yorkshire.

✠ HODGSON, Oswald Arthur
4/3/4393, 24/6/15; North'd. Fus., 12/12/15; 2/Lieut.
Killed in action 16/4/17.

HODGSON, Robert Daniel
K/2204, 30/11/14; R. Lanc. R., 19/12/14, secd. M.G.C.; F; Major; w(3); M(3).
Stedham Rectory, Midhurst.

HODGSON, Thomas
6/4/6012, 2/9/15; 9th Lond. R., 21/10/15; SWA,F; Capt.; M.C.
c/o F. J. Manning Esq., St. Michael's House, Basinghall Street, E.C. (Now in India.)

HODSON, Hubert Selwyn
Sq/1216, 14/9/14; Staff. Yeo., 23/12/14; Capt.; Inj.
2 Dr. Johnson's Buildings, Temple, E.C. 4.

HODSON, Robert Benedict
4/6/5/4972, 19/7/15, L/C.; L'pool. R., 6/6/16; F; Capt.; w; M(1).
Chezmoi, Aintree, Liverpool.

HODSON, Sidney
6/1/5851, 26/8/15; dis. med. unfit, 31/12/15.

✠ HODSON, Sydney
6/1/8928, 15/1/16, L/C.; No. 14 O.C.B., 30/10/16; K.R. Rif. C., 24/1/17; F; 2/Lieut.; w(2).
Killed in action 21/3/18.

HOGAN, Basil Harry
6/7608, 19/11/15; E. York. R., 18/12/16; F; Lieut.; w.
4a Louisville Road, Balham, S.W. 17.

HOGAN, Donald Vincent
6/5/C/8288, 10/12/15; No. 7 O.C.B., 11/8/16; trfr. 18th Lond. R., 2/2/17, M.G.C.; F; Pte.; w(2).
3 Blackrock Road, Cork, Ireland.

HOGAN, John Ross
A/14021, 16/9/18; demob. 22/1/19.
Cotterbrook, New Barnet, Hertfordshire.

HOGAN-FLEMING, Arthur George
D/2911, 10/2/15; Hamps. R., 29/4/15, Lab. Corps; Lieut.
Cissbury Villa, Old Shoreham Road, Hove, Sussex.

HOGG, Alfred Robert
A/13957, 6/9/18; No. 11 O.C.B., 24/1/19; General List, 8/3/19; 2/Lieut.
c/o Messrs. Cornabe, Eckford & Coy., Chefoo, North China.

HOGG, Arthur Cyril
D/10022, 27/11/16; trfr. Essex R., 11/4/17; F; Cpl.
23 Hartington Street, Derby.

HOGG, James Noel
K/C/2490, 29/12/14, C.Q.M.S.; R.A.S.C., 15/11/15; F; Lieut.
1 Albert Road, Birkdale, Lancashire.

HOGG, John Kenneth
B/12704, 8/3/18; No. 1 O.C.B., 6/9/18; trfr. 14th Lond. R., 6/1/19.
46 Manor Road, N. 16.

✠ HOGG, Lewis Stephen
B/633, 26/4/12; R.W. Fus., 12/9/14; Capt.
Killed in action 25/9/15.

HOGG, Richard John Jefferson
4/5/4829, 13/7/15, L/C.; E. Surr. R., 15/10/15; Lieut.; M.C.
59 Elm Park Gardens, S.W.

HOGGART-HILL, Rowland James
B/Sq/10532, 17/1/17; A.S.C., C/S, 1/5/17; R.A.S.C., 28/6/17; F; Lieut.
Brook Hall Cottage, Winslow, Buckinghamshire.

HOLBERTON, Thomas Edmund
Sq/394, 31/3/09; dis. 3/4/11; R.H.A., 20/4/15; Lieut.; M.C. and Bar, M(2).
Elstree School, Hertfordshire.

✠ HOLBOURN, Cyril Ralph
A/14086, 2/10/18;
Died 1/11/18.

HOLBROOK, Ernest
D/9981, 22/11/16; R.F.A., C/S, 23/2/17; R.F.A., 21/7/17; F; Lieut.
22 Miers Street, Swansea.

HOLBROOK, John William
A/D/13036, 4/5/18; No. 15 O.C.B., 15/10/18; Notts. & Derby. R., 17/3/19; 2/Lieut.
The Manor House, Tollerton, Nr. Nottingham.

HOLBROOK, Vincent Stanley
4/6/4973, 19/7/15, L/C.; R.A., C/S, 5/2/16; dis. med. unfit, 8/8/16; R.F.C., 8/12/16, R.A.F.; F; Flying Officer.
c/o Messrs. Martin & Martin, 16 Market Place, Reading, Berkshire. (Now in India.)

HOLCROFT, Norman
C/1/Sq/8270, 9/12/15; R.A., C/S, 26/10/16; R.F.A., 21/4/17; F; Lieut.
6 Heath Villas, Halifax, Yorkshire.

HOLDCROFT, Victor Cecil
6/5/6693, 7/10/15, L/C.; K.R. Rif. C., 6/7/16; F; Capt.; w; M(1).
P.O. Box 488, Johannesburg, South Africa.

HOLDEN, Benjamin
B/10770, 19/2/17; R.F.C., C/S, 16/4/17; R.F.C., 14/6/17, R.A.F.; 2/Lieut.
Sunnyside, Wolston, Nr. Coventry.

✠ HOLDEN, Cecil Alexander Naldrett
B/9868, 6/11/16; No. 14 O.C.B., 5/3/17; Lein. R., 26/6/17, Indian Army; F,I; Lieut.; g.
Killed in action 27/5/19.

HOLDEN, Eustace Arthur Theodore Adolphus
4/5/4797, 12/7/15; Dorset R., 19/11/15; M; Lieut.
9 Stradbroke Road, Highbury New Park, N. 5.

✠ HOLDEN, Harold
6/5/6045, 3/9/15; N. Lan. R., 16/7/16; F; 2/Lieut.
Killed in action 20/9/17.

HOLDEN, Ralph Ainsworth
A/B/D/11970, 6/9/17; R.A., C/S, 7/2/18; R.G.A., 2/9/18; 2/Lieut.
5 John Street, Bedford Row, W.C. 1.

HOLDEN, Robert Wynne
A/13087, 20/5/18, L/C.; trfr. K.R. Rif. C., 7/7/19; Cpl.
168 Castle Hill, Reading, Berkshire.

✠ HOLDEN, William Leak
6/4/6857, 15/10/15; No. 14 O.C.B., 30/9/16; Manch. R., 24/10/16; 2/Lieut.
Killed in action 4/1/17.

HOLDSWORTH, Conrad
B/D/11983, 10/9/17; trfr. 28th Lond. R., 20/3/18.
7 St. Stephen's Crescent, Bayswater, W. 2.

HOLDSWORTH, Harold
D/11155, 30/4/17; No. 14 O.C.B., 10/8/17, att. R.F.C. and York. and Lanc. R.; F,It,E; Lieut.
Claremont, Nab Wood, Shipley, Yorkshire.

✠ HOLDSWORTH, Vavaseur Mervyn
C/443, 8/11/09; dis. 29/10/12; 22nd Lond. R., 2/4/15; 2/Lieut
Killed in action 20/12/15.

HOLDWAY, Henry Charles
6/3/6526, 30/9/15; N. Lan. R., 7/9/16; F; Capt.; g.
25 London Road, Twickenham.

HOLE, Herbert Wray
D/Sq/11562, 28/6/17; No. 1 Cav. C/S, 1/12/17; Hamps. R., 27/8/18; 2/Lieut.
Anglo-Persian Oil Coy., Mohammeruh, Persian Gulf, via Bombay.

APPENDIX II.—RECORDS OF RANK AND FILE.

HOLGATE, John William
6/5/5225, 30/7/15; R.E., 26/12/15; F; Lieut.
163 Holyroad, Prestwich, Manchester.

HOLGATE-SHAW, Richard
B/D/11984, 10/9/17; No. 17 O.C.B., 5/4/18; Sea. Highrs., 11/2/19; 2/Lieut.
Crantock, Finchley Road, Golders Green, N.W. 11.

HOLLAND, Charles Henry Hayman
B/1255, 23/9/14; R.W. Surr. R., 20/10/14, att. Glouc. R. and R.A.F.; G,M; Capt.; w.
Keston, Westbury Road, New Malden, Surrey.

HOLLAND, Harold Ernest
B/279, 19/6/08; dis. 18/6/09; rej. Sq/813, 3/8/14; trfr. 13th Lond. R., 7/8/14; 13th Lond. R., 30/9/14; F; Capt.; w; M.C., M(2) c/o T. W. Holland Esq., 9 Bedford Row, W.C. 1. (Now in California).

HOLLAND, Hugh Delano
Sq/1215, 14/9/14; R. Regt. of Cav., 15/9/14, 1st R. Drag.; Lieut.
57 Cadogan Gardens, S.W. 3.

HOLLAND, Percy Estcourt
B/815, 3/8/14, L/C.; R.A.S.C., 28/10/14; F; Capt.; w.
Junior Carlton Club, Pall Mall, S.W. 1. (Now in France).

✠ HOLLAND, Ralph Bertram
A/812, 3/8/14; R.W. Kent R., 2/9/14; F; Capt.
Killed in action 2/10/16.

HOLLAND, Richard
B/E/13606, 24/7/18; R. Marines, 18/9/18; Lieut.
Ashbourne, Derbyshire.

HOLLAND, Robert Pembrey
D/10245, 29/12/16, L/C.; No. 14 O.C.B., 5/5/17; Manch. R, 28/8/17; 2/Lieut.; p.
Whitemere, Davenport, Stockport, Cheshire.

HOLLAND, Talbot William
B/816, 3/8/14; R.N.V.R., 16/8/14; Lieut.
Combe Cottage, Wilmington, Kent.

HOLLEBONE, Harold Trench
4/3/4045, 7/6/15; R.F.A., 2/9/15.
4 Shaftesbury Road, Southsea.

✠ HOLLES, Frederick Tetherly Noel
K/B/2407, 21/12/14; E. Lan. R., 22/4/15; E,M; 2/Lieut.
Died 11/9/16.

HOLLIDAY, Julius Oliver
6/5/8416, 15/12/15; No. 7 O.C.B., 11/8/16; R. Muns. Fus., 18/12/16, R.A.F.; F; Lieut.; w.
Foxcombe Cottage, Upper Weston, Bath.

HOLLINS, Frank Hubert
K/E/2265, 7/12/14; Rif. Brig., 17/3/15, att. K.R. Rif. C.; F; Major.
Greyfriars, Preston, Lancashire.

HOLLINS, Harold
A/13060, 13/5/18; No. 5 O.C.B., 8/11/18, Nos. 20 & 12 O.C.Bs.; Rif. Brig., 17/3/19; 2/Lieut.
Brookdale, Alderley Edge, Cheshire. (Now in Switzerland.)

HOLLINS, William
2/3848, 31/5/15; E. Surr. R., 2/9/15, Midd'x. R., Lab. Corps; F; Capt.; w.
64 Albacore Crescent, Lewisham, S.E. 13.

HOLLOM, Leslie Percy Gilbert
4/3730, 24/5/15; W. Kent. Yeo., 30/4/15, att. E. Kent. R.; 2/Lieut.; w.
Hutwa House, Princes Road, Blackheath, S.E. 13.

HOLLOND, Raymond Claude
B/1626, 9/10/14; Rif. Brig., 12/12/14; F; Capt.; w, Inv; M(1).
Leiston Old Abbey, Leiston, Suffolk.

HOLLOWAY, George James Warner
K/A/2215, 30/11/14; W. York. R., 20/2/15, att. North'd. Fus.; G,E,F; Capt.; w-p.
Hill House, Amberley, Gloucestershire.

HOLLOWAY, Harold Hugh
6/1/8803, 10/1/16; R.A., C/S, 4/8/16; R.G.A., 26/11/16; F; Lieut.; g.
21 Trafalgar Road, Moseley, Birmingham.

HOLLOWAY, Rupert
6/2/8482, 20/12/15; No. 8 O.C.B., 4/8/16; K.R. Rif. C., 21/11/16; 2/Lieut.
88 West Side, Clapham Common, S.W. 4.

HOLLOWELL, James Hirst
B/11419, 1/6/17; A.S.C., C/S, 1/9/17; R.A.S.C., 27/10/17; F; Lieut.; w.
434 Royal Exchange, Manchester.

HOLLOWELL, Richard William
A/B/D/12183, 2/11/17; R.F.A., C/S, 15/3/18; R.F.A., 15/2/19; 2/Lieut.
12 St. Michael's Avenue, Northampton.

HOLLY, Stanley Gordon
D/10680, 6/2/17; trfr. 16th Lond. R., 9/3/17.
Hamm Court Farm, Weybridge, Surrey.

HOLMAN, Clifford Evans
C/1020, 7/8/14; Glouc. R., 12/9/14, R.F.C., R.A.F.; Capt.
Woodside, Buckhurst Hill, Essex.

HOLMAN, Eric
6/1/6809, 14/10/15, L/C.; No. 11 O C.B., 7/5/16; R.F.C., 4/9/16, R.A.F.; F; Lieut.
198 Mansel Road, Small Heath, Birmingham.

HOLMAN, Kenneth James
D/10801, 28/2/17, L/C.; R.A., C/S, 18/7/17; trfr. R.G.A., 18/2/18.
Tregenna, Camborne, Cornwall.

HOLME, Henry Atkinson
6/3/6951, 21/10/15; R.A., C/S, 29/1/16; dis. to R. Mil. Coll., 29/8/16; R. Sco. Fus., 1/5/17; F; Lieut.; w.
Thrimley, Hackthorpe, Penrith, Cumberland.

HOLME, Joseph Johnson
4/3777, 27/5/15, L/C.; North'd. Fus., 12/8/15; F; Lieut.; w.
6 Chester Street, Newcastle-on-Tyne.

✠ HOLMES, Akehurst Wilson
Sq/3133, 29/3/15; dis. to R Mil. Academy, 11/5/16; R.G.A., 23/11/16; 2/Lieut.
Died of wounds 28/7/17.

HOLMES, Edward Allen
6/3/5299, 2/8/15, L/C.; York. & Lanc. R., 6/1/16; Lieut.; w,p.
Hathersage, Peak of Derbyshire.

HOLMES, Edward John
B/D/13605, 24/7/18, L/C.; demob. 19/5/19.
8 Livingstone Road, Southampton.

HOLMES, Ernest Bowden
2/3482, 3/5/15; N. Lan. R., 17/8/15; Lieut.
High Croft, Duffield, Derby.

HOLMES, Frank Edmund
6/5/6858, 15/10/15, Sgt.; Manch. R., 4/9/16, att. Yorks. L.I. and Lab. Corps; F; Lieut.; w.
29 Manley Road, Whalley Range, Manchester.

HOLMES, Frederick Harrold Scott
D/13891, 23/8/18; trfr. K.R. Rif. C., 7/4/19.
Barclay's Bank House, Dartford, Kent.

HOLMES, Harold
6/1/6527, 30/9/15, Sgt.; Manch. R., 4/9/16, R.A.F.; Lieut.; w.
Denton, Ben Rhydding, Yorkshire.

HOLMES, James Carlton
D/14043, 19/9/18; No. 18 O.C.B., 10/2/19; Rif. Brig., 18/3/19; 2/Lieut.
63 Weston Road, Strood, Rochester, Kent.

HOLMES, Joseph William Mounteney
D/E/13760, 7/8/18, L/C.; No. 22 O.C.B., 20/9/18; E. Kent R., 5/2/19; 2/Lieut.
4 Stone Buildings, Lincoln's Inn, W.C. 2.

✠ HOLMES, Oswald Matthews
2/6/5300, 2/8/15; Yorks. L.I., 1/11/15; 2/Lieut.; w.
Died of wounds 25/8/17

HOLMES, Robert Howard
B/12758, 14/3/18; No. 6 O.C.B., 6/9/18; demob.
1 Portland Place, Pitville, Cheltenham.

HOLMES, Valentine
A/10827, 2/3/17, Cpl.; R.A., C/S, 10/8/17; R.F.A., 6/1/18; 2/Lieut.

HOLMES, Ward
D/11124, 30/4/17; No. 12 O.C.B., 10/8/17; Bedf. R., 27/11/17; Lieut.; w.
Wathorpe, Stamford, Lincolnshire.

✠ HOLMES, Wilfred Bertram
2/9728, 16/10/16; No. 14 O.C.B., 27/12/16; Ches. R., 27/3/17; F; 2/Lieut.
Killed in action 20/9/17.

✠ HOLMS, William
6/7769, 23/11/15; No. 9 O.C.B., 8/3/16; High. L.I., 6/7/16; F; 2/Lieut.
Killed in action 16/9/16.

✠ HOLROYD, Clifford
6/2/8360, 13/12/15, L/C.; No. 14 O.C.B., 30/10/16; W. Rid. R., 24/1/17; F; 2/Lieut.
Killed in action 3/5/17.

APPENDIX II.—RECORDS OF RANK AND FILE.

HOLROYD, *Edward Hermann Henderson*
6/5/C/6528, 30/9/15; No. 8 O.C.B., 4/8/16; trfr. 16th Lond. R., 6/12/16, Lab. Corps; F; Cpl.
17 Burngreave Road, Sheffield, Yorkshire.

HOLROYD, *Walter*
A/11247, 14/5/17; No. 16 O.C.B., 5/10/17; N. Cyc. Bn., 12/3/18; 2/Lieut.
c/o Mrs. T. Waters, West View, Morpeth, Northumberland.

HOLT, *Alcimus Harrison*
B/10331, 4/1/17, L/C.; No. 20 O.C.B., 7/6/17; S. Lan. R., 25/9/17; F; Lieut.
Branksome, Sunnyhurst, Darwen, Lancashire.

HOLT, *Charles William*
D/13871, 21/8/18; trfr. K.R. Rif. C., 7/4/19.
50 Shorndean Street, Catford, S.E. 6.

HOLT, *Frank*
B/10978, 2/4/17; No. 12 O.C.B., 10/8/17; Bord. R., 27/11/17; F; Lieut.; w.
c/o John Holt & Coy. Ltd., Royal Liver Buildings, Liverpool.

HOLT, *Fred Whitehead*
D/13843, 16/8/18; demob. 20/3/19.
4 Woodland Avenue, Cliftonville, Belfast.

HOLT, *James*
C/D/12292, 7/12/17; No. 17 O.C.B., 10/5/18; Ches. R., 2/2/19; 2/Lieut.
1 Wythenshawe Road, Northenden, Manchester.

HOLT, *John*
E/14027, 18/9/18; R.G.A , C/S, 1/11/18; demob.
Naden, North Promenade, St. Annes-on-the-Sea.

HOLT, *Norman Charles*
C/9970, 20/11/16; No. 14 O.C.B., 30/1/17; 8th Lond. R., 25/4/17, att. M.G.C.; Lieut.
Arundel, Archar Road, Southampton.

HOLT, *Rodney Gill*
4/4279, 17/6/15; E. Lan. R., 9/12/15, att. R.F.C. and R.A.F.; F; Capt. & Flt. Cmdr.
38 Whitelow Road, Chorlton-cum-Hardy, Manchester.

HOLTON, *Charles Henry Stroud*
2/3442, 1/5/15; R.F.A., 12/10/15; F; Capt.; w.
The Bungalow, 46 St. Georges Park Avenue, Chalkwell Park, Westcliff-on-Sea, Essex.

HOLTON, *George William*
Sq/3599, 13/5/15; R.A.S.C., 24/8/15; Lieut.
Maidley House, Witney, Oxon.

HOLWILL, *John Henry Ivor*
6/3/8216, 7/12/15, L/C.; No. 14 O.C.B., 28/8/16, M.G.C., C/S; M.G.C., 28/12/16; Lieut.
Kersbrook, Sketty Road, Swansea.

HOME, *George*
B/12417, 18/1/18; R.F.A., C/S, 15/3/18; R.G.A., 3/2/19; 2/Lieut.

✠ HOMER, *William Howard Claude*
6/2/7354, 10/11/15; Glouc. R., 4/8/16; Lieut.; M.C.
Killed in action 26/4/18.

HOMEWOOD, *Charles Jesse*
6/5/5935, 1/9/15; L'pool. R., 23/4/16, Manch. R.; F; Capt.
41 Longland Road, Wallasey, Cheshire.

HONE, *Herbert Ralph*
3/3388, 26/4/15; 18th Lond. R., 15/7/15, att. M. of Munitions; F; Capt.; w; M.C.
77 Hollingbury Park Avenue, Brighton. (Now in Uganda)

HONE, *Percival William*
6/3/8568, 31/12/15; R.F.C., C/S, 8/10/16; R.F.C., 2/5/17; 2/Lieut.
Colebrook House, Winchester, Hampshire.

HOOD, *John Alexander*
6/Sq/5852, 26/8/15; R.A.S.C., 27/11/15; Capt.; M(1).
Fletching, Uckfield, Sussex.

✠ HOOD, *John William*
3/6/8693, 4/1/16; R.A., C/S, 7/7/16; R.G.A., 11/10/16; Lieut.
Died 15/11/18.

HOOK, *Charles Wilfrid Theodore*
6/5/6734, 11/10/15; E. Kent. R., 10/6/16; M,I ; Capt.
c/o The Commissioners for the Port of Calcutta, Strano Road, Calcutta.

✠ HOOK, *Duncan*
H/1935, 22/10/14; Lan. Fus., 16/11/14; G; Lieut.
Killed in action 7/8/15.

HOOK, *Gerald Joseph Keenan*
C/12570, 6/2/18; R.F.A., C/S, 17/5/18; R.F.A., 12/3/19; 2/Lieut.
24 Whalley Grove, Whalley Range, Manchester.

✠ HOOK, *Robin*
H/1929, 22/10/14; Lan. Fus., 16/11/14; G; 2/Lieut.
Killed in action 7/8/15.

HOOKE, *Harold George*
D/12986, 26/4/18; No. 11 O.C.B., 4/10/18, No. 15 O.C.B.; Midd'x. R., 16/3/19; 2/Lieut.
23 Creighton Avenue, Muswell Hill, N. 10.

HOOKE, *Henry Martyn*
H/K/2111, 15/11/14; R. Fus., 4/1/15, att. T.M. Bty.; F; Capt.; w(2).
Junior Carlton Club, Pall Mall, S.W. 1.

HOOKE, *Robert James Trevor*
B/C/12681, 4/3/18, L/C.; H. Bde. O.C.B., 6/9/18; Gds. M.G.R., 10/3/19; 2/Lieut.
39 Eaton Place, S.W. 1.

HOOKER, *Frederick Richard*
C/10141, 7/12/16; No. 14 O.C.B., 6/4/17; 7th Lond. R., 31/7/17, att. 16th Lond. R. and Norf. R.; E,P; Capt.; w.
Park Hill, Ewell, Surrey.

HOOKEY, *Reginald Edward*
6/3/9406, 9/2/16; R.A., C/S, 23/6/16; R.G.A., 27/9/16; F; Lieut.
c/o Mrs. Lawton, Beeston Moss, Tarporley, Cheshire.

HOOKHAM, *George Edward*
4/6/Sq/4885, 15/7/15, Sgt.; No. 2 Cav. C/S, 31/3/16; R. Glouc Huss., 6/9/16; E; Capt.
11 Ford Park Road, Matley, Plymouth.

HOOKINS, *Cuthbert Walter*
B/13642, 26/7/18; demob. 20/3/19.
19 Station Road, Liscard, Cheshire.

✠ HOOPER, *Bernard Keith*
2/3778, 27/5/15; 9th Lond. R., 25/9/16; 2/Lieut.
Killed in action 26/9/17.

HOOPER, *Bernard Leslie*
A/324, 23/7/08; 20th Lond. R., 19/3/09; F; Lt.-Col.
17 Dartmouth Row, S.E. 10.

HOOPER, *Charles Arthur*
4/3/3967, 3/6/15; Interpretership, 12/7/15.
36 Endsleigh Gardens, Ilford.

HOOPER, *Charles Randolph*
Sq/3333, 21/4/15; York. Huss., 25/6/15; Lieut.

HOOPER, *Christopher John*
3/9615, 14/9/16; No. 14 O.C.B., 26/11/16; Dorset R., 28/2/17, att. Linc. R.; F; Lieut.
Langton, Blandford, Dorset.

HOOPER, *Edwin Russell*
6/Sq/8217, 7/12/15; No. 1 Cav. C/S, 12/10/16; 5th Huss., 16/2/17, att. North'd. Huss. and North'd. Fus.; F; Lieut.; w.
4 Northumberland Avenue, Putney, S.W. 15.

HOOPER, *Geoffrey Michael*
C/53, 7/4/08; 11th Lond. R., 10/5/13; Capt.; w(2); M.C.
Newlands, Snakes Lane, Woodford Green.

HOOPER, *Richard Beverley*
A/10932, 18/3/17; R.F.C., C/S, 4/5/17; R.F.C., 14/6/17, R.A.F.; Lieut.; w.
Ferndale, Court Oak Road, Harborne, Birmingham.

HOOPER, *William John Deverell*
6/5/8814, 10/1/16; R.E., C/S, 2/7/16; trfr. R.F.A., 20/10/16; F.
Prospect House, Swainswick, Nr. Bath.

✠ HOOPS, *Harry Albert Mostyn*
6/4/6013, 2/9/15; No. 7 O.C.B., 3/7/16; R. Ir. Fus., 3/11/16, att. R. Ir. Rif.; 2/Lieut.
Killed in action 16/8/17.

HOOPS, *Reginald Hastings*
6/1/8417, 15/12/15; No. 14 O.C.B., 30/10/16; Shrop. Yeo., 24/1/17, att. R.W. Fus.; F,It; Lieut.
119 Albany Road, Cardiff.

✠ HOOTON, *Edward Cedric*
D/1419, 29/9/14; R. War. R., 19/12/14; F; Lieut.
Killed in action 27/6/16.

HOOTON, *George Eastwood*
C/13369, 21/6/18; trfr. 14th Lond. R., 6/12/18, Gord. Highrs.; L/C.
31 Lime Grove, Long Eaton, Derbyshire.

HOPE, *Arthur Edward*
6/4/6014, 2/9/15; 7th Lond. R., 27/11/15, att. T.M. Bty.; F; Capt.
Eversleigh, Langley Park Road, Sutton, Surrey.

APPENDIX II.—RECORDS OF RANK AND FILE.

HOPE, Edward Lepine
1/9648, 27/9/16, L/C.; No. 14 O.C.B., 27/12/16; Suff. R., 25/4/17, Camb. R., 26/10/18; F; Lieut.; w.
29 Westerfield Road, Ipswich.

✠ HOPE, Herbert Alfred
6/7408, 13/11/15, Sgt.; R.F.C., C/S, 8/10/16; R.F.C., 26/2/17; 2/Lieut. Died of wounds 28/7/17.

HOPE, John Brookfield Alban
6/5/6850, 16/10/15; Bord. R., 24/10/16; Lieut.; p; M(1).
200 Coppice Street, Meerneth, Oldham.

HOPE, Maurice St. John
B/70, 10/4/08; dis. 5/4/11; City of Lond. Yeo., 20/11/15, att. Tank Corps; Lieut. Burlington House, Piccadilly, W. 1.

HOPE, Selwyn Peter
4/3419, 29/4/15, Sgt.; Gren. Gds., 28/9/15; F; Lieut.; Inv.
20 Castle Street, Liverpool. (Now in New Zealand).

✠ HOPE-WALLACE, James
B/266, 1/6/08; dis. 30/5/10; North'd. Fus.; Lieut.
Killed in action 15/9/17.

HOPEWELL, Philip Handley
D/13864, 20/8/18; trfr. 14th Lond. R., 6/12/18.
Jardine, Dale Road, Purley, Surrey.

HOPKIN-JAMES, David Kynvelyn John
B/13551, 19/7/18; demob. 24/1/19.
The Vicarage, Cowbridge, Glamorganshire.

HOPKINS, Arthur Leslie
A/12484, 29/1/18; No. 2 O.C.B., 7/6/18; R.W. Surr. R., 6/2/19; 2/Lieut. Sidney Sussex College, Cambridge.

✠ HOPKINS, Arthur Mackern
F/1801, 16/10/14; S. Lan. R., 14/12/14; Lieut.; w.
Died of wounds 18/11/16.

HOPKINS, Arthur Williams
3/3372, 24/4/15; Dorset R., 28/7/15, att. R. War. R., and Oxf. and Bucks. L.I.; F; Capt.; Inv.
The Cottage, Chalfont St. Giles, Buckinghamshire.

HOPKINS, Edward Augustus
C/B/13269, 12/6/18; demob. 5/2/19.
Pamber Heath Parsonage, Basingstoke.

HOPKINS, Ernest Lewis
C/4, 1/4/08; dis. 31/3/10; C.S.M.; R.A.F.
35 Onslow Gardens, Muswell Hill, N. 10.

HOPKINS, George Joseph
6/2/7103, 1/11/15; dis. med. unfit, 27/11/17.
Lancaster House, Compton Road, Canonbury, N. 1.

HOPKINS, Leslie Walter
4/3/4188, 14/6/15; Welch. R., 4/10/15, M.G.C.; M; Major.
18 Wilbury Villas, Hove, Sussex.

HOPKINS, Lindsay
B/1084, 2/9/14; High. L.I., 12/9/14, R.A.S.C.; Capt.; M(1).

HOPKINS, Richard
A/10745, 16/2/17; No. 20 O.C.B., 5/5/17; K.R. Rif. C., 28/8/17; GermSWA,S; Lieut.; w.
Box 515, QueQue, Southern Rhodesia, South Africa.

HOPKINS, Sydney Charles
6/1/7921, 29/11/15, L/C.; Mon. R., 22/11/16, att. Shrop. L.I. and Welch R.; F; Capt.; w.
1 Windsor Terrace, Uplands, Swansea, South Wales.

HOPKINS, William
6/1/7262, 8/11/15; N. Lan. R., 4/8/16; M; Lieut.; w.
Royal Societies Club, St. James Street, S.W.

HOPKINSON, Harry Grenville
6/Sq/7922, 29/11/15, L/C.; No. 1 Cav. C/S, 12/10/16; 4th Drag., 16/2/17; F; Lieut.; w.
44 High Street, Grantham, Lincolnshire.

✠ HOPSON, Albert Edward
4/3/5074, 26/7/15; Durh L.I., 3/1/16; Lieut.
Killed in action 11/4/18.

HORDER, Ivan Kingsley
B/13607, 24/7/18; demob. 23/1/19.
12/13 Henrietta Street, W.C. 2.

HORDERN, Herbert Radcliffe
6/5332, 2/8/15; Ir. Gds., 26/8/15; Lieut.; w.
Throwley House, Faversham, Kent.

HORE, Charles Leonard
6/1/6086, 6/9/15; N. Lan. R., 25/1/16; F; Capt.; w(2); M.C., M(1). 28 Milton Road, Highgate, N. 6.

✠ HORE, Ruthven Pomfret
K/E/2283, 8/12/14; Dorset R., 6/3/15, att. Welch R.; F; 2/Lieut.
Died of wounds 2/10/15.

✠ HORLEY, Engelbert Lutyens Rothwell
H/2580, 4/1/15; Manch. R., 22/5/15; 2/Lieut.; w.
Killed in action 4/9/17.

HORLOCK, Alfred George
D/2854, 4/2/15; E. Kent R., 23/4/15, att. R.A.F.; F; Lieut.; w; M(1). Rockfield, 64 Frances Road, Windsor, Berkshire.

HORN, Devid
6/5/6765, 11/10/15; Brit. W.I.R., 18/6/16, att. Midd'x. R.; E,F; Capt. c/o Messrs. Anderson, Kenross, Scotland.

HORN, Edgar Cuthbert
6/Sq/5623, 16/8/15; R.A., C/S, 24/1/16; R.F.A., 23/6/16; F; Lieut.; w. 31 Cornfield Road, Eastbourne.

HORN, Edward George
B/13486, 8/7/18; No. 22 O.C.B., 23/8/18; Bedf. & Herts. R., 13/2/19; 2/Lieut.
The Laurels, 17 Queen's Avenue, Porthcawl, Glamorganshire.

HORNBY, John Heald
6/4/Sq/5151, 29/7/15; 3rd Cty. of Lond. Yeo., 1/12/15, secd. Tank Corps; Lieut.
The Limes, Amyand Park Gardens, Twickenham.

HORNBY, Richard Arthur
D/12907, 8/4/18, L/C.; demob. 13/2/19.
247 St. Pauls Road, Preston, Lancashire.

HORNE, Edwin Chancellor
D/13729, 2/8/18; trfr. K.R. Rif. C., 7/4/19; Pte.
Studley House, 57 Hanworth Road, Hounslow.

✠ HORNE, Herbert George Macmillan
4/3/5111, 26/7/15; 19th Lond. R., 11/11/15, R.F.C.; F; 2/Lieut.
Killed in action 13/4/17.

HORNE, Lindsay Austin
K/B/2445, 28/12/14, Cpl.; R.W. Surr. R., 31/3/15, secd. R.E., att. Bedf. R.; F; Capt.; M.C.
Standard Bank of South Africa Ltd., 10 Clements Lane, E.C. (Now in Sudan.)

HORNE, Robert Cecil
3/3122, 27/3/15; R. Suss. R., 19/6/15; Lieut.
24 Oxford Street, Southampton.

HORNE, William Henry Dennis
B/13671, 29/7/18; dis. med. unfit, 4/3/19.
2 Clarence Gardens, Church End, Finchley, N. 3.

HORNER, Harry
6/3/8777, 1/1/16; No. 5 O.C.B., 14/8/16; Manch. R., 21/11/16; F,It,E,M; Capt.; M.B.E., M(1).
13 Dobroyd Street, Crumpsall, Manchester. (Now in India).

HORNER, John Kenneth Julian
6/4/5476, 9/8/15; Ches. R., 1/1/16; F; Lieut.; w.
11 Orford Road, Walthamstow.

HORNER, Walter Reginald
6/4/6356, 20/9/15; dis. med. unfit, 26/9/16.

✠ HORRABIN, Maurice Pinney
C/9963, 20/11/16, L/C.; No. 14 O.C.B., 30/1/17; E. Kent R., 25/4/17; F; 2/Lieut. Missing believed killed 30/11/17.

HORRELL, Joseph Betts
2/9789, 25/10/16, L/C.; No. 14 O.C.B., 30/1/17; R. Dub. Fus., 29/5/17; F; Lieut.; w-g; M.C.
R.I.C., Manorhamilton, Co. Leitrim, Ireland.

HORRIDGE, Frederick Randolph
C/D/12048, 27/9/17; Tank Corps C/S, 25/1/18; Tank Corps, 8/10/18; 2/Lieut. 11 Ducie Avenue, Bolton, Lancashire.

HORSFALL, Robert Eric
D/10864, 12/3/17; No. 11 O.C.B., 5/7/17; N. Lan. R., 30/10/17; Lieut. St. Andrew's Avenue, Ashton-on-Ribble, Preston.

HORSFIELD, Thomas
6/4/Sq/4130, 10/6/15; R.A., C/S, 29/1/16; R.F.A., 11/3/17; F; Lieut.; w. 55 Wickham Road, Brockley, S.E. 4.

HORSFORD, Frederick Cecil
2/3849, 31/5/15; R.F.A., 12/10/15; Lieut.

APPENDIX II.—RECORDS OF RANK AND FILE.

HORSFORD, Jack Tucker
4/1/4189, 14/6/15; R.W. Surr. R., 10/9/15; F; Lieut.
19b The Langeway, Winchmore Hill, N.

☦ HORSLEY, Ralph Neville
6/3/7454, 15/11/15, L/C.; Worc. R., 4/8/16; F; 2/Lieut.
Killed in action 27/8/17.

HORSLEY, William Ewart
6/2/7675, 22/11/15; W. Rid. R., 22/11/16; F; Capt.
1 Leicester Terrace, Halifax, Yorkshire.

HORTON, Henry
B/Sq/12323, 28/12/17, L/C.; No. 2 Cav. C/S, 11/4/18; R. Regt. of Cav., 18/10/18; 2/Lieut.
Wilsford, Pewsey, Wiltshire.

HORTON, Keith John Hoult
D/Sq/12948, 19/4/18; trfr. 14th Lond. R., 6/12/18.
c/o The Anglo-South American Central Club, 1 Queens Gate, S.W.7.

HORTON, Leslie Thornton
Sq/427, 25/5/09; dis. 15/8/10.
17 Bedford Row, W.C.1.

HORWILL, Frank Gregson
6/8795, 8/1/16; R.A., C/S, 9/6/16; R.F.A., 8/9/16; F; Lieut.
24 Windermere Road, Muswell Hill, N.10.

HOSACK, Kenneth Murray
A/13010, 1/5/18; No. 22 O.C.B., 7/6/18, No. 11 O.C.B.; General List, 8/3/19; 2/Lieut.

HOSEGOOD, Frank
6/9439, 12/2/16; R.A., C/S, 9/6/16; R.F.A., 23/9/16; F; Lieut.
Holmsley, Holway, Taunton.

HOSKEN, William Wesley
4/2/4310, 17/6/15; 7th Lond. R., 4/6/16; Lieut.
c/o James Hosken, 7 & 8 Idol Lane, E.C.

HOSKING, Richard Courtenay
C/Sq/13208, 5/6/18; No. 11 O.C.B., 31/1/19; General List, 8/3/19; 2/Lieut.
Rose Cottage, Byrne, Richmond, Natal, South Africa.

HOSKINS, Henry John
C/13300, 17/6/18, L/C.; trfr. 14th Lond. R., 6/12/18, Gord. Highrs.; Cpl.
41 Effingham Road, Hornsey, N.8.

☦ HOTCHKIS, Gilbert
4/3/4462, 28/6/15; Gord. Highrs., 1/1/16; 2/Lieut.
Killed in action 23/4/17.

HOTHAM, Thomas Burn
C/14269, 6/11/18; trfr. K.R. Rif. C., 25/4/19.
39a Brunswick Avenue, Beverley Road, Hull.

☦ HOUGHAM, Bertram William
K/C/2393, 17/12/14, L/C.; R.W. Kent. R., 13/6/15, att. R. Berks. R.; F; Capt.; M.C.
Killed in action 6/9/18.

HOUGHTON, Francis Cyril
C/10594, 22/1/17, L/C.; R.A., C/S, 6/6/17; R.G.A., 1/10/17; F; 2/Lieut.; w.
Barclay's Bank Ltd., Barton-on-Humber.

HOUGHTON, Harold
D/A/12892, 9/4/18; R.E., C/S, 11/10/18; demob. 27/1/19.
10 Lime Street, Southport, Lancashire.

HOUGHTON, John Benedict
3/3162, 1/4/15; Yorks. L.I., 28/7/15, M.G.C., att. M. of Munitions; F; Lieut.
Standon Road, Puckeridge, Nr. Ware, Hertfordshire.

HOUGHTON, Matthew Murtaugh
C/14239, 28/10/18; demob. 30/1/19.
2 York Road, Ilford, Essex.

☦ HOUGHTON, Noel
A/1048, 31/8/14, Sgt.; Notts. & Derby. R., 5/5/15; Lt.-Col.; M(1)
Killed in action 13/9/17.

HOUGHTON, William
A/K/2121, 16/11/14; R.E., 30/1/15; F; Major.
10 The Drive, Walthamstow, E.17.

☦ HOUGHTON, William
K/2385, 17/12/14; R. Fus., 18/12/14, att. R.W. Fus.; 2/Lieut.
Killed in action 9/4/16.

HOUSE, Donald Victor
A/13034, 4/5/18; R.A., C/S, 26/7/18; R.G.A., 7/4/19; 2/Lieut.
73 Newsham Drive, Liverpool.

☦ HOUSECROFT, Harold
A/900, 5/8/14; E. Surr. R., 15/8/14; 2/Lieut.
Killed in action 19/11/14.

☦ HOUSEHOLD, Ernest Scott
6/1/8172, 6/12/15; No. 14 O.C.B., 30/10/16; Essex R., 24/1/17; 2/Lieut.
Died 22/7/17.

☦ HOUSTON, Kenneth D'Aguilar
A/1735, 15/10/14; 18th Lond. R., 18/3/15; Capt.; w.
Killed in action 24/3/18.

HOWARD, Alexander Newman
1/3543, 10/5/15, L/C.; Cold. Gds., 5/7/15; Lieut.; M.C.
Lynch House, Totteridge, Hertfordshire.

HOWARD, Arthur Henry
Sq/1136, 10/9/14; York. Huss., 10/9/14, att. W. York. R.; F; Capt.; O.B.E., M.C., M(1).
Brightwalton Rectory, Wantage.

HOWARD, Charles Edward
B/2752, 21/1/15, L/C.; K.R. Rif. C., 3/6/15; Lieut.; w(3), p.
Sundial, Cooden, Bexhill, Sussex.

☦ HOWARD, Douglas Edward
6/4/5301, 2/8/15; R. Lanc. R., 12/6/16; 2/Lieut.
Killed in action 20/9/17.

HOWARD, Ernest Dudley
K/C/6/3/2378, 17/12/14, Cpl.; R.F.C., 21/7/16, R.A.F.; F; Lieut.; w.
25 Charlbury Road, Oxford.

HOWARD, Geoffrey
E/1514, 1/10/14; R. Fus., 27/11/14, att. R.F.C.; Lieut.
24 Inverness Terrace, W.2.

HOWARD, George Wren
D/1400, 29/9/14, L/C.; K.R. Rif. C., 17/12/14; F,It; Capt.; M.C.
11 Briardale Gardens, Hampstead, N.W.3.

HOWARD, Guy Bertram Charles
B/272, 11/6/08; dis. 10/6/09; rej. A/1178, 14/9/14, L/C.; K.R. Rif. C., 18/11/14, R.E.; Capt.; w.
45 Leadenhall Street, E.C.

HOWARD, Henry Southey
D/1401, 29/9/14; R. War. R., 6/3/15; 2/Lieut.
The Corner House, Cobham, Surrey.

HOWARD, John Gulliver
6/2/6399, 23/9/15; Midd'x. R., 1/6/16, R.E.; F; Lieut.; M.C.
c/o H. A. Thorne Esq., Eastney, Kent.

HOWARD, Kingsley Newman
K/A/3/2229, 3/12/14, C.Q.M.S.; A.S.C., C/S, 1/9/16; R.A.S.C., 25/10/16; F; Capt.
7 Meadow Way, Weald Village, Harrow.

HOWARD, Langley Walter
1/4/3283, 15/4/15; North'd. Fus., 2/10/15, att. Durh. L.I.; Lieut.; w(2).
99 Airedale Avenue, Chiswick, W.4.

HOWARD, William Reginald
F/1765, 16/10/14; L'pool. R., 13/11/14, emp. M. of Nat. Service; Capt.

HOWARD-JONES, Glyn Howard. See JONES, G. H.

HOWARTH, Albert Frank
6/5/5442, 6/8/15; R.A., C/S, 13/10/16; R.F.A., 3/2/17; F,It; Lieut.
Breckside, Upper Faul Road, Maidstone.

HOWARTH, Herbert
D/11143, 30/4/17, Sgt.; demob. 29/1/19.
Palmer's School, Grays, Essex.

HOWDEN, Sidney Sleight
4/4150, 10/6/15; R.F.A., 7/10/15.
248 Cleethorpe Road, Grimsby.

HOWE, Albert Percy
E/2700, 18/1/15; R. Fus., 29/4/15, att. 11th Lond. R.; F; Lieut.
14 Alma Square, St. John's Wood, N.W.8.

HOWE, Frank William
B/13496, 9/7/18; demob. 30/1/19.
35 Addington Road, Bow, E.3.

HOWE, Harold Wilberforce
D/11137, 30/4/17; Garr. O.C.B., 5/10/17; Lab. Corps, 15/12/17, att. Rif. Brig. and Midd'x. R.; F; 2/Lieut.
7 Ox Lane, Harpenden.

HOWE, Harry Thomas
D/Sq/10915, 26/3/17, L/C.; No. 2 Cav. C/S, 11/1/18; R. Regt. of Cav., 22/6/18; 2/Lieut.
Dovedale, 9 Milton Road, West Bridgford, Nottinghamshire.

APPENDIX II.—RECORDS OF RANK AND FILE.

HOWE, Ivan Albert
6/5/5899, 30/8/15; R.G.A., 16/12/15; F; Major.
19 Eustace Street, Dublin, Ireland.

HOWE, Norman
6/4/6015, 2/9/15; R. Fus., 6/7/16; 2/Lieut.; w.

HOWE, Wilfred
6/4/5624, 16/8/15, Cpl.; W. York. R., 9/6/16, att. R.E.; F; Capt.
121 Upperthorpe Road, Sheffield, Yorkshire.

HOWELL, Arthur Hendrick Lewes
6/1/7923, 29/11/15, L/C.; Suff. R., 22/11/16, emp. M. of Labour; F; Lieut.; w.
c/o Capt. James Williams, Narbeth, Pembrokeshire.

HOWELL, Arthur Joseph Wareham
D/13929, 30/8/18; demob. 30/1/19.
Fern Villa, Long Lane, Church End, Finchley, N. 3.

HOWELL, George Frederick
6/1/8940, 17/1/16; K.R. Rif. C., 25/9/16; Capt.; w.
Devonshire House, Bexhill.

HOWELL, Harold John
6/4/5792, 23/8/15; No. 4 O.C.B., 7/3/16; R.F.C., 6/7/16.
The Villas, Bolsover, Chesterfield.

HOWELL, Idrys Llewelyn
6/8694, 4/1/16; R.A., C/S, 26/5/16; R.G.A., 30/8/16; F,It,E; Lieut.
35 Kensington Avenue, Victoria Park, Manchester.

HOWELL, Kenneth
A/11263, 14/5/17; trfr. Class W. Res., 15/4/18.
Pendennis, Clytha Park, Newport, Monmouthshire.

HOWELL, Norman Gwenwyn
F/1826, 16/10/14; R.G.A., 13/11/14; E; 2/Lieut.
c/o E. Davey Esq., Tower House, Dunmow, Essex.

HOWELL, Owen Bulmer
Sq/278, 18/6/08; dis. 17/6/09; R.F.C., 31/7/16, R.N.A.S., R.A.F.; Lieut.
35 Ovington Square, S.W. 3.

✠ HOWELL, Richard David
6/3/8988, 18/1/16; No. 13 O.C.B., 4/11/16; Welch R., 28/2/17; 2/Lieut.; M.C.
Killed in action 15/9/18.

HOWELL, Roland A.
F/1825, 16/10/14; R.A.S.C., 3/11/14; Lieut.
All Saints Vicarage, Derby.

HOWELL, Wilfred John
1/3639, 17/5/15, L/C.; R.W. Surr. R., 28/7/15; Capt.; w.

HOWELL-JONES, Howell Griffith
6/1/8679, 30/12/15, L/C.; R.W. Fus., 4/9/16; Lieut.

HOWELLS, David John
4/8637, 3/1/16; R.A., C/S, 14/9/16; R.F.A., 12/2/17; Lieut.
Bryn Hywel, Close Road, Morriston.

HOWELLS, James Aubrey
B/10344, 4/1/17, Sgt.; demob. 3/2/19.
Wootton, Woodstock, Oxon.

HOWELLS, Morgan Thomas
6/2/5302, 2/8/15, L/C.; Mon. R., 16/6/16; Lieut.
Babell Lyr, Ynysddn, Nr. Newport, Monmouthshire.

HOWELLS, Philip Ivor
6/4/7295, 8/11/15; Devon. R., 7/7/16; I,M; Lieut.
21 St. George Street, Swansea

HOWES, Herbert Henry
H/1873, 16/10/14; dis. 28/10/14.

HOWE-SUGG, Frank Reginald
6/2/9378, 8/2/16, Cpl.; Garr. O.C.B., 12/12/16; Manch. R., 10/3/17; Lieut.
The Studio, 12 St. Mary's Place, Newcastle-on-Tyne.

HOWIE, John Struthers
4/3/3968, 3/6/15; R.F.A., 13/9/15; F; Major; w(3), g; M.C.
c/o John Tucker Esq., 27 Chancery Lane, W.C. 2. (Now in Serbia.)

HOWIS, Arthur Wilfrid Heriot
C/10379, 8/1/17; No. 20 O.C.B., 7/6/17; trfr. 28th Lond. R., 11/8/17; F; Pte.
37 Wearbay Crescent, Folkestone.

HOWITT, Thomas Henry
A/11273, 14/5/17, L/C.; A.S.C., C/S, 1/9/17; R.A.S.C., 27/10/17; 2/Lieut.
Constitutional Club, Nottingham.

HOWLETT, Henry Evan
4/5/4672, 8/7/15; 7th Lond. R., 27/11/15, att. 10th Lond. R.; F,P,E; Staff Lieut.
103 Riverview Gardens, Barnes, S.W.13.

HOWLING, Gordon William
6/4/8135, 3/12/15; R.A., C/S, 23/6/16; R.G.A., 11/10/16; F; Major; M(1).
5 Portland Villas, Gravesend.

HOWORTH, Reginald Francis Park
4/6/1/4909, 16/7/15; K.R. Rif. C., 15/1/16; F; Lieut.; w; M.C
Fordell, Coniston Road, Blackburn.

HOYLAND, Harold Allan Dilke
K/H/2118, 16/11/14; Interpretership, 13/2/15; G; Major; M.B.E., Chevalier of the Royal Greek Order of the Redeemer, Serbian Order of the White Eagle (5th Class), M(2).
British Vice Consulate, Patras, Greece.

✠ HOYLE, William
6/2/8391, 14/12/15; No. 8 O.C.B., 4/8/16; E. York. R., 21/11/16; 2/Lieut.
Killed in action 9/4/17.

✠ HOYTE, Raymond Wilson
4/1/4074, 7/6/15; Notts. & Derby. R., 1/9/15; Lieut.
Killed in action 21/3/18.

HUBAND, Kenneth George
A/14327, 30/12/18; demob. 10/1/19.
Martyn Leigh, Station Road, Yardley, Birmingham.

✠ HUBBARD, Alfred William
4/2/3969, 3/6/15; R.W. Fus., 10/9/15; M; 2/Lieut.; M(1).
Killed in action 25/1/17.

HUBBARD, George Edward
6/5/5900, 30/8/15; trfr. R.G.A., 26/9/16; F; Cpl.
34 Bedford Square, W.C.1

HUBBARD, Henry
C/D/A/12071, 1/10/17; demob. 31/1/19.
North Devon Villa, Grange Park Road, Leyton, N.E.

HUCKER, James Reginald
4/1/3970, 3/6/15, L/C.; E. Surr. R., 19/8/15; F; Capt.; w; M.C., M(1).
20 Allfarthing Lane, Wandsworth, S.W. 18.

HUCKER, Thomas William
4/1/4589, 2/7/15, L/C.; E. Surr. R., 19/8/15; F; Staff Capt.; M.C., Croix de Guerre (Belge), M(2).
41d Spencer Park, Wandsworth Common, S.W. 18.

HUCKETT, William Henry
F/1854, 16/10/14; Durh. L.I., 10/12/14, Yorks. L.I.; 2/Lieut.
Strathmore, Lambert Road, Grimsby.

HUDD, Owen
D/12917, 10/4/18, L/C.; No. 21 O.C.B., 4/10/18, No. 18 O.C.B.; Wilts. R., 17/3/19; 2/Lieut.
Foghamshire Nursery, Chippenham, Wiltshire.

HUDDART, Lancelot Arthur
B/10966, 30/3/17; No. 12 O.C.B., 10/8/17; Bord. R., 27/11/17; F; Lieut.; w.
Hensingham Road, Whitehaven, Cumberland.

HUDDART, Richard Melvil Fane
K/E/2366, 17/12/14; R.E., 27/2/15; F; Capt.; w; M.C.
12 Lingfield Road, Wimbledon, S.W. 19.

HUDDLESTON, Norman Charles
4/5/4711, 9/7/15; Manch. R., 17/12/15, att. Intelligence Corps; F; Lieut.
Redclyffe, Hale, Cheshire.

✠ HUDLESTON, Harold Robert
3/3346, 22/4/15; Midd'x. R., 21/6/15; 2/Lieut.
Died of wounds 2/7/16.

HUDSON, Aelfric Henry
A/945, 5/8/14; 1st Lond. R., 28/9/14; F; Capt.; w.
Borden Vicarage, Stansted, Essex.

HUDSON, Charles
4/3/4573, 1/7/15; Yorks. L.I., 1/10/15; F; Capt.; M.B.E.
Bell House, Bierley Lane, Bradford, Yorkshire.

HUDSON, Charles Frederick
6/7735, 22/11/15; dis. med. unfit, 26/5/16.
Essenden, Tivoli Crescent, Brighton.

HUDSON, Eric Carew
B/950, 5/8/14; D. of Corn. L.I., 9/9/14, M.G.C.; F,S; Major; M.C., M(1).
3 Finch Lane, London, E.C. (Now in Hong Kong).

HUDSON, Frank
K/E/1/2288, 10/12/14, Cpl.; R.F.C., 9/7/15, R.A.F.; Capt.; M.C., M(1).

APPENDIX II.—RECORDS OF RANK AND FILE.

✠ HUDSON, *Godfrey*
A/1336, 26/9/14, L/C.; R.W. Kent. R., 14/11/14, M.G.C.; Major;
M.C. *Killed in action* 12/4/18.

HUDSON, *Herbert Ringer*
6/Sq/9430, 11/2/16; No. 1 Cav. C/S, 6/12/16; 1st Lanc.,
16/4/17; Lieut. *Wighton, Norfolk.*

HUDSON, *Hugh Persse*
C/10623, 26/1/17; R.W. Surr. R., 9/3/17; S; Lieut.
P.O. Box 287, Durban, Natal, South Africa.

HUDSON, *John Robert*
6/5/8173, 6/12/15; R.A., C/S, 14/7/16; R.G.A., 8/11/16; F;
Capt. *20 Clyde Road, Alexandra Park, N. 22.*

HUDSON, *Thompson*
6/Sq/6801, 13/10/15; No. 1 Cav. C/S, 24/4/16; Suff. Yeo.,
27/8/16, Indian Army; I,P; Lieut.; M(1).
31st D.C.O. Lancers, c/o Thos. Cook & Son, Bombay.

HUDSON, *Victor Reginald*
6/7736, 22/11/15; dis. med. unfit, 9/6/16.
6 Cannon Place, Brighton.

HUGGAN, *Robert Elliot-*
B/13415, 1/7/18; trfr. R. Highrs., 16/4/19; L/C.
136 Rawlinson Street, Barrow-in-Furness.

✠ HUGGETT, *Sydney George*
B/11420, 1/6/17; No. 14 O.C.B., 5/10/17; R. Suss. R., 26/2/18;
2/Lieut. *Killed in action* 18/9/18.

HUGGINS, *Arthur Percy*
6/B/8289, 10/12/15; R.F.A., C/S, 10/11/16; R.F.A., 16/9/17; F;
Lieut.
c/o Geo. F. Huggins & Coy. Ltd., Port of Spain, Trinidad, British West Indies.

HUGHES, *Alwyn Rigby*
3/9617, 15/9/16, L/C.; No. 14 O.C.B., 27/12/16; Dorset R.,
27/3/17, att. Hamps. R.; E,P; Lieut.; w.
23 Rutland Avenue, Sefton Park, Liverpool.

HUGHES, *Arthur George*
6/5/5981, 2/9/15; D. of Corn. L.I., 13/6/16; F; Capt.; w.
Cavendish Hull, Beckett Park, Leeds.

HUGHES, *Arthur Price*
6/2/5585, 12/8/15; R.W. Fus., 6/1/16; Capt.; w.
27 Hampstead Hill Gardens, N.W. 3.

HUGHES, *Basil*
K/F/2361, 9/12/14; R.E., 10/2/15; F; Major.
The Conifers, Woldingham, Surrey.

HUGHES, *Cecil Harold*
C/11513, 18/6/17; A.S.C., C/S, 1/9/17; R.A.S.C., 27/10/17; F;
Lieut. *Nat. Prov. & Union Bank Ltd., Westcliff-on-Sea.*

✠ HUGHES, *Cyril Ralph*
C/1335, 26/9/14; N. Lan. R., 24/11/14; Lieut.
Killed in action 4/7/16

HUGHES, *David Thomas*
D/13896, 23/8/18; demob. 24/1/19.
22 Alexandra Road, Winshill, Burton-on-Trent.

HUGHES, *Edmund John*
6/5/6529, 30/9/15; dis med. unfit, 22/5/16; Lab. Corps, 24/2/18;
Lieut. *2 Brynhyfryd, Aberdare, Glamorganshire.*

HUGHES, *Ednyfed Wynne*
6/8454, 17/12/15; R.A., C/S, 26/5/16; R.G.A., 18/8/16, secd
R.E.; F; Capt.; M(1). *Llys Elen, Pen-y-grves, North Wales.*

HUGHES, *Edward Mountfort*
6/1/7924, 29/11/15; Dorset R., 21/11/16, R.E.; F; Lieut.
Fernhurst, Blundellsands, Liverpool.

HUGHES, *Emrys*
6/2/5383, 5/8/15, Sgt.; R.A., C/S, 26/5/16; R.G.A., 30/8/16; F;
Capt.; M(2). *Dale House, Delph, Nr. Oldham, Lancashire.*

✠ HUGHES, *Eric James Walrond*
C/369, 20/3/09; dis. 9/3/12; Notts. & Derby. R., att. M.G.C;
Capt. *Killed in action* 20/9/17.

HUGHES, *Ernest Charles*
A/924, 5/8/14; Ches. R., 19/9/14, M.G.C.; F; Major; M.C.
c/o Messrs. Brunner Mond & Coy. Ltd., 2 Old Court House Corner, Calcutta, India.

HUGHES, *Frederick*
E/1561, 6/10/14; Devon. R., 9/12/14; F,M,I; Lieut.
c/o Cox & Coy., 16 Charing Cross, S.W. 1.

HUGHES, *Frederick Max*
B/12390, 15/1/18; demob. 29/1/19.
8 Fairholme Road, Great Crosby, Liverpool.

HUGHES, *Godfrey Roydon*
K/B/2106, 16/11/14; Hamps. R., 13/3/15; E,F; Lieut.; w.
Champabarie Tea Estate, Medley P.O. via Juri, Sythet, India.

HUGHES, *Harry Halmshaw*
6/2/7551, 17/11/15; Midd'x. R., 4/7/16, att. T.M. Bty.; F,S;
Capt.; w.; M(1). *Breeze Hill, Wistaston, Crewe, Cheshire.*

HUGHES, *Hugh Lewellyn*
6/3/7356, 10/11/15; No. 11 O.C.B., 7/5/16; Mon. R., 4/9/16; F;
Lieut.; w(2); M(1). *Ty Celyn, Pontypool Road, Monmouthshire.*

HUGHES, *James Allan*
6/3/6203, 13/9/15; R. Dub. Fus., 1/6/16, att. N. Lan. R.; M,SR;
Lieut.; M.C. *Elgin, Ontario, Canada.*

✠ HUGHES, *John*
4/2/4076, 7/6/15; R. War. R., 5/9/15; Lieut.; w; M.C.
Killed in action 9/10/17.

✠ HUGHES, *John Arthur*
E/1671, 12/10/14; R.W. Fus., 13/10/14; Lieut.
Died of wounds 26/1/15.

HUGHES, *John Edward*
A/14336, 30/12/18; No. 11 O.C.B., 24/1/19; demob. 6/2/19.
36 Cumberland Mansions, Bryanston Square, W. 1.

HUGHES, *John Edwyn*
6/1/8806, 10/1/16; No 14 O.C.B., 26/11/16; R.W. Fus., 27/3/17;
F; 2/Lieut. *Tegfan, Everard Road, Colwyn Bay.*

✠ HUGHES, *John Meirion*
6/5/6503, 28/9/15; S. Lan. R., 22/1/16, att. R.A.F.; F; Lieut.
Killed in action 16/6/18.

HUGHES, *Leonard Victor*
6/Sq/6377, 20/9/15; No. 2 Cav. C/S, 31/3/16; Wilt. Yeo.,
19/8/16; 2/Lieut. *Coulston Rectory, Westbury, Wiltshire.*

HUGHES, *Michael Wyndham*
C/267, 2/6/08; dis. 1/6/09. *14a Electric Avenue, Brixton, S.W.*

HUGHES, *Morris*
A/11932, 30/8/17; R.E., C/S, 11/11/17; R.E., 21/12/17; F;
2/Lieut. *83 Crowbridge Road, Cardiff, South Wales.*

HUGHES, *Percy Bartlett*
6/Sq/7320, 8/11/15; No. 1 Cav. C/S, 2/8/16; West. & Cumb.
Yeo., 27/11/16; Lieut. *54 West Bank Road, Birkenhead.*

HUGHES, *Reginald Frank*
A/10497, 15/1/17; R.G.A., C/S, 16/5/17; R.G.A., 17/9/17;
2/Lieut. *2 Wallingford Avenue, W. 10.*

HUGHES, *Reginald Hamilton*
6/Sq/5937, 1/9/15; A.S.C., C/S, 1/5/16; R.A.S.C., 4/6/16; F;
Lieut.; Inj. *Davies Benachi & Coy., Orleans House, Liverpool.*

HUGHES, *Stanislaus Thomas*
6/3/8638, 3/1/16; R.A., C/S, 4/8/16; R.G.A., 24/11/16; F;
Lieut.; w. *Cornfield Villas, Linthorpe Road, Middlesbrough, Yorkshire.*

HUGHES, *Thomas William*
C/A/12086, 4/10/17; R.F.C., C/S, 15/2/18; trfr. R.A.F.,
15/2/18. *Grove House, Caerwys, Flintshire.*

HUGHES, *Vernon Hugh*
4/2/4338, 21/6/15; R.G.A., 8/10/15, R.A.F.; F; Lieut.; Italian
Silver Medal for Military Valour.
680 Madison Avenue, New York City, U.S.A.

HUGHES, *William Charles*
B/10544, 17/1/17; No. 11 O.C.B., 5/7/17; R.W. Fus., 30/10/17;
F; Lieut. *1 Park Villas, Mold, North Wales.*

HUGHES, *William Henry*
6/5/5936, 1/9/15, L/C.; L'pool. R., 1/6/16; F; Lieut.; w.
12 Meddowcroft Road, Wallasey, Cheshire.

✠ HUGHES-HUGHES, *William Montagu*
A/478, 5/4/10, L/C.; Welch R., 12/9/14; F; Capt.
Killed in action 25/9/15.

HUGHES-JONES, *John Trevor*
E/1501, 1/10/14; R.A.O.C., 22/1/15; F; Major; O.B.E., M(2).
21 Bentley Road, Princes Park, Liverpool

APPENDIX II.—RECORDS OF RANK AND FILE.

HUGMAN, *Robert Llewellyn*
6/4/9355, 7/2/16; No. 11 O.C.B., 7/5/16; M.G.C., 4/9/16; Lieut.; M.C.
c/o H. V. Ellis Esq., *19 St. Andrew's Mansions, Dorset Street, Portman Square, W. 1.*

HULL, *Edward*
A/14135, 10/10/18; trfr. 14th Lond. R., 6/12/18.

HULL, *Wilfrid*
6/5/7014, 26/10/14; Bord. R., 4/9/16, att. 16th Lond. R.; F; Lieut.; Inv. *2 Ribblesdale Place, Preston, Lancashire.*

HULME, *Robert Lawrence*
4/1/4574, 1/7/15; 2nd Lond. R., 3/12/15; F; Major; M.C., M(2)
89 Clifton Road, Prestwich, Manchester. (Now in South America).

HULSE, *James Frederic Ewart*
A/10034, 29/11/16; trfr. R.F.A., 27/4/17; Pte.
Green Bank Farm, Gatley, Cheshire.

HULTON, *John Barnes*
E/14093, 2/10/18; demob. 10/1/19.
Mayfield, Albany Road, Douglas, Isle of Man.

HUMBERT, *Charles*
Sq/601, 22/1/12; dis. 29/10/12; rej. Sq/892, 5/8/14; 11th R. Regt. of Cav., 12/9/14, 10th Huss.; Lieut.; w.
Troy Orchard, West Hyde, Nr. Rickmansworth, Hertfordshire.

✠ HUMBERT, *Ernest Graham Johnston*
C/A/907, 5/8/14, L/C.; R. Berks. R., 20/10/14, att. Hamps. R.; G; Lieut. *Died of wounds 8/6/15.*

HUMBLE, *William Franklin*
K/Sq/2312, 10/12/14, L/C.; York. Huss., 19/3/15, att. W. York R.; F; Capt.; w(2). *Westfield, Ilkley, Yorkshire.*

HUMPHREY, *Frederick George*
A/10608, 22/1/17; No. 20 O.C.B., 7/6/17; L'pool. R., 25/9/17, emp. M. of Labour; 2/Lieut.
Gernant, The Walk, Merthyr Tydfil, South Wales.

HUMPHREY, *Gwilym Pritchard*
4/1/5011, 22/7/15; D. of Corn. L.I., 1/6/16, Som. L.I., Dorset R.,; M; Lieut. *Hendrewaelod, Glan Conway, North Wales.*

HUMPHREY, *Norman*
2/3779, 27/5/15; York. R., 10/9/15, R.W. Fus., S. Wales Bord.; 2/Lieut.

HUMPHREY, *Sydney Knight Forbes Phillips*
6/D/9261, 29/1/16, L/C.; R.N.A.S., 23/2/17, R.A.F.; Lieut.

HUMPHREY, *William Henry Eustace*
K/2970, 25/2/15; R.E., 4/3/15; Major.
Kenton, Great Marlow.

HUMPHREY-MOORE, *Montague Edwin*
6/1/7233, 5/11/15; Manch. R., 4/8/16; Lieut.; w.
Casteldar, Webster Gardens, Ealing, W. 5.

HUMPHREYS, *Herbert Philip Wynne*
K/Sq/2492, 31/12/14; R.F.A., 27/2/15; F; Capt.; w(2); M.C.
Thornby Vicarage, Tow Law, Durham.

HUMPHREYS, *Humphrey Dight*
D/10552, 17/1/17; R.F.C., C/S, 13/3/17; R.F.C., 19/4/17, R.A.F.; Lieut. *1 Knowsley Road, Cressington Park, Liverpool.*

HUMPHREYS, *John David*
4/Sq/4339, 21/6/15; R.G.A., 20/11/15; F; Capt.
Alexandra Buildings, Hong Kong.

HUMPHREYS, *Rhys*
4/2/4673, 8/7/15; Welch R., 30/8/15; 2/Lieut.

✠ HUMPHREYS, *Richard Grain*
4/1/4646, 5/7/15; K.R. Rif. C., 5/11/15; 2/Lieut.
Killed in action 28/9/17.

HUMPHREYS, *William Herbert*
B/E/13566, 19/7/18; No. 22 O.C.B., 20/9/18; R.W. Fus., 5/2/19; 2/Lieut. *5 Hamilton Street, Hoole, Chester.*

✠ HUMPHREYS, *William Thomas*
K/A/2186, 26/11/14, L/C.; R. Fus., 13/3/15; Capt.
Killed in action 4/10/18.

HUMPHRIES, *Ernest Augustus*
C/D/14277, 8/11/18; demob. 30/5/19.
2 Foster Road, Chiswick, W. 4

HUMPHRISS, *Alfred Ernest*
6/3/8174, 6/12/15, Sgt.; M.G.C., 24/10/16; Lieut.

HUMPHRY, *John McNab*
6/1/6284, 16/9/15, L/C.; No. 9 O.C.B., 6/3/16; Arg. & Suth'd. Highrs., 6/7/16; F; Lieut.; w(2); M.C., Croix de Guerre (French). *Sudan Club, Khartoum, Sudan.*

HUNT, *Archibald*
C/D/12049, 27/9/17; No. 11 O.C.B., 5/4/18; trfr. 28th Lond. R., 6/9/18. *Parsonage Street, Halstead, Essex.*

HUNT, *Arthur Adrian*
5/4/5007, 21/7/15; R.E., 21/12/15; F,M; Lieut.
The Crescent, Crescent Road, Burgess Hill, Sussex.

HUNT, *Charles Anthony*
C/11486, 14/6/17; Garr. O.C.B., 5/10/17; Lab. Corps, 15/12/17, att. R. Suss. R.; F; 2/Lieut.
17 Gwendolen Avenue, Putney, S.W. 15.

HUNT, *Charles William Stanley*
A/Sq/12485, 29/1/18; No. 1 Cav C/S, 3/9/18; 3rd R. Regt. of Cav., 12/3/19; 2/Lieut.
7 Montrell Road, Streatham Hill, S.W. 2.

✠ HUNT, *Claude Holdsworth*
Sq/379, 24/3/09; dis. 16/9/11; rej. K/2289, 10/12/14, L/C.; R.F.A., 4/1/15; Capt.; w; M(1). *Died of wounds 2/4/17.*

HUNT, *Cyril George*
A/11647, 12/7/17; No. 14 O.C.B., 7/12/17; E. Surr. R., 28/5/18; 2/Lieut. *22 Park Road, East Twickenham.*

✠ HUNT, *David Reginald*
A/10507, 15/1/17; R.F.C., C/S, 16/4/17; R.F.C., 16/5/17, R.A.F.; F; 2/Lieut. *Killed in action 18/8/18.*

HUNT, *Edward Geoffrey*
6/1/7144, 2/11/15, L/C.; No. 11 O.C.B., 7/5/16; Midd'x. R., 4/9/16; Lieut.; w. *Waverley Court, Camberley.*

HUNT, *Eric Bernard Kenneth*
4/1/4221, 14/6/15; R.W. Kent R., 5/11/15, Lab. Corps; F; Capt.; w. *15 Kenilworth Avenue, Wimbledon, S.W. 19.*

HUNT, *George William*
C/12602, 13/2/18, L/C.; R.E., C/S, 16/6/18; R.E., 9/2/19; 2/Lieut. *Ryecroft, Park Road, Watford.*

HUNT, *Herbert Richard van Hoytema*
6/5/8175, 6/12/15; M.G.C., 24/10/16; F; Lieut.; w.
Farnsfield, Nr. Southwell, Nottinghamshire.

HUNT, *John Durell*
C/D/14216, 23/10/18; trfr. K.R. Rif. C., 29/5/19.
Ryecroft, Park Road, Watford

HUNT, *John Willets Bertram*
Sq/660, 19/11/12, L/C.; Linc. Yeo., 19/1/15, M.G.C.; E,P,F; Capt. *New University Club, 57 St. James Street, S.W. 1.*

HUNT, *Lionel Neil*
6/2/B/6791, 13/10/15; R.A., C/S, 29/12/16; R.G.A., 27/3/17; F; 2/Lieut.; w. *Arbury, 23 Gordon Road, Wanstead, E. 11.*

HUNT, *Martin Meadows*
F/1796, 16/10/14; Paymaster, 7/12/14; F; Capt.
Newholme, West Hill, Putney, S.W. 15.

HUNT, *Oliver Graham*
Sq/304, 29/6/08; dis. 17/1/10; R. Lanc. R., 23/10/14; Capt.; w; M(1). *36 Albion Street, W.*

HUNT, *Percival Godwin*
2/3492, 6/5/15; Yorks. L.I., 28/7/15, M.G.C.; F; Lieut.; w.
2 Mill Lane, West Hampstead, N.W. 6

HUNT, *William Arthur*
A/B/13950, 4/9/18; No. 24 O.C.B., 15/11/18; Tank Corps, 22/3/19; 2/Lieut. *4 Courtfield Gardens, Ealing, W. 13.*

✠ HUNTER, *Alec Guy Bayntum Field*
C/13270, 12/6/18; No. 22 O.C.B., 23/8/18; *Died 16/12/18.*

HUNTER, *Bertrand Robert*
A/13088, 20/5/18; trfr. Class W. Res., 19/11/18.

HUNTER, *Clarence Dyall*
C/11487, 14/6/17; Garr. O.C.B., 28/12/17; 1st Lond. R., 22/6/18, att. 29th Lond. R.; 2/Lieut.
30 Cann Hall Road, Leytonstone, E. 11.

APPENDIX II.—RECORDS OF RANK AND FILE.

HUNTER, Edmund Kent
6/5/7676, 22/11/15; No. 14 O.C.B., 28/8/16; Norf. R., 22/11/16, M.G.C.; F; Lieut.
39 Panmuir Road, West Wimbledon, S.W. 20.

HUNTER, Eric Aloysius Joseph
6/3/6461, 27/9/15; No. 9 O.C.B., 8/3/16; High. L.I., 4/8/16; F,E; Lieut.; w.
12 Oxford Terrace, Kelvinside North, Glasgow.

HUNTER, Ernest Langton
2/6/6506, 29/9/15; R.F.A., C/S, 26/3/16; R.F.A., 1/9/16; Lieut.
The Shanty, Stormont Road, Highgate, N. 6.

HUNTER, Ernest Samuel
C/Sq/10843, 7/3/17; No. 19 O.C.B., 9/11/17; R. Ir. Regt., 26/3/18; F; 2/Lieut.
Fieldhead, Brighouse, Yorkshire.

HUNTER, Gerald Arthur
3/9618, 18/9/16, Cpl.; No. 14 O.C.B., 5/3/17; Dorset R., 26/6/17, R.A.F.; Lieut.; w.
Edgemoor, Broad Lane, Hale, Cheshire.

✠ HUNTER, Godfrey Jackson
Sq/858, 4/8/14; 5th Lanc., 15/8/14; 2/Lieut.
Killed in Dublin riots 26/4/16.

HUNTER, Hugh Stewart
B/376, 22/3/09; dis.
33 Museum Street, W.C. 1.

HUNTER, John
K/2477, 28/12/14; Glouc. R., 27/3/15, Intelligence; F; Capt.; M(1).
5 Holly Bush Lane, Harpenden, Hertfordshire.

HUNTER, John
6/1/8677, 4/1/16, L/C.; L'pool. R., 25/9/16, att. No. 10 O.C.B., Inst; F; Capt.; w; M.C.
1 St. Annes Churchyard, Manchester.

HUNTER, Murland
E/2990, 1/3/15; dis. 21/12/15; R.N.A.S., R.A.F.; NR; Capt.
13 Blenheim Road, Bedford Park, W. 4.

HUNTER, Robert Henry Stuart
3/6/8639, 3/1/16; R.F.C., 7/8/16; F; Capt.
7 Woodfield Park Drive, Leigh-on-Sea, Essex, (Now in F.M.S.)

HUNTER, Robert Leslie
A/13011, 1/5/18; No. 1 O.C.B., 8/11/18; Arg. & Suth'd. Highrs., 17/3/19; 2/Lieut.
Newlands House, Polmont, Stirlingshire, N.B.

HUNTER, Simon
C/14115, 9/10/18; demob. 30/1/19.
Sowerby Grange, Northallerton, Yorkshire.

HUNTER, Thomas Stevenson
6/4/9565, 28/3/16; A.S.C., C/S, 27/10/16; R.A.S.C., 20/12/16; F; Lieut.
Woodford, Dumfries, N.B.

HUNTER, William Irvine
B/12334, 31/12/17, Cpl.; demob. 5/2/19.
9 South Gillsland Road, Edinburgh.

✠ HUNTER, William Stuart
6/4/8943, 17/1/16; No. 8 O.C.B., 4/8/16, M.G.C., C/S; Linc. R., 18/12/16; F; Capt.
Killed in action 31/7/17.

HUNTER-BLAIR, James. See BLAIR, J. H.

HUNTINGTON, John Francis
B/2628, 2/1/15; 22nd Lond. R., 13/3/15; F,S,E; Lieut.
Formo, Malvern, Worcestershire.

HUNTINGTON, John Wright
4/3/4463, 28/6/15; Yorks. L.I., 11/11/15; F; Lieut.; w(3).
Ousedene, Goole, Yorkshire.

HURLEY, Henry Alfred
4/2/4603, 5/7/15; 18th Lond. R., 29/10/15, att. 19th Lond. R.; F,S,P; Capt.
c/o National Safe Deposit Coy. Ltd., 1 Queen Victoria Street, E.C. 4.

HURNDALL, Robert Kenneth Featherstone
6/Sq/7925, 29/11/15, L/C.; No. 1 Cav. C/S, 24/4/16; North'd. Huss., 28/7/16, M.G.C.; Lieut.

HURST, A. R. B. See BURNETT-HURST, A. R.

✠ HURST, John Julian
4/3731, 24/5/15; 22nd Lond. R., 16/11/15; Lieut.
Killed in action 31/10/17.

HURST, Joseph Gerard
6/5/7417, 12/11/15, L/C.; Yorks. L.I., 24/10/16; F; Lieut.; w.
The Mickering, Aughton, Nr. Ormskirk, Lancashire.

HURST, Mervyn Colvin
6/D/12012, 17/9/17, L/C.; No. 13 O.C.B., 5/4/18; Essex R. 29/10/18, att. Lab. Corps; 2/Lieut.
Asheldham Chase, Southminster, Essex.

✠ HURST, Richard Henry
D/10387, 8/1/17, L/C.; No. 14 O.C.B., 7/6/17; L'pool. R., 25/9/17, att. Norf. R.; E,P,F; 2/Lieut.
Killed in action 29/9/18.

✠ HURSTBOURNE, Walter Hirsch
4/4311, 17/6/15; R.F.A., 26/11/15; 2/Lieut.
Killed in action 23/6/17.

HURTZIG, George Harry Gubb
B/11394, 30/5/17; R.E., C/S, 30/9/17; R.E., 9/11/17; Germ.E&WA.
c/o Standard Bank of South Africa, 10 Clements Lane, E.C.

✠ HUSBAND, Peter Ross
6/8529, 29/12/15; No. 9 O.C.B., 8/3/16; R. Highrs., 6/7/16; 2/Lieut.
Killed in action 25/9/16.

HUSS, Thomas Charles Sebastin
4/3405, 26/4/15; dis. 26/4/15; Welch R., 8/6/15; S,F,It; Lieut.; p by Turks and escaped, re-captured by "U" Boat.
Evelyn Street, Bute Docks, Cardiff.

HUSSEY, Glen Owen
B/1668, 10/10/14; R. Fus., 10/2/15; 2/Lieut.

✠ HUSSEY, Harold Edward
B/820, 4/8/14; dis. 4/9/14; Devon. R., 5/8/16, att. Manch. R.; 2/Lieut.
Killed in action 25/3/17.

HUSSEY, Reginald Edward
D/10021, 27/11/16; R.A., C/S, 9/3/17; R.F.A., 5/8/17, R.A.F.; F; Lieut.
Folkestone House, Grange Gardens, Cardiff.

HUSTLER, Colonel Bedford
6/4/D/8938, 12/1/16; No. 14 O.C.B., 30/10/16; 9th Lond. R., 24/1/17, R.E.; F; Capt.
18 Church Street, Castleford, Yorkshire.

HUTCHENS, William Edward
D/9990, 22/11/16; R.A., C/S, 9/3/17; R.F.A., 5/8/17, att. H.A.C.; G,F,E; Lieut.; w.
56 Belsize Park Gardens, Hampstead, N.W.

HUTCHESON, Hugh Francis
A/11899, 23/8/17; No. 14 O.C.B., 7/12/17; Arg. & Suth'd. Highrs., 28/5/18, att. Linc. R.; 2/Lieut.
Denbigh Mansions Hotel, 39 Charlwood Street, S.W. 1.

✠ HUTCHESON, John
A/1969, 26/10/14; Notts. & Derby. R., 3/12/14; 2/Lieut.
Killed in action 8/9/15.

HUTCHINGS, Samuel Frank
6/1/9048, 21/1/16, L/C.; No. 14 O.C.B., 26/11/16; Devon. R., 27/3/17, att. Hamps. R.; Lieut.
4 Megla Villas, Warberry Road, Torquay.

HUTCHINGS, William Stanley
6/4/9188, 28/1/16; No. 8 O.C.B., 4/8/16; Manch. R., 21/11/16; Lieut.
New Road, Bideford, North Devonshire.

HUTCHINS, Frederick Henry
4/1/4464, 28/6/15, Sgt.; 11th Lond. R., 25/9/16, att. 4th Lond R. and R.A.O.C.; F; Capt.; w.
96 Streathbourne Road, Upper Tooting, S.W. 17.

HUTCHINS, William
C/12229, 16/11/17, Sgt.; No. 22 O.C.B., 7/6/18; Hamps. R., 11/2/19; 2/Lieut.
4 Beaconsfield Road, Basingstoke, Hampshire

HUTCHINSON, Charles Reginald Herbert
C/10814, 2/3/17; R.F.A., C/S, 22/6/17; trfr. R.F.A., 20/10/17.
29 Springfield Crescent, Lidget Green, Bradfora.

HUTCHINSON, Denis Fawcett
D/12097, 8/10/17, Cpl.; No. 11 O.C.B., 7/6/18; Devon. R., 5/2/19; 2/Lieut.
Glenluce, Dinas Powis, Glamorganshire.

✠ HUTCHINSON, Edgar Francis
K/F/2335, 14/12/14; York. R., 12/3/15; 2/Lieut.
Died of wounds 24/5/15.

HUTCHINSON, Edward Thomas
6/7677, 22/11/15; dis. med. unfit, 9/6/16; Lab. Corps, 23/8/17; F; Lieut.
Carisbrooke Road, Knighton, Leicester.

APPENDIX II.—RECORDS OF RANK AND FILE.

HUTCHINSON, *Francis Egerton*
6/4/7455, 15/11/15; A.S.C., C/S, 8/5/16; R.A.S.C., 11/6/16; Lieut.

HUTCHINSON, *Francis Graham*
B/D/Sq/12024, 20/9/17; No. 2 Cav. C/S, 11/4/18; 6th R. Regt of Cav., 15/2/19; 2/Lieut.
Tiger's Head, Southend, Catford, S.E. 6.

HUTCHINSON, *Godfrey Cresswell*
Sq/2065, 12/11/14; R.F.A., 24/11/14; F; Lieut.
35 Ovington Square, S.W. 3.

HUTCHINSON, *Herbert John*
D/13844, 16/8/18; demob. 4/2/19.
4 Lenham Road, Lee, S.E. 12.

HUTCHINSON, *Hubert Gerald*
H/1956, 26/10/14; R. Marines, 30/11/14, R.F.C.; w.
20 Arundel Gardens, W. 11.

✠ HUTCHINSON, *John Clifford*
6/3/5454, 7/8/15; E. Surr. R., 3/1/16; Lieut.
Killed in action 22/3/18.

HUTCHISON, *Ernest William Andrew Kennedy*
Sq/2983, 27/2/15; R.A.S.C., 10/6/15; F; Capt.; Inj.
c/o Sir C. R. McGrigor Bart. & Coy., 39 Panton Street, S.W. 1.

HUTCHISON, *Legh Richmond*
K/D/2469, 28/12/14; R.A.S.C., 23/3/15, Hamps. R., M.G.C.; F; Major; w; M.C.
Maddox Farm, Little Bookham, Surrey.

HUTH, *Noel H. P.*
6/Sq/6147, 9/9/15, L/C.; R.G.A., 23/12/15; F; Capt.
243 Goldhurst Terrace, N.W. 6.

HUTSON, *Douglas James*
1/3437, 1/5/15; N. Mid. Div. Cyc. Coy., 17/9/15, M.G.C.; Lieut.; w.
Alderley House, Park Avenue, Wisbech.

✠ HUTSON, *Harry Austen*
K/A/2494, 31/12/14; Lan. Fus., 6/4/15; Capt.; w.
Killed in action 28/5/18.

HUTSON, *Stanley Herbert*
1/3714, 22/5/15; N. Mid. Div. Cyc. Coy., 21/9/15; F,It; Lieut.
West Parade, Wisbech, Cambridgeshire.

HUTTON, *Archibald Winder*
K/A/2485, 28/12/14; Sea. Highrs., 22/1/15; ✠,SR; Capt.; w(2); M.C., M(1).
c/o Messrs. Shaw Wallace, & Coy., P.O. 14, Madras, India.

HUTTON, *David*
6/5/5384, 5/8/15; Gord. Highrs., 22/11/15; F; Lieut.; M.C.
15 Lonsdale Street, Belleknowes, Dunedin, New Zealand.

HUTTON, *Herbert Malcolm*
B/9892, 10/11/16; R.F.C., C/S, 13/3/17; R.F.C., 19/4/17, R.A.F.; Lieut.
3 Lyndewode Road, Cambridge.

HUTTON, *Sydney*
B/11329, 21/5/17; No. 10 O.C.B., 5/10/17; War. Yeo., 26/2/18; 2/Lieut.
Kineton, Warwickshire.

HUTTON, *Thomas James*
B/12339, 1/1/18; No. 12 O.C.B., 10/5/18; trfr. 28th Lond. R., 18/11/18.
Wayside, Streetly, Birmingham.

HUXLEY, *Roy Hammond*
C/Sq/9925, 15/11/16, Sgt.; No. 2 Cav. C/S, 11/4/18; 6th R. Regt. of Cav., 18/10/18; 2/Lieut.
Hillside, Turners Hill, Worth, Sussex.

HUXSTER, *John Nunn*
A/11604, 5/7/17, L/C.; No. 14 O.C.B., 4/1/18; S. Lan. R., 25/6/18; F; 2/Lieut.
Tangley, Guernsey Grove, Herne Hill, S.E. 23.

HUXTABLE, *John Ridd*
D/10397, 8/1/17; No. 20 O.C.B., 7/6/17; Durh. L.I., 25/9/17; F; Capt.; w.
Poyers, Wrafton, Barnstaple, North Devonshire.

HUXTABLE, *William Richard*
F/1712, 15/10/14; W. Rid. R., 25/1/15, att. R.A.S.C.; F; Capt.; w(2); M(1).
c/o Tredegar Coy., 60 Fenchurch Street, E.C.

✠ HYATT, *Valentine*
A/11288, 16/5/17; R.F.C., C/S, 2/8/17; R.F.C., 8/9/17; F; 2/Lieut.
Killed in action 24/3/18.

HYDE, *Arthur Reginald*
A/10711, 12/2/17, L/C.; R.G.A., C/S, 21/11/17; R.G.A., 29/4/18; F; 2/Lieut.
22 Hilldown Road, Streatham, S.W. 16.

HYDE, *Bryan*
B/13672, 29/7/18; trfr. K.R. Rif. C., 25/4/19.
Bredbury Hall, Nr. Stockport, Cheshire.

HYDE, *Cyril James*
4/5012, 22/7/15; trfr. N. Lan. R., 9/6/16; Lan. Fus., 29/8/17; F; Lieut.; w.
Junior Army and Navy Club, Horse Guards Avenue, Whitehall, S.W. 1.

HYDE, *Edward Forester*
A/10516, 15/1/17; No. 21 O.C.B., 5/5/17, Garr. O.C.B.; Lab. Corps, 18/8/17, 1st Lond. R.; F; Lieut.; w.
13 Dryden Mansions, W. 14.

HYDE, *Henry Barry*
6/5333, 2/8/15; dis. 18/8/15.

HYDE, *William Denis*
6/4/9578, 5/5/16; R.A., C/S, 7/8/16; R.F.A., 3/12/16; w.
Clayton House, Chester.

✠ HYLAND, *Albert Clive*
Sq/515, 4/11/10; dis. 13/11/13; rej. Sq/2099, 16/11/14, Cpl.; R.A.S.C., 28/1/15, att. E. Kent R.; F; Capt.
Died of wounds 10/8/18.

HYLAND, *James Columba*
B/A/Sq/12313, 17/12/17; trfr. 28th Lond. R., 13/9/18, R.A.S.C.; Pte.
1 Linenhall Street, Banbridge, Co. Down.

HYLTON-GARDNER, *Guy Stanley*
Sq/A/11605, 5/7/17; No. 2 Cav. C/S, 13/7/17; 3rd Huss., 14/12/17.
48 Grosvenor Square, W.

HYNES, *Charles Stanley*
C/12640, 22/2/18; Sig. C/S, 14/6/18; R.E., 24/3/19; 2/Lieut.
10 Perham Road, Barons Court, W. 14.

HYSLOP, *Andrew John*
4/2/4340, 21/6/15; R.W. Surr. R., 17/1/16; Lieut.
35 Milk Street, E.C.

I'ANSON, *William Mangles*
K/F/3/2387, 17/12/14, L/C.; trfr. Class W. Res., 3/2/17.
Bardencroft, Saltburn-by-the-Sea, Yorkshire.

IBBETSON, *Ernest Frederick Ilford*
6/3/5725, 19/8/15; dis. med. unfit, 22/5/16.
29 Addiscombe Grove, Croydon, Surrey.

IBBETSON, *Francis George*
4/3/4170, 12/6/15; General List, 21/4/16; Lieut.
3 Addiscombe Grove, Croydon, Surrey.

IBBOTSON, *James Gordon*
A/11627, 9/7/17; No. 14 O.C.B., 9/11/17; Glouc. R., 30/4/18; F; 2/Lieut.
26 Claremont Road, Highgate, N. 6.

✠ IBBS, *John Thomas*
6/2/7527, 16/11/15; Worc. R., 4/9/16; 2/Lieut.
Died of wounds 20/3/17.

ICKRINGILL, *Clifford Stanley*
6/1/8812, 10/1/16; R.E., C/S, 5/8/16; R.E., 21/10/16; F; Lieut.; w.
Inglehurst, Rawdon, Nr. Leeds, Yorkshire.

IDDON, *George Gastall*
6/5/8548, 30/12/15, Sgt.; S. Lan. R., 18/12/16; Lieut.
Harding Mount, Northumberland Avenue, Bispham, Nr. Blackpool.

IDLE, *Francis Park*
D/11130, 30/4/17; No. 12 O.C.B., 10/8/17; 7th Lond. R., 27/11/17, att. 1st Lond. R.; F; Lieut.
8 Lewisham Hill, S.E. 13. (Now in Canada)

IDRIS, *John Hugh Williams*
H/2/1830, 16/10/14, Cpl.; 19th Lond. R., 29/5/15, att. 6th Lond. R.; Capt.; M.C.
4 St. Albans Villas, Highgate Road, Highgate, N.W. 5.

ILES, *Noel Lancelot*
6/5/7610, 19/11/15; R.A., C/S, 29/9/16; R.F.A., 20/1/17; Lieut.; M.C.
Park Farm, Fairford, Gloucestershire.

ILLINGWORTH, *Robert Leslie*
H/2685, 14/1/15, L/C.; Notts. & Derby R., 13/6/15, att. American Forces; F; Capt.; D.S.O., M.C. and Bar, M(2).
43 Bryanston Street, Marble Arch, W. 1.

ILLINGWORTH, *Vivian Richard*
B/12794, 18/3/18; No. 18 O.C.B., 20/9/18; R.W. Fus., 17/3/19; 2/Lieut.
Arnside, St. Athan, Nr. Cardiff, South Wales.

APPENDIX II.—RECORDS OF RANK AND FILE.

IMESON, *Cecil Charles*
6/2/7678, 22/11/15; No. 8 O.C.B., 4/8/16, M.G.C., C/S.; M.G.C., 28/10/16, Tank Corps; Lieut.

IMLACH, *Alan George*
6/5/8641, 3/1/16; R.A., C/S, 7/8/16; R.G.A., 9/12/16; F; Lieut.
49 Allerton Road, Mossley Hill, Liverpool

IMRAY, *Robin Sydney*
B/11985, 10/9/17; R.E., C/S, 25/11/17; R.E., 22/2/18; 2/Lieut.

Im THURN, *Richard Foster*
Sq/410, 28/4/09; 18th Huss., 1/11/14; F; Lieut.
9 Hereford Square, S.W.

INCE, *Percy Douglas*
A/14010, 16/9/18; No. 11 O.C.B., 24/1/19; General List, 8/3/19; 2/Lieut.
Three Houses Factory Ltd., St. Philip, Barbados, British West Indies.

INCE, *Sidney Monk*
6/2/6438, 25/9/15; Notts. & Derby. R., 4/9/16; F; Lieut.
147 Osborne Road, Forest Gate, E.7.

INCH, *Alexander Campbell*
B/12772, 15/3/18, L/C.; R.E., C/S, 23/8/18; demob.
Kirktonhill Manse, Dumbarton, Scotland.

INGALL, *Joseph Marsden*
E/14109, 7/10/18; R.G.A., C/S, 1/11/18; R.G.A., 13/4/19; 2/Lieut.
25 Palmerston Road, Southsea.

INGHAM, *John Burnell*
B/13582, 22/7/18, L/C.; trfr. K.R. Rif. C., 25/4/19, M.G.C.; Cpl.
38 Marlborough Road, Manningham, Bradford.

INGLE, *Alan*
6/4/9131, 22/1/16; No. 8 O.C.B., 4/8/16; North'd. Fus., 21/11/16; F; Lieut.; p.
c/o H. Ingle & Sons Ltd., Wellington Street, Leicester.

INGLEBY, *Robert John*
A/11224, 7/5/17; No. 14 O.C.B., 7/9/17; W. York. R., 17/12/17, emp. M. of Labour; 2/Lieut.; w.
120 East Parade, Heworth, York.

INGLESANT, *Harold Edwin*
B/11421, 1/6/17; No. 11 O.C.B., 9/11/17; Leic. R., 30/4/18, 19th Lond. R.; P; Lieut. Atlas House, Housefain Street, Leicester

INGLIS, *Cecil George*
6/5/5938, 1/9/15; L'pool. R., 1/6/16; F; 2/Lieut.
Knockgrink, Oswestry, Salop.

INGLIS, *Gordon*
C/1717, 15/10/14; 9th Lond. R., 12/1/15, Gren. Gds.; F; Lieut.
Cavendish Club, 119, Piccadilly, W.1.

INGLIS, *Patrick Charles*
6/8642, 3/1/16; R.A., C/S, 24/1/16; R.F.A., 23/6/16; Lieut.; M.C.
Grianach, Nairn, N.B.

☨ INGLIS, *Robert Anderson*
C/10142, 8/12/16; R.F.C., C/S, 13/3/17; R.F.C., 19/4/17; F; 2/Lieut.
Killed in action 21/9/17.

INGOLDBY, *Frederick John Millar*
C/60, 8/4/08; Linc. R., 1/11/08; Capt.
9 Willow Road, Hampstead Heath, N.W.3.

INGOLDSBY, *Arthur James*
6/5/C/9005, 19/1/16; No. 14 O.C.B., 30/10/16; 23rd Lond. R, 24/1/17; S,E,P,F; Capt.; w; M.C.
Bank of Ireland, Navan, Co. Meath, Ireland.

INGRAM, *Herbert Alfred*
6/2/8483, 20/12/15, L/C.; No. 2 O.C.B., 14/8/16; W. York. R., 27/3/17; Lieut.

INMAN, *William St. John*
B/13417, 1/7/18; demob. 21/12/18.
Torrington, West Cliffe, Roker, Sunderland, Co. Durham.

☨ INSKIP, *Sydney Hope Elsdale*
B/1290, 23/9/14; R. Marines, 29/9/14; G; Lieut.
Killed in action 23/4/18.

INSTON, *Edward Clay*
A/13971, 6/9/18; demob. 23/1/19.
7 Drury Road, Harrow-on-the-Hill.

☨ IONIDES, *Ambrose Constantine*
D/1488, 29/9/14, Cpl.; K.R. Rif. C., 5/1/15; F; Lieut.
Killed in action 16/10/15.

IRBY, *Greville Northey*
1/3307, 19/4/15; Oxf. & Bucks. L.I., 19/6/15; Lieut.

IRELAND, *Edgar Henry*
4/6/4697, 8/7/15, L/C.; 7th Lond. R., 14/12/15; F; Lieut.
Beecholme, Nacton Road, Ipswich.

IRELAND, *Humphrey John*
4/Sq/4169, 10/6/15, L/C.; R.F.A., 19/12/15; Lieut.; M(1).

IRVINE, *James Robert*
A/14328, 30/12/18; No. 11 O.C.B., 24/1/19; General List, 8/3/19; 2/Lieut.
c/o Chartered Bank of India, Australia & China, 38 Bishopsgate, E.C.2.

☨ IRVINE, *Reginald Arthur James*
4/3850, 31/5/15; trfr. 14th Lond. R., 17/3/16; F; Pte.
Killed in action 6/9/16.

☨ IRVINE-WATSON, *John*
6/Sq/6967, 22/10/15; R.A., C/S, 29/1/16; R.F.A., 6/7/16; F; 2/Lieut.; w(2).
Killed in action 13/8/17.

IRVING, *Gilmour Dundas*
4/1/4222, 14/6/15; 19th Lond. R., 6/11/15; F; 2/Lieut.; Inv.
282 Elgin Avenue, Maida Vale, W.9.

IRVING, *Robert Daniel*
4/2/4046, 7/6/15; R.W. Surr. R., 3/10/15; F,It; Capt.; w.
3 Coquet Terrace, Heaton, Newcastle-on-Tyne.

ISAAC, *John Palmer*
C/10412, 8/1/17; No. 14 O.C.B., 5/5/17; R. Suss. R., 28/8/17; F; 2/Lieut.; w; M.C.
East Marden, Chichester.

ISAAC, *Walter James Paige*
B/10333, 4/1/17; No. 14 O.C.B., 7/6/17; trfr. 28th Lond. R., 10/8/17.
Court Wick, Littlehampton, Sussex.

☨ ISAAC, *William James*
2/3483, 3/5/15; 19th Lond. R., 19/8/15; 2/Lieut.
Killed in action 26/4/16.

☨ ISARD, *Cyril Beckford*
C/377, 24/3/09; 10th Lond. R., 10/2/13; Capt.
Killed in action 15/8/15.

ISARD, *Oswald Clark*
C/774, 2/3/14; Norf. R., 12/9/14, R.G.A.; Lieut.
Camans, Tonbridge.

ISBELL, *Arthur Thomas*
D/10198, 15/12/16; R.F.C., 13/3/17; R.F.C., 19/4/17, R.A.F.; F; Lieut.; p,w.
Lower Gilli, Llanvitherine, Abergavenny.

ISGAR, *Francis Cook*
C/Sq/13399, 28/6/18; demob. 22/1/19.
Wainbridge Mark, Nr. Highbridge, Somerset

ISHERWOOD, *John*
D/E/13921, 26/8/18; demob. 10/1/19.
11 King Street, Blackburn.

ISHERWOOD, *Robert Rentoul*
4/Sq/4223, 14/6/15, L/C.; R.H.A., 10/12/15; Lieut.; M(1).
58 Lancaster Gate, Hyde Park, W.

ISITT, *Sidney Clivebrook Roberts*
Sq/1527, 5/10/14, Cpl.; York. Huss., 11/2/15, Ir. Gds.; 2/Lieut.
5 Dorset Road, Bexhill-on-Sea.

☨ ISSOTT, *John Thomas*
C/12050, 27/9/17, L/C.;
Died 20/4/18.

☨ IVATTS, *Selwyn*
6/5/8176, 6/12/15; R.A., C/S, 4/8/16; R.F.A., 10/11/16; 2/Lieut.; M.C.
Killed in action 8/10/17.

IVE, *Arthur Charles*
C/10793, 26/2/17, L/C.; R.G.A., C/S, 15/8/17; R.G.A., 31/12/17; F; Lieut. Mabel House, Harefield Road, Uxbridge, Middlesex.

IVENS, *Henry James*
6/5/5358, 3/8/15; R.F.A., 22/10/15, att. R.A.F.; F; Lieut.; w; M.C. Copt Hall, Chipperfield, Kings Langley, Hertfordshire.

IVES, *Wilfried Shepheard*
D/13761, 7/8/18; demob. 5/3/19. 9 Havelock Road, Norwich

IVESON, *James Albert*
4/5/5112, 26/7/15; R.G.A., 27/11/15; F; Capt.; w; M.C.
Fieldhead, Newby, Nr. Scarborough, Yorkshire

APPENDIX II.—RECORDS OF RANK AND FILE.

IVIMEY, Corrie
6/2/6821, 14/10/15, L/C.; 10th Lond. R., 25/9/16; F; Capt.; w; M.C. 1 Manor Crescent, East Molesey, Surrey.

IVISON, Horace Garnar
B/11986, 10/9/17; Sig. C/S, 14/12/17; R.E., 24/5/18, att. R.G.A.; F; 2/Lieut. 7 Blenheim Crescent, South Croydon, Surrey.

IZARD, Walter Wallace
C/6, 1/4/08; dis. 11/11/10. 10 The Paragon, Blackheath, S.E. 3.

IZOD, Ronald Eric
A/13035, 4/5/18; demob. 29/1/19.
Fernbank Cottage, Felpham, Sussex.

✠ JACK, Douglas Peacock
6/1/D/5742, 20/8/15; No. 14 O.C.B., 27/12/16; E. Kent. R., 25/4/17; 2/Lieut.; w. Killed in action 18/9/18.

JACK, Norman Price
B/12736, 11/3/18; No. 20 O.C.B., 20/9/18; Midd'x. R., 17/3/19; 2/Lieut. St. Helens, Lansdowne Road, N. 3.

JACK, Oswald Gordon Pearce
6/3/7799, 24/11/15; L/C.; M.G.C., 24/10/16; E,P; 2/Lieut.; w.
21 Springfield Avenue, Muswell Hill, N. 10.

JACKMAN, John
4/Sq/5113, 26/7/15, L/C.; R.A., C/S, 31/3/16; R.F.A., 7/8/16; E; Capt. Noumea, Phillips Avenue, Exmouth, Devonshire.

JACKS, Walter Raymond
A/11277, 14/5/17; Indian Army, 10/10/17; 2/Lieut.

JACKSON, Alexander Logan
6/9092, 24/1/16; No. 9 O.C.B., 8/3/16; Arg. & Suth'd. Highrs., 6/7/16, att. N. Lan. R.; Lieut.
Beechwood, Arbroath, Forfarshire.

✠ JACKSON, Arthur Graham
B/11326, 21/5/17; No. 14 O.C.B., 5/10/17; 13th Lond. R., 26/2/18; F; 2/Lieut. Killed in action 6/10/18.

✠ JACKSON, Cecil Thomas
2/3197, 8/4/15; N. Lan. R., 2/11/15, R.A.F.; E; Lieut.
Killed in action 31/8/18.

JACKSON, Charles Parry
H/2/2851. 26/12/14, Sgt.; trfr. 28th Lond. R., 8/4/18.
2a Wellington Street, S.E.18.

JACKSON, Clement
4/5/4674, 8/7/15; R.G.A., 7/10/15; F; Capt.; M.C.
Ambersgate, Oxford Road, Moseley, Birmingham.

JACKSON, Colin Ralph
C/13344, 21/6/18; trfr 14th Lond. R., 5/12/18.
23 Abingdon Road, Leicester.

JACKSON, Cranworth Franklin
6/Sq/9109, 24/1/16; Devon. Yeo., 5/7/16, 11th Lond. R.; Lieut.; M(2).

JACKSON, Cyril
B/10095, 4/12/16, Sgt.; R.F.A., C/S, 28/12/17; R.G.A., 17/6/18; F; 2/Lieut. 12 Whitmore Road, Beckenham, Kent.

✠ JACKSON, Cyril Robert Howard
6/5/6302, 17/9/15; R.F.C., 6/7/16, R.A.F.; It; Lieut.
Killed in action 16/8/18.

✠ JACKSON, Ernest
3/3851, 31/5/15; R.E., 9/7/15; Major; w; D.S.O., M.C.
Died of wounds 15/4/18.

JACKSON, Frances William Jex
A/93, 16/4/08, C.Q.M.S.; A.S.C., C/S, 1/9/16; R.A.S.C., 25/10/16; F; Capt. The Pines, Ashtead, Surrey.

JACKSON, Francis Gorham
6/8177, 6/12/15; R.E., 24/4/16; E; Major; M(2).
F.C. Central del Uruguay, Monte Video, Uruguay.

✠ JACKSON, Frank Egerton
C/11445, 4/6/17; dis. med. unfit, 27/11/17; R.N.V.R., R.A F.; Capt. Died 11/6/20.

JACKSON, Frederick Lloyd
2/4/3284, 15/4/15; R.F.A., 1/7/15; 2/Lieut.

✠ JACKSON, George Dewar
6/4/5834, 26/8/15; Gren. Gds., 2/10/15; 2/Lieut.
Killed in action 14/9/16.

JACKSON, George Ernest
E/B/14244, 28/10/18; demob. 25/3/19.
The Rectory, Haselbeck, Northamptonshire.

JACKSON, Harold Warters
D/E/B/13935, 2/9/18; demob. 5/2/19.
40 Bank Street, Sheffield.

JACKSON, Henry
C/13301, 17/6/18; trfr. 14th Lond. R., 6/12/18, Gord. Highrs.; Pte.
St. Aubins, Priory Road, West Bridgford, Nottinghamshire.

JACKSON, Horace Arthur
6/1/8935, 17/1/16; No. 8 O.C.B., 4/8/16; K.R. Rif. C., 21/11/16; F; Capt.; w(2). 69 Kingsgate Street, Winchester.

JACKSON, James Frederick
6/3/5477, 9/8/15; Rif. Brig., 27/11/15; F; Capt.; Inv.
Homerville, Woodside Road, New Malden.

✠ JACKSON, James Herbert
B/10599, 22/1/17; No. 11 O.C.B., 5/7/17; trfr. 28th Lond. R., 12/9/17; F; Pte. Killed in action 27/3/18.

JACKSON, John George
6/3/5793, 23/8/15; Welch R., 2/7/16; F; 2/Lieut.
The White Cot, Kingsand, Plymouth.

JACKSON, John Herbert
6/3/8559, 31/12/15; No. 8 O.C.B., 4/8/16; Oxf. & Bucks. L.I., 21/11/16, att. Glouc. R.; F; Lieut.; w; M(1).
Downley, High Wycombe.

JACKSON, John Owen
B/11188, 7/5/17; A.S.C., C/S, 1/9/17; trfr. 28th Lond. R., 25/2/18. Arley, Port Hill, Shrewsbury.

JACKSON, Joseph Barrow
B/10952, 30/3/17, Cpl.; R.F.A., C/S, 17/12/17; R.F.A., 3/6/18; F; 2/Lieut. Applethwaite, Keswick

JACKSON, Leonard Edmund Selmes
Sq/2133, 19/11/14, L/C.; R.F.A., 11/3/15; Capt.; w; M.B.E., M(1). 3 North Park, Eltham, S.E. 9.

JACKSON, Leslie Singleton
6/5/5261, 31/7/15, L/C.; L'pool. R., 13/12/15; Lieut.; w.
6 Dewery Avenue, Elton Park, Aintree, Liverpool.

✠ JACKSON, Noel Bower
B/10088, 4/12/16; No. 14 O.C.B., 5/5/17; Notts. & Derby. R., 28/8/17; F; 2/Lieut. Killed in action 6/12/17.

JACKSON, Percy William
6/5/7456, 15/11/15, L/C.; E. Kent. R., 4/9/16, att. L'pool. R ; I; Lieut. 170 Godintan Road, Ashford, Kent.

JACKSON, Philip Nevill
C/13189, 3/6/18; trfr. 14th Lond. R., 6/12/18.
Grove Hill, Filey, East Yorkshire.

JACKSON, Reginald
6/Sq/5980, 1/9/15, L/C.; R.F.A., 6/12/15; F,It; Lieut.; w; M(2). 70 Oxford Road, Moseley, Birmingham

JACKSON, Rex William
6/9034, 20/1/16; R.F.A., C/S, 9/6/16; R.F.A., 8/9/16; S,F; Lieut.; w; Serbian Cross of Charity.
c/o B.O.C., Clive Street, Calcutta.

JACKSON, Robert Ernest
4/5/4698, 8/7/15; 3rd Lond. R., 17/10/15, 1st Lond. R.; F; Staff Capt.; M.C. 30 Wimborne Road, Southend-on-Sea.

JACKSON, Robert Victor
B/D/13608, 24/7/18; trfr. 6th R. Regt. of Cav., 11/6/19, 4th Drag. Gds.; Pte. Little Hallingbury, Bishop's Stortford.

JACKSON, Thomas
6/2/8088, 1/12/15; No. 8 O.C.B., 4/8/16; R.A.O.C., 7/12/16; F,M,I; Capt.
Graystock, Westwood Avenue, Linthorpe, Middlesborough.

JACKSON, Thomas Heath
6/5/5285, 31/7/15, Cpl.; Manch. R., 19/12/15; Lieut.; w.
74 Devon Street, Bewick, Manchester.

JACKSON, Tom Cyril
6/4/6328, 20/9/15; Essex R., 20/1/16; Lieut.; M.C.
Haxted, Edenbridge, Kent.

APPENDIX II.—RECORDS OF RANK AND FILE.

JACKSON, *Walter Wade*
Sq/3347, 22/4/15; R.F.A., 26/8/15; F; Lieut.; g, Inv.
Cayton, York Road, St. Albans, Hertfordshire.

JACKSON, *William Arthur*
4/5/6/5006, 20/7/15; dis. med. unfit, 8/8/16.

✠ JACKSON, *William Brabazon Mather*
K/E/2247, 7/12/14; ; Notts. & Derby. R., 27/3/15; Capt.
Killed in action 27/4/17.

✠ JACKSON, *William John Humphrey*
C/10581, 19/1/17, L/C.; No. 14 O.C.B., 5/7/17; R. Innis. Fus., 30/10/17; 2/Lieut.
Died of wounds 26/3/18.

✠ JACOB, *John Victor Reed*
1/3695, 20/5/15; R.G.A., 11/8/15, att. R.A.F.; F; Lieut.
Died 16/3/19.

JACOB, *Lionel Ernest Brooksby*
3/3389, 26/4/15; 8th Lond. R., 7/8/15; F; Capt.; *M.C.*, M(2).
38 Alleyn Road, Dulwich, S.E. 21.

✠ JACOBI, *Walter Thomas*
4/6/4932, 19/7/15, L/C.; R. War. R., 27/11/15; F; 2/Lieut.; w.
Died of wounds 21/10/16.

JACOBS, *Alfred Joseph*
D/12108, 11/10/17; Tank Corps, C/S, 25/1/18; Tank Corps, 8/10/18; 2/Lieut.
268 Hagley Road, Edgbaston, Birmingham.

JACOBS, *Bertram*
D/12930, 15/4/18; H. Bde. O.C.B., 4/10/18; Gds. M.G.R., 10/3/19; 2/Lieut.
North View, Whickham-on-Tyne.

JACOBS, *Claude Chapman*
K/5/A/C/2128, 19/11/14, C.S.M.; R.A.O.C., 5/11/16; F; Lieut.
10 Mark Lane, E.C. 3.

JACOBS, *William James*
6/Sq/9035, 20/1/16; R.A., C/S, 9/6/16; R.G.A., 13/9/16; S; Lieut.
11 Landsdowne Terrace, Eastbourne.

JACOBY, *Adolph*
3/3390, 26/4/15, L/C.; S. Wales Bord., 20/11/15; F; Lieut.
4 Demesne Road, Wilbraham Road, Fallowfield, Manchester.

JAGER, *George Harold*
C/13285, 14/6/18; Tank Corps, C/S, 2/8/18; Tank Corps, 5/3/19; 2/Lieut.
6 Marsham Lane, Gerrards Cross.

JAGGAR, *Joah*
C/Sq/12656, 27/2/18, L/C.; No. 2 Cav. C/S, 7/11/18; R. Regt. of Cav., 12/3/19; 2/Lieut.
Carr House, Shelley, Nr. Huddersfield.

JAGGER, *John Hubert*
A/10934, 28/3/17; R.G.A., C/S, 26/9/17; R.G.A., 18/2/18; 2/Lieut.

JAGO, *Cecil Frederick*
C/14250, 30/10/18; demob. 13/12/18.
22 Coleridge Road, Crouch End, N. 8.

JAKEWAY, *George Burton*
6/3/8218, 7/12/15; No. 14 O.C.B., 26/11/16; Mon. R., 27/3/17. att. S. Wales Bord.; F; Lieut.
65 Victoria Avenue, Newport, Monmouthshire.

JAMES, *Abraham Thomas*
6/1/8245, 8/12/15, L/C.; No. 5 O.C.B., 14/8/16; R.W. Fus., 21/11/16; Capt.
Ornia Villa, New Quay, Cardiff.

JAMES, *Algernon Finlay*
K/F/2261, 7/12/14; W. York. R., 7/1/15; F; Lieut.; w.
c/o Lond. West. & Parr's Bank Ltd., Irongate, Derby. (Now in Australia.)

JAMES, *Charles Alexander Marshall*
K/C/2517, 31/12/14; R. Suss. R., 31/3/15, Tank Corps, emp. M. of Labour; Capt.
5 Cumberland Gate, New Gardens.

JAMES, *David Emrys*
B/Sq/12864, 26/3/18; demob. 20/3/19.
Dalcoed, Croxton, Neath.

JAMES, *Dennis Cory*
A/984, 5/8/14, L/C.; Worc. R., 7/11/14, secd. R.F.C.; F; Major; w; O.B.E., Legion d'Honneur, Italian Medal, M(1).
20 Woodville Gardens, Ealing, W. 5.

JAMES, *Edgar*
4/3732, 24/5/15; Devon. R., 24/9/15; M,I; Lieut.; w.
Westfield, Southampton

✠ JAMES, *Enoch Lewis*
6/1/8246, 8/12/15; No. 5 O.C.B., 14/8/16; R.W. Fus., 21/11/16; F; 2/Lieut.
Killed in action 18/2/17.

JAMES, *Ernest Alfred*
4/6/1/5167, 29/7/15; R.G.A., 14/12/15; Lieut.; w.
Rosaldene, Gravel Road, South Farnborough, Hampshire.

JAMES, *Francis Trevor*
6/2/8219, 7/12/15; R.E., C/S, 21/10/16; R.E., 13/1/17; F; Lieut.; w; M.C.
65 Gwydr Crescent, Swansea.

✠ JAMES, *Frank*
6/2/5560, 12/8/15; S. Wales Bord., 4/1/16; F; Lieut.
Killed in action 1/11/18.

JAMES, *Frederick*
D/1422, 29/9/14, Cpl.; Manch. R., 3/3/15, M.G.C.; F; Lieut.; w.
19 Bishopsthorpe Road, Sydenham, S.E. 26.

JAMES, *Frederick Powell*
6/2/B/8313, 11/12/15; R.A., C/S, 24/11/16; R.A., 12/5/17; Lieut.

JAMES, *Frederick Titus*
6/3/8920, 14/1/16; trfr. Linc. R., 30/6/16; F; Pte.
18 Old Carter Gates, Grimsby.

JAMES, *George Lionel*
E/2867, 5/2/15; Welch R., 22/4/15, secd. Lab. Corps; Lieut.; w.

✠ JAMES, *Gwilym Christopher Bowring*
3/9611, 6/9/16; No. 14 O.C.B., 26/11/16; S. Wales Bord., 27/3/17; Lieut.
Died of wounds 23/11/17.

JAMES, *Harold Edgar*
6/4/6663, 7/10/15; trfr. R.G.A., 17/11/16.
Claverdon, Cedar Road, Sutton, Surrey.

JAMES, *Harold Leighton*
3/3780, 27/5/15; R.F.A., 29/10/15; Lieut.
63 Albert Road, Alexandra Park, N. 22.

JAMES, *Herbert*
3/3337, 22/4/15, L/C.; N. Lan. R., 15/9/15; Capt.
44 Venner Road, Sydenham, S.E. 26.

JAMES, *Howard Arthur*
4/3/4224, 14/6/15; Manch. R., 18/10/15; F; Lieut.; w.
1 Rusham Road, Wandsworth Common, S.W. 12.

JAMES, *John Henry*
4/1/4280, 17/6/15; R.G.A., 11/8/15.
Nancotham House, Redruth, Cornwall.

JAMES, *Lambert William*
6/D/3/5478, 9/8/15, C.S.M.; R.A.F., C/S, 1/7/18; dis. med. unfit, 14/12/18.
School House, Harlington, Dunstable.

JAMES, *Matthew Vallance Theodore*
B/12418, 18/1/18; No. 23 O.C.B., 7/6/18; Midd'x. R., 5/2/19; 2/Lieut.
Oakhurst, St. Catherine's Road, Ruislip, Middlesex.

JAMES, *Philip Vallance*
D/Sq/10646, 2/2/17; No. 14 O.C.B., 5/10/17; E. Surr. R., 30/4/18; F; 2/Lieut.; w.
4 Briar Road, Pollards Hill, Norbury, S.W. 16.

JAMES, *Reginald Vye*
4/3/4394, 24/6/15; Durh. L.I., 21/12/15, secd. R.F.C., R.A.F.; Lieut.; w; D.F.C.

JAMES, *Richard Bush*
Sq/1088, 3/9/14; R.G.A., 7/11/14, R. Horse Gds.; F; Capt.; w; M(1).
7 Montpelier Terrace, Cheltenham.

JAMES, *William*
6/4/7457, 15/11/15, Sgt.; M.G.C., 25/9/16; F; Lieut.
27 Pendarren Street, Aberdare, South Wales.

JAMES, *William Thomas*
6/2/6575, 2/10/15; No. 7 O.C.B., 7/4/16; 8th Lond. R., 4/8/16, att. 17th Lond. R.; F; Capt.; w; M.C.
St. George's Church Path, Upper Deal, Kent.

JAMESON, *Andrew St. Clair*
K/C/2071, 12/11/14; Sea. Highrs., 13/1/15; Lieut.; w.
16 Coates Crescent, Edinburgh.

JAMESON, *Thomas William*
6/1/7991, 29/11/15; dis. med. unfit, 1/6/17.

JAMIESON, *Archibald Dick*
B/11670, 16/7/16; No. 11 O.C.B., 9/11/17; Gord. Highrs., 26/3/18; F; 2/Lieut.
17 Torphichen Street, Edinburgh.

APPENDIX II.—RECORDS OF RANK AND FILE.

JAMIESON, Thomas Thomson
A/11628, 9/7/17; No. 14 O.C.B., 9/11/17; R. Scots, 30/4/18; F; 2/Lieut.
81 Duke Street, Leith, Scotland.

JAMISON, William
6/3/7046, 28/10/15; No. 8 O.C.B., 4/8/16; Suff. R., 27/11/16.
54 Cartwright Gardens, Russell Square, W.C. 1.

JANE, Francis Hammond
D/A/12978, 24/4/18; R.E., C/S, 11/10/18; demob. 28/1/19.
1540 Hawthorn Avenue, Portland, Onegan, U.S.A.

JANES, Denys Frank
B/Sq/12324, 28/12/17; No. 1 Cav. C/S, 3/9/18; R. Regt. of Cav., 12/3/19; 2/Lieut.
Ravensleigh, Hindes Road, Harrow-on-the-Hill.

JANNINGS, Alfred Gordon
C/10182, 13/12/16, L/C.; No. 14 O.C.B., 6/4/17; R. War. R., 31/7/17; F; 2/Lieut.; w(2).
53 St. George's Road, Golders Green, N.W. 11.

JANSON, Arthur Dearman
H/1736, 15/10/14; dis. med. unfit, 6/11/14.

JANSON, Frederick Ernest
Sq/378, 24/3/09; dis. 23/3/13; joined 28th Lond. R., -/9/14; R Jersey Militia, 9/2/15, R.A.O.C.; Capt.; M.B.E.
80 Eaton Terrace, S.W. 1.

JAQUES, Charles Norman
C/14202, 21/10/18; demob. 23/1/19.
Stamore, St. Albans Avenue, Weybridge, Surrey.

JARDINE, David Wallace
B/10313, 4/1/17; R.G.A., C/S, 6/6/17; R.G.A., 1/10/17; Lieut.
Rhinds House, Baillieston, Glasgow.

JARMAN, Sydney Leopold
A/Sq/C/14047, 23/9/18; No. 11 O.C.B., 31/1/19; General List, 8/3/19; 2/Lieut.
35 Nelson Road, Great Yarmouth.

JARRENS, Reginald
6/5/6046, 3/9/15; Manch. R., 6/7/16; F; 2/Lieut.; w.
21 Holland Road, Wallasey, Cheshire.

JARRETT, Maurice
A/13012, 1/5/18, L/C.; demob. 3/2/19.
Grove Road, Sydney, Gloucestershire.

JARVIS, Basil James
6/4/8111, 2/12/15; No. 8 O.C.B., 4/8/16; Linc. R., 21/11/16; Lieut.
Connaught Club, Marble Arch, W.

JARVIS, John Norman
A/D/11972, 6/9/17, L/C.; No. 17 O.C.B., 5/4/18; L'pool. R., 24/9/18; 2/Lieut.
3 Ormonde Street, Wallasey, Cheshire.

JAY, Stanley
6/3/7510, 15/11/15; K.R. Rif. C., 6/7/16, att. M. of Munitions; F; Lieut.; Inv; M.B.E.
25 Chatsworth Avenue, Wimbledon, S.W. 20

JEANS, Gerald Mark
B/9880, 8/11/16; No. 14 O.C.B., 6/4/17; Wilts. R., 31/7/17; F; Lieut.; w(3).
King Hall, Milton, Pewsey, Wiltshire.

JEFFCOCK, Thomas Roy
K/B/2112, 16/11/14; dis. med. unfit, 17/12/14.
Welham Hall, Retford, Nottinghamshire.

JEFFCOCK, William Henry Claude
F/1872, 16/10/14, Cpl.; York. & Lanc. R., 10/2/15, W. York. R.; F; Lieut.; w.
The Cottage, Bawtry, Nr. Doncaster.

JEFFERIES, Laurence
D/11179, 4/5/17; A.S.C., C/S, 1/9/17; R.A.S.C., 27/10/17; F; 2/Lieut.
3 Cranley Gardens, Palmers Green, N. 13.

JEFFERIES, Leonard Stanton
4/3/4395, 24/6/15; R. War. R., 29/11/15; Lieut.; w; M(1).
45 Cowper Road, Hanwell, W. 7.

JEFFERSON, Harry Dixon
B/13914, 27/8/18; demob. 23/1/19.
6 Ridge Terrace, Bedlington, Northumberland.

JEFFERSON, Robert James
C/Sq/14298, 12/11/18; demob. 7/1/19.
Springfield, Bigrigg, Cumberland.

JEFFERY, Donald Leslie
4/2/3267, 15/4/15; R.F.A., 12/10/15; 2/Lieut.

JEFFERY, Edgar John Walter
C/10482, 12/1/17; R.F.A., C/S, 29/6/17; R.F.A., 7/1/18; P,E; Lieut.
77 Ashburton Avenue, Addiscombe, Surrey.

✠ JEFFERY, George Reginald
Sq/709, 15/4/13; dis. 2/9/14; 20th Huss.; 2/Lieut.
Killed in action 13/2/16.

✠ JEFFREY, Roland Edward
6/B/7104, 1/11/15; No. 11 O.C.B., 7/5/16; R.F.C., 4/9/16; 2/Lieut.
Killed in action 25/5/17.

✠ JEFFREYS, Alec Harry
C/1151, 14/9/14; North'd. Fus., 7/12/14; Capt.
Killed in action 6/11/16.

✠ JEFFRIES, Thomas
6/2/8569, 31/12/15, L/C.; No. 14 O.C.B., 30/10/16; 3rd Lond. R., 28/2/17; F; 2/Lieut.
Killed in action 14/8/17.

JEFFS, Charles Hubert
6/3/5811, 24/8/15; Bord. R., 7/6/16, R.A.F.; F; Lieut.; s.d.p.
The Close, Holton-le-Clay, Nr. Grimsby, Lincolnshire. (Now in Egypt).

JELLICOE, John Andrew
H/1992, 29/10/14; North'd. Fus., 2/3/15, Indian Army; F,I; Capt.
28 Brandling Park, Newcastle-on-Tyne.

JEMMETT, Eric Rowntree
4/3694, 20/5/15; Linc. R., 28/11/15, emp. M. of Munitions; F; Lieut.
64 Northcote Road, Sidcup, Kent.

JEMMETT, William Bartram
6/3/Sq/7384, 11/11/15; R.F.A., C/S, 4/8/16; R.F.A., 22/12/16; Lieut.
Elwich, Hythe, Kent.

✠ JENKINS, Aneurin
6/5/C/7490, 15/11/15, L/C.; trfr. M.G.C., 29/12/16; S. Wales Bord.; 2/Lieut.
Killed in action 13/4/18.

✠ JENKINS, Beavan Pendleton
D/A/12441, 22/1/18; R.F.C., C/S, 21/5/18; R.A.F., 5/7/18; F; Lieut.
Died of wounds as Prisoner of War 20/10/18.

JENKINS, Edward
B/E/13567, 19/7/18, L/C.; No. 22 O.C.B., 20/9/18; R. Fus., 14/2/19; 2/Lieut.
Park House, Warwick Park, Tunbridge Wells, Kent.

JENKINS, Edward Basil Terence
B/1696, 13/10/14, Cpl.; R. Fus., 10/2/15; F; Capt.; w.
232 Strand, W.C. 2

JENKINS, Frederick Albert
5/1/8361, 13/12/15; No. 5 O.C.B., 14/8/16; R.N.V.R., 21/11/16; F; Lieut.; M.C.
75 Musgrove Road, S.E. 14

JENKINS, George Kirkhouse
1/3812, 27/5/15; Welch R., 16/9/15; E,P; Lieut.; Inv.
36 Park Place, Cardiff.

JENKINS, Ivor Bramhall
D/11081, 18/4/17, L/C.; No. 14 O.C.B., 10/8/17; Welch R., 27/11/17; F; Lieut.
c/o Nat. Prov. Band, Ltd., Birmingham.

✠ JENKINS, James Temple
6/3/9134, 25/1/16, L/C.; No. 14 O.C.B., 30/10/16; Sea. Highrs., 24/1/17; 2/Lieut.
Killed in action 20/9/17.

JENKINS, Nathaniel Llewelyn
C/13328, 19/6/18; No. 22 O.C.B., 25/8/18; S. Wales Bord., 5/2/19; F; 2/Lieut.
Birkwood, Lower Bourne, Farnham, Surrey.

JENKINS, Robert
Sq/2971, 25/2/15; R.A.S.C., 3/5/15, att. Rif. Brig.; F; Capt.
36 Westwood Road, Southampton.

JENKINS, Robert Christmas Dewar
C/14251, 30/10/18; trfr. K.R. Rif. C., 17/4/19.
42 St. Dunstan's Road, West Kensington, W. 6.

JENKINS, Stanley
A/11286, 14/5/17; No. 16 O.C.B., 5/10/17; Welch R., 12/3/18; 2/Lieut.
Melsonby, Pencisely, Llandaff, South Wales.

JENKINS, Wilfrid Lawson
D/E/13822, 9/8/18; demob. 10/1/19.
116 Cromwell Road, S.W. 7.

✠ JENKINS, William
B/11671, 16/7/17; No. 14 O.C.B., 9/11/17; Dorset R., 30/4/18; 2/Lieut.
Killed in action 11/10/18

APPENDIX II.—RECORDS OF RANK AND FILE.

✠ JENKS, Alan Robert Constantine
B/752, 23/1/14; R.E., 8/9/14; Major; M.C., M(1).
Killed in action 31/7/17.

JENKS, Percy Legh
A/11250, 14/5/17; No 14 O.C.B., 7/9/17; Glouc. R., 17/12/17; F; 2/Lieut.
Danesbury, Belle Vue, Shrewsbury.

JENKYN, Frank Alfred
6/1/6016, 2/9/15; North'd. Fus., 22/6/16, att. Essex R.; Lieut.
c/o Millers Ltd., West Africa House, Kingsway, W.C.

JENNER, Arthur Leonard
1/3457, 3/5/15; W. York. R., 28/7/15, M.G.C.; F; Lieut.; w; M.C. and Bar.
28 West Lodge Avenue, West Acton, W. 3.

JENNER, John Geoffrey Wilder
A/D/13013, 1/5/18; demob. 30/5/19.
75 Grove Lane, Denmark Hill, S.E. 5.

JENNER, Ronald Vivian
6/1/9321, 5/2/16; M.G.C., C/S, 25/11/16; M.G.C., 24/3/17, R.E. Sigs.; F; Lieut.
3 Belgrave Mansions, S.W. 1.

JENNINGS, Arthur Louis
H/1997, 1/11/14, L/C.; Devon. R., 9/4/15; 2/Lieut.
22 Trebovir Road, S.W. 5.

JENNINGS, Charles
B/2067, 12/11/14; Leic. R., 13/11/14; F; Major; p.
c/o Messrs. Holt & Coy., 3 Whitehall Place, S.W. 1. (Now in Egypt.)

JENNINGS, Edgar Ernest
6/2/8455, 17/12/15; R.A., C/S, 4/8/16; R.G.A., 1/11/16; Lieut.
77 Whittington Road, Bowes Park, N. 22.

JENNINGS, Sidney Augustus
6/1/9046, 21/1/16; R.A., C/S, 4/8/16; R.G.A., 1/11/16; F; Lieut.
21 Boscastle Road, Highgate, N.W. 5.

JENNINGS, Walter Henry
6/2/9511, 16/2/16, Sgt.; R.F.A., C/S, 18/5/17; R.F.A., 20/10/17; 2/Lieut.; w.
Bemvinda, Queens Road, Kingston Hill.

JENRICK, Philip Henry
C/1241, 23/9/14; R. Berks. R., 28/12/14, M.G.C.; Capt.; w.

JEPHSON, Basil Leslie
6/2/5625, 16/8/15; 12th Lond. R., 20/12/15, 16th Lond. R.; F; Lieut.
Rosenhallas, Redhill, Surrey.

JEPSON, Thomas
4/5/4716, 9/7/15; dis. med. unfit, 1/8/16.
Sunshine Villa, The Avenue, Halton, Leeds.

JERAM, Charles Mayvore
C/11726, 23/7/17; A.S.C., C/S, 1/11/17; R.A.S.C., 25/1/18; S; Capt.
29 Sutton Court, Chiswick, W. 4.

JERDEIN, Edward Stanton
C/13209, 5/6/18; No. 22 O.C.B., 5/7/18; R.A.S.C., 22/11/18; 2/Lieut.
70a High Street, St. John's Wood, N.W.

JERMYN, Keppel
6/5/6372, 18/10/15; No. 8 O.C.B., 4/8/16; W. York. R., 24/10/16, secd. Indian Army; Lieut.; w.
Grammar School, Shoreham, Sussex.

JERRARD, Francis Douglas Slade
6/8456, 17/12/15; A.S.C., C/S, 15/5/16; R.A.S.C., 18/6/16; Lieut.
4 Tavistock Square, W.C. 1.

JERRETT, Harold
6/8570, 31/12/15; L'pool. R., 26/1/16, secd. S. Lan. R.; F; Lieut.; Inv.
Culcheth, 29 Kingsway, Wallasey, Cheshire.

JERROME, Henry Abraham
6/1/6992, 26/10/15, L/C.; 4th Lond. R., 10/6/16; Lieut.

JERVOIS, Francis
A/12430, 21/1/18; trfr. 28th Lond. R., 17/5/18.
Mervne, Youghal, Co. Cork, Ireland.

JESPER, Norman McKay
4/6/5168, 29/7/15; Gren. Gds., 17/11/15; F; Lieut.; w(2); M.C.
49 St. George's Road, Harrogate.

JESPER, Sydney Watson
B/13464, 5/7/18; trfr. K.R. Rif. C., 25/4/19.
49 St. George's Road, Harrogate.

✠ JESSEL, Victor Albert Villiers
B/2713, 18/1/15; Durh. L.I., 18/5/15; 2/Lieut.
Killed in action 6/4/17.

JESSEMAN, Bertram Frederick
6/3/7047, 28/10/15; Mon. R., 15/6/16; F; Lieut.; g.
Oakdene, Somerset Road, Newport, Monmouthshire.

JESSEMAN, Ivor Reginald
6/3/7458, 15/11/15; Garr. O.C.B., 12/12/16; Worc. R., 10/2/17; Lieut.
Oakdene, Somerset Road, Newport, Monmouthshire.

JESSIMAN, John Murray
6/7872, 26/11/15; A.S.C., C/S, 28/2/16; R.A.S.C., 7/5/16, R.E., Lab. Corps; M,Persia,Siberia; Capt.
The Rythe, Esher, Surrey.

✠ JESSON, Robert Wilfrid Fairey
C/518, 18/11/10; Wilts. R., 1/9/14; Major; w.
Killed in action 22/2/17.

JESSON, Thomas Touchet
F/2847, 1/2/15; Worc. R., 29/4/15; Lieut.
Beausite, Upper Wyche, Malvern, Worcestershire.

JESSOP, Cecil Owen
D/12966, 22/4/18; demob. 31/1/19.
81 Fitzjohn's Avenue, Hampstead, N.W. 3.

JESSOP, Joseph Wilfrid
6/4/9214, 31/1/16; No. 14 O.C.B., 26/11/16; R. War. R., 27/3/17; F; Lieut.; w.
Elford, Olton, Birmingham.

JEUDWINE, James Gordon
Sq/157, 18/4/08; dis. 17/4/12; R.G.A., 19/8/17; F; Lieut.
Sleaford, Lincolnshire.

JEWELL, Charles Leonard
B/13519, 12/7/18; demob. 23/1/19.
19 Litchdon Street, Barnstaple, North Devonshire.

JEWELL, Frederick Ernest
4/3/4225, 14/6/15; Devon. R., 4/11/15; F; Lieut.; w.
Trafalgar Lawn, Barnstaple, North Devonshire.

JEWELL, Richard Albert
6/2/7206, 4/11/15; trfr. R.G.A., 1/12/16; F; Bdr.
2 Ross Street, Newport, Monmouthshire.

JEWSON, Frederick Dunbar
6/5/C/8290, 10/12/15, L/C.; No. 14 O.C.B., 30/10/16; Mon. R., 28/2/17, att. Shrop. L.I.; F; Lieut.
8 Conan Mansions, West Kensington, W. 14.

JEWSON, Percy William
D/11151, 30/4/17; No. 14 O.C.B., 10/8/17; Worc. R., 27/11/17; F; 2/Lieut.
The Lindens, Lime Tree Road, Norwich.

JEX, Cyril Francis
6/4/6717, 9/10/15; R.F.C., 13/8/16, R.A.F.; F; Lieut.
20 Erskine Hill, Hendon, N.W. 4.

JILLINGS, Basil Ridley
B/K/2617, 7/1/15; R.W. Fus., 10/4/15, att. R.F.C. and R.A.F.; M,I,E; Lieut.
Claremont, Brighton Road, Purley, Surrey.

JINMAN, Charles Harris
B/11701, 19/7/17; R.E., C/S, 16/12/17; R.E., 29/3/18; 2/Lieut
Woodroydon, Leamington Road, Southend, Essex.

JOBSON, Donald Robert
A/11933, 30/8/17; No. 14 O.C.B., 7/12/17; W. Rid. R., 28/5/18, att. Lan. Fus.; F; 2/Lieut.
13 Crown Terrace, Scarborough.

JOBSON, Edward Merryne Frost
6/5/6621, 4/10/15; S. Notts. Huss., 3/1/16.
27 Beverley Terrace, Cuttercoats, Northampton.

JOEL, William Frederic
B/11422, 1/6/17; No. 14 O.C.B., 7/9/17; L'pool. R., 17/12/17; F; 2/Lieut.
108 Argyle Road, West Ealing.

JOELS, Edwin James
3/3852, 31/5/15; N. Staff. R., 7/10/15; E,F; Lieut.; w.
9 Wood Vale, Forest Hill, S.E. 23.

JOHN, Sydney
B/10135, 6/12/16; No. 21 O.C.B., 5/5/17; R.W. Fus., 28/8/17; E,P; Lieut.; w.
29 Morris Street, Morriston, Swansea.

✠ JOHN, Wilbur Arnold
Sq/2891, 9/2/15; Suss. Yeo., 23/4/15, R.A.F.; F; Lieut.
Killed in action 1/8/18.

JOHN, William David
B/10547, 17/1/17; No. 20 O.C.B., 7/6/17; Mon. R., 17/12/17, att. Yorks. L.I.; F; Lieut.; g.
30 Rosslyn Road, Maindw, Newport, Monmouthshire.

APPENDIX II.—RECORDS OF RANK AND FILE.

JOHNS, James Frederick
3/3853, 31/5/15, L/C.; York. R., 10/9/15; Capt.; w.

JOHNS, Nicholas Allen
A/1174, 14/9/14; R.W. Kent R., 20/10/14, M.G.C.; F; Major; M.C. and Bar. Woodendale, Beckenham, Kent.

JOHNSON, Alwyn Henry Elphinstone
4/5/5075, 26/7/15; No. 11 O.C.B., 7/5/16; Ches. R., 4/9/16; F; Lieut. 34 Cressida Road, Highgate, N. 19.

JOHNSON, Arthur Gerald
E/1597, 6/10/14; Essex R., 2/12/14; Lieut.; w.
146 Hainault Road, Leytonstone, E. 11.

JOHNSON, Arthur Samuel
6/2/6184, 13/9/15; No. 1 O.C.B., 25/2/16; 25th Lond. R., 8/7/16, 10th Lond. R., R.E.; F; Lieut.
c/o British Bank of South America Ltd., Calle 400, Bartolomé Mitre, Buenos Aires, Argentina.

JOHNSON, Basil Henry
4/3198, 8/4/15, Sgt.; Herts. R., 2/7/15; F; Lieut.; w.
55 Sloane Gardens, S.W. 1.

✠ JOHNSON, Cecil Marland
C/11447, 4/6/17; R.F.C., C/S, 2/8/17; R.F.C., 8/9/17, R.A.F.; F; 2/Lieut. Killed in action 6/6/18.

JOHNSON, Cecil Paroixien
6/4/9254, 2/2/16; L/C.; M.G.C., C/S, 1/1/17; M.G.C., 25/4/17.
2 Whitehall Court, S.W. 1

JOHNSON, Charles Campbell
4/Sq/5145, 26/7/15, Cpl.; No. 2 Cav. C/S, 31/3/16; Dorset Yeo., 19/8/16; P; Lieut. Saxon Lodge, Clifton Place, Brighton.

JOHNSON, Charles Leopold Hamilton
C/11446, 4/6/17; R.F.C., C/S, 2/8/17; R.F.C., 9/1/18; 2/Lieut.

JOHNSON, Clifford Fallowfield
4/9699, 9/10/16; No. 14 O.C.B., 27/12/16; Som. L.I., 25/4/17; F; Lieut.; w. The Manse, Bibury, Gloucestershire.

JOHNSON, Clive Henry
C/11050, 16/4/17; No. 14 O.C.B., 5/10/17; R.W. Surr. R., 30/4/18; F; Lieut.
Wanganni, Alexandra Road, Hunstanton, Norfolk.

JOHNSON, Clyde Heywood
K/E/2527, 31/12/14; R.E., 6/3/15, att. R.A.F.; F; Staff Capt.; w.
R.A.F. Club, 13 Bruton Street, W.

JOHNSON, Cuthbert Rowland Ingram
6/1/6087, 6/9/15; North'd. Fus., 4/1/16; w.
Edgeborough Lodge, Guildford.

JOHNSON, Edward Cyril
6/5/7873, 26/11/15; R.A., C/S, 7/8/16; R.G.A., 8/11/16; Lieut.
The Myrtles, Merlin Road, Blackburn.

JOHNSON, Eric Digby
F/1943, 22/10/14; E. Surr. R., 7/1/15, R.F.C.; F; Capt.; A.F.C., M(1). Westmorland House, Tunbridge Wells.

JOHNSON, Ernest
6/Sq/6443, 26/9/15, L/C.; No. 2 Cav. C/S, 31/3/16; Fife and Forfar Yeo., 19/8/16, att. R. Scots Fus.; F; Lieut.
Mui-y-don, 11 Walnut Street, Southport, Lancashire.

JOHNSON, Ernest Edward
2/3114, 25/3/15; R.W. Surr. R., 18/6/15, att. Lab. Corps; F,It; Lieut.; w. 46 Bungalow Road, South Norwood, S.E.

JOHNSON, Ernest Roland
A/13991, 11/9/18; trfr. Class W. Res., 19/11/18.
2 Ferndale Avenue, East Boldon, Co. Durham.

JOHNSON, Francis Hannam
B/12706, 8/3/18; R.E., C/S, 23/8/18; demob.
Algoa House, Tomline Road, Felixstowe.

✠ JOHNSON, George Arthur Moxey Tuker
4/3336, 21/4/15, L/C.; 19th Lond. R., 6/11/15; 2/Lieut.
Killed in action 21/5/17.

JOHNSON, George Crawford
B/E/13568, 19/7/18; No. 22 O.C.B., 20/9/18; Leic. R., 14/2/19; 2/Lieut. Uplands, Market Harborough.

JOHNSON, George Harold Burgoyne. See BORGOYNE-JOHNSON, H. G.

JOHNSON, George Wilfrid
6/2/5334, 2/8/15; Hamps. R., 30/10/15.
Alleyn's Grammar School, Stevenage.

JOHNSON, George William
B/227, 14/5/08; dis. 13/5/10. Hildenborough, Tonbridge.

✠ JOHNSON, George William
6/2/5508, 9/8/15; Durh. L.I., 6/7/16, M.G.C.; F; Capt.
Killed in action 24/4/18.

JOHNSON, Harold Cecil John
B/1300, 24/9/14, Cpl.; R.A.O.C., 10/12/14; F,M; Major, D.A.D.O.S.; O.B.E., M(1).
Beauvale, P.O. Besters, Natal, South Africa.

JOHNSON, Harold George Burgoyne. See BURGOYNE-JOHNSON, H. G.

JOHNSON, Henry Andrew
6/4/6329, 20/9/15; York. R., 6/7/16; Lieut.
The Vicarage, Great Harwood, Blackburn

✠ JOHNSON, John Chapman
F/1894, 16/10/14, Sgt.; R. War. R., 13/3/15; 2/Lieut.
Killed in action 8/7/15.

✠ JOHNSON, Laurence Bertrand
1/9753, 18/10/16; No. 14 O.C.B., 27/12/16; Som. L.I., 25/4/17; 2/Lieut. Died of wounds 15/4/18.

JOHNSON, Leslie Hayes
A/D/13014, 1/5/18; No. 16 O.C.B., 18/10/18, No. 14 O.C.B.; Arg. & Suth'd. Highrs., 17/3/19; 2/Lieut.
14 Campbell Road, Hanwell, W. 7.

✠ JOHNSON, Leslie Nethercote
6/5/6018, 2/9/15; Notts. & Derby. R., 25/1/16; 2/Lieut.; w; M.C.
Killed in action 3/6/17.

JOHNSON, Leslie Vincent
3/3308, 19/4/15; R.F.A., 3/10/15. Barnfield, Bromley, Kent.

JOHNSON, Marcus Labron
6/4/8818, 10/1/16; No. 8 O.C.B., 4/8/16; S. Lan. R., 21/11/16, att. M.G.C.; F; Lieut.; Inv.
35 Guilford Street, Russell Square, W.C. 1.

JOHNSON, Ramsay Gelling
6/5/7843, 25/11/15; R.A., C/S, 15/9/16; R.F.A., 12/1/17; F; Lieut.; w. 17 Athol Street, Douglas, Isle of Man.

JOHNSON, Reginald
2/6/7737, 22/11/15, L/C.; 9th Lond. R., 4/8/16; Lieut.; w.

JOHNSON, Reginald Sidney
2/3433, 30/4/15; Durh. L.I., 11/7/15, secd. Indian Army; Capt.; w; M.C. Stafford Lodge, Stafford Road, Croydon.

JOHNSON, Richard Harold
D/E/13762, 7/8/18; No. 20 O.C.B., 20/9/18; E. York. R., 14/2/19; 2/Lieut. 19 Park Avenue, Hull.

JOHNSON, Sydney Charles
B/11702, 19/7/17; No. 11 O.C.B., 9/11/17; Worc. R., 30/4/18; F; 2/Lieut.; g; M.C.
Elmscroft, Yardley Wood Road, Moseley, Birmingham.

JOHNSON, Sydney Joseph
6/4/5774, 23/8/15; R.A.S.C., 6/11/15.
Fairlawn, Churchfield, Woodford

JOHNSON, Wilfred Guy
6/4/9320, 4/2/16; A.S.C., C/S, 7/8/16; R.A.S.C., 10/9/16, R.G.A.; F,It; Lieut.; M(1).
c/o Messrs. Johnson & Akam Ltd., Harris Street, Bradford.

✠ JOHNSON, William Dixon
C/10596, 22/1/17; trfr. 8th Lond. R., 26/2/17; F; Pte.
Killed 17/8/17.

JOHNSON, William Dudley
A/14133, 8/10/18; demob. 22/1/19.
1 Norfolk Square, Great Yarmouth.

JOHNSON, William Ralph
6/4/8337, 13/12/15; No. 11 O.C.B., 7/5/16; L'pool. R., 4/9/16; F; Lieut.; w; Portuguese Military Cross, Military Order of Avis, 5th Class, M(1).
The Cottage, Thomas Lane, Knotty Ash, Liverpool. (Now in Portugal.)

✠ JOHNSTON, Alexander Francis
6/3/5434, 5/8/15; 11th Lond. R., 4/6/16; 2/Lieut.
Killed in action 10/9/16.

JOHNSTON, Arthur Stewart
B/11339, 21/5/17, L/C.; R.E., C/S, 4/11/17; R.E., 1/2/18; F; 2/Lieut.; M.C. Box 108, Germiston, Transvaal, South Africa.

APPENDIX II.—RECORDS OF RANK AND FILE.

✠ JOHNSTON, Donald Clark
E/1580, 6/10/14; Bedf. R., 8/10/14, R.W. Surr. R., att. Sco. Rif.;
F; Capt.; w. Died of wounds 13/9/18.

JOHNSTON, Donald Vaughan
D/E/13730, 2/8/18; No. 22 O.C.B., 22/11/18; R.W. Fus., 15/2/19;
2/Lieut. Bank House, Newtown, Montgomeryshire.

JOHNSTON, Edwin David
6/2/7679, 22/11/15, L/C.; High. L.I., 25/9/16; F; Lieut.; w.
14 Falkland Mansions, Hyndland, Glasgow.

✠ JOHNSTON, Frank
C/1152, 14/9/14; Shrop. L.I., 19/9/14; Lt.-Col.; w.
Died of wounds 31/5/18.

JOHNSTON, George Adam
4/3/4418, 24/6/15; Essex R., 7/11/15, att. Oxf. & Bucks. L.I.; F;
Lieut.; w(2); M.C., M(1).
Asthore, 27 Alwyne Road, Wimbledon, S.W.19.

JOHNSTON, George Douglas
6/5/7770, 23/11/15; R.A., C/S, 23/6/16; R.G.A., 27/9/16; F;
Capt. 10 Old Square, Lincoln's Inn, W.C.2.

JOHNSTON, Henry Vincent
6/1/5707, 19/8/15; R. Lanc. R., 29/6/16; F; 2/Lieut.
Fern Bank, Etterly, Carlisle.

JOHNSTON, John Alexander
6/2/6017, 2/9/15; R. Innis. Fus., 17/1/16; F,S,P; Major; M.C.,
M(1).
The Beeches, Moy, Co. Tyrone, Ireland. (Now in Egypt).

JOHNSTON, John Rodney
6/4/6088, 6/9/15; E. Surr. R., 11/1/16, Herts. R.; F; Lieut.; w;
M.C., M(1). 23 St. Lawrence Road, Brixton, S.W.9.

JOHNSTON, Robert Tordiff
A/11919, 24/8/17, L/C.; H. Bde. O.C.B., 9/11/17; Lan. Fus.,
26/3/18; F; 2/Lieut. Nether Henton, Low Road, Carlisle.

JOHNSTON, Samuel Frederick Sinclair
Sq/288, 22/6/08; dis. 21/6/09; R.A.S.C., -/9/14; F; Capt.; M(1).
4 King's Bench Walk, Temple, E.C.4.

✠ JOHNSTON, Thomas Peacock
4/Sq/4354, 19/6/15, L/C.; Shrop. Yeo., 19/8/15, R.F.C.; Lieut.
Killed in action 20/5/17.

JOHNSTONE, Charles Arthur
F/1907, 16/10/14; R. Suss. R., 15/11/14, Dorset R.; w.

JOHNSTONE, Douglas Francis
6/2/6357, 20/9/15; No. 11 O.C.B., 7/5/16; 9th Lond. R., 4/9/16;
Lieut.; w. 23 Grove Road, Surbiton, Surrey.

✠ JOHNSTONE, George Smith
6/4/7459, 15/11/15; No. 9 O.C.B., 8/3/16; K.O. Sco. Bord.,
6/7/16, att. Portuguese Army; Lieut. Killed in action 26/8/18.

JOHNSTONE, Harold Bruce
E/1569, 6/10/14; Cam'n. Highrs., 5/11/14; Capt.; w(2).
The Pass, Callander, N.B.

✠ JOHNSTONE, Richard Michael
B/1198, 14/9/14; High. L.I., 5/10/14; Capt.
Killed in action 25/3/18.

JOHNSTONE-WILSON, Clive
6/6735, 11/10/15; A.S.C., C/S, 8/5/16; R.A.S.C., 18/6/16; F,It;
Lieut. 4 Marina Court, Bexhill-on-Sea.

JOINER, William George
B/D/11987, 10/9/17; R.F.A., C/S, 15/3/18; R.F.A., 17/10/18;
2/Lieut. 7 Lutterworth Road, Northampton.

JOLLIFFE, Alexander
D/11132, 30/4/17; No. 12 O.C.B., 10/8/17; R. War. R., 27/11/17;
It; Lieut.; Special Medal.
Meadow Cottage, Willaston, Birkenhead, Cheshire. (Now in India).

JOLLY, Herbert
C/10196, 15/12/16, L/C.; No. 14 O.C.B., 6/4/17; E. Lan. R.,
31/7/17, att. Manch. R.; 2/Lieut.
Grunewald, Lostock Park, Bolton, Lancashire.

JOLLYE, Henry Patrick Lynch
A/9819, 30/10/16; No. 14 O.C.B., 27/12/16; K.R. Rif. C., 27/3/17;
S,F; Lieut. Manila Electric Coy., Manila, Phillipine Islands.

JOLLYE, Stanley Arthur
Sq/3069, 18/3/15, L/C.; N. Som. Yeo., 25/6/15, Tank Corps; F;
Capt.; w. Brooklands, Marlowes, Hemel Hempsted.

JOLOWICZ, Herbert Felix
D/1475, 29/9/14; Bedf. R., 10/2/15; G,E,F; Lieut.
70 Compayne Gardens, West Hampstead, N.W.6.

JOLOWICZ, Paul
D/9916, 15/11/16, L/C.; R.W. Surr. R., 9/3/17, Lab. Corps;
Lieut. 34 Old Change, E.C.

JOLY, Richard Reginald
C/14203, 21/10/18; demob. 19/12/18.
141 Castle Street, Salisbury, Wiltshire.

JONES, Alan Vaughan
C/13397, 25/6/18; No. 3 O.C.B., 10/2/19; R.W. Fus., 17/3/19;
2/Lieut. Frondeg, Radyr, Nr. Cardiff.

JONES, Alfred Bamber
6/5/5939, 1/9/15; L'pool. R., 21/4/16, att. Ches. R.; M; Lieut.;
p. Nyroca, 10 Monk Road, Liscard, Cheshire.

JONES, Alfred Thomas
A/10276, 1/1/17; dis. med. unfit, 21/5/17.
Bryn, 121 Woodwarde Road, Dulwich, S.E.22.

✠ JONES, Arthur Ewart
K/2257, 7/12/14; Welch R., 8/12/14; 2/Lieut.
Killed in action 8/8/15.

JONES, Arthur Joseph
2/3456, 3/5/15; 10th Lond. R., 29/9/15.
159 Hither Green Lane, Lewisham, S.E.13.

JONES, Arthur Linley
E/1610, 6/10/14; Dorset R., 27/2/15.

JONES, Arthur Llewelyn
6/4/6420, 23/9/15; E. Surr. R., att. K.R. Rif. C.; F; Lieut.;
g, w; M.C. 19 Redcliffe Gardens, Ilford, Essex.

JONES, Arthur Richard
C/10625, 26/1/17; No. 11 O.C.B., 5/7/17; R.F.C., 27/11/17,
Ches. R.; S; 2/Lieut. 55 Bedford Road, Rock Ferry, Cheshire.

JONES, Arthur Wilfred Bamford
6/5656, 16/8/15; R.W. Fus., 1/6/16, K. Af. Rif.; Germ.EA;
Lieut.
Gellygaer Rectory, Glamorganshire, South Wales. (Now in West Africa.)

JONES, Besil Portier
A/1124, 7/9/14, L/C.; Midd'x. R., 23/12/14, secd. R.F.C., R.A.F.;
Lieut.

JONES, Carlton Gwynne
4/6/5/4902, 15/7/15; No. 7 O.C.B., 6/4/16; R.W. Fus., 4/8/16;
F; Lieut.; Inv.; M.C.
c/o V. Hadfield Jones Esq., 34c Nevern Place, Earls Court, S.W.5.

JONES, Ceulanytt Emlyn
6/2/7588, 18/11/15; dis. med. unfit, 26/9/16.
Metropolitan Theological College, Newington.

✠ JONES, Charles Arnold
6/2/7926, 29/11/15; A.S.C., C/S, 1/9/16; R.A.S.C., 25/10/16,
Manch. R., R. Berks. R.; F; 2/Lieut. Died of wounds 1/5/18.

✠ JONES, Charles David
2/9785, 25/10/16; No. 14 O.C.B., 27/12/16; W. Rid. R., 27/3/17,
att. British Portuguese Mission; 2/Lieut. Died 7/3/18.

JONES, Clifford Erskine
C/D/13236, 7/6/18; No. 11 O.C.B., 24/1/19; General List, 8/3/19;
2/Lieut.
c/o D. A. Arderne Esq., 141 Longmarket Street, Capetown, South Africa.

JONES, Cyril
4/6/Sq/4933, 19/7/15; R.F.A., 13/1/16, att. T.M. Bty., R.E.;
Lieut.; w. Chelston, Mumbles, South Wales.

JONES, Cyril McLean
D/10899, 21/3/17; No. 11 O.C.B., 5/7/17; E. Surr. R., 30/10/17;
2/Lieut. 12 Guilford Avenue, Surbiton.

JONES, David Edward
6/5/5940, 1/9/15; L'pool. R., 23/4/16.

JONES, David John
B/11395, 30/5/17; No. 11 O.C.B., 9/11/17; trfr. Class W. Res.,
26/2/18. 50 Oakfield Street, Cardiff.

APPENDIX II.—RECORDS OF RANK AND FILE.

JONES, David Laurence
6/6185, 13/9/15; R.A., C/S, 9/6/16; R.F.A., 30/9/16; Lieut.; w.
15 Russell Square, W.C. 1

JONES, David Trevor
E/1512, 1/10/14; R.W. Fus., 16/2/15; 2/Lieut.
75 Savoy Chambers, Cairo, Egypt.

JONES, David Wilson
6/3/8712, 5/1/16; R.A., C/S, 23/6/16; R.G.A., 27/9/16, att. R.E.; F; Lieut.; w. Knelston, Reynoldston, Swansea.

✠ JONES, Edward Earle
K/2735, 18/1/15; York. R., 12/3/15; 2/Lieut.
Died of wounds 1/8/16.

JONES, Edward George Arnold
4/1/4514, 28/6/15; York. & Lanc. R., 23/9/15, R.A.F.; F; Lieut.; Inv; M.C., M(1). St. Mary de Crypt Rectory, Gloucester.

JONES, Edward Oliver
1/3781, 27/5/15; R.W. Fus., 9/11/15, att. R.W. Surr. R.; F; Lieut. Lark Hill, Conway, North Wales.

✠ JONES, Edward Stanley
4/1/4542, 1/7/15, Sgt.; R.A.O.C., 7/1/17; Lieut.
Died 28/11/18.

JONES, Edwin Hevin
C/D/13394, 24/6/18; trfr. R.A.M.C., 30/5/19.
26 Pool Street, Carnarvon, North Wales.

✠ JONES, Eric
4/5/4710, 9/7/15; L'pool. R., 19/12/15; F; 2/Lieut.
Killed in action 2/7/16.

JONES, Ernest
A/2760, 21/1/15; E. Lan. R., 3/6/15.
5 Bridgefield Street, Radcliffe, Lancashire.

JONES, Ernest Lionel
6/1/8592, 3/1/16; No. 5 O.C.B., 14/8/16; R. Fus., 21/11/16; F; Capt.; Inv; M.C. 47 Wembdon Road, Bridgewater, Somerset.

JONES, Ernest Pryce
C/D/12252, 27/11/17; No. 5 O.C.B., 10/5/18, No. 14 O.C.B.; Hamps. R., 3/2/19; 2/Lieut. York House, Cosham, Hampshire.

JONES, Evan Claude Llewellyn
6/1/7015, 26/10/14; No. 11 O.C.B., 7/5/16; R.W. Fus., 4/9/16, att. R. Innis. Fus.; Lieut.
Maes-yr-haf, Cefn-Coed Road, Roathlake, Cardiff.

✠ JONES, Evelyn Llewellyn Hustler
F/2612, 7/1/15; R.W. Fus., 11/5/15; G,E,P; 2/Lieut.
Killed in action 26/3/17.

✠ JONES, Felix Ernest
4/3/4131, 10/6/15, C.Q.M.S.; Oxf. & Bucks. L.I., 12/12/15; Lieut.; w; M.C. Killed in action 16/8/17.

JONES, Frederick Buttenshaw
5/3/6471, 27/9/15; No. 7 O.C.B., 18/5/16; Lond. Div. Cyc. Coy., 4/9/16, Army Cyc. Corps; F; Lieut.; M(1).
123 Torridon Road, Catford, S.E. 6.

✠ JONES, Frederick Thomas Averary
2/3674, 17/5/15; Hereford R., 23/7/16; 2/Lieut.; w.
Died of wounds 5/12/17.

JONES, Geoffrey
6/1/8505, 23/12/15; No. 8 O.C.B., 4/8/16; Welch R., 21/11/16; F; 2/Lieut.
c/o A. G. Jones, Esq., Mentenottle, Crown Park, Cork.

JONES, George Angus Champion
K/A/2504, 31/12/14; E. Surr. R., 23/4/15, R.E. Sigs.; F; Capt.
7 Bury Street, St. Mary Axe, E.C. 3.

✠ JONES, George James
B/1695, 13/10/14, L/C.; Lan. Fus., 9/1/15, R.F.C.; F; Capt.
Killed in action 7/4/17.

JONES, Gerald Francis
C/1153, 14/9/14, Sgt.; D. of Corn. L.I., 7/1/15, R.E.; F,It; Major; O.B.E., Croci di Guerra, M(2).
329 High Holborn, W.C. 1.

✠ JONES, Gerald Spencer Evans
C/12571, 6/2/18; Died 7/3/18.

JONES, Glyn Howard
6/1/9036, 20/1/16; No. 8 O.C.B., 4/8/16; T.F. Res., 7/10/16; Lieut.; O.B.E. 48 Strathavna Road, Wallasey, Cheshire

✠ JONES, Griffith Morris
6/3/5853, 26/8/15; West. & Cumb. Yeo., 23/10/15.
Died 13/12/18.

✠ JONES, Griffith Vaughan
6/5/6910, 18/10/15; No. 14 O.C.B., 27/9/16; No. 2 O.C.B.; Shrop. L.I., 25/4/17; F; 2/Lieut.; w.
Died of wounds as Prisoner of War, 24/4/18.

JONES, Gwynne Mervyn
6/2/6227, 13/9/15, L/C.; E. Kent R., 15/4/16, att. N. Lan. R.; Capt.; M.C.

JONES, Harold Austin
4/5/4798, 12/7/15, L/C.; Suff. R., 1/6/16; Lieut.; w.

JONES, Harold Lavender
6/2/6089, 6/9/15, L/C.; E. Kent R., 9/6/16; Staff Capt.; M.C

JONES, Harry Percival
E/14054, 23/9/18; demob. 29/1/19.
9 York Avenue, Wolverhampton.

✠ JONES, Harry Reynolds
A/11227, 7/5/17; R.F.C., C/S, 1/6/17; R.F.C., 4/7/17; 2/Lieut.
Killed in action 17/3/18.

JONES, Harry William
D/10687, 7/2/17; R.F.C., C/S, 13/3/17; R.F.C., 19/4/17; 2/Lieut.
136 Dawes Road, Fulham, S.W. 6.

JONES, Henry Aubrey
D/11867, 16/8/17; No. 3 O.C.B., 8/2/18; Norf. R., 30/7/18; F; 2/Lieut. 27 Leander Road, Thornton Heath, Surrey.

JONES, Henry Francis Gordon
6/3/7844, 25/11/15; No. 8 O.C.B., 4/8/16; trfr. 16th Lond. R., 6/12/16, Army Pay Corps; F; Pte.; w.
The Cote, Northwick Road, Evesham, Worcestershire.

JONES, Henry Gilman
A/10820, 2/3/17; A.S.C., C/S, 1/9/17; R.A.S.C., 27/10/17; F; Lieut. 8 Bexley Square, Salford.

JONES, Henry Gwynne
D/10000, 24/11/16; No. 14 O.C.B., 6/4/17; R.W. Fus., 31/7/17; Lieut.; w(2).
The Nook, Victoria Avenue, Porthcawl, Glamorganshire.

JONES, Henry William
5/4/4751, 12/7/15, Cpl.; Devon. R., 5/10/15; F,It; Major; w; M.C. 90 Grosvenor Road, Westminster, S.W. 1.

JONES, Herbert
6/6785, 11/10/15; dis. to re-enlist in R.A.S.C., 19/12/15.

JONES, Herbert Alan Reid
6/4/7992, 29/11/15; Devon. R., 15/3/17; F; 2/Lieut.
Carreg Llwyd, Oswestry, Salop

JONES, Herbert Augustus
A/11649, 12/7/17; No. 19 O.C.B., 9/11/17; K.R. Rif. C., 26/3/18, att. R.E.; SR; 2/Lieut. 93 Walm Lane, Cricklewood, N.W. 2.

JONES, Hugh David
6/4/7177, 3/11/15; R.W. Fus., 24/10/16; Lieut.; w.

JONES, Hugh Hughes
1/3573, 10/5/15, L/C.; R.A.S.C., 24/1/16; M; Capt.
c/o Oficina General, F.C. Sud, Plaza Constitution, Buenos Aires

JONES, Humphrey Edward
6/2/7178, 3/11/15; No. 11 O.C.B., 7/5/16; R.W. Fus., 4/9/16; F; Lieut.; g. c/o Technical College, Durban, South Africa.

JONES, Isaac
6/4/8643, 3/1/16; No. 14 O.C.B., 29/8/16; R.W. Fus., 22/11/16.
East Lynne, Holyhead Road, Bangor.

JONES, James Greer
6/5/9006, 19/1/16; No. 5 O.C.B., 14/8/16; Lein. R., 21/11/16; F; Lieut.; Inv.
Mount Charles, Slane, Co. Meath, Ireland. (Now in British Columbia).

JONES, James Ivor Morgan
B/12737, 11/3/18; No. 20 O.C.B., 20/9/18; S. Wales Bord., 17/3/19; 2/Lieut.
Maes-yr-Houl, Cymmer, Porth, Glamorganshire.

✠ JONES, James Thomas
6/1/6622, 4/10/15; 20th Lond. R., 14/7/16; 2/Lieut.
Died of wounds 24/8/17.

APPENDIX II.—RECORDS OF RANK AND FILE.

JONES, John Edward
C/10605, 22/1/17; R.F.C., C/S, 4/5/17; R.F.C., 14/6/17, R.A.F.; F; 2/Lieut.
22 King Street, Leigh, Lancashire.

JONES, John Elias
E/14160, 14/10/18; R.G.A., C/S, 1/11/18; R.G.A., 13/4/19; 2/Lieut.
146 High Street, Portmadoc, North Wales.

JONES, John Ewart Sibbering
B/9897, 10/11/16, Sgt.; No. 14 O.C.B., 9/11/17; Welch R., 30/4/18; F; Lieut.
8 Church Place, Porthcawl, Glamorganshire.

JONES, John Ferdinand
6/Sq/7680, 22/11/15; R.A., C/S, 24/1/16; R.F.A., 31/1/16; Lieut.

JONES, John Hugh Oscar
6/2/9475, 14/2/16; R.F.C., 7/7/16; F; Capt.; Croix de Guerre, Order of the Belgian Crown.
Isbury House, Marlborough, Wiltshire.

JONES, John Lees
4/5/4699, 8/7/15, L/C.; R.F.A., 1/12/15; S; Lieut.; Inv.
2 Albert Road, Whalley Range, Manchester.

✠ JONES, John Llewelyn Thomas
6/2/7234, 5/11/15; 3rd Lond. R., 4/8/16; F; Capt.; w.
Killed in action 16/8/17.

JONES, John Parry
6/5/7418, 12/11/15, L/C.; R.N.V.R., 8/9/16; North Sea; Lieut.
Westview, Breck Road, Wallasey, Cheshire.

JONES, John Pugh
A/10700, 13/2/17; No. 11 O.C.B., 5/7/17; Hunt. Cyc. Bn., 30/10/17, Bedf. R.; Lieut.
1 Church Street, Bishop's Castle, Shropshire.

JONES, John Richard
6/2/9067, 21/1/16; No. 14 O.C.B., 30/10/16; R.M.L.I., 28/2/17; F; Lieut.
c/o Chief Constable, Bodlondeb, Dolgelley, North Wales.

JONES, Joseph Arthur Eddy
B/13915, 24/8/18; No. 13 O.C.B., 10/2/19; demob. 22/4/19.
39 Frederick Street, Werneth, Oldham.

JONES, Joseph Harold Parry
6/2/6603, 4/10/15; Welch R., 1/6/16, M.G.C.; F; Capt.
Cantley, Connaught Avenue, Chingford, Essex.

JONES, Joseph Llewellyn
6/2/D/5561, 12/8/15, Cpl.; dis. to R. Mil. Coll., 3/11/16; K.R. Rif. C., 29/8/17.

JONES, Kenneth Leslie
6/4/9144, 25/1/16; No. 14 O.C.B., 30/10/16; Welch R., 28/2/17, att. R.N. Div.; F; Capt.; w; M.C.
37 Romilly Park, Barry, Glamorganshire.

JONES, Lawrence Evelyn
Sq/419, 21/5/09; Bedf. Yeo., 28/4/13, M.G.C.; F; Major; w-p; M.C., M(1).
15 Cleneland Gardens, W.2.

JONES, Leslie William
6/1/6892, 18/10/15; No. 11 O.C.B., 7/5/16; Devon. R., 4/9/16, Indian Army; P,Afghan; Lieut.
55 Lyndhurst Drive, Leyton, E.10.

JONES, Lewis William Neville
4/5/5114, 26/7/15; R.W. Fus., 4/8/16, 4th Lond. R., Indian Army; F,I; Lieut.; w.
The Poplars, Buckley, Chester.

JONES, Lionel Baker
4/3854, 31/5/15; Welch R., 16/9/15, R.F.C., R.A.F.; F,E,P; Lieut.; M.C.
Brynfield, Reynoldston, Glamorganshire, South Wales.

JONES, Llewelin Hopkin
6/Sq/5283, 31/7/15; R.A.S.C., 27/11/15; Capt.
Blaermant, Pontordine, Glamorganshire.

JONES, Nevile Marriott
6/4/5/4934, 19/7/15; R. Highrs., 10/1/16, att. R. Fus.; Germ.EA,F; Capt.; w(2).
Grosvenor House, Upper Maudlin Street, Bristol. (Now in West Africa.)

JONES, Norman Harry
6/5/9505, 15/2/16; R.A., C/S, 1/9/16; R.G.A., 10/12/16, att. R.A.F.; F; Lieut.
119 Herbert Road, Woolwich, S.E.18.

✠ JONES, Owen Morris
6/1/7927, 29/11/15; No. 2 O.C.B., 14/8/16; R.W. Fus., 18/12/16; Lieut.
Killed in action 31/10/18.

JONES, Penry Lottyn
6/Sq/6169, 11/9/15; Lond. Div. Eng., 13/12/15.
Pentwyn, Raven Hill, Swansea.

✠ JONES, Percival Halley
1/3163, 1/4/15; E. Surr. R., 10/7/15, 7th Lond. R.; F; Capt.; M.C.
Killed in action 9/3/18.

JONES, Percy
6/3/7528, 16/11/15, L/C.; No. 11 O.C.B., 7/5/16; 7th Lond. R., 4/9/16, att. T.M. Bty.; F; Lieut.; w.
46 College Road, Whalley Range, Manchester.

JONES, Philip Francis
6/5/8026, 30/11/15, L/C.; No. 14 O.C.B., 27/9/16; 15th Lond. R., 24/1/17, att. Midd'x. R., emp. M. of Munitions; F; Lieut.; w.
Selattyn, Purley Downs Road, Purley, Surrey.

JONES, Ralph Mansel
6/1/5743, 20/8/15; North'd. Fus., 1/6/16; Lieut.
Hilltop, Tyrfran Villas, Llanelly.

JONES, Reginald Austin
6/5/5361, 3/8/15; Welch R., 22/1/16.

JONES, Richard Granville
A/14320, 30/12/18; demob. 10/1/19.
Lancing, 42 Belgrave Road, Wanstead, E.11.

JONES, Richard Lewis
C/D/12051, 27/9/17, L/C.; R.A., C/S, 15/3/18; R.F.A., 24/10/18; 2/Lieut.
59 Warren Road, Morriston, Swansea.

✠ JONES, Robert Nelson
4/1/4604, 5/7/15; North'n. R., 12/11/15, M.G.C.; Lieut.
Killed in action 31/7/17.

✠ JONES, Robert Rowland Akrill. See AKRILL-JONES, R. R.

JONES, Ronald Charles
A/13020, 2/5/18; No. 1 O.C.B., 8/11/18, No. 3 O.C.B.; S. Staff. R., 19/3/19; 2/Lieut.
180 Newhampton Road East, Wolverhampton.

JONES, Ronald Henry
B/10972, 2/4/17, L/C.; No. 12 O.C.B., 10/8/17; Bord. R., 27/11/17; 2/Lieut.
27 Meteor Road, Westcliffe-on-Sea.

JONES, St. John Henry Maurice
B/11988, 10/9/17, L/C.; R.F.C., C/S, 26/11/17, No. 19 O.C.B.; R. War R., 3/3/19; 2/Lieut.
99 Wolfington Road, West Norwood, S.E.27.

JONES, Sidney Presland
2/3505, 6/5/15; 7th Lond. R., 2/7/15; Lieut.
Heathcote, Unthank Road, Norwich.

JONES, Stanley Wynn
D/12908, 8/4/18; No. 5 O.C.B., 8/11/18, Nos. 20 & 11 O.C.B.; demob. 17/2/19.
16 Prince's Avenue, Great Crosby, Liverpool. (Now in Ceylon).

✠ JONES, Sydney James
2/3458, 3/5/15; R.W. Kent R., 14/7/15; Lieut.
Killed in action 15/9/16.

✠ JONES, Thomas
6/Sq/9204, 31/1/16; R.A., C/S, 26/10/16; R.F.A., 27/2/17; 2/Lieut.
Killed in action 31/7/17.

JONES, Thomas Anthony W.
Sq/1339, 26/9/14; R.F.A., 5/10/14; Lieut.
Windwhistle, Meonstoke, Bishops Waltham, Hampshire.

✠ JONES, Thomas Bertram
5/5/5226, 30/7/15;
Died 26/10/15.

✠ JONES, Thomas Esmor
6/1/7296, 8/11/15; R.W. Fus., 4/9/16; Lieut.; w.
Killed in action 6/4/18.

JONES, Thomas Ifor
6/1/6237, 14/9/15; R.A.S.C., 9/2/16, R.W. Fus.; F,S; Lieut.
Ty Mawr, Rumney, Cardiff.

JONES, Thomas James
C/A/D/12052, 27/9/17; R.E., C/S, 12/5/18; R.E., 27/9/18; 2/Lieut.
White House, Russell Hill, Purley, Surrey.

✠ JONES, Thomas Lewis
6/2/7357, 10/11/15; Worc. R., 4/8/16; Lieut.
Died of wounds 10/10/18.

APPENDIX II.—RECORDS OF RANK AND FILE.

JONES, Thomas Roberts
6/4/7071, 29/10/15, L/C.; R.W. Fus., 4/9/16, K. Af. Rif.; F,Germ.EA; Lieut. 13 North Villas, Camden Town, N.

JONES, Trevor Tyrwhitt Palmer
A/10696, 14/2/17; R.A., C/S, 22/6/17; trfr. R.F.A., 8/10/17.
48 Barons Court Road, West Kensington, W. 14.

JONES, Valentine William Fowles
C/13370, 21/6/18; trfr. 14th Lond. R., 6/12/18; Cpl.
Yatesfield, Nailsworth, Gloucestershire.

✠ JONES, Vavasor
6/4/5/4857, 15/7/15; No. 11 O.C.B., 7/5/16; R.W. Fus., 4/9/16; 2/Lieut. Killed in action 19/5/17.

JONES, Victor Berwyn
4/Sq/4396, 24/6/15, L/C.; R.A., C/S, 24/1/16; R.F.A., 16/6/16; F; Lieut.; w-g.
Lindisfarne, Langley Road, Watford, Hertfordshire.

JONES, Victor Robert
B/13621, 24/7/18; trfr. R. Highrs., 2/5/19.
Post Office, Presteign, Radnorshire.

JONES, Walter
12123, 15/10/17; No. 18 O.C.B., 10/5/18; Wilts. R., 4/2/19; 2/Lieut. 6 High Street, Malmesbury, Wiltshire.

✠ JONES, Walter Truran
6/2/6873, 18/10/15, L/C.; Manch. R., 1/6/16; F; 2/Lieut.
Killed in action 12/10/16.

JONES, Watkin John Brynmor
6/5/6839, 14/10/15; No. 7 O.C.B., 6/4/16; R. Lanc. R., 4/8/16, M.G.C.; Lieut. Wyndham House, Dowlais, Glamorganshire.

JONES, Wilfred Edwards
6/4/9216, 31/1/16; No. 14 O.C.B., 26/11/16; R. Lanc. R., 28/2/17; F; Lieut.; w-g. 3 Brunswick Square, Penrith, Cumberland.

JONES, William
B/11720, 19/7/17; trfr. R.G.A., 9/11/17.
23 Humphrey Terrace, Caeran, Glamorganshire.

✠ JONES, William Bartholomew
6/1/7263, 8/11/15, L/C.; M.G.C., 25/9/16; 2/Lieut.; w.
Killed in action 27/5/18.

JONES, William Edward
5681, 16/8/15; 23rd Lond. R., 12/1/16, att. 29th Lond. R.; F; Lieut.; w(2). 118 West Side, Clapham Common, S.W. 4.

JONES, William Edward
6/4/6228, 13/9/15; R.A.M.C., 16/12/15; Capt.
4 Abbey Square, Chester.

JONES, William Harold
4/3/5115, 26/7/15; Shrop. L.I., 24/11/15, secd. M.G.C.; Lieut.; w. Cathorp Police House, Cnwys Road, Cardiff.

JONES, William Henry
6/4/8064, 1/12/15; No. 5 O.C.B., 14/8/16; N. Lan. R., 21/11/16; Lieut. Derrygolan, Kilbeggan, Co. Westmeath.

✠ JONES, William Henry
A/10506, 15/1/17; No. 14 O.C.B., 7/6/17; York. R., 25/9/17; 2/Lieut. Killed in action 27/5/18.

JONES, William Herbert
2/2962, 24/2/15, Cpl.; Worc. R., 21/10/15; Capt.
Ivy House, New Barnet, Hertfordshire.

JONES, William Hindmarsh
6/5/7419, 12/11/15; L'pool. R., 24/10/16, secd. M.G.C.; F; Lieut. 45 Glenwyllin Road, Waterloo, Liverpool.

JONES, William Jefferiss
6/4/9394, 9/2/16; No. 8 O.C.B., 4/8/16; K.R. Rif. C., 21/11/16; F; Lieut.; Inv. Birklands, Clevedon, Somerset.

JONES, William Poole Lester
6/9927, 13/11/16, Cpl.; R.F.C., C/S, 8/3/17; R.F.C., 9/5/17, R.A.F.; F; Lieut.
3 Suffield Chambers, 79 Davies Street, Berkeley Square, W. 1.

JONES, Wyndham
6/2/8027, 30/11/15; No. 8 O.C.B., 4/8/16, M.G.C., C/S; M.G.C., 23/11/16. Cartef, Cwmavon, Nr. Port Talbot.

JOPE, Francis Edward
6/3/5407, 5/8/15; trfr. R.A.M.C., 10/3/16.
60 Baxter Avenue, Southend-on-Sea.

JORDAN, Frank Hugh Dormer
6/4/8965, 17/1/16; R.A., C/S, 4/8/16; R.G.A., 26/11/16; 2/Lieut.

JORDAN, John Paul
Sq/870, 4/8/14; R.G.A., 4/11/14; F; Lt.-Col.; M.C., Croix de Guerre (Belge), Order of Leopold (Belge), M(2).
93 South Croxted Road, Dulwich, S.E. 21.

JORDAN, Richard
6/2/8065, 1/12/15; No. 14 O.C.B., 6/9/16; Worc. R., 28/2/17; F; Lieut.; Inj. Kestle, St. Thomas, Launceston, Cornwall.

JORDAN, Victor Frederick
6/1/9110, 24/1/16; No. 13 O.C.B., 4/11/16; North'd. Fus., 28/2/17; F; 2/Lieut.; w. 32 Handsworth Wood Road, Birmingham.

JORDAN, Victor Stuart
B/10775, 19/2/17; R.A., C/S, 29/6/17; R.F.A., 22/1/18; F; Lieut.; g. Broad Marston, Stratford-on-Avon.

✠ JOSCELYNE, Clement Percy
2/9692, 5/10/16; No. 14 O.C.B., 30/1/17; Suff. R., 29/5/17; 2/Lieut. Died of wounds 10/10/17.

✠ JOSELAND, Frederick Osborn
4/6/5/4858, 15/7/15; 12th Lond. R., 19/12/15; 2/Lieut.
Killed in action 21/10/16.

✠ JOSEPH, William Franklin George
H/1684, 12/10/14; R. Berks. R., 17/3/15; F; 2/Lieut.
Killed in action 27/5/18.

JOULE, John Wilfred
Sq/2816, 29/1/15; Notts. Yeo., 13/7/15; Lieut.

JOULE, Robert Jackson
Sq/K/2714, 18/1/15, L/C.; Notts. & Derby. Yeo., 10/7/15; Lieut. Holly Bank, Paynes Lane, Pinner.

✠ JOWETT, Harold Crossley
D/10235, 29/12/16; No. 14 O.C.B., 5/5/17; Lan. Fus., 28/8/17; 2/Lieut. Killed in action 1/9/18.

✠ JOWETT, James Atkinson- See ATKINSON-JOWETT, J.

JOWETT, Priestly
4/5/4799, 12/7/15; W. York. R., 18/10/15, emp. M. of Labour; Lieut.; w; M.C. 13 Belmont Bridge, Skipton.

JOWITT, Robert Lionel Palgrave
A/D/11886, 20/8/17; No. 23 O.C.B., 5/4/18; trfr. 28th Lond. R., 17/8/18. Chilland, Nr. Winchester.

✠ JOYCE, Philip Soloman
6/1/6939, 20/10/15; R.F.C., 2/6/16; Lieut.
Missing believed killed 6/3/17.

JOYCE, Thomas Michael
6/5/7028, 27/10/15; No. 7 O.C.B., 3/7/16; R.N.V.R., 21/11/16, att. Tank Corps; F; Lieut.
29 Rathmines Road, Rathmines, Dublin.

JOYNSON, Sydney Davies
6/2/9460, 14/2/16; No. 14 O.C.B., 26/11/16; R. Berks. R., 27/3/17, att. Som. L.I.; I; Lieut.
Longcroft House, Woodgreen, Wednesbury, South Staffordshire.

✠ JOYNT, Albert William Lane
F/1821, 16/10/14; Dorset. R., 20/10/14, M.G.C.; Lieut.
Killed in action 26/2/16.

✠ JOYNT, Ivor William
C/505, 4/11/10; dis. med. unfit, 1/7/14.

JUDD, Alfred Cecil
6/2/7928, 29/11/15; R.A., C/S, 26/10/16, M.G.C., C/S; Tank Corps, 26/7/17, Indian Army; F,I; Lieut.
18 Wolseley Gardens, Chiswick, W. 4.

JUDSON, Henry Lawrence
F/1800, 16/10/14, L/C.; Oxf. & Bucks. L.I., 9/3/15; F; Lieut.

JULYAN, William Leopold
1/9640, 26/9/16; No. 14 O.C.B., 27/12/16; D. of Corn. L.I., 25/4/17; F; Lt.-Col.; M(2).
Meledor, Grampound Road S.O., Cornwall.

APPENDIX II.—RECORDS OF RANK AND FILE.

KANE, *Michael Harry Kirkpatrick*
6/2/6822, 14/10/15; R. Dub. Fus., 1/6/16, R.A.F.; F; Lieut.; w; M.C. University College Hospital, Gower Street, W.C. 1.

✠ KANN, *Edward Henry*
D/1525, 5/10/14; N. Lan. R., 19/11/14, R.F.C.; Lieut.
Killed in action 21/10/17.

KAPP, *Edmond Xavier*
K/H/2251, 7/12/14; R. Suss. R., 31/3/15; F; Capt.; M(1).
Studio, 72 West End Lane, N.W. 6. (Now in Austria).

KARSTEL, *Claude Adolphus*
6/4/6090, 6/9/15; North'd. Fus., 8/7/16, secd. Tank Corps; Lieut.
c/o Fowlie & Boden, 29-35 City Road, E.C.

✠ KATZ, *Sampson Goldstone*
C/1622, 9/10/14; R. Lanc. R., 10/3/15; F; Lieut.
Died of wounds 19/7/18.

KAY, *Cecil*
D/13833, 14/8/18; demob. 30/5/19.
82 Wynyerd Road, Hillsboro', Sheffield.

KAY, *Charles Bagnall*
A/D/11912, 27/8/17; No. 4 O.C.B., 5/4/18; M.G.C., 12/11/18; 2/Lieut. The Lodge, Bramley, Leeds, Yorkshire.

KAY, *George Alban*
6/5/6047, 3/9/15; A.S.C., C/S, 18/9/16; R.A.S.C., 22/10/16.
48 Alexandra Road, South Shore, Blackpool.

KAY, *George Leonard*
C/13201, 5/6/18, L/C.; trfr. 14th Lond. R., 6/12/18.
Highercroft, Lower Dorwen, Lancashire.

✠ KAY, *Melville Herbert*
4/6/3/4886, 15/7/15, L/C.; Durh. L.I., 21/12/15; 2/Lieut.
Killed in action 5/11/16.

KAY, *Wilfred Percival Heath*
A/14321, 30/12/18; No. 11 O.C.B., 25/1/19; General List, 8/3/19; 2/Lieut.
18 Tividale Street, Tipton, Staffordshire.

KAYE, *Bertram David*
D/10920, 26/3/17, L/C.; No. 14 O.C.B., 5/7/17; R. Scots, 30/10/17, att. Sco. Rif.; F; 2/Lieut.
74 Blackford Avenue, Edinburgh.

✠ KAYE, *Eric Priestley*
4/5/4675, 8/7/15; W. Rid. R., 29/10/15; 2/Lieut.
Killed in action 3/5/17.

KAYE, *George Hartley Carr*
4/6/2/4974, 19/7/15, L/C.; York. & Lanc. R., 10/1/16; F; Lieut.; Inv. Cluny, St. James Park, Harrogate.

KAYE, *William Herbert*
6/1/8484, 20/12/15; trfr. R.G.A., 17/11/16.
7 Marlborough Road, Blackheath, S.E.

KEADY, *Thomas Pakenham*
6/4/6285, 16/9/15; R.E., C/S, 18/3/16; R.E., 6/7/16, secd. R.F.C.; Lieut.

KEANE, *Edmond Patrick*
6/5/9007, 19/1/16; No. 5 O.C.B., 14/8/16; Muns. Fus., 21/11/16, R. Ir. Rif.; F,It; Lieut.; Inv.
Milltown Castle, Charleville, Co. Cork. Ireland.

KEANE, *John Francis*
A/11205, 7/5/17, Sgt.; demob. 31/1/19.
78 Parchmore Road, Thornton Heath, Surrey. (Now in Paris).

KEARNEY, *John*
6/5/7333, 9/11/15; dis. med. unfit, 22/9/16.
South Main Street, Bandon, Co. Cork, Ireland.

KEARNEY, *Maurice*
6/5/D/5854, 26/8/15, Sgt.; No. 7 O.C.B., 3/7/16; demob. 19/5/19.
Ballinamona House, Tullamore, King's Co., Ireland.

KEATES, *William Albert*
6/4/7845, 25/11/15; No. 14 O.C.B., M.G.C., C/S; M.G.C., 28/12/16; F; Lieut.; M.C.
55 South Park Road, Wimbledon, S.W. 19. (Now in Buenos Aires).

KEATING, *Arthur Patrick*
3/3855, 31/5/15; Bedf. R., 10/9/15, Suff. R.; Lieut.
17 Upper Market Street, Woolwich, S.E. 18

KEATING, *Henry Charles*
4/1/5038, 22/7/15, L/C.; York. R., 20/1/16, Tank Corps; Lieut.; w. 88 Sanderville Mansions, Maida Vale, W. 9.

KEATS, *Claude Achille*
6/4/8983, 18/1/16; No. 14 O.C.B., 26/11/16; Ches. R., 30/10/17, att. R.F.C. and Lab. Corps; F; Lieut.; cr.
33 Cauldon Road, Shelton, Stoke-on-Trent, Staffordshire.

KEAYS, *William St. John Vivian*
D/10666, 5/2/17; R.F.A., C/S, 29/6/17; R.F.A., 2/2/18; 2/Lieut.

✠ KEBBLEWHITE, *Fred Edgar*
B/2792, 26/1/15; Notts. & Derby. R., 24/6/15, R.F.C.; 2/Lieut.; w. Killed in action 14/8/17.

✠ KEEBLE, *Alfred Ernest*
4/2/4647, 5/7/15; R. Fus., 12/10/15, M.G.C.; Capt.
Died of wounds 5/8/18.

KEEBLE, *Eric John*
D/13899, 23/8/18; trfr. K.R. Rif. C., 7/4/19.
16 The Rise, Palmers Green, N. 13.

KEEBLE, *Raymond Harry Lancelot*
4/9700, 9/10/16; No. 14 O.C.B., 30/1/17; Som. L. I., 29/5/17; Lieut. Washford, Taunton, Somerset.

KEECH, *Arthur Francis*
B/11672, 16/7/17; No. 14 O.C.B., 9/11/17; Notts. & Derby. R., 30/4/18; 2/Lieut. The Old Bank, Alton, Hampshire.

KEEGAN, *Alfred Thomas*
B/11351, 25/5/17; No. 16 O.C.B., 5/10/17; R. Muns. Fus., 12/3/18, Rif. Brig., R.W. Kent. R., att. R.A.F.; F; Lieut.
Rosegreen, Clonmel, Co. Tipperary, Ireland.

KEEGAN, *Edwin Robert*
B/2062, 12/11/14, Cpl.; R.A.S.C., 23/4/15, emp. R. Sco. Fus.; Lieut.; M(1).

✠ KEEGAN, *Patrick George*
C/14171, 12/10/18; Died 3/11/18.

✠ KEELER, *Oscar Alan*
6/3/8834, 10/1/16, Sgt.; 7th Lond. R., 27/8/16; 2/Lieut.; M.C
Killed in action 20/9/17.

KEELY, *Reginald Philipps*
6/5/7829, 29/11/15; No. 14 O.C.B., 27/9/16; 7th Lond. R., 24/1/17, 11th Lond. R., R.A.F.; F; Capt.; M(1).
8 Warrington Gardens, Maida Vale, W. 9.

KEELY, *Thomas Calder Southwell*
4/2/4377, 21/6/15; L'pool. R., 7/10/15, att. Leic. R., Ches. R and 19th Lond. R.; F,M,E,P; Lieut.; w.
7 Netherton Road, St. Margarets, Twickenham.

KEEN, *Lionel Charles*
6/3/6441, 25/9/15; R.A.S.C., 4/12/15, R.F.C.; F; Lieut.; Inj.
Cremyll, Victoria Avenue, Southend-on-Sea. (Now in F.M.S.).

✠ KEEN, *William Allan*
K/C/2184, 26/11/14; Midd'x. R., 14/3/15, att. W. Som. Yeo and Som. L.I.; E,P,F; Capt. Died of wounds 5/9/18.

KEENE, *William John Augustus*
4/1/3902, 31/5/15; 2nd Lond. R., 5/10/15, R.F.C., R.A.F.; F; Lieut. Opposite Palmers Green Station, G.N. Rly., N. 13.

KEEP, *Herbert Stanley*
C/11727, 23/7/17; No. 14 O.C.B., 7/12/17; North'n. R., 28/5/18; F; 2/Lieut.; M.C.
School House, Arlesey, Nr. Hitchin, Hertfordshire.

✠ KEEP, *John Drummond*
D/11829, 9/8/17; No. 3 O.C.B., 8/2/18; 5th Lond. R., 30/7/18; 2/Lieut. Killed in action 13/10/18

KEFFORD, *Henry Withers*
6/1/7460, 15/11/15; R.A., C/S, 26/5/16; R.G.A., 19/11/16, emp. M. of Food; Lieut.
Fairview, Love Lane, Pinner, Middlesex.

KEIG, *Stanley Robertson*
6/3/8326, 10/12/15, L/C.; L'pool. R., 24/1/17; F; Lieut.
c/o A. Robertson Esq., Woodside Terrace, Douglas, Isle of Man.

KEIGHLEY, *Fred*
K/H/2384, 17/12/14, L/C.; 3rd Lond. R., 20/4/15, R.A.S.C.; F; Capt. 54 Stockwell Park Crescent, S.W. 9.

KEIGHTLEY, *John William*
D/10204, 18/12/16; No. 14 O.C.B., 6/4/17; Lan. Fus., 31/7/17, att. Sco. Rif.; F; 2/Lieut.; w.
3 Celtic Street, Princes Park, Liverpool.

APPENDIX II.—RECORDS OF RANK AND FILE.

☩ KEILLER, George Weston
6/3/7461, 15/11/15, L/C.; R.E., 13/3/16; Capt.
Died 9/3/19.

KEIR, Laurence
10685, 7/2/17; R.G.A., C/S, 26/9/17; R.G.A., 18/2/18; 2/Lieut.
Hamston House, Kensington Court, W.8.

KEITH, Cecil Graham
B/3027, 9/3/15, Sgt.; Gren. Gds., 17/11/15; F; Staff Capt.; M.C., M(1). 11 Stafford Terrace, Kensington, W.8.

KEITH, Neville Yorke
C/10354, 5/1/17, L/C.; No. 14 O.C.B., 7/6/17; Indian Army, 25/9/17. 73 Gunterstone Road, Barons Court, W.14.

☩ KEITH, Noel
B/876, 4/8/14; York. & Lanc. R., 12/9/14, Army Cyc. Corps, M.G.C., att. L'pool. R.; F; Capt. Killed in action 22/5/17.

KELK, Basil Milner
6/2/5303, 2/8/15; Notts. & Derby. R., 4/12/15, secd. Indian Army; Lieut.

KELLAWAY, Frederick Stewart
6/2/6091, 6/9/15; No. 2 Cav. C/S, 18/5/16; Worc. Yeo., 6/9/16; Lieut. Killarney, The Watering, St. Austell, Cornwall.

KELLEHER, Daniel Joseph
6/5/6067, 6/9/15; R. Ir. Regt., 6/7/16, Som. L.I.; F; Capt.; w; M(1). 14 Sunday's Well Road, Cork, Ireland.

KELLETT, John Robert
B/D/12317, 21/12/17; R.F.C., C/S, 5/4/18; R.F.C., 23/9/18, R.A.F.; F; Lieut.
Barleyhill House, Kingscourt, Co. Cavan, Ireland.

KELLETT, William Arthur
A/10694, 14/2/17; R.E., C/S, 16/6/17; R.E., 7/9/17; F; Lieut.
87 Newgate Street, Bishop Auckland, Co. Durham.

KELLIE, Donald Fores
A/635, 25/4/12; 22nd Lond. R., 29/8/14, att. R.E.; M,I; Capt.; M(1). Camelot, Renfrew Road, Kingston Hill, Surrey.

KELLY, Arthur Lindsay
6/1/8532, 29/12/15; No. 8 O.C.B., 4/8/16; K.R. Rif. C., 21/11/16; F; Capt.; O.B.E., M(1).
Hockley Lands, Worplesdon, Guildford.

KELLY, Austin McEvoy
C/14270, 31/10/18; trfr. K.R. Rif. C., 7/4/19.
2 Achill Road, Drumcondra, Dublin.

KELLY, Charles
6/5/8112, 2/12/15; No. 14 O.C.B., 28/8/16; 8th Lond. R., 22/11/16; F; Capt.; w; M.C. and Bar.
108 Clyde Road, West Didsbury, Manchester.

KELLY, Denis Patrick
6/5/C/7358, 10/11/15, Sgt.; No. 7 O.C.B., 3/7/16; dis. to re-enlist in R. Dub. Fus., 19/1/17.
Main Street, Mohill, Co. Leitrim, Ireland.

KELLY, Donald Fores. See KELLIE, D. F.

KELLY, Gavin
D/12984, 25/4/18; No. 16 O.C.B., 18/10/18; demob.
140 South Circular Road, Rialto, Dublin.

KELLY, George Herbert
D/11563, 28/6/17, L/C.; No. 19 O.C.B., 9/11/17; E. Kent R., 30/4/18; 2/Lieut.
36 Wilmington Avenue, Grove Park, Chiswick, W.4.

KELLY, Gerald Hubert
2/3229, 12/4/15, L/C.; Wilts. R., 6/8/15; F; Lieut.; w.
Camelot, Renfrew Road, Coombe Warren, Kingston Hill, Surrey.

KELLY, James Francis William
B/11325, 21/5/17; No. 14 O.C.B., 5/10/17; 18th Lond. R., 26/2/18; 2/Lieut. 5 Dalmeny Avenue, N.7

☩ KELLY, James Sheil
D/10220, 20/12/16, L/C.; No. 14 O.C.B., 5/5/17; Lan. Fus., 28/8/17; F; 2/Lieut. Died of wounds 29/3/18.

☩ KELLY, Oscar Raphael
6/3/5855, 26/8/15; North'd. Fus., 1/6/16, R.F.C.; 2/Lieut.
Killed 2/5/17.

KELLY, Raymond Maxwell
4/5/5057, 22/7/15; 8th Lond. R., 9/10/15; F; Capt.; Inv. w.
49 Storey Square, Barrow-in-Furness, Lancashire.

KELLY, Robert Charles
D/13763, 7/8/18, L/C.; trfr. K.R. Rif. C., 7/4/19.
63 Cranhurst Road, Cricklewood, N.W.2.

KELLY, William Dunphy
A/14322, 30/12/18; dis. med. unfit, 7/2/19.
Deanfield, Waterside, Londonderry, Ireland.

KELSEY, Edmund Dixon Parkin
D/11127, 30/4/17, L/C.; A.S.C., C/S, 1/2/18; R.A.S.C., 26/4/18; lt; 2/Lieut. Lyndhurst, Chester Road, Poynton, Stockport

KELSEY, Frederic
4/1/5013, 22/7/15; R.F.A., 26/11/15; Capt.; w(2); M(1).
Montala, Queen Place, West Drive, Boscombe, Bournemouth.

☩ KELSEY, Leon De Barr
3/3366, 22/4/15; 23rd Lond. R., 11/6/15; 2/Lieut.
Killed in action 16/9/16.

☩ KEMBLE, Cyril Stewart
6/4/5775, 23/8/15; No. 14 O.C.B., 30/10/16; Suff. R., 24/1/17, att. R. Berks. R.; 2/Lieut. Killed in action 27/5/18.

☩ KEMP, Basil Aubrey
6/4/3/7180, 3/11/15; No. 14 O.C.B., 30/9/16; Midd'x. R., 24/10/16; 2/Lieut. Killed in action 3/5/17.

KEMP, Charles John Murray
D/11160, 2/5/17, L/C.; R.E., 14/12/17; 2/Lieut.
2 Boclair Gardens, Bearsden, Nr. Glasgow.

KEMP, Cyril Armitage
H/1946, 22/10/14; R.F.A., 13/7/15; M,Afghan; Lieut.
25 Leyland Road, Lee, S.E.12

KEMP, George William Hodgert
F/1763, 16/10/14; R.A.S.C., 21/10/14; Lieut.
The Croft, Aldershot.

KEMP, Harry John
D/1385, 29/9/14; N. Lan. R., 24/12/14, L'pool. R., R.E., att. American Army; F; Capt. 84 St. George's Road, S.W.1

KEMP, James
B/D/13503, 10/7/18; demob. 30/5/19.
West Dene, Balfour Road, Southport, Lancashire.

KEMP, John Henry Bryning
6/5/9546, 21/2/16; R.A., C/S, 7/8/16; trfr. R.F.A., 13/10/16; R.F.A.; F; 2/Lieut. 63 Woolstone Road, Forest Hill, S.E.23.

KEMP, Leslie James
2/3640, 17/5/15; R.W. Surr. R., 21/8/15, att. Linc. R.; F; Capt.; w; M.C., M(1). 8 Arodene Road, Brixton Hill, S.W.2.

KEMP, Norman
4/6/6486, 27/9/15; R.A., C/S, 31/3/16; R.G.A., 2/8/16; F; Lieut.; w. Slindon, Hadley Road, New Barnet, Hertfordshire.

☩ KEMP, Reginald
C/10601, 22/1/17; No. 14 O.C.B., 7/6/17; Manch. R., 25/9/17; F; 2/Lieut. Killed in action 26/8/18.

KEMP, Walter Thomas
3/3348, 22/4/15, L/C.; Midd'x. R., 12/1/16, Lab. Corps; F; Lieut. 27 Lampton Road, Hounslow.

KENDAL, John Michael Angerstein
K/Sq/2268, 7/12/14; Norf. Yeo., 23/2/15; Capt.
974 The Paragon, Blackheath, S.E.

KENDALL, Arthur
6/1/6766, 11/10/15; No. 11 O.C.B., 7/5/16; E. Kent R., 4/9/16; F; 2/Lieut.; w. Hatherdon, Andover, Hampshire.

KENDALL, Charles Wye
C/811, 3/8/14; Interpreter, 25/9/14, R.A.S.C., Tank Corps; F; Capt. 9 Lordship Park, N.16.

KENDALL, Reginald George Gunton
B/13552, 19/7/18; trfr. 28th Lond. R., 13/11/18.
101 Underhill Road, Dulwich, S.E.22.

KENDERDINE, John Edwin
6/1/7681, 22/11/15; R.E., C/S, 25/9/16; R.E., 31/1/17; F; 2/Lieut.; Inv. 24 Bluff, Yokohama, Japan.

KENDLE, Henry Maydwell
F/1844, 16/10/14; Wilts. R., 18/12/14, R.A.F.; WA; Capt.; Inv.
c/o Messrs. H. L. Slater Ltd., Harter Street, Manchester.

APPENDIX II.—RECORDS OF RANK AND FILE.

KENDRICK, Reginald Arthur
A/D/12486, 29/1/18; R.A.F., C/S, 21/5/18; R.A.F., 29/1/19; 2/Lieut. Tamhorn Park, Nr. Lichfield, Staffordshire.

KENISTON, James Roy
10660, 5/2/17; R.A., C/S, 7/6/17; R.F.A., 8/12/17; 2/Lieut.; M(1).

KENNARD, Alan Spencer Gaskell
A/425, 24/5/09; dis. 11/11/10; Hamps. Yeo., 26/8/14; F; Capt.; M(1). Charlton Mackrell, Taunton, Somerset.

KENNARD, Cecil Henry
B/13418, 1/7/18; demob. 25/1/19. 47 Linver Road, S.W.6.

KENNARD, Leonard Maurice
Sq/2925, 15/2/15; R.A.S.C., 26/4/15, att. R.W. Kent R.; F; Lieut.; M.C. Estancia Albion, Pascanas F.C.C.A., Argentina.

KENNAWAY, Henry James
6/8136, 3/12/15; Life Gds., 22/3/16; Lieut.; w. Kenwood Park, Auchterarder, Perthshire.

KENNEDY, Algernon Thomas
B/11054, 16/4/17; R.A., C/S, 6/8/17; R.F.A., 12/1/18. 24 Upper Brook Street, W.1.

KENNEDY, Aubrey Leo
Sq/493, 11/5/10; dis. 2/2/12; Yorks. L.I., Scots. Gds.; Lieut.; M.C., M(2).

KENNEDY, Cyril Noble
A/10946, 29/3/17; No. 12 O.C.B., 10/8/17; Bord. R., 27/11/17; 2/Lieut. Wythop Vicarage, Bass Lake, Cockermouth, Cumberland.

KENNEDY, David Dobbin
D/10011, 24/11/16, L/C.; No. 14 O.C.B., 7/6/17; Midd'x. R., 25/9/17, att. E. Kent R. and E. Surr. R.; I,M; 2/Lieut. 106 Warwick Road, Kensington, W.14.

KENNEDY, Edward William Hugh
E/1570, 6/10/14, Sgt.; Wilts. R., 21/1/15, Bord. R., Hamps. R., R.F.C., R.A.F.; G,F; Major; w. Tytherley South, Ewell Road, Surbiton, Surrey.

KENNEDY, Edwin Sturrock
1/3856, 31/5/15, L/C.; R.A.S.C., 4/11/15; Lieut. The Pines, Broughty Ferry, Scotland.

KENNEDY, Patrick Joseph
C/14256, 12/10/18; demob. 4/3/19. 21 Haddington Road, Dublin.

KENNEDY, Richard Maurice Edward
6/1/D/6940, 20/10/15, L/C.; No. 6 O.C.B., 15/2/17; R.F.C., 23/5/17, R. Fus.; Staff Lieut.; cr. Fryers House, Branghing, Nr. Ware, Hertfordshire.

KENNEDY, Robert Kenneth Atthill
6/9506, 15/2/16; R.A., C/S, 9/6/16; R.F.A., 15/12/16, R.H.A.; F; Lieut.; w; M.C. Kilmacurragh, Rathdrum, Co. Wicklow.

✠ KENNEDY, Walter Louis
6/2/6400, 23/9/15; R. Suss. R., 1/6/16; 2/Lieut.
Killed in action 3/9/16.

✠ KENNEDY, William
K/A/2467, 28/12/14; High. L.I., 31/3/15, att. Welch R.; Lt.-Col.; w(2); M.C. Killed in action 23/11/17.

KENNEDY, William
6/5/5941, 1/9/15, Sgt.; L'pool. R., 20/1/16; F; Lieut.; g-w. Fanhaven, Aughton, Ormskirk, Lancashire.

KENNEDY, William Theodore
K/F/2275, 7/12/14, Cpl.; Rif. Brig., 29/4/15, att. High. L.I.; F; Capt. Almeley, Eardisley, Hereford.

KENNERLEY, Juba Elgar
6/Sq/6186, 13/9/15; trfr. R.F.A., 23/6/16; F; Gnr.
7 Marlborough Place, St. Johns Wood Park, N.W.8. (Now in Burma.)

KENNIE, Thomas
4/4167, 10/6/15; E. York. R., 29/10/15, secd. R.F.C., R.A.F.; F; Capt. 3 Belsize Park Gardens, Hampstead, N.W.3.

KENNING, Albert Lewis
E/1543, 6/10/14; R.H.A., 23/3/15, att. R.F.C.; E; Lieut.; cr.
38 Cholmeley Park, Highgate.

KENNINGTON, Allan
6/3/8640, 3/1/16; Ches. R., 25/9/16, M.G.C., Notts. & Derby. R.; F; Lieut. Cwichan Station, Vancouver Island, Canada.

KENNY, James
6/2/6993, 25/10/15; No. 7 O.C.B., 3/7/16; R. Marines, 24/10/16; w. Moystown, Belmont, Kings Co., Ireland.

✠ KENNY, Laurence Henry
A/1371, 26/9/14; Suff. R., 12/12/14; 2/Lieut.
Killed in action 26/6/16

KENNY, Thomas Joseph
D/10785, 23/2/17, L/C.; R.G.A., C/S, 31/8/17; R.G.A., 25/2/18; It; 2/Lieut. 16 Manhattan Mansions, Holloway, N.7.

KENSHOLE, Edward Harold
6/1/7589, 18/11/15; Mon. R., 4/9/16, att. Welch R.; F; Lieut.
Courtland Terrace, Merthyr Tydfil.

KENSHOLE, George Herbert
C/13371, 21/6/18; demob. 29/1/19.
Bryn-Awel, Hengoed, Nr. Cardiff

KENSHOLE, Thomas Reginald
B/10768, 19/2/17, L/C.; No. 14 O.C.B., 10/8/17; L'pool. R., 27/11/17; F; Lieut.; M.C. Bryncemydd, Caerphilly, Glamorganshire.

KENSHOLE, William Trevor
C/13246, 8/6/18; demob. 29/1/19.
12 Courtland Terrace, Merthyr Tydfil, South Wales.

KENT, Arthur
E/K/2548, 4/1/15, L/C.; Dorset R., 29/4/15, att. Wilts. R. and R.E. Sigs.; F; Lieut.; Inv.
The Forge, Hampstead Norris, Newbury.

KENT, Arthur Charles
B/168, 20/4/08, Sgt.; dis. 10/4/09. 176 Victoria Street, S.W.1

KENT, Charles Russell
D/13872, 21/8/18; demob. 30/5/19.
28 Stroud Green Road, Finsbury Park, N.4.

KENT, Clifford George William
B/13487, 8/7/18; demob. 7/5/19.
3 Symington Street, St. James, Northampton.

KENT, Douglas George
4/6/5/4935, 19/7/15; R. Lanc. R., 20/1/16, Devon. R.; Lieut.
Sussex Lodge, Beckenham, Kent.

KENT, Richard Courtenay
C/11514, 18/6/17; No. 10 O.C.B., 5/10/17; R. Muns. Fus., 26/2/18; F; 2/Lieut. 64 Hollybank Road, Drumcondra, Dublin.

KENT, Robert Douglas
4/1/4226, 14/6/15; R.W. Kent R., 5/11/15; F; Lieut.; w, g; M.C., M(1). Calle Colon 74, Valencia, Spain.

KENTISH, Edgar
A/11650, 12/7/17; trfr. R.F.C., 13/12/17.
79 Burnt Ash Hill, Lee, S.E.

KENWARD, Edward William
6/2/7179, 3/11/15, L/C.; Glouc. R., 4/8/16, att. Lan. Fus.; Lieut
41a Grovehill Road, Redhill, Surrey.

KENWARD, John Howell
Sq/3823, 29/5/15, Cpl.; Bedf. Yeo., 26/9/15, att. York. Drag Yeo.; Lieut. The Warren, Piltdown, Nr. Uckfield, Sussex

KENYON, Ernest
C/10402, 8/1/17; trfr. 8th Lond. R., 9/3/17.
98 Saltergate, Chesterfield

KENYON, Geoffrey
B/Sq/13419, 1/7/18; demob. 9/1/19.
Plainville, Haxby, York.

KEOGH, John William
C/10349, 5/1/17; No. 20 O.C.B., 5/5/17; R. Ir. Fus., 27/11/17, R. Muns. Fus.; 2/Lieut.
24 Moundfield Road, Stamford Hill, N.16

KEPPEL-JONES, Charles
6/4/8362, 13/12/15, L/C.; Lovat's Scouts, 5/8/16, Tank Corps; F; Capt.; M.C. P.O. Box 7372, Johannesburg, South Africa

KER, Launcelot
F/B/290, 22/6/08; dis. 21/6/09; rej. C/10478, 12/1/17, L/C.; R.G.A., C/S, 15/8/17; R.G.A., 24/6/18; 2/Lieut.
Merrywood, Ballard's Lane, Church End, Finchley, N.3.

✠ KER, Laurence Arthur
K/F/2264, 7/12/14; R. Sco. Fus., 17/3/15; 2/Lieut.
Died 4/4/15.

APPENDIX II.—RECORDS OF RANK AND FILE.

KERBY, Albert Maurice
4/6/4859, 15/7/15; R.F.A., 27/8/15; Lieut.; w(2); D.S.O., M.C., M(2).
The Elms, Smeeton, Leicester.

KERLEY, Henry Leslie Hugh
A/11971, 6/9/17; No. 14 O.C.B., 4/1/18; R. Suss. R., 25/6/18; F; 2/Lieut.
Riverdale, Alfriston, Sussex.

✠ KERNAGHAN, Graham Hemery
K/H/2314, 10/12/14; R.W. Fus., 4/1/15, Yorks. L.I.; Lieut.
Killed in action 1/7/16.

KERR, John
B/13553, 19/7/18; trfr. R. Highrs., 2/5/19.
Dunsmure, Broughty Ferry W., Dundee.

KERR, John Joseph
6/9518, 16/2/16; dis. med. unfit, 6/10/16.
Gortalowny, Cookstown, Co. Tyrone, Ireland.

KERR, Ian Collow. Now COLLOW, John Pocock
6/2/9461, 14/2/16; No. 8 O.C.B., 4/8/16; trfr. Class W. Res., 22/1/17.
15 The Heys, Thongsbridge, Nr. Huddersfield, Yorkshire.

KERR, Ronald George Augustus
D/Sq/12918, 10/4/18; trfr. Gren. Gds., 6/11/18.
27 Hereford Square, S.W.

KERR, Stanley Alexander Turner
4/3251, 12/4/15; North'd. Fus., 31/7/15; Lieut.

KERRIDGE, Burnard Fred
D/13673, 29/7/18; demob. 21/12/18.
The Crest, Beech Hill, Luton, Bedfordshire.

KERSHAW, Harold Austin
6/4/5304, 2/8/15; R. Lanc. R., 9/6/16; F; Lieut.; w; M(1).
Clare House, Clare Road, Halifax.

KERSHAW, James Leonard
6/8695, 4/1/16; R.F.A., C/S, 21/7/16; R.F.A., 27/10/16; F; Lieut.; w; M.C.
Fairlands, Castleford, Yorkshire.

KERSLAKE, Sidney Samuel
6/4/5360, 4/8/15; Essex R., 16/11/15, att. Wilts. R., E. York. R. and York. R.; Lieut.
Kent Lodge, Herbert Road, Hornchurch.

KESHAN, John Howard
B/12013, 17/9/17; R.E., C/S, 16/11/17; R.E., 19/4/18; 2/Lieut.
c/o J. H. Keshan Esq., 28 Terrapin Road, Bedford Hill, S.W.

KESTIN, John
6/3/8247, 8/12/15; No. 5 O.C.B., 14/8/16; Sea. Highrs., 21/11/16, att. Arg. & Suth'd. Highrs.; F,Turkey; Lieut.; w.
Watch Oak, Langton Green, Tunbridge Wells, Kent.

KETCHELL, Jack
A/10534, 17/1/17; No. 21 O.C.B., 5/5/17; K.R. Rif. C., 28/8/17, att. Lab. Corps.; F; Capt.; g.
Lyminge, Kent.

KETCHLEY, Clement Percival Guy
6/8835, 10/1/16; R.A., C/S, 4/8/16; R.G.A., 12/11/16; Lieut.
Farnborough, Bath.

KETLEY, Ernest Wilfred
6/6/6953, 21/10/15, L/C.; No. 11 O.C.B., 7/5/16; Lovats Scouts, 5/9/16; I,Persia; Staff Capt.
The Laurels, Meare Green, Stoke St. Gregory, Nr. Taunton, Somerset.

KETLEY, Robert Roy
C/14204, 21/10/18; dis. med. unfit, 23/2/19.
Mossley Hall, Congleton, Cheshire.

KETTLE, Lancelot Sydney
A/B/12159, 25/10/17, Sgt.; No. 15 O.C.B., 10/5/18; Bedf. and Herts. R., 3/2/19; 2/Lieut.
27 Alexandra Road, Finsbury Park, N.4.

KEWIN, Thomas
6/8930, 15/1/16; No. 9 O.C.B., 8/3/16; High. L.I., 6/7/16; F; Lieut.; w; M.C.
43 Queensborough Gardens, Glasgow w.

KEY, George Vernon
C/D/14155, 14/10/18; demob. 30/5/19.
Oak Hill, Cromford, Nr. Matlock, Derby.

KEYS, Francis Herbert
6/5/8644, 3/1/16, L/C.; E. Surr. R., 6/7/16, att. R.W. Surr. R. and Ches. R.; I; Lieut.
147 Church Road, Canonbury, N.1.

KIDD, Albert Amos
6/2/5991, 2/9/15, L/C.; K.R. Rif. C., 21/4/16; K. Af. Rif.; F,Germ.EA; Lieut.; w; M.C.
Carnarvon, Western Australia.

KIDDLE, John Ivory
D/13764, 7/8/18; trfr. K.R. Rif. C., 7/4/19; Pte.
52 Chestnut Grove, Birkenhead, Cheshire.

KIEK, Herman Louis
E/1510, 1/10/14, Cpl.; Rif. Brig., 26/2/15; Lieut.; w.
4 Holland Park, W.11.

KILDUFF, William
6/3/6055, 28/8/15; dis. 9/3/16.

KILFORD, William George
6/5/7264, 8/11/15, L/C.; No. 8 O.C.B., 4/8/16; North'd. Fus., 24/10/16, att. R.E.; F; Lieut.; w.
Thrapston Road, Brampton, Huntingdonshire.

KILGOUR, Harvey Nicol
A/C/12528, 1/2/18, Cpl.; demob. 29/1/19.
964 Sauchiehall Street, Glasgow.

KILGOUR, William Watson
K/F/2336, 14/12/14; Arg. & Suth'd. Highrs., 8/4/15; F; Capt.
24 Onslow Road, Richmond

KILLEY, James Brown
6/5/7738, 22/11/15; No. 14 O.C.B., 28/8/16; L'pool. R., 22/11/16; F; Capt.
18 Marmion Road, Sefton Park, Liverpool.

KILNER, John Washington
C/440, 5/11/09; dis. 13/2/12; 11th Lond. R., 28/3/15; F,G,E; Capt.; w; M(1).
Longview, Wenakhee, Washington, U.S.A.

KILPATRICK, James
4/5/4752, 12/7/15; R. Sco. Fus., 6/12/15, M.G.C.; Lieut.
Struan, Lugar, Ayrshire.

KILPATRICK, John Auld
6/5/7359, 10/11/15; R.E., C/S, 3/7/16; R.E., 15/9/16; F; Capt.; w; M.C., M(1).
Kair Leil, St. Quivox Road, Prestwick, Ayrshire.

KIMBERLIN, Leonard
C/10609, 22/1/17; No. 14 O.C.B., 7/6/17; E. Lan. R., 25/9/17, att. Essex R.; I; Lieut.
Glenmore, Brooksville Avenue, Brondesbury, N.W.6.

KINAHAN, John Hickson
6/1/8418, 15/12/15; No. 7 O.C.B., 11/8/16, M.G.C., C/S; M.G.C., 28/12/16; F; Lieut.; p.
Beaupare, Co. Meath, Ireland.

KINDER, Gerald
B/11703, 19/7/17; No. 14 O.C.B., 4/1/18; W. York. R., 25/6/18; 2/Lieut.
Carlton House, East Grinstead, Sussex.

KING, Alec Scott
C/13252, 10/6/18; trfr. 14th Lond. R., 6/12/18.
17 Cwmdonkin Terrace, Swansea, South Wales.

KING, Ambrose George William Shallcross
4/5169, 29/7/15; R.A., C/S, 24/1/16; R.G.A., 19/6/16; F; Capt.; g; Croix de Guerre (French).
The Orchard, Lymm, Cheshire.

KING, Anthony Highmore
A/822, 4/8/14; E. Surr. R., 15/8/14, att. M. of Nat. Service; F; Lieut.; w.
1 Harcourt Buildings, Temple, E.C.4.

KING, Archdale Arthur
6/3/8028, 30/11/15; dis. med. unfit, 26/9/16.
St. Saviour's Clergy House, Poplar, E.14.

KING, Arnold
C/11448, 4/6/17, L/C.; A.S.C., C/S, 1/10/17; R.A.S.C., 30/11/17; M; Lieut.
c/o Nat. Prov. & Union Bank Ltd., 30 Cheapside, E.C.2.

KING, Charles Alfred
F/1869, 16/10/14; Midd'x. R., 13/3/15; F,E,S; Lieut.
40 Longstone Road, Furzedown Drive, Streatham, S.W.17.

KING, Charles Francis
B/721, 23/6/13; Ches. R., 11/9/14, Welch R.; Lt.-Col.; w(3); D.S.O. and Bar, M.C., M(3).

KING, Charles Henry Claude
4/4341, 21/6/15; R.F.A., 5/11/15; F; Lieut.; w.
35 Old Deer Park Gardens, Richmond, Surrey.

KING, Cyril George
3/4/5116, 26/7/15; 11th Lond. R., 10/1/16, att. 20th and 22nd Lond. R.; F; Lieut.; w; M.C.
35 Botley Road, Oxford.

KING, Denys Penkivil
C/Sq/13348, 25/6/18; demob. 6/1/19.
School House, Clifton College, Bristol.

APPENDIX II.—RECORDS OF RANK AND FILE.

KING, Donald Buckley
6/5/5262, 31/7/15, L/C.; L'pool. R., 13/12/15, R.A.F.; Capt.;
p. The Moorings, Rock Ferry, Cheshire.

KING, Eric Harold
D/1469, 29/9/14, L/C.; 8th Lond. R., 29/5/15, att. K.O. Sco.
Bord.; Lieut. Glenroy, Maidenhead.

KING, Frederic George
4/3/4419, 24/6/15; R.A.S.C., 9/10/15; F,G,E; Capt.
c/o Jonathan King Ltd., 304 Essex Road, N.

KING, Frederick Allison
B/12810, 20/3/18; No. 1 O.C.B., 6/9/18, No. 3 O.C.B.; Worc. R., 17/3/19; 2/Lieut.
The Cottage, St. Julian's Avenue, Ludlow, Salop.

KING, Frederick William
6/8485, 20/12/15; Glouc. R., 24/1/17; F; Capt.; w(3).
Darlington Villa, Bisley Road, Stroud, Gloucestershire.

KING, George Mark
6/Sq/5352, 3/8/15; Berks. Yeo., 20/10/15, secd. M.G.C.; E,P; Lieut.
York House, Headroomgate Road, St. Annes-on-the-Sea, Lancashire.

KING, George Sidney
6/5/C/5708, 19/8/15; trfr. M.G.C., 6/12/16.
Dryden House, Heaton Moor, Nr. Stockport.

KING, Harold Edgar
A/12529, 1/2/18; R.F.A., C/S, 14/6/18; R.G.A., 4/4/19; 2/Lieut.
Croyde, Brighton Road, Sutton, Surrey.

KING, Harold Thomas Elstone
6/2/5435, 5/8/15; Norf. R., 4/9/16; P; Capt.; w.
235 High Street, Berkhamsted, Hertfordshire

✠ KING, Harry
A/2569, 4/1/15; Worc. R., 4/1/15; Capt.
Killed in action 3/9/16.

✠ KING, Henry Arthur
D/Sq/1447, 29/9/14, L/C.; R.F.A., 13/10/15; 2/Lieut.; M.C.
Killed in action 1/7/17.

KING, Horace Henry
A/11241, 11/5/17; trfr. Class W. Res., 9/7/17.
Altarnum, Launceston, Cornwall.

KING, Hugh
K/D/2101, 16/11/14; Sea. Highrs., 27/2/15, att. R.E.; F,It; Capt.;
M.C. and Bar. Balmacneil, Ballinling, Perthshire.

✠ KING, Hugh Denham
F/3051, 15/3/15; R.W. Surr. R., 8/7/15, 10th Lond. R.; 2/Lieut
Killed in action 13/3/17.

KING, Jefford
A/Sq/12544, 5/2/18, L/C.; No. 1 Cav. C/S, 3/9/18; 4th R. Regt. of Cav., 12/3/19; 2/Lieut.
c/o Edward Moore & Sons, 3 Crosby Square, E.C. 3.

KING, John Louis
6/5/5794, 23/8/15; R.F.C., C/S, 6/9/16; R.F.C., 25/1/17, R.A.F.;
F; Lieut.
c/o Lond. Joint City & Mid. Bk. Ltd., Commerce House, Oxford Street, W. 1.

KING, John Walter
Sq/3641, 17/5/15; R.G.A., 28/10/15; Lieut.; w; M(1).

KING, Kenneth Arthur
4/6/D/4753, 12/7/15; trfr. Essex R., 1/5/17.
26 Prince of Wales Road, Norwich.

KING, Norman Wright
6/4/6330, 20/9/15; Camb. R., 4/8/16, R.E.; F; Lieut.; M.C. and Bar.
St. Quentin, Queen's Road, Bury St. Edmunds.

✠ KING, Percy
B/10839, 5/3/17, L/C.; A.S.C., C/S, 1/9/17; R.A.S.C., 27/10/17;
F; 2/Lieut. Died 15/8/20.

KING, Reginald Duncan
4/1/3903, 31/5/15; Hamps. R., 2/10/15; w.

✠ KING, Reginald Graham
6/3/8604, 3/1/16, L/C.; Dorset R., 22/11/16; 2/Lieut.
Killed in action 23/3/18.

KING, Reginald John L'Ecuyer
B/13474, 5/7/18, L/C.; demob. 23/1/19.
77 Hortington Road, Stockton-on-Tees.

✠ KING, Richard
F/1833, 16/10/14; S. Lan. R., 4/11/14; 2/Lieut.
Died of wounds 18/4/16.

KING, Robert Reginald
6/Sq/9447, 12/2/16; R.F.C., C/S, 8/10/16; R.F.C., 4/4/17,
R.A.F.; Lieut. 29 Fosse Road Central, Leicester.

KING, Samuel Henry
6/4/1/5170, 29/7/15; R.F.A., 22/12/15; M,P; Lieut.
12 Queen's Road, Southport.

KING, Sidney Ernest Edwin
C/11799, 2/8/17; No. 14 O.C.B., 4/1/18; S. Lan. R., 25/6/18; F;
Lieut.; w. 218 Evering Road, Clapton, E. 5.

✠ KING, Simmonds
K/H/2102, 16/11/14; Herts. R., 6/3/15; F; Lieut.
Killed in action 31/7/17.

KING, Stanley Jesse
6/3/6303, 18/9/15; 7th Lond. R., 14/12/15, att. R. Fus. and Indian
Army; S,I; Capt. Shirbourn, Shepherds Hill, Highgate, N. 6.

KING, William
A/10305, 1/1/17, L/C.; R.G.A., C/S, 7/11/17; R.G.A., 29/4/18;
M; 2/Lieut. The Elms, Irlam Road, Flexton, Manchester.

KING, William Arthur
B/2064, 12/11/14; 1st Lond. R., 19/2/15.
Rippleside, Nr. Barking, Essex.

KING, William Charles Holland
6/1/7611, 19/11/15, L/C.; No. 14 O.C.B., 26/11/16; R. Scots, 28/2/17; Lieut.
6 Wychcombe Studios, England's Lane, N.W. 3.

KING, William Percy
B/9860, 6/11/16, Sgt.; Sigs. C/S, 28/4/17; R.E., 14/9/17; 2/Lieut.
2 The Parade, High Road, Kilburn, N.W.

KING, William Samuel Dinham
D/12949, 19/4/18; No. 21 O.C.B., 4/10/18; Devon. R., 16/3/19;
2/Lieut. 9 Regents Park, Exeter.

✠ KING, William Thomas
A/11246, 14/5/17; No. 16 O.C.B., 5/10/17; R.W. Kent R., 12/3/18; 2/Lieut.
Killed in action 29/8/18.

✠ KING-CHURCH, Cyril Edward
A/432, 17/6/09; 7th Lond. R., 9/8/10; F; Capt.
Killed in action 25/9/15.

✠ KINGDON, Arthur Francis
H/1984, 29/10/14; York. & Lanc. R., 15/1/15; Capt.; w.
Killed in action 9/10/17.

KINGDON, Hubert William
B/2716, 18/1/15, Cpl.; Hamps. R., 15/5/15, R.A.F.; G,E; Capt.
Charlton, Biggin Hill, Kent.

KINGDON, William Tremlett
D/10250, 29/12/16; trfr. 16th Lond. R., 26/2/17.
Dowhayne, Cheriton Fitzpaine, Crediton, Devonshire.

KINGHAM, John Thomas Gordon
K/2143, 19/11/14; dis. 21/12/14; Rif. Brig., 29/8/17; F; Lieut.;
g. Bath Club, Dover Street, W. 1.

KINGHORN, Douglas Curtis
4/4281, 17/6/15; R.A.S.C., 9/10/15; Lieut.; M.B.E.
Ardoch, Prenton, Cheshire.

KING-LEWIS, Arthur
B/13583, 22/7/18; trfr. K.R. Rif. C., 25/4/19.
Nunwell House, Bromyord, Herefordshire.

KINGS, Wilfred
6/8645, 3/1/16; R.A., C/S, 14/7/16; R.F.A., 13/10/16; F,P;
Lieut. 29 Bridge Street, Rugby, Warwickshire.

KINGSTON, Harold Abercrombie
4/9703, 9/10/16; dis. med. unfit, 2/10/17.
Pinckbeck Road, Spalding, Lincolnshire.

✠ KINGSTON, William
6/5/8248, 8/12/15; No. 7 O.C.B., 11/8/16; R. Muns. Fus., 18/12/16, att. R. Ir. Rif.; 2/Lieut.; M.C.
Killed in action 16/8/17.

KINGWILL, Frederick Joseph
Sq/2943, 18/2/15, L/C.; N. Som. Yeo., 25/6/15, Tank Corps;
Capt. 67 Overhill Road, East Dulwich, S.E. 22.

APPENDIX II.—RECORDS OF RANK AND FILE.

KINLOCH, Robert Parlane
6/8549, 30/12/15; R.A., C/S, 26/5/16; R.G.A., 30/8/16; F; Major; w(2); M.C., Croix de Guerre (Belge).
Kirkton Cottage, Cardross, Dumbartonshire.

KINNEAR, Charles Maxwell
K/2321, 14/12/14; dis. 14/12/14.
Eastbury Avenue, Northwood.

KINNERSLEY, Norman Stuart
1/4/5204, 29/7/15; R F.A., 13/12/15; F; Capt.; M.C.
34 Charlton Road, Keynsham, Somerset.

KINNISON, Clive Hastings
D/1490, 29/9/14, L/C.; 9th Lond. R., 8/1/15, M.G.C., Tank Corps; F; Major; w; M.C. and Bar.
Hurst Place, Bexley, Kent.

KINSLEY, Herbert Randells
6/2/7739, 22/11/15, L/C.; No. 5 O.C.B., 14/8/16; K.R. Rif. C, 21/11/16; Lieut.; M.C., M(1).
46 Anson Road, Tufnell Park, N.7.

KINSMAN, Francis Geoffrey
B/12707, 8/3/18; No. 18 O.C.B., 20/9/18; Lan. Fus., 18/3/19; 2/Lieut.
Ivanhoe, 108 Mount Pleasant Road, Wallasey, Cheshire.

✠ KIPPAX, James Elliot
C/10631, 30/1/17; No. 20 O.C.B., 7/6/17; E. Lan. R., 25/9/17; 2/Lieut.
Killed in action 22/9/18.

✠ KIPPS, George Stewart
4/6/Sq/4887, 15/7/15, Sgt.; A.S.C., C/S, 1/9/16; R.A.S.C., 25/10/16, att. Worc. R.; Lieut.
Killed in action 22/8/18.

KIRBY, Arthur Charles
C/13329, 19/6/18; trfr. K.R. Rif. C., 7/4/19.
10 Clifton Street, Barry, South Wales.

KIRBY, Arthur George
1/9641, 26/9/16; No. 14 O.C.B., 26/11/16; North'n. R ;, 27/3/17; F; Lieut.
Cliffe House, Barrow-on-Soar, Leicestershire.

KIRBY, Basil William
K/F/2347, 14/12/14, Cpl.; Dorset R., 2/6/15, att. R.A.F.; M,E; Capt.
Parkside, Parkside Avenue, Ipswich, Suffolk.

KIRBY, Bernard Burrows
2/3600, 13/5/15; Glouc. R., 21/8/15; F; Capt.; M.C., M(1).
Shenley, Hertfordshire.

✠ KIRBY, Leslie Jack
A/12442, 22/1/18; No. 14 O.C.B., 7/6/18; N. Staff. R., 6/2/19; 2/Lieut.
Died 16/7/19.

KIRBY, Reginald Marriott
6/3/5835, 26/8/15; Worc. R., 29/11/15; S; Lieut.; w; M(1).
107 Morton Terrace, Gainsborough, Lincolnshire.

KIRK, David Lewis
6/4/9307, 4/2/16, L/C.; A.S.C., C/S, 27/10/16; R.A.S.C., 20/12/16; Lieut.
17 Greenhill Gardens, Edinburgh.

KIRK, Geoffrey John Craisdale
4/3/4420, 24/6/15; R.G.A., 15/10/15; F; Lieut.; w.
Llanishen, Cardiff.

✠ KIRK, Ronald Leslie
A/11887, 20/8/17; No. 14 O.C.B., 7/12/17; 7th Lond. R., 28/5/18; EA,F; 2/Lieut.
Killed in action 1/9/18.

KIRK, Rupert
4/5003, 20/7/15; Manch. R., 6/11/15; Lieut.; Inj.
256 Manchester Road, Droylsden, Manchester.

KIRKBY, Geoffrey Richard
A/12443, 22/1/18; Sig. C/S, 14/6/18; trfr. 14th Lond. R., 6/1/19.
Shippon Vicarage, Abingdon, Berkshire.

KIRKHAM, Harry William Thomas
6/4/7376, 11/11/15; Oxf. & Bucks. L.I., 4/9/16, att. R. War. R.; 2/Lieut.

KIRKMAN, Frank
C/11515, 18/6/17; No. 14 O.C.B., 5/10/17; York. & Lanc. R., 26/2/18; Capt.
26 Oak Road, Newton Park, Leeds.

KIRKPATRICK, John
D/11162, 2/5/17; trfr. 28th Lond. R., 28/8/17, Cpl.; Arg. and Suth'd. Highrs., 5/3/19; F; 2/Lieut.; w-g; M.B.E.
The Chase, Chigwell Row, Essex. (Now in Persia).

KIRKPATRICK, Thomas Roger
E/1673, 12/10/14; R. Suss. R., 27/11/14; p.
2 Wellington Place, Hastings.

KIRKWOOD, Ernest Robert
1/3420, 29/4/15; Dorset R., 28/7/15; 2/Lieut.
Mookwi River Ranche, Sindia, Southern Rhodesia.

✠ KIRKWOOD, William John
3/3506, 6/5/15, Cpl.; York. R., 28/7/15; 2/Lieut.
Killed in action 11/11/15.

KIRLEW, Thomas Oliver
H/2637, 11/1/15, L/C.; Notts. & Derby. R., 5/5/15; F; Capt.; w.
30 Arlington Road, Eastbourne, Sussex.

KISCH, Augustus Maitland
D/10994, 4/4/17; R.A., C/S, 15/12/17; R. Fus., 31/7/18; 2/Lieut.
11 Crawford Gardens, Cliftonville, Margate.

KISS, Thomas Eric Babington
6/2/6187, 13/9/15; No. 4 O.C.B., 7/3/16; Linc. R., 13/7/16; F; 2/Lieut.; w.
Brianwood, Lumley Avenue, Skegness, Lincolnshire.

KISSAN, Edgar Duguid
H/2013, 2/11/14, L/C.; Bedf. R., 10/2/15, L'pool. R.; S,F; Capt.
11 Cranley Gardens, Palmers Green, N.13.

KITCHIN, Clifford Henry Benn
6/3/6128, 9/9/15; R. War. R., 7/7/16, att. M.G.C.; F; Lieut.; w.
Holmwood, Boar's Hill, Oxford.

KITCHIN, Francis Ellerton
B/9891, 10/11/16, L/C.; M.G.C., C/S, 14/3/17; M.G.C., 26/8/17; F,It; Lieut.
c/o 224 Slade Road, Erdington, Birmingham.

KITTON, John Herbert
B/13674, 29/7/18; trfr. K.R. Rif. C., 25/4/19, M.G.C.
5 Wyvell Road, Forest Hill, S.E.23.

KITTOW, John Hugh
4/3/4227, 14/6/15; D. of Corn. L.I., 16/11/15; F; Capt.
Ardeley, Stevenage, Hertfordshire.

KITTS, Archibald Eustace
D/12124, 15/10/17; H. Bde. O.C.B., 8/2/18; R. Suss. R., 30/7/18; Capt.

✠ KNAPMAN, Allen Arthur
6/4/8836, 10/1/16; No. 14 O.C.B., 26/11/16; Arg. & Suth'd. Highrs., 27/3/17; I; 2/Lieut.
Died 1920.

✠ KNAPP, Oswald Reed
4/3/4465, 28/6/15; Welch. R., 7/10/15; 2/Lieut.
Died of wounds 13/9/16.

KNEE, Percival Hebden
B/11396, 30/5/17, L/C.; R.A., C/S, 15/12/17; R.G.A., 1/7/18; F; 2/Lieut.
Ingram House, Bloomfield Avenue, Bath.

KNEEN, Edwyn Corlett
A/13999, 13/9/18; demob. 23/1/19.
Glevcrutcherry, Douglas, Isle of Man.

KNIGHT, Alfred Martyn
3/7072, 29/10/15, L/C.; No. 11 O.C.B., 7/5/16; Midd'x. R., 4/9/16; F; Lieut.; w.
50 Park Avenue, Bush Hill Park, Enfield.

KNIGHT, Arthur Albert Eustace
4/9723, 13/10/16; No. 14 O.C.B., 30/1/17; trfr. Devon. R., 20/4/17, R. War. R.; Pte.; p.
Moorlands, St. Marychurch, Torquay.

KNIGHT, Charles Henry
6/5/8220, 7/12/15; No. 14 O.C.B., 27/9/16; R. Suss. R., 24/1/17; F; Lieut.; w; M.C.
Cumballa, Gravel Lane, Wilmslow, Cheshire.

✠ KNIGHT, Clarence Raymond Wentworth
6/9545, 19/2/16; R.F.C., 18/3/16; F,NR; Lieut.
Killed in action 21/6/19.

KNIGHT, Edmund
A/B/D/12179, 1/11/17; A.S.C., C/S, 4/3/18; R.A.S.C., 28/4/18; F; 2/Lieut.
11 Ambleside Avenue, Bradford.

KNIGHT, Edward Spurin
6/1/8461, 18/12/15; No. 14 O.C.B., 30/10/16; 12th Lond. R., 28/2/18; F; Lieut.; D.S.O., M(1).
c/o Barclay's Bank Ltd., Bishops Waltham, Hampshire.

KNIGHT, Ewart Draper
A/9856, 6/11/16, L/C.; R.E., C/S, 8/4/17; R.E., 29/6/17; Lieut.
63 Leeside Crescent, Golders Green, N.W.

KNIGHT, Frederick William
B/E/14152, 11/10/18; demob. 31/3/19.
19 Ridgeway Place, Wimbledon, S.W.19.

APPENDIX II.—RECORDS OF RANK AND FILE.

✠ KNIGHT, Gerald Featherstone
A/1334, 26/9/14; Devon. R., 4/11/14, att. Glouc. R., R.F.C., R.A.F.; F; Capt.; p, escaped; M.C. Died 30/10/19.

✠ KNIGHT, Gerald Robert Frank
K/B/2114, 16/11/14; Essex R., 27/1/15, att. Oxf. & Bucks. L.I.; F; Capt. Died of wounds 17/8/17.

KNIGHT, Henry
A/10485, 12/1/17; No. 14 O.C.B., 7/6/17; L'pool. R., 25/9/17 att. Devon. R.; P,F; 2/Lieut.
138 Liscard Road, Wallasey, Cheshire.

KNIGHT, Horace Geoffrey
4/3581, 13/5/15; Glouc. R., 26/7/15, att. M. of Labour; F; Lieut.; w.
Kentisbury House, Little Ilford, Essex.

✠ KNIGHT, John Oswald
6/2/6893, 18/10/15; R.W. Kent R., 4/9/16; F; 2/Lieut.
Killed in action 31/10/16.

KNIGHT, Lionel Ranken
B/1099, 7/9/14; L'pool. R., 19/9/14.

KNIGHT, Richard Cassteels
B/13420, 1/7/18; trfr. K.R. Rif. C., 7/4/19.
Woodcroft, Midhurst, Sussex.

KNIGHT, Stanley Gordon
5/6/7891, 27/11/15; Linc. R., 25/9/16, att. M. of Munitions; F,G; Lieut.; w.
118 Balfour Road, Ilford, Essex.

✠ KNIGHT, William Bernard
A/87, 14/4/08; dis. 13/4/12; rej. A/1119, 7/9/14; N. Staff. R., 15/8/14; 2/Lieut. Killed in action 21/4/15.

KNIGHT, William Frederick
A/10037, 29/11/16; No. 14 O.C.B., 30/1/17; Manch. R., 29/5/17, att. R.E. Sigs, L'pool. R. and K.R. Rif. C.; F; Lieut.
17 Ragdale Road, Bulwell, Nottinghamshire.

KNIGHT, William Kircher
Sq/3822, 29/5/15, Cpl.; R.F.A., 18/8/15; F,E,P; Lieut.
Haybrook, Kings Road, Horsham, Sussex.

KNIGHTON, George Francis
6/5/9497, 15/2/16; No. 14 O.C.B., 27/9/16; Notts. & Derby. R., 18/12/16; F; Capt. 101 Whitaker Road, Derby.

KNIGHTON, Thomas
6/5/7612, 19/11/15, L/C.; No. 11 O.C.B., 16/5/16; Notts. and Derby. R., 4/9/16, att. M.G.C.; Lieut.

✠ KNIGHTS-SMITH, Philip Arnold
6/Sq/6092, 6/9/15; trfr. Bedf. Yeo., 6/3/16.

KNOBEL, Gerald William
B/2017, 5/11/14, Sgt.; North'd. Fus., 17/3/15; E,F; Lieut.
Ex-Officers Club, 31 Leinster Gardens, Lancaster Gate, W. 2.

KNOTT, Douglas Cedric
H/2054, 9/11/14; Hamps. R., 27/2/15; Lieut.; w; M.C.
Scriventon, Speldhurst, Tunbridge Wells, Kent.

✠ KNOTT, Frederic William
6/1/7048, 28/10/15, L/C.; York. R., 5/5/16; F; 2/Lieut.
Killed in action 7/6/17.

KNOWLES, Edward Frith
A/11888, 20/8/17, Sgt.; demob. 28/1/19.
Ryecroft, Ossett, Yorkshire.

KNOWLES, Frederick George Yalden
Sq/2619, 7/1/15, L/C.; R.A.S.C., 13/4/15; F,S,P; Lieut.
Heath Hall, Thursley, Surrey.

KNOWLES, George
Sq/3544, 10/5/15; R.F.A., 27/7/15; Lieut.; w; M.C.

KNOWLES, John Yalden
A/9842, 3/11/16; R.W. Surr. R., 9/3/17, att. Lab. Corps; F; Lieut. Heath Hall, Thursley, Surrey.

KNOWLES, Samuel
6/Sq/8530, 25/12/15, L/C.; R.A., C/S, 15/9/16; R.F.A., 22/1/17; F; 2/Lieut.; w. The Cove, West Derby, Liverpool.

✠ KNOWLSON-WILLIAMS, Henry William
6/8760, 6/1/16; R.F.C., C/S, 8/10/16; R.F.C., 26/2/17; 2/Lieut.
Killed 11/7/17.

KNOX, Ernest Moore
A/14315, 1/11/18; demob. 10/1/19.
41 Ulsterville Avenue, Belfast, Ireland.

KNOX, George Latham
A/Sq/14126, 4/10/18; demob. 21/1/19.
Brookvale, Stillorgan, Co. Dublin, Ireland.

✠ KNOX, John Lawrence
6/4/7105, 1/11/15; No. 7 O.C.B., 3/7/16; R. Suss. R., 21/11/16; 2/Lieut. Killed in action 20/11/17.

KNOX-WILSON, George Reginald
K/4/D/2137, 19/11/14, C.Q.M.S.; R.A.O.C., 10/12/16; E; Lieut.; Inv. 55 Ashburnham Mansions, Chelsea, S.W. 10

KNOX-WILSON, James Percival
A/10202, 18/12/16, L/C.; R.W. Surr. R., 9/3/17, Lab. Corps; F; Capt. 52 Ashburnham Mansions, Chelsea, S.W. 10.

KNUBLEY, Miles Ponsonby
6/1/9496, 15/2/16, L/C.; No. 14 O.C.B., 26/11/16; Wilts. R., 27/3/17, att. York. & Lanc. R. and R.E.; S,F; Capt.; Inv.
Steeple Ashton Vicarage, Trowbridge.

KNUCKEY, Bryant Woodward
A/10281, 1/1/17; R.F.C., C/S, 16/4/17; R.F.C., 16/5/17, R.A.F.; F; Lieut. Nunpean, Redruth, Cornwall

KNUDSEN, Duncan Joures
C/9795, 27/10/16; No. 14 O.C.B., 30/1/17; Manch. R., 25/4/17; F; Lieut.; w. 24 Edge Lane, Chorlton-cum-Hardy, Manchester.

KOCKANSKI, Marcel Leon
Sq/1133, 9/9/14, L/C.; R.A.S.C., 28/11/14; Capt.

KOE, Dugby Latimer Francis
A/2, 1/4/08; dis. 31/3/12. 35 Blessington Road, S.E. 13.

✠ KOE, Philip Stephen
A/3070, 18/3/15, L/C.; York. & Lanc. R., 27/8/15; F; 2/Lieut.
Killed in action 31/7/16.

✠ KOHNSTAM, Oscar Jacob Charles
E/1555, 6/10/14; N. Staff. R., 31/3/15, M.G.C.; F; 2/Lieut.
Killed in action 29/6/16.

KREUGER, Oscar Fredrik
F/1919, 16/10/14, Cpl.; Yorks. L.I., 26/2/15; F; Lieut.
131 West End Lane, West Hampstead, N.W. 6.

KROHN, Raleigh William
C/D/12258, 29/11/17; No. 3 O.C.B., 9/8/18; R. Fus., 5/3/19; 2/Lieut. c/o Messrs. Krohn Bros. Ltd., Funchal, Madeira.

KUSEL, Reginald
Sq/792, 8/5/14; R.F.A., 10/10/14; Capt.; Croce di Guerra, M(2).
70 Talgarth Mansions, Barons Court, W.

✠ KYLE, Stewart Leslie
6/1/C/6148, 9/9/15; R.F.C., C/S, 16/4/17; trfr. 19th Lond. R., 1/6/17; R.N.A.S.; Sub. Lieut. Drowned -/4/18.

KYLE, Sigvard Holm
6/D/8178, 6/12/15; Garr. O.C.B., 12/12/16; North'n. R., 10/3/17, Worc. R.; Capt. County Hall, Aylesbury, Buckinghamshire.

LABES, Frederick Gerrard Thomas
6/3/5408, 5/8/15; trfr. Hamps. R., 7/7/16; M.G.C., 25/3/17; F Lieut. c/o Messrs. Shaw, Wallace & Coy., P.O. Box 203, Bombay

LABORDE, Edward Dalrymple
A/14087, 2/10/18; demob. 31/1/19.
c/o Colonial Office, Downing Street, S.W. 1.

LACEY, Horace Marsden
B/12419, 18/1/18; No. 2 O.C.B., 10/5/18; trfr. 14th Lond. R., 6/1/19, Gord. Highrs.; Pte. 37 Oakhill Road, Putney, S.W.

LACEY, Kenneth Charles Warner
6/Sq/7552, 17/11/15; No. 2 Cav. C/S, 31/3/16; Devon. Yeo., 19/8/16; F,It; Capt.; M.C., M(1).
Budore, Delungra, New South Wales, Australia.

LACEY, William Cecil
B/12682, 4/3/18, Cpl.; trfr. K.R. Rif. C., 13/5/19.
67 Elmhurst Mansions, Edgeley Road, Clapham.

LACHLAN, Aubrey Graves
C/9936, 17/11/16; No. 14 O.C.B., 30/1/17; E. Kent R., 25/4/17; Lieut. 65 Gondar Gardens, West Hampstead, N.W. 6.

LACHLAN, Hugh Robert
6/4/9528, 18/2/16; No. 14 O.C.B., 26/11/16; trfr. 16th Lond. R., 11/4/17.

APPENDIX II.—RECORDS OF RANK AND FILE.

LACY, *James Frank*
6/5/7740, 22/11/15; No. 7 O.C.B., 11/8/16; R. Ir. Regt., 18/12/16, att. R. Innis. Fus.; F; Lieut.; w.
    Ardmore, Albion Street, New Brighton, Cheshire.

LADD, *William Bernard Hamilton*
4/4342, 21/6/15; R.W. Fus., 17/12/15; E,P; Lieut.; w.
    8 St. James Gardens, Swansea.

LA FONTAINE, *Cecil Walter*
A/14111, 30/9/18; No. 11 O.C.B., 24/1/19; General List, 8/3/19; 2/Lieut.
    10 Nottingham Place, W.1.

LAHAYE, *Guy Foster*
4/6/Sq/4627, 5/7/15, L/C.; No. 1 Cav. C/S, 24/4/16; trfr 13th Lond. R., 14/6/16; F,S,P; Pte.
    c/o Mrs. Hamnett, 52 Boileau Road, Ealing, W.5.

LAING, *Charles Hilary Cope*
C/A/11745, 26/7/17; R.A., C/S, 25/1/18; R.G.A., 23/9/18; 2/Lieut.
    Thornton House, Horncastle.

✠ LAIRD, *Colin*
6/5/5942, 1/9/15; L'pool. R., 13/12/15; Capt.
    Killed in action 20/9/17.

LAKE, *Athelstan*
A/10462, 12/1/17, L/C.; No. 14 O.C.B., 5/7/17; Essex R., 30/10/17; E; Capt.
    21 Brittania Road, Westcliff-on-Sea.

LAKE, *Evelyn George*
D/11830, 9/8/17; A.S.C., C/S, 12/11/17; R.A.S.C., 6/1/18; 2/Lieut.
    65 Tranquil Vale, Blackheath.

✠ LAKE, *Frank Gilbert*
C/1349, 26/9/14, Sgt.; Herts. R., 6/8/15; Lieut.
    Killed in action 31/7/17.

✠ LAKE, *Geoffrey William*
D/13765, 7/8/18;
    Died 10/11/18.

LAKE, *George Douglas*
C/11449, 4/6/17; A.S.C., C/S, 1/11/17; R.A.S.C., 25/1/18; F; 2/Lieut.
    Brookfield House, Mortimer, Berkshire.

LAKE, *Henry Vivian*
B/2615, 7/1/15; Hamps. R., 3/6/15, Worc. R.; M,Persia,SR; Capt.; M(1).
    Mountside, Rayleigh, Essex.

LAKE, *Ivan*
6/3/5541, 10/8/15, L/C.; Wessex Div. Cyc. Coy., 16/9/15, Army Cyc. Corps, att. Som. L.I.; F; Capt.; w.
    The Strand, Falmouth, Cornwall.

✠ LAKE, *Reginald St. George*
C/998, 5/8/14, L/C.; Oxf. & Bucks. L.I., 9/3/15; Lieut.
    Killed in action 17/11/16.

✠ LAKE, *William Addison*
6/1/5726, 19/8/15, L/C.; No. 14 O.C.B., 30/9/16; R. Marines, 24/10/16; 2/Lieut.
    Killed in action 10/12/17.

✠ LAKEMAN, *John Pearse*
6/4/9153, 25/1/16; No. 8 O.C.B., 4/8/16; North'd. Fus., 21/11/16; 2/Lieut.
    Died of wounds 20/4/17.

LAKEMAN, *Stephen*
1/3642, 17/5/15; 3rd Lond. R., 10/8/15; F; Lieut.; w(2).
    29 Bishops Road, Highgate, N.6. (Now in India).

LAKER, *Frederick George*
2/9783, 25/10/16; No. 21 O.C.B., 5/5/17; 13th Lond. R., 28/8/17; Lieut.

LAKIN-SMITH, *William Hawkes*
4/1/4369, 21/6/15; R.A.S.C., 6/11/15; Lieut.
    Holmwood, Somerset Road, Edgbaston, Birmingham.

✠ LAMAISON, *Leonard William Henry*
D/1389, 29/9/14, L/C.; R. War. R., 15/3/15; Lieu.t
    Killed in action 2/7/16.

LAMARQUE, *Reginald Alvin*
A/10050, 29/11/16; No. 14 O.C.B., 27/12/16; North'd. Fus., 27/3/17; Lieut.
    Kokine, Orpington, Kent.

LAMB, *Arthur Cardain*
6/1/8221, 7/12/15; R.F.A., C/S, 31/3/16; R.F.A., 14/8/16; Capt.
    3 Greenway, Berkhamsted.

LAMB, *Christopher Walter*
1/9742, 16/10/16; No. 14 O.C.B., 27/12/16; E. York. R., 25/4/17; F; Lieut.; w.
    16 St. Leonard's Road, Hull.

LAMB, *Edward*
B/12358, 3/1/18; No. 11 O.C.B., 10/5/18; Sco. Rif., 3/2/19; 2/Lieut.

✠ LAMB, *Francis Cardno*
6/3/1/7385, 11/11/15; R.F.C., 7/7/16; 2/Lieut. *Killed 7/9/16.*

LAMB, *Francis Robert*
K/E/2082, 13/11/14; R. Marines, 31/5/15; F; Lieut.; Croix de Guerre (French), Croix de Guerre (Belgian), M(2).
    3 Greenway, Berkhamsted, Hertfordshire. (Now in Hong Kong).

LAMB, *Frank Edward*
6/8471, 20/12/15; trfr. R.A.S.C., 2/7/16.

✠ LAMB, *Frank Müller*
4/6/1/4888, 15/7/15; Notts. & Derby R., 9/1/16; F; Lieut.; w(2).
    Killed in action 21/3/18.

LAMB, *John Edward Stewart*
6/1/5682, 16/8/15; K.R. Rif. C., 15/1/16; Lieut.
    32 Whitstable Road, Canterbury.

LAMB, *John William*
6/Sq/9384, 8/2/16; R.F.A., C/S, 4/8/16; R.F.A., 9/12/16; Lieut.
    c/o A. W. S. Brown Esq., Penchircle, Bromley, Kent. (Now in South Africa.)

✠ LAMB, *Launcelot Rupert*
K/B/2397, 17/12/14; dis. 27/1/15; R. Lanc. R., 14/8/15; S; Lieut.
    Killed in action 25/5/17.

LAMB, *Norman Ernest*
C/11746, 26/7/17; No. 14 O.C.B., 4/1/18; R. Fus., 25/6/18; F; 2/Lieut.; w.
    Wellsmere, 36 St. Julian's Avenue, Newport, Monmouthshire.

LAMBE, *Laurence Joseph*
6/3/8874, 12/1/16; A.S.C., C/S, 1/9/16; R.A.S.C., 25/10/16, R.F.C.; F; Lieut.; w.
    Glenview, Hollyford, Tipperary.

LAMBERT, *Arthur*
D/9999, 24/11/16; No. 14 O.C.B., 30/1/17; E. Kent R., 29/5/17; att. R.W. Kent R.; I; Capt.
    Gilsland, Mill Road, Deal.

LAMBERT, *Cecil Osmund*
4/3134, 29/3/15; Lan. Fus., 30/7/15, 3rd Lond. R.; Lieut.; M(1).
    c/o Wm. Roskett & Coy., 1 Grays Inn Square, W.C.1.

LAMBERT, *Charles Frederick*
6/1/7993, 29/11/15, L/C.; R.A., C/S, 14/7/16; R.G.A., 4/10/16; 2/Lieut.
    85 Chetwynd Road, N.W.5.

LAMBERT, *Frank Arthur*
4/3/4228, 14/6/15; dis. 8/9/15.

✠ LAMBERT, *Geoffrey Fontaine*
C/1238, 23/9/14, L/C.; Herts. R., 2/3/15; 2/Lieut.
    Died of wounds 15/4/16.

LAMBERT, *Robert Blaikie*
D/10236, 29/12/16; No. 11 O.C.B., 5/7/17; Glouc. R., 30/10/17; It; Lieut.; Croce di Guerra.
    29 Clarenden Road, Redland, Bristol.

LAMBERT, *Thomas William Henry*
A/13129, 27/5/18; trfr. 14th Lond. R., 6/12/18, Gord. Highrs.
    39 Forthbridge Road, Lavender Hill, Clapham Common, S.W.11.

LAMBERT, *Victor Francis*
C/Sq/B/12253, 27/11/17, Cpl.; R.A., C/S, 26/7/18; R.F.A., 7/4/19; 2/Lieut.
    Lismore, 43 Hawthorne Road, Deane Bolton, Lancashire.

LAMBERT, *William Ashcroft*
D/E/B/13936, 2/9/18; demob. 5/2/19.
    54 Bank Street, Sheffield.

LAMBKIN, *Daniel Vincent*
1/3857, 31/5/15; R. Sco. Fus., 8/9/15, R.F.A.; Lieut.

LAMBKIN, *Douglas Raymond*
6/4/6286, 16/9/15; No. 7 O.C.B., 3/7/16; R. Dub. Fus., 3/11/16; Lieut.; M.C.
    1 Barnhill Villas, Dalkly, Dublin.

LAMMIN, *James*
B/1202, 14/9/14; R. Fus., 5/10/14, M.G.C.; F; Lieut.; Inv.
    Carter House, Deal, Kent. (Now in South Africa).

LAMONBY, *Harold*
C/13400, 28/6/18; trfr. 14th London. R., 6/12/18.
    9 Stanton Road, Wimbledon, S.W.19.

LAMOTTE, *Bonamy*
E/1552, 6/10/14; E. Surr. R., 9/11/14; Lieut.

APPENDIX II.—RECORDS OF RANK AND FILE.

LAMPREY, Richard Arthur
C/Sq/10616, 25/1/17; dis. to R. Mil. Coll., 14/1/18; 21st Lancers, 20/12/18; I; Lieut.
Hythe Road, Ashford, Kent. (Now in India).

✠ LANAWAY, Francis Charlton
A/11189, 7/5/17; No. 12 O.C.B., 10/8/17; R. Suss. R., 17/12/17, att. R. Fus.; 2/Lieut. *Killed in action 21/8/18.*

✠ LANCASTER, Cuthbert Buxton
C/Sq/10794, 26/2/17; trfr. 28th Lond. R., 14/8/17; F; Pte.; w(2), g; M(1). *Died -/9/21.*

LANCASTER, Douglas Arthur
C/10991, 4/4/17, Sgt.; No. 14 O.C.B., 8/3/18; E. Kent R., 10/9/18; 2/Lieut.
Rydal, 3 Becton Terrace, Victoria Road North, Southsea, Hampshire.

✠ LANCASTER, Eric Edward
6/5/C/8007, 30/11/15; No. 8 O.C.B., 4/8/16; trfr. 16th Lond. R., 1/12/16; F; Pte. *Killed in action 16/5/17.*

LANCASTER, John Carlyle
6/2/6716, 9/10/15, Cpl.; R. Lanc. R., 24/10/16, M.G.C.; F; Capt.; w; M.C. Market Square, Penrith, Cumberland.

LANCASTER, Norman Rutherford
C/11516, 18/6/17; No. 14 O.C.B., 9/11/17; N. Lan. R., 30/4/18; 2/Lieut. Green Bank, Manchester Road, Burnley.

LANCASTER, Percy Noel
3/3199, 8/4/15; R. Ir. Rif., 21/5/15; 2/Lieut.
17 St. James Mansions, West Hampstead.

LANCASTER, Samuel Laban
2/3782, 27/5/15; Notts. & Derby. R., 17/9/15, emp. M. of Labour; Lieut.; w.

LAND, Edward Taylor
B/10913, 26/3/17; A.S.C., C/S, 30/6/17; R.A.S.C., 25/8/17; S,NR; Lieut. Services Club, 19 Stratford Place, W.1.

LAND, William Walker
A/13984, 9/9/18; demob. 30/1/19.
Bolehill, Ellesmere Road, Chorlton-cum-Hardy, Manchester.

LANDLESS, Jeffrey Wardlaw Lawson
D/13919, 28/8/18; trfr. K.R. Rif. C., 7/4/19.
12 Cambridge Avenue, Great Crosby, Liverpool.

LANDON, George Simpson
6/3/5440, 6/8/15, L/C.; Lond. Div. Cyc. Coy., 14/8/16, att. Manch. R.; F; Lieut.; w.
31 Montrose Avenue, Kilburn, N.W.6.

LANE, Cyril Francis
2/9683, 2/10/16; R.A., C/S, 11/1/17; R.G.A., 8/4/17; 2/Lieut.; w. Inglewood, Shipley, Yorkshire.

LANE, Douglas Harvey
C/11064, 16/4/17; R.A., C/S, 28/12/17, No. 1 Cav. C/S; demob.
Glen Wathen, Church End, Finchley, N.3.

LANE, Douglas Wakeford
D/10023, 27/11/16, Sgt.; R.F.C., C/S, 16/4/17; R.F.C., 14/6/17, R.A.F.; Lieut.

LANE, Edward de L. B.
6/4/5147, 28/7/15; K.R. Rif. C., 7/10/15; 2/Lieut.
7 Cameron Road, Croydon.

LANE, Henry Walker
B/2926, 15/2/15; R.E., 16/6/15; F,E,P; Capt.
c/o P. Lane Esq., 1 Arboretum Road, Worcester.

LANE, Richard Graham
E/2793, 26/1/15; R.G.A., 12/5/15, att. T.M. Bty.; E,F; Capt.; M(1). 26 Rosecroft Avenue, Hampstead, N.W.3.

LANE, Rupert James Howard
C/11488, 14/6/17; R.F.C., C/S, 2/8/17; R.F.C., 8/9/17, R.A.F., R.A.S.C.; NR; Lieut. Benhall, Ross-on-Wye, Herefordshire.

LANE, Stuart Nassau
6/1/D/6287, 16/9/15; trfr. R.G.A., 17/11/16; F; Gnr.
Melville, Glasnevin, Dublin, Ireland.

LANE, William
D/B/C/12109, 11/10/17; trfr. 28th Lond. R., 26/4/18.
Old Hillsborough Road, Lisburn, Co. Down, Ireland.

LANE, William Charles Newton
D/E/13852, 16/8/18; No. 22 O.C.B., 20/9/18; Manch. R., 14/2/19; 2/Lieut. Normanhurst, Hoscote Park, West Kirby, Cheshire.

✠ LANE-HALL, Robert
C/9953, 20/11/16, L/C.; No. 14 O.C.B., 30/1/17; North'n. R., 25/4/17; 2/Lieut. *Killed in action 27/5/18.*

✠ LANE-JOYNT, Albert William. See JOYNT, A. W. L.

LANG, David Marshall
6/4/5885, 30/8/15; Gord. Highrs., 25/9/16; Lieut.; w.
C. M. College, Islington, N.

LANGDON, Glanville
F/1823, 16/10/14; Manch. R., 10/12/14, att. Bord. R.; F,It; Capt.; M.C. Lanherne, Grosvenor Place, Newquay, Cornwall.

LANGDON, Herbert
6/4/8137, 3/12/15; No. 14 O.C.B., 30/10/16; Som. L.I., 24/1/17; F; Lieut.
c/o Lond. Cty. West. & Parr's Bank Ltd., Williton, Somerset.

✠ LANGDON, Lawrence
K/B/2529, 31/12/14; Hamps. R., 31/3/15; Lieut.
Died of wounds 14/3/16.

LANGLANDS, James
H/1961, 26/10/14; R.W. Kent R., 14/11/14, R.F.C.; F; Lieut.; w. Darenth Court, Darenth, Nr. Dartford, Kent.

LANGLER, George Ernest
C/11057, 16/4/17; No. 12 O.C.B., 10/8/17; Som. L.I., 27/11/17; P,F; 2/Lieut. Courtenay Park, Newton Abbot, Devonshire.

LANGLEY, Hubert Francis Grace
D/1410, 29/9/14; dis. 17/3/15; R.F.A., 20/5/17; Lieut.
10 Warwick Square, W.

LANGLEY-WEBB, Henry James
A/10487, 12/1/17; R.A., C/S, 7/9/17; trfr. R.F.A., 23/3/18.
Lulworth House, Spaker, Melksham, Wiltshire.

LANGRIDGE, Arthur Bracy
4/6/2/15, 1/4/08, R.Q.M.S.; R.A.F., 8/11/18; Sqd. Ldr.
St. Andrews Vicarage, Hillingdon, Nr. Uxbridge, Middlesex.

LANGRIDGE, Cecil
4/2972, 25/2/15, Sgt.; K.R. Rif. C., 17/11/15; Lieut.
41 London Road, Wembley, Middlesex.

LANGTON, Charles Hamilton
4/1/4078, 7/6/15; R. Suss. R., 13/11/15; Lieut.
34 Compton Avenue, Brighton, Sussex.

LANGTON, Cuthbert George
4/3349, 22/4/15; No. 9 O.C.B., 8/3/16; High. L.I., 6/7/16; F; Lieut. 2 Porchester Houses, Porchester Road, W.2.

LANGTON, Herbert Allan Guy
6/5/5509, 9/8/15; R.G.A., 21/10/15; F; Lieut.
c/o Finch, Turner & Taylor, 84 Cannon Street, E.C.4.

LANGTRY, Ross Lyle
6/4/9215, 31/1/16; Welch R., 18/12/16; F; Lieut.; g.
22 Rectory Chambers, Church Street, Chelsea, S.W.3.

LANKSHEAR, Alfred John
D/11564, 28/6/17; trfr. Class W. Res., 12/6/18; G; Pte.
127 Highbury Quadrant, Highbury, N.5.

LANNING, Reginald Charles Douglas
6/3/7106, 1/11/15; trfr. M.G.C., 16/10/16.
c/o Mrs. Harvey, Cholsey, Berkshire.

✠ LAPTHORN, Owen Heckford
4/6/Sq/4575, 1/7/15, L/C.; R.A., C/S, 31/3/16; R.F.A., 11/8/16; 2/Lieut. *Killed in action 29/5/17.*

LAPWORTH, Claude
6/2/6824, 14/10/15, L/C.; No. 11 O.C.B., 16/5/16; R. Suss. R., 4/9/16; F; Capt.; p; M(1).
Hillside, Court Hill, Chipstead, Surrey.

✠ LARCOMBE, Archibald Herbert
6/3/9542, 15/2/16; No. 5 O.C.B., 14/8/16; W. Rid. R., 21/11/16; 2/Lieut.; w. *Died 26/10/18 as Prisoner of War.*

LARCOMBE, Francis Maxwell
C/14205, 21/10/18; trfr. K.R. Rif. C., 25/4/19.
c/o M. Brownjohn Esq., 20 Campden House Chambers, Kensington, W.

✠ LARGE, Ernest Lynton
Sq/287, 20/6/08; dis. 19/6/10; 5th Lond. R.; Capt.
Died of wounds 21/5/15.

LARKCOM, Eric Herbert L. Jacobs-
3/3230, 12/4/15; dis. to R. Mil. Academy, 25/2/16; R.E., 26/8/16; Lieut.; w. 1 Harcourt Buildings, Temple, E.C.4.

APPENDIX II.—RECORDS OF RANK AND FILE.

LARKIN, Cyril Gaisford
6/2/6401, 23/9/15; No. 11 O.C.B., 16/5/16; R.F.C., 4/9/16, E. Surr. R. 128 Merton Hall Road, Merton Park, S.W. 19.

LARKIN, George Edwin
6/5/6019, 2/9/15; No. 7 O.C.B., 3/7/16; R. Dub. Fus., 24/10/16, R. Ir. Regt.; S,P,F; Lieut.
Oldville, Sandymount Avenue, Ballsbridge, Co. Dublin.

LARKING, Edwin Victor
F/1926, 22/10/14; E. Kent R., 26/11/14, R.G.A.; Lieut.
Kimberley House, Buckingham.

LARKWORTHY, Eric Gordon
D/Sq, 29/9/14, L/C.; R.F.A., 19/2/15; F; Capt.; w.
The White House, Brondesbury Park, N.W. 6.

LARMAN, George Edward
B/9862, 6/11/16; No. 14 O.C.B., 30/1/17; R. Fus., 29/5/17; F; 2/Lieut.; Inv. Oak House, Wimborne Road, Southend-on-Sea.

LARQUE, Edmund
A/11606, 5/7/17; R.E., C/S, 16/12/17; R.E., 29/3/18; 2/Lieut.
Southend, Upton Lane, Barnwood.

LARSSON, Edward Bengt
13108, 16/5/18; R.E., C/S, 20/8/18; R.E., 8/4/19; 2/Lieut.
31 Oxford Road, Putney, S.W.

LART, Edmund Louis Bertrand
4/4502, 28/6/15; Dorset R., 28/11/15; F; Capt.; w(2).
Meltham Mills, Nr. Huddersfield, Yorkshire.

LASCELLES, Francis William
Sq/1094, 5/9/14; Suss. Yeo., 5/10/14; Capt.; M.C.
5 Bryanston Square, W.

✠ LASCELLES, Harold Leslie
K/2698, 14/1/15; York. R., 23/7/15, R.F.C.; Lieut.
Killed 11/3/17.

LATHAM, Arthur Selby
6/2/5544, 12/8/15; No. 7 O.C.B., 6/4/16; R. Lanc. R., 16/7/16; F; Lieut.; w,p; M.C. 25 Cotswold Road, Westcliff-on-Sea.

LATHAM, Gerald Alfred Butler
6/Sq/9111, 24/1/16; No. 1 Cav. C/S, 12/10/16; 5th Huss., 16/2/17, att. York. Huss. Yeo.; Lieut.; w(2).
28 York Road, Harrogate, Yorkshire.

LATHAM, John Christmas
6/1/6994, 25/10/15, L/C.; Linc. R., 4/9/16, Yorks. L.I., R.F.C., R.A.F.; F; Capt.; w. 6 Sydney Grove, Hendon, N.W. 4.

LATHAM, Leslie Wyndham
C/10187, 13/12/16; trfr. R.F.A., 17/4/17; I.
Gibson Road, Handsworth, Birmingham.

✠ LATHAM, Percy
H/K/3052, 15/3/15; Hamps. R., 15/5/15; G; 2/Lieut.
Killed in actoin 20/8/15.

LATHAM, Robert
6/4/3/8761, 6/1/16; R.A., C/S, 1/12/16; R.G.A., 1/5/17; F; Lieut. Farncombe House, Worthing.

LATIMER, Dennis
6/4/8807, 10/1/16; R.F.C., C/S, 6/9/16; R.F.C., 25/1/17, R.A.F.; F; Capt.; p; M.C., D.F.C. Kirtle House, Knutsford, Cheshire.

LaTROBE-BATEMAN, Frederick George
A/10734, 15/2/17; R.A., C/S, 22/6/17; R.F.A., 15/12/17; Lieut.
22 Caernarvon Road, Norwich, Norfolk.

✠ LATTA, Robert William Campbell
6/4/9567, 4/4/16, L/C.; No. 13 O.C.B., 4/11/16 Sea. Highrs., 28/2/17; F; 2/Lieut. Died of wounds 22/10/17.

✠ LATTER, Francis Robinson
A/749, 1/12/13; R. W. Kent R., 3/9/14; Capt.
Died of wounds 3/5/17.

LAUDER, Thomas James
B/13590, 19/7/18; No. 13 O.C.B., 10/2/19; trfr. K.R. Rif. C., 7/4/19. Old Park, Lydney, Gloucestershire.

LAUGHTON, Reginald James
B/E/13512, 11/7/18; No. 22 O.C.B., 20/9/18; demob. 8/1/19.
35 Albert Hall Mansions, Kensington Gardens, S.W.

LAUGHTON, Roger
6/8522, 29/12/15; R.A., C/S, 9/6/16; R.G.A., 16/9/16; Lieut.; M(1).

✠ LAUNCETON, Roy
6/2/5627, 16/8/15; Midd'x. R., 21/4/16; Capt.; M.C.
Killed in action 24/3/18.

LAURENCE, Basil Stanley
B/12801, 19/3/18; No. 2 O.C.B., 20/9/18; R. Fus., 19/3/19; 2/Lieut. 7 Royal Exchange, E.C. 2.

LAVENDER, Edward Price
6/3/5479, 9/8/15; Notts. & Derby. R., 14/10/15; F; Lieut.; g.
Hughenden, Walsall, Staffordshire.

LAVENDER, Harold Thomas
B/13504, 10/7/18, L/C.; trfr. R. Highrs., 16/4/19; L/C.
Hughenden, Walsall, Staffordshire.

LAVER, John Arthur
6/2/7682, 22/11/15; R. Fus., 25/9/16, R.W. Surr. R., Midd'x. R.; F; Lieut.; Inv.
La Bonanza, Port of Spain, Trinidad, British West Indies.

LAVERACK, Fred William Reid
6/1/8392, 14/12/15; No. 13 O.C.B., 4/11/16; R. Fus., 28/2/17; F; Lieut.; g. Winislea, 49 Barrington Road, Crouch End, N. 8.

LAW, Charles
F/2817, 29/1/15; Devon. R., 22/4/15; F; Lieut.
c/o Fleet Rectory, Nr. Holbeach, Lincolnshire.

LAW, Eric William
6/3/5539, 9/8/15; R.A.S.C., 4/12/15; WA; Lieut.
41 Heriot Row, Edinburgh.

LAW, Louis Stephen
6/3/7107, 1/11/15; No. 9 O.C.B., 8/3/16; High. L.I., 5/7/16, K.O. Sco. Bord.; F; Staff Capt.; w. Inv.
69 Egerton Gardens, S.W. 3.

LAW, Robert John
4/1/4466, 28/6/15; Gord. Highrs., 7/10/15, secd. High. L.I., emp. M. of Labour; F; Lieut.; w.
9 Boscombe Road, Shepherds Bush, W. 12.

✠ LAWDER, Arthur William Charles
6/5/6623, 4/10/15; R.A., C/S, 29/1/16; R.F.A., 6/7/16; 2/Lieut.
Died of wounds 15/4/17.

LAWES, Robert Francis
A/12454, 22/1/18; No. 20 O.C.B., 7/6/18; R. Berks. R., 5/2/19; 2/Lieut. 9 Mount Pleasant Road, Ealing, W. 5.

LAWFORD, Eric Cazenove
B/10134, 6/12/16; trfr. 16th Lond. R., 27/4/17.
Sabrang Estate, Teluk Anson, Perak, Federated Malay States.

LAWFORD, Wingate
F/335, 4/12/08; dis. 28/6/10.

LAWLEDGE, Eric Colen
4/2/4605, 5/7/15; R. War. R., 24/11/15; F; Lieut.; w.
529 City Road, Edgbaston, Birmingham

✠ LAWLESS, Barry Joseph Anthony
4/3/4397, 24/6/15; 12th Lond. R., 31/10/15, att. T.M. Bty.; 2/Lieut. Killed in action 17/7/17.

LAWLESS, Francis
6/5/6379, 22/9/15, L/C.; L'pool. R., 1/6/16, Linc. R.; F; Capt.; w; D.S.O., M(2).
c/o White Star Line, Piazza della Borsa 21, Naples, Italy.

LAWRENCE, Aubrey Trevor
A/271, 3/6/08; dis. 2/6/10; emp. M. of Munitions; M.B.E.
1 Essex Court, Temple, E.C. 4.

✠ LAWRENCE, Charles Alfred
4/1/4001, 3/6/15; Bedf. R., 10/9/15; F; Capt.; M.C.
Killed in actoin 24/4/18.

LAWRENCE, Clifford Alfred Thomas
4/3/3971, 3/6/15; E. Surr. R., 10/9/15; Lieut.
Cranleigh, Woberton Avenue, Kingston Hill, Surrey.

LAWRENCE, Colin Hudson
6/3/8363, 13/12/15; No. 14 O.C.B., 26/11/16; York. & Lanc. R., 27/3/17, R.F.C., R.A.F.; F; Lieut.; cr(3).
Ingfield, Ossett, Yorkshire.

LAWRENCE, Leslie Frederick Warwick
A/12545, 5/2/18; No. 15 O.C.B., 7/6/18; R.W. Kent R., 5/2/19; 2/Lieut. Springhurst, Wiverton Road, Sydenham, S.E. 26.

LAWRENCE, Reuben Richard Samuel
6/1/6034, 2/9/15; No. 7 O.C.B., 6/4/16; D. of Corn. L.I., 22/6/16; I; Capt. Holly Lodge, Hill Lane, Southampton.

APPENDIX II.—RECORDS OF RANK AND FILE.

LAWRENCE, Stanley
3/3696, 20/5/15; R.W. Surr. R., 16/8/15.
18 Wolverton Avenue, Kingston Hill.

LAWRENCE, William Henry Arthur
6/3/8419, 15/12/15, L,'C.; No. 14 O.C.B., 28/8/16; Essex R., 22/11/16, att. Rif. Brig.; F,I; Lieut.
81 Belsize Lane, Hampstead, N.W. 3.

LAWRIE, Roy Cyril
A/Sq/11954, 3/9/17; trfr. R.F•A., 14/12/17.
St. Joseph, Trinidad, British West Indies.

LAWSON, Donald Alexander
B/12853, 25/3/18; R.E., C/S, 23/8/18; demob.
Morven, Canonbie Road, S.E. 23.

LAWSON, Eric William
6/2/8364, 13/12/15, Sgt.; No. 10 O.C.B., 5/10/17; L'pool. R., 26/2/18; F; 2/Lieut.
7 Woodland Grove, Newton Road, Leeds.

LAWSON, Gavin
1/2927, 15/2/15, Sgt.; Gord. Highrs., 24/6/16; F; Capt.
The Manse, Wigtown, Wigtownshire.

✠ LAWSON, Revd. Henry Heaton
A/10492, 12/1/17; Army Chaplains Dept., 27/4/17, att. North'n R.; Capt.
Killed in action 24/3/18.

LAWSON, John
4/1/4079, 7/6/15; Notts. & Derby. R., 5/9/15, att. Lab. Corps; F; Lieut.; w; M(1).
13 Elms Road, Clapham Common, S.W. 4.

✠ LAWSON, Joseph Percy
6/1/5735, 17/8/15; R. Lanc. R., 4/1/16; 2/Lieut.
Killed in action 8/8/16.

LAWSON, Thomas Mattock
C/14206, 21/10/18; trfr. K.R. Rif. C., 7/4/19; Pte.
Stanley Street, Workington, Cumberland.

LAWSON, William Strong
6/4/8330, 11/12/15; L'pool. R., 18/12/16, att. M.G.C.; F; Lieut.; w.
25 Oldfield Road, Wallasey, Cheshire.

✠ LAWTON, Eric Reginald
6/5/7590, 18/11/15; No. 14 O.C.C., 30/9/16; Manch. R., 24/10/16; 2/Lieut.
Killed in action 10/8/17.

LAWTON, Geoffrey Wilfred
C/12572, 6/2/18; No. 21 O.C.B., 5/7/18; R. Berks. R., 3/3/19; 2/Lieut.
Wayside, Shinfield, Reading.

LAWTON, John Frederick
C/D/12246, 23/11/17; No. 6 O.C.B., 7/6/18; Essex R., 4/2/19; 2/Lieut.
Maglona, Derby Road, South Woodford, Essex.

LAX, Martin Bernard
B/13440, 3/7/18; demob. 30/1/19.
17 Hilton Road, Harehills Lane, Leeds, Yorkshire.

LAY, Frederick Charles
5/4/5117, 26/7/15; Oxf. & Bucks. L.I., 19/12/15, att. M.G.C.; F; Lieut.; w(2).
228 Abingdon Road, Oxford.

LAY, Harry Tradescant
A/10301, 1/1/17; H. Bde., O.C.B., 6/3/17; Bord. R., 29/5/17; Lieut.; w.

LAYFIELD, Alan
6/5/5305, 2/8/15, Sgt.; L'pool. R., 27/10/15, att. T.M. Bty.; F,NR; Capt.; w(2); M.C., M(1).
33 Calderstones Road, Liverpool.

LAYLAND, James Muir
B/10118, 6/12/16; A.S.C., C/S, 1/9/17; R.A.S.C., 27/10/17; F; 2/Lieut.; w.
Milborne Wick, Milborne Port, Somerset.

LAYTON, Eric Charles
C/558. 17/3/11; dis. 18/8/13; joined Midd'x R., Sgt.; R.W. Kent R., 5/7/16; F,M; Lieut.; M(1).
Lee Crofts, Caterham Valley, Surrey. (Now in Ceylon).

✠ LAZARUS, Ralph Louis
4/3/4048, 7/6/15; E. Kent R., 10/9/15, Lab. Corps; F; Capt.; w.
Died 30/11/20.

LEA, Edward
6/5/7420, 12/11/15; R.A., C/S, 21/7/16; R.G.A., 1/11/16, R.A.O.C.; S,F; Lieut.
Construction Department, General Electric Company, Schenectady, New York City, U.S.A.

LEA, Geoffrey Lulham
4/4824, 13/7/15, Cpl.; Leic. R., 6/10/15; F; Capt.; w(2).
Leahurst, Stoney Gate Road, Leicester.

LEA, Richard Henry Madure
B/9853, 6/11/16, Cpl.; No. 14 O.C.B., 5/5/17; K.R. Rif. C., 28/8/17; Lieut.; p.

LEA, Thomas Shelton
4/6/5148, 29/7/15; N. Div. Cyc. Coy., 17/9/15, R.E., Rif. Brig.; E,F; Lieut.; w.
96 Sparkenhoe Street, Leicester.

LEA, William
3/9625, 20/9/16, L/C.; No. 14 O.C.B., 27/12/16; Dorset R., 25/4/17, Norf. R., Indian Army; F; Capt.
Commercial Union Assurance Coy. Ltd., 29 Dalhousie Square, Calcutta, India.

LEACH, Frederick Francis
3/3309, 19/4/15; D. of Corn. L.I., 12/5/15; F; Lieut.; w(2).
Capel Curig, Moss Hall Grove, Finchley, N. 12.

LEACH, Harold
6/Sq/7235, 5/11/15, L/C.; No. 1 Cav. C/S, 24/4/16; Devon Huss., 29/5/16; Lieut.; w.

LEACH, Leslie Arthur
D/12919, 10/4/18; No. 5 O.C.B., 8/11/18, No. 20 O.C.B.; R.W. Surr. R., 17/3/19; 2/Lieut.
Durley, 45 Penerley Road, Catford, S.E. 6.

LEACH, Murray Thompson
6/5/6035, 4/9/15, L/C.; L'pool. R., 20/11/15; F; Capt.; M.C. and Bar.
32 Mersey Lane South, Rock Ferry, Cheshire.

✠ LEADBITTER, Francis John Graham
6/4/8875, 12/1/16; No. 8 O.C.B., 4/8/16; K.R. Rif. C., 21/11/16; 2/Lieut.
Killed in action 5/3/17.

LEADER, Leonard William Leader
F/1868, 16/10/14; Conn. Rang., 7/11/14, R. Innis. Fus.; Lieut.; w(2); M(2).
Stake Hill, Clonbanin, Banteen, Co. Cork.

LEADER-WILLIAMS, Basil Conrad
6/5/5385, 5/8/15; Rif. Brig., 20/11/15; I; Lieut.
Palazzo Atenasis, Taormina, Sicily.

LEADLEY, Douglas Gordon
6/3/5510, 9/8/15, L/C.; Yorks. L.I., 15/10/15; S,P; Major; M.C., M(1).
16 London Road, Reading.

LEAH, Thomas
6/5/6926, 19/10/15, L/C.; North'd. Fus., 21/4/16; Lieut.
West Street, Stonebroom, Alfreton.

✠ LEAH, Wilfred Reginald
6/5/6437, 25/9/15; No. 7 O.C.B., 6/4/16; R. Lanc. R., 16/7/16; F; 2/Lieut.
Killed in action 9/9/16.

LEAKE, Victor George
B/10611, 25/1/17; No. 14 O.C.B., 5/7/17; Shrops. L.I., 30/10/17; F; Lieut.; w.
St. Davids, Llanyre, Llandridod Wells.

LEAMING, John Stapleton
F/1794, 16/10/14, L/C.; R. Fus., 10/2/15; Lieut.

LEAN, Leslie John Lawrance
A/12487, 29/1/18, L/C.; demob. 23/1/19.
34 Paddenswick Road, W. 6.

LEAN, William Frank
4/9724, 13/10/16; No. 14 O.C.B., 30/1/17; W. York. R., 29/5/17, att. T.M. Bty.; F; Capt.; w; M(1).
Home Park House, Saltash, Cornwall.

LEAR, Colin Dunlop
6/9588, 17/6/16; R.A., C/S, 12/10/16; R.G.A., 19/12/16; F; Lieut.
McCreary, Manitoba, Canada.

LEARMOND, George Thomas
6/Sq/6767, 11/10/15; No. 2 Cav. C/S, 1/9/16; R. Regt. of Cav., 20/12/16, R.A.F.; F; Lieut.
c/o Nat. Bank of India Ltd., Bishopsgate, E.C. 2.

LEASK, Henry William
6/4/6288, 16/9/15; 8th Lond. R., 13/7/16, emp. M. of Munitions; Lieut.; w.
Sheriff Brae, Forres, N.B.

LEATHAM, William Edward
1/3858, 31/5/15; Gord. Highrs., 10/9/15, emp. M. of Nat. Service; Lieut.; w.

LEATHER, Arthur Bowring
C/11489, 14/6/17, L/C.; R.A., C/S, 15/12/17; R.G.A., 13/5/18; F; 2/Lieut.
Royston, Aigburth, Liverpool.

✠ LEATHES, Robert Herbert de Mussenden
Sq/4/3254, 15/4/15, L/C.; R.F.A., 29/9/15; 2/Lieut.
Killed in action 18/4/17.

APPENDIX II.—RECORDS OF RANK AND FILE.

✠ LEBISH, Frank Roland
6/4/6402, 23/9/15, L/C.; dis. to R. Mil. Academy, 7/9/16; R.F.A., 6/7/17; 2/Lieut.   Died of wounds 25/7/17.

✠ LeBLOND, Royston Cecil Gamage de Plessis
B/1111, 7/9/14; Rif. Brig., 25/9/14; Capt.   Died 17/5/15.

LeBRASSEUR, James Ashhurst
A/431, 15/6/09; dis. 14/6/13.
                 40 Carey Street, Lincoln's Inn Fields, W.C. 2.

LEDBURY, Nelson Herbert Reginald
B/D/12195, 6/11/17; Tank Corps C/S, 1/3/18; Tank Corps, 4/3/19; 2/Lieut.   The Beeches, Trowbridge, Wiltshire.

LEDEBOER, Claude
C/14278, 8/11/18; No. 11 O.C.B., 24/1/19; General List, 8/3/19; 2/Lieut.   c/o B.P.G., Mafeking, South Africa.

LEE, Alfred Charles
6/2/6462, 27/9/15; No. 7 O.C.B., 7/4/16; Yorks. L.I., 21/7/16; F; 2/Lieut.; Inv.   Seaton House, Ranelagh Road, Weymouth

LEE, Arthur John
6/1/7145, 2/11/15, L/C.; No. 11 O.C.B., 8/5/16; R.G.A., 3/7/16; It,E,P,S; Capt.; Medal " Al Valore Militare."
                                   Kettlewell, Woking.

LEE, Bernard Matthew
B/Sq/12683, 4/3/18, Cpl.; trfr. K.R. Rif. C., 13/5/19.
                          50 Alwyn Road, Wimbledon, S.W. 19.

LEE, Clarence Octavius
D/10386, 8/1/17; R.A.O.C., 29/3/17; Lieut.
                         82 Scotts Lane, Shortlands, Kent.

LEE, Edward
6/5/6048, 3/9/15; R.A.S.C., 6/12/15, R.E.; F,SR; Capt.
Lane Rigg, The Heads, Keswick, Cumberland. (Now in India).

LEE, Harold William
4/4151, 10/6/15, L/C.; E. York. R., 20/12/15; F; Capt.
                    Bempton, Bridlington, East Yorkshire.

LEE, Harry Geoffrey
A/11216, 7/5/17; No. 16 O.C.B., 5/10/17; K.R. Rif. C., 12/3/18, R.A.F.; 2/Lieut.   29 Church Road, Moseley, Birmingham.

LEE, Henry
6/3/B/8179, 6/12/15; Garr. O.C.B., 23/5/17; Lab. Corps,14/7/17; Lieut.   24 Kensington Mansions, W.

LEE, Henry Boswell
6/1/6341, 20/9/15, Cpl.; R.E., 17/3/16, R.F.C., R.A.F.; F; Lieut.   Maplefield, Amersham Common, Buckinghamshire.

LEE, Henry Charles Cyril
C/3350, 22/4/15, C.Q.M.S.; demob. 22/2/19.
                         Tremayne, Bloomfield Gardens, Bath.

LEE, John Cuthbert
6/5/6033, 4/9/15, L/C.; No. 5 O.C.B., 14/8/16; R. Marines, 21/11/16; Lieut.; M(1).
                    Antondale, Hoghton Street, Southport.

LEE, Michael John Stanislaus
6/1/5586, 12/8/15, L/C.; No. 7 O.C.B., 3/7/16; R. Marines, 24/10/16; Lieut.

LEE, Reginald Arthur
6/Sq/5562, 12/8/15; R.A., C/S, 24/1/16; R.G.A., 19/6/16; F; Lieut.; p.   West Tarring Rectory, Worthing, Sussex.

LEE, Richard Stuart
6/3/7049, 28/10/15; 20th Lond. R., 4/8/16; Lieut.
                         137 West Side, Clapham Common, S.W.

LEE, Samuel
6/5/5480, 9/8/15; R. Ir. Fus., 20/11/15.
                             93 Townsend Street, Belfast.

LEE, Thomas Harry
C/13401, 28/6/18, L/C.; trfr. K.R. Rif. C., 7/4/19.
                     Bryn Gwenyn, Talycafn, S.O., North Wales.

✠ LEE, William Robert Charles Paul
C/722, 23/6/13; R. Fus., 15/8/14, att. R.W. Fus.; F; 2/Lieut.
                                 Killed in action 10/7/15.

LEE-BOOKER, Roland
K/2503, 31/12/14; S. Lan. R., 20/5/15; Lieut.; w.
                          Swarthdale, Carnforth, Lancashire.

✠ LEECE, Edwin Stanley
4/1/4398, 24/6/15; L'pool. R., 29/11/15; Lieut.
                                  Died of wounds 13/12/17.

LEECH, Donald Collins
D/11831, 9/8/17, L/C.; No. 14 O.C.B., 4/1/18; Essex R., 25/6/18, att. Gren. Gds.; F; Lieut.; g.
                         28 Queens Road, Chelmsford, Essex.

LEECH, Samuel Brice
2/9695, 6/10/16; No. 14 O.C.B., 27/12/16; E. York. R., 25/4/17; 2/Lieut.   The Grammar School, Campden, Gloucestershire.

LEECH, William Charles
D/12979, 24/4/18, L/C.; trfr. K.R. Rif. C., 13/5/19.
                The Grammar School, Campden, Gloucestershire.

LEEDS, Geoffrey Norman
4/2/4648, 5/7/15, Sgt.; R. Fus., 30/12/15, Tank Corps; F; Lieut.
                      20 Tivoli Crescent, Brighton, Sussex.

LEE-JONES, Reginald Wynne
B/11356, 28/5/17; R.F.C., C/S, 26/11/17, No. 6 O.C.B.; dis. med. unfit, 7/12/18.   Luzon, Brixham, South Devonshire.

LEES, Charles Joseph Denis
6/9057, 20/1/16; dis. to re-enlist in R.F.C., 22/8/16.

LEES, Christopher John
4/5/4889, 15/7/15; R.G.A., 29/10/15; F; Lieut.
        c/o N. E. W. Millington Esq., Berfield, Bramhall, Cheshire

LEES, Noah
6/5/5227, 30/7/15; L'pool. R., 3/1/16; F; Lieut.
                               1a Egerton Road, Blackpool.

LEES, Oscar Russell
5/6/5263, 31/7/15; R. Lanc. R., 3/1/16; F; 2/Lieut.
                    Westhill House, Middleton Road, Oldham.

LEES, Robert Cowan
4/4132, 10/6/15; R.F.A., 3/11/15; F,NR; Lieut.; w(2), g; M.C
                         Avenue House, Pershore, Worcestershire.

LEES, William Donald
C/12554, 6/2/18; No. 22 O.C.B., 7/6/18; Midd'x. R., 12/2/19; 2/Lieut.   Covered Way, Sharps Lane, Ruislip, Middlesex.

LEES-BARTON, Joseph. See BARTON, J. L.

✠ LEETE, John Hurstwaite William
A/1184, 14/9/14; Lan. Fus., 19/9/14; F; Capt.
                                    Killed in action 21/1/16.

LEFFMAN, Frank Emil
B/K/6/D/346, 23/2/09, C.S.M.; No. 5 O.C.B., 5/7/18; R.W. Surr. R., 3/3/19; 2/Lieut.
           c/o Cox & Coy., 17 Tower Royal, Cannon Street, E.C. 4.

LEFROY, Anthony Langlois Massy
H/1964, 26/10/14, Cpl.; Devon. R., 24/3/15; Lieut.

LEFROY, Edward Jeffry
B/1253, 23/9/14; Wilts. R., 16/11/14, R.E.; F; Capt.; w.
                 7 Fitz James Avenue, West Kensington, W. 14.

✠ LEGG, William Norman
K/2298, 10/12/14, Cpl.; Shrops. L.I., 18/6/15; Lieut.
                                   Died of wounds 24/3/16.

LEGG, William Wickham
A/277, 18/6/08; dis. 17/6/10.   43 Charlwood Street, S.W. 1.

LEGGAT, Wilson
6/5/6736, 11/10/15, L/C.; N. Lan. R., 25/9/16, secd. Indian Army; F,I; Capt.; w.   Gairnieston, Turriff, Aberdeenshire.

LEGGE, Geoffrey Edward
4/3904, 31/5/15; L'pool. R., 3/6/15, Manch. R.; I; Lieut.
                           11 & 12 Foster Lane, London

LEGGE, Reginald James
4/3231, 12/4/15; R.A.S.C., 16/8/15; R.F.A.; P,F; Staff Major.
                      Department of Education, Jerusalem, Palestine.

✠ LEGGE, William Herman
4/3733, 24/5/15; R.A., C/S, 24/1/16; dis. to re-enlist in R.F.C., 22/8/16; R.N.V.R., att. R.F.C.; Sub. Lieut.   Killed 19/2/17.

✠ LEGGETT, William Evers
D/1393, 29/9/14, L/C.; Midd'x. R., 27/11/14; 2/Lieut.
                                   Killed in action 29/7/16.

LEGH, Arthur Herbert
6/1/8582, 1/1/16, Cpl.; Ches. R., 4/8/16; Lieut.; M.C.
                6 Cowper Road, Berkhamsted, Hertfordshire.

LeGROS, Lewis William
4/5/4676, 8/7/15; E. Lan. R., 7/10/15, secd. R.E. Sigs.; Lieut.

APPENDIX II.—RECORDS OF RANK AND FILE.

✠ LEHFELDT, William Robert Alexander
4/1/4467, 28/6/15; Notts. & Derby. R., 18/10/15; Lieut.
                            Died of wounds 11/10/16.

LEIGH, Percy
6/2/7360, 10/11/15; R.F.C., 16/6/16, R.A.F.; F; Lieut.; Inj.
              Elmfield, Park Avenue, Grimsby.

LEIGH, Walter
4/2/4282, 17/6/15, L/C.; 11th Lond. R., 29/9/15; Staff Capt.; M(1).

LEIGH-HUNT, Gerard Robert Townshend
C/13327, 19/6/18; No. 22 O.C.B., 23/8/18; R. Fus., 13/2/19; 2/Lieut.   14 Victoria Road, Kensington, W. 8.

LEIGHTON, Eric James Harlow
6/2/5335, 2/8/15; R.F.C., C/S, 6/9/16; R.F.C., 16/3/17, Essex R.; P; Lieut.
     Hilaimont, 4 Ailsa Road, Westcliff-on-Sea. (Now in Bombay).

LEIGHTON, Herbert Melville
C/10575, 19/1/17; No. 14 O.C.B., 16/3/17; Special List, 25/4/17, S. Pers. Rif.; Persia; Capt.
                51a Queens Road, Watford, Hertfordshire.

LEIGHTON, E. John Blair
E/1575, 6/10/14; R.G.A., 10/3/15.
              14 Priory Road, Bedford Park, W. 4.

LEITCH, Walter
6/1/7800, 24/11/15; trfr. 18th Lond. R., 14/9/16.

LEITH, James
F/1867, 16/10/14; Hamps. R., 27/2/15, secd. R.F.C., R.A.F.; Capt.; M.C.

LELAND, Charles Henry
C/A/12053, 27/9/17; R.F.C., C/S, 18/1/18; R.F.C., 6/3/18, R.A.F.; 2/Lieut   1 Mary's Road, Drogheda, Ireland.

✠ LeMARCHANT, Spencer Henry
B/503, 4/11/10, Sgt.; R. Fus., 9/9/14; 2/Lieut.
                     Died of wounds 25/5/15.

Le MAY, Raleigh
B/D/12212, 11/11/17; trfr. Class W. Res., 14/3/18; Order of S. Stanislaus (Class II.).   Denmark House, Tonbridge, Kent.

LEMERLE, Augustus Lewis
4/3212, 12/4/15; Bedf. R., 3/6/15, R.E.; G,E,M,I; Major; M(1).
      c/o Cox & Coy., 16 Charing Cross, S.W. 1.

Le MESSURIER, Hugh Arnott
K/2441, 28/12/14; Oxf. & Bucks. L.I., 30/11/14; Capt.
                      40 Windsor Road, Ealing.

LeMESURIER, Hubert Francis Augustine
A/1657, 9/10/14; Ches. R., 23/12/14; F; Major; w, w-p; M.C.
             Lingmoor, Howbeck Road, Birkenhead.

✠ LEMON, Adrian Leigh
Sq/511, 4/11/10, L/C.; Drag. Gds., 15/8/14; Lieut.
                     Killed in action 29/11/17.

LENANTON, Harold Arthur
6/A/8646, 3/1/16, Sgt.; M.G.C., C/S, 6/7/17; M.G.C., 19/12/17; F; 2/Lieut.; M.C.
        Queensthorpe, Queensthorpe Road, Sydenham, S.E.

LENEY, Bertram
C/11490, 14/6/17, L/C.; R.A., C/S, 25/1/18; demob.
                Orpines, Wateringbury, Kent.

LENNON, George Homan
6/5/7820, 24/11/15; No. 8 O.C.B., 4/8/16; Lein. R., 25/4/17; F; Lieut.; w; M(1).   Hotwell Enfield, Co. Meath, Ireland.

LENNOX, Henry Hutchinson
6/3/9008, 19/1/16, L/C.; R.A., C/S, 4/8/16; R.F.A., 27/10/16; F,lt; Capt.; w; M.C.
   Thatched House Club, St. James Street, S.W.1. (Now in China).

LEONARD, Allan Lancefield Parratt
6/Sq/5436, 5/8/15, L/C.; No. 2 Cav. C/S, 1/9/16; R. Regt. of Cav., 20/12/16; Lieut.; w.
        1 St. Andrews Terrace, Regent Square, Northampton.

LEONARD, Herbert William
6/Sq/8089, 1/12/15, L/C.; No. 2 Cav. C/S, 1/9/16; R. Regt. of Cav., 20/12/16.
        1 St. Andrew's Terrace, Regent Square, Northampton.

LEONARD, Hugh Robert
Sq/367, 19/3/09; dis. 18/3/13; rej. Sq/1340, 26/9/14, L/C.; 2nd Lovats Scouts. 5/2/15; E,S,F; Lieut.
               15 Park Avenue, Hampstead, N.W. 11.

LEONARD, Richard Wilton
6/9421, 10/2/16; A.S.C., C/S, 1/5/16; trfr. R.A.S.C., 17/7/16.
           4 Whiteford Road, Mannamead, Plymouth.

LEONARD, Stuart Berrington
6/5/C/9112, 24/1/16; No. 14 O.C.B., 30/10/16; E. Kent R., 28/2/17, att. Notts. & Derby. R.; F; Lieut.
                  3 Boileau Road, Ealing, W. 5.

LEPINE, Charles Alexander
1/3859, 31/5/15; Yorks. L.I., 29/7/15; F; Capt.
          Violet Dale, Carew Road, Wallington, Surrey.

LEPINGWELL, Roderick Arthur
A/512, 4/11/10; dis. med. unfit, 16/1/13.
           Bracklyn, Malden Road, Wallington, Surrey.

LEPPER, Frank Ewart
C/D/10841, 7/3/17, L/C.; demob. 14/10/19.
          Fairholme, 70 Croxted Road, Dulwich, S.E. 21.

LE PREVOST, Alfred Paul Harrison
B/2725, 18/1/15, Sgt.; Notts. & Derby. R., 12/7/15, K.R. Rif. C.; Lt.-Col.; w(2); D.S.O. and Bar, M(1).
      c/o Messrs. George Atherton & Coy., Liverpool.

Le QUESNE, Frank Philip
B/11051, 16/4/17, L/C.; R.E., C/S, 25/11/17; R.E., 22/2/18; P; 2/Lieut.
    14 Le Geyt Street, St. Helier, Jersey, Channel Islands.

LESCHALLAS, Beaumont
F/1841, 16/10/14; R. Berks. R., 4/11/14.
                  Highams, Windlesham, Surrey.

LESLIE, Alan
C/1157, 14/9/14, L/C.; R.F.A., 21/11/14; F; Capt.; w.
               Goldsmith Building, Temple, E.C. 4.

LESLIE, Bernard Alexander
K/E/2159, 23/11/14; N. Staff. R., 3/2/15, att. R. Lanc. R.; Capt.; w.

LESSER, Albert
C/14140, 11/10/18; trfr. Class W. Res., 14/12/18.
              15 Sunbury Road, Anfield, Liverpool.

LESTER, Dudley Emerton
6/2/6556, 30/9/15; E. Kent R., 4/1/16; Lieut.
                      40 Biggin Street, Dover.

✠ LESTER, John Beaumont
C/627, 29/3/12, L/C.; Hamps. R., 12/9/14, K.R. Rif. C.; Capt.
                   Killed in action 16/9/16.

LeSUEUR, Arthur William Payne
4/6/2/4975, 19/7/15; R.A.S.C., 27/11/15; F; Lieut.
Inglewood, Shore Road, Uplands, Victoria, British Columbia, Canada.

✠ LETHEM, John
6/2/5511, 9/8/15; R.F.A., 23/11/15; 2/Lieut.
                     Killed in action 1/12/17.

LETTS, Arthur Bertram Davis
D/13731, 2/8/18; trfr. K.R. Rif. C., 7/4/19.
      10 Girdlers Road, Brook Green, West Kensington, W. 14.

LETTS, Egerton Michael
E/1609, 6/10/14, Cpl.; Oxf. & Bucks. L.I., 20/2/15, R.F.C.; F; Lieut.; w.   98 Great Russell Street, W.C. 1.

✠ LEVENE-DAVIS, John
4/6/3/4936, 19/7/15;   Died 18/1/16.

LEVER, James Darcy
6/Sq/8647, 3/1/16; No. 2 Cav. C/S, 5/1/17; R. Regt. of Cav., 7/7/17, Staff. Yeo.; P; Lieut.
              The Grove, Thornton Hough, Cheshire.

LEVERINGTON, James Robert
B/11347, 23/5/17; R.G.A., C/S, 10/10/17; R.G.A., 1/7/18; 2/Lieut.   Norma House, Sunny Bank, South Norwood, S.E. 25.

LEVERSON, Basil Alfred David
B/1032, 24/8/14; N. Lan. R., 12/9/14; F; Capt.; w(2).
                        18a Marloes Road, W. 8.

LEVERSON, Elmer James
C/10188, 13/12/16; trfr. 8th Lond. R., 9/3/17.
           4 Stanhope Terrace, Hyde Park Gardens, W. 2

LEVETT, Edward George
A/2740, 21/1/15; Essex R., 29/4/15; 2/Lieut.
            High Firs, Brenchley, Paddock Wood, Kent.

APPENDIX II.—RECORDS OF RANK AND FILE.

✠ LEVETT, *Richard Henry*
A/2710, 18/1/15; R.W. Kent R., 29/4/15; 2/Lieut.
Died 20/8/16.

LEVITT, *Joseph Beales*
E/14161, 14/10/18; demob. 10/1/19.
Dashwood, Station Road, March, Cambridgeshire.

LEVY, *Douglas Oscar*
6/D/6768, 11/10/15; trfr. Class W. Res., 29/11/16.

LEVY, *Frederick David*
C/1155, 14/9/14; 21st Lond. R., 19/10/14, R.A.F.; F,S,E,P; Lieut.
38 Porchester Square, Hyde Park, W. 2.

LEVY, *Percy Philip*
6/4/7399, 12/11/15, L/C.; No. 11 O.C.B., 7/5/16; Oxf. & Bucks. L.I., 4/9/16, att. Intelligence Corps; F; Lieut.; Croix de Guerre (Belge), M(1).
3 Lymington Road, N.W. 6.

LEWCOCK, *Francis James*
2/3443, 1/5/15; R.F.A., 27/10/15; F; Capt.; g.
23 Doughty Street, Mecklenburgh Square, W.C. 1.

LEWELL, *John Kindred*
5/6/6810, 14/10/15, Sgt.; R.A., C/S, 29/1/16; Norf. R., 24/7/16; E,P; Lieut.
Cedars Farm, Springfield Lane, Ipswich, Suffolk.

LEWELLIN, *Llewellyn*
C/10362, 5/1/17; trfr. 8th Lond. R., 9/3/17.

LEWES, *John Ponsonby Powell*
C/Sq/14299, 12/11/18; demob. 22/1/19.
Abermead, Llanforian, Aberystwyth.

LEWIN, *Claude John*
6/1/D/5563, 12/8/15, L/C.; No. 14 O.C.B., 26/11/16; Som. L.I., 28/2/17; F; Lieut.; w; M.C.
10 Elmsleigh Road, Weston-super-Mare, Somerset.

LEWIN, *Harry William*
C/13210, 5/6/18; R.E., C/S, 25/8/18; demob. 21/12/18.
Fulham, Blairhill, Coatbridge, Scotland.

LEWIS, *Alan Dix*
K/2333, 14/12/14; Dorset R., 2/6/15, att. R.F.C., R.A.F.; F,S,P; Lieut.
Chase Side, Winchmore Hill, N. 21.

LEWIS, *Alexander Cameron*
C/14185, 18/10/18; No. 11 O.C.B., 24/1/19; General List, 8/3/19; 2/Lieut.
Box 46, Johannesburg, South Africa.

✠ LEWIS, *Alfred Drysdale*
6/3/5795, 23/8/15; Bord. R., 28/12/15, R.E.; F; Lieut.; w.
Killed in action 23/3/18.

LEWIS, *Brian Lander*
Sq/798, 25/5/14; Innis. Drag., 15/8/14, att. 3rd Cty. of Lond Yeo.; Lieut.

LEWIS, *Charles Bertram*
6/4/9175, 27/1/16; R.A., C/S, 7/8/16; R.G.A., 1/11/16; S; Lieut
1 Dempster Terrace, St. Andrews, Scotland.

LEWIS, *Charles Cecil Courteney*
B/1320, 26/9/14, Cpl.; Hamps. R., 22/12/14, R.W. Fus., Manch. R., Indian Army; I,M; Capt.
Churchill, Sutton, Surrey.

LEWIS, *Charles Parker*
B/12708, 8/3/18; No. 6 O.C.B., 6/9/18, Nos. 1 & 3 O.C.B.; Ches R., 18/3/19; 2/Lieut.
Granton House, Queens Road, Coventry.

LEWIS, *Cyril Frederic*
6/2/5512, 9/8/15; R.F.A., 12/1/16, secd. R.F.C.; Lieut.
37 Marlborough Road, Wimbledon Park, S.W. 19.

LEWIS, *Daniel John*
1/3643, 17/5/15; R. War. R., 28/7/15; F; Capt.; w.
c/o Messrs. Johnson, Stokes & Master, Solicitors, Hong Kong.

LEWIS, *David Charles*
6/5/7683, 22/11/15; R.A., C/S, 31/3/16; R.G.A., 6/7/16; F; Major.
Bryrrhos, Treboeth, Swansea.

LEWIS, *David Greswolde*
A/10746, 16/2/17; R.F.C., C/S, 16/4/17; R.F.C., 14/6/17, R.A.F.; F; Lieut.; p.
Melvin Hall, Goiders Green, N.W.

LEWIS, *David Thomas*
6/7146, 2/11/15, L/C.; No. 6 O.C.B., 17/4/16; R. War. R., 4/9/16; F; Lieut.; Inv.
278 Kingsbury Road, Erdington, Birmingham.

LEWIS, *Denis Foster*
6/4/9173, 27/1/16; Dental Surgeon, 7/10/16; Capt.
Leicester Lodge, 43 Station Road, Clacton-on-Sea.

✠ LEWIS, *Denys Mervyn*
6/4/6358, 20/9/15; Worc. R., 25/9/16; F; 2/Lieut.
Killed in action 25/4/17.

LEWIS, *Edward Harold*
6/1/9087, 24/1/16; R.A., C/S, 18/8/16; R.F.A., 12/1/17.
Wellfield, Aberavon, Port Talbot.

✠ LEWIS, *Edward Pugh*
D/Sq/9997, 24/11/16; R.F.C., C/S, 13/3/17; R.F.C., 19/4/17; 2/Lieut.
Killed in action 6/10/17.

LEWIS, *Ernest Lytle*
B/13477, 30/6/18; trfr. 16th Lond. R., 13/9/18.
32 Waldegrave Park, Twickenham.

✠ LEWIS, *George Hardy*
B/779, 27/3/14; E. Surr. R., 15/8/14; Capt.
Died of wounds 28/9/15.

✠ LEWIS, *Gerald Sidney*
B/799, 25/5/14; Midd'x. R., 12/9/14; F; Capt.
Killed in action 7/7/16.

✠ LEWIS, *Harold*
4/5/5039, 22/7/15; M.G.C., 4/8/16; 2/Lieut.
Died of wounds 12/5/17.

LEWIS, *Harold Arthur*
B/13441, 3/7/18; trfr. K.R. Rif. C., 7/4/19, att. R.E.
Eversfield, Connaught Avenue, Chingford.

LEWIS, *Harold Brayam*
4/3/5076, 26/7/15; R.W. Kent R., 27/12/15; Lieut.

LEWIS, *Harold Langford*
A/185, 1/5/08; dis. 30/4/10.
78 Gladstone Road, Watford, Hertfordshire.

LEWIS, *Harry Parker*
6/3/5409, 5/8/15.
32 Waldegrave Park, Twickenham.

LEWIS, *Hedley Wallace*
B/13675, 29/7/18; trfr. K.R. Rif. C., 7/4/19.
6 Sloane Street, S.W. 1.

LEWIS, *Henry Steedman*
K/H/2502, 31/12/14, L/C.; R. Suss. R., 31/3/15, Tank Corps; F; Major; w; M.C. and Bar, M(1).
Eccentric Club, Ryder Street, St. James. (Now in Brazil).

LEWIS, *Hywel Glyn*
6/2/5336, 2/8/15; Som. L.I., 23/11/15, Tank Corps; F; Capt.
Lurganbrae, Shawkill, Co. Dublin.

LEWIS, *James Charles*
6/3/8180, 6/12/15; A.S.C., C/S, 22/5/16; R.A.S.C., 25/6/16; Lt.-Col.; O.B.E., M(2).
21 St. Margaret's Road, Brockley, S.E. 4.

LEWIS, *James Scourfield*
B/12400, 8/1/18, L/C.; No. 18 O.C.B., 10/5/18; Welch R., 3/2/19; 2/Lieut.
6 Broniestyn Terrace, Aberdare, Glamorganshire.

LEWIS, *James William*
6/2/9544, 19/2/16; No. 13 O.C.B., 4/11/16; Lan. Fus., 28/2/17; F; Capt.; w; M.C. and Bar.
76 Moston Lane, Harpurhey, Manchester.

LEWIS, *John Cecil*
A/D/B/12532, 2/2/18; No. 13 O.C.B., 9/8/18; R.W. Fus., 5/3/19; 2/Lieut.
Glasfryn, Heathfield, Swansea.

✠ LEWIS, *John Charles*
6/5/8113, 2/12/15; Mon. R., 22/11/16, Shrops. L.I.; Capt.
Killed 4/12/17.

LEWIS, *John Cyril Morgan*
6/1/6094, 6/9/15; No. 4 O.C.B., 7/3/16; R.W. Fus., 14/7/16; F; Capt.; M.C.
Morgan's Terrace, Pembroke.

LEWIS, *John Samuel*
D/12996, 29/4/18; No. 5 O.C.B., 8/11/18, No. 20 O.C.B.; Welch R., 4/2/19; 2/Lieut.
35 Pemberton Street, Llanelly, N. Wales.

LEWIS, *John William*
6/Sq/5564, 12/8/15, L/C.; Worc. R., 19/12/15, R.G.A.; F; Capt.
25 Elmhurst Road, Bruce Grove, N. 17.

LEWIS, *Leonard Cyril St. Alban*
2/3092, 22/3/15; Welch R., 20/8/15; Lieut.
St. John's College, Oxford

APPENDIX II.—RECORDS OF RANK AND FILE.

LEWIS, Lewis Charles
B/13643, 26/7/18; demob. 21/12/18.
Malvern House, Richmond Road, Abertillery, Monmouthshire.

✠ LEWIS, Reginald Walter Morton
6/3/6444, 25/9/15, L/C.; No. 11 O.C.B., 7/5/16; Worc. R. 4/9/16; Lieut. Died 3/10/18.

✠ LEWIS, Robert Frederick
6/1/7741, 22/11/15; No. 8 O.C.B., 4/8/16; K.R. Rif. C., 21/11/16, att. T.M. Bty.; 2/Lieut. Killed in action 20/9/17.

✠ LEWIS, Robert George
6/2/6664, 7/10/15; M.G.C., 25/9/16; Lieut.
Killed in action 23/9/18.

LEWIS, Robert William
6/1/8696, 4/1/16; No. 14 O.C.B., 26/11/16; L'pool. R., 27/3/17, secd. R.A.O.C.; Lieut.
Lyndale, Laurel Road, Fairfield, Liverpool.

LEWIS, Roger
C/1884, 16/10/14; dis. 31/10/14; R.W. Fus., 31/10/14; F; Staff Capt.; w; M(1). Belmont, Bangor, North Wales.

LEWIS, Stuart H.
B/671, 26/11/12; R.W. Kent R., 15/8/14; Capt.; w; M(1). Netherton, Westcombe Park Road, Blackheath, S.E. (Now in Shanghai).

LEWIS, Sydney Hubert
D/13886, 21/8/18; trfr. K.R. Rif. C., 7/4/19.
10 Northcote Street, Roath, Cardiff

LEWIS, Thomas Arthur
6/8989, 18/1/16; R.A.S.C., 10/4/16; S; Lieut.
45 Bullingham Mansions, W.1.

LEWIS, Thomas William
2/3783, 27/5/15; R. Mar. Art., 30/8/15; Lieut.; Croix de Guerre (Belge), Ordre de la Couronne (Belge), M(1).
4 The Causeway, Teddington, Middlesex.

LEWIS, Tom Chilton
D/11159, 2/5/17; A.S.C., C/S, 1/10/17; R.A.S.C., 30/11/17; F,E; Lieut. 34 Ashburton Avenue, Croydon, Surrey.

LEWIS, Trevor Kempthorne
6/D/Sq/9356, 7/2/16; No. 1 Cav. C/S, 31/7/17; R. Regt. of Cav., 22/2/18; F; 2/Lieut. Maesyrhaf, Neath, South Wales.

✠ LEWIS, Wallenstein Ryan
Sq/3135, 29/3/15; R.E., 24/4/15; Capt. Died of wounds 25/3/18

LEWIS, William Augustus
6/4/7462, 15/11/15, Sgt.; R.A., C/S, 26/10/16; R.F.A., 5/5/17; F; Lieut.; w. Mount Pleasant, Rumney, Nr. Cardiff.

LEWIS, William Lester
6/5/C/8066, 1/12/15, Cpl.; No. 14 O.C.B., 30/10/16, M.G.C., C/S; M.G.C., 24/2/17, Tank Corps; F; Lieut.; w.
11 Yy Gwyn Road, Pontypridd, Glamorganshire.

LEWIS, William Pitt
C/14228. 25/10/18; demob. 22/1/19.
Belvoir House, Newport, Monmouthshire.

LEWIS-PHILIPPS, Hugh William
5/9590, 20/6/16; No. 14 O.C.B., 27/9/16; Pemb. Yeo., 24/1/17, secd. M.G.C.; Lieut. Clyngwynne, Whitland, South Wales.

LEWORTHY, Archibald Joseph
B/10718, 12/2/17, L/C.; R.A., C/S, 3/9/17; R.F.A., 9/2/18; 2/Lieut.
The Chalet, Chaworth Road, West Bridgford, Nottinghamshire.

LEY, Edward M.
Sq/126, 18/4/08; dis. 17/4/09; K.R. Rif. C., 9/9/14; F,S; Major; w(2); D.S.O., M(2). Colombo Club, Ceylon.

LEYLAND, Stanley
C/13302, 17/6/18; trfr. 14th Lond. R., 6/12/18, Gord. Highrs.; Sgt. 3 Cambridge Terrace, Waterloo, Liverpool.

LEYSHON, Frederick Stanley
B/10530, 17/1/17; R.E., 10/9/17; Lieut.
Fairlawns, Heathcote Road, St. Margaret's-on-Thames, Middlesex.

LEYSON, Thomas
4/9623, 20/9/16; No. 14 O.C.B., 5/3/17; S. Wales Bord., 26/6/17; Lieut. Pencynor, Aberdulais, Glamorganshire.

✠ LIBBY, Alfred Thomas
6/3/5513, 9/8/15, Cpl.; E. Surr. R., 28/12/15; Lieut.
Killed in action 20/9/17.

LIDDELL, Frederic Volence
6/4/6403, 23/9/15; trfr. M.G.C., 3/11/16.

LIDDELL, Geoffrey Oswald
6/5/8067, 1/12/15, Sgt.; R.A., C/S, 4/8/16; R.F.A., 27/10/16; F; Lieut.; w; M.C.
The Headlands, Kimbolton Road, Bedford.

LIDDERDALE, Eustace Henry
6/2/5514, 9/8/15, L/C.; R.A.S.C., 13/2/16; EA; Lieut.
Woodland House, Boxmoor, Hertfordshire.

LIDDLE, Edward Marcus
B/A/12224, 13/11/17; R.F.C., C/S, 15/2/18; trfr. R.A.F., 15/2/18.
Lisgoole, Hungerford Road, Crewe, Cheshire.

LIDDLE, Henry Weddell
6/5/8915, 7/1/16; No. 8 O.C.B., 4/8/16; K.R. Rif. C., 21/11/16; F; 2/Lieut.; w-p. Clifton Manor, York.

LIDDON, John Henry Churchill
6/4/8138, 3/12/15; No. 14 O.C.B., 30/9/16; Som. L.I., 24/10/16; F; 2/Lieut.; w. Silver Street House, Taunton, Somerset.

LIDINGTON, Arthur Douglas
A/10714, 12/2/17; R.F.A., C/S, 29/6/17; R.F.A., 28/12/17; 2/Lieut.

LIGHT, Alwyn Henry
6/1/Sq/6694, 7/10/15, L/C.; R.A., C/S, 28/4/16; R.G.A., 8/8/16; Lieut.

✠ LIGHTBODY, Wilfrid Petre
D/1396, 29/9/14, Sgt.; Norf. R., 27/11/14; Lieut.
Killed in action 26/9/15.

LIGHTBURN, John Edward
3/3784, 27/5/15; Manch. R., 9/9/15; F; Lieut.
Springfield, Stockton Heath, Warrington.

✠ LILICO, Percy
C/11491, 14/6/17; R.F.C., C/S, 23/10/17; R.F.C., 12/12/17, R.A.F.; 2/Lieut. Killed 16/2/18.

✠ LILLEY, Edmund Arthur Howe
4/3697, 20/5/15; Bedf. R., 10/9/15, att. T.M. Bty.; Lieut.
Killed in action 31/7/18.

LILLEY, John Louis St. George
6/5/6737, 11/10/15; R.F.C., C/S, 25/2/16; trfr. 13th Lond. R., 15/6/16, Cpl.; R.E., 1/9/17; F,S,Germ.EA; Lieut.
c/o T. Mason, Esq., 3-5 Rood Lane, E.C.

LILLEY, Samuel Frederick
B/2668, 12/1/15, Sgt.; Notts. & Derby. R., 7/6/15; F; Capt.; M.C. 11 Winterbrook Road, Herne Hill, S.E. 24.

LILLEY, Walter Eaden
C/13384, 24/6/18; No. 22 O.C.B., 23/8/18; Suff. R., 13/2/19; 2/Lieut. Holmleigh, West Road, Cambridge.

LILLEY, William Galpin
6/2/5901, 30/8/15; Notts. & Derby. R., 4/8/16, Indian Army; F,I; Capt.; w. c/o Messrs. Cox & Coy., Bombay.

LILLICRAP, Claude Ernest Henry
4/3/5118, 26/7/15; R.F.C., C/S, 28/12/16; R.F.C., 3/4/17, R.A.F; Capt. Courtnay House, 24 Collings Park, Mannamead, Plymouth.

LILLIE, William Henry George
6/6581, 2/10/15, Sgt.; trfr. 13th Lond. R., 2/5/16.
3 Conyers Avenue, Birkdale, Southport.

LIMA, Theodore George Alexander
4/4576, 1/7/15; Welch R., 4/1/16, S. Wales Bord.; F,SR; Lieut.; w; M.C.
c/o National Bank of Turkey, Constantinople.

LIMBERY-BUSE, Richard Geoffrey King
K/D/2371, 17/12/14; R. Suss. R., 31/3/15, att. R. War. R.; F; Lieut.; w(2).
25 St. Johns Road, Tunbridge Wells, Kent. (Now in California).

LIMMER, Laurence James
6/3/5796, 23/8/15; K.R. Rif. C., 15/1/16; Capt.; w.
255 Finchley Road, Hampstead, N.W.

LINAKER, Ellis Edward
D/10240, 29/12/16; trfr. R.G.A., 24/4/17.
Charlesbye, Ormskirk, Lancashire.

✠ LINCEY, Charles Edgar
6/2/5767, 21/8/15, Cpl.; R. Lanc. R., 31/12/15; 2/Lieut.
Killed in action 31/7/16.

237

APPENDIX II.—RECORDS OF RANK AND FILE.

LINCOLN, *Alfred*
6/1/6095, 6/9/15; R.A., C/S, 7/8/16; R.F.A., 3/12/16; Lieut.; *w*.
11 Salisbury Street, Hull.

LINDEMERE, *Victor*
K/C/3/2075, 13/11/14, Sgt.; R.A.S.C., 8/6/15; F; Capt.; M(1).
Carholme, Wargrave, Berkshire.

LINDLEY, *Frank Riley*
F/1767, 16/10/14, Sgt.; Linc. R., 27/11/14; F; Major; *w*; *M.C.*, M(1).
Abbeville, Parson Street, Hendon, N.W.

LINDLEY, *John*
B/10098, 4/12/16; No. 14 O.C.B., 5/3/17; Manch. R., 26/6/17; F; Lieut.; *w*.
c/o Peel Mills Ltd., Chamber Hall, Bury, Lancashire.

✠ LINDLEY, *John Bennett*
6/3/5437, 5/8/15; R.F.A., 3/11/15, att. T.M. Bty.; F; 2/Lieut.
Died of wounds 19/5/17.

LINDSAY, *Arthur Samuel*
C/A/11773, 30/7/17, L/C.; Garr. O.C.B., 8/3/18; Lab. Corps, 4/9/18, att. R.A.S.C.; F; 2/Lieut. *122 Ladbroke Grove, W.*

LINDSAY, *John Forrest*
B/96, 16/4/08; dis. 15/4/11; rej. A/1077, 2/9/14; 1st Lond. R., 5/10/14, secd. R.F.C., R.A.F.; Capt.; *A.F.C.*
2 Cranley Place, S.W.7.

LINDSELL-STEWART, *Antony William James*
4/2/4468, 28/6/15; N. Staff. R., 7/10/15, att. Yorks. L.I.; F; Capt.; *w*(2). *Sleaford House, The Grove, Denmark Hill, S.E.5.*

✠ LINDSEY, *Douglas*
F/1861, 16/10/14, Sgt.; Dorset R., 2/6/15; Lieut.
Killed in action 17/12/17.

✠ LINDSEY, *Paul*
6/5/C/7613, 19/11/15; No. 14 O.C.B., 30/10/16; Oxf. & Bucks L.I., 28/2/17; 2/Lieut. *Killed in action 2/6/17.*

LINEKAR, *John Clarence*
6/4/8837, 10/1/16; No. 8 O.C.B., 4/8/16; L'pool. R., 21/11/16; F; Lieut. *7 Portland Street, Abertillery, Monmouthshire.*

LINFORD, *Vivian Haldane Bruce*
D/A/12987, 26/4/18; trfr. 14th Lond. R., 6/12/18.
13 Oak Avenue, Chorlton-cum-Hardy, Manchester.

LINFORD, *William Alan Milroy*
6/2/5337, 2/8/15; North'n. R., 13/12/15; Lieut.
Downsend, Nr. Leatherhead, Surrey.

LING, *George Malcolm*
A/10306, 1/1/17; R.F.C., C/S, 13/3/17; R.F.C., 19/4/17, att Devon. R.; E,F; Lieut.; *w*; M(1) .
49 Grosvenor Road, Handsworth, Birmingham.

LINGARD, *Claude Frank*
C/476, 24/3/10; dis. 23/4/14; R.E., 1/10/14; Lieut.; *w*.

LINGEMAN, *Eric Ralph*
A/Sq/11295, 16/5/17; No. 14 O.C.B., 10/5/18; dis. to Indian Tr Coll., 11/9/18; Indian Army, 15/4/19; 2/Lieut.
12 Ave. Pierre I de Serbie, Paris.

LINGEMAN, *Frank Edgar*
C/1683, 12/10/14; Lan. Fus., 8/4/15; Lieut.; *w*; Croix de Guerre (French), M(1).

LINGHAM, *George Alexander*
D/10438, 10/1/17; R.F.C., C/S, 13/3/17; R.F.C., 19/4/17, R.A.F.; F; Lieut.; *D.F.C.*
Riverina, Elm Road, Earley, Berkshire.

LINNELL, *William Howes*
A/10868, 14/3/17; R.G.A., C/S, 15/8/17; R.G.A., 31/12/17; F; Lieut. *Tower House, Carfax, Oxford.*

LINSCOTT, *Edward John Crews*
C/11518, 18/6/17; No. 16 O.C.B., 5/10/17; D. of Corn. L.I., 12/3/18; 2/Lieut. *27 Prospect Terrace, Newton Abbot.*

LINTERN, *Richard Turner*
4/4577, 1/7/15; R.F.A., 18/10/15; F,SR; Capt.; *w*.
Helenlia, St. Notts, Lanarkshire, N.B.

LINTON, *Arthur Cyril*
4/4133, 10/6/15; 19th Lond. R., 2/11/15; F; Lieut.; *w*.
Latimer, Hope P.O., Jamaica, British West Indies.

LINTON, *Leonard*
6/2/5657, 16/8/15; trfr. 22nd Lond. R., 2/5/16.
Ashfield Villas, Stockton-on-Tees.

LINTON, *William John*
6/5/C/9009, 19/1/16; No. 7 O.C.B., 4/11/16; R. Ir. Rif., 28/2/17; F; Lieut.; *w*; *M.C.* *Ulster Bank Ltd., Sorabane.*

✠ LION, *Neville Isidore*
F/3/2982, 27/2/15; R. Marines, 28/5/15; Lieut.
Killed 29/4/17.

LION, *Stanley Percy*
4/5/6/4860, 15/7/15; dis. med. unfit, 6/5/16.
9 Princes Street, Hanover Square, W.1.

LIPP, *George Allan Stuart*
6/1/9113, 24/1/16; M.G.C., C/S, 25/11/16; M.G.C., 24/3/17; F,NR; Lieut.; *w*; *M.C.*, Croix de Guerre.
Vlottenburg, Cape Province, South Africa.

LIPSCOMB, *Sidney George*
H/2/2611, 7/1/15, L/C ; 3rd Lond. R., 20/4/15; F; Capt.; g, *w*; *M.C.* *71 Gladstone Park Gardens, Cricklewood, N.W.2.*

✠ LISBY, *Leslie Norman*
3/3121, 27/3/15, L/C.; R. Suss. R., 19/6/15; Lieut.
Died of wounds 5/11/17.

LISTER, *Cecil Jack*
A/13120, 24/5/18; demob. 11/11/19.
Ashbourne Lodge, 26 George Lane, Lewisham, S.E.13.

LISTER, *Edward Arthur*
4/3698, 20/5/15, Cpl.; York. R., 1/11/15; F; Lieut.; *w*.
12 Lansdowne Road, Bridlington, Yorkshire.

LISTER, *William Rayner*
6/2/6435, 25/9/15; trfr. 6th Lond. R., 4/8/16.
The Lodge, Terrington Street Clerments, Kings Lynn.

LISTER-TIBBETS, *Joseph*. See TIBBETTS, J. L.

✠ LITTEN, *Raymond*
C/854, 4/8/14; R. Berks. R., 12/9/14; F; Capt.
Killed in action 1/7/16.

LITTLE, *David Allen*
C/D/14255, 24/10/18; trfr. R. Regt. of Cav., 11/6/19.
Belfast Bank, Central Branch, Belfast.

LITTLE, *Edward*
6/5/C/8648, 3/1/16. L/C.; No. 14 O.C.B., 30/10/16; Oxf. and Bucks. L.I., 28/2/17; F; Lieut.; *p.*
Middleton Stoney, Bicester, Oxon.

LITTLE, *Henry Hamilton*
Sq/1954, 26/10/14; Denb. Huss., 3/11/14, secd. M.G.C.; Capt.; *M.C.*

LITTLE, *John Douglas*
C/12621, 18/2/18, L/C.; No. 22 O.C.B., 7/6/18; Ches. R., 11/2/19; 2/Lieut. *Eihandune, Hoylake, Cheshire.*

✠ LITTLE, *Norman James Richard*
3/3351, 22/4/15, L/C.; R. Fus., 8/7/15; Lieut.; M.(1).
Killed in action 13/3/17.

LITTLE, *Raymond Brooke*
2/3507, 6/5/15; R.E., 20/7/15, secd. Tank Corps; E,F; Capt.; M(1). *21 Ladbroke Gardens, W.11.*

LITTLE, *Rudolf Alexander*
6/8857, 11/1/16; R.A., C/S, 9/6/16; R.F.A., 23/9/16; Lieut.; *w*.
Barnhill, Moffat, Dumfries.

LITTLE, *Wilfrid Joseph Hamilton*
Sq/593, 27/11/11; dis. 10/10/13; R. War. R., 3/12/14; Major; *w*.
125 Merton Hall Road, Wimbledon, S.W.19.

LITTLEHALES, *Alan Douglas*
6/1/8929, 15/1/16; No. 14 O.C.B., 30/10/16, M.G.C., C/S; M.G.C., 25/1/17, Tank Corps; F; Lieut.; *w*, *Inj*.
17 Fawdry Street, Wolverhampton.

LITTLEJOHN, *Frederick Miller*
6/3/A/9158, 26/1/16, Sgt.; demob. 25/1/19.
116 Hanover Street, Edinburgh.

LITTLEWORTH, *Aubrey Guy*
6/Sq/7207, 4/11/15; trfr. Bedf. Yeo., 13/6/16.
Lavender Cottage, Torquay.

LITTON, *William Roy Upton*
K/2201, 30/11/14; dis. med. unfit, 17/12/14; General List, 10/5/16, att. War. Office; Capt.
Woolmer Lodge, Liphook, Hampshire.

LIVERMORE, *Stanley Ronald*
6/3/C/8649, 3/1/16; No. 14 O.C.B., 30/10/16, M.G.C., C/S; M.G.C., 30/1/17, Tank Corps; F; Capt.; *w*.
2 Manor Street, Braintree, Essex.

APPENDIX II.—RECORDS OF RANK AND FILE.

LIVESEY, Herbert
6/3/7614, 19/11/15; S. Lan. R., 4/9/16, att. 12th Lond. R.; F;
Lieut.; w. Glasgow House, Cluvel, Accrington.

LIVINGSTON, David Clark Hall
D/13855, 19/8/18; trfr. K.R. Rif. C., 7/4/19.
Lalunt, 12 Chase Green Avenue, Enfield, Middlesex.

LIVINGSTONE, Kenneth Gilbert
K/H/2463, 28/12/14, Sgt.; Midd'x. R., 23/7/15; F; Capt.; w(2).
33 Queensborough Terrace, W. 2.

LIVINGSTONE, Stanley
6/2/5481, 9/8/15; Midd'x. R., 1/6/16, att. Derby Cyc. Bn.; F;
Lieut. 36 Clavering Avenue, Castelnau, Barnes.

LIVOCK, James Edgar
B/A/11704, 19/7/17; No. 22 O.C.B., 7/6/18; York. R., 11/2/19;
2/Lieut. Hazelcroft, Boxwell Road, Berkhamsted, Hertfordshire.

LLEWELLYN, George Henry
D/E/13712, 31/7/18; R.G.A., C/S, 2/10/18; R.G.A., 11/4/19;
2/Lieut. 41 Sladefield Grove, Washwood Heath, Birmingham.

LLEWELYN, William Eustace
6/1/7265, 8/11/15, L/C.; No. 5 O.C.B., 14/8/16; R. Marines,
21/11/16; F; Lieut. Fairwater, Pantyffynon, South Wales.

LLEWELLYN-DAVIES, Alan Howell Pryce
6/1/9419, 9/2/16; No. 14 O.C.B., 30/10/16, M.G.C., C/S;
M.G.C., 25/1/17; Lieut.; w.

LLOYD, Albert Lawrence
4/3/4002, 3/6/15; Essex R., 21/10/15, secd. Lab. Corps; Capt.
43 Paddenswick Road, Ravenscourt Park, W. 6.

LLOYD, Arthur Sneyd
C/D/14217, 23/10/18; trfr. K.R. Rif. C., 13/5/19.
Bronllys, Aberystwyth.

LLOYD, Charles Evan
D/E/13676, 29/7/18; No. 22 O.C.B., 20/9/18; Oxf. & Bucks.
L.I., 5/2/19; 2/Lieut. The Vicarage, New Hinksley, Oxford.

LLOYD, Charles Harry Percival
6/2/8797, 10/1/16; dis. med. unfit, 26/9/16.
15 St. George's Terrace, Kemptown, Brighton.

LLOYD, Ebenezer Edge
6/1/6463, 27/9/15, Sgt.; W. York. R., 21/4/16; F,It; Lieut.;
M.C., M(1). 59 Chestnut Street, Southport, Lancashire.

LLOYD, Edward Albert
4/3860, 31/5/15, Sgt.; Midd'x. R., 5/2/16, att. R. Berks. R.;
F,S,SR; Lieut.; w. 98 East Dulwich Grove, S.E. 22.

LLOYD, Frederick William
Sq/886, 5/8/14; R.A.S.C., 5/10/14; F; Capt.; Inv; M(1).
Green Room Club, W.C. (Now in New York)

LLOYD, George Moss
K/E/2282, 8/12/14, Cpl.; R. Lanc. R., 17/3/15; Lieut.

LLOYD, Humphrey
B/C/12315, 21/12/17; trfr. 28th Lond. R., 4/10/18.
Plas Tregyan, Llamgwyllog, Anglesey.

LLOYD, James Becket
B/10720, 12/2/17, Sgt.; demob. 18/2/19.
c/o Hughes & Lloyd, 31 North John Street, Liverpool.

LLOYD, John Bebb
B/12709, 8/3/18; No. 14 O.C.B., 23/8/18; demob. 3/1/19.
Russell House, Silver Street, Edmonton, N. 8

LLOYD, John Davies Knatchbull
C/14310, 30/11/18; demob. 27/12/18.
Plas Trefaldwyn, Montgomery, North Wales.

LLOYD, Lionel Walter
4/1/5119, 26/7/15; dis. med. unfit, 8/8/16.
Summer Hill, Dyke Road, Brighton.

LLOYD, Philip Franklin
C/11747, 26/7/17; Sigs. C/S, 14/12/17; R.E., 24/5/18, att
R.F.A.; F; 2/Lieut.
Export Dept., British Thomson Houston Coy. Ltd., Rugby.

LLOYD, Rae Llewelyn
6/Sq/5306, 2/8/15, L/C.; R.F.A., 22/10/15; Lieut.; M.C.
16 Campden Hill Gardens, W. 8.

LLOYD, Reginald John
A/14088, 2/10/18; No. 11 O.C.B., 24/1/19; General List, 8/3/19;
2/Lieut. Broughton Lodge, St. Georges Road, Cheltenham.

LLOYD, Standish Edward Graham
6/Sq/5992, 2/9/15; R.A., C/S, 24/1/16; R.F.A., 22/12/16; F;
Lieut. 16 Campden Hill Gardens, W.8. (Now in Argentina).

LLOYD, Thomas Chadwick
6/7771, 23/11/15; R.N.A.S., 3/1/16, R.A.F.; Capt.
12a Elgin Court, Maida Vale.

LLOYD, William Gambold
6/1/8393, 14/12/15; No. 8 O.C.B., 4/8/16, M.G.C., C/S; R.W.
Fus., 18/12/16; F; 2/Lieut.; w(2).
Longstone, Letterston, Pembrokeshire.

LLOYD-BLOOD, Lancelot Ivan Neptune
6/5/6093, 6/9/15; R. Dub. Fus., 29/1/16; F; Capt.; w(2); M.C.,
M(1).
c/o Standard Bank of South Africa, Mombasa, Kenja Colony.

LLOYD-DAVIS, Edward Hanbury Carington
4/2/4312, 17/6/15; Shrops. L.I., 28/10/15; F; Lieut.; w.
Brewood, Staffordshire.

LLOYD-GREAME, Sir Philip
A/446, 12/11/09; dis. 30/10/11; rej. A/897, 5/8/14; York. R.;
Major; K.B.E., M.C. 8 Wetherby Place, S.W. 7.

LLOYD-JONES, Robert William Arnold
C/9941, 17/11/16; No. 14 O.C.B., 30/1/17; E. Kent R., 29/5/17,
R. Suss. R.; Capt.
198 Rishton Lane, St. Lever, Bolton, Lancashire.

LLOYD-MOSTYN, Ievan
K/6/2086, 13/11/14; R.W. Fus., 17/5/15; Lieut.

LLOYD-REES, Wilfred
6/Sq/7208, 4/11/15, Cpl.; No. 2 Cav. C/S, 22/2/17; R. Regt. of
Cav., 7/7/17, 9th Lancers; F; Lieut.
Eglwysilan Rectory, Abertridwr, Nr. Cardiff, South Wales.

✠ LLOYDS, Cyril Edwin Fowler
6/4/6624, 4/10/15; R.G.A., C/S, 28/2/17; R.G.A., 22/7/17; F;
2/Lieut.; w. Died 9/1/19.

LLOYDS, Walter Harry Richardson
B/10762, 19/2/17; No. 12 O.C.B., 10/8/17; S. Staff. R., 27/11/17;
2/Lieut.; M.C.
5 Somerset Road, Handsworth Wood, Birmingham.

LLOYD-WILLIAMS, Wynne
D/A/12110, 11/10/17; R.F.C., C/S, 18/1/18; R.F.C., 6/3/18,
R.A.F.; 2/Lieut. 22 Ferners Road, Oswestry, Salop.

LOADER, Robert Arthur
D/B/13812, 12/8/18; No. 24 O.C.B., 15/11/18; Tank Corps,
22/3/19; 2/Lieut. 83 Pinner Road, Harrow, Middlesex.

LOBEL, Alfred
F/1839, 16/10/14; R.A.O.C., 8/2/15; G,E; Major.
Services Club, Stratford Place, W.

LOCK, Robert Bartholomew
D/E/13796, 9/8/18; No. 22 O.C.B., 20/9/18; Essex R., 5/2/19;
2/Lieut. c/o National Bank of South Africa, London Wall, E.C

LOCKE, Albert Edward
A/10461, 12/1/17; No. 20 O.C.B., 5/5/17; 8th Lond. R., 28/8/17;
F; Lieut. 16 Clissold Road, Clissold Park, N. 16.

LOCKE, Henry Oscar
4/1/4047, 7/6/15; R. Ir. Fus., 7/10/15, emp. M. of Labour; F;
Lieut.; Inv. 6 Heath Hurst Road, Hampstead, N.W. 3.

✠ LOCKETT, Clifford Vincent
6/2/6530, 30/9/15, L/C.; No. 7 O.C.B., 7/4/16; Essex R.,
17/7/16, att. Rif. Brig.; F; Lieut.; w. Died of wounds.

LOCKETT, Louis Hudson
D/3028, 11/3/15, Sgt.; Midd'x R., 1/7/15; F; Major; M.C., M(1).
64 Londsdale Road, Barnes, S.W. 13.

LOCKHART, Frederick Ramsdale
6/1/6859, 15/10/15; Manch. R., 4/9/16, M.G.C.; F; Lieut.
Hartley College, Alexandra Park, Manchester.

LOCKHART, William Alan
6/2/7615, 19/11/15; dis. to R. Mil. Academy, 7/9/16; R.G.A.,
6/6/17, att. Intelligence Corps; F; Capt.
The Ridge, Kingsdown Road, Epsom.

LOCKS, John Leonard
B/12832, 22/3/18; R.F.A., C/S, 26/7/18; R.F.A., 5/4/19; 2/Lieut.
Gainsborough Lodge, Leytonstone, Essex.

LOCKWOOD, Donald Dawson
A/10699, 13/2/17; R.F.C., C/S, 13/3/17; R.F.C., 19/4/17,
R.A.F.; F; Lieut. Croft Grove, Milnsbridge, Huddersfield.

APPENDIX II.—RECORDS OF RANK AND FILE.

✠ LOCKYER, Stanley Watkins
C/14207, 21/10/18; Died 6/11/18.

LODGE, Aubrey Frederick
E/14061, 25/9/18; No. 22 O.C.B., 22/11/18; R. War. R., 19/2/19; 2/Lieut. 12 Hawkwood Road, Boscombe, Hampshire.

LODGE, Bernard Hutchings
4/6/5/4861, 15/7/15; 12th Lond. R., 19/12/15, R.A.F.; F; Lieut 9 Hoole Road, Chester.

LODGE, Christopher Fyers.
H/1962, 26/10/14; Worc. R., 13/3/15, R.F.C.; F; Lieut.; p. Aish, South Brent, South Devonshire.

LODGE, John Weighill
6/2/8181, 6/12/15; No. 14 O.C.B., 27/9/16; Mon. R., 18/12/16, att. R.W. Fus.; P,F; Lieut.; w; M.C. The Limes, Staplegrove, Taunton, Somerset.

LODGE, Leslie King
6/8598, 1/1/16; R.F.A., C/S, 26/5/16; R.G.A., 13/9/16; F; Lieut. Ivy Lodge, Boston Avenue, Southend-on-Sea, Essex.

LODGE, Thomas Arthur
A/1125, 7/9/14; 24th Lond. R., 25/11/14; Capt.; w; O.B.E., M(2). Blythe Lawn, Angel Road, Thames Ditton.

LOFTHOUSE, William Alexander
C/13253, 10/6/18; No. 22 O.C.B., 5/7/18; Education Officer, 8/12/18; Capt. Dunedin, Walton Road, Altrincham, Cheshire.

LOGAN, John Alexander
6/1/7994, 29/11/15, L/C.; No. 14 O.C.B.; R.W. Fus., 24/10/16, att. No. 15 O.C.B., Inst; F; Lieut.; Inv. Technical College, Durban, Natal, South Africa.

✠ LOGAN, William Alexander Ross
6/5/5943, 1/9/15; L'pool. R., 1/6/16, M.G.C.; F; Lieut. Died 19/2/19.

✠ LOMAS, Harold
K/E/2192, 26/11/14; Manch. R., 3/3/15. Killed 1/7/16.

LOMAS, Lewis Edward
4/4152, 10/6/15; R.F.C., 4/9/16, R.A.F.; F; Lieut. Rosedene, Hertford Heath, Hertfordshire.

LOMAS, Robert Stuart
A/B/D/12169, 29/10/17; R.A., C/S, 15/3/18; R.F.A., 8/3/19; 2/Lieut. Butley Cottage, Prestbury, Cheshire.

✠ LOMAX, John
6/2/5338, 2/8/15; Leic. R., 31/12/15, D. of Corn. L.I., att. R. War. R.; 2/Lieut. Killed in action 18/8/16.

LOMER, Arthur George Thomas
6/3/5320, 4/8/15; Notts. & Derby. R., 15/11/15; F; Lieut.; M.C. 78 Crawley Road, Horsham, Sussex.

LONDON, Arthur Frank
B/2832, 1/2/15; Notts. & Derby. R., 11/6/15; Lieut.

LONDON, Frank James
4/4229, 14/6/15; Wilts. R., 23/4/16; F; Lieut.; w, p. 47 Highbury Quadrant, N. 5.

LONDON, Harold Ernest George
C/Sq/11059, 16/4/17, L/C; No. 2 Cav. C/S, 11/1/18; R. Regt. of Cav., 22/6/18; 2/Lieut. 15 Leaside Avenue, Muswell Hill, N. 10.

LONERAGAN, O'Donald
4/6/Sq/4469, 28/6/15; R.F.A., 23/9/15; F; Major; M.C., Croix de Guerre (Belge). c/o New South Wales Bank, Threadneedle Street, E.C.

LONERGAN, Ernest James Henry Mousley-
Sq/1692, 13/10/14; R.H.A., 5/2/15; Lieut.

LONERGAN, Francis
Sq/1693, 13/10/14; R.H.A., 5/2/15; 2/Lieut. Cressingham Park, Nr. Reading.

LONG, Alfred
6/4/8913, 14/1/16; A.S.C., C/S, 27/10/16; R.A.S.C., 20/12/16; F,It; Lieut.; M(1). Medina House, Park Gate, Nr. Southampton.

LONG, Charles
4/3/4112, 5/6/15; trfr. Class W. Res., 25/7/16 Lacton Farm, Westwell, Kent.

LONG, Charles Bernard
6/5/8182, 6/12/15; No. 5 O.C.B., 14/8/16; Cold. Gds., 20/11/16.

LONG, Charles Edward
6/4/8853, 11/1/16, L/C.; 7th Lond. R., 23/6/16; F,SWA; Lieut. 8 Bentinck Terrace, St. Johns Wood, N.W. 8.

LONG, George Oliver
B/11366, 28/5/17; No. 14 O.C.B., 9/11/17; Wilts. R., 30/4/18; F; 2/Lieut. 30 Richmond Park Avenue, Bournemouth.

LONG, Harold Noble
6/Sq/8457, 17/12/15; No. 1 Cav. C/S, 18/8/16; Essex Yeo., 27/11/16; F; Lieut. Ringshall Hall, Stowmarket, Suffolk.

✠ LONG, Horace Victor
6/2/6359, 20/9/15; No. 11 O.C.B., 7/5/16; R.F.C., 4/9/16. Died of wounds 16/7/17.

LONG, James Ronald
6/5/8183, 6/12/15; No. 5 O.C.B., 14/8/16; Cold. Gds., 20/11/16; 2/Lieut. The Bushes, Iron Bridge, Shropshire.

LONG, Robert Joseph Mudie
4/6/Sq/4470, 28/6/15, L/C.; R.F.A., 16/11/15; Lieut.; M(1). 3 Upper Bedford Place, W.C.

LONG, Victor Edwin
4/1/4399, 24/6/15; trfr. Hamps. Yeo., 17/3/16. Down End, Fareham.

LONGDEN, Winton Spence
6/Sq/7684, 22/11/15, L/C.; No. 2 Cav. C/S, 1/9/16; Bedf. Yeo., 27/1/17, att. York. Drag.; F; Lieut.; Inv. Lynrode Farm, Dersingham, Norfolk.

✠ LONGHURST, Harold
A/1026, 24/8/14; R. Berks. R., 3/9/14; Lt.-Col.; w. Killed in action 12/10/17.

✠ LONGLEY, Frank Arthur John
6/3/6968, 22/10/15; 7th Lond. R., 4/9/16, att. K.R. Rif. C.; F; 2/Lieut. Killed in action 18/6/17.

LONGSDON, Robert Cyril
A/Sq/14066, 27/9/18; demob. 8/1/19. Norman Court, Salisbury, Wiltshire.

LONGSTAFF, John
4/3/4421, 24/6/15; R.W. Fus., 31/10/15; E; Capt. Barclay's Bank House, Fleet, Hampshire.

LONGTON, Edward Harold
C/12631, 19/2/18; R.A., C/S, 17/5/18; R.F.A., 8/3/19; 2/Lieut. Mavis Bank, Feniscliffe, Blackburn, Lancahsire.

✠ LONGTON, Edward John
H/2041, 9/11/14; Essex R., 30/12/14; 2/Lieut. Killed in action 6/6/15.

LONGWORTH, Thomas
6/5/6204, 13/9/15, L/C.; Manch. R., 4/9/16; F; Lieut.; p. 25 Brook Road, Flixton, Manchester.

LORD, William Thomas
6/1/8114, 2/12/15, L/C.; R. Berks. R., 30/5/17; F; Lieut.; M.C., M.M. Box 149, Randfontein, Transvaal, South Africa.

LONSDALE, John Frederick
C/13254, 10/6/18; No. 22 O.C.B., 5/7/18; Midd'x. R., 5/2/19; 2/Lieut. 43 Oakley Street, Chelsea, S.W. 3.

✠ LOOKER, Leonard Davies
6/4/8838, 10/1/16; No. 14 O.C.B., 27/9/16; R.W. Surr. R., 18/12/16; 2/Lieut. Killed in action 1/8/17.

LOOSEMORE, Alfred
D/A/297, 24/6/08; dis. 23/6/13. Beechwood, Tiverton, Devonshire.

LORD, Chadwick
C/13303, 17/6/18; R.E., C/S, 18/10/18. 9 Jubilee, Shan, Nr. Oldham, Lancashire.

LORD, Charles George
4/3421, 29/4/15; Notts. & Derby. R., 3/8/15; R.A.F.; F; Capt.; M.C., M(1). Mile Ash, Derby.

✠ LORD, Evelyn Geoffrey
6/3/8784, 7/1/16; No. 14 O.C.B.; M.G.C., 24/10/16; Lieut.; w. Died 25/6/18.

LORD, Henry Douglas
A/1372, 26/9/14, L/C.; Hamps. R., 14/12/14; F,S; Capt. Selwood, Alleyn Park, Dulwich, S.E.

LORD, John
A/12488, 29/1/18; No. 16 O.C.B., 7/6/18; Manch. R., 6/2/19; 2/Lieut. 16 Alphonsus Street, Old Trafford, Manchester.

APPENDIX II.—RECORDS OF RANK AND FILE.

LORDAN, Jeremiah Patrick
D/Sq/10675, 3/2/17, Cpl.; No. 1 Cav. C/S, 1/9/17; R. Regt. of Cav., 22/2/18, Indian Army; F; Lieut.; M(1).
Leap, Skibbereen, Co. Cork, Ireland.

LORDEN, Henry Matthew
F/1860, 16/10/14, L/C.; 4th Lond. R., 24/12/14; Capt.; w.
Ravenswood, West Hill, Putney, S.W. 15.

LORDON, Francis Patrick Cyril
A/11651, 12/7/17; No. 19 O.C.B., 9/11/17; R. Marines, 30/4/18; Lieut.
R.M.L.I., c/o G.P.O., London.

LORENZEN, Christian Carl
4/4003, 3/6/15; Manch. R., 6/12/15; F; Lieut.; w.
Dalkeith, Bishop's Avenue, East Finchley, N. 2.

LORIMER, Arthur Roderick
A/10038, 29/11/16; No. 14 O.C.B., 10/8/17; N. Cyc. Bn., 27/11/17. M.G.C.; F; Lieut.
2 Chesterfield Mansions, Highgate Village, N. 6.

LORIMER, Henry George Smallwood
6/2/7147, 2/11/15; Rif Brig., 4/9/16; F; Lieut.; M.C.
c/o Barker & Coy. Ltd., Singapore, Straits Settlements.

✠ LORIMER, Hugh Cowan
4/6/2/4937, 19/7/15; D. of Corn. L.I., 12/12/15; w.
Died 27/11/18.

LORIMER, Robert
6/1/6995, 25/10/15; No. 9 O.C.B., 8/3/16; Arg. & Suth'd. Highrs., 6/7/16; Lieut.
22 Dublin Street, Edinburgh.

✠ LORING, Charles Michael
F/K/2534, 31/12/14; R. War. R., 31/3/15; F; 2/Lieut.
Killed in action 3/9/16.

✠ LOTAN, William Desmond Guthrie
6/5/5515, 9/8/15; No. 1 O.C.B., 6/3/16; R.F.C., 6/7/16; 2/Lieut.
Killed 10/12/16.

LOTON, James Joseph
6/5/C/8896, 13/1/16; No. 2 O.C.B., 14/8/16; trfr. R.G.A 16/2/17.

LOUDAN, Stirling Mouat
6/2/8271, 9/12/15; No. 13 O.C.B., 4/11/16; R. Berks. R., 28/2/17; F; Lieut.; w-p.
Secretary, Diplomatic Travel Bureau, Modane Gare, Savori, France.

LOUDEN, William George Martin
B/12391, 15/1/18, L/C.; demob. 19/1/19.
202 Brownhill Road, Catford, S.E. 6.

LOUGH, Jack
4/3/4000, 3/6/15; Manch. R., 18/10/15; Lieut.
125 Wimbledon Park Road, S.W.

LOUND, John Draycott
6/9385, 8/2/16; dis. med. unfit, 26/9/16.

LOVE, Alfred Francis
6/1/8029, 30/11/15; No. 8 O.C.B., 4/8/16; K.R. Rif. C., 24/10/16; F; Staff Lieut.
Crown Office, Royal Courts of Justice, Strand, W.C.

LOVE, Claude Gordon
D/Sq/10849, 7/3/17; No. 14 O.C.B., 5/10/17; R.W. Surr. R., 26/2/18; F; Lieut.; w.
Airhil, Schull, Co. Cork.

LOVE, Herbert Nisbet
6/2/7266, 8/11/15; R.W. Kent R., 4/8/16, att. R.A.F.; F; Lieut; w.
12 Spencer Road, Cottenham Park, S.W. 20.

✠ LOVE, James Ellis
6/3/D/8030, 30/11/15; No. 14 O.C.B., 30/10/16; Manch. R., 28/2/17; F; 2/Lieut.
Killed in action 2/9/18.

LOVEDAY, Francis Alfred
6/Sq/7930, 29/11/15; No. 1 Cav. C/S, 6/12/16; Wilts. Yeo., 16/4/17, 2nd Cty. of Lond. Yeo., att. M.G.C.; Germ.SWA,P,F; Lieut.; Croix de Guerre (Belge), Ordre de Chevalier de la Couronne.
The Corner Cottage, Mundesley, Norfolk.

LOVEDAY, Frederick Charles
D/13732, 2/8/18; demob. 30/1/19.
112 Barry Road, S.E. 22.

LOVEDAY, Sidney George
C/778, 27/3/14; Midd'x. R., 5/9/14; I; Capt.
The Corner Cottage, Mundesley, Norfolk.

LOVEGROVE, George Cole
6/5/5438, 5/8/15; R.A.S.C., 8/11/15; S; Lieut.
Cedarholme, Church Gardens, Osterley, Middlesex.

✠ LOVELL, John Cuthbert
H/2053, 9/11/14; Sco. Rif., 5/1/15; F; Lieut.; w.(2).
Killed in action 1/8/17.

✠ LOVELL, Robert Clifford
6/1/7297, 8/11/15; No. 1 O.C.B., 6/9/16; R.F.C., 25/1/17; F; 2/Lieut.
Killed in action 26/1/18.

LOVELY, William Stanley
A/14089, 2/10/18; demob. 29/1/19.
21 Worthington Street, Dover, Kent.

LOVEMORE, Robert Baillie
6/4/9432, 11/2/16, Sgt.; 3rd Lond. R., 23/6/16, att. R.F.C. and R.A.F.; Germ.SWA & EA,E,F; Lieut.; w; D.S.O., M(2).
Sundridge, P.O. Franklin, East Griqualand, South Africa.

LOW, David William Beveridge
1/3041, 13/3/15, Sgt.; Cam'n. Highrs., 1/5/16, att. 14th Lond. R.; F,S,P; Lieut.
160 High Road, Wood Green, N.W.

LOW, John Claud Nelson
1/3644, 17/5/15; Bedf. R., 10/9/15, M.G.C.
Homelands, The Avneue, Grove Park, Lee, S.E. 12.

LOW, Robert
D/12950, 19/4/18; No. 16 O.C.B., 18/9/18; L'pool. R., 17/3/19; 2/Lieut.
36 Rosslyn Street, St. Michaels, Liverpool.

LOW, William Loveridge
1/3645, 17/5/15, L/C.; York. & Lanc. R., 14/11/15, att. Rif. Brig.; F; Capt.
Northcroft, North Road, Berkhamsted, Hertfordshire. (Now in Canada).

LOWE, Charles Conyers
6/5/7108, 1/11/15; M.G.C., 25/9/16; Lieut.
Stamford, Lincolnshire.

LOWE, George Desmond Hudson
1/3331, 21/4/15, Sgt.; Midd'x. R., 3/8/15, att. R. Suss. R.; F; Lieut.; w.
Grosvenor Cottage, Denton, Nr. Canterbury, Kent.

LOWE, John
D/14041, 20/9/18; No. 18 O.C.B., 10/2/19; trfr. 5th Lond. R., 7/3/19.
24 West Holmes Gardens, Musselburgh, Scotland.

LOWE, John Longton
6/5/8068, 1/12/15, L/C.; No. 14 O.C.B., M.G.C., C/S; M.G.C., 28/12/16; Lieut.
Winwich, Nr. Warrington, Lancashire.

LOWE, Reginald Arthur Grierson
B/13488, 8/7/18; demob. 23/1/19.
The Round Hill, South Benfleet, Essex.

✠ LOWE, Ronald Charles
6/1/6860, 15/10/15, L/C.; L'pool. R., 22/11/16; Lieut.
Died of wounds 18/8/18 as Prisoner of War.

LOWE, Rouxville Mark
6/8583, 3/1/16; R.A., C/S, 26/5/16; R.G.A., 30/8/16; F; Capt.; w.
55 Manchester Street, W. 1.

✠ LOWE, Thomas Henry
4/1/4628, 5/7/15; Bord. R., 23/12/15; 2/Lieut.
Killed in action 23/4/17.

✠ LOWE, William Earl Bridson
4/3972, 3/6/15; dis. 3/6/15; E. Lan. R.; Capt.; M.C. and Bar
Killed in action 28/5/18.

LOWINSKY, Rupert Esmond
B/1208, 14/9/14; York. & Lanc. R., 23/11/14, Lab. Corps; Lieut.; w.
Tittenhurst, Sunnyhill, Berkshire.

LOWINSKY, Thomas Edward
A/1275, 23/9/14; R.W. Kent R., Scots. Gds.; Lieut.
Tittenhurst, Sunnyhill, Berkshire.

LOWLES, John Geoffrey Nelson
6/3/7073, 29/10/15, Cpl.; No. 14 O.C.B., 27/12/16; E. Kent. R., 27/3/17; 2/Lieut.; w.

LOWN, Charles Robert
4/3/4471, 28/6/15, Cpl.; Linc. R., 3/9/15, secd. M.G.C.; F,E; Lieut.; w(2).
62 Toll Garell, Beverley, East Yorkshire.

LOWNDES, Ernest Alfred
A/1662, 10/10/14; Yorks. L.I., 20/12/14; F; Capt.; Inj.
Towpath House, Staines.

LOWNDES, George Alfred Norman
6/5/8536, 30/12/15; 16th Lond. R., 6/6/16, emp. M. of Labour; Capt.; w(2); M.C.
Cottingham Rectory, Nr. Hull.

APPENDIX II.—RECORDS OF RANK AND FILE.

LOWNDES, *Sidney Edwin*
4/6/4976, 19/7/15; 3rd Lond. R., 14/12/15; Lieut.
103 Grove Lane, Denmark Hill, S.E.

LOWRIE, *James*
A/10370, 5/1/17; No. 14 O.C.B., 5/5/17; R. Highrs., 28/8/17; F; Lieut.; *M.C.*
Blegbie, Humbie, East Lothian.

LOWRY, *Charles George*
C/12630, 11/2/18; No. 7 O.C.B., 5/7/18; R. Ir. Regt., 3/3/19; 2/Lieut.
Bachelors Lodge, Navan, Co. Meath.

LOWRY, *Graham Leonard Bayley*
C/906, 5/8/14; N. Staff. R., 12/9/14; Lieut.; *M.C.*

LOWRY, *Henry*
6/1/6665, 7/10/15; No. 9 O.C.B., 6/3/16, R.A., C/S; R.G.A., 3/7/16; Lieut.
Huntley, Greenisland, Co. Antrim.

LOWRY, *Hugh Vernon*
3/3574, 10/5/15, Cpl.; R. Innis. Fus., 22/1/16, att. M.G.C.; F; Lieut.
Sidney Sussex College, Cambridge.

✠ LOWRY, *Joseph Ewart*
D/10881, 8/3/17; No. 14 O.C.B., 7/9/17; R. Ir. Regt., 17/12/17; Lieut.
Killed in action 25/8/18.

✠ LOWRY, *Sidney Henry*
B/946, 5/8/14; Herts. R., 1/10/14; Capt.; *M.C.*
Killed in action 31/7/17.

LOWSON, *George Frederick*
1/3699, 20/5/15, Sgt.; E. York. R., 14/12/15, secd. Army Cyc. Corps; F,It; Lieut.; *p.*
8 Prince Street, Bridlington, East Yorkshire.

LOWSON, *Noel Leslie*
6/1/7616, 19/11/15; trfr. R.G.A., 16/10/16.
16 Westborough, Scarborough.

✠ LOWTH, *John Leslie*
6/9357, 7/2/16; No. 5 O.C.B., 14/3/16; North'd. Fus., 6/7/16; 2/Lieut.
Killed in action 4/10/17.

LOWTHER, *Clifford Jack*
B/12869, 13/3/18; R.G.A., C/S, 20/9/18; trfr. R.G.A., 20/9/18.

✠ LOWY, *Walter Albert*
D/1526, 5/10/14; Hamps. R., 13/11/14; S; Capt.
Died of wounds 3/9/18.

✠ LOXLEY, *Arthur Harry*
4/1/4080, 7/6/15; N. Staff. R., 5/9/15, att. Yorks. L.I.; 2/Lieut.
Killed in action 9/4/17.

LOYNES, *Octavius John*
C/13237, 7/6/18; No. 22 O.C.B., 5/7/18; R.A.F., 20/11/18; F; 2/Lieut.
Wyverstone Rectory, Stowmarket.

✠ LUBBOCK, *Harold*
Sq/103, 18/4/08; W. Kent. Yeo., 27/3/11, Gren. Gds., R.F.C.; Lieut.
Killed 24/4/18.

LUCAS, *Frederick James*
K/C/2258, 7/12/14, L/C.; W. Rid. R., 11/5/15; F; Capt.
White Cottage, Totteridge, High Wycombe.

✠ LUCAS, *William Herbert*
B/927, 5/8/14; N. Staff. R., 12/9/14; Lieut.
Died of wounds 21/1/16.

LUCHFORD, *Cyril Gordon*
4/2/5077, 26/7/15; North'd. Fus., 6/7/16; F; Lieut.; *w*; *M.C.*
Walmer, Quernmore Road, Bromley, Kent.

LUCIE-SMITH, *John Alfred*
A/347, 24/2/09; dis. 29/3/10; R. Dub. Fus.; G,S; Major; O.B.E., M(2).
56 Wickham Road, Brockley, S.E. 4. (*Now in British West Indies*).

LUCK, *Cecil George John*
K/H/2364, 15/12/14, L/C.; Sea. Highrs., 6/3/15, R.E.; F,It,NR; Capt.; *w*; *M.C.* and Bar, Order of S. Stanislaus 3rd Class (Russia).
Summerland, Magdalen Road, Bexhill-on-Sea. (*Now in Canada*).

LUCKHAM, *Cyril Godfrey Frank*
6/2/8300, 11/12/15, Cpl.; R.A., C/S, 24/11/16; R.F.A., 16/3/17; F; Lieut.; *w.*
Oakhurst, Broadway, Dorchester, Dorset.

LUCKHOFF, *Charles Ferdinon*
4/5014, 22/7/15, L/C.; L'pool. R., 7/10/15, Wilts. R.; 2/Lieut.; *w.*

LUCKING, *Cyril Dudley*
4/2/5120, 26/7/15; R.G.A., 1/12/15; F; Capt.; Croix de Chevalier de l'Ordre de la Couronne (Belge), Croix de Guerre (Belge), M(1).
Lackham House, 15 Oxford Road, Colchester.

LUDLOW, *Richard Robert*
6/1/6969, 22/10/15, L/C.; D. of Corn. L.I., 5/7/16; F; 2/Lieut.; *w.*
4 Paper Buildings, Temple, E.C. 4.

LUGG, *James Clifford*
C/10175, 11/12/16; No. 14 O.C.B., 6/4/17; Ches. R., 31/7/17; F; Staff Capt.; *w.*
c/o Lloyds Bank Ltd., Broadway, Worcestershire.

LUKER, *Frederick George*
A/13030, 3/5/18, L/C.; demob. 19/12/18.
Thornhill Road, Streetly, Nr. Birmingham.

LUKYN, *Clarence Hannan*
6/4/9088, 24/1/16; No. 14 O.C.B.; Midd'x. R., 18/12/16, att. T.M. Bty.; F; Lieut.
49 Charing Cross, S.W. 1.

✠ LUMB, *Joseph William*
C/10372, 5/1/17; No. 14 O.C.B., 5/5/17; W. Rid. R., 28/8/17; F; 2/Lieut.; *w*; *M.C.*
Died of wounds 30/10/18.

LUMB, *Stanley Clifford*
6/2/7209, 4/11/15; General List, 4/8/16, R.A.F.; F; Lieut.; Inv.
Brinsworth, Nr. Rotherham, Yorkshire.

LUMBY, *Christopher Dittmar Rawson*
4/2/4503, 28/6/15; Manch. R., 2/9/15; F; Lieut.; *w*(2).
c/o The Times, Printing House Square, E.C.

LUMLEY, *Archie Basil*
K/6/A/2076, 13/11/14, Cpl.; dis. med. unfit, 6/6/16.
4 Chester Place, Regents Park, N.W. 1.

LUMSDEN, *John Arthur*
D/E/13838, 14/8/18; R.A., C/S, 2/10/18; R.G.A., 11/4/19; 2/Lieut.
Fircroft, Uppingham.

LUMSDEN, *Victor Nelson*
6/3/6874, 18/10/15; No. 11 O.C.B., 7/5/16; Camb. R., 4/9/16; Lieut.; *w.*
c/o National Bank of South Africa, Circus Place, E.C. 2.

LUNAN, *Reuben Miles*
6/Sq/8729, 5/1/16, L/C.; No. 2 Cav. C/S, 5/1/17; R. Regt. of Cav., 7/7/17.
c/o Messrs. Cochrane & McPherson, Advocates, Aberdeen.

LUNBERG, *Charles Mashiter*
C/10156, 8/12/16; No. 14 O.C.B., 5/5/17; L'pool. R., 29/8/17; F; 2/Lieut.
11 Bundoran Road, Aigburth, Liverpool.

LUND, *Richard Henry*
4/1/4649, 5/7/15; R.F.A., 2/10/15; F; Lieut.; g. *w.*
24 Bilton Grove Avenue, Harrogate.

LUNGHI, *Charles Albert*
1/3700, 20/5/15; L'pool. R., 1/9/15, secd. R.F.C., R.A.F.; Lieut.
56 Long Acre, W.C.

LUNN, *John Septimus*
A/11934, 30/8/17; No. 14 O.C.B., 4/1/18; S. Lan. R., 25/6/18; F,SR; Capt.; *w.*
c/o F. J. Smith Esq., The School, Market Bosworth, Nuneaton.

LUNT, *Edward Lysons*
B/3004, 4/3/15; R. Marines, 28/5/15; F,S; Capt.
Lyndale, Old Trafford, Manchester. (*Now in Buenos Aires*).

LUNT, *Ralph Marshall*
6/5/5944, 1/9/15; L'pool. R., 1/6/16, Indian Army; F; Capt.; *w*; Croix de Guerre.
c/o Cox & Coy., Bombay.

LUNT, *William*
6/5/C/8650, 3/1/16; R.A.O.C., 25/10/16; S; Lieut.
Christleton, Chester.

LUPTON, *Arthur Wright*
4/2/4578, 1/7/15; Yorks. L.I., 11/11/15; Lieut.; *w*; *M.C.*
15 Bootham, York.

LUPTON, *Ralph Henry*
K/B/2388, 17/12/14, Cpl.; R. Suss. R., 31/3/15; Capt.; *M.C.*, M(1).
43 Waterpark Road, Preston, Cheshire.

LUSCOMBE, *Alfred*
D/Sq/C/13797, 9/8/18; No. 11 O.C.B., 31/1/19; General List, 8/3/19; 2/Lieut.
Newlands, Graaf Remet, South Africa.

LUSCOMBE, *John Hilton*
6/Sq/6685, 7/10/15, L/C.; No. 1 Cav. C/S, 23/4/17; Derby. Yeo., 24/8/17; Lieut.
Pine Cottage, Elmfield Avenue, Teddington.

APPENDIX II.—RECORDS OF RANK AND FILE.

LUSH, *Harold Charles*
D/11832, 9/8/17; H. Bde. O.C.B., 9/11/17; Cold. Gds., 28/5/18; F; 2/Lieut.   *15 Sussex Square, Hyde Park, W.2.*

LUTKENS, *Edgar*
A/11889, 20/8/17; R.A., C/S, 7/2/18; R.G.A., 2/9/18; 2/Lieut. *c/o W. Arnold Esq., 157 Abbey Road, Barrow-in-Furness.*

LUTTRELL, *John Frederick*
C/10800, 28/2/17; No. 11 O.C.B., 5/7/17; 7th Lond. R., 30/10/17. att. Lab. Corps; F; Lieut.   *51 Kings Road, Willesden, N.W. 10.*

LYAL, *John Coutts*
6/3/6852, 16/10/15; Midd'x. R., 6/7/16; Lieut.; w(2); M.C.   *33 Park Avenue, Wood Green, N. 22.*

LYALL, *Frank Gerald*
B/Sq/10123, 6/12/16, Sgt.; No. 1 Cav. C/S, 1/9/17; R. Regt. of Cav., 22/2/18; 2/Lieut. *Saltby Waltham, Melton Mowbray.*

LYALL, *Robert Vincent*
C/14218, 23/10/18; trfr. K.R. Rif. C., 7/4/19.   *Swallowbeck, Lincoln.*

LYDE, *Herbert William*
B/11673, 16/7/17, Cpl.; R.A., C/S, 7/2/18; demob. *Eckington, Southam Road, Hall Green, Birmingham.*

LYELL, *Angus Chambers*
B/3029, 11/3/15, Sgt.; K R. Rif. C., 17/11/15; F; Capt.; M.C.   *1 Fleet Street, E.C.*

LYELL, *Donald Chambers*
2/4/5063, 24/7/15; trfr. R.G.A., 15/12/16; F; Gnr.   *13 Poulton's Square, Chelsea, S.W. 3.*

LYELL, *Walter H.*
3/3180, 6/4/15; Gord. Highrs., 18/6/15; Lieut.; Albert Medal. *British Linen Bank House, Montrose, N.B.*

✠ LYLE, *Geoffrey Samuel LaWarre*
A/1191, 14/9/14; Oxf. & Bucks. L.I., 14/12/14; 2/Lieut. *Died of wounds 29/4/17.*

✠ LYLE, *James Vernon*
6/1/6996, 25/10/15; No. 9 O.C.B., 8/3/16; R.F.C., 6/7/16; 2/Lieut. *Killed in action 23/1/17.*

LYLE, *Oliver*
A/1012, 6/8/14; High. L.I., 12/9/14, emp. M. of Munitions; F; Capt.; w; O.B.E., M(1), m(1). *Oak Royd, Kingswood, Tadworth, Surrey.*

LYLE, *Robert Henry*
B/11016, 11/4/17, Sgt.; R.A., C/S, 17/12/17; R.F.A., 3/6/18; 2/Lieut. *27 Castle Terrace, Edinburgh.*

LYNCH, *Humphrey Eric Hylton*
F/2734, 18/1/15; R. Ir. Rif., 25/5/15, Indian Army; F,M,P; Capt.; w; M.C. *Apartado 380, San José, Costa Rica.*

LYNCH, *James Patrick*
D/13713, 23/7/18; trfr. Gord. Highrs., 29/5/19.

LYNCH, *Patrick Robert*
6/5/C/8401, 15/12/15; trfr. 19th Lond. R., 18/5/17; Pte. *Enagh House, Virginia, Co. Cavan.*

LYNCH, *Stephen Hugh*
6/5/5902, 30/8/15; R.F.A., 17/12/15; F,S; Lieut.; *Inj.* *6 Seaview House, Donnybrook, Dublin.*

✠ LYNCH-STANTON, *Eric Margrave*
6/2/5658, 16/8/15; 3rd Lond. R., 30/12/15; 2/Lieut. *Killed in action 9/5/17.*

✠ LYNDALL, *Joseph Gwynne*
6/4/6695, 7/10/15; No. 11 O.C.B., 7/5/16; K.R. Rif. C., 4/9/16; F; 2/Lieut. *Killed in action 3/5/17.*

LYNESS, *William*
Sq/3025, 26/2/15; L/C.; Notts. & Derby. Yeo., 21/7/15, att. Notts. & Derby. R.; F; Lieut. *146 Queen's Drive, Glasgow, S. 5.*

LYNN, *David Crawford*
D/14075, 28/9/18; trfr. 14th Lond. R., 6/12/18. *Pallion, Sunderland.*

LYON, *Charles Benton*
Sq/1955, 26/10/14; N. Som. Yeo., 7/1/15, 21st Lancers; Lieut. *Banbury, Fairford, Gloucestershire.*

LYON, *Max*
D/13696, 31/7/18; trfr. K.R. Rif. C., 7/4/19, R.A.O.C. *102 North Marine Road, Scarborough.*

LYON, *Reginald John*
F/2632, 7/1/15; E. Lan. R., 18/2/15; Lieut.; w. *53 Eardley Crescent, Earls Court, S.W. 5.*

LYONS, *Albert Leonard*
D/13697, 31/7/18; Cpl.; demob. 4/1/19. *16 Carlton Hill, N.W. 8.*

LYONS, *Charles Frederick*
C/1156, 14/9/14; E. Surr. R., 14/12/14; Lieut.; w.

LYONS, *Patrick Joseph*
6/8762, 6/1/16; dis. med. unfit, 3/3/16. *Kittaboe, Bally Rannis, Co. Mayo.*

✠ LYONS, *Vincent Aloysius*
6/8763, 6/1/16; No. 9 O.C.B., 8/3/16; High. L.I., 6/7/16; 2/Lieut. *Died of wounds 23/8/17.*

LYONS-DAVIS, *Frederick James*
C/10613, 25/1/17; R.E., 5/7/17, att. R.A.F.; Lieut. *23 Victoria Avenue, Cardiff.*

LYS, *William Frederick*
A/Sq/12546, 5/2/18, Cpl.; No. 1 Cav. C/S, 3/9/18; R. Regt. of Cav., 12/3/19; 2/Lieut. *Bere Regis, Wareham, Dorset.*

LYSAGHT, *William Daniel Joseph*
6/5/7409, 13/11/15; 18th Lond. R., 24/10/16, att. R.A.F.; F; Lieut.; g. *90 Lewin Road, Streatham, S.W. 16.*

LYSTER, *Frederick John*
6/5/6129, 9/9/15; Interpreter, 22/6/16; S; Lieut.; M(1), Order of the Redeemer (Greek). *c/o A. J. Lyster Esq., Imperial Ottoman Bank, Constantinople.*

LYTH, *Tom Bruce*
D/2953, 18/2/15, L/C.; York. & Lanc. R., 12/7/15; F; Lieut.; w(2). *Heworth, Hyrst, York, Yorkshire.*

LYTH, *Walter Rowe*
A/11629, 9/7/17; No. 14 O.C.B., 9/11/17; York. & Lanc. R., 30/4/18; F; 2/Lieut. *7 Heworth Green, York, Yorkshire.*

MABEY, *Charles Henry Cecil*
4/6/Sq/4864, 15/7/15, Cpl.; No. 2 Cav. C/S, 31/3/16; Devon. Yeo., 19/8/16, att. Devon. R.; F; Lieut. *The Cottage, Streatham Park, S.W. 16.*

MABEY, *Harold Victor*
4/6/Sq/4579, 1/7/15, L/C.; No. 2 Cav. C/S, 31/3/16; Devon. Yeo., 19/8/16, att. Devon. R. and Manch. R.; F,It; Lieut. *150a Vauxhall Bridge Road, Westminster, S.W.1.*

McADAM, *Arthur*
6/5/7635, 20/11/15; No. 11 O.C.B., 7/5/16; 22nd Lond. R., 4/9/16; Lieut. *57 Meath Road, Ilford.*

MACADAM, *Edward Hughes*
A/14337, 30/12/18; No. 11 O.C.B., 24/1/19; General List, 8/3/19; 2/Lieut. *36 Cumberland Mansions, Bryanston Square, W.*

McADAM, *James Stanley*
A/14345, 6/1/19; demob. 30/1/19. *Parkfield, Blackley, Manchester.*

McAFEE, *Alan Rodman*
6/1/6840, 14/10/15; dis. to re-enlist in R.N.V.R., 3/9/16; R.N.A.S., 1/4/17, R.A.F.; F; Capt.; D.F.C. *4c Bickenhall Mansions, Baker Street, W.1.*

✠ MACAN, *Hugh O'Donoghue*
1/3508, 6/5/15; E. Surr. R., 28/7/15; Capt. *Died of wounds 1/9/18.*

MACAN, *Leslie FitzGerald*
B/12753, 13/3/18; No. 3 O.C.B., 9/8/18, No. 11 O.C.B.; General List, 8/3/19; 2/Lieut. *Milford, Co. Donegal.*

MACARTHUR, *Don Jessel*
A/11635, 10/7/17; No. 2 Cav. C/S, 11/1/18; R. Regt. of Cav., 18/10/18; 2/Lieut.

McARTHUR, *James*
D/13677, 29/7/18; demob. 21/12/18. *33 Glasgow Road, St. Ninians, By Stirling, Scotland.*

McARTHUR, *Valentine*
C/972, 5/8/14; R. Berks. R., 12/9/14, emp. M. of Munitions; Major; w(2); M.C. *29 The Boltons, S.W. 10.*

McARTHY, *John Maitland*
A/14329, 30/12/18; No. 11 O.C.B., 6/2/19; General List, 8/3/19; 2/Lieut. *12 North Park Terrace, Edinburgh. (Now in Rhodesia)*

APPENDIX II.—RECORDS OF RANK AND FILE.

✠ MACAULAY, Bruce Wallace
6/3/9393, 9/2/16; No. 5 O.C.B., 14/8/16; Sea. Highrs., 21/11/16; 2/Lieut. *Killed in action 3/5/17.*

McAULEY, Francis James
6/5/7241, 6/11/15; No. 11 O.C.B., 7/5/16; L'pool. R., 4/9/16, att. R.F.C.; F; Lieut. *19 Vectis Road, Tooting, S.W. 17.*

McBEAN, Malcolm
6/2/6557, 30/9/15; No. 11 O.C.B., 8/5/16; Bord. R., 4/9/16, Tank Corps; F; Capt. *Thomas McBean & Coy., Warwick Chambers, Corporation Street, Birmingham.*

MACBRIDE, Colin Campbell
12573, 6/2/18. *2 Biarritz Court, Crowstone Road, Westcliff-on-Sea.*

McBRYDE, William Orr
C/13238, 7/6/18; No. 22 O.C.B., 5/7/18; Essex R., 5/2/19; 2/Lieut. *Corrie, Epping, Essex.*

MacCABE, Ernan Hugh Joseph
A/11297, 16/5/17; No. 10 O.C.B., 5/10/17; R. Muns. Fus., 26/2/18; F; 2/Lieut. *Killeshandra, Co. Cavan.*

MACCABE, Frederic
C/12593, 12/2/18; No. 11 O.C.B., 6/2/19; General List, 8/3/19; 2/Lieut. *23 Grosvenor Street, Liscard, Cheshire.*

McCAFFREY, James
6/5/8891, 13/1/16; No. 5 O.C.B., 14/8/16; M.G.C., 30/11/16, Tank Corps; F; Capt.; M.C. *4th Tank Bn., Woognet Camp, Wareham, Dorset.*

McCALL-McCOWAN, David
6/2/9519, 16/2/16, Sgt.; No. 14 O.C.B., 30/10/16; R. Highrs., 24/1/17, att. R. Suss. R.; I,M,P; Lieut. *c/o D. McCowan Esq., 9 Park Circus Place, Glasgow, N.B.*

✠ McCALLUM, Duncan
4/6/2/4938, 19/7/15, L/C.; E. Surr. R., 17/12/15; Capt. *Killed in action 22/9/17.*

McCALLUM, Hugh
D/13834, 14/8/18; demob. 21/2/19. *20 Caird Drive, Patrickhill, Glasgow.*

McCANN, Arthur John Hedley
6/5/8785, 7/1/16; dis. med. unfit, 8/8/16. *Stalleen House, Donore, Co. Meath.*

McCARTHY, Herbert John
6/2/5516, 9/8/15; Bord. R., 16/12/15, att. Lab. Corps; F,S; Lieut.; w(2). *49 Highbury Park, N. 5.*

McCARTHY, Norman Hardress
6/3/8140, 3/12/15; R.F.A., C/S, 4/8/16; R.F.A., 15/12/16; 2/Lieut.; w.

McCARTHY-BARRY, Leo James. See BARRY, L. J. M.

McCAUSLAND, Bernard George
3546, 10/5/15; Yorks. L.I., 31/7/15; F; Capt.; g. *The Glebe, Carshalton, Surrey. (Now in Buenos Aires).*

McCAUSLAND, Connolly John H.
E/2544, 4/1/15; Yorks. L.I., 12/4/15; F; Capt.; M.C. *The Glebe, Carshalton, Surrey.*

MacCLYMONT, Colin Alexander
A/10280, 1/1/17, L/C.; R.A., C/S, 16/3/17; R.G.A., 4/8/17; F; 2/Lieut. *30 Addison Avenue, Holland Park, W.*

McCOAN, Colin Kenneth
B/13609, 24/7/18; demob. 24/1/19. *Kinfauns, Port Talbot, Glamorganshire.*

McCOLL, John
B/13622, 16/7/18; demob. 20/3/19. *2 North Avenue, Yoker, Glasgow.*

McCOLLOUGH, Ronald Laurence
H/2010, 2/11/14; dis. med. unfit, 2/11/14; 1st Drag. Gds., 13/11/14; Lieut.

McCOMAS, Reginald
K/2928, 15/2/15; dis. 30/4/15; 22nd Lond. R., 19/8/15; 2/Lieut *Homestead, Hoddesdon, Hertfordshire.*

McCOMBE, Robert Thomas
C/B/13338, 20/6/18; demob. 24/4/19. *Crescent Lodge, Dundalk, Co. Louth.*

McCONECHY, Ronald McLeod
A/12455, 22/1/18; No. 20 O.C.B., 7/6/18; R. Highrs., 5/2/19; 2/Lieut. *Woodthorpe, Sydenham Hill Road, Sydenham Hill, S.E. 26.*

McCONKEY, James Norman Townsend
C/13339, 20/6/18, Cpl.; trfr. K.R. Rif. C., 7/4/19. *Clovelly, Carlan, Ireland.*

McCONNELL, Edward Huron
6/2/8786, 7/1/16; M.G.C., 25/9/16; Lieut. *Caxton Publicity Coy., Clun House, Surrey Street, Strand, W.C.*

McCONNELL, George Roland Begley
A/14313, 1/11/18; demob. 13/2/19. *203 North Circular Road, Dublin.*

McCONNELL, Reginald James
C/13271, 12/6/18, L/C.; trfr. K.R. Rif. C., 7/4/19. *Rodney, 69 Anglesea Road, Ballsbridge, Co. Dublin.*

McCORKINDALE, Douglas Taylor
6/2/9340, 4/2/16, L/C.; No. 14 O.C.B., 26/11/16; Sco. Rif., 27/3/17; Lieut.

McCORMACK, Brian Hugh
D/11119, 30/4/17; R.F.C., C/S, 1/6/17; R.F.C., 4/7/17, R.A.F.; 2/Lieut. *289 Hagley Road, Birmingham.*

MacCORMACK, William George
D/11565, 28/6/17; R.F.C., C/S, 23/10/17; R.F.C., 12/12/17, R.A.F.; 2/Lieut. *Dunluce, Kenilworth Road, Dublin.*

✠ McCOURT, Cyril Douglas
4/2/4400, 24/6/15, L/C.; 12th Lond. R., 24/12/15; F; 2/Lieut. *Killed in action 8/10/16.*

McCOWAN, Alexander Bruce
C/13330, 19/6/18, L/C.; demob. 29/1/19. *Newstead, 20 Woodlands Road, Aigburth, Liverpool.*

McCOY, Herbert George
6/1/7933, 29/11/15; No. 8 O.C.B., 4/8/16; K.R. Rif. C., 21/11/16; F; Lieut.; w. *Oxcroft, London Road, High Wycombe.*

McCOY, James Patrick
6/4/5628, 16/8/15, Sgt.; R.E., 1/11/15; F,S,E,P,M; Major; M(1). *Herschel, Cape Province, South Africa.*

McCRACKEN, Albert Henry
4/4135, 10/6/15; 17th Lond. R., 25/8/15, M.G.C.; F,M,I; Major; M(1). *28 Roxborough Park, Harrow, Middlesex.*

McCREA, Francis Wylam Wetherall
6/D/9462, 14/2/16, L/C.; No. 14 O.C.B., 5/7/17; Devon. R., 30/10/17; F,S; Lieut.; Inj. *Pathini Tea Estate, Medley P.O. (Via Juri), Sylhet, India.*

McCREA, Frederick Haughton Gower
D/Sq/10749, 22/1/17; No. 1 Cav. C/S, 1/9/17; R. Regt. of Cav., 22/2/18; 2/Lieut. *Ardevin, Bray, Co. Wicklow, Ireland.*

McCREATH, Cecil Angus
6/2/6531, 30/9/15; No. 1 O.C.B., 6/9/16; R.F.C., 25/1/17, R.A.F.; Lieut. *School House, Roxeth Hill, Harrow-on-the-Hill.*

✠ McCREDIE, John Forrest
6/2/6738, 11/10/15; No 14 O.C.B.; M.G.C., 24/10/16; F; 2/Lieut. *Killed in action 30/11/17.*

MacCULLOCH, Andrew
D/Sq/13678, 29/7/18; dis. med. unfit, 14/12/18. *62 Sherbrooke Avenue, Maxwell Park, Glasgow.*

McCULLOCH, George Torance
6/3/6421, 23/9/15; L'pool. R., 21/1/16; F; Lieut.; M(1). *Overton House, Westkilbride, Ayrshire.*

✠ McCULLOCH, James Arthur
C/421, 21/5/09; dis. 1/11/13; rej. B/1254, 23/9/14; Lan. Fus. 27/10/14; F; Capt. *Killed in action 27/9/18.*

McCULLOCH, William Andrew
6/1/D/6504, 28/9/15, Sgt.; R.F.C., C/S, 13/3/17; R.F.C., 19/4/17, R.A.F.; F; Lieut.; w. *Gerrardstown, Donabate, Co. Dublin.*

McDERMOTT, Francis
4/4153, 10/6/15; R.W. Surr. R., 14/11/15, att. Ches. R., R. Berks. R. and Welch R., Indian Army; F; Lieut. *c/o Messrs. Cox & Coy., Bombay, India.*

MacDERMOTT, George
A/262, 27/5/08; dis. 26/5/10.

McDERMOTT, Gerald
K/C/2253, 7/12/14; R.A.S.C., 6/2/15; F; Capt.; M.C., M(1). *Brackenhill Platt, Boro' Green, Kent.*

APPENDIX II.—RECORDS OF RANK AND FILE.

MACDIARMID, *Duncan Stewart*
B/14071, 27/9/18; demob. 6/2/19.
                       Carisbroke, Helensburgh, N.B.

MACDONALD, *Alastair Somerled*
D/1450, 29/9/14; Durh. L.I., 8/1/15; Capt.

✠ McDONALD, *Archibald Joseph*
6/Sq/7029, 27/10/15; No. 1 Cav. C/S, 24/4/16; Lovats Scouts, 28/7/16; Lieut.   Died 3/11/18.

MACDONALD, *Archibald Walker*
6/3/9329, 7/2/16; No. 14 O.C.B., 30/1/17; R. Highrs., 25/4/17, att. American Army; F; Lieut.
                       59 *Magdalen Green, Dundee.*

MACDONALD, *Charles John*
D/9994, 24/11/16; R.F.A.; C/S, 9/3/17; R.F.A., 1/10/17; F; 2/Lieut.   57 *Hazellville Road, N. 19.*

MacDONALD, *Douglas Stuart*
6/3/9239, 1/2/16; No. 8 O.C.B., 4/8/16; Gord. Highrs., 21/11/16; Lieut.; w(2).

MACDONALD, *Geoffrey Ernest*
4/5/5171, 29/7/15; R.A.S.C., 28/8/15, Strathcona's Horse; F; Capt.; w; M.C.   93 *Harrow Street, Winnipeg, Canada.*

McDONALD, *Ian*
6/8924, 14/1/16; No. 9 O.C.B., 8/3/16; R. Scots, 6/7/16; F; Lieut.; w-g.   *Sunnylaw Manse, Bridge of Allan, Stirlingshire.*

MACDONALD, *John Alexander*
B/12773, 15/3/18, L/C.; H. Bde. O.C.B., 9/8/18; Scots Gds., 4/3/19; 2/Lieut.   *The Inglenook, Walton-on-Thames.*

McDONALD, *John Currie*
Sq/717, 12/6/13; Essex R., 27/11/14; Welch. R.; Capt.; M.C.
                        12 *Tokenhouse Yard, E.C.*

✠ MACDONALD, *Lachlan*
6/4/9145, 25/1/16; R.F.C., 6/7/16; Lieut.   Killed 19/1/18.

✠ McDONALD, *Norman*
4/1/4230, 14/6/15; N. Lan. R., 5/9/15; 2/Lieut.
                       Died of wounds 25/12/16.

MacDONALD, *Ranald*
C/11069, 16/4/17; R.F.C., C/S, 4/5/17; R.F.C., 14/6/17, R.A.F.; Lieut.; p; M.B.E.
          Ennerdale, Fernwood Road, Newcastle-on-Tyne.

MACDONALD, *Ronald Alexander*
A/11913, 27/8/17; R.E., C/S, 11/11/17; R.E., 21/12/17; F; Lieut.; p.   *Glencoe, Orchard Park, Giffnock, Glasgow.*

✠ MACDONALD, *Somerled*
4/1/4231, 14/6/15, L/C.; Cam'n. Highrs., 7/10/15, Indian Army; S,E,P; Lieut.   Died.

McDONALD, *William Charles George*
A/11652, 12/7/17; A.S.C., C/S, 1/11/17; R.A.S.C., 25/1/18; F; Lieut.   266 *Elgin Avenue, W. 9.*

McDONALD, *William Ian*
B/12738, 11/3/18, L/C.; No. 17 O.C.B., 9/8/18; demob. 28/12/18. c/o Col. A. W. McDonald D.S.O., *Blaram, Spean Bridge, Scotland.*

✠ MacDONNAGH, *William John*
3/3392, 26/4/15; Midd'x. R., 10/9/15; 2/Lieut.
                       Killed in action 11/9/16.

McDONNELL, *Charles William*
B/10808, 28/2/17, L/C.; R.G.A., C/S, 10/10/17; R.G.A., 18/3/18; F; 2/Lieut.   26 *Kinnaird Road, Wallasey, Cheshire.*

✠ MacDONNELL, *John Henry O'Connell de Courcy*
A/2794, 26/1/15; Manch. R., 11/5/15, Conn. Rang., att. Lein. R.; F; Capt.; w.   Died of wounds 14/10/18.

MacDONNELL, *Randal Anthony Mary Joseph de Courcy*
4/1/4283, 17/6/15; Manch. R., 5/12/15, att. R. Berks. R.; F; Lieut.; w, g, p.   4 *Marlborough Crescent, Bedford Park, W. 4.*

McDONNELL, *William*
B/11044, 11/4/17; A.S.C., C/S, 30/6/17; R.A.S.C., 25/8/17; Lieut.

McDOUGALL, *Alan Houston*
B/12754, 13/3/18; No. 2 O.C.B., 20/9/18, H. Bde. O.C.B.; demob. 29/1/19.   100 *Park Avenue South, N. 8.*

✠ MacDOUGALL, *Allen*
B/1248, 23/9/14; R. Fus., 19/10/14; Capt.
                       Killed in action 4/8/16.

McDOWELL, *Cecil Thomas Jeffrey*
C/448, 16/11/09; R.F.A., 31/1/13; F,It; Staff Capt.; M.C., M(2).
                   Springhaven, Stanmore, Middlesex.

McDOWELL, *Ernest John Paul*
A/12489, 28/1/18; No. 6 O.C.B., 7/6/18; R. Fus., 4/2/19; 2/Lieut.   60 *East Hill, Wandsworth, S.W. 18.*

McDOWELL, *John James*
D/A/11579, 2/7/17, L/C.; A.S.C., C/S, 1/2/18; R.A.S.C., 26/4/18; F; Lieut.   3 & 4 *Station Road, Darlington.*

✠ MACE, *Alfred Reginald*
6/4/5482, 9/8/15; R.A.S.C., 11/10/15; EA; Capt.; Inv.
                        Died 19/10/19.

MACE, *Ernest Joseph Humphrey*
C/Sq/7995, 29/11/15, Cpl.; No. 2 Cav. C/S, 1/9/16; R. Regt. of Cav., 20/12/16; Capt.   128/9 *Cheapside, E.C.*

McELDERRY, *Samuel Burnside Boyd*
A/13031, 3/5/18; R.F.A., C/S, 19/8/18; demob.
                   Civil Service, Hong Kong.

McELHAW, *Joseph Ignatius*
4/1/4543, 1/7/15; Glasgow Yeo., 2/10/15, secd. M.G.C.; S; Lieut.; w; M.C., French Croix de Guerre.
               Loretto, Clydeshore, Dumbarton.

McELWAINE, *Percy Alexander*
6/5/5993, 2/9/15; R. Ir. Rif., 4/8/16; F; Lieut.
            Soufriere, St. Lucia, British West Indies.

MacELWEE, *Henry Kennedy*
A/2647, 11/1/15; R.A.S.C., 7/5/15; F,M,I,Persia; Capt.
      Lawrence Studios, 12 Lawrence Street, Chelsea.

McEWAN, *Duncan Watson*
K/A/2481, 28/12/14; Arg. & Suth'd. Highrs., 31/3/15; F; Lieut.
                 9 *Eglinton Drive, Glasgow, W.*

MacEWAN, *Henry George*
B/C/12684, 4/3/18; H. Bde. O.C.B., 7/6/18; Scots. Gds., 4/2/19; 2/Lieut.
        8 *Rosslyn Terrace, Kelvinside, Glasgow, W.*

McEWAN, *Thomas Doig*
Sq/2876, 8/2/15, L/C.; Suss. Yeo., 10/5/15; Capt.
         Conservative Club, St. James Street, S.W.

MacFARLANE, *Basil Hall*
B/D/13854, 5/8/18; No. 18 O.C.B., 17/2/19; trfr. 5th Lond. R., 7/3/19.

McFARLANE, *James Robb*
D/10959, 30/3/17, Sgt.; R.F.A., C/S, 24/8/17; R.F.A., 21/1/18; F; Lieut.   9 *Westover Road, Wandsworth, S.W. 18.*

MACFARLANE, *James Waddell*
K/E/2341, 14/12/14; Arg. & Suth'd. Highrs., 29/4/15, High. L.I.; Capt.   c/o *Bank of Scotland, Edinburgh.*

MACFARLANE, *John*
K/2412, 21/12/14; Sgt., R.A.O.C.; F,It.
  c/o *The Green Room Club, 46 Leicester Square, W.C.*

✠ McFARLANE, *William Hannah*
4/3/4009, 5/6/15; Arg. & Suth'd. Highrs., 17/9/15; F; Lieut.; w.   Killed in action 27/5/18.

MACGILLIVRAY, *Alister Duncan*
A/13048, 8/5/18; No. 1 O.C.B., 8/11/18, No. 11 O.C.B.; General List, 8/3/19; 2/Lieut.   24 *Windsor Road, Ealing Common, W. 5.*

McGOVERN, *Frank*
6/5/6049, 3/9/15; No. 11 O.C.B., 7/5/16; S. Lan. R., 4/9/16; 2/Lieut.   *Oakfield, Hough Green, Nr. Widnes.*

McGOVERN, *John*
B/13489, 8/7/18; No. 22 O.C.B., 23/8/18; Midd'x. R., 13/2/19; 2/Lieut.   9 *North Grove, South Tottenham, N. 15.*

McGOWAN, *Ivor Alexander Whitworth*
Sq/1338, 26/9/14; R.F.A., 1/10/14; Lieut.; M.C.
                   2 *Curzon Road, Weybridge.*

McGRANE, *Christopher*
6/5/6532, 30/9/15; No. 7 O.C.B., 3/7/16; R. Dub. Fus., 24/10/16. R.F.C., R.A.F.; F; Lieut.
        B.S.A. Police, Rusapi, Southern Rhodesia.

✠ McGRANE, *Peter Leo*
6/5/6533, 30/9/15; No. 7 O.C.B., 3/7/16; R. Ir. Regt., 3/11/16, att. R. Innis. Fus.; 2/Lieut.   Killed in action 20/5/17.

APPENDIX II.—RECORDS OF RANK AND FILE.

McGREGOR, David Allan
C/11471, 11/6/17; R.F.C., C/S, 23/10/17; R.F.C., 12/12/17 R.A.F.; Lieut. Morningside, Fairfield, Manchester.

MACGREGOR, Devid James
6/2/7298, 8/11/15; trfr. 16th Lond. R., 11/8/16; Midd'x. R., 27/6/17, att. T.M. Bty.; F,It; 2/Lieut.
117 Windsor Road, Forest Gate, E. 7.

McGREGOR, Gilbert Ney
6/5/6289, 16/9/15, L/C.; No. 14 O.C.B., 30/10/16; Sea. Highrs., 24/1/17; Lieut. Redlands, Breage, Nelston, Cornwall.

MACGREGOR, Peter
6/8595, 3/1/16; No 9 O.C.B., 8/3/16; Arg. & Suth'd. Highrs., 23/7/16; 2/Lieut. Albyn Lodge, Bridge of Allan.

McGRUER, Alexander Gruer
6/1/5692, 16/8/15; No. 4 O.C.B., 7/3/16; Cam'n. Highrs., 13/7/16; F; Lieut.; w-p; M.C.
Braelea, York Drive, Inverness. (Now in South Africa).

✠ McGUSTY, George Ross
B/1204, 14/9/14; R. Ir. Rif., 14/11/14; F; Lieut.
Died of wounds 14/6/16.

McHALE, Francis Joseph
D/10385, 8/1/17, L/C.; No. 14 O.C.B., 7/6/17; E. Lan. R., 25/9/17, att. Wilts. R.; Lieut.
Lyndhurst, Lambton Road, Worsley, Lancashire.

✠ MACHELL, Humphrey Gilbert
A/11276, 14/5/17; No. 14 O.C.B., 7/9/17; Bord. R., 17/12/17; 2/Lieut. Died 12/6/18.

MACHIN, Basil Montague
6/1/5710, 19/8/15; No. 4 O.C.B., 7/3/16; W. Rid. R., 13/7/16; F; Capt.; w. Lindisfarne, Newhouse Park, St. Albans.

MACHIN, Charles Willis
6/2/6097, 6/9/15; dis. med. unfit, 8/8/16.
Weston House, Trentham Road, Longton, Stoke-on-Trent.

MACHIN, Harold Stanley
D/1459, 29/9/14, L/C.; R. Suss. R., 14/12/14, Leic. R., Linc. R., Indian Army; M; Capt.; Inv; M(l).
33 Durham Road, Wimbledon, S.W. 20.

MACHIN, Jack Francis
A/13173, 31/5/18; No. 1 O.C.B., 8/11/18; Glouc. R., 16/3/19; 2/Lieut. 10 City Road, Birstol.

MACHIN, Raymond John
A/10286, 1/1/17; No. 14 O.C.B., 5/3/17; W. Rid. R., 26/6/17, att. Durh. L.I., High. L.I., and Worc. R.; F; Capt.; w(3); M.C.
Canvey Island, South Benfleet, Essex.

MACHON, Harold Cyril
4/1/5143, 26/7/15; trfr. H.A.C., 22/5/16.

MACINDOE, Robert Gourlay
6/8967, 17/1/16; No. 9 O.C.B., 8/3/16; High. L.I., 6/7/16; Lieut.; w. 18 Belhaven Terrace, Glasgow.

✠ McINNES, Percy Norman Leopold
6/2/5347, 2/8/15; York. R., 15/11/15; F; 2/Lieut.
Died of wounsds 20/7/16.

McINTOSH, Donald
C/13318, 17/6/18; No. 11 O.C.B., 24/1/19; General List, 8/3/19; Germ.SWA; 2/Lieut.
4 St. Matthews Road, Belgravia, East London, South Africa.

MacINTOSH, Douglas William
3/3647, 17/5/15; Leic. R., 20/8/15; Cam'n. Hgihrs., secd. R.F.C., R.A.F.; F,It; Lieut.
R.A.F. Club, Bruton Street, W. 1. (Now in India).

MACINTOSH, Walter Graham
6/4/8897, 13/1/16, Sgt.; 7th Lond. R., 8/7/16; F; Lieut.; w.
c/o Hirsch, Loulson & Coy. Ltd., P.O. Box 196, Port Elizabeth, South Africa.

✠ McINTYRE, Frederic Malcolm
Sq/4/4650, 5/7/15; Hamps. R., 12/7/15; R.E.; 2/Lieut.
Died of wounds 2/5/16.

MacINTYRE, Robert Hamilton
6/1/6130, 9/9/15, L/C.; Midd'x. R., 1/6/17; 2/Lieut.
75 Kingscourt Road, Streatham, S.W. 16.

McINTYRE, William Bertram
6/9240, 1/2/16; R.A., C/S, 26/5/16; R.G.A., 30/8/16; Lieut.; M.C. 30 Lombard Street, E.C.

McISAAC, William Laxon
6/8805, 8/1/16; R.A., C/S, 26/5/16; R.G.A., 18/8/16; F; Lieut.; Inv. Ryde Grammar School, Ryde, Isle of Wight.

McIVER, Lewis
A/11890, 20/8/17; R.F.C., C/S, 26/11/17; R.F.C., 23/1/18; Lieut. Mount Meryla, Moss Vale, New South Wales, Australia.

McJANNET, Henry Gordon
A/C/D/12140, 22/10/17; No. 19 O.C.B., 10/5/18; trfr. 28th Lond. R., 25/9/18. 47 Castle Road, Bedford.

McKANE, Robert William
6/5/9289, 3/2/16; R.A., C/S, 7/8/16; R.G.A., 19/12/16; Lieut.
Iveagh, 31 Osborne Park, Belfast.

MACKANESS, Arthur William
D/13766, 7/8/18; demob. 29/1/19. Cawston Farm, Rugby.

McKAY, Donald McGavin Kerr
6/3/9190, 28/1/16, L/C.; Arg. & Suth'd. Highrs., 22/11/16; F; Lieut. Manse of Durisdeer, Thornhill, Dumfrieshire, N.B.

MACKAY, George Frederick
6/Sq/6697, 7/10/15; No. 7 O.C.B., 6/4/16; R.F.C., 6/7/16, Lein. R.; F; Lieut.; w. 52 Fisherton Street, Salisbury.

MACKAY, John Roy
6/5/6666, 7/10/15; dis. med. unfit, 8/8/16.
Dorrie Kintail, Kyle of Lochalsh, Scotland.

McKAY, Joseph
A/14011, 11/9/18; demob. 30/1/19.
Clerihan, Clonmel, Co. Tipperary.

MACKAY, Robert Donald
6/2/6205, 13/9/15; 12th Lond. R., 8/6/16, att. 11th Lond. R.; P; Lieut. 3k Bickenhall Mansions, Baker Street, W. 1.

McKAY, William Legge
C/12574, 6/2/18; trfr. Class W. Res., 25/6/18.
507 Alexandra Parade, Dennistown, Glasgow.

✠ MACKAY, William Gidden
K/B/2202, 30/11/14; Gord. Highrs., 6/2/15; 2/Lieut.
Killed in action 25/9/15.

McKECHNIE, Ronald
6/Sq/9463, 14/2/16; N. Som. Yeo., 2/8/16, att. E. Surr .R.; F,It; Lieut.; M.C.
P.O. Fort Victoria, Rhodesia, South Africa.

✠ McKEEVER, James Holden
Sq/1979, 7/10/14; Ches. R., 19/5/15; Lieut.
Died of wounds 20/9/17.

McKELLAR, James Jeffrey Livingstone
A/14314, 1/11/18; trfr. K.R. Rif. C., 7/4/19.
St. Marnocks, Portmarnock, Co. Dublin.

McKELVIE, Alistair Campbell
F/1786, 16/10/14; Suff. Yeo., 15/1/15, att. Suff. R.; Capt.

McKENNA, Francis
D/Sq/C/12893, 9/4/18; No. 11 O.C.B., 31/1/19; General List, 8/3/19; 2/Lieut.
61 Albert Drive, Crosshill, Glasgow. (Now in U.S.A.).

McKENZIE, Charles Duncan
D/11868, 16/8/17; No. 14 O.C.B., 7/12/17; Sea. Highrs., 28/5/18; F; 2/Lieut. c/o Nat. Bank of India, 26 Bishopsgate, E.C. 2.

MacKENZIE, Clifton Alexander
B/10773, 17/2/17, L/C.; No. 14 O.C.B., 5/7/17; Sea. Highrs, 30/10/17; E,F; 2/Lieut.
23 Croxteth Grove, Sefton Park, Liverpool.

McKENZIE, Cyril
B/1327, 26/9/14; E. Lan. R., 14/12/14; F; Capt.; w; D.S.O., M.C., M(l). Langton Lodge, Hendon, N.W. 4.

MACKENZIE, Donald
4/4049, 7/6/15; 22nd Lond. R., 29/10/15, R.F.C., R.A.F.; F; Lieut.
11 Criffel Avenue, Streatham Hill, S.W. 2. (Now in Mexico).

MACKENZIE, Donald Alexander
6/1/6251, 16/9/15, L/C.; R.F.A., C/S, 23/6/16; R.F.A., 2/10/16; F; Capt.; M.C.
Hawkley Hall, Worsley Mesnes, Wigan, Lancashire.

MacKENZIE, Donald Stewart
6/9533, 16/2/16; R.A., C/S, 23/6/16; R.G.A., 27/9/16; F; Staff Capt. Kildrummy Manse, Mossat, Aberdeenshire.

APPENDIX II.—RECORDS OF RANK AND FILE.

MACKENZIE, Duncan
C/Sq/13190, 3/6/18; demob. 15/1/19.
Kings Sutton, Nr. Banbury, Oxon.

MACKENZIE, Fleming
6/1/6823, 14/10/15; No. 9 O.C.B., 8/3/16, M.G.C., C/S; M.G.C., 25/1/17.
32 Lancaster Gate, W. 2.

MACKENZIE, George Lyon
6/5/9306, 4/2/16; R.A., C/S, 4/8/16; R.G.A., 3/11/16; Lieut.
Craig Lee, Broughty Ferry.

MacKENZIE, Hugh
6/3/9303, 4/2/16; R.A., C/S, 4/8/16; R.G.A., 24/11/16; It,E; Lieut.; M(1).
1 The Pryors, East Heath Road, Hampstead, N.W. 3.

✠ MACKENZIE, Ivan Emilio Mario
6/8966, 17/1/16; R.F.C., 2/6/16; Capt.   Killed 12/10/17.

MACKENZIE, Kenneth
C/1882, 16/10/14; Sea. Highrs., 27/2/15, secd. R.F.C.; Lieut.

MACKENZIE, Kenneth
4/2/4190, 14/6/15; Sea. Highrs., 28/9/15, R.A.F.; F; Lieut.; w(2).
Dunninald, Montrose, Scotland. (Now in Shanghai).

MACKENZIE, Kenneth Howard
K/D/2209, 30/11/14, Sgt.; Sea. Highrs., 21/5/15, secd. M.G.C.; Lieut.; w.
Locksley, Formby, Nr. Liverpool.

McKENZIE, Lewis Charles
4/3/4117, 8/6/15, L/C.; Manch. R., 18/10/15; F; Lieut.; w; M(1).
30 Gwendolen Avenue, Putney, S.W.

✠ MACKENZIE, Melville
6/4/7181, 3/11/15; dis. med. unfit, 21/2/16.   Died.

MACKENZIE, Murdo
6/Sq/7617, 19/11/15; No. 2 Cav. C/S, 1/9/16; Surr. Yeo., 27/1/17; 2/Lieut.
Guy's Hospital, S.E.

MACKENZIE, Noel Donald George
A/12463, 22/1/18; No 2 O.C.B., 7/6/18; Norf. R., 5/2/19; 2/Lieut.
15 Churchill Road, Newtown, Great Yarmouth.

McKENZIE-HILL, William Edward
6/2/9358, 7/2/16; No. 8 O.C.B., 4/8/16; Sea. Highrs., 21/11/16; 2/Lieut.; w.
The Lodge, Beaminster, Dorset.

McKEON, James Michael
A/11630, 9/7/17; R.G.A., C/S, 27/12/17; R.G.A., 17/6/18; F; 2/Lieut.
Office of Public Works, 51 St. Stephen's Green East, Dublin.

MACKERETH, Michael
6/2/D/6206, 13/9/15; R.A., C/S, 29/12/16; R.F.A., 25/5/17; F; Lieut.; w.
Belmont, Ulverston, Lancashire.

McKERNAN, Oscar Towers
B/11423, 1/6/17; No. 14 O.C.B., 5/10/17; R. Fus., 10/9/18; 2/Lieut.
232 Burnley Road, Accrington, Lancashire.

McKEVITT, Philip John
3/3164, 1/4/15, Sgt.; Lan. Fus., 13/8/15; F; Capt.; w; M.C. M(1).
c/o 150 Severn Street, Hull, Yorkshire.

MACKEY, J. Robert Conn
6/5/Sq/6131, 9/9/15; North'd. Fus., 20/12/15; F,S; Lieut.; w(2).
Porto Novo, West Africa.

MACKEY, Milburn Vincent
K/H/2103, 16/11/14; dis. to R. Mil. Coll., 28/12/14; Gord. Highrs., 12/5/15; Lieut.
Highlands, Maidstone, Kent.

MACKIE, David Matthew
6/4/8808, 10/1/16; R.F.C., 10/9/16, R.A.F.; Lieut.

McKIE, James
4/5/4828, 7/7/15, L/C.; No. 9 O.C.B., 8/3/16; High. L.I., 4/8/16; Lieut.; w.
51 Cambridge Road, W.

MACKIE, John Baillie
C/D/12247, 21/11/17; No. 10 O.C.B., 10/5/18; trfr. 28th Lond. R., 11/10/18.
118 Ledard Road, Langside, Glasgow.

MACKIE, Reginald Charles
6/3/8205, 7/12/15, L/C.; R.A., C/S, 19/1/17; R.F.A., 2/6/17; F; Lieut.; w.
35 Forest Road, Aberdeen.

MACKIE, Robert Walter
A/13039, 6/5/18; trfr. 14th Lond. R., 6/12/18.
Park Cottage, Castle Cary, Somerset.

McKIE, Roger Alexander
H/2743, 21/1/15, L/C.; Arg. & Suth'd. Highrs., 29/4/15, Worc. R.; Capt.
c/o James Bec Esq., 16 Rutland Square, Edinburgh.

McKINLAY, Charles Alexander
D/10883, 19/3/17; No. 11 O.C.B., 5/7/17; Hunt. Cyc. Bn., 30/10/17; Lieut.
8 Grange Road, Canonbury, N. 1.

MacKINNON, Claude Alexander
6/1/5817, 26/8/15, L/C.; R. Highrs., 25/11/15; Lieut.
75 Clifton Crescent, Peckham, S.E. 15.

MacKINNON, Donald Archibald Whyte
C/12239, 19/11/17; R.F.A., C/S, 15/3/18; demob.
102a High Road, Streatham, S.W. 16.

MACKINNON, Mervyn Alexander
B/1121, 7/9/14, L/C.; Durh. L.I., 27/11/14; F; Major; w; M.C., M(1).
Junior Constitutional Club, Piccadilly, W.

✠ MACKINNON, Neil Alexander
4/3/6/4191, 14/6/15; No. 13 O.C.B., 4/11/16; Suff. R., 28/2/17; Lieut.
Killed in action 19/9/18.

McKINNON, Norman
A/13050, 7/5/18; No. 9 O.C.B., 8/11/18; York. & Lanc. R., 6/2/19; 2/Lieut.
10 Rubislaw Terrace, Aberdeen.

McKINNON, Sydney Frederick
A/13071, 15/5/18; No. 1 O.C.B., 8/11/18; High. L.I., 17/3/19; 2/Lieut.
1 Albyn Terrace, Aberdeen, Scotland.

McKINNON-WOOD, Hugh. See WOOD, H. McK.

MACKINTOSH, Hugh Kinghorn
6/5/C/8184, 6/12/15; No. 14 O.C.B., 30/10/16; 1st Lond. R., 28/2/17; w.
Wellwood, Broomelknowe, Edinburgh.

✠ MACKLE, Austin Ignatius
6/5/7386, 11/11/15; No. 11 O.C.B., 7/5/16; Bord. R., 4/9/16, L'pool. R.; Lieut.
Killed 11/8/18.

MACKLEY, Ernest
6/3/7874, 26/11/15; Leic. R., 25/9/16; F; Lieut.
Melton Mowbray, Leicestershire.

MACKNESS, Douglas Charles
A/11607, 5/7/17; Garr O.C.B., 28/12/17; Arg. & Suth'd. Highrs., 18/5/18; 2/Lieut.
The Sheiling, Hornchurch Road, Romford, Essex.

McKNIGHT, Richard Alexander
6/2/6875, 18/10/15, L/C.; Ches. R., 24/10/16, Manch. R.; Lieut.; w.
77 Allerton Road, Mossley Hill, Birmingham.

McLACHLAN, Alexander
Sq/399, 5/4/09; dis. 5/3/10.

McLACHLEN, Robert Jessie
D/13945, 1/9/18; demob. 22/1/19.
27 Rue-des-Pyramides, Paris.

McLAGLAN, Cyril Rochford
B/12383, 12/1/18, L/C.; H. Bde. O.C.B., 5/7/18; trfr. 28th Lond. R., 26/9/18.
Ashleigh, 628 High Road, Gunnersbury.

McLAGLAN, Lewis M. R.
K/2457, 28/12/14; K.R. Rif. C., 27/3/15, R.A.S.C.; F; Lieut.; w.
Ashleigh, 628 High Road, Gunnersbury.

McLARE, William Murray
6/4/6068, 6/9/15, L/C.; North'd. Fus., 1/6/16; F; Lieut.; p.
Brewery House, Chester le Street, Co. Durham.

MACLAREN, John Rayner
B/11674, 16/7/17; A.S.C., C/S, 1/11/17; R.A.S.C., 25/1/18; F; 2/Lieut.
The Bungalow, Bishopsteignton, South Devonshire.

McLAREN, William Stanley
6/3/8070, 1/12/15; No. 14 O.C.B., 26/11/16; Essex R., 28/2/17; Lieut.
Glendale, Swanage Road, Southend.

McLARNON, Thomas Steed
A/B/C/D/12141, 22/10/17; No. 19 O.C.B., 10/5/18; trfr. 28th Lond. R., 28/10/18.
Dunsenaine, Hadley Road, New Barnet.

McLAUGHLIN, Gerard Cuthbert
K/D/2586, 4/1/15, Cpl.; Lan. Fus., 25/4/15; Lieut.; w.

MACLAURIN, James Cockburn
D/13813, 12/8/18; demob. 29/1/19.
Ardrech, 9 Spence Street, Maryhill Park, Glasgow

APPENDIX II.—RECORDS OF RANK AND FILE.

MACLEAN, Donald Douglas
3/3646, 17/5/15; R.A.S.C., 30/7/15; Lieut.
40 Park Lane, Croydon, Surrey.

McLEAN, John Alexander Stewart
4/3/4021, 7/6/15; Sco. Rif., 27/8/15, Oxf. & Bucks. L.I.; F; Capt.; w.
38 Garry Street, Cathcart.

McLEAN, Robert Chesney
6/5/C/8386, 11/12/15; No. 14 O.C.B., 30/10/16, M.G.C., C/S; M.G.C., 30/1/17, Tank Corps; Lieut.
23 Victoria Grove, Heaton Chapel, Manchester.

✠ **MacLEHOSE, Norman Crawford**
B/665, 19/11/12; 8th Lond. R., 23/12/13; Lieut.
Killed in action 26/5/15.

McLELLAN, Bernard Vincent Harry
Sq/655, 1/11/12; R.A.S.C., 7/10/14; Lieut.
Aspenden, Buntingford, Hertfordshire.

McLENNAN, Harold
6/2/6464, 27/9/15; L/C.; R.F.A., C/S, 17/3/16; R.G.A., 6/7/16; F; Lieut.; M.C., M(1).
19 Chesterford Gardens, Hampstead, N.W. 3.

MacLEOD, Arnold Frank
4/6/3/4862, 15/7/15; Midd'x. R., 18/12/15; F; Lieut.; w.
2 Fonthill Road, Aberdeen, N.B.

McLEOD, Harvey
6/5/5945, 1/9/15, L/C.; L'pool. R., 20/1/16; Lieut.

MacLEOD, John Mackay
4/6/3/4890, 15/7/15; L/C.; Gord. Highrs., 22/11/15; F; Capt.; w(2).
Caixa 16, St. Vincent, Cape Verde Islands.

MACLEOD, Norman Murray
6/2/6558, 30/9/15; Indian Army, 18/6/17; P,I; Lieut.
c/o Mrs. H. A. Macleod, 221 St. Margarets Road, St. Margarets-on-Thames, Middlesex.

MACLEOD-BROWN, James
6/7537, 16/11/15; trfr. R. Highrs., 25/1/16; w.
7 Cleveland Road, Ealing, W. 13.

McLOUGHLIN, John
C/10068, 1/12/16; No. 14 O.C.B., 5/3/17; R. Muns. Fus., 26/6/17, R. Ir. Regt.; F; 2/Lieut.; w.
2 Zonview Terrace, North Strand, Limerick, Ireland.

✠ **MACLUCKIE, Reginald William**
D/2693, 14/1/15, L/C.; Arg. & Suth'd. Highrs., 31/3/15, att. W. York. R.; Capt.
Killed in action 11/8/16.

McMAHON, Harold Edward
C/10408, 8/1/17; No. 14 O.C.B., 7/6/17; R. Innis. Fus., 25/9/17; Lieut.

MacMAHON, Percy Andrew M.
D/2749, 21/1/15; R. Lanc. R., 23/2/15; 2/Lieut.
14 Dolman Road, Aston Manor.

MacMAHON, Thomas Francis
6/2/5709, 19/8/15, Cpl.; Ir. Gds., 16/2/15; F; Capt.; w; M.C., M(1).
57 Windle Street, St. Helens, Lancashire.

McMAHON, William John Alexander
6/5/8731, 5/1/16, L/C.; M.G.C., C/S, 25/11/16; M.G.C., 24/3/17; Lieut.
Ballenahinch, Richhill, Co. Armagh, Ireland.

MacMAHON, William Percy Dartrey
B/12854, 25/3/18; R. Marines, 10/5/18; 2/Lieut.
10 Goldsmid Road, Brighton, Sussex.

MacMANUS, James Clive Denys
6/5/7465, 15/11/15, L/C.; R. War. R., 25/9/16, att. Yorks. L.I.; F; Lieut.; w; M(1).
10 Liverpool Terrace, Worthing, Sussex.

McMICHAEL, John James
6/5/6096, 6/9/15, L/C.; No. 9 O.C.B., 6/3/16; R. Fus., 6/7/16; F; Lieut.
Daldowie, Monifirth, Forfarshire, Scotland

MACMILLAN, Alastair
6/8249, 8/12/15; No. 9 O.C.B., 8/3/16; Sea. Highrs., 6/7/16; w.
2 Roseleigh Avenue, Highbury, N. 5.

✠ **MACMILLAN, Edwin James**
4/4118, 8/6/15; R. Ir. Fus., 16/11/15; 2/Lieut.
Killed in action 12/1/17.

MacMILLAN, Emerson Augustus
D/13865, 20/8/18; No. 11 O.C.B., 24/1/19; trfr. R.E., 27/2/19; NR; C.S.M.; p.
180 Ontario Street, St Catherines, Ontario, Canada.

McMILLAN, John Knox
6/7819, 24/11/15; No. 9 O.C.B., 8/3/16; Arg. & Suth'd. Highrs., 28/7/16, att. Cam'n. Highrs.; F; Lieut.; w.
Glandore, Baily, Co. Dublin.

MACMILLAN, Maurice Harold
H/1643, 9/10/14; K.R. Rif. C., 19/11/14, Gren. Gds.; Lieut.; w(3).
52 Cadogan Place, S.W. 1.

McMILLAN, Robert
C/14165, 14/10/18; demob. 5/2/19.
36 Bertrand Road, Bolton, Lancashire.

McMINN, Robert Martin
D/9903, 13/11/16, L/C.; R.A., C/S, 2/3/17; R.G.A., 28/5/17; I; Lieut.
Kildoon, Clifford Road, Nr Barnet, Hertfordshire.

McMORRAN, Robert Alexander Colles
A/14338, 30/12/18; No. 11 O.C.B., 24/1/19; General List, 8/3/19; 2/Lieut.

McMURCHY, Daniel
B/C/D/12203, 8/11/17; No. 10 O.C.B., 10/5/18; Sco. Rif., 3/2/19; 2/Lieut.
Lyndene, 5 Woodend Drive, Jordanhill, Glasgow.

McMURDO, Montagu Scott
6/2/6505, 28/9/15; No. 7 O.C.B., 3/7/16, No. 14 O.C.B.; R. Ir. Rif., 26/7/17; F; Lieut.; w.
105 Upper Richmond Road, Putney, S.W.

✠ **McMURTRIE, John**
K/2795, 26/1/15; R.E., 29/5/15; Major; w; M.C.
Killed in action 26/7/17.

MACNABB, Hugh
1/3136, 29/3/15, Sgt.; Lovats Scouts, 5/8/16, att. L'pool. R.; I; Staff Capt.
Millfield, Blackwaterfoot, Isle of Annan, Scotland.

MACNAMARA, Brian Cameron
B/1357, 26/9/14, L/C.; Durh. L.I., 27/11/14; F; Capt.; w(3).
31 Rollscourt Avenue, Herne Hill, S.E. 24.

McNAUGHT, Kenneth Grahame
6/2/D/6252, 16/9/15; No. 14 O.C.B., 27/12/16; Dorset R., 27/3/17; Lieut.
24 Coolhurst Road, Crouch End, N.

MACNAUGHTON, Hamish Colin
D/11101, 21/4/17, L/C.; R.A., C/S, 24/8/17; R.F.A., 4/2/18; It; 2/Lieut.
Elcombe House, De Parys Avenue, Bedford.

MacNAY, Harold Francis
67/8985, 18/1/16; R.A., C/S, 26/5/16; R.F.A., 1/9/16; 2/Lieut.
49 Firth Park Road, Sheffield.

McNEIGHT, William Herbert
A/11608, 2/7/17; No. 19 O.C.B., 9/11/17; R. Ir. Regt., 6/3/18; F; 2/Lieut.
110 North Circular Road, Dublin, Ireland.

MacNEIL, Neil Harcourt
F/1776, 16/10/14, Sgt.; High. L.I., 27/11/14, R.A.F.; F; Capt.; w; M.C., M(2).
Kyllachy, Natimuk, Victoria, Australia.

McNIVEN, Edward Allan Hugh
1/3422, 29/4/15; Railway Transport Officer, 14/1/17, Wilts. R.; F; Lieut.
Manningford Abbots, Mailbrough, Wiltshire.

McPHEE, Donald
B/13520, 12/7/18; demob. 20/3/19.
Ardenvohr, Silverwells Crescent, Bothwell, Nr. Glasgow, Scotland.

McPHEE, Thomas
D/10249, 29/12/16, L/C.; R.E., C/S, 16/6/17; R.E., 7/9/17; 2/Lieut.
Ardenvohr, Silverwells Crescent, Bothwell, Nr. Glasgow, Scotland.

MACPHERSON, Charles Fowkes
D/10650, 2/2/17; R.F.C., C/S, 16/4/17; R.F.C., 16/5/17, R.A.F.; F; Lieut.
Priestwell House, Dufftown, Banffshire, Scotland.

MACPHERSON, Ewen
A/13154, 29/5/18; No. 22 O.C.B., 5/7/18; E. Surr. R., 11/2/19; 2/Lieut.
Charity Commission, Ryder Street, S.W. 1.

MACPHERSON, James Esslemont
6/Sq/7685, 22/11/15, Cpl.; R.F.A., C/S, 4/8/16; R.F.A., 10/11/16; F; Lieut.; Inv.
Scarborough, Tobago, British West Indies

MACPHERSON, James Henry
6/1/6959, 22/10/15; No 9 O.C.B., 8/3/16; Cam'n. Highrs., 23/7/16; S; Lieut.; M.C.
84 Embleton Road, Lewisham, S.E. 13.

APPENDIX II.—RECORDS OF RANK AND FILE.

✠ McPHERSON, Leonard Alfred
4/5/6/4863, 15/7/15; R.H.A., 10/11/15, R.F.C.; F; 2/Lieut.
Killed in action 28/7/17.

McQUAID, Eugene Ward
D/12922, 4/4/18; R.A.F., C/S, 16/10/18; demob. 24/1/19.
Court View, Cootehill, Co. Cavan, Ireland.

McQUEEN, Norman
A/1277, 23/9/14; Arg. & Suth'd. Highrs., 10/10/14; F; Major; D.S.O. and Bar. Legion of Honour, M(4).
Caledonian Club, St. James Square, S.W.1.

McQUEEN, Samuel Brown
B/11675, 16/7/17; M.G.C., C/S, 2/11/17; M.G.C., 25/6/18; F; 2/Lieut. 11 Cambridge Avenue, Great Crosby, Liverpool.

MacRAE, Donald Edgar
4/Sq/4284, 17/6/15, L/C.; R.H.A., 10/11/15, R.A.V.C.; E,I; Capt. Los Galponas, Corres Mandisovi, Entre Rios, Argentina.

McSWEENY, Donal Hugh
6/1/6625, 4/10/15; N. Lan. R., 25/1/16; Lieut .
53 Balham Park Road, Balham, S.W.

MacTAGGART, John Keith
C/14292, 11/11/18; demob. 30/1/19.
118 Sutton Court, Chiswick, W. 4.

MACTAGGART, Murdoch Islay
6/2/6188, 13/9/15; No. 9 O.C.B., 8/3/16; Cam'n. Highrs., 23/7/16; S; Lieut.; w.
Rungamuttee Tea Estate, Mal P.O., Jalparguri, Dooars, India.

McVEAN, Alexander
6/2/5/6803, 14/10/15; R.F.A., 28/12/15; Lieut.
Bellanoch, Foxley, Glasgow.

McVICKER, Robert Brian
D/13798, 9/8/18; demob. 25/1/19.
20 Mornington Avenue, West Kensington.

MACVIE, Adam
B/11349, 22/5/17; A.S.C., C/S, 1/9/17; R.A.S.C., 27/10/17; Lieut.

McWEENEY, Cecil Brazil
1/9759, 18/10/16; No. 14 O.C.B., 27/12/16; R. Dub. Fus., 25/4/17; Lieut. 4 St. Stephens Green, Dublin.

✠ McWHINNIE, Charles Routledge
B/3042, 14/3/15; R.W. Surr. R., 18/6/15; Lieut.
Died of wounds 1/7/18.

McWILLIAMS, Cecil Moore
6/Sq/8396, 14/12/15; R.F.A., C/S, 4/8/16; R.F.A., 10/11/16; F; 2/Lieut.; g.
Manor Hastings, Walmer, Port Elizabeth, South Africa.

McWILLIAMS, Owen John
C/14172, 16/10/18; demob. 19/12/18.
12 Park Beau Terrace, St. Ives, Cornwall.

McWILLIAMS, William Robert
6/5/8732, 5/1/16; No. 7 O.C.B., 11/8/16; R. Innis. Fus., 18/12/16; F; Capt.; Inj.
Rose House, Coyle's Place, Belfast, Ireland.

MADDEN, Charles Hulbert
C/9957, 20/11/16; No. 14 O.C.B., 30/1/17; Som. L.I., 29/5/17; F; Capt.; M.C. and Bar.
Seahaven, Shoreham-by-Sea, Sussex.

MADDEN, Henry Erle
A/B/D/12142, 22/10/17; No. 9 O.C.B., 10/5/18; Sco. Rif., 3/2/19; 2/Lieut. 9 Overdale Street, Langside, Glasgow.

✠ MADDEN, Hubert William
C/10615, 22/1/17; dis. med. unfit, 2/8/17. Died 2/12/18.

MADDISON, Sidney Philip
A/11251, 12/5/17, L/C.; No. 14 O.C.B., 5/10/17; Devon. R., 26/2/18, att. R.W. Fus.; 2/Lieut.
1 Brett Villas, Horn Lane, Acton, W. 3.

MADDOCK, George Henshall
B/13538, 17/7/18; demob. 22/1/19.
95 Brooklyn Street, Crewe.

MADDOCK, William
6/1/D/5517, 9/8/15; No. 14 O.C.B., 26/11/16; Mon. R., 27/3/17, att. S. Wales Bord., S. Staff. R. and M.G.C.; F,It,S; Lieut.; g.
Llanarthney, Hornsey Rise, N. 19.

MADDY, Alfred Arnold
D/11110, 25/4/17; R.E., C/S, 7/10/17; R.E., 1/2/18; F; 2/Lieut
36 Trothy Road, Bermondsey, S.E. 1.

MADGE, Sidney Joseph
E/14005, 13/9/18; No. 22 O.C.B., 22/11/18; E. Kent R., 15/2/19; 2/Lieut. 69 Oakfield Road, Stroud Green, N. 4.

MAELOR-JONES, William Harold
6/4/9217, 31/1/16; No. 8 O.C.B., 4/8/16, M.G.C., C/S; M.G.C., 23/11/16, Tank Corps; F; Lieut.; g, w.
Newton Vicarage, Pickering, Yorkshire.

MAGEE, Andrew Victor
D/14042, 20/9/18; demob. 24/1/19.
12 Montgomerie Street, Kelvinside, Glasgow.

MAGER, George Edmund
K/2367, 17/12/14; R.F.A., 6/2/15; F; Major; w; M.C., M(1).
12 Denbigh Gardens, Richmond, Surrey.

MAGINN, William
C/13191, 3/6/18; demob. 13/12/18.

MAGRATH, Harry William
C/1159, 14/9/14; K.R. Rif. C., 28/11/14; F; Capt.; g; M.C.
Union Club, Trafalgar Square, W.C.

MAGRATH, William Christopher McClean
A/10738, 15/2/17; R.F.A., C/S, 22/6/17; R.F.A., 17/11/17; F; Lieut.; g; M(1).
1 Eglington Terrace, Phibsborough, Dublin, Ireland. (Now in India).

MAHAFFY, Robert Pentland
B/191, 4/5/08; dis. 3/5/13; Devon. R., 12/12/14, 2nd Lond. R.; F; Major; w. 2 Paper Buildings, Temple, E.C. 4.

MAHON, Charles Vivian
D/Sq/10525, 15/1/17, Sgt.; No. 2 Cav. C/S, 11/4/18; R. Regt. of Cav., 18/10/18, att. R.A.S.C.; 2/Lieut.
1 Victoria Terrace, Ennis, Co. Clare, Ireland.

MAHONY, Henry Erward
D/1470, 29/9/14; dis. med. unfit, 27/11/14.
6 Grafton Square, Clapham, S.W. 4.

MAHONY, John Joseph
6/5/5410, 5/8/15; trfr. R.G.A., 7/7/16; R.G.A., -/12/17; F; Lieut. 57 St. Charles Square, Ladbroke Grove, W.

MAISEY, William Allan
6/2/7210, 4/11/15, Sgt.; R.F.A., C/S, 4/5/17; R.F.A., 1/10/17; F; Lieut.; M.C. Roman Road Farm, Ashley, Whitfield, Dover.

MAISTER, Hugh Charles Langley
B/12833, 22/3/18; No. 21 O.C.B., 4/10/18; Yorks. L.I., 17/3/19; 2/Lieut. Swinton, Masham, Via Ripon, Yorkshire.

MAITH, Albert Edward
6/1/6997, 25/10/15, Sgt.; R.A., C/S, 7/8/16; R.G.A., 18/10/16; Capt. Park House, Balmoral Terrace, Newcastle.

MAITLAND, Alexander Wood
6/4/9579, 8/5/16, L/C.; R.A., C/S, 29/12/16; R.F.A., 9/6/17; F; Lieut.; w; M.C., M(1). 22 Manchester Road, Bury.

MAITLAND, Charles
D/E/13737, 2/8/18; No. 22 O.C.B., 20/9/18; R. Highrs., 5/2/19; 2/Lieut. Kinburn West, St. Andrews, Fife, N.B.

MAITLAND, William Macdonald
K/F/2248, 7/12/14, L/C.; R. Dub. Fus., 22/4/15, secd. R.E.; F; Lieut.; w(2). 31 Byron Road, Ealing Common, W. 5.

MAITLAND-MAKGILL-CRICHTON, Andrew Gavin
H/2042, 9/11/14, Cpl.; Cam'n. Highrs., 17/12/14; F; Lt.-Col.; D.S.O., M.C., M(1). 17a Great Cumberland Place, W. 1.

MAJOR, Arthur William
6/1/6998, 25/10/15; M.G.C., 4/8/16; F; Lieut.; w.
Mounts Bay, 106 Upper Walthamstow Road, E. 17.

MAJOR, John Robert
B/12739, 11/3/18; R.F.A., C/S, 17/5/18; R.F.A., 15/2/19; 2/Lieut.
Whyte House, Ramsey, Huntingdonshire.

MAJOR, Lancelot Bruce. See BRUCE-MAJOR, L.

MAKGILL-CRICHTON, Andrew Gavin Maitland
See MAITLAND-MAKGILL-CRICHTON, A. G.

✠ MAKINS, Hugh
Sq/117, 18/4/08; dis. 16/10/11, rej. 1209, 14/9/14; 16th Lond. R, 26/9/14; F; Capt. Died of wounds 4/11/15.

MALBY, Herbert Francis
4/1/4343, 21/6/15; R.A., C/S, 12/1/17; R.F.A., 19/5/17; F; Capt.; M.C. Beaumont, Westcliff Park Drive, Westcliff-on-Sea.

APPENDIX II.—RECORDS OF RANK AND FILE.

MALCOLM, Douglas
Sq/1008, 6/8/14; Leic. Yeo., 26/8/14.
Bath Club, Dover Street, W.

MALCOLM, Roy Alexander
A/13951, 4/9/18; demob. 23/1/19.
Ardeen, Cowper Road, Worthing.

MALCOMSON, John Fraser
6/9114, 24/1/16; trfr. 9th Lond. R., 29/3/16.
Dolforgan Hotel, Exmouth, Devonshire.

MALDEN, John William
A/10890, 15/3/17; R.A., C/S, 29/6/17; R.G.A., 2/12/17; F; 2/Lieut.
The Lodge, Mereworth Road, Tunbridge Wells.

✠ MALET, Hugh Arthur Grenville
Sq/766, 16/2/14; Dorset R., 15/8/14, K.O. Sco. Bord.; Lieut.
Killed in action 18/4/15.

MALLABAR, John Frederick
D/13856, 19/8/18; trfr. K.R. Rif. C., 7/4/19.
Rosslyn, The Avenue, Watford, Hertfordshire.

MALLER, Frank
K/A/2451, 28/12/14; R. Dub. Fus., 20/4/15; 2/Lieut.
43 Millais Road, Enfield.

MALLETT, Ernest Tresilian
C/10396, 8/1/17; No. 14 O.C.B., 5/5/17; N. Lan. R., 28/8/17; F; Lieut.; w; M.C.
6 Graham Road, Hendon, N.W. 4.

MALLETT, William Newman
4/1/4285, 17/6/15; Welch R., 5/11/15, att. Army Cyc. Corps; F; Capt.; w; M(1).
1 Gresham Street, E.C. 2.

MALLINSON, Percy Russell
4/3734, 24/5/15; Bedf. R., 10/9/15, R.F.C., R.A.F.; F; Lieut.
13 The Grove, Wandsworth Common, S.W. 18.

MALLOCK, Rawlin Richard Maconchy
H/1914, 16/10/14; dis. med. unfit, 29/11/14.

✠ MALLORY, John Charles
4/2/4192, 14/6/15; North'd. Fus., 1/6/16; 2/Lieut.
Killed in action 23/4/17.

MALONE, Francis Laurence Gerard
B/13644, 23/7/18; demob. 30/1/19.
64 Moyne Road, Rathmines, Dublin.

✠ MALONEY, Adrian Edwin
6/5/8876, 12/1/16; No. 5 O.C.B., 14/8/16; R.N.V.R., 21/11/16; F; Sub. Lieut.
Killed in action 8/3/18.

MALTBY, Charles Thomas
D/10336, 4/1/17; A.S.C., C/S, 1/5/17; R.A.S.C., 28/6/17; F; Lieut.
7 Kingsway, Monument Park, Wigan, Lancashire.

MALTBY, Raymond Allen Lionel
B/2680, 12/1/15; Durh. L.I., 26/2/15, R.E.; F; Capt.; g(2).
139 Claremont Road, Forest Gate, Essex.

✠ MALTON, Michael Innes
C/9800, 27/10/16; M.G.C., C/S, 1/2/17; E. Kent R., 26/6/17; 2/Lieut.; w.
Killed in action 22/8/18.

MALZER, Kurt Reinhold
C/11472, 11/6/17; No. 2 Cav. C/S, 13/7/17; R. Regt. of Cav., 5/8/18; 2/Lieut.
c/o Union Castle Coy., 3/4 Fenchurch Street, E.C.

MAMMATT, Edward Martin
B/11370, 28/5/17; No. 14 O.C.B., 5/10/17; Leic. R., 26/3/18; F; 2/Lieut.
Priorfield, Ashby-de-la-Zouch, Leicestershire.

✠ MANATON, George Aubrey
4/4313, 17/6/15; dis. med. unfit, 26/11/15. Died -/8/18.

MANDER, Reginald James Josiah
B/Sq/A/12377, 10/1/18; No. 23 O.C.B., 7/6/18; K.O. Sco. Bord., 5/2/19; 2/Lieut.
20 Clifton Avenue, Church End, Finchley, N. 3.

MANES, Leopold Joseph Ferdinand
6/5/6559, 30/9/15; R.G.A., 14/12/15; F; Lieut.
30 Wilbury Crescent, Hove, Sussex.

MANIFOLD, Alfred Frederick Clarendon
C/12259, 29/11/17, L/C.; No. 6 O.C.B., 7/6/18; R. Ir. Rif., 4/2/19; 2/Lieut.
Glenbrook, Bray, Co. Wicklow. (Now in East Africa.)

✠ MANISTY, Henry Scott
Sq/642, 9/5/12, L/C.; R.E., 23/10/14; Lieut.; w; M.C.
Killed in action 16/10/17.

MANLEY, Anthony Deverell
A/10291, 1/1/17; No. 14 O.C.B., 6/4/17; R. Dub. Fus., 31/7/17; 2/Lieut.
Caldecott House, Heyford, Banbury, Oxon.

MANLEY, Gerald Arthur Churchill
B/10761, 17/2/17; R.F.C., C/S, 16/4/17; R.F.C., 16/5/17, R.A.F.; F; Lieut.; p.
Davenport Avenue, Hessle, East Yorkshire.

MANLEY, Gordon Noel
B/13554, 19/7/18; demob. 30/1/19.
St. Dunstan's Vicarage, Canterbury.

MANN, Arthur Reginald
1/3489, 4/5/15, Sgt.; R.F.A., 30/7/15; Lieut.

✠ MANN, Besil Stamforth
A/2022, 2/11/14; W. Rid. R., 22/4/15; Capt.
Killed in action 27/11/17.

MANN, Charles
6/3/8862, 12/1/16; R.A., C/S, 4/8/16; R.G.A., 1/11/16; F; Lieut.; g.
Lumsden Aberdeenshire.

MANN, David Mann
1/3648, 17/5/15; R. Highrs., 11/8/15, Tank Corps; F; Capt.; M.C.
Gladstone Place, Kirriemuir, Forfarshire, Scotland.

MANN, Dudley Stuart
B/12774, 15/3/18; No. 3 O.C.B., 6/9/18; Midd'x. R., 17/3/19; 2/Lieut.
643 Fulham Road, S.W. 6.

MANN, Francis Alfred Wharton
6/2/6739, 11/10/15; No 11 O.C.B., 7/5/16; R.F.C., 4/9/16, R.A.F.; F; Lieut.; w.
83 Huskisson Street, Liverpool.

MANN, Frederick Farrell
6/4/8394, 14/12/15; No. 11 O.C.B., 7/5/16; trfr. R.F.A., 8/12/16.
62 Queensborough Terrace, Bayswater, W. 2.

MANN, George Ernest
6/4/5659, 16/8/15; E. Surr. R., 24/12/15, att. E. Kent R. and Manch. R.; M,I; Lieut.; w; M.C. 81 Kimberley Road, S.E. 15.

MANN, Harold Loveys
D/11833, 9/8/17, L/C.; Sigs. C/S, 15/2/18; R.E., 19/7/18; S; Lieut.
Pinewood, The Grove, Coulsdon, Surrey. (Now in Straits Settlements).

MANN, James Wallace
C/11519, 18/6/17; trfr. 28th Lond. R., 24/9/17.

✠ MANN, Laurence John
6/4/9082, 24/1/16; No. 2 O.C.B., 14/8/16; North'd. Fus., 18/12/16; 2/Lieut.
Killed in action 12/7/17.

✠ MANN, Percy Charles
6/1/9192, 29/1/16; No. 13 O.C.B., 4/11/16; K.R. Rif. C., 28/2/17; 2/Lieut.
Killed in action 31/7/17.

MANN, Richard
4/4119, 8/6/15, L/C.; Lan. Fus., 25/9/15, M.G.C.; F; Lieut.
Swaton Vicarage, Billingborough, Lincolnshire.

MANN, Robert Arthur
6/1/6954, 21/10/15, L/C.; York. R., 24/4/16, att. R. Lanc. R.; Lieut.; w.

MANN, Sydney Frederick George
2/6/D/Sq/6534, 30/9/15, Cpl.; R.A., C/S, 2/3/17; R.F.A., 30/7/17; Lieut.
75 Ashgrove Road, Goodmayes.

✠ MANN, Theodore John Lewis
6/3/7148, 2/11/15, L/C.; R.A., C/S, 31/3/16; R.F.A., 5/8/16; 2/Lieut.
Died of wounds 28/4/18.

MANN, Thomas Basil Duncombe
A/305, 29/6/08; 22nd Lond. R., 14/10/09, 10th Lond. R.; G,F; Major; w.
c/o Lond. City & Mid. Bank, Ltd., Bromley, Kent.

MANNERS, Joseph Edward
4/5/4865, 15/7/15, L/C.; K.R. Rif. C., 6/7/16; F; Lieut.; g.
2 Heath Mansions, Putney, S.W. 15. (Now in Western Australia).

MANNERS, Walwyn Stanley
C/12555, 4/2/18; R.E., C/S, 12/5/18; R.E., 27/9/18; 2/Lieut.
c/o. E. & T. Pink Ltd., Staple Street, Borough, S.E. 1.

✠ MANNING, Albert George Walter
A/10965, 30/3/17; No. 12 O.C.B., 10/8/17; trfr. 28th Lond. R., 25/2/18; F; Pte.
Died of wounds 30/9/18.

APPENDIX II.—RECORDS OF RANK AND FILE.

MANNING, Charles Rosedale Upwood
6/2/5339, 2/8/15; North'n. R., 26/12/15; Lieut.

MANNING, Frederick Edwin Alfred
6/1/8458, 17/12/15, L/C.; No. 8 O.C.B., 4/8/16, M.G.C., C/S; M.G.C., 28/10/16, Tank Corps; F,NR; Major; w(2); M.C., Orders of S. Stanislaus and S. Vladimir (Russia).
5 The Gardens, East Dulwich, S.E. 22.

MANNING, George Howell Coad
C/859, 4/8/14.

MANNING, James Frederick Charles
B/Sq/12710, 8/3/18; No. 2 Cav. C/S, 26/6/18; demob. 24/1/19.
Esthlon, Newmarket.

✠ MANNING, John Carlton
6/1/7267, 8/11/15; No. 11 O.C.B., 7/5/16; Ches. R., 4/9/16; 2/Lieut. Died of wounds 17/2/17.

MANNING, William
6/2/5660, 16/8/15; E. Kent R., 25/12/5; S; Capt.; Greek Medal for Military Merit. 16 St. Lawrence Road, Tinsley, Sheffield.

MANNING, William Leopold
C/11748, 26/7/17; A.S.C., C/S, 1/11/17; R.A.S.C., 25/1/18; F; Lieut. 26 High Street, Colchester.

MANNING, William Maurice
10643, 2/2/17, L/C.; No. 11 O.C.B., 5/7/17; 22nd Lond. R., 30/10/17; F; 2/Lieut.
Nilla Park, 31 Warrior Square, Southend-on-Sea.

MANSEL-CAREY, David Vernon Mansel
6/3/8982, 15/1/16; No. 8 O.C.B., 4/8/16; Devon. R., 21/11/16; F; Lieut. Chesterton, Uppingham, Rutland.

MANSEL-EDWARDS, Ronald Ivor
A/10935, 24/3/17; R.F.C., C/S, 4/5/17; R.F.C., 14/6/17, R.A.F.; NR; Lieut. The Turret, Bath Road, Hounslow.

MANSFIELD, Arthur
F/3053, 15/3/15, L/C.; R.W. Surr. R., 3/6/15, R. Ir. Rif., R.E.; E,S,P; Capt.; Inv. 5 High Street, Godalming.

MANSFIELD, Frederick William
6/3/7742, 22/11/15; No. 14 O.C.B., 28/8/16; Mon. R., 22/11/16, att. Manch. R.; Lieut.; w; M(1).
47 Broadway, Leigh-on-Sea, Essex.

MANSFIELD, Henry
C/10159, 11/12/16; No. 14 O.C.B., 5/5/17; York. & Lanc. R., 28/8/17; 2/Lieut.; w.
5 Grosvenor Terrace, Hornsea, East Yorkshire.

MANSFIELD, Herbert Charles
6/7686, 22/11/15; dis. med. unfit, 26/9/16.
41 St. Alban's Road, Leicester.

MANSFIELD, Leonard George
6/3/5483, 9/8/15; R.A.S.C., 6/9/15; I,M; Capt.
37 Selborne Road, Denmark Hill, S.E.

MANSHIP, George
E/2833, 1/2/15, Cpl.; R. Berks. R., 14/5/15, R.E.; Lieut.; M(1)

MANSON, Albert Geoffrey Baradaile
A/1288, 23/9/14; Lan. Fus., 14/12/14; Lieut.

MANSON, Charles Henry
6/4/6740, 11/10/15; No. 11 O.C.B., 7/5/16; N. Staff. R., 4/9/16, att. Manch. R. and R. Guernsey L.I.; F; Capt.
3 George Place, Guernsey, Channel Islands.

MANSON, Edward Beresford
C/Sq/9931, 15/11/16; R.G.A., C/S, 16/2/17; R.G.A., 18/5/17; Lieut.

MANSON, Neville Borrodaile
A/585, 20/11/11; 22nd Lond. R., 28/8/14, R.F.C.; F; Capt.; w(2). Charnwood, Worple Road, Epsom, Surrey.

MANTELL, John Heathcote
4/3/4544, 1/7/15; Notts. & Derby. R., 17/12/15; Lieut.
Heather View, Harpenden, Hertfordshire.

✠ MANTELL, John Paul
C/12641, 22/2/18; Died 9/6/18.

✠ MANTLE, Alexander
F/2655, 11/1/15; 7th Lond. R., 22/4/15; Lieut.
Killed in action 23/5/17.

MANTLE, Frank Mitchell
6/5/7299, 8/11/15; Leic. R., 4/8/16, att. R. Devon. Yeo.; F; Lieut. Woodland, Knighton Grange Road, Leicester.

MAPLESON, Cecil Horsley
D/1444, 29/9/14; R.A.O.C., 22/1/15; F,M; Major, D.A.D.O.S.; M(1). Wyham House, Dover.

MARAIS, Guillaume Hermanus
C/12241, 22/11/17; No. 5 O.C.B., 6/9/18, No. 11 O.C.B.; General List, 8/3/19; 2/Lieut.
Royal Colonial Institute, Northumberland Avenue, W.C.1.

✠ MARCH, Alfred John Jethro
C/12087, 4/10/17; Sigs. C/S, 14/12/17; R.E., 24/5/18; F; 2/Lieut. Died 24/10/18.

MARCH, George Frederick
6/2/8069, 1/12/15; No. 8 O.C.B., 4/8/16; dis. med. unfit, 13/9/16.

MARCHANT, Frederick Stanley
6/5/C/5903, 30/8/15; dis. to R. Mil. Coll., 2/11/16; R. Innis. Fus., 12/9/17; Lieut.
2 Greenmount Road, Terenure, Dublin.

MARCHANT, James John
6/4/7529, 16/11/15; No. 11 O.C.B., 7/5/16; Devon. R., 4/9/16; Lieut. 61 Coplestone Road, East Dulwich, S.E. 15.

MARCKX, Maurice Cressy-
E/2796, 26/1/15; N. Lan. R., 21/5/15, att. Intelligence Corps.; F; Capt.; w. 3 Broad Walk, Buxton, Derbyshire.

MARCY, Frederick Nichols
H/2/1747, 15/10/14, Sgt.; Shrop. L.I., 2/5/15, Tank Corps; F; Capt. 8b Oxford and Cambridge Mansions, Hyde Park, W. 2.

MARCY, Frederick Rupert
6916, 19/10/15, Sgt.; No. 14 O.C.B., 7/12/17; Shrop. L.I., 26/6/18; F; 2/Lieut. 312 Goldhawk Road, Ravenscourt Park, W.

MARDON, William James Thomas
6/3/8651, 3/1/16, L/C.; No. 14 O.C.B., 28/8/16; Glouc. R., 18/12/16, att. R.A.F.; F; Lieut.
Devonia, Bovey Tracey, Devonshire.

MARE-MONTEMBAULT, Max John J. G.
Sq/3054, 15/3/15; North. Som. Yeo., 25/6/15, R.F.C.; Lieut.; w, p; M.C., M(1).
c/o The Honble. Mrs. Cook, Baynords, Cranleigh, Surrey.

MARKBY, Ralph Freeling
C/477, 5/4/10; L'pool. R., 3/10/15; Lieut.; w.
34 Bolton Gardens, S.W. 5.

MARKEY, Reginald John
D/10747, 20/1/17; No. 14 O.C.B., 5/7/17; Lein. R., 30/10/17; P,E; 2/Lieut. 8 Terenure Park, Dublin.

MARKHAM, William Henry Edgcombe
D/10644, 2/2/17; No. 14 O.C.B., 5/7/17; 9th Lond. R., 30/10/17; F; Lieut.; g. 47 Bedford Road, Harrow, Middlesex.

MARKS, Godfrey Davis
4/3861, 31/5/15; Durh. L.I., 17/12/15, R.F.C., R.A.F.; Lieut.
3 Twyford Crescent, Acton Hill, W. 3.

MARKS, Henry James
B/12755, 13/3/18; No. 3 O.C.B., 6/9/18; Hamps. R., 17/3/19; 2/Lieut. The Nutshell, South Park, Reigate.

MARKS, Herbert Henry
C/1158, 14/9/14; Durh. L.I., 27/11/14, att. R.A.F. and Intelligence; F; Lieut.; M.C. 79 Warrington Crescent, Maida Vale, W. 9.

MARKS, Robert Ferguson
D/12894, 9/4/18; No. 16 O.C.B., 18/10/18; demob. 7/2/19; NR.
208 Main Street, Wishaw, Scotland.

MARLAND, Alfred
A/11609, 5/7/17, L/C.; No. 14 O.C.B., 9/4/17; N. Cyc. Bn., 30/4/18, att. North'd. Fus.; Lieut.
68 Deansgate Arcade, Manchester.

MARLEY, Cuthbert David
6/1/6626, 4/10/15; Durh. L.I., 25/1/16; F; Capt.; w.
Marton Grove, Darlington.

✠ MARLOW, Albert Leopold Craddock
6/3/7847, 25/11/15; No. 8 O.C.B., 4/8/16; K.R. Rif. C., 21/11/16; 2/Lieut. Died of wounds 4/4/17.

MARLOW, Arthur Herbert
B/10766, 19/2/17, L/C.; R.G.A., C/S, 22/6/17; R.G.A., 25/11/17; lt; 2/Lieut. 21 Stimson Avenue, Northampton.

MARLOW, Horace Alfred
6/1/5587, 12/8/15; No. 7 O.C.B., 3/7/16; R.N.V.R., 21/11/16; F; Sub. Lieut.; g; M.C.
71 Upper Beechwood Avenue, Ranelagh, Dublin.

APPENDIX II.—RECORDS OF RANK AND FILE.

MARMENT, Harry Baden
C/13304, 17/6/18, L/C.; demob. 19/2/19.
12 High Street, Ascot, Berkshire.

MARNHAM, Arthur Ewart
Sq/661, 19/11/12; R.F.A., 28/8/14, R.G.A.; F; Lt.-Col.; M.C., Order of Leopold, Croix de Guerre (Belgian), M(2).
The Chauntry, Burnham Abbey, Buckinghamshire.

MARQUARDT, Charles Sherman Patrick
6/4/7268, 8/11/15; R.F.C., C/S, 13/3/17; R.F.C., 19/4/17.
10 Effra Mansions, Brixton Hill.

MARR, George Millar
2/9781, 25/10/16; R.A., C/S, 3/4/17; R.G.A., 25/6/17; Lieut.
75 Buchanan Street, Glasgow.

MARRIAGE, Edward Burtt
6/8291, 10/12/15; A.S.C., C/S, 10/4/16; R.A.S.C., 14/5/16; Lieut.
Twyford Mill, Banbury, Oxon.

MARRION, Walter William
C/13242, 7/6/18; No. 22 O.C.B., 5/7/18; R.A.S.C., 15/2/19; 2/Lieut.
14 St. Judes Road, Wolverhampton, Staffordshire.

MARRIOTT, Cecil Henry
E/1497, 1/10/14, L/C.; 5th Lond. R., 7/2/15; F; Capt.
25 Esmond Road, Bedford Park, W. 4.

MARRIOTT, John Percival
A/11274, 14/5/17, L/C.; No. 14 O.C.B., 7/12/17; Shrop. L.I., 25/6/18; 2/Lieut.
Ellesmere, Kings Acre Road, Hereford

MARRIS, Hugh Maclaren
6/3/8580, 1/1/16, L/C.; No. 14 O.C.B., 30/10/16; Shrop. L.I., 28/2/17; F; Lieut.; w; M.C.
22 Avenue Road, South Norwood, S.E. 25.

MARRS, Theodore Arthur
C/9954, 20/11/16; M.G.C., C/S, 14/3/17, Garr. O.C.B.; R.W. Fus., 15/12/17; F; 2/Lieut.
47 Bingham Road, Sherwood, Nottinghamshire.

MARS, Lionel Jackson
K/Sq/2702, 18/1/15, L/C.; York. Huss., 20/4/15, att. R.A.F.; F; Lieut.; w; M.B.E.
23 Mowbray Road, Brondesbury, N.W. 6.

MARS, Walter Herbert
C/13239, 7/6/18; R.F.A., C/S, 26/7/18; General List, 8/3/19; 2/Lieut.
c/o Nat. Bank of South Africa Ltd., London Wall, E.C

MARSDEN, Arthur Whitehead
B/D/12348, 31/12/17; R.A.F., C/S, 19/4/18; trfr. R.A.F.
The Ferns, Coseley, Bilston, Staffordshire.

MARSDEN, Claud Eric David
B/11989, 10/9/17; R.F.C., C/S, 6/12/17; R.F.C., 4/2/18; 2/Lieut
142 Broadhurst Gardens, N.W. 6.

✠ MARSDEN, Harold
6/5/8292, 10/12/15; No. 14 O.C.B., 28/8/16; L'pool. R., 18/12/16; 2/Lieut.
Died of wounds 14/8/17.

MARSH, Ernest John
B/78, 13/4/08; dis. 12/4/09.
71 East India Dock Road, E.

✠ MARSH, Francis Bedford
4/4134, 10/6/15; R.W. Surr. R., 21/11/15, att. M.G.C.; F; 2/Lieut.
Died of wounds 5/10/16.

✠ MARSH, Frank Sydney
6/1/8459, 18/12/15; No. 8 O.C.B., 4/8/16; R. Marines, 21/11/16; F; 2/Lieut.
Missing believed killed 28/4/17.

MARSH, George Fletcher Riley
C/13305, 17/6/18; trfr. 14th Lond. R., 6/12/18.
4 The Crescent, Bedford.

MARSH, Hector Charles
4/3/5040, 22/7/15; 11th Lond. R., 4/6/16; Lieut.; w.
Jamesville, Crow Hill, Broadstairs.

MARSH, Roderick Phillipson
6/7931, 29/11/15; R.A., C/S, 7/8/16; trfr. R.F.A., 20/10/16.
Field Lane, Letchworth, Hertfordshire.

MARSH, Stanley George
B/10565, 19/1/17; No. 11 O.C.B., 5/7/17; Midd'x. R., 30/10/17, M.G.C.; F; 2/Lieut.
28 Chretien Road, Northenden, Manchester.

MARSHALL, Albert Wilfrid Cornwallis
6/Sq/6487, 27/9/15, L/C.; dis. 23/4/16; Lab. Corps, 28/9/16; E,P; Lieut.
c/o Forbes, Forbes & Campbell, Forbes Buildings, Bombay, India.

MARSHALL, Angus
1/3545, 10/5/15; N. Lan. R., 21/8/15; Lieut.; w.

MARSHALL, Arthur Courland
A/10514, 15/1/17; A.S.C., C/S, 1/5/17; R.A.S.C., 28/6/17; F; Lieut.; M(1).
Crane Lodge, Cranford, Middlesex.

MARSHALL, Cecil Leycester
6/4/7772, 23/11/15; No. 14 O.C.B., 28/8/16, M.G.C., C/S; M.G.C., 25/1/17; F; Lieut.; w.
5 Cosbycote Avenue, Herne Hill, S.E. 24.

MARSHALL, Claude William
F/3/2991, 1/3/15, L/C.; Rif. Brig., 18/6/15; F; Lieut.; w(2).
6 Elm Street, Ipswich.

MARSHALL, Clifford James
C/11492, 14/6/17; No. 10 O.C.B., 5/10/17; Inland Water Transport, 14/1/18, R.E.; M; Lieut.
Wincliff, King's Avenue, Woodford Green Essex.

MARSHALL, Frederick
B/11350, 19/5/17; No. 10 O.C.B., 5/10/17; Norf. R., 26/2/18, att. Indian Army; E; 2/Lieut.
3 Mapperley Park Drive, Nottingham.

MARSHALL, Frederick Charles
6/7361, 10/11/15; No. 14 O.C.B., 27/9/16; Oxf. & Bucks. L.I., 24/1/17; F; Lieut.; w.
26 Brackley Road, Beckenham, Kent.

MARSHALL, George Frederick
D/11141, 30/4/17; No. 22 O.C.B., 22/11/18; R. War. R., 15/2/19; 2/Lieut.
Sledmere, Lichfield Street, Four Oaks, Worcestershire.

MARSHALL, Harold Percy
E/14117, 9/10/18; No. 22 O.C.B., 22/11/18; demob. 18/1/19.
92 Haslemere Road, Thornton Heath, Surrey.

MARSHALL, Henry George
H/2012, 2/11/14, L/C.; Bord. R., 18/3/15; I,Afghan; Major.
Hawse End, Keswick, Cumberland.

✠ MARSHALL, John
B/9875, 8/11/16, L/C.; No. 14 O.C.B., 30/1/17; 9th Lond. R., 25/4/17; F; 2/Lieut.
Killed in action 26/9/17.

MARSHALL, John Dalrymple Calder
4/2/4472, 28/6/15, Cpl.; Cam'n. Highrs., 3/12/15, Indian Army; S,M; Capt.
c/o Messrs. Cox & Coy., Bombay, India.

MARSHALL, Kenneth Murray
2/3785, 27/5/15; N. Staff. R., 5/9/15; 2/Lieut.

MARSHALL, Norman Vectis
6/1/5727, 19/8/15; R. Suss. R., 14/12/15; F; Lieut.; w.
Keri, Barnham, Sussex.

MARSHALL, Philip Harold
Sq/132, 18/4/08; dis. 31/12/09.

✠ MARSHALL, Robert Wilson
6/3/8730, 5/1/16; No. 14 O.C.B., 30/10/16; Arg. & Suth'd. Highrs., 28/2/17, att. Sea. Highrs.; M,E; 2/Lieut.
Killed in action 29/5/18.

MARSHALL, Stanley
6/5/Sq/8608, 3/1/16; R.A., C/S, 7/8/16; R.G.A., 24/11/16; F; Lieut.
The Old Hall, Sefton, Nr. Liverpool.

MARSHALL, William
2/3813, 27/5/15, L/C.; R.W. Fus., 31/10/15, att. R. Scots; Lieut.
Latchmere, Ham Common, Richmond, Surrey.

✠ MARSHALL, William Cornelius
A/10261, 29/12/16; No. 20 O.C.B., 5/5/17; L'pool. R., 28/8/17; 2/Lieut.
Killed in action 29/9/18.

MARSHALL, William James
D/10940, 26/3/17; R.A., C/S, 24/8/17; R.F.A., 21/1/18; F, Lieut.
Dudley Avenue, Whalley Range, Manchester.

MARSH-SMITH, Eric Cecil
2/9689, 4/10/16, L/C.; M.G.C., C/S, 1/2/17, No. 12 O.C.B.; Indian Army, 25/9/17; I,M,Persia; 2/Lieut.
46 Castle Hill Avenue, Folkestone, Kent. (Now in Ceylon).

✠ MARSTON, Arthur Bright
2/3424, 29/4/15; R.W. Surr. R., 21/8/15; 2/Lieut.
Died of wounds 14/7/16.

MARSTON, Henry Lancaster
4/2/4286, 17/6/15; Manch. R., 2/1/16, E. Lan. R., R.F.C., R.A.F.; F; Capt.
10 St. Johns Road, Clydach-on-Tawe, Glamorganshire.

APPENDIX II.—RECORDS OF RANK AND FILE.

MARTIN, Alan Smiles
6/1/7687, 22/11/15, L/C.; 22nd Lond. R., 25/9/16, 24th Lond. R.; Lieut.

✠ MARTIN, Alfred John
1/3649, 17/5/15; E. Surr. R., 10/9/15; F; 2/Lieut.
Killed 4/8/16.

MARTIN, Arthur Campbell
B/225, 13/5/08; dis. 12/5/12; R. Fus., 1/1/15; F; Capt.
9 New Square; Lincoln's Inn, W.C. 2.

MARTIN, Arthur John
Sq/693, 7/2/13, L/C.; York. Huss., 20/1/15; Capt.
British Legation, Peking, China.

MARTIN, Charles Daniel
K/A/2402, 21/12/14; Essex R., 16/3/15; G,E,P; Capt.
238 Edgware Road, Hyde Park, W. 2.

MARTIN, Colin Livingstone
B/12406, 17/1/18; No. 21 O.C.B., 10/5/18; R. Berks. R., 2/2/19; 2/Lieut.
Taplow Grammar School, Buckinghamshire.

MARTIN, Cyril Arthur Joseph
6/9146, 25/1/16; R.F.A., C/S, 9/6/16; R.G.A., 16/9/16; F; Lieut.; g; M.C.
Oulton Rectory, Lowestoft.

MARTIN, Ernest Leonard
6/2/7591, 18/11/15, Cpl.; No. 14 O.C.B.; E. Kent R., 24/10/16. att. Indian Army; I; Capt.
19 Morley Road, Lewisham, S.E. 13.

MARTIN, Frederick James
A/11610, 5/7/17; Lab. Corps, 25/9/17; F; Inv.
Gardenia, Grange Terrace, Exmouth, Devonshire.

MARTIN, John Mary Joseph
6/5/8506, 22/12/15; No. 7 O.C.B., 11/8/16; R. Dub. Fus., 18/12/16; F; Lieut.; p.
3 Waldamer Terrace, Dundrum, Co. Dublin.

MARTIN, John Bromley Lewis
F/1772, 16/10/14, Cpl.; Cold. Gds., 7/7/15; F; Lieut.; w.
Odiam Farm, Stone-in-Oxney, Nr. Ashford, Kent.

MARTIN, John Ede
B/13539, 17/7/18; trfr. 28th Lond. R., 13/11/18.

MARTIN, Kenneth Harvey
6/9386, 8/2/16; R.F.A., C/S, 21/7/16; R.F.A., 10/11/16; F; Lieut.; w.
4 Codrington Place, Clifton, Bristol. (Now in Shanghai).

MARTIN, Lawrence Alfred Dunkley
C/14260, 1/11/18; demob. 29/1/19.
Filey, Sandy Lane, Wallington, Surrey.

MARTIN, Maximilian Victor
4/6/5/4891, 15/7/15; trfr. 13th Lond. R., 25/9/16; F; Pte.; Inv.
Maydencroft, Ampthill. (Now in Brazil).

MARTIN, Maxwell Manley Sawdy
C/13372, 21/6/18, L/C.; demob. 12/3/19.
5 Napier Terrace, Mutley, Plymouth.

MARTIN, Robert Eric
B/9857, 6/11/16, L/C.; No. 14 O.C.B., 5/3/17; 13th Lond. R., 26/6/17, att. 10th Lond. R.; F; Lieut.; w.
18 Cranley Gardens, Muswell Hill, N. 10.

MARTIN, Robert Francis Joseph
D/11580, 2/7/17; No. 19 O.C.B., 9/11/17; trfr. Class W. Res., 1/2/18.
64 Shrewsbury Road, Oxton, Birkenhead.

MARTIN, Ronald Clifford
D/13873, 21/8/18.
23 Rivercourt Road, Hammersmith, W. 6

✠ MARTIN, Sidney Grant
4/2/4193, 14/6/15; R.F.A., 10/12/15; 2/Lieut.
Died of wounds 18/4/17.

MARTIN, Thomas Arthur McMurray
B/12359, 3/1/18; No. 12 O.C.B., 10/5/18; R. Highrs., 3/2/19; 2/Lieut.
c/o F. G. McMurray, Esq., 8 Eagle Place, Piccadilly, W.

MARTIN, Walter Frederick
A/Sq/13061, 13/5/18; demob. 9/1/19.
Attleton, 45 Harbord Street, Fulham, S.W. 6.

MARTINDELL, Ernest Walter
A/1688, 12/10/14; Notts. & Derby. R., 10/12/14, att. L'pool. R. and Manch. R.; F; Capt.
Chelston, Ashford, Middlesex.

MARTYN, James Vivian
6/4/8139, 3/12/15; No. 1 O.C.B., 6/9/16; R.F.C., 25/1/17, R.A.F.; F; Capt.
105 Aber Rhondda Road, Porth, South Wales.

MARTYR, Edward Gordon Waring
4/1/4083, 7/6/15, L/C.; Durh. L.I., 8/10/15, att. No. 5 O.C.B. Inst; Major.
37 Bramston Road, Harlesden, N.W. 10.

✠ MARTYR, Leonard Justin
C/D/12072, 1/10/17; R.F.C., C/S, 18/1/18; R.F.C., 6/3/18, R.A.F.; 2/Lieut.
Died 11/3/21.

MARWOOD, Donal Joseph
B/13645, 20/7/18, Sgt.; trfr. R. Highrs., 16/4/19.
7 Mount Pleasant Square, Ranelagh, Dublin.

MARX, Claude Maurice
6/2/5459, 7/8/15; dis. med. unfit, 31/12/15.
65 Compayne Gardens, Hampstead, N.W.

✠ MARYON, John William
6/2/6848, 16/10/15; trfr. 5th Lond. R., 13/3/16; F.
Died 1918.

MASCHMAYER, Douglas Herman
6/5/7211, 4/11/15; K.R. Rif. C., 4/6/16; 2/Lieut.
Alverstone Road, Mapperley Park, Nottinghamshire.

MASCHWITZ, Herbert Charles
B/11357, 28/5/17; No. 14 O.C.B., 7/9/17; S. Staff. R., 17/12/17 Worc. R., M.G.C.; Germ.EA,F; 2/Lieut.
83 Fountain Road, Birmingham. (Now in South Africa).

MASLEN, Gerald Leonard
6/Sq/5611, 16/8/15, L/C.; R.F.A., 31/12/15, att. R.A.F.; F; Lieut.; w.
53 North Gate, Regents Park, N.W. 8.

MASON, Alec
6/4/5994, 2/9/15; E. Surr. R., 1/6/16, att. R. Fus.; F; Lieut.; w(2); M(1).
Eton Lodge, Hampton Hill, Middlesex.

✠ MASON, Arthur Edmund
D/10895, 16/3/17; No. 12 O.C.B., 10/8/17; 8th Lond. R., 27/11/17; F; 2/Lieut
Killed in action 8/8/18.

MASON, Colin Morley
4/3526, 6/5/15; 22nd Lond. R., 29/10/15; att. Devon. R.; M; Capt.
1 Voss Court, Streatham Common, S.W. 16.

MASON, Cuthbert Francis
D/11749, 16/8/17; No. 14 O.C.B., 4/1/18; 7th Lond. R., 25/6/18; 2/Lieut.
62 Biddulph Mansions, Paddington, W.

MASON, Denis Herbert Finch
2/9686, 2/10/16; No. 14 O.C.B., 30/1/17; trfr. 14th Lond. R., 25/5/17.
Lane End's House, Macclesfield.

MASON, Frank Reginald
D/12125, 15/10/17; H. Bde. O.C.B., 8/2/18; Welch Gds., 30/7/18; Lieut.
Orford, Harpenden, Hertfordshire.

MASON, Harold Charles Ernest
4/1/4344, 21/6/15; Oxf. & Bucks. L.I., 26/9/15, Indian Army; F,I; Lieut.; w(2).
The Tilt House, Beaconsfield, Buckinghamshire.

✠ MASON, Harold Victor Hardey. See HARDEY-MASON, H. V.

MASON, Henry Alexander
A/10302, 1/1/17; R.F.C., C/S, 13/3/17; R.F.C., 3/5/17, R.A.F.; F; Capt.
Bentley Mill, Nr. Doncaster.

✠ MASON, Henry Victor
10697, 14/2/17, Sgt.; H. Bde. O.C.B., 9/8/18; Scots Gds., 5/3/19; 2/Lieut.
Died 20/4/20.

✠ MASON, James Philip
4677, 8/7/15; E. Surr. R., 7/10/15; 2/Lieut.
Killed in action 9/4/17.

MASON, John Walter
D/12967, 22/4/18; No. 8 O.C.B., 18/10/18; demob.
The Tilt House, Beaconsfield, Buckinghamshire.

✠ MASON, Kenneth Ralph
F/1898, 16/10/14, Cpl.; Suff. R., 28/11/14; F; 2/Lieut.
Killed in action 21/6/15.

✠ MASON, Lancelot William Hart
6/1/7996, 29/11/15; W. York. R., 4/8/16; 2/Lieut.
Killed in action 14/4/17.

MASON, Nicholas Haddon
6/4/7801, 24/11/15, L/C.; K.R. Rif. C., 21/11/16; Lieut.; w(3).

MASON, Richard Norman Rollet
6/9176, 27/1/16; A.S.C., C/S, 16/10/16; R.A.S.C., 19/11/16; Lieut.
Cedar House, Rotherham, Yorkshire.

APPENDIX II.—RECORDS OF RANK AND FILE.

MASON, Samuel Reginald
6/6360, 20/9/15; S. Staff. R., 25/9/15; 2/Lieut.
Nat Prov. & Union Bank House, 1 Victoria Road, Aston Manor, Birmingham.

MASON, Stanley Walter
A/10618, 25/1/17; No. 14 O.C.B., 7/6/17; Manch. R., 25/9/17, secd. M.G.C.; F; Lieut. 19 Station Road, Greenhithe, Kent.

MASON, Syrett John
6/2/5411, 5/8/15; Suff. R., 14/11/15, att. R.W. Surr. R. and R.A.F.; F; Lieut.; w. Box 70, Haileybury, Ontario, Canada.

MASON, Thomas
6/1/9331, 7/2/16, L/C.; No. 13 O.C.B., 4/11/16; R. Fus., 28/2/17; F,lt; Major; Croix de Guerre (Belgian), M.C.
The Elms, Wickhamford, Evesham, Worcestershire.

✠ MASON, Wilfred Howard
3/3673, 17/5/15; R.E., 8/5/15; 2/Lieut.
Killed in action 9/3/17.

MASSEY, Everard Ernest
1/3310, 19/4/15, L/C.; R.A.S.C., 12/7/15; M; Major; M.B.E., M(2). Hampden Club, London, N.W. 1.

✠ MASSEY, John Hamon
K/F/2348, 14/12/14; R.F.A., 27/2/15; F; Capt.; w; M.C., Croix de Guerre (French). Killed in action 27/5/18.

MASTER, Reginald Arthur
E/1600, 6/10/14; S. Wales Bord., 21/10/14; F; Capt.; w(2); M(1). Grove Farm Cottage, South Harrow.

MASTERS, Clive Percy
A/11235, 9/5/17; No. 16 O.C.B., 5/10/17; 19th Lond. R., 12/3/18, att. R.A.F.; 2/Lieut. 402 Central Park Road, East Ham, E. 6.

MASTERS, Percy Edgar Howard
A/10954, 29/3/17, Cpl.; R.F.A., C/S, 17/12/17; R.F.A., 3/6/18; F; 2/Lieut. 141 Wentworth Road, Golders Green, N.W. 11.

MASTERS, Reginald William
4/Sq/5142, 26/7/15, L/C.; R.A.S.C., 6/10/15, R. Ir. Rif.; F; Capt.; Inv. a/British Vice-Consul, Bogota, Colombia, South America.

MASTERTON, Ronald John
6/8898, 13/1/16; No. 9 O.C.B., 8/3/16; R. Highrs., 6/7/16; Lieut. Belmont, New Town, Ashford.

MASUREL, Gaston Francis Vivian
C/A/12286, 3/12/17; R.F.C., C/S, 15/2/18, No. 9 O.C.B.; demob. 78 Temple Fortune Lane, Hampstead, N.W. 3.

MATCHAM, Henry David Laird
F/3079, 19/3/15, L/C.; R.N.D., 2/8/15; F; Lieut.; w(2).
The Croft, Cliffsea Grove, Leigh-on-Sea, Essex.

MATHER, Alfred Lushington
Sq/176, 29/4/08; dis. 28/4/09.

MATHER, Leonard Wright
6/5/6752, 7/10/15; No. 7 O.C.B., 6/4/16; North'd. Fus., 17/7/16, secd. R.F.C.; Lieut. Padock Road, Audlem, Cheshire.

MATHESON, Robert
4/5/4800, 12/7/15; North'n. R., 13/12/15; F; Capt.; Inv.; M.C.
12 Salisbury Road, Leicester.

MATHEWS, Charles Jehu
B/D/12014, 17/9/17; R.F.C., C/S, 26/11/17; dis. med. unfit, 2/6/19. White Lodge, Bushy Park Road, Rathgar, Dublin.

MATHEWS, Norman Hugh
6/3/6132, 9/9/15, L/C.; Suff. R., 1/6/16, M.G.C.; F; Capt.; w.
12 Savile Row, W. 1.

MATHEWS, Thomas Gurney
6/Sq/8441, 16/12/15, L/C.; A.S.C., C/S, 27/10/16; R.A.S.C., 20/12/16; Lieut. Holmsdale, Lansdown Road, Worthing.

MATHEWS, Wilfrid Clarkson
K/E/2395, 17/12/14; R.E., 10/3/15; E,P; Capt.
7 Cannon Street, Birmingham.

✠ MATHIAS, John Harold Tudor
6/1/7932, 29/11/15; No. 14 O.C.B., 28/8/16; Welch R., 18/12/16; 2/Lieut.; w. Killed in action 25/11/17.

MATHIAS, William Douglas
3/9626, 21/9/16; No. 14 O.C.B., 5/3/17; trfr. R.F.A., 16/5/17.
The Garth, Pontypridd, South Wales.

MATHIESON, Douglas
K/B/2205, 30/11/14; R. Highrs., 7/1/15; Lieut.
50 Princes Gate, S.W. 7.

✠ MATHIESON, John
E/1582, 6/10/14, L/C.; Arg. & Suth'd. Highrs., 14/12/14, att Sea. Highrs.; 2/Lieut. Killed in action 5/8/18.

MATTHEWS, Alonzo Morgan
B/13456, 3/7/18; trfr. K.R. Rif. C., 25/4/19, R.E. Sigs.; Pte.
Dolphin, Landore, Swansea, South Wales

MATTHEWS, Basil Hugh
6/Sq/6207, 13/9/15; No. 2 Cav. C/S, 31/3/16; Oxf. Huss. Yeo., 19/8/16; F; Capt.; w.
Elmhurst, Church Avenue, Sidcup, Kent. (Now in South India).

MATTHEWS, Bertie John Andrew
A/9845, 3/11/16, L/C.; R.G.A., C/S, 18/7/17; R.G.A., 9/12/17; F; Lieut. West Park, Tamerton Foliot, South Devonshire.

MATTHEWS, Cecil Stanley St. Clair
6/4/7464, 15/11/15; Oxf. & Bucks. L. I., 4/9/16, att. Durh. L.I.; F; Capt. 68 Wenham Drive, Westcliff-on-Sea.

MATTHEWS, Edward Francis
A/1171, 14/9/14; Wilts. R., 27/11/14; Lieut.

MATTHEWS, Gaspard Hewett
C/B/12666, 27/2/18; No. 11 O.C.B., 23/8/18; General List. 8/3/19; 2/Lieut. Thornton Hale, Aysgarth, Yorkshire.

MATTHEWS, Henry Salter
6/3/7511, 15/11/15; dis. med. unfit, 31/5/16.
134 Gordon Hill, Enfield.

MATTHEWS, Herbert George William
4/6/Sq/4866, 15/7/15; R.F.C., 11/8/16, R.N.V.R.; Sub. Lieut.
Westfield, Bloomfield Road, Bath.

MATTHEWS, Horace Arthur
B/13626, 25/7/18; demob. 29/1/19.
112 West Wycombe Road, High Wycombe, Buckinghamshire.

MATTHEWS, Hugh Trevor
6/Sq/6718, 9/10/15, L/C.; No. 1 Cav. C/S, 24/4/16; Ches. Yeo., 28/7/16, R.A.F.; F; Lieut.; w.
Wayside, Hoylake, Cheshire.

MATTHEWS, Laurence Dore
4/2/5205, 29/7/15; Devon. R., 8/6/16; M; Lieut.
46 Alexandra Road, St John's Wood, N.W. 8.

MATTHEWS, Norman Louis
B/13466, 5/7/18; demob. 29/1/19.
45 Tyrwhitt Road, St. John's, Brockley, S.E. 4.

MATTHEWS, Pryce
B/D/12220, 12/11/17; Tank Corps C/S, 12/4/18; Tank Corps, 20/3/19; 2/Lieut. Lulworth House, Spa Road, Milksham, Wiltshire.

MATTHEWS, Reginald Percy
D/12939, 17/4/18; No. 11 O.C.B., 4/10/18; Midd'x. R., 17/3/19; 2/Lieut. 66 Alexandra Park Road, Muswell Hill, N. 10.

MATTHEWS, Stanley Norris
D/13733, 2/8/18; demob. 23/1/19.
Kent House, 33 Redington Road, Hampstead, N.W. 3.

MATTHEWS, Trevor Jocelyn
B/351, 4/3/09; dis. 22/6/10.

MATTHEWS, Victor James
C/801, 25/5/14; S. Lan. R., 18/9/14, att. Manch. R.; G,I,M; Lieut. 46 Alexandra Road, St. Johns Wood, N.W. 8.

✠ MATTHEWS, William Henry
D/10879, 12/3/17; R.G.A., C/S, 6/6/17; R.G.A., 1/10/17; 2/Lieut. Killed in action 28/9/18.

MATTINGLEY, Eric Graham
K/F/2501, 31/12/14; Lan. Fus., 22/4/15, R.A.F.; F; Lieut.; w.
Rowetts Farm, East Church, Isle of Sheppey, Kent.

MATTISON, John George
D/12931, 15/4/18; Sigs. C/S, 31/5/18; demob.
36 First Avenue, Mortlake, S.W. 14.

MATTISON, William
6/1/5728, 19/8/15, L/C.; Linc. R., 1/6/16; F; Capt.; w(2).
116 De la Pole Avenue, Hull.

✠ MAUD, Frederick
6/3/D/6911, 18/10/15, L/C.; M.G.C., C/S, 1/7/17; M.G.C., 29/3/17; F; 2/Lieut. Killed in action 20/9/17.

APPENDIX II.—RECORDS OF RANK AND FILE.

MAUDE, Charles Raymond
E/1642, 9/10/14; N. Lan. R., 5/11/14; Major; O.B.E., M.C., M(2). The Barns, Eastcote, Middlesex.

MAUDE, Evelyn John
Sq/180, 30/4/08; dis. 29/4/10.

✠ MAUDE, John William Ashley
K/2170, 26/11/14; K.R. Rif. C., 15/12/14; 2/Lieut.
Killed in action 24/8/15.

MAUGHAN, Archibald Dickson Kilgour
D/12888, 5/4/18; No. 2 O.C.B., 20/9/18; Gds. M.G.R., 10/3/19; 2/Lieut. c/o J. Strachan Esq., Netherley, Dallar, N.B.

MAUGHAN, Rupert William
A/Sq/12459, 21/1/18; No. 1 Cav. C/S, 3/9/18; 4th R. Regt. of Cav., 13/3/19; 2/Lieut. Pantile Farm, Hawkins, Nr. Folkestone.

MAUGHAN, William Bainbridge
C/10178, 12/12/16; trfr. R.F.A., 17/4/17.
13 Harris Street, Middlesborough.

MAUL, Gerald Broughton
B/1106, 7/9/14; Oxf. & Bucks. L.I., 17/11/14; Capt.
44 Paulton's Square, Chelsea, S.W.3

MAULE, Edward George Frederick
B/10983, 2/4/17; R.F.A., C/S, 17/12/17; Durh. L.I., 11/9/18; 2/Lieut. Godmanchester, Huntingdonshire.

MAULE, Harry Carteret
B/1041, 26/8/14; N Staff. R., 2/10/14, att. N. Lan. R. and No. 5 O.C.B. Inst.; F; Capt.; w.
The Bungalow, East Bergholt, Suffolk.

MAUNDER, Harold Frederick
6/3/6404, 23/9/15; trfr. 13th Lond. R., 5/5/16.
Red House, Addlestone, Surrey.

✠ MAURICE, Sterling
Sq/156, 18/4/08; dis. 17/4/10; rej. Sq/817, 4/8/14; R.E., 1/9/14; 2/Lieut.; M(1). Died of wounds 11/5/15.

MAW, John Sidney
A/13976, 9/9/18; trfr. K.R. Rif. C., 7/4/19.
13 St. John's Hill, Shrewsbury, Shropshire.

MAWER, Walter Leslie
C/11493, 14/6/17; No. 16 O.C.B., 5/10/17; Linc. R., 12/3/18, secd. M.G.C.; F; Lieut. 40 Silver Street, Lincoln.

MAWER, William
6/5/8006, 29/11/15; R.F.A., C/S, 15/7/16; trfr. L'pool. R., 25/10/16. 197 Beacon Lane, Liverpool.

MAWLE, Norman William Reginald
6/2/7362, 10/11/15; 20th Lond. R., 4/9/16, att. R.A.F.; F; Lieut; w(3); D.F.C. 14 Oxford Road, Banbury, Oxon.

MAWN, Alfred Ernest
E/6/1554, 6/10/14, Sgt.; R.A.O.C., 24/5/16; F; Lieut.; Inv.
8 Sylvia Gardens, Wembley, Middlesex.

MAXTED, Godfrey Vincent John
4/3786, 27/5/15, L/C.; R.N.A.S., 9/12/15, E. York. R., att. R.A.F.; F; Lieut. Ellaughton, Brough, East Yorkshire.

✠ MAXWELL, Arthur Edwin
A/C/D/B/12184, 1/11/17; R.E., C/S, 14/4/18; R.E., 15/8/18; 2/Lieut. Died 18/3/20.

MAXWELL, David Henry
A/D/13062, 13/5/18, Sgt.; trfr. K.R. Rif. C., 23/5/19; R. Marines, 3/9/20; NR; Lieut.; M.S.M., Silver Medal of S. Anne.
14 Highfield Avenue, Hendon, N.W.11.

MAXWELL, Ernest William
4/9606, 29/8/16; No. 14 O.C.B., 10/1/17; 15th Lond. R., 25/4/17, att. and Lond. R.; F; Lieut.; w.
Westoe Villa, South Shields, Co. Durham.

MAXWELL, Frederic Mackenzie
Sq/565, 5/4/11; dis. 30/3/14; City of Lond. Yeo., M.G.C.; Capt.

MAXWELL, George Sydney
6/5/Sq/5809, 23/8/15; R.A., C/S, 8/11/16; R.F.A., 21/4/17; F; Lieut.; w. c/o Bain, Calera, Tanderagh, Co. Armagh, Ireland.

MAXWELL, Herbert Percy
6/1/5820, 26/8/15; E. York. R., 18/6/16; EA; Lieut.
White House, Purston, Nr. Pontefract, Yorkshire.

MAXWELL, Robert
D/E/13698, 29/7/18; No. 22 O.C.B., 20/9/18; R. Scots, 5/2/19; 2/Lieut. 22 Queensberry Terrace, Edinburgh.

✠ MAXWELL, Robert Greenwood
K/H/2516, 31/12/14; Sea. Highrs., 20/3/15; M; Capt.
Killed in action 7/1/16.

MAXWELL-LAWFORD, Francis
6/4/5412, 5/8/15; Suff. R., 19/1/16, Midd'x. R.; F; Capt.; w; M(1). 1st Suffolk Regt., India.

MAY, Charles Henry
A/914, 5/8/14; R. Suss. R., 12/9/14, Tank Corps; Capt.; M.C.
Pine Lodge, Byfleet Road, Weybridge.

MAY, Frank
A/10731, 12/2/17, L/C.; No. 14 O.C.B., 7/6/17; 7th Lond. R., 25/9/17, att. 14th Lond. R.; F; Lieut.; w.
Vogelfontein P.O., Delport's Hope, Cape Colony, South Africa.

MAY, Frederick William John
6/8395, 14/12/15; R.F.A., C/S, 9/6/16; R.F.A., 28/8/16; F; Lieut.; M.C. Caldecott Farm, Abingdon, Berkshire.

MAY, Harry Michael
D/10230, 29/12/16; No. 14 O.C.B., 5/5/17; Ches. R., 28/8/17; 2/Lieut.; w. 59 St. Pauls Road, Tottenham, N.17.

MAY, Henry William
3/3071, 18/3/15; E. Surr. R., 31/12/15, M.G.C.; F; Capt.
Tigh-na-bruiach, Duluain Bridge, Grantoun-on-Spey.

MAY, Herbert James
4/2/4232, 14/6/15; Essex R., 21/4/16, emp. M. of Munitions; Lieut. Puckerton Lodge, Pepys Road, Raynes Park, S.W.19.

MAY, Jonathan
D/13699, 31/7/18; trfr. Gord. Highrs., 6/5/19.
Willow Dene, Park Crescent, Milton, Portsmouth.

MAY, Percy Robert
Sq/396, 31/3/09; dis. 20/3/11.

MAY, Reginald William
B/10102, 4/12/16; R.F.A., C/S, 14/7/17; trfr. Class W. Res., 14/3/18. 70 Belgrave Road, Warwick Square, S.W.1.

✠ MAY, Richard Trelawny
A/904, 5/8/14; R. Suss. R., 12/9/14; Capt.; M(1).
Killed in action 7/7/16.

✠ MAY, William Ernest Edward Frederick
4/2/4606, 5/7/15; 22nd Lond. R., 14/12/15; F; 2/Lieut.
Killed in action 24/11/16.

MAYBURY, Arthur Harrison
D/11869, 16/8/17; No. 3 O.C.B., 8/2/18; R. Berks. R., 30/7/18; 2/Lieut. Graty, The Green, Wanstead, Essex.

MAYCOCK, Martin George
C/14208, 21/10/18; trfr. K.R. Rif. C., 7/4/19.
5 Muister Yard, York.

MAYER, Alfred
1315, 26/9/14; 22nd Lond. R., 27/9/14; Capt.
32 Pembridge Gardens, W.2.

✠ MAYER, John Stuart
4/3973, 3/6/15; Manch. R., 6/12/15, att. T.M. Bty.; F; Lieut.
Killed in action 29/1/18.

MAYES, Thomas Frederick
D/13778, 7/8/18; demob. 18/2/19.
Harden-Dene, 2 Victoria Parade, Morecambe

MAYHEW, Herbert Alfred
B/1266, 23/9/14; L'pool. R., 10/11/14; F; Capt.; w.
135 Lauderdale Mansions, Maida Vale.

MAYNARD, George
6/Sq/5696, 18/8/15; R.F.A., 28/10/15, emp. M. of Munitions; M; Lieut.; Inv. 140 Waldegrave Road, Preston Park, Brighton.

MAYNARD, Herbert Arthur Vernon
B/1656, 9/10/14; R.W. Fus., 7/11/14; Lieut.; w.
70 St. Georges Road, Warwick Square.

MAYNE, Thomas Gordon
4/3862, 31/5/15; N. Staff. R., 5/9/15, att. Yorks. L.I.; F; Capt.
9 Sea Lawn, Dawlish, South Devonshire.

✠ MAYSON, Frank Eric Hutton
4/3/4081, 7/6/15; Yorks. L.I., 13/12/15; 2/Lieut.
Killed in action 28/8/16.

APPENDIX II.—RECORDS OF RANK AND FILE.

✠ MAZENGARB, George Richard Bostock
K/F/2583, 4/1/15; E. Surr. R., 31/3/15; F; 2/Lieut.
Killed in action 29/7/16.

MEACHER, Arthur Augustine
6/Sq/5711, 19/8/15; R.A.S.C., 9/10/15; G,E,M; Capt.
St. Margarets, Hemel Hempsted, Hertfordshire.

MEAD, Alan Phillips
Sq/851, 4/8/14; 16th Lanc., 15/8/14, att. M.G.C.; F; Lieut.; w; M.C.
St. Marys, Teddington, Middlesex.

✠ MEAD, Christopher
C/454, 20/12/09; E. Surr. R., 15/8/14; Lieut.
Killed in action 28/9/15.

MEAD-BRIGGS, Henry
E/14181, 14/10/18; demob. 10/1/19.
158 Edmund Street, Birmingham.

MEADE, James Christopher
6/2/8031, 30/11/15; No. 13 O.C.B., 4/11/16; Bedf. R., 28/2/17; F,It; Lieut.
7 Cedars Road, Beckenham, Kent.

MEADE, Joaquin Philip
B/C/12711, 8/3/18; No. 11 O.C.B., 24/1/19; demob. 6/2/19.
Manche & Coy., 86 Gresham House, Old Broad Street, E.C.

✠ MEADE, Richard Gilbert Trevor
Sq/833, 4/8/14; R. Regt. of Cav., 12/9/14, M.G.C.; 2/Lieut.
Died of wounds 10/10/17.

MEADOWS, Edgar William
6/5/5452, 7/8/15, L/C.; N. Lan. R., 6/12/15; F; Lieut.; w.
3 Sutton Road, Heaton Norris, Stockport.

MEADOWS, Francis Edward
6/3/7050, 28/10/15; W. Rid. R., 6/6/16; F; Lieut.; w.
35 Duke Road, Chiswick, W.

MEADOWS, George Denis
D/11807, 9/8/17, L/C.; No. 14 O.C.B., 4/1/18; M.G.C., 25/6/18; F; 2/Lieut.
122 Nightingale Lane, S.W.12. (Now in U.S.A.).

MEADOWS, William
C/10365, 5/1/17; trfr. R.G.A., 27/4/17.
7 Bank Street, Cherry Tree, Blackburn.

MEAKIN, Bernard
Sq/3232, 12/4/15, L/C.; R.A.S.C., 16/8/15; F; Capt.
Dorlaston Hall, Stone, Staffordshire.

MEAKIN, Frank Percival
6/4/6361, 20/9/15; No. 11 O.C.B., 7/5/16; 20th Lond. R., 4/9/16, att. Tank Corps; F; Lieut.; w.
14 Dorset Mansions, 390 Lillie Road, S.W. 6.

MEARS, Arnold de Quincey
6/3/8968, 17/1/16; Garr. O.C.B., 15/1/17; E. Kent R., 10/3/17; Lieut.
Little Bardfield Rectory, Braintree, Essex. (Now in Japan).

MEARS, Richard Alic Fielders
4/2/5121, 26/7/15; Notts. & Derby. R., 6/7/16, att. R.A.F.; F; Lieut.
12 Polstead Road, Oxford.

MEASURES, Leonard John
3/3787, 27/5/15, L/C,; R.A.S.C., 16/10/15; S; Capt.
Keystone, Huntingdonshire.

MEDHURST, Charles Frederick
D/11020, 11/4/17; R.G.A., C/S, 12/9/17; R.G.A., 22/4/18; F; 2/Lieut.
c/o Nat. Prov. Bank of England Ltd., Leamington Spa.

MEDILL, Thomas Herbert
B/E/13588, 22/7/18; R.G.A., C/S, 2/10/18; R.G.A., 11/4/19; 2/Lieut.
Rostrevor, Hill Crest Road, Purley, Surrey.

MEDWAY, Leonard John
B/10335, 4/1/17; R.A., C/S, 27/4/17; R.G.A., 1/9/17; F; Lieut.
22 Colliton Street, Dorchester, Dorset.

✠ MEDWORTH, Frank Oswald
C/1892, 16/10/14; Manch. R., 24/11/14; Capt.; w; M.C.
Killed in action 13/5/18.

✠ MEECHAM, Daniel Jeffreys
6/4/7463, 15/11/15; R.W Fus., 4/9/16; 2/Lieut.
Killed in action 27/3/17.

MEEKE, Bernard Dawe
4/2/3974, 3/6/15; R.G.A., 18/8/15; F; Lieut.; M(l).
Libury Hall Fruit Farm, Nr. Ware, Hertfordshire.

✠ MEEKE, William Stanley
A/956, 5/8/14; Midd'x. R., 15/8/14; F; Capt.; M.C.
Killed in action 1/7/16.

MEERING, Sydney Edward
6/1/D/6133, 9/9/15; No. 6 O.C.B., 15/2/17; R.F.C., 25/4/17, R.A.F.; F; Lieut.
c/o Aldous & Campbell, Lower Bland Street, S.E.

MEERS, Charles Harry
6/Sq/6465, 27/9/15, L/C.; Derby. Yeo., 24/8/17; S; 2/Lieut.
13 Hervey Road, Blackheath, S.E. 3.

✠ MEES, Ian Rudolf
C/10063, 1/12/16; R.F.C., C/S, 16/4/17; R.F.C., 16/5/17, R.A.F.; Lieut.
Killed 14/11/18.

MEGGY, Ernest Radvers
A/12517, 31/1/18; No. 2 O.C.B., 7/6/18; Essex R., 5/2/19; 2/Lieut.
St. Venant, Broomhill Road, Woodford Green.

MEGLAUGHLIN, John Greenacre
B/13523, 12/7/18; demob. 14/5/19.
Rockhurst, West Hoathly, Sussex.

MEIKLE, Lawrence Avondale
4/3327, 19/4/15; N. Cyc. Bn., 7/9/15, att. Manch. R., North'd. Fus.; F; Lieut.; g.
Winscombe, Pinner, Middlesex.

MEIKLEM, William Halliday
A/D/11935, 30/8/17, Sgt.; demob. 22/1/19.
6 Stanley Avenue, Norwich.

MEIKLEREID, Kenneth
6/Sq/6722, 9/10/15; No. 1 Cav. C/S, 24/4/16; Worc. Yeo., 27/9/16; E,P; Lieut.; w.
Knighton, 32 Rodway Road, Bromley, Kent.

MELLOR, Harry Albinson
6/2/5904, 30/8/15, L/C.; No. 2 Cav. C/S, 18/5/16; Worc. Yeo., 6/9/16, secd. M.G.C. and Tank Corps; F; Lieut.; w.
15 Beaufort Road, Edgbaston, Birmingham.

MELLOR, Samuel Hall
6/1/5604, 14/8/15, L/C.; trfr. R. Berks. R., 21/7/16.
14 Woodland Crescent, Muswell Hill Road, N. 10.

✠ MELVILLE, Henry Colquhoun
A/1634, 9/10/14; Notts. & Derby. R., 10/2/15; 2/Lieut.
Killed in action 14/2/16.

MELVILLE, William George
A/12460, 27/1/18; R.F.A., C/S, 26/7/18; R.G.A., 8/4/19; F; 2/Lieut.
51 Whitbread Road, Brockley, S.E. 4.

MELVILLE-BERGHEIM, Charles Melville
B/603, 24/1/12; dis. 25/4/13.

MENDEL, Bernard Francis
6/3/5807, 23/8/15; Linc. R., 25/12/15, att. Gord. Highrs.; F; Lieut.; w.
81 Avenue Road, Regents Park, N.W. 8.

MENDL, Anthony Lionel
C/939, 5/8/14, L/C.; Interpreter, 13/11/14.
27 Victoria Square, S.W. 1.

MENDL, Louis Ernest
D/1415, 29/9/14; R.A.S.C., 25/11/14; F,Sp; Capt.
Reform Club, Pall Mall, S.W.

MENNELL, John Smith
A/D/12534, 31/1/18; R.F.C., C/S, 21/5/18; trfr. R.A.F.
8 Haddon Place, Leeds.

MENY-GILBERT, Marcel Arthur
1/3423, 29/4/15; Worc. R., 7/10/15; Lieut.
41 Keith Road, Shepherds Bush, W. 12.

MENZIES, Charles Edward Kenneth
A/1195, 14/9/14; R. Highrs., 27/11/14; F; 2/Lieut.; Inv.
St. Stephens Club, Westminster, S.W. 1.

MENZIES, James Joseph Walter
4/1/4004, 3/6/15; L'pool. R., 7/10/15; 2/Lieut.
118 Abbey Road, West Hampstead, N.W. 6.

MENZIES-JONES, Llewellyn Frederick
4/3268, 15/4/15; E. Surr. R., 28/7/15; F; Capt.
Ravenswood, Kingston Hill, Surrey.

MERCER, Ernest Cedric
C/9958, 20/11/16; No. 14 O.C.B., 30/1/17; Dorset R., 29/5/17, att. R.A.F.; Lieut.
4 Alexandra Drive, Aintree, Liverpool.

APPENDIX II.—RECORDS OF RANK AND FILE.

MERCER, Frank
6/5/5979, 1/9/15; N. Lan. R., 24/10/16, att. T.M. Bty. and Admiralty; F; Lieut.; w.
14 Saville Road, Stoneycroft, Liverpool.

MERCER, William Trevor
A/10504, 15/1/17; R.G.A., C/S, 1/5/17; R.G.A., 1/8/17; Lieut.
c/o Standard Bank of South Africa Ltd., 10 Clements Lane, E.C.

MERCHANT, Alexander Walker
6/4/6769, 11/10/15; No. 11 O.C.B.; 20th Lond. R., 4/9/16, R.F.C., R.A.F.; F; Capt.; Inv.
Burgoyne, Elm Park Road, Winchmore Hill, N.21.

MEREDITH, James
4/2/4629, 5/7/15, Sgt.; R.A., C/S, 7/8/16; R.F.A., 3/12/16; F; Lieut.; M.C., M(1).
Comberton Road, Kidderminster.

✠ MEREDITH, Owen Watkin Wynn Hardinge
6/2/8365, 13/12/15; R.F.C., C/S, 8/10/16; R.F.C., 16/3/17; F; 2/Lieut. Died of wounds 20/11/17 as Prisoner of War.

✠ MEREDITH-THOMAS, Stanley
D/10415, 10/1/17; R.A., C/S, 8/6/17; R.F.A., 23/2/18; 2/Lieut.
Died 13/12/18.

MERIVALE, Bernard
Sq/264, 30/5/08; dis. 29/5/11.

MERNAGH, Laurence Reginald
A/D/11955, 3/9/17; No. 20 O.C.B., 8/3/18; Essex R., 10/9/18, att. Bedf. R.; F; Lieut. 6 Grosvenor Road, Highbury, N.5.

MERRICKS, Lionel Marten
4/3863, 31/5/15; D. of Corn. L.I., 1/11/15, secd. M.G.C.; F,M,P; Lieut. 38 Devizes Road, Swindon, Wiltshire.

MERRIKIN, Alec Edward
4/2/4082, 7/6/15; North'd. Fus., 11/8/15; 2/Lieut.

MERRILEES, Alexander Charles Belbin
6/8652, 3/1/16; No. 9 O.C.B., 8/3/16; Arg. & Suth'd. Highrs, 6/7/16; F; Lieut. 8 Wellesley Grove, Croydon, Surrey.

MERRIMAN, John Richard
6/5/C/7512, 15/11/15, trfr. R.G.A., 10/11/16.
1 Northfield Road, Stamford Hill, N.16.

✠ MERRIMAN, William Robert Hill
A/202, 6/5/08; dis. 5/5/13; Rif. Brig.; 2/Lieut.
Killed in action 15/8/16.

MERRITT, Walter
A/2929, 15/2/15; R.A.O.C., 27/5/15; F; Capt.
19 Molyneux Park, Tunbridge Wells.

MERRY, Douglas Gerald
6/5/C/7773, 23/11/15; No. 14 O.C.B., 30/10/16; E. Kent R., 28/2/17; M,I; Lieut. 18 Bushnell Road, S.W.17.

MESSUM, Alexander Wilson
3/3311, 19/1/15, L/C.; S. Lan. R., 2/9/15; Lieut.

✠ METCALF, David
6/4/7363, 10/11/15, L/C.; 7th Lond. R., 10/6/16; Lieut.
Killed in action 20/4/18.

✠ METCALF, Lester
4/1/4287, 17/6/15; R. Lanc. R., 21/1/16; 2/Lieut.
Killed in action 8/8/16.

METCALF, Rowland Garratt
3/5206, 29/7/15; R. Lanc. R., 2/1/16; F; Capt.; w(2).
9 The Avenue, Durham.

METCALFE, Albert Thomas
F/2958, 22/2/15; Shrop. L.I., 21/6/15, M.G.C.; F; Lieut.; w.
Upwey, Cornwall Road, Sutton, Surrey.

METCALFE, George Arthur
A/12518, 31/1/18, L/C.; No. 18 O.C.B., 9/8/18; R. Ir. Rif., 6/3/19; It; 2/Lieut.; Italian Bronze Medal.
Hawthornden House, Kusch, Belfast.

✠ METCALFE, Harry
6/5/5518, 9/8/15; Notts. & Derby. R., 26/12/15; 2/Lieut.
Killed in action 4/4/17.

METCALFE, John Francis
2/3650, 17/5/15; Essex R., 7/11/15; 2/Lieut.; Inv. Sub. Lieut., R.N., att. R.N.A.S. 60 Old Park Road, Palmers Green, N.13.

METCALFE, John Joseph
K/D/2144, 19/11/14; Essex R., 7/3/15, R.A.F.; Capt.

METCALFE, Ralph Ismay
D/10925, 26/3/17; R.F.C., C/S, 4/5/17; R.F.C., 13/7/17, R.A.F.; F; Flt. Cmdr.; M(1). 23 Carlton Road, Putney, S.W.15.

METHERELL, Harold Donovan
6/5/C/5851, 16/10/15; trfr. R.G.A., 10/11/16.
Durleston, Merchant Street, Bognor.

METHVEN, Malcolm David
Sq/786, 8/5/14; 10th Lond. R., 28/8/14, R.A.F.; F; Lt.-Col.; O.B.E., M(3).
Chiltern, Eastbury Avenue, Northwood, Middlesex.

METTAM, Edward John Hubert
6/5/6696, 7/10/15; No. 8 O.C.B., 4/8/16; K.O. Sco. Bord., 21/11/16, att. Bord. R.; 2/Lieut.

MEW, Philip William Theodore
6/4/6069, 6/9/15; R.A.S.C., 8/11/15; F; Capt.
102 Upper Thames Street, E.C.

✠ MEYER, Alan Wallace
6/5/7822, 24/11/15; trfr. R.G.A., 6/10/16; 2/Lieut.
Died 11/3/18.

MEYER, Bernard Henry
6/Sq/8071, 1/12/15; R.A., C/S, 15/9/16; R.F.A., 6/2/17; WA,F; Lieut.; g. 19 Longton Avenue, Sydenham, S.E.26.

✠ MEYER, Llewellyn
6/4/6229, 13/9/15; Durh. L.I., 21/12/15; 2/Lieut.
Killed in action 11/6/16.

MEYRICK, Basil George
B/10113, 4/12/16, L/C.; R.G.A., C/S, 25/4/17; R.G.A., 18/3/18; F; Lieut., D.A.P.M.
Royal Canadian Mounted Police, Regina, Canada.

MEYRICK, Edric Gladstone
4/3975, 3/6/15; Midd'x. R., 10/12/15; F; Lieut.; w.
32 West End Lane, Hampstead, N.W.6.

MEYRICK, William Charles Frederick
4/3/4401, 24/6/15, L/C.; Devon. R., 8/6/16; Capt.; w(2); M C.
Moure Wise, Falmouth.

MEYSEY-THOMPSON, Hubert Charles
C/980, 5/8/14, L/C.; R. Berks. R., 20/10/14, K.R. Rif. C.; F; Capt.; w. 74 Oxford Terrace, Hyde Park, W.2.

MICHELL, Cyril Leslie
K/H/2307, 10/12/14; R. Suss. R., 31/3/15; F; Capt.; w; M.C.
Normanhurst, Main Road, Romford, Middlesex.

MICHELL, Frank William
6/5/7934, 29/11/15; R.F.C., 2/6/16, R.A.F.; Lieut.

MICHELL, Frederick Charles
6/2/7269, 8/11/15; trfr. 13th Lond. R., 2/5/16; 13th Lond. R.; F,S; Capt.
The Grove, Crows Nest, St. Cleer, Nr. Lickard, Cornwall.

MICHELL, John Henry
Sq/2978, 25/2/15, L/C.; Norf. Yeo., 7/6/15, Indian Army; G,E,P; Capt.
The Rectory, St. Sennen R.S.O., Cornwall. (Now in India).

MICHELSON, Alfred
A/12, 1/4/08; Interpreter, 8/9/14, att. Indian Army and Manch. R.; F; Capt. Cavendish Club, 119 Piccadilly, W.1.

MICHIE, George Bennet Thomson
6/9560, 1/3/16; M.G.C., C/S, 6/12/16; M.G.C., 30/1/17; F; Capt.; Inj. The Manse, Gourock, Scotland.

MICKLEM, Edward Romilly
6/5/9115, 24/1/16; R.F.A., C/S, 4/8/16; R.G.A., 26/11/16; F; Lieut. Mansfield College, Oxford.

MICKLEWOOD, Ernest Philip
6/6344, 20/9/15; R.F.A., 7/11/15; SWA,F; Major; M(1).
15 Beechwood Avenue, N.10. (Now in South Africa).

✠ MICKLEWRIGHT, James
C/11520, 18/6/17; R.E., C/S, 11/11/17; R.E., 21/12/17; F; 2/Lieut.; g. Killed in action 3/11/18.

MIDDLE, Reginald John
6/1/6627, 4/10/15; Som. L.I., 25/1/16; Capt.
The Cottage, Gilestone, St. Athan, Glamorganshire.

MIDDLETON, Clifford
A/1193, 14/9/14; Midd'x. R., 5/10/14; F; Staff Capt.; w(2).
24 Portland Place, W.1.

MIDDLETON, Frank Garside
B/2764, 21/1/15; R.F.A., 18/11/15; F; 2/Lieut.; Inv.
1 Chestnut Street, Southport, Lancashire.

MIDDLETON, George Paton
A/13130, 27/5/18; R.F.A., C/S, 26/7/18; demob.
13 Mount Stuart Street, Shautlands, Glasgow. (Now in Northern Rhodesia).

APPENDIX II.—RECORDS OF RANK AND FILE.

MIDDLETON, Hector Rowland
B/13610, 23/7/18; demob. 31/1/19.
2 High Street, Bushey.

MIDDLETON, John Ellis
6/2/7688, 22/11/15; R.E., C/S, 21/10/16; R.E., 13/1/17; Lieut.
Alandale, 7 Redcar Road, Blackpool.

MIDDLETON, Noel
A/10518, 15/1/17; Garr. O.C.B., 23/4/17; High. L.I., 16/6/17, att. Sea. Highrs.; Staff Lieut.
78 Oxford Terrace, Hyde Park, W. 2.

MIDDLETON, Thomas Percy
B/2738, 16/1/15; R.F.A., 16/5/15, secd. R.F.C., R.A.F.; F; Flt Cmdr,; D.F.C.
5 Rue Gretry, Paris.

MIDGLEY, Eric Lee
C/13277, 12/6/18; No. 24 O.C.B., 15/11/18; Tank Corps 23/3/19; 2/Lieut.
39 Dunkeld Road, Ecclesall, Sheffield.

MIDGLEY, Thomas Arthur
D/13700, 31/7/18; trfr. 14th Lond. R., 6/12/18.
30 Bedford Row, W.C. 1.

MILBANK, George Acclon
D/1432, 29/9/14; R.F.A., 1/10/14; Capt.; w.
c/o H. M. Paine Esq., 5 Beckenhall Mansions, W. 1.

MILBURN, John Davison
A/2046, 9/11/14; R. Highrs., 27/2/15; 2/Lieut.
Gwyzance, Acklington, Northumberland.

MILDENSTEIN, George
D/13874, 21/8/18; trfr. K.R. Rif. C., 7/4/19.
25 Hatherley Street, Princes Avenue, Liverpool.

MILES, Brinley Richard
B/12740, 11/3/18; No. 2 O.C.B., 20/9/18; R.W. Fus., 17/3/19; 2/Lieut.
Bryn Awel, Shotton, Chester.

MILES, Charles William
3/3702, 20/5/15, Cpl.; N. Lan. R., 15/9/15; F; Capt.
Savage Club, 6 Adelphi Terrace, W.C. 2.

✠ MILES, Gordon
4/1/4659, 5/7/15; York. R., 20/1/16; F; Lieut.
Killed in action 9/10/16.

✠ MILES, Leonard Percy
2/3459, 3/5/15; Dorset R., 28/7/15; 2/Lieut.
Killed in action 7/10/16.

MILES, Richard
A/14079, 30/9/18; trfr. K.R. Rif. C., 25/4/19, M.G.C.
Odstock, Instow, North Devonshire. (Now in Argentina).

✠ MILES, Robert William
F/1799, 16/10/14; Notts. & Derby. R., 28/11/14; Capt.
Killed in action 1/6/17.

MILES, William Harold
B/12775, 15/3/18; No. 20 O.C.B., 20/9/18, No. 18 O.C.B.; R.W. Kent R., 18/3/19; 2/Lieut.
37a Anerley Park, Anerley, S.E. 20.

MILES, William Henry
H/1959, 26/10/14; Som. L.I., 27/10/14; Capt.; w; M(1).

MILES, William John
B/9871, 6/11/16; No. 14 O.C.B., 6/4/17; N. Lan. R., 31/7/17; 2/Lieut.; w.
60 Anwell Street, E.C. 1.

MILLAR, David William Mackay
C/13211, 5/6/18; demob. 30/1/19.
Welton, Brough, East Yorkshire.

MILLAR, Eric George
4/2/4867, 15/7/15; E. Kent R., 14/9/15; I; Lieut.
28 Pembroke Gardens, Kensington, W. 8

✠ MILLAR, George William
B/D/12196, 5/11/17; No. 2 O.C.B., 10/5/18;
Died 30/10/18.

MILLAR, Robert Strachan Christie
C/10162, 11/12/16, L/C.; No. 14 O.C.B., 5/7/17; Indian Army, 30/10/17.
St. John's Mount, Bodinham Road, Hereford.

MILLARD, Gilbert
C/13192, 3/6/18, L/C.; demob. 4/3/19.
36 Mayfield Road, Sanderstead, Surrey.

MILLEN, Charles Reginald
6/1/8733, 5/1/16; No. 14 O.C.B., 26/11/16; 8th Lond. R., 27/3/17, secd. K. Af. Rif., Rif. Brig.; F,EA; Capt.; w; M.C., M(1).
33 Elm Park Avenue, Ranelagh, Dublin.

MILLEN, James Alec
6/1/5683, 16/8/15; R.W. Kent R., 15/1/16; M,I; Lieut.
Newton House, Newton Road, Faversham.

MILLEN, William James
D/11566, 28/6/17; R.F.C., C/S, 23/10/17; R.F.C., 29/12/17, R.A.F.; It; Lieut.
3 Nelson Street, Dublin, Ireland.

MILLER, Alan Eustace
Sq/1588, 6/10/14, Cpl.; 2nd Lovats Scouts, 23/2/15; Capt.
The Orchard, Meopham, Kent.

MILLER, Albert Edward
B/11397, 26/5/17; No. 11 O.C.B., 9/11/17; S. Staff. R., 30/4/18; 2/Lieut.

MILLER, Alexander
A/B/C/12143, 15/10/17; R.F.A., C/S, 15/3/18; R.F.A., 21/10/18; 2/Lieut.
c/o Mrs. Henderson, 77 New Street, Rothes, Elgin.

MILLER, Arthur William
D/11150, 26/4/17, L/C.; R.G.A., C/S, 27/12/17; R.G.A., 17/6/18; 2/Lieut.
10 Princes Road, Stamford, Lincolnshire.

MILLER, Cecil William Davies
6/8839, 10/1/16; R.A., C/S, 23/6/16; R.G.A., 27/9/16; 2/Lieut
Bond Vista, 52 Madeira Road, Streatham, S.W. 16.

MILLER, Cyril Frederick
A/11240, 8/5/17; R.F.C., C/S, 1/6/17; R.F.C., 4/7/17; resigned and rej. A/D/14080, 30/9/18;demob. 30/5/19.
Water Orton, Nr. Birmingham.

MILLER, David
B/11042, 9/4/17; R.F.C., C/S, 1/6/17; R.F.C., 4/7/17, R.A.F.; F; Lieut.; w-p.
Hill Farm, Hadleigh, Suffolk.

MILLER, Douglas Owen D'Elbon
Sq/770, 2/3/14; R.F.A., 27/10/15; Lieut.; M.C., M(1).

MILLER, Eric Douglas
4/6/5/4939, 19/7/15; R.A.S.C., 8/10/15; F; Capt.; M(1).
239 High Road, Kilburn, N.W. 6.

✠ MILLER, George Gibbs
6/1/7236, 5/11/15, L/C.; No. 11 O.C.B., 7/5/16; Manch. R., 4/9/16, R.E.; F,S; Lieut.; M(1)
Died 18/11/18.

MILLER, George Thurlow
B/11373, 28/5/17; No. 10 O.C.B., 5/10/17; R.W. Surr. R., 26/2/18; 2/Lieut.
No. 1 Flat, 11 Wyndham Crescent, Junction Road, N. 19.

MILLER, Henry Francis Swainson
D/10015, 27/11/16; No. 20 O.C.B., 5/5/17; L'pool. R., 25/9/17; 2/Lieut.

MILLER, Hugh
6/8141, 3/12/15; dis. med. unfit, 26/5/16.

MILLER, John
D/10928, 24/3/17; R.G.A., C/S, 15/8/17; R.G.A., 31/12/17; 2/Lieut.

MILLER, John McIntyre
C/14186, 18/10/18; dis. 5/2/19.
32 Burn Valley Road, West Hartlepool.

MILLER, Leonard James
6/7689, 22/11/15; No. 9 O.C.B., 8/3/16; Sea. Highrs., 6/7/16, att. E. Lan. R.; Lieut.
53 Kings Road, Peckham, S.E. 15.

MILLER, Louis Gerard
A/12444, 21/1/18; R.E., C/S, 16/6/18; trfr. 14th Lond. R., 6/12/18.
115 Earlshall Road, Eltham, S.E. 9.

MILLER, Maurice
6/4/8142, 3/12/15; A.S.C., C/S, 15/5/16; R.A.S.C., 18/6/16, att. R.G.A.; F; Lieut.
Cedars, Doebank, Sutton Coldfield.

MILLER, Paul Tennant
B/1108, 7/9/14; S. Wales Bord., 15/10/14, R.W. Fus.; Capt.; w.

MILLER, Percival Alexander
6/3/9520, 16/2/16, L/C.; No. 14 O.C.B., 27/9/16; S. Lan. R., 18/12/16; F; Capt.; w. g.
Acting Traffic Manager, Southern Railways of Peru, Arequipa, Peru, South America.

MILLER, Percy Frederick
B/Sq/10551, 17/1/17; R.F.A., C/S, 17/12/17; R.F.A., 3/6/18; F; 2/Lieut.
13 Coombe Gardens, New Malden, Surrey. (Now in Germany).

MILLER, Percy John
6/9218, 31/1/16; R.E., C/S, 18/3/16; R.E., 2/6/16, Lab. Corps; Capt.; M.C.
Municipal and County Club, Whitehall Court, S.W.

APPENDIX II.—RECORDS OF RANK AND FILE.

MILLER, Percy William
 6/4/8366, 13/12/15, Sgt.; A.S.C., C/S, 1/3/17; R.A.S.C., 27/4/17. M.G.C.; E,P; Lieut.
 Eccentric Club, Ryder Street, St. James, S.W.

MILLER, Robert Ernest
 C/13255, 10/6/18; trfr. 28th Lond. R., 13/11/18.
 156 Boundaries Road, Balham, S.W. 12.

MILLER, Thomas Oswald
 B/11990, 10/9/17; A.S.C., C/S, 1/11/17; R.A.S.C., 25/1/18; 2/Lieut.

✠ MILLER, William Edward
 6/3/6098, 6/9/15; 7th Lond. R., 19/11/15; 2/Lieut.
 Died of wounds 17/7/16.

MILLER-WILLIAMS, Eustace James
 6/2/5519, 9/8/15, L/C.; R.F.A., C/S, 17/3/16; R.F.A., 17/7/16; F; Lieut.; w.
 Penty Park, Clarbeston Road S.O., Pembrokeshire.

MILLIGAN, Derrick Warden
 H/1974, 26/10/14, Cpl.; Cam'n. Highrs., 27/3/15, R.A.S.C.; F; Lieut.
 Polmood, Broughton, Peebleshire.

✠ MILLIGAN, George Barry
 6/Sq/5776, 23/8/15, L/C.; R.F.A., 1/12/15; Lieut.; w.
 Killed in action 24/3/18.

MILLIGAN, Walter Humphreys
 6/Sq/8764, 6/1/16; R.F.A., C/S, 4/8/16; R.F.A., 12/1/17, att. T.M. Bty.; F; Lieut.; g.
 Oldcourt, Athlone, Ireland.

MILLIKEN, Ernest Norman
 6/4/5448, 7/8/15, L/C.; R.A.S.C., 8/11/15; Lieut.; M.B.E.
 208 Felixstowe Road, Ipswich.

✠ MILLIKEN, Frank Stevens
 6/5/5946, 1/9/15; L'pool. R., 1/6/16; F; 2/Lieut.
 Died of wounds 4/5/17.

MILLIKEN, Kenneth Edward
 A/98, 16/4/08; dis. 15/4/09; E. Surr. R.; Capt.
 c/o Cox & Coy. ("T" Branch), 16 Charing Cross, S.W. 1.

✠ MILLS, Ben Holt
 6/5/5759, 21/8/15; Manch. R., 21/12/15; 2/Lieut.
 Died of wounds 29/4/17.

MILLS, Cecil
 4/4194, 14/6/15; North'd. Fus., 9/6/16; F; Lieut.
 97 Lynton Road, Acton, W. 3.

MILLS, Daniel William
 D/11858, 13/8/17; M.G.C., C/S, 10/11/17; Tank Corps, 27/3/18; 2/Lieut.
 c/o Messrs. Blyth, Green, Jourdain & Coy., 47 King William Street, E.C.

MILLS, Edward
 E/13993, 11/9/18; demob. 10/1/19.
 Darley Dale, 48 Westmoreland Road, Urmston, Nr. Manchester.

MILLS, Frederick George
 1/3547, 10/5/15, L/C.; 8th Lond. R., 25/7/15; F; Lieut.; w; M(1).
 25 College Road, Ripon, Yorkshire.

MILLS, George Alfred
 Sq/1630, 9/10/14, Cpl.; York. Huss., 18/2/15; Capt.
 Dildawn, Woldingham, Surrey.

MILLS, Harry
 C/10406, 8/1/17; No. 14 O.C.B., 5/5/17; York. & Lanc. R., 28/8/17; F; Lieut.; g.
 62 Shaftmoor Lane, Acocks Green, Warwickshire.

MILLS, Horace Algernon William
 6/5/9521, 16/2/16; No. 8 O.C.B., 4/8/16; North'd. Fus., 21/11/16; F; Lieut.
 c/o G. Mills Esq., Bullard, King & Coy., Shipowners, 14 St. Mary Axe., E.C. (Now in South Africa).

✠ MILLS, John Birchall
 6/3/7364, 10/11/15; R.W. Fus., 4/8/16; 2/Lieut.
 Died of wounds 16/4/17.

MILL, Loighton
 A/Sq/C/12783, 20/1/18; R.E., C/S, 16/6/18; trfr. 14th Lond. R., 6/12/18.
 6 Lily Crescent, Jesmond, Newcastle-on-Tyne.

MILLS, Richard Charles
 6/2/8796, 8/1/16; R.A., C/S, 23/6/16; R.G.A., 27/9/16; F; Capt.; w; M(1).
 Department of Economics, Sydney University, Sydney, New South Wales, Australia.

MILLS, Thomas Trevenen
 B/10557, 19/1/17; R.F.C., C/S, 13/3/17; dis. med. unfit, 2/10/17.

✠ MILLSON, Alvan Ewen Abram
 B/1719, 15/10/14; R. Fus., 10/12/15; Capt.
 Killed in action 9/4/17.

MILLWARD, George Thomas
 B/13442, 3/7/18; demob. 29/1/19.
 2 Horncop Villas, Kendall, Westmorland.

✠ MILNE, Alexander Richard
 D/1425, 29/9/14; Herts. R., 28/10/14; F; Capt.
 Killed in action 31/7/17.

MILNE, Harold James
 6/5/9494, 15/2/16; No. 8 O.C.B., 4/8/16; Gord. Highrs., 18/12/16; F; Capt.; w; M.C.
 Auchtercrag, Ellon, Aberdeenshire.

MILNE, John
 A/13101, 22/5/18; No. 22 O.C.B., 5/7/18; R. Scots., 12/2/19; 2/Lieut.
 The Sheiling, Corstorphine, Midlothian.

MILNER, Frank Lewis
 C/11066, 16/4/17; R.F.C., C/S, 2/8/17; R.F.C., 8/9/17, R.A.F.; Lieut.
 31 Penkett Road, Liscard, Cheshire.

MILNER, John Sowerby
 F/3/2902, 11/2/15; R.W. Surr. R., 18/6/15; Lieut.; w.
 64 Quarrenden Street, Parsons Green, S.W. 6.

MILNER, William Townsend
 6/4/5565, 12/8/15; R.W. Surr. R., 11/11/15; 2/Lieut.

MILNES, Percy James
 B/11473, 11/6/17; Garr. O.C.B., 5/10/17; Worc. R., 15/12/17; Lieut.

MILROY, Arthur John Wallace
 Sq/113, 18/4/08; dis. 17/4/09.
 The Oart House, Farnham, Surrey.

MILTON, Frederick Albert
 1/Sq/9743, 16/10/16; R.A., C/S, 23/1/17; R.G.A., 9/9/17; Lieut.; M(1).
 42 Ordnance Road, St. Johns Wood, N.W.

MILTON, Harman Clarence Fairn
 6/Sq/5856, 26/8/15; R.F.A., C/S, 4/8/16; R.F.A., 9/12/16; Lieut.; w.
 Penlee, Carbis Bay, Cornwall.

MILTON, Herbert Reginald
 B/10577, 19/1/17; R.F.C., C/S, 13/3/17; R.F.C., 19/4/17, R.A.F.; Lieut.
 Sunny South, The Mount, Guildford, Surrey.

MILTON, Lewis
 6/3/7405, 12/11/15, L/C.; No. 11 O.C.B., 16/5/16; Glouc. R., 4/9/16; Germ.WA,F; 2/Lieut.; w.
 13 St. Ronan's Avenue, Redland, Bristol.

MILTON, Walter Henry
 A/D/13015, 1/5/18; R.E., C/S, 21/7/18, No. 11 O.C.B.; General List, 8/3/19; 2/Lieut.
 4 London Road, Northfleet, Kent.

MILWARD, Victor Walton
 D/13937, 2/9/18; demob. 29/1/19.
 144 Redlam, Witton, Blackburn.

MINCHIN, Thomas William
 3/3788, 27/5/15, Sgt.; Gren. Gds., 17/11/15; F; Capt.; w(2); D.S.O., M(2).
 Grantmoore, Bracknell, Berkshire.

MINETT, Aidan
 D/13845, 16/8/18; trfr. Gord. Highrs., 6/5/19, att. Cam'n. Highrs.
 Adlington Vicarage, Nr. Chorley, Lancashire.

MINETT, Oswald
 D/13846, 16/8/18; trfr. Gord. Highrs., 6/5/19, att. Cam'n. Highrs.
 Adlington Vicarage, Nr. Chorley, Lancashire.

MINSHALL, Thomas Herbert
 4/2944, 18/2/15; R.E., 16/3/15; F; Colonel, Asst. Director of Labour and Controller of Salvage G.H.Q.; D.S.O., M(2).
 9 Melbury Road, Kensington, W. 14.

MINTER, William Murton
 D/11154, 28/4/17, Sgt.; M.G.C., C/S, 7/12/17; M.G.C., 25/6/18; 2/Lieut.
 1 Summer Hill, Harbledown, Canterbury.

MINTON, Robert Samuel
 A/10987, 2/4/17; Garr. O.C.B., 23/5/17; Lab. Corps, 18/8/17, Devon. R.; 2/Lieut.
 10a Eaton Place, Kemp Town, Brighton.

MISKIN, Charles Leonard
 F/1750, 16/10/14, L/C.; H.A.C., 15/1/15, R.W. Kent R.; F; Staff Capt.; g; m(1).
 3 Penywern Road, Earls Court, S.W. 5.

MISKIN, Frank
 K/2834, 1/2/15; R.W. Kent. R., 4/2/15, Midd'x. R., Suff. R., York. R.; F,NR; Lt.-Col.; M.C.
 Loose, Nr. Maidstone.

APPENDIX II.—RECORDS OF RANK AND FILE.

MISKIN, *William*
H/2835, 1/2/15, L/C.; R.W. Kent R., 22/5/15, Midd'x. R., Suff. R.; F; Capt.   *Bolsham Lodge, Elmstead, Ashford, Kent.*

MISSING, *Claude Marler Stonhouse*
C/9924, 15/11/16; No. 14 O.C.B., 30/1/17; Dorset R., 29/5/17, att. Som. L.I. and W. Rid. R.; Afghan; Capt.
    c/o Lond. Joint City & Mid. Bank Ltd., Lewisham, S.E. 13.

MITCHELL, *Alexander Millar*
C/13382, 24/6/18; demob. 30/1/19.
    Dun-Edin, Castlebar Park Road, Ealing, W. 5.

MITCHELL, *David Cecil*
6/9484, 15/2/16; Chaplain, 16/5/16.
    St. Andrews Manse, Peebles.

MITCHELL, *David Cumming*
6/8886, 13/1/16; No. 9 O.C.B., 8/3/16; Arg. & Suth'd. Highrs., 6/7/16; Lieut.   *Bannockburn House, Bannockburn.*

MITCHELL, *Edward Grose Harper*
6/2/7553, 17/11/15, Cpl.; Rif. Brig., 25/9/16, att. No. 6 O.C.B. Inst; F; Capt.; w.
    The Cottage, Burley-in-Wharfedale, Nr. Leeds, Yorkshire.

MITCHELL, *Edward William*
Sq/3393, 26/4/15, Cpl.; R. Horse Gds., 2/10/15; F; Lieut.; M(1).
    Traveller's Club, Pall Mall, S.W. 1.

✠ MITCHELL, *Frank*
6/1/7300, 8/11/15; No. 11 O.C.B., 7/5/16; M.G.C., 4/9/16; 2/Lieut.   Killed in action 12/5/17.

MITCHELL, *Frederick Alexander*
B/13555, 19/7/18; trfr. R. Highrs., 16/4/19; L/C.
    c/o Crawford, 206 Battlefield Road, Langside, Glasgow.

MITCHELL, *Frederick George*
6/2/8072, 1/12/15; No. 8 O.C.B., 4/8/16; Dorset R., 21/11/16; Lieut.; w.   *169 Anerley Road, Anerley, S.E. 20.*

MITCHELL, *George*
B/1104, 7/9/14; Hamps. R., 27/11/14; F,S; Capt.; w.
    49 Duke Street, St. James, S.W. 1.

MITCHELL, *James Farey*
6/5/8599, 3/1/16; Special List, 24/7/16, R.A.S.C.; P; Capt.
    P.O. Box 1280, Alexandria, Egypt.

✠ MITCHELL, *John Horsley*
6/5/7409, 12/11/15; R.F.A., C/S, 31/3/16; R.G.A., 11/8/16; 2/Lieut.   Killed in action 19/5/17.

MITCHELL, *Robert Cowan*
6/3/9255, 2/2/16; A.S.C., C/S, 27/10/16; trfr. R.G.A., 12/1/17.

MITCHELL, *Robert Henry*
C/13373, 21/6/18; No. 22 O.C.B., 23/8/18; R. Suss. R., 13/2/19; 2/Lieut.   *Rookwood, Cuckfield, Haywards Heath.*

MITCHELL, *Warwick*
B/11376, 25/5/17; No. 14 O.C.B., 9/11/17; W. Rid. R., 30/4/18; Lieut.   *Falcon House, 399 Wakefield Road, Huddersfield.*

MITCHELL, *William Frank*
4/1/5041, 22/7/15; Oxf. & Bucks. L.I., 30/11/15; 2/Lieut.
    The Lodge, Leek Wootton, Warwickshire.

✠ MITCHELL, *William Holford*
2/3460, 3/5/15; E. Surr. R., 3/9/15; Lieut.   Drowned 15/4/17.

MITCHESON, *George Guy*
6/4/9481, 16/2/16; R.F.A., C/S, 18/8/16; R.F.A., 22/12/16; Lieut.   *Hall End Hall, Tamworth*

MITCHISON, *Gilbert Richard*
Sq/761, 23/1/14; 2nd Drag. Gds., 15/8/14, att. R.E. Sigs.; F,It; Major; Croix de Guerre (French).   *17 Cheyne Walk, S.W. 3.*

MITFORD, *Culling Eardley*
A/B/C/12144, 22/10/17; dis. med. unfit, 22/2/18.
    2 Kidderpore Avenue, Hampstead, N.W. 3.

MITFORD, *Edward Bawden*
4/1/4515, 28/6/15; R.W. Fus., 17/12/15, att. R. War. R.; F,It; Capt.; M.C. and Bar.   *Huish's Grammar School, Taunton, Somerset.*

MITTON, *Alexander Warren Dury*
Sq/2004, 2/11/14; Staff. Yeo., 12/12/14; Lieut.; w.
    Rouge Dragon, Park Row, S.W. 1.

MOBBS, *Charles Graily*
6/1/6290, 16/9/15; North'n. R., 24/10/16; Lieut.
    43 Billing Road, Northampton.

MOBBS, *Eric Charles*
A/12503, 29/1/18; R.E., C/S, 18/5/18; R.E., 27/9/18; 2/Lieut.
    1 Athelstane Road, Bow, E. 3.

MOBERLY, *Arthur Hamilton*
B/570, 20/7/11; 21st Lond. R., 7/4/14, emp. M. of Labour; Capt.; w(2).   *48 Hampstead Way, N.W. 4.*

MOCKETT, *Vere Brooks*
Sq/411, 5/5/09; dis. 31/7/11; E. Kent R., 21/8/14; M,I; Staff Capt.; M.B.E., M(2).   *1 Kings Bench Walk, Temple, E.C. 4.*

MODLIN, *Frederick Walesby*
6/2/6894, 18/10/15; M.G.C., C/S, 31/10/16; M.G.C., 28/12/16; Lieut.   *Marston House, Ampthill Road, Bedford.*

MOFFAT, *Rennie John*
C/10351, 5/1/17, Sgt.; trfr. Class W. Res., 12/3/18; M.B.E.
    50 Lightcliffe Road, Palmers Green, N. 13.

MOFFATT, *Alexander*
6/9072, 21/1/16; No. 9 O.C.B., 8/3/16; High. L.I., 23/7/16; Lieut.   *5 Marshall Place, Perth.*

MOFFATT, *Harold Midgley*
B/13467, 5/7/18; trfr. K.R. Rif. C., 7/4/19.
    Barley Close, Belgrave Road, Gloucester.

MOFFETT, *Thomas Henry*
6/5/C/6721, 9/10/15; trfr. 8th Lond. R., 26/2/17.
    1 Bennetts Hill, Oxton, Birkenhead.

MOFFITT, *George Storey*
6/3/6877, 18/10/15; North'd. Fus., 4/8/16; Lieut.
    Field House, Acklington, Northumberland.

MOGRIDGE, *Edward Cole*
H/2/2909, 13/2/15, L/C.; No. 3 O.C.B., 25/2/16; Hereford R., 4/9/16, att. Bedf. R., Suff. R., Shrop. L.I. and 23rd Lond. R.; F.E.P; Capt.; w.
    618 High Road, Chiswick, W. 4. (Now in West Africa).

MOIR, *William Charles James*
B/C/12685, 4/3/18, L/C.; trfr. 14th Lond. R., 6/12/18.
    c/o Dr. Barton, 2 Belgrave Square, Darwen, Lancashire.

MOLD, *Charles Trevor*
C/14279, 8/11/18; No. 11 O.C.B., 24/1/19; General List, 8/3/19; 2/Lieut.   *700 Calle Saimiento, Buenos Aires.*

MÖLLER, *Arthur Christian*
B/1223, 16/9/14; R. Lanc. R., 22/9/14, War Office; F,S; Capt.
    110 Arran Road, Catford, S.E., 6.

MOLLET, *Charles*
H/2930, 15/2/15; Dorset R., 2/6/15, R. Berks. R.; F; Staff Capt.; M.C. and Bar, M(1).   *37 Rue du Ranelagh, Paris XVI, France.*

MOLLET, *Paul*
A/14030, 18/9/18; No. 11 O.C.B., 6/2/19; General List, 8/3/19; 2/Lieut.   *16 Rue Levavasseur, Dinard, France.*

MOLLISON, *Hugh Reid*
6/D/9051, 18/1/16; R.E., 4/11/16; Lieut.
    114 Queens Road, Aberdeen.

MOLLOY, *Frederico George*
A/14067, 27/9/18; demob. 23/1/19.
    Mayfair Chambers, Little Grosvenor Street, W. 1.

✠ MOLLOY, *Henry Edmund*
6/3/5857, 26/8/15; Oxf. & Bucks. L.I., 26/1/16; 2/Lieut.
    Killed in action 22/8/17.

MOLSON, *Harold Elsdale*
Sq/949, 5/8/14; K.R. Rif. C., 16/9/14; Capt.; w.
    Goring Hall, Worthing.

MOLYNEUX, *Esmond John*
B/13421, 1/7/18; trfr. 14th Lond. R., 6/12/18.
    Brantwood, Reigate Road, Ewell, Surrey.

MONCUR, *Francis Kerr*
6/8969, 17/1/16; No. 9 O.C.B., 8/3/16; Sea. Highrs., 23/7/16, att. R.F.C., R.A.F.; Lieut.   *77 Viewforth, Edinburgh.*

MONEY, *Allan Campbell*
C/1531, 6/10/14; dis. 30/10/14.
    7 Lower Ward, Windsor Castle.

MONEY, *Arthur Walter Kyrle*
C/368, 20/3/09; dis. 11/2/10; R. War. R., 10/6/15, att. Lan. Fus.; Lieut.

MONEY, *Cyril Moore Chiozza*
6/2/6725, 9/10/15; R.F.A., C/S, 7/7/16; R.G.A., 13/10/16, emp. M. of Labour; Lieut.; w.   *3 Trossachs Road, East Dulwich, S.E. 22.*

APPENDIX II.—RECORDS OF RANK AND FILE.

✠ MONEY, *Duncan Goff*
6/3/D/6974, 23/10/15; No. 6 O.C.B., 15/2/17; R.F.C., 25/4/17; 2/Lieut. *Killed in action* 16/2/18.

MONEY, *George Jessep*
6/4/9206, 31/1/16; A.S.C., C/S, 4/9/16; R.A.S.C., 8/10/16; F; Lieut. 118 *Barons Court Road, W.* 14.

✠ MONEY, *Roy Granville Kyrle*
4/2/4022, 7/6/15; E. Kent R., 7/10/15; 2/Lieut.; w. *Killed in action* 9/4/17.

MONFRIES, *James Drummond Carmichael*
6/2/5629, 16/8/15, L/C.; trfr. Class W. Res., 25/7/16.

MONIER-WILLIAMS, *Roy Thornton*
A/36½, 15/3/09; dis. 2/7/12; E. Kent R., 9/9/14; F; Major; O.B.E., M(2). *Lamb Building, Temple, E.C.* 4.

MONK, *Maurice Percival*
C/13332, 19/6/18; trfr. 14th Lond. R., 6/12/18.
c/o Messrs. Graham, Rowe & Coy., *Mersey Chambers, Old Church Yard, Liverpool.*

MONKHOUSE, *Allan*
B/D/13646, 26/7/18, Sgt.; R.E., 23/1/19; NR; Capt.; Order of S. Anne. 9 *Chestnut Avenue, Chorlton-cum-Hardy, Manchester.*

MONKHOUSE, *Allan Cuthbertson*
D/13767, 7/8/18; demob. 24/1/19.
14 *Queen Anne's Road, York.*

MONKHOUSE, *Basil*
A/10712, 9/2/17; R.F.C., C/S, 13/3/17; R.F.C., 19/4/17, R.A.F.; Lieut. 4 *Gloucester Road, Birkdale, Southport.*

MONKHOUSE, *Charles Cosmo*
6/Sq/7149, 2/11/15; R.F.A., C/S, 31/3/16; R.G.A., 2/8/16; Lieut.; M.C. *The Downs, Dale Road, Purley, Surrey.*

MONRO, *Henry Ramsay*
B/12325, 27/12/17; No. 13 O.C.B., 10/5/18; R. Highrs., 3/2/19; 2/Lieut. *Calder Cottage, Allerton, Liverpool.*

MONRO, *John Robert Hale*
B/E/13463, 5/7/18; A.S.C., C/S, 1/10/18; demob. 27/12/18.
Raylands, Maidenhead.

MONROE, *William*
6/8998, 19/1/16; R.F.A., C/S, 26/5/16; trfr. R.F.A., 28/8/16.
Glen View, Plymouth Road, Penarth.

MONSELL, *Charles Noel*
B/80, 13/4/08; dis. 12/4/12.

MONSELL, *John Robert*
H/B/95, 16/4/08, Sgt.; 12th Lond. R., 12/4/15; F; Capt.
19 *Poulton Square, Chelsea, S.W.*

MONTAGU-STUART-WORTLEY, *Edward Thomas*
A/C/D/13131, 24/5/18; demob. 30/1/19.
Wortley Hall, Sheffield.

MONTEITH, *Robert*
C/10812, 21/2/17; No. 11 O.C.B., 5/7/17; R. Ir. Rif., 30/10/17; F; Lieut.; p; M.C. 98 *York Street, Belfast.*

MONTGOMERIE, *Gordon Rainsford*
6/3/7530, 16/11/15; A.S.C., C/S, 27/10/16; R.A.S.C., 20/12/16; F; Lieut.; *Inv.*
9 *Walpole Gardens, Strawberry Hill, Middlesex.*

✠ MONTGOMERY, *Albert Barr*
4/5/4754, 12/7/15, Sgt.; Worc. R., 29/9/15; Capt.
Died of wounds 17/8/17.

MONTGOMERY, *Charles Auber*
3/3328, 19/4/15, L/C.; R.W. Surr. R., 8/7/15, 8th Lond. R.; Lieut. *Byways, Exmouth.*

MONTGOMERY, *Denis Hugh*
6/2/D/7334, 9/11/15, L/C.; R.F.C., C/S, 13/3/17; R.F.C., 19/4/17, R.A.F.; Lieut.
11 *Abbey Road, St. Johns Wood, N.W.* 8.

MONTGOMERY, *Gilbert*
6/3/6331, 20/9/15, L/C.; K.R. Rif. C., 1/6/16; F,EA; Major, D.A.A.G.; w; M(2). 1 *Sunningdale, Clifton, Bristol.*

MONTGOMERY, *James*
A/10947, 24/3/17; R.F.C., C/S, 1/6/17; R.F.C., 4/7/17, R.A.F.; Lieut. *High Street, Ballymana, Co. Antrim.*

MONTGOMERY, *James*
C/13340, 14/6/18; demob. 23/1/19.
30 *Lower Beechwood Avenue, Ranelagh, Dublin.*

MONTGOMERY, *Martin*
6/5/5453, 7/8/15; N. Lan. R., 2/11/15; Capt.; M(1).
21 *Oak Drive, Denton, Manchester.*

MONTGOMERY, *Robert Lindsey*
6/5/7365, 10/11/15; R.F.A., C/S, 29/1/16; trfr. R.F.A., 18/8/16.
58 *Risbygate Street, Bury St. Edmunds.*

✠ MONTROSE-EKIN, *Leslie* See EKIN, L. M.

MONYPENNY, *Robert D'Arbley Gybbon*
Sq/923, 5/8/14; Essex R., 15/8/14, att. Indian Army; F,I; Capt.; w. 74 *Kensington Gardens Square, Bayswater, W.* 2.

MOODIE, *Donald Arthur Birbeck*
6/4/9116, 24/1/16, Cpl.; Ir. Gds., 20/8/16; F; Lieut.; M.C.
Native Dept., Umtali, Southern Rhodesia.

MOODY-STUART, *Mark Sprot*
4/Sq/5122, 26/7/15; R.F.A., 22/10/15; F; Capt.; M.C.; M(1).
Usine Sainte Madeleine, Trinidad, British West Indies.

MOON, *Cyril Edward*
B/9864, 6/11/16; No. 14 O.C.B., 5/5/17; Oxf. & Bucks. L.I., 28/8/17; F,It; Lieut.; M(1).
St. Chrysostom's Vicarage, Handsworth, Staffordshire.

MOON, *Henry William*
6/5/8143, 3/12/15, L/C.; Yorks. L.I., 4/8/16; Lieut.
c/o *Matheson & Coy. Ltd., 3 Lombard Street, E.C.*

✠ MOON, *Leonard James*
K/E/2090, 16/11/14; Devon. R., 10/2/15; Lieut.
Died 23/11/16.

MOON, *Thomas Godfrey*
D/13847, 14/8/18; trfr. K.R. Rif. C., 7/4/19.
56 *Shirburn Terrace, Consett, Co. Durham.*

MOONEY, *Edward James*
6/1/6628, 4/10/15; Notts & Derby. R., 6/7/16, att. Admiralty; F; Lieut.; w. 71 *Molineux Street, Derby.*

MOONEY, *Edwin*
6/1/6975, 23/10/15, L/C.; No. 11 O.C.B., 7/5/16; 13th Lond. R., 4/9/16; Lieut.; M(1). 64 *Avenue Hill, Leeds.*

MOORAT, *Samuel Arthur Joseph*
2/3461, 3/5/15; trfr. 5th Lond. R., 17/3/16.
25 *Pembroke Gardens, Kensington, W.* 8.

MOORE, *Arthur Sidney*
D/11834, 9/8/17, L/C.; No. 3 O.C.B., 8/2/18; Notts. & Derby. R., 30/7/18; 2/Lieut.
The Orchard, Castle Hill, Duffield, Nr. Derby.

MOORE, *Arthur Walter*
C/11474, 11/6/17; A.S.C., C/S, 1/9/17; R.A.S.C., 27/10/17; Lieut.
c/o *Anglo South American Club, 1 Queens Gate, S.W.* 7.

MOORE, *Bernard Joseph*
B/13422, 1/7/17; demob. 25/3/19.
27 *Hill Street, Hinckley, Leicestershire.*

✠ MOORE, *Clive Goulding*
B/1259, 23/9/14; R. Fus., 19/10/14, R.F.C.; F; Lieut.
Killed in action 15/8/17.

MOORE, *Corbett Spencer Dickin*
4/5/4758, 12/7/15; dis. med. unfit, 22/5/16.
12a *Victoria Square, S.W.* 1.

MOORE, *Edward Alan*
B/880, 5/8/14; Midd'x. R., 12/9/14; Capt.; w(2).
Hillcroft, Shawfield Park, Bromley, Kent.

MOORE, *Edward George*
A/11265, 12/5/17; Garr. O.C.B., 5/10/17; Lab. Corps, 15/12/17, R.A.O.C.; Lieut. *Denewood, West Moors, Dorset.*

MOORE, *Ernest Arthur*
6/3/6719, 9/10/15, L/C.; E. Kent R., 7/7/16; M; Lieut.
Bath Parade, Cheltenham.

MOORE, *Ernest Reginald*
A/D/12547, 4/2/18; R.F.C., C/S, 21/5/18; trfr. R.A.F.
23 *Chapel Street, East Stonehouse, Plymouth.*

MOORE, *Francis*
4/2/4607, 5/7/15; 3rd Lond. R., 8/12/15, M.G.C.; F; Capt.
16 *Harriet Street, Derby.*

MOORE, *Frank*
6/3/6362, 20/9/15, L/C.; K.R. Rif. C., 1/6/16; F; 2/Lieut.; g.
52 *Cabra Park, Dublin.*

MOORE, *Frank Reginald*
6/5/5886, 30/8/15; R.E., 20/11/15; Lieut.
Bank House, Buckley, Nr. Chester.

APPENDIX II.—RECORDS OF RANK AND FILE.

MOORE, Harold Augustus
6/Sq/7554, 17/11/15; No 2 Cav. C/S, 1/9/16; 14th R. Regt. of Cav., 20/12/16; I; Lieut.
9 Talgarth Mansions, Barons Court, W. 14.

MOORE, Harold Brooks
D/11100, 21/4/17; No. 14 O.C.B., 7/9/17; Yorks. L.I., 17/12/17, att. W. Rid. R.; 2/Lieut.
The Chalet, Warwick Drive, Hale, Cheshire.

MOORE, Ivon Stanley
B/C/12686, 4/3/18; No. 12 O.C.B., 5/7/18; Dorset R., 4/3/19; 2/Lieut.
33 Blandford Road, St. Albans, Hertfordshire.

MOORE, John Stephen
6/7743, 22/11/15; dis. 23/11/15.

MOORE, Johnson, Ashworth
A/D/11936, 30/8/17; R.F.A., C/S, 15/3/18; R.G.A., 4/11/18; 2/Lieut.
17 Alder Grange, Rawtenstall, Lancashire.

MOORE, Joseph Reginald
4/1/3905, 31/5/15; Linc. R., 27/10/15; F; Lieut.; Inv.
96 Grosvenor Road, Highbury, N. 5.

MOORE, Joseph Scott-
6/7690, 22/11/15; R.A.O.C., 19/4/16; Lieut.; m(1).
19 Ridgway Place, Wimbledon, S.W. 19.

MOORE, Ronald Nicholas
C/10850, 6/3/17; No. 14 O.C.B., 10/8/17; Indian Army, 27/11/17.

MOORE, Thomas
6/3/8293, 10/12/15, L/C.; R.A.O.C., 9/11/16; Lieut.
Darenthdale, Shoreham, Kent.

✠ MOORE, Ulich Augustus
4/5/4755, 12/7/15; Conn. Rang., 20/11/15; Lieut.; w.
Killed in action 22/3/18.

MOORE, Wilfred Henry
B/11705, 19/7/17; No. 14 O.C.B., 4/1/18; Norf. R., 25/6/18, att. Ir. Guards; Lieut.
Westview, Broughton, Kettering.

✠ MOORE, William Henry Helme
A/1049, 31/8/14; K.R. Rif. C., 3/10/14; F; Lieut.
Killed in action 19/10/15.

MOORE, William James Sago
4/1/4580, 1/7/15; W. York. R., 18/10/15; F; Capt.; M.C.
43 First Avenue, Doncaster Road, Rotherham.

MOORE, William Shaw
A/14330, 30/12/18; demob. 10/1/19.
89 Leyland Road, Southport.

MOORE-BAYLEY, John
D/11007, 2/4/17; A.S.C., C/S, 1/11/17; demob. 29/1/19.
Barnt Green, Nr. Birmingham.

MOORES, Edward Charles Joseph
4/5/C/4801, 12/7/15.
3 East India Avenue, E.C.

✠ MOORHOUSE, Arthur
4/9725, 13/10/16; No. 14 O.C.B., 30/1/17;
Died 12/3/17.

✠ MORANT, William Hedley
Sq/734, 11/11/13; 6th R. Regt. of Cav., 9/9/14, North'd. Fus.; 2/Lieut.
Killed in action 25/10/16.

MORBEY, Cyril Ellis
A/Sq/13078, 17/5/18; demob. 10/1/19.
The Quench, Great Barton, Bury St. Edmunds, Suffolk.

MORCOM, Philip Denniss
C/D/14229, 25/10/18; trfr. Gord. Highrs., 6/5/19.
Stuart House, Liskeard, Cornwall.

MORCOMBE, Percy Reginald
6/2/5870, 28/8/15; S. Wales Bord., 1/6/16; F,S; Lieut.
c/o Holt & Coy., 3 Whitehall Place, S.W. 1.

MORDEN, Sydney Herbert
6/8697, 4/1/16; trfr. Class W. Res., 26/6/16; R.E., 11/6/17, War Office; Capt.
St. Stephens Club, Westminster, S.W. 1.

MORE, Jasper Frederick
A/390, 31/3/09; dis. 20/3/11.
17 South Eaton Place, S.W. 1.

MORE, Thomas
H/2/2770, 25/1/15, L/C.; Cam'n. Highrs., 7/5/15, War Office; F; Lieut.; M.B.E.
c/o Lindsay, Jamieson & Haldane, 24 St. Andrews Square, Edinburgh.

MOREHEAD, William Forde
C/9932, 15/11/16; No. 14 O.C.B., 5/3/17; R. Muns. Fus., 26/6/17; Lieut.
Holt & Coy., Whitehall Place, S.W. 1.

MORETON, Raymond Laurence
B/3005, 4/3/15; 11th Lond. R., 15/5/15; G,E; 2/Lieut.; Inv.
12 Sergeant's Inn, Temple, E.C. 4.

MORFORD, Howard Frederick
6/Sq/7856, 26/11/15, L/C.; No. 1 Cav. C/S, 2/8/16; Surr. Yeo., 27/11/16; S; Lieut.
c/o Chartered Bank of India, Australia & China, 38 Bishopsgate, E.C. (Now in Cochin China).

MORGAN, Alfred Hastings
6/Sq/6786, 12/10/15; R.F.A., C/S, 31/3/16; R.F.A., 7/8/16; Lieut.; w.
26 Hartington Place, Edinburgh.

MORGAN, Christopher Leslie
4/1449, 29/9/14, Sgt.; Midd'x. R., 3/6/15, Wilts. R., R.E.; F; Lieut.
280 Brixton Hill, S.W. 2.

MORGAN, David
6/2/9037, 20/1/16; R.F.A., C/S, 10/11/16; R.F.A., 2/3/17; Lieut.; M.B.E.
18 Marlborough Road, Cardiff.

MORGAN, Dennis Hugh
C/D/12248, 22/11/17; No. 8 O.C.B., 18/10/18; Welch R., 17/3/19; 2/Lieut.
Garthowen, Whitchurch, Glamorganshire.

✠ MORGAN, Edward Leslie
6/Sq/9117, 24/1/16; R.F.A., C/S, 4/8/16; R.F.A., 27/10/16; 2/Lieut.
Died of wounds 9/11/17.

MORGAN, Eric John
6/H/1903, 16/10/14, Sgt.; Shrop. Yeo., 24/10/16, Indian Army; I; Capt.
107 Endlesham Road, Balham, S.W. 12.

MORGAN, Frank Thomas
6/3/5484, 9/8/15; Som. L.I., 28/10/15, att. Hamps. R.; M,I,P,F; Capt.; Inv.
Merton House, Penmaenmawr, North Wales.

MORGAN, Frederick Charles Cyril
4/6/2/5172, 29/7/15; R.E., 5/9/15; F; Lieut.; Inj.
Sandringham House, Croft Road, Thame.

MORGAN, Henry William
B/10206, 18/12/16; R.A., C/S, 3/4/17; R.F.A., 15/9/17; Lieut.
Forest Hall, Forestfach, Nr. Swansea.

MORGAN, Ieuan Honddu
B/10543, 17/1/17; No. 14 O.C.B., 5/7/17; R.W. Fus., 30/10/17; F; Lieut.
Bwlchgwyn Vicarage, Wrexham.

MORGAN, Ifor Milwyn
B/11706, 19/7/17, L/C.; demob. 22/1/19.
Southdown, Le Breos Avenue, Swansea.

MORGAN, John Campbell
6/2/7270, 8/11/15; No. 5 O.C.B., 14/8/16; North'd. Fus., 21/11/16, att. North'n. R.; F; Lieut.; w; M.C.
88 Colchester Road, Leyton, E. 10.

MORGAN, John Griffith
6/9379, 8/2/16; R.F.A., C/S, 21/7/16; R.F.A., 8/12/16; Lieut.
Tan-y-Bryn, Brynmawr, Breconshire, South Wales.

✠ MORGAN, John James
6/Sq/5520, 9/8/15; R.F.A., 29/12/15; F; 2/Lieut.
Killed in action 7/4/17.

MORGAN, John Richard Victor
6/4/8970, 17/1/16; No. 14 O.C.B., 26/11/16; trfr. 16th Lond. R., 11/4/17.
The Vicarage, North Shoebury, Essex.

MORGAN, John Stephen Raymond
B/10127, 6/12/16; R.F.C., C/S, 13/3/17; R.F.C., 19/4/17.
153 Russell Road, Moor Green, Birmingham.

✠ MORGAN, Joseph Anthony Philip Cyril Patrick
3/3165, 1/4/15; Shrop. L.I., 30/6/15, att. R.F.C.; Lieut.
Killed in action 30/5/17.

MORGAN, Kevern Ivor I. W.
6/2/7997, 29/11/15; Mon. R., 18/12/16; Lieut.
7 Clarence Terrace, Swansea.

MORGAN, Laurence Llewellyn
B/12818, 20/3/18; No. 8 O.C.B., 20/9/18; demob.
21 Sketty Avenue, Sketty. Swansea. (Now in France).

MORGAN, Mark Swinfen
6/3/5797, 23/8/15; Welch R., 18/12/15; F; Capt.; w.
168 Haverstock Hill, N.W. 3.

✠ MORGAN, Ralph Lewis
6/3/5777, 23/8/15, L/C.; Welch R., 18/12/15; F; 2/Lieut.
Killed in action 14/1/17.

APPENDIX II.—RECORDS OF RANK AND FILE.

MORGAN, Randall Courtenay
6/2/8090, 1/12/15; Shrops. L.I., 24/1/17, att. Ches. R.; F; Lieut.; w(2).
30 Welwell Road, Exeter.

✠ MORGAN, Sidney Herbert
6/1/5566, 12/8/15; E. Surr. R., 21/4/16, att. T.M. Bty.; 2/Lieut.
Killed in action 4/4/17.

MORGAN, Talusin Merfyn
6/4/5521, 9/8/15; R.N.A.S., 5/4/16.
Telynfa, Aberdare.

MORGAN, Tennyson Dudley
4/Sq/4195, 14/6/15; R.A.S.C., 22/11/15.
Primrose Club, St. James, S.W.

MORGAN, Thomas Douglas
4/6/5/4995, 19/7/15; R.W. Fus., 21/12/15, M.G.C., R.A.M.C.; F; Capt.; Inv.
Brookhurst, 16 Newry Park, Chester.

MORGAN, Thomas Edwin
A/9832, 1/11/16, L/C.; R.E., C/S, 8/4/17; R.E., 29/6/17; F; Lieut.; w-p.
75 Chancery Lane, W.C. 2.

MORGAN, William Leslie
B/11330, 18/5/17; No. 14 O.C.B., 5/10/17; R.W. Fus., 26/2/18; 2/Lieut.
Garth Owen, Merches Gardens, Cardiff.

MORGAN, William Russell
6/4/6667, 7/10/15; R.A., C/S, 14/7/16; R.G.A., 4/10/16; Lieut.; w.

✠ MORGAN-BROWN, Nigel Martin
D/1453, 29/9/14; North'd. Fus., 13/11/14; 2/Lieut.
Died 31/10/15.

MORIARTY, Dennis
6/4/7894, 24/11/15; 15th Lond. R., 24/10/16, Manch. R., Indian Army; F,I; Lieut.; Inv.
2/67th Punjabis, c/o Cox & Coy., Bombay.

✠ MORICE, Norman Archibald
A/1180, 14/9/14; E. York. R., 3/10/14; Lieut.
Died of wounds 11/3/16.

✠ MORISON, John Sinclair
4/3/4523, 30/6/15; R.F.C., 6/7/16; 2/Lieut.
Killed in action 13/10/16.

MORLEY, Charles
Sq/889, 5/8/14; dis. med. unfit, 31/8/14.
53 Great Cumberland Place, W.

MORLEY, Francis Howard
A/10859, 10/3/17, Sgt.; demob. 25/1/19.
6 Hillside Crescent, St. James Lane, Muswell Hlil, N. 10.

MORLEY, John
C/11084, 19/4/17; trfr. North'd. Fus., 13/8/17; F; Sgt.; p.
16 Gordon Square, Whitley Bay, Northumberland.

MORLEY, Reginald Mills
F/E/2901, 11/2/15, Cpl.; Lan. Fus., 4/6/15; F; Lieut.; w(2).
14 St. Peter's Square, Manchester.

MORLEY, Richard James
6/2/5588, 12/8/15; L/C.; M.G.C., C/S, 25/10/16; M.G.C., 24/2/17; 2/Lieut.
29 Manor Court Road, Hanwell, W. 7.

MORLEY, Rollo Streatfield
F/3030, 9/3/15, Sgt.; Lan. Fus., 18/8/15; F; Capt.; w-p.
Fir Corner, Broadwater, Worthing.

MORREY, Joseph
1/9746, 17/10/16, Sgt.; M.G.C., C/S, 28/3/17; Special List, 16/7/17.
16 Nicholas Street, Chester.

MORRICE, Ronald Leslie Seaton
6/5/5947, 1/9/15; L'pool. R., 1/6/16, R.A.F.; Lieut.

MORRIS, Alan Gordon
D/13701, 31/7/18; demob. 30/5/19.
38 Kingsley Road, Bedford.

✠ MORRIS, Allan Duncan
F/2892, 9/2/15; S. Wales Bord., 21/6/15; F; Lieut.
Killed in action 30/8/18.

MORRIS, Broughton Aspinwall
6/2/7212, 4/11/15; No. 9 O.C.B., 4/3/16; R. Scots, 23/7/16, att. Gord. Highrs.; F; Lieut.
1718 Richmond Terrace, West New Brighton, Stalen Island, New York, U.S.A.

MORRIS, Charles Joseph A.
6/4/9290, 3/2/16; No. 7 O.C.B., 11/8/16; R. Dub. Fus., 18/12/16; F; Lieut.
1 Greenmount Road, Terenure, Dublin.

MORRIS, David
6/5/C/8144, 3/12/15; No. 14 O.C.B., 30/10/16; Mon. R., 24/1/17; F; Lieut.; w.
6 Aubrey Road, Cymmer, Porth, Glamorganshire.

MORRIS, Frank
D/13848, 16/8/18; trfr. K.R. Rif. C., 7/4/19.
40 Farnaby Road, Bromley, Kent.

MORRIS, Frank Mosedale
4/Sq/4504, 28/6/15; R.G.A., 10/11/15; Lieut.; M(1).
20 Old Buildings, Lincoln's Inn, W.C. 2.

MORRIS, George Dixon
6/1/6895, 18/10/15; Devon. R., 4/8/16, R.F.C.; F; Lieut.
Briarsley, The Avenue, Wanstead, Essex.

✠ MORRIS, George Mackelvey
3/3864, 31/5/15, L/C.; L'pool. R., 21/4/16; 2/Lieut.
Died of wounds 7/9/16.

MORRIS, Guy Safford
6/2/5458, 7/8/15; 20th Lond. R., 28/11/15; F; Lieut.; w.
c/o Rev. H. S. Morris, Twyford Vicarage, Nr. Winchester, Hampshire. (Now in Ceylon).

MORRIS, Harold Courtenay
6/3/5798, 23/8/15; Mon. R., 14/6/16; 2/Lieut.

MORRIS, Harold John
6/1/9418, 10/2/10; No. 14 O.C.B., 30/10/16; Shrops. L.I., 24/1/17; F; Lieut.
Didsbury College, Manchester.

MORRIS, Harry Lloyd
3/3181, 6/4/15; R.E., 16/6/15, emp. M. of Munitions; Lieut.

MORRIS, Henry
K/Sq/2356, 14/12/14; R.A.S.C., 2/3/15; Capt.
13 Gordon Street, Gordon Square, W.C.

MORRIS, Idwal Thomas
A/10048, 29/11/16; No. 14 O.C.B., 30/1/17; R. Fus., 29/5/17, att. Sea. Highrs.; It,S,F; Lieut.
c/o A. King Davies Esq., Maesteg, Glamorganshire.

MORRIS, John Talwin
Sq/357, 11/3/09; Dorset Yeo., 10/10/14; Capt.; w.
The Firs, Witley, Reading.

MORRIS, John Turner
K/D/2252, 7/12/14; R. War. R., 28/12/14, R.E., att. Admiralty; F; 2/Lieut.
88 Fitzjohns Avenue, Hampstead, N.W. 3 (Now in Barbados)

✠ MORRIS, Lionel Bertram Frank
2/3601, 13/5/15; R.W. Surr. R., 20/8/15, att. R.F.C.; 2/Lieut.
Died of wounds 17/9/16 as Prisoner of War.

MORRIS, Richard Vivian
2/3115, 25/3/15; R. Suss. R., 3/6/15, R.E.; F; Capt.
c/o Crown Agents for the Colonies, Malay States Dept., Millbank, S.W. 1.

MORRIS, Robert John
6/2/7618, 19/11/15, Cpl.; Mon. R., 25/9/16; F; Lieut.
5 Osterley Terrace, Briton Ferry, Glamorganshire.

✠ MORRIS, Robert Williams
4/3/4422, 24/6/15; trfr. Hants. Car. Yeo., 21/7/16, Hamps. R.; F; Pte.
Killed in action -/9/17.

MORRIS, Victor Mayfield
D/A/11835, 9/8/17; Dental Surgeon, 14/3/18; Capt.
6 Windhill, Bishop's Stortford.

MORRIS, William James
6/3/7366, 10/11/15; No. 11 O.C.B., 7/5/16; Welch R., 4/9/16, R.W. Fus.; Lieut.
1 Aberdare Road, Mountain Ash.

MORRISON, Bertie Charlton
6/Sq/8800, 10/1/16, L/C.; A.S.C., C/S, 27/10/16; R.A.S.C., 20/12/16; Lieut.
Greetham House, Nr. Horncastle, Lincolnshire.

MORRISON, Brian Harford
6/7998, 29/11/15; trfr. 101st Prov Bn., 7/4/16.
The Hut, St. Albans, Hertfordshire.

MORRISON, Douglas Cato
H/1704, 13/10/14, L/C.; R.G.A., 8/5/15, R.E.; F; Lieut.; g.
District Judge, Halfa, Sudan.

MORRISON, Dudley
C/12671, 1/3/18; trfr. Gord. Highrs., 10/1/19.
San Remo, Church Road, Wavertree, Liverpool.

✠ MORRISON, Duncan Craig
4/1/4288, 17/6/15; Arg. & Suth'd. Highrs., 5/11/15; 2/Lieut.
Killed in action 10/4/17.

MORRISON, Geoffrey
1/2649, 11/1/15; Bord. R., 10/7/15; F; Lieut.
1 St. Michael's House, Cornhill, E.C. 3.

APPENDIX II.—RECORDS OF RANK AND FILE.

MORRISON, Hugh
Sq/303, 29/6/08; dis. 28/6/09.
c/o James Finlay & Coy., 34 Leadenhall Street, E.C.

MORRISON, James Gray Stevens
4/2/3270, 15/4/15; R.W. Surr. R., 18/6/15; F; Capt.; w.
Bank of Montreal, Lethbridge, Alta, Canada.

MORRISON, John
H/2/2640, 11/1/15; Sea. Highrs., 18/4/15, Intelligence; F; Capt.; M.C., M(2).
3 Morton Terrace, Greenock, Scotland. (Now in Constantinople).

MORRISS, William Nelson
B/D/13679, 29/7/18; trfr. K.R. Rif. C., 12/6/19; Sgt.
7 Brunswick Park Road, New Southgate, N. 11.

MORROW, Charles William
4/1/5042, 22/7/15; Lan. Fus., 22/12/15; F; Lieut.; w.
The Knoll, Atwick Road, Hornsea, East Yorkshire.

MORROW, George Leslie
6/Sq/6021, 2/9/15; R.F.A., C/S, 31/3/16; dis. med. unfit, 1/9/16.
Brent Lodge, Doctors Commons Road, Berkhamsted, Hertfordshire.

MORSE, Charles George Hugh
B/9, 1/4/08; R.A.M.C., 16/9/12; F; Major.
Sherborne, Chessel Avenue, Boscombe, Hampshire.

✠ MORSE, Christopher Charles
A/11074, 26/3/17; R.F.C., C/S, 1/6/17; R.F.C., 4/7/17; 2/Lieut.
Killed in action 14/11/17.

MORSE, John Phillip
A/2708, 18/1/15; E. Surr. R., 5/6/15, emp. M. of Munitions; 2/Lieut.; w.
Rushmere, Beechwood Road, Sanderstead, Surrey.

MORT, John Harold
4/3/4005, 3/6/15; N. Lan. R., 7/10/15; Lieut.
64 Barrowford Road, Colne, Lancashire.

MORTIMER, Alan Lee
6/5/5522, 9/8/15, L/C.; W. York. R., 19/7/16, R.E.; Lieut.; w.
134 Tempest Road, Leeds.

MORTIMER, Gilbert Leslie
A/10703, 12/2/17; R.G.A., C/S, 26/9/17; R.G.A., 18/2/18; 2/Lieut.

MORTIMER, Herbert Clifford
C/9796, 27/10/16; R.W. Surr. R., 9/3/17, att. Lab. Corps, R.E.; Capt.
1 Dr. Johnson's Buildings, Temple, E.C. 4.

MORTIMORE, Foster Richard
4/1/4630, 5/7/15; Devon. R., 7/12/15, secd. K. Af. Rif.; Lieut.

✠ MORTIMORE, Harry Limner
6/1/5589, 12/8/15; E. Surr. R., 8/6/16; F; Capt.
Died of wounds 20/9/17.

✠ MORTON, Arthur Darley
A/11271, 12/5/17; No. 14 O.C.B., 5/10/17; 21st Lond. R., 26/2/18; 2/Lieut.
Killed in action 24/8/18.

MORTON, Cecil James
6/1/6629, 4/10/15; Yorks. L.I., 8/7/16; F; Lieut.; w(3).
72 Lennard Road, Penge, S.E. 20.

MORTON, Charles Edward
2/3789, 27/5/15; Indian Army, 18/6/17; Capt.

MORTON, Charles Frederick Alexander
B/12373, 7/1/18, L/C.; No. 15 O.C.B., 7/6/18; 7th Lond. R., 5/2/19; 2/Lieut.
27 The Avenue, Kew Gardens, Surrey.

MORTON, George Bond
C/676, 24/1/13, Sgt.; R. Fus., 12/9/14; Capt.; w; M.C.

MORTON, Harold Trestrail
Sq/710, 6/5/13, L/C.; E. Rid. of York. Yeo., 22/9/14, R. Horse Gds.; F; Capt.
Llaunden House, Chesham, Buckinghamshire.

MORTON, John Darnley Mitford
6/5/5590, 12/8/15; York. & Lanc. R., 26/12/15; Lieut.; M.B.E
52 Warton Street, Lytham, Lancashire.

MORTON, John Stuart
A/14317, 30/12/18; demob. 11/1/19.
20 Queen Street, Edinburgh.

MORTON, Keith Douglas
C/A/13185, 31/5/18; demob. 29/1/19.
c/o Mrs. Simpson, 9 Borden Road, Jordanhill, Glasgow.

MORTON, Montague Cecil
C/14187, 18/10/18; demob. 30/1/19.
73 Brondesbury Villas, N.W. 6.

MORTON, Thomas Trestrail
Sq/2540, 4/1/15, Cpl.; York. Huss., 3/8/15, W. York. R., R.A.F.; F; Capt.; w. Inj.   Hall Place, St. Albans, Hertfordshire.

MORTON, Thomas William
4/5/4717, 9/7/15; E. Lan. R., 9/12/15; E,P; Staff Lieut.
3 Carlyle Road, West Bridgford, Nottingham.

MOSCROP, Samuel Frederic
B/12420, 17/1/18; No. 21 O.C.B., 10/5/18; L'pool. R., 2/2/19; 2/Lieut.
33 York Avenue, Great Crosby, Liverpool.

MOSELEY, Cyril Kaye
4/6/4996, 19/7/15; Yorks. L.I., 15/10/15, M.G.C.; F; Lieut.; w(2), g.
24 Park Lane, Wakefield. (Now in Southern Rhodesia).

MOSELEY, Edwin Francis Walter
H/1963, 26/10/14; 3rd Lond. R., 3/4/15, att. Lab. Corps; F; Capt.
Buildwas Abbey, Iron-bridge, Shropshire.

MOSELEY, Geoffrey
A/1019, 7/8/14; York. R., 3/10/14; Capt.
7 Holland Park, W.

MOSER, Hugh Shedden
K/C/2313, 10/12/14; 17th Lond. R., 25/3/15; F,S,P; Capt.; M.C.
Firlands, Fürzefield Road, Reigate, Surrey.

MOSES, Charles Robert
B/10117, 6/12/16; No. 21 O.C.B., 5/5/17; Camb. R., 28/8/17, att. Bord. R.; I,S; Lieut.
62 Yale Court, West Hampstead, N.W. 6.

MOSES, Fletcher Wade
D/12895, 9/4/18; No. 11 O.C.B., 4/10/18; trfr. 28th Lond. R., 1/11/18.
115 Cedar Street, Haverhill, Mass., U.S.A.

MOSEY, Harold Yeoman
B/12712, 8/3/18; R.E., C/S, 23/8/18; R.E., 8/4/19; 2/Lieut.
Beachfield Cliff Road, Leigh-on-Sea, Essex.

✠ MOSLEY, Arthur Roy
K/F/2781, 25/1/15; Yorks. L.I., 12/4/15; F; Lieut.; w.
Died of wounds 23/11/17.

✠ MOSS, Cyril James
K/2149, 19/11/14; Suff. R., 12/5/15; 2/Lieut.
Died of wounds 19/8/16.

✠ MOSS, Hamilton
6/3/9315, 4/2/16; No. 5 O.C.B., 14/8/16; W. Rid. R., 21/11/16; F; Capt.; M.C.
Killed in action 31/5/18.

MOSS, Laurence Montague
B/E/13457, 3/7/18, L/C.; R.A.F., 21/9/18; Lieut.
18 Victoria Mansions, Willesden Green, N.W. 10.

MOSS, Samuel
2/9766, 23/10/16; No. 14 O.C.B., 15/5/17; R.F.C., 28/8/17, R.A.F.; F; Lieut.
Hollies, Vale Street, Denbigh.

MOSS, William Lionel Henry
K/Sq/2410, 21/12/14; R.A.S.C., 1/3/15; S,F; Capt.
c/o Gailey & Roberts, Nairobi, British East Africa.

MOSSE, Ewen Field Cameron
6/5/8420, 15/12/15; R.A., C/S, 7/7/16; R.G.A., 27/9/16; Lieut., w.
Landour, Ferndale Road, Woking.

MOSSMAN, Percy Matthew
6/2/8145, 3/12/15; Worc. R., 18/12/16, att. Suff. R.; P; Lieut.
6 Brancaster Road, Streatham, S.W. 16.

MOSSOP, Richard Grosvenor
K/B/2478, 28/12/14, L/C.; Wilts. R., 28/7/15, secd. Nigeria Regt.; Lieut.

MOTT, Grey Egerton T.
K/Sq/2679, 14/1/15, L/C.; York. Huss., 24/4/15, 1st Drag. Gds.; Lieut.
207 Ashley Gardens, Westminster, S.W. 1.

MOTTLEY, Herbert Williams
6/2/7271, 8/11/15, Sgt.; No. 11 O.C.B., 7/5/16; Yorks. L.I., 4/8/16; S,F; Capt.; M.C.
8 Fitzjohn Avenue, Barnet.

MOTTRAM, Arthur William
B/12374, 7/1/18, Sgt.; demob. 30/1/19.
Westwood, Tillington, Stafford.

MOUL, Frank Douglas
B/13556, 19/7/18; demob. 29/1/19.
5 Blakesley Avenue, Ealing, W. 5.

MOULD, Frederick Victor
B/13490, 8/7/18; trfr. K.R. Rif. C., 7/4/19.
38 Streatham Place, Streatham Hill, S.W. 2.

MOULDEN, John William
4/1/5043, 22/7/15; North'd. Fus., 24/1/16; F; Lieut.; w.
The Grange, Beckett Park, Leeds.

APPENDIX II.—RECORDS OF RANK AND FILE.

MOULDING, James
6/1/D/6668, 7/10/15; dis. to R. Mil. Coll., 3/11/16; Devon. R., 12/9/17; Lieut.; Italian Silver Medal for Valour.
2 Marlborough Road, Exeter.

MOUNSEY, Jasper Percy
K/B/2520, 31/12/14; Lan. Fus., 22/4/15, secd. K. Af. Rif.; F,Germ.EA; Capt.; w. 128 Victoria Terrace, Littlehampton.

MOUNSEY, Thomas William
6/5/6787, 12/10/15; trfr. 1st Lond. R., 14/2/17; F; Pte.
Eamont Lodge, Penrith, Cumberland.

MOUNT, Ralph
6/3/6770, 11/10/15; trfr. R.G.A., 6/10/16, R.A.F.; F; Sgt.
25 Bisterne Avenue, Walthamstow, E. 17.

MOUNTAIN, Charles Frederick Johnson
D/1397, 29/9/14; R.A.S.C., 11/11/14, att. R.A.F.; G,E; Capt.
Phœnix House, 4/5 King William Street, E.C.

MOUNTAIN, Frank
6/2/6876, 18/10/15; Yorks. L.I., 9/6/16; F; Capt.; w.
44 Bond Street, Wakefield, Yorkshire.

MOUNTFORD, George Burleigh
E/1616, 9/10/14, Cpl.; R. Suss. R., 2/4/15; Capt.; M.C.

MOUNTFORD, Leslie Warden
D/13746, 2/8/18; trfr. K.R. Rif. C., 25/4/19, M.G.C.
Yew Tree Farm, Shendley Lane, Northfield, Birmingham.

MOUNTFORT, Charles
2/Sq/9782, 25/10/16; No. 1 Cav. C/S, 1/9/17; R. Regt. of Cav., 22/2/18; F; 2/Lieut. Elsinore, Highgate, Walsall.

MOWATT, Ernest Johnson
6/2/8091, 1/12/15; No. 7 O.C.B., 11/8/16; R. Dub. Fus., 18/12/16, att. Hamps. R.; Lieut. 282 Croxted Road, Herne Hill, S.E.

MOWATT, John
6/3/9084, 24/1/16; No. 13 O.C.B., 4/11/16; North'd. Fus., 28/2/17; F; Lieut.; w(2). 40 Percy Road, Ravenscourt Park, W. 12.

MOWFORTH, Haydn
6/2/7425, 13/11/15; No. 9 O.C.B., 8/3/16; Cam'n. Highrs., 7/7/16, Indian Army; I,M; Lieut.
46 Belvoir Street, Hull, East Yorkshire.

MOXEY, John Llewellyn
B/682, 24/1/13; R. Fus., 15/8/14; F; Capt.; w(2).
Framingham Hall, Nr. Norwich.

✠ MOXON, Hugh Cecil
6/9147, 25/1/16; Bedf. R., 8/2/16; 2/Lieut.
Died of wounds 19/7/17.

MOY, Cecil Eric
4/2/3269, 15/4/15; 16th Lond. R., 25/8/15, att. T.M. Bty.; F; Capt.; w, g; M.C. 24 Criffel Avenue, Streatham Hill, S.W. 2.

MOZLEY, Dudley Edward
F/2711, 18/1/15, L/C.; Glouc. R., 9/6/15, att. R.A.F.; F; Capt.; w; M.C. Blanche Farm House, South Mimms, Middlesex.

MUCKLE, James Smith
B/11359, 21/5/17; trfr. R.G.A., 21/9/17.
Breeze Mount, Donaghadee, Co. Down.

MUDD, John
B/A/D/12185, 1/11/17, L/C.; No. 17 O.C.B., 16/3/18; Shrop. L.I., 3/2/19; 2/Lieut. 72 Wyle Cop, Shrewsbury.

MUDDELL, Woodford Alan
4/Sq/5044, 22/7/15; R.A.S.C., 23/10/15, R.W. Surr. R.; F; Capt. Thornton, Aslockton, Nottinghamshire.

MUDDIMER, Ernest
A/12445, 21/1/18; No. 4 O.C.B., 7/6/18; Leic. R., 6/3/19; 2/Lieut. 26 De Montfort Street, Leicester.

✠ MUDDOCH, Jasper Milton
Sq/3651, 17/5/15; Shrop. Yeo., 19/8/15; 2/Lieut.
Killed in action 30/11/17.

MUDFORD, Harold Ernest
Sq/1130, 9/9/14; dis. to R. Mil. Coll., 28/12/14; Bedf. R., 12/5/15; Staff Capt.; w; M(1).

MUFF, Frank
6/4/8146, 3/12/15; W. Rid. R., 18/12/16; Lieut.; w; M.C.
42 Waterhouse Street, Lindley, Huddersfield.

MUFF, William Roland
C/10361, 5/1/17; No. 21 O.C.B., 5/5/17; York. & Lanc. R., 28/8/17; F; Lieut.; g-p.
65 Vineyard Hill Road, Wimbledon Park, S.W. 19.

✠ MUIR, Alexander Brisbain
6/2/9510, 15/2/16; No. 14 O.C.B., 26/11/16; Arg. & Suth'd. Highrs., 28/2/17; F; 2/Lieut. Killed in action 20/9/17.

MUIR, Godfrey George
11956, 3/9/17; R. Suss. R., 3/2/19; 2/Lieut.
1 Lessing Street, Honor Oak Park, S.E. 23.

MUIR, Jamieson
2/9673, 2/10/16; No 14 O.C.B., 26/11/16; Worc. R., 27/3/17; S; Lieut.; w. Michaelston House, St. Teath R.S.O., Cornwall.

MUIR, Robert Dunlop
D/14230, 25/10/18; demob. 24/1/19.
57 Dalziel Drive, Maxwell Park, Glasgow.

✠ MUIRDEN, Norman Hadley
A/11211, 7/5/17; R.F.C., C/S, 1/6/17; R.F.C., 1/8/17, R.A.F.; F; Lieut. Died of wounds 8/8/18 as Prisoner of War.

MUIRHEAD, Alexander Henry
F/2696, 14/1/15; R. Dub. Fus., 22/4/15, R. Suss. R.; Capt.; w.

✠ MUIRHEAD, John
6/2/5413, 5/8/15; R.F.C., 6/7/16; 2/Lieut.
Killed in action 16/3/17.

MUIRHEAD, Norman
C/D/12277, 3/12/17; No. 20 O.C.B., 10/5/18; trfr. 28th Lond. R., 14/10/18. Stamford House, Redford Road, Leamington.

MUIR-SMITH, Hugh
6/4/7182, 3/11/15, L/C.; Midd'x. R., 4/9/16, M.G.C.; F; Lieut.; w. 121 London Road, Leicester.

MUIR-SMITH, William
6/4/7466, 15/11/15, L/C.; R.W. Surr. R., 18/12/16; F,It; Lieut.
Riversdale, 8 Upperton Road, Eastbourne.

MULGAN, Geoffrey William Douglas
D/10642, 1/2/17, L/C.; R.G.A., C/S, 18/7/17; R.G.A., 17/12/17; 2/Lieut. 65 Carlisle Mansions, Carlisle Place, S.W. 1.

MULKERN, Hugh Alfred
6/3/7051, 28/10/15; Essex R., 4/9/16; Capt.; w; M.C.
New Oxford and Cambridge Club, Stratton Street, W.

MULLER, Louis
C/986, 5/8/14; dis. 5/9/14; Essex R., 2/5/15; Lieut.; w.
132 Delaware Road, Maida Vale, W. 9.

MULLIN, Richard Ballantine. See BALLANTINE, R. W. H.

✠ MULLINS, Henry Joseph
A/10736, 12/2/17; trfr. 16th Lond. R., 23/3/17; F; Pte.
Killed in action 16/8/17.

MULLINS, Hugh Thomas
Sq/187, 1/5/08; dis. 1/7/11.
18 Lyndhurst Gardens, Hampstead, N.W. 3.

MULVEY, Francis
4/5/4759, 12/7/15, Sgt.; R.A.S.C., 11/11/15; Capt.
The Cottage, Ballards Lane, Church End, Finchley, N. 3.

MUMFORD, Ernest Leslie
D/12932, 15/4/18, L/C.; demob. 23/1/19; F; M(1).
Lyford, Park Farm Road, Kingston-on-Thames.

MUMFORD, Harold Youell
A/13155, 29/5/18; trfr. 14th Lond. R., 6/12/18, Gord. Highrs.
15 Brookview Road, Streatham Park, S.W. 16.

MUMFORD, Henry Alexander
D/Sq/13840, 14/8/18; No. 1 O.C.B., 8/11/18, No. 11 O.C.B.; General List, 8/3/19; 2/Lieut.
62 Gothic Avenue, Toronto, Canada.

MUMFORD, Leslie Franklin
A/1285, 23/9/14; Midd'x. R., 27/10/14, Essex R.; P; Capt.; M(1).
14 Onslow Crescent, South Kensington, S.W. 7.

MUMFORD, Thomas John
2/2742, 21/1/15; Shrop. L.I., 8/7/15, 8th Lond. R., att. 6th Lond. R.; F; Staff Capt.; M.C., M(1).
Charwelton Hall, Byfield, Northamptonshire.

MUMMERY, Ernest Vale
Sq/3371, 24/4/15; R.F.A., 18/8/15; F,It; Lieut.
Dengewell Hall, Wix, Nr. Manningtree, Essex.

MUMMERY, John Pascho
4/5/4678, 8/7/15, L/C.; Surr. Yeo., 3/11/15, R.W. Surr. R.; F,It; Lieut.; Order of the Crown and Croix de Guerre (Belgian).
50 Devonshire Road, Bexhill-on-Sea.

MUNBY, Joe Douglas
A/11611, 5/7/17; A.S.C., C/S, 1/2/18; R.A.S.C., 25/4/18; F; 2/Lieut. Colvin, The Garlands, Scarborough.

APPENDIX II.—RECORDS OF RANK AND FILE.

MUNDAY, Leonard
D/10009, 24/11/16; Garr. O.C.B., 23/4/17; Suff. R., 14/7/17, emp. M. of Labour; Lieut.   40 Church Street, Edmonton.

✠ MUNDEN, John Arnold
2/3200, 8/4/15; Som. L.I., 10/7/15; F; 2/Lieut.; w.
Killed in action 27/8/16.

MUNDY, Frank Waring
6/1/6363, 20/9/15; Bucks. Huss., 26/12/15, secd. R.F.C., R.A.F.; Lieut.

MUNDY, Percy Charles Dryden
K/F/2294, 10/12/14; R. Suss. R., 6/6/15, att. K.R. Rif. C.; F; Capt.; Inv.; m(1).   The Nutshell, Burley, New Forest.

MUNNION, Cecil Ernest Forwood
6/2/7935, 29/11/15; No. 2 O.C.B., 14/8/16; K.R. Rif. C., 18/12/16; S,F; Lieut.; w; M.C.
6 Ormonde Terrace, Primrose Hill, N.W. 8.

MUNRO, Gordon Ross
A/13132, 27/5/18; No. 1 O.C.B., 8/11/18, No. 11 O.C.B.; General List, 8/3/19; EA; 2/Lieut.
21 Soper Road, Berea, Johannesburg, Transvaal, South Africa.

MUNRO, Hector
K/2704, 18/1/15; Cam'n. Highrs., 23/2/15; F; Capt.
6 Connaught Avenue, Chingford, Essex.

MUNRO, Henry Hugh
K/Sq/2593, 4/1/15; R.F.A., 27/2/15, R.E.; F; Capt.
Cia Salitrera Astwrias, Valparaiso, Chile.

✠ MUNRO, John Clegg
B/10590, 17/1/17; No. 14 O.C.B., 5/7/17; Worc. R., 30/10/17; F; 2/Lieut.   Died 9/11/18.

MUNRO, Malcolm William
A/12519, 30/1/18; H. Bde. O.C.B., 8/4/18; Welch Gds., 2/2/19; 2/Lieut.   176a Upper Richmond Road, East Sheen, S.W. 14.

MUNRO, Robert Dormond
C/13306, 17/6/18; No. 22 O.C.B., 23/8/18; Sco. Rif., 12/2/19; 2/Lieut.   Caledonian Club, St. James Square, S.W. 1.

MUNSEY, Laurence George Hensman
6/1/7936, 29/11/15; R.A.O.C., 26/4/16; S; Lieut.
Norsdal Crown Road, Kingston Hill, Surrey.

MURCH, Jack
6/5/6741, 11/10/15; 7th Lond. R., 24/10/16, att. R.A.F.; F; Lieut.   23 Fortis Green Avenue, Fortis Green, N.

MURCH, James Howard
D/13866, 20/8/18; dis. med. unfit, 14/12/18.
The Fessenden School, West Newton, Mass., U.S.A.

✠ MURDOCH, James Gorden
D/1408, 29/9/14, L/C.; S. Lan. R., 27/11/14; Lieut.
Died of wounds 22/9/15.

✠ MURDOCH, Ronald Hamilton
6/5/5948, 1/9/15; L'pool. R., 1/6/16; 2/Lieut.
Killed in action 28/10/16.

MURFITT, William Frederick Clay
6/3/5414, 5/8/15; K.R. Rif. C., 15/1/16; F; Lieut.
Haddenham Lodge, Hampstead Way, N.W.

✠ MURGATROYD, Hugh Lester
H/2014, 2/11/14; Leic. R., 11/1/15, att. Lan. Fus.; F; Capt.; M.C.   Died of wounds 27/9/18.

MURGATROYD, Norman Arthur
6/8654, 3/1/16; R.F.A., C/S, 23/6/16; R.F.A., 27/10/16; Lieut.
Park Drive, Huddersfield.

MURISON, Alfred Ross
A/11631, 9/7/17; trfr. R.F.C., 17/3/18, R.A.F.; Cpl.
Rector, Thurso Academy, Thurso.

✠ MURLY-GOTTO, James
6/4/5661, 16/8/15; R.E., 12/11/15; F; Lieut.; M(1).
Died of wounds 20/8/16.

MURPHY, Bertram Burke
6/1/5591, 12/8/15; R. Dub. Fus., 10/12/15, att. R. Fus.; Lieut.
Irish Land Commission, Upper Merrion Street, Dublin.

✠ MURPHY, Christopher Trevor Elias
6/2/8914, 12/1/16, L/C.; R.A., C/S, 4/8/16; R.G.A., 1/11/16; Lieut.   Died of wounds 8/5/18.

MURPHY, Daniel Joseph
D/11567, 22/6/17; No. 13 O.C.B., 5/4/18; M.G.C., 29/10/18; 2/Lieut.   Devonshire Villa, Youghal, Co. Cork, Ireland.

MURPHY, John Herbert F.
6/5/5264, 31/7/15; No. 11 O.C.B., 7/5/16; L'pool. R., 4/9/16; 2/Lieut.
Sunnyside House, Slough Green, Nr. Widnes, Lancashire.

✠ MURPHY, John Patrick
H/1947, 22/10/14, Cpl.; Hamps. R., 15/5/15; E,P; Capt.
Died 28/3/20.

✠ MURPHY, Leo Joseph
D/10748, 22/1/17; R.F.C., C/S, 13/3/17; R.F.C., 19/4/17; F; 2/Lieut.   Killed in action 29/5/17.

MURPHY, Paul
3/2992, 1/3/15; Midd'x. R., 31/8/15; Capt.
Beck Isle, Pickering, Yorkshire.

MURPHY, Searles
A/9979, 22/11/16; No. 14 O.C.B., 5/3/17; Arg. & Suth'd. Highrs., 26/6/17; F; Lieut.   Westcote, Ripon.

MURPHY, Thomas Arthur
C/12642, 18/2/18; R.F.A., C/S, 17/5/18; R.F.A., 8/3/19; 2/Lieut.
Club House Hotel, Kilkenny, Ireland.

MURRAY, Albert Frederick
6/5/9522, 16/2/16; 7th Lond. R., 23/6/16; F; Capt.; w.
St. Andrews College, Grahamstown, South Africa.

MURRAY, Alexander MacLeod
6/1/5778, 23/8/15, L/C.; R.G.A., 1/1/16; M,P; Lieut.; Inv; M(1).
Holy Trinity Vicarage, Upper Tooting, S.W. 17. (Now in Jerusalem).

MURRAY, Anthony Stoddard
6/3/9489, 15/2/16; No. 14 O.C.B., 30/10/16; Arg. & Suth'd. Highrs., 28/2/17; 2/Lieut.; p.   18 Woodside Crescent, Glasgow.

MURRAY, Archibald
4/6/Sq/4868, 15/7/15, L/C.; E. Kent Yeo., 6/9/15, Herts. Yeo.; Lieut.   28 St. Johns Wood Road, N.W.

MURRAY, Bernard Alleyne
Sq/607, 13/2/12, Sgt.; Notts. & Derby Yeo., 13/9/14, att. R.E. Sigs.; S,P; Capt.; M.C.
Nynehead, Austen Way, Gerrard's Cross, Buckinghamshire.

MURRAY, Charles John
4/6/Sq/4869, 15/7/15; E. Kent Yeo., 6/9/15, Herts. Yeo.; Lieut
28 St. Johns Wood Road, N.W.

MURRAY, Charles Stewart
6/9424, 10/2/16; No. 5 O.C.B., 14/3/16; R. Scots, 4/8/16, att. Bord. R.; Capt.

MURRAY, Colin Fraser
C/13240, 7/6/18; No. 11 O.C.B., 24/1/19; General List, 8/3/19; 2/Lieut.   P.O. Box 7, Rustenburg, Transvaal, South Africa.

MURRAY, Felix Thomas
A/11013, 5/4/17; No. 12 O.C.B., 10/8/17; R. Suss. R., 27/11/17; 2/Lieut.   Court House, Dundalk, Co. Louth.

MURRAY, Harry
C/14252, 30/10/18; trfr. K.R. Rif. C., 7/4/19.
120 Northcroft Road, West Ealing, W. 13.

MURRAY, James Ainslie
6/2/9442, 11/2/16; R.A., C/S, 26/10/16; R.F.A., 11/3/17; F; Lieut.   8 Royal Terrace, Edinburgh.

MURRAY, James Hamilton
6/2/8222, 7/12/15, Sgt.; demob. 5/2/19.
Millfield Lodge, Berkhamsted.

MURRAY, John
B/11676, 16/7/17; No. 11 O.C.B., 9/11/17; L'pool. R., 30/4/18; 2/Lieut.
c/o Inspector of Taxes, Mealhouse Lane, Bolton.

MURRAY, John George
B/A/10314, 4/1/17; R.E., C/S, 13/1/18; trfr. K.R. Rif. C., 7/4/19.   Kirklinton Villa, Kirklinton, Carlisle.

MURRAY, John Joseph
6/1/9291, 3/2/16; No. 8 O.C.B., 4/8/16, M.G.C., C/S; M.G.C., 23/11/16, Tank Corps; F; Capt.; M.C.
30 Fair Street, Drogheda, Co. Louth, Ireland.

MURRAY, Richard Marr
6/3/7301, 8/11/15; No. 9 O.C.B., 8/3/16; R. Scots, 23/7/16; F; Capt.; M.C.   66 Childebert Road, Balham, S.W. 17.

MURRAY, Vivian Royston
6/4/7401, 12/11/15; No. 9 O.C.B., 8/3/16; Cam'n. Highrs., 6/7/16; Lieut.
c/o British South African Coy., 2 London Wall Buildings, E.C.

APPENDIX II.—RECORDS OF RANK AND FILE.

MURRAY, William Carrington
6/5/C/8421, 15/12/15; No. 7 O.C.B., 4/11/16; trfr. R.F.A., 10/4/17; F; g. w.
Clomantogh Rectory, Woodsgift, Co. Kilkenny.

MURRAY-DIXON, Charles Edward Trevelyan
A/1283, 23/9/14; Leic. R., 27/11/14; F; Major; M.C., M(2).
Swithland Rectory, Loughborough, Leicestershire.

MURRAY-JOHNSON, Francis Kinloch
Sq/417, 21/5/09, Sgt.; R. Regt. of Cav., 16/9/14, 1st Drag. Gds.; F,I; Staff Capt.; w.
13 Cadogan Court, S.W. 3.

MURRAY-SMITH, John Edward
Sq/1089, 3/9/14; R. Horse Gds., 28/10/14; F; Major; w.
Gumley Hall, Market Harborough.

MURTON, Ernest
A/216, 11/5/08; dis. 10/5/12; R.N.V.R., 16/7/17; Lieut.
Lloyds, Royal Exchange, E.C. 3.

MUSGRAVE, Egerton Fitzwallis
6/3/8185, 6/12/15; L/C.; 7th Lond. R., 22/11/16, att. R. Fus.; F; Lieut.; w.
Cedar Creek Ranch, Shawnigan V.I., British Columbia, Canada.

✠ MUSGRAVE, Joseph Baxter
4/4371, 21/6/15; Ches. R., 7/1/16, att. R. War. R.; F; Capt.; w; M.C.
Died 16/3/20.

MUSGRAVE, Leonard
A/14019, 8/9/18; No. 13 O.C.B., 10/2/19; trfr. K.R. Rif. C., 25/4/19.
18 Wesley Road, Armley, Leeds.

MUSKETT, Lionel Herbert
B/1641, 9/10/14, L/C.; K.R. Rif. C., 15/2/15; Lieut.
Montrose, Kings Road, Richmond.

MYERS, Carl
C/12281, 17/11/17; trfr. R.E., 13/5/18; F; Spr.
40 Ashland Road, Sheffield.

MYERS, Cyril Joel
4/1/4345, 21/6/15; Essex R., 10/10/15, att. R. War. R.; Lieut.; w.
117 Sutherland Avenue, Maida Vale, W. 9.

MYHILL, Henry Thurgood
6/4/8367, 13/12/15; Worc. R., 18/12/16, att. M.G.C.; Lieut.; w.
Fairycroft, Saffron Walden.

MYHRE, Einer
C/13331, 19/6/18; R.E., C/S, 1/11/18; demob. 27/1/19
Grote House, Blackheath.

✠ MYLES, Alfred Thomas Charles
A/11002, 4/4/17; No. 12 O.C.B., 10/8/17; L'pool. R., 27/11/17; 2/Lieut.
Killed in action 2/7/18.

MYLES, Ernest William Riddle
A/13174, 31/5/18; trfr. 14th Lond. R., 6/12/18.
Wellbank, Arbroath, N.B.

MYLES, William Arthur
A/D/13016, 1/5/18; dis. med. unfit, 21/5/19.

✠ MYTTON, Richard Devereux Hugh
4/5/4802, 12/7/15; 1st Lond. R., 24/12/15; 2/Lieut.
Died of wounds 3/10/16.

NAISH, Reginald Neville Thomson
1/3093, 22/3/15; Sea. Highrs., 23/6/15; Lieut.
Bickley Farm, Milverton, Somerset.

MALDER, Reginald Fielding
6/1/6604, 4/10/15; R. Dub. Fus., 1/6/16, Tank Corps; Lieut.; w, p.
21 Onslow Gardens, S.W. 7.

NALDRETT, Harold Carter
B/1210, 14/9/14; Essex R., 23/12/14, R.F.C.; G,F; Lieut.; w.
3 Temple Gardens, Temple, E.C. 4.

NANSON, John Furness
B/12834, 22/3/18; dis. med, unfit, 9/11/18.
Haverbrack, Milnthorpe, Westmoreland.

NAOROJI, Karesasp Ardeshir Dadabhai
D/A/13977, 9/9/18; No. 17 O.C.B., 5/12/18, No. 23 O.C.B.; Indian Army, 30/11/19; F; 2/Lieut.
Bhuj, Cutch, India.

NAPIER, Ivan Robert
B/1040, 26/8/14; Cam'n. Highrs., 13/10/14, secd. M.G.C.; Lieut.; M(2).
68 Knightsbridge, Hyde Park, S.W. 1.

NAPIER, John Rupert Haslem
5/2/5630, 16/8/15; trfr. 5th Lond. R., 14/4/16.
Upton House, Ward, Eastry, Kent.

NAPIER, Robert Archibald
Sq/498, 14/6/10; dis. 13/6/14; R.E. Kent Yeo., 29/10/14, att. E. Kent R.; Lieut.; w.
33 Hill Street, Knightsbridge, S.W. 7.

NAPIER, Ronald Church Dixon
6/Sq/7109, 1/11/15, L/C.; No. 2 Cav. C/S, 31/3/16; Devon. Yeo., 6/9/16; F; Capt.; M.C.
Falcon Mine, Umouma, Southern Rhodesia.

NARUP, Einar Studdart
D/9982, 22/11/16; A.S.C., C/S, 30/6/17; R.A.S.C., 25/8/17; F; 2/Lieut.
Sunnybank, Mumbles, Glamorganshire.

NASH, Christopher Shore
6/1/5799, 23/8/15; Gren. Gds., 24/10/15; F; Lieut.; w(2); M.C.
Cannon Lodge, Hampstead, N.W. 3.

NASH, George Nathaniel
6/Sq/8899, 13/1/16; R.A., C/S, 9/6/16; R.G.A., 13/9/16; NR,SR; Capt.; p; Order of S. Stanislaus 2nd Class (Twice), 3rd Class (Once), Order of S. Anne.
54 St. Ann's Road, Stamford Hill, N. 16.

NASH, Harry Thomas Pritchard
B/12741, 11/3/18; R.A., C/S, 17/5/18; R.F.A., 15/2/19; 2/Lieut.
31a Wix Lane, Clapham Common, S.W. 4.

NASH, Leslie Chessborough Fleetwood
A/333, 1/12/08; dis. 30/11/13; Rif. Brig., 11/9/14; F; Capt.; g.
6 Raymond Buildings, Grays Inn, W.C.

NASH, William Rowland
6/2/8115, 2/12/15; trfr. R.G.A., 1/12/16; R.G.A., 2/9/17; Lieut.
Fleur-de-lis. Cardiff.

NASH-WILLIAMS, Victor Erle. See WILLIAMS, V. E. N.

✠ NASMITH, Arthur Plater
C/852, 4/8/14; Bord. R., 12/9/14; F; Capt.; D.S.O., M(2).
Killed in action 23/4/17.

NASMITH, Reginald
A/836, 4/8/14; High. L.I., 11/9/14, M.G.C.; F,NR; Major; w; D.S.O., M.C., Croix de Guerre (French), M(4).
Glen of Rothes, Rothes, Morayshire. (Now in Mesopotamia).

NATHAN, Charles Joseph
3/3406, 26/4/15; R.F.A., 3/9/15; Lieut.; w.
88 Gracechurch Street, E.C. 3.

NATHAN, Edward
D/E/13799, 9/8/18; No. 22 O.C.B., 25/9/18; demob.
Rosemount, Rickmansworth.

NATHAN, Gilbert Grace
C/1721, 15/10/14; 9th Lond. R., 6/2/15, att. T.M. Bty.; F; Lieut.; w, g.
Bank of New South Wales, 29 Threadneedle Street, E.C.

NAUHEIM, Richard Felix
1640, 9/10/14; Dorset R., 22/4/15, R.A.S.C.; Lieut.
17 Clarendon Court, Maida Vale, W. 9.

NAUNTON, Hugh Parker
C/462, 21/2/10; dis. 20/2/14; rej. C/1917, 16/10/14, L/C.; Suff. R., 12/12/14, E. Surr. R., R. Fus.; F; Capt.; w; D.S.O., M(1).
Hurstleigh, Redhill, Surrey.

NAYLER, Clifford Harry
D/12392, 15/1/18; No. 21 O.C.B., 10/5/18; trfr. 28th Lond. R., 7/10/18.
79 Bloomfield Road, Gloucester.

NAYLOR, Frank Bertram
6/3/8765, 6/1/16; R.E., C/S, 2/9/16; R.E., 18/11/16; F; Lieut.; w.
Hazel Royd, Girlington, Bradford, Yorkshire.

NAYLOR, Mark Charlton
4/4154, 10/6/15; dis. med. unfit, 8/8/16.
9 Brackley Road, Chiswick, W. 4.

NEAL, Archibald Bird
6/1/6253, 16/9/15; No. 1 O.C.B., 25/2/16; Essex R., 8/7/16; Lieut.; M.C.
Regora, Berkhamsted Avenue, Wembley Hill.

NEAL, George John
C/11750, 26/7/17; No. 14 O.C.B., 4/1/18; R. Fus., 25/6/18; F; 2/Lieut.; w.
19 Belgrave Road, Wanstead, Essex.

NEAL, James Douglas O'Dowd
B/13429, 2/7/18; demob. 23/1/19.
24 Drayton Gardens, S.W. 10.

NEALE, Douglas Herbert
4/3271, 15/4/15, Cpl.; L'pool. R., 30/10/15, M.G.C.; F; Lieut.
32 Streathbourne Road, Upper Tooting, S.W. 17.

NEALE, Gordon Seward
C/Sq/9971, 20/11/16; No. 1 Cav. C.S, 1/9/17; R. Regt. of Cav., 22/2/18; 2/Lieut.
East Grafton, Marlborough, Wiltshire.

APPENDIX II.—RECORDS OF RANK AND FILE.

NEALE, Harold Charles
B/11377, 28/5/17; No. 14 O.C.B., 5/10/17; 13th Lond. R., 26/2/18; 2/Lieut.   24a Louisville Road, S.W. 17.

NEALE, Nelson
6/1/8422, 15/12/15; R.E., C/S, 12/5/18; R.E., 27/9/18; 2/Lieut.
Tresta, Lavernock Road, Penarth, Glamorganshire.

NEALE, Norman William
C/1899, 16/10/14, Sgt.; K.R. Rif. C., 21/4/16; F; 2/Lieut.; w.
Connaught House, Ballards Lane, Church End, Finchley, N. 3.

NEALE, Ralph Stanley
3/3166, 1/4/15; Dorset R., 10/7/15; Lieut.; w.
Pickett, South Parrott, Miderton, Somerset.

NEAME, Barry
Sq/3548, 10/5/15, L/C.; Notts. Yeo., 2/9/15, att. R. Glouc. Huss.; E,S; Lieut.; Inv; M(2).   376 Clapham Road, S.W. 9.

NEATE, Edward George
C/13383, 24/6/18; trfr. 14th Lond. R., 6/12/18.
Fairview, Highfield Road, Sutton, Surrey.

✠ NEATE, Nelson Rayner
A/869, 4/8/14; R. Fus., 12/9/14, att. H.A.C.; F; Capt.; w(2); M.C.   Killed in action 3/5/17.

NEAVE-HILL, Wilfred
Sq/1677, 12/10/14; North'n. Yeo., 24/2/15; E,P; Capt.
5 Princes Terrace, Palace Court, W. 2.

NEEDHAM, Henry Ernest
A/11252, 14/5/17; No. 14 O.C.B., 7/9/17; R.W. Kent R., 17/12/17; 2/Lieut.
Crombie Lodge, Hatherley Road, Sidcup, Kent.

✠ NEEDHAM, Joseph Walter David
6/D/7074, 29/10/15, L/C.; R.F.C., C/S, 13/3/17; R.F.C., 19/4/17; 2/Lieut.   Died of wounds 12/11/17.

NEELY, Clive William
Sq/149, 18/4/08; dis. 17/4/09.

✠ NEGRETTI, Norman Charles Achille
6/3/5712, 19/8/15; Midd'x. R., 1/6/16; F; 2/Lieut.
Killed in action 30/1/17.

NEGRETTI, Paul Ernest
6/3/7774, 23/11/15, Sgt.; Garr. O.C.B., 12/12/16; R.F.C., 16/1/17, R.A.F.; Capt.   Ovingdean, Woking, Surrey.

NEGUS, William Martyn Ewings
E/1536, 6/10/14; R.N.V.R., 8/1/15; E; Lieut.
The Lawn, Walton-on-Thames.

NEILL, Archibald Frederick
B/10538, 17/1/17; No. 14 O.C.B., 7/6/17; W. Kent Yeo., 25/9/17; F; Lieut.; Inv.
17 Estcourt Terrace, Headingley, Leeds.

NEILL, Arthur
6/4/7467, 15/11/15; No. 11 O.C.B., 7/5/16; W. Rid. R., 4/9/16; Lieut.   Midlands, Rutland Road, Harrogate, Yorkshire.

✠ NEILL, Robert Kirkpatrick
6/1/7875, 26/11/15; North'd. Fus., 24/1/17; 2/Lieut.
Killed in action 16/8/17.

NEILSON, Henry Vere
F/2908, 13/2/15; Notts. & Derby. R., 22/6/15; F; Lieut.
Lyddington House, Lyddington, Uppingham, Rutland.

NEILSON, Richard Smith
2/9784, 25/10/16; No. 14 O.C.B., 5/3/17; Sco. Rif., 26/6/17, Sco. Horse; F; Lieut.; w.   Ardrohr, Coatbridge.

NEL, Joseph Rose
D/Sq/11836, 9/8/17; No. 14 O.C.B., 4/1/18; Som. L.I., 25/6/18; 2/Lieut.
c/o Standard Bank of South Africa Ltd., Lombard Street, E.C.

NELIGAN, Maurice Victor
6/5/9012, 19/1/16; R.A., C/S, 7/8/16; R.F.A., 17/11/16; Lieut.; w; M(1).   Bank House, Ballymahon, Co. Longford, Ireland.

✠ NELL, Basil Frank
3703, 20/5/15, L/C.; R.E., 23/7/15; Major.   Died 22/12/18.

NELSON, Henry Ince
6/9433, 11/2/16; R.F.A., C/S, 23/6/16; R.F.A., 23/9/16, att. R.A.F.; F; Lieut.; w.   Netherwood, Blundellsands, Liverpool.

NELSON, Roland Hugh
K/2320, 11/12/14; dis. 15/1/15.

NELSON, Walter Lawrence
4/3509, 6/5/15; R.A.S.C., 15/5/15; Capt.
Netherwood, Blundellsands, Nr. Liverpool.

NELSON, William Lucas
4/3865, 31/5/15; 22nd Lond. R., 16/11/15, secd. M.G.C.; Lieut.
Avondale, Penton Hook, Staines, Middlesex.

NESBITT, David
B/13468, 5/7/18; demob. 24/1/19.
Millisle, Donaghadee, Co. Down, Ireland.

NESBITT, Thomas
6/3/9395, 9/2/16; No. 13 O.C.B., 4/11/16; North'd. Fus., 28/2/17, att. Ches. R.; F; Lieut.; w.
Millisle, Donaghadee, Co. Down, Ireland.

NESS, Arthur Carmichael
A/13175, 31/5/18; demob. 23/1/19.
c/o Duncan Fox & Coy., Cunard Buildings, Liverpool.

NETHERCOTT, Alan George
3/4907, 17/7/15; Essex R., 7/11/15; Lieut.; w; M.C.
107 Porters Grange Avenue, Southend.

NETTING, Ewart Arthur
D/10656, 5/2/17; No. 11 O.C.B., 5/7/17; Devon. R., 30/10/17; P.F; 2/Lieut.
27 Holmesdale Road, Hampton Wick, Middlesex.

NETTLETON, Stanley
D/11555, 25/6/17; R.E., C/S, 11/11/17; R.E., 21/12/17; F,It; Lieut.   Kelvingrove, 42 Dunmore Road, Wimbledon, S.W. 19.

NEVE, Noel Wilfrid
3/3462, 3/5/15; North'd. Fus., 5/8/15.

✠ NEVE, Walter Gregory
3116, 25/3/15, L/C.; E. Kent R., 17/10/15; E,S; 2/Lieut.
Killed in action 25/8/17.

NEVETT, Richard Brian
A/12520, 31/1/18, L/C.; No. 13 O.C.B., 7/6/18; N. Staff. R, 5/2/19; 2/Lieut.   Rossall College, Nr. Fleetwood, Lancashire.

NEVILLE, Arthur Smith
D/13734, 2/8/18; trfr. K.R. Rif. C., 7/4/19.
54 Hampton Road, Redland, Bristol.

✠ NEVILLE, Frank Septimus
C/1013, 6/8/14; North'n. R., 12/9/14; Capt.; w; M(1).
Died of wounds 24/11/17.

NEVILLE, George John Ernest
Sq/194, 5/5/08; dis. 31/12/09.

NEVILLE, George Robertson
4/3/4423, 24/6/15; North'd. Fus., 22/6/16; F; Lieut.
East Hall Farm, Feltwell, Nr. Brandon, Norfolk.

✠ NEVILLE, Henry George
6/1/6070, 6/9/15; No. 11 O.C.B., 7/5/16; R.F.C., 4/9/16; 2/Lieut.
Died of wounds 15/5/17.

NEVILLE, Leslie Robin
9119, 24/1/16; R.F.C., 11/8/16, R.A.F.; Lieut.; w.

✠ NEVILLE, William Sim
B/2747, 21/1/15; R.G.A., 10/4/15; 2/Lieut.
Killed in action 25/9/16.

NEW, George Francis
A/13063, 13/5/18; No. 1 O.C.B., 8/11/18; Hamps. R., 16/3/19; 2/Lieut.   Soles Hill, Chilham, Kent.

NEW, Stanley Wilson
B/12421, 18/1/18; No. 13 O.C.B., 7/6/18; R.W. Kent R., 5/2/19; 2/Lieut.   86 Dawlish Road, Leyton, E. 10.

NEWALL, Nathan
6/3/9479, 14/2/16, L/C.; Arg. & Suth'd. Highrs., 22/11/16; Lieut.
18 St. Marks Crescent, Regents Park Road, N.W. 1.

NEWBERRY, Francis James
1/9762, 20/10/16, L/C.; No. 14 O.C.B.; Midd'x. R., 29/5/17, R.A.S.C.; F; Lieut.; Inv.
Danesbury, Flower Lane, Mill Hill, N.W. 7.

NEWBERRY, Victor Lionel
C/11800, 2/8/17; No. 5 O.C.B., 7/9/17; R.E., 17/12/17; F; 2/Lieut.
The Glen, Oakwood, Via Inverell, New South Wales, Australia.

NEWBERRY, William John
6/1/6845, 15/10/15, L/C.; No. 14 O.C.B., 27/9/16; R.W. Kent R., 24/1/17; F; Lieut.; w.   Stoke Poges, Buckinghamshire.

APPENDIX II.—RECORDS OF RANK AND FILE.

NEWBERY, Robert Edwin
B/9904, 13/11/16, L/C.; M.G.C., C/S, 14/3/17; M.G.C., 26/8/17; F; Lieut.; M.C.
Roslin, Rookery Road, Staines, Middlesex.

NEWBERY, Sidney
6/7075, 29/10/15; No. 14 O.C.B.; M.G.C., 25/9/16; F; Lieut.; w.
Montrave, The Mount, Caversham, Reading.

NEWBOLD, Henry Charles
B/2659, 12/1/15; R.F.A., 16/5/15; Lieut.
Holywell, Holywell Hill, St. Albans, Hertfordshire.

NEWBY, Walter Clifford
D/11837, 9/8/17; No. 3 O.C.B., 8/2/18; W. York. R., 30/7/18; 2/Lieut.
24 Cecil Avenue, Horton Park, Bradford, Yorkshire.

✠ NEWCOMB, Cyril
K/D/2528, 31/12/14; R. Fus., 25/1/15; 2/Lieut.
Killed in action 25-28/9/15.

NEWCOMBE, Frederick George
6/8653, 3/1/16; R.F.A., C/S, 26/5/16; R.G.A., 30/8/16; F; Lieut.; M.C.
128 Mildred Avenue, Watford, Hertfordshire.

NEWELL, Adrian Leonard
D/10639, 1/2/17; R.F.C., C/S, 13/3/17; R.F.C., 19/4/17; Lieut.
Heywood, Cobham, Surrey.

NEWELL, John Beaumont
D/11568, 28/6/17; No. 19 O.C.B., 9/11/17; E. Kent R., 26/3/18; F; 2/Lieut.
65 Hill Top Avenue, Cheadle Hulme, Cheshire.

NEWENHAM, George Alexander
6/5/9407, 9/2/16; No. 1 O.C.B., 6/9/16; R.F.C., 5/2/17, R.A.F.; Lieut.; w-p.
Parkowen, Summerhill South, Cork, Ireland.

NEWINGTON, Alfred
B/12379, 12/1/18; No. 14 O.C.B., 7/6/18; trfr. 28th Lond. R., 18/10/18.
8 Lee Terrace, Blackheath, S.E. 3.

✠ NEWINGTON, John
A/496, 12/5/10; dis. 11/5/11; E. Surr. R., att. Ches. R.; Lieut.
Killed in action 22/2/15.

✠ NEWLAND, Edward Albert
C/11774, 30/7/17; No. 14 O.C.B., 4/1/18; R. Fus., 25/6/18; 2/Lieut.
Killed in action 23/10/18.

NEWLING, George Arthur
6/1/7691, 22/11/15, L/C.; No. 14 O.C.B.; R. Marines, 24/10/16; F; Staff Capt.; w(2); M.C. and Bar, M(1).
2 Ranelagh Avenue, Barnes, S.W. 13.

NEWLING, Philip Tudor
D/1440, 29/9/14, L/C.; Remount Depot, 30/12/14, R.F.C.; Lieut.; w.

NEWMAN, Charles Francis
8936, 17/1/16; R.A., C/S, 9/6/16; R.G.A., 16/9/16; F,M; Lieut.; w.
Ivydene, Farnborough, Kent.

NEWMAN, Douglas
K/B/2154, 23/11/14; Suff. R., 16/3/15; Lieut.
16 Church Street, Ipswich.

NEWMAN, Frank Harlow
C/10974, 2/4/17; M.G.C., C/S, 31/8/17; Tank Corps, 27/3/18; F; 2/Lieut.; Inv.
Park View, Port Talbot, Glamorganshire.

NEWMAN, Frank James
6/3/5523, 9/8/15; R.F.A., 2/12/15; 2/Lieut.; Inv.
Grootsfontein School of Agriculture, Middleberg, Cape Province, South Africa.

NEWMAN, Frederick Henry
6/4/5995, 2/9/15, Sgt.; No. 14 O.C.B., 27/12/16; 8th Lond. R., 28/2/17, K.R. Rif. C.; F; Lieut.; M(1).
29 Aberdare Gardens, N.W. 6.

NEWMAN, George Emeny
4/4346, 21/6/15; R.F.A., 4/10/15; F,I; Lieut.
Cliff House, Warwick Park, Tunbridge Wells.

NEWMAN, Henry Augustus Alexander
A/430, 15/6/09; dis. 14/6/13; rej. B/11707, 19/7/17; No. 14 O.C.B., 9/11/17; Oxf. & Bucks. L.I., 30/4/18; 2/Lieut.
Lyndhurst, Radlett, Hertfordshire.

NEWMAN, Herbert George
4/1/3976, 3/6/15; R. Fus., 10/9/15.
20 Maygrove Road, Kilburn, N.W. 6.

NEWMAN, Herbert John Greatrex
A/2877, 8/2/15; Lan. Fus., 25/5/15, R.F.C., R.A.F.; F; Major; w(2); M.B.E., M(1).
Beechurst, Hickman Road, Sparkbrook, Birmingham.

NEWMAN, James William Eldridge
6/4/7592, 18/11/15, Cpl.; E. Kent R., 25/9/16, att. Midd'x. R., Tank Corps; F; Lieut.
53 Oakfield Road, Croydon, Surrey.

NEWMAN, Richard Arthur
6/C/6122, 23/9/15; No. 13 O.C.B., 4/11/16; R. Suss. R., 28/2/17; F; Lieut.; w.
80 Haddington Road, Dublin.

NEWSAM, Frank Aubrey
2/4424, 24/6/15; R. Ir. Fus., 7/10/15, Indian Army; F,I; Lieut.; M.C., M(1).
10 Ladbroke Gardens, Notting Hill, W. 11.

NEWSON, William Hill
B/729, 11/11/13, Sgt.; Gord. Highrs., 18/11/14; F; Major; w; M.C., M(1).
34 Clarence Gate Gardens, N.W. 1.

NEWSTEAD, Willie
A/11287, 14/5/17; demob. 14/2/19.
Muckleton Hill Farm, Stanhoe, Norfolk.

NEWTH, Frederick Douglas
6/2/7213, 4/11/15; 13th Lond. R., 2/9/16; F,S,P; Lieut.; M(1).
43/44 Percival Street, Clerkenwell, E.C.

NEWTON, Arthur Watson
9263, 3/2/16, L/C.; No. 5 O.C.B., 14/8/16; S. Wales Bord., 21/11/16; F; Capt.; M(1).
52 St. Enoch Square, Glasgow.

NEWTON, Charles Hotham
D/13779, 7/8/18; demob. 31/3/19.
8 Tithebarn Road, Southport, Lancashire.

NEWTON, Dan Taylor
A/11269, 14/5/17; No. 10 O.C.B., 5/10/17; 11th Lond. R., 26/2/18; 2/Lieut.
16 Queensdown Road, Clapton, E. 5.

NEWTON, Duncan Stuart Campbell
3/6/9118, 24/1/16; R.F.C., 7/8/16; R.A.F.; Lieut.
49 Cotswold Road, Westcliff-on-Sea, Essex.

NEWTON, Frank Leslie
6/4/8368, 13/12/15, L/C.; Hamps. R., 18/12/16; F; Lieut.; w.
Bincleaves, Westerham, Kent.

NEWTON, Giles Fendall
C/1629, 9/10/14; R.W. Surr. R., 28/11/14, R.F.A.; F; Lieut.
Conservative Club, St. James, S.W.

NEWTON, Leonard Arthur
C/883, 5/8/14; Bord. R., 12/9/14, att. No. 1 O.C.B. Inst; F; Capt.; w, Inv.
Westbourne, Emsworth.

NEWTON, Robert
D/11097, 23/4/17; R.G.A., C/S, 31/8/17; R.G.A., 6/1/18; F; 2/Lieut.
54 Eldon Place, Newcastle-on-Tyne.

NEWTON, Sydney James Nicholas
6/4/6310, 18/9/15; No. 14 O.C.B., 30/9/16; Glouc. R., 24/10/16; F; Lieut.; w.
93 Cornwall Gardens, Queens Gate, S.W. 7. (Now in British West Indies).

NEY, Reginald Osborne
6/3/7341, 10/11/15, L/C.; Midd'x. R., 2/9/16, Rif. Brig., att. Lab. Corps; F; Lieut.; w.
Rooklands, Rye, Sussex. (Now in Africa).

✠ NIBLETT, Arthur Hilton
A/785, 20/4/14; Midd'x. R., 4/10/14, R.E.; 2/Lieut.
Died of wounds 21/9/16.

NIBLETT, Basil Morton
F/1922, 22/10/14; W.orc. R., 13/11/14; F; Capt.; w; M(1).
Redmarley Rectory, Gloucester.

NICHOLAS, Archibald John
4/3866, 31/5/15; R.W. Fus., 12/8/15; F; Lieut.
Belmont, Aberavon, Glamorganshire.

NICHOLAS, Edric Morgan
C/A/11775, 30/7/17; R.F.C., C/S, 15/2/18; R.F.C., 13/3/18, R.A.F.; F; Lieut.; p.
The Grange, Maesteg, South Wales.

NICHOLAS, Ernest Noel
6/4/5858, 26/8/15; trfr. 16th Lond. R., 2/5/16.
6 Johnson Mansions, Queens Club Gardens, West Kensington, W. 14.

NICHOLAS, Frank James
6/3/5800, 23/8/15; Glouc. R., 1/6/16, Hamps. R.; F; Lieut.; w.
Pershore, Worcestershire.

NICHOLAS, Percy Edgar
A/E/13964, 6/9/18; No. 22 O.C.B., 22/11/18; demob. 18/1/19.
13 Dunston Road, Golders Green, N.W.

APPENDIX II.—RECORDS OF RANK AND FILE.

NICHOLAS, *Wilfrid Lawrence John*
B/513, 4/11/10, Sgt.; E. Kent R., 14/8/14, att. R.W. Surr. R., secd. R.F.C.; F; Capt.; w(2); M.C., M(2).
  c/o The Barma Corporation Ltd., Namtu, Northern Shan States, Burma.

NICHOLL, *Edwin Anthony*
6/5/5340, 2/8/15; R.A.S.C., 8/11/15; F,It; Capt.; M(1).
  129 Newington Butts, Kennington, S.E. 11.

✠ NICHOLL-CARNE, *Osmond Whitlock*
6/2/9487, 15/2/16; No. 13 O.C.B., 4/11/16; Welch R., 28/2/17; 2/Lieut. Killed in action 1/8/17.

NICHOLLS, *Charles*
4/6/5/5173, 29/7/15; R.E., 5/10/15; F; Capt.; M.C.
  14 New Hill, Goodwick, Pembrokeshire. (Now in Cyprus).

NICHOLLS, *Eugene John Henry Cathcart*
6/5/8223, 7/12/15; Linc. R., 28/7/16, att. S. Lan. R.; EA,SWA,F; Capt.; w.
  c/o H. C. Nicholls Esq., City Club, Cape Town, South Africa.

NICHOLLS, *Frank*
D/1381, 29/9/14; Manch. R., 3/3/15; F,It; Capt.; w; D.S.O., M.C., M(1). Hill Bank, Spring Grove, Loughton, Essex.

✠ NICHOLLS, *Lionel*
6/1/6376, 21/9/15, L/C.; 8th Lond. R., 6/6/16; 2/Lieut.
  Killed in action 26/8/16.

NICHOLS, *Basil George*
4/3735, 24/5/15; R.F.A., 27/10/15, att. R.A.F.; F,It; Lieut.; w.
  233 Lavender Hill, S.W. 11.

✠ NICHOLS, *Douglas William Lane*
A/1373, 26/9/14; R.W. Surr. R., 27/11/14; Capt.; M.C.
  Killed in action 20/8/16

NICHOLS, *Francis Gerald*
1/9635, 25/9/16; No. 14 O.C.B., 26/11/16; E. York. R., 27/3/17; F; Lieut.; w, p. Ocean House, Great Tower Street, E.C. 3.

NICHOLS, *Harold Salter*
E/1517, 1/10/14; R.W. Surr. R., 10/8/15, R.F.C., R.A.F.; Lieut.
  56 Welbeck Street, Cavendish Square, W. 1.

NICHOLS, *Harry Archie*
A/10299, 1/1/17; R.F.A., C/S, 22/6/17; trfr. R.F.A., 25/9/17.
  36 St. Andrews Street, Cambridge.

NICHOLS, *Henry Leon*
6/Sq/5598, 12/8/15; R.F.A., 15/10/15; Lieut.; M.C. and Bar, M(1). Quince House, Bishops Nympton, North Devonshire.

NICHOLS, *Oretie Stanley*
3824, 29/5/15; R.F.A., C/S, 4/8/16; R.F.A., 10/11/16; F; Lieut.; M.C. 3 Beach Houses, Royal Crescent, Margate.

NICHOLS, *Richard Floyd*
E/14166, 14/10/18; No. 11 O.C.B., 24/1/19; General List, 8/3/19; 2/Lieut. Goldsithney, Marazion, Cornwall.

✠ NICHOLSON, *Arthur Harry*
6/5/7999, 29/11/15; No. 8 O.C.B., 4/8/16; Manch. R., 21/11/16; 2/Lieut. Died of wounds 9/4/17.

NICHOLSON, *Claude John Hartshorne*
C/1160, 14/9/14; Suff. R., 30/9/14, General List; F; Lieut.; w.
  74 Portland Place, W. 1.

NICHOLSON, *Clifford*
6/Sq/6605, 4/10/15; 2nd Life Guards, 3/2/16; F; 2/Lieut.
  Horkston Manor, Barton-on-Humber, Lincolnshire.

NICHOLSON, *Frederick Cecil Guy*
6/1/5415, 5/8/15, L/C.; R. Lanc. R., 27/12/15, att. M.G.C.; M; Capt.
  30 Clyfford Crescent, Newport, Monmouthshire. (Now in French West Africa).

NICHOLSON, *Geoffrey*
6/1/D/6630, 4/10/15, L/C.; No. 14 O.C.B., 27/12/16; North'd. Fus., 27/3/17; F; Lieut.; w.
  Halliwell Dene, Hexham, Northumberland.

NICHOLSON, *Joseph Arthur*
A/10036, 29/11/16; R.A., C/S, 27/4/17; R.G.A., 1/9/17; F; Capt. Patterdale, London Road South, Lowestoft.

NICHOLSON, *Norwood*
4/6/5/4977, 19/7/15; R.A.S.C., 1/9/15; Capt.
  Edale Morgate, Rotherham.

NICHOLSON, *Philip William*
A/14098, 4/10/18; No. 11 O.C.B., 27/1/19; General List, 8/3/19; 2/Lieut. c/o Mrs. Percy, Victoria Lodge, Raynes Park.

NICHOLSON, *William Dixon*
6/5/5949, 1/9/15, L/C.; L'pool. R., 1/6/16; F; Lieut.
  35 Newsham Drive, Newsham Park, Liverpool.

NICHOLSON, *William Henry*
4/3906, 31/5/15; trfr. Fife & Forfar Yeo., 9/3/16, K.O. Sco. Bord.; F; w. p. 23 Conington Road, Lewisham, S.E. 13.

NICHOLSON, *William Hubert*
6/1/6698, 7/10/15; No. 4 O.C.B., 7/3/16; North'd. Fus., 14/7/16; F; Lieut.; w.
  Anick Grange, Hexham, Northumberland. (Now in Switzerland).

✠ NICKEL, *George Gaston*
5/5348, 2/8/15, Sgt.; L'pool. R., 27/12/15; F; 2/Lieut.
  Killed in action 31/7/17.

NICOL, *Arthur Murray*
6/5/6771, 11/10/15; No. 9 O.C.B., 8/3/16; Bord. R., 6/7/16, R.A.S.C.; F; Capt.
  8 Hughenden Terrace, Kelvinside, Glasgow. W.

NICOLL, *Leonard Vere*
1589, 6/10/14; R. Suss. R., 9/3/15; F; Lieut.; w.
  Bidicote, Gerrards Cross, Buckinghamshire.

NICOLL, *William Macdonald*
B/13506, 10/7/18; demob. 27/1/19.
  164 Alexander Street, Dundee.

NICOLLE, *Roland*
6/3/8900, 13/1/16; R.A., C/S, 7/8/16; R.F.A., 17/11/16, att. R.F.C., R.A.F.; Lieut.; w.
  105 Boyne Road, Lewisham, S.E. 13.

NIELD, *Arnold*
B/10367, 5/1/17; dis. med. unfit, 10/4/17.
  The Cottage, Latchford West, Warrington, Lancashire.

✠ NIGHTINGALE, Sir *Edward Manners*
6/9130, 24/1/16; R.A.O.C., 12/4/16. Died.

NIGHTINGALE, *Ernest*
D/11870, 16/8/17; R.E., C/S, 11/11/17; R.E., 21/12/17; F; Lieut. Bernam, Myra Road, Fairhaven, Lytham, Lancashire.

NIGHY, *James Terence*
B/A/D/11677, 16/7/17; H. Bde. O.C.B., 5/4/18; E. Surr. R., 3/2/19; 2/Lieut. 43 The Brent, Dartford, Kent.

NINER, *Bertie Collins*
6/2/9523, 16/2/16; R.A., C/S, 10/11/16; R.G.A., 1/5/17; Capt.
  c/o Anglo South American Bank Ltd., Old Broad Street, E.C. 2.

NINNIS, *George Elvey Howard*
B/11424, 1/6/17; A.S.C., C/S, 1/11/17; R.A.S.C., 25/1/18; F; 2/Lieut. 5 Leopold Road, East Finchley, N. 2.

NINNIS, *Robert Douglas Kyallmark*
6/Sq/9148, 25/1/16; No. 2 Cav. C/S, 5/1/17; 2nd Huss., 30/4/17; Lieut. The Elms, Leigham Avenue, Streatham, S.W. 16.

✠ NISBET, *Douglas Guille*
A/1053, 31/8/14; S. Wales Bord., 21/10/14; Lieut.; w.
  Killed in action 10/6/16

✠ NIVEN, *James*
6/9120, 24/1/16; R.E., 27/5/16; 2/Lieut.
  Killed in action 3/5/17.

✠ NIVEN, *John*
6/8864, 12/1/16; R.F.A., C/S, 21/7/16; R.F.A., 27/10/16; 2/Lieut. Killed in action 13/5/17.

NIVISON, *John*
6/2/8990, 18/1/16; R.A.O.C., 19/9/16; Lieut.
  Deema, Upper Sea Road, Bexhill-on-Sea.

NIX, *Bertram Deen*
3/3352, 22/4/15; Leic. R., 28/7/15, Army Cyc. Corps; M,P; Capt.; w; M(1). 27 Lushington Road, Eastbourne.

NIXON, *Anthony Leo*
C/10173, 11/12/16; No. 12 O.C.B., 7/9/17; Lab. Corps, 20/10/17; 2/Lieut. Overseas Club, General Buildings, Aldwych, W.C. 2.

✠ NIXON, *Arthur William Lennox*
6/5/7110, 1/11/15, L/C.; R.F.C., 2/8/16; 2/Lieut.
  Killed in action 1/6/17.

NIXON, *Charles Fuller*
6/9121, 24/1/16; 2nd Life Guards, 11/4/16.
  Stansted, Mountfitchet, Stansted R.S.O., Essex.

NIXON, *Frederick Henry*
D/2820, 30/1/15; R.E., 7/7/15; F; Capt.
  12 Emperors Gate, South Kensington, S.W. 7.

APPENDIX II.—RECORDS OF RANK AND FILE.

NIXON, Maurice Allan
2/3233, 12/4/15; Shrop. L.I., 30/6/15, North'n. R.; Lieut.
c/o Turf Club, Cairo.

✠ NIXON, Noel Charles Frederick
B/1261, 23/9/14; Bedf. R., 20/10/14; Capt.
Killed in action 24/3/18.

NIXON-SMITH, Percival
C/12054, 27/9/17, L/C.; No. 6 O.C.B., 5/4/18; Gds. M.G.R., 12/11/18; 2/Lieut.
53 St. James Road, S.W.17.

NOAKES, Eric John Wickham
F/1857, 16/10/14, Sgt.; 6th Lond. R., 3/3/15, secd. Indian Army; Capt.

NOAKES, Geoffrey Bertram
B/Sq/10779, 19/2/17; No. 1 Cav. C/S, 1/9/17; R. Regt. of Cav., 22/2/18, att. R.A.S.C.; SR; Lieut.
c/o N. R. Smith Esq., Fairoaks, Sacramento Co., California, U.S.A.

NOAKES, Stanley Leopold
4/5/4903, 15/7/15; R.W. Kent R., 4/9/16; F; 2/Lieut.; w.
45 Capel Road, Forest Gate, Essex.

NOAKES, Sydney Neville
C/13361, 27/6/18; No. 22 O.C.B., 23/8/18; E. Kent R., 13/2/19; 2/Lieut.
Selsdon Park, Nr. Croydon.

✠ NOBLE, Alfred T. L.
4/1/4402, 24/6/15; R.W. Surr. R., 8/1/16; F; 2/Lieut.; w.
Died 5/3/19.

✠ NOBLE, Archibald Francis
B/508, 4/11/10; Ches. R., 11/9/14; Capt.; M(1).
Killed in action 21/5/16.

NOBLE, Brian Henry Heywood
A/11256, 14/5/17; H. Bde. O.C.B., 7/9/17; trfr 28th Lond. R., 25/2/18, att Rif. Brig.; F.
4 Abercrombie Square, Liverpool.

NOBLE, Ernest Philip
6/1/5567, 12/8/15, L/C.; S. Lan. R., 8/6/16, att. Hamps. R.; F; Capt.; Inv.
110 Flixton Road, Urmston, Manchester.

NOBLE, Herbert George
1/3549, 10/5/15; R. Fus., 10/9/15, War Office; F; Lieut.; w.
24 Moorgate Street, E.C. 2.

NOBLE, John Wood
B/12369, 4/1/18; R.F.A., C/S, 15/3/18; R.F.A., 10/10/18; 2/Lieut.
Sherbrooke, Dobcross, Nr. Oldham, Lancashire.

NOBLE, Richmond Samuel Howe
6/1/9186, 28/1/16; No. 7 O.C.B., 11/8/16; R. Ir. Rif., 21/11/16; F; 2/Lieut.; w.
Lisnatore, Suffolk, Dunmurry, Co. Antrim, Ireland.

NOBLE, Robert
B/10325, 4/1/17; trfr. 16th Lond. R., 23/3/17.
4 Park Place, St. James Street, S.W. 1.

NOCK, Alan Robert
6/1/5662, 16/8/15; R. War. R., 27/1/16, R.A.F.; F; Capt.; D.F.C.
79 Hall Road, Handsworth, Birmingham.

NOCK, Harry Clayton
A/B/12170, 29/10/17, L/C.; No. 8 O.C.B., 7/6/18; R. War. R., 5/2/19; 2/Lieut.
79 Hall Road, Handsworth, Birmingham.

NOCK, Malcolm Martin
C/13241, 7/6/18; No. 11 O.C.B., 24/1/19; General List, 8/3/19; 2/Lieut. c/o A. E. Aspinall Esq., 15 Seething Lane, E.C. 3.

✠ NOEL, Francis Methuen
6/4/8116, 2/12/15; No. 8 O.C.B., 4/8/16; Devon. R., 21/11/16; F; Capt.; M(1).
Killed in action 26/10/17.

NOLAN, Henry Grattan
6/4/9219, 31/1/16; dis. to re-enlist in Canadian Army; Canadian Infantry; F; Capt.; w; M.C., M(1).
University College, Oxford.

NOLAN, James Gregory
C/13362, 27/6/18; trfr. K.R. Rif. C., 25/4/19.
Holmsdene, Victoria Road, Bridlington, Yorkshire.

NOLAN, James Vincent
6/4/Sq/4940, 19/7/15; R.A.S.C., 4/10/15; S,E,P,F; Lieut.
Ulcombe, St. John's Road, Orpington, Kent.

NOON, Leonard
C/73, 13/4/08; dis. 12/4/12.

NOON, Ronald Ernest
6/3/8794, 6/1/16; No. 14 O.C.B., 26/11/16; L'pool. R., 28/2/17; F; Capt.; M.C.
14 Garston Old Road, Cressington, Liverpool.

NORDON, Charles Louis
A/B/C/D/12145, 22/10/17; demob. 6/1/19.
Cross Keys House, 56, Moorgate Street, E.C. 2.

NORIE-MILLER, Stanley
B/1030, 24/8/14; R. Highrs., 12/9/14; F; Capt.; w(2); M.C., M(1).
Cleeve, Perth, Scotland.

NORLAND, Richard Felix   See NAUHEIM, R. F.

NORMAN, Burford Noel
B/174, 29/4/08; dis. 28/4/09; R.A.M.C.; Capt.; M.C.
University College, Gower Street, W.C. 1.

NORMAN, Cyril Augustus
6/4/7468, 15/11/15; No. 11 O.C.B., 7/5/16; Glouc. R., 4/9/16; Lieut.

NORMAN, Edward James
C/12672, 1/3/18; No. 14 O.C.B., 5/7/18; Dorset R., 4/3/19; 2/Lieut.
18 Orion Road, Rodwell, Weymouth.

NORMAN, Frank Kendall
Sq/881, 5/8/14, L/C.; R.A.S.C., 14/11/14; F; Major; M.C., Croix de Guerre (French).
The New Beacon, Sevenoaks.

✠ NORMAN, Gilford William
6/2/6982, 25/10/15; Notts. & Derby. R., 1/6/16, att. Leic. R.; 2/Lieut.
Killed in action 25/9/16.

NORMAN, Raymond Thomas
1908, 16/10/14, L/C.; Ches. R., 14/5/15, att. T.M. Bty.; E,P,F; Lieut.; Croix de Guerre (Belgian).
Spring Hill, Wellingborough, Northamptonshire.

NORMAN, Richard Douglas
3/3407, 26/4/15; 23rd Lond. R., 18/8/15, Rif. Brig.; F,P; Capt.; w(2).
53 Tivoli Crescent, Brighton.

NORRIS, Charles Grayson
B/12855, 25/3/18; R.F.A., C/S, 26/7/18; R.F.A., 7/4/19; 2/Lieut.
Poplar Gate, Stonehouse, Gloucestershire.

NORRIS, Frank Leslie
B/560, 5/4/11; dis. 23/2/12; York. & Lanc. R., att. No. 17 O.C.B. Inst; F,It,M; Capt.; Inv; M.C.
Langley Lodge, Surbiton. (Now in Mesopotamia).

NORRIS, Harry
C/13222, 6/6/18; R.E., C/S, 25/8/18; demob. 21/12/18.
130 Bradford Street, Haulgh, Bolton, Lancashire.

NORRISH, Frank
6/2/7183, 3/11/15; 20th Lond. R., 4/8/16, Indian Army; F,Afghan; Capt.; M.C.
c/o Cox & Coy., Bombay, India.

NORRISH, Harold Sydney
4/1/6/4473, 28/6/15; dis. med. unfit, 8/8/16.
1 Avenue Road, Anerley, S.E. 20.

NORTH, Alfred Lionel
A/11284, 14/5/17; No. 14 O.C.B., 5/10/17; Lan. Fus., 26/2/18; F; Capt.; w; M(1).
30 Park Crescent, Undercliffe, Bradford, Yorkshire.

NORTH, Eric Harrison
B/1701, 13/10/14; Midd'x. R., 10/2/15, 4th Huss.; F; Lieut.
Killinghall, Nr. Harrogate

NORTH, Vivian Gordon
C/1350, 26/9/14; K.R. Rif. C., 14/6/15, Welch Gds., Gds. M.G.R.; F; Lieut.; g.
Lemon Well, Eltham, S.E. 9.

NORTHCOTE, Beauchamp
6/4/5439, 5/8/15; W. York. R., 18/12/16, att. T.M. Bty.; F; Lieut.; g, w.
13 Gwendwr Road, West Kensington, W. 14.

NORTHCOTE, Dudley Stafford
B/758, 23/1/14; Oxf. & Bucks. L.I., 26/11/14; F,M; Lieut.; w.
23 Royal Avenue, Chelsea, S.W. 3.

✠ NORTHCOTE, James Fitz-Gaulfiel
6/4/6423, 23/9/15; W. York. R., 24/10/16; 2/Lieut.
Killed in action 9/10/17.

NORTHCOTE, Otho Stuart Irwin
B/718, 18/6/13; Suff. R., 11/9/14, att. L'pool. R.; F; Capt.; w(5)
Bridford, Devonshire.

NORTHCOTT, John Frayer
Sq/3790, 27/5/15, L/C.; Worc. Yeo., 13/11/15; Lieut.
Sheering Hall Farm, Harlow, Essex.

NORTHEN, Harold
Sq/128, 18/4/08; dis. 17/4/09.   61 The Drive, Hove, Sussex.

NORTHEY, Henry Doidge
B/A/13647, 26/7/18; trfr. K.R. Rif. C., 7/4/19, R.A.S.C.
Hillside, Okehampton, Devonshire.

APPENDIX II.—RECORDS OF RANK AND FILE.

NORTHRIDGE, *John Henry*
A/C/12467, 25/1/18; No. 21 O.C.B., 4/10/18; R. Ir. Rif., 17/3/19; 2/Lieut.
    Liscubba House, Rossmone, Ballineen, Co. Cork, Ireland.

NORTHWOOD, *John William*
B/11398, 30/5/17; No. 14 O.C.B., 5/10/17; R.W. Surr. R., 26/2/18; F; 2/Lieut.
    35 Sherwood Road, Addiscombe, Croydon, Surrey.

NORTON, *Frederick Raymond*
6/Sq/5905, 30/8/15, L/C.; No. 2 Cav. C/S, 1/9/16; R. Regt. of Cav., 20/12/16; Lieut.
    112 Bennerley Road, New Wandsworth, S.W. 11.

NORTON, *George William*
B/A/12218, 15/11/17; No. 11 O.C.B., 14/2/19; General List, 8/3/19; 2/Lieut.
    c/o R. E. Carr Esq., Sylvan Mount, Sylvan Road, Upper Norwood, S.E. 19.

✠ **NORTON,** *Hugh*
A/1173, 14/9/14; R. Lanc. R., 4/11/14, R.F.C.; Lieut.
    Killed in action 24/3/17.

NORTON, *Reginald Arthur*
D/13736, 2/8/18; trfr. K.R. Rif. C., 7/4/19.
    229 High Street, Watford, Hertfordshire.

✠ **NORTON,** *Tom Edgar Grantley*
Sq/130, 18/4/08; E. Surr. R., 16/10/14; 2/Lieut.
    Killed in action 20/4/15.

NORWELL, *Francis Alan*
6/4/6414, 23/9/15; trfr. Lond. Elec. Eng., 10/4/16; Sgt.
    41 Park Vale Road, Leicester.

NOTLEY, *Harold Francis Hopton*
C/10567, 19/1/17; dis. med. unfit, 29/12/17.
    Ablington House, Barnham, Sussex.

NOTLEY, *Stanley Guy*
Sq/970, 5/8/14; R.F.A., 2/11/14; F,S,E,P,It; Capt.; M.C., M(1).
    Stanton Street, Bernard, Pewsey, Wiltshire

NOTT, *George Arnold*
B/10752, 21/2/17; R.F.C., C/S, 13/3/17; R.F.C., 19/4/17, R.N.V.R.; North Sea; Sub. Lieut.
    Kyrewood, Tenbury, Wells, Worcesterhsire

NOTT, *James*
6/2/8032, 30/11/15; Worc. R., 22/11/16; F; Lieut.; M(1).
    Kyrewood, Tenbury, Wells, Worcestershire.

NOTT-BOWER, *Charles Cecil*
A/606, 13/2/12; dis. 13/11/13.

NOTT-BOWER, *Reginald Everett*
C/1062, 2/9/14; Rif. Brig., 19/9/14, att. K.R. Rif. C.; F; Major; w.
    1 Friar Street, Reading, Berkshire.

NOTT-BOWER, *William Guy*
D/13887, 23/8/18; demob. 19/12/18.
    2 Ashford House, Wimbledon Common, S.W. 19.

NOTTIDGE, *Thomas*
Sq/481, 8/4/10; Life Guards, 12/9/14, Berks. Yeo., att. Imp. Camel Corps; F,E,P; Capt.
    21 Walpole Street, Chelsea, S.W.

NOTTINGHAM, *Bertram Daniel*
6/1/7890, 27/11/15; No. 14 O.C.B., 27/9/16; 20th Lond. R., 18/12/16; F; Capt.; w; M.C., M(1).
    37 Elm Road, East Sheen, S.W.

✠ **NOTTON,** *Cyril George*
4/5/4803, 12/7/15; No. 11 O.C.B., 7/5/16; Norf. Yeo., 5/9/16; P; 2/Lieut.
    Killed in action 3/12/17.

NOWELL, *H. Norman*
Sq/2158, 23/11/14; Nott. Yeo., 13/3/15; Lieut.
    18 Springfield Road, Hampstead, N.W. 8.

NOYCE, *Frederick John*
C/12033, 24/9/17; R.E., C/S, 4/11/17; R.E., 1/2/18; 2/Lieut.
    c/o Nat. Bank of South Africa Ltd., Circus Place, London Wall, E.C. 2.

NOYES, *Henry*
C/9920, 15/11/16; No. 14 O.C.B., 30/1/17; Dorset R., 29/5/17; I; Lieut.
    37 Morlais Street, Roath Park, Cardiff.

NUDDS, *Gerald Arthur Hugh*
C/12088, 4/10/17; R.F.C., C/S, 26/11/17; R.F.C., 23/1/18, R.A.F.; F; Lieut.; w.
    Milden House, Dorchester, Wallingford, Berkshire.

NUGENT, *James Joseph*
6/5/C/7030, 27/10/15; No. 7 O.C.B., 3/7/16; trfr. City of Lond. Yeo., 19/1/17, M.G.C., att. 14th Huss.; M,Persia; Pte.
    Barratogher House, Rathowen, Westmeath, Ireland.

✠ **NUGENT,** *Raymond Henry*
6/Sq/9094, 24/1/16; R.A., C/S, 13/10/16; R.F.A., 25/2/17; 2/Lieut.
    Killed in action 25/11/17.

NUNN, *Howard*
6/4/7513, 15/11/15; Leic. R., 25/9/16, att. Indian Army; F,I; Lieut.
    23 Bishops Road, Highgate, N. 6.

NUNN, *Sidney Charles*
5801, 23/8/15; 12th Lond. R., 19/12/15; F; Capt.; w(2).
    33 Hartley Street, Ipswich.

✠ **NUNNELEY,** *Wilfred Herbert*
A/10744, 16/2/17; No. 11 O.C.B., 5/7/17; Essex R., 30/10/17; F; Capt.; M.C.
    Killed in action 24/4/18.

NUNNERLEY, *Richard*
D/10199, 15/12/16; R.W. Surr. R., 9/3/17, Lab. Corps; F; Lieut.; w.
    25 Scarisbrick Street, Southport, Lancashire.

✠ **NUNNERLEY,** *Willson Kenwick*
B/10776, 19/2/17; R.F.C., C/S, 13/3/17; R.F.C., 19/4/17; 2/Lieut.
    Killed in action 5/12/17.

NUTTALL, *Franklin Harold*
A/10079, 1/12/16; No. 14 O.C.B., 26/1/17; E. Kent R., 29/5/17, att. Hamps. R. and R.W. Kent R.; Afghan; Lieut.
    Ebon House, Manchester Road, Bury, Lancashire.

NYE, *Edward Kingsworth*
D/11838, 9/8/17, L/C.; No. 3 O.C.B., 8/2/18; E. Kent R., 30/7/18; F; Lieut.
    11 Champion Grove, Denmark Hill, S.E. 5.

NYE, *Gerald*
B/34, 3/4/08; dis. 2/4/10; enlisted in R. Fus., -/9/14; F; Cpl.
    Camperdown, Wallington, Surrey.

OADES, *Bertie Clifford*
C/14271, 6/11/18; demob. 17/3/19.
    23 London Road, Salisbury.

OAKELEY, *John Edmund Eckley*
4/3/4403, 24/6/15; Hereford R., 18/12/15, att. Ches. R.; F,It; Capt.; M.C.
    Kingsthorne, Hawthorn Park, Wilmslow, Cheshire.

OAKLEY, *Bernard*
6/4/4978, 19/7/15; 3rd Lond. R., 27/11/15; F; Lieut.; w.
    30 Burnt Ash Hill, Lee, S.E. 12.

✠ **OAKLEY,** *Christopher Herbert*
4/3791, 27/5/15; 22nd Lond. R., 16/11/15; Capt.; M.C.
    Died of wounds 2/9/18.

OAKLEY, *Gilbert Coleman*
Sq/1639, 9/10/14; R.G.A., 21/10/14; F,I,M; Lieut.
    16 Glebe Road, Bromley, Kent.

✠ **OAKLEY,** *Henry Bernard*
6/3/7111, 1/11/15; Rif. Brig., 25/9/16; 2/Lieut.
    Killed in action 3/5/17.

OAKLEY, *Robert Phelps*
6/Sq/7321, 9/11/15, Cpl.; No. 1 Cav. C/S, 24/4/16; Linc. Yeo., 28/7/16, att. Leic. R. and Linc. R.; F; Lieut.
    Hillmorton, Parkstone, Dorset.

OAKS, *Cecil George.* See OCHS, C. G.

OATES, *Reginald Lambert*
4/1/5174, 29/7/15; E. Surr. R., 23/12/15; F; Lieut.; Inv.
    62 Genesta Road, Westcliff-on-Sea.

OATES, *William Richard*
C/9799, 27/10/16, L/C.; No. 14 O.C.B., 7/6/17; W. York. R., 25/9/17, R.E.; G,F; Lieut.
    Rock Cottage, Blackwtaer, Scorrier, Cornwall.

OATRIDGE, *Ronald William*
A/10303, 1/1/17, L/C.; No. 21 O.C.B., 5/5/17; N. Lan R, 28/8/17, S. Lan. R., York. & Lanc. R.; F; Lieut.
    45 South Parade, Deal, Kent.

OATWAY, *Alfred Edwin*
D/13930, 30/8/18; trfr. K.R. Rif. C., 7/4/19.
    39 High Street, Hemel Hempstead, Hertfordshire.

O'BEIRNE, *Alphonsus Rudolph*
6/5/7802, 24/11/15; trfr. 18th Lond. R., 15/9/16.
    The Flanker, Drumsna, Co. Leitrim, Ireland.

O'BRIEN, *Charles Henry Wingate*
D/13904, 26/8/18; trfr. K.R. Rif. C., 7/4/19.
    Hazel Bank, Priory Road, Hornsey, N. 8.

APPENDIX II.—RECORDS OF RANK AND FILE.

O'BRIEN, Gerard
6/2/7744, 22/11/15; No. 7 O.C.B., 3/7/16; R. Muns. Fus., 3/11/16, att. R. Innis. Fus.; 2/Lieut.; D.S.O.   Killed in action 22/3/18.

O'BRIEN, Henry
6/6699, 7/10/15; E. Kent R., 9/6/16, att. T.M. Bty.; M; Lieut.
54 Meadowcroft Road, Palmers Green, N. 13.

O'BRIEN, James Patrick
C/13360, 27/6/18; trfr. 14th Lond. R., 6/12/18.
Church Avenue, Baltinglass, Co. Wicklow, Ireland.

O'BRIEN, Maurice Barry
D/1380, 26/9/14, Sgt.; 18th Lond. R., att. R.A.F.; F; Major.
68 Victoria Street, Westminster, S.W. 1.

O'BRIEN, Richard Andrew
B/E/13569, 18/7/18; No. 22 O.C.B., 20/9/18; demob. 18/1/19.
c/o Lt.-Col. A. McMann, c/o Holt & Coy., 3 Whitehall Place, S.W. 1.

✠ O'BRYEN, Myles Wheeler. See WHEELER-O'BRYEN, M.

O'CALLAGHAN, Cyril Tait
Sq/107, 18/4/08; dis. 17/4/12; N. Som. Yeo., -/5/14, 1st R. Drag., 10th Huss.; F; Capt.; M.C., M(1).
97 Eaton Square, S.W. 1.

O'CARROLL, Claude St. John
A/10425, 10/1/17; No. 6 O.C.B., 7/4/17; R. Dub. Fus., 31/7/17; F; Lieut.; g.   40 St. Giles, Oxford.

O'CARROLL, Geoffrey Charles William
4/1/5207, 29/7/15; D. of Corn. L.I., 2/9/16; F; Lieut.; w.
10 Pembroke Road, Dublin.

OCHS, Cecil George
K/H/2426, 21/12/14; 3rd Lond. R., 23/4/15; F; Staff Lieut.; Inv.   27 Collingham Gardens, S.W. 5.

O'CONNOR, James
A/11304, 18/5/17; trfr. 28th Lond. R., 1/10/17.
Castle, Blackrock, Dublin, Ireland.

ODAM, Frank Moore
6/1/7272, 8/11/15; trfr. R.A.V.C., 14/4/16.
The Firs, Newborough, Peterborough.

ODDY, Alfred Edgar
D/E/13895, 23/8/18; demob. 11/1/19.
Moorlands Hall, Birkinshaw, Bradford.

ODDY, Edward Alexander Hargreaves
6/1/8698, 4/1/16; K.R. Rif. C., 28/2/17, att. Rif. Brig.; F; Lieut.; p.   8 York Place Mansions, W. 1.

O'DEA, John Frederick
6/1/9122, 24/1/16; No. 8 O.C.B., 4/8/16; K.R. Rif. C., 21/11/16; Lieut.   28 Berkhamsted Avenue, Wembley.

✠ ODELL, William Ward
6/2/6424, 23/9/15; No 11 O.C.B., 7/5/16; Notts. & Derby. R., 4/9/16; 2/Lieut.; w; M.C.   Killed in action 4/10/17.

ODGERS, Lindsey Noel Blake
D/1462, 29/9/14; Midd'x. R., 13/11/14, R.E.; F; Capt.; w(3); M.C., M(1).   The Garth, North Finchley, N. 12.

ODGERS, Walter Blake
6/7803, 24/11/15; R.A.S.C., 28/3/16; F; Capt.
2 Mitre Court Buildings, Temple, E.C. 4.

ODLING, Aldo George
D/13881, 21/8/18; trfr. K.R. Rif. C., 25/4/19.
Casella 37, Carrara, Italy

ODLING, Cedric Jameson
6/9464, 14/2/16; R.F.A., C/S, 23/6/16; R.F.A., 11/8/16; F; Capt.; g; M(1).   132 New North Road, N. 1.

ODOM, George Crawford
4/1/4379, 21/6/15; L'pool. R., 7/10/15, M.G.C.; F; Lieut.; p; M.C., M(1).   70 Broadway, Peterborough.

O'DONNELL, Archibald
3/3867, 31/5/15; 1st Lond. R., 8/12/15.
28 Paddington Street, W. 1.

O'DONNELL, George William
6/5/8901, 13/1/16; No. 2 O.C.B., 14/8/16; R. Dub. Fus., 18/12/16, Hamps. R.; S; Lieut.; Inj.
25 Anglesea Road, Ballsbridge, Dublin.

O'DONOGHUE, John James
D/13714, 23/7/18; demob. 25/1/19.
3 Madden's Buildings, Cork.

O'DONOGHUE, John Kingston
D/10649, 2/2/17; No. 11 O.C.B., 5/7/17; 18th Lond. R., 30/10/17; 2/Lieut.   Cable Terrace, Valentia Island, Ireland.

O'DONOVAN, Gerald Patrick
4/1/4085, 7/6/15; Worc. R., 5/9/15; F,NR; Capt.; w(3); M C and Bar, Croix de Guerre (French), M(2).
Dulverton House, Cedars Road, Hampton Wick.

O'DONOVAN, Peter
C/12575, 6/2/18; No. 7 O.C.B., 5/7/18; R. Dub. Fus., 2/3/19; 2/Lieut.   13 Grace Park Gardens, Drumcondra, Dublin, Ireland

O'DOWD, Joseph
2/3234, 12/4/15, Sgt.; R.A.S.C., 21/10/15; S; Lieut.
No. 7 Flat, 24 Powis Square, Notting Hill, W. 11.

✠ OERTLING, Lewis John Francis
H/1885, 16/10/14, Sgt.; Bedf. R., 24/7/15, R.A.F.; F; Capt.
Died of wounds 8/8/18.

O'FARRELL, Anthony Clarke
D/10674, 9/2/17; R.E., C/S, 4/11/17; R.E., 1/2/18; Lieut.
Lisnacusha, Lanesboro', Co. Longford, Ireland.

✠ O'FERRALL, Brendan Hynds
6/5/8092, 1/12/15; R.F.A., C/S, 4/8/16; R.F.A., 10/11/16; 2/Lieut.   Killed in action 16/8/17.

OFFORD, Percival Guy
6/1/5684, 16/8/15; trfr. R.G.A., 7/7/16; R.G.A., 30/5/17; F; Lieut.   85 Portsdown Road, W. 2.

O'FLANAGAN, Patrick Louis
6/3/9010, 19/1/16; No. 7 O.C.B., 11/8/16; trfr. M.G.C., 15/12/16; F; Gnr.   135 Altona Terrace, North Circular Road, Dublin.

O'FLYNN, Roy Lockwood.
3/3175, 6/4/15; Midd'x. R., 28/8/15; F; Lieut.
63 Uxbridge Road, Ealing, W. 5.

✠ O'GALLIGAN, Thomas Netterfield
C/10856, 9/3/17; R.F.C., C/S, 4/5/17; R.F.C., 14/6/17, R.A.F.; Lieut.   Died 27/3/21.

OGDEN, Douglas Hartley
K/1/A/2185, 26/11/14, Sgt.; R.F.C., C/S, 8/10/16; R.F.C., 26/2/17, R.A.F.; Lieut.   Inchkeith, Bushey Hall Road, Watford

OGDEN, Frederick Perry
4/3/5175, 29/7/15; R. War. R., 4/12/15, att. Norf. R.; F,P; Lieut.; w.
c/o Revd. J. C. Wilcox, 9 Wiltshire Road, Brixton, S.W. 9.

OGDEN, William
B/13443, 3/7/18, L/C.; trfr. R. Highrs., 2/5/19; Cpl.
60 Beaconsfield Street, Bolton, Lancashire.

OGDEN, William Arthur Spencer
6/1/6912, 18/10/15; No. 2 O.C.B., 14/8/16; Bedf. R., 18/12/16; F; Lieut.; w(2).   The Manse, Dunstable.

✠ OGILVIE, William Edmond
F/1824, 16/10/14; Bord. R., 11/1/15; 2/Lieut.
Killed in action 27/9/15.

OGILVIE, William Farquhar
6/1/5906, 30/8/15; 9th Lond. R., 14/12/15, emp. M. of Munitions; Lieut.; w.

OGILVY, Frederick Allsworth
E/13982, 9/9/18; No. 22 O.C.B., 22/11/18; R. Berks. R., 15/2/19; 2/Lieut.   25 St. Marks Road, Windsor

OGLE, Frank
6/1/8466, 20/12/15; M.G.C., C/S, 24/10/16; M.G.C., 23/11/16, Tank Corps; P; Lieut.
Denstone College, Rocester, Staffordshire.

✠ OGSTON, James
6/8774, 7/1/16; No. 9 O.C.B., 8/3/16; R. Scots., 6/7/16; 2/Lieut.
Died of wounds 15/9/16.

O'HARA, Cecil Alfred
6/6825, 14/10/15, L/C.; R.A., C/S, 26/10/16; R.F.A., 5/5/17; F,E; Lieut.   96 Esmond Road, Bedford Park, W. 4

O'HARA, James A. Columbkille
6/5/8073, 1/12/15; No. 7 O.C.B., 11/8/16; R. Innis. Fus., 18/12/16, att. Indian Army; Lieut.
Main Street, Blessington, Co. Wicklow, Ireland.

O'HARA, Leo
6/4/9551, 23/2/16; No. 7 O.C.B., 11/8/16; trfr. R.F.A., 3/11/16; Gnr.   5 Royal Marine Road, Kingstown, Co. Dublin.

O'HARA, Thomas Alphonsus
6/9562, 6/3/16; dis. 18/8/16.

✠ O'HARE, Henry
D/10943, 27/3/17; R.A., C/S, 3/11/17.   Died 28/11/17.

APPENDIX II.—RECORDS OF RANK AND FILE.

☩ OHLMANN, Gerrard Alexander Louis
F/1726, 15/10/14; Dorset R., 27/2/15, att. R. Fus.; 2/Lieut.
Killed in action 29/9/15.

O'KEEFE, Henry Joseph
4/3736, 24/5/15; R.E., 27/9/15; Staff Capt.
Fairoak, Esher, Surrey.

OKELL, George
F/3/2836, 1/2/15; Welch R., 22/6/15; F; Lieut.; w.
Ross, Herefordshire.

OKELL, John Duncan
1/3712, 20/5/15; R.G.A., 23/9/15; F; Capt.; w(2); M(1).
14 Glan Aber Park, Chester.

O'KELLY, Edward Canning
6/5/C/6942, 20/10/15; No. 7 O.C.B., 3/7/16; trfr. M.G.C., 3/11/16, Tank Corps; F, C.S.M.; Croix de Guerre (French)
Cannings, Ramelton, Co. Donegal, Ireland.

O'KELLY, Xavier Francis
6/5/C/6941, 20/10/15; No. 7 O.C.B., 3/7/16; trfr. M.G.C., 3/11/16, Tank Corps; F; Cpl.
Cannings, Ramelton, Co. Donegal, Ireland.

OLDACRE, Francis Harold Arthur
K/F/2255, 7/12/14; R. Berks. R., 23/3/15, secd. M.G.C.; Lieut.
28 King Street, Cheapside, E.C. 2.

OLDEN, Albert Edwin
B/11306, 21/5/17; No. 16 O.C.B., 5/10/17; Leic. R., 12/3/18; F; 2/Lieut.
Kinfare, Bason's Lane, Langley, Nr. Birmingham.

OLDFIELD, Albert Reginald
4/4086, 7/6/15, Sgt.; Manch. R., 24/12/15; F; Capt.; M.C. and Bar.
105 Oxford Road, Macclesfield.

OLDFIELD, Clement Victor
Sq/480, 8/4/10; dis. 29/10/12.
10 Farquhar Road, Upper Norwood, S.E. 19.

☩ OLDFIELD, Fred
4/2/4425, 24/6/15; N. Staff. R., 8/11/15; 2/Lieut.
Killed in action 29/6/17.

☩ OLDFIELD, Laurel Cecil Francis
A/1214, 14/9/14; Rif. Brig., 3/3/15; F; Capt.
Killed in action 25/9/15

OLDLAND, Victor Urry
A/B/12146, 22/10/17, L/C.; R.F.A., C/S, 1/3/18; R.G.A., 14/10/18; 2/Lieut.
132 Oxford Road, Gloucester.

O'LEARY, John Joseph
B/D/12318, 21/12/17; R.F.C., C/S, 5/4/18; trfr. R.A.F., 5/4/18.
33 Arran Quay, Dublin, Ireland.

OLIPHANT, Kenneth Morton
C/1314, 26/9/14; Herts. R., 2/3/15; F; Capt.; M.C., M(1).
44 Lambolle Road, N.W. 3.

OLIPHANT, Nathan
6/5/C/9292, 3/2/16; No. 7 O.C.B., 4/11/16; trfr. R.F.A., 10/4/17.
Grahamsland, Castlefinn, Co. Donegal, Ireland.

OLIPHANT, Ronald Wynne
2/6/7937, 29/11/15, Sgt.; No. 14 O.C.B., 5/5/17; Indian Army, 19/10/17.

OLIVEIRA, Benjamin Ernest Graeme
A/9816, 30/10/16, L/C.; dis. med. unfit, 26/4/17.

OLIVER, Charles Aldworth
K/2663, 12/1/15; Ches. R., 6/2/15; F; Lieut.; w; M.C., M(2).
214 Hamlet Gardens, Ravenscourt Park, W. 6.

OLIVER, Douglas Harold
6/1/5568, 12/8/15, Sgt.; R.F.C., C/S, 13/3/17; R.F.C., 19/4/17, R.A.F.; F; Capt.; M.C.
Thrale Hall Hotel, Streatham, S.W. 16

OLIVER, Edward Victor
D/1398, 29/9/14; R.A.O.C., 22/1/15; F; Major, D.A.D.O.S.; O.B.E., M(2).
1 Millbank, S.W. 1.

OLIVER, Edwin Hamerton
D/B/C/12134, 18/10/17; R.F.A., C/S, 13/2/18; R.G.A., 21/10/18; Lieut.
c/o Revd. John Oliver, The Manse, Maryhill, Glasgow.

OLIVER, George Scott
A/D/13051, 7/5/18; No. 9 O.C.B., 8/11/18; High. L.I., 17/3/19; 2/Lieut.

OLIVER, Gilbert
6/1/9359, 7/2/16; No. 2 O.C.B., 28/8/16; D. of Corn. L.I., 24/10/16; F; Lieut.; w; M.C.
St. John's Rectory, North Bay, Ontario, Canada

OLIVER, Kenneth Mander
6/1/7876, 26/11/15; No. 11 O.C.B., 7/5/17; Glouc. R., 4/9/16, att. T.M. Bty.; F,It; Capt.; w; M.C.
66 Fitzharre's Avenue, Bournemouth. (Now in Nigeria).

OLIVER, Robert Denis
C/D/12235, 16/11/17; No. 17 O.C.B., 10/5/18; Bord. R., 2/2/19; 2/Lieut.
23 Carshalton Road, Blackpool, Lancashire.

OLIVER, Walter Stanley Victor
H/K/2418, 21/12/14; Lan. Fus., 28/4/15, R.F.C., R.A.F.; F,P; Lieut.; w.
Belmont, Mill Hill School, Mill Hill, N.W. 7.

OLLEY, Reginald James Miall
6/8127, 30/11/15; dis. med. unfit, 8/8/16; R.N.R.; Paymaster Lieut.; F; Inv.
Spring Cottage, 26 Lynmouth Road, Stamford Hill, N. 16.

OLLIVER, Vallance Irwin
3/3550, 10/5/15; S. Staff. R., 28/7/15, R.A.F.; Lieut.
12 Richmond Terrace, Brighton.

O'LOUGHLIN, Edward Joseph Aloysius
D/13784, 30/7/18; trfr. K.R. Rif. C., 25/11/19.
9 Stanley Street, Bury, Lancashire.

O'MALLEY, Edward Sansom Charles
A/11612, 5/7/17; A.S.C., C/S, 1/10/17; R.A.S.C., 23/11/17; It; Lieut.
c/o Hendee Mfg. Coy., 366 Euston Road, N.W. 1.

O'MALLEY, Francis
6/4/9123, 24/1/16, L/C.; No. 5 O.C.B., 14/8/16; Manch. R., 21/11/16; Lieut.
13 Stradbroke Road, Highbury New Park, N. 5.

☩ O'NEILL, Frederick
4/1/4608, 5/7/15; Oxf. & Bucks. L.I., 18/11/15, R. Dub. Fus.; 2/Lieut.
Killed in action 13/11/16.

O'NEILL, Harold Ernest
6/5/8663, 3/1/16; R.A., C/S, 26/10/16; R.G.A., 19/2/17; F; Lieut.; w.
29 Seafield Drive, Wallasey, Cheshire.

☩ O'NEILL, Thomas
5/6/9011, 19/1/16; No. 2 Cav. C/S, 1/1/17; 2nd R. Regt. of Cav., 7/7/17, att. Dorset Yeo.; 2/Lieut.
Died 29/5/19.

ONGLEY, Arthur Sydney
6/5/5386, 5/8/15; R.W. Kent R., 1/6/16; F; Lieut.; w.
189 Ivydale Road, Waverley Park, S.E. 15.

OPENSHAW, Herbert Stanley
H/2/3015, 8/3/15; Essex R., 3/6/15, E. Surr. R.; Capt.; w; M.C., M(1).

OPENSHAW, Kay Harold
D/2932, 15/2/15; Hamps. R., 30/7/15; F; Lieut.
Highfield, Radwell, Weymouth.

OPENSHAW, Percy Austin
D/12951, 19/4/18; demob. 11/1/19.
Belmont Park, S.E. 13.

OPENSHAW, Sydney Noel
D/2443, 28/12/14; Lan. Fus., 6/4/15, Indian Army; F,I; Capt.; w.
c/o Messrs. Cox & Coy., 16 Charing Cross, S.W. 1.

ORCHARD, Arthur Frederick
D/10840, 7/3/17; No. 11 O.C.B., 5/7/17; E. Surr. R., 30/10/17; 2/Lieut.
43 Priory Road, Kew, Surrey.

☩ ORCHARD, Ernest Frank Gordon
A/2762, 21/1/15; L'pool. R., 13/4/15; F; Capt.; M(2).
Died of wounds 1/8/17.

ORCHARD, John Dennis
A/14090, 2/10/18; demob. 20/3/19.
Post Office, Porthcawl, South Wales.

ORCHARD, Walter Donald
6/1/5713, 19/8/15; trfr. Dorset R., 8/3/16, Sgt.; Rif. Brig., 28/3/17, att. T.M. Bty.; F; Lieut.; p.
Terra Nova, Milton Road, Weymouth.

ORCHARD, William Charles
B/10316, 4/1/17, L/C.; No. 20 O.C.B., 7/6/17; Som. L.I., 25/9/17; 2/Lieut.
Beckington House, Wells Road, Bath.

ORD, Harold
C/1180J, 2/8/17; R.F.C., C/S, 26/11/17; R.F.C., 23/1/18, R.A.F.; Lieut.
24 Savernake Road, N.W. 3.

ORD, Simon Dodd
4/1/4084, 7/6/15, L/C.; Essex R., 29/9/15; M,F; Capt.; M.C.
Wendover, Buckinghamshire.

ORD, W. E. B. See BLACKETT-ORD, W. E.

ORDISH, John Edward
6/5/7076, 29/10/15; No. 7 O.C.B., 7/4/16; N. Lan. R., 17/7/16, att. M. of Labour; F; Lieut.
Wildmere, Oak Lane, West Derby, Liverpool.

APPENDIX II.—RECORDS OF RANK AND FILE.

O'REILLY, James
6/5/C/6772, 11/10/15; No. 14 O.C.B., 30/10/16; Linc. R., 25/4/17, att. Tank Corps; F; Lieut.
16 Clarence Road, Mottingham, Eltham, Kent.

O'REILLY, Joseph Patrick
6/D/9293, 3/2/16; No. 7 O.C.B., 4/11/16; R. Muns. Fus., 28/2/17, F; Lieut.; M.C.
1 Royal Marine Terrace, Bray, Co. Wicklow, Ireland.

O'REILLY, John Patrick Stephen
6/5584, 12/8/15; R.A., C/S, 21/7/16; trfr. 18th Lond. R., 6/4/17.
22 Clanricarde Gardens, Kensington, W. 2.

ORGAN, Samuel Bowerman
C/14316, 13/12/18; No. 3 O.C.B., 10/2/19; Glouc. R., 19/3/19; 2/Lieut.
40 Northumberland Road, Redland, Bristol.

O'RIORDAN, Henry Michael
t/8186, 6/12/15; No. 7 O.C.B., 11/8/16; R. Muns. Fus., 18/12/16; Capt.; O.B.E.
6 Morrison Island, Cork, Ireland.

ORME, Duncan Halford
6/8224, 7/12/15; R.F.A., C/S, 23/6/16; R.F.A., 19/8/16; F; 2/Lieut.
Ty Dedwydd, Bakewell, Derbyshire

☩ ORMOND, Alexander
6/3/7469, 15/11/15; L/C.; Manch. R., 6/9/16; F; 2/Lieut.
Killed in action 30/9/16.

ORMOND, Augustine James
C/Sq/A/D/11475, 11/6/17; Garr. O.C.B., 8/3/18; Lab. Corps., 4/9/18; 2/Lieut.
c/o Mrs. P. Swatton, Uryheid, Natal, South Africa.

ORMSBY, Bernard Hamilton
K/2452, 28/12/14; North'd. Fus., 30/12/14; F; Capt.; Inv. w.
32 St. Mary's Place, Newcastle-on-Tyne.

ORMSBY, George Vandeleur
A/1185, 14/9/14; R.F.A., 23/9/14; F; Major; w; M(5).
48 Beaufort Mansions, Chelsea, S.W. 3.

ORR, Kenric Ernest Rhodes
B/A/12360, 3/1/18; No. 12 O.C.B., 10/5/18; demob. 30/1/19.
Meadow Bank, Prestwich, Nr. Manchester.

☩ ORR, Robert Watson
B/2085, 13/11/14; 18th Lond. R., 5/3/15; 2/Lieut.
Killed in action 25/9/15.

ORRELL, Walter Gregory
B/12713, 8/3/18; No. 18 O.C.B., 20/9/18; Lan. Fus., 17/3/19; 2/Lieut.
Entre Rios, Woodhey, Rock Ferry, Cheshire.

ORRETT, Edgar James Phillips
A/11283, 14/5/17; No. 16 O.C.B., 5/10/17; K.R. Rif. C., 12/3/18; 2/Lieut.
Bradford House, Solihull, Birmingham.

ORRETT, Frank Claude
4/4289, 17/6/15; trfr. Fife & Forfar Yeo., 13/3/16.
17 Warrington Crescent, Maida Vale, W. 9

ORRITT, Frederick Arthur
5/6/7804, 24/11/15; Manch. R., 4/9/16; F; 2/Lieut.
142 Sussex Road, Southport, Lancashire.

ORR-LEWIS, John Duncan
A/13066, 14/5/18; demob. 10/1/19.
White Webbs, Enfield, Middlesex.

ORTON, Noel Barry
6/4/9038, 20/1/16; dis. to re-enlist in K.R. Rif. C., 19/5/16.

ORTON, Richard Osborn
D/10427, 10/1/17; No. 20 O.C.B., 7/6/17; trfr. 28th Lond. R., 3/8/17.
79 Middlesboro' Road, Coventry.

O'RYAN, John Mortimer
6/1/7877, 26/11/15; dis. med. unfit, 22/8/16.

OSBORN, George Dunraven
1/9749, 18/10/16; R.A., C/S, 1/2/17; trfr. R.F.A., 25/5/17.
52 Creffield Road, Ealing, W. 5

OSBORN, Marmaduke Alfred
6/3/8925, 14/1/16; R.F.A., C/S, 4/8/16; R.F.A., 27/10/16; resigned and re-enlisted in R.F.A.; F,It; Gnr.
14 Clifton Avenue, Church End, Finchley, N. 3.

OSBORNE, David Robert
B/1264, 23/9/14; Cpl.; North'd. Fus., 6/12/14.
4 Brick Court, Temple, E.C. 4.

☩ OSBORNE, Frederick William
6/3/8225, 7/12/15; L/C.; No. 14 O.C.B., 30/9/16; K.R. Rif C., 24/10/16; 2/Lieut.
Killed in action 23/4/17.

OSBORNE, Henry Charles
Sq/3353, 22/4/15; R.F.A., 29/6/15; F,M; Capt.; w; M.C.
Gunnong, Jugrawah, Coolac, New South Wales, Australia.

☩ OSBORNE, Henry Douglas
B/11335, 21/5/17; No. 14 O.C.B., 5/10/17; E. Kent R., 25/2/18; 2/Lieut.
Died 24/2/19.

OSBORNE, Kenneth Edward
A/12147, 22/10/17; dis. med. unfit, 9/10/18.
7 Hartfield Road, Eastbourne, Sussex.

OSBORNE, Reginald John
4/5/5176, 29/7/15; trfr. H.A.C., 7/4/16; E,P.
62 Elm Road, Leigh-on-Sea, Essex.

OSBORNE, Sidney Herbert
A/11613, 5/7/17; dis. med. unfit, 1/1/18.
Mackenzie House, Kinnear Road, Edinburgh

OSBORNE, Thomas
A/10393, 8/1/17; R.F.A., C/S. 4/5/17; R.F.A., 28/10/17; Lieut
7 Brookfield Park, Highgate Road, N.W. 5.

OSBORNE, Vernon William
B/10520, 15/1/17, L/C.; R.F.A., C/S, 18/5/17; R.F.A., 17/11/17; 2/Lieut.
Sapong Estate, Tluon, British North Borneo

☩ O'SHEA, Dermot Timothy
6/4/9193, 29/1/16; No. 14 O.C.B., 30/10/16, M.G.C., C/S; M.G.C., 24/2/17. Tank Corps; 2/Lieut.; w.
Killed in action 10/8/18.

O'SHEA, John
6/5/8274, 9/12/15; R.A., C/S, 23/9/16; R.G.A., 9/12/16; Lieut
Henro Street, Killarney, Ireland.

O'SHEA, Reginald Cecil Morell
C/D/13286, 14/6/18, L/C.; demob. 30/5/19.
Hanover House, Hanover Place, Canterbury, Kent.

☩ OSMAN, Eric Edward
4/6/5149, 29/7/15; R. Innis. Fus., 9/10/15; 2/Lieut.
Killed in action 25/7/17.

OSTREHAN, Laurence Brudenell
6/1/6999, 25/10/15; trfr 13th Lond. R., 9/6/16; F,S,P; Cpl.; w.
Hallow, Worcester. (Now in Sumatra).

OSTROROG, Stanislaus John
Sq/3602, 13/5/15; R.G.A., 22/7/15.
5 Netherton Grove, Chelsea, S.W. 10.

O'SULLIVAN, Denis Joseph
6/5/C/8881, 12/1/16; No. 7 O.C.B., 4/11/16; R. Muns. Fus., 28/2/17, att. T.M. Bty.; F; Lieut.
Langford Street, Killorghin, Co. Kerry, Ireland.

O'SULLIVAN, John Francis Blake
A/2741, 21/1/15, L/C.; Conn. Rang., 2/6/15; Lieut.; w.
53 Burlington Road, Bayswater, W. 2.

O'SULLIVAN, John Joseph
6/5/6798, 13/10/15; trfr. 18th Lond. R., 14/9/16.

O'SULLIVAN, Timothy Adolphus
6/5/8486, 20/12/15; R.A., C/S, 9/6/16; R.G.A., 13/9/16; F; Lieut. Education Officer, Alor Star, Kedah, Malay Peninsula.

O'SULLIVAN, William Bradley
6/5/C/8487, 20/12/15; R.A., C/S, 8/11/16; R.G.A., 2/2/17; Lieut.
High School for Boys, Croydon, Surrey.

O'SULLIVAN-BEARE, Donal Barry
A/Sq/13107, 16/5/18; trfr. 28th Lond. R., 24/8/18; rej. A/Sq/C/14129, 8/10/18; No. 13 O.C.B., 25/1/19; trfr. R. Regt. of Cav., 11/6/19, att. R.G.A. and M.G.C.; I; Sgt.
c/o King & Coy., 9 Pall Mall, S.W. 1.

OTTAWAY, Robert John
6/1/8369, 13/12/15, Sgt.; No. 14 O.C.B., 9/11/17; Bedf. R., 30/4/18; 2/Lieut.
Ferndale, Hexham Road, New Barnet, Hertfordshire.

OTTLEY, Richard Charles Drewry
C/Sq/D/13656, 27/7/18; demob. 23/1/19.
1 Park Street, Bath.

OUGHTON, Harold Charles
6/4/6332, 20/9/15; M.G.C., 25/9/16; F,It; Lieut.
Crantock, 26 Malbrook Road, Putney, S.W. 15.

OUNSWORTH, Harry Norman Baker
4/9719, 10/10/16; No. 14 O.C.B., 30/1/17; trfr. R.E. 18/5/17.
13 Ampthill Road, Liverpool.

APPENDIX II.—RECORDS OF RANK AND FILE.

OVERELL, *Eric Vernon*
3/A/2744, 21/1/15, Sgt.; M.G.C., C/S, 25/11/16; M.G.C., 24/3/17; F; Lieut.; *Inv.* 3 Clarence Terrace, Leamington Spa.

OVERMASS, *Walter Seaton Taylor*
C/13333, 19/6/18; *trfr.* R. Fus., 6/7/18.
18 Wood Street, Cheapside, E.C. 2.

OVERTON, *Isle Grant*
D/E/13780, 7/8/18; No. 22 O.C.B., 20/9/18; Hamps. R., 5/2/19; 2/Lieut. 10 Stokewood Road, Bournemouth.

OVINGTON, *Warwick Parker John.* See SUTHERLAND, *Warwick Parker*

OWEN, *Arthur Lewis Scott*
4/1/4233, 14/6/15; R.E., 4/8/15; Lieut.
Cefnwifed, Newtown, Montgomeryshire.

OWEN, *Arthur Trevor*
6/3/7421, 12/11/15; N. Lan. R., 25/9/16, R.E.; F; 2/Lieut.
Myrtle Bank, Dalmorton Road, New Brighton, Cheshire.

OWEN, *David Alexander*
B/9912, 13/11/16, L/C.; No. 14 O.C.B., 6/4/17; Wilts. R, 31/7/17; Capt. 13 St. Georges Street, W.

OWEN, *Edward Bernard*
C/D/14280, 8/11/18; demob. 23/10/19.
28 Cranes Drive, Surbiton, Surrey.

OWEN, *Edward James*
6/1/9450, 14/2/16; No. 14 O.C.B., 26/11/16; 1st Cty. of Lond. Yeo., 27/3/17, att. Midd'x. R.; F; Lieut.; *w*.
Brockhurst, Shifnal, Shropshire.

OWEN, *Griffith Richard*
C/10759, 21/2/17; No. 14 O.C.B., 7/6/17; S. Lan. R., 25/9/17, att. R.W. Surr. R.; I; Lieut.; *w*.
c/o Williams & Owen, Palace Street, Carnarvon, North Wales.

OWEN, *Henry Campbell Roderick*
4/Sq/4651, 5/7/15; Dorset Yeo., 20/10/15, att. R.F.C.; F; Capt.
Harton Road, Four Oaks, Warwick.

✠ OWEN, *Horre Solle*
6/4/7470, 15/11/15; Manch. R., 4/9/16; 2/Lieut.
Killed in action 23/11/16.

OWEN, *Hugh Ellis*
6/3/8996, 19/1/16; R.F.A., C/S, 4/8/16; R.F.A., 10/11/16; F; Lieut. Hendre, The Common, Pontypridd, South Wales.

OWEN, *Hugh John*
2/2855, 4/2/15; R.A.O.C., 14/6/15; S; Capt.; *Inv.*
The Cottage, Pwllheli, North Wales.

✠ OWEN, *Humphrey Francis*
K/F/2453, 28/12/14; R.W. Fus., 9/7/15; F; Lieut.; *w*.
Killed in action 22/3/18.

✠ OWEN, *Iorwerth ap Roland*
6/4/5631, 16/8/15; No. 11 O.C.B., 16/5/16; R.F.C., 4/9/16; 2/Lieut. Killed in action 7/5/17.

OWEN, *John Francis*
B/10545, 17/1/17; No. 20 O.C.B., 7/6/17; trfr. 28th Lond. R., 3/8/17; F; L/C. Monarvon, Deane Road, Liverpool.

OWEN, *John Hugh Lloyd*
B/9852, 6/11/16; No. 14 O.C.B., 30/1/17; L'pool. R., 29/5/17; F; Lieut.; *w*. 47 Osborne Road, The Brook, Liverpool.

OWEN, *John Peredur*
B/K/2390, 17/12/14; R.W. Fus., 13/3/15; F; Lieut.; *M.C.*, M(1).
The Palace, Abergwili S.O., Carmarthenshire, South Wales.

OWEN, *Joseph Arthur John*
4/2/4380, 21/6/15; North'd. Fus., 6/9/15; F; Lieut.
123 Cooks Road, Kennington Park, S.E. 17.

OWEN, *Leslie Edward*
6/9305, 4/2/16; R.F.C., 28/4/16, R.A.F.; Lieut.
14 Thurlstone Road, West Norwood, S.E. 27.

OWEN, *Owen Hugh*
B/12856, 22/3/18; No. 8 O.C.B., 20/9/18; demob.
Penybout, Llanbedr, Merioneth, North Wales.

OWEN, *Owen Llewelyn*
B/2055, 9/11/14; R. War. R., 5/3/15, R.F.C., R.A.F.; Lieut.; *w*.

✠ OWEN, *Philip Charles*
A/969, 5/8/14; Shrop. L.I., 5/10/14; 2/Lieut.
Killed in action 25/9/15.

OWEN, *Philip Henry Ashington*
B/11399, 30/5/17; trfr. 28th Lond. R., 17/9/17.
Steep Hill, Harrow-on-the-Hill, Middlesex.

OWEN, *Thomas Alexander*
D/2945, 18/2/15; Midd'x. R., 22/4/15; F; Capt.; *w*; M(1).
68 Inverness Terrace, W. 2.

OWEN, *Trevor Thomas*
4/4136, 10/6/15; L'pool. R., 7/10/15; F; Capt.; *w*.
30 Grove Road, Pontardawe, Glamorganshire, South Wales.

✠ OWEN, *William David*
A/10515, 15/1/17; No. 20 O.C.B., 7/6/17; Welch R., 25/9/17; 2/Lieut. Died 11/10/18.

OWEN, *William Norman*
B/10332, 4/1/17; R.F.C., C/S, 13/3/17; R.F.C., 19/4/17, R.A.F.; F; Lieut. Derwent, 12 Groes Road, Grassendale, Liverpool.

OWEN, *William Stanley*
6/4/7692, 22/11/15, L/C.; No. 14 O.C.B.; Mon. R., 22/11/16; F; Lieut.; *w*. Brooklands Villa, 24 Brooklands Terrace, Swansea.

OWEN, *William Tom Frederick*
6/2/B/8550, 30/12/15, Sgt.; R.F.A., C/S, 6/7/18; R.F.A., 3/4/19; 2/Lieut. 96 Moor Street, Burton-on-Trent.

✠ OWEN, *William Vandeleur*
B/C/D/12025, 20/9/17; No. 3 O.C.B., 10/5/18; R. Scots., 29/10/18; 2/Lieut. Died 12/11/18.

OWENS, *Benjamin Johnson*
A/13145, 24/5/18; No. 5 O.C.B., 8/11/18; S. Lan. R., 17/3/19; 2/Lieut. 40 Jolliffe Street, Princes Park, Liverpool.

OWEN-SMITH, *Gilbert*
C/D/12260, 29/1/17; No. 19 O.C.B., 10/5/18, No. 11 O.C.B.; General List, 8/3/19; 2/Lieut.
c/o Commissioner of Customs and Excise, Pretoria, South Africa.

OXENHAM, *Edward John Baron*
K/C/2087, 14/11/14; R.A.O.C., 22/1/15; F,It; Major, D.A.D.O.S.; M.C., M(2). 32 Arran Road, Catford, S.E. 6.

✠ OXLEY, *Herman Grant*
2/3792, 27/5/15; K.R. Rif. C., 10/8/15; Lieut.; *w*.
Killed in action 4/11/18.

OXLEY, *Hubert Hearfield*
C/13272, 12/6/18, L/C.; demob. 30/1/19.
208 Kew Road, Richmond, Surrey.

OXLEY, *William Edward Alan*
6/2/7938, 29/11/15; No. 13 O.C.B., 4/11/16; York. R., 28/2/17; F; 2/Lieut.; *w*.
Municipal School of Art, Margaret Street, Birmingham.

PADDON, *Leslie*
4/6/5/4941, 19/7/15; Leic. R., 6/12/15; F; Lieut
44 King William Street, E.C. 4.

PADFIELD, *Leonard*
A/2590, 4/1/15; Norf. R., 26/3/15, Tank Corps; F; Major; *w*; M.C., M(1). Hawkwell Rectory, Hockley, Essex.

PADMORE, *Arthur*
E/2814, 29/1/15; Midd'x. R., 3/6/15; F; Lieut.
49 Ritherdon Road. S.W. 17.

PAFFORD, *John Henry Pyle*
B/12714, 8/3/18; No. 7 O.C.B., 9/8/18; Wilts. R., 8/3/19; 2/Lieut. Holt, Trowbridge, Wiltshire.

✠ PAGE, *Arthur Herbert*
A/1920, 22/10/14; Suff. R., 12/12/14; F; 2/Lieut.
Killed in action 19/7/16.

PAGE, *Arthur Stanley*
6/5/8655, 3/1/16; R.A., C/S, 9/6/16; R.G.A., 13/9/16; F; Lieut.
140 Hill Lane, Southampton.

PAGE, *Arthur Valentine*
A/3912, 31/5/15; No. 14 O.C.B., 26/11/16; Shrop. Yeo., 27/3/17; P; 2/Lieut.; *w*. 52 Maryland Road, Bowes Park, N. 22.

PAGE, *Cecil Grantham*
D/1492, 29/9/14; Bord. R., 29/9/14, att. L'pool. R., Lan. Fus., emp. M. of Labour; F; Major; *w*; M.C.
6 Tite Street, Chelsea, S.W. 3.

PAGE, *Geoffrey Verdon*
A/12469, 25/1/18; No. 11 O.C.B., 9/8/18; E. Kent R., 5/3/19; 2/Lieut. 35 Wyatt Park Road, Streatham Hill, S.W. 2.

PAGE, *George Nelson*
6/Sq/6773, 11/10/15; No. 2 Cav. C/S, 31/3/16; Bedf. Yeo., 6/9/16. Colonial Institute, Northumberland Avenue, W.C.

APPENDIX II.—RECORDS OF RANK AND FILE.

PAGE, Gordon Coles
6/4/6208, 13/9/15; R.F.A., C/S, 17/3/16; R.F.A., 7/8/16; F; Lieut. 1 Abingdon Court, Kensington. W.8.

PAGE, Gordon Shepherd
11195, 7/5/17; R.F.C., C/S, 1/6/17; R.F.C., 4/7/17, R.A.F.; Lieut. 10 Lynford Gardens, Seven Kings, Essex.

✠ PAGE, Meaburn Staniland
B/10368, 5/1/17, L/C.; No. 20 O.C.B., 7/6/17; Linc. R., 25/9/17; F; 2/Lieut. Killed in action 21/3/18.

PAGE, Norman Urbane
B/12857, 25/3/18; trfr. Gord. Highrs., 6/5/19.

PAGE, Reginald Knightley
C/13334, 19/6/18; trfr. 14th Lond. R., 6/12/18, Gord. Highrs.; Sgt. Copford, London Road, Bishops Stortford, Hertfordshire.

PAGE, Richmond Francis
6/8991, 18/1/16; A.S.C., C/S, 15/5/16; R.A.S.C., 18/6/16; F; Lieut. c/o Messrs. Morgan's Brewery Coy. Ltd., Norwich

PAGET, Jack
D/2797, 26/1/15; Lan. Fus., 22/4/15, emp. M. of Labour; Lieut.; w. 145 West End Lane, West Hampstead, N.W.6.

PAGETT, Sydney Gill
6/1/5663, 16/8/15; Yorks. L.I., 8/7/16; F; Lieut.; g. Lond. Joint City & Mid. Bank Ltd., Boroughbridge, Yorkshire.

PAIN, Godfrey Smorthwaite
1/3652, 17/5/15; E. Surr. R., 10/9/15; F; 2/Lieut. Holly Bank, Avenue Road, Sevenoaks, Kent.

PAIN, Sydney Parker
6/2/7214, 4/11/15, L/C.; No. 11 O.C.B., 16/5/16; E. Kent R., 4/9/16, att. Shrop L.I.; S; Lieut.; Inv. Westward Ho! Deal, Kent.

PAINE, Arthur Thomas Worship
A/809, 31/7/14; North'd. Fus., 18/9/14; Capt.; w(2). Mill Lawn, Reigate, Surrey.

PAINE, James Nevin Desmond
B/12715, 8/3/18; No. 4 O.C.B., 6/9/18; R.W. Kent R., 19/3/19; 2/Lieut. 24 Thornton Hill, Wimbledon, S.W.19.

✠ PAINE, John James
6/5/7939, 29/11/15; R.F.C., 14/8/16. Died 13/4/19.

PAINTER, Robert Turnbull
K/2636, 7/1/15; Shrop. L.I., 2/1/15, R.A.S.C.; Lieut.; M(1). 4 Willow Avenue, Barnes, S.W.13.

PAKENHAM, Thomas Compton
4/4023, 10/6/15; Cold. Gds., 30/9/15, secd. M.G.C.; Lieut.; M C. Woldingham Cottage, Woldingham Court, Woldingham, Surrey.

PALAMOUNTAIN, William Bennett
B/11708, 19/7/17; trfr. R.F.C., 13/12/17.

✠ PALETHORPE, Edwin Donald
6/Sq/6488, 27/9/15; R.F.A., C/S, 14/4/16; R.F.A., 7/8/16, att R.H.A.; F; 2/Lieut. Killed in action 9/10/17.

PALK, Sydney Arthur
K/A/2509, 31/12/14; Lan. Fus., 1/3/15; F; Capt.; w(2); M.C. 42 High Street, Sidcup, Kent.

✠ PALLANT, Herbert Charles
4/1/4253, 14/6/15, L/C.; R. Innis. Fus., 1/9/15, Indian Army; F,I; Capt. Died 21/2/20.

PALLETT, Ernest Edward
4/4652, 5/7/15, Sgt.; D. of Corn. L.I., 23/4/16; Lieut.

PALMER, Arthur Leonard
Sq/7077, 29/10/15, L/C.; A.S.C., C/S, 28/2/16; R.A.S.C., 7/5/16; F; Capt.; w; M(1) Bower Hinton, Martock, Somerset

PALMER, Charles Courtney
6/1/7693, 22/11/15, Cpl.; R. Marines, 24/10/16; F; Lieut.; w. 1 Southwark Street, Southwark, S.E.1.

PALMER Charles Edward
D/10908, 26/3/17; No. 14 O.C.B., 5/7/17; W. York. R., 30/10/17. att. Yorks. L.I.; F; Lieut.; w. 1 Brookfield Mansions, West Hill, Highgate, N.6.

PALMER, Edward Leopold
B/10310, 2/1/17, L/C.; No. 20 O.C.B., 5/5/17; Linc. R., 28/8/17; w. 19 Linden Avenue, Wembley Hill, Middlesex.

✠ PALMER, Edwin
6/C/5387, 5/8/15; No. 11 O.C.B., 16/5/16; trfr. 2nd Lond R., 10/11/16; F; Cpl. Killed in action 15/6/17.

PALMER, Eric Trestrail
A/Sq/14008, 13/9/18; demob. 14/1/19. Native Affairs Department, Salisbury, Rhodesia.

PALMER, Ernest Bevan
2/3094, 22/3/15; E. Surr. R., 9/8/15, L'pool. R.; F; Lieut.; w; M(1). 28 Kirkstall Road, Streatham Hill, S.W.2.

PALMER, Ernest Henry
4/3510, 6/5/15; R.A.O.C., 19/7/15; Capt.; O.B.E., M.B.E., M(2) 36 North Side, Wandsworth Common, S.W.18.

PALMER, Frederick George
4/5/Sq/4760, 12/7/15; No. 2 Cav. C/S, 1/9/16; Surr. Yeo., 10/1/17; S; Lieut.; Inv. Tottenhill, King's Lynn, Norfolk.

PALMER, Frederick Owen
6/3/7302, 8/11/15, L/C.; No. 11 O.C.B., 7/5/16; Devon. R., 4/9/16; I,P; Lieut.; Inv. Handel House, Gervis Place, Bournemouth

PALMER, Frederick Walter
C/14141, 11/10/18; trfr. K.R. Rif. C., 7/4/19. 6 Dewbury Street, Poplar, E.14.

PALMER, Hedley
D/13875, 21/8/18; demob. 29/1/19. Homelea, King's Road, Clacton-on-Sea.

PALMER, Hubert Grayling
6/1/8840, 10/1/16; No. 8 O.C.B., 4/8/16; R.W. Surr. R., 21/11/16; Lieut.; w. 14 Eaton Gardens, Hove, Sussex.

PALMER, Jack Cyril Gordon
3/4120, 8/6/15, L/C.; demob. 3/2/19. Lynton, St. John's, Woking.

PALMER, James Valentine
D/E/13861, 19/8/18; No. 22 O.C.B., 22/11/18; Glouc. R., 5/2/19; 2/Lieut. 17 Royal York Crescent, Clifton, Bristol.

PALMER, Maurice Llewelyn
D/13715, 31/7/18; trfr. K.R. Rif. C., 7/4/19. Terceira, Selden Road, Worthing.

PALMER, Nelson George
6/2/5907, 30/8/15; 7th Lond. R., 15/11/15; Lieut. 10 Berwyn Road, Herne Hill, S.E.24

PALMER, Norman St. Clair
6/4/8336, 13/12/15, L/C.; Herts. R., 18/12/16; Lieut.; p. Claybury, Bushey, Hertfordshire.

PALMER, Ronald Frank
C/14209, 21/10/18; demob. 29/1/19. Kenilworth, Grove Road, Sutton, Surrey

PALMER, Seymour Charles
6/1/7335, 9/11/15; dis. to re-enlist R.N.A.S., 2/6/16, R.A.F. Barclay Perkins & Coy. Ltd., Brewery, Park Street, Southwark, S.E.1.

✠ PALMER, Walter Harvey
6/4/6861, 15/10/15; Manch. R., 4/9/16; F; 2/Lieut.; w. Killed in action 23/4/17.

PALMER, William Claud Michel
B/10109, 4/12/16; No. 14 O.C.B., 5/3/17; Suff. R., 26/6/17, att. M.G.C.; F; Lieut.; w(2). Hill Crest, Epping, Essex.

PALMER, William Gordon
6/1/8799, 10/1/16; R.A., C/S, 7/8/16; R.F.A., 3/12/16; F; Lieut.; w. 24 Fairholme Road, West Kensington, W.14.

PALMER, William Herbert
C/10180, 13/12/16, L/C.; No. 14 O.C.B., 5/3/17; Midd'x. R., 26/6/17; F; Capt. 20 Perceval Avenue, Hampstead, N.W.3.

PALMER-STONE, Dominic Anthony Edgar Stuart
2/9670, 3/10/16; R.F.C., C/S, 13/3/17; R.F.C., 19/4/17, R.A.F.; Lieut. St. George's College, Woburn Park, Weybridge, Surrey.

PALMOUR, Frederick John Clifford
A/11255, 14/5/17, L/C.; R.E., C/S, 4/11/17; R.E., 1/2/18; Lieut. The Hedges, Bulford Village.

PAMMENT, Oscar Rokeby
C/10640, 1/2/17; C.Q.M.S.; demob. 1/5/19. 15 Spencer Gardens, Eltham, S.E.9.

PANK, John Reginald
B/13533, 15/7/18; No. 22 O.C.B., 23/8/18; Midd'x. R., 13/2/19; 2/Lieut. Oakleigh Park, Middlesex.

APPENDIX II.—RECORDS OF RANK AND FILE.

✠ PANTING, Arnold Clement
B/1904, 16/10/14; R.W. Surr. R., 10/2/15, R. Muns. Fus.; 2/Lieut. *Killed in action 13/1/17.*

PANTON, John Hubert
6/5/4/5887, 30/8/15; No. 7 O.C.B., 6/4/16; D. of Corn. L.I., 22/6/16; Lieut.

PARAMOR, William
D/13768, 7/8/18; demob. 13/12/18.
144 Addison Way, Golders Green, N.W. 4.

PARBURY, Herbert Victor
K/2806, 28/1/15; R.F.A., 21/3/15, att. Intelligence; F,E; Lieut.
Oakwood, Headley, Surrey.

✠ PARDEY, William Leslie
4/5/4722, 9/7/15; S. Lan. R., 21/11/15; F; 2/Lieut.
Died of wounds 16/9/16.

PARDOE, John Frederick
A/13978, 9/9/18; demob. 31/1/19.
Ingledene, Aberdare, South Wales.

PARFITT, James Frank
3/4/4087, 7/6/15, Cpl.; trfr. 8th Lond. R., 16/3/17.

PARIS, Albert Vernon
4/Sq/4234, 14/6/15; City of Lond. Yeo., 5/9/15, att. R.F.C. and 12th Lancers; M,E,F; Lieut.; w.
c/o P.O. Box 72, Calcutta, India.

PARISOT, Eugène Oscar William La Valette
B/13465, 5/7/18; trfr. K.R. Rif. C., 7/4/19.
Vale Cottage, Whyteleafe, Surrey.

PARISOTTI, Louis
1/3868, 31/5/15; York. R., 2/9/15, Indian Army; Lieut.; w.
5 Inverness Place, W. 2.

PARK, Gilbert
B/10328, 4/1/17; R.W. Surr. R., 20/3/17; F.
Victoria House, Northumberland Square, North Shields.

PARK, Leslie
B/2837, 1/2/15; Dorset R., 2/6/15, att. R. Berks R. and Indian Army; F,I; Lieut.; w.
West Riding Bank Chambers, Cleckheaton, Yorkshire.

PARK, Robert Spencer
C/397, 3/4/09; dis. 25/4/12.

PARKE, Charles Herbert
2/3511, 6/5/15, L/C.; E. Surr. R., 24/10/15; Lieut.
Mon Plaisir, Latchmere Road, Kingston.

PARKER, Arnold Clifford
C/11751, 26/7/17; A.S.C., C/S, 1/11/17; R.A.S.C., 25/1/18; F; 2/Lieut.
Lond. Cty. West. & Parrs Bank Ltd., Marylebone Branch, 1 Stratford Place, W. 1.

PARKER, Arthur Dennis Clifton
A/B/12446, 22/1/18; No. 8 O.C.B., 7/6/18; 20th Lond. R., 5/2/19; 2/Lieut. *St. Olave, Church Road, Forest Hill, S.E. 23.*

PARKER, Arthur Gilmour
4/6/5/4906, 16/7/15; W. York. R., 31/12/15, R.G.A.; Lieut.

PARKER, Charles Shirecliffe Kenyon
6/4/7215, 4/11/15, Sgt.; R.A., C/S, 7/7/16; R.G.A., 13/9/16; F; Capt. *217 Ryrie Buildings, Toronto, Ontario, Canada.*

PARKER, Cyril Brian Denis
6/5/C/5996, 2/9/15; trfr. R.G.A., 17/11/16; F; Gnr.
58 Kenilworth Square, Rathgar, Dublin

✠ PARKER, Frederick Richard
1/3312, 19/4/15; Wilts. R., 10/7/15; F; 2/Lieut.
Killed in action 19/7/16.

PARKER, George Alexander
D/11111, 25/4/17; No. 12 O.C.B., 10/8/17; R.W. Fus., 27/11/17; E; Lieut. *15 Eaton Road, Chester.*

PARKER, George Wilfrid
A/10029, 28/11/16; R.G.A., C/S, 14/3/17, R.G.A., 6/7/17, emp. M. of Labour; F; Lieut. *Hillcrest, Colsgate Hill, Ripon.*

PARKER, George William Chorley
6/5/7471, 15/11/15; R.F.A., C/S, 31/3/16; R.F.A., 5/8/16, att. T.M. Bty.; F,It; Capt.; M(1). *261 Newport Road, Cardiff.*

PARKER, Harold Thomas
3/6/3869, 31/5/15; dis. med. unfit, 22/5/16.
44 Kelmsiott Road, Wandsworth Common, S.W. 11.

PARKER, Henry Tyrrel
6/3/5765, 21/8/15; Midd'x. R., 24/10/16; F; 2/Lieut.; w.
Wytcott, Murray Road, Northwood, Middlesex.

PARKER, Hugh
4/Sq/5/3/4609, 5/7/15, L/C.; M.G.C., C/S, 6/12/16; M.G.C., 30/1/17, Tank Corps; Lieut.
The Grange, Carleton, Skipton, Yorkshire.

PARKER, Hugh Medows Pottinger
A/12530, 1/2/18; No. 5 O.C.B., 7/6/18, No. 14 O.C.B.; E. Kent R., 4/2/19; 2/Lieut. *47 Southbrook Road, Lee, S.E. 12*

PARKER, John Nowell
6/5/5307, 2/8/15; L'pool. R., 27/12/15; Lieut.; w.
Wolmsley House, Ormskirk, Lancashire.

PARKER, Leslie Middleton
C/13212, 5/6/18; demob. 29/1/19.
9 The Grove, Uplands, Swansea.

PARKER, Noel Middlemore
A/10283, 1/1/17, L/C.; R.A., C/S, 7/11/17; R.G.A., 29/4/18; S; 2/Lieut. *37a Highbury New Park, N. 5.*

PARKER, Reginald Frank
E/1598, 6/10/14, Sgt.; Manch. R., 7/1/15; F,It; Staff Capt.; O.B.E., M.C., M(3). *12 New Court, Carey Street, W.C. 2.*

PARKER, Sidney James
4/3463, 3/5/15; dis. 3/5/15.

PARKER, Thomas Dalby Septimus
D/11546, 21/6/17, L/C.; H. Bde. O.C.B., 7/12/17; Scots Gds., 28/5/18; 2/Lieut.

PARKER, Thomas Gordon Vincent
6/4/7112, 1/11/15; No. 11 O.C.B., 7/5/16; 7th Lond. R., 29/5/16; F; Lieut.; w(2). *West Hill, Grahamstown, South Africa.*

PARKER, Vincent Henry Goodhand
4/3313, 19/4/15; R.F.A., 9/7/15, R.F.C., R.A.F.; 2/Lieut.

PARKER, William
4/2/4290, 17/6/15, L/C.; Gren. Gds., 17/11/15; F; Capt.
Ashburnham, Steephill, Streatham, S.W. 16.

PARKER, William Alonzo
6/5/7303, 8/11/15; No. 5 O.C.B., 14/8/16; M.G.C., 28/10/16, Tank Corps; F; Lieut.; w; M(1).
95 Carisbrook Street, Queens Park, Manchester

PARKES, Arthur Fraser
4/6/5208, 29/7/15; R.F.A., 8/11/15; F; 2/Lieut.
9 Nevern Mansions, Nevern Square, S.W. 5.

PARKES, Bernard Joseph
B/10371, 5/1/17; R.F.C., C/S, 13/3/17; R.F.C., 19/4/17, R.A.F.; Lieut. *Earlsbury Grange, Trinity Road, Birmingham.*

PARKES, Henry Alfred
1/4/5209, 29/7/15, L/C.; S. Lan. R., 8/6/16, Wilts. R., Dorset R.; F; Lieut.; Inv. *5 Sefton Avenue, Congleton, Cheshire.*

PARKES, John Read
4/6/2/4997, 19/7/15, L/C.; S. Lan. R., 13/7/16, Lan. Fus.; F; Lieut.; w. *13 Sydney Street, Basford, Stoke-on-Trent*

PARKES, James William
B/12811, 20/3/18, L/C.; No. 3 O.C.B., 6/9/18; R. War. R., 17/3/19; 2/Lieut.
Stanshope, Warwick Road, Solihull, Warwickshire.

PARKES, Thomas
D/13702, 31/7/18; demob. 23/1/19. *21 Graham Street, S.W. 1.*

PARKHOUSE, Charles William
B/10846, 7/3/17; R.A., C/S, 29/6/17; R.G.A., 2/12/17; Lieut.; M(1). *96 Leadenhall Street, E.C. 3.*

PARKIN, Anthony Deane
E/2771, 25/1/15, L/C.; Notts. & Derby. R., 30/6/15; F; Capt.; w(2); M.C. *Mount Pleasant, Borough Green, Kent.*

PARKIN, Joseph Donald
B/1628, 9/10/14, L/C.; North'd. Fus., 28/1/15; Lieut.

PARKIN, Reginald Charles
1/2772, 25/1/15, L/C.; 20th Lond. R., 27/8/15; Lieut.
Westbank, Borough Green, Kent.

PARKINSON, Arthur Muir
4/2/5177, 29/7/15, Sgt.; R.E., 9/5/16; F,It; Lieut.
1105 Chester Road, Stretford, Manchester.

APPENDIX II.—RECORDS OF RANK AND FILE.

PARKINSON, *Edward Marshall*
Sq/2838, 1/2/15; North'd. Fus., 22/3/15; Capt.; M.C., M(1).

PARKINSON, *Frank*
A/10727, 10/2/17; Special List, 25/6/17; 2/Lieut.
                      3 *Albert Road, Saltaire, Yorkshire.*

✠ PARKINSON, *Oswald Wright*
4/3252, 13/4/15; E. Lan. R., 28/4/15; 2/Lieut.; *w*.
                      Killed in action 1/2/17.

PARKS, *Frank Herbert Hamilton*
6/4/8147, 3/12/15; No. 8 O.C.B., 4/8/16; Linc. R., 21/11/16; F; Capt.   47 *Mostyn Avenue, Wembley Hill, Middlesex.*

PARLE, *John Audley*
6/5/5950, 1/9/15, L/C.; No. 11 O.C.B., 7/5/16; L'pool. R., 4/9/16; Capt.; *w*; M.C.   90 *Edge Lane, Liverpool.*

PARMENTER, *Fred*
F/2773, 25/1/15; Bord. R., 12/5/15, Indian Army; F,I,P; Capt.; *w*; M(1).   *Camden Lodge, Brentwood.*

PARNELL, *John Landemann*
E/2568, 4/1/15; Wilts. R., 29/4/15, att. T.M. Bty. and American Army; F; Staff Capt.   *Calmore, Nr. Southampton, Hampshire.*

PARNELL, *Leslie Carleton*
6/2/9507, 15/2/16; R.N.R., 26/7/16; Lieut.
                      Calmore, Nr. Southampton, Hampshire.

PARNELL, *Roderick Harry*
D/12952, 19/4/18, L/C.; R.E., C/S, 23/8/18; General List, 8/3/19; 2/Lieut.   *Burmah Oil Coy. Ltd., Rangoon, Burma.*

PARNELL, *Thomas*
D/11120, 30/4/17, Sgt.; R.F.A., C/S, 25/1/18; R.F.A., 15/7/18; I; Capt..   11 *St. Augustine's Mansions, S.W. 1.*

PARNIS, *William Hamilton*
6/3/5779, 23/8/15; E. Kent R., 23/11/15, M.G.C.; F; Capt.; *w*; M.C.   *Cratloe, Faversham, Kent.*

PARR, *Henry*
B/13423, 1/7/18; demob. 21/12/18.
                37 *South John Street, St. Helens, Lancashire.*

PARR, *James Stanley*
C/A/11494, 14/6/17, L/C.; No. 5 O.C.B., 7/6/18, No. 14 O.C.B.; Midd'x. R., 5/2/19; 2/Lieut.
                10 *Leighton Road, Old Trafford, Manchester, Lancashire.*

✠ PARR-DUDLEY, *Walter*
A/11225, 7/5/17; No. 12 O.C.B., 10/8/17; R. Fus., 27/11/17; 2/Lieut.   Killed in action 5/4/18.

PARRETT, *Alexander Burgess*
A/13133, 27/5/18; No. 1 O.C.B., 8/11/18; D. of Corn. L.I., 16/3/19; 2/Lieut.   *Lamon Villa, Daniel Road, Truro, Cornwall.*

PARRISH, *Frank William*
F/3/2946, 18/2/15, Cpl.; K.R. Rif. C., 28/7/15; Lieut.; *w, p*.
                Highlands, Nr. Romford, Essex.

PARRISH, *John*
C/14293, 11/11/18; demob. 27/12/18.
                Heath Farm, Beacontree, Romford, Essex.

PARRISS, *John Westwood*
6/6826, 14/10/15; dis. med. unfit, 12/5/16.

PARRITT, *Leslie Jonnaux*
B/13648, 26/7/18; demob. 29/1/19.
                14 *Stanhope Gardens, Highgate, N. 6.*

PARRY, *Arthur Haydon*
B/1103, 7/9/14; Rif. Brig., 19/9/14; Capt.; *w*(2).

PARRY, *Charles Norman*
D/11581, 2/7/17; No. 19 O.C.B., 9/11/17; Sea. Highrs., 30/4/18; F; 2/Lieut.; *w*.   *Earnslaw, Malvern.*

PARRY, *Edward Arthur*
6/4/9220, 31/1/16, Sgt.; No. 14 O.C.B., 7/6/17; Notts. & Derby. R., 25/9/17, att. Wilts. R.; I; Capt.
                14 *Sussex Square, Hyde Park, W. 2.*

✠ PARRY, *Frank Meredith*
3/3551, 10/5/15, L/C.; Hamps. R., 7/10/15; 2/Lieut.
                  Killed in action 15/9/16.

✠ PARRY, *George Owen*
6/1/6955, 21/10/15; No. 11 O.C.B., 7/5/16; R.W. Fus., 4/9/16; F; Lieut.; *g*   Died 13/4/20.

PARRY, *Griffith Wynn Vaughan*
6/1/7619, 19/11/15; R.F.A., C/S, 4/8/16; R.F.A., 22/12/16; F; Lieut.; *w*.   *Knowbury Vicarage, Ludlow, Salop.*

PARRY, *John Griffith Montagu*
6/4/8571, 31/12/15; No. 8 O.C.B., 4/8/16; K.R. Rif. C., 18/12/16; 2/Lieut.

PARRY, *John Mathias Baden*
C/13402, 28/6/18; trfr. 14th Lond. R., 6/12/18, Gord. Highrs.
                14 *Kingsland Road, Victoria Park, Cardiff.*

PARRY, *Robert William*
A/10058, 30/11/16; No. 14 O.C.B., 30/1/17; trfr. R.G.A., 25/4/17.
                High School for Boys, Newport Road, Cardiff.

PARRY, *Stephen*
6/5/5228, 30/7/15; R.G.A., 5/10/15; F; Capt.
              c/o Miss Parry, Leamington House, Tulbrook, Liverpool.

PARRY, *Thomas Howard*
C/D/12254, 27/11/17; No. 18 O.C.B., 10/5/18; Welch R., 3/2/19; 2/Lieut.
              18 *Cwm Terrace, Cwm, Nr. Newport, Monmouthshire.*

✠ PARRY, *William Norman Maule*
E/2543, 4/1/15; 3rd Lond. R., 20/4/15; 2/Lieut.; *w*.
              Died of wounds 19/8/17 as Prisoner of War.

PARRY, *Willis Harvey*
D/11839, 9/8/17; No. 3 O.C.B., 8/2/18; trfr. 28th Lond. R., 2/8/18.   *Phœnix House, Lalgarth, Brecon.*

PARSON, *Claude Arthur*
B/10732, 15/2/17, Sgt.; R.A., C/S, 6/8/17; R.F.A., 12/1/18; F; Lieut.   50 *Bonningham Street, West Bromwich.*

PARSON, *Douglas Gerald*
4/3425, 29/4/15; dis. 29/4/15; rej. 4/3/3737, 24/5/15; No. 14 O.C.B., 30/10/16; R. Lanc. R., 24/1/17; Lieut.

PARSONS, *Albert Henry*
6/2/6489, 27/9/15; No. 6 O.C.B., 5/10/16; Wilts. R., 24/1/17; Lieut.; *w*.   207 *Upper Richmond Road, Putney, S.W. 15.*

PARSONS, *Arthur William*
3/3354, 22/4/15, L/C.; Shrop. L.I., 8/7/15; Lieut.

PARSONS, *Eustace Russell*
6/4/Sq/4155, 10/6/15; R.G.A., 28/9/15, R.A.F.; F; Lieut.
              Leutchine, Burlington Road, Swanage.

PARSONS, *George*
6/3/7031, 27/10/15; Bedf. R., 25/1/16; Lieut.
              Ferndale, Granville Road, St. Albans, Hertfordshire.

✠ PARSONS, *George Jonathan*
A/10985, 2/4/17; No. 14 O.C.B., 10/8/17; R. Fus., 27/11/17; F; 2/Lieut.   Died of wounds 31/8/18.

PARSONS, *Gordon Maxim*
B/12812, 20/3/18; No. 2 O.C.B., 20/9/18; York. R., 17/3/19; 2/Lieut.   54 *Spencer Place, Leeds, Yorkshire.*

PARSONS, *Grenville Vaughan*
C/D/12249, 23/11/17, L/C.; R.E., C/S, 16/6/18; R.E., 1/11/18; 2/Lieut.   34 *Golds Hill Road, Handsworth, Birmingham.*

PARSONS, *John Francis*
B/E/13623, 24/7/18; A.S.C., C/S, 1/10/18; demob. 27/12/18.
              Tubney House, Abingdon, Berkshire.

PARSONS, *Joshua*
4/3/3977, 3/6/15; S. Lan. R., 6/9/15; Lieut.; *w*.
              12 *Warwick Avenue, Paddington, W. 2.*

PARSONS, *Lionel Cuthbert*
6/1/6134, 9/9/15; Som. L.I., 24/1/16; Lieut.

PARSONS, *Robert*
C/D/12268, 30/11/17; No. 4 O.C.B., 10/5/18; Essex R., 4/2/19; 2/Lieut.   149 *Grosvenor Road, Highbury, N. 5.*

PARSONS, *William Walter*
A/11003, 4/4/17; No. 14 O.C.B., 5/10/17; Leic. R., 26/2/18; F; Lieut.; *w*.   65 *Albert Street, Rugby.*

PARSONSON, *Charles Leonard*
B/D/12742, 11/3/18, L/C.; demob. 30/5/19.
              15 *Maidenstone Hill, Greenwich, S.E. 10.*

PARTINGTON, *Edward Noel*
H/2903, 11/2/15; Ches. R., 24/5/15; F; Lieut.
              Deva Lodge, Prestatyn, North Wales.

APPENDIX II.—RECORDS OF RANK AND FILE.

PARTINGTON, John Laughton
B/2893, 9/2/15; R.E., 16/4/15; F; Major; M.C., M(1).
The Grange, Norton, Worcestershire.

PARTINGTON, Wilfred George
B/12865, 26/3/18; R.F.A., C/S, 17/5/18; demob.
11 Halden Road, Westhill, Wandsworth, S.W. 18.

PARTON, Ernest George
E/1538, 6/10/14, L/C.; 13th Lond. R., 15/12/14; Capt.
1a Clanricarde Gardens, W. 2.

PARTRIDGE, Alfred Thomas
6/5/C/8656, 3/1/16; R.F.C., C/S, 28/12/16; R.F.C., 4/4/17, R.A.F.; Lieut.
Carlton, Palmers Avenue, Grays, Essex.

PARTRIDGE, Cuthbert
4/6/5/1979, 19/7/15; R.G.A., 21/12/15.
The Bank, Ebbw Vale, Monmouthshire.

PARTRIDGE, Cyril
C/10834, 5/3/17; trfr. R.F.A., 25/5/17.
Grangefield, Earls Barton, Northamptonshire.

✠ PARTRIDGE, Henry Treneman
E/3077, 18/3/15, L/C.; R. Suss. R., 20/7/15, R.A.F.; E; Lieut.
Killed 14/7/18.

PARTRIDGE, James Reginald
6/1/9231, 1/2/16; R.F.A., C/S, 4/8/16; dis. med. unfit, 6/10/16.
17 Lower Bridge Street, St. George's, Canterbury.

✠ PARTRIDGE, Robert Henry
F/1806, 16/10/14; Norf. R., 19/11/14; G,E,P; Capt.
Died 4/9/17.

PASCOE, Albert Leopold
6/5/7555, 17/11/15, Sgt.; No. 7 O.C.B., 3/7/16; R. Innis. Fus., 3/11/16, att. R.F.C.; F; Lieut.
18 Oak Hill Road, Putney, S.W. 15.

PASMORE, Ivan Wallace
C/9950, 20/11/16, L/C.; No. 14 O.C.B., 6/4/17; Special List, 14/6/17; Capt.
Sperazu, High Street, Exeter.

PASSMORE, Douglas Gordon
C/12230, 15/11/17; H. Bde. O.C.B., 8/3/18; Leic. R., 27/8/18; F; Lieut.
2 The Chase, Clapham Common, S.W. 4.

PATCHETT, Norman
6/2/5524, 9/8/15; No. 4 O.C.B.; W. Rid. R., 13/7/16; F; Lieut.; w.
75 Upper Rushton Road, Thornbury, Bradford.

PATCHETT, Sidney North
A/B/C/12186, 2/11/17; Tank Corps C/S, 22/2/18; Tank Corps, 3/3/19; 2/Lieut.
75 Upper Rushton Road, Thornbury, Bradford.

PATERSON, Alfred
6/5/6943, 20/10/15; North'd. Fus., 6/7/16, att. R. Ir. Regt.; F; Lieut.; p.
107 Kingsley Avenue, West Ealing, W. 13.

✠ PATERSON, Arthur Cecil
4/6/5/4942, 19/7/15, Cpl.; Durh. L.I., 18/12/16, Intelligence; F; 2/Lieut.
Killed in action 22/4/18.

PATERSON, Frank Sydney
K/2430, 21/12/14; dis. 21/12/14; R.E.; Lieut.
Tudor House, West Overcliff Drive, Bournemouth.

PATERSON, George Andrew
B/12835, 22/3/18; R.E., C/S, 23/8/18; R.E., 17/12/18; 2/Lieut.
Parkhall, Dalmuir, Dumbartonshire.

PATERSON, George Ernest
H/2602, 7/1/15; R.F.A., 12/3/15; Lieut.
122 Edith Road, West Kensington, W. 14.

PATERSON, George Frederick
6/4/9124, 24/1/16; No. 7 O.C.B., 11/8/16; R. Innis. Fus., 18/12/16, secd. Indian Army; F; Lieut.; w.
2/5th Royal Gurkhas, Abbottabad, N.W.F.P., India.

PATERSON, Harold Rose
C/12034, 24/9/17, L/C.; R.F.A., C/S, 15/3/18; R.F.A., 10/10/18; 2/Lieut.
56 Fox Grove Road, Beckenham, Kent.

PATERSON, Hugh Dennis
A/13055, 10/5/18; No. 1 O.C.B., 8/11/18; 7th Lond. R., 17/3/19; 2/Lieut.
79 Danecroft Road, Herne Hill, S.E. 24.

✠ PATERSON, James
6/8841, 10/1/16; No. 9 O.C.B., 8/3/16; Sco. Rif., 23/7/16; F; 2/Lieut.; w.
Died of wounds 20/9/17.

PATERSON, John Cochran
B/Sq/C/12393, 15/1/18; No. 12 O.C.B., 5/7/18; R. Sco. Fus., 3/3/19; 2/Lieut.
79 Muswell Road, Muswell Hill, N. 10.

PATERSON, Richard John
4/5210, 29/7/15; Hamps. R., 8/7/16, R.A.F.; Lieut.; w.

PATERSON, Robert
C/11450, 4/6/17; No. 14 O.C.B., 4/1/18; Sco. Rif., 25/6/18; F; 2/Lieut.; w.
99 Milbrae Road, Langside, Glasgow.

PATERSON, Thomas
E/14094, 2/10/18; R.G.A., C/S, 1/11/18; demob.; O.B.E.
17 Spring Hill, Sheffield.

PATERSON, William
6/8851, 10/1/16; No. 9 O.C.B., 8/3/16; Gord. Highrs., 6/7/16.
York Place, U.P. Church, Perth.

PATERSON-BROWN, Alan Moray
C/12622, 18/2/18; R.A.F., C/S, 21/5/18; R.A.F., 24/3/19; E; 2/Lieut.
Gorno Grove, Gateside, N.B.

PATEY, Samuel
B/E/13611, 24/7/18; R.G.A., C/S, 2/10/18; R.G.A., 11/4/19; 2/Lieut.
42 Finsbury Square, E.C. 2.

PATON, James Richard
4/3793, 27/5/15; 11th Lond. R., 29/9/15; S; Lieut.
31 Dornton Road, South Croydon.

PATON, Percival Edward
K/C/Sq/2243, 3/12/14, Cpl.; York. Huss., 29/6/15, secd. M.G.C.; Lieut.
Baronga, Bennett Street, Neutral Bay, Sydney, New South Wales, Australia.

PATON, Robert Michael
C/352, 8/3/09; dis. 7/3/13; rej. K/D/6/3/2126, 14/11/14, Sgt.; Garr. O.C.B., 24/4/17; Worc. R., 16/6/17, Ches. R., att. Brit. W.I. Regt.; P; Lieut.
35a St. James Street, S.W. 1.

PATRICK, William Donald
6/8787, 7/1/16; No. 9 O.C.B., 8/3/16; R.F.C., 6/7/16, R.A.F.; Lieut.
Toftshill, Dabey, Ayrshire.

PATTERSON, George Malcolm
6/1/7402, 12/11/15, L/C.; R.A., C/S, 25/8/16; R.G.A., 19/12/16; Lieut.
Dauphin Hill, St. Andrews, Fife.

PATTERSON, Vancouver
B/589, 27/11/11; dis. 4/4/13.
55 Manchester Street, W. 1.

PATTINSON, Howard Alan
6/2/6560, 30/9/15; E. Surr. R., 8/6/16, att. Notts. & Derby. R., Indian Army; F,I; Major; w; M.C., M(1).
c/o Messrs. Cox & Coy., Bombay, India.

PATTISSON, Charles Hoel
C/13407, 29/6/18; A.S.C., C/S, 31/8/18; R.A.S.C., 22/11/18; 2/Lieut.
Morgraunt, West Byfleet, Surrey.

PATTISSON, Walter Merriman
2/4137, 10/6/15, Cpl.; R.A.S.C., 24/1/16; Capt.
Dalegarth, Stevenage, Hampshire.

PAUL, Bickerstaff George
B/1722, 15/10/14; Essex R., 3/12/14; F; Staff Capt.; M(1).
48 Windsor Road, Forest Gate, Essex.

PAUL, Cyril Arthur James
A/14012, 16/9/18; trfr. K.R. Rif. C., 7/4/19.
Glenbrook, Essenden Road, Belvedere, Kent.

PAUL, Frank Oscar
6/8488, 20/12/15; R.A., C/S, 14/4/16; R.G.A., 17/7/16; Capt.
Overchurch Hill, Upton, Birkenhead.

PAUL, William Cyril
4/2/5078, 26/7/15, L/C.; D. of Corn. L.I., 1/6/16, Lab. Corps; Lieut.; M.C.

PAULL, Clarence Vivian
D/10774, 19/2/17, L/C.; R.F.A., C/S, 22/6/17; R.F.A., 17/11/17; Lieut.
Havelock, Camborne, Cornwall.

✠ PAULL, Frederick Major
K/B/2414, 21/12/14, L/C.; Notts. & Derby. R., 7/5/15; G; 2/Lieut.
Killed in action 28/11/15.

PAULLEY, Harold
K/D/2505, 31/12/14; Norf. R., 3/6/15; E,P; Lieut.
Kingsland, Newcastle, Staffordshire.

PAUMIER, Ronald Hodgson
1/3314, 19/4/15; North'd. Fus., 27/11/15.
7 Essex Road, Acton, W. 3.

PAVER-CROW, Richard George
6/8971, 17/1/16; A.S.C., C/S, 1/5/16; R.A.S.C., 4/6/16; S,F; Lieut.
Ornhams Hall, Boroughbridge, Yorkshire.

APPENDIX II.—RECORDS OF RANK AND FILE.

PAVIERE, Horace Duncan
K/E/2274, 7/12/14; Glouc. R., 17/2/15; Lieut.; w.
44 St. Giles, Oxford

☥ PAVITT, Reginald James
6/Sq/6981, 25/10/15, L/C.; No. 2 Cav. C/S, 31/3/16; R.E. Kent Yeo., 19/8/16; F; Lieut. Killed in action 9/8/18.

PAWSON, Albert Guy
Sq/299, 25/6/08; dis. 31/12/09.
Christ Church, Oxford.

PAWSON, Arthur Clive
Sq/175, 29/4/08; dis. 28/4/09.

PAXTON, Charles Henry
E/6/2688, 14/1/15, Cpl.; Lovat's Scouts, 5/8/16, att. M.G.C.; Lieut.

PAY, Lionel Thomas
C/9949, 20/11/16; A.S.C., C/S, 12/3/17; R.A.S.C., 7/5/17; 2/Lieut.; M(1). 14 Wickham Gardens, Brockley, S.E. 4.

PAYNE, Allen
D/13920, 28/8/18; demob. 19/2/19.
134 Ravensbourne Avenue, Shortlands, Kent.

PAYNE, Arnold Cyril
6/B/9149, 25/1/16; Sgt.; demob. 24/1/19.
17a St. Georges Street, Northampton.

PAYNE, Benjamin William
6/4/9165, 26/1/16; R.E., 14/7/16; Lieut.

PAYNE, James Grahame
4/5/5058, 24/7/15; No. 2 Cav. C/S, 18/5/16; Notts. & Derby. Yeo., 6/9/16; E,P; Lieut.
53 Buckingham Road, Aylesbury, Buckinghamshire.

PAYNE, Kenneth Sampson
6/2/6209, 13/9/15; trfr. Lond. Div. Cyc. Coy., 4/3/16.
33 Ferntower Road, Canonbury, N. 1.

PAYNE, Martin Sylvester
4/2/4156, 10/6/15; Linc. R., 20/10/15; F; Lieut.
The Vicarage, Gosberton, Spalding, Lincolnshire.

PAYNE, Reginald Arthur
6/3/6432, 24/9/15; No. 11 O.C.B., 7/5/16; Midd'x. R., 4/9/16, Indian Army; F,I; Lieut.; w(2). 33rd Punjabi Depôt, India.

PAYNE, Reginald Theobald
B/13526, 15/7/18; demob. 29/1/19.
17a St. George's Street, Northampton.

PAYNE, Richard Ino
A/13079, 17/5/18; demob. 29/1/19.
46 Wakehurst Road, Wandsworth Common, S.W. 11.

PAYNE, Sydney Edgar
4/5/C/4804, 12/7/15; C.Q.M.S.; Garr. O.C.B.; Lab. Corps, 8/5/18; F; 2/Lieut.
c/o Mrs. Park, 92 Fellows Road, Hampstead, N.W. 3. (Now in South Africa).

PAYTON, William Seymour Emilius
A/13032, 3/5/18; dis. to re-enlist in Gren. Gds., 6/2/19.
11 Exeter Road, Brondesbury, N.W. 2.

PEACEY, Arthur Frederic
6/2/A/6561, 30/9/15; R.F.C., C/S, 1/6/17; R.F.C., 26/7/17, R.A.F.; F; Flt. Cmdr.; D.F.C., M(2).
The Wold, Charlton Kings, Cheltenham. (Now in U.S.A.).

PEACEY, Prescott Dare
6/4/7556, 17/11/15; R. Dub. Fus., 24/4/16; Lieut.; w.
Collingsbourne, Liverpool Road, Kingston.

PEACEY, Reginald John Freeman
6/4/7557, 17/11/15, L/C.; R. Dub. Fus., 24/4/16; Germ.SWA,F; Capt. The Hollies, Aulaby Park, Hull.

PEACOCK, Arthur Harcourt
B/10106, 4/12/16; trfr. 19th Lond. R., 6/7/17.

PEACOCK, Henry Maurice
B/10363, 5/1/17; dis. med. unfit, 29/5/17.
7 West Street, Epsom, Surrey.

☥ PEACOCKE, Gerald Fergusson
6/1/D/6333, 20/9/15; trfr. E. Kent R., 26/1/17. Killed.

PEACOCKE, Tully Lloyd Courtenay
1/3072, 17/3/15; R.E., 22/5/15.
Lynton, Bromley Grove, Shortlands, Kent.

☥ PEAKE, Henry Wright
A/848, 4/8/14; Essex R., 15/8/14; Capt.
Killed in action 3/7/16.

PEAKE, Herbert Sidney
C/11784, 3/8/17; trfr. R.F.C., 13/12/17, R.A.F.; Cpl.
Meadowside, Hampton Wick, Kingston-on-Thames.

PEAKE, Walter
6/2/7216, 4/11/15; E. Kent R., 9/6/16; F; Major; M.C., M(1).
27 Christchurch Road, Southend-on-Sea.

PEAKMAN, Henry Joseph Simeon
D/11182, 4/5/17; No. 16 O.C.B., 5/10/17; Leic. R., 12/3/18; 2/Lieut. 123 College Road, Moseley, Birmingham.

PEARCE, Alfred Spicer Deane
B/11678, 16/7/17; No. 14 O.C.B., 9/11/17; Devon. R., 30/4/18; F; 2/Lieut. Rew, Ashburton, South Devonshire.

PEARCE, Alfred Tom
C/10784, 23/2/17; R.F.A., C/S, 22/6/17; R.F.A., 17/11/17; F; 2/Lieut.; w; M.C. Brentor, Warwick Road, Hale, Cheshire.

PEARCE, Arthur
C/12287, 4/12/17; R.E., C/S, 10/3/18; trfr. 30th Lond. R., 21/7/18. Pilton House, Barnstaple, North Devonshire.

☥ PEARCE, Arthur Carlton
F/1866, 16/10/14; R.A.S.C., 19/11/14, att. Notts. & Derby. R.; F; Capt. Killed in action 22/7/18.

PEARCE, Christopher Maurice Hussey
H/2573, 4/1/15, Cpl.; Cold. Gds., 7/7/15; Capt.; w.
Ripley Court, Surrey.

☥ PEARCE, Edward Sydney Charles
A/10191, 13/12/16; R.F.C., C/S, 13/3/17; R.F.C., 29/5/17; F; 2/Lieut. Missing 31/3/18.

PEARCE, Henry Joseph
6/3/8187, 6/12/15; R.E., C/S, 2/9/16; R.E., 18/11/16; F; Lieut.; g; M.C. and Bar.
161 Dorchester Road, Weymouth. (Now in Hong Kong).

PEARCE, John Edward
K/D/2322, 14/12/14; R.E., 8/2/15; F; Major; M(1).
Highfield, Verne Road, Weymouth.

PEARCE-BATTEN, William Hubert
B/11362, 28/5/17; No. 10 O.C.B., 5/10/17; D. of Corn. L.I., 26/2/18, att. M.G.C.; 2/Lieut.

PEARKES, Percy Walter
6/1/Sq/8275, 9/12/15; R.N.A.S., 31/10/16.
2 Coventry Road, Ilford, Essex.

☥ PEARS, Charles Martin
D/10476, 12/1/17; R.F.C., C/S, 13/3/17; R.F.C., 19/4/17; F; 2/Lieut. Killed in action 23/11/17.

PEARS, Thomas Winfield
2/3704, 20/5/15; R.M.L.I., 30/8/15; Lieut.
23 Queen Anne's Grove, Bedford Park, W. 4.

PEARSE, Ensor Stanbury
Sq/922, 5/8/14, L/C.; R.F.A., 7/10/14, R.N.A.S., R.A.F.; F; Major. P.O. Addo, Cape Province, South Africa.

PEARSE, Harry Marrs
Sq/951, 5/8/14, L/C.; R.F.A., 7/10/14; F,It; Capt.; w(2); M(2).
P.O. Addo, Cape Province, South Africa.

☥ PEARSE, Kenneth Herbert
C/1351, 26/9/14; E. Surr. R., 23/12/14, att. Hamps. R.; G; 2/Lieut. Killed in action 6/8/15.

PEARSE, Leslie Henry
6/3/7745, 22/11/15, L/C.; No. 14 O.C.B., 30/10/16; E. Surr. R., 28/2/17; Lieut.; p.
Flat 2, 77 Kensington Gardens Square, W. 2.

PEARSE, William Henry
3/3870, 31/5/15, Sgt.; R.A., C/S, 26/10/16; R.G.A., 5/1/17; F; Capt.; w.
17 Prebend Mansions, Chiswick, W. 4. (Now in Malay).

PEARSON, Alec Thomas
B/12015, 17/9/17; E. Kent R., 30/7/18, att. R. Suss. R.; NR; Capt. Park House, Appledore, Kent.

PEARSON, Arthur Donald
6/5/6852, 15/10/15; W. Lanc. Div. Cyc. Coy., 5/8/16, R. Bucks. Huss.; F; Lieut.; w.
55 Cambridge Avenue, Great Crosby, Liverpool. (Now in Singapore).

PEARSON, Compton Edwin
A/14037, 20/9/18; demob. 29/1/19.
Hallgarth, Nr. Pershore, Worcestershire.

APPENDIX II.—RECORDS OF RANK AND FILE.

PEARSON, George
3/3653, 17/5/15; 18th Lond. R., 10/8/15; F; Lieut.
12 Queens Road, Harrogate.

PEARSON, Harold Fellows
K/1/2404, 21/12/14, L/C.; No. 11 O.C.B., 7/5/16; Midd'x. R., 4/8/16; F; Capt.; M.C. 11 Burgess Hill, Hampstead, N.W. 2.

PEARSON, Herbert Nichols
C/12623, 18/2/18; No. 2 O.C.B., 20/9/18; demob.
Pendleton, Ulverston, Lancashire.

PEARSON, Hugh G.
Sq/2157, 23/11/14; W. Kent Yeo., 29/4/15, att. Gds. M.G.R.; Lieut. 129 Kings Road, Brighton.

✠ PEARSON, James
6/3/7052, 28/10/15; No. 11 O.C.B., 7/5/16; M.G.C., 4/9/16; Lieut. Died of wounds 28/3/18.

PEARSON, John Alexander
E/14118, 9/10/18; R.G.A., C/S, 1/11/18; demob.
7 Fifth Avenue, Kelvinside, Glasgow.

PEARSON, Joseph Powell
4/3/4631, 5/7/15; No. 4 O.C.B., 7/3/16; R.W. Fus., 21/6/16, att. S. Wales Bord.; F; Lieut. 9 Princes Avenue, Nuneaton.

✠ PEARSON, Oliver Charles
6/5/6405, 23/9/15; R.F.C., 25/9/16; F; 2/Lieut.
Killed in action 10/9/17.

✠ PEARSON, Thomas Raleigh
4/3738, 24/5/15; K.R. Rif. C., 10/8/15; 2/Lieut.
Died of wounds 2/7/16.

✠ PEARSON, Wilfrid Hearne
A/10909, 26/3/17; No. 14 O.C.B., 5/7/17; N. Cyc. Bn., 30/10/17, M.G.C.; F; 2/Lieut. Killed in action 29/9/18.

PEARSON, William Ellis
6/3/8033, 30/11/15; No. 14 O.C.B., 28/8/16; North'd. Fus., 22/11/16; Lieut. 17 Hextol Terrace, Hexham-on-Tyne.

PEAT, James Henry
F/1769, 16/10/14, L/C.; Midd'x. R., 2/3/15; 1st Life Guards; F; Lieut.; w. Cranmer, Mitcham, Surrey.

PEBODY, Leonard Gardner
6/5/8100, 2/12/15, L/C.; No. 8 O.C.B., 4/8/16; Yorks. L.I., 21/11/16; F,It; Lieut.
Ash Cottage, Stoke Goldington, Newport Pagnell, Buckinghamshire.

✠ PECK, Edwin Robert Richmond
6/3/5599, 13/8/15; Suff. R., 20/1/16; 2/Lieut.; M.C.
Killed in action 3/5/17.

PECK, Kenneth
A/11614, 5/7/17, L/C.; No. 14 O.C.B., 7/12/17; L'pool. R., 28/5/18; F; 2/Lieut.
9 Hawkshead Street, Southport, Lancashire.

✠ PECKHAM, Arthur Nyton
Sq/120, 18/4/08; dis. 16/4/12; Indian Army; I,M; 2/Lieut.
Killed 14/2/18.

✠ PECKSTON, Robert Henry
6/2/5632, 16/8/15, L/C.; North'd. Fus., 9/6/16; 2/Lieut.
Died 22/10/17.

PEDDAR, Reginald Vardy
2/3073, 18/3/15, L/C.; R.W. Surr. R., 29/7/15, War Office; Lieut.; w.

PEDDER, Reginald Stanley
2/3464, 3/5/15; Lan. Fus., 28/7/15, Ches. R., R.E.; S,F; Capt.; Inv. 5 York Avenue, Sefton Park, Liverpool.

PEDERSEN, Harold
C/Sq/14300, 12/11/18; demob. 22/1/19.
Fredheim, Linden Grove, West Hartlepool.

PEDGRIFT, Frederick Walter
4/3/6/4088, 7/6/15, Sgt.; Dorset R., 25/9/16; Lieut.; w.
56 Manville Road, Balham, S.W. 17.

PEEK, Francis Edward
F/2748, 21/1/15; W. York. R., 28/7/15, Yorks. L.I.; 2/Lieut.; w.

PEEK, Patrick Charles
2/9777, 24/10/16; trfr. 16th Lond. R., 18/4/17.
Woodley Hall, Boscombe Cliff Road, Bournemouth.

PEEL, Edward Orrell
A/10294, 1/1/17; R.F.C., C/S, 13/3/17; R.F.C., 19/4/17, R.A.F.; F; Lieut.; w. North View, Daisy Hill, Bradford.

PEEL, Edward Percy
6/4/5592, 12/8/15, Sgt.; R.F.A., C/S, 17/3/16; R.F.A., 13/7/16; F; Capt. 30 Lawn Terrace, Blackheath, S.E 3.

PEEL, Robert
Sq/151, 18/4/08; dis. 17/4/09; rej. C/1161, 14/9/14; 16th Lond. R., 26/9/14; S; Major; O.B.E., Serbian Order of the White Eagle, M(2). 4 New Square, Lincoln's Inn, W.C. 2.

PEELE, Richardson
4/1/5211, 29/7/15; R.F.A., C/S, 31/3/16; R.G.A., 2/8/16; F; Capt. 4 Sunny Bank, Springbank West, Hull, Yorkshire.

✠ PEERLESS, Cuthbert Henry
6/4/9136, 21/1/16; No. 8 O.C.B., 4/8/16; R. Suss. R., 18/12/16; 2/Lieut. Died 12/5/18.

PEERLESS, Herbert Read
3/3355, 22/4/15; Notts. & Derby. R., 11/6/15; Lieut.

PEERS, Kenneth Edleston
6/1/8699, 4/1/16, L/C.; No. 14 O.C.B., 26/11/16; Ches. R., 28/2/17; F; Lieut.; w. Millthwaite, Wallasey, Cheshire.

PEGGE, Wilfred John
6/3/9448, 10/2/16; No. 14 O.C.B., 30/10/16; L'pool. R., 28/2/17; F; Lieut.; w; M.C.
Oaklands Drive, Ashton-on-Mersey, Cheshire.

PEGLER, Lionel
A/1615, 9/10/14; Essex R., 13/10/14; Capt.; w.
The Mount, Chepstow.

PEIRCE, Edgar James
2/3235, 12/4/15; R.E., 23/7/15; Lieut.; M(1).

PELL, William John
D/E/13907, 26/8/18; demob. 11/1/19.
70 Springfield Road, Brighton.

PELLEGRINI, Agostino Raffaello
B/Sq/A/12378, 11/1/18; No. 19 O.C.B., 7/6/18; R. Suss. R., 3/2/19; 2/Lieut. 45 Hollingbury Park Avenue, Brighton.

PELLEW, George
6/9465, 14/2/16; R.E., 27/5/16; F; Capt.; w,g(2); M.C.
Box 153, Roodepoort, Transvaal, South Africa.

PEMBERTON, Clement
Sq/4/4012, 5/6/15; Norf. Yeo., 22/9/15, att. 1st Lanc.; Lieut.
Castle Hill Farm, Norwich Road, Ipswich, Suffolk.

PEMBERTON, Harold Charles
H/3016, 8/3/15, L/C.; Lan. Fus., 13/6/15; F; Capt.; D.S.O., Croix de Guerre (French).
St. Cynes, 10 Upper Brighton Road, Surbiton, Surrey.

PEMBERTON, Joseph Desmond
6/8902, 13/1/16; No. 9 O.C.B., 8/3/16; R. Ir. Rif., 6/7/16, secd. Indian Army; Lieut.

PEMBERTON, Percy Roy Lafont
D/12923, 12/4/18; R.F.A., C/S, 26/7/18; R.F.A., 7/4/19; 2/Lieut.
The Mount, Bean's Combe, Wood Road, Bournemouth.

PEMBERTON, Richard Oliver Walpole
Sq/545, 10/2/11; dis. 22/2/12; Suff. Yeo.; Capt.

PEMBERTON, Warwick Geoffrey Travers
Sq/577, 13/11/11; dis. 18/8/13. 34/36 Gresham Street, E.C. 2.

PEMBO, Charles Montague
D/6/1394, 29/9/14, Sgt.; demob. 21/1/19.
38 Dewhurst Road, West Kensington, W. 14.

PEMBROKE, Sydney Keith
1952, 22/10/14; Manch. R., 28/11/14; Lieut.; w.
Glenesk Pond Road, Blackheath, S.E.

PEMBROOK, John Gilbert
4/1/4610, 5/7/15; Kent. Cyc. Bn., 11/11/15; I; Lieut.
15 Burgate Street, Canterbury.

PENBERTHY, Eric Hillman
6/3/7775, 23/11/15, L/C.; 5th Lond. R., 23/6/16; Lieut.; w.
3 Grosvenor Square, W. 1.

PENDERGAST, Thomas
6/5/C/7620, 19/11/15; trfr. M.G.C., 6/12/16.
39 St. George's Road, Bolton, Lancashire.

PENDLEBURY, John Arnold
6/3/7304, 8/11/15; trfr. R.G.A., 7/7/16; R.G.A.; 2/Lieut.
27 Priory Avenue, High Wycombe, Buckinghamshire.

✠ PENDRIGH, Alexander Conrad Cuthbertson
6/4/7113, 1/11/15, Sgt.; Devon. R., 4/8/16; 2/Lieut.
Died of wounds 17/8/17.

PENFOLD, Marchant Eric Harvey
C/12576, 6/2/18; No. 6 O.C.B., 7/6/18; trfr. 28th Lond. R., 12/9/18. H.M. Dockyard, Sheerness

APPENDIX II.—RECORDS OF RANK AND FILE.

PENGELLEY, Walter Murray
B/Sq/A/11721, 19/7/17, L/C.; No. 2 Cav. C/S, 11/4/18; 6th R. Regt. of Cav., 18/10/18; 2/Lieut.

PENGILLY, Albert Rennie
C/12035, 24/9/17; R.F.C., C/S, 26/11/17; R.F.C., 23/1/18, R.A.F.; F; Lieut.; D.F.C.
San Joao da Madeira, Portugal. (Now in Mexico).

PENLINGTON, Harry Napier
6/3/5859, 26/8/15; Worc. R., 23/12/15, R.A.F.; Capt.
Rushenholme, Hemsworth, Nr. Wakefield.

PENLINGTON, Herbert William
6/3/8117, 2/12/15, Sgt.; A.S.C., C/S, 27/10/16; R.A.S.C., 20/12/16; F; Lieut. Worsboro Common, Barnsley, Yorkshire.

✠ PENMAN, Rowland Arthur
6/4/9256, 2/2/16; No. 8 O.C.B., 4/8/16, M.G.C., C/S; M.G.C., 28/12/16; 2/Lieut. Killed in action 16/6/17.

PENN, Frederick John
B/13557, 19/7/18; demob. 29/1/19.
Maypole Farm, East Grinstead, Salisbury, Wiltshire.

PENNEY, Keith Brodie
4/5/4756, 12/7/15; W. York. R., 16/12/15, emp. M. of Munitions; F; Lieut.; w.
Grove Lodge, Rossmore Avenue, Parkstone, Dorset.

✠ PENN-GASKELL, W. P. See GASKELL, W. W. P.

PENNIALL, Sidney Ernest
6/3/6631, 4/10/15, L/C.; Norf. R., 1/6/16; F; Lieut.
52 York Road, Great Yarmouth.

PENNING, Albert Leonard
D/11142, 30/4/17; R.F.C., C/S, 1/6/17; R.F.C., 4/7/17, R.A.F.; Lieut.

PENNINGTON, Ernest
6/2/7558, 17/11/15; dis. med. unfit, 8/8/16.
Stoneleigh, Orrell, Nr. Wigan, Lancashire.

PENNINGTON, John
D/10004, 24/11/16; No. 14 O.C.B., 30/1/17; L'pool. R., 25/4/17; F; Lieut.; w. Raby, 3 Glen Park Road, Wallasey, Cheshire.

PENNINGTON, Stanley Muncaster
6/8331, 11/12/15; R.E., C/S, 2/9/16; R.E., 18/11/16; F; Lieut.; M.C., M(1). 10 Merton Road, Bootle, Liverpool.

PENNY, George Stephen
6/9589, 17/6/16; R.F.A., C/S, 6/9/16.
St. Pauls School, West Kensington, W.

PENNY, Harold George Yelverton
B/12422, 18/1/18; Sigs. C/S, 31/5/18; trfr. 5th Lond. R., 24/3/19
10 Oakley Street, Chelsea, S.W. 3.

PENNY, Thomas Edward
6/2/6811, 14/10/15, L/C.; Herts. R., 21/4/16; F; Lieut.; w.
Grays, Dr. Commons Road, Berkhamsted, Hertfordshire.

PENRICE, Walter
4/5/4712, 9/7/15, L/C.; L'pool. R., 3/1/16; F; Lieut.; w, g.
Redcliffe, Green Lawn, Rock Ferry, Birkenhead. (Now in Singapore).

PENROSE, Donald Michael
A/636, 25/4/12, Sgt.; Essex R., 2/12/14; G,E,P; Capt.; Inv.
Avonmore, Epping, Essex.

PENRY, Henry Alexander
D/3031, 11/3/15, C.Q.M.S.; R.A.O.C., 25/8/16; F; Capt.; M(1).
Roden House, Wem, Salop.

PEPPER, Frederick Arthur
6/3/5369, 1/8/15, L/C.; R.F.A., 3/11/15; F,It; Lieut.
16 Julian Road, Folkestone.

PERCIVAL, Arthur Ernest
A/1000, 5/8/15; Bedf. R., 3/9/14, Essex. R.; Lt.-Col.; w; D.S.O., M.C., Croix de Guerre (French), M(3).
Sprangewell, Ware.

PERCIVAL, Leonard George
B/10094, 4/12/16; No. 14 O.C.B., 5/3/17; R. Marines, 26/6/17, att. R.A.F.; Lieut. 19 Elsie Road, East Dulwich, S.E. 22.

PERCIVAL, Victor William
D/10376, 8/1/17, L/C.; R.G.A., C/S, 25/4/17; R.G.A., 19/8/17; F; Lieut. Limbrook, Dore, Sheffield.

PERCY, Percy Algernon
A/10308, 1/1/17; No. 14 O.C.B., 6/4/17; R.W. Kent R., 31/7/17, att. W.O.; F,It; Lieut.; w; M(1). 61 Fleet Street, E.C. 4.

PEREIRA, Horace Alvarez de Courcy
B/3017, 8/3/15, L/C.; R.A.O.C., 27/5/15; F; Capt.
Probate Registry, Newcastle-on-Tyne.

PERKES, Henry Midgeley
B/Sq/D/12326; 28/12/17; No. 2 Cav. C/S, 26/6/18; dis. 14/1/19.
2 Riverview, Lower Road, Belvedere, Kent.

PERKINS, Arnold Smallman
6/5/C/7422, 12/11/15; No. 14 O.C.B.; trfr. R.G.A., 29/12/16.

PERKINS, Arthur Desmond Knox
6/8700, 4/1/16; R. Ir. Fus., 16/8/16, att. R.F.C.; Lieut.
Park House, Youghal, Co. Cork, Ireland.

PERKINS, Frederick William
K/F/2563, 4/1/15; E. Lan. R., 22/4/15.
139 Oxford Street, W.1.

PERKINS, Frederick William
D/10600, 22/1/17; R.A., C/S, 29/6/17; R.G.A., 2/12/17; F; 2/Lieut. 60 Lowlands Road, Harrow.

PERKINS, George Herbert
6/4/5816, 24/8/15; Midd'x. R., 1/6/16, R.E.; F; Lieut.
The Hollies, Lightwood Road, Bearwood, Birmingham.

PERKINS, Gerard Henry
1/3167, 1/4/15; Notts. & Derby. R., 25/9/15, York. R.; F; Capt.; w(2); M.C. 19 Church Street, Stratford-on-Avon.

PERKINS, Harry Dunbar
A/D/13134, 27/5/18, Sgt.; General List, 12/5/19; NR; 2/Lieut.; M.B.E. c/o Toplis & Harding, 28 Old Jewry, E.C.

PERKINS, Hubert Barry
6/4/7114, 1/11/15; Mon. R., 4/8/16, att. S. Staff. R.; F; Lieut.; Inv. 47 Holland Park Avenue, W. 11.

PERKINS, Richard Nugent
C/13273, 12/6/18; trfr. 14th Lond. R., 6/12/18, Gord. Highrs.
Woodford, Eaton Crescent, Swansea.

PERKINS, Wilfrid George Albert
6/1/5780, 4/9/15; R.F.A., C/S, 17/3/16; R.F.A., 13/7/16; F; Lieut.; w. c/o Hydrographic Department, Admiralty.

PERKINS, William Aubrey
6/4/C/5062, 24/7/15; dis. med. unfit.
30 Kendrick Road, Reading.

PERKS, Bernard
2/81, 13/4/08, C.S.M.; dis. med. unfit, 19/3/18; m.
39 Barkston Gardens, Earls Court, S.W. 5.

PERKS, Frank Arnold
4/3/4235, 14/6/15; Worc. R., 23/12/15, att. R. War. R.; F; Lieut.; Inv. Hob Hill, Alvechurch, Birmingham.

PERKS-MORRIS, Fitzgerald Arthur Hay Frank
6/Sq/7305, 8/11/15; R.F.C., 16/6/16; w.
Southleigh, Ashgrove, Worthing.

PEROWNE, Francis Leslie
6/Sq/5750, 21/8/15, L/C.; R.F.A., 26/11/15; F; 2/Lieut.; g.
Fakenham, Norfolk.

PERRETT, Edward Francis
C/14212, 21/10/18; trfr. K.R. Rif. C., 7/4/19.
The Lodge, Punchbowl Lane, Dorking.

PERRETT, Maurice Copeland
6/1/6827, 14/10/15, L/C.; No. 14 O.C.B.; Glouc. R., 24/10/16, Lieut.

✠ PERRIN, Gilbert Dennis
B/1211, 14/9/14; S. Staff. R., 21/10/14; F; Capt.; w(2).
Killed in action 13/11/16.

PERRIN, James Frederick
4/1/4123, 27/5/15; 12th Lond. R., 6/6/16; E,P; Lieut.
57 Underhill Road, East Dulwich, S.E. 22.

PERRIN, Roland Eugène
6/Sq/7805, 24/11/15, Cpl.; No. 1 Cav. C/S, 6/12/16; S. Notts. Huss. Yeo., 16/2/17; Lieut.
The Vicarage, North Lonsdale, British Columbia.

PERROTT, Herbert Charles
A/13135, 27/5/13; R.A., C/S, 26/7/18; R.G.A., 11/4/19; 2/Lieut
1 Kings Avenue, Bromley, Kent.

PERROTT, William Noel
B/12361, 3/1/18; No. 22 O.C.B., 7/6/18; R. Fus., 12/2/19; NR; 2/Lieut.
c/o Messrs. Waller Neale & Houlston, 3 & 4 Clements Inn, Strand, W.C. 2.

✠ PERRY, Brian
A/Sq/1937, 22/10/14, Sgt. Died 18/8/15.

APPENDIX II.—RECORDS OF RANK AND FILE.

✠ PERRY, Cecil Robert
6/2/6022, 2/9/15; R.A.S.C., 21/1/16, att. D. of Corn L.I.;
P,E; Lieut. Died 24/10/19.

PERRY, Denis
A/D/Sq/11957, 3/9/17; No. 20 O.C.B., 7/6/18; trfr. 28th Lond. R., 2/10/18.
Barrington, Kings Road, Berkhamsted, Hertfordshire.

PERRY, Ernest Smith
D/E/13880, 21/8/18; demob. 23/1/19.
47 Richmond Avenue, Wimbledon, S.W.19.

PERRY, Frederick William Abbott
6/3/5758, 21/8/15; R.M.L.I., 19/12/15.
170 Gleneagle Road, Streatham, S.W.16.

PERRY, Grahame Herbert
4/2/4050, 7/6/15; dis. med. unfit, 17/11/15.
Kelham College, Newark-on-Trent.

PERRY, Isaac Geoffrey Batten
B/332, 1/12/08; dis. 30/11/12; rej. B/1096, 7/9/14; 11th Lond. R., 19/9/14; Capt.; Inj. 125 Victoria Street, S.W.1.

PERRY, Percival John
4/1/4385, 21/6/15; R.E., 28/7/15; Capt.; M(1).
Mayfield House, Wolverhampton.

PERRY, Stanley
B/13444, 3/7/18; demob. 23/1/19.
P.O. Box 583, Bulawayo, Southern Rhodesia.

PERRY, William
K/Sq/2343, 14/12/14; R.A.S.C., 2/3/15; Capt.
Tryandall, Wolverhampton.

PERRY-GORE, John Christopher
C/10619, 25/1/17; Garr. O.C.B., 5/10/17; Lab. Corps, 25/1/18; 2/Lieut.
Tackley Rectory, Oxfordshire.

PERRYMAN, Francis Spencer
6/2/6071, 6/9/15; Midd'x. R., 1/6/16; F; Lieut.; w; M(1).
70 Queens Avenue, Church End, Finchley, N.3.

PERTWEE, Ernest Charles Guy
6/1/5714, 19/8/15; L/C.; No. 2 Cav. C/S, 31/3/16; Oxf. Huss., 6/9/16, att. Oxf. & Bucks. L.I.; Lieut.
Torcloso, War Coppice, Caterham.

✠ PETER, Pomeroy John
B/10382, 9/1/17; L/C.; No. 14 O.C.B., 5/7/17; W. Kent Yeo., 30/10/17; 2/Lieut. Killed in action 19/9/18.

PETERKIN, Lionel Denis
D/12111, 11/10/17; No. 2 O.C.B., 8/2/18; High. L.I., 13/8/18; 2/Lieut. c/o W. India Centre, 15 Seething Lane, E.C.3.

PETERS, Arthur Bowden
6/2/6562, 30/9/15; L/C.; No. 11 O.C.B., 7/5/16; R.F.C., 4/9/16, R.A.F.; 2/Lieut. The Links, Worth, Nr. Sandwich, Kent.

PETERS, Arthur Stanley
6/3/7016, 26/10/15; E. Kent R., 7/7/16, att. N. Lan. R. and War Office; F; Lieut.; w(2).
106 Osborne Road, Forest Gate, Essex.

PETERS, Clement Alexander Knight
K/E/2391, 17/12/14; Lan. Fus., 3/4/15; Capt.

✠ PETERS, Gerard
6/1/7367, 10/11/15, L/C.; Glouc. R., 4/9/16; 2/Lieut.
Died 24/2/17.

PETHEBRIDGE, Frank
B/A/11722, 19/7/17; L/C.; No. 6 O.C.B., 5/4/18; Devon. R., 12/11/18, att. W. Rid. R.; F; 2/Lieut.
Barclay's Bank Ltd., Maidenhead, Berkshire.

PETIT, Charles Russell
H/1681, 12/10/14; Midd'x. R., 7/11/14, emp. M. of Munitions, 1/7/17; Lieut. Oakmead, Harrow.

PETRE, Louis John
C/D/12240, 20/11/17; No. 15 O.C.B., 10/5/18; dis. med. unfit, 2/1/19.

PETRIE, George Norman
A/B/C/Sq/12160, 25/10/17; No. 1 Cav. C/S, 3/9/18; R. Regt. of Cav., 12/3/19; 2/Lieut.
Rosserick House, Ballina, Co. Mayo, Ireland.

PETRIE, Robert Fairlie
A/853, 4/8/14; R. Fus., 3/9/14, Lab. Corps; Lieut.; w.
7 Cambalt Road, Putney, S.W.15.

PETTIFORD, Payne Harry
6/5/6606, 4/10/15; N. Lan. R., 27/12/15; F.S.P; Capt.; M(1).
Lynton, Woodlands Avenue, Hornchurch, Essex.

PETTIT, John Hallam
6/1/7150, 2/11/15; No. 14 O.C.B., 28/8/16; North'n. R., 22/11/16; 2/Lieut. Wavney House, Mere Road, Leicester.

PETTS, Cyril Edward
6/5/6577, 2/10/15, L/C.; No. 11 O.C.B., 7/5/16; Notts. and Derby. R., 4/9/16; 2/Lieut.
Glenwood, South Darley, Nr. Matlock.

PEZARO, Louis
D/12936, 15/4/18; No. 8 O.C.B., 18/10/18; K.R. Rif. C., 17/3/19; 2/Lieut. 16 Manstone Road, Cricklewood, N.W.2.

PHAREZ, Eric Alfred
A/13090, 20/5/18; No. 24 O.C.B., 18/11/18; Tank Corps, 22/3/19; 2/Lieut. 102 Upper Tulse Hill, S.W.2.

PHELPS, Albert Edward
D/11547, 21/6/17; Garr. O.C.B., 28/12/17; Lab. Corps, 18/5/18; 2/Lieut.
Royal Exchange Assurance, 29/30 High Holborn, W.C.1.

PHELPS, Alfred Cooper
6/3/7053, 28/10/15; R.E., 17/2/16; Capt. 6 The Hythe, Staines.

PHELPS, Leslie Herbert
4/3182, 6/4/15; Linc. R., 8/7/15, att. R.A.F.; F,NR; Lieut.; w.
Glastonbury, Somerset.

PHELPS, Thomas Tettrell
Sq/940, 5/8/14; 1st Cty. of Lond. Yeo., 1/10/14, att. Intelligence; Major. 8 Orme Court, Bayswater, W.2.

✠ PHILBRICK, Edward Hooper
6/9360, 7/2/16; R.A., C/S, 31/5/16; R.F.A., 17/12/16; Lieut.; w.
Died 6/11/18.

✠ PHILCOX, Cecil Ernest
3/3369, 21/4/15, Cpl.; S. Staff. R., 27/7/15; F; Lieut.; M.C., M(1). Died 24/5/17.

PHILCOX, Herbert John
B/12327, 28/12/17; No. 22 O.C.B., 7/6/18; R. Suss. R., 11/2/19; 2/Lieut. 38 Approach Road, Margate.

PHILIP, Albert
6/9316, 4/2/16; dis. to re-enlist in R.E., 22/6/16.
95 Mile End Avenue, Aberdeen, Scotland.

PHILIP, John Douglas Macintosh
6/4/8903, 13/1/16; 7th Lond. R., 8/7/16; F; Lieut.; w.
P.O. Box 523, Pretoria, South Africa.

PHILIPP, Reginald Gladstone
B/A/11709, 19/7/17; R.E., C/S, 10/2/18; R.E., 31/5/18; F; 2/Lieut.
246 Coombe Lane, Wimbledon, S.W.20. (Now in Upper Assam).

PHILLIPPS, Richard Alexander
K/F/2262, 7/12/14; R. War. R., 26/2/15, att. T.M. Bty.; F; Capt. c/o G. A. Witt, 36 Lime Street, E.C.3.

PHILLIPS, Alfred Henry
C/D/11460, 5/6/17; Indian Army, 8/10/18; 2/Lieut.
Singleton House, Stourbridge.

✠ PHILLIPS, Arthur Blakeway
4679, 8/7/15; 12th Lond. R., 12/11/15; 2/Lieut.
Killed in action 19/6/16.

PHILLIPS, Arthur Herbert
6/2/7217, 4/11/15; No. 11 O.C.B., 7/5/16; W. York. R., 4/9/16; F; Lieut. Brooklands, Stockton Lane, York.

PHILLIPS, Aubrey Wyndham
6/3/8272, 9/12/15; R.E., C/S 2/9/16; R.E., 18/11/16; F; Lieut.
Bleak House, Northwick, Cheshire.

✠ PHILLIPS, David Charles
6/1/5729, 19/8/15; R.W. Fus., 14/6/16, att. S. Wales Bord.; 2/Lieut. Killed in action 16/8/17.

PHILLIPS, Douglas James
A/10979, 2/4/17; No. 12 O.C.B., 10/8/17; N. Cyc. Bn., 27/11/17, att. M.G.C.; 2/Lieut. Pitcairn, Basingstoke, Hampshire.

PHILLIPS, Douglas Middleton Parnham
D/1431, 29/9/14, Sgt.; Midd'x. R., 17/11/14; Lieut.
68 Brook Street, W.1.

PHILLIPS, Edward Blakeway
6/5/8611, 3/1/16; R.F.A., C/S, 7/8/16; trfr. R.F.A., 9/10/16.
Hanwood, Shrewsbury.

PHILLIPS, Ewart Haydn
4/2/5079, 26/7/15; N. Staff. R., 29/11/15; F; Lieut.; w.
Claremont, Hillside Park, Bargoed, Glamorganshire.

PHILLIPS, George Edward
6/4/2/6099, 6/9/15; L/C.; E. Kent R., 4/9/16; 2/Lieut.
Albert House, Sandown, Isle of Wight.

APPENDIX II.—RECORDS OF RANK AND FILE.

PHILLIPS, *Gordon*
D/11158, 2/5/17; No. 14 O.C.B., 5/10/17; Manch. R., 26/2/18, att. Durh. L.I.; F; 2/Lieut.
22 *Church Lane, Prestwich, Manchester.*

PHILLIPS, *Harry Vaughan*
F/1729, 15/10/14; North'd. Fus., 3/11/14, emp. M. of Nat. Ser.; Capt.

PHILLIPS, *Hubert*
K/C/2079, 13/11/14, L/C.; Essex R., 9/3/15; F; Lieut.
11 *Rossiter's Hill, Frome, Somerset.*

PHILLIPS, *Jack George*
4/3335, 21/4/15; 4th Lond. R., 28/5/15.

PHILLIPS, *John Percival*
6/1/7115, 1/11/15; dis. med. unfit, 8/8/16.
Cross House, Cardigan.

PHILLIPS, *Lawrence Frederick*
4/5/4404, 24/6/15, Sgt.; Yorks. L.I., 7/10/15; 2/Lieut.; w.
189 *Willesden Lane, N.W.* 6

PHILLIPS, *Lewis*
A/11632, 9/7/17; trfr. R.G.A., 16/1/18.
404 *St. Annes Road, Harringay, N.*

PHILLIPS, *Lionel Beart*
1/3512, 6/5/15; R.W. Fus., 24/8/15, R.E.; F; Capt.
Bryncoed, Radyr, Glamorganshire.

PHILLIPS, *Percy Tyrell Spencer*
Sq/178, 29/4/08; dis. 28/4/12; R.F.A., -/12/14, R.A.M.C.; F; Major; w; M(1). *Great Buddow, Chelmsford, Essex.*

PHILLIPS, *Philip Hamilton*
H/2/3032, 11/3/15; trfr. 13th Lond. R., 5/9/15.
Peveril, Golders Green, N.W. 4.

PHILLIPS, *Rees Frederick*
4/3409, 25/4/15, Sgt.; D. of Corn. L.I., 20/8/15, Lab. Corps; F; Capt.; w; M.C., M(1). *Tanlan, Forestfach, Swansea.*

✠ PHILLIPS, *Richard Glyndwr*
4/2/4024, 7/6/15; R.G.A., 2/10/15; Lieut.
Killed in action 27/8/17.

PHILLIPS, *Robert Stanley*
C/12089, 4/10/17; No. 11 O.C.B., 10/5/18; 7th Lond. R., 3/2/19; 2/Lieut. 127 *Gloucester Road, Kensington, W.*

PHILLIPS, *Royston Edward Rosevear*
8912, 13/1/16, Sgt.; demob. 23/1/19.
Chevithorne, Tiverton, North Devonshire

PHILLIPS, *Stephen Thomas*
6/5/6023, 2/9/15; No. 11 O.C.B., 16/5/16; R.W. Fus., 4/9/16, Devon. R.; F; Lieut.; M.C.
4 *Vittoria Street, Llanelly, South Wales.*

PHILLIPS, *Thomas Charles*
C/10573, 17/1/17; R.G.A., 1/3/18; F; Lieut.
23 *Canadian Avenue, Catford, S.E.* 6.

PHILLIPS, *William Edward*
3/3552, 10/5/15; R.W. Fus., 21/8/15, M.G.C., R.A.F.; F,It; Lieut.; w *Druslwyn, Ferndale, South Wales.*

PHILLIPS, *William George*
6/5/5888, 30/8/15; No. 11 O.C.B., 7/5/16; Welch R., 4/9/16, att. R.W. Fus., Indian Army; F,P,E; Lieut.; w; M(1).
4 *James Street, Pontardulais, Glamorganshire.*

PHILLIPS, *William Gruffydd*
D/Sq/12876, 3/4/18; demob. 24/1/19.
Box 1031, Johannesburg, Transvaal, South Africa.

PHILPOT, *Frederick Harold*
6/9221, 31/1/16; dis. 26/5/16. Schoolmaster, Royal Navy.
The College, Cheltenham.

PHILPOTT, *Harold*
A/14068, 27/9/18; trfr. 14th Lond. R., 6/12/18.
Little Appley, Ryde, Isle of Wight.

✠ PHIPPS, *Arthur Coryn*
4/6/1/4943, 19/7/15; E. Ang. Div. Cyc. Coy., 25/9/16, Army Cyc. Corps; F; 2/Lieut. *Killed in action 13/4/18.*

PHYTHIAN-ADAMS, *William John*
B/1257, 23/9/14; R. Fus., 20/10/14; F; Lt. Col.; D.S.O., M.C, M(2). *British School of Archæology, P.O. Box 357, Jerusalem.*

✠ PICKARD, *Lawrence Delafons*
6/3/C/9425, 10/2/16; No. 14 O.C.B., 26/11/16; R.W. Surr. R., 27/3/17; F; 2/Lieut. *Killed in action 10/8/17.*

PICKEN, *Andrew Maurice*
A/D/11891, 20/8/17; No. 3 O.C.B., 8/2/18; High. L.I., 30/7/18; F; Lieut. *Libberton Manse, Carnwath, Lanarkshire, Scotland.*

PICKEN, *James Craigie*
K/B/2459, 28/12/14; High. L.I., 22/4/15; F; Capt.; w, p; M.C.
Manse of Libberton, Carnwath, Lanarkshire, Scotland.

PICKER, *Charles Edward*
6/1/9159, 26/1/16, L/C.; No. 13 O.C.B., 4/11/16; North'd. Fus., 28/2/17; Lieut.; w.

PICKETT, *Thomas William Harold*
4/5/5123, 26/7/15; Rif. Brig., 3/12/15, att. Hamps. R., R.E.; E,P; Lieut. 1 *Paulton's Square, Chelsea, S.W.* 3

PICKETT, *William Richard*
K/C/2358, 14/12/14, Sgt.; R.F.A., 9/7/15; F; Capt.
Meon House, Meonstoke, Hampshire.

PICKFORD, *Harold Langley*
A/12548, 5/2/18; No. 4 O.C.B., 7/6/18; Som. L.I., 3/3/19; 2/Lieut.
108 *Fernside Road, Wandsworth Common, S.W.* 12. (*Now in Siam*).

PICKFORD, *Stanley*
6/5/7940, 29/11/15; R.F.C., 25/9/16, R.A.F.; F,It; Lieut.
Dental Hospital, Oxford Road, Manchester.

PICKFORD, *William Lewis*
6/2/7848, 25/11/15; Manch. R., 18/12/16; F; Lieut.
108 *Fernside Road, Wandsworth Common, S.W.* 12.

PICKLES, *Charles Ernest*
6/5/C/6774, 11/10/15; trfr. R.F.A., 10/11/16.
105 *Camp Road, Leeds.*

✠ PICKOP, *James Taylor Greer*
B/1832, 16/10/14; R. Fus., 23/1/15; F; Lieut.; w(2).
Died of wounds 21/6/17.

✠ PICKSTONE, *Charley*
B/10124, 6/12/16; R.F.C., C/S, 13/3/17; R.F.C., 19/4/17; 2/Lieut. *Killed in action 3/9/17.*

✠ PICTON, *James Allanson*
F/1762, 16/10/14; E. Surr. R., 17/3/15; F; Lieut.; M.C.
Killed in action 23/7/17.

PICTON, *Sydney Charles*
6/8809, 10/1/16; R.A., C/S, 26/5/16; R.G.A., 30/8/16; F; Capt.; w; M(1). *Melbourne House, Melbourne Grove, East Dulwich, S.E.* 22.

PIDCOCK, *Richard George*
D/11548, 21/6/17, L/C.; No. 14 O.C.B., 7/12/17, No. 4 O.C.B.; K.R. Rif. C., 28/5/18; F; 2/Lieut.; w.
Bramcote, Scarborough.

PIDGEON, *Alonzo James*
4/5/4757, 12/7/15; 1st Lond. R., 15/11/15; F; 2/Lieut.
11 *Forest Glade, Leytonstone, E.* 11.

PIERCE, *Harry West*
B/D/12214, 12/11/17, Cpl.; No. 1 O.C.B., 10/5/18; R. Lanc. R., 29/10/18; Lieut.
Houseboat, Changsha, The Bridge, Portumna, Co. Galway, Ireland.

PIERCE, *Wilfred Ernest*
6/5/7000, 25/10/15; Lpool. R., 1/6/16; F; Lieut.
The Buff House, Hightown, Liverpool.

PIERCE, *William Harold*
6/5/5951, 1/9/15; L'pool. R., 23/4/16; F; Capt.; M(1).
9 *Welfield Place, Princes Park, Liverpool.*

PIERCY, *Arthur*
K/F/2334, 14/12/14; Ches. R., 3/2/15; Capt.
c/o Messrs. Matheson & Coy., Ltd., 3 Lombard Street, E.C. 3.

PIERCY, *Henry Roy Cauden*
A/12148, 22/10/17; R.F.C., C/S, 18/1/18; R.F.C., 6/3/18, R.A.F.; 2/Lieut. *Mostyn, Park Hill, Moseley, Birmingham.*

PIERSON, *Alan Roach*
K/F/2340, 14/12/14; R.A.O.C., 8/2/15; F; Major; w.
Highview, Maidstone Road, Chatham.

PIERSON, *Norman Stanley*
D/14016, 12/9/18; No. 18 O.C.B., 10/2/19; R. Fus., 18/3/19; 2/Lieut.

✠ PIERSSENÉ, *Frederick Andrew*
4/6/5/4944, 19/7/15; R. Suss. R., 4/12/15, att. R. Fus.; F; Lieut. *Died of wounds 6/9/18.*

PIGGINS, *Charles Redvers*
B/12858, 25/3/18; No. 18 O.C.B., 9/2/19, No. 20 O.C.B.; R Berks. R., 17/3/19; 2/Lieut.
15 *Richmond Road, Bearwood, Birmingham.*

APPENDIX II.—RECORDS OF RANK AND FILE.

✠ PIGGOTT, Arthur Alfred
C/1080, 2/9/14; North'd. Fus., 19/9/14; F; Lieut.
             Killed in action 26/9/15.

PIKE, Henry
Sq/1295, 24/9/14, Cpl.; R.A.S.C., 13/1/15; Capt.; M(1).
           45 Waterloo Road, Bedford.

PIKE, Herbert Twyneham
4/1/4347, 21/6/15, att. R.E.; F; Lieut.; w.
     62 Enmore Road, Woodside, South Norwood, S.E. 25.

PIKE, John Percy
6/3/8463, 18/12/15; R.E., C/S, 21/8/16; R.E., 3/11/16; M; Lieut.; M(1). *37 Holmdene Avenue, Herne Hill, S.E. 24.*

PIKE, Kenneth Twyneham
6/1/5997, 2/9/15, L/C.; No. 14 O.C.B.; M.G.C., 24/10/16, att. Chinese Lab. Corps; E,P,F; Lieut.; M.C.
  62 Enmore Road, South Norwood, S.E. 25. (Now in Brazil).

PILCHER, Hector. See BOND, H.

PILE, John William
H/2/4/1991, 29/10/14, L/C.; R.G.A., 15/4/15.
           34 Great St. Helens, E.C. 3.

PILKINGTON, John Edward
D/11131, 30/4/17; A.S.C., C/S, 1/9/17; R.A.S.C., 27/10/17; F; 2/Lieut.; M.C. *Leecross House, Dobcross, Yorkshire.*

PILKINGTON, Wilfrid
4/1/4653, 5/7/15; R.F.A., 2/10/15, Indian Army; F; Capt.; g(2); M.C. *6 Holmefield View, Barrowford, Nr. Nelson, Lancashire.*

PILKINGTON, William Alan
1/3236, 12/4/15; Shrop. L.I., 30/6/15, att. Ches. R.; F; Lieut.; w.
            Hayfield, Nr. Stockport.

PILLING, James
C/14311, 30/11/18; No. 3 O.C.B., 10/2/19; E. York R., 18/3/19; 2/Lieut.
  Beaufort House, Station Road, Golcar, Nr. Huddersfield.

PILLMAN, Charles Henry
A/1027, 24/8/14; 4th Drag. Gds., 15/8/14; F; Capt.; M.C
         11 Hart Street, Mark Lane, E.C.

✠ PINCHIN, George Harold
A/1374, 26/9/14, Sgt.; Bedf. R., 24/7/15; Lieut.
           Died of wounds 27/11/17.

PINCOTT, John William
4/6/3814, 27/5/15.

PINHEY, Harold Townley
4/4157, 10/6/15; Devon. R., 18/12/15, att. E. Kent R.; I,M; Lieut.
    c/o Nat. Bank of India Ltd., 26 Bishopsgate, E.C. 2.

✠ PINK, Alan Luis
3/3315, 19/4/15; dis. to R. Mil Coll., 8/11/15; Rif. Brig., 19/7/16, att. R.A.F.; F; Lieut. *Killed in action 30/10/18.*

PINNINGTON, Frederick
6/4/6669, 7/10/15; Devon. R., 4/8/16; Lieut.; w.
        South View, Fyldesby, Nr. Manchester

PINNOCK, Harold George
2/3484, 3/5/15; R.E., 27/8/15; Lieut.
         29 Princes Avenue, Finchley, N. 3.

PIPER, John Daniel
4/2/4611, 5/7/15; E. Kent R., 23/9/15, att. Midd'x. R., R.W. Kent R. and R. Suss. R.; F; Lieut.; w; M.C.
    41 Baldry Gardens, Streatham Common, S.W. 16.

PIPER, Leonard James
4/3578, 2/5/15; N. Lan. R., 9/9/15; F; Capt.
   Waverley, 35 Westcombe Park Road, Blackheath, S.E. 3.

PIPER, Malcolm James
4/3577, 2/5/15, Cpl.; North'd. Fus., 6/7/16, M.G.C.; F; Lieut.; w.
   Waverley, 35 Westcombe Park Road, Blackheath, S.E. 3.

PIPER, Reginald Eustace
3/4025, 7/6/15; Norf. R., 7/10/15, Indian Army; F,P; Staff Capt.; w, Inv. *17 St. Augustine's Avenue, South Croydon*

PIPON, Arthur Roach Thomas
D/Sq/1477, 29/9/14; R. Navy, -/6/15, R.N.A.S., R.A.F.; Capt.; D.S.C. *Woodhaven, Walton-on-Thames, Surrey.*

PIRIE, Alexander
B/A/11991, 10/9/17; dis. med. unfit, 18/2/18.
        170 High Street, Kirkcaldy, Scotland.

PIRIE, Allan Grant
H/2616, 7/1/15; R. War. R., 31/5/15; F; Capt.; w.
          12 Golden Square, Aberdeen.

PIRKIS, Frederick Chandos Lyne
2550, 4/1/15; R.F.A., 27/2/15; Lieut.; w.
    Oxford and Cambridge Club, Pall Mall, S.W. 1.

PIRKIS, George Cecil Middleton Lyne
3/3654, 17/5/15; York. & Lanc. R., 1/6/16, M.G.C.; F; Capt.; w.
         2 Church Street, Greenwich

PITCAIRN, Arthur Alexander
6/7941, 29/11/15, L/C.; No. 14 O.C.B.; Sea. Highrs., 24/1/17; F; Capt.   *65 London Wall, E.C. 2.*

PITCHER, Maurice Albert
C/9962, 20/11/16, L/C.; No. 14 O.C.B., 5/3/17; Dorset R., 26/6/17; F; Lieut.; w.
  c/o Messrs. E. Pitcher & Coy., 3 Clerkenwell Road, E.C. 1

PITHER, Frank Eugene
4/3272, 15/4/15; dis. to R. Mil. Coll., 13/5/15; R.A.S.C., 15/9/15; F; Lieut.   *10 Steeles Road, N.W. 1.*

✠ PITHER, Harold Francis
K/A/2399, 17/12/14; R. Dub. Fus., 22/4/15; 2/Lieut.
          Killed in action 6/7/16.

PITMAN, Edwin Earl
C/12577, 6/2/18; No. 18 O.C.B., 9/8/18; R. Fus., 6/3/19; 2/Lieut.
  Oban, Ellesmere Road, Chorlton-cum-Hardy, Manchester.

PITT, Frank
6/1/8489, 20/12/15, Sgt.; Manch. R., 16/7/16, att. Indian Army; Lieut.; M.C., M(1). *6 Bradley Terrace, Dipton, Co. Durham.*

PITT, Gordon Henry
Sq/612, 29/2/12; Notts & Derby. Yeo., 24/9/14, att. R.F.C., R.A.F.; Capt.; w; M(2).
  St. Agatha's Lodge, Gerrard's Cross, Buckinghamshire.

PITT, Jack Moffatt
I/3871, 31/5/15; R. Suss. R., 11/9/15, att. Tank Corps, Bedf. Yeo.; Lieut.

PITTARD, Robert Marmaduke
6/3/7001, 25/10/15, L/C.; Worc. R., 4/9/16; F; Lieut.; w; M.C.
        139 Cathedral Road, Cardiff.

PITT-LEWIS, George Francis
B/2676, 12/1/15, Cpl.; Devon. R., 2/7/15; F; Capt.; w; M.C.
   c/o Coward & Coy., 30 Mincing Lane, E.C. 3.

✠ PITT-PITTS, Edward Crewdson Pitt
D/11569, 28/6/17; No. 14 O.C.B., 9/11/17; E. Kent R., 30/4/18; 2/Lieut.   *Killed 17/10/18.*

✠ PITT-PITTS, Walter John
B/10523, 15/1/17; R.F.C., C/S, 13/3/17; R.F.C., 19/4/17, R.A.F.; F; Lieut.   *Killed in action 9/8/18.*

PITTS, Benjamin Alec
A/D/11892, 20/8/17, L/C.; R.F.A., C/S, 15/3/18; R.F.A., 11/3/19; 2/Lieut. *4 Swires Road, Undercliffe, Bradford.*

PITTS, George Allen
6/1/A/8523, 29/12/15; No. 14 O.C.B., 30/10/16; Oxf. & Bucks L.I., 24/1/17; F; 2/Lieut.; Inv.
  The School House, Horton-in-Ribblesdale, Settle, Yorkshire.

✠ PIZEY, Noel Martin
6/Sq/5873, 28/8/15; Devon. Yeo., 25/12/15, att. R.F.C.; Lieut.
        Died of wounds 27/7/17.

PLACE, George Herbert
D/12909, 8/4/18; No. 21 O.C.B., 4/10/18, No. 18 O.C.B.; trfr. 5th Lond. R., 3/3/19. *32 Blackburn Road, Rushton, Nr. Blackburn.*

PLAFORD, Robert Ballantyne
3/3656, 17/5/15; 19th Lond. R., 17/8/15, att. 23rd Lond. R., Indian Army; F,S,I.; Capt.; Inv.
 c/o The Alliance Bank of Simla Ltd., Quetta, Baluchistan.

✠ PLAISTOWE, Alan
H/1985, 29/10/14; Worc. R., 14/2/15; Capt.; w; M(2).
         Killed in action 24/4/17.

PLAISTOWE, Gordon Christian
B/12776, 15/3/18; No. 23 O.C.B., 9/8/18; Essex R., 4/3/19; 2/Lieut. *21 Oakleigh Park Drive, Leigh-on-Sea, Essex.*

✠ PLAISTOWE, Richard Reeves
H/2807, 28/1/15; Norf. R., 4/6/15; Lieut.; w.
         Killed in action 19/4/17.

PLANT, Arthur Eddie
4/3/4426, 24/6/15; dis. med. unfit, 22/5/16.
    Wycombe House, Wilbraham Road, Chorlton

APPENDIX II.—RECORDS OF RANK AND FILE.

☨ PLANT, George Bede Hornby
Sq/4090, 7/6/15, L/C.; Norf. Yeo., 21/9/15; Lieut.; M.C.
Killed in action 18/9/18.

PLANT, John Christopher George
2/3655, 17/5/15; Norf. R., 24/9/15, att. Leic. R.; M; Lieut.; Inv
Moorfield, Burket Road, Woodbridge, Suffolk. (Now in South Africa).

PLANT, Percival William
6/1/6896, 18/10/15; Notts. & Derby. R., 6/10/16, att. R.F.C., R.A.F.; Lieut. Bank House, Etwal, Derby.

PLATT, Charles Beckett
6/8000, 29/11/15; R.A., C/S, 26/5/16; R.G.A., 30/8/16.
26 Kings Avenue, Clapham Park, S.W. 4.

PLATT, Percy
C/9960, 20/11/16; No. 14 O.C.B., 5/5/17; Lan. Fus., 28/8/17; F;
Lieut. Varden House, Wilmslow, Cheshire.

PLATT, Thomas Glyn
F/2730, 18/1/15; R.W. Kent R., 8/7/15; Lieut.; w(2).
Combe Martin, Bexley, Kent.

PLATTS, Gilbert Latimer
B/10309, 2/1/17; R.F.C., C/S, 13/3/17; R.F.C., 19/4/17, R.A.F.;
Lieut. Hazlewood, Venner Road, Sydenham, S.E. 26.

PLAXTON, Harold Henry
A/Sq/D/11914, 27/8/17; No. 2 Cav. C/S, 11/4/18; 6th R. Regt. of Cav., 8/10/18; 2/Lieut. 16 Scalby Road, Scarborough.

PLAYER, Ernest William
1/3237, 12/4/15; N. Staff. R., 10/7/15; Lieut.
141 Lyneham Road, Lavender Hill, S.W. 11.

PLAYER, John Geoffrey
6/3/8423, 15/12/15; No. 14 O.C.B., 30/10/16; Worc. R., 29/5/17, att. R. War. R.; F; Lieut.; w-p.
28 York Road, Edgbaston, Birmingham.

PLAYFORD, Redvers Samuel
B/12836, 22/3/18; No. 14 O.C.B., 23/8/18; demob. 24/1/19.
Potter Heigham, Great Yarmouth, Norfolk.

PLAYNE, Norman
D/13882, 21/8/18; trfr. K.R. Rif. C., 7/4/19.
9 Stanley Street, Bedford.

☨ PLEWMAN, Charles Edward
6/5/6210, 13/9/15; No. 4 O.C.B., 7/3/16; L'pool R., 13/7/16;
Lieut.; M.C. Killed in action 9/4/18.

☨ PLEYDELL-BOUVERIE, Samuel Wilfred
4/5124, 26/7/15; 19th Lond. R., 2/11/15; F; 2/Lieut.
Killed in action 15/9/16.

PLINCKE, John Frederick
A/52, 7/4/08; E. Surr. R., 28/2/11, att. Dorset R.; M,S; Capt.;
M(1). Lismore Lodge, 31 Cole Park Road, Twickenham.

PLOMMER, George Frederick
6/2/6291, 16/9/15; dis. med. unfit, 31/3/16.
Red House, Whitstable, Kent.

PLOUGHMAN, Harry William
6/2/7274, 8/11/15; dis. to re-enlist in Australian Army, 8/12/16.

PLOWDEN, Archibald Hugo Chicheley
6/5/6135, 9/9/15; No. 3 O.C.B., 25/2/16; Devon. R., 19/7/16;
Lieut.; w.

☨ PLOWMAN, Thomas Room
A/9829, 1/11/16; No. 14 O.C.B., 27/12/16; 15th Lond. R., 25/4/17, att. 2nd Lond. R.; F; Lieut.; w. Died 1/1/20.

☨ PLUM, Robert Bagshaw
6/8842, 10/1/16; R.F.A., C/S, 21/7/16; R.F.A., 27/10/16; 2/Lieut.
Died of wounds 2/10/17.

PLUMB, William Thomas
B/500, 12/7/10; trfr. Lond. Elec. Eng., 18/3/13.
95 Tuskar Street, East Greenwich, S.E. 10. (Now in Southern Rhodesia).

PLUMER, Arthur Frederick
A/Sq/13064, 13/5/18; trfr. 14th Lond. R., 6/12/18, Gord. Highrs.
The Bungalow, Shoreham Road, Otford, Kent.

PLUNKETT, John Joseph Archer
A/11289, 16/5/17; No. 14 O.C.B., 5/10/17; 9th Lond. R., 26/2/18, att. 18th Lond. R.; F; 2/Lieut.
173 Stroud Green Road, Finsbury Park, N.4.

PLUNKETT, Leo Randal
B/11372, 28/5/17; No. 14 O.C.B., 7/9/17; R. Dub. Fus., 17/12/17;
2/Lieut. Plunkett Bros., Island Bridge Maltings, Dublin, Ireland.

POAD, Kenneth
C/14240, 28/10/18; demob. 24/1/19.
Ousefield, Fulford, York.

POCHIN, Victor Robert
6/Sq/9233, 1/2/16; Leic. Yeo., 16/8/16, 1st Life Gds., Gds.
M.G.R.; F; Lieut. Barkby Hall, Leicester.

POCOCK, Arthur Aynsley
A/1911, 16/10/14, Cpl.; North'd. Fus., 28/1/15; F; Capt.; w;
M.C. 147 Leadenhall Street, E.C. 3.

POCOCK, Charles Arthur
3553, 10/5/15; Hamps. R., 18/8/15; F,G; Lieut.; Inv.
11a Oxford Road, Kilburn, N.W. 6.

☨ POCOCK, Charles Arthur
4/1/4612, 5/7/15; R. War. R., 4/12/15; 2/Lieut.
Killed in action 8/5/17.

POCOCK, Hugh Shellshear
4/1/5080, 26/7/15; R.E., 17/10/15; E,M,I; Capt.; M(1).
1 The Parade, Kilburn Priory, N.W. 6.

POCOCK, John Grahame
C/1082, 2/9/14; Devon. R., 16/9/14; w(2).

POCOCK, Leonard Walter
1/3554, 10/5/15; R. Innis. Fus., 9/8/15, att. R.F.C.; F; Lieut.;
cr. Elmwood, Southwood Road, New Eltham.

POCOCK, Leslie James
A/10936, 28/3/17; No. 11 O.C.B., 5/7/17; Indian Army, 30/10/17;
I,Afghan; Lieut.; Inj. Westbrook, Morgan Road, Reading.

POCOCK, Maurice Stuart
D/11582, 2/7/17; R.G.A., C/S, 10/10/17; R.G.A., 18/3/18; F;
Lieut. Surbiton Hall, Kingston-on-Thames.

PODD, Geoffrey Kemp
6/9426, 10/2/16; R.E., 15/7/16; F; Lieut.; w; M.C.
c/o P. O. Gilgil, Kenya Colony, British East Africa.

☨ PODMORE, Edward Glanville
6/5/5365, 3/8/15; L'pool. R., 1/1/16; 2/Lieut.
Killed in action 25/9/16.

☨ POGGI, Arthur Rupert
6/5/7472, 15/11/15; No. 11 O.C.B., 7/5/16; trfr. L'pool. R., 6/10/16, R. Fus., 1st Lond. R.; F; Cpl.
Killed in action 2/4/18.

POINTER, Giles Arthur
K/D/4/2083, 13/11/14, L/C.; R. War. R., 29/10/15; 2/Lieut.
Godalming, Nr. Guildford, Surrey.

POLAND, Francis Rexford
Sq/388, 24/3/09; 24th Lond. R., 21/12/12.
110 Queen Victoria Street, E.C. 4.

☨ POLAND, Guy Bernard
A/10729, 12/2/17; No. 11 O.C.B., 5/7/17; 24th Lond. R., 30/10/17; 2/Lieut.
Killed in action 21/3/18.

☨ POLAND, Henry Arthur
B/663, 19/11/12; R.W. Kent R., 14/8/14; F; Lieut.
Killed in action 18/4/15.

POLAND, Kenneth Gordon
A/11615, 5/7/17, L/C.; H. Bde. O.C.B., 4/1/18; Cold. Gds., 25/6/18, emp. Gds. M.G.R.; 2/Lieut.

POLAND, Raymond Denham
A/C/Sq/D/9735, 16/10/16; R.A., C/S, 4/2/18; R.G.A., 1/8/18;
Lieut. Inveresk, Tower Road, Orpington, Kent.

POLDEN, Herbert Elwyn Russell
D/13781, 7/8/18; demob. 23/1/19.
Cranleigh, New Malden, Surrey.

POLEY, Albert Edwin
Sq/976, 5/8/14. Willow Bank, Uxbridge Road, Hampton Hill.

POLGE, Arthur Herbert
4/1/3978, 3/6/15, L/C.; Durh. L.I., 8/10/15; F; Lieut.; w(2).
Elladene, 7 Dornton Road, South Croydon, Surrey. (Now in Sweden).

POLHILL, Cecil Charles
4/5/Sq/4904, 16/7/15; Dorset Yeo., 4/11/15; Lieut.
Howbury Hall, Bedford.

☨ POLLAK, Harry L.
F/2599, 7/1/15, L/C.; R. Marines, 4/4/15.
Killed in action /10/16.

POLLARD, Ernest Cyril
6/2/6607, 4/10/15; trfr. 14th Lond. R., 3/11/16.
St. Just, Ventnor, Isle of Wight.

POLLARD, George
4/3/4007, 3/6/15, L/C.; L'pool. R., 30/11/15, att. T.M. Bty.;
F; Lieut.; w; M(1). 346 Colne Road, Burnley, Lancashire.

287

APPENDIX II.—RECORDS OF RANK AND FILE.

POLLETT, Lionel Williams
6/5/5388, 5/8/15, L/C.; North'd. Fus., 21/4/16; F; Lieut.; w.
269 Waterloo Street, Burton-on-Trent.

POLLOCK, Guy Cameron
C/318, 30/6/08; dis. 29/6/09.
21 Drayton Court, South Kensington.

POLLOCK, Humphrey Rivers
B/776, 27/3/14; trfr. R.A.M.C., 14/8/14; R.A.M.C., 12/1/15; F; Capt.
12 Gloucester Terrace, Cranley Gardens, South Kensington, S.W. 7.

POLLOCK, Norman Fleming
B/Sq/D/12795, 18/3/18; trfr. 6th R. Regt. of Cav., 11/6/19, 4th Drag. Gds.
82 Main Street, Cavan, Ireland.

POLLOCK, Robert
Sq/235, 20/5/08; dis. 25/2/10.

PONSFORD, Henry
4/5/4632, 5/7/15, L/C.; R.A., C/S, 24/1/16; trfr. 5th Lond. R., 31/3/16; Gord. Highrs., 1/3/17; F; Lieut.; w.
Church View House, Moretonhampstead, Devonshire. (Now in Burma).

PONSONBY, Victor C.
A/426, 24/5/09; Herts. Yeo., 1/1/11; Capt.; M.C., M(2).

✠ PONTER, Harry William Francis
4/3/4325, 19/6/15, L/C.; R.W. Surr. R., 14/11/15; Lieut.
Killed in action 3/9/18.

POOLE, Victor Durrand
4/3/5152, 29/7/15; E. Surr. R., 23/4/16; Lieut.
Surrey Hall, Surrey Road, Cliftonville, Margate.

POOLE, Vincent McDonald
4/3/6/4581, 1/7/15, Cpl.; Arg. & Suth'd. Highrs., 18/12/16; Lieut.
45 Brigstock Road, Thornton Heath, Surrey.

POOLEY, Harold Tracy
1/9741, 16/10/16; R.A., C/S, 23/1/17; R.G.A., 26/5/17; F; Lieut.; g.
c/o Royal Colonial Institute, Northumberland Avenue, W.C.

POPE, Cecil Morville
3/3137, 29/3/15; Durh. L.I., 28/7/15, Lab. Corps; Lieut.
38 Harold Road, Leytonstone, E. 11.

✠ POPE, Edwin Albert
6/7746, 22/11/15; R.F.C., 13/5/16; 2/Lieut.
Killed in action 27/2/17.

✠ POPE, Harold Edward
Sq/2878, 8/2/15; R.G.A., 19/3/15; F; Capt.; M.C. and Bar.
Killed in action 24/8/18.

POPE, Harold Joseph
6/7275, 8/11/15; R.A., C/S, 23/6/16; R.G.A., 27/9/16; F; Lieut
151 Chamberlayne Road, Willesden, N.W. 10.

POPE, Herbert Montagu
Sq/592, 27/11/11; dis. med. unfit, 4/8/14; R.A.M.C.; F,M; Capt.; w.
Stanfield House, Pontefract, Yorkshire.

POPE, John Wilson
C/11802, 2/8/17; R.F.C., C/S, 23/10/17; R.F.C., 12/12/17, R.A.F.; F; 2/Lieut.
10 Rossdale Road, Putney, S.W. 15.

✠ POPE, Percy Paris
F/1827, 16/10/14; Welch R., 6/3/15; 2/Lieut.
Killed in action 1/10/15.

POPE, Sydney Leo Gregory
6/5/5781, 23/8/15, L/C.; R.F.C., 2/6/16, R.A.F.; Lieut.

POPPLEWELL, Frederick Ewart
C/11785, 4/8/17; trfr. 28th Lond. R., 6/3/18; F; w.
Brynmor, Pinford Lane, Halton, Nr. Leeds.

PORDAGE, Ernest John William
4/1/4582, 1/7/15; R. Mar. Art., 19/11/15; F; Lieut.; M(1).
18 Bethel Street, Norwich.

✠ PORKESS, Walter Henderson
Sq/3104, 21/3/15, L/C.; Notts. & Derby. Yeo., 21/7/15, att. R.F.C.; Lieut.
Killed in action 10/2/17.

PORTEOUS, Cecil John Montague
D/Sq/12953, 19/4/18; A.S.C., C/S, 1/11/18; R.A.S.C., 13/3/19; 2/Lieut.
Lauriston Castle, Montrose.

PORTEOUS, Percival
B/11992, 10/9/17, L/C.; R.F.A., C/S, 7/2/18; R.F.A., 21/10/18; 2/Lieut.

PORTEOUS, William Ford
4/6/4892, 15/7/15, L/C.; Midd'x. R., 18/11/15, secd. M.G.C.; Lieut.; p; M.C.
106 Alexandra Road, St. Johns Wood, N.W. 8.

PORTER, Adrian Russell
D/3008, 4/3/15, L/C.; York. R., 29/4/15; Lieut.

PORTER, Algernon
D/12126, 15/10/17; No. 4 O.C.B., 10/5/18; R.W. Kent R., 4/2/19; 2/Lieut.
Sungei Yukang Estate, near Sungei Patani, Kedah, Straits Settlements.

PORTER, Aubrey Harry
A/B/12171, 29/10/17; R.E., C/S, 13/1/18; R.E., 26/4/18; 2/Lieut.
Woodside House, Cardross, Dumbartonshire.

PORTER, Charles Robert
4/3705, 20/5/15; R.E., 25/11/15; F; Lieut.; w.
c/o Tees Conservancy Commissioners, Middlesbrough, Yorkshire.

PORTER, Claude Ludovic
D/3007, 4/3/15, Sgt.; York. R., 29/4/15; Lieut.

PORTER, Clement Wilfred
A/1627, 9/10/14; North'd. Fus., 21/1/15; Lieut.
90 Edith Road, West Kensington, W. 14.

✠ PORTER, Frederick Ernest Gilchrist
D/1428, 29/9/14; N. Lan. R., 27/11/14; Capt.
Died of wounds 3/11/16.

PORTER, Frederick William
D/10018, 27/11/16, L/C.; R.E., 18/6/17; F; Lieut.
Scotgate House, Goole, Yorkshire.

PORTER, George Joseph
C/12657, 27/2/18; No. 17 O.C.B., 8/8/18; R. War. R., 5/3/19; 2/Lieut.
143 Lightwoods Road, Bearwood, Birmingham.

PORTER, Henry Spencer Holmes
6/5/C/8877, 12/1/16; No. 7 O.C.B., 4/11/16; trfr. 1st Cty. of Lond. Yeo., 5/3/17; P; Sgt.
Brookview, Demamanagh, Strabane, Tyrone, Ireland.

PORTER, Herbert
B/325, 24/7/08; dis. 23/7/12; rej. Sq. 1292, 24/9/14, S.Q.M.S.; emp. M. of Munitions; O.B.E.
77 Beaconsfield Road, Blackheath, S.E. 3.

PORTER, John Copestake
Sq/109, 18/4/08; dis. 17/4/12; rej. Sq/1341, 26/9/14, Farr. Sgt.; Special List, 28/12/14; F; Lt.-Col.
Caithness Lodge, Epsom.

PORTER, Maurice Shirley
6/2/9434, 11/2/16; No. 14 O.C.B., 26/11/16; Shrop. L.I., 27/3/17; F; Lieut.; w.
56 Saxby Street, Leicester.

PORTER, Richard Paitson
4/5/4719, 9/7/15; Manch. R., 6/12/15; F; Capt.; w; M.C., M(1).
Aurora Schoolhouse, General Delivery, Regina, Sask., Canada.

PORTER, Robert Guy
B/11365, 28/5/17, L/C.; R.G.A., C/S, 27/12/17; R.G.A., 17/6/18; F; 2/Lieut.
Hill Lodge, Clay Hill, Enfield, Middlesex.

PORTER, Robert Howie
Sq/142, 18/4/08; dis. 17/4/10; rej. Sq/1880, 16/10/14; R.F.A., 20/10/14, R.A.S.C.; F; Capt.
Austin Friars House, Austin Friars, E.C.

PORTER, Thomas
Sq/121, 18/4/08; dis. 18/4/13.

PORTER, Thomas Newnham Saunders
A/13958, 6/9/18; demob. 22/4/19.
The Hawthornes, Southey Street, Nottingham.

PORTER, Thomas William
3/3367, 22/4/15, L/C.; Shrop. L.I., 8/7/15, 8th Lond. R.; F; Capt.; M.C.
The Larches, Trinity Road, Wood Green, N. 22.

PORTER, William Herbert
D/10229, 29/12/16; Garr. O.C.B., 23/5/17; Lab. Corps. 14/7/17; Lieut.

POSKITT, Frederick Richard
A/14000, 13/9/18; demob. 29/1/19.
61 Manor Park Road, N.W. 10.

✠ POSNETT, William Leonard
C/9793, 27/10/16; No. 14 O.C.B., 27/12/16; 13th Lond. R., 27/3/17; 2/Lieut.
Killed in action 22/6/17.

POSTGATE, William Havelock
D/10869, 13/3/17; No. 11 O.C.B., 5/7/17; Durh. L.I., 3/10/17, att. Wilts. R.; F; Lieut.; w.
Fell View, Cockermouth, Cumberland.

APPENDIX II.—RECORDS OF RANK AND FILE.

POTT, *Francis Cecil*
6/4/6490, 27/9/15, L/C.; K.R. Rif. C., 1/6/16; Lieut.

POTTAGE, *Cecil Fredrick*
B/12859, 25/3/18; No. 20 O.C.B., 20/9/18; demob.
46 Woodside Park Road, North Finchley, N. 13.

POTTER, *Alfred Howard*
B/13680, 29/7/18; trfr. K.R. Rif. C., 7/4/19.
12 Crookston Road, Eltham, S.E. 9.

POTTER, *Arthur Cyril*
A/604, 13/2/12; 25th Lond. R., R. War. R., M.G.C.; F,E,P; Capt.
128 Maida Vale, W. 9.

POTTER, *Charles Gerald*
6/3/7116, 1/11/15, L/C.; 8th Lond. R., 4/8/16; F; Capt.
33 Harvard Road, Chiswick, W. 4.

POTTER, *Edward*
B/13424, 1/7/18; demob. 25/1/19.
25 Plaistow Grove, West Ham, E. 15.

POTTER, *Ernest Harold*
6/5/8587, 3/1/16; A.S.C., C/S, 17/7/16; R.A.S.C., 8/5/17; E; Lieut.
Court Downs Cottage, Court Downs Road, Beckenham, Kent.

✠ POTTER, *Francis George*
6/5/7776, 23/11/15, L/C.; Worc. R., 4/9/16; F; 2/Lieut.
Killed in action 24/4/17.

POTTER, *Gilbert John Reginald*
4/3/5212, 29/7/15; R.F.A., 26/11/15, R.A.F.; F; Lieut.; w.
Wytham, Oxford.

POTTER, *Harold*
B/13445, 3/7/18; trfr. K.R. Rif. C., 7/4/19.
22 Park Avenue, West Budsford, Nottinghamshire.

POTTER, *Henry William Morgan*
A/862, 4/8/14; Midd'x. R., 15/8/14; F; Capt.; w; M.C., M(2).
Ashburton, Tatsfield, Nr. Westerham, Kent.

POTTER, *Herbert Frederick*
D/10241, 29/12/16; No. 2 O.C.B., 5/5/17; Essex R., 28/8/17; F; Lieut.; w.
9 Trinity Street, Colchester.

POTTER, *Percy*
6/Sq/8701, 4/1/16; No. 2 Cav. C/S, 1/9/16; 8th R. Regt. of Cav., 20/12/16; F; Lieut.
40 Broadway, Westminster, S.W. 1.

POTTER, *Reginald Francis*
A/1078, 2/9/14, Sgt.; 7th Lond. R., 28/9/14, M.G.C.; F; Capt.
The Hermitage, East Molesey, Surrey.

POTTER, *Robert Blair McCabe*
D/10168, 11/12/16, Sgt.; R.G.A., C/S, 15/8/17; R.G.A., 31/12/17; F; Lieut.
32 York Road, West Norwood, S.E. 27.

POTTER, *Stephen Meredith*
D/12997, 29/4/18; H. Bde. O.C.B., 4/10/18; Cold. Gds., 9/3/19; 2/Lieut.
36 Old Park Avenue, S.W. 12.

POTTER, *William Edward Henry*
6/2/7942, 29/11/15; R.A., C/S, 4/8/16; R.G.A., 12/11/16; Lieut.
The Hut, Kingham, Oxon.

POTTER, *William Thomas*
E/14006, 13/9/18; demob. 10/1/19.   13 Edgar Street, Worcester.

POTTINGER, *Joseph Hector*
6/3/7218, 4/11/15; R.F.C., C/S, 16/4/17; R.F.C., 16/5/17.
16 Thorndale Road, Waterloo, Liverpool.

✠ POTTS, *Arnold Leslie Leopold*
4/3/4505, 28/6/15; Durh. L.I., 17/12/15; 2/Lieut.
Killed in action 5/11/16.

✠ POTTS, *Charles*
6/3/9408, 9/2/16; No. 14 O.C.B., 30/10/16; Ches. R., 28/2/17; F; 2/Lieut.; w.
Died of wounds 11/6/17.

POTTS, *Donald Stuart*
D/9989, 22/11/16; No. 14 O.C.B., 5/3/17; R. Highrs., 26/6/17; F; Lieut.; w.
Borrowdale, Warren Road, Blundellsands, Liverpool.

POTTS, *John Robert*
6/5/5525, 9/8/15; R.G.A., 2/11/15, L'pool. R., emp. M. of Labour; F; Lieut.
Langley House, 66 Daisy Bank Road, Victoria Park, Manchester.

POTTS, *Wilfrid Calder*
D/B/Sq/12138, 19/10/17; No. 11 O.C.B., 22/1/19; General List, 8/3/19; 2/Lieut.
Comodoro, Rivadavia, Chubut, Patagonia, Argentina.

✠ POULTNEY, *John Bernard*
4/3657, 17/5/15; R. War. R., 2/7/15, S. Lan. R.; 2/Lieut.; w; M(1).
Killed in action 18/2/17.

POUNCY, *Joseph Robert*
D/11133, 26/4/17; No. 11 O.C.B., 10/8/17; Hamps. R., 27/11/17; F; Lieut.; g-p.
Birnam, Twyford, Nr. Winchester.

POUND, *Allen Leslie*
A/10053, 29/11/16; No. 14 O.C.B., 30/1/17; R. Fus., 29/5/17; Lieut.
62 Oxford Street, W. 1.

POUNDALL, *William Lloyd*
B/A/12328, 27/12/17; No. 2 O.C.B., 7/6/18; trfr. 14th Lond. R., 6/12/18, Gord. Highrs.; Pte.
19 Fernleigh Road, Winchmore Hill, N. 21.

POWDITCH, *Bernard Hirst*
4/1/4372, 21/6/15; trfr. R.F.A., 5/5/16; F.
c/o Dr. H. Rubra, 66 Crouch Hall Road, Crouch End, N. 8.

POWE, *Arthur Blancy*
6/9241, 1/2/16; R.A., C/S, 26/5/16; R.G.A., 30/8/16; F; Lieut.
Esplanade, Wynnum South, Queensland, Australia.

POWE, *Harold David*
1/3872, 31/5/15; C.Q.M.S.; R.G.A., C/S, 10/10/17; dis. med. unfit.
7b Peterborough Villas, S.W. 6.

POWELL, *Albert Arthur*
D/10678, 6/2/17, Sgt.; demob. 11/1/19.
Avisjorde, 255 Melfort Road, Norbury, S.W.

POWELL, *Alfred Thomas*
B/13649, 26/7/18; demob. 31/1/19.
Upton Bishop, Ross-on-Wye.

POWELL, *Arthur Henry*
A/11937, 30/8/17; R.A., C/S, 4/2/18; R.G.A., 26/8/18; 2/Lieut.
34 Princethorpe Road, Sydenham, S.E. 26.

POWELL, *Arthur Lunniss*
B/Sq/12843, 21/3/18; No. 2 Cav. C/S, 7/11/18; 4th R. Regt. of Cav., 13/3/19; 2/Lieut.
Pen-Carrig, Caeran Park, Newport, Monmouthshire.

POWELL, *Cecil Waring*
A/D/12490, 28/1/18; R.A.F., C/S, 19/4/18; R.A.F., 23/11/18; 2/Lieut.
Elmcroft, Muswell Hill Road, Muswell Hill, N. 10.

POWELL, *Charles Edmonds*
B/2667, 12/1/15; R.E., 27/3/15; G,P; Lieut.
South Lawn, Bickley, Kent.

POWELL, *Charles Henry*
B/2879, 8/2/15, L/C.; Notts. & Derby. R., 30/7/15; F; Capt.
Clovelly, Queens Road, High Wycombe.

POWELL, *Charles Vernon*
6/3/8878, 12/1/16; R.A., C/S, 4/8/16; R.G.A., 3/11/16; F; Lieut.; w; M.C.
2 Monk Street, Monmouth.

POWELL, *Conrad Martin*
D/10907, 26/3/17; R.F.C., C/S, 4/5/17; R.F.C., 14/6/17, R.A.F.; F; Lieut.
38 Alcester Road, King's Heath, Birmingham.

✠ POWELL, *Dafydd Emrys*
2/3117, 25/3/15; R.W. Fus., 17/8/15; M.G.C.; F; Lieut.
Killed in action 28/3/18.

✠ POWELL, *Eric Limbery*
K/B/2530, 31/12/14, Sgt.; R.A.S.C., 25/10/15, R.F.A.; Lieut.
Killed in action 6/4/18.

POWELL, *Frederick Arthur*
6/2/5633, 16/8/15, L/C.; Midd'x. R., 27/1/16; S; Lieut.
26 King Edward's Gardens, Acton Hill, W. 3.

✠ POWELL, *Frederick William*
6/5/6149, 9/9/15; R. Dub. Fus., 1/6/16; 2/Lieut.
Died 20/1/17.

✠ POWELL, *Harold Osborne*
Sq/667, 26/11/12; 4th Drag. Gds., 14/8/14; F; 2/Lieut.
Killed in action 31/10/14.

POWELL, *Harry Creswell*
1/3555, 10/5/15; Dental Surgeon, 16/7/15; Capt.
41 Bellerton Road, Knowle, Bristol.

POWELL, *Herbert Hugh*
6/1/8004, 30/11/15, Sgt.; demob. 3/2/19.
36 Wallbutton Road, Brockley, S.E. 4.

✠ POWELL, *James Stanley*
C/10588, 22/1/17;
Died 5/4/17.

POWELL, *John*
B/13612, 24/7/18; No. 11 O.C.B., 24/1/19; General List, 8/3/19; 2/Lieut.
c/o Major Graham, Hilston Park, Monmouth.

APPENDIX II.—RECORDS OF RANK AND FILE.

✠ POWELL, Maurice
Sq/395, 31/3/09; Surr. Yeo., 18/1/13, R.F.A.; Lieut.
Killed in action 5/7/17

POWELL, Owen Geoffrey
F/1759, 16/10/14; Hamps. R., 27/1/15, R.F.C., R.A.F.; F; Lieut.;
Inv.   Rowley, Huxtable Hill, Torquay. (Now in Uganda).

POWELL, Roger
6/5802, 23/8/15; Hamps. R., 23/12/15, att. R.A.F.; P; Lieut.
Charity Farm, Chiddingly, Sussex.

POWELL, Ronald Arthur
E/1602, 6/10/14; Hamps. R., 24/11/14, War Office; Capt.
28 Stafford Terrace, Kensington, W.8.

POWELL, Ronald Vannock
4/1/4761, 12/7/15, L/C.; Scots. Gds., 2/9/15; Lieut.; w(2);
M.C., M(1).   East Park, Handcross, Sussex.

✠ POWELL, Scott
A/899, 5/8/14; R. Dub. Fus., 22/8/14; M; Capt.; M(1).
Died of wounds 4-5/4/16.

POWELL, Vivian Alfred
6/1/2227, 3/12/14; R.F.C., C/S, 16/4/17; R.F.C., 10/5/17, att.
R.E.; 2/Lieut.   Hill Garden, Torquay.

POWELL, Walter Lionel
6/4/6024, 2/9/15; R.W. Fus., 4/11/16; F; 2/Lieut.; w.
The Eagles, Newtown, Montgomeryshire, North Wales.

POWELL, William Basil Stewart
D/11570, 28/6/17; A.S.C., C/S, 1/9/17; R.A.S.C., 13/3/18; E,P;
Lieut.   Usk Glendale, Rhodesia, South Africa.

POWER, Edgar Arthur
D/13876, 21/8/18; trfr. K.R. Rif. C., 7/4/19.
127 North Street, Brighton, Sussex.

✠ POWERS, Bernard Alexander
4/3979, 3/6/15; Midd'x. R., 2/12/15, att. R.F.C.; F; Lieut.
Killed in action 25/9/17.

POWLES, Edward Paulet
E/1515, 1/10/14; Rif. Brig., 30/11/14, K.R. Rif. C.; Capt.
42 Warwick Gardens, Kensington, W.14.

✠ POWLES-CURTIS, Arthur John
D/2670, 12/1/15; L'pool. R., 25/5/15, K.R. Rif. C.; Capt.
Died of wounds 11/9/16.

POWYS, Atherton Richard Norman
B/261, 26/5/08; dis. 25/5/09; rej. B/A/D/11752, 26/7/17; R.A,
C/S, 15/3/18; R.G.A., 8/2/19; 2/Lieut.
6 Lincoln's Inn Fields, W.C. 2.

POYNTON, Brian Osborne
A/13089, 20/5/18; No. 11 O.C.B., 24/1/19; General List, 8/3/19,
2/Lieut.   665 Essenwood Road, Berea, Durban, Natal, South Africa.

POYSER, Charles Langford
6/9595, 30/6/16; R.A., C/S, 1/9/16; R.G.A., 24/12/16; Lieut.
21 Queens Road, Monkseaton, Northumberland.

POYSER, Kenneth Elliston
B/860, 4/8/14; Yorks. L.I., 12/9/14, N. Lan. R.; F,It; Lt.-Col.;
w; D.S.O., M(3).   3 Hare Court, Temple, E.C.

PRAGNELL, D. William Alan
A/10080, 1/12/16; A.S.C., C/S, 26/2/17; R.A.S.C., 7/5/17;
Lieut.; M.B.E.   22 St. Pauls Churchyard, E.C. 4.

PRANCE, Arthur Leigh
D/12098, 5/10/17; H. Bde. O.C.B., 8/2/18; Welch Gds., 24/9/18;
F; Lieut.   Oakfield Road, Ashtead, Surrey.

PRATLEY, Frank Alan
A/13979, 9/9/18; trfr. K.R. Rif. C., 7/4/19.
Fairholme, Mill Road, Epsom.

PRATT, Bernard William Harries
Sq/772, 2/3/14, L/C.; R.A.S.C., 17/1/15; S; Lieut.
Roughton, Caerleon, Monmouthshire.

PRATT, Bickerton
B/89, 16/4/08; dis. 15/4/10.
Roughton, Caerleon, Monmouthshire.

PRATT, Edward Spencer
Sq/358, 12/3/09; dis. 3/4/11.

PRATT, Frederic James
6/3/5850, 26/8/15; Manch. R., 1/6/16; F; Lieut.; w.
Broome Estate, Bangi, Selangor, Federated Malay States.

PRATT, Guy Warwick
A/9846, 3/11/16; trfr. M.G.C., 14/3/17.
3 Grand Drive, Leigh-on-Sea.

PRATT, Henry Godwin
4/6/5/4945, 19/7/15; Welch R., 4/1/16, R.A.F.; F,S,SR; Lieut.;
w; M(2).   6 Risca Road, Newport, Monmouthshire.

PRATT, John Lhind
6/9556, 28/2/16; R.A., C/S, 26/5/16; R.G.A., 30/8/16; F; Capt.;
M(1).   3 Dr. Johnson's Buildings, Temple, E.C. 4.

PRATT, John Rupert Bailic
6/1/5685, 16/8/15; 12th Lond. R., 30/12/15, secd. M.G.C., att.
R.A.F.; F; Lieut.
c/o Mrs. White, Wavertree, 21 Sydenham Hill, S.E. 26.

PRATT, Leonard Webster
K/C/2386, 17/12/14; W. Rid. R., 11/3/15; F; 2/Lieut.; w.
Highcliffe House, Bradford, Yorkshire.

PRATT, Stuart Harvey
K/B/2091, 16/11/14, L/C.; R. Fus., 13/3/15, att. R. Scots., secd.
R.F.C., R.A.F.; F; Capt.; w, Inj; M(1).
The Bungalow, Albion Road, Sutton, Surrey.

PRATT, William Lyyn
C/11753, 26/7/17; A.S.C., C/S, 12/11/17; R.A.S.C., 6/1/18;
M,Persia; Lieut.
Lond. Joint City & Midland Bk. Ltd., Cirencester.

✠ PREBBLE, John
4/Sq/4089, 7/6/15, L/C.; R.F.A., C/S, 28/4/16; R.F.A., 26/8/16;
F; 2/Lieut.   Killed in action 21/6/17.

PREECE, Sydney George
11900, 23/8/17, Cpl.; No. 5 O.C.B., 7/6/18, No. 14 O.C.B.; R.
Berks. R., 5/2/19; 2/Lieut.
78 Belmont Road, Maidenhead, Berkshire.

PREEDY, Arthur Edward
6/2/5416, 5/8/15; Devon. R., 4/12/15, att. R. Lanc. R.; F; Staff
Capt.; w.   The Palace, Hampton Court, Middlesex.

PREEDY, Bernard
A/2931, 15/2/15; 1st Lond. R., 8/4/15; F; Lieut.; w(3); M.C.
90 White Lion Street, N. 1.

✠ PRENTICE, Oliver
6/3/7276, 8/11/15; 1st Lond. R., 18/12/16, att. Lan. Fus.; F;
2/Lieut.   Killed in action 27/3/18.

PRESCOTT, Francis Arthur
3/3556, 10/5/15; Bord. R., 7/8/15, att. R.F.C., R.A.F.; Lieut.
74 Cromwell Avenue, Highgate, N. 6.

PRESCOTT, George Aylward
6/5/7559, 17/11/15; No. 7 O.C.B., 3/7/16, M.G.C., C/S; M.G.C,
28/10/16, Tank Corps; F,SR; Capt.; M.C.
12 Upper Leeson Street, Dublin.

PRESLAND, Herbert Purcell
A/1282, 23/9/14; R.A.S.C., 29/10/14; Lieut.
8 Bexley Road, Belvedere, Kent.

PRESTAGE, Thomas Thompson
A/11616, 30/6/17; No. 11 O.C.B., 9/11/17; L'pool. R., 30/4/18;
NR; Lieut.   Customs & Excise, Custom House, Dublin.

PRESTON, Charles Edmund
B/12813, 20/3/18; No. 2 O.C.B., 20/9/18; Norf. R., 19/3/19;
2/Lieut.   Christchurch Lodge, Eaton, Norwich, Norfolk.

PRESTON, Clifford William
A/10902, 21/3/17; trfr. Class W. Res., 27/9/18.
Montague Road, Berkhamsted.

PRESTON, George Arthur Chevallier
B/700, 12/3/13; dis. 4/8/14.

PRESTON, John Basil
D/11859, 13/8/17; No. 3 O.C.B., 8/2/18; Lan. Fus., 27/8/18, att.
S. Lan. R.; 2/Lieut.   51 East Mount, Barrow-in-Furness.

PRESTON, Julius Hervey
D/10214, 18/12/16; No. 14 O.C.B., 6/4/17; Sea. Highrs., 31/7/17,
R.A.F.; F; Lieut.   130 Lloyd Avenue, Providence, Rhode Island, U.S.A.

PRESTON, Stanley Howard
6/8294, 10/12/15; R.F.C., 5/5/16, R.A.F.; F; Capt.; A.F.C.
Ambleside, Bunbury Road, King's Norton, Birmingham.

PRESTON, Thomas
6/Sq/8992, 18/1/16; No. 2 O.C.B., 6/9/16; 101st Tr. Res. Bn.,
23/1/17, S. Persian Rif.; Persia; Capt.; M(1).
43 Belgrave Road, Darwen, Lancashire. (Now in Uganda).

PRESTWICH, Herbert
A/D/11893, 20/8/17; No. 3 O.C.B., 8/2/18; Manch. R., 30/7/18;
2/Lieut.   Brookside, Singleton Road, Kersal, Manchester.

APPENDIX II.—RECORDS OF RANK AND FILE.

PRETTY, Arnold Herbert Falk
Sq/486, 25/4/10; dis. 18/8/13; 22nd Lond. R., 18/6/15, cmp. M. of Nat. Serv.; Lieut.; w(2).

✠ PRETYMAN, Maurice William
C/850, 4/8/14; R.E., 2/9/14; 2/Lieut.
Killed in action 12/8/15.

PREVOST, Peter Guillaume
D/E/13826, 12/8/18; R.G.A., C/S, 2/10/18; R.G.A., 10/3/19; 2/Lieut.
c/o Sir C. R. McGrigor Bart & Coy., 39 Panton Street, W.1.

PREW, Robert James
C/12296, 10/12/17, Sgt.; demob. 9/1/19.
89 Shaftesbury Avenue, Montpelier, Bristol.

PRICE, Arthur Rees
E/1564, 6/10/14, L/C.; Devon. R., 3/12/14; E,P; Staff Capt.; M(1).
61 Carey Street, Lincoln's Inn, W.C.2.

✠ PRICE, Charles
6/2/7322, 6/11/15, Cpl.; S. Lan. R., 15/7/16; 2/Lieut.
Died of wounds 18/7/17.

PRICE, Clifford James
B/9900, 13/11/16; No. 14 O.C.B., 5/3/17; R.N.V.R., 26/6/17; F; Sub. Lieut.
Boulsdon, Newent, Gloucestershire.

PRICE, Cormell Edward William
6/3/5417, 5/8/15, Sgt.; R. Suss. R., 24/10/16; P,F; Capt.; w.
c/o Rudyard Kipling Esq., Batemans, Burwash, Sussex. (Now in India).

PRICE, Donald Gwilliam
D/11107, 23/4/17, L/C.; No. 14 O.C.B., 5/10/17; Manch. R., 26/2/18, att. N. Lan. R.; F; 2/Lieut.
New Inn Chambers, King Street, Gloucester.

PRICE, Evan Arthur
B/11400, 29/5/17; No. 14 O.C.B., 5/10/17; Welch R., 26/2/18; F; 2/Lieut.
Oakdene, Cwmfelinfach, Near Newport, Monmouthshire.

PRICE, George
C/13307, 17/6/18; R.E., C/S, 18/10/18; demob.
5 Cromwell Road, Mexborough, Nr. Rotherham, Yorkshire.

PRICE, George Kenneth
6/5/5952, 1/9/15, Sgt.; L'pool. R., 20/1/16; F; Lieut.; w.
63 Green Bank Road, Devonshire Park, Birkenhead.

PRICE, Glyn Morlais
4/3815, 27/5/15; Welch R., 5/11/15, att. Pemb. Yeo.; F; Lieut.
49 Stanwell Road, Penarth, Nr. Cardiff.

PRICE, John Rhys Lymington
D/Sq/13853, 16/8/18; demob. 22/1/19.
Wisborough Park, Billingshurst, Sussex.

PRICE, John William
F/3055, 15/3/15; 4th Lond. R., 28/7/15; Lieut.; w(2).
20 Darnley Road, Grays, Essex.

PRICE, Joseph Edelsten
C/13385, 24/6/18; trfr. 14th Lond. R., 6/12/18.
225 Great Cheetham Street, Higher Broughton, Manchester.

PRICE, Lionel Lewis
K/A/2175, 26/11/14; R.W. Fus., 26/5/15; F; Lieut.; Inv.
54 Fairhazel Gardens, N.W.6.

✠ PRICE, Paul Adrian Edward
6/3/5418, 5/8/15; R.G.A., 27/10/15; F; 2/Lieut.
Killed in action 23/4/17.

PRICE, Percy Harold
2/3603, 13/5/15; R. Fus., 3/9/15.
Holmleigh, Walton-on-Thames.

PRICE, Rees Thomas
6/2/6306, 17/9/15; S. Wales Bord., 4/9/16; F; Lieut.
Eastnor House, Cimla Road, Neath, South Wales.

PRICE, Robert Bernard
C/459, 31/1/10; R.A.M.C., 26/7/12; F; Capt.; D.S.O., M(3).
30 Copers Cope Road, Beckenham, Kent.

PRICE, William Edward
F/1941, 22/10/14; Welch R., 3/12/14; Major; O.B.E., M(2).
19 St. Pauls Road, Clifton, Bristol. (Now in Bombay).

PRICHARD, John Holden
A/12491, 28/1/18; No. 16 O.C.B., 7/6/18; R. Lanc. R., 5/2/19; 2/Lieut.
45 Tennyson Street, Princes Park, Liverpool.

PRICHARD, William Hugh
B/11344, 19/5/17, L/C.; R.A., C/S, 30/11/17; trfr. R.F.A., 21/5/18.
Arden, Pwllheli, Carmarthenshire.

PRIDAY, Cyril Arthur
A/10865, 10/3/17, Sgt.; H. Bde. O.C.B., 8/2/18; Oxf. & Bucks. L.I., 30/7/18, att. Notts. & Derby. R.; F; 2/Lieut.
2 Vanburgh Terrace, Blackheath, S.E.3.

PRIDE, Robert
C/12293, 6/12/17, L/C.; No. 10 O.C.B., 10/5/18; R. Scots, 3/2/19; 2/Lieut. 4 Oakwood Terrace, West Park Road, Dundee.

PRIDEAUX, Robert Armstrong
C/12578, 6/2/18; H. Bde. O.C.B., 7/6/18; trfr. 28th Lond. R., 16/11/18.
158 Llandaff Road, Cardiff.

PRIDEAUX, Robert Flemyng
6/1/8250, 8/12/15; R.A., C/S, 29/9/16; R.G.A., 31/1/17; I; Lieut.
The Guildhall, Shrewsbury.

PRIDEAUX, Vernon Harry
6/3/7777, 23/11/15; Devon. R., 25/9/16, att. M.G.C.; I,E,F; Lieut.
8 Short Park Road, Peverell, Plymouth, Devonshire.

PRIDEAUX, Vivian Francis
K/F/2514, 31/12/14; R.W. Fus., 14/4/15; S; Lieut.
4 Boyle Street, Savile Row, W.1. (Now in Trinidad).

PRIDEAUX, William Reginald Bray
E/1613, 6/10/14; Wilts. R., 25/10/14, R. Berks. R., Lab. Corps; F; Capt.
The Prairie, Baldock, Hertfordshire.

PRIDHAM, Cyril Norman
4/2/5125, 26/7/15; E. Surr. R., 9/11/15; F; Capt.
21 Victoria Street, Paignton, South Devonshire.

PRIESTLEY, Charles Henry
6/4/8370, 13/12/15, L/C.; Suff. R., 24/10/16, secd. M.G.C.; Lieut
Waterdale, Doncaster.

PRIESTLEY, Henry Robert James
B/D/12213, 12/11/17; No. 3 O.C.B., 10/5/18; trfr. 28th Lond. R., 1/11/18.
99 Lexham Gardens, Kensington.

PRING, Alec
6/3/6828, 14/10/15, L/C.; R.F.A., C/S, 4/8/16; R.F.A., 12/1/17; Lieut.; w.
Calcets, Arundel, Sussex.

PRING, Hugh Oliver
3/3658, 17/5/15; Som. L.I., 24/10/15; F; Capt.; M.C., Order of the Crown of Roumania, M(1).
76 Bishops Road, Bayswater, W.2.

✠ PRINGLE, Charles Eric
E/2839, 1/2/15; N. Lan. R., 8/7/15; 2/Lieut.
Killed in action 10/7/16.

PRINGLE, George Taylor
6/3/9166, 26/1/16; R.A., C/S, 7/8/16; R.G.A., 18/10/16; F; 2/Lieut.; Inv.
20 St. Ann's Drive, Giffnock, Glasgow.

✠ PRINGLE, Hubert Alexander Montgomerie
2/3095, 22/3/15;
Died 30/4/15.

PRINGLE, William Blair
6/8295, 10/12/15; No. 9 O.C.B., 8/3/16; Arg. & Suth'd. Highrs., 6/7/16, W. Rid. R.; I; Staff Capt.
4 St. Johns Wood Terrace, Dundee.

PRINSEP, Thomas Arthur Levett
D/10002, 24/11/16; R.W. Surr. R., 9/3/17; S; Lieut.
Barton-under-Needwood, Burton-on-Trent.

PRIOR, Godfrey Kemeys
4/5/C/5126, 26/7/15, Sgt.; No. 14 O.C.B., 30/1/17; Durh. L.I., 25/4/17; F,It; Lieut.; g.
11 Bedford Row, W.C.1.

PRITCHARD, Benjamin John
B/12693, 6/3/18; No. 23. O.C.B., 9/8/18; K.R. Rif. C., 14/3/19, Indian Army, 23rd Lond. R.; Lieut.
143 Louisville Road, Upper Tooting, S.W.17.

✠ PRITCHARD, Charles Frederick
D/9926, 15/11/16; R.F.C., C/S, 13/3/17; R.F.C., 19/4/17; 2/Lieut.
Killed in action 17/9/17.

PRITCHARD, Douglas Leonard
6/3/7032, 27/10/15; No. 9 O.C.B., 8/3/16; Gord. Highrs., 3/8/16. Tank Corps; F; Lieut.; w.
11 Clive Street, P.O. Box 120, Calcutta, India.

✠ PRITCHARD, John Eric Stirling
6/Sq/7943, 29/11/15; R.F.A., C/S, 31/3/16; R.F.A., 2/8/16; 2/Lieut.
Died of wounds 27/10/17.

PRITCHARD, Percy John
A/B/D/12172, 29/10/17, L/C.; No. 21 O.C.B., 4/10/18; R. War. R., 17/3/19; 2/Lieut. 4 Redings Road, Moseley, Birmingham,

APPENDIX II.—RECORDS OF RANK AND FILE.

PRITCHARD, Thomas Archer
6/5/3/8251, 8/12/15; No. 3 O.C.B., 28/8/16; M.G.C., C/S; M.G.C., 9/12/16, Tank Corps, Indian Army; F,I; Lieut.
Ormeside, Springfield Road, Abergavenny, Monmouthshire.

PROBY, Granville
Sq/483, 8/4/10; Bedf. Yeo., 3/10/11; Capt.; w.
126a, St. James Court, Buckingham Gate, S.W.1.

PROBYN, Alfred Hugh
B/13540, 17/7/18; trfr. K.R. Rif. C., 7/4/19.
Eddington, High Road, Whetstone, N.20.

PROCTER, Alfred Paul
6/3/7403, 12/11/15, L/C.; R. Lanc. R., 4/8/16; Lieut.; M.C.

PROCTER, George Eric
1/3096, 22/3/15; R.G.A., 16/8/15; F; Lieut.; Inv.
64 Marlborough Road, Watford.

PROCTER, John Clifford
F/2763, 21/1/15; Glouc. R., 29/4/15; F; Capt.; M.C., M(1).
The Grange, Ilkley, Yorkshire.

PROCTER, Victor Charles
6/5/7473, 15/11/15; trfr. R.G.A., 21/7/16.
Alchester, Farnham Road, Guildford.

PROCTOR, Thomas Augustus Hugh
A/11191, 5/5/17; R.F.C., C/S, 1/6/17; R.F.C., 1/8/17, R.W. Fus., att. K.R. Rif. C. and Rif. Brig. R.A.F.; E; Lieut.
39 Hallewell Road, Edgbaston, Birmingham.

PROLE, John Cyril
6/9387, 8/2/16; dis. med. unfit, 2/6/16.
13 Tredegar Road, Ebbw Vale, Monmouthshire.

PROSSER, Cecil Ernest Gotterell
6/3/8734, 5/1/16; R.A., C/S, 23/6/16; R.G.A., 27/9/16; Lieut.
Llanishen, Nr. Cardiff.

PROSSER, Donald Sydney
6/2/5569, 12/8/15, L/C.; North'd. Fus., 21/4/16; F; Lieut.; M(1).
6 Harvist Road, N.W.6.

PROSSER, Wynford
B/10319, 4/1/17; trfr. 13th Lond. R., 16/2/17.
145 Clifton Street, Roath, Cardiff.

PROUD, Ernest Barton
A/10510, 15/1/17; No. 14 O.C.B., 5/5/17; S. Staff. R., 28/8/17; F; Lieut.; g.
5 Victoria Avenue, Bishops Auckland.

PROUDFOOT, Reginald
A/1272, 23/9/14, Sgt.; R.A.O.C., 4/6/15; Capt.; M(1).
97 Hill Lane, Southampton.

✠ PROUGHTEN, Charles Ernest
A/10494, 12/1/17; No. 14 O.C.B., 7/6/17; Surr. Yeo., 25/9/17; 2/Lieut.
Killed in action 23/5/18.

✠ PROUT, Douglas William
A/1912, 16/10/14; R. Berks. R., 27/11/14; 2/Lieut.
Killed in action 3/9/16.

PROUT, Edward Archibald
A/Sq/1528, 5/10/14; R. Berks. R., 30/11/14, Notts. Yeo.; Major

PRUDEN, William Colin
6/D/7593, 18/11/15; R.F.C., C/S, 28/12/16; R.F.C., 12/4/17, R.A.F.; Lieut.
6 Queen Street, Weymouth.

✠ PRUST, Henry Royston
6/5/7806, 24/11/15, Sgt.; Yorks. L.I., 6/7/16; Capt.; w(2).
Killed in action 20/11/17.

PRUST, Thomas Walter
6/2/5351, 2/8/15; Midd'x. R., 1/6/16; Capt.
2 Windsor Terrace, Swansea.

PRYER, Edward John
6/1/6632, 4/10/15; No. 11 O.C.B., 7/5/16; 7th Lond. R., 4/9/16, 19th Lond. R., Midd'x. R.; F; Lieut.; w(2), g; M(1).
59 Culverley Road, Catford, S.E.6.

PRYOR, Ernest Langman
4/6/2/4998, 19/7/15, L/C.; R.N.V.R., 21/11/16; F; Sub. Lieut.
Harford Lodge, 21 Vanbrugh Fields, Blackheath, S.E.3.

PRYS-JONES, Trevor Berwyn
A/13146, 24/5/18; No. 5 O.C.B., 8/11/18, No. 20 O.C.B.; R.W. Fus., 17/3/19; 2/Lieut.
Bryn Tegid, Pontypridd, Glamorganshire.

PUCKERING, Walter Ernest
C/B/12297, 7/12/17; No. 22 O.C.B., 7/6/18; trfr. Class W. Res., 2/11/18.
Solicitor, Pocklington, Yorkshire.

PUDDEPHATT, Claude Harold
D/13849, 16/8/18; trfr. K.R. Rif. C., 7/4/19.
11 Lexham Gardens, Amersham Common, Buckinghamshire.

PUDSEY, Edgar Harold
6/4/9125, 24/1/16; No. 8 O.C.B., 4/8/16; Wilts. R., 21/11/16, att. Devon. R.; S; Lieut.; Inv.
Lond. Joint City & Mid. Bk. Ltd., Coleford, Gloucester.

PUGH, Edward Pryce Hugh
C/10593, 8/1/17; No. 14 O.C.B., 7/6/17; Manch. R., 25/9/17; Lieut.

PUGH, Eric Victor
C/13223, 31/5/18; demob. 23/1/19.
90 Vaughan Road, New Brighton, Cheshire.

✠ PUGH, Henry Loyn
4/5/4870, 15/7/15; S. Wales Bord., 7/10/15; 2/Lieut.
Died of wounds 11/9/16.

PUGH, Maurice Henry
B/12423, 18/1/18; R.A., C/S, 24/5/18; R.G.A., 3/3/19; 2/Lieut.

PUGH, Stanley Thomas
6/3/7778, 23/11/15, L/C.; R.A., C/S, 7/8/16; R.G.A., 17/6/17; Lieut.
11 Foxfield Road, Great Meols, Cheshire.

PULLAN, Cyril Frank
F/1809, 16/10/14; E. Surr. R., 7/11/14, emp. M. of Munitions; Lieut.; w.

PULLAN, John William
D/E/13823, 12/8/18; R.G.A., C/S, 2/10/18; R.G.A., 11/4/19; 2/Lieut.
82 Westbourne Avenue, Hull.

PULMAN, Gerald Charles
H/1931, 22/10/14; 3rd Lond. R., 16/1/15, R.A.F.; Capt.; w.

PULMAN, Herbert Ernest Ambler
6/5/5265, 31/7/15; L'pool. R., 6/12/15; F; Lieut.; w.
50 Princess Street, Manchester.

✠ PUMPHREY, Hubert
6/2/9449, 14/2/16; No. 8 O.C.B., 4/8/16; Ches. R., 21/11/16; F; 2/Lieut.; w.
Killed in action 26/4/18.

PUNCHARD, Norman Alfred
B/12867, 27/3/18; No. 20 O.C.B., 20/9/18; R.W. Surr. R., 17/3/19; 2/Lieut.
14 St. Augustine's Avenue, South Croydon, Surrey.

PUNT, Alfred Arthur
6/3/7017, 26/10/15; No. 7 O.C.B., 7/4/16; 9th Lond. R., 17/7/16, R.A.F.; F,P; Lieut.; w.
73 Balham Park Road, S.W.12.

PURDON, John Rutledge
6/5/8252, 8/12/15; No. 7 O.C.B., 11/8/16; R. Ir. Rif., 18/12/16.
69 Scottish Provident Buildings, Belfast.

✠ PURKIS, Harold Arthur
6/4/5998, 2/9/15; M.G.C., 4/8/16; 2/Lieut.
Killed in action 28/7/17.

PURRY, Philip Stephen
3/3238, 12/4/15, Sgt.; Midd'x. R., 7/9/15; I,M; Capt.
51 Parliament Hill, Hampstead, N.W.3.

PURSSELL, Frederick John
B/13613, 24/7/18; demob. 5/2/19.
Small Dean Farm, Wendover, Buckinghamshire.

✠ PUSCH, Ernest John
4/3394, 26/4/15; R. War. R., 5/9/15; 2/Lieut.
Killed in action 8/8/16.

✠ PUTNAM, Edmund
D/10343, 4/1/17; R.A., C/S, 27/4/17; R.G.A., 1/9/17; 2/Lieut.
Died 16/4/18.

PYCRAFT, Harry George
A/10073, 1/12/16; No. 14 O.C.B., 30/1/17; L'pool. R., 25/4/17, M.G.C.; F; Lieut.
40 Admiral Street, Liverpool. (Now in India).

PYE, Charles Edward
6/2/7747, 22/11/15; No. 8 O.C.B., 4/8/16; Dorset R., 21/11/16, Devon. R.; F; Lieut.
27 Orion Road, Weymouth.

PYE, Herbert Garnet Wakeley
4/Sq/4700, 8/7/15, L/C.; R.F.A., 27/10/15, R.F.C.; F; Capt; g; M.C.
Clonsillagh, London Road, West Malling, Kent. (Now in Chile).

PYE, Lawrence Knell
4/Sq/4248, 14/6/15, L/C.; R.F.A., 8/9/15; M; Capt.; M(1).
The Kyns Court, Cobham, Surrey.

PYE, Simeon
6/5/6100, 6/9/15, L/C.; K.R. Rif. C., 23/4/16; F; Lieut.
Montrose, Wellington Road, Brighton.

APPENDIX II.—RECORDS OF RANK AND FILE.

PYLE, Desmond Elliot
B/12726, 14/3/18; H. Bde. O.C.B., 9/8/18; Scots Gds., 5/3/19; 2/Lieut.

✠ PYM, Francis Leslie Melville
B/944, 5/8/14; Linc. R., 12/9/14, Ir. Gds.; Lieut.
Killed in action 2/7/16.

✠ PYM, John Walter
4/4583, 1/7/15, L/C.; 9th Lond. R., 21/4/16; 2/Lieut.
Killed in action 7/7/16.

PYM, Robert Jenkins
6/Sq/7237, 5/11/15; No. 1 Cav. C/S, 24/4/16; R. Devon. Yeo., 1/6/16, 2nd Life Gds.; F; Lieut.
Lower Umkomaas, Natal, South Africa.

PYMAN, Geoffrey Lee
C/937, 5/8/14; Yorks. L.I., 12/9/14; F,It; Major; D.S.O., M.C., Croce di Guerra, M(4).   *50 Avenue Road, N.W. 8.*

PYMAN, Robert Lauder
C/10358, 5/1/17; trfr. R.G.A., 25/4/17.
35 Copers Cope Road, Beckenham, Kent.

✠ PYMAN, Ronald Lee
C/966, 5/8/14; Midd'x. R., 15/8/14; F; Lieut.
Killed in action 3/5/17.

PYMAN, William Haigh
D/1436, 29/9/14; R.F.A., 6/11/14, emp. M. of Shipping; Lieut.
57 Bishopsgate, E.C. 2.

PYNE, George Joslin
C/D/12036, 24/9/17; No. 13 O.C.B., 5/4/18; M.G.C., 29/10/18; 2/Lieut.   *Denver House, Topsham, Devonshire.*

✠ QUAILE, Robert Ernest Browne
B/11425, 24/5/17; No. 16 O.C.B., 5/10/17; R. Innis. Fus., 12/3/18; 2/Lieut.   *Killed in action 3/10/18.*

QUANCE, John Stanley
C/Sq/B/11451, 4/6/17; No. 2 Cav. C/S, 11/4/18; 5th R. Regt. of Cav., 18/10/18; 2/Lieut.
9 Gloucester Road, Birkdale, Nr. Southport, Lancashire.

QUARTERMAINE, Alfred John
6/4/7117, 1/11/15; E. Ang. Div. Cyc. Coy., 4/9/16, Army Cyc. Corps; F; Lieut.
71 Edenbridge Road, Bush Hill Park, N.

✠ QUEKETT, John
6/1/6913, 18/10/15; No. 9 O.C.B., 8/3/16; R. Highrs., 23/7/16; F; 2/Lieut.   *Killed in action 31/7/17.*

QUEKETT, Reginald Scott
6/1/7944, 29/11/15; No. 11 O.C.B., 7/5/16; R. Highrs., 4/9/16, R.A.F., emp. M. of Munitions; F; Lieut.; w.
Junior Army and Navy Club, Whitehall, S.W. 1.

QUILTER, Keith Molyneux
4/1/4381, 21/6/15, Sgt.; R.G.A., 8/11/15; Lieut.

✠ QUILTER, Roy Molyneux
A/955, 5/8/14; Bedf. & Herts. R., 19/9/14; F; Capt.; M(1).
Killed in action 19/4/16.

QUIN, Francis Noel
Sq/2880, 8/2/15; Bucks. Huss., 7/10/15; 2/Lieut.
22 Kingscliffe Gardens, Wimbledon Park, S.W. 19.

✠ QUIN, Leslie William Whitworth
6/1/7054, 28/10/15, L/C.; North'd. Fus., 24/4/16; Capt.; M.C.
Killed in action 24/4/17.

QUINEY, Charles Cyril
C/13308, 17/6/18; trfr. 14th Lond. R., 6/12/18, Gord. Highrs.; Pte.
Bickleigh, Guildersfield Road, Streatham, S.W. 16. (Now in Brazil).

QUINN, James
6/5/7474, 15/11/15; No. 9 O.C.B., 8/3/16; R. Sco. Fus., 6/7/16; F; Lieut.; w; M.C. and Bar.
Martin Cottage, Auchinleck, Ayrshire.

QUINNEY, Harold
D/3033, 11/3/15, Sgt.; L'pool. R., 21/6/15, Lan. Fus.; Capt.; w.
14 Lichfield Grove, Church End, Finchley, N. 3.

QUINT, Sidney Tyers
K/F/2278, 7/12/14; S. Lan. R., 24/2/15; F; Capt.; w(2); M(1).
South African Officers' Club, Grosvenor Square, W. 1.

QUIRKE, Raymond Fitzwilliam
6/4/5693, 17/8/15, Sgt.; R.A., C/S, 31/3/16; R.G.A., 2/8/16, att. R.A.F.; Capt.; O.B.E.   *22 Compton Avenue, Brighton.*

RABAGLIATI, Herman Victor
Sq/479, 8/4/10; dis. 5/7/11; R.F.C., R.A.F.; F; Capt.
3 New Court, Carey Street, W.C. 2.

RABY, John Nettleton
B/10769, 16/2/17; R.F.C., C/S, 16/4/17; R.F.C., 16/5/17.
Hendra, St. Germans, Cornwall.

RABY, Thomas David
B/11710, 19/7/17; R.F.C., C/S, 23/10/17; R.F.C., 26/2/18, R.A.F.; F; Lieut.; w.   *16 Kent House Road, Sydenham, S.E. 26.*

RABY, Victor Harry
6/7945, 29/11/15, L/C.; 7th Lond. R., 24/10/16, att. 22nd Lond. R.; F; Capt.; M.C., M(1).
16 Pelham Road, South Woodford, Essex.

✠ RACINE, Ernest Guy
6/5/7786, 24/11/15, Sgt.; L'pool. R., 24/10/16; 2/Lieut.
Killed in action 9/4/17.

RACKHAM, George Mutimer
B/Sq/12016, 17/9/17; No. 1 Cav. C/S, 16/5/18; 4th R. Regt. of Cav., 14/2/19; 2/Lieut.   *Hill House, Hethel, Norwich.*

RACKOWE, Alexander Daudet
C/14219, 23/10/18; No. 11 O.C.B., 24/1/19; General List, 8/3/19; 2/Lieut.

RADBONE, Victor James
D/12896, 9/4/18; R.E., C/S, 23/8/18; R.E., 8/4/19; 2/Lieut.
83 Cannon Street, E.C. 4.

RADCLIFFE, David Ernest
B/D/13521, 12/7/18; trfr. K.R. Rif. C., 27/5/19.
Penmark Place, Rhoos, Nr. Cardiff.

✠ RADCLIFFE, Ernest Charles Derwentwater
6/5/8118, 2/12/15; No. 8 O.C.B., 4/8/16; R.W. Fus., 21/11/16; 2/Lieut.   *Killed in action 31/7/17.*

RADCLIFFE, Geoffrey Reynolds
Sq/232, 16/5/08; dis. 15/5/09; rej. Sq/935, 5/8/14, Cpl.; 23rd Lond. R., 14/11/14; Capt.; w.
Radcliffe Observatory, Oxford.

✠ RADCLIFFE, John Douglas Henderson
A/943, 5/8/14; K.R. Rif. C., 12/9/14; F; Capt.
Died of wounds 30/7/15.

RADCLYFFE, Edward John Dilston
B/11401, 28/5/17, L/C.; No. 2 O.C.B., 9/11/17; Hunts. Cyc. Bn., 26/3/18, att. Bedf. R.; 2/Lieut.   *4 Holly Terrace, N. 6.*

RADFORD, William
A/12504, 28/1/18; No. 21 O.C.B., 7/6/18; Oxf. & Bucks. L.I., 4/2/19; 2/Lieut.   *6 Ferme Park Mansions, Hornsey, N. 8.*

RADFORD, William Vincent
6/2/8273, 9/12/15; R.F.C., 13/9/16, R.A.F.; F,It; Lieut.
Kenilworth Road, Coventry.

RADLOFF, Heinrich
4/5015, 22/7/15, L/C.; 11th Lond. R., 21/10/15, att. R.F.C.; Lieut.   *c/o J. Flanagan & Son, 5 Fenchurch Street, E.C. 3.*

RAE, Norman Dunbar
H/2684, 14/1/15; York. & Lanc. R., 5/5/15; F; Lieut.
13 Carlton Drive, Shipley, Yorkshire.

RAE, William
6/3/7219, 4/11/15; No. 9 O.C.B., 8/3/16; High. L.I., 23/7/16, att. Tank Corps; F; Capt.; w.   *28 Queen Street, Dumfries.*

RAE, William Wilson
2057, 9/11/14; R.A.S.C., 20/3/15; F,S; Capt.
38 Addison Gardens, Kensington, W. 14.

RAGGETT, Frank Sydney
C/12603, 13/2/18; trfr. K.R. Rif. C., 7/4/19.
68 Perryn Road, Acton, W. 3.

RAILTON, Eric Pownall
6/5/5686, 16/8/15; York. & Lanc. R., 4/9/16, att. Chinese Lab. Corps; F; Lieut.   *Chefoo, Northern China.*

RAINE, Thomas Foster
B/10129, 6/12/16; No. 20 O.C.B., 5/5/17; E. Kent R., 28/8/17; 2/Lieut.; w.   *54 Lyncroft Gardens, West Hampstead, N.W. 6.*

✠ RAISTRICK, John William
6/1/6970, 22/10/15, L/C.; No. 11 O.C.B., 7/5/16; W. York. R., 4/9/16; 2/Lieut.   *Killed in action 19/5/17.*

RAIT, Donald McCulloch
D/12998, 29/4/18; No. 16 O.C.B., 18/10/18; Midd'x. R., 17/3/19; 2/Lieut.   *20 Queens Road, Hendon, N.W. 4.*

APPENDIX II.—RECORDS OF RANK AND FILE.

RAIT, Robert
Sq/144, 18/4/08; dis. 17/4/11.
Milton, Haine Road, Beckenham, Kent.

RALFS, Clifford Eric
6/7560, 17/11/15; dis. med. unfit, 8/8/16.
Barbizon, West End Avenue, Pinner, Middlesex.

✠ RALFS, Francis Arthur
F/1766, 16/10/14; R. Fus., 20/2/15; att. Lan. Fus.; Lieut.
Died of wounds 16/9/16.

✠ RALPHS, Walter Joel
K/B/2329, 14/12/14; R.F.A., 30/12/14; F; Capt.
Died of wounds 16/7/16.

✠ RAM, Percival John
4/5609, 16/8/15, L/C.; Manch. R., 26/10/15; F; 2/Lieut.
Killed in action 1/7/16.

RAMBAUT, Hugh Calder
Sq/775, 27/3/14, Sgt.; Bedf. Yeo., 14/1/15, att. 8th Huss.; F; Lieut.
Radcliffe Observatory, Oxford.

RAMSAY, Arthur Douglas
4/2759, 21/1/15; R.A.S.C., 7/4/15; Capt.
Howletts, Canterbury, Kent.

✠ RAMSAY, Keith Winton
K/H/2284, 8/12/14, L/C.; K.R. Rif. C., 8/4/15; Lieut.
Killed in action 3/5/16.

RAMSAY, Robert Guy
4/3/4027, 7/6/15; Sco. Rif., 27/8/15; 2/Lieut.
Homelea, Maybole, Ayrshire.

RAMSAY, William Aubrey
6/1/3292, 16/9/15; Oxf. & Bucks. L.I., 1/6/16, Indian Army; F,I,E; Capt.; p.
c/o Revd. W. Ramsay, Radclive, Buckinghamshire. (Now in Egypt).

RAMSAY-ANDERSON, James
C/D/12278, 3/12/17; R.E., C/S, 16/6/18, No. 11 O.C.B.; General List, 8/3/19; 2/Lieut.

RAMSBOTHAM, Herewald
A/863, 4/8/14; Bedf. R., 12/9/14; F; Major, D.A.A.G.; O.B.E., M.C., M(3).
3/4 Lothbury, E.C. 2.

RAMSBOTTOM, Laurance
C/D/12301, 11/12/17; R.F.A., C/S, 17/5/18; R.F.A., 15/2/19; 2/Lieut.
38 Irwell Street, Radcliffe, Manchester.

RAMSDEN, Henry
4/3/4910, 17/7/15; Manch. R., 18/10/15; F; Lieut.; g.
Rose Cottage, Cemetery Road, Lidget Green, Bradford, Yorkshire.

RAMSDEN, Norman
A/10078, 1/12/16; R.F.C., C/S, 13/3/17; R.F.C., 19/4/17, R.A.F.; Lieut.
5 Kings Mount, Birkenhead.

RAMSDEN, Robert Charles Plumptre
B/13491, 8/7/18; No. 22 O.C.B., 23/8/18; Notts. & Derby. R., 13/2/19; 2/Lieut.
Wigthorpe Hill, Worksop.

RAMSEY, Leonard Allan
6/1/5634, 16/8/15; E. Kent R., 7/7/16; I,M; Capt.
4 Esplanade, Dover, Kent.

RAMSEY, Richard Neville
C/D/12073, 1/10/17; No. 8 O.C.B., 5/4/18; 14th Lond. R., 8/10/18; 2/Lieut.
The Hollies, London Road, Hampton, Middlesex.

RAMSEY, Walter James
C/63, 8/4/08; R.A.S.C., 17/6/11; F; Major.
5 Grange Road West, Jarrow.

RANCE, Cecil Joseph
A/13176, 31/5/18; demob. 29/1/19.
415 High Road, Chiswick, W. 4.

RANCE, Douglas Gordon
B/13507, 10/7/18; demob. 29/1/19.
24a St. Martins, Stamford, Lincolnshire. (Now in British East Africa).

RAND, Carl
A/B/C/12161, 25/10/17; Garr. O.C.B., 8/3/18; Lab. Corps, 4/9/18; 2/Lieut.
Oakwood, Shipley, Yorkshire.

RANDALL, Bertie Charles
4/3/6/4506, 28/6/15; dis. med. unfit, 8/8/16; rej. D/11808, 9/8/17; dis. med. unfit, 3/12/17.
4 Park Road, Cromer, Norfolk.

RANDALL, Charles William
6/8884, 13/1/16; trfr. Class W. Res., 15/7/16.
Seafield, Blundellsands, Liverpool.

✠ RANDALL, Frank Horace
6/3/8314, 11/12/15; No. 2 O.C.B., 14/8/16; Norf. R., 18/12/16; 2/Lieut.
Killed in action 18/7/17.

RANDALL, Leslie Ernest
F/2904, 11/2/15, L/C.; 22nd Lond. R., 8/6/15, Indian Army; F,S,P,I,E; Capt.
Coonoor, 10 Avenue Road, South Norwood Park, S.E. 25. (Now in India).

RANDALL, Sidney Walter
C/10185, 13/12/16; R.F.C., C/S, 13/3/17; R.F.C., 19/4/17; 2/Lieut.
Died 3/10/17.

RANDALL, Stuart Hume
6/7368, 10/11/15; R.F.A., C/S, 9/6/16; R.F.A., 30/9/16; F; Lieut.; g.
104 Stapleton Hall Road, Stroud Green, N. 4.

RANDALL, William Haselwood
B/10104, 4/12/16; R.W. Surr. R., 9/3/17; 2/Lieut.
Kesama, Dunmow, Essex.

RANDELL, George
C/11521, 18/6/17; R.F.C., C/S, 2/8/17; R.F.C., 8/9/17, R.A.F.; 2/Lieut.; Inj.
6 Theresa Place, Bristol Road, Gloucester.

RANFT, Rudolph Cecil
C/10317, 4/1/17; R.A., C/S, 29/6/17; R.G.A., 2/12/17; lt; 2/Lieut.
Rushmere, 33 Canadian Avenue, Catford, S.E. 6.

RANGER, Cecil Argill
D/1461, 29/9/14; Norf. R., 26/3/15; I; Capt.
179 Queen Victoria Street, E.C. 4.

RANKIN, Andrew Fulton
B/11679, 16/7/17; Tank Corps, C/S, 2/11/17; Tank Corps, 25/6/18; 2/Lieut.
Westray, Birkenhead Road, Meols, Cheshire.

✠ RANKIN, Frederick Alan
6/2/7246, 6/11/15; No. 11 O.C.B., 16/5/16; Bord. R., 4/9/16; 2/Lieut.
Killed in action 23/4/17.

RANKIN, Reginald John
6/2/8511, 29/12/15; R.F.C., 7/7/16.
County School, Bridgend, Glamorganshire.

✠ RANSDALE, Alfred Charles
C/11495, 14/6/17; No. 19 O.C.B., 9/11/17; N. Lan. R., 30/4/18; 2/Lieut.
Killed in action 1/9/18.

RANSOM, Christopher
B/11993, 10/9/17; Tank Corps, C/S, 23/11/17; Tank Corps, 8/10/18; 2/Lieut.
Newlands, Hitchin, Hertfordshire.

✠ RANSON, Charles Sherriff
6/4/8904, 13/1/16, L/C.; 13th Lond. R., 18/12/16; 2/Lieut.
Killed in action 16/8/17.

RANSON, Harold
6/5/6334, 20/9/15; Arg. & Suth'd. Highrs., 31/10/16; F,I; Lieut.; w.
9 Normanhurst Road, Streatham Hill, S.W. 2.

RAPHAEL, Osmond Philip
4/5/4806, 12/7/15, L/C.; 8th Lond. R., 20/10/15; F; Lieut.; w; m.
The Warren, Northwood.

RAPLEY, Frederic Ardern
D/10431, 10/1/17, L/C.; R.F.A., C/S, 22/6/17; R.F.A., 17/11/17.
Moorgate Hall, Finsbury Pavement, E.C. 2.

RAPLEY, Harold Charles
C/10181, 13/12/16; R.W. Surr. R., 9/3/17, Lab. Corps; F; Capt.; M(1).
Monkton Cottage, Monks Risboro', Buckinghamshire.

✠ RAPOPORT, John Lindsay
6/5/9022, 19/1/16, L/C.; No. 2 O.C.B., 14/8/16; Rif. Brig., 18/12/16; 2/Lieut.; w.
Killed in action 27/5/18.

RAPSON, Douglas Sibree
6/1/7336, 9/11/15; No. 14 O.C.B., 26/11/16; Shrop Yeo., 27/3/17, att. R.A.F.; E,F; Lieut.
206 Leigh Road, Leigh-on-Sea, Essex.

RAPSON, Harold Arthur
D/13814, 12/8/18; trfr. K.R. Rif. C., 7/4/19.
32 Kings Road, Wimbledon, S.W. 19.

RASHLEIGH, Henry Pelham
C/40, 6/4/08; 10th Lond. R., 16/11/12, 9th Lond. R.; Capt.
Riseley, Horton Kirby, Kent.

RATCLIFF, Samuel Geoffrey
B/Sq/11346, 23/5/17; No. 1 Cav. C/S, 28/2/18; R. Regt. of Cav., 28/8/18; 2/Lieut.
Mowden Hall, Hatfield Peverel, Essex.

APPENDIX II.—RECORDS OF RANK AND FILE.

✠ RATCLIFF-GAYLARD, Eric Ronald
4/3557, 10/5/15, Cpl.; D. of Corn. L.I., 5/7/15; F; 2/Lieut.
Killed in action 19/7/16.

✠ RATHBONE, John Ernest Vivian
4/3148, 31/3/15, Sgt.; Dorset R., 11/6/15; Lieut.; w.
Killed in action 4/6/18.

RATHBONE, Maurice
A/11653, 12/7/17; No. 14 O.C.B., 9/11/17; R. Fus., 30/4/18; 2/Lieut.

RATLIFF, Derwent William
A/2894, 9/2/15; R.F.A., 30/3/15; Lieut.; w.

RATTO, Frank Louis
6/4/8972, 17/1/16; No. 8 O.C.B., 4/8/16; R.W. Fus., 21/11/16; F; Capt.; g; M.C.
4 Elm Court, Temple, E.C. 4.

✠ RATTON, Wilfrid Holroyd
A/455, 21/12/09; 22nd Lond. R., 12/7/12; 2/Lieut.
Died 9/7/15.

RAVEN, Charles Henry
6/8034, 30/11/15; A.S.C., C/S, 6/3/16; R.A.S.C., 7/5/16; Lieut.
38 Dartmouth Row, Blackheath, S.E 10.

RAVEN, Edward Earle
6/4/6841, 14/10/15; Chaplain, 1/1/17.
St. Mary's Clergy House, Provost Street, W 1.

RAVEN, Henry Vincent
6/5/7946, 29/11/15; Suff. R., 25/9/16, att. Camb. R., Suff. R.; F; Capt.; w(3).
Homecote, Royelle Road, Parkstone, Dorset.

RAVEN-HILL, Lucien Ennar
B/2074, 12/11/14; Kent Cyc. Bn., 17/3/15, Indian Army; Capt.

RAVN, Walter Alfred
6/D/8735, 5/1/16; trfr. 19th Lond. R., 25/5/17.
49 Avonmore Road, West Kensington, W. 14.

RAWCLIFFE, Wallace Bernard
6/4/5289, 1/8/15; Hamps. R., 24/10/15; 2/Lieut.
50 Poulton Street, Kirkham, Lancashire.

RAWES, Frederick Renshaw
6/2/9446, 14/2/16; No. 8 O.C.B., 4/8/16; Manch. R., 21/11/16; F; 2/Lieut.; w.
Brooklyn, Stainton, Penrith, Cumberland.

RAWES, Glennie
B/D/11994, 10/9/17; No. 21 O.C.B., 5/4/18; R.W. Surr. R., 24/9/18; 2/Lieut.
c/o Rawes & Coy., Rua da Nova Affandega, Oporto, Portugal.

RAWLE, John
Sq/536, 13/1/11; dis. 5/2/13; rej. Sq/982, 5/8/14; 4th Drag. Gds., 15/8/14; F; Lieut.
New University Club, St. James, S.W. 1.

RAWLE, Thomas Frederick
K/H/2350, 14/12/14; S. Wales Bord., 24/2/15; F; Lieut.; w; M.C.
Herongate House, Brentwood, Essex.

RAWLES, Cecil Howard Lancaster
6/8585, 3/1/16; A.S.C., C/S, 22/5/16; R.A.S.C., 25/6/16; Lieut.
107 Priory Road, West Hampstead, N.W.

✠ RAWLINGS, Leonard Justly
E/1551, 6/10/14; General List, 10/2/15; North'n. R.; F; 2/Lieut.
Killed in action 7/11/16.

RAWLINS, Arthur Rae Denby
2947, 18/2/15; Durh. L.I., 23/2/15, Lab. Corps; Capt.; w.
The Moorings, Bray-on-Thames.

✠ RAWLINS, Gerald Edmund Adair
C/605, 13/2/12, Cpl.; R. Fus., 11/9/14; Capt.
Killed in action 7/7/16.

RAWLINS, Reginald Sparrow Pyhsent
Sq/975, 5/8/14; S. Wales Bord., 23/10/14, att. R.W. Fus.; Capt.; M.C.
11 West Halkin Street, Belgrave Square, S.W. 1.

RAWLINSON, Arthur Richard
B/995, 5/8/14; R.W. Surr. R., 1/9/14; Lieut.
10 Burghley Road, Wimbledon, S.W. 19.

✠ RAWLINSON, Curwen Vaughan
K/2109, 16/11/14; Dorset R., 16/12/14; 2/Lieut.
Killed in action 22/5/15.

RAWLINSON, Harold
6/2/9047, 21/1/16; No. 14 O.C.B., 30/10/16, M.G.C., C/S.; M.G.C., 30/1/17; Lieut.
241 Edge Lane, Liverpool.

RAWLINSON, John
B/10337, 4/1/17; M.G.C., C/S, 4/5/17; Tank Corps, 29/9/17; F; 2/Lieut.; w; M.C.
Holmlea, Egerton Park, Worsley, Lancashire.

RAWNSLEY, George Tennant
6/4/9091, 24/1/16; No. 8 O.C.B., 4/8/16; Rif. Brig., 24/10/16; F; 2/Lieut.
11 Valencia Bungalows, Eccleston Park, Nr. Prescott, Lancashire.

RAWSON, Charles Herbert
D/2913, -/2/15; Midd'x. R., 22/4/15; F; 2/Lieut.; w.
Holmwood, Ashfield Road, Leicester.

RAWSON-SHAW, Thomas
Sq/1092, 5/9/14; Suss. Yeo., 27/10/14, 1st Life Gds.; F; Lieut.
Slindon, Nr. Arundel, Sussex.

RAY, Francis William
C/14305, 27/11/18; No. 3 O.C.B., 10/2/19; L'pool. R., 19/3/19; 2/Lieut.
12 Lancaster Avenue, Sefton Park, Liverpool.

RAY, Frank Hubert
6/1/5664, 16/8/15; trfr. R.G.A., 16/10/16.

RAYDEN, Lionel Grahame
6/2/7078, 29/10/15; 8th Lond. R., 4/8/16, att. M.G.C.; F; Lieut.
c/o Thomas Fox & Coy. Ltd., 2 New Broad Street, E.C. 2.

RAYMOND, Percy James
4/1/4405, 24/6/15; 10th Lond. R., 1/11/15; Lieut.
11 Wightman Road, Harringay, N. 4.

RAYMOND-BARKER, Aubrey Basil
6/1/6150, 9/9/15, L/C.; R.F.C., 26/5/16, R.A.F.; Lieut.; w

✠ RAYMOND-BARKER, Cecil Langton. See BARKER, C. L. R.

RAYMONT, William Hodge
C/Sq/11522, 18/6/17, L/C.; No. 2 Cav. C/S, 21/1/18; demob. 17/1/19.
4/6 Hemwoods Arcade, Johannesburg, South Africa.

✠ RAYNBIRD, Leonard Barton
6/2/D/5665, 16/8/15, L/C.; No. 14 O.C.B., 30/1/17; Hamps. R., 25/4/17; F,It; Lieut.
Died.

RAYNE, William George. See COWIE, W. G.

✠ RAYNER, Haydn Eric William
6/2/5635, 16/8/15; Oxf. & Bucks. L.I., 16/11/15; 2/Lieut.
Killed in action 17/3/17.

RAYSON, Alexander Arnold
D/1421, 29/9/14; Suff. R., 7/3/15; Lieut.
25 Belsize Avenue, Hampstead, N.W. 3.

RAZZELL, Albert Maurice
D/11871, 16/8/17; No. 3 O.C.B., 8/2/18; R.W. Kent. R., 30/7/18; F; Lieut.; M.C.
67 Ceres Road, Plumstead, S.E. 18.

REA, Reginald Riviere
K/B/2309, 10/12/14; R. Dub. Fus., 1/2/15; Lieut.

REA, William George
6/3/8657, 3/1/16; No. 2 O.C.B., 14/8/16; Ir. Gds., 18/12/16; F; g-w.
6 Clarendon Place, Gravesend, Kent.

READ, Alfred Burgess
A/D/11938, 30/8/17; H. Bde., O.C.B., 5/4/18; Welch Gds., 24/9/18; 2/Lieut.
4 Longstone Road, Eastbourne.

READ, Cecil Finlay
F/1789, 16/10/14; R. Suss. R., 15/11/14; 2/Lieut.

READ, Ewart Kingsley
B/10111, 4/12/16; No. 14 O.C.B., 5/3/17; Essex R., 26/6/17; Lieut.
87 Church Hill, Walthamstow, E. 17.

✠ READ, Harry Esmond
Sq/1017, 7/8/14; Linc. Yeo., 25/11/14, att. R.F.C.; Capt.
Killed in action 10/8/17.

READ, Horace Samuel
D/11872, 16/8/17, L/C.; No. 3 O.C.B., 8/2/18; 7th Lond. R., 30/7/18; 2/Lieut.
116 Chestnut Avenue, Forest Gate, E. 7.

READ, John
A/Sq/13177, 31/5/18, L/C.; demob. 20/1/19.
Ibsley, Ringwood, Hampshire.

READ, Maurice Rix
A/50, 7/4/08; dis. 6/4/11; R.W. Surr. R., 15/9/14, M.G.C.; F; Lieut.; w.
c/o J. S Moon Esq., 172 Barcombe Avenue, S.W. 2. (Now in India).

APPENDIX II.—RECORDS OF RANK AND FILE.

READ, Ralph Sidney
C/11754, 26/7/17, L/C.; Sigs. C/S, 14/12/17; R.E., 24/5, 18; 2/Lieut.

READ, Richard Spencer
B/Sq/10579, 19/1/17, L/C.; No. 2 Cav. C/S, 11/1/18; demob. 3/2/19.　　　Black Diamond Coy., British Columbia.

READ, Sidney
3/6/7748, 22/11/15, L/C.; 5th Lond. R., 4/8/16, Intelligence Corps; F,NR; Lieut.; M.B.E., M.C., M(1).
117 Fawnbrake Avenue, Herne Hill, S.E. 24.

READ, William
3/3513, 6/5/15, Cpl.; 13th Lond. R., 22/9/15; Lieut.; w; M.C., M(1).　　　Clifton, Alton Road, Croydon, Surrey.

READE, John Bacon
6/5/9550, 23/2/16; R.A., C/S, 7/8/16; R.F.A., 3/12/16; F; Lieut.; w.　　　5 Bingham Road, Bournemouth.

REAH, John
6/Sq/8709, 5/1/16; No. 1 Cav. C/S, 2/8/16; E. Rid. Yeo., 27/11/16; F; Capt.; Merite Agricole.
Newlands, Gosforth, Newcastle-on-Tyne.

RECORDON, David Aubrey
1/2026, -/9/14; K.R. Rif. C., 3/6/15, att. R.A.F.; F; Lieut.; w.
97 High Street, Berkhamsted, Hertfordshire.

REDDEN, Frederick Adam Corrie
B/234, 18/5/08; dis. 1/11/13; rej. B/1434, 29/9/14, C.Q.M.S.; Garr. O.C.B., 27/8/17; Worc. R., 27/11/17, att. Chinese Lab Corps; F; 2/Lieut.　　　17 Victoria Street, S.W.1.

REDFERN, Norman
6/1/8932, 15/1/16; No. 2 O.C.B., 14/8/16; Rif. Brig., 18/12/16, att. T.M. Bty.; F; Lieut.; w; M.C.　Bank of England, E.C. 2.

REDGRAVE, Charles Reginald
3/5359, 3/8/15, Sgt.; Linc. R., 28/12/15, M.G.C.; S; Major; M.C.　　　30 Blythwood Road, Crouch Hill, N. 4.

REDGRAVE, Percy Rutherford
D/11140, 30/4/17, L/C.; Garr. O.C.B., 30/11/17; Lab. Corps, 23/2/18; F; 2/Lieut.
Eastney, 13 Buckingham Road, South Woodford, Essex.

REDHOUSE, Harold Edward
4/2/5127, 26/7/15; Midd'x. R., 28/11/15; F; Lieut.
17 Westbourne Gardens, Folkestone.

REDMAN, Robert
Sq/3395, 26/4/15; R.H.A., 10/11/15; Lieut.
4 Albion Terrace, Gravesend.

REDMAN, Roy
6/1/8001, 29/11/15; R.A., C/S, 7/8/16; R.G.A., 18/10/16; F; Staff Lieut.
Albert Cottage, Higher Bank Road, Fulwood, Preston, Lancashire.

REDSHAW, Douglas Samuel
B/13541, 17/7/18; trfr. 7/4/19.
51 Cambridge Mansions, S.W. 11.

REDSTONE, Alfred George
A/11959, 3/9/17; R.F.C., C/S, 26/11/17; R.F.C., 6/3/18; 2/Lieut.
57 Atherley Road, Southampton.

REDWOOD, Frederick Arthur
B/11309, 21/5/17; No. 14 O.C.B., 7/9/17; Shrop. L.I., 17/12/17; 2/Lieut.　　　8 Harcourt Terrace, Salisbury.

REECE, Francis Bertram
B/10537, 17/1/17; trfr. Class W. Res., 25/5/17.

REECE, George Macaulay Stevenson
Sq/613, 29/2/12; dis. to re-enlist in Regular Army, 1/4/13.
33 Duke Street, St. James, S.W. 1.

REED, Arthur Eric
B/13614, 24/7/18; trfr. R. Suss. R., 7/5/19.
1 Wesley Villas, Frome, Somerset.

REED, Arthur Weston
2/3097, 22/3/15, L/C.; E. Surr. R., 8/8/15; F; Lieut.; w.
176 Barcombe Avenue, Streatham Hill, S.W. 2.

REED, Charles Arundel
A/14048, 23/9/18; demob. 6/1/19.　97 Alwa Road, Bournemouth.

REED, Charles James Johnson
E/2798, 26/1/15; R.E., 12/6/15; F; Capt.; w; M.C., M(1).
Coham, Highampton, North Devonshire.

REED, Ian Francis
D/11583, 2/7/17; dis. med. unfit, 1/2/19.
Crellow, South Road, Stithians, Cornwall.

REED, Thomas
6/B/3/8742, 6/1/16; Garr. O.C.B., 19/2/17; Midd'x. R., 14/4/17; NR; Capt.; M.B.E., Order of S. Stanislaus.
Crown Road, Chesterfield.

REES, David Edmunds
4/3873, 31/5/15; North'n. R., 17/6/15.
Garth Hall, Abertridwr, Cardiff.

REES, David Ivor
6/D/8442, 16/12/15; No. 14 O.C.B., 30/10/16; Welch R., 28/2/17
Trem-y-Wawr, Burry Point.

REES, David Kenvyn
D/11094, 20/4/17, L/C.; No. 14 O.C.B., 10/8/17; S. Wales Bord., 27/11/17; F; 2/Lieut.　　　Ely, Cardiff.

REES, Evan Gwyn
A/13166, 29/5/18; R.E., C/S, 21/7/18; R.E., 18/1/19; 2/Lieut.
Wellfield, Aberavon, Port Talbot, South Wales.

REES, Francis Llewelyn
A/12535, 31/1/18; R.A., C/S, 17/5/18; R.G.A., 3/4/19; 2/Lieut.
Menai, Delwyn Avenue, Hengoed, Via Cardiff.

REES, Henry Draver
6/5/7475, 15/11/15; R.W. Fus., 4/8/16, att. 4th Lond. R.; F; Capt.　　　1 Teilo Street, Cardiff.

REES, Hubert Leonard
D/2840, 1/2/15; 24th Lond. R., 7/5/15; F,S.P; Capt
136 Denmark Hill, S.E. 5.

REES, Lionel William
6/2/8551, 30/12/15; M.G.C., 25/9/16; F; Major.
c/o National Bank of South Africa Ltd., P.O. Box 434, Pretoria, South Africa.

REES, Rees
6/5/6710, 8/10/15, L/C.; R.W. Fus., 4/8/16, att. S. Lan. R.; F; Capt.; g.　15 Rockingham Terrace, Briton Ferry, South Wales.

REES, Richard Eric Bowen
4/5/4762, 12/7/15; R.W. Fus., 23/1/16; Lieut.; M.C.
c/o Bevan, 28 The Promenade, Swansea.

REES, Vernon Walters
6/2/6335, 20/9/15; Mon. R., 7/11/16, att. Manch. R.; Lieut.
Pacific Villa, Briton Ferry, South Wales.

REES, William
6/3/9323, 5/2/16; No. 2 O.C.B., 14/8/16; W. Rid. R., 18/12/16; F; Lieut.;　Brynpedol, Brynammon, Carmarthenshire.

REES, William Lewis
6/5/C/6742, 11/10/15; trfr. M.G.C., 3/11/16; M.
36 Romilly Road, Barry, Glamorganshire.

REES, W. L. See LLOYD-REES, W.

REEVE, Albert
6/1/5593, 12/8/15; E. Surr. R., 19/1/16; I; Capt.
24 Twisden Road, Highgate Road, N.W. 5.

REEVE, Charles Robert
4/5/4893, 15/7/15; R. Fus., 24/12/15; Suff. R.; Lieut.
Gisleham Lodge, Gisleham, Nr. Lowestoft.

REEVE, Francis Henry Ernest
3/3558, 10/5/15; North'd. Fus., 5/8/15, R.A.F.; Capt.; w.

✠ REEVE, Gilfrid Montier
D/1438, 29/9/14; Essex R., 27/11/14; F; Capt.; w.
Killed in action 8/7/16.

✠ REEVE, Herbert
2/3514, 6/5/15, L/C.; R. Suss. R., 21/8/15.　Died 8/2/17.

✠ REEVE, Walter James
6/1/5308, 2/8/15; Devon. R., 24/6/16; M; Lieut.
Died 29/11/18.

REEVE-BALL, Lionel Arthur
4/3/4051, 7/6/15; dis. 11/8/15.

REEVES, Bernard George
4/1/4110, 7/6/15; trfr. 15th Lond. R., 23/8/16, att. Tank Corps; F; Cpl.　　　194a West End Lane, Hampstead, N.W. 6.

REEVES, Brian
K/B/2234, 3/12/14, L/C.; R.W. Fus., 13/3/15; F,It; Major; M.C., M(1).　62 Kensington Park Road, W. 11. (Now in Italy)

REEVES, Cecil Gilbert
6/5/7018, 26/10/15; Oxf. & Bucks. L.I., 10/6/16; F,It; Capt.; M.C., M(1).
Headquarters, Bucks. Bn., O. & B.L.I., Market Place, Aylesbury.

REEVES, Charles Ernest
A/9818, 30/10/16, L/C.; No. 14 O.C.B., 30/1/17; R. Fus., 29/5/17; F; Lieut.; w.　　　28 Colville Square, W. 11.

APPENDIX II.—RECORDS OF RANK AND FILE.

REEVES, Charles Westcott
4/3201, 8/4/15; R.A.S.C., 30/8/15; F; Capt.
Bramshaw, Uplands Park, Enfield, Middlesex.

REEVES, Cordlandt Cedric
D/Sq/10658, 5/2/17; R.A., C/S, 10/8/17; R.G.A., 13/5/18; 2/Lieut. Mansfield, Hazelgrove Road, Hampstead, N.W. 6.

REEVES, Philip Arthur
A/875, 4/8/14; R. Fus., 5/10/14, Army Cyc. Corps; Lieut.

REEVES, William Harold
6/D/9398, 9/2/16; R.A., C/S, 26/10/16, Garr. O.C.B.; Lab. Corps, 2/11/18; 2/Lieut. Langford, Nr. Bristol.

REFFELL, Edward
6/5/D/A/8552, 30/12/15, Cpl.; R.F.C., C/S, 1/2/17; R.F.C., 12/4/17, R.A.F.; E; Lieut.; cr.
Burwood, Caterham Valley, Surrey.

REFFITT, Frank
6/4/2/7184, 3/11/15; dis. med. unfit, 8/8/16.
Ringshall, Nr. Berkhamsted.

REID, Alexander Arthur
A/11030, 2/4/17; No. 14 O.C.B., 10/8/17; N. Cyc. Bn., 27/11/17.
Danmore, Willaston, Nr. Chester.

REID, Andrew
B/10342, 4/1/17; R.W. Surr. R., 22/3/17.

✠ REID, Duncan F. Cunningham
Sq/1091, 4/9/14; Interpreter, 4/9/14, att. R.F.C.; 2/Lieut.
Killed in action 19/12/15.

REID, Edward Dutton
C/13213, 5/6/18; R.E., C/S, 1/11/18; demob.
Sefton, Inveresk Place, Coatbridge, Scotland.

REID, Harry Farquharson Begg
D/2948, 18/2/15; R.E., 11/4/15; Capt.

REID, Hugh Courtney
K/2141, 19/11/14; Wilts. R., 27/11/14; w(2).
71 Holbein House, Sloane Square, S.W. 1.

✠ REID, James
6/4/7561, 17/11/15; No. 9 O.C.B., 8/3/16; High. L.I., 6/7/16; 2/Lieut. Died of wounds 1/2/17.

REID, James Henry W.
6/5/7849, 25/11/15, Sgt.; Suss. Yeo., 18/5/16; Lieut.
2 Field Road, Forest Gate, E. 7.

REID, John
1/3706, 20/5/15; R. Highrs., 27/8/15, att. Sea. Highrs.; F; Lt.-Col.; M.C. and Bar, M(1).
Southcourt, St. Andrews, Scotland.

REID, John Claud Alexander
6/1/6293, 16/9/15; trfr. R.F.A., 29/9/16.
Gortahurh, Lellerbreen, Enniskillen.

REID, Kenneth
6/4/7306, 8/11/15; High. L.I., 24/10/16; F; Lieut.; w, w-p.
King's Bay, Tobago, British West Indies.

REID, Robert John
6/3/9547, 22/2/16, L/C.; No. 14 O.C.B., 26/11/16; R. Scots., 28/2/17; F; Lieut. 61 Falcon Road, Edinburgh

REID, Thomas Standish
6/2/6799, 13/10/15; No. 7 O.C.B., 3/7/16; trfr. M.G.C., 29/12/16

REID, Walter Lewis
C/11755, 26/7/17; A.S.C., C/S, 1/11/17; R.A.S.C., 25/1/18; F; 2/Lieut. El Nido, Puerto Orotava, Teneriffe, Canary Islands.

REID, Walter Stewart
6/8658, 3/1/16; No. 9 O.C.B., 8/3/16; High. L.I., 6/7/16; F; Lieut.; w. 12 Blackburn Road, Ayr, Scotland.

REIDY, Joseph
6/5/7034, 27/10/15; R. Muns. Fus., 4/8/16; Lieut.
2 York Terrace, Killarney, Ireland.

REILLY, John McKelvie
6/5/7807, 24/11/15; R. Ir. Rif., 4/8/16, R.A.F.; S,P; Lieut.
36 Rosemount Gardens, Antrim Road, Belfast, Ireland.

REILLY, Thomas Joseph
6/1/9191, 29/1/16; No. 8 O.C.B., 4/8/16; R. Dub. Fus., 18/12/16, Indian Army; 2/Lieut.; w.

REINER, Arthur Veitch
6/1/5309, 2/8/15, L/C.; E. Surr. R., 13/12/15; F,It; Capt.; w(2).
Ferriby, Sutton, Surrey.

REIS, Charles
C/1718, 15/10/14; dis. 2/1/15.

REISS, Geoffrey Algernon Charles
H/1993, 29/10/14. Whatcroft Hall, Northwick, Cheshire.

REISS, Richard Leopold
B/48, 7/4/08; dis. 6/4/11; N. Lan. R., 13/2/15; G,M; Capt.; w
55 Oakley Square, N.W. 1.

RELPH, Harry
B/Sq/12687, 4/3/18, Sgt.; No. 1 Cav. C/S, 3/9/18; R. Regt. of Cav., 12/3/19; 2/Lieut. c/o Fraser & Neave Ltd., Singapore.

RELTON, Frederick Ernest
6/1/9373, 8/2/16; R.A., C/S, 23/6/16; R.G.A., 27/9/16, emp. M of Munitions; 2/Lieut.; w. The Grange, Becketts Park, Leeds.

REMINGTON, Edward Nicholson A.
H/1988, 29/10/14; R. Berks. R., 1/2/15, R.F.C., R.A.F.; Lieut.
Jesmond, Laburnum Road, Maidenhead.

RENDALL, Alexander Burnell
B/330, 25/11/08; dis. 16/10/11.

RENDALL, Robert Harry Motyer
D/13703, 31/7/18; demob. 29/1/19. 20 Vicarage Road, Rugby.

RENNIE, Clement Seaman
6/3/9198, 31/1/16; R.A., C/S, 26/10/16; trfr. 14th Lond. R., 2/3/17. 11 Wilton Hill, Hawick, N.B.

RENNIE, John George
6/2/8553, 30/12/15; R.A., C/S, 4/8/16; R.G.A., 29/11/16.

RENSHAW, Charles Evelyn
6/5/6863, 15/10/15; Bord. R., 4/8/16; F; Lieut.; w(3).
Ashbeck Ghyll, Underbank, Sedbergh, Yorkshire.

RENTON, Buller Alfred
B/12424, 17/1/18; demob. 23/1/19.
18 First Avenue, Hove, Sussex.

✠ RENTOUL, Alexander
4/4/4291, 17/6/15; Yorks. Huss., 15/10/15, R.F.C.; Lieut.
Killed in action 27/3/18.

RESTALL, Reginald
D/13704, 31/7/18; demob. 20/3/19.
44 Holmbush Road, Putney Hill, S.W. 15.

RETIEF, Paul Johannes
6/4/9222, 31/1/16; 7th Lond. R., 5/8/16, Indian Army; Lieut.
c/o Mrs. Dowling, 2 Rotherwood, Madeira Road, Streatham, S.W. 16.

RETTIE, George Kelly
C/10851, 6/3/17, Sgt.; demob. 23/1/19.
37 Fawnbrake Avenue, Herne Hill, S.E. 24.

RETTIE, Joseph Morrison
C/11000, 31/3/17, L/C.; No. 14 O.C.B., 10/8/17; Gord. Highrs., 27/11/17; 2/Lieut. Morley's Hotel, Trafalgar Square, W.C.

REVELS, David Henry
6/Sq/9294, 3/2/16; R.A., C/S, 7/8/16; R.F.A., 17/11/16; F; Lieut.; g, w(2).
Tullyhappy House, Jerretts Pass, Co. Armagh, Ireland.

REVETT, Henry John
A/B/Sq/12173, 29/10/17, L/C.; R.F.C., C/S, 15/2/18, No. 1 Cav. C/S; R. Regt. of Cav., 13/3/19; 2/Lieut.
1 Queens Gate, S.W. 1.

REVILL, Henry Hamilton
6/4/6775, 11/10/15; No. 7 O.C.B., 7/4/16; York & Lanc. R., 4/8/16, att. E. York. R.; F; Lieut.; w(2); M.C.
16 Castle Gate, Newark-on-Trent, Nottinghamshire.

REW, Noel Ackroyd
6/4/9361, 7/2/16; R.E., C/S, 5/8/16; R.E., 20/10/16; F; Capt.; g. 219 High Street, Berkhamsted, Hertfordshire.

REYNETTE-JAMES, Rupert Bernard
A/13959, 6/9/18; trfr. K.R. Rif. C., 7/4/19.
Lansdowne, The Avenue, Worcester Park, Surrey.

REYNOLDS, Alfred Norman
6/7562, 17/11/15; dis. 24/11/15.

REYNOLDS, Edward Lionel
B/11363, 28/5/17; R.F.C., 14/1/18; 2/Lieut.
The Gabled House, Farnham Common, Slough, Buckinghamshire.

REYNOLDS, Eric James
C/715, 27/5/13; W. York R., 11/9/14; F; Capt.; w(2); M.C.
7 Dry Hill Park Road, Tonbridge, Kent.

APPENDIX II.—RECORDS OF RANK AND FILE.

REYNOLDS, Felix Cossey
B/12349, 31/12/17, L/C.; No. 15 O.C.B., 10/5/18; Suff. R., 2/2/19; 2/Lieut.
    Denham, Diss, Norfolk.

REYNOLDS, Francis Edmond
Sq/2799, 26/1/15, L/C.; York. Huss., 20/4/15, R.A.M.C.; Capt
    R. Coll. of Physicians Laboratory, Edinburgh.

REYNOLDS, Frederick
B/10334, 4/1/17; No. 20 O.C.B., 7/6/17; Welch R., 25/9/17, M.G.C.; F; Lieut.   3 Plassey Street, Penarth, South Wales.

REYNOLDS, George William Morris
B/11315, 21/5/17; dis. 26/10/17; 2/Lieut.
    28 Shepherds Hill, Highgate, N. 6.

REYNOLDS, Kenneth Charles Rees
C/14231, 25/10/18; trfr. K.R. Rif. C., 7/4/19.
    Fairholme, Strawberry Hill, Middlesex.

REYNOLDS, Lewis Frank
B/9884, 8/11/16, L/C.; H. Bde. O.C.B., 6/3/17; Cold. Gds., 26/6/17; Lieut.; w.
c/o Standard Bank of South Africa; 10 Clements Lane, E.C. 4.

REYNOLDS, Lionel William
B/11711, 19/7/17, Sgt.; demob. 30/1/19.
    10 High Street, Rye, Sussex.

✠ REYNOLDS, Richard Frederic
Sq/2745, 21/1/15, Cpl.; No. 2 Cav. C/S, 31/3/16; Hants. Yeo., 19/8/16.

REYNOLDS, Thomas Edward Stewart
6/3/8035, 30/11/15; No. 8 O.C.B., 4/8/16; E. Surr. R., 21/11/16; F; Lieut.; M.C.   Percy House, High Street, Eltham, S.E. 9.

REYNOLDS, Walter Hugh
6/4/7476, 15/11/15; Worc. R., 4/9/16; F,It; Lieut.; w(2); M.C.
Park Place, Park Mill S.O., Glamorganshire.

REZIN, William Herbert B.
4/2/4052, 7/6/15, L/C.; Notts. & Derby. R., 17/9/15, secd. M.G.C.; Lieut.; w; M(2).
    3 Rowan Avenue, Urmston, Manchester.

RHEAM, George Turner Tatham
A/14105, 7/10/18; demob. 23/1/19.
    Raven's Croft, Warlingham, Surrey.

✠ RHODES, Eric Ralph
A/14013, 16/9/18.   Died 29/10/18.

RHODES, Ernest George
6/8371, 13/12/15; R.A., C/S, 14/7/16; R.G.A., 17/12/16; F; Lieut
146 Lordship Road, Stoke Newington, N. 16.

RHODES, John Heaton
D/1384, 29/9/14; dis. med. unfit, 31/10/14; rej. Sq/3138, 29/3/15; R.A.S.C., 5/7/15; S; Lieut.
c/o Messrs Rhodes, Ross & Godley, 178 Hereford Street, Christchurch, New Zealand.

RHODES, John Wilfrid
D/10001, 24/11/16; No. 14 O.C.B., 30/1/17; R.F.C., 29/5/17, R.A.F.; Lieut.   Moorlands, Sherburn-in-Elmet, Yorkshire.

RHODES, Rushforth
D/11098, 21/4/17; Garr. O.C.B., 5/10/17; Lab. Corps, 15/12/17; Lieut.
Meadow View, New Road, Horsforth, Nr. Leeds, Yorkshire.

RHODES, Wilfred
C/13290, 15/6/18; R.E., C/S, 18/10/18; demob.
Blind Lane Farm, Kirkburton, Nr. Huddersfield.

RHODES, William Albert
D/E/13824, 12/8/18; No. 22 O.C.B., 20/9/18; E. York. R., 14/2/19; 2/Lieut.
    Hillcot, Rusworp Lane, Whitby, Yorkshire.

✠ RICE, Albert George
D/10867, 13/3/17; No. 14 O.C.B., 5/7/17; trfr. 28th Lond. R., 3/9/17; F; Pte.   Died of wounds 3/9/18.

✠ RICE, Arnold Hamilton
C/10350, 5/1/17; R.F.C., C/S, 16/4/17; R.F.C., 16/5/17; 2/Lieut
    Killed in action 29/11/17

✠ RICE, Edgar William
4/1/5081, 26/7/15; N. Lan. R., 26/12/15; 2/Lieut.
    Killed in action 9/8/16.

RICE, James Howard
6/Sq/D/6364, 20/9/15; trfr. 2nd Cty. of Lond. Yeo., 31/5/17.
    Wolferton Rectory, Kings Lynn.

RICE-JONES, Benjamin Rowland
K/D/2210, 30/11/14; R.G.A., 1/5/15; F; Lieut.; w.
    5 Harrington Street, Liverpool.

RICE-OXLEY, Francis Bouyon
4/5/4654, 5/7/15; Durh. L.I., 5/1/16; F; Lieut.
Northdene, 8 Chatsworth Road, West Norwood, S.E. 27.

RICE-OXLEY, Frederick William
6/D/3488, 4/5/15, L/C.; R.F.C., C/S, 13/3/17; R.F.C., 19/4/17.
    Conisbro', Watford, Hertfordshire.

RICE-OXLEY, George Kenneth
K/A/2531, 31/12/14; R.A.S.C., 24/5/15, att. R.F.C.; Lieut.
    Conisbro', Watford, Hertfordshire.

RICH, Eric Ralph
6/2/6535, 30/9/15; No. 11 O.C.B., 7/5/16; S. Staff. R., 4/9/16; F; Lieut.; w.   43 Quarrenden Street, Parsons Green, S.W. 6.

RICH, Sidney Hedley Oliver
6/4/7531, 16/11/15; W. Som. Yeo., 2/9/16, Som. L.I.; F; Lieut.; w.
c/o Royal Mail Steam Packet Coy., Edificio Britanico, Buenos Aires, Argentina.

RICHARD, Archibald Henry
D/12910, 8/4/18; No. 16 O.C.B., 18/10/18; Rif. Brig., 17/3/19; 2/Lieut.   Castries, St. Lucia, British West Indies.

RICHARDS, Archibald Ivor
6/Sq/6829, 14/10/15; trfr. R.F.A., 2/6/16; R.F.A., 30/7/17; Lieut.; w; M(1).
The Bungalow, Kinmel Park, Abergele, North Wales.

RICHARDS, Benjamin Phillip
1/3118, 25/3/15; Dorset R., 23/7/15, M.G.C.; Lieut.; w.

✠ RICHARDS, Bruce Carlton
6/5/5867, 28/8/15; R.F.A., 16/11/15; Lieut.
    Killed in action 11/7/17.

RICHARDS, Dudley John Edgcome
C/12673, 1/3/18; No 3 O.C.B., 6/9/18; Notts. & Derby. R., 17/3/19; 2/Lieut.   The Vicarage, Maryport, Cumberland.

RICHARDS, Ernest George
4/3707, 20/5/15; R.E., 5/10/15; S; Lieut.
    Owen House, Tor Hill Road, Torquay.

RICHARDS, Francis Charles Montagu
B/91, 16/4/08; dis. 15/4/10.

RICHARDS, Gerald Seymour
6/5/D/9538, 18/2/16; No. 13 O.C.B., 4/11/16; Bedf. R., 28/2/17, att. R.E.; F; Lieut.; w.   49 Surbiton Road, Southend, Essex.

RICHARDS, Gordon Brinley
C/1686, 12/10/14; 1st Lond. R., 13/11/14, R.A.S.C.; F; Capt.; Chevalier de l'Ordre de la Couronne, Croix de Guerre (Belge).
    40 Chancery Lane, W.C. 2.

RICHARDS, Harold Gordon
4/6/5/4946, 19/7/15; R.E., 23/5/16; 2/Lieut.
    7 Glebe Road, Barnes, S.W. 3.

RICHARDS, Harold William
B/10910, 24/3/17; R.A., C/S, 4/1/18; R.F.A., 5/8/18; F; 2/Lieut.
The Lynn, 16 Devonshire Road, Handsworth Wood, Birmingham.

RICHARDS, James Guy
6/3/5310, 2/8/15; R.F.A., 1/12/15; F; Lieut.; w.
    35 Ladbroke Gardens, Notting Hill, W. 11.

RICHARDS, John Griffiths
4/3/4121, 8/6/15; Manch. R., 2/1/16; F; Lieut.; w.
    43 Wellington Square, Hastings.

✠ RICHARDS, John William
4/1/4026, 7/6/15; R.M.L.I., 30/8/15.   Killed -/12/16.

RICHARDS, Leonard John
4/6/2/4999, 19/7/15; Midd'x. R., 29/10/15, R. Suss. R., att. Glouc. R.; F,It,E; Lieut.
    c/o Lloyds Bank Ltd., 296 High Holborn, W.C. 1.

RICHARDS, Martin Joseph
B/10059, 1/12/16; A.S.C., C/S, 1/5/17; R.A.S.C., 28/6/17.
    Innistone, Westbury Road, Woodside Park, N.

RICHARDS, Norman Carlyle
B/11368, 23/5/17; R.E., C/S, 16/12/17; R.E., 29/3/18; F; 2/Lieut.
    3 Waterloo Road, Newport, Monmouthshire.

RICHARDS, Richard John
B/Sq/12329, 27/12/17, L/C.; No. 2 Cav. C/S, 11/4/18; 6th R. Regt. of Cav., 18/10/18; 2/Lieut.
    Bryerlseyfryd, Talybrut on Usk, Breconshire.

APPENDIX II.—RECORDS OF RANK AND FILE.

✠ RICHARDS, *Ronald Henry*
K/B/2389, 17/12/14; R. Suss. R., 21/5/15; 2/Lieut.
Killed in action 2/6/16.

✠ RICHARDS, *R. H. W. B.* See BRINSLEY-RICHARDS, *R. H. W*

✠ RICHARDS, *Stanley Earl*
4/5/4680, 8/7/15, L/C.; Mon. R., 21/11/15; 2/Lieut.
Died of wounds 29/8/16.

RICHARDS, *Thomas Powell*
6/2/6608, 4/10/15; R.W. Fus., 8/6/16; F; Lieut.; *w*.
12 Dee Side, Promenade, West Kirby.

RICHARDS, *Vivyan Warren*
A/11213, 5/5/17; Garr. O.C.B., 23/7/17; Yorks. L.I., 15/9/17; 2/Lieut. The Bryn, Monkhams Drive, Woodford Green, Essex.

RICHARDS, *William*
6/1/7947, 29/11/15, L/C.; M.G.C., 24/10/16; F; Major; *w*; M.C.
28 Disraeli Road, Ealing, W. 5.

RICHARDS, *William Islwyn*
6/Sq/1/6365, 20/9/15; M.G.C., C/S, 25/10/16; M.G.C., 24/2/17, Tank Corps; Lieut. 52 Drayton Gardens, West Ealing, W. 13.

RICHARDS, *William Rodger Gilmour*
4/1/4382, 21/6/15; Suff. Yeo., 25/9/16; Lieut.
19 Blakesley Avenue, Ealing, W. 5.

✠ RICHARDSON, *Allan William*
C/745, 1/12/13; R. Ir. Rif., 11/9/14; G; Lieut.
Killed in action 11/8/15.

✠ RICHARDSON, *Archer Stuart*
C/639, 9/5/12; dis. 1/6/14; R.G.A., 4/5/17; 2/Lieut.
Killed in action 25/6/17.

RICHARDSON, *Arthur Antonio*
6/6897, 18/10/15; dis. 14/1/16.

RICHARDSON, *Arthur William*
6/1/8974, 17/1/16; No. 14 O.C.B., 30/10/16; R. Suss. R., 28/2/17; F; Capt.; *w*; M.C. Wayside, Pembury, Kent.

RICHARDSON, *Arthur Wray*
6/Sq/8524, 29/12/15; R.A., C/S, 4/8/16; R.G.A., 12/11/16; Lieut.; *w*; M(1). Ravensworth, Potters Bar, Middlesex.

RICHARDSON, *Bertram Charles Heastey*
D/13857, 19/8/18; demob. 7/4/19.
28 St. John's Avenue East, Bridlington, Yorkshire.

RICHARDSON, *Cyril*
2/9776, 24/10/16; No. 14 O.C.B., 5/5/17; W. Rid. R., 28/8/17; F; Lieut. 22 Beresford Avenue, Newland, Hull, East Yorkshire.

RICHARDSON, *Ernest Gilbert*
H/2/3006, 4/3/15. Cpl.; R.G.A., 17/11/15, R.A.F.; F; Lieut.
104 Tollington Park, N. 4.

RICHARDSON, *George Crane*
6/5/7694, 22/11/15; Bedf. R., 22/11/16, att. North'n. R. and R W. Surr. R.; F; Lieut.; *w*. 5 High Street, St. Albans, Hertfordshire.

RICHARDSON, *James*
C/13341, 20/6/18; R.E., C/S. 18/10/18.
c/o F. Bernard Newman, Probyn, Cornwall.

RICHARDSON, *Joe Brook*
6/8315, 11/12/15; R.A., C/S, 9/6/16; R.G.A., 13/9/16; F; Capt.; *w*(2). The Firs, Cole Park Road, Twickenham.

RICHARDSON, *John Charles Ryder*
C/1163, 14/9/14; K.R. Rif. C., 3/10/14; F; Lieut.
The Beeches, Saxmundham, Suffolk.

RICHARDSON, *John McGowan*
C/11728, 23/7/17; No. 14 O.C.B., 4/1/18; R.W. Surr. R., 25/6/18; 2/Lieut. 228 South Norwood Hill, S.E. 25

RICHARDSON, *Richard Henry*
6/5/5954, 1/9/15, L/C.; trfr. L'pool. R., 10/4/16.
9 Victoria Road, Waterloo, Liverpool.

RICHARDSON, *Roland Alexander*
E/2774, 25/1/15; Devon. R., 31/5/15, Indian Army; E,P,SR; Capt.
Homestead, Four Elms, Edenbridge, Kent.

RICHARDSON, *Sidney Hugh*
4/5/4613, 5/7/15, L/C.; R.A.S.C., 8/10/15; F; Lieut.
34 Elvaston Place, Queens Gate, S.W. 7.

RICHARDSON, *Thomas Arthur*
6/3/5808, 23/8/15; Linc. R., 14/11/15; F; Capt.; *w*.
184 Legsby Avenue, Grimsby, Lincolnshire.

RICHARDSON, *William Horton*
D/11180, 3/5/17; No. 14 O.C.B., 9/11/17; Bedf. R., 30/4/18; F; Lieut.; *w*. Buccleugh, Clarence Road, St. Albans, Hertfordshire.

RICHARDSON, *William Phillips*
C/13274, 12/6/18; demob. 23/1/19.
Leathley, Otley, Yorkshire.

RICHFORD, *Oliver Barrett*
6/9512, 16/2/16; A.S.C., C/S, 1/5/16; R.A.S.C., 4/6/16, att. R.G.A.; F; Lieut. East Sutton, Nr. Maidstone, Kent.

RICHFORD, *Robert Miller*
3/3078, 19/3/15, L/C.; E. Kent R., 3/6/15, Midd'x. R.; F; Major; *w*. Stone House, Chelsfield, Kent.

RICHMAN, *William Henry*
6/1/8443, 16/12/15; R.A., C/S, 7/8/16; R.G.A., 18/10/16, emp. M. of Labour; Lieut. 1 Rose Hill Gardens, Jarvis Brook, Sussex.

RICHMOND, *Alan Cecil*
B/12350, 1/1/18; R.E., C/S, 21/7/18.
93a Golders Green Road, N.W. 4.

RICHMOND, *John Philip*
K/D/2376, 17/12/14; 9th Lond. R., 12/2/15, Indian Army; F,I,M,Afghan; Capt. c/o National Bank of India, Bombay, India.

RICKARD, *Edward Martin*
6/3/7307, 8/11/15, Sgt.; A.S.C., C/S, 27/10/16; dis. med. unfit, 2/3/17. 23 Beech Road, Horsfield, Bristol.

RICKARDS, *Aubrey Robert Maxwell*
6/2/6633, 4/10/15, Sgt.; R.F.C., 7/8/16, R.A.F.; F; Lieut.; *w-p*; M(1). Daubney House, Fairford, Gloucestershire.

RICKARDS, *George Somers*
C/12579, 6/2/18; demob. 4/2/19.
44 Narcissus Road, West Hampstead, N.W. 6.

RICKARDS, *Philip John*
B/13650, 26/7/18; trfr. 14th Lond. R., 6/12/18.
44 Narcissus Road, West Hampstead, N.W. 6.

RICKARDS, *William Henry*
4/6/5/4871, 15/7/15; trfr. R.F.A., 14/4/16.

RICKETT, *Cedric Arthur Lacy*
4/3794, 27/5/15; E. Surr. R., 4/12/15, K.R. Rif. C.; Lieut.; *w*.
52 Anerley Park, S.E. 20.

RICKETT, *Cyril Lacy*
3/3202, 8/4/15, Cpl.; Notts. & Derby. R., 25/10/15; F; Lieut.
52 Anerley Park, Anerley, S.E. 20.

RICKS, *Vincent Joseph*
6/5/8424, 15/12/15; No 7 O.C.B., 11/8/16; R. Dub. Fus., 18/12/16; F; Lieut.; *w*. 20 Salisbury Road, Cressington, Liverpool.

RIDDELL, *John Geoffry*
B/11008, 3/4/17; A.S.C., C/S, 12/11/17; R.A.S.C., 6/1/18; F; 2/Lieut. Whitebank, Whitefields Road, Solihull.

RIDDELL, *Walter Buchanan*
6/Sq/5266, 31/7/15; No. 1 Cav. C/S, 24/4/16; Oxf. Huss., 28/7/16; *w*. Kenwood, Elm Road, Prenton, Cheshire.

RIDDING, *Reginald*
K/A/2427, 21/12/14; R. Suss. R., 31/3/15; F; Capt.; Inj.; M.B.E. c/o Lond. Westminster and Parr's Bank Ltd., 21 Lombard Street, E.C.

RIDDLE, *Cecil Brimble*
2/3434, 1/5/15; Durh. L.I., 9/6/15, R.A.F.; Capt.

RIDER, *Henry*
6/5/7850, 25/11/15, L/C.; R.A., C/S, 13/10/16; R.F.A., 19/5/17; F; Lieut. 3 Moorgate Terrace, Rotherham, Yorkshire.

RIDER, *Henry Sawyer*
6/2/5419, 5/8/15; R. Marines, 10/11/15; Lieut.; *w*.
1 Elliott Street, The Hoe, Plymouth.

RIDER, *John L. Wase*
4/5/4805, 12/7/15, L/C.; 1st Lond. R., 19/11/15; Lieut.
1 Lansdowne Road, W. 11.

RIDGE, *James Henry*
6/7948, 29/11/15; R.A., C/S, 26/10/16; R.G.A., 19/2/17; F; Capt.; *w*(2). 24 Shrubbery Avenue, Kidderminster.

RIDGER, *Arthur Loton*
E/1532, 6/10/14; R.N.V.R., 14/10/14; G,F; Lt. Cmdr.; M(1).
46 Finchley Road, N.W. 8.

APPENDIX II.—RECORDS OF RANK AND FILE.

RIDGER, *Ernest Edwin*
H/1996, 30/10/14; R. Fus., 2/11/14; Capt.; *w*.
63 *Vanburgh Park, Blackheath, S.E.* 3.

RIDING, *George Albert*
6/2/5570, 12/8/15, L/C.; North'd. Fus., 21/4/16; Lieut.; *w*.
37 *Kensington Road, Victoria Park, Manchester.*

RIDLER, *Arthur Whitaker*
6/Sq/8843, 10/1/16; R.A., C/S, 4/8/16; R.G.A., 24/11/16; F;
Lieut. *The Bungalow, Hoborne Farm, Christchurch, Hampshire.*

RIDLER, *Francis James*
D/10416, 10/1/17; R.A., C/S, 27/4/17; R.G.A., 1/9/17; 2/Lieut
35 *Dartmouth Park Road, Highgate Road, N.W.* 5.

RIDLEY, *Albert George*
A/10070, 1/12/16; R.G.A., C/S, 28/2/17; R.G.A., 23/6/17; I,M;
Lieut. 46 *Andalus Road, Stockwell, S.W.* 9.

RIDLEY, *Basil White*
C/549, 24/2/11; S. Lan. R., 11/9/14, Durh. L.I.; F; Lt.-Col.; *w*;
D.S.O., M.C., Italian Silver Medal for Military Valour, M(2).
Oaklea, Sanderstead, Surrey.

RIDLEY, *Ernest Oswald*
6/3/6336, 20/9/15; Herts. R., 4/8/16, att. Tank Corps; F; Lieut.
18 *Clorane Gardens, Hampstead, N.W.* 3.

RIDLEY, *Geoffrey Paul*
B/13527, 15/7/18; demob. 25/1/19.
Chesterholme, Park Road, Ipswich.

RIDLEY, *Geoffrey William*
C/548, 24/2/11; R. Suss. R., 6/2/14; G,E,P; Major, D.A.A.G.;
w; O.B.E., Order of the Nile, M(2).
The Manor House, West Hoathby, Sussex.

✠ RIDLEY, *Lancelot Edwin*
K/B/2173, 26/11/14, L/Sgt.; R. Berks. R., 9/3/15; Lieut.
Killed in action 19/8/16.

RIDSDALE, *John Stables*
6/3/5803, 23/8/15; R. Lanc. R., 9/6/16; F; Lieut.
Windyridge, Luttrell Road, Four Oaks, Warwickshire.

RIES, *Howard Neville*
6/9388, 8/2/16; dis. to R. Mil. Coll., 27/4/16; Rif. Brig., 27/10/16;
Lieut.; *w*; M(1). 3 *Fitzjohns Avenue, Hampstead, N.W.* 3.

✠ RIGBY, *Francis John*
A/552, 24/2/11; Sea. Highrs., 14/8/14; F,M; Capt.; M.C., M(1).
Killed in action 21/1/16.

RIGBY, *Frank Bernard*
C/13354, 26/6/18; trfr. 14th Lond. R., 6/12/18.
32 *Etna Road, St. Albans, Hertfordshire.*

RIGDEN, *Brian Cawes*
6/3/5449, 7/8/15, L/C.; Oxf. & Bucks. L.I., 15/10/15, Indian
Army; F,It; Capt.; *w*; M.C. and Bar. M(1).
c/o F. S. Saunders Esq., Field Place, Horsham. (Now in India).

RILEY, *Alfred Arnold*
6/2/7151, 2/11/15; Midd'x. R., 4/8/16; F; Capt.; *w*; M.C.
47 *Northfield Road, Stamford Hill, N.* 16.

RILEY, *Arthur*
A/14339, 30/12/18; No. 11 O.C.B., 24/1/19; General List, 8/3/19;
2/Lieut. 15 *Hale Gardens, Acton, W.* 3.

RILEY, *Arthur Godfrey*
4/1/5178, 29/7/15; R. Fus., 4/12/15, M.G.C.; Capt.; M.C.
Lyncot, Ravensbourne Park, Catford, S.E. 6.

RILEY, *Cyril Reginald*
4/5/4807, 12/7/15; Oxf. & Bucks. L.I., 24/11/15; F; Capt.; *w*.
20 *Park Road, Banbury, Oxon.*

RILEY, *Frederic Charles*
4/3426, 29/4/15; R.G.A., 8/9/15; F,E; Lieut.; *w*.
5 *Newmarket Road, Norwich.*

✠ RILEY, *Herbert Angus*
4/2/4158, 10/6/15; L'pool. R., 30/11/15; 2/Lieut.
Killed in action 28/6/16.

RILEY, *Herbert George*
4/5/4681, 8/7/15; Leic. R., 6/12/15; F; Capt.
25 *Horsefair Street, Leicester.*

RILEY, *James Conly Hunter*
C/11466, 8/6/17; No. 10 O.C.B., 5/10/17; Lan. Fus., 26/2/18;
2/Lieut. *The Anchorage, Clayton-le-Morris, Nr. Accrington.*

RILEY, *Milton Ewart*
5/C/9722, 12/10/16; No. 14 O.C.B., 27/12/16; E. Lan. R., 27/3/17;
F; Lieut.; M.C. *Elm Bank, St. Silas Road, Blackburn, Lancashire.*

RILEY, *Riley*
4/1/3980, 3/6/15, L/C.; R.G.A., 6/10/15; F; Lieut.
29 *Threadneedle Street, E.C.* 2.

RILEY, *William Franklin*
6/1/6634, 4/10/15; R.A., C/S, 17/3/16; trfr. R.F.A., 10/11/16.
Lyncott, Ravensbourne Park, Catford, S.E. 6.

RIMINGTON, *Herbert Percival*
4/4028, 7/6/15, L/C.; M.G.C., C/S, 1/3/17, No. 14 O.C.B.; R.W
Kent R., 31/7/17; F; 2/Lieut.; *p*.
102 *Maidstone Road, Rochester, Kent.*

RIMINGTON, *William*
B/12314, 17/12/17; R.E., C/S, 14/4/18; R.E., 15/8/18.

✠ RING, *Leslie Gordon*
6/4/6425, 23/9/15, L/C.; 3rd Lond. R., 21/4/16; Lieut.
Killed in action 18/9/18.

RISELEY, *Frank Lorymer*
A/11939, 30/8/17, L/C.; H. Bde. O.C.B., 7/12/17; Gren. Gds.,
28/5/18; F; Lieut. *The Oak, Stoke Bishop, Bristol.*

RITCHIE, *Ernest Edgar*
4/3427, 29/4/15, L/C.; E. Lan. R., 16/7/15, Army Cyc. Corps;
F,E; 2/Lieut.; *w*. *Bowling Park House, Rorby Lane, Bradford.*

RITCHIE, *Keneth James*
3/3559, 10/5/15; Herts. R., 25/7/15, att. No. 13 O.C.B., Inst; F;
Capt.; *w*(2); M(1). *Burcote, Berkhamsted, Hertfordshire.*

✠ RITCHIE, *William Lancelot*
6/3/6743, 11/10/15; No. 11 O.C.B., 7/5/16; Camb. R., 4/9/16;
2/Lieut. Died of wounds 1/8/17.

RITCHIE, *William Thackeray Denis*
Sq/409, 28/4/09; Leic. Yeo., 8/3/11; Capt.
The End House, Berkeley Place, Wimbledon, S.W.

✠ RIVERS, *George Claude*
A/2045, 9/11/14; E. Surr. R., 5/1/15; F; 2/Lieut.
Killed in action 21/8/16.

RIVERS, *Vernon Huntley*
C/12604, 13/2/18; H. Bde. O.C.B., 7/6/18; trfr. 14th Lond. R.,
4/1/19. *Lynmouth, Denmark Road, Reading.*

RIVIERE, *Augene Gonzague*
C/704, 9/4/13; N. Lan. R., 11/8/14; F,M; Staff Capt.; *w*;
M.B.E., M.C., M(1). *Wells, Somerset.*

RIVINGTON, *Henry Gibson*
D/E/13900, 23/8/18; demob. 21/12/18.
27 *Chancery Lane, W.C.* 2.

RIX, *Arthur Herbert*
4/Sq/4633, 5/7/15; E. Rid. Yeo., 5/10/15; Capt.
Ipoh, Perak, Federated Malay States.

RIX, *Evelyn Harry*
E/14241, 28/10/18; No. 11 O.C.B., 24/1/19; General List, 8/3/19;
2/Lieut. *Anglo-South American Club, 1 Queens Gate, S.W.* 7.

RIXON, *James Chaston*
6/4/6670, 7/10/15; dis. to re-enlist in R.E., 18/4/16.
1 *Bonnington Square, S.W.* 8.

ROACH, *Bremer Henry*
6/1/Sq/7697, 22/11/15; R.A., C/S, 8/11/16; R.F.A., 11/3/17; F;
Staff Lieut. 143 *Petherton Road, Highbury, N* 5.

ROARK, *Edmund Charles*
B/Sq/12362, 31/12/17; No. 1 Cav. C/S, 16/5/18; R. Regt. of Cav.,
14/2/19; 2/Lieut. *Kingswalden Buy, Hitchin, Hertfordshire.*

ROBARTS, *Percy Wilfred*
6/1/A/6635, 4/10/15; Garr. O.C.B., 12/12/16; Suff. R., 26/2/17;
2/Lieut. *Atherton, Sawbridgeworth, Hertfordshire.*

ROBBINS, *Alan Pitt*
D/10876, 16/3/17; Garr. O.C.B., 5/10/17; Lab. Corps, 15/12/17;
2/Lieut. 20 *Bernard Gardens, Wimbledon, S.W.* 19.

ROBBINS, *Eric*
6/3/8047, 1/12/15; North'd. Fus., 24/1/17, emp. M. of Labour;
F; Lieut.; *w*. 1 *Norwich Road, Ipswich, Suffolk.*

ROBBINS, *Samuel Alexander*
4/3708, 20/5/15; R. Fus., 29/11/15; F; Lieut.
Rolvenden, Foots Cray Road, New Eltham, S.E. 9.

ROBERTS, *Albert Percy*
A/11268, 12/5/17; No. 14 O.C.B., 5/10/17; Dorset R., 26/2/18,
att. R.F.C. and R.A.F.; F; Lieut.
Fairlight, 45 Francis Road, Watford, Hertfordshire. (Now in Burma).

ROBERTS, *Albert Samuel*
K/D/2355, 14/12/14; Ches. R., 21/7/15; F.
The Poplars, Bredhurst, Nr. Chatham, Kent.

APPENDIX II.—RECORDS OF RANK AND FILE.

ROBERTS, Archibald Morriss
6/3/9058, 21/1/16; W. York. R., 22/11/16; F; Lieut.
Oak Hill Lodge, Frognal, Hampstead, N.W. 3.

ROBERTS, Arthur Beaver Llewelyn
C/382, 24/3/09; dis. 31/8/11.

ROBERTS, Arthur Glynn
6/5/5953, 1/9/15, Sgt.; L'pool. R., 20/1/16; F; Lieut.; M.C.
29 Radcliffe Road, Winchmore Hill, N. 21.

ROBERTS, Charles Clifton
E/14162, 14/10/18; R.G.A., C/S, 1/11/18; R.G.A., 10/3/19; 2/Lieut. *Lamb Building, Temple, E.C. 4. (Now in Nyassaland).*

ROBERTS, David Ewart
C/13386, 24/6/18; demob. 29/1/19.
10 Hilda Street, Barry, Glamorganshire.

ROBERTS, Douglas Leslie
6/5/8434, 16/12/15; R.A., C/S, 4/8/16; R.F.A., 10/11/16; F; Lieut.; g. *Hill House, Narbeth, South Wales.*

ROBERTS, Eric Mark
1/3168, 1/4/15; North'd. Fus., 1/7/15; F; Capt.; w; M.C.
Cranleigh, Hampton Road, Worcester Park, Surrey.

ROBERTS, E. C. B. See BLACK-ROBERTS, E. C.

ROBERTS, Geoffrey Darling
B/843, 4/8/14; Devon. R., 1/9/14; Capt.
19 Berkeley Street, Piccadilly, W. 1.

✠ ROBERTS, Griffith Evans
6/4/5485, 9/8/15; No. 11 O.C.B., 7/5/16; Bord. R., 4/9/16; 2/Lieut. *Killed in action 7/6/17.*

ROBERTS, Harold
6/9591, 22/6/16, L/C.; A.S.C., C/S, 27/10/16; R.A.S.C., 20/12/16; Lieut.; M(1). *33 Caudray Road, Southport, Lancashire.*

ROBERTS, Henry Glanville
3/3874, 31/5/15; Worc. R., 20/1/16; Capt.; w.
3 Andrews Buildings, Penarth, South Wales.

ROBERTS, Herbert Frederick
B/13497, 8/7/18; trfr. 14th Lond. R., 6/12/18, Gord. Highrs.
44 Derby Lane, Stoneycroft, Liverpool.

ROBERTS, Hugh Trevor
5/Sq/5636, 16/8/15, L/C.; R.F.A., 26/11/15; F; Lieut.; w.
c/o S.L.L.D. Coy. Ltd., P.O. Box 447, Calcutta, India.

✠ ROBERTS, H. O. B. See BODVEL-ROBERTS, H. O.

ROBERTS, James Edmond
6/5/8444, 16/12/15; No. 8 O.C.B., 4/8/16, M.G.C., C/S; M.G.C., 23/11/16, Tank Corps; F; Lieut. *40 Gladstone Road, Chester.*

ROBERTS, Jeremiah Williams
B/9890, 10/11/16; Garr. O.C.B., 23/5/17; dis. med. unfit, 29/10/17
Arcuaig, Pwllheli, North Wales.

✠ ROBERTS, John Herbert
6/7695, 22/11/15; R.A. C/S, 24/1/16; R.F.A., 23/6/16, R.A.F.; Germ.SWA,F,It; Lieut.; w. *Killed in action 24/9/18.*

ROBERTS, John Meiric
4/3/5128, 26/7/15, Cpl.; Welch R., 5/5/16; F,P; Capt.; w.
9 St. Peter's Square, Ruthin, North Wales.

ROBERTS, John Prichard
4/5/4727, 9/7/15; Manch. R., 17/12/15; F; Lieut.; w(2).
Rydal Mount, Churton Road, Rhyl, North Wales.

ROBERTS, John Theodore Cyril
5/4/8958, 18/1/16; No. 2 O.C.B., 14/8/16; Bord. R., 18/12/16; F; Lieut. *Dinton House, Whitley Park, Wigan.*

ROBERTS, Joseph
6/Sq/7308, 8/11/15, L/C.; R.A., C/S, 21/7/16; R.F.A., 30/9/16; F; Capt.; M(1). *Ballure, Heswall, Cheshire.*

✠ ROBERTS, Leon Rees
6/2/5571, 12/7/15; trfr. 5th Lond. R., 17/3/16; F; Pte.
Killed in action 4/10/16.

ROBERTS, Percival Alfred
6/3/7696, 22/11/15; Mon. R., 24/1/17; F; Lieut.; w(2).
28 Riverview Gardens, Strawberry Hill, Twickenham.

ROBERTS, Percy Easthope
6/5/6864, 15/10/15, L/C.; No. 11 O.C.B., 7/5/16; 1st Lovatt's Scouts, 5/9/16, att. Tank Corps; F; Lieut.
36 Belgrave Street, Liscard, Cheshire.

✠ ROBERTS, Reuben
A/2709, 18/1/15; R.A.O.C., 4/6/15; F; Capt.
Killed in action 8/7/16.

ROBERTS, Robert Davies
B/E/13570, 19/7/18; R.G.A., C/S, 2/10/18; demob.
c/o Dr. Ll. Roberts, The Field, Pontypridd, South Wales.

ROBERTS, Robert Ellis
6/4/8572, 31/12/15; No. 2 O.C.B., 14/8/16; Welch R., 18/12/16; Lieut. *12 Wexford Road, Wandsworth Common, S.W.12.*

ROBERTS, Stanley Reginald
4/5/4808, 12/7/15; R.W. Fus., 6/12/15; Lieut.

ROBERTS, Sydney Charles
K/F/2263, 7/12/14, L/C.; K.O. Sco. Bord., 8/4/15; G; Lieut.; w(2); M.C., M(1). *43 Evington Drive, Leicester.*

ROBERTS, Sydney Robert
2/3618, 13/5/15, C.Q.M.S.; demob. 22/2/19.
72 Waterloo Road, Ashton, Preston.

ROBERTS, Thomas Edmund
A/12549, 4/2/18, L/C.; No. 1 O.C.B., 9/8/18; N. Lan. R., 5/3/19; 2/Lieut. *88 Palmerston Road, Bowes Park, N. 22.*

ROBERTS, Thomas Llewelyn Lunt
C/12302, 10/12/17; No. 11 O.C.B., 7/6/18; R.W. Fus., 5/2/19; 2/Lieut. *65 Upper Tichborne Street, Leicester.*

ROBERTS, Vincent Helliwell
D/12937, 15/4/18; No. 16 O.C.B., 18/10/18; R.W. Fus., 17/3/19; 2/Lieut. *Bryn Eithin, Northop, Flintshire.*

✠ ROBERTS, Victor George
6/1/8579, 2/1/16; No. 14 O.C.B., 30/10/16; Welch R., 28/2/17; F; 2/Lieut. *Killed in action 27/7/17.*

ROBERTS, Wilfrid Straughan
3/3550, 10/5/15; Hamps. R., 14/8/15; E,P; Lieut.; p.
5 Tonbridge Road, Maidstone.

ROBERTS, William Arthur
Sq/3739, 24/5/15, Cpl.; Worc. Yeo., 29/10/15; Lieut.
Canterbury House, Princes Square, Harrogate.

ROBERTS, William Gower
B/D/A/12027, 20/9/17; R.F.C., C/S, 15/2/18; R.A.F., 18/11/18; 2/Lieut. *2 Gwydir Gardens, Swansea.*

ROBERTS, William Henry
C/10564, 19/1/17; Garr. O.C.B., 23/5/17; Lab. Corps, 14/7/17; Lieut. *17 Llandaff Road, Canton, Cardiff.*

ROBERTS, William James
6/4/8817, 10/1/16; No. 8 O.C.B., 4/8/16; S. Lan. R., 24/10/16; F; Lieut. *3 Home Lea, Victoria Park, Wavertree, Liverpool.*

ROBERTS, William Nefydd
6/2/7563, 17/11/15; No. 13 O.C.B., 4/11/16; R.W. Fus., 28/2/17; Lieut. *67 Woodland Gardens, Muswell Hill, N. 10.*

ROBERTSHAW, A. J. Illingworth
4383, 21/6/15; Manch. R., 6/1/16, att. W. Rid. R.; Lieut.

ROBERTSON, Douglas Dickson
C/13355, 26/6/18, L/C.; trfr. K.R. Rif. C., 7/4/19.
9 Queen Mary Avenue, Crosshill, Glasgow.

ROBERTSON, George James
2/9769, 23/10/16; No. 14 O.C.B., 27/12/16; Gord. Highrs., 25/4/17; F; Lieut.; p. *The Manse, Strathkinness, St. Andrews, Fife.*

ROBERTSON, George Michael Warton
4/2/4406, 24/6/15, Sgt.; Midd'x. R., 5/2/15; F; Lieut.; w.
2 Clyde Mansions, Gondar Gardens, N.W. 6.

ROBERTSON, Harry Summers
K/A/2401, 21/12/14; High. L.I., 17/3/15, Lab. Corps; Capt.
c/o Dalgleish & Coy., 7/8 Great Winchester Street, E.C. 2.

✠ ROBERTSON, Helenus Macaulay
B/276, 17/6/08; dis. 31/12/09; rej. B/1010, 6/8/14, Sgt.; R.W. Fus., 13/1/15; Capt. *Killed in action 26/1/16.*

ROBERTSON, Joseph Albert
A/11901, 23/8/17; No. 14 O.C.B., 7/12/17; Arg. & Suth'd. Highrs., 28/5/18; Germ.SWA; 2/Lieut.
10 Schimer Street, Southwick, Sunderland.

✠ ROBERTSON, Laurence Grant
H/1987, 29/10/14, L/C.; R.A.O.C., 8/2/15; K.O. Sco. Bord.; F; Lieut. *Killed in action 30/7/16.*

APPENDIX II.—RECORDS OF RANK AND FILE.

ROBERTSON, Leslie William Rose
K/B/2107, 16/11/14, L/C.; 25th Lond. R., 12/3/15, R.F.A.; I,F; Lieut. Clermiston, Burghley Road, Wimbledon, S.W. 19.

ROBERTSON, Lionel Gallwey-
4/2/3273, 15/4/15; Suff. R., 8/7/15, att. Essex R., R.A.F.; F; Lieut. 14 Eaton Terrace, S.W. 1.

✠ ROBERTSON, Norman Cairns
E/1638, 9/10/14; Hamps. R., 20/2/15; F; Capt.; p.
Died 20/6/17 as Prisoner of War.

ROBERTSON, Patrick James
D/E/13908, 26/8/18, L/C.; demob. 10/1/19.
1a Netheral Gardens, Hampstead, N.W.

✠ ROBERTSON, Ralph R.
4/5005, 20/7/15, L/C.; Hamps. R., 24/10/15, R.F.C.; 2/Lieut.
Killed 11/5/17.

ROBERTSON, Robert
D/11556, 25/6/17, L/C.; No. 14 O.C.B., 4/1/18; E. Kent R., 25/6/18. 7 London Lane, Bromley, Kent.

ROBERTSON, Robert J.
2/8659, 3/1/16; Scots Gds., 24/3/16; Capt.
c/o High Commissioner for New Zealand, Victoria Street, S.W.

✠ ROBERTSON, Walter Raymond
4/2/5082, 26/7/15; Bord R., 2/1/16; 2/Lieut.
Killed in action 1/7/16.

ROBERTSON, Wilfrid Edmond
B/2572, 4/1/15, Cpl.; S. Wales Bord., 2/6/15, att. M.G.C.; F; Lieut. Woodthorpe Lodge, Alvaston, Nr. Derby.

ROBERTSON, William Adrian
6/8332, 11/12/15; dis. med unfit, 31/5/16; rej. D/B/11584, 2/7/17, L/C.; demob. 5/2/19. 1 Alton Road, Oxton, Cheshire.

ROBEY, Gilbert Leonard
6/B/8766, 6/1/16; No. 8 O.C.B., 4/8/16; N. Staff. R., 21/11/16; F; Lieut. 35 Trafalgar Place, Devonport, South Devonshire.

ROBEY, Harold Gordon
C/10165, 11/12/16; No. 14 O.C.B., 5/3/17; K.O. Sco. Bord., 26/10/17, secd. R.F.C., R.A.F.; F; Lieut.; w(2); M(1).
The Bank House, Surrey Street, Lowestoft.

ROBINS, Charles Henry
1/3659, 17/5/15; Durh. L.I., 28/7/15; Lieut.; w.
Manor House, Buckland, Tring.

ROBINSON, Alexander Okell
6/5/5267, 31/7/15; L'pool. R., 6/12/15, M.G.C.; Major.
37 Thorndale Road, Waterloo, Liverpool.

ROBINSON, Arthur
D/10447, 10/1/17, L/C.; R.A., C/S, 27/4/17; R.G.A., 1/9/17; F; Lieut. 26 West Avenue, Leicester.

ROBINSON, Arthur Hartley
6/1/6927, 19/10/15; R. Berks. R., 4/9/16; F; Lieut.; w.
16 Grosvenor Gardens, Cricklewood.

✠ ROBINSON, Arthur Pearson
B/D/11995, 10/9/17, Sgt.; demob. 10/1/19. Died -/6/20.

ROBINSON, Bernard Hollanby
C/11756, 26/7/17; A.S.C., C/S, 1/11/17; R.A.S.C., 25/1/18; F; 2/Lieut. Lucknow, Holly Park, Finchley, N. 3.

ROBINSON, Bertie Stuart
A/14323, 30/12/18; demob. 10/1/19.
555 Finchley Road, Hampstead, N.W. 3.

ROBINSON, Charles William
C/11452, 4/6/17; No. 14 O.C.B., 5/10/17; Yorks. L.I., 26/2/18, York. & Lanc. R.; F; 2/Lieut.; w.
135 Hampstead Road, N.W. 1.

ROBINSON, Cooper
6/Sq/5782, 23/8/15; R.A.S.C., 9/10/15.
Kettlewell, Skipton, Yorkshire.

ROBINSON, Edgar Cyril
6/2/8372, 13/12/15, Sgt.; trfr. R.F.C., 13/12/17.
17 Upper Dicconson Street, Wigan, Lancashire.

ROBINSON, Edward Backhouse
6/D/9597, 11/7/16; R.A., C/S, 24/11/16; R.F.A., 5/6/17; F; Lieut.; w. Chadsmore, Malvern. (Now in Ceylon).

ROBINSON, Edward John
B/13446, 3/7/18; demob. 1/2/19.
Tithebarn Street, Poulton-le-Fylde, Nr. Preston, Lancashire.

ROBINSON, Edward Stanley Gotch
K/F/2325, 14/12/14; North'n. R., 6/3/15; F; 2/Lieut.; w(2).
34 Kensington Park Road, W. 11.

ROBINSON, Edward Stanley Kemp
Sq/525, 3/12/10; demob. 31/3/20.
133 Castelnau, Barnes, S.W. 13.

✠ ROBINSON, Frank
C/991, 5/8/14; North'd. Fus., 19/9/14; F; Lieut.; w.
Died of wounds 7/7/16.

ROBINSON, Frederic Oscar Clayton
C/12231, 16/11/17; R.F.A., C/S, 29/3/18; demob.
Secunderabad Club, Secunderabad, India.

✠ ROBINSON, George Sidney
6/1/6636, 4/10/15; trfr. Class W. Res., 7/8/16; re-enlisted E Kent R.; Pte. Died of wounds 26/4/18.

ROBINSON, Harold
6/3/5420, 5/8/15; Linc. R., 1/6/16, Indian Army; F,I,SR; Capt.; w. c/o Cox & Coy., Bombay, India.

✠ ROBINSON, Harold Percival
6/5/7152, 2/11/15; No. 11 O.C.B., 7/5/16; L'pool. R., 4/9/16; 2/Lieut. Killed in action 31/7/17.

✠ ROBINSON, Horace Victor George
6/2/7949, 29/11/15, L/C.; Worc. R., 22/11/16; F; 2/Lieut.
Killed in action 24/10/17.

✠ ROBINSON, Houghton
4/6/3/4894, 15/7/15; dis. to R. Mil. Coll., 3/11/16. Died.

ROBINSON, Hugh
6/4/9169, 26/1/16; R.A., C/S, 26/10/16; R.G.A., 5/1/17; F; Lieut. Holmleigh, 13 Lynton Road, Heaton Moor, Stockport.

ROBINSON, Hugh Falkland
6/Sq/6151, 9/9/15; No. 2 Cav. C/S, 31/3/16; Oxf. Huss. Yeo., 19/8/16, att. Lan. Huss.; F; Lieut.
Box 3228, Johannesburg, South Africa.

✠ ROBINSON, Hugh Thomas Kay
K/E/2380, 17/12/14; R. Suss. R., 31/3/15; Lt.-Col.; D.S.O., M(1).
Killed in action 26/4/18.

✠ ROBINSON, John
1/3604, 13/5/15; S. Wales Bord., 31/7/15; 2/Lieut.
Killed in action 1/7/16.

ROBINSON, John Speir
6/3/8660, 3/1/16; A.S.C., C/S, 27/10/16; R.A.S.C., 20/12/16.
Lynhales, Kington, Hereford.

✠ ROBINSON, Joseph
1/3329, 19/4/15, L/C.; North'd. Fus., 10/7/15; F; 2/Lieut.; w.
Died of wounds 11/10/16.

ROBINSON, Lennard
6/3/5389, 5/8/15; York. & Lanc. R., 26/12/15, Life Gds., att. Gds. M.G.R. and Welch Gds.; F; Lieut.

ROBINSON, Lindsay King
6/3/5311, 2/8/15, L/C.; York. & Lanc. R., 14/11/15, Life Gds.; F; Lieut.; g.
Yatala, Union Street, North Sydney, Sydney, Australia.

ROBINSON, Noel Oswald
B/10887, 19/3/17, Sgt.; No. 2 O.C.B., 20/9/18; Gds. M.G.R., 10/3/19; 2/Lieut. Lynton, Alderley Edge, Cheshire.

ROBINSON, Norman Vaughan
4/6/4980, 19/7/15; R. Fus., 3/1/16, Rif. Brig.; F; Lieut.; w(2); M.C. Craig-y-don, Milford Haven, South Wales.

ROBINSON, Percy
C/13193, 3/6/18; No. 22 O.C.B., 5/7/18; Notts. & Derby. R., 11/2/19; 2/Lieut. 12 Sneinton Hollows, Nottingham.

ROBINSON, Ronald Eric
4/6/Sq/4634, 5/7/15; No. 2 Cav. C/S, 18/5/16; Bedf. Yeo., 6/9/16, att. R.F.C.; S,E; Lieut. 293a Willesden Lane, N.W. 2.

ROBINSON, Thomas Peter
6/2/1/6800, 13/10/15; No. 7 O.C.B., 6/4/16; R. Dub. Fus., 6/7/16; 2/Lieut.

✠ ROBINSON, William Alfred Layton
4/5512, 16/8/15, Sgt.; R.W. Surr. R., 16/11/15; F; 2/Lieut.; w.
Killed in action 26/6/17.

ROBINSON, William Arthur
C/D/12269, 29/11/17; No. 2 O.C.B., 10/5/18; Interpreter, 31/10/18; 2/Lieut. 365 Church Road, Leyton, E. 10.

ROBINSON, William Barry
1/3605, 13/5/15; S. Wales Bord., 31/7/15, att. Welch R.; F; Lieut. 8 Vicarage Terrace, Kendal, Westmoreland.

ROBINSON, William Buckton
B/10556, 19/1/17, L/C.; A.S.C., C/S, 1/11/17; R.A.S.C., 25/1/18; F; Lieut. 33 Moorfield, High West Jesmond, Newcastle.

APPENDIX II.—RECORDS OF RANK AND FILE.

ROBINSON, William Collingwood
4/1/4635, 5/7/15; Notts. & Derby. R., 4/11/15, R.A.F.; F;
Lieut.; w.
Hayworthingham Grange, Spilsby, Lincolnshire. (Now in New Zealand).

ROBINSON, William George
C/Sq/10580, 19/1/17, L/C.; No. 1 Cav. C/S, 31/7/17; R. Regt. of Cav., 22/2/18, att. North'd. Huss.; F; 2/Lieut.
56 Venner Road, Sydenham, S.E. 26.

ROBINSON, William John Scott
6/4/7477, 15/11/15; No. 9 O.C.B., 8/3/16; K.O. Sco. Bord., 27/7/16; 2/Lieut.; w.
Cluden, Annan, Scotland.

ROBINSON, William Willmore
6/2/6211, 13/9/15; Devon. R., 7/7/16, Indian Army; P; Lieut.
95 Brownhill Road, Catford, S.E. 6.

ROBISON, Norman Douglas
6/5/9073, 21/1/16; R.F.C., 14/8/16.
56 Gordon Road, Wanstead, Essex.

ROBOTHAM, Harry Peat
6/4/6491, 27/9/15, L/C.; Glouc. R., 24/4/16, att. R.F.C.

ROBSON, Emmerson John
A/11212, 7/5/17; No. 14 O.C.B., 7/9/17; Shrop. L.I., 17/12/17; 2/Lieut.
321 Green Lanes, Finsbury Park, N. 4.

ROBSON, Henry George Sydney
4/5/4872, 15/7/15; Durh. L.I., 1/1/16, att. R.F.C.; F; Lieut.
Kirklands, Eaglescliffe, Co. Durham. (Now in America).

ROBSON, Ian Galbraith
Sq/14304, 5/11/18; demob. 24/1/19.
Irthington, Dumbarton, Scotland.

ROBSON, John George
A/13178, 31/5/18; No 22 O.C.B., 5/7/18; Education Officer, 8/12/18; Capt.
8 Brookfield Park, N.W. 5.

ROBSON, John Ord
D/A/11840, 9/8/17; A.S.C., C/S, 1/2/18; R.A.S.C., 26/4/18; 2/Lieut.
Union Club, P.O. Box 1138, Johannesburg, South Africa.

ROBSON, Ronald Milner
D/12954, 19/4/18, L/C.; demob. 18/3/19.
69 Cambridge Road, Southport.

ROBSON, Stephen Arthur
B/12351, 31/12/17; No. 12 O.C.B., 10/5/18; R. Fus., 3/2/19; 2/Lieut.
30 Southend Road, Grays, Essex.

ROBSON, Thomas Frederick
6/4/6671, 7/10/15; Yorks. L.I., 6/7/16; Lieut.; w.

ROBSON, William Archibald
E/14072, 27/9/18; demob. 11/1/19.
42 Turner Street, Redcar, Yorkshire.

ROBY, Henry
6/1/5648, 16/8/15; North'd. Fus., 20/12/15, att. M.G.C.; F; Lieut.
29 Rosthwaite Road, West Derby, Liverpool.

ROCH, Ernest Twining
6/1/7878, 26/11/15; R.W. Fus., 21/11/16, R.E.; F; Lieut.
Public Works Department, Karachi Buildings, Karachi, India.

ROCHE, George Walter
C/14272, 6/11/18; trfr. K.R. Rif. C., 7/4/19.
26 Lambourne Road, Clapham, S.W. 4.

ROCHE, John Wilson
C/11496, 14/6/17; No. 14 O.C.B., 9/11/17; Norf. R., 28/5/18; F; 2/Lieut.
Beaumont, Badminton Grove, Ebbw Vale, Monmouthshire.

ROCHE, William Joseph
E/3060, 16/3/15; R. Ir. Regt., 20/8/15; F; Lieut.; w,p.
Oriel Lodge, 59 Upper Richmond Road, S.W. 13.

ROCHFORD, Walter
6/3/8861, 12/1/16; No. 14 O.C.B., 30/10/16, M.G.C., C/S; M.G.C., 30/1/17, Tank Corps; F; Lieut.
Twinford Hall, Nr. Broxbourne, Hertfordshire.

✠ ROCHFORT, Arthur D'Oyly
6/8702, 4/1/16; R.A., C/S, 23/6/16; R.G.A., 30/9/16, R.A.F.; E; Lieut.
Died 31/10/18.

RODDICK, George
C/12580, 6/2/18, L/C.; H. Bde. O.C.B., 7/6/18; Scots Gds., 4/2/19; 2/Lieut.
21 Dover Road, Birkdale, Lancashire.

RODDICK, James Albert
2/3465, 3/5/15, L/C.; Hamps. R., 2/10/15, W. Rid. R.; F; Major; D.S.O., M.C., M(2).
68 Park Lane, Croydon, Surrey.

RODEN, Sampson William
6/1/9335, 7/2/16, L/C.; No. 14 O.C.B., 26/11/16; Shrop. L.I., 28/2/17; Lieut.
Melbourne Cottage, Wilden, Nr. Stourport.

RODERICK, Benjamin
6/2/7185, 3/11/15, L/C.; No. 11 O.C.B., 7/5/16; Welch R., 4/9/16; F; Lieut.
Ashbrook House, Aberdare, South Wales.

RODGER, Will Ashton
K/F/2461, 28/12/14, Sgt.; Welch R., 11/4/15; F,S; Capt.
24 Strathtay Road, Banner Cross, Sheffield.

RODGERS, Arthur
4/2/4507, 28/6/15; 11th Lond. R., 21/10/15; Lieut.; w.

RODGERS, Gilbert
4/2/5129, 26/7/15; W. Rid. R., 22/7/16; Lieut.; w.

RODGERS, James William
C/D/12074, 1/10/17, Cpl.; demob. 1/2/19.
15 Pitkerro Road, Dundee.

✠ RODGERS, John Richard
4/2/4262, 15/6/15; Hamps. R., 16/10/15, att. Tank Corps; Lieut
Killed in action 20/11/17.

RODWELL, Arthur Christopher
B/10125, 6/12/16, L/C.; R.A., C/S, 27/4/17; R.G.A., 1/9/17; Lieut.
16 Victoria Mansions, Queens Club Gardens, West Kensington, W. 14.

RODWELL, John George
4/3/4236, 14/6/15; Midd'x. R., 10/9/15; F; Lieut.
120 Shooters Hill Road, Blackheath, S.E. 3.

ROE, Adolphus Edgar
4/1/6/4237, 14/6/15; Dorset R., 11/11/15, att. R.A.O.C.; M; Capt.
4 Ranworth Mansions, 23 Compayne Gardens, N.W.

ROEBUCK, Edmund de Laval Willis
6/1/8947, 17/1/16, Cpl.; No. 14 O.C.B., 30/10/16; Linc. R, 24/1/17; F; Lieut.; p.
Bank of England, E.C.

ROGER, Alan
B/12837, 22/3/18; H. Bde. O.C.B., 9/8/18; trfr. 14th Lond. R., 7/12/18, R. Fus.; NR; Pte.
Deepdene, Seal Hollow Road, Sevenoaks, Kent.

✠ ROGERS, Cecil Victor de Burgh
6/1/6255, 16/9/15; R.F.C., 21/7/16, R.A.F.; F; 2/Lieut.
Missing presumed killed 21/4/17.

ROGERS, Clive
A/14049, 23/9/18; No. 11 O.C.B., 24/1/19; General List, 8/3/19; 2/Lieut.
P.O. Addo District, Uitenhage, South Africa.

ROGERS, Edward Charles
C/13387, 24/6/18; trfr. 14th Lond. R., 6/12/18.
St. Helen, 8 Goddington Road, Frendsbury, Rochester, Kent.

ROGERS, Ernest Stanley
D/11184, 4/5/17, L/C.; No. 14 O.C.B., 5/10/17; 7th Lond. R. 26/2/18; 2/Lieut.
West Nicholson, Rhodesia.

ROGERS, Frank Cecil
D/10819, 21/2/17; No. 11 O.C.B, 5/7/17; North'd. Fus., 30/10/17; F; 2/Lieut.; w.
7 Eskin Street, Keswick, Cumberland.

ROGERS, George James Arthur
B/10100, 4/12/16, Cpl.; R.G.A., C/S, 28/3/17; R.G.A., 22/7/17; F; Lieut.
3 Telford Avenue, Streatham Hill, S.W. 2.

ROGERS, George William Hope
6/1/7404, 12/11/15; R. Fus., 24/1/17; F; Lieut.; p-w.
54 Raffles Road, Birkenhead.

ROGERS, Griffith William
D/12877, 3/4/18; No. 8 O.C.B., 18/10/18; demob. 20/2/19.
17 Severn Street, Leicester.

ROGERS, Henry Izod
C/10411, 8/1/17; No. 20 O.C.B., 7/6/17; E. Lan. R., 25/9/17; F; 2/Lieut.
St. Michael's Rectory, Stamford, Lincolnshire.

ROGERS, Hubert John Mackarness
D/12911, 8/4/18; demob. 4/3/19.
Ye Bath Cottage, Bexley, Kent.

ROGERS, James Aubrey
6/4/7564, 17/11/15; No. 11 O.C.B., 7/5/16; Linc. R., 4/9/16; F; Lieut.
17 Mecklenberg Street, Leicester.

✠ ROGERS, John Davenport
A/61, 8/4/08; dis. 7/4/09.
Died 27/8/14.

ROGERS, John Emrys
4/9698, 9/10/16; No. 14 O.C.B., 27/12/16; Linc. R., 25/4/17; F; Lieut.; w(2); M.C.
17 Severn Street, Leicester.

APPENDIX II.—RECORDS OF RANK AND FILE.

✠ ROGERS, Leonard Neville
E/2775, 25/1/15; North'd. Fus., 4/5/15; F; Capt.
Killed in action 11/8/17.

ROGERS, Oliver
4/5/6/4723, 9/7/15; trfr. R.G.A., 26/9/16; R.F.A., 12/8/18; Lieut.

✠ ROGERS, Percy Alexander Mackarness
6/1/6254, 16/9/15; W. York. R., 7/1/16; F; Lieut.
Killed in action 9/10/17.

ROGERS, Percy Miller Maclean
C/11776, 30/7/17; No. 14 O.C.B., 4/1/18; Midd'x. R., 10/9/18, att. R. Fus.; 2/Lieut. 53 Friends Road, Croydon, Surrey.

ROGERS, Ronald Clayton
B/12364, 3/1/18, Sgt.; No. 5 O.C.B., 6/9/18, No. 8 O.C.B.; R. Suss. R., 16/3/19; 2/Lieut.
88 Beaconsfield Road, Brighton, Sussex.

✠ ROGERS, Sidney Frederick
C/10990, 29/3/17; R.E., 9/7/17; 2/Lieut. Killed 31/12/17.

ROGERS, Sydney
3/9619, 18/9/16, L/C.; No. 14 O.C.B., 27/12/16; Sco. Horse Yeo., 25/4/17; Lieut. Chemis, Dawlish Road, Brondesbury, N.W. 2.

ROGERS, William Edwin
4/5/4725, 9/7/15, L/C.; L'pool. R., 15/4/16; Lieut.
4 Rivington Road, Seacombe, Wallasey, Cheshire.

ROGERSON, Stanley
3/3660, 17/5/15; Glouc. R., 21/8/15, Army Cyc. Corps; F; Lieut.; w. Ivydene, Oakfield Road, East Cowes, Isle of Wight.

ROGERS-TILLSTONE, Ernest Monkhouse
4/3322, 19/4/15; R.G.A., 1/6/15; F,S,SR; Major; D.S.O., M.C., M(3). Tinogasta, F.C.A. del N., Argentina.

ROLFE, Eustace William Somerville
4/3/4427, 24/6/15; W. Rid. R., 9/2/16; 2/Lieut.
The Rectory, Kirk Bramwith, Doncaster.

✠ ROLFE, Wilfred Edwin
D/6/9172, 27/1/16; No. 14 O.C.B., 26/11/16; Oxf. & Bucks. L.I., 28/2/17; 2/Lieut. Killed in action 22/8/17.

ROLLAND, John Francis
Sq/224, 13/5/08; dis. 12/5/12; rej. Sq/929, 5/8/14, Cpl.; E. Rid. York. Yeo., 23/9/14; Lieut.; w; M(1).

ROLLIT, Dorrell Kaye
1/3373, 24/4/15; 9th Lond. R., 22/9/15; F; Lieut.; w.
37 Ambleside Drive, Southend-on-Sea.

✠ ROLSTON, Leslie Hicks
6/1/6700, 7/10/15; R.A., C/S, 31/3/16; R.G.A., 2/8/16; F; Lieut.
Died of wounds 1/4/18.

ROMER, Charles Robert Ritchie
C/1715, 15/10/14; K.R. Rif. C., 2/1/15; F; Capt.; w; O.B.E., M(2). 43 Scarsdale Villas, Kensington, W. 8.

✠ ROMER, Guy Frederick
A/2100, 16/11/14; Midd'x. R., 10/2/15; 2/Lieut.
Died of wounds 3/5/16.

ROMER, Harold George
B/1251, 23/9/14; 22nd Lond. R., 27/9/14; Capt.
6 Mechlin Mansions, Brook Green, W. 6.

ROMILLY, Frederic Carnegie
A/1981, 27/10/14; R.G.A., 12/11/14; Lieut.
44 Wilton Crescent, Knightsbridge, S.W. 1.

RONALD, Warwick
4/Sq/4545, 1/7/15; R.A.S.C., 22/11/15, att. R.F.C., R.A.F.; Lieut.
Highbury, Sewardston, West Chingford, Essex.

RONALD, William Douglas
D/2678, 8/1/15; High. L.I., 26/2/15; Lieut.
Highbury, Sewardston, West Chingford, Essex.

✠ RONCA, Edward Henry
D/11841, 9/8/17, L/C.; No. 14 O.C.B., 4/1/18; E. Kent R., 25/6/18; F; 2/Lieut. Killed in action 17/10/18.

✠ ROOK, Reuben Victor
6/5/7088, 30/10/15; 20th Lond. R., 4/9/16; F; Capt.; w.
Killed 30/8/18.

ROOKS, Henry Courtenay
D/13705, 31/7/18; No. 11 O.C.B., 24/1/19; General List, 8/3/19; 2/Lieut. 75 Picton Street, Port of Spain, Trinidad, British West Indies.

ROONEY, Thomas
4/4292, 17/6/15; No. 11 O.C.B., 7/5/16; R.W. Kent R., 4/9/16; F,It; Capt.; M.C. and Bar. 10/11 Stonecutter Street, E.C. 4.

✠ ROOT, Harold Walter
3/3332, 21/4/15, Cpl.; Som. L.I., 4/10/15, M.G.C.; F; Lieut.; w-p. Died of wounds 22/3/18 as Prisoner of War.

ROPER, Edward Magee
1/9765, 20/10/16; No. 14 O.C.B., 27/12/16; Suff. R., 27/3/17; Lieut.; w.

ROPER, Henry Leslie
A/13136, 27/5/18; trfr. K.R. Rif. C., 7/4/19.

✠ ROSCOE, Richard Lang
B/1258, 23/9/14; R. Fus., 19/10/14; F; Capt.; w; M.C., M(1).
Died of wounds 4/2/17.

ROSCOW, Walter Ainger
A/11902, 23/8/17, L/C.; No. 14 O.C.B., 7/12/17; York. & Lanc. R., 28/5/18, att. E. York. R.; F; 2/Lieut.
Eccles-by-Sea, Lessingham, Norfolk.

ROSE, Arthur George
D/10221, 20/12/16, L/C.; R.A., C/S, 29/6/17; R.G.A., 2/12/17; F; 2/Lieut. Wayside, Kineton Road, Olton, Warwickshire.

ROSE, Bernard Marlow
C/12279, 29/11/17; No. 21 O.C.B., 4/10/18; R. Berks. R., 17/3/19; 2/Lieut. 95 Caversham Road, Reading.

ROSE, Duke Conway
Sq/2872, 3/2/15; Pemb. Yeo., 3/4/15; E; Lieut.
Hernewood, Mumbles, South Wales.

ROSE, Edward Cranfield
1/3316, 19/4/15; R.F.A., 10/9/15; Lieut.; p; M(1).

✠ ROSE, Geoffrey Craig
A/960, 5/8/14; Sea. Highrs., 15/8/14, att. Gord. Highrs.; 2/Lieut.
Died of wounds 13/2/15.

ROSE, Harry Cecil
C/29, 3/4/08; R.A.S.C., 28/9/10; E,S; Major; M(2).
Faringdon, Berkshire.

ROSE, Howard John
6/1/8119, 2/12/15; R. Suss. R., 18/12/16; F; Capt.
Hertford College, Oxford.

ROSE, Hubert Alan
6/1/7950, 29/11/15; No. 14 O.C.B., 30/10/16; R. Scots, 24/1/17; F; Lieut.; g. 10 Old Square, Lincoln's Inn, W.C. 2.

ROSE, Kenneth Woodhouse
C/13403, 28/6/18; trfr. 14th Lond. R., 6/12/18.
The Mount, Halesowen, Nr. Birmingham, Worcestershire.

ROSE, Leonard Gordon
D/10448, 10/1/17; R.A., C/S, 27/4/17; R.G.A., 1/9/17; Lieut.
31 Vernon Street, Lincoln.

ROSE, Lewis
B/2658, 12/1/15; Sea. Highrs., 2/6/15.
The Rannoch, Thorntonhall, Glasgow.

ROSE, Reginald George
B/2037, 9/11/14; Essex. R., 17/3/15; 2/Lieut.; w.

ROSE, William Alexander
6/3/8682, 4/1/15; R.A., C/S, 4/8/16; R.G.A., 12/11/16; F; Lieut.
7 Gainsborough Street, Plymouth Green, Manchester.

ROSE, William Harold
B/10673, 9/2/17; R.A., C/S, 22/6/17; R.F.A., 18/11/17; F; Lieut.
161 High Road, Streatham, S.W. 16.

ROSEDALE, Thorold Honyel Pelly
D/13769, 7/8/18; trfr. 14th Lond. R., 6/12/18, Gord. Highrs.; Sgt.
7 Gloucester Street, Victoria, S.W. 1.

ROSE-TROUP, John Montgomery
B/507, 4/11/10; R.W. Surr. R., 13/4/12; F; Capt.; w.
Wyndham Cottage, Roxeth Hill, Harrow, Middlesex.

ROSEWARNE, John Noel
A/12505, 29/1/18; No. 21 O.C.B., 7/6/18; D. of Corn. L.I., 4/2/19; 2/Lieut. 8 Clifton Gardens, Truro, Cornwall.

ROSHER, Leslie
4/1/4327, 19/6/15; R.F.A., 30/9/15; Capt.; M.C.
42 Ranelagh Gardens, Barnes, S.W. 13.

ROSS, Alexander Lewis
4/1/5016, 22/7/15, L/C.; R.A.S.C., 1/1/16; I,M,Persia; Capt.; M.B.E., M(2). 9 Serle Street, Lincolns Inn, W.C. 2.

ROSS, Alfred James
4/4293, 17/6/15; R.F.A., C/S, 31/3/16; R.F.A., 20/8/16; F; Lieut.; w. 2 Dinsdale Road, Blackheath, S.E. 3.

ROSS, Charles Percy
4/6/5/4584, 1/7/15; Suff. R., 23/8/15; Lieut.
Kelvin, Baxwell Road, Berkhamsted.

APPENDIX II.—RECORDS OF RANK AND FILE.

ROSS, Colin Trevor
6/3/7055, 28/10/15, L/C.; K.R. Rif. C., 21/4/16; F; Lieut.
7 Livingston Avenue, Sefton Park, Liverpool.

ROSS, Cyril
B/11402, 30/5/17; No. 14 O.C.B., 9/11/17; L'pool. R., 30/4/18; F; Lieut.; w.
19 Glen Park Road, New Brighton, Cheshire.

✠ ROSS, Donald Neil Campbell
A/Sq/9844, 3/11/16; R.A., C/S, 1/2/17; R.F.A., 16/6/17; 2/Lieut.
Died of wounds 3/11/17.

✠ ROSS, George Augustus Bellair
6/3/7808, 24/11/15; L'pool. R., 23/6/16, att. R.A.F.; F; Lieut.; w.
Killed in action 1/6/18.

ROSS, George John Josiah
6/4/6309, 18/9/15, Sgt.; R.W. Kent R., 9/6/16, S. Wales Bord., Notts. & Derby. R.; F; Lieut.; g.
15 The Drive, Purfleet, Essex.

ROSS, George Montague
B/12363, 29/12/17; No. 7 O.C.B., 10/5/18; Lein. R., 29/10/18; F; 2/Lieut.
59 Henry Street, Limerick, Ireland.

✠ ROSS, Harold
4/9714, 11/10/16, L/C.; No. 16 O.C.B., 5/5/17; Lan. Fus., 28/8/17; F; 2/Lieut.
Died of wounds 8/4/18 as Prisoner of War.

ROSS, Ian Hamilton
C/14142, 11/10/18; No. 11 O.C.B., 24/1/19; General List, 8/3/19; 2/Lieut.
606 West 122nd Street, New York City, U.S.A.

ROSS, John Adams
B/13591, 19/7/18; demob. 30/1/19.
Amphorlie, Castlehead, Paisley.

ROSS, John Colin
C/12624, 18/2/18; No. 21 O.C.B., 5/7/18; trfr. 28th Lond. R., 22/8/18.
Pen-y-Parc, Tredegar, Monmouthshire.

ROSS, John Harold
6/4/5730, 19/8/15; W. York. R., 11/12/15; F; Lieut.
15 Bromley Road, Shipley, Yorkshire

ROSS, Thomas
6/3/9207, 31/1/16; No. 14 O.C.B., 30/10/16; R.N.V.R., 28/2/17; F; Sub. Lieut.; g.
17 Dundonald Road, Glasgow, W.

ROSS, William David
C/12605, 13/2/18; No. 10 O.C.B., 5/7/18; Cam'n. Highrs., 4/3/19; 2/Lieut.
37 Lewisham Park, S.E. 13.

ROSSI, Joseph Arthur
4/1/4238, 14/6/15; R.F.C., 4/9/16, R.A.F.; F; Capt.; w.
Larchwood, Thorpe St. Andrew, Norwich.

ROSSITER, Arthur Rawlinson
6/3/B/7951, 29/11/15; demob. 13/2/19; R.Q.M.S.
New Oxford and Cambridge Club, Stratton Street, W. 1.

ROSSITER, George Hugh Blagdon
6/3/8188, 6/12/15, L/C.; Som. L.I., 25/9/16; F; Capt.; w.
71/74 Little Britain, E.C 1.

ROSSITER, Leslie Anthony
6/3/7594, 18/11/15, L/C.; E. Surr. R., 4/8/16; F; Lieut.
51 Sutton Lane, W. 4

ROSS-TODD, Robert Cecil
B/13571, 19/7/18; trfr. 14th Lond. R., 6/12/18.
14 Princes Square, W. 2.

ROTH, Reginald Arthur
6/D/8005, 30/11/15; R.F.C., C/S, 13/3/17; R.F.C., 19/4/17.
30 Thorney Hedge Road, Gunnersbury, W. 4.

ROTHBAND, Baron Harold
C/1924, 22/10/14; Lan. Fus., 24/2/15; F; Capt.; w.
32 Broadway, Withington, Manchester

✠ ROTHE, Sidney Ernest Orme
4/6/2/4947, 19/7/15, L/C.; Midd'x. R., 21/4/16; F; 2/Lieut.
Killed in action 13/11/16.

ROTHERHAM, Charles Ludlam
C/11065, 12/4/17; R.G.A., C/S, 12/9/17; R.G.A., 4/2/18; F, Lieut.
Parsonage, Parsonage Road, Herne Bay, Kent.

ROTHWELL, Thomas
6/4/9409, 9/2/16; No. 7 O.C.B., 11/8/16; R. Innis. Fus., 18/12/16; F,E,P; Lieut.; w; M.C.
Barnahask, Newtownbarry, Co. Wexford, Ireland.

ROTHWELL, William Edmund
2/3466, 3/5/15; Lan. Fus., 7/9/15, R.F.C., R.A.F.; Lieut.; w; M(1).

ROUGHLEY, Edward
4/3/4093, 7/6/15; S. Lan. R., 28/7/15; F; Capt.
The Hawthorns, Lawton Road, Rainhill, Lancashire.

ROULSTON, Francis William Henry
H/1983, 29/10/14, Sgt.; R. Berks. R., 2/10/15; F; 2/Lieut.
Home Garth, Blenheim Road, Wakefield.

ROUQUETTE, Louis Prestwich
6/2/5341, 2/8/15; R.G.A., 15/11/15, att. Indian Army; P,S; Capt.; Lion and Sun (Persia).
Bray, Berkshire.

ROURKE, Ian Victor
B/13492, 8/7/18; trfr. K.R. Rif. C., 7/4/19.
Bebington, Tudor Road, New Barnet, Hertfordshire.

ROUSE, Aubyn Redmond
2039, 9/11/14, L/C.; R. Berks. R., 10/2/15; 2/Lieut.; w.
Endyon, Walton-on-Thames.

ROUSE, George
6/4/5213, 29/7/15; R.A.S.C., 21/10/15; S; Major.
6 Greenbank, Waterloo, Nr. Liverpool.

ROVER, Frederick Harold
1/3875, 31/5/15; Oxf. & Bucks. L.I., 15/10/15; F,It; Lieut.
45 Richmond Road, Ilford, Essex.

ROWAN, Edgar William James
6/1/5715, 19/8/15, L/C.; Midd'x. R., 1/6/16; Lieut.

ROWBOTHAM, Harold
6/2/D/6672, 7/10/15; No. 6 O.C.B., 15/2/17; R.F.C., 3/4/17, R.A.F.; F; Lieut. 41 Sudworth Road, New Brighton, Cheshire.

ROWE, Benjamin
6/5/5229, 30/7/15; No. 7 O.C.B., 7/4/16; Manch. R., 17/7/16, att. N. Lan. R.; F; Lieut. 53 Lansdowne Road, Bromley, Kent.

ROWE, Clarence Stuart
6/4/7387, 11/11/15; trfr. R.F.A., 5/8/16.
The Grange, Somersham, Huntingdonshire.

ROWE, Digby Scarth
A/9813, 30/10/16; No. 14 O.C.B., 30/1/17; North'd. Fus., 25/4/17; F; Capt. 53 Lansdowne Road, Bromley, Kent.

ROWE, Harry Sibley
4/Sq/4092, 7/6/15, L/C.; Bedf. Yeo., 26/9/15, North'd. Fus.; F; Lieut.; w, g; M.C. and Bar. Windrush Manor, Burford, Oxon.

ROWE, Reginald Graham
6/9454, 14/2/16; R.A., C/S, 25/10/16; M.G.C., 24/2/17; F; Lieut.; w.
Oakland House, Brittania Square, Worcester.

✠ ROWE, Stafford Gordon Garnett Godfrey Thomas
4/3/5179, 29/7/15; Dorset R., 8/12/15; F; Lieut.
Killed in action 10/11/17.

ROWE, Stanley Ernest
6/5/7427, 15/11/15; trfr. R.G.A., 29/9/16; R.G.A., 18/11/17; F; Lieut.
53 Lansdowne Road, Bromley, Kent.

✠ ROWE, Thomas
B/1708, 15/10/14, L/C.; L'pool. R., 31/10/14; F; 2/Lieut.
Killed in action 23/5/16.

ROWE, Thomas Garfield
4/3317, 19/4/15; Bord. R., 2/12/15; 2/Lieut.
1 Regent Square, Penzance.

ROWE, Victor Gordon
6/5/7428, 15/11/15; North'd. Fus., 4/9/16, att. Bord. R.; F,I; Lieut.; g.
Lorretto, 17 North Road, Clapham, S.W. 4.

ROWE, William Page
6/1/6256, 16/9/15; Garr. O.C.B., 24/4/17; Lab. Corps, 16/6/17; F; 2/Lieut.
c/o Bank of New Zealand, Auckland, New Zealand.

ROWELL, George
F/2993, 1/3/15; North'd. Fus., 12/5/15, emp. R.E.; Lieut.; w; M(1).

ROWLAND, Hugh Mortimer
Sq/162, 18/4/08; dis. 31/12/09; rej. Sq/1005, 6/8/14, Sgt.; N. Som. Yeo., 3/4/15; Capt.
Land Registry, Lincoln's Inn Fields, W.C. 2.

ROWLAND, John Leslie Francis
A/D/11973, 6/9/17; No. 4 O.C.B., 5/4/18; Mon. R., 12/11/18; 2/Lieut. Bank House, Tredegar, Monmouthshire.

ROWLAND, John Turrenne
6/Sq/8036, 30/11/15; R.F.A., C/S, 18/2/16; R.F.A., 15/12/16; Lieut.; w.

✠ ROWLAND, William Charles Roche
6/3/8037, 30/11/15; No. 2 O.C.B., 14/8/16; W. Rid. R., 18/12/16; Lieut.
Killed in action 4/11/18.

APPENDIX II.—RECORDS OF RANK AND FILE.

ROWLAND, William John Wickham
A/11303, 18/5/17; R.F.A., C/S, 28/12/17; trfr. R.F.A., 12/7/18.
Shabbington, Thame, Oxon.

ROWLANDSON, Edward
D/1466, 29/9/14; dis. med. unfit, 4/11/14.
22 Priory Road, Bedford Park, W. 4.

ROWLEY, George Henry
A/10275, 1/1/17; No. 21 O.C.B., 5/5/17; Notts. & Derby. R., 28/8/17, att. R.A.M.C.; F,It; Lieut. 50 Osmaston Road, Derby.

ROWSE, Eric Anthony Ambrose
6/3/6830, 14/10/15; trfr. 14th Lond. R., 2/5/16; F,S,P; Pte.; w; M.M. Clifton Ville, Newquay, Cornwall.

ROWSE, Ivan Ambrose
6/3/6744, 11/10/15; R.W. Surr. R., 4/9/16; F; Lieut.; w. Clifton Ville, Newquay, Cornwall. (Now in West Africa).

ROWSE, Reginald Montague
A/10873, 14/3/17; R.G.A., C/S, 12/9/17; R.G.A., 4/2/18; 2/Lieut.
44 Villiers Road, Southall, Middlesex.

✠ ROWSON, Stanley
H/2/2581, 4/1/15; Lan. Fus., 12/5/15; 2/Lieut.
Killed in action 29/9/16.

✠ ROXBURGH, Alan Cameron
4/Sq/4239, 14/6/15; Notts. & Derby. Yeo., 2/9/15, R.F.C.; S,E,P; Lieut. Died of wounds 27/11/17.

ROXBURGH, Andrew
A/13033, 3/5/18, L/C.; demob. 29/1/19.
271 Clifton Road, Rugby, Warwickshire.

ROXBURGH, Thomas Archibald
6/Sq/6831, 14/10/15, L/C.; R.A., C/S, 24/1/16; R.F.A., 15/6/16; F; Major; M.C.
Walkerswood, Jamaica, British West Indies.

ROY, Charles Fleming
B/11403, 30/5/17; R.E., C/S, 30/9/17; R.E., 9/11/17; Germ.WA; 2/Lieut.
c/o S. Sinclair Esq., Elenbrook, Shanklin, Isle of Wight.

ROY, Thomas James
6/8253, 8/12/15; No. 9 O.C.B., 8/3/16; trfr. R.E., 4/8/16; F; Spr. 65 Harberton Road, Highgate, N. 19.

✠ ROYDEN, Thomas Utting
6/5/5268, 31/7/15, Sgt.; K.R. Rif. C., 23/4/16; 2/Lieut.
Killed in action 14/11/16.

ROYLE, Douglas Arthur
3/9729, 16/10/16; No. 14 O.C.B., 30/1/17; Manch. R., 25/4/17; F; Lieut.; w. 9 Chudleigh Road, Twickenham.

ROYLE, John Charles Fanshawe
D/12955, 19/4/18; R.A.O.C., 20/10/18; Lieut.
Eaton Mascott Hall, Shrewsbury.

ROYLE, Stanley Edward Alfred
6/3/7749, 22/11/15; E. Surr. R., 18/12/16, att. R.A.F.; F; Lieut.; w. St. Bernard, Brighton Road, Purley.

ROYLE, Vernon Peter
6/9257, 2/2/16; R.A.O.C., 25/4/16; S; Lieut.
Clougha, Radlett, Hertfordshire.

RUANE, John Edward
4/2/4091, 7/6/15, L/C.; Camb. R., 29/10/15; F; Lieut.; w.
Kingswood, 22 Coventry Road, Ilford, Essex.

RUAULT, Claude
D/1482, 29/9/14; Midd'x. R., 27/10/14, att. R.N.V.R., R.N.A.S. and R.A.F.; F,It; Capt.; Corona d'Italia.
17 Southampton Street, Holborn, W.C.

RUBIN, Albert Reginald
6/3/6898, 18/10/15; dis. med. unfit, 8/8/16.
Khandalla, Flamstead Avenue, Wembley Hill.

RUCK, Denniss Alfred Walter
3/3467, 3/5/15, L/C.; Leic. R., 10/9/15, Ches. R.; F; Lieut.; w.
c/o Standard Bank of South Africa Ltd., Port Elizabeth, South Africa.

RUCKER, Arthur Nevil
C/1162, 14/9/14; dis. med. unfit, 19/9/14; Suff. R., 4/12/15; F; Lieut.; w(2). Everington House, Newbury, Berkshire.

RUCKER, John Hamilton
Sq/3749, 24/5/15, L/C.; Bedf. Yeo., 26/9/15, att. Lothian and Border Horse Yeo.; Lieut. Cudham Hall, Nr. Sevenoaks, Kent.

RUDD, Herbert Edward
B/13615, 24/7/18, L/C.; demob. 23/1/19.
10 Pembroke Road, Widmore, Bromley, Kent.

RUDD, Noel Bateman
K/E/2271, 7/12/14; Norf. R., 25/2/15, Indian Army; I,M,Persia; Capt. The Mount, Thorpe Hamlet, Norwich.

RUDD, Stanley
6/2/4614, 5/7/15, Cpl.; R.A., C/S, 26/5/16; R.G.A., 30/8/16; Lieut.; w.

RUDDOCK, James Herbert
4/3876, 31/5/15, Cpl.; R.F.A., 28/12/15; F; Capt.; g.
287 High Street, Lincoln.

✠ RUDDOCK, Joseph John
2/5908, 30/8/15; R. Lanc. R., 3/1/16; F; Lieut.; w.
Died of wounds 5/6/18.

RUDDOCK, Thomas
1/3183, 6/4/15; E. Surr. R., 23/7/15, E. Kent R., R. War. R.; Lieut.

RUDGE, Ernest Nouaille
A/D/11974, 6/9/17, L./C.; No. 17 O.C.B., 5/4/18; trfr. 28th Lond. R., 11/7/18. Heatherset, St. Georges Hill, Weybridge.

RUDRA, Ayit Amil
A/D/14074, 18/9/18; No. 17 O.C.B., 5/12/18; Indian Army, 30/11/19; 2/Lieut. St. Stephens College, Delhi, India.

RUFF, Horace Haynes
A/13156, 27/5/18; demob. 30/1/19.
63 Vincent Square, Westminster, S.W. 1.

RUFFEL, William Guy
4/3740, 24/5/15; R.G.A., 8/9/15; Lieut.; w. Stebbing, Essex.

RULE, Geoffrey Charles Spurway
6/4/6305, 17/9/15; D. of Corn. L.I., 13/6/16; Lieut.

RULE, Robert
6/1/6609, 4/10/15; R. Lanc. R., 14/7/16; Lieut.
33 Melling Road, Southport.

RUMBALL, Harold George Victor
6/4/9025, 20/1/16; R.A., C/S, 26/10/16; R.G.A., 19/2/17; F,It; Lieut. 177 Ongar Road, Brentwood, Essex.

✠ RUNDLE, Horace Liberty
3396, 26/4/15; Devon. R., 28/7/15; F; 2/Lieut.
Killed in action 20/7/16.

✠ RUNDLE, Stanley
4/6/4981, 19/7/15; R.A.S.C., 11/11/15; Lieut.
Died of wounds 30/4/18 as Prisoner of War.

RUNHAM, Walter Keith
2/3397, 26/4/15; N. Staff. R., 28/7/15, S. Wales Bord.; F; Capt.; w; M.C. and Bar, M(1).
Ellesmere, Apsley, Hemel Hempsted, Hertfordshire.

RUNTZ, Ernest Munro
D/1452, 29/9/14; E. Surr. R., 9/3/15, secd. M.G.C.; F; Major; M(1). 20 Gayfere Street, S.W. 1.

RUSHTON, Gerald Arnold
6/4/6865, 15/10/15; No. 4 O.C.B., 7/3/16; N. Lan. R., 15/7/16; F; Lieut. Caerleon, Elmsley Road, Mosley Hill, Liverpool.

RUSHTON, Wilfred Oates
E/2776, 25/1/15; Lan. Fus., 20/4/15; Capt.; w(2); M.C.
Morningside, Wigan, Lancashire.

RUSSELL, Arthur James
B/12814, 20/3/18, L/C.; H. Bde. O.C.B., 9/8/18; Scots. Gds., 5/3/19; 2/Lieut.
1 Cardigan Court, Cardigan Road, Richmond, S.W.

RUSSELL, Claude
B/K/1313, 26/9/14, Sgt.; Essex R., 3/2/15; F; Lieut.
85 Barrowgate Road, Chiswick, W. 4.

RUSSELL, Daniel George
4/Sq/4442, 26/6/15; R.F.A., 24/9/15; F,E,P; Major; w,g; M.C.
Week Farm, Ventnor, Isle of Wight.

RUSSELL, Edgar James
D/10419, 10/1/17; No. 20 O.C.B., 7/6/17; S. Wales Bord., 25/9/17; F; 2/Lieut.; w.
Riversdale, Morriston, Glamorganshire.

✠ RUSSELL, Edward
A/1126, 7/9/14; Notts. & Derby. R., 27/11/14; Lieut.
Killed in action 1/7/16.

RUSSELL, Frederick Roger
B/A/11019, 11/4/17; R.A., C/S, 25/1/18; R.G.A., 22/7/18; F; 2/Lieut · Kingerby, Malvern.

RUSSELL, Guy
E/1519, 1/10/14, L/C.; R.A.S.C., 8/2/15; Capt.

APPENDIX II.—RECORDS OF RANK AND FILE.

RUSSELL, Hedley Ernest Freshfield
6/1/6701, 7/10/15; General List, 4/8/16, R.F.C., R.A.F.; F;
Capt. 126 High Street, Huntingdon, Huntingdonshire.

RUSSELL, Henry
3/3795, 27/5/15; Hamps. R., 25/8/15; E,P; Capt.; w.
114 Barlow Moor Road, West Didsbury, Manchester.

RUSSELL, James Percy
4/2/4254, 14/6/15; Manch. R., 28/9/15; F; Staff Lieut.; w; M(1).
1 Princes Terrace, Palace Court, Bayswater, W. 2.

RUSSELL, James Smith Thompson
6/2/7079, 29/10/15; No. 9 O.C.B., 8/3/16; Arg. & Suth'd. Highrs,
23/7/16; F; Lieut. Schoolhouse, Glenboig, Scotland.

RUSSELL, John Albert
E/1578, 6/10/14; S. Staff. R., 23/2/15, att. Glouc. R.; F,S; Capt.;
w(2); M.C. 35 Ladbroke Grove, W. 11.

RUSSELL, John Austin Rutter
6/2/6847, 16/10/15; dis. med. unfit, 8/8/16.
Melrose, Manor Road, West Worthing, Sussex.

RUSSELL, Percy
6/1/7056, 28/10/15; No. 11 O.C.B., 7/5/16; Devon. R., 4/9/16,
att. Indian Army; I,P; Lieut.
Steers House, Holcombe Rogers, Nr. Wellington, Somerset.

RUSSELL, Philip George
A/11187, 7/5/17; No. 12 O.C.B., 10/8/17; Yorks. L.I., 27/11/17;
F; Lieut. The Brae, Malton, Yorkshire.

RUSSELL, Reginald James Kingston
6/Sq/7879, 26/11/15, L/C.; No. 1 Cav. C/S, 2/8/16; Lothian and
Bord. Horse Yeo., 27/11/16; S; Capt.; M(2).
73 Cromwell Road, Wimbledon, S.W. 19.

RUSSELL, Richard
D/A/11116, 21/4/17; R.A., C/S, 25/1/18; R. Regt. of Cav.;
2/Lieut. Seafield, Bonmahon, Co. Waterford, Ireland.

RUSSELL, Rupert
D/12878, 3/4/18; R.F.A., C/S, 26/7/18; R.F.A., 7/4/19; 2/Lieut.
4 Mount Crescent, Malton, Yorkshire.

RUSSELL, Spencer Cowper
4/3741, 24/5/15; dis. 24/5/15.

RUSSELL, Warren Augustus
A/14101, 3/10/18; demob. 30/1/19.
School House, Groombridge, Sussex.

RUSSELL-JONES, Gregson
D/12956, 19/4/18; No. 11 O.C.B., 4/10/18; demob. 21/1/19.
22 Oakdale Road, Waterloo, Liverpool.

RUSSELL-SMITH, William
E/1617, 9/10/14; Bedf. R., 27/11/14; Essex R.; F,E,P; Capt.
1 Aubert Park, Highbury, N. 5.

RUST, Francis Holyoake
4/1/4474, 28/6/15; Essex R., 21/10/15; F; Lieut.
White House, Rattlesden, Bury St. Edmunds, Suffolk.

RUST, James
B/13425, 1/7/18; trfr. 14th Lond. R., 6/12/18.
34 Belvidere Crescent, Aberdeen, Scotland.

RUST, Ronald Harry
C/11453, 4/6/17, L/C.; R.G.A., C/S, 23/1/18; R.G.A., 9/7/18;
2/Lieut. Bank House, Kelvedon, Essex.

RUTHERFORD, Cecil Moore
6/1/9295, 3/2/16; No. 7 O.C.B., 4/11/16; R. Dub. Fus., 28/2/17,
att. R.A.F.; F; Lieut. 9 Micklefield Road, Wavertree, Liverpool.

RUTHERFORD, Eric James Wilson
A/13980, 9/9/18; demob. 31/1/19.
Halliford Lodge, Upper Halliford, Middlesex.

RUTHERFORD, Ralph Urquhart
F/2959, 22/2/15, Sgt.; Rif. Brig., 18/6/15; Lieut.; w.
Solorno Court, Banstead, Surrey.

RUTHERFORD, Walter
H/1916, 16/10/14, L/C.; Devon. R., 24/3/15; F; Lieut.
196 Ashley Gardens, S.W. 1.

RUTLAND, Arthur John
6/4/6294, 16/9/15; E. Ang. Div. Cyc. Coy., 28/8/16, Essex R.,
att. Nigeria R.; W. & EA; Lieut.
27 Court Lane, Dulwich Village, S.E. 21.

RUTLAND, Harold Fred
A/14038, 20/9/18; demob. 27/1/19.
27 Court Lane, Dulwich Village, S.E. 21.

RUTLAND, James Hart
B/12425, 17/1/18; No. 13 O.C.B., 7/6/18; Glouc. R., 5/2/19;
2/Lieut. 113 Louisville Road, Balham, S.W. 17.

RUTTER, Jack Gibson
B/12716, 8/3/18; No. 5 O.C.B., 6/9/18; E. Surr. R., 17/3/19;
2/Lieut. Londesborough Lodge, Worcester Park, Surrey.

RUTTER, Walter Harry
E/14119, 9/10/18; demob. 10/1/19.
119 Merton Hale Road, Wimbledon, S.W. 19.

RUTTLE, William Ernest Patrick
D/12971, 3/4/18; No. 11 O.C.B., 4/10/18; Lein. R., 17/3/19;
2/Lieut. 39 Brown Street, Portlaw, Co. Waterford, Ireland.

RUTTLEDGE, Eric Peter Knox
B/12312, 17/12/17; R.F.A., C/S, 15/3/18; R.H. & R.F.A., 11/3/19;
2/Lieut. c/o Lloyds Bank Ltd., Cambridge.

RYAN, Curteis Fraser Maxwell Norwood
A/595, 27/11/11; R.E., 1/9/14; F; Major; w; D.S.O., M.C,
M(3). Treasury Chambers, Whitehall, S.W. 1.

✠ RYAN, Edward St. John Norwood
A/941, 5/8/14; E. Surr. R., 5/10/14; F; Capt.; M.C.
Killed in action 22/10/18.

✠ RYAN, Finlay Francis
6/5/6592, 4/10/15; L'pool. R., 4/9/16; Capt.; M.C.
Killed in action 25/6/17.

✠ RYAN, George Joshua Kroenig
K/D/2223, 2/12/14, Sgt.; dis. med unfit, 15/9/18. Died.

RYAN, Jack
6/2/7388, 11/11/15; dis. med. unfit, 26/9/16.
78 Pepys Road, Wimbledon, S.W. 19.

✠ RYAN, Warwick John Norwood
Sq/989, 5/8/14; Dorset Yeo., 19/12/14; 2/Lieut.
Killed in action 5/9/16.

RYAN, William James
6/5/5637, 16/8/15; No. 1 O.C.B., 25/2/16; 11th Lond. R., 8/7/16,
att. R.A.F.; F; Lieut. 27 Hampton Road, Redland, Bristol.

RYDER, Frank
C/D/12270, 29/11/17; A.S.C., C/S, 16/9/18; R.A.S.C., 10/11/18;
2/Lieut. Hawthorns, Warmley, Gloucestershire.

RYDER, Frederick Keet
4/1/4348, 21/6/15; Hamps. R., 16/10/15, att. M.G.C.; E,P,F;
Lieut. Copthorne, 38 Archers Road, Southampton.

RYDER, Stanley Ralph Stewart
6/5/6702, 7/10/15, L/C.; No. 11 O.C.B., 7/5/16; 20th Lond. R.,
4/9/16, secd. M.G.C.; Lieut.

RYDING, John Thackeray
6/3/7035, 27/10/15; K.R. Rif. C., 1/6/16; Lieut.
36 Ashburton Avenue, Croydon, Surrey.

RYLE, Edward Hewish
6/1/6072, 6/9/15; dis. med. unfit, 16/3/16.
11 Sumner Place, S.W. 7.

RYOTT, Thomas Gurney
A/401, 19/4/09; dis. 1/11/11.

RYVES, Thomas Evan
6/5/8491, 20/12/15; R.F.A., C/S, 15/9/16; R.F.A., 12/1/17;
2/Lieut. 7 Richmond Park Road, Clifton, Bristol.

SAALFELD, Albert Edward
4/6/3816, 27/5/15, L/C.; dis. to R. Mil. Academy, 11/5/16;
R.G.A.; F; Lieut. 12 St. James Square, S.W. 1.

✠ SACH, Charles Burleigh
6/4/6101, 6/9/15; 13th Lond. R., 24/12/15; F; 2/Lieut.
Killed in action 1/7/16.

SACKETT, Gilbert Henry
D/10665, 5/2/17; Garr. O.C.B., 23/5/17; Lab. Corps, 14/7/17;
2/Lieut. c/o F. Sackett Esq., Lond. & Lanc. Insurance Coy. Ltd., 66
Cornhill, E.C. 3.

SACRÉ, Francis Claud
A/13126, 27/5/17; demob. 29/1/19.
28 Lambolle Road, Hampstead, N.W. 3.

SADDLETON, William Henry
6/2/6257, 16/9/15; Durh. L.I., 21/12/15, secd. M.G.C.; Lieut.;
w. 3 Melrose Mansions, Walm Lane, Cricklewood, N.W. 10.

APPENDIX II.—RECORDS OF RANK AND FILE.

SADLER, Alfred Victor
6/4/9177, 27/1/16; No. 13 O.C.B., 4/11/16; W. York. R., 28/2/17, att. M.G.C.; F; Lieut. 34 Molineux Street, Derby.

SADLER, Bernard Eustace
C/12658, 27/2/18; R.A.F., C/S, 30/5/18; R.A.F., 11/10/18; F; 2/Lieut. 72 Shakespeare Road, Hanwell, W.7.

SADLER, Cecil Molineux
6/5/7880, 26/11/15; Worc. R., 18/12/16; F; Capt.
The Bungalow, Hassocks, Sussex.

SADLER, Leonard Mountford
D/13770, 7/8/18; demob. 19/12/18.
Breydon, Oakhill Gardens, Woodford Green, Essex.

SADLER, Michael Charles Stanley
6/3/6366, 20/9/15; Derby. Yeo., 2/12/15; Lieut.; M.C.
Walpole House, Burton-on-Trent.

SAFFORD, Archibald
B/1358, 26/9/14; R.A.S.C., 30/11/14; Capt.; M.C.

SAINSBURY, Eric John
4/5/4763, 12/7/15, Sgt.; R.A., C/S, 31/3/16; R.G.A., 2/8/16; Lieut.; w; M.B.E., Croix de Guerre (French).
33 Clonmel Road, Fulham, S.W.6.

SAINSBURY, Nelson Horatio Ethelbert
10439, 10/1/17; trfr. Hamps. Yeo., 16/5/17.
Frost Hill, Overton, Nr. Basingstoke, Hampshire.

SAINT, Percy Errington Wales
6/5/5390, 5/8/15; R.A.S.C., 11/11/15, R.E.; F; Lt.-Col.
Tai Cluwdd, Ruabon, Denbighshire.

SAINT, Roland Cyril
A/11654, 12/7/17; No. 11 O.C.B., 9/11/17; Bord. R., 30/4/18; F; 2/Lieut. 135 Warwick Road, Carlisle.

ST. AUBYN, John Kenilworth
2/3742, 24/5/15, Sgt.; 7th Lond. R., 8/7/16; Lieut.; w.

ST. GEORGE, H. E. See VON-HEYDER, H.

ST. HILL, Harry
B/3061, 16/3/15; Devon. R., 11/6/15, att. R.A.F.; F; Lieut.
Te Hira, Rugby.

ST. JOHN-SMITH, Jack Eric
C/12582, 6/2/18; No. 3 O.C.B., 9/8/18; N. Staff. R., 4/3/19; 2/Lieut. Gorse Cottage, Bowes Road, Walton-on-Thames.

✠ ST. LEGER, William Brett
6/2/7187, 3/11/15; Cold. Gds., 5/3/16; Lieut.; w; M.C.
Killed in action 27/4/18.

ST. LEGIER, Gerald William
6/3/7084, 30/10/15, L/C.; Devon. R., 4/9/16; p; M.C.
5 Grosvenor Road, Gunnersbury, W.7.

SAINTON, Philip Prosper
6/1/8397, 14/12/15; R. Suss. R., 4/9/16, secd. M.G.C.; 2/Lieut.
14 Melcombe Court, Dorset Square, N.W.1.

SALATHIEL, Trevor Snell
B/Sq/D/12777, 15/3/18; No. 18 O.C.B., 20/9/18; trfr. 5th Lond. R., 7/2/19. Bryn Martin, Caerphilly, South Wales.

SALE, John Francis
B/6/6426, 23/9/15; R.G.A., 10/11/16. The Orchard, Atherstone.

✠ SALE, Richard Lander
Sq/3796, 27/5/15, L/C.; R. Horse Gds., 2/10/15; Lieut.
Died of wounds 15/1/18.

SALEW, Louis George Leslie
A/D/12447, 22/1/18; R.A.F., C/S, 19/4/18; F,I; Lieut.
c/o Major G. A. Salew, S. & T. Corps Supply Depot, Jubbulpore.

✠ SALISBURY, Robert Cecil
6/5/5269, 31/7/15; L'pool. R., 13/12/15; Capt.
Killed in action 22/3/18.

SALLAI, Charles Greenslade
6/5/7118, 1/11/15; R.N.V.R., 21/11/16, Indian Army; F,P; Capt.
2/76th Punjabis. c/o Cox & Coy., Bombay, India.

SALMON, Joseph Eric
3/3172, 6/4/15, Sgt.; Dorset R., 30/6/15; F; Lieut.; w.
Upway, The Drive, Sevenoaks, Kent.

SALMON, Ronald Cedric
6/4/8373, 13/12/15; 13th Lond. R., 22/11/16, att. Rif. Brig.; F; Capt. c/o Overseas Club, Aldwych, W.C.

SALMOND, James Bell
4/1/4546, 1/7/15; R. Highrs., 17/11/15; F; Capt.
Springbank, Arbroath, Scotland.

SALMOND, Theodore David Eric
B/12796, 18/3/18; No. 18 O.C.B., 20/9/18, No. 11 O.C.B.; General List, 8/3/19; 2/Lieut.
Oatlands, Victoria Parade, Pwllheli, North Wales.

SALT, Alfred Cyril Josiah
6/Sq/8148, 3/12/15; L/C.; No. 2 Cav. C/S, 21/10/16; 1st R. Regt. of Cav., 20/12/16, att. Drag. Gds., Indian Army; F,I; Capt. c/o Alliance Bank of Simla, Quetta, Baluchistan, India.

SALT, Cyril
B/658, 1/11/12; dis. 11/12/12; R.N.D.
36 Rockmount Road, Norwood, S.E.19.

SALTER, George Edward
B/10311, 2/1/17, L/C.; No. 21 O.C.B., 5/5/17; Dorset R., 28/8/17; F; 2/Lieut.
3 Empress Avenue, Woodford Green, Essex.

SALTER, Harry
A/13960, 6/9/18; demob. 6/1/19. 2 Penn Road, Holloway, N.7.

SALTON, Alexander John
6/8525, 29/12/15; R.F.C., 7/7/16, R.A.F.; F; Capt.
Portland House, West Hartlepool.

SALTON, George Logan
6/Sq/9529, 16/2/16; No. 2 Cav. C/S, 1/9/16; 11th R. Regt. of Cav., 20/12/16, 10th Huss., R.F.A.; F; Major; M(1).
Bellevue, Wellington Road, Taunton, Somerset.

SALVESEN, Philip
6/5/C/6050, 3/9/15; No. 7 O.C.B., 7/4/16; dis. med. unfit, 30/12/16. 39 Kenmore Road, Liverpool.

SAMBROOK, Henry Fabian
6/Sq/5836, 26/8/15; R.E., 18/1/16; Lieut.
Craneton, Bickley, Kent.

SAMMAN, Charles Frederick Galloway
B/D/12017, 17/9/17; No. 18 O.C.B., 10/5/18; trfr. 28th Lond. R., 2/11/18. Ilton Vicarage, Ilminster, Somerset.

SAMPSON, Caryl
4/1/4655, 5/7/15; trfr. H.A.C., 24/7/16.

SAMPSON, Ernest Wyatt
D/13800, 9/8/18; No. 11 O.C.B., 24/1/19; General List, 8/3/19; 2/Lieut.
c/o Standard Bank of South Africa Ltd., 10 Clements Lane, E.C.4.

SAMPSON, Frank
6/Sq/6832, 14/10/15; R.F.A., C/S, 31/3/16; R.F.A., 5/8/16; F; Lieut. Ferndale, Manor Road, Sutton Coldfield, Warwick.

SAMPSON, Fredric Harold
6/1/7952, 29/11/15, L/C.; No. 8 O.C.B., 4/8/16; R. War. R., 21/11/16; Lieut.

SAMPSON, Geoffrey Marquick
1/3661, 17/5/15; trfr. H.A.C., 12/5/16.

✠ SAMPSON, Hugh Delane
C/Sq/10392, 8/1/17; A.S.C., C/S, 1/5/17; R.A.S.C., 28/6/17; 2/Lieut. Died of wounds 2/9/17.

SAMS, Charles Egbert Reynolds
A/14340, 30/12/18; demob. 23/1/19.
61 Eardley Crescent, Earls Court, S.W.5.

SAMUEL, Archibald
6/1/9039, 20/1/16; R.A., C/S, 4/8/16; R.G.A., 12/11/16; Lieut.
Pwll, Llanelly, South Wales.

SAMUEL, Cecil Harry
A/894, 5/8/14; Lan. Fus., 19/9/14; F,S; Capt.
12 Hanover Terrace, N.W.1.

SAMUEL, David Sydney
D/10891, 16/3/17; R.E., 9/6/17; F; Lieut.
Tanlan, Llanelly, South Wales.

SAMUEL, Tristram Albert Seton
6/4/8316, 11/12/15, L/C.; 15th Lond. R., 22/11/16; F; 2/Lieut.; w; M.C. North Hill House, Torpoint, Cornwall.

✠ SAMUELS, George Bernard
4/1/4255, 14/6/15; Durh. L.I., 18/10/15, R.F.C.; F; 2/Lieut.
Died 22/10/16.

SAMUELS, Sydney Morris
D/9986, 22/11/16; No. 14 O.C.B., 6/4/17; R. Fus., 31/7/17, Indian Army; F,It; Lieut.; M.C. and Bar. 156 Aldersgate Street, E.C.

SAMUELSON, Geoffrey Lionel
B/1105, 7/9/14; E. Kent R., 3/10/14; Capt.; w; M(1).
Bodicote Grange, Banbury, Oxon.

SAMUELSON, Vivian Francis
K/E/2130, 19/11/14; R.W. Surr. R., 27/1/15; Capt.; w; M.C., M(1).

APPENDIX II.—RECORDS OF RANK AND FILE.

✠ SANCTUARY, *Charles Lloyd*
B/1054, 31/8/14; Suff. R., 19/9/14; Capt.; *w*; M.C.
　　　　　　　　　　　　　　　Died of wounds 15/11/16.

SANDEMAN, *Gerald*
A/1375, 26/9/14; R.F.A., 5/10/14; F; Major; M(1).
　　　　　　　　　　　　　　　5 Courtfield Gardens, S.W. 5.

SANDER, *Eric Henry Lancelot*
2/3606, 13/5/15; Midd'x. R., 21/8/15; F,It; Capt.; *w*; M.C.
　　　　　　　　　　　　21 Tunstall Road, East Croydon, Surrey.

SANDERS, *Allan Dudley Clarke*
A/13072, 15/5/18, L/C.; trfr. K.R. Rif. C., 7/4/19, M.G.C.; L/C
　　　　　　　　　　　　6 Preston Road, Leytonstone, E. 11.

SANDERS, *Guy*
Sq/3184, 6/4/15; R.F.A., 31/5/15; Capt.; *w*.
　　　　　　　　　　9 Livingstone Mansions, Queens Club Gardens, W. 14.

SANDERS, *Henry Percy Stanley*
D/Sq/13771, 7/8/18; demob. 30/5/19.
　　　　　　　　　　Manor House, Tunstall, Catterick, Yorkshire.

SANDERS, *Patrick Donald*
6/5/5955, 1/9/15; R.G.A., 30/11/15; F; Lieut.; *w*.
　　　　　　　　　　　　　Driftway, Nr. Epsom, Surrey.

✠ SANDERS, *William Alfred Thomas*
6/1/6304, 18/9/15; 13th Lond. R., 19/12/15; 2/Lieut.
　　　　　　　　　　　　　　Killed in action 9/9/16.

SANDERS, *William Rutherford*
1/3675, 17/5/15; trfr. 5th Lond. R., 24/3/16.
　　　　　　　　Drayton, Dudsbury Avenue, Ferndown, Wimborne.

✠ SANDERSON, *Charles Buswell*
6/1/8425, 15/12/15; trfr. Class W. Res., 4/12/16; R.A.F.; F;
2/Lieut. 　　　　　　Died of wounds 17/10/18 as Prisoner of War.

SANDERSON, *Elliot Albert*
E/14055, 23/9/18; demob. 10/1/19.
　　　　　　Heath Park Lodge, Leighton Buzzard, Bedfordshire.

✠ SANDERSON, *Eric Harward*
2/9676, 2/10/16, Cpl.; R.A., C/S, 12/1/17; R.F.A., 5/6/17;
2/Lieut. 　　　　　　　　　　Killed in action 24/9/18.

SANDERSON, *Geoffrey Ernest*
4/9717, 11/10/16; R.G.A., C/S, 17/2/17; R.G.A., 18/5/17; Lieut.
　　　　　　　　　　　The Gables, Hessle, East Yorkshire.

SANDERSON, *James*
C/11757, 26/7/17; A.S.C., C/S, 1/11/17; R.A.S.C., 25/1/18; S;
Lieut. 　　　　　　Dunmow House, Newmarket, Cambridgeshire.

SANDERSON, *James Ross*
C/D/14253, 30/10/18; trfr. 6th R. Regt. of Cav., 11/6/19.
　　　　　　　　　　41 Marlborough Hill, St. Johns Wood, N.W. 8.

✠ SANDERSON, *Lancelot*
Sq/315, 30/6/08; dis. 31/8/11; Camel Corps; M(1).
　　　　　　　　　　　　　　　　Died -/4/16.

SANDERSON, *Roland Crisp*
B/C/12219, 14/11/17; No. 11 O.C.B., 1/2/19; General List,
8/3/19; 2/Lieut.
c/o Lond. & S. West. Bank Ltd., 170 Fenchurch Street, E.C. 3.

SANDERSON, *Victor Stewart*
D/11873, 16/8/17; No. 3 O.C.B., 8/2/18; 11th Lond. R., 30/7/18;
F; 2/Lieut. 　　　　　　　　7 Monahan Avenue, Purley, Surrey.

SANDIFORD, *Hubert Cecil*
C/10833, 3/3/17, L/C.; R.G.A., C/S, 20/6/17; R.G.A., 18/11/17;
Lieut. 　　　　　　　Glenside, Bankhall Lane, Hale, Cheshire.

SANDOE, *John*
C/11777, 30/7/17; R.E., C/S, 7/10/17; R.E., 11/1/18; F; 2/Lieut.
　　　　　　　　Stand 3028, Muir Avenue, Brakpan, South Africa.

SANDS, *George Edward*
C/13356, 24/6/18; demob. 29/1/19.
　　　　　　　　　20 Casewick Road, West Norwood, S.E. 27.

SANDYS, *Henry Claude Congreve*
2/9691, 4/10/16; R.A., C/S, 15/3/17; R.F.A., 8/9/17; F; 2/Lieut.
　　　　　　　　　　　Raglan House, Brooklands, Cheshire.

SANFORD, *John Collins*
D/2664, 12/1/15, L/C.; Oxf. & Bucks. L.I., 21/7/15, att. M.G.C.;
F; Lieut. 　　　　　　　Athol Lodge, Wallington, Surrey.

SANGSTER-GREEN, *George Cecil Lewis*
6/1/7057, 28/10/15; R.A.S.C., 9/11/16; M; Lieut.
　　　　　　　c/o E. C. Pullan Esq., 36 Bloomsbury Square, W.C.

SANKEY, *Geoffrey Barham*
C/474, 16/3/10; Kent Cyc. Bn., 4/12/14; I; Major, D.A.A.G.
　　　　　　　　　　　　　　44 Russell Square, W.C. 1.

SANSOM, *Albert Edward*
6/1/6776, 11/10/15; Indian Army, 18/6/17; Lieut.
　　　　　　　　　　　Kingsmead Avenue, Worcester Park.

SANSOM, *Frederick Arthur*
H/2584, 4/1/15; Bedf. R., 31/3/15; F; Lieut.
　　　　　　　　　　　Poundstock, Bude, North Cornwall.

SAPSED, *Arthur Harold*
6/3/6442, 25/9/15; No. 2 Cav. C/S, 31/3/16; Notts. & Derby.
Yeo., 6/9/16; S,E; Lieut.
　　　　　　　　　　　43 Bellingham Road, Catford, S.E. 6.

SARA, *Stanley Eric*
A/D/13021, 1/5/18; R.E., C/S, 11/10/18; demob. 27/1/19.
　　　　　　　　　　　Newnham Lodge, Belvedere, Kent.

✠ SARGEANT, *Bernard Theobald*
6/1/9557, 29/2/16; No. 14 O.C.B., 30/10/16; 8th Lond. R.,
24/1/17; F; 2/Lieut. 　　　　　　Killed in action 5/4/17.

SARGENT, *Cyril Grosvenor*
C/11045, 13/4/17; trfr. Norf. R., 9/7/17.
　　　　　　　　Morningthorpe Manor, Long Stratton, Norfolk.

SARGENT, *Evelyn Fitzgerald*
2/3141, 29/3/15, L/C.; K.R. Rif. C., 8/9/15; Lieut.; *w*, *p*; M.C.
　　　　　　　　　　　Raglan, Dane Road, Seaford, Sussex.

SARGENT, *John Herbert*
6/8374, 13/12/15; R.N.V.R., 26/12/15.
　　　　　　　　　Glengariff, Tussell Hill, Purley, Surrey.

SARGINSON, *Frederick William*
6/8002, 29/11/15; R.F.A., C/S, 1/3/16; R.F.A., 6/7/16; F,It;
Lieut. 　　　　　　P.O. Box 5043, Johannesburg, South Africa.

✠ SARSON, *Herbert William Phillips*
4/3877, 31/5/15; Yorks. L.I., 29/7/15; 2/Lieut.
　　　　　　　　　　　　　　Died of wounds 20/10/15.

✠ SARTORIS, *Charles Frederick*
C/1036, 24/8/14; Leic. R., 12/9/14, att. R. Fus.; G; Lieut.
　　　　　　　　　　　　　　Killed in action 25/6/15.

SARZANO, *Carlos*
4/5/4873, 15/7/15; S. Notts. Huss. Yeo., 28/12/15.

SATCHELL, *Hugh Glanville*
6/2/9362, 7/2/16; No. 5 O.C.B., 14/8/16; R. Scots, 21/11/16,
secd. R.E.; F; Lieut.; *w*.
　　　　　　　Charlbury, Castle Bar Road, Ealing, W. 5.

SATOW, *Hugh Ralph*
4/1/4159, 10/6/15; R.A.S.C., 8/7/15; F; Major; C.B.E., O.B.E.
Ordre de la Couronne (Belge). Paskers Lane, Shenfield, Essex.

SAUL, *Edward Royston*
6/2/9440, 10/2/16; No. 8 O.C.B., 4/8/16; R.A.M.C., 16/9/16; I;
Capt. 　　　　　c/o Holt & Coy., 3 Whitehall Place, S.W. 1.

SAULEZ, *Robert George Rendall*
Sq/2194, 26/11/14; R.A.S.C., 18/12/15; E,P; Capt.; M.1).
　　　　　　Willingale, Ongar, Essex. (Now in India).

✠ SAUMAREZ, *Reginald Stafford*
A/457, 10/1/10; dis. 9/1/14; rej. A/842, 4/8/14; 22nd Lond. R.,
29/8/14; F; Capt.; M.C. 　　　　　Killed in action 23/3/18.

SAUNDERS, *Cecil Edward Arthur*
3/3709, 20/5/15, L/C.; North'd. Fus., 26/8/15; Lieut.
　　　　　　Sutherland House, London Street, Hyde Park, W. 2.

SAUNDERS, *Edward Eliot*
6/4/6367, 20/9/15, L/C.; D. of Corn. L.I., 1/6/16; F; Lieut.; *w*;
M(1).
Thys Ziyir Doorns, P.O. Buckingham, West Transvaal, South
Africa.

✠ SAUNDERS, *Frank William*
C/6/9167, 26/1/16; No. 14 O.C.B., 30/10/16; Arg. & Suth'd.
Highrs., 28/2/17; Lieut. 　　　　　Killed in action 1/8/18.

SAUNDERS, *Guy Farewell*
6/2/9540, 18/2/16; Suff. Yeo., 13/7/16, secd. K.Af. Rif.; EA;
Capt. 　　　147 Clarence Gate Gardens, Regents Park, N.W.

SAUNDERS, *Hilary Aidan St. George*
6/1/9534, 18/2/16; Welch Gds., 16/6/16; F; Lieut.; M.C.
　　　　　　　36 Abingdon Mansions, Kensington, W. 8.

SAUNDERS, *James Restell Ernest*
4/1/5180, 29/7/15; retd. to 13th Lond. R., 13/1/16.
　　　　　　　Kinsfarms Lodge, The Woodlands, Isleworth.

✠ SAUNDERS, *Reginald Arthur*
C/644, 18/6/12; R.F.A., R.F.C.; F; Lieut.; M.C., M(1).
　　　　　　　　　　　　　Killed in action 14/3/16.

APPENDIX II.—RECORDS OF RANK AND FILE.

✠ SAUNDERS, Robert
4/4294, 17/6/15; No. 14 O.C.B.; M.G.C., 25/9/16; 2/Lieut.
Killed in action 26/10/17.

SAUNDERS, Thomas William
C/9922, 15/11/16; No. 14 O.C.B., 6/4/17; L'pool. R., 28/8/17, F; Lieut.; p. 111 Arundel Road, Sefton Park, Liverpool.

SAUNDERS, William Henry
6/1/6751, 9/10/15, L/C.; No. 11 O.C.B., 7/5/16; Suff. R., 4/9/16; W,A,F; Lieut.
Elder Grove, Newton Road, Ashton-on-Ribble, Preston, Lancashire.

SAUNDERS, William Morley
C/Sq/10606, 22/1/17, L/C.; No. 1 Cav. C/S, 1/9/17; R. Regt. of Cav., 9/5/18; 2/Lieut. Wennington Hall, Nr. Lancaster.

SAUNDERS-JACOBS, Ruskin Atkinson
B/12778, 15/3/18; R.E., C/S, 23/8/18; demob.
195 Romford Road, Forest Gate, E 7.

SAUNDRY, John Baynard Hingston
6/4/6637, 4/10/15, C.Q.M.S.; demob. 1/5/19.
c/o Mrs. Hill, 30 Lithos Road, Hampstead, N.W. 3.

SAVAGE, Basil
C/13395, 24/6/18; trfr. 14th Lond. R., 6/12/18.
Blandford House, Iffley Road, Oxford.

SAVAGE, Cyril Albert
B/12838, 22/3/18; R.F.A., C/S, 26/7/18; demob.
159 Creswell Road, Clowne, Chesterfield, Derbyshire.

✠ SAVAGE, Frederick Quinton
4/3468, 3/5/15; Wilts. R., 12/5/15, att. T.M. Bty.; F; Lieut.; w(2). Killed in action 20/9/17.

SAVAGE, George John
C/12261, 29/11/17; R.E., C/S, 10/2/18; R.E., 31/5/18; 2/Lieut.
73 Hereford Road, Bayswater, W. 2.

SAVAGE, Reginald James
C/12643, 22/2/18; No. 3 O.C.B., 6/9/18; trfr. 14th Lond. R., 6/12/18. 56 Perham Road, Barons Court, W. 14.

SAVERY, Robert Churton
6/2/5666, 16/8/15; R.F.C., 4/8/16, R.A.F.; F; Capt.; D.F.C.
The Willows, Westcott, Dorking, Surrey.

SAVILL, Herbert Stewart
6/2/9524, 16/2/16; R.A., C/S, 26/10/16; R.G.A., 24/2/17; Lieut.
Southfleet, Buckhurst Hill, Essex.

SAVILL, Mervyn
B/1879, 16/10/14; 24th Lond. R.; Capt.; w; M.C.

SAVORY, Alec John
6/9054, 22/1/16; No. 2 Cav. C/S, 31/3/16; S. Notts. Huss., 19/8/16; Lieut. Ryburgh, Norfolk.

SAVORY, Guy Victor George
A/Sq/9810, 30/10/16; No. 1 Cav. C/S, 31/7/17; R. Regt. of Cav., 22/2/18, att. 2nd Drag. Gds.; F; 2/Lieut.
Highfield, Ryburgh, Norfolk.

SAVORY, Hubert Dolobran
Sq/1980, 27/10/14; Oxf. Huss., 11/2/15; Lieut.
9 Tokenhouse Yard, E.C. 2.

SAW, Henry William
B/183, 30/4/08; dis. 29/4/11; C. of Lond. Vol.; Major.
70 Queen Street, E.C. 4.

SAWBRIDGE, Bartle Frere
1/3515, 6/5/15; 5th Lond. R., 5/8/15; F; Capt.; w(2).
Thelnetham Rectory, Diss, Norfolk.

SAWDAY, Albert Ernest
Sq/4/3285, 15/4/15; dis. med. unfit, 16/11/15.
Coargard, Elphinstone Road, Hastings

SAWTELL, Ellis John
6/2/8558, 31/5/15; L/C.; No. 14 O.C.B., 27/9/16; K.R. Rif. C., 24/1/17; F; Capt. Kingweston, Taunton, Somerset.

SAWTELL, Leonard Alan
6/3/A/6164, 11/9/15, Sgt.; Midd'x. R., 31/10/16; F; Lieut.
4 Chalfont Avenue, Wembley Hill, Middlesex.

✠ SAWYER, Robert Fulwell
A/10075, 1/12/16; No. 14 O.C.B., 30/1/17; K.R. Rif. C., 29/5/17; 2/Lieut. Died of wounds 24/8/17.

✠ SAWYER, Sidney William
4/3878, 31/5/15; R. Fus., 29/11/15. Died 30/6/20.

SAXBY, John Edward
C/10163, 11/12/16; R.G.A., C/S, 15/8/17; R.G.A., 31/12/17; F; 2/Lieut. 31 Cliftonville Avenue, Margate.

SAYER, Geoffrey Latimer
6/5/9536, 18/2/16; No. 14 O.C.B., 30/10/16; Lanc. Huss. Yeo., 24/1/17, att. Lan. Fus.; F; Lieut.; w; M.C.
c/o Messrs. Wookay, Sayer & Thorold, Bank Plain, Norwich, Norfolk.

✠ SAYER, Robert Bramwell
4/2/4615, 5/7/15, L/C.; R. Fus.; 2/Lieut.
Died of wounds 19/2/17.

SAYER, Walter
D/A/11025, 11/4/17, Sgt.; demob. 7/2/19.
13 Hollingbourne Gardens, West Ealing, W. 13.

SAYER, William Arnold
4/3907, 31/5/15; R. Fus., 7/10/15, secd. R.E.; Major, D.A.Q.M.G.; M(1).

SAYERS, Eldred Frank
B/611, 1/3/12; dis. 11/9/14; W. Af. F.F.; Lieut.
D. C. Kaballa, Sierra Leone Protectorate, British West Africa.

SAYERS, John Gilbert
B/12860, 25/3/18; No. 23 O.C.B., 9/8/18; W. Rid. R., 4/3/19; 2/Lieut. 23 Brookfield Road, Highgate, N.W. 5.

SAYLES, James Patterson
6/5/7825, 24/11/15; No. 7 O.C.B., 11/8/16; R. Ir. Rif., 18/12/16; F; 2/Lieut.; w.
Cardigan House, Cardigan Drive, Cliftonville, Belfast, Ireland.

SCAIFE, Leslie
6/2/5526, 9/8/15; Durh. L.I., 21/12/15; 2/Lieut.
Home Farm, North Wootton, Kings Lynn.

SCAMMELL, Wilfrid Stanley
B/1977, 26/10/14; Worc. R., 14/11/14; F; Capt.; w; M.C., M(1).
5 Royal York Crescent, Clifton, Bristol.

SCANDRETT, Alfred Joseph
A/11617, 3/7/17; No. 14 O.C.B., 7/12/17; R. Ir. Rif., 28/5/18; F; 2/Lieut. 17 Woodcot Avenue, Bloomfield, Belfast, Ireland.

SCANLAN, Thomas Henry
6/2/6536, 30/9/15; R. Dub. Fus., 4/9/16, R.F.C., R.A.F.; F; Lieut. 33 Kildare Street, Dublin.

SCARFE, Cyril George
6/2/6297, 27/9/15, L/C.; Notts. & Derby. R., 1/6/16, Leic. R.; F; Lieut.; w(2), p. 5 Durrell Road, S.W. 6.

SCARFF, William John
1/3318, 19/4/15; N. Lan. R., 8/7/15; F; Lieut.; w.
Quay House, Rowhedge, Near Colchester.

SCARLETT, John Charles Dameron
6/2/8573, 31/12/15, Sgt.; R.F.A., C/S, 18/5/17; R.F.A., 20/10/17; F; Lieut.; p.
c/o Morgan, Hayes & Coy., 14 Place Vendome, Paris.

SCARLETT, John Frederick
B/11361, 22/5/17; No. 14 O.C.B., 5/10/17; Norf. R., 30/5/18, att. Gren. Gds. and R. Ir. Regt.; P; 2/Lieut.
Orchard Mount, Ashburton, South Devonshire.

SCARR, Kenneth Roy
6/3/5839, 26/8/15; E. Kent R., 9/6/16; Capt.; w.
Junior House, Warwick School, Warwick.

SCARSBROOK, Reginald George
D/10919, 22/3/17, Cpl.; R.G.A., C/S, 15/8/17; R.G.A., 31/12/17; 2/Lieut. 94 Hampton Street, Birmingham.

SCHAEFFER, Harold G.
2/3398, 26/4/15, Sgt.; No. 5 O.C.B., 14/8/16; K.R. Rif. C., 21/11/16; F; Capt. 51 Onslow Gardens, Muswell Hill, N. 10.

✠ SCHIFF, Mortimer Edward Harold
4/3185, 6/4/15, Sgt.; Suff. R., 17/10/15; Capt.
Killed in action 26/9/17.

SCHLEE, Robert
B/557, 17/3/11; dis. 30/3/13; Rif. Brig.; Capt.; w.

✠ SCHLOTEL, Charles Henry Cooper
4/3274, 15/4/15, Sgt.; D. of Corn. L.I., 16/9/15; F; Capt.; M.C. M(2). Died 21/3/19.

SCHLOTEL, Lyle Cooper
4/3149, 31/3/15, Sgt.; R.G.A., 9/8/15; F; Capt.; M.C.
2 Anglesea Road, Kingston-on-Thames.

SCHMITZ, Hubert Oswald
Sq/531, 13/1/11; dis. 16/10/11.
Belmont, Atkins Road, Clapham Park, S.W. 12.

APPENDIX II.—RECORDS OF RANK AND FILE.

SCHMITZ, *John Hubert.* Now ELLIOT-LAWSON, J. H.
Sq/2868, 5/2/15; R.H.A., 19/8/15; Lieut.; w.
56 Cleveland Square, Hyde Park, W. 2.

SCHOFIELD, *Alfred*
6/5/B/5421, 5/8/15, Sgt.; R.G.A., C/S, 28/2/17; R.G.A., 26/5/17, R.A.F.; F; Lieut.; w(2).
Oxf. & Camb. Musical Club, 6 Bedford Square, W.C. 1.

SCHOFIELD, *Allan*
6/4/8855, 11/1/16, L/C.; No. 14 O.C.B.; M.G.C., 25/9/16; F; Capt.; w(2).
21 Anlaby Road, Hull.

SCHOFIELD, *Arthur*
D/11842, 9/8/17; No. 2 O.C.B., 5/4/18; Oxf. & Bucks. L.I., 12/11/18, Welch R.; F; 2/Lieut.
Sunnydene, Highgate Road, Walsall.

SCHOFIELD, *Gerald William*
D/13772, 7/8/18; demob. 7/4/19. 140 Roundthorn Road, Oldham.

SCHOFIELD, *James*
6/5/5270, 31/7/15; L'pool. R., 13/12/15; F; Lieut.; w.
8 Preston Road, Hesketh Park, Southport, Lancashire.

SCHOFIELD, *James Douglas*
A/Sq/12492, 28/1/18; No. 1 Cav. C/S, 16/5/18; 5th R. Regt. of Cav., 14/2/19; 2/Lieut.
Cote House, Micklehurst, Mossley, Nr. Manchester.

✠ SCHOLEFIELD, *Arthur Hoyle*
4/1/4616, 5/7/15; 19th Lond. R., 12/11/15; 2/Lieut.
Killed in action 18/5/17.

SCHOLEFIELD, *Leslie Cotterill*
2/3000, 2/3/15, Cpl.; North'n. R., 4/8/16, att. Suff. R.; Lieut.; w.

SCHOLTE, *Frederick Lewellen*
Sq/H/1989, 29/10/14; R.F.C., 8/3/15, R.A.F.; F; Lt.-Col.; O.B.E., M(1).
1 Burgess Hill, Hampstead, N.W. 2.

SCHON, *Basil*
A/968, 5/8/14, Cpl.; dis. to re-enlist in School of Musketry, Bisley, 3/5/15; C.S.M.I.
St. Winifred's, Walmer, Kent.

SCHON, *James Geoffrey*
A/992, 5/8/14, L/C.; R.E., 24/10/14, R.N.V.R.; F; Capt.; w; M.C., M(1).
St. Winifred's, Walmer, Kent. (Now in Siam).

SCHREIBER, *Patrick Quintin Robert*
A/14024, 18/9/18; trfr. K.R. Rif. C., 7/4/19.
Netley, Constitution Hill, Woking.

SCHULTZ, *Carl James.* See GREGG, *James.*

✠ SCHWABACHER, *Frederick Adolph*
Sq/1015, 6/8/14; R.A.S.C., 19/9/14; F; Lieut.; w.
Died —/4/20.

SCLATER, *Thomas Ward*
6/4/6673, 7/10/15; 7th Lond. R., 10/6/16, att. R.F.C., R.A.F.; Lieut.; w.
16 Warrenden Park Crescent, Edinburgh.

✠ SCOBIE, *James*
6/7750, 22/11/15; No. 9 O.C.B., 8/3/16; Gord. Highrs., 24/7/16; 2/Lieut.
Died of wounds 2/8/17.

SCOLES, *Robert Walter*
2/3098, 22/3/15; R.W. Kent R., 30/6/15, R.F.C.; w.
34 Foxgrove Road, Beckenham, Kent.

SCOTLAND, *Alexander Paterson*
6/Sq/8879, 12/1/16; Intelligence Corps, 10/7/16; F; Capt.; O.B.E., M(2).
11 Bryanston Mansions, York Street, W. 1.

SCOTT, *Adrian Gilbert*
B/1265, 23/9/14, Sgt.; R.E., 6/12/14; G,E,P; Major; M.C., M(2).
9 Well Walk, Hampstead, N.W. 3.

SCOTT, *Charles Edward*
A/11200, 7/5/17; No. 14 O.C.B., 7/9/17; Yorks. L.I., 17/12/17; F; 2/Lieut.
The Mount, Marple, Cheshire.

SCOTT, *Charles Marriott Oldrid*
C/76, 13/4/08; dis. 12/4/10. 2 Deans Yard, Westminster, S.W.1.

SCOTT, *Charles Paley*
C/11049, 16/4/17, L/C.; R.G.A., C/S, 12/9/17; R.G.A., 4/2/18; F; 2/Lieut.
4 Harcourt Buildings, Temple, E.C. 4.

✠ SCOTT, *Clifford*
6/3/8703, 4/1/16; R.A., C/S, 7/8/16; R.F.A., 17/11/16; F; 2/Lieut.
Killed in action 2/8/17.

SCOTT, *Douglas Walter*
B/D/12839, 22/3/18; demob. 14/10/19.
Springfield, Granville Road, High Barnet.

SCOTT, *Edward Guy*
Sq/3879, 31/5/15, Sgt.; A.S.C., C/S, 27/10/16; R.A.S.C., 20/12/16; S; Lieut.
c/o Standard Bank of South Africa Ltd., Durban, South Africa.

SCOTT, *Edward Taylor*
Sq/3066, 18/3/15; R.F.A., 9/6/15; F; Lieut.; p.
The Firs, Fallowfield, Manchester.

SCOTT, *Ernest Penfold*
6/9592, 26/6/16; R.A., C/S, 26/10/16; R.G.A., 5/1/17; F; Lieut.
36 George Street, Dumfries, Scotland.

SCOTT, *Frank Pilkington*
K/Sq/2273, 7/12/14, Sgt.; E. Rid. Yeo., 31/3/15, R.F.C., R.A.F.; Capt.
Savoy Hotel, Strand, W.C. 2.

SCOTT, *George*
6/3/9270, 3/2/16, L/C.; No. 14 O.C.B., 25/8/16; R. Highrs., 22/11/16; Lieut.; M.C.
Gerrichrew, Comrie, Perthshire.

✠ SCOTT, *Gilbert Ernest Josiah*
E/2800, 26/1/15, Sgt.; K.R. Rif. C., 17/11/15; Capt.
Killed in action 25/3/18.

SCOTT, *Guy Harden Guillum*
6/Sq/D/A/7595, 18/11/15, Sgt.; trfr. Class W. Res., 1/2/17.
41 Lexham Gardens, W. 8.

SCOTT, *Harold Richard*
A/587, 20/11/11; dis. 19/11/15.

✠ SCOTT, *Henry Arthur*
4/2/4029, 7/6/15, L/C.; R.E., 1/11/15; F; 2/Lieut.
Killed in action 8/4/17.

SCOTT, *Henry Garnock*
D/E/13681, 29/7/18, L/C.; No. 22 O.C.B., 22/11/18; K.O. Sco. Bord., 15/2/19; 2/Lieut.
School House, Gavington, Duns, Berwickshire.

SCOTT, *Henry James*
4/1/4053, 7/6/15, Sgt.; R.A., C/S, 26/10/16; R.G.A., 5/1/17; F; Capt.
7 Vernham Road, Plumstead, S.E. 18.

SCOTT, *Herbert Guy*
C/10152, 8/12/16; A.S.C., C/S, 1/5/17; trfr. 28th Lond. R., 14/8/17.

SCOTT, *Herman Alexander*
A/2777, 25/1/15; R.A.S.C., 24/5/15; 2/Lieut.
134 Gloucester Terrace, Hyde Park, W. 2.

SCOTT, *Hugh Gallie*
Sq/1906, 16/10/14; dis. 16/11/14.
20 Gresham Road, Brixton, S.W. 9.

✠ SCOTT, *James Yuill*
B/865, 4/8/14; Bord. R., 12/9/14; Rif. Brig.; Lieut.
Killed in action 3/9/16.

SCOTT, *John*
1/3169, 1/4/15; N. Lan. R., 8/7/15, M.G.C.; F,NR; Lieut.
Montrose, Winchmore Hill, N. 21.

SCOTT, *Kenneth*
4/5/4819, 12/7/15; A.S.C., C/S, 20/3/16; R.A.S.C., 4/3/17; F; Lieut.
Heath Park, Blairgowrie, Perthshire, N.B.

SCOTT, *Kenneth*
B/12330, 27/12/17, L/C.; demob. 29/1/19.
69 Alexandra Road, Blackburn, Lancashire.

SCOTT, *Leslie George*
4/5/5017, 22/7/15, L/C.; 11th Lond. R., 21/10/15, secd. M.G.C.; Lieut.; M(1).
c/o High Commissioner for South Africa, 32 Victoria Street, S.W. 1.

SCOTT, *Leslie Mayne Stevenson*
A/D/13157, 29/5/18; trfr. 27/5/19.
c/o S. J. Passmore Esq., 2 Paper Buildings, Temple, E.C. 4.

SCOTT, *Malcolm Robert Charles*
6/9599, 17/7/16; R.N.V.R., 6/10/16; Lieut.
35 New Broad Street, E.C. 1.

✠ SCOTT, *Nigel Dennistoun*
B/3034, 9/3/15, L/C.; R.W. Surr. R., 18/6/15, R.F.C.; 2/Lieut.
Killed 19/4/16.

SCOTT, *Norman Carson*
A/11655, 12/7/17; R.F.C., C/S, 23/10/17; R.F.C., 12/12/17, R.A.F.; 2/Lieut.
81 Woodwarde Road, Dulwich, S.E. 22.

SCOTT, *Peter*
6/1/9077, 22/1/16, Sgt.; R.F.A., C/S, 18/5/17; R.F.A., 20/10/17; E,P; 2/Lieut.
4 Quarry Bank, Heswall, Cheshire.

SCOTT, *Ralph Montagu*
6/9598, 11/7/16; R.A., C/S, 26/10/16; R.G.A., 19/2/17; w.
6 Staple Inn, W.C. 2.

APPENDIX II.—RECORDS OF RANK AND FILE.

SCOTT, Robert Noel Adie
C/10838, 5/3/17; No. 14 O.C.B., 10/8/17; R. War. R., 27/11/17; lt; Lieut.; w.
The Hollies, St. Margarets, Twickenham.

✠ SCOTT, Ronald Burrell Ind
4/6/5/4895, 15/7/15; 1st Lond. R., 19/12/15; F; 2/Lieut.
Killed in action 9/9/16.

SCOTT, Stephen Robert
6/2/5594, 12/8/15; 12th Lond. R., 24/12/15; Lieut.; w.
San Remo, East Acton Lane, W. 3.

SCOTT, William
B/10733, 14/2/17; R.A., C/S, 29/6/17; R.G.A., 2/12/17; F; 2/Lieut.
7 Broad Street, Bury, Lancashire.

SCOTT, William Donald
C/10857, 9/3/17; No. 14 O.C.B., 5/7/17; Som. L.I., 30/10/17; F, 2/Lieut.; p.
7 St. Michael's Road, Bedford.

SCOTT, William Noble
A/10806, 28/2/17; L/C.; R.G.A., C/S, 6/6/17; R.G.A., 1/10/17; F; Lieut.
Aspley Lodge, Stonebridge Park, N.W. 10.

SCOTTS, Wilfrid Claud
3/3880, 31/5/15; trfr. Class W. Res., 29/8/16.
Renby, Priory Road, Hornsey, N. 8.

SCOUGAL, Joseph
C/12659, 27/2/18, L/C.; No. 10 O.C.B., 5/7/18; North'd. Fus., 3/3/19; 2/Lieut.

SCOVELL, Charles John
6/2/7779, 23/11/15; No. 14 O.C.B., 28/8/16; Hamps. R., 18/12/16; F; Lieut.; w. Pascholm, Peppard Common, Henley-on-Thames.

SCOVELL, Thornton Sydney
C/370, 20/3/09; dis. 20/3/13.

SCRAGG, Frank
C/12610, 13/2/18; R.F.A., C/S, 17/5/18; R.F.A., 18/3/19; 2/Lieut.
Linton, 240 Upton Lane, Forest Gate, E. 7.

SCRATCHLEY, James Sivewright
6/2/7119, 1/11/15; R.A., C/S, 31/3/16; R.G.A., 6/7/16; Lieut.
Elmsell Rectory, Ipswich.

✠ SCRATTON, Geoffrey Howell
H/2648, 11/1/15; Arg. & Suth'd. Highrs., 22/3/15, att. R. Highrs.; Lieut.; M.C.
Killed in action 1/8/17.

SCRATTON, Humphrey John Howel
4/1/4547, 1/7/15; R.W. Surr. R., 22/10/15, R. Fus.; 2/Lieut.

SCRIVEN, Ambrose
Sq/145, 18/4/08; dis. 17/4/09.
Cobham, Surrey.

SCRIVEN, Arthur Edward
D/13827, 12/8/18; trfr. K.R. Rif. C., 7/4/19.
4 Drayton Road, West Ealing, W. 13.

SCRIVEN, Edward Gordon
B/12743, 11/3/18; No. 4 O.C.B., 6/9/18, No. 18 O.C.B.; demob.
2a Vereker Road, West Kensington.

SCRIVEN, Henry Wilfred Ambrose
B/10572, 19/1/17; dis. med. unfit, 12/4/17.
Tudor Court, Cobham, Surrey.

✠ SCRIVENER, John Sydney
6/5/5872, 28/8/15; No. 1 O.C.B., 25/2/16; Lan. Fus., 7/7/16; F; 2/Lieut.
Killed in action 2/12/17.

SCRIVENER, Walter Reginald Buckingham
A/12470, 24/1/18; R.F.A., C/S, 17/5/18; demob.
6 Plashet Road, Upton Manor, E. 13.

SCRIVENOR, John Brooke
A/10150, 8/12/16, Sgt.; Sig. C/S, 9/6/17; R.E., 4/11/17; F; 2/Lieut.
Ardmore, Tring, Hertfordshire. (Now in F.M.S.)

SCRUBY, Cecil
D/1489, 29/9/14; 4th Lond. R., 3/7/15, att. Rif. Brig.; Lieut.
Norfolk House, Bishops Stortford.

SCRUBY, Frank Sutherland
A/11, 1/4/08; Aldenham School O.T.C., 16/6/09; Camb. R., 18/6/15; F; Major; O.B.E., M(l).
62 Hallowell Road, Northwood, Middlesex.

SCRUTON, Jack
D/12879, 3/4/18; No. 24 O.C.B., 15/11/18; Tank Corps, 22/3/19; 2/Lieut.
18 New Walk Terrace, York.

SCRUTTON, Frank Seymour
K/C/2239, 3/12/14, L/C.; Manch. R., 6/4/15, Army Cyc. Corps, Tank Corps, Lab. Corps; F; Lieut.
50 Calthorpe Road, Birmingham.

SCUTT, Cecil
6/4/8492, 20/12/15; No. 14 O.C.B., 6/4/17; Bedf. R., 31/7/17; 2/Lieut.; w.
Preston, Nr. Weymouth.

SCUTT, George Buckhurst Martin
H/1883, 16/10/14; Worc. R., 28/12/14, secd. M.G.C.; F; Lieut.; w. 38 Hastings Road, West Ealing, W.13. (Now in India).

SCUTT, John Alfred Homer
6/4/9410, 9/2/16; No. 14 O.C.B., 30/10/16; Hamps. R., 27/3/17; F; Lieut.; M.C.
House of the Sacred Mission, Kelham, Newark-on-Trent.

SEABROOK, George Frederick
D/13801, 9/8/18; demob. 7/2/19.
18 Shoebury Road, Burgess Road, East Ham, E 6.

✠ SEABROOK, Harry Spencer
4/3/4138, 10/6/15; Notts. & Derby. R., 5/9/15; 2/Lieut.
Killed in action 12/7/16.

SEAGAR, Harry Bernard
4/1/3981, 3/6/15; Notts. & Derby. R., 14/9/15, York. R.; Lieut.
10 Stuart, Gravesend, Kent.

SEAGER, Arthur Tom
6/1/8038, 30/11/15; M.G.C., C/S, 25/10/16; M.G.C., 24/2/17; Lieut.; w.

SEAGER, John Arnold
B/12208, 8/11/17; A.S.C., C/S, 4/3/18; R.A.S.C., 28/4/18; 2/Lieut.
Sunnyside, 81 Steade Road, Sheffield.

SEALE, John Carteret Hyde
Sq/218, 11/5/08; dis. 31/12/09. 34 Duke Street, St. James, S.W. 1.

SEALE, Peter Rickard
C/12611, 11/2/18; trfr. R.A.F., 4/5/18, Sgt.; R. Dub. Fus.; Lieut
The Star Printing Works Ltd., 229-8th Avenue West, Calgary, Alberta, Canada.

SEALEY, Stanley Forster
C/12606, 13/2/18; No. 1 O.C.B., 6/9/18; Midd'x. R., 17/3/19; 2/Lieut.
Springcroft, Shepherd's Hill, Highgate, N. 6.

SEAR, Walter George Lane
6/3/5391, 5/8/15; Durh. L.I., 17/11/15; Capt.; w; M.C.
c/o Debenhams Ltd., 91 Wimpole Street, W. 1.

SEARL, Arthur Andrew Forbes
6/3/7565, 17/11/15, L/C.; No. 14 O.C.B.; M.G.C., 24/10/16; F; Lieut.; w; M(l).
95 Hamilton Road, Wimbledon, S.W. 19.

SEARLE, Frederick Norman
6/D/6025, 2/9/15; dis. to re-enlist Army Pay Corps, 27/7/17.
56 Kings Hall Road, Beckenham, Kent.

SEARLE, Sidney John
6/1/9437, 12/2/16, Cpl.; R.A., C/S, 26/10/16; R.G.A., 26/5/17; F; Lieut.; w.
4 Stanmore Road, Leytonstone, E. 11.

SEARLE, Thomas
6/7277, 8/11/15; A.S.C., C/S, 27/10/16; R.A.S.C., 20/12/16; Lieut.
Claygate House, Whittlesea.

SEARLE, Wallis Walter
6/3/7596, 18/11/15; trfr. M.G.C., 29/11/16.
St. Michael's College, Tunbridge Wells.

SEARLES, Eric Edward James
D/12968, 22/4/18; No. 16 O.C.B., 18/10/18; E. Kent R., 17/3/19; 2/Lieut.
The Cottage, Ramsgate, Kent.

SEARLES, Geoffrey William
6/1/7953, 29/11/15, L/C.; No. 14 O.C.B., 28/8/16; E. Kent R, 18/12/16; F; Capt.; g.
38 Madeira Road, Margate.

SEARS, Herbert
6/4/9126, 24/1/16; No. 8 O.C.B., 4/8/16; North'd. Fus. 21/11/16; F; Lieut.
Belwood, Brookside, Chesterfield.

SEARSON, Charles Moore
4/2/5045, 22/7/15; trfr. R.A.S.C., 12/5/16.
Sunnyside, Lymm, Cheshire.

SEARSON, Harold Ernest
6/2/D/5342, 2/8/15, L/C.; R.F.C., C/S, 1/2/17; R.F.C., 12/4/17, R.A.F.; F; Lieut.; D.F.C.
Air Ministry, Kingsway, W.C. 2. (Now in Egypt).

SEATON, George Stuart
A/11958, 3/9/17; A.S.C., C/S, 1/11/17; R.A.S.C., 25/1/18; P; Lieut.
9 Pall Mall, S.W. 1.

SEATON, William Dunham
3/2994, 1/3/15; Midd'x. R., 26/7/15; F; Lieut.
Experimental Station, Porton, Salisbury.

APPENDIX II.—RECORDS OF RANK AND FILE.

SEAVER, George Fenn
Sq/2973, 25/2/15; R.A.S.C., 25/5/15; F; Lieut.
Cam Vicarage, Dursley, Gloucestershire. (Now in Rhodesia).

SEAWARD, Sydney Widmer
4/Sq/4384, 21/6/15; R.F.A., 21/10/15; F; Lieut.
The Bay House, Gerrard's Cross, Buckinghamshire.

SECCOMBE, Samuel Simpson
3/3561, 10/5/15; Essex R., 29/7/15; S,E; Capt.; M.C. and Bar.
22 St. Mary's Street, Stamford, Lincolnshire.

SECKER, Berkeley
C/Sq./11005, 3/4/17, L/C.; No. 2 Cav. C/S, 11/1/18; R. Regt. of Cav., 22/6/18; 2/Lieut.
Malvern Link, Worcestershire.

SEDCOLE, Frederick
6/4/8554, 30/12/15; R.A., C/S, 4/8/16; R.G.A., 26/11/16; F; Lieut.; g.
7 Wentworth Road, Golders Green, N.W. 11.

SEDDING, Edmund
A/11193, 7/5/17; No. 12 O.C.B., 10/8/17; dis. med. unfit, 1/10/18.

SEDDON, Eric Arthur
A/B/12429, 18/1/18; R.F.A., C/S, 26/4/18; R.F.A., 8/3/19; 2/Lieut.

SEDDON, William D'Arcy
D/A/12969, 22/4/18; R.E., C/S, 16/6/18; trfr. K.R. Rif. C., 7/4/19.
21 Prince Edward Mansions, Palace Court, W. 2.

SEDGWICK, Harold
A/13080, 17/5/18; No. 22 O.C.B., 5/7/18; R. War. R., 5/2/19; 2/Lieut.
The Brewery House, Watford, Hertfordshire.

SEDGWICK, Leslie
H/2808, 28/1/15; E. Surr. R., 8/9/15, R.F.C., R.A.F.; S,E; Flt. Cmdr.
4 South End House, Montpelier Road, Twickenham.

SEDGWICK, Rupert William
B/E/13572, 19/7/18; No. 22 O.C.B., 20/9/18; R.W. Kent R., 5/2/19; 2/Lieut.
Ednothington, Hollingbourne, Kent.

✠ SEEAR, Christopher Charles
3/3469, 3/5/15; Railway Transport Officer, 10/9/15; F.
Died 30/10/19.

SEEBER, Harold Charles Rundle
6/8324, 11/12/15; dis. to R. Mil. Coll., 29/8/16; R.A.S.C., 1/5/17. secd. Indian Army; Lieut.
78 St. Andrews Road, Southsea, Hampshire.

SEED, George Percy
A/10502, 15/1/17; No. 14 O.C.B., 7/6/17; Lan. Fus., 25/9/17; F; 2/Lieut.
19 Crescent Road, Hale, Cheshire.

✠ SEED, James Parrott
D/10896, 19/3/17; No. 14 O.C.B., 5/7/17; Hamps. R., 30/10/17; 2/Lieut.
Killed in action 17/6/18.

SEED, William Harold
5/6/5956, 1/9/15; No. 14 O.C.B.; L'pool. R., 24/10/16; Lieut.
20 Elleray Park Road, Wallasey, Cheshire.

SEEL, Edward Horace
A/11960, 3/9/17, Cpl.; demob.
The Nook, Vernon Road, Leigh-on-Sea.

SEELEY, Charles Gage
Sq/3516, 6/5/15; R.E., 16/6/15; M,E,P; Capt.; M(1).
c/o F. H. Seeley Esq., 18 Fleet Street, E.C. 4. (Now in Australia).

SEELEY, Lawrence Arthur
4/3817, 27/5/15; E. Surr. R., 1/10/15; F; Lieut.; w.
2 South Square, Gray's Inn, W.C. 2.

SEELEY, Marcel Gerald
F/2949, 18/2/15; Bedf. R., 7/4/15, Cold. Gds.; w.

✠ SEERY, Laurence William
6/5/8427, 15/12/15; No. 7 O.C.B., 5/10/16; Lein. R., 28/2/17, R.A.F.; F; Capt.; w.
Died 28/11/20.

SEERY, Michael
6/Sq/8426, 15/12/15; No. 1 Cav. C/S, 6/12/16; 1st R. Regt. of Lanc., 16/4/17; 2/Lieut.
Sheepsdown House, Delsin, Westmeath, Ireland.

SEFI, Antonio Gabriel
6/1/6537, 30/9/15; Wilts. R., 4/9/16; S; Lieut.
136-7 Palmerston House, Bishopsgate, E.C. 2.

SELBIE, William Philip
H/2690, 14/1/15; E. Surr. R., 29/4/15; F,It; Capt.; w; M.C.
10 Rowsley Avenue, Hendon, N.W. (Now in India).

SELBY, Charles Montague
A/Sq/12448, 21/1/18; No. 1 Cav. C/S, 16/5/18; R. Regt. of Cav. 14/2/19; 2/Lieut.
Oakside, Shinfield, Reading.

✠ SELBY, Gerard Prideaux
B/696, 10/3/13; R.A.M.C., 30/7/14, att. Lan. Fus.; Capt.; w.
Killed in action 26/9/16.

SELBY, Harry Prideaux
Sq/129, 18/4/08; dis. 17/4/11; Suff. R., 11/12/14; Capt.; w.
90 Claverton Street, St. Georges Square, S.W. 1.

SELBY, Leslie James
4/3881, 31/5/15, Cpl.; 11th Lond. R., 21/10/15, emp. M. of Munitions; Lieut.

SELDEN, Leonard
4/3428, 29/4/15; 1st Lond. R., 8/12/15, R. Suss. R.; F; Lieut.; w(3); M.C., M(1).
26 Pleydell Avenue, Stamford Brook, W. 6.

SELIGMAN, Gerald
E/1596, 6/10/14, L/C.; R.A.O.C., 8/2/15; EA; Lieut.
27 Campden Hill Square, W. 8.

SELLAR, Frederick Charles
C/13404, 28/6/18; trfr. 28th Lond. R., 13/11/18.
The Belvedon, Runcorn, Cheshire.

SELLER, John Reginald
6/5/C/8926, 14/1/16; No. 14 O.C.B., 26/11/16; Arg. & Suth'd. Highrs., 27/3/17; 1,M; Lieut.
The Braes, Sleights S.O., Yorkshire.

✠ SELLERS, Philip
4/1/5214, 29/7/15; dis. to R. Mil. Coll., 28/1/16; Worc. R., att. R.F.C.; 2/Lieut.
Died 23/3/17.

SELLICK, Sebastian Emerson
C/12581, 6/2/18; R.F.A., C/S, 17/5/18; R.F.A., 18/3/19; 2/Lieut.
51 Oxford Street, Weston-super-Mare.

SELMON, Howard Russell
C/13405, 28/6/18, L/C.; demob. 23/1/19.
2 Barton Crescent, Mannamead, Plymouth.

SELTMAN, Charles Theodore
6/D/9127, 24/1/16; Garr. O.C.B., 12/12/16; Suff. R., 10/2/17; F; Lieut.
24 Fulbrooke Road, Cambridge.

✠ SELWYN, Colin Redgrave
H/1942, 22/10/14; Som. L.I., 4/11/14; Lieut.; w.
Killed in action 22/8/17.

SELWYN, Wilfred
6/3/7153, 2/11/15; R.F.C., 18/8/16, R.A.F.; F; Capt.; D.F.C.
Toadmoor, Nr. Stroud, Gloucestershire.

SEMPLE, John Edward Stewart
6/3/6944, 20/10/15; 7th Lond. R., 4/8/16; F; Lieut.; w(2).
18 Dryburgh Road, Putney, S.W. 15.

SENTON, Reginald Mayhew
6/5/7698, 22/11/15; No. 14 O.C.B., 27/9/16; R. Lanc. R., 18/12/16; F; Lieut.; w.
Shirley, 302 Norwich Road, Ipswich.

SERBY, William Francis
1/3517, 6/5/15; R.W. Surr. R., 28/7/15; Lieut.; w.
209 Ashmore Road, Maida Hill, W. 9.

SERGEANT, Cyril Charles
A/10937, 28/3/17; R.F.C. C/S, 2/8/17; R.F.C., 12/8/17, R.A.F.; F; Lieut.
Westcliffe, Essex Road, Leyton, Essex.

SERGEANT, Cyril Winsley Holroyd
6/4/5861, 26/8/15; E. Surr. R., 10/1/16; M; Lieut.; w.
The Cottage, Oserick, Yorkshire.

SERGEANT, Frederick Cavendish Hilton
C/11012, 2/4/17, L/C.; R.A., C/S, 7/9/17; R.F.A., 2/2/18; 2/Lieut.
4 Bentley Road, Princes Park, Liverpool.

SETH-SMITH, Hugh Eric
Sq/402, 21/4/09; dis. 28/6/10; R. Ir. Rif., 21/10/14; F; Staff Capt.; w; M.C.
Elm Park, Killylea, Co. Armagh, Ireland.

✠ SEVERS, Alfred George
4/2/4103, 7/6/15; Midd'x. R., 10/9/15, R.F.C.; F; 2/Lieut.
Killed in action 28/3/17.

SEVERS, William Frederick
C/11729, 23/7/17; No. 14 O.C.B., 4/1/18; trfr. 28th Lond. R., 22/9/18.

SEWARD, Edgar Cecil
B/11723, 19/7/17; A.S.C., C/S, 1/10/17; R.A.S.C., 30/11/17; 2/Lieut.
50 Guildford Avenue, Surbiton.

SEWARD, Eric John
B/Sq/12018, 17/9/17; No. 1 Cav. C/S, 28/2/18; R. Regt. of Cav., 28/8/18; 2/Lieut.
6 Northwick House, St. Johns Wood Road, N.W. 8.

APPENDIX II.—RECORDS OF RANK AND FILE.

SEWARD, William Ronald
6/Sq/9230, 1/2/16; R.F.A., C/S, 9/6/16; R.F.A., 8/9/16; Lieut.; w(2).
12 Westbourne Road, Penarth, Cardiff.

SEWELL, Edward Owen
A/837, 4/8/14; S. Lan. R., 11/9/14; F; Major; w(4); M.C. and Bar, Croix de Guerre, M(3).
Watermillock, Radlett, Hertfordshire.

SEWELL, Thomas Jackson Elliott
6/8609, 3/1/16; R.F.A., C/S, 23/6/16; R.G.A., 27/9/16; F; Major; w; M.C., M(1).
Claremont House, Kirkley Cliff, Lowestoft.

SEXTON, Cornelius Arthur
A/11267, 12/5/17, Sgt.; demob. 11/1/19.
Rydal Cottage, Berkhamsted.

SEXTON, Frederick
A/10737, 12/2/17; trfr. 19th Lond. R., 18/4/17.

SEYMOUR, Arthur
6/5/6777, 11/10/15; W. York. R., 4/8/16; Lieut.; M(1).
14 Scarcroft Road, York.

✠ SEYMOUR, Bertram
6/2/6778, 11/10/15, Cpl.; No 8 O.C.B., 4/8/16, M.G.C., C/S; M.G.C., 23/11/16; 2/Lieut.
Killed in action 31/7/17.

SEYMOUR, Ernest Ralph
A/10489, 12/1/17; R.F.C., C/S, 13/3/17; R.F.C., 19/4/17, R.A.F.; F; Lieut.
The Haven, Dunton Green, Nr. Sevenoaks, Kent.

✠ SEYMOUR, Francis
A/810, 3/8/14; K.R. Rif. C., 11/9/14; F; Lieut.
Killed in action 30/7/15.

SEYMOUR, Lionel
C/1352, 26/9/14, L/C.; Herts. R., 2/3/15; Capt.; O.B.E.. m.
Longedge, East Molesey, Surrey.

SEYMOUR, Stanley Frank
6/8793, 8/1/16; trfr. 23rd Lond. R., 14/7/16.

SHACKEL, Richard Frank Wellesley
B/E/13616, 24/7/18; No. 22 O.C.B., 20/9/18; demob. 17/1/19.
100 Burnt Ash Road, Lee, S.E. 12.

SHACKLETON, Jonas Tom
B/13785, 10/8/18; demob. 24/1/19.
Woodside, Farfield Road, Shirley, Yorkshire.

SHADDICK, Clifford Ramiro
B/637, 29/4/12; dis. med. unfit, 18/8/13.

SHAKESPEAR, George Albert
Sq/2960, 22/2/15; R.A.S.C., 13/4/15; G,E,P; Capt.
c/o Sir C. R. McGrigor Bart. & Coy., 39 Panton Street, Haymarket, S.W. 1.

SHAKESPEARE, Geoffrey Hithersay
H/1986, 29/10/14; Norf. R., 23/10/14, R.A.S.C.; G,E,P; Capt.
20 Woodlands Road, Redhill, Surrey.

SHAND, Eric David
F/3036, 11/2/15, L/C.; 9th Lond. R., 3/7/15; Lieut.
4 Wemyss Road, Blackheath, S.E. 3.

SHAND, Philip Morton
D/A/11146, 30/4/17; R.F.A., C/S, 25/1/18.
1 Edwarde's Place, Kensington, W. 8.

SHAND, Randolph Charles Reid
6/4/9223, 31/1/16, L/C.; No. 5 O.C.B., 14/8/16; Welch Gds., 21/11/16; F; Lieut.; M.C.
c/o Rust, Trowbridge & Coy., Port of Spain, Trinidad, British West Indies.

SHANKS, Frederick
C/Sq/13347, 25/6/18; demob. 8/1/19.
Denfield House, Arbroath.

✠ SHANN, Alan Webster
6/1/9377, 8/2/16; No. 14 O.C.B., 30/10/16; W. York. R., 24/1/17; 2/Lieut.
Killed in action 27/11/17.

SHANNON, Alfred Drury
A/11282, 12/5/17; R.F.C., C/S, 1/6/17; R.F.C., 4/7/17, R.A.F.; Lieut.
4 Collingwood Villas, Stoke Devonport.

SHAPLAND, Arden Francis Terrell
C/13357, 26/6/18; trfr. 14th Lond. R., 6/12/18.
Penstone, Lancing, Sussex.

SHAPLEY, Ronald Norman
2/3239, 12/4/15; 8th Lond. R., 23/7/15; F; Lieut.; M.C., M(1).
5 St. James Terrace, Holland Park, W. 11.

SHARDLOW, Cecil Francis
4/2/4160, 10/6/15; R.W. Fus., 30/9/15, Tank Corps; F; Lieut.; w.
Fernbank, Huyton, Nr. Liverpool.

SHARKEY, William Joseph
D/1460, 29/9/14; Essex R., 11/12/14; G,F; Capt.
11 Iona Drive, Glasnevin, Dublin.

SHARLAND, Herbert Neville
6/2/D/6745, 11/10/15; No. 14 O.C.B., 30/10/16; E. Kent R., 24/1/17; F; Lieut.; w.
Carn Brae, London Road, Bromley, Kent.

SHARMAN, Edward Melfort
B/12426, 17/1/18; No. 8 O.C.B., 5/7/18; North'n. R., 4/3/19; 2/Lieut.
Doddington Road, Wellingborough, Nothamptonshire.

✠ SHARP, Charles Gordon
K/B/2409, 21/12/14; North'd. Fus., 27/3/15; 2/Lieut.
Died of wounds 5/2/16.

SHARP, Gerald Ernest
A/14346, 6/1/19; trfr. K.R. Rif. C., 7/4/19.
112 Princes Avenue, Hull.

SHARP, Herbert Victor
B/10426, 10/1/17; A.S.C., C/S, 9/4/17; R.A.S.C., 3/6/17, R.A.M.C.; F; Capt.
17 College Road, Harrow-on-the-Hill.

SHARP, John Stanley
A/349, 24/2/09; dis. 28/2/13.

SHARP, Joseph Trayton Jack
4/5/C/5059, 24/7/15; M.G.C., C/S, 6/12/16; trfr. 28th Lond. R., 25/2/18; F; Pte.
10 The Crescent, Sutton, Surrey.

SHARP, Robert
B/12815, 20/3/18; No. 4 O.C.B., 6/9/18; Bord. R., 16/3/19; 2/Lieut.
Barton Vicarage, Tirril, Penrith, Cumberland.

SHARP, Robert Hampton
6/3/7629, 20/11/15; trfr. R.F.A., 5/5/16.
21 Springfield Gardens, Clapton Common, E. 5.

SHARP, Sydney Reginald Courtney
6/2/9363, 7/2/16; No. 8 O.C.B., 4/8/16; K.R. Rif. C., 21/11/16; F; 2/Lieut.; w.
61 Gayton Road, Harrow.

SHARP, William Henry Cartwright
A/13102, 22/5/18; demob. 23/1/19.
2 Garden Court, Temple, E.C. 4.

SHARP, William Reginald
A/11192, 7/5/17, L/C.; No. 14 O.C.B., 9/11/17; R. Suss. R., 30/4/18; 2/Lieut.
93 Beaconsfield Villas, Brighton.

SHARPE, Charles Donald Reynolds
K/F/2458, 28/12/14; R. Berks. R., 9/3/15; F; Capt.
Kingsclere, Acraman's Road, Southville, Bristol.

SHARPE, Cyril Peter
4/2/3281, 15/4/15, Cpl.; Oxf. & Bucks. L.I., 8/10/15; F; Staff Capt.
Kingsclere, Acraman's Road, Southville, Bristol.

SHARPE, Eric George
Sq/2673, 12/1/15; R.F.A., 2/4/15, emb. R.E.; F,S,E,P; Capt.; g. w; M.C., M(1).
Calcetto, Rushington, Sussex. (Now in Chile).

SHARPE, Frank George Granville
6/2/9304, 4/2/16; No. 14 O.C.B., 26/11/16; Norf. R., 27/3/17, att. Bedf. R.; F; Lieut.; w.
Kingsclere, Acraman's Road, Southville, Bristol.

✠ SHARPE, Guy Crawford
K/Sq/2672, 12/1/15; R.F.A., 2/4/15; F,S,E,P; Lieut.; g.
Died.

SHARPE, Reginald Lawford
B/698, 10/3/13, Cpl.; 1st Lond. R., 27/9/15; G,E,F; Capt.; w.
c/o Crawford, Bayley & Coy., Bombay, India.

SHARPE, Roy Collingwood
C/12607, 13/2/18; No. 23 O.C.B., 5/7/18; Midd'x. R., 3/3/19; 2/Lieut.
10 Highbury Crescent, N. 5.

SHARPE, Samuel Stuart
Sq/3099, 22/3/15; R.G.A., 1/6/15; Lieut.; w.
1 Fernwood Avenue, Streatham, S.W. 16.

SHARPE, Sidney Ughtred
B/10086, 4/12/16; R.G.A., C/S, 25/4/17; R.G.A., 19/8/17, att. R.A.F.; F; Capt.; M.C.
St. Ives, Berkhamsted, Hertfordshire.

SHARPE, Wilfred
B/170, 27/4/08; dis. 26/4/10.
14 Kemplay Road, Hampstead, N.W. 3.

SHARPE, William Henry Sharpe
Sq/3364, 22/4/15; R.N.A.S., 22/5/15; Capt.
c/o Edmund Hodgkinson Esq., 124 Chancery Lane, W.C. 2.

APPENDIX II.—RECORDS OF RANK AND FILE.

SHARPE, William Seaford
K/E/2317, 10/12/14; 1st Lond. R., 14/2/15; Capt.; w.
4 Church Road, Highgate, N.6.

SHARPLES, Sidney Carson
C/13309, 17/6/18; No. 11 O.C.B., 24/1/19; General List, 8/3/19; 2/Lieut. 9 Darley Road, Sugmour Grove, Manchester.

SHARPLEY, Roger
C/10828, 2/3/17; trfr. 32nd Lond. R., 6/7/17.
Westnor, Louth, Lincolnshire.

SHARRATT, Niel Wilcock
A/13943, 2/9/18; trfr. K.R. Rif. C., 25/4/19.
16 Mauldreth Road, Heaton Mersey, Manchester.

✠ SHAW, Alexander Morton
Sq/524, 28/11/10; dis. 4/8/14; York. R.; Capt.
Killed in action 10/4/18.

SHAW, Arthur Trevor Ryan
K/2280, 7/12/14; dis. med. unfit, 7/1/15.

SHAW, Bertram Wadsworth
6/2/7194, 27/10/15, Cpl.; No. 1 Cav. C/S, 31/7/17; R. Regt. of Cav., 22/2/18; 2/Lieut.
590 Holderness Road, Hull, Yorkshire.

SHAW, Charles Courtenay
E/1619, 9/10/14, Sgt.; North'd. Fus., 27/1/15.
88 Lansdowne Place, Hove.

SHAW, Colin Mackenzie
C/13214, 5/6/18, L/C.; trfr. 14th Lond. R., 6/12/18.
57 Mount Ararat, Richmond, Surrey.

SHAW, Eric Dennis Penrhyn
C/14294, 11/11/18; No. 11 O.C.B., 24/1/19; General List, 8/3/19; 2/Lieut.
c/o The Smithfield and Argentine Meat Coy. Ltd., 46 Reconquista, Buenos Aires, Argentina.

SHAW, Frank
A/10044, 29/11/16; No. 14 O.C.B., 30/1/17; Manch. R., 25/4/17, secd. M.G.C.; Lieut.
48 Foxhall Road, Nottingham.

✠ SHAW, F. A. See SCHWABACHER, F. A.

SHAW, George Frederick
6/5/5957, 1/9/15; L'pool. R., 1/6/16, Indian Army; F,I; Capt.
Sefton, The Drive, Headlands, Kettering.

SHAW, George Henry
D/A/11843, 9/8/17, L/C.; No. 6 O.C.B., 10/5/18; Norf. R., 3/2/19; 2/Lieut. 71 Kennington Park Road, S.E. 11.

SHAW, George Victor
B/13447, 3/7/18; No. 11 O.C.B., 24/1/19; General List, 8/3/19; 2/Lieut. 5 Western Street, Bedford.

SHAW, George Whitlaw
4/6/5/4982, 19/7/15; Manch. R., 11/12/15, att M.G.C.; E,F; Lieut.; w. Threlkeld, 14 Kings Drive, Heaton Moor, Stockport.

SHAW, George William
6/1/5731, 19/8/15; dis. to re-enlist in R.N.V.R., 3/9/16.
The Schools, Tetsworth, Oxon.

SHAW, Gilbert Shuldham
D/1481, 29/9/14, L/C.; R.F.A., 6/10/14; 2/Lieut.

✠ SHAW, Giles Havergal
4/4585, 1/7/15; Bedf. R., 28/7/15; Lieut.
Killed in action 11/4/17.

SHAW, Harold John
6/5/8120, 2/12/15; R.F.A., C/S, 4/8/16; R.F.A., 10/11/16; F; Lieut.; g(2). 17 Highfield South, Rock Ferry, Cheshire.

SHAW, Harry Nicholas
6/4/8555, 30/12/15; No. 14 O.C.B., 28/8/16; Notts. & Derby. R., 18/2/16; F; Capt.; g.
42 Parkhill Road, Belsize Park, Hampstead. N.W. 3.

SHAW, Herbert
B/10592, 20/1/17, Sgt.; demob. 5/2/19.
14 St. Leonard's Road, Hove, Sussex.

SHAW, James
C/11778, 30/7/17; No. 14 O.C.B., 7/12/17; K.O. Sco. Bord., 28/5/18; 2/Lieut. Larch Villa, Annan, Scotland.

SHAW, John Beetham
6/5/8661, 3/1/16; No. 8 O.C.B., 4/8/16; North'd. Fus., 24/10/16; F; Lieut. Esk Dale, Bingham, Nottinghamshire.

SHAW, John Ford
A/12493, 28/1/18; demob. 29/1/19.
7 Addison Road, Bedford, Park, W. 4.

SHAW, John Leslie
C/14143, 11/10/18; demob. 29/1/19.
Thornycroft, Chelford, Cheshire.

SHAW, Joseph Taylor
6/4/5638, 16/8/15, L/C.; York. R., 12/1/16; F,It; Capt.; w; D.S.O., M(1). Holmecroft, Bromley Road, Shipley, Yorkshire.

SHAW, Leslie
6/5/C/7954, 29/11/15, Sgt.; No. 14 O.C.B., 5/7/17; L'pool. R., 30/10/17; F; Lieut.
Beechfield, Woodlands Park, Altrincham, Cheshire.

✠ SHAW, Ronald Percy
6/9089, 24/1/16; M.G.C., C/S, 25/10/16; M.G.C., 24/2/17; 2/Lieut.; w. Killed in action 22/3/18.

SHAW, Sydney Vernon
A/10855, 6/3/17; H. Bde. O.C.B., 18/8/17; Cold. Gds., 27/11/17; Lieut. Sunnyside, Clifford Road, New Barnet, Hertfordshire.

✠ SHAW, William Bernard
F/1757, 16/10/14; R. Suss. R., 13/11/14; Lieut.; w.
Killed in action 12/4/17.

✠ SHAW, William Cobley
6/3/7059, 28/10/15, L/C.; No. 14 O.C.B.; Wilts. R., 24/10/16; F; 2/Lieut. Killed in action 6/9/17.

SHAW, William Edmund Dale
6/1/7532, 16/11/15, Sgt.; York. & Lanc. R., 25/9/16, att. Yorks. L.I.; F; Lieut. Holmefield, Longwood, Huddersfield.

SHAW, William Kenneth
C/10832, 3/3/17, L/C.; R.F.A., C/S, 24/8/17; R.F.A., 4/2/18; F; Lieut. 2 The Crescent, Street Lane, Roundhay, Leeds.

SHAWCROSS, Anthony Tuer
A/14025, 18/9/18; demob. 23/1/19. 15 Belsize Park, N.W. 3.

SHAXBY, Richard Underdown
C/487, 25/4/10, Sgt.; dis. 24/4/15; R.A.O.C., 16/5/15; F; Capt.
H.M. Inspector of Factories, Home Office, Whitehall, S.W. 1.

SHEARD, Francis Edward Sandbach
6/3/7881, 26/11/15; No. 8 O.C.B., 4/8/16, M.G.C., C/S; M.G.C., 23/11/16, Tank Corps; F; Lieut.; w.
27 Albert Road, Southport, Lancashire.

SHEARER, Frank Chiffelle
A/10459, 12/1/17; No. 14 O.C.B., 5/5/17; Indian Army, 28/8/17.
8 Oakfield Road, Stroud Green, N.

SHEARING, Beverley James
B/13558, 19/7/18; No. 11 O.C.B., 24/1/19; General List, 8/3/19; 2/Lieut. 75 Silverton Road, Berea, Durban, Natal, South Africa.

SHEARLOCK, Frank Ernest
D/11585, 2/7/17; No. 14 O.C.B., 9/11/17; D. of Corn. L.I., 30/4/18; F; 2/Lieut.
103 Northolt Road, South Harrow, Middlesex.

✠ SHEARMAN, Ambrose Augustus
1/3203, 8/4/15; N. Staff. R., 8/7/15, 7th Lond. R.; Capt.
Died of wounds 20/4/18.

SHEARMAN, John
A/1276, 23/9/14; R.A.S.C., 14/11/14; F; Capt.; M(1).
Meadowside, Wintaston, Nantwich, Cheshire.

SHEARME, Frank Edward Cecil
K/H/2935, 17/2/15; W. Rid. R., 29/4/15; F,I; Capt.; w(2); M.C., M(1). 44 Loughborough Park, S.W. 9.

SHEARME, Valentine Edward
4/3/4054, 7/6/15; D. of Corn. L.I., 4/11/15, secd. R.E. Sigs.; F; Lieut. Wilboldero, Herne Bay, Kent.

SHEATE, Reginald Edward John Ewart
6/Sq/9543, 19/2/16; R.F.A., C/S, 18/8/16; trfr. R.F.A., 2/3/17; R.F.A., 8/4/19; F; 2/Lieut.; w.
Magnolia House, Cheddar, Somerset.

SHEATHER, Ronald William Ernest
6/5/C/8189, 6/12/15; No. 14 I.C.B., 30/10/16; R.W. Surr. R., 28/2/17; F; 2/Lieut.; b. Homelea, Teddington, Middlesex.

SHEEL, Edgar William
A/C/D/11941, 30/8/17; No. 21 O.C.B., 10/5/18; Res. of Off., 2/2/19; 2/Lieut. 41 Carfield Avenue, Meersbrook, Sheffield.

✠ SHEEPSHANKS, William
6/1/7019, 26/10/15, L/C.; No. 11 O.C.B., 7/5/16; K.R. Rif. C., 4/9/16; 2/Lieut. Killed in action 10/7/17.

APPENDIX II.—RECORDS OF RANK AND FILE.

☖ SHEFFIELD, *Lancelot Hull*
F/2841, 1/2/15, L/C.; Dorset R., 2/6/15; M; Capt.
Killed in action 25/3/17.

☖ SHEFFIELD, *Ralph David*
H/2/2984, 27/2/15; 3rd Lond. R., 20/4/15; F; 2/Lieut.
Killed in action 16/6/17.

SHELDON, *Harold George*
A/1038, 26/8/14; Essex R., 4/9/14, Indian Army; Lieut.; w.
7 *Woodlands Crescent, Muswell Hill, N. 10.*

SHELDON, *Harold Stephen*
6/3/B/7220, 4/11/15; Garr. O.C.B., 30/11/17; Essex R., 26/3/18, att. R.A.F.; Lieut.
23 *Frederica Road, Chingford, Essex.*

SHELDRAKE, *Thomas Wentworth Swinborne*
6/3/6230, 13/9/15; R.G.A., 14/12/15; Lieut.

SHELLEY, *Charles Edgar*
4/5/4701, 8/7/15; W. York. R., 12/11/15; F,I; Capt.; w-g.
40 *Cleave Road, Gillingham, Kent.*

☖ SHELLEY, *Ernest Bowen*
F/2995, 1/3/15, Sgt.; dis. to R. Mil. Coll., 27/8/15; Gren. Gds.; Capt.; w.
Killed in action 12/9/18.

SHELLEY, *Percy John*
B/2844, 1/2/15, L/C.; Hamps. R., 30/5/15; Lieut.; w.
16 *Fitzalan Road, Littlehampton, Sussex.*

☖ SHELLEY, *Philip John*
4/2/4349, 21/6/15; R.A., C/S, 24/1/16; R.F.A., 23/6/16; 2/Lieut.
Killed in action 31/7/17.

SHELSWELL, *Geoffrey Henry*
1/6/3562, 10/5/15, L/C.; R.F.A., C/S, 31/3/16; R.F.A., 5/8/16; M,1; Capt.
Assistant District Commissioner, c/o The Secretariat, Zanzibar, East Africa.

☖ SHELTON, *Charles*
C/640, 9/5/12; Norf. R., 11/9/14; F; Capt.; M.C.
Killed in action 22/10/16.

☖ SHELTON, *John Parker*
A/381, 24/3/09; dis. 4/3/11; rej. B/2801, 26/1/15, L/C.; Hamps. R., 15/5/15; P; 2/Lieut.; w.
Killed in action 19/4/17.

SHELTON, *Leonard Jarvis*
6/2/5486, 9/8/15; S. Staff. R., 4/1/16; F; Lieut.; p.
St. Chether, Park Road, East, Wolverhampton, Staffordshire.

SHELTON, *Leslie*
B/12427, 17/1/18; No. 13 O.C.B., 10/5/18; dis. med. unfit, 4/1/19.
47 *Glencairn Buildings, Joubert Street, Johannesburg, South Africa.*

SHENTON, *Geoffrey James Henry*
4/Sq/3982, 3/6/15, Cpl.; R.H.A., 28/9/15; E; Capt.; M.C.
The Grange, Little Sutton, Sutton Coldfield, Birmingham.

☖ SHEPARD, *Cyril Harry*
Sq/123, 18/4/08; dis. 17/4/12; rej. H/2950, 18/2/15; Devon. R., 29/4/15; F; 2/Lieut.
Killed in action 1/7/16.

☖ SHEPHARD, *Stuart Norman*
A/9854, 6/11/16; R.F.C., C/S, 13/3/17; R.F.C., 19/4/17; 2/Lieut.
Killed 17/2/18.

SHEPHERD, *Charles Herbert Boutflower*
K/E/2447, 28/12/14; Manch. R., 7/4/15, M.G.C.; F; Major; w; M.C.
195 *Iffley Road, Oxford.*

SHEPHERD, *Edward Clifford Malden*
6/4/6295, 16/9/15, L/C.; No. 14 O.C.B.; M.G.C., 25/9/16, Tank Corps; Lieut.

SHEPHERD, *Francis Michie*
Sq/2858, 6/2/15, L/C.; R.F.A., 28/4/15; F,M,Afghan; Major; w.
18 *Kensington Gate, W. 8.*

SHEPHERD, *George Hubbard Gelston*
K/E/2187, 26/11/14, Cpl.; Oxf. & Bucks. L.I., 15/5/15, att. R.A.F.; F; Lieut.; w.
Glyndowr, Abingdon, Berkshire.

SHEPHERD, *Godfrey Harcourt*
1/3882, 31/5/15; Midd'x. R., 10/9/15, emp. M. of Munitions; Lieut. - c/o *Bank of Liverpool Ltd., 7 Water Street, Liverpool.*

SHEPHERD, *James Chiene*
6/5/5271, 31/7/15; L'pool. R., 27/12/15, emp. M. of Labour; Lieut.; w.

SHEPHERD, *John Gelston*
K/E/2188, 26/11/14; Oxf. & Bucks. L.I., 15/5/15; Lieut.
Glyndowr, Abingdon, Berkshire.

SHEPHERD, *Roscoe Harcourt*
4/1/4111, 8/6/15; Midd'x. R., 10/9/15, R.F.C.; F,P; Staff Lieut.; w.
8 *The Park, Sidcup, Kent. (Now in France).*

SHEPHERD, *Tom Seymour Gelston*
D/13877, 21/8/18; trfr. K.R. Rif. C., 7/4/19.
Glyndowr, Abingdon, Berkshire.

SHEPHERDSON, *Leslie William*
4/5/5060, 24/7/15; Durh. L.I., 17/12/15; F,It; Capt.; M.C .and Bar.
Croft Cottage, Crawley, Sussex.

SHEPPARD, *Sydney Victor*
2/3518, 6/5/15, L/C.; Midd'x. R., 25/9/15, att. E. York. R.; F,I; Lieut.; w.
16 *Ampthill Square, Regents Park, N.W. 1.*

SHEPPARD, *William Henry*
A/13049, 8/5/18; No. 1 O.C.B., 8/11/18; Som. L.I., 16/3/19; 2/Lieut.
11 *Seymour Road, Bath.*

SHERATON, *Richard Frederick Wilfrid*
6/5/7597, 18/11/15; W. Som. Yeo., 21/11/16, R.A.F.; F,E,It; Lieut.
35 *Duke Street, Brighton.*

☖ SHERIDAN, *William Nicholas*
4/1/4240, 14/6/15; R. Ir. Rif., 4/10/15; 2/Lieut.
Killed in action 1/9/16.

SHERIDAN-SHEDDEN, *George Alfred*
Sq/2871, 3/2/15; Pemb. Yeo., 3/4/15, secd. M.G.C.; E,P,F; Lieut.; M.C.
24 *Newfoundland Road, Gudalpa, Cardiff.*

SHERMAN, *Charles Henry*
C/12506, 29/1/18; R.A., C/S, 17/5/18; R.G.A., 3/4/19; 2/Lieut.
16 *Bulstrode Avenue, Hounslow.*

SHERREN, *Edward Herbert*
4/5/4764, 12/7/15, Sgt.; K.R. Rif. C., 28/11/15; F; Lieut.
Kingsdale, Stanmore, Middlesex.

SHERRIFF, *George James*
6/1/9187, 28/1/16; R.A., C/S, 14/7/16; R.G.A., 4/10/16; Capt.; m.
Netherley, Dumfermline, Fifeshire.

SHERWELL, *George Egbert Ferriday*
6/8464, 18/12/15; dis. 2/5/16; R.N.R.; Paymaster Sub. Lieut.
134 *Bridge Street, Gainsborough, Lincolnshire.*

☖ SHERWOOD, *Hamilton Stanley*
B/11323, 19/5/17; No. 14 O.C.B., 7/9/17; Shrop. L.I., 17/12/17, F; 2/Lieut.
Killed in action 29/8/18.

SHERWOOD, *Herbert William Thelwell*
A/13057, 10/5/18, L/C.; demob. 7/4/19.
Amroth, Friern Watch Avenue, Woodside Park, N. 12

SHERWOOD, *John*
K/D/2434, 19/12/14; R.G.A., 23/2/15; F; Capt.; M(1).
21 *Park Road, Ipswich.*

SHERWOOD-SMITH, *Arthur Denis*
A/11961, 3/9/17; Intelligence Corps, 12/12/17; F; 2/Lieut.
c/o *Messrs. Grindlay & Coy., 54 Parliament Street, S.W. 1.*

☖ SHERYER, *Harold John*
4/3145, 30/3/15, L/C.; Hamps. R., 13/11/15; Lieut.
Died of wounds 5/8/17.

SHIELDS, *Clifford*
6/4/7478, 15/11/15, L/C.; No. 11 O.C.B., 16/5/16; North'd. Fus 4/9/16, att. Leic. R., and Lan. Fus.; F; Capt.; M(1).
125 *St. George's Road, Westminster, S.W. 1.*

SHIELDS, *Douglas Gordon*
E/1576, 6/10/14; R. Scots., 7/12/14; Lieut.

SHIELDS, *Frank Raymond*
A/11294, 16/5/17; Garr. O.C.B., 5/10/17; Lab. Corps, 15/12/17; F; 2/Lieut.
St. James the Great Vicarage, Bethnal Green Road, E. 1.

SHILLITO, *James Trueman*
6/2/6368, 20/9/15; No. 11 O.C.B., 7/5/16; M.G.C., 4/9/16; F; Lieut.; w.
8 *Palace Road, Kingston-on-Thames.*

SHILTON, *Arnold Victor*
6/2/6746, 11/10/15; Oxf. & Bucks. L.I., 8/6/16, att. R. Innis. Fus.; Lieut.

SHILVOCK-WRIGHT, *William Edward*
D/12889, 3/4/18; R.F.A., C/S, 6/7/18; R.F.A., 3/4/19; 2/Lieut.
Laredo, Warwick Road, Solihull, Warwickshire.

SHIMMIN, *Ernest Creer*
6/2/5343, 2/8/15, L/C.; Mon. R., 16/6/16; F; Lieut.; w.
7 *Christian Road, Douglas, Isle of Man.*

☖ SHIMMIN, *Thomas Edwin*
2/3743, 24/5/15; N. Cyc. Bn., 12/7/15, R.F.C.; 2/Lieut.
Killed 22/4/17.

SHIPP, *Frederick Arthur*
C/11454, 4/6/17, Sgt.; No. 16 O.C.B., 22/3/18; Norf. R., 12/11/18; F; 2/Lieut.
Beechurst, Knighton Road, Leicester.

APPENDIX II.—RECORDS OF RANK AND FILE.

SHIPTON, Edmund Pond
B/10807, 28/2/17; No. 14 O.C.B., 10/8/17; Glouc. R., 27/11/17; It; 2/Lieut.   17 Tyne Road, Bishopston, Bristol.

SHIRLAW, William Kenneth Johnstone
C/11779, 30/7/17; R.F.C., C/S, 23/10/17; R.F.C., 4/11/17, R.A.F.; 2/Lieut.   The Hall Green, Upholland, Nr. Wigan, Lancashire.

SHIRLEY, Cecil Annesley
4/3/3985, 3/6/15; R.G.A., 29/9/15; F; Capt.
             82 Taybridge Road, Clapham Common, S.W. 4.

✠ SHIRREFF, Francis Gordon
B/2566, 4/1/15; R. Berks. R., 2/6/15; F; 2/Lieut.
                             Killed in action 1/7/16.

SHOESMITH, Herbert
A/12449, 22/1/18, Cpl.; No. 5 O.C.B., 8/11/18; R.W. Kent R., 17/3/19; 2/Lieut.   48 Prospect Road, Southborough, Kent.

✠ SHOOBERT, Neil
C/1242, 23/9/14, L/C.; Midd'x. R., 10/2/15; F; Lieut.
                             Killed in action 31/7/17.

SHOOBERT, Wilfrid Harold
F/2712, 18/1/15; Rif. Brig., 29/4/15; F; Lieut.; w(2).
           c/o Messrs. King, King & Coy., Bombay, India.

SHOOSMITH, Charles Eric
D/12112, 10/10/17; No. 20 O.C.B., 10/5/18; Interpretership, 31/10/18; NR; Lieut.
    c/o A. Gibson Esq., Estliansky, Branksome Park, Bournemouth.

SHOOSMITH, Robert Osborn
1/3056, 15/3/15; R. Suss. R., 23/4/15; att. M.G.C.; E,P,F; Lieut.; w.   Box 661, Durban, Natal, South Africa.

SHORE, John Henry
6/9296, 3/2/16; No. 7 O.C.B., 11/8/16; R. Dub. Fus., 18/12/16, R. War. R.; F; Lieut.   Parc-na-silla, Shankill, Co. Dublin.

✠ SHORT, Francis Leslie
B/520, 18/11/10, dis. 23/12/13; R.W. Kent R., 15/8/14; Capt.
                                     Died 3/6/16.

SHORT, Fred John Sharer. Now SHORT-SHORT, F. J.
4/5/4702, 8/7/15; Yorks. L.I., 14/10/15, S. Lan. R., L'pool. R., Linc. R.; F; Major; w(3); M(1).
            Junior Army & Navy Club, Whitehall Court, S.W. 1.

SHORT, Leonard Highton
1/3884, 31/5/15; Durh. L.I., 8/10/15, att. R.A.F.; F; Capt.; w; M.C.   2 Norbury Court Road, Norbury, S.W. 16.

✠ SHORT, Walter
6/1/8039, 30/11/15; No. 8 O.C.B., 4/8/16; Yorks. L.I., 21/11/16; F; Capt.   Killed in action 20/7/18.

SHORTER, Frank Arthur
6/4/5312, 2/8/15; trfr. 14th Lond. R., 2/5/16; F,S,E,P; Pte
                 School House, Clewer Green, Windsor.

✠ SHORTER, Lewis Victor Henry
B/9887, 9/11/16; No. 14 O.C.B., 30/1/17; E. Kent R., 29/5/17; M,I; Lieut.   Died 14/11/19.

SHORTHOSE, Thomas Hartshorne
D/13802, 9/8/18; trfr. K.R. Rif. C., 25/4/19, R.A.O.C.; Pte.
               Stickworth Hall, Arreton, Isle of Wight.

SHORTING, John Carl Nicholas
C/14273, 6/11/18; trfr. K.R. Rif. C., 25/4/19; Pte.
             P.O. Box 381, Swift Current, Saskatchewan, Canada.

✠ SHORTO, Martin Hubert
K/F/2359, 14/12/14; S. Lan. R., 24/2/15, R.E.; Lieut.
                            Killed in action 27/7/17.

SHOULER, Alfred John
6/2/7699, 22/11/15; No. 8 O.C.B., 4/8/16; North'n. R., 21/11/16; F; Capt.   Barclay's Bank Ltd., Peterborough.

SHOVELTON, Leslie
6/7955, 29/11/15; R.A.M.C., 30/12/15; I; Capt.
               Kirkee, Croft Road, Evesham, Worcestershire.

SHOWAN, Percy Bernard
6/3/8788, 7/1/16; R.A., C/S, 4/3/16; R.G.A., 12/11/16; F; Lieut.; w(2).   Inglenook, Appleton, Widnes, Lancashire.

SHRIMPTON, George Ernest
A/11249, 12/5/17; No. 14 O.C.B., 5/10/17; Devon. R., 26/2/18, att. M.G.C.; F; Lieut.
             28 Old Queen Street, Westminster, S.W. 1.

SHUBROOK, Charles William Richard
A/11207, 5/5/17, L/C.; No. 14 O.C.B., 5/10/17; 7th Lond. R., 26/2/18; F; 2/Lieut.   839 Garrett Lane, Tooting, S.W. 17.

SHUBROOK, Maurice Arthur
D/9988, 22/11/16; No. 14 O.C.B., 5/3/17; trfr. 19th Lond. R., 5/7/17.

SHUCKBURGH, Robert Shirley
A/239, 22/5/08; dis. 21/5/10; enlisted R.H.A.; R.G.A., -/9/17; F; Capt.; M(1).   70 Clifton Hill, N.W. 8.

SHURMUR, Stanley Emberick
4/1/4428, 24/6/15; A.S.C., C/S, 17/7/16; R.A.S.C., 20/8/16; F,M; Capt.; M.B.E., M(2).
                    Rivenside Works, Upper Clapton, E. 5.

SHUTE, Francis Scott Wilkinson
6/2/6102, 6/9/15; N. Staff. R., 21/4/16; F; Lieut.; M.C.
   c/o Dr. G. S. Shute, Granby Place, Northfleet, Kent. (Now in Australia).

✠ SHUTT, Herbert Cecil
H/1990, 29/10/14; R. Sco. Fus., 30/12/14; Lieut.
                             Killed in action 13/11/16.

✠ SHUTTLEWORTH, Richard Welbury
D/10005, 24/11/16; No. 14 O.C.B., 5/3/17; Lan. Fus., 26/6/17, R.A.F.; F; 2/Lieut.; w.   Killed 16/8/18.

SIBBALD, Samuel James Ramsay
A/11940, 30/8/17; trfr. York. R., 5/12/18.
          The Manse, Crathie, Ballater, Aberdeenshire.

✠ SIBLEY, Desmond Wilkie
6/4/6674, 7/10/15; R.F.C., C/S, 8/10/16; R.F.C., 26/2/17, R.A.F.; F,E; Lieut.   Killed -/-/20.

SIBLEY, George Vincent
C/14188, 18/10/18; demob. 29/1/19.
            Station Stones, Fochriw, Via Cardiff, South Wales.

SICH, Percy Bertram Wardell
4/4161, 10/6/15; 17th Lond. R., 4/9/16; F; Lieut.
                  Norfolk House, The Mall, Chiswick, W. 4.

SIDDALLS, Francis Spearman
B/11712, 19/7/17; No. 14 O.C.B., 9/11/17; E. Lan. R., 30/4/18; 2/Lieut.   Draycott, Temple Ewell, Dover.

SIDDELEY, Frederic
6/4/7479, 15/11/15, L/C.; No. 11 O.C.B., 16/5/16; North'd. Fus., 4/9/16; F; Lieut.; w; M.C.
                    41 Mount Park Road, Ealing, W. 5.

SIDDELEY, Norman Goodier
2/9688, 4/10/16; No. 14 O.C.B., 26/11/16; R. Fus., 27/3/17; Lieut.; w.   Hill Orchard, Minden, Nr. Coventry, Warwickshire.

SIDES, Henry Edmund
A/13125, 24/5/18; No. 11 O.C.B., 14/2/19; General List, 8/3/19; 2/Lieut.   41 Rue des Martyrs, Paris, France.

SIDNEY, Thomas
K/3062, 16/3/15; dis. 16/3/15; rej. 6/9586, 15/6/16; R.A., C/S, 4/8/16; R.G.A., 1/11/16; w.

✠ SIKES, Robert Gordon
6/Sq/8880, 12/1/16; No. 1 Cav. C/S, 2/8/16; Leic. Yeo., 27/11/16, att. 4th Huss.; F; Lieut.   Died 22/2/19.

SILLITOE, Cyril Arthur
C/13256, 10/6/18; No. 22 O.C.B., 5/7/18; Suff. R., 12/2/19; 2/Lieut.   23 Ritherdown Road, S.W. 17.

SILVER, Gordon
B/D/13542, 15/7/18; trfr. K.R. Rif. C., 29/5/19.
                 120 Ridley Road, Forest Gate, Essex.

SILVESTER, Sidney Bartlett
D/10664, 3/2/17; R.G.A., C/S, 25/4/17; R.G.A., 1/10/17; 2/Lieut.
            Kinlough, Purley Downs Road, Purley, Surrey.

SILVESTER, Victor Marlborough
B/12365, 2/1/18, L/C.; No. 6 O.C.B., 7/6/18; trfr. 28th Lond. R., 26/9/18.   The Vicarage, Wembley.

SIM, Stuart Grant
6/5/5272, 31/7/15, Sgt.; L'pool. R., 27/10/15, att. M.G.C.; F, Capt.; w(2).   83 Edith Road, West Kensington, W. 14.

✠ SIM, William George
D/11156, 28/4/17; No. 9 O.C.B., 10/8/17; R. Highrs., 17/12/17; 2/Lieut.   Killed in action 14/10/18.

APPENDIX II.—RECORDS OF RANK AND FILE.

SIMCOCK, Frank Barton
6/5/6051, 3/9/15; R. Lanc. R., 9/6/16, att. 6th Lond. R.; F;
Lieut.; w.   Allandale, Marshland Road, Brooklands, Cheshire.

SIMCOX, William Martin
C/11523, 18/6/17; No. 16 O.C.B., 5/10/17; R. War. R., 12/3/18;
F; 2/Lieut.   Kyotts Lake, Hall Green, Birmingham.

SIMKINS, Rupert Mann
B/12370, 3/1/18; demob. 7/1/19.   3 Podsmead Road, Gloucester.

SIMMANCE, John Audley
4/2/3275, 15/4/15; R.W. Surr. R., 10/7/15, att. R.F.C.; F; Capt.;
w.
c/o J. F. Simmance Esq. Knowle Tooth, Hurstpierpoint, Sussex.
(Now in East Africa).

SIMMIE, James McWilliam
D/12880, 3/4/18; No. 21 O.C.B., 4/10/18, No. 18 O.C.B.; trfr. 5th
Lond. R., 3/3/19.   8 Ross Avenue, Inverness.

SIMMONDS, Frederick Daniel
D/11549, 21/6/17; No. 14 O.C.B., 9/11/17; Bedf. R., 30/4/18.
25 Lordship Lane, East Dulwich, S.E. 22.

SIMMONDS, Hugh Henry Dawes
K/Sq/2570, 4/1/15; Herts. Yeo., 15/3/15; M,P; Capt.

✠ SIMMONS, Arthur Donald
D/10898, 17/3/17; R.F.C., C/S, 4/5/17; R.F.C., 14/6/17, R.A.F.;
2/Lieut.   Killed 26/2/19.

SIMMONS, Bernard Frank
A/14347, 6/1/19; trfr. K.R. Rif. C., 7/4/19.
Hillside, Woodville Road, New Barnet, Hertfordshire.

SIMMONS, Edwin John
6/4/7154, 2/11/15; No. 14 O.C.B.; trfr. R.G.A., 17/11/16; R.G.A.,
2/9/17; F; Lieut.; M.C.
Norfolk House, Alderbrook Road, Clapham Common, S.W. 12.

SIMMONS, Frederick David
4/3/4094, 7/6/15, Sgt.; Dorset R., 25/9/16, Indian Army; I,M,E,P;
Capt.   49 Hillier Road, Wandsworth Common, S.W. 11.

SIMMONS, Frederick Thomas
D/12980, 24/4/18; No. 8 O.C.B., 18/10/18; demob.
Clovelly, Alan Road, Withington, Manchester.

SIMMONS, John Ayscough
B/689, 7/2/13; Ches. R., 11/9/14; Major; w(3); D.S.O., M.C.,
M(2).

SIMMONS, Stephen
Sq/1918, 16/10/14; R.F.A., 19/12/14; Lieut.
81 Babington Road, Streatham, S.W. 16.

✠ SIMMONS, Sydney Noel
Sq/404, 23/4/09; dis. 23/4/13; enlisted R. Wilts. Yeo., -/8/14; R.
Wilts. Yeo., 7/12/15; F; Lieut.; w.   Died of wounds 27/10/16.

SIMNER, Percy Reginald O. A.
C/1164, 14/9/14; W. Rid. R., 19/11/14, W. York. R.; F; Lt.Col.;
D.S.O. and Bar, M(4).
7 Prince of Wales Terrace, Kensington, W. 8.

SIMON, Arthur Powell
D/E/13706, 31/7/18; No. 22 O.C.B., 20/9/18; Oxf. & Bucks. L.I.,
5/2/19; 2/Lieut.   Endcliffe, Beaconsfield, Buckinghamshire.

SIMON, Frank Cecil
D/E/13913, 26/8/18; demob. 10/1/19.
51 Belsize Park, N.W. 3.

✠ SIMON, Marcel André
3/7186, 3/11/15, L/C.; No. 14 O.C.B., 27/9/16; R. Berks. R.,
18/12/16; 2/Lieut.   Killed in action 29/4/17.

SIMONDS, Charles Cabourn Bannister
4/3/750, 24/5/15; R.E., 11/7/15; Lieut.
Norwood House, Sleaford Road, Boston, Lincolnshire.

SIMONS, Edward Gayle
6/2/6538, 30/9/15, Sgt.; North'd. Fus., 4/9/16; F,It; Lieut.; M(1).
The Manse, Pennel Grove, Lincoln.

SIMONS, Evelyn John
1/3408, 26/4/15; E. Surr. R., 8/7/15, 7th Lond. R., R.A.S.C.; F;
Lieut.   Hagley, Bull Lane, Gerrard's Cross, Buckinghamshire.

SIMONS, Geoffrey Richard
4/3/4407, 24/6/15; Durh. L.I., 21/12/15; R.A.F.; S,E; Lieut.
c/o Craigmore, Godstone Road, Rotherham, Yorkshire.

✠ SIMPKIN, Arthur Wilson
1/2905, 11/2/15, Cpl.; Notts. & Derby. R., 25/9/15, York. R., att.
W. York. R.; F; Capt.; w.   Killed in action 30/9/18.

SIMPKIN, Frederick Vaughan Guy
10938, 28/3/17; No. 14 O.C.B., 5/10/17; Manch. R., 26/2/18;
2/Lieut.   12 Mount Road, Hinckley, Leicester.

SIMPKIN, Harry
B/10705, 12/2/17, L/C.; R.A., C/S, 29/6/17; R.G.A., 2/12/17;
F; Lieut.; g.   7 St. Helena Road, Westbury Park, Bristol.

✠ SIMPKIN, Harry Hargreaves
1/2974, 25/2/15, L/C.; Notts. & Derby. R., 25/9/15, W. York.
R.; F; Capt.   Killed in action 22/3/18.

SIMPKINS, Ernest Henry
4/3744, 24/5/15; Norf. R., 16/11/15, M.G.C.; F; Lieut.; w.
Church Lea, 10 Church Hill, Walthamstow, E. 17.

SIMPSON, Alan
6/4/8885, 13/1/16; No. 8 O.C.B., 4/8/16; K.R. Rif. C., 18/12/16;
F; Lieut.; p.   Winwick, Warrington, Lancashire.

SIMPSON, Bertie Leon
A/1889, 16/10/14; Oxf. & Bucks. L.I., 27/11/14; Capt.

✠ SIMPSON, Cecil Barclay
6/3/9499, 15/2/16; No. 14 O.C.B., 30/10/16; Sea. Highrs., 28/2/17;
2/Lieut.   Killed in action 7/10/17.

SIMPSON, Charles Abercrombie
6/4/8997, 19/1/16; A.S.C., C/S, 27/10/16; R.A.S.C., 20/12/16; I;
Lieut.; M(1).   2 Matilda Road, Pollokshields, Glasgow.

✠ SIMPSON, Cyril Woodhouse
F/1731, 15/10/14, L/C.; Leic. R., 13/11/14; Lieut.; w.
Killed in action 14/7/16.

SIMPSON, Eric Tracy
F/1793, 16/10/14, Sgt.; Manch. R., 1/2/15, M.G.C.; F; Capt.; w.
12 Hartington Mansions, Eastbourne.

SIMPSON, Ernest Dawes. See SIMPSON, Thomas Ernest William
Dawes

SIMPSON, Ernest Frederick
6/3/8093, 1/12/15; No. 14 O.C.B., 30/10/16; Ches. R., 28/2/17;
F; Lieut.; w.
Blake House, Seagry Road, Cambridge Park, Wanstead.

SIMPSON, Henry William
B/11404, 29/5/17; No. 14 O.C.B., 5/10/17; Norf. R., 26/2/18;
2/Lieut.   70 High Street, Bridlington, East Yorkshire.

SIMPSON, Herbert Muir
A/13158, 29/5/18; No. 22 O.C.B., 5/7/18; Sco. Rif., 12/2/19;
2/Lieut.   27 Mansion House Road, Langside, Glasgow.

SIMPSON, Hugh Burton
K/Sq/2396, 17/12/14, L/C.; R.A.S.C., 2/3/15, R.F.A.; F; Lieut.;
w.   4 Richmond Road, Headingley, Leeds.

SIMPSON, Hugh Hallgate
6/3/6212, 13/9/15, L/C.; 15th Lond. R., 4/6/16; Lieut.
88 Thornton Avenue, Chiswick, W. 4.

SIMPSON, James
6/5/5230, 30/7/15; trfr. R.E., 14/7/16; R.W. Kent R., 1/5/19; I;
2/Lieut.   79 Aigburth Road, Sefton Park, Liverpool.

SIMPSON, James Herbert
A/11962, 3/9/17; H. Bde. O.C.B., 7/12/17; Gren. Gds., 28/5/18;
Lieut.   Rendcombe College, Cirencester.

SIMPSON, John Edward Alan
K/D/2444, 28/12/14; R.G.A., 8/9/15, R.F.A.; Lieut.

SIMPSON, Joseph Norman
4/5/4809, 12/7/15, L/C.; R. Scots., 26/10/15; Lieut.; w.

SIMPSON, Leonard
Sq/2539, 4/1/15; R.W. Surr. R., 13/1/15; 2/Lieut.
15 Greenway, Berkhamsted, Hertfordshire.

SIMPSON, Maurice Muir
1/3204, 8/4/15, L/C.; High. L.I., 19/9/15, Yorks. L.I.; F; Capt.;
w; M.C.   Pinehurst, Tilford, Farnham, Surrey.

SIMPSON, Philip William
A/1685, 12/10/14; E. Surr. R., 8/4/15, North'n. R., Suff. R., Bedf.
R., R. War. R.; E,I,M; Capt.
Loftus Hotel, Templeton Place, S.W. 5.

APPENDIX II.—RECORDS OF RANK AND FILE.

SIMPSON, Robert Gordon
6/8493, 20/12/15; No. 9 O.C.B., 8/3/16; R. Scots. 25/7/16; F;
Lieut.; g, w; M.C.   23 Douglas Crescent, Edinburgh.

SIMPSON, Ronald Maitland
F/1771, 16/10/14; Yorks. L.I., 10/2/15, secd. Sigs.; F; Lieut.
                               89 Lancaster Gate, W. 2.

SIMPSON, Thomas Ernest William Dawes
6/Sq/7544, 17/11/15; R.A., C/S, 29/1/16, A.S.C., C/S; R.A.S.C.,
25/2/17; F; Capt.; w; M(1).   4/5 King William Street, E.C. 4.

SIMPSON, Thomas Ivan
6/4/9154, 25/1/16; No. 14 O.C.B., 30/10/16; Mon. R., 28/2/17;
Lieut.   Tynemouth, Clytha Park, Newport, Monmouthshire.

SIMS, Eric Thomas George
6/4/8772, 6/1/16; No. 14 O.C.B., 26/11/16; Welch R., 28/2/17;
Lieut.   Land Agent, Abbey Road, Neath, South Wales.

SIMS, George William
B/13426, 1/7/18; demob. 23/1/19.
          Wistaria, Osborne Road, East Cowes, Isle of Wight.

✠ SINCLAIR, Gerald John
D/1491, 29/9/14, L/C.; dis. to R. Mil. Coll., 28/12/14; R. Highrs.,
16/6/15; Capt.; w.   Killed in action 18/4/18.

SINCLAIR, John Duff
B/12744, 11/3/18; R.E., C/S, 14/4/18; R.E., 15/8/18; 2/Lieut.;
Russian Medal of St. George and Order of S. Stanislaus.
                            Acharn, Milngavie, Glasgow.

SINCLAIR, Paul
6/3/9427, 10/2/16; trfr. 15th Lond. R., 28/9/16.
                St. Auslem's Vicarage, Davies Street, W. 1.

SINKINSON, Alfred Peveril le Mesurier
B/713, 6/5/13; R. Fus., 14/8/14, att. Lan. Fus.; F; Major,
D.A.A.G.; O.B.E., M(1).   49 Haverstock Hill, N.W. 3.

✠ SIORDET, Gerald Caldwell
Sq/464, 23/2/10; dis. 13/6/10; Rif. Brig., 27/1/15, att. R. Lanc. R.;
2/Lieut.; M.C.   Killed in action 9/2/17.

SIPPE, Charles Blackburn
A/2881, 8/2/15; Linc. R., 29/4/15, att. Suff. R., and M.G.C.; F;
Lieut.; w, Inj.   12 Farquhar Road, Upper Norwood, S.E. 19.

✠ SISTERSON, Norman Hele
6/3/9249, 2/2/16; No. 8 O.C.B., 4/8/16; North'd. Fus., 21/11/16,
att. Linc. R.; 2/Lieut.   Killed in action 16/4/18.

SKAE, George Pierce Malcolm
4/2/5130, 26/7/15, L/C.; R.A.S.C., 4/12/15; F; Capt.; M(1).
                      The Club, George Row, Northampton.

✠ SKEET, John Richard
6/4/5838, 26/8/15; 2nd Lond. R., 20/12/15; Lieut.; w.
                                Killed in action 27/4/18.

SKERRITT, Francis Greenfield
B/13493, 8/7/18; No. 22 O.C.B., 23/8/18; Notts. & Derby. R.
13/2/19; 2/Lieut.   35 Ebury Road, Nottingham.

SKERTCHLEY, Ernest William
C/12625, 18/2/18; No. 16 O.C.B., 5/7/18; trfr. 28th Lond. R.,
12/9/18, K.R. Rif. C.; L/C
            Kenwyn, Station Road, Borrowash, Nr. Derby.

SKETCH, Hubert James
6/9466, 14/2/16; R.F.A., C/S, 23/6/16; R.F.A., 28/8/18; Lieut.;
w.   Johnston, Pembrokeshire.

SKEVINGTON, Arthur Johnson
6/5/7621, 19/11/15; No. 8 O.C.B., 4/8/16; Linc. R., 21/11/16;
F; Lieut.; w(2).

SKIDMORE, John Hadley
6/D/9739, 16/10/16; No. 14 O.C.B., 30/1/17; Shrops. L.I., 25/4/17;
F; Lieut.; w.   Cleveland Street, Cherry Orchard, Shrewsbury.

SKINNER, Alfred Ernest Lionel
Sq/2882, 8/2/15, Cpl.; Norf. Yeo., 7/6/15, R.F.C.; E,M; Capt.;
M.C., M(1).   34 Old Bond Street, W. 1.

SKINNER, Frank Hollamby
6/4/7514, 15/11/15, Sgt.; No. 11 O.C.B., 7/5/16; 8th Lond. R.,
4/9/16, Indian Army; F,I; Capt.
                            c/o Cox & Coy., Bombay, India.

SKINNER, James Hay McInnes
A/1287, 23/9/14, L/C.; Oxf. & Bucks. L.I., 20/10/14, M.G.C.; F;
Major; resigned and rej. A/11301, 16/5/17, Cpl.; No. 5 O.C.B.,
7/9/17; Cam'n. Highrs., 30/10/17; w.
                              Lycrome, Chesham, Buckinghamshire.

SKINNER, John William
D/B/12135, 18/10/17; R.F.A., C/S, 15/3/18; R.F.A., 1/1/19;
2/Lieut.   c/o J. H. Skinner Esq., 64 Basinghall Street, E.C. 2.

SKINNER, Reginald Thomas
F/3035, 9/3/15; Notts. & Derby. R., 11/6/15; F; Lieut.; w.
                3 Upper George Street, Bryanston Square, W. 1.

SKINNER, Walter Reginald Thynne
6/1/6296, 16/9/15; Midd'x. R., 1/6/16; F; Lieut.; w.
                        30 Fellows Road, Hampstead, N.W. 3.

SKIRROW, Philip Wilson
A/12494, 28/1/18; No. 13 O.C.B., 7/6/18; Welch R., 5/2/19;
2/Lieut.   4 The Grove, Swansea.

SLADE, Alfred John
1/9733, 16/10/16, L/C.; M.G.C., C/S, 1/3/17; M.G.C., 25/6/17;
Lieut.   The Pass, Tower Road, Worthing.

✠ SLADE, Robert Gordon
4/3/6/4011, 5/6/15; R.F.A., 11/9/15; Lieut.
                                Killed in action 18/4/18.

SLADE, Ronald Crawford
D/11096, 16/4/17; No. 9 O.C.B., 10/8/17; K.O. Sco. Bord.,
17/12/17; 2/Lieut.; M.C.
            Llanarthney, Clytha Park, Newport, Monmouthshire.

✠ SLADE, Stewart Harold
6/9156, 26/1/16; No. 8 O.C.B., 13/3/16, M.G.C., C/S; M.G.C.,
28/10/16, Tank Corps; Lieut.   Killed in action 21/8/18.

SLATER, John Wynn
6/3/6213, 13/9/15; A.S.C., C/S, 28/2/16; R.A.S.C., 29/3/16;
Lieut.   44 Bloomsbury Street, W.C. 1.

SLATER, Joseph Emile
A/12495, 28/1/18; No. 14 O.C.B., 7/6/18; demob. 29/1/19.
                    23 Blenheim Crescent, South Croydon, Surrey.

SLATER, Robert
4/3883, 31/5/15, L/C.; R. Lanc. R., 29/11/15, Lab. Corps; Lieut.
                              Natosa, Preston, Lancashire.

SLATER, Robert Cecil
6/Sq/6788, 12/10/15; R.F.A., C/S, 4/8/16; R.F.A., 22/12/16; F;
Capt.; w.   38 Corn Exchange, Leeds, Yorkshire.

✠ SLATTERY, Duncan Vincent
4/1/4435, 24/6/15; Hamps. R., 4/12/15, R.F.C.; 2/Lieut.
                                          Killed 3/3/17.

SLATTERY, Udolpho Wolfe
C/2056, 9/11/14, L/C.; R.W. Kent R., 5/3/15; Lieut.

SLAUGHTER, Frederick William
6/1/9364, 7/2/16, Cpl.; No. 14 O.C.B., 26/11/16; R.M.L.I., 28/2/17,
secd. M.G.C.; Lieut.
                    c/o G. A. Newling Esq., 16 Brookwood Avenue, Barnes.

SLEE, Edwin Sheppard
A/10184, 13/12/16; No. 20 O.C.B., 7/6/17; Manch. R., 25/9/17;
F; Lieut.; w.
                    Oakdene, Kings Road, Alexandra Park, Manchester.

SLEIGHT, Kenneth Richard
6/1/7810, 24/11/15, L/C.; No. 14 O.C.B., 27/9/16; 20th Lond. R.,
24/1/17; F; Lieut.; w.
                      The Vicarage, Towcester, Northamptonshire.

SLINGSBY, Stanley Victor
B/12717, 8/3/18; No. 2 O.C.B., 20/9/18; demob.
                    Hartlands, Wellington Road, Enfield, Middlesex.

SLOAN, Archibald
4/3/4408, 24/6/15, L/C.; Essex R., 7/11/15; F; Capt.
                                  Thorshavn, Faroe Islands.

SLOAN, Frank
C/10195, 15/12/16; No. 14 O.C.B., 6/4/17; Manch. R., 31/7/17;
F; Lieut.   33 Buller Road, Longsight, Manchester.

✠ SLOAN, Harold Alexander
6/4/9013, 19/1/16; R.A., C/S, 7/8/16; R.G.A., 18/10/16; 2/Lieut.
                                    Killed in action 21/1/17.

SLOMAN, Harold Newman Penrose
1/9647, 27/9/16; No. 14 O.C.B., 26/11/16; Rif. Brig., 28/2/17; F;
Lieut.; w; M.C.   Public Schools Club, W.

SMAIL, Harry William
6/5/7700, 22/11/15; R.A., C/S, 7/8/16; R.F.A., 17/11/16; F,
Capt.; M.C.   19 Bolton Road, Port Sunlight, Cheshire.

SMAIL, Herbert Morgan
6/2/9527, 16/2/16; No. 8 O.C.B., 4/8/16; D. of Corn. L.I.,
21/11/16; F; Lieut.; p.
                        4 Balmyle Road, Broughty Ferry, Scotland.

APPENDIX II.—RECORDS OF RANK AND FILE.

SMALL, Oswald Clifford
D/11550, 21/6/17, Sgt.; R.E., C/S, 4/11/17; R.E., 1/2/18; 2/Lieut.
c/o O. F. Small Esq., 38 Brantwood Road, Luton, Bedfordshire.

SMALLDRIDGE, Francis William
D/12099, 8/10/17, Cpl.; demob. 26/5/19.
77 Ellesmere Road, Berkhamsted.

SMALLEY, Albert George
6/3/6593, 4/10/15; W. Rid. R., 6/6/16, R.A.F.; F; Lieut.
Marlborough House, Pall Mall, S.W.1.

SMALLEY, William George
B/13448, 3/7/18; demob. 18/2/19.
Earle Cottage, Earlestown, Lancashire.

SMALLMAN, Bertie Strong
1/3563, 10/5/15; R.F.A., 19/9/15, R.F.C.; F,S,E; Lieut.; w(2).
Eliot Lodge, Albemarle Road, Beckenham, Kent.

✠ SMALLWOOD, Eric Butter
D/2999, 2/3/15, Sgt.; Herts. R., 11/6/15; Capt.; M.C.
Killed in action 7/1/17.

SMALLWOOD, Thomas Noble
4/5/4721, 9/7/15; Ches. R., 6/12/15, att. M.G.C., R.E.; F;
Lieut.; w(2); M.C.
Springbank, Loney Street, Macclesfield. (Now in Malaya).

SMART, Donald Percy
A/10082, 1/12/16; trfr. R.G.A., 19/2/17.
30 Landrock Road, Crouch End, N.8.

✠ SMART, Eustace Fowler
A/916, 5/8/14; Lein. R., 12/9/14; F; Lieut.
Killed in action 8/2/16.

SMART, Thomas Fraser Mackenzie
4/5/4810, 12/7/15, L/C.; North'd. Fus., 17/9/15; F; Major;
O.B.E., m. 81 Beaconsfield Road, Blackheath, S.E.3.

SMEE, Rosslyn
Sq/540, 27/1/11; dis. 31/3/14; rej. Sq/1676, 12/10/14, Cpl.; Bedf.
Yeo., 16/12/14, att. 15th Huss.; F; Lieut.
6 Wildwood Road, Golders Green, N.W.4.

SMELLIE, James Kirkwood
B/12007, 13/9/17, L/C.; R.F.C., C/S, 26/11/17.
38 Garturk Street, Queens Park, Glasgow.

SMELTZER, John Bertie
4/2/4196, 14/6/15; Shrops. L.I., 10/9/15, M.G.C.; F; Major;
M.C. and Bar, M(1). 55 South Park Road, Wimbledon, S.W.19.

SMERDON, Harry Maurice
4/6/4948, 19/7/15; Devon. R., 11/1/16, att. D. of Corn. L.I;
I,P; Capt.; w. Bemerton, St. Marychurch, Torquay.

✠ SMETHURST, Frederick James
6/5/5999, 2/9/15; No. 4 O.C.B., 7/3/16; S. Lan. R., 15/7/16;
Capt.; w; M.C. Killed in action 30/11/17.

SMETHURST, Robert Merton
C/13388, 24/6/18; demob. 23/1/19.
Holmlea, 48 Bignor Street, Cheetham, Manchester.

SMITH, Alexander Cormack
C/14189, 18/10/18; No. 11 O.C.B., 24/1/19; General List, 8/3/19;
2/Lieut. Box 4303, Johannesburg, South Africa.

SMITH, Alfred William Exton
6/2/9365, 7/2/16, Cpl.; No. 14 O.C.B., 26/11/16; R. Suss. R.,
27/3/17; Lieut. Lennor Lodge, Carlisle Road, Eastbourne.

SMITH, Alic Halford
Sq/190, 4/5/08; dis. 3/5/11.

✠ SMITH, Allison Gould
B/1011, 6/8/14; N. Lan R., 12/9/14; Capt.; w; M.C.
Killed in action 18/4/18.

SMITH, Arthur Alborough
K/B/Sq/2155, 23/11/14, L/C.; R.A.S.C., 23/3/15, Hamps. R.;
F,I; Capt. The Priory, Little Horkesley, Nr. Colchester.

SMITH, Arthur Bertrand Burgess
6/2/8296, 10/12/15, Cpl.; No. 14 O.C.B., 28/8/16; Hamps. R.,
24/10/16; F; 2/Lieut.
Whitehaven, Fernleigh Drive, Leigh-on-Sea.

SMITH, Arthur Kirke
C/181, 30/4/08; dis. 29/4/09; Indian Army; M; Lieut.
c/o Messrs. Little & Coy., Apollo Street, Bombay.

SMITH, Arthur Woodward
6/1/5667, 16/8/15; dis. to enter R. Navy, 30/6/16.
34 Rewsland Park Road, Newport, Monmouthshire.

SMITH, Basil Powy
Sq/1559, 6/10/14, L/C.; York. Huss., 31/12/14, att. W. Rid. R.;
F; Capt. 13 Hereford Road, Bayswater, W.

SMITH, Benjamin Roxburgh
6/1/8736, 5/1/16; R.F.C., 11/8/16, R.A.F.; Lieut.; D.F.C. and Bar.

SMITH, Cecil William Montague
6/2/6189, 13/9/15; Manch. R., 4/8/16, secd. K. Af. Rif.; F,EA;
Lieut.; w.
106 Woodlands Avenue, Wanstead Park, E.11. (Now in East Africa).

SMITH, Charles James
D/2622, 7/1/15; R. Fus., 26/3/15, E. York. R.; G,E,F; Capt.;
M.C., M(1). 9 Winchester Road, Highams Park, E.4.

SMITH, Charles Love
D/2555, 4/1/15; Manch. R., 7/4/15; F; Capt.; w; M(1).
724 South Catalina Avenue, Redondo Beach, California, U.S.A.

SMITH, Charles Raymond
1/3100, 22/3/15, L/C.; Midd'x. R., 27/7/15; F,It,S; Lieut.; w(2).
Leaholme, Springfield Road, Leicester.

SMITH, Charles Westwood
1/3362, 17/5/15; N. Staff. R., 28/7/15; F; Capt.; p.
28 West Avenue, Clarendon Park, Leicester.

SMITH, Christopher Patrick
6/5/7036, 27/10/15, L/C.; dis. to R. Mil. Coll., 29/8/16; R. Ir.
Regt., 1/5/17, secd. M.G.C.; Lieut.
Grallagh House, Thurles, Co. Tipperary, Ireland.

SMITH, Clarence Castle
Sq/3429, 29/4/15, L/C.; E. Rid. Yeo., 5/10/15, att. E. York. R.;
F; Lieut.; w(2).
The Moorings, 18 Western Gardens, Ealing, W.5.

SMITH, Clinton Basden
B/11374, 28/5/17, L/C.; R.G.A., C/S, 23/1/18; R.G.A., 29/7/18;
2/Lieut. 10 Gleneagle Road, Mannamead, Plymouth.

SMITH, Denis Langford
4/1/4617, 5/7/15; trfr. H.A.C., 8/12/15.

SMITH, Douglas
6/4/6078, 2/9/15; D. of Corn. L.I., 1/6/16; 2/Lieut.
Park View, Penylan Road, Cardiff.

SMITH, Edgar Lionel
6/3/7753, 22/11/15; No. 8 O.C.B., 4/8/16; Dorset R., 21/11/16;
F; 2/Lieut. Langholme, Avenue Road, Weymouth.

SMITH, Edward Archibald
3/4/3282, 15/4/15; R.E., 15/7/15; Lieut.; M.C.
Andover Vicarage, Hampshire.

SMITH, Edward Montague
H/1933, 22/10/14; R.E., 9/1/15, att. Portuguese Army; F; Major;
g; M.C., Portuguese Military Order of the Avis, M(2).
The Rectory, Longfield S.O., Kent. (Now in Brazil).

✠ SMITH, Eric Drummond
3/6/6231, 13/9/15; Notts. & Derby. R., 4/9/16, att. York. & Lanc.
R.; 2/Lieut. Killed in action 4/10/17.

SMITH, Ernest
6/1/6239, 16/9/15; 1st Lond. R., 19/12/15; F; Lieut.
94 Inderwick Road, Hornsey, N.8.

SMITH, Fidelis Joseph
6/5/8605, 3/1/16; R.A., C/S, 7/8/16; R.G.A., 8/11/16; F; Lieut.;
w. Carlton, Nr. Snaith, Yorkshire.

SMITH, Francis George
C/488, 25/4/10; dis. 24/4/14.

SMITH, Francis Jermyn
6/2/5527, 9/8/15, L/C.; E. York. R., 11/6/16; F; Capt.; w.
Anchor Chambers, Nene Quay, Wisbech.

✠ SMITH, Frank William Howard
4/3885, 31/5/15, L/C.; 19th Lond. R., 6/11/15; Lieut.
Died of wounds 4/12/17.

SMITH, Frederick
6/2/8494, 20/12/15, L/C.; No. 14 O.C.B., 30/10/16; R. War. R.,
24/1/17; F; Lieut.; w; M(1). 15 Styvechale Avenue, Coventry.

SMITH, Frederick Elmore Vernon
A/12550, 4/2/18; No. 14 O.C.B., 7/6/18; trfr. 28th Lond. R.,
18/10/18, R.A.O.C.; Lt; Cpl.
280a Northdown Road, Cliftonville, Margate.

APPENDIX II.—RECORDS OF RANK AND FILE.

SMITH, Frederick James Gemmell
K/H/2508, 31/12/14; Lan. Fus., 8/4/15, Bord. R., L'pool. R.; F;
Major; w(3). 42 Castelnau Gardens, Barnes, S.W. 13.

SMITH, Frederic Norman
2/3485, 3/5/15; R.A.S.C., 5/7/15; G; Lieut.
Asst. Solicitor, Town Hall, Birkenhead, Cheshire.

SMITH, Frederick Radford
6/8513, 29/12/15; R.F.A., C/S, 21/7/16; R.F.A., 13/10/16; F;
Lieut.; M(1). 34 Buxton Gardens, Acton Hill, W. 3.

SMITH, Geoffrey Howard
4/1/4055, 7/6/15; York. R., 8/9/15; Lieut.; w.

SMITH, George
D/12924, 12/4/18; No. 5 O.C.B., 8/11/18; demob.
Bodryn, Mostyn Road, Colwyn Bay, North Wales.

SMITH, George Henry
6/4/6638, 4/10/15; L/C.; dis. to re-enlist in R.M.A., 5/5/16;
R.G.A., -/4/17; F; Lieut.; M(1).
c/o Bank of Liverpool & Martin's Ltd., 7 Water Street,
Liverpool.

SMITH, George Young
B/11321, 19/5/17, L/C.; No. 14 O.C.B., 9/11/17; Lan. Fus.,
30/4/18; 2/Lieut. Elmbrie House, Sully, Nr. Cardiff.

SMITH, Gerald Edward Roberts
A/356, 11/3/09; dis. 10/3/13.
The Datcha, Kingston Road, Teddington.

SMITH, Gilbert Freeman
C/12660, 27/2/18; No. 17 O.C.B., 5/7/18; demob. 4/2/19.
Aviemore, Nant Hall Road, Prestatyn.

SMITH, Graham
6/5/7956, 29/11/15; Suff. R., 22/11/16; F; Lieut.; w.
White Cottage, Cedar Avenue, Chelmsford.

SMITH, Graham Gould
6/5/6000, 2/9/15; Oxf. & Bucks. L.I., 14/7/16; Lieut.
Horbling Hall, Folkingham.

SMITH, Harold
6/3/7480, 15/11/15, L/C.; W. Rid. R., 13/7/16; F; Capt.
14 Fitzjohn's Avenue, Barnet, Hertfordshire.

SMITH, Harold
6/1/7882, 26/11/15; No. 14 O.C.B., 26/11/16, No. 2 O.C.B.;
General List, 27/3/17, att. S. Persia Rif.; Persia; Major; M(1).
22 Althorp Road, St. James, Northampton.

SMITH, Harold George
C/12626, 18/2/18; No. 3 O.C.B., 9/8/18; R. Fus., 4/3/19; 2/Lieut.
70 Geoffrey Road, Brockley, S.E. 4.

SMITH, Harold John
A/B/12162, 25/10/17; R.E., C/S, 13/1/18; R.E., 31/5/18; 2/Lieut.
62 Charles Street East, Toronto, Canada.

SMITH, Harold John Emrys
A/D/12450, 22/1/18; R.F.C., C/S, 19/4/18; R.A.F., 30/10/18; F;
2/Lieut. Cartief, Rowantree Road, Enfield, Middlesex.

SMITH, Harold Machin
4/1/3986, 3/6/15, L/C.; Notts. & Derby. R., 10/9/15; F; Capt.;
M(1). 48 Full Street, Derby.

SMITH, Harold Meredith
C/9915, 14/11/16; R.G.A., C/S, 21/11/17, A.S.C., C/S; R.A.S C.,
27/7/18; 2/Lieut.

✠ SMITH, Harold Robert
2/3582, 13/5/15; R.W. Kent R., 28/7/15; F,It; Capt.; w; M.C.
Killed in action 7/11/18.

SMITH, Harri
C/Sq/10786, 23/2/17; R.F.A., C/S, 17/12/17; R.F.A., 3/6/18; F;
2/Lieut. 10 Glenhurst Road, Shipley, Yorkshire.

SMITH, Harry Gordon
C/13194, 3/6/18; trfr. 14th Lond. R., 6/12/18.
The Priory, Lanark, Scotland.

SMITH, Harwood Thomas
6/3/8502, 22/12/15, Cpl.; No 14 O.C.B., 30/10/16; E. Surr. R.,
28/2/17; F; Lieut.; w, p.
2 Glenure Road, Eltham Park, S.E. 9.

SMITH, Henry
D/12988, 26/4/18; R.E., C/S, 23/8/18; demob.
Ingleside, Carleton, Poulton-le-Fylde, Nr. Preston.

SMITH, Henry Arthur Neville
6/2/5349, 2/8/15; D. of Corn. L.I., 27/11/15; I,E,P; Lieut.; w.
c/o Mrs. Pickett, The Red House, Old Shoreham, Sussex.

SMITH, Henry Gordon
6/1/8662, 3/1/16; No. 5 O.C.B., 14/8/16; Suff. R., 21/11/16,
Shrops. L.I.; S; Lieut.
East Greer, Great Bradley, Nr. Newmarket.

SMITH, Henry Montagu Campbell
B/10463, 12/1/17; No. 14 O.C.B., 7/6/17; Midd'x. R., 25/9/17;
F; Lieut.; w.
Ingleside, 230 London Road, Twickenham, Middlesex.

✠ SMITH, Herbert Bennett
6/2/6833, 14/10/15; W. Som. Yeo., 5/8/16, att. Som. L.I.; F;
2/Lieut. Killed in action 17/7/17.

SMITH, Hubert Niemann
E/2722, 18/1/15; R.E., 9/4/15; Lieut.
Bridgeham Cottage, Nr. Horley, Surrey

SMITH, Hugh Scott
A/B/12163, 25/10/17, L/C.; No. 15 O.C.B., 5/7/18; demob.
3/2/19. Rye Croft, Grove Road, Wanstead, Essex.

SMITH, Jack Hayden
B/13592, 19/7/18; demob. 30/1/19.
St. Mark's College, Chelsea, S.W.

SMITH, James
A/D/11963, 3/9/17; H. Bde. O.C.B., 8/3/18; Welch Gds.,
27/8/18; Lieut. 8 New Square, Lincoln's Inn, W.C. 2.

SMITH, James
A/14341, 30/12/18; demob. 11/1/19.
35 Windsor Gardens, North Shields.

SMITH, James Holt
6/2/8789, 7/1/16; R.A., C/S, 23/6/16; R.G.A., 27/9/16; F;
Capt.; M.C. 108 Davenport Street, Bolton.

SMITH, John
C/10407, 8/1/17; trfr. 30th Lond. R., 2/3/17; Garr. O.C.B.,
-/5/17; Lab. Corps, 17/7/17; F; 2/Lieut.
Windyridge, Mellor, Blackburn.

✠ SMITH, John Adams
6/4/7377, 9/11/15; North'd. Fus., 1/6/16; 2/Lieut.; w(2); M.C.
Died of wounds 28/4/17.

SMITH, John Cecil
4/Sq/4682, 8/7/15; E. Rid. Yeo., 15/10/15, R.F.C.
Southminster, Essex.

SMITH, John Leonard
4/9715, 11/10/16; No. 14 O.C.B., 6/4/17; N. Lan. R., 31/7/17;
F; Lieut. Hindover Nurseries Egg Farm, Seaford, Sussex.

✠ SMITH, John Rankin Donald
6/8860, 12/1/16; No. 9 O.C.B., 8/3/16; R. Sco. Fus., 3/8/16;
2/Lieut. Killed in action 31/7/17.

SMITH, Kenneth Stuart
4/3320, 19/4/15; R. Fus., 28/7/15; F; Capt.; w(3).
18 Western Gardens, Ealing, W. 5. (Now in U.S.A.).

SMITH, Laurence Butler
6/8973, 17/1/16; R.F.A., C/S, 9/6/16; R.F.A., 27/10/16; F;
Lieut.; w. Knutton House, Tewitwell Road, Harrogate.

SMITH, Leslie Tildero
F/1858, 16/10/14; General List, 10/2/15, Yorks. L.I.; 2/Lieut.
Killed in action 16/9/16.

SMITH, Louis Percy
6/5/7601, 19/11/15, L/C.; R.W. Surr. R., 4/8/16, att. R.A.F.;
F; Lieut. 9 Ruskin Mansions, Queens Club Gardens, W. 14.

SMITH, Malcolm
6/1/7002, 25/10/15, L/C.; W. York. R., 4/8/16, att. L'pool. R.;
Lieut. 39 Lupers Street, St. Georges Square, S.W. 1.

SMITH, Marmaduke Roy
6/4/6320, 20/9/15, L/C.; Som. L.I., 11/12/15, Devon. R.; M;
Lieut.; M.C., M(1).
Higher Northcote, Sheldon, Craddock, Cullompton, Devonshire.

SMITH, Matthew Arnold Bracy
B/9858, 6/11/16; R.W. Surr. R., 9/3/17, Lab. Corps; F; Lieut.;
w.
c/o Messrs. Frederick Smith & Coy. Ltd., Salford, Manchester.

-SMITH, Norman
6/5/5273, 31/7/15; L'pool. R., 6/12/15; w
Westela, Downhills Road, Blundelsands, Liverpool.

SMITH, Percival Edwin
D/11844, 9/8/17; No. 3 O.C.B., 8/2/18; R. War. R., 30/7/18;
2/Lieut. Mottisfont, Romsey, Hampshire.

APPENDIX II.—RECORDS OF RANK AND FILE.

SMITH, Percy Bourdon
Sq/1337, 26/9/14; R.E., 9/1/15; F; Capt.; w; M.C., M(1).
Junior Navy and Army Club, Horseguards Avenue, S.W.1.

SMITH, Percy Campbell
6/2/6594, 4/10/15; North'd. Fus., 23/4/16; F; Lieut.; w; O.B.E.
Whitemeads, Royston Grove, Hatch End.

✠ SMITH, Percy Lloyd
6/5/7883, 26/11/15; No 13 O.C.B., 4/11/16; W. York. R., 28/2/17; 2/Lieut.
Killed in action 3/5/17.

SMITH, Ralph Edward
4/Sq/4006, 3/6/15, Cpl.; R.F.A., 6/10/15; F; Lieut.; g.
Dunstad House, Langley Mill, Nottinghamshire.

SMITH, Ralph Fell
D/11103, 23/4/17; Sigs. C/S, 11/8/17; R.E., 25/1/18; 2/Lieut.
18 Glenton Road, Lee, S.E. 13.

✠ SMITH, Reginald
4/2/4618, 5/7/15; E. Surr. R., 6/7/16, R.F.C.; F; Lieut.
Killed in action 20/12/16.

✠ SMITH, Reginald Frederick
6/5/7957, 29/11/15; No. 14 O.C.B.; 15th Lond. R., 22/11/16; 2/Lieut.
Killed in action 14/5/17.

SMITH, Reginald Frederick Jermyn
6/2/6258, 16/9/15; Durh. L.I., 21/12/15; F; Lieut.
The Cottage, Russell Road, Buckhurst Hill, Essex.

SMITH, Reginald John
C/14144, 11/10/18; trfr. K.R. Rif. C., 7/4/19.
12 Festing Grove, Southsea, Portsmouth, Hampshire.

SMITH, Robert Bernard
6/4/3941, 17/1/16; R.F.A., C/S, 18/8/16; R.G.A., 26/11/16; 2/Lieut.
The Mount, Heckmondwike, Yorkshire.

SMITH, Ronald
D/2694, 14/1/15, Sgt.; Bedf. R., 24/7/15; F; Lieut.
7 Fig Tree Court, Temple, E.C.4.

SMITH, Rowland Sidney
4/5/4683, 8/7/15; Dorset R., 19/11/15, Indian Army; I,E,P; Lieut.; w.
57 Romilly Road, Cardiff.

SMITH, Sidney Lawrence
4/2/5001, 20/7/15; R.H.A., 1/11/15; F,P,E; Capt.
15 Belmont Road, Tottenham, N.15.

SMITH, Stafford Wilson
C/D/14145, 11/10/18; trfr. 6th R. Regt. of Cav., 11/6/19.
27 Waverley Road, Exmouth, Devonshire.

SMITH, Stanley
B/11307, 21/5/17; trfr. R.E., 30/7/17; F; Pnr.
Brandon House, Houghton de Skerne, Darlington.

SMITH, Stewart Archer
5/8664, 3/1/16, L/C.; E. Surr. R., 1/6/16; F; Capt.
43 Charing Cross, S.W.1.

SMITH, Sydney
C/10604, 22/1/17; Garr. O.C.B., 5/10/17; Lab. Corps, 15/12/17; F; 2/Lieut.
Rotherwick, Truro Road, St. Austell, Cornwall.

SMITH, Sydney Thorpe
1/3799, 27/5/15; R.G.A., 4/10/15; E,P; Capt.
Belvedere, 192 Eastern Esplanade, Thorpe Bay, Essex.

SMITH, Thomas
D/11099, 18/4/17; No. 14 O.C.B., 10/8/17; Durh. L.I., 27/11/17; F; Lieut.
Edgton House, Low Fell, Gateshead-on-Tyne.

SMITH, Victor Walter George
D/11105, 23/4/17; No. 12 O.C.B., 10/8/17; 11th Lond. R. 27/11/17, att. 8th and 9th Lond. R.; Lieut.
The Moorings, Shirley Road, Southampton.

SMITH, Walter Charles Sydney
4/6/3/B/4983, 19/7/15; No. 14 O.C.B., 5/5/17; E. Lan. R., 28/8/17, R.A.F.; F; Lieut.
136 Hagden Lane, Watford.

SMITH, Walter John Lindley
B/11405, 29/5/17; M.G.C., C/S, 24/8/17; Tank Corps, 30/1/18, 2/Lieut.
1 Springfield Avenue, Muswell Hill, N.10.

SMITH, Walter Richard
6/3/5313, 2/8/15; R.A.S.C., 9/10/15; Capt.

SMITH, Wilfred Brook
C/11524, 18/6/17; No. 14 O.C.B., 3/10/17; W. York .R., 26/2/18; F; 2/Lieut.
Park House, Deighton, Huddersfield.

SMITH, Wilfred Samuel Christopher
6/2/6563, 30/9/15, L/C.; No. 1 O.C.B., 6/9/16; R.F.C., 25/1/17, R.A.F.; F; Capt.
10 All Saints Terrace, Cheltenham, Gloucestershire.

✠ SMITH, William
6/7809, 24/11/15; R.F.A., C/S, 21/7/16; R.F.A., 30/9/16; 2/Lieut.
Died of wounds 8/6/17.

SMITH, William Allan
B/2687, 14/1/15; dis. 26/2/15.

SMITH, William Aris
C/11730, 23/7/17; No. 24 O.C.B., 28/12/17; Tank Corps, 22/10/18; 2/Lieut.
Lancaster House, High Road, Tottenham, N.17.

SMITH, William Henry Ferdinand
A/10279, 1/1/17; No. 14 O.C.B., 6/4/17; N. Lan. R., 31/7/17; F; 2/Lieut.
Keighley, Coombe Dingle, Bristol.

SMITH, William Henry Stewart
C/12055, 27/9/17, L/C.; A.S.C., C/S, 12/11/17; R.A.S.C., 6/1/18; 2/Lieut.
The Woodlands, Habberby, Kidderminster.

SMITH, William Humphrey
C/925, 5/8/14, Sgt.; Yorks. L.I., 20/12/14; F; Capt.; w.
55 Wellington Road, St. Johns Wood, N.W.8.

SMITH, William John
A/14318, 30/12/8; demob. 11/1/19.
Newton, Collessie, Fife, Scotland.

✠ SMITH, William Joseph
6/5/C/9317, 4/2/16; No. 7 O.C.B., 4/11/16; Lein. R., 28/2/17; 2/Lieut.
Killed in action 31/7/17.

SMITH, William Stanley
4/5/5004, 17/7/15; S. Lan. R., 6/1/16, att. M.G.C.; F; Lieut.; w.
10 Bukenham Road, New Brighton, Cheshire.

SMITH, William Thomas
B/13593, 19/7/18; No. 13 O.C.B., 10/2/19; trfr. Gord. Highrs., 6/5/19.
11 Trewhitt Road, Heaton, Newcastle-on-Tyne.

SMITH-HOWARD, Henry Wilfrid Howard
2/3607, 13/5/15; R. Suss. R., 21/8/15; E,P,F; Lieut.; w.
33 Macaulay Road, Clapham Common, S.W.4.

✠ SMITH-HOWARD, Kenneth Overend
6/2/6337, 20/9/15; R. Suss. R., 1/6/16; F; 2/Lieut.
Killed in action 16-17/10/16.

SMITH-SAVILLE, James Rupert
C/10138, 7/12/16; No. 20 O.C.B., 5/5/17; E. Lan. R., 28/8/17; F; Lieut.; w.
54 Lancaster Place, Blackburn, Lancashire.

SMITION, Arthur Cornelius
6/1/6595, 4/10/15; dis. to re-enlist in R. Ir. Fus., 18/8/16.

SMYLY, Alexander Ferguson
A/1376, 26/9/14; S. Staff. R., 27/11/14; F; Capt.; w.
Heathfield, Windlesham, Surrey.

SMYLY, William Henry
6/5/B/6103, 6/9/15; R.A., C/S, 30/11/15; R.F.A., 5/8/18; 2/Lieut.

SMYTH, Charles Stuart
6/8398, 14/12/15; A.S.C., C/S, 8/5/16; R.A.S.C., 11/6/16; F; Lieut.
26 Maybury Mansions, Marylebone Street, W.1.

SMYTH, George Joseph
6/5/9309, 4/2/16; trfr. L'pool. R., 21/7/16.

SMYTHE, Alexander William
F/2600, 7/1/15, Sgt.; R.F.A., 2/4/15; Capt.; w(2); M.C.

SMYTHE, Alfred John
6/3/5572, 12/8/15; dis. med. unfit, 8/8/16.
14 Felsberg Road, Brixton Hill, S.W.2.

SMYTHE, Cyril Richard
D/10629, 29/1/17; R.F.C., C/S, 13/3/17; R.F.C., 29/5/17, R.A.F.; Lieut.
The Hollies, Hampton Hill.

✠ SMYTHIES, Ernest Dudley
4/3/4095, 7/6/15, Sgt.; K.R. Rif. C., 25/9/15, R.E.; F; Staff Capt.; w.
Died 16/7/18.

SNAPE, Sidney Frank
4/3/5083, 26/7/15; R. War. R., 12/11/15; F; Lieut.; w.
Rockside, Broadway, Coventry.

SNELGAR, John Thomas
B/1739, 15/10/14, L/C.; Wilts. R., 10/2/15; F,M,I; Capt.; w; M.B.E., M(1).
12 Kitchener Road, Thornton Heath, Surrey.

APPENDIX II.—RECORDS OF RANK AND FILE.

SNELGROVE, William Charles
A/B/D/12153, 24/10/17; No. 4 O.C.B., 10/5/18; Som. L.I., 4/2/19; 2/Lieut.
Dreamland Park, Margate.

✠ SNELL, Francis Saxon
F/1764, 16/10/14; R. Berks. R., 27/11/14; 2/Lieut.
Killed in action 11/7/16.

✠ SNELL, Herbert
6/4/9139, 12/1/16; No. 14 O.C.B., 27/9/16; 22nd Lond. R., 18/12/16, att. Lan. Fus.; 2/Lieut.
Killed in action 7/4/17.

SNELL, Ivan Edward
Sq/687, 31/1/13; dis. 4/8/14; 14th Lond. R., R. Highrs.; Capt ; w; M.C., M(3).
5 Rutland Gate, S.W.7.

SNELL, Robert Stuart
6/1/6427, 27/9/15; trfr. North'n. R., 19/2/17; F.
Aberdeen Lodge, Clifton Hill, Brighton.

SNELLGROVE, Gladstone Rudolph
6/2/5344, 2/8/15; Hamps. R., 16/10/15; 2/Lieut.
67/68 Upper St. James Street, Newport, Isle of Wight.

SNELLING, Eric Ernest
6/5862, 26/8/15; 12th Lond. R., 19/12/15; F; Lieut.; w.
Malvern, 74 Central Hill, Upper Norwood, S.E. 19.

SNELLING, Walter Carbery
2/3399, 26/4/15; Wilts. R., 28/7/15; Lieut.
10 Highview Road, Upper Norwood, S.E. 19.

SNEYD, Robert Stuart
A/310, 25/6/08; dis. 25/6/09.
Bray St. Germans, Cornwall.

SNODGRASS, Curtis Lamond
Sq/3057, 15/3/15, Cpl.; Bedf. Yeo., 27/7/15, M.G.C.; F,NR; Lieut.; g; M.C., Russian Order of St. Anne.
323 Fulton Building, Pittsburg, U.S.A.

SNOOK, Reginald
B/13449, 1/7/18; trfr. Gord. Highrs., 6/5/19.
120 Longfellow Road, Worcester Park, Surrey.

SNOW, Herbert Joseph
C/12271, 29/11/17, Sgt.; No. 6 O.C.B., 6/9/18; K.R. Rif. C., 17/3/19; 2/Lieut.
5 Shemball Street, Walthamstow, Essex.

SNOWBALL, John Stanley
K/B/2174, 23/11/14; S. Staff. R., 19/2/15, M.G.C.; F,E; Major; M.C., M(1).
1 Oriel Crescent, Scarborough.

SNOWDEN, Arthur Jackson
4/3/4139, 10/6/15, L/C.; Devon. R., 7/10/15; Lieut.; w.
The Chantry, Stanmore, Middlesex.

SNOWDEN, Arthur Owen
C/13275, 12/6/18; demob. 22/1/19.
Hildershaw House, St. Peters, Broadstairs.

SNOWDEN, Rowley Chaplin
F/3018, 8/3/15, Sgt.; Bedf. R., 25/8/15, att. R. War. R.: F; Lieut.; w.
Windlesham Cottage, Windlesham, Surrey.

✠ SNOWDEN, Sidney Frank
4/6/5/4896, 15/7/15, L/C.; 1st Lond. R., 19/12/15; 2/Lieut.
Killed in action 15/9/16.

✠ SNOWDEN, Stanley Jackson
D/1483, 29/9/14; Midd'x. R., 27/10/14; Capt.; w.
Killed in action 26/3/17.

SNOWDON, Gilbert Cecil
6/5345, 2/8/15, L/C.; North'd. Fus., 6/7/16; F; Lieut.; p.
5 Parkville, Heaton, Newcastle-on-Tyne.

✠ SNOWDON, Henry Frederick
B/275, 17/6/08; dis. 16/6/09; 1st Lond. R.; Lieut.
Killed in action 6/10/16.

SOAMES, Arthur Lancelot
A/10265, 29/12/16; R.A.S.C., 27/2/17; F; Lieut.
Richmond House, Laleham Road, Shepperton.

SOAMES, John Beecroft
Sq/418, 21/5/09; dis. med. unfit, 30/10/12.
45 Lexham Gardens, W. 8.

SOAR, Arthur Cobden
A/10257, 29/12/16; R.E., C/S, 4/6/17; R.E., 24/8/17; F; Lieut.
Dilkusha, Park Road, Cheam, Surrey.

SOAR, Edward Drover
6/2/6747, 11/10/15; No. 11 O.C.B., 7/5/16; R.F.C., 4/9/16, R.A.F.; F,It; Lieut.
St. Colomb, Barnmead Road, Beckenham, Kent.

SOAR, Leonard Charles
A/11656, 12/7/17, Sgt.; R.E., C/S, 11/10/18; demob.
258 Croxted Road, Herne Hill, S.E. 24.

SODDY, Leslie
6/2/9467, 14/2/16; R.A., C/S, 26/10/16; R.G.A., 9/3/17; F; Lieut.; w.
22 Upperton Gardens, Eastbourne.

SODEN, Frank Ormond
A/1279, 23/9/14; S. Staff. R., 27/11/14, R.F.C., R.A.F.; F; Capt.; D.F.C.
18 Preston Park Avenue, Brighton, Sussex.

SOFFE, Tom Morgan
C/13287, 14/6/18; trfr. 14th Lond. R., 6/12/18.
Stone Farm, Fawley, Nr. Southampton, Hampshire.

SOLLY, Alan Richard Jones
B/12394, 14/1/18; No. 14 O.C.B., 7/6/18; E. Kent R., 6/2/19; 2/Lieut.
Maylond, Manor Way, Beckenham, Kent.

SOLLY, Reginald Charles
B/E/13573, 19/7/18; No. 23 O.C.B., 20/9/18; R. Fus., 5/2/19; 2/Lieut.
7 Cunningham Park, Harrow.

✠ SOLOMAN, Edmund John
H/3064, 16/3/15; R.M.L.I., 22/5/15; S. Lan. R., 5/9/16; F; 2/Lieut.
Killed in action 2/8/17.

SOLOMAN, Geoffrey Dudley
B/2050, 9/11/14; Worc. R., 13/3/15, 10th Lond. R.; 2/Lieut.
21 Holland Road, Kensington, W. 14.

✠ SOLOMON, John Howard
6/3/8844, 10/1/16; 7th Lond. R., 27/8/16; 2/Lieut.
Died of wounds 21/4/17.

SOLOMON, William Ewart Gladstone
2019, 2/11/14; Welch. R., 9/1/15; G,M; Capt.
Principal, Sir J. J. School of Art, Bombay, India.

SOMERS, Charles Dudley
C/100, 17/4/08; dis. 16/4/09.
Aldburgh, Suffolk.

SOMERSET, E. J. See SONNENSCHEIN, E. J.

✠ SOMERSET, Noel Harry Plantagenet
C/465, 23/2/10; dis. 31/7/11; rej. 4/Sq/4140, 10/6/15; R.A.S.C., 15/9/15; E,P; Capt.
Died -/9/21.

SOMERVILLE, George
A/D/13981, 9/9/18; demob. 30/5/19.
Estrella, Sheepcote Road, Harrow.

SOMERVILLE, James Morton
E/14194, 18/10/18; demob. 11/1/19.
22 Robertson Street, Greenock, N.B.

SOMMERFIELD, Harold George
6/8665, 3/1/16; R.F.A., C/S, 9/6/16; R.F.A., 30/9/16; E,P; Lieut.
Hanthorpe, Woodhouse Road, North Finchley, N. 12.

SOMMERVILLE, William Douglas
4/1/4475, 28/6/15; R.G.A., 8/10/15; F; Lieut.
Rushton House, Taunton, Somerset. (Now in U.S.A.).

SONGER, Manford Charles
C/13195, 3/6/18; No. 22 O.C.B., 5/7/18; Essex R., 11/2/19; 2/Lieut.
21 St. Albans Road, Colchester, Essex.

SONNENBERG, Mervyn Julian
3/6/9242, 1/2/16; R.F.C., 7/7/16; 2/Lieut.
Box 190, Bulawayo, Southern Rhodesia.

SONNENSCHEIN, Edward Jamie
6/1/7622, 19/11/15; No. 2 O.C.B., 6/9/16; General List, 29/12/16; 2/Lieut.
4 Lion Hill Place, Lansdown, Bath. (Now in Egypt).

SONNENTHAL, Arthur
B/9876, 8/11/16; No. 20 O.C.B., 5/5/17; Rif. Brig., 28/8/17; F; 2/Lieut.; w.
90 Avenue Road, N.W. 3.

SOPER, Roland George
6/2/7337, 9/11/15, L/C.; dis. to re-enlist in R. Marines, 2/5/16.
Lo Casa, Thornbury Avenue, Southampton.

SOPER, Ronald Garland
B/E/2049, 9/11/14, L/C.; North'd. Fus., 17/9/15; F; Lieut.; w.
16 Cheniston Gardens, Kensington, W. 8.

SOPER, Sydney James
A/10500, 15/1/17; No. 21 O.C.B., 5/5/17; R. Innis. Fus., 28/8/17; 2/Lieut.
12 Whitefield Terrace, Plymouth.

SOPER, Vivian
E/1544, 6/10/14, L/C.; Dorset R., 21/2/15, R.A.F.; I,M; Lieut.
16 Cheniston Gardens, Kensington, W. 8.

✠ SOTHAM, Ralph Clifford
4/3797, 27/5/15, Cpl.; R.W. Kent R., 18/9/15, R.F.C.; I,F; Lieut.
Killed in action 9/1/18.

APPENDIX II.—RECORDS OF RANK AND FILE.

SOTHCOTT, Raymond
K/2495, 31/12/14; Essex R., 2/5/15; G,E,P; Capt.; w.
6 Essex Street, Strand, W.C. 2.

SOUCHON, Joseph Louis
A/Sq/11296, 16/5/17; dis. med. unfit, 5/6/18.
Scotwood, Sunningdale, Berkshire.

✠ SOUTAR, Frank Henderson
K/F/2305, 10/12/14; R. Highrs., 31/3/15; M; 2/Lieut.; M(1).
Killed in action 21/1/16.

SOUTER, James Gordon
E/13994, 11/9/18; R.G.A., C/S, 1/11/18; R.G.A., 13/4/19; 2/Lieut.
School House, New Machor, Aberdeen.

SOUTH, Bernard Guy
D/13738, 2/8/18; trfr. K.R. Rif. C., 7/4/19.
113 Dalston Lane, E. 8.

SOUTHAM, Thomas Alfred
3/9731, 16/10/16; dis. med. unfit, 26/1/18.

SOUTHAM, Thomas Roger Seymour
C/Sq/13346, 25/6/18; demob. 8/1/19.
The Homestead, Longor, Nr. Shrewsbury.

SOUTHERN, Laurence John Cumberbatch
Sq/1128, 9/9/14, L/C.; Bedf. Yeo., 31/12/14; Lieut.; w(2).
7 Mincing Lane, E.C. 3.

✠ SOUTHERN, Thomas William
6/2/8714, 5/1/16, Cpl.; No. 14 O.C.B., 30/10/16; E. York. R., 24/1/17; F; Capt.; M.C.
Killed in action 29/9/18.

SOUTHGATE, Compton
B/1100, 7/9/14; North'd. Fus., 19/9/14; F,I; Staff Capt.; M.C., M(1).
Abbot's Croft, Chappel, Essex. (Now in India).

✠ SOUTHON, John Edward
6/4/5837, 26/8/15; No. 1 O.C.B., 25/2/16; 17th Lond. R., 8/7/16; 2/Lieut.; M.C.
Killed in action 3/12/17.

SOUTHON, Wilfred Lansdell
6/2/7369, 10/11/15, L/C.; Essex R., 4/9/16, Rif. Brig.; F; Lieut.; w.
6 The Promenade, High Street, Sutton, Surrey.

SOUTHWELL, Martin Grew
6/3/7389, 11/11/15; No. 14 O.C.B., 28/8/16; Worc. R., 22/11/16, att. M.G.C.; F; Lieut.; w.
19 Kempshott Road, Streatham, S.W.16.

SOUTHWOOD, Stuart Walter
B/1249, 23/9/14; Worc R., 20/10/14, att. Durh. L.I., R.A.F.; G,F; Capt.; w; M.C., M(1).
5 Carlton Vale, Maida Vale, N.W. 6.

SOWARD, Donald
B/12395, 14/1/18; No. 13 O.C.B., 10/5/18; D. of Corn. L.I., 3/2/19; 2/Lieut.
c/o Chartered Bank of India, 38 Bishopgate, E.C.2.

✠ SOWERBY, Frank Douglas
Sq/1016, 6/8/14; 4th Huss., 15/8/14, att. Lan. Fus.; 2/Lieut.; Legion of Honour.
Died of wounds 1/8/16.

SOWERBY, James Philip
6/3/5392, 5/8/15; North'd. Fus., 4/1/16, Durh. L.I.; F; Lieut.; w.
39 Scholes Lane, Prestwich, Lancashire.

SOWERBY, Robert William
D/13850, 16/8/18; demob. 20/3/19. 11 Ranelagh Road, Wembley.

✠ SOWINSKI, Joseph Ladislas
Sq/3139, 29/3/15; R.F.A., 12/7/15; Lieut.; M.C., M(1).
Killed in action 28/11/17.

✠ SOWTER, Francis Ingle
6/6539, 30/9/15, Sgt.; No. 14 O.C.B., 28/8/16; E. Kent R., 22/11/16; F; 2/Lieut.
Killed in action 9/8/17.

✠ SPAFFORD, Alfred Douglas Dale
K/A/2507, 31/12/14; R. Scots., 3/4/15; Capt.
Killed in action 13/11/16.

SPAIN, Ernest Sidney
6/5/5909, 30/8/15; trfr. 2nd Lond. Yeo., 29/3/16.

SPARGO, William Henry
6/1/6369, 20/9/15, L/C.; L'pool. R., 21/1/16, R.A.F.; F; Lieut.; w.
411 Old Chester Road, Rock Ferry, Cheshire.

SPARK, Alfred John
6/3/7780, 23/11/15; R.F.A., C/S, 31/3/16; R.F.A., 5/8/16; I,M,NR; Capt.; M(1).
10 Brookside Terrace, Sunderland.

SPARKS, Gurth Caral Leonard
A/1333, 26/9/14, L/C.; R.W. Kent R., 7/3/15; Lieut.
61 Melrose Road, Southfields, S.W.

SPARKS, Walter
K/C/2362, 17/12/14, L/C.; R. Ir. Fus., 31/3/15; F; Capt.; w; M.C., Croix de Guerre (Belge).
Well Cottage, Doghurst Lane, Shepestead, Surrey.

SPARROW, Alan Burnaby
K/A/2181, 26/11/14; Hamps. R., 13/3/15, E. York. R., M.G.C.; F,M; Capt.; w(2).
c/o Lloyds Bank Ltd., Hythe, Kent.

✠ SPARROW, Walter Burnaby
K/A/2214, 30/11/14, L/C.; Hamps. R., 13/3/15, M.G.C.; S; Lieut.
Killed in action 1/9/18.

SPARSHOTT, Charles Henry
4/2/4141, 10/6/15; S. Staff. R., 15/7/15, York. R.; F,It; Capt.; w. Italian Silver Medal.
Weybread Vicarage, Harleston, Norfolk.

SPARSHOTT, Rowland
B/9851, 6/11/16; No. 14 O.C.B., 5/5/17; 8th Lond. R., 28/8/17, secd. M.G.C.; Lieut.

✠ SPARTALI, Cyril
K/D/2127, 19/11/14; R. Berks. R., 29/1/15; 2/Lieut.
Killed in action 13/10/15.

SPAWFORTH, Gilbert Caffin
D/9974, 21/11/16; No. 14 O.C.B., 30/1/17; K.R. Rif. C., 29/5/17, emp. M. of Shipping; 2/Lieut.; M.C.
67 Parliament Hill, N.W. 3.

SPEAR, Charles Oscar
K/Sq/2433, 16/12/14; R.E., 31/3/15, R.G.A.; F; Capt.; w(2).
Claverton, Stoke Bishop, Nr. Bristol.

SPEAR, Reginald
B/13508, 10/7/18; No. 22 O.C.B., 23/8/18; General List, 8/3/19; 2/Lieut.
2025 Walnut Street, Philadelphia.

SPEDDING, Robert Kewley
6/1/8541, 30/12/15; No. 14 O.C.B., 30/10/16, M.G.C., C/S; M.G.C., 25/1/17, Tank Corps; F; Capt.
Saxon House, Cleethorpes, Lincolnshire.

SPEED, Ralph Henley
Sq/3074, 18/3/15; R.A.S.C., 19/5/15; F; Capt.; O.B.E., M(3).
c/o Erasmic Ltd., Warrington, Lancashire.

SPEIGHT, George
6/2/9483, 15/2/16; No. 14 O.C.B., 26/11/16; Yorks. L.I., 27/3/17; 2/Lieut.; w.
Mulberry House, Littleport, Nr. Ely, Cambridgeshire.

SPEIGHT, Harold Clifford
B/12756, 13/3/18, Sgt.; trfr. K.R. Rif. C., 13/5/19; Sgt.
Woodland View, Thorpe Hesley, Rotherham.

SPELMAN, Clement Franklin Rix
C/13247, 7/6/18; trfr. 14th Lond. R., 6/12/18.
Eccles-on-Sea, Lessingham, Norwich.

SPELMAN, Dudley William
6/1/6983, 25/10/15, L/C.; No. 14 O.C.B., 28/8/16; R. Fus., 18/12/16; w.
111 Minard Road, Catford, S.E. 6.

✠ SPENCE, Alec William
C/1045, 27/8/14; Midd'x. R., 12/9/14, R.F.C.; 2/Lieut.
Killed 25/4/17.

SPENCE, Matthew Robert Cuthbert
D/E/13739, 31/7/18; No. 22 O.C.B., 20/9/18; R. Lanc. R., 14/2/19; 2/Lieut.
28 Regent Street, Lancaster.

SPENCE, Robert Readdle
4/3/5181, 29/7/15; Arg. & Suth'd. Highrs., 5/11/15, att. R.W. Fus.; F,I; Capt.; w.
126 Cumming Drive, Mount Florida, Glasgow.

SPENCE, William Hustwich
6/5573, 12/8/15; Lond. Div. Cyc. Coy., 24/6/16.
116 Elms Road, Clapham Road, S.W. 4.

SPENCER, Charles Edward
A/10505, 15/1/17; R.G.A., C/S, 9/5/17; R.G.A., 2/9/17; F; Lieut.
40 Farnaby Road, Bromley, Kent.

SPENCER, John Clive
4/4314, 17/6/15; Devon. R., 4/12/15; Lieut.

SPENCER, Kelvin Tallent
A/10251, 29/12/16, Cpl.; R.E., C/S, 1/7/17; R.E., 21/9/17; F; 2/Lieut.; M.C.
The Hall, Harmondsworth, Middlesex.

✠ SPENCER, Mowbray Bertram Stovell. See STOVELL-SPENCER, M. B.

SPENCER, Philip Corbett
C/D/12257, 19/11/17, L/C.; trfr. D. of Corn. L.I., 10/5/19.
Summerfield Court, West Bromwich.

✠ SPENCER, Sydney Gurton
A/791, 8/5/14; R. Berks. R., 25/8/14; F; Capt.
Killed in action 13/10/15.

APPENDIX II.—RECORDS OF RANK AND FILE.

SPENCER, Walter
C/1058, 31/8/14; R. Fus., 5/10/14; F; Capt.; w.
2 Portland Place, W..1.

SPENCER, Wilfred Edward Chetwode
K/C/2474, 28/12/14; R. Suss. R., 31/3/15, Indian Army; F; Capt.; w. Bank House, Oatmeal Row, Salisbury. (Now in India).

SPENCER-PHILLIPS, Percy Terrell. See PHILLIPS, P. T. S.

SPENCER-SMITH, Michael
C/1060, 31/8/14; 12th Lond. R., 16/9/14, K.R. Rif. C.; F,NR; Lt.-Col.; D.S.O., M.C., M(2). Norman House, Stansted, Essex.

SPENDLOVE, Walter William
A/11023, 10/4/17; No. 14 O.C.B., 10/8/17; N. Cyc. Bn., 27/11/17, M.G.C.; F; 2/Lieut. 128 Fox Lane, Palmers Green, N.

SPENLOVE-SPENLOVE, Francis A.
6/2/6564, 30/9/15; dis. med. unfit, 8/8/16.

☨ SPENS, Walter Thomas Patrick
K/2621, 7/1/15; R. Scots, 5/3/15; F; Lieut.; w(2).
Died 18/2/17.

SPERO, Cecil Neville
4/1/3276, 15/4/15, L/C.; K.R. Rif. C., 29/10/15; Lieut.; w.

SPERO, Leopold
1/3608, 13/5/15; K.R. Rif. C., 10/8/15; F; Lieut.; w.
24 Ormonde Mansions, 100a Southampton Row, W.C.1.

SPICE, William Bernard
6/1/7515, 15/11/15; Dorset R., 4/9/16, att. K.R. Rif. C.; F; Lieut. 21 Dalkeith Road, West Dulwich, S.E. 21.

☨ SPICER, Filmer Blake
4/1/3984, 3/6/15; E. Kent R., 5/9/15, att. M.G.C.; 2/Lieut.
Died of wounds 6/10/16.

☨ SPICER, Ronald Murray
6/Sq/5749, 21/8/15; E. Rid. Yeo., 5/10/15; 2/Lieut.
Died 31/5/16.

☨ SPIELMANN, Harold Lionel Isidore
A/1022, 8/8/14; Manch. R., 14/10/14; G; Capt.
Killed in action 12-13/8/15.

SPIERS, Stanley Victor
C/9937, 17/11/16, Sgt.; R.G.A., C/S, 28/3/17; R.G.A., 22/7/17; F; Lieut. Clydesdale, Argyle Road, Woodside Park, N.12.

SPILLER, William Eli
B/10130, 6/12/16, L/C.; R.F.A., C/S, 24/2/17; R.F.A., 21/7/17; 2/Lieut.

SPINK, Henry Makinson
6/4/7309, 8/11/15; North'd. Fus., 25/9/16; F; Capt.; w'2); M.C., M(1). 5 Addingham Road, Mossley Hill, Liverpool.

SPINK, John Norman
6/5/7120, 1/11/15; General List, 5/9/16; F; Staff Lieut.
17 Piccadilly, W.1.

SPINK, William Donald
6/4/8810, 10/1/16; No. 14 O.C.B., 30/10/16; Midd'x. R., 28/2/17, secd. M.G.C.; P; Lieut. 57 Church Road, Richmond, Surrey.

SPINNEY, Arthur
A/10519, 15/1/17; No. 20 O.C.B., 7/6/17; Notts. & Derby. R., 25/10/17; F; Lieut.; w. The Green, Theydon Bois, Essex.

SPINNEY, Arthur Rawdon
6/3/Sq/7058, 28/10/15; No. 1 Cav. C/S, 2/8/16; Staff. Yeo., 27/11/16; E,P; Lieut.
Newborough Vicarage, Burton-on-Trent. (Now in Palestine).

SPITTAL, Charles James
K/D/2420, 21/12/14; R.E., 8/2/15; Capt.

SPOONER, Charles
6/1/7481, 15/11/15; No. 14 O.C.B., 28/8/16; R. Berks. R., 18/12/16; w.
Clive House, The Bishops Avenue, East Finchley, N. 2.

SPOONER, Harold
6/4/5131, 26/7/15; dis. med. unfit, 8/8/16.
Clive House, The Bishops Avenue, East Finchley, N. 2.

SPRAGUE, Ivor Percival
6/8317, 11/12/15; Welch R., 15/4/16; S; 2/Lieut.
1 Wellesley Villas, Wellesley Road, Chiswick, W. 4.

SPRAGUE, William Nathaniel
Sq/1611, 7/10/14; General List, 10/12/14; F; Major.
Park Hill, Frant, Sussex.

SPRAKE, Geoffrey Guy
D/11551, 21/6/17, Cpl.; R.G.A., C/S, 23/1/18; R.G.A., 29/7/18; 2/Lieut. Bungay, Suffolk.

SPRAKE, Percy Jeans
D/11571, 28/6/17, Cpl.; R.G.A., C/S, 23/1/18; R.G.A., 29/7/18; 2/Lieut. Bungay, Suffolk.

SPRANGER, Herbert Arthur
4/5084, 26/7/15; R. War. R., 1/1/16; F; Lieut.; w.
Medwyn, 114 Hill Lane, Southampton.

☨ SPRATT, David Herbert
6/5/D/6779, 11/10/15, L/C.; No. 14 O.C.B., 5/3/17; Midd'x. R., 26/6/17, att. L'pool. R.; 2/Lieut. Killed in action 20/9/17.

SPREULL, James Manly
K/E/2306, 10/12/14; High. L.I., 7/7/15; P,F; Capt.
Caledonian Club, St. James Square, S.W.1.

SPRINGTHORPE, Gerald William
A/9847, 3/11/16; R.G.A., C/S, 21/4/17; R.G.A., 1/8/17; Lieut.

SPRULES, Robert George Wallbutton
K/C/2066, 12/11/14; R.A.O.C., 8/2/15; F; Major; M(1).
Highways, Harpenden, Hertfordshire.

☨ SPURWAY, Sidney Macdonald
6/5/6780, 11/10/15; No. 1 O.C.B., 6/9/16; R.F.C., 25/1/17; F, 2/Lieut. Killed in action 21/9/17.

SQUAREY, Robert Owen
A/1377, 26/9/14; R.E., 10/10/14; F; Major; M.C., m.
The Red House, Epsom, Surrey.

SQUIER, Guy Worrin
D/9921, 15/11/16, L/C.; No. 14 O.C.B., 5/3/17; Midd'x. R., 26/6/17; Lieut. Fairview Avenue, Stanton-le-hope, Essex.

SQUIER, Norman
C/11497, 14/6/17, Sgt.; No. 1 O.C.B., 8/3/18; K.R. Rif. C., 27/8/18; F; 2/Lieut. 66 Swiss Avenue, Chelmsford, Essex.

☨ SQUIRE, Wallace Henry
6/2/7960, 29/11/15, Sgt.; No. 14 O.C.B., 28/8/16; E. Kent R. 24/10/16; 2/Lieut. Died of wounds 9/4/17.

SQUIRE, William Mountjoy
1/9747, 17/10/16, Cpl.; R.G.A., C/S, 28/3/17; R.G.A., 22/7/17; F; Capt. Yokohama United Club, Yokohama, Japan.

SQUIRES, Charles Stephenson
Sq/882, 5/18/14; dis. med. unfit, 8/9/14.

☨ SQUIRES, Sidney Charles
3/4/5146, 27/7/15; R. War. R., 13/11/15; F; Lieut.; Croix de Guerre (Belge). Killed in action 29/10/18.

STABLES, Edward
5/6899, 18/10/15; R.A., C/S, 18/8/16; R.G.A., 9/12/16; F; Lieut.
Sinnington, 50 Overton Drive, Wanstead, E. 11.

☨ STABLES, Harold Rolleston
A/563, 5/4/11; R. Fus., 14/8/14, att. Ches. R.; Lieut.
Killed in action 15/11/14.

STABLES, Horace Alfred
2/3356, 22/4/15, L/C.; R. Fus., 29/11/15; Lieut.; w.

STADDON, Charles Eric
4/3/4056, 7/6/15; R.W. Kent R., 18/9/15; M,I,Afghan; Capt.
Withycombe, Studley Road, Luton, Bedfordshire.

STADDON, John Wilfrid
1/3519, 6/5/15; E. Surr. R., 2/9/15; F; Lieut.; w.
Withycombe, Studley Road, Luton, Bedfordshire.

STAFFORD, John Joseph
6/5/6540, 30/9/15; R. Dub. Fus., 1/6/16; Lieut.

STAFFORD, Steven Nestor
A/13073, 8/5/18; No. 1 O.C.B., 8/11/18; demob.
St. Germains, Terenure Road, Dublin, Ireland.

STAGG, Frederick Louis
D/Sq/12999, 29/4/18; No. 2 Cav. C/S, 7/11/18; 6th R. Regt. of Cav., 13/3/19; 2/Lieut.
c/o Kilburn, Brown & Coy., 42-45 New Broad Street, E.C.

STAGG, Wilfrid Hill
3/9734, 16/10/16; R.A., C/S, 23/3/17; R.G.A., 1/7/17; Lieut.
Rose Hill, Sandhurst Road, Tunbridge Wells.

☨ STAHLSCHMIDT, Frederick Arthur Durns
B/1950; Oxf. & Bucks. L.I., 24/10/14; Lieut.
Killed in action 9/5/17.

APPENDIX II.—RECORDS OF RANK AND FILE.

STAINER, Alfred Charles
A/Sq/13179, 31/5/18; demob. 1/2/19.

✠ STAINER, Claude Hamilton
6/3/6675, 7/10/15; No. 7 O.C.B., 6/4/16; E. Surr. R., 4/8/16; 2/Lieut.   Killed in action 15/11/16.

STAINTON, John Armitage
Sq/760, 23/1/14; Arg. & Suth'd. Highrs., 14/8/14, att. Cam'n. Highrs.; F; Capt.; w.   10 Hyde Park Street, W. 2.

STAIR, Vernon
C/67, 9/4/08; dis. 8/4/10; rej. D/11113, 24/4/17; trfr. Class W. Res., 21/12/17.   Flat 4, 8 Colville Gardens, Bayswater, W. 11.

STALBERG, Ivan Isaac
6/3/8767, 6/1/16; No 5 O.C.B., 14/8/16; Midd'x. R., 21/11/16; F,It; Lieut.   Bramley, Bramley Avenue, Coulsdon, Surrey.

STALEY, John James
C/13310, 17/6/18; R.E., C/S, 18/10/18; demob.
    Church House, Highley, Nr. Kidderminster.

STALEY, Ralph
6/9224, 31/1/16; No. 8 O.C.B., 4/8/16; Ches. R., 21/11/16; Lieut.; w(2).   25 High Street, Bognor, Sussex.

STALLARD, Henry Thomas
E/14176, 16/10/18; demob. 10/1/19.
    52 Devonshire Road, Greenwich, S.E. 10.

STALLARD, Richard Joseph
6/2/7566, 17/11/15; R.N.A.S., 31/10/16; Flt. Sub. Lieut.
    Newton Rectory, Folkingham, Lincolnshire.

STALLEY, George Albert
6/4/7482, 15/11/15; dis. med. unfit, 8/8/16; Colonial Auxiliary Forces, Trinidad; Lieut.
c/o Messrs. T. Geddes Grant Ltd., Port of Spain, Trinidad, British West Indies.

STAMFORD-COLEMAN, Philip Noel
D/13901, 26/8/18, L/C.; trfr. K.R. Rif. C., 21/6/19.
    The Limes, Glade Road, Marlow, Buckinghamshire.

STAMMERS, Sidney Robert
B/1073, 2/9/14; W. York. R., 12/9/14, R.F.C., R.A.F.; F; Major; A.F.C.   52 Coleman Street, E.C. 2.

STAMP, Clive Blatspiel
6/1/6074, 6/9/15, Sgt.; R.F.C., C/S, 28/12/16; R.F.C., 12/4/17, R.A.F.; Lieut.   38 Knightrider Street, E.C. 4.

✠ STAMP, Douglas Blatspiel
Sq/789, 8/5/14; E. York. R., 14/8/14; Lieut.; w.
    Died of wounds 10/4/16

STANBROOK, Stephen John
1/3440, 1/5/15; E. Surr. R., 10/7/15; Lieut.; w.
    16 Newington Green Mansions, Stoke Newington, N. 16

STANCOURT, Rupert Fred Cecil
B/13528, 15/7/18; trfr. K.R. Rif. C., 25/4/19.
    Aban Court Hotel, Harrington Gardens, S.W. 7.

STANDFORD, Victor Henry
C/13276, 12/6/18; trfr. 14th Lond. R., 6/12/18.
    3 Lower Lemon Villas, Truro, Cornwall.

✠ STANDRICK, Jones Harold
4/1/3987, 3/6/15; 18th Lond. R., 17/9/15; Capt.
    Died of wounds 21/2/18.

STANDRING, William George
A/12471, 24/1/18; R.E., C/S, 12/5/18; R.E., 27/9/18; 2/Lieut.
    13 Heswall Road, Aintree, Liverpool

STANFIELD, Charles Joseph
B/10760, 17/2/17; R.F.C., C/S, 13/3/17; R.F.C., 19/4/17, R.A.F.; Lieut.; w.

STANFORD, Bernard Arthur
6/1/6703, 7/10/15; 17th Lond. R., 4/9/16; F,S,P; Lieut.; w.
    Treherne, Beccles, Suffolk.

✠ STANFORD, Frederick Edward
A/11916, 27/8/17.   Died 9/1/18.

STANGER, Frank Railton
H/1960, 26/10/14; Suff. R., 23/12/14, Indian Army; P; Capt.
    Riverdale, St. Pauls Cray, Kent. (Now in India).

✠ STANGER, Nevill Bentlif
K/H/2299, 10/12/14; S. Lan. R., 24/2/15, att. Gord. Highrs.; F; 2/Lieut.   Died of wounds 5/10/15.

STANHAM, Charles Taylor
D/1455, 29/9/14, L/C.; E. Kent R., 9/2/15, secd. K. Af. Rif.; EA; Lieut.   Dartmouth Grove House, Blackheath, S.E. 10.

STANHAM, Reginald George
B/1055, 31/8/14; Leic. R., 12/9/14, E. Kent R.; Lieut.; w.
    Dartmouth Grove House, Blackheath, S.E. 3.

STANIER, Edwin Gordon
C/11498, 14/6/17; No. 16 O.C.B., 5/10/17; trfr .R.F.C., 20/2/18.
    Bankcroft, Douglas Road, Harpenden, Hertfordshire.

STANIER, Harold Allan
6/4/7310, 8/11/15; No. 14 O.C.B.; Glouc. R., 18/12/16, att. Manch. R.; F; Lieut.; w.
    Bankcroft, Douglas Road, Harpenden, Hertfordshire.

STANISTREET, Harold Lindsay
K/4/2302, 10/12/14, Sgt.; D. of Corn. L.I., 20/8/15, att. R.A.F.; F; Capt.   Dunolly, 11 Woodstock Road, Croydon, Surrey.

STANLEY, Albert Edward
4/5/4811, 12/7/15; Linc. R., 26/10/15; Lieut.
    35 Trinity Lane, Louth, Lincolnshire.

✠ STANLEY, Arthur Kinnaird
6/3/7085, 30/10/15; Glouc. R., 4/8/16; Lieut.
    Killed in action 15/6/18.

STANLEY, Victor William
6/2/7751, 22/11/15; No. 8 O.C.B., 4/8/16; Manch. R., 21/11/16; Lieut.   33 Mayflower Road, Clapham Road, S.W. 9.

STANNARD, Alfred Maurice
D/13863, 19/8/18; trfr. 14th Lond. R., 6/12/18.
    44 Ashbourne Avenue, Golders Green, N.W. 4.

STANNARD, Stewart Reginald
B/9911, 13/11/16, L/C.; No. 14 O.C.B., 6/4/17; Essex R., 31/7/17, att. Norf. R.; F; Lieut.; w.
    34 Denholme Road, Maida Hill, W. 9.

STANSFIELD, Edward Maryons
K/H/2523, 31/12/14, L/C.; Lan. Fus., 22/4/15, secd. K. Af. Rif.; F,EA; Capt.; w.   Prescote, St. Edwards Road, Southsea.

✠ STANSFIELD, Fred Noel
K/F/2496, 31/12/14; Midd'x. R., 24/4/15; F; Capt.; w.
    Killed in action 2/12/17.

STANSFIELD, Wilfrid Willard Hartley
B/13469, 5/7/18; No. 22 O.C.B., 23/8/18; Education Officer, 8/12/18, M.G.C., att. R. Suss. R.; Capt.
    Brighton Grammar School, Brighton.

STANTON, Horace Mills Alderson
4/1/4162, 10/6/15, L/C.; R.A., C/S, 24/1/16; R.F.A., 16/6/16; I,M; Lieut.   Market Deeping, Lincolnshire.

STANTON, Reginald
D/E/13747, 2/8/18, L/C.; No. 22 O.C.B., 20/9/18; R. Muns. Fus., 14/2/19; 2/Lieut.   83 Coleraine Road, Blackheath, S.E. 3.

✠ STANTON, Robert Greenhow Openshaw
4/1/4241, 14/6/15; R.M.L.I., 19/12/15; Lieut.
    Died of wounds 28/4/18.

✠ STANWAY, Gerald
6/2/6971, 22/10/15; No. 11 O.C.B., 7/5/16; S. Staff. R., 4/9/16; F; 2/Lieut.   Died of wounds 5/10/17.

STANWAY, Percy Anderton
6/3/B/6565, 30/9/15; No. 14 O.C.B., 30/1/17; E. Kent R., 25/4/17; F; 2/Lieut.   Blackwall, Hinschill, Ashford, Kent.

STAPLES, Henry Arthur
D/2757, 21/1/15; 18th Lond. R., 3/6/15; F; Capt.; M.C.; M(1).
    19 Birchwood Road, Tooling Common, S.W. 17.

STAPLETON, Michael William
D/10892, 5/3/17; trfr. R.F.A., 23/6/17; F; Bdr.
    121 Strand Road, Sandymount, Dublin, Ireland.

✠ STAPLEY, Lawrence D'Arcy
6/2/5766, 21/8/15; Suff. R., 24/10/15; 2/Lieut.
    Killed in action 12/10/16.

STARES, John William Chester
4/3/4295, 17/6/15; Hamps. R., 4/10/15; F; Capt.; w.
    Portchester, Hampshire.

STARK, John Ernest
C/10160, 11/12/16; trfr. 16th Lond. R., 27/4/17.
    Hawthornden, Holbrook Road, Leicester.

STARK, Rudolph Clarence Symons
6/1/7188, 3/11/15; N. Lan. R., 25/9/16, att. R.A.F.; F; 2/Lieut.; w.   Toronto House, Wallasey, Cheshire.

APPENDIX II.—RECORDS OF RANK AND FILE.

STARKEY, *Digby Mounteney*
6/2/7311, 8/11/15; No. 8 O.C.B., 4/8/16; trfr. R. Suss. R., 1/12/16.
    62 *Central Hill, Norwood, S.E. 19.*

☩ STARLING, *Frederick Leslie*
K/E/2236, 3/12/14; 3rd Lond. R., 20/4/15; 2/Lieut.
    Killed in action 13/9/16.

STARLING, *Sidney William*
6/5/7516, 15/11/15, L/C.; R. War. R., 4/8/16; F; Lieut.
    138 *Yardley Wood Road, Moseley, Birmingham.*

STARTIN, *Hugh Adkin*
6/3/Sq/7221, 4/11/15; Midd'x. R., 4/9/16, att. Indian Army; Lieut.
    14 *Lowlands Road, Harrow.*

STATHAM, *George Wellington*
B/11680, 16/7/17; A.S.C., C/S, 1/11/17; R.A.S.C., 25/1/18;
2/Lieut. 56 *Queens Road, St. Johns Wood, N.W. 8.*

STATHER-DUNN, *Harry*
6/4/6819, 14/10/15; 3rd Lond. R., 13/2/16; 2/Lieut.
    1 *Regency House, Westminster, S.W. 1.*

STAUFFER, *Byron Reginald*
4/2/4197, 14/6/15; R.F.A., 8/10/15; Lieut.; w.
    Mount Charles, St. Austell, Cornwall.

STAVELEY, *Tom*
A/1076, 2/9/14; E. Lan. R., 19/9/14; Lieut.

STEAD, *John*
6/3/5393, 5/8/15, L/C.; R.E., 20/11/15; F; Capt.
    7 *Albany Road, Sharrow, Sheffield.*

STEADMAN, *Eric*
6/1/9297, 3/2/16; R.F.C., 16/6/16, R.A.F.; Lieut.
    21 *Ferguson Drive, Strandtown, Belfast, Ireland.*

STEAINS, *Leslie*
A/11223, 7/5/17, L/C.; R.A., C/S, 16/11/17; R.G.A., 15/4/18;
Lieut. *Greeba, Harborough Road, Ashton-on-Mersey, Cheshire.*

☩ STEARNS, *Patrick Chillingworth*
6/4/8121, 2/12/15, L/C.; No. 8 O.C.B., 4/8/16; K.R. Rif. C.,
21/11/16; 2/Lieut. *Killed in action 4/12/17.*

STEAVENSON, *Dudley Vaughan*
E/14007, 13/9/18; R.G.A., C/S, 1/11/18; demob.
    1 *Des Voeux Road, Central, Hong Kong.*

STEBBINGS, *Charles Goff*
6/4/9020, 20/1/16; A.S.C., C/S, 27/10/16; R.A.S.C., 20/12/16; P,
Lieut. *Burgate, Leighton Buzzard, Bedfordshire.*

STEDMAN, *Archibald George*
6/3/7623, 19/11/15; S. Lan. R., 4/9/16; F; Lieut.; w.
    West Street, Midhurst, Sussex

STEDMAN, *Ernest*
6/8602, 3/1/16; R.A., C/S, 26/5/16; R.G.A., 30/8/16, att. R.E.;
F; Lieut. *Sandbrook House, Orrell, Wigan.*

STEDMAN, *Noel Warneford*
A/14081, 30/9/18; demob. 29/1/19. *Little Cote, Oxshott, Surrey.*

☩ STEED, *Alan Davidson*
4/2/4656, 5/7/15; trfr. 15th Lond. R., 6/3/16, 5th and 16th Lond.
R.; F,P; Pte. *Killed in action 30/4/18.*

STEED, *Percy*
6/4/9178, 27/1/16; No. 14 O.C.B., 30/10/16; Oxf. & Bucks. L.I.,
28/2/17; F; Lieut.; w. *Warborough, Wallingford, Berkshire.*

STEEDS, *Geoffrey Graham*
4/3/4429, 24/6/15; R.A.S.C., 27/11/15, 16th. Lond. R.; F;
Lieut. *Barkby Firs, Syston, Near Leicester.*

STEEL, *Charles Reedman*
A/12496, 29/1/18; No. 15 O.C.B., 7/6/18; Gord. Highrs., 4/2/19;
2/Lieut.
 16 *Brookfield, West Hill, Highgate, N. 6. (Now in Sweden).*

STEELE, *Eric*
Sq/652, 1/11/12; 18th Lond. R., 24/6/14; F; Lieut.
    Bankside, Arterberry Road, Wimbledon, S.W. 19.

STEELE, *Herbert Walter*
6/3/5732, 19/8/15; 3rd Lond. R., 18/1/16, R.A.F.; Lieut.

STEELE, *Hugh Biden*
B/2996, 1/3/15, Sgt.; R. Berks. R., 23/4/16; Capt.
    11 *St. Martin's Court, W.C. 2.*

STEELE, *John Grahame*
B/13470, 5/7/18; demob. 4/3/19.
    77 *Portsmouth Road, Woolston, Southampton.*

STEELE, *Richard Philip*
3/3470, 3/5/15; York. & Lanc. R., 28/7/15, Indian Army; F,I,P;
Lieut. *Tockwith, York.*

STEELE, *William Bryce*
C/12627, 18/2/18; No. 21 O.C.B., 5/7/18; York. R., 3/3/19;
2/Lieut. *Lyndhurst, Bitterne Grove, Bitterne Park, Southampton.*

STEEPLE, *Stephen*
6/4/5863, 26/8/15, L/C.; R. Lanc. R., 31/12/15; Lieut.; w.
    20 *Balmoral Road, Blackpool.*

STEGGALL, *John Sterndale*
6/7156, 2/11/15; dis. med. unfit, 11/8/16.
    Banghurst Rectory, Basingstoke.

STEINER, *Leslie Howard*
Sq/1530, 5/10/14; North'd. Yeo., 9/3/15.
    4 *Jasper Road, Upper Norwood, S.E. 19.*

STENNETT, *Frederick George Melville*
D/B/13815, 12/8/18; No. 24 O.C.B., 15/11/18; Tank Corps,
22/3/19; 2/Lieut. 26 *Silver Street, Gainsborough, Lincolnshire.*

STEPHEN, *James Karran*
C/10982, 30/3/17; Garr. O.C.B., 23/5/17; Lab. Corps, 14/7/17;
Lieut. *Bella Vista, Victoria Road, Douglas, Isle of Man.*

STEPHEN, *Noel Campbell*
Sq/124, 18/4/08; dis. 17/4/09; R.N.V.R., R.N.A.S.
    93 *Cornwall Gardens, Queens Gate, S.W. 7.*

STEPHEN, *Ronald James*
6/5/7888, 27/11/15, L/C.; Hamps. R., 24/10/16, att. Essex R.; F;
Lieut. *The Croft, 31 Bracken Avenue, Nightingale Lane, S.W. 12.*

STEPHEN, *Stephen Dicran*
D/10904, 20/3/17, L/C.; No. 12 O.C.B., 10/8/17; Lan. Fus.,
27/11/17; S,F; 2/Lieut. 8 *Hesketh Road, Southport, Lancashire.*

STEPHENS, *Claude Raymond*
B/13617, 24/7/18; demob. 29/1/19. 34 *Cranbrook Road, Bristol.*

STEPHENS, *Cyril Ridgway*
F/2733, 18/1/15, L/C.; Manch. R., 3/6/15; F; Lieut.; w.
    2 *Argyle Avenue, Victoria Park, Manchester.*

☩ STEPHENS, *Fred Orlando*
6/1/7884, 26/11/15; W. York. R., 4/8/16; Lieut.
    Killed in action 24/4/18

STEPHENS, *Geoffrey Duncan*
Sq/556, 17/3/11; dis. 16/10/11.

STEPHENS, *Gilbert Henry*
D/E/13835, 14/8/18; R.A., C/S, 2/10/18; demob.
    33 *Wonford Road, Exeter.*

STEPHENS, *Harold Stanley*
4/2/4296, 17/6/15; R.A.S.C., 11/10/15; F; Capt.; w.
    Kyltrasna, Clinton Road, Redruth, Cornwall.

STEPHENS, *Herbert Victor Stanley*
C/11780, 30/7/17; No. 14 O.C.B., 4/1/18; Devon. R., 25/6/18,
Cold. Gds.; F; Capt.; w. *The Square, Launceston, Cornwall.*

STEPHENS, *Ivor David Powell*
6/4/8094, 1/12/15; No. 8 O.C.B., 4/8/16; Yorks. L.I., 21/11/16;
F; Lieut.; w. 48 *Lime Grove, New Malden, Surrey. (Now in India).*

STEPHENS, *Joseph*
6/3/6406, 23/9/15; dis. med. unfit, 23/7/16; R.N.V.R.; Asst.
Paymaster. *Beulah Spa Hotel, Upper Norwood, S.E.*

☩ STEPHENS, *Kyrle Nalder*
4/6/5215, 29/7/15; R.A.S.C., 15/11/15; 2/Lieut.
    Died 31/12/17.

STEPHENS, *Nigel Daubeny*
D/13782, 7/8/18; trfr. K.R. Rif. C., 7/4/19.
    17 *Elers Road, Ealing, W. 13.*

STEPHENSON, *Albert Ernest*
4/5/4765, 12/7/15; Linc. R., 22/10/15; Lieut.; w(2).

STEPHENSON, *Herbert Charles*
6/4/6781, 11/10/15; R.A., C/S, 31/3/16; R.G.A., 11/8/16; F;
Lieut. 8 *The Park, Mitcham, Surrey.*

STEPHENSON, *Hugh Percival*
Sq/1220, 14/9/14; K.R. Rif. C., 17/11/14; F; Capt.
    Primrose Club, Park Place, St. James, S.W. 1.

STEPHENSON, *John*
1/3798, 27/5/15; Durh. L.I., 8/9/15; F; Capt.; M.C.
St. Colomb, 58 *Barnmead Road, Kent House, Beckenham, Kent.*

APPENDIX II.—RECORDS OF RANK AND FILE.

STEPHENSON, Joseph William
A/13137, 27/5/18; R.A., C/S, 26/7/18; R.G.A., 10/4/19; 2/Lieut.
Kilmarnock, Guildford, Surrey.

STEPHENSON, Paul
4/6/2/4949, 19/7/15, L/C.; Notts. & Derby. R., 8/7/16; Lieut.

STEPHENSON, Reginald Aubrey
K/A/2438, 28/12/14; Essex R., 10/10/15; Lieut.; w.
Meadow Cottage, White Hill, Berkhamsted, Hertfordshire.

STEPHENSON, Reginald James
6/Sq/9366, 7/2/16, L/C.; No. 1 Cav. C/S, 18/8/16; Linc. Yeo., 27/11/16; P; Lieut.; w.
Brasted House, Althorpe, Doncaster.

STEPHENSON, William Dalton
6/Sq/9229, 1/2/16, Cpl.; No. 1 Cav. C/S, 18/8/16; Linc. Yeo., 27/11/16, 9th Lanc.; F; Capt.; w; D.C.M.
Eastgate House, Marham, Downham, Norfolk.

STEPHENSON, William Sprott
B/1667, 10/10/14; R. Fus., 13/11/14; w.

STERNBERG, William Ernest Charles
B/13427, 1/7/18; demob. 23/1/18.
149 Dairy House Road, Derby.

STERNDALE, Reginald Marcus
C/1056, 31/8/14; N. Lan. R., 16/9/14; Lieut.

STERRETT, Henry Robert
6/2/5441, 5/8/15, Sgt.; E. Kent R., 21/4/16; 2/Lieut.

STEVENS, Douglas Wilfrid
H/2809, 28/1/15, L/C.; Notts. & Derby. R., 13/6/15; F; Capt.; M.C., M(1).
Gwynfe House, Llangadock, Carmarthenshire.

STEVENS, Edred Marshall
6/9128, 24/1/16; R.F.A., C/S, 7/7/16; R.F.A., 13/10/16; F; Major.
Messrs. Burt, Myrtle & Coy., Batavia, Java, Dutch East Indies.

STEVENS, Edward Charles
4/1/4548, 1/7/15; N. Lan. R., 5/1/16.
38 Heath Street, Hampstead, N.W. 3.

STEVENS, Edward Denys
4/5/Sq/4684, 8/7/15; No. 2 Cav. C/S, 31/3/16; Oxf. Huss., 19/8/16, att. R.E. and R.A.F.; F; Lieut.; w(2).
26 Montalt Road, Woodford Green, Essex. (Now in Rhodesia).

STEVENS, Esca George Somerville
A/942, 5/8/14; R.A.S.C., 27/8/14; F,NR; Major; M(2).
Caledonian Club, St. James Square, S.W. 1.

✠ STEVENS, George Kellner
4/2/4030, 7/6/15; Linc. R., 20/8/15; 2/Lieut.
Killed in action 4/6/16.

STEVENS, Gordon
6/1/8297, 10/12/15; R.E., C/S, 2/7/16; R.E., 15/9/16; S; Capt.; M.B.E.
Oldbury, Bower Mount Road, Maidstone, Kent.

STEVENS, Gordon Edward Witherden
6/5/7781, 23/11/15; No. 14 O.C.B., 28/8/16; E. Kent R., 18/12/16, R.F.C.; F; Lieut.; M.C.
Uppertoes, Bobbing, Sittingbourne, Kent.

STEVENS, Henry Norman
4/2/5046, 22/7/15; E. York. R., 29/11/15, K. Af. Rif.; F,EA; Lieut.
Warleigh, 131 Palace Road, Tulse Hill, S.W. 2.

✠ STEVENS, Leonard Frank
6/1/7121, 1/11/15; E. Surr. R., 4/8/16, att. N. Staff. R.; Lieut.
Killed in action 25/3/18.

STEVENS, Leslie Alfred Emile
C/10754, 17/2/17; No. 20 O.C.B., 7/6/17; Devon. R., 25/9/17; F,It; Lieut.; w.
Station House, Devonport, Devonshire.

STEVENS, Richard Carnegie des Coux
C/14254, 30/10/18; demob. 30/1/19.
Winchet Hall, Goudhurst, Kent.

✠ STEVENS, Richard Henry Barkwood
B/11338, 21/5/17, L/C.; R.F.C., C/S, 23/10/17; R.F.C., 12/12/17, R.A.F.; F; 2/Lieut.
Killed 30/5/18.

STEVENS, Robert William
6/1/9564, 20/3/16; No. 13 O.C.B., 4/11/16; R.W. Kent R., 28/2/17; F,E; Major; w.
11bis Rue Lord Byron, Paris (VIII.), France.

STEVENS, Victor George
6/1/6639, 4/10/15; No. 14 O.C.B.; trfr. R.G.A., 15/11/16; R.E., 16/2/17; F; Lieut.
St. Ives, Huntingdonshire.

STEVENS, William Hargreaves
6/3/6235, 11/9/15; No. 11 O.C.B., 7/5/16; Devon. R., 4/9/16, att. R. Berks. R.; F; Lieut.; M.C.
31 Highwood Avenue, North Finchley, N. 12.

STEVENS, William Thomas
6/3/7126, 2/11/15; No. 11 O.C.B., 16/5/16; E. Kent R., 4/9/16; F; Lieut.; w, w-p; M.C.
38 Rockbourne Road, Forest Hill, S.E. 23.

STEVENS, Wilmot Driffield
6/Sq/9021, 20/1/16; R.A., C/S, 21/7/16; R.G.A., 2/11/16; Lieut.
Nunthorpe S.O., Yorkshire.

STEVENSON, Alan
H/2/2565, 4/1/15; Sea. Highrs., 7/5/15; 2/Lieut.
5 Balcombe Street, Dorset Square, N.W. 1.

STEVENSON, Arthur
4/3/4096, 7/6/15, L/C.; Notts. & Derby. R., 5/9/15; F; Capt.; w(2); M.C., M(1).
c/o Messrs. Wm. Forbes, Stuart & Coy. Ltd.; 33 Monument Street, E.C.

STEVENSON, Frederick Burton
K/H/Sq/2193, 26/11/14; dis. 28/12/14; Leic. R., 26/8/15; 2/Lieut.; w.
Halygolle Estate, Yakantota, Ceylon.

STEVENSON, James Hamilton
4/3205, 8/4/15; Railway Transport Officer, 10/5/15; F,Lt; Capt.
Westdale, Hoylake, Cheshire.

STEVENSON, Ralph
6/8190, 6/12/15; No. 9 O.C.B., 8/3/16; Arg. & Suth'd. Highrs., 23/7/16; Lieut.
Coro Linn, Clydebank, Dumbartonshire.

STEVENSON, Samuel Brown
6/5/8495, 20/12/15, L/C.; A.S.C., C/S, 4/9/16; R.A.S.C., 8/10/16; F; Lieut.
Newstead, Chinley, Derbyshire.

STEVENSON, William Francis James Felix
1/3103, 21/3/15; dis. 20/5/15.

STEVENSON-REECE, George Macaulay. See REECE, G, M. S.

STEVINSON, Harold Butterworth
6/2/8298, 10/12/15; No. 11 O.C.B., 7/5/16; Lan. Fus., 4/9/16; Lieut.
St. Michaels, Bexley, Kent.

✠ STEWARD, Harold North
Sq/153, 18/4/08; dis. 29/11/09.

STEWARD, John Reginald O'Bryen
Sq/803, 13/7/14; Linc. Yeo., 27/1/15, att. Indian Army; Lieut.
Marlborough Lodge, Weston, Bath.

✠ STEWART, Alexander Charles
1951, -/10/14; Army Cys. Corps; Capt.
Killed in action 12/4/18.

STEWART, Alexander John Campbell
A/Sq/12507, 29/1/18; No. 1 Cav. C/S, 16/5/18; R. Regt. of Cav., 14/2/19; 2/Lieut.
21 Falkland Avenue, Church End, Finchley, N. 3.

STEWART, Archibald MacKenzie
6/2/5768, 21/8/15, L/C.; Tr. Res. Bn., 4/1/16; Lieut.
35 DeVere Gardens, Ilford, Essex.

STEWART, Charles
4/5/4766, 12/7/15, Cpl.; Devon. R., 8/6/16; F; Capt.; M(1).
Jemima Estate, Mambau, Negri Sembilan, F.M.S.

STEWART, Charles Alan Francis
6/1/8318, 11/12/15; No. 8 O.C.B., 4/8/16; Manch. R., 24/10/16; Lieut.
Somers Arms Hotel, Eastnor, Nr. Ledbury, Hereford.

STEWART, Charles Edward
6/4/9298, 3/2/16; R.F.A., C/S, 18/8/16; R.F.A., 27/1/17, att. R.F.C.; 2/Lieut.; w. 3 Upper Sheviard Street, Dublin, Ireland.

STEWART, David
B/13651, 24/7/18; demob. 23/1/19.
73 Richmond Grove, Manchester, S.E.

STEWART, Frank. See SCRAGG, F.

STEWART, George Vernon
3/3357, 22/4/15; att. R.F.C., R.A.F.; Lieut; w.
1 Kirklee Gardens, Glasgow, W.

✠ STEWART, Hugh Duncan
Sq/3609, 13/5/15; R.F.A., 18/8/15; Major; M.C.
Killed in action 12/10/18.

✠ STEWART, Humphrey
B/805, 13/7/14; R. Berks. R., 31/8/14; F; Capt.; M(1).
Killed in action 3/7/16.

APPENDIX II.—RECORDS OF RANK AND FILE.

✠ STEWART, James
6/5/5958, 1/9/15, L/C.; L'pool. R., 23/4/16; 2/Lieut.
   Killed in action 28/10/16.

STEWART, John Allison
C/11525, 18/6/17, L/C.; No. 10 O.C.B., 5/10/17; Arg. & Suth'd. Highrs., 26/2/18, att. High. L.I.; F; 2/Lieut.
   1 Quail Road, Ayr, Ayrshire.

STEWART, John Deans
C/14173, 16/10/18; demob. 19/12/18.
   New Church College, Devonshire Street, N.1.

STEWART, John Herdman
C/13374, 21/6/18; No. 22 O.C.B., 23/8/18; Oxf. & Bucks. L.I., 13/2/19; 2/Lieut.
   Hollybush, Shiplake-on-Thames, Oxon.

STEWART, Robert
A/13965, 6/9/18; No. 22 O.C.B., 22/11/18; R. Scots, 5/2/19; 2/Lieut.
   29 Moresby Road, Upper Clapton, E.5.

STEWART, Robert Barnes
6/3/9411, 9/2/16; R.F.A., C/S, 4/8/16; R.F.A., 1/12/16, R.A.F.; F; Lieut.; w.
   Windsor Lodge, Craigmore, Isle of Bute.

STEWART, Robert Paul
D/13740, 2/8/18; trfr. R. Highrs., 16/4/19.
   29 Moresby Road, Upper Clapton, E.5.

STEWART, Vivian
6/1/9441, 11/2/16; No. 14 O.C.B., 26/11/16; Lan. Fus., 27/3/17; Lieut.
   Wykeham, Burgess Hill, Sussex.

STEWART, William McKenzie
D/13816, 9/8/18; demob. 31/1/19.
   36 York Road, New Southgate, N.11

STIDSTON, Horace Mark
6/7701, 22/11/15; R.A., C/S, 9/6/16; R.G.A., 16/9/16; F,S; Capt.; w.
   201 Ferme Park Road, Crouch End, N.8.

STIEBEL, Arthur
K/E/2344, 14/12/14; R.W. Kent R., 19/2/15; F; Lieut.; w.
   1 Sussex Place, Hyde Park, W.2.

✠ STIEBEL, Ernest Arthur
6/1/8040, 30/11/15; dis. med. unfit. 8/8/16.   Died 1917.

STILES, Edwin Francis
6/3/6407, 23/9/15; A.S.C., C/S, 13/3/16; R.A.S.C., 10/4/16; Lieut.
   36 Station Road, Harlesden, N.W.10.

STILES, Malcolm Chester
B/D/12026, 20/9/17; No. 20 O.C.B., 5/4/18; General List, 8/10/18, R.W. Kent R., R Suss. R.; WA; 2/Lieut.
Gonville, Clarendon Road, Wallington, Surrey. (Now in West Africa).

STILLIARD, Rupert John
6/2/6834, 14/10/15; No. 11 O.C.B., 7/5/16; L'pool. R., 4/9/16; F; Lieut.
   The Cloisters, Windsor Castle.

STILLWELL, William Arthur
6/4/6370, 20/9/15; R.F.C., C/S, 25/2/16; R.F.C., 5/2/17, 16th Lond. R.; F; Lieut.
   Park Corner Farm, Little Chart, Ashford, Kent.

STIMSON, Sidney
6/3/5528, 9/8/15, L/C.; E. Surr. R., 28/12/15; 2/Lieut.; w.
   36 Friar Street, Reading, Berkshire.

STINSON, Henry John Edwin
D/1387, 29/9/14, Sgt.; R.G.A., 17/5/15; F; Lieut.; M.C. and Bar.
   Arundel House, Arundel Street, Strand, W.C.2.

STIRLING, Adam Keith
6/4/8905, 13/1/16; No. 14 O.C.B., 30/10/16; M.G.C., 29/3/17; Lieut.

STIRLING, Charles McKidd
6/4/9569, 11/4/16; A.S.C., C/S, 1/9/16; R.A.S.C., 25/10/16; I,Afghan; Major; M.B.E.
   8 Grange Terrace, Edinburgh.

STIRLING, John Ashwell
D/1441, 29/9/14, L/C.; Bord. R., 24/11/14; F; Lieut.; M.C., M(1).
   2 Vanbrugh Park Road, Blackheath, S.E.3.

STIRLING, Robert Ingleton
D/11185, 4/5/17, L/C.; No. 14 O.C.B., 5/10/17; Manch. R., 26/2/18, M.G.C.; F; 2/Lieut.
   Fernroyd, Prestwich, Manchester.

STIRRUP, Thomas Cyril
6/4/7189, 3/11/15; York. & Lanc. R., 4/8/16; F; Capt.; M.C.
   34 Wellington Street, Blackburn, Lancashire.

STOBART, James Douglas
Sq/391, 31/3/09; dis. 22/12/11; Hamps. Yeo., 23/12/14; Capt.

STOBBS, George Drury
B/10755, 17/2/17, L/C.; R.G.A., C/S, 12/9/17; R.G.A., 11/2/18; F; 2/Lieut.   Illovo, 136 Thurlow Park Road, Dulwich, S.E.21.

STOCK, Arthur Roy
C/961, 5/8/14; Ayr. Yeo., 19/9/14; Lieut.

STOCK, Ewart Elliot
B/10555, 19/1/17; R.F.C., C/S, 13/3/17; R.F.C., 19/4/17, R.A.F.; F; Lieut.; w; M.C.
   Wastdale, Radlett, Hertfordshire.

✠ STOCK, James Mulock Thompson
B/1632, 9/10/14, L/C.; E. Lan. R., 3/1/15; F; Capt.
   Killed in action 15/11/16.

STOCKDALE, Percy
A/10270, 1/1/17; No. 14 O.C.B., 6/4/17; Manch. R., 31/7/17; F; Lieut.; w.   Osborne Villa, 1 Osborne Road, Oldham, Lancashire.

STOCKDALE, Stanley Reginald
6/1/6782, 11/10/15; Hamps. R., 14/7/16; M.Persia; Lieut.
   Harlech Road, Blundellsands, Liverpool.

STOCKMAN, Ralph Herbert
6/4/7567, 17/11/15, L/C.; Suff. R., 24/10/16, secd. R.E.; F; Lieut.
   The Briars, Torrington Park, North Finchley.

STOCKS, Andrew Denys
B/12019, 17/9/17, L/C.; H. Bde. O.C.B., 4/1/18; Cold. Gds., 25/6/18; Lieut.; O.B.E.   8 Old Square, Lincoln's Inn, W.C.2.

✠ STOCKTON, James Godfrey
C/532, 13/1/11; Oxf. & Bucks. L.I., 31/8/14; Capt.
   Killed in action 22/8/17.

STOCKWELL, John Oldham
C/9794, 27/10/16, L/C.; R.W. Surr. R., 9/3/17, att. Suff. R.; Lieut.
   Chancellor Cottage, Sheringham, Norfolk.

STOER, Edmund Maxwell
B/10973, 1/3/17; No. 14 O.C.B., 5/10/17; R. Ir. Regt., 26/2/18; F; 2/Lieut.; M.C.   37 Queens Gardens, Lancaster Gate, W.2.

STOGDON, John
H/3040, 12/3/15, L/C.; Wilts. R., 28/7/15; Lieut.; w-p; M.C. and Bar.
   c/o R. J. Neville Esq., 7 Fig Tree Court, Temple, E.C.4.

STOKER, Alexander Frederick
D/10243, 29/12/16; No. 21 O.C.B., 5/5/17; Lan. Fus., 28/8/17; Lieut.; w.
   5 Howard Drive, Grassendale, Liverpool.

STOKES, Alan
B/12690, 4/3/18; R.F.A., C/S, 26/7/18; R.F.A.; 2/Lieut.
   Laverstock, Boscombe, Bournemouth. (Now in Rhodesia).

STOKES, Denny O'Connor Crane
A/12551, 4/2/18; H. Bde. O.C.B., 8/4/18; Welch Gds., 24/9/18; 2/Lieut.
   42 Kensington Park Gardens, W.11.

✠ STOKES, Harold
6/4/8906, 13/1/16, Sgt.; No. 14 O.C.B., 28/8/16; M.G.C., C/S; M.G.C., 9/12/16, Tank Corps; 2/Lieut.
   Killed in action 20/11/17.

✠ STOKES, Henry John Edgar
6/3/5606, 14/8/15, L/C.; R.F.C., C/S, 1/2/17; R.F.C., 12/4/17, R.A.F.; Lieut.
   Killed 19/11/19.

✠ STOKES, John Godfrey
A/B/D/12187, 1/11/17; No. 7 O.C.B., 10/5/18; R. Ir. Fus., 29/10/18, att. R. Ir. Rif.; F; 2/Lieut.; w.
   Killed in Ireland 1921.

✠ STOKES, John Hill
B/646, 18/6/12; R.W. Kent R., 14/8/14, att. R. Berks. R.; F; Capt.; M.C., M(2).
   Died of wounds 22/3/15.

STOKES, Joseph
B/13513, 10/7/18; No. 22 O.C.B., 23/8/18; demob. 16/1/19.
   250 Bristol Road, Edgbaston, Birmingham.

✠ STOKES, Leicester Henry
6/4/9299, 3/2/16; No. 14 O.C.B., 29/9/16; 18th Lond. R., 24/1/17; 2/Lieut.
   Killed in action 31/10/17.

STOKES, Norman
4/5/6/4812, 12/7/15; R.F.A., C/S, 31/3/16; R.F.A., 5/8/16; Lieut.
   The Lodge, Princes Gardens, Cliftonville, Margate

STOKES, Stanley Graham
C/Sq/11526, 18/6/17; trfr. M.G.C., 28/9/17.
   21 Great St. Helens, E.C.3.

✠ STOKES-REES, Philip George
6/D/8574, 31/12/15; R.N.A.S., 31/10/16, R.A.F.   Killed 1918.

329

APPENDIX II.—RECORDS OF RANK AND FILE.

✠ STOLLERY, John Cecil
A/677, 24/1/13; R. Fus., 14/8/14, att. R. War. R.; F; 2/Lieut.
Killed in action 24/5/15.

✠ STONE, Arthur
Sq./274, 15/6/08; dis. 14/6/09; Lan. Fus., 28/10/14; F; Lt. Col.;
D.S.O. *Killed in action 5/10/18.*

STONE, Francis LeStrange
Sq/291, 23/6/08; dis. 22/6/09; rcj. Sq/ 1028, 24/8/14; 3rd Huss.,
15/8/14; Lieut.; M.C.
2 Vanbrugh Terrace, Blackheath, S.E. 3.

STONE, Gerald Graham Holmes
K/C/2179, 26/11/14; 15th Lond. R., 2/4/15; Capt.
9 Sheffield Terrace, W. 8.

STONE, Herbert George
Sq/2842, 1/2/15, L/C.; R.A.S.C., 1/7/15; F; Capt.
Kenmore, Aberfeldy, Perthshire, N.B. (Now in Buenos Aires).

STONE, John Leonard
B/1250, 23/9/14; Worc. R., 20/10/14; G; Capt.; w, p; M(2).
50 Shooters Hill Road, Blackheath, S.E.

STONE, Norman
B/12352, 31/12/17; No. 7 O.C.B., 10/5/18; R. Suss. R., 29/10/18,
att. W. Rid. R.; F; 2/Lieut. *33 Lower Road, S.E. 16.*

STONE, Ralph Browning Leckie
6/8254, 8/12/15; A.S.C., C/S, 27/3/16; R.A.S.C., 1/5/16; Lieut.
Cumnor, The Drive, Sydenham, S.E.

✠ STONE, Richard
C/11455, 4/6/17; R.F.C., C/S, 2/8/17; R.F.C., 8/9/17, R.A.F.;
F; Lieut. *Killed in action 9/8/18.*

✠ V.C. STONE, Walter Napleton
K/A/2030, 9/11/14; dis. to R. Mil. Coll., 29/12/14; R. Fus.; F
Capt.; Victoria Cross. *Killed in action 30/11/17.*

STONEHAM, Douglas William
6/Sq/6676, 7/10/15; No. 1 Cav. C/S, 24/4/16; Suff. Yeo., 28/7/16,
att. Norf. Yeo.; E,F; Capt.
Rover Villa, High Street, Kingston-on-Thames. (Now in Canada).

STONEHOUSE, Harry
6/1/7278, 8/11/15; R. Lanc. R., 4/8/16; F; Lieut.; w.
Lymehurst, Market Drayton, Salop.

STONEMAN, Arthur Cyril
K/2598, 6/1/15; R.G.A., 2/3/15; F; Lieut.
1 Furzehatt Villas, Plymstock, South Devonshire.

STORER, Richard Samuel
C/1720, 15/10/14; Herts. R., 25/3/15; R.N.V.R.; Lieut
Vicar's Moor, 27 Kidderpore Avenue, Hampstead, N.W. 3.

STOREY, Theophilus Monckton Milnes
Sq/1523, 2/10/14; Linc. Yeo., 8/1/15, att. 21st Lanc. and 13th
Huss.; I; Lieut.
Junior Naval and Military Club, 96 Piccadilly, W. 1.

✠ STORRAR, Andrew Wynne
6/5/7702, 22/11/15; R. Dub. Fus., 4/8/16, att. T.M. Bty.; 2/Lieut.
Killed in action 16/8/17.

✠ STORRS, Francis Edmund
Sq/328, 10/11/08; dis. 16/6/11; R.N.V.R., 2/12/16; Lieut.;
Russian Order of S. Anne. *Died 10/11/18.*

STORY, Charles
A/E/13966, 6/9/18; demob. 10/1/19.
67 Bridge Lane, Golders Green, N.W.

STORY, Duncan
C/1034, 24/8/14; R. War. R., 12/9/14; F; Capt.; w; M.C.
48 Esmond Road, W. 4.

STORY, Henry Harle
K/C/2464, 28/12/14; R. Suss. R., 31/3/15, Sco. Rif.; F; Capt.;
M.C., M(1).
42 Harley Terrace, Gosforth, Newcastle-on-Tyne. (Now in India).

STOTT, Gerard
A/13180, 31/5/18, Sgt.; General List, 4/2/19, att. R.E.; NR;
2/Lieut. *4 Windsor Road, Ealing, W. 5.*

STOTT, Jack
A/12531, 31/1/18; No. 19 O.C.B., 7/6/18; Manch. R., 4/2/19;
2/Lieut. *Clevedon, 205 Green Lane, Great Lever, Bolton.*

STOTT, Millie Dow
A/838, 4/8/14; Bord. R., 11/9/14; F,S; Capt.; M.C.
36 Sea Road, Bexhill-on-Sea.

STOTT, Walter Davies
A/11260, 12/5/17; No. 10 O.C.B., 5/10/17; Lan. Fus., 26/2/18;
2/Lieut.; M.C.
Fox Hill, Liverpool Road, Patricroft, Manchester.

✠ STOTT, William Ernest
D/10941, 24/3/17; No. 12 O.C.B., 10/8/17; Lan. Fus., 27/11/17;
F; 2/Lieut. *Killed in action 8/8/18.*

STOTT, William Henry
6/5/7080, 29/10/15; trfr. R.G.A., 6/10/16.
Mapledene, Egerton Park, Rock Ferry.

STOTTNER, Kathburt Henry
6/2/7958, 29/11/15, Cpl.; trfr. Midd'x. R., 9/3/17.
Lond. & Brazilian Bank, 7 Tokenhouse Yard, E.C. 2.

✠ STOVELL-SPENCER, Mowbray Bertram
K/A/2480, 28/12/14; Worc. R., 9/3/15; 2/Lieut.
Killed in action 4/8/15.

STOVES, Howard Trevelyan
A/10064, 1/12/16; No. 14 O.C.B., 30/1/17; E. Kent R., 29/5/17;
Lieut. *Stoneycroft, Southport, Lancashire.*

STOW, James Lindsay
K/E/2151, 20/11/14, Cpl.; K.R. Rif. C., 26/2/15; F; Capt.; w.
Horris Hill, Newbury, Berkshire.

STOWELL, Leonard Hamilton
6/1/5394, 5/8/15, Cpl.; R.F.C., 14/4/16; S,E; Capt.
26 Kensington Road, Weston-super-Mare.

STRACHEY, John Francis
4/5/B/4430, 24/6/15; dis. med. unfit, 28/3/18.

✠ STRAHAN, Geoffrey Bennock
D/1443, 29/9/14, L/C.; 10th Lond. R., 28/3/15; G; 2/Lieut.
Killed in action 31/8/15.

STRAHAN, William Roscoe
D/1395, 29/9/14, Cpl.; 18th Lond. R., 3/6/15, att. Midd'x. R.;
F; Capt. *28 City Road, Norwich.*

STRANG, Robert Maurice
D/11126, 28/4/17; R.F.C., C/S, 1/6/17; R.F.C., 4/7/17, R.A.F.;
F; Lieut.; cr; Croix de Guerre (Belge).
Rossie, Salisbury Avenue, Finchley, N. 3.

STRANG, William Fleming
C/12232, 15/11/17; H. Bde. O.C.B., 8/3/18; Welch Gds., 27/8/18;
2/Lieut. *Bosfield, West Kilbride, Lanarkshire.*

STRANGE, Bailey
Sq/3368, 22/4/15, L/C.; Linc. Yeo., 8/7/15, R.F.C., R.A.F.; F;
Lieut.; w. *Briar Cottage, Greenway, Berkhamsted.*

STRANGE, Christopher Gilbert
2/9772, 23/10/16; No. 14 O.C.B., 5/3/17; Dorset R., 26/6/17,
att. R.F.C.; Lieut.
North Farm, Spettisbury, Blandford, Dorset.

STRANGE, Cresswell
6/4/8866, 12/1/16; No. 8 O.C.B., 4/8/16; N. Lan. R., 21/11/16;
F; Capt. *Kirkham Grammar School, Kirkham, Lancashire.*

STRANGE, Lennard Francis
4/4549, 1/7/15; Bord. R., 5/1/16; Lieut.

✠ STRANGE, Lionel Cresswell
6/5/8191, 6/12/15; No. 14 O.C.B., 30/10/16; Essex R., 24/1/17;
2/Lieut. *Died of wounds 22/7/17.*

STRANGER, William
2/3174, 6/4/15; R.W. Surr. R., 18/6/15; Lieut.; w; M.C.
c/o Standard Bank of South Africa, Clements Lane, E.C.

✠ STRATHERN, Tom Dalrymple
1/3321, 19/4/15, L/C.; York. R., 9/12/15; 2/Lieut.
Killed in action 8/7/16.

STRAUSS, Henry George
A/911, 5/8/14; dis. med unfit, 21/8/14.
1 Tanfield Court, Temple, E.C. 4.

✠ STRAUSS, Victor Arthur
Sq/2961, 22/2/15, L/C.; R.A.S.C., 24/5/15, R.F.C.; Lieut.
Killed in action 27/11/16.

STREAT, Edward Raymond
6/5/5231, 30/7/15; Manch. R., 21/12/15; F; Lieut.; w.
Heatherleigh, Mottram Road, Stalybridge.

STREATFIELD, Edward Philip
B/12861, 25/3/18; No. 2 O.C.B., 20/9/18; Gds. M.G.R., 10/3/19;
2/Lieut. *Rocklers, London Road, Maidstone, Kent.*

STREATHER, Norman
C/A/12233, 15/11/17; R.F.C., C/S; trfr. R.A.F., 15/2/18.
Glencairn, Four Oaks, Warwickshire.

STREET, Arthur William
4/3/4520, 29/6/15, L/C.; Hamps. R., 24/10/15, secd. M.G.C.;
E; Major; w; M.C., M(1).
5 Sunnydale Gardens, The Hale, Mill Hill, N.W. 7.

APPENDIX II.—RECORDS OF RANK AND FILE.

✠ STREET, *Herbert Duke*
6/1/7155, 2/11/15, L/C.; No. 11 O.C.B., 7/5/16; R. Suss. R., 4/9/16; 2/Lieut. *Died 26/3/19.*

STREET, *Ralph Hope*
6/4/8948, 17/1/16, L/C.; No. 14 O.C.B., 30/10/16; Notts. and Derby. R., 24/1/17; F; Capt.; w.
Kinsmansdale, Moretonhampstead, Devonshire.

STRETCH, *Leonard Gordon*
C/14261, 1/11/18; No. 11 O.C.B., 24/1/19; General List, 8/3/19; 2/Lieut.
c/o W. Stretch Esq., Ash Lea, Uttoxeter, Staffordshire.

STRIBLING, *Bertram Hooper*
6/1/7782, 23/11/15; No. 8 O.C.B., 4/8/16; Wilts. R., 21/11/16; F; w.
London Hospital, Whitechapel, E. 1.

STRICKLAND, *Donald*
F/1790, 16/10/14, Sgt.; R.A.O.C., 8/2/15; G,E,F; Major; M(1)
Engadine, Dartford Road, Dartford, Kent.

STRICKLAND, *Frederick William*
C/13288, 14/6/18; R.E., C/S; demob.
The Cottage, Prinfield Road, Staines.

STRICKLAND, *William Joseph*
B/13509, 10/7/18; No. 22 O.C.B., 23/8/18; L'pool. R., 13/2/19; 2/Lieut.
262 Walton Road, Liverpool.

STRIDE, *Basil Hugh*
A/12497, 28/1/18; R.F.A., C/S, 17/5/18; R.G.A., 3/3/19; 2/Lieut.
Homeacre, Leigh Woods, Somerset.

STRINGER, *Cecil Burgess*
D/11175, 2/5/17; R.F.C., C/S, 1/6/17; R.F.C., 4/7/17; F; Lieut.; w.
47 Mountfield Road, Finchley, N. 3.

STRINGER, *Charles John McNair*
Sq/567, 29/5/11; dis. 25/6/12; rej. Sq/1291, 24/9/14; R.A.S.C., 5/12/14, att. Norf. R.; S,F; Capt.
47 Selbourne Road, Hove, Sussex.

STRINGER, *Francis Randolph Perceval*
A/329, 23/11/08; dis. 12/11/12.

STRINGER, *Miles Beaconsfield*
D/10894, 19/3/17; No. 14 O.C.B., 10/8/17; Hunt. Cyc. Bn., 27/11/17; 2/Lieut.
Seaforth, Craneswater Avenue, Southsea, Hampshire.

STRINGFELLOW, *Geoffrey F.*
B/1083, 2/9/14; Durh. L.I., 19/9/14; Lieut.; w(2); M.C., M(1).
Enderfield, Chislehurst.

STROLOGO, *Reginald Charles*
C/1165, 14/9/14; Leic. R., 27/11/14, North'd. Fus.; Capt.

✠ STRONG, *Arthur Penton*
6/5/6945, 20/10/15, L/C.; North'd. Fus., 21/4/16; Lieut.
Killed in action 26/10/17.

STRONG, *Charles Herbert*
6/Sq/D/6812, 14/10/15, Cpl.; No. 1 O.C.B., 8/3/17; R.F.C., 9/5/17, R.A.F., att North'd. Fus.; F; Lieut.; w.
28 Western Road, Hove, Sussex.

STRONG, *Herbert Richard*
F/1819, 16/10/14, L/C.; Midd'x. R., 10/2/15; F; Lieut.; w(2); M.C.
Redlands, Chislehurst Road, Bickley, Kent.

STRONG, *James Rowland*
6/4/6946, 20/10/15; D. of Corn. L.I., 8/7/16, M.G.C.; I,F,F; Lieut.
2 Cromwell Crescent, Stanwix, Carlisle.

✠ STRONG, *James William*
B/2535, 1/1/15; Lan. Fus., 1/4/15; Lieut.
Killed in action 11/6/16.

✠ STROSS, *David*
Sq/3101, 22/3/15; R.F.A., 21/8/15; 2/Lieut. *Killed 12/3/17.*

STROUD, *Douglas Aikenhead*
6/5/7598, 18/11/15; 8th Lond. R., 29/7/16, R.A.S.C.; F; Lieut.; w.
44 Blenheim Gardens, Wallington, Surrey.

STROUD, *George Mannering*
4/3/4826, 13/7/15; Indian Army, 23/11/16; Lieut.
Ivanhoe, Holmfield Road, Stoneygate, Leicester.

STROUD, *William Frederick*
6/3/5868, 27/8/15; No. 1 O.C.B., 25/2/16; 20th Lond. R., 7/7/16, att. T.M.Bty.; F,S,P; Lieut.; M(1).
2 Locks Hill, Frome, Somerset.

STROUTS, *Edward Murton*
A/31, 3/4/08; dis. 2/4/11.
28 Palace Street, Westminster, S.W. 1

STROVER, *Herbert Ivel*
1/3240, 12/4/15; Shrop. L.I., 30/6/15, M.G.C.; F; Capt.; w(2); M.C.
St. Ivels, Sandy, Bedfordshire. (*Now in France*).

STROVER, *Herbert Kimberley*
D/12925, 3/4/18; trfr. 28th Lond. R., 8/11/18.
St. Ivels, Sandy, Bedfordshire.

STRUGNELL, *George Kenneth*
A/13138, 27/5/18; demob. 29/1/19.
30 Carholme Road, Forest Hill, S.E.23.

STRUGNELL, *Milton Arthur*
K/E/2290, 10/12/14, Sgt.; Bedf. R., 24/7/15; Lieut.
192 Portsdown Road, Maida Vale, W.9.

✠ STRUTT, *Anthony Herbert*
E/3019, 8/3/15; Notts. & Derby R., 22/7/15; F; Lieut.; g-w.
Killed in action 27/4/18.

STRUTT, *Edward Jolliffe*
F/1895, 16/10/14; Essex R., 6/11/14; Capt.
30 Walpole Street, Chelsea, S.W. 3.

STRUTT, *John James*
A/414, 7/5/09; dis. 11/11/10. Whitelands, Witham, Essex.

STUART, *Charles*
A/10725, 12/2/17; No. 11 O.C.B., 5/7/17; E. Surr. R., 30/10/17; Lieut.; w.

STUART, *Douglas Ernest Offord*
6/4/5864, 26/8/15; No. 14 O.C.B., 26/11/16; trfr. 14th Lond. R., 11/4/17; F; Pte.; w.
65 Vanbrugh Park, Blackheath, S.E. 3.

STUART, *Eric Mansfield*
1/9636, 25/9/16; No. 14 O.C.B., 26/11/16; Worc. R., 27/3/17, Ches. R.; S; Lieut.; w; M.C.
The Woodlands, Woodsley, Stourbridge.

STUART, *Frederick Charles*
A/11222, 7/5/17; No. 16 O.C.B., 5/10/17; Norf. R., 12/3/18; F, Lieut.
Nat. Prov. & Union Bank of England Ltd., 157 Regent Road, Salford, Manchester.

STUART, *Hector*
3/3210, 10/4/15, Cpl.; Midd'x. R., 21/6/15, Suff. R.; F; Capt.
12 Tatam Road, Stonebridge Park, N.W. 10.

STUART, *Ian St. Clare*
C/11086, 20/4/17; L/C.; R.A., C/S, 7/9/17; Special List, 1/10/18; 2/Lieut.
12 Charles Street, Knightsbridge, S.W. 7.

STUART, *John Patrick*
4/2/4097, 7/6/15; North'd. Fus., 6/9/15, secd. Indian Army; Lieut.; w.

STUART, *Robert Scott*
B/12797, 18/3/18; No. 1 O.C.B., 6/9/18; demob.
12 Trelawney Road, Cotham, Bristol.

✠ STUART, *Thomas Charles*
D/11572, 25/6/17; R.F.C., C/S, 23/10/17; R.F.C., 12/12/17, R.A.F.; 2/Lieut. *Died 12/12/18.*

✠ STUART, *Vernon Douglas*
Sq/350, 1/3/09; dis. 28/2/13; R.G.A.; Lieut.; w; M.C.
Killed in action 29/9/18.

STUBBS, *Arthur Duncan*
A/11298, 15/5/17; R.F.C., C/S, 2/8/17; R.F.C., 8/9/17; R.A.F.; F,It,NR; Lieut.
92 Cedar Road, Southampton.

STURGESS, *George*
A/D/13082, 17/5/18; dis. med. unfit, 19/5/19.
2 Earle Street, Earlestown, Lancashire.

STURMAN, *Ralph*
D/12127, 15/10/17, Cpl.; No. 12 O.C.B., 20/9/18, No. 11 O.C.B.; General List, 8/3/19; 2/Lieut.
c/o Major E. A. Sturman, G.P.O., Pretoria, South Africa.

STURT, *Edmund Anthony*
4/3564, 10/5/15, Cpl.; R. War. R., 8/7/15, M.G.C.; Lieut.; w.

STURTON, *Thomas Walter*
D/11123, 26/4/17; A.S.C., C/S, 1/9/17; R.A.S.C., 27/10/17; F; 2/Lieut.
The Croft, Statham, Warrington.

STUTFIELD, *Rupert*
H/2656, 11/1/15; R.W. Surr. R., 22/4/15; 2/Lieut.
Grove House, Hampton.

SUFFILL, *Thomas Lionel*
D/B/12136, 17/10/17, Sgt.; No. 5 O.C.B., 5/4/18; High. L.I., 29/10/18; 2/Lieut.
Chevat, Cartuke, Scotland.

APPENDIX II.—RECORDS OF RANK AND FILE.

✠ SUGDEN, *John Paget*
6/4/6073, 6/9/15, Cpl.; W. Rid. R., 6/6/16; 2/Lieut.
Killed in action 8/8/17.

SUGDEN, *Kaye Aspinall Ramsden*
Sq/138, 18/4/08; dis. 31/12/09.

SUKER, *John Cecil*
6/4/9227, 31/1/16; R.A., C/S, 7/8/16; R.G.A., 19/11/16; F;
Capt.; g. *40 North John Street, Liverpool.*

SULLIVAN, *Arthur John*
6/5/7483, 15/11/15, L/C.; R. War. R., 4/8/16; F,It; Capt.; M(2).
96 Westeria Gardens, Chiswick, W. 4.

SULLIVAN, *Bernard Ponsonby*
K/B/2217, 30/11/14; dis. 10/2/15. *Middlewych, St. Albans.*

✠ SULLIVAN, *Cyril Charles Lloyd*
4/1/3983, 3/6/15; Linc. R., 5/9/15; 2/Lieut.
Killed in action 16/6/17.

SULLIVAN, *Joseph Bennet*
F/2660, 12/1/15; Sea. Highrs., 20/3/15, att. M. of Munitions;
F,M; Lieut.; w(2).
Kajang, Selangor, Federated Malay States.

SUMMERBELL, *Lawrence James*
6/2/7279, 8/11/15, L/C.; Linc. R., 4/8/16, Notts. & Derby. R,
R.A.F.; F; Lieut.; w. *192 Holland Road, Kensington. W.*

SUMMERFIELD, *Mark*
6/1/7959, 29/11/15, L/C.; K.R. Rif. C., 4/8/16; F; Capt.; w.
M.C., M(1).
*Nat. Bank of South Africa Ltd., Circus Place, London Wall,
E.C. (Now in South Africa).*

SUMMERS, *Malcolm de Vere*
D/11164, 2/5/17; R.F.C., C/S, 1/6/17; R.F.C., 4/7/17, R.A.F.,
Lieut.; cr. *19 Abbeville Road, Clapham Park, S.W. 4.*

SUMMERSON, *Athanasius John*
12745, 11/3/18; No. 6 O.C.B., 6/9/18; Oxf. & Bucks. L.I., 16/3/19;
2/Lieut. *38 Thorncliffe Road, Oxford.*

SUMNER, *Cecil Carol Winton*
E/14149, 11/10/18; demob. 10/1/19.
St. Pauls Vicarage, Gateshead-on-Tyne.

SUMSION, *Charles Corbett*
A/D/13040, 6/5/18, Cpl.; demob. 6/6/19.
Lothian House, Stroud Road, Gloucester.

SUMSION, *Wilfrid Henry*
6/1/9472, 14/2/16; No. 13 O.C.B., 4/11/16; Hamps. R., 28/2/17;
F; Lieut. *Lothian House, Stroud Road, Gloucester.*

SUNDERLAND, *Harold*
B/D/12401, 16/1/18; R.F.C., C/S, 19/4/18; trfr, R.A.F.
Lawton House, Kent Road, Harrogate.

SUNDIUS-SMITH, *Basil Knightley*
B/9901, 13/11/16; R.A., C/S, 23/3/17; R.G.A., 18/6/17; F;
Lieut. *3 Courtenay Terrace, Portslade, Sussex.*

SUNDQUIST, *John*
6/2/6934, 20/10/15, L/C.; 8th Lond. R., 4/9/16; F; Lieut.; w.
13 Seafield Road, Hove, Sussex.

SUNDT, *Frank Harold*
1/9760, 18/10/16; No. 14 O.C.B., 30/1/17; Dorset R., 25/4/17;
F; Lieut.
c/o Messrs. Cox & Coy., F. Branch, Charing Cross, S.W. 1.

SURGEY, *Frank*
4/3/4554, 26/6/15; E. Ang. Div. Cyc. Coy., 1/9/15, R.F.C.,
R.A.F.; F; Lieut.; w.
2 The Chine, Grange Park, Winchmore Hill, N. 21.

SURSHAM, *Ernest Albert*
6/1/9508, 15/2/16; Cold. Gds., 10/6/16, emp. Gds. M.G.R.;
Lieut.; w. *8 West Heath Drive, N.W. 3.*

✠ SUTCLIFFE, *Charles Geoffrey Fielden*
4/1/5132, 26/7/15; Yorks. L.I., 18/6/16, att. Som. L.I.; F; Capt.
Died 9/12/19.

✠ SUTCLIFFE, *Fred Malcolm*
6/1/7533, 16/11/15, Sgt.; 8th Lond. R., 4/9/16; F; 2/Lieut.
Killed in action 29/5/17.

SUTCLIFFE, *Hubert Thomas*
A/13017, 1/5/18; No. 1 O.C.B., 8/11/18; Manch. R., 18/3/19;
2/Lieut. *45 Church Street, Harlesyke, Nr. Burnley, Lancashire.*

SUTCLIFFE, *Joseph Hedley*
F/1875, 16/10/14, L/C.; Essex R., 7/3/15; Capt.
Ashen Croft, Ilkley, Yorkshire.

SUTCLIFFE, *Norman*
D/1383, 29/9/14, Sgt.; York. & Lanc. R., 5/5/15; F; Capt.
St. Martins, Malvern.

SUTCLIFFE, *Sextus Edward*
6/4/5910, 30/8/15; North'd. Fus., 1/6/16, R.F.C., R.A.F.; F;
Lieut.; w(2).
Cuba House, 10 Trinity Road, Bridlington, Yorkshire.

SUTHERLAND, *Warwick Parker*. Now OVINGTON, W. P. J.
C/10154, 8/12/16; No. 14 O.C.B., 5/5/17; R.F.C., 28/8/17,
R.A.F.; 2/Lieut. *28 Dorset Square, N.W. 1.*

✠ SUTTON, *Arthur Eldred Barker*
6/4/8333, 11/12/15; No. 14 O.C.B., 28/8/16; L'pool. R., 18/12/16,
R.A.F.; Lieut. *Died 4/7/18.*

SUTTON, *Bertine Entwisle*
Sq/1218, 14/9/14; West. & Cumb. Yeo., 19/10/14, R.A.F.; F;
Capt.; w; D.S.O., O.B.E., M.C., M(1).
24 Wellington Square, Chelsea, S.W. 3.

SUTTON, *Frank Stanley Bolton*
K/B/2346, 14/12/14, Cpl.; dis. 4/6/15.
Diamond's Farm, Horeham Road, Sussex.

SUTTON, *Fraser*
6/3/8226, 7/12/15; No. 8 O.C.B., 4/8/16, M.G.C., C/S; M.G.C.,
23/11/16, Tank Corps; F; Capt.; w.
Thornhill, Hale Road, Hale, Cheshire.

SUTTON, *Jack Cyril*
6/1/6677, 7/10/15; No. 14 O.C.B.; 18th Lond. R., 24/10/16,
Manch. R., Indian Army; F,I,Persia; Lieut.; M.C.
23 Parsons Green, S.W. 6. (Now in India).

SUTTON, *John*
B/12798, 18/3/18; trfr. R.A.F., 2/7/18.
3 Alexandra Avenue, Newtown, Great Yarmouth.

SUTTON, *Lawrence Hope*
6/2/D/6214, 13/9/15, Cpl.; R.F.C., C/S, 13/3/17; R.F.C.,
19/4/17, R.A.F.; F; Lieut. *29 Birch Grove, Acton, W. 3.*

✠ SUTTON, *Percy Turner*
6/5/8584, 3/1/16; R.A., C/S, 4/8/16; R.G.A., 1/11/16; F;
Lieut.; w. *Killed in action 24/8/18.*

SUTTON, *Vane Laprimaundaye*
A/12521, 31/1/18, Cpl.; No. 21 O.C.B., 5/7/18; trfr. 28th Lond.
R., 19/11/18. *37 Forest Hill Road, Hove, Sussex.*

SUTTON, *William*
6/Sq/7190, 3/11/15, Cpl.; No. 1 Cav. C/S, 12/10/16; Linc. Yeo.,
16/2/17, att. Linc. R.; F; Lieut.
Wilcote Grange, Charlbury, Oxon.

SUTTON, *William George Leslie*
D/14017, 12/9/18; demob. 24/1/19.
The School House, Cwmcarn, Crosskeys, Monmouthshire.

SWAILES, *Harry*
A/10468, 12/1/17; R.A., C/S, 24/8/17, No. 8 O.C.B.; Midd'x. R.,
29/5/18. *12 Grendon Avenue, Coppice, Oldham, Lancashire.*

SWAIN, *Arthur Bernard*
6/3/8192, 6/12/15, L/C.; No. 14 O.C.B., 28/8/16; North'n. R.,
21/11/16; F; Lieut.; w-p.
22 Howard Road, Upminster, Essex.

SWAIN, *Arthur George*
6/2/7003, 25/10/15; No. 11 O.C.B., 7/5/16; W. Som. Yeo.,
5/9/16, att. Som. L.I.; 2/Lieut.
31 Hemingford Road, Cambridge.

SWAINE, *Harold*
6/5/6436, 25/9/15, L/C.; N. Lan. R., 16/11/16; F; Capt.
269 Park Lane, Macclesfield.

SWAINE, *Robert Obank*
A/D/11894, 20/8/17, L/C.; trfr. Class W. Res., 15/4/18.
23 Cleveland Road, Heaton, Bradford.

SWAINE, *Thomas Charles Lethbridge*
K/2557, 4/1/15; R.G.A., 27/2/15, R.A.F.; F; Capt.
c/o Lond. Cty. West. & Parr's Bank, 1 St. James Square, S.W. 1.

SWAN, *Lionel Maynard*
B/580, 13/11/11, Sgt.; Dorset R., 20/2/15; Lieut.; w; M(1).
1 The Grange, Maitland Park, N.

SWANN, *Alfred*
D/E/13917, 10/8/18; R.G.A., C/S, 1/11/18; demob.
Fairlie Villa, Avenue Road, Kings Lynn, Norfolk.

SWANN, *Geoffrey*
6/8193, 6/12/15; A.S.C., C/S, 24/4/16; R.A.S.C., 28/5/16; F;
Lieut. *Ludwick Corner, Hatfield.*

SWANN, *Horace Arthur*
5422, 5/8/15, Sgt.; R.F.A., C/S, 7/7/16; R.F.A., 27/10/16; F;
Capt.; M(1). *15 St. Albans Road, Watford, Hertfordshire.*

APPENDIX II.—RECORDS OF RANK AND FILE.

SWANSON, *Robert Gilbert*
6/2/8590, 3/1/16, L/C.; No. 8 O.C.B., 4/8/16; Yorks. L.I., 21/11/16; F; Capt. 23 *St. Marys, York.*

SWASH, *Stanley Victor*
6/9318, 4/2/16; R.F.A., C/S, 9/6/16; R.F.A., 8/9/16; F; Capt.; w; M.C. and Bar. 151 *Richmond Road, Cardiff.*

SWEENEY, *Michael*
1/3565, 10/5/15; R.A., C/S, 24/1/16; R.F.A., 16/6/16; M; Capt. 31 *Campden House Road, Kensington, W. 8.*

✠ SWEETMAN, *Richard Rodney Stephen*
E/2618, 7/1/15; R.F.A., 19/1/15; Capt. *Killed in action* 1/7/16.

SWIFFEN, *John Dennis*
A/11942, 30/8/17; R.F.C., C/S, 30/11/17; trfr. 28th Lond. R., 21/6/18. *Arden, Barnt Green, Worcestershire.*

SWIFT, *Eustace Musker*
D/13803, 9/8/18; dis. 21/1/19.
c/o *Mallet & Swift, Box 179, Kimberley, South Africa.*

SWIFT, *Harold*
6/3/7222, 3/11/15, L/C.; W. York. R., 4/9/16, Tank Corps; F; Lieut.
c/o *Morrhouse & Wainwright, Woodside Dyeworks, Horsforth, Nr. Leeds.*

✠ SWIFT, *Humphrey Morris*
6/4/6152, 9/9/15, L/C.; Welch R., 1/6/16; 2/Lieut.
Killed in action 16/11/17.

SWINBURNE, *John Evelyn*
D/11573, 28/6/17; R.F.C., C/S, 23/10/17; R.F.C., 12/12/17, R.A.F.; 2/Lieut. 14 *Saltoun Road, Brixton, S.W. 2.*

SWINDELLS, *Herbert Rowland*
1/3710, 20/5/15; Wilts. R., 28/7/15, E. Lan. R.; F,I; Lieut.; w.
Hendre, Carisbrooke Road, Leicester. (Now in Rhodesia).

SWINDELLS, *Samuel*
6/5/7517, 15/11/15, L/C.; No. 11 O.C.B., 7/5/16; Bord. R., 4/9/16, att. R. Innis. Fus. and Indian Army; F; Capt.; w.
The Esplanade, New Ferry, Cheshire.

SWINDEN, *William Mather*
B/10433, 10/1/17; R.G.A., C/S, 26/6/17; R.G.A., 25/11/17; F; 2/Lieut.; M(1). 45 *Lancaster Park, Richmond, Surrey.*

SWINFORD, *Cecil William*
C/11527, 18/6/17; No. 16 O.C.B., 5/10/17; R.E. Kent Yeo., 28/5/18; 2/Lieut. *Minster House, Minster, Isle of Thanet, Kent.*

SWINSON, *Reginald Barnes*
A/13056, 10/5/18; No. 1 O.C.B., 8/11/18, No. 3 O.C.B.; E. Surr. R., 20/3/19; 2/Lieut. *Swastika, The Ridgeway, Sutton, Surrey.*

SWITHINBANK, *Crossley*
B/632, 25/4/12; 1st Lond. R., 27/9/14; 2/Lieut.
Maybanks, Rudgwick, Sussex.

✠ SWORD, *Frederick William*
E/2653, 11/1/15; Rif. Brig., 3/6/15. *Killed* -/5/17.

SYCAMORE, *William Abdy*
6/8255, 8/12/15; Lond. Elec. Eng., 12/8/16; Lieut.
White Lodge, Brightlingsea, Essex.

SYFRET, *Stephen Henry McEwen*
C/11528, 18/6/17; dis. med. unfit, 2/10/17.
c/o *Standard Bank of South Africa, Clements Lane, E.C. 4.*

SYKES, *Alexander Richard*
C/1043, 26/8/14; L'pool. R., 19/9/14; Major; D.S.O., M.C., M(2). 46 *Great Russell Street, W.C. 1.*

SYKES, *Carlton*
6/5/6750, 9/10/15, L/C.; Leic. R., 6/7/16; Lieut.
Hull and East Riding Club, Hull, East Yorkshire.

✠ SYKES, *James Martyn Strickland*
6/5/6001, 2/9/15; No. 2 O.C.B., 25/2/16; Gord. Highrs., 6/7/16; 2/Lieut. *Killed in action* 13/11/16.

SYKES, *Oliver Heywood*
K/B/2156, 23/11/14; dis. 23/4/15.

SYKES, *Stanley William*
A/893, 5/8/14; dis. 8/8/14; Intelligence Corps.; F; Capt.; O.B.E., M.C., M(3). *Authors Club, St. James Street, S.W. 1.*

SYKES, *Thomas Lionel Talbot*
K/F/2291, 10/12/14; R. Ir. Fus., 31/3/15, R.A.F.; Lieut.

SYLVESTER, *Arthur Edgar*
6/3/6783, 11/10/15; Notts. & Derby. R., 25/12/15, secd. M.G.C.; Lieut. 1 *Ladbroke Gardens, W. 11.*

SYMCOX, *William Arthur*
B/12353, 31/12/17, L/C.; trfr. Rif. Brig., 24/3/19.
31 *Dulwich Village, S.E. 21.*

SYMES, *Cecil Lindley*
B/11633, 9/7/17; Garr. O.C.B., 28/12/17; Worc. R., 22/6/18; 2/Lieut. 23 *Berkeley Square, Clifton, Bristol.*

SYMINGTON, *Laurence Hugh Gales*
6/3/6439, 25/9/15, Sgt.; No. 14 O.C.B., 28/8/16; Sea. Highrs., 18/12/16; F,E; Lieut.
54 *Hailsham Avenue, Streatham Hill, S.W. (Now in Portugal).*

SYMINTON, *Hazle*
6/5/5959, 1/9/15, L/C.; R.A., C/S, 6/10/16; R.G.A., 12/11/16; F; Lieut. *Kirkcarswell, Castle Douglas, Kirkcudbrightshire, N.B.*

SYMON, *Charles James Ballaarat*
6/4/7223, 4/11/15; Cold. Gds., 5/3/16; Lieut.; M.C.
30 *Thurloe Place, S.W. 7.*

SYMOND, *Ronald Tudor*
6/4/8845, 10/1/16; No. 14 O.C.B., 27/9/16, M.G.C., C/S; L'pool. R., 27/3/17, R.A.F.; F; Lieut.; M.C.
101 *Ullet Road, Liverpool.*

SYMONDS, *Charlie Vincent*
2/3241, 12/4/15, R.Q.M.S.; demob. 10/2/19.
The Mount, Swanage, Dorset.

SYMONS, *Hubert Alford*
6/5/8445, 16/1/16; R.F.A., C/S, 4/8/16; R.F.A., 22/12/16; Lieut.; w *Octavian, Taunton Road, Bridgwater.*

✠ SYMONS, *Thomas Stewart*
K/E/2352, 15/12/14; R. Suss. R., 31/3/15, R.A.F.; F; Capt.; D.F.C. *Killed* 29/9/18.

SYMPSON, *Thomas Mansel*
Sq/2705, 18/1/15; E. Rid. Yeo., 2/3/15, M.G.C.; E,P,F; Lieut.
Estancia, Maxia Louisa, San Marcos, F.C.C.A., Argentina.

SYNGE, *Harold Millington*
B/10101, 4/12/16; Garr. O.C.B., 19/3/17; High. L.I., 12/5/17, R.A.S.C.; S; 2/Lieut. 5 *Lancaster Street, Lancaster Gate, W. 2.*

SYVRET, *Stanley de Beaudenis*
6/4/5356, 31/7/15; R. Sco. Fus., 7/10/15; Lieut.; w.

TAAFFE, *Charles Reddington O'Reilly*
6/1/6104, 6/9/15; Manch. R., 21/12/15; Lieut.; w.
Stapleton Rectory, Bristol.

TABBUSH, *Cecil Wilfred*
A/K/1286, 23/9/14, Sgt.; Midd'x. R., 8/7/15; F; Capt.; w.
Warnford Court, Throgmorton Street, E.C.

TABERNACLE, *Ernest Malcolm John*
6/5/D/6002, 2/9/15; R.F.A., C/S, 24/11/16; R.F.A., 7/4/17; F; Lieut. *New Cottage, Potters Bar, Middlesex.*

TACON, *George Lublin*
4/3663, 17/5/15; Glouc. R., 21/8/15, att. D. of Corn. L.I.; E,S; Capt. *Christchurch, New Zealand.*

TADMAN, *Ralph*
D/10627, 24/1/17; No. 14 O.C.B., 5/7/17; Devon. R., 30/10/17; 2/Lieut.; p. 41 *Atherfold Road, Clapham, S.W. 9.*

TAFFS, *Arthur Leslie*
A/11293, 16/5/17; dis. to R. Mil. Coll., 14/1/18; R. Berks. R., 20/12/18; M,Persia; Lieut.
Middle Green, Slough, Buckinghamshire.

TAFT, *Charles Frederick James*
6/1/7157, 2/11/15, L/C.; W. York. R., 4/8/16; F; Capt.; w; M.C. *Chartered Accountant, Burton Road, Derby.*

TAHOURDIN, *Raoul John Liddon*
6/6704, 7/10/15; Indian Army, 29/6/16; E; Capt.
Weycroft Lodge, Wimbledon

TAIT, *Charles Kingsley*
6/1/7885, 26/11/15, L/C.; R.F.C., 7/8/16, M.G.C.; F; Capt.
29 *Scotland Street, Edinburgh.*

TAIT, *Hugh Nimmo*
A/14069, 27/9/18; demob. 13/12/18.
16 *Pandova Road, West Hampstead, N.W. 6.*

APPENDIX II.—RECORDS OF RANK AND FILE.

TAIT, James
6/5/7783, 23/11/15; dis. to R. Mil. Coll., 29/8/16; Midd'x. R., 12/9/17; F; Lieut.   14 Vicarage Road, Eastbourne.

TAIT, William Raitt
E/14120, 9/10/18; General List, 7/3/19; 2/Lieut.
Queen Street, Newport, Fife, Scotland.

TALBOT, Charles Reginald
D/10635, 30/1/17, L/C.; demob. 29/1/19.
23 Palm Hill, Birkenhead.

TALBOT, Frank Heyworth
A/14050, 23/9/18; demob. 6/1/19.
Broadclough, 39 Lansdowne Road, Tottenham, N.7.

TALBOT, Frank Sydney
A/10274, 1/1/17; No. 1 Cav. C/S, 5/7/17, No. 12 O.C.B.; R. War. R., 27/11/17; F; Lieut.; g.
41 Hartington Road, Leicester.

TALBOT, Horace William Bass
B/13584, 22/7/18; demob. 23/1/19.
35 Glenfield Road, Leicester.

TALBOT, John Ward
6/5/7061, 29/10/15; Devon. R., 7/7/16; 2/Lieut.
37 Glenfield Road, Leicester.

TALBOT, Richard Warner
C/9944, 17/11/16, Cpl.; demob. 23/1/19.
13 The Avenue, Gravesend.

✠ TALBOT, Theophilus Edwin
6/Sq/7004, 25/10/15, Cpl.; R.A., C/S, 26/9/16; R.F.A., 5/5/17; 2/Lieut.   Died of wounds 21/3/18.

TALBOYS, Cyril Clifford
F/2997, 1/3/15; R.W. Surr. R., 2/6/15, Nigeria Regt.; EA; Capt.
La Rocque, Abbey Road, Rhos, Colwyn Bay. (Now in West Africa).

✠ TALLENT, Cecil Albert
6/4/7191, 3/11/15; dis. to re-enlist in R.F.C., 23/7/16; R.F.C; 2/Lieut.   Killed 4/11/17.

TALLENT, George Henry Louis
1/3566, 10/5/15; Bedf. R., 10/9/15, att. Norf. R.; E; Lieut.; p.
30 Highfield Avenue, Golders Green, N.W.4.

TAMBLING, Harold George
6/2/D/6026, 2/9/15, L/C.; R.F.C., C/S, 16/11/16; R.F.C, 16/3/17, R.A.F.; Lieut.;. p.

TAMBLYN, James Frederick
4/1/4619, 5/7/15, L/C.; E. Surr. R., 29/12/15; F,It; Major; w; M.C. and Bar, Croix de Guerre (French), M(1).
c/o Mrs. H. Madge, 2 Pembridge Square, Notting Hill Gate, W.2.

TAME, Thomas Roland
B/12862, 25/3/18; R.A.F., C/S, 25/3/19; demob. 27/3/19.
4 Darrell Road, Caversham, Reading.

TANNER, William Stanley
6/3/6492, 27/9/15; No. 7 O.C.B., 7/4/16; Hamps. R., 17/7/16, secd. M.G.C.; Lieut.; w; M(1). 55 St. Davids Road, Southsea.

TAPP, Eric George Raikes
A/Sq/10052, 29/11/16; trfr. 14th Lond. R., 2/3/17.
2 Glenesk Road, Eltham, Kent.

TAPPIN, Wallace Henry
6/3/5443, 7/8/15, L/C.; North'n. R., att. N. Staff. R.; F,I,S; Lieut.; w.   Elmhurst, 95 Albert Road, Ilford, Essex.

TARRAN, Percy James
4/4984, 19/7/15; 12th Lond. R., 12/1/16; F; Lieut.; w.
49 Delaware Mansions, Maida Vale, W.9.

TARRANT, James Augustine
B/13916, 24/8/18; demob. 29/1/19.
22 Hall's Crescent, Rochdale Road, Manchester.

TARRANT, Sydney Ernest
1/3664, 17/5/15; R.F.A., 20/9/15; F; Lieut.; M.C.
Hendre, Llandudno Junction, North Wales.

TATHAM, Christopher Kemplay
B/231, 15/5/08; 1st Lond. R., 6/7/10; G,F; Lt.-Col.
3 Hare Court, Temple, E.C.4.

TATHAM, Eric Walter
C/13196, 3/6/18; trfr. 14th Lond. R., 6/12/18, Gord. Highrs., att. R.A.S.C.; Pte.
23 Albany Road, St. Leonards-on-Sea, Sussex.

TATHAM, Guy Thomas Percy
D/A/11574, 28/6/17; R.A.M.C., 4/2/18; Capt.
90 The Grove, Ealing, W.5.

TATTERSALL, John
6/2/8496, 20/12/15; No. 14 O.C.B., 30/10/16, M.G.C., C/S; M.G.C., 25/1/17, Tank Corps, emp. M. of Labour; F; Lieut.; w.
Greenfield, Lytham, Lancashire.

TAVENER, Letson Alfred
A/9830, 1/11/16; No. 14 O.C.B., 27/12/16; North'd. Fus., 27/3/17; F; Lieut. 80 Westbourne Road, Penarth, Nr. Cardiff.

TAVENER, Warwick Harold
D/13707, 31/7/18; trfr. Gord. Highrs., 6/5/19.
80 Westbourne Road, Penarth.

TAVERNER, Wilfrid Alan
B/12396, 14/1/18; No. 15 O.C.B., 7/6/18; Essex R., 4/2/19; 2/Lieut.   Gews, Broomfield Road, Chelmsford, Essex.

TAYLER, Harold Crompton
6/4/7312, 8/11/15; R.F.A., C/S, 31/3/16; R.F.A., 6/7/16.
c/o B. A. Western Railway, River Plate House, E.C.2.

TAYLER, James Richard
Sq/2883, 8/2/15, L/C.; Wilts. R., 3/4/15; F; Lieut.; w(2); M.C., M(1).
Parsonage Farm, Catherington, Nr. Horndean, Hampshire.

TAYLER, John Cross
6/1/6136, 9/9/15; Midd'x. R., 6/7/16; F; Lieut.; w.
Nash Court, Nr. Margate, Kent.

TAYLOR, Alan Linnell
C/12056, 27/9/17, L/C.; Indian Army, 8/10/18, Bedf. R.; 2/Lieut
The Limes, Newport Pagnell, Buckinghamshire.

TAYLOR, Albert Richard
6/D/9740, 16/10/16; trfr. Army Pay Corps, 4/12/16; Sgt.
St. Annes, Town Walls, Shrewsbury.

TAYLOR, Alfred Miles
6/4/6027, 2/9/15, L/C.; Notts. & Derby. R., 4/1/16, att. Lab. Corps; F; Lieut.
c/o T. Jordan Esq., The Hollies, Horsley Woodhouse, Nr. Derby.

TAYLOR, Angus McKinnon
B/13543, 17/7/18; trfr. 14th Lond. R., 6/12/18.

TAYLOR, Archibald James
4/1/4636, 5/7/15; R.W. Surr. R., 7/12/15; Lieut.
3 Fairfax Road, Bedford Park, W.4.

TAYLOR, Arthur Stanley
A/11257, 14/5/17; No. 14 O.C.B., 7/9/17; Glouc. R., 17/12/17, att. Hamps. R.; F; 2/Lieut. 82 Fonthill Road, Hove, Sussex.

TAYLOR, Bernard Archie
6/4/8980, 18/1/16; R.F.C., 21/7/16, R.A.F.; F; Major; Inj; M.B.E., Croix de Guerre (French).
Tangmere, Gatwick, Horley, Surrey.

TAYLOR, Bryon Samuel William
B/11036, 9/4/17; R.F.C., C/S, 4/5/17; R.F.C., 13/7/17, R.A.F.; F; Lieut.; D.F.C.
Barclays Bank Ltd., Leominster, Herefordshire.

TAYLOR, Charles
6/5/7886, 26/11/15; R.A., C/S, 15/9/16; R.G.A., 3/12/16; F; Capt   Normanby, The Park, Grimsby.

TAYLOR, Charles
B/12779, 15/3/18; No. 20 O.C.B., 20/9/18; R. Berks. R., 17/3/19; 2/Lieut.   Rodiey, Abingdon, Berkshire.

Taylor, Charles Albert
K/H/542, 3/2/11, Sgt.; R.A.O.C., 17/5/15; F; Capt.
5 Ravenstone Street, Balham, S.W.12.

TAYLOR, Charles Dewhurst
C/12644, 22/2/18; No. 17 O.C.B., 5/7/18; R. Lanc. R., 3/3/19; 2/Lieut. Whitegate, Wrea Green, Kirkham, Lancashire.

TAYLOR, Charles Edgar
A/10045, 29/11/16; R.W. Surr. R., 9/3/17; F; Lieut.; g.
Aberglaslyn, 67 Park Road, Peterborough.

TAYLOR, Charles Reginald
K/D/2488, 31/12/14; 5th Lond. R., 11/2/15; Lieut.
87 Knightsbridge, S.W.1.

TAYLOR, Christian Edward
A/11006, 2/4/17; No. 12 O.C.B., 10/8/17; Yorks. L.I., 27/11/17; F; Lieut.; p.   Parkhurst, Oakdane, Bradford.

TAYLOR, Christopher Charles
E/2542, 4/1/15, L/C.; 3rd Lond. R., 20/4/15, emp. M. of Labour; F; Lieut.; w; M(1).
Junior Constitutional Club, Piccadilly, W.1.

APPENDIX II.—RECORDS OF RANK AND FILE.

TAYLOR, David
6/Sq/7628, 13/11/15; No. 2 Cav. C/S, 31/3/16; Lan. Huss. Yeo., 19/8/16, att. L'pool. R. and Tank Corps; F; Lieut.
27 Greasby Road, Wallasey, Cheshire.

TAYLOR, Edward
E/13995, 11/9/18, L/C.; demob. 23/1/19.
12 Holly Gardens, Low Fell, Co. Durham.

TAYLOR, Eric Henry
C/14146, 3/10/18; demob. 16/1/19.
76 Waterloo Road, Dublin, Ireland.

TAYLOR, Eric Howard
6/2/7313, 8/11/15; No. 14 O.C.B.; Oxf. & Bucks. L.I., 24/10/16, R. Fus., North'd. Fus. att. R.A.F.; F; Lieut.
East Franklands, Haywards Heath, Sussex.

TAYLOR, Ernest Henry
2/3206, 8/4/15, L/C.; N. Lan. R., 19/8/15, att. R.E. Sigs.; F; Lieut.; w(2).
Solicitor, Yorkshire Street, Rochdale, Lancashire.

TAYLOR, E. S. Sedley
A/1122, 7/9/14; S. Staff. R., 8/10/14, att. Bedf. R.; 2/Lieut.

✠ TAYLOR, Francis Maurice
C/781, 27/3/14; R. Fus., 11/9/14; Lieut.
Killed in action 15/7/16.

TAYLOR, Frank
6/5/8095, 1/12/15, L/C.; L'pool. R., 4/9/16, emp. M. of Labour; F; Lieut.
Hawthorn Cottage, Little Sutton, Chester.

TAYLOR, Frank William
B/12800, 18/3/18; demob. 21/12/18.
118 Hill Lane, Southampton.

✠ TAYLOR, Frederick Cecil
6/3/7811, 24/11/15; No. 8 O.C.B., 4/8/16; R. Ir. Rif., 21/11/16; Capt.
Killed in action 22/8/18.

✠ TAYLOR, Frederick George
6/3/6748, 11/10/15; North'd. Fus., 4/8/16; 2/Lieut.; w.
Died 21/7/17.

TAYLOR, Frederick Harold
A/D/11657, 12/7/17; trfr. 28th Lond. R., 8/4/18.
Kilmacrevan, Co. Donegal, Ireland.

TAYLOR, Frederick Risdon Lanceley
A/B/D/12188, 1/11/17; A.S.C., C/S, 4/3/18; R.A.S.C., 28/4/18, att. R.A.F.; F; 2/Lieut.
8 Westbourne Crescent, Hyde Park, W. 2.

TAYLOR, Frederick Thomas
F/1855, 16/10/14; Manch. R., 10/12/14; S,F; Capt.; w(2); M.C. and Bar.
36 High Street, Newport Pagnell, Buckinghamshire.

TAYLOR, Gerard Thorn
B/10373, 5/1/17; R.W. Surr. R., 9/3/17; F; Capt.
c/o Taylor, Hoare & Jelf, 12 Norfolk Street, Strand, W.C. 2. (Now in Ceylon).

TAYLOR, Gordon Crosland
H/1975, 26/10/14; R. Suss. R., 31/3/15, emp. M. of Labour; Lieut.; w.
42 Lancaster Gate, W. 2.

TAYLOR, Henry Leslie Jardine
K/B/2036, 9/11/14; 3rd Lond. R., 24/4/15, 21st Lond. R.; F,S; Capt.
Woodhay, Windlesham, Surrey.

TAYLOR, Henry Rosser
F/2843, 1/2/15, L/C.; S. Wales Bord., 1/6/15; F; Capt.
2 Dock Chambers, Bute Docks, Cardiff.

✠ TAYLOR, Henry William
6/3/7624, 19/11/15, L/C.; North'd. Fus., 4/8/16; 2/Lieut.
Died 29/5/17.

TAYLOR, Herbert Norman
6/7961, 29/11/15; No. 9 O.C.B., 8/3/16; High. L.I., 5/7/16; F; Lieut.; w.
25 Danes Drive, Scotstown, Glasgow.

TAYLOR, Herbert Owen
6/2/7962, 29/11/15; No. 14 O.C.B., 28/8/16; W. York. R., 22/11/16; F; 2/Lieut.
Fairhaven, Lawles Terrace, Eastbourne.

TAYLOR, Howard Dalton
6/1/6493, 27/9/15; R.W. Fus., 6/7/16; F; Lieut.; w(2); M.C.
12 Cwrtyvil Road, Penarth, South Wales.

TAYLOR, Jack Francis Mahon
C/13311, 17/6/18; trfr. 14th Lond. R., 6/12/18.
10 Meynell Crescent, South Hackney, E. 9.

TAYLOR, James Douglas
C/14147, 3/10/18; demob. 24/1/19.
76 Waterloo Road, Dublin.

TAYLOR, John Alexander
A/13121, 24/5/18; demob. 7/2/19.
Tredegar House, 25 New Road, Chatham, Kent.

TAYLOR, John Holmes
4/1/4586, 1/7/15; K.R. Rif. C., 17/11/15, R.A.F.; F,E; 2/Lieut.; w.
65 Altenburg Gardens, Clapham Common, S.W. 11.

TAYLOR, John Joseph Valentine
6/1/5889, 30/8/15, L/C.; Herts. R., 13/1/16, Camb. R.; F; Capt.; w.
Northoe, Hoddesdon, Hertfordshire.

TAYLOR, John Norman
C/32, 3/4/08; dis. 2/4/10.

✠ TAYLOR, John Ogilvie
2/3277, 15/4/15, L/C.; E. Kent R., 22/9/15; Capt.
Killed in action 3/5/17.

✠ TAYLOR, John Yates
4/5/4720, 9/7/15; E. Lan. R., 21/11/15, R.F.C.; Lieut.
Killed in action 6/7/17.

TAYLOR, Kenneth Walsham
4/1/3913, 31/5/15; Durh. L.I., 8/10/15; F; Lieut.; w.
Ixworth Court, 22 Palace Road, Streatham Hill, S.W.

TAYLOR, Leonard
1/3886, 31/5/15, Sgt.; R.W. Kent R., 1/11/15; Capt.

TAYLOR, Leonard Charles
6/2/6566, 30/9/15, L/C.; L'pool. R., 6/6/16; Capt.
59 Chalsey Road, Brockley, S.E. 4.

TAYLOR, Luke
D/1382, 29/9/14, L/C.; N. Lan. R., 9/1/15.
Hawley Grange, Dartford, Kent.

✠ TAYLOR, Maurice William
6/5/6003, 2/9/15, L/C.; R. Ir. Fus., 25/8/16; 2/Lieut.; w; M.C.
Killed in action 12/4/18.

TAYLOR, Michael Eden
B/13510, 10/7/18; demob. 30/1/19.
9 Broad Street, Leominster, Herefordshire.

TAYLOR, Patrick
6/2/8096, 1/12/15; No. 7 O.C.B., 3/7/16; R. Ir. Regt., 3/11/16, att. R. Innis. Fus. and R.A.V.C.; F; Lieut.; w.
32 Sutherland Place, Bayswater, W. 2.

TAYLOR, Percy Charles
6/5/7889, 27/11/15; R. Lanc. R., 4/8/16; F; Capt.; w.
55 Westbere Road, N.W. 2.

TAYLOR, Reginald George
D/2933, 15/2/15; K.R. Rif. C., 25/5/15, R.F.C., R.A.F.; F; Capt.; w; M(1).
Via Lauro 1a, Milan, Italy.

TAYLOR, Richard Herbert
4/2/5133, 26/7/15; No. 7 O.C.B., 7/4/16; Welch R., 4/8/16; Lieut.; w.
Holly House, Pontypridd.

TAYLOR, Richard William
6/3/5366, 3/8/15; R.G.A., 27/11/15; F,E,P; Lieut.
The Gables, Syston, Leicester.

TAYLOR, Robert Arthur
A/C/13122, 23/5/18; demob. 7/2/19.
Post Office, Bracebridge, Lincoln.

TAYLOR, Robert Collingwood
4/6/1/4985, 19/7/15; dis. med. unfit, 22/5/16.
Millswood, South Brent, South Devonshire.

TAYLOR, Robert Leslie
C/Sq/12294, 6/12/17, L/C.; demob. 24/1/19.
Rolleston, Sea Road, Wallasey, Cheshire.

TAYLOR, Robert Miller
4/2/4297, 17/6/15; R.E., 28/8/15; F; Major; w(2); M.C., Croix de Guerre (French), M(1).
c/o Oliver, 19 Windsor Street, Glasgow, W.

✠ TAYLOR, Roger Cecil
A/1741, 15/10/14; S. Staff. R., 24/11/14; Lieut.
Killed in action 4/10/17.

TAYLOR, Ronald Gillies
6/3/6541, 30/9/15; No. 9 O.C.B., 8/3/16; K.O. Sco. Bord., 16/7/16, R.F.C., R.A.F.; E,F; Lieut.; w.
Messrs. Anglo-Mexican Petroleum Coy. Ltd., Casilla 951, Concepcion, Chile, South America.

TAYLOR, Samuel
A/1740, 15/10/14; S. Staff. R., 24/11/14; F; Lieut.
Pouchen End, Boxmoor, Hertfordshire.

✠ TAYLOR, Samuel Alexander
6/5/8428, 15/12/15; No. 7 O.C.B., 11/8/16; R. Innis. Fus., 18/12/16, att. T.M. Bty.; 2/Lieut.
Killed in action 16/8/17.

APPENDIX II.—RECORDS OF RANK AND FILE.

TAYLOR, Stephen John
E/14028, 16/9/18; demob. 10/1/19.
19 Meads Street, Eastbourne.

TAYLOR, Thomas
C/10798, 22/2/17; No. 20 O.C.B., 7/6/17; L'pool. R., 25/9/17; F; 2/Lieut.
20 Victoria Avenue, Crosby, Nr. Liverpool.

TAYLOR, Walter
E/1590, 6/10/14; R.F.A., 12/10/14; F; Major; M.C., M(1).
Newlands, Leigham Court Road, Streatham, S.W.16.

TAYLOR, Webley Charles
6/2/6567, 30/9/15; trfr. W. York. R., 14/7/16.
Mrs. E. L. Taylor, China Inland Mission, Newington Green, N. (Now in China).

✠ TAYLOR, William Bruce
6/4/5668, 16/8/15; W. York. R., 6/7/16; 2/Lieut.
Died of wounds 17/4/17.

TAYLOR, William Henry
6/Sq/6371, 20/9/15, L/C.; No. 2 Cav. C/S, 1/1/17; Notts. and Derby. Yeo., 30/4/17, Herts. Yeo.; Lieut.
Drummonds Bank, 49 Charing Cross, S.W.1.

TAYLOR, William John
6/4/6105, 6/9/15, Sgt.; K.R. Rif. C., 5/5/16; F,It; Major; w(2).
Kinnersley, Granville Road, Barnet, Hertfordshire.

TAYLOR, William Lawrence
C/Sq/10822, 28/2/17, L/C.; No. 2 Cav. C/S, 11/1/18; 6th R. Regt. of Cav., 22/6/18; 2/Lieut.
Galleywood, Essex.

TAYLOR, William Leighton
6/2/7338, 9/11/15; Glouc. R., 4/8/16; F; Lieut.; w.
6 Bisenden Road, Croydon, Surrey.

TAYLOR, William Reginald
6/Sq/8666, 3/1/16; No. 2 Cav. C/S, 1/9/16; 9th R. Regt. of Cav., 20/12/16, att. 7th Huss.; M; Lieut.
Rolleston, Wallasey, Cheshire.

TAYLOR, William Robinson
6/4/5354, 31/7/15; E. Surr. R., 1/10/15, Indian Army; I; Staff Capt.
152 Hartfield Road, Wimbledon, S.W. (Now in India).

TAYLOR, Winthrop James Crosland-
F/3044, 15/3/15, Cpl.; R.N.V.R., 13/7/15; F; Lieut.; M.C.
The Gables, Wistaston, Nr. Crewe.

TAYLOR-JONES, William
6/2/7370, 10/11/15; Manch. R., 4/8/16; F,It; Lieut.
Rydal Mount, Prestwich, Manchester.

TAYLOUR, Alfred Robert
A/597, 11/1/12; 1st Lond. R., 27/9/14; F; Capt.; M(1).
5 New Square, Lincoln's Inn, W.C.2.

TAYNTON, Harry
6/2/9471, 14/2/16; Shrop. Yeo., 25/9/16; F; Lieut.
8 Henderson Road, Wandsworth Common, S.W.18.

TEAL, Fred Whiteley
D/Sq/10019, 27/11/16; No. 10 O.C.B., 5/10/17; Norf. R., 26/2/18; F; Lieut.; w.
The Lumb, Triangle, Nr. Halifax, Yorkshire.

TEARE, Robert Victor
Sq/3821, 29/5/15, L/C.; R.A.S.C., 29/7/15, R.E.; S; Major.
Paragon House, Dewsbury, Yorkshire.

TEBBUTT, Ernest
A/E/13967, 6/9/18; demob. 30/1/19.
Wellfield, Derby Road, Widnes, Lancashire.

TEBBUTT, Vivian Francis
6/2/5669, 16/8/15; North'n. R., 6/1/16; F; Lieut.; w.
14 Meriden Street, Coventry. (Now in India).

TEE, Frederick Walter
6/4/6232, 13/9/15; Durh. L.I., 21/12/15, att. T.M. Bty.; F,Germ.SWA; Capt.; w.
P.O. Box 640, Bloemfontein, South Africa.

✠ TEED, Henry Samuel
1/3520, 6/5/15, L/C.; R. Berks. R., 6/8/15; 2/Lieut.
Killed in action 24/7/16.

TEED, Thomas Westcott
B/756, 23/1/14; S. Staff. R., 11/9/14, att. Surr. Yeo. and Norf. Yeo., Army Cyc. Corps; F,E,P; Capt.; w.
73 Fawnbrake Avenue, Herne Hill, S.E.24.

TEEHAN, Patrick
6/8768, 6/1/16; Indian Army, 31/5/16; I,M; Capt.
New Ross, Ireland.

TEESDALE, Marmaduke
A/10190, 13/12/16, L/C.; H. Bde. O.C.B., 6/3/17; Suff. R., 26/6/17; F; Lieut.
The Gables, Walton-on-the-Hill, Surrey.

TELFER, William
A/13103, 22/5/18, L/C.; No. 8 O.C.B., 18/10/18; Yorks. L.I., 16/3/19; 2/Lieut.; M.C.
c/o State Assurance Coy., Dale Street, Liverpool.

TELFORD, Thomas
C/10203, 18/12/16; No. 20 O.C.B., 5/5/17; L'pool. R., 28/8/17; F; Lieut.; w.
5 Hood Crescent, Haverton Hill on Tees, Durham.

TEMPERLEY, Norman
C/97, 16/4/08; dis. 15/4/09.

TEMPEST, Ewart Vincent
3/3887, 31/5/15; W. York. R., 10/9/15; F; Capt.; w; D.S.O., M.C., M(3).
Pendragon, Lister Lane, Bradford, Yorkshire.

TEMPEST, John Ernest Edward
6/3/8769, 6/1/16; dis. med. unfit, 8/8/16.
Valley House, 112 Cardigan Street, Headingley, Leeds.

✠ TEMPLE, Edgar
2/3471, 3/5/15; S. Staff. R., 28/7/15, W. York. R., att. York R.; Lieut.
Killed in action 10/9/17.

TEMPLE, Percy
H/2/2574, 4/1/15, L/C.; R. Scots, 2/5/15; F; 2/Lieut.
82 Braybrooke Road, Hastings.

TEMPLER, Edmund Reginald
6/1/6720, 7/10/15; 20th Lond. R., 4/8/16; Lieut.

TENBOSCH, Lyman
Sq/1132, 9/9/14; Essex R., 16/9/14; Major; w.

TENCH, Richard John Ferdinand
4/Sq/4298, 17/6/15, L/C.; R.N.V.R., 29/11/15.
Woodside, Wallis Road, Waterlooville, Hampshire.

✠ TENNANT, Philip Eyre
6/5/C/8429, 15/12/15; No. 7 O.C.B., 4/11/16; Conn. Rang., 28/2/17, att. Lein. R.; 2/Lieut.
Killed in action 31/7/17.

TENNENT, John
B/12382, 14/1/18; No. 1 Cav. C/S, 16/5/18; 6th Drag., 14/2/19; 2/Lieut.
P.O. Box 12, Picksburg, Orange Free State, South Africa.

TENNENT, John Harvey
A/2/2907, 13/2/15, Cpl.; Rif. Brig., 17/7/15, att. R.A.F.; F; Capt.; M.C., M(1).
Eliot Vale House, Blackheath, S.E.3.

TENNENT, Maurice Balliscombe
A/11874, 16/8/17, L/C.; No. 14 O.C.B., 4/1/18; Rif. Brig., 25/6/18; 2/Lieut.
Eliot Vale, Blackheath, S.E.3.

✠ TERRELL, Arthur Clive
F/1874, 16/10/14; Midd'x. R., 20/2/15; 2/Lieut.
Died of wounds 20/4/17.

TERRELL, Arthur Koberwein á Beckett
146, 18/4/08; dis. 31/12/09; rej. 1134, 9/9/14, L/C.; R.F.A., 20/11/14; F; Capt.; w.
9 Beach Street, Penang, Straits Settlements.

✠ TERRELL, Claude Romako á Beckett
Sq/263, 27/5/08; dis. 26/5/12; R.F.A., 12/1/16; Capt.; M.C.
Died of wounds 10/6/17.

TERRELL, Thomas
6/1/5529, 9/8/15; R.N.V.R., 19/9/16.

✠ TERRY, Charles Warwick
B/E/D/13577, 19/7/18.
Died 5/11/18.

TERRY, Geoffrey Rouse
6/Sq/8846, 10/1/16; No. 2 Cav. C/S, 1/9/16; 11th R. Regt. of Cav., 20/12/16, North'd. Huss., att. North'd. Fus., R.A.F.; F; Lieut.
100 Cromwell Road, Hove, Sussex.

✠ TERRY, Leonard Alfred Hardwick
H/1707, 14/10/14, L/C.; R.E., 27/2/15, R.F.C.; Capt.
Killed in action 31/8/17.

✠ TERRY, Leslie Ryder
4/4350, 21/6/15; R. War. R., 17/10/15; Lieut. Died 7/8/19.

TERRY, Thomas Bertram
6/Sq/7089, 31/10/15, L/C.; No. 2 Cav. C/S, 1/9/16; 14th Huss., 20/12/16; M; Capt.
Fetterangus, Beresford Road, West Southbourne, Bournemouth.

TESTER, Leslie
1/3610, 13/5/15; York. & Lanc. R., 28/7/15; F,It; Capt.; M.C., M(2).
The Treasury, Lagos, Nigeria, West Africa.

APPENDIX II.—RECORDS OF RANK AND FILE.

TETLEY, John
6/8593, 3/1/16; R.A.O.C., 15/5/16; Lieut.
County Hall, Spring Gardens, S.W. 1.

TETLEY, Samuel
6/2/9267, 3/2/16, L/C.; No. 14 O.C.B., 26/11/16; W. York. R., 27/3/17; 2/Lieut. 136 Otley Road, Headingley, Leeds.

✠ TETLOW, Joseph
6/4/6075, 6/9/15, Cpl.; No. 11 O.C.B., 7/5/16; K.R. Rif. C., 4/9/16; Lieut.; w. Killed in action 25/8/18.

✠ TETLOW, Kenneth Burgess
6/1/7314, 8/11/15; No. 14 O.C.B.; Worc. R., 22/11/16; 2/Lieut.
Killed in action 21/3/18.

TEUTEN, Percy Theodore
1/3888, 31/5/15, Cpl.; A.S.C., C/S, 27/10/16; R.A.S.C., 20/12/16; M; Capt.; M(1). 104 Airedale Avenue, Chiswick, W. 4.

TEWSON, Edward George
A/9821, 31/10/16; R.G.A., C/S, 28/2/17; R.G.A., 26/5/17; Lieut.

THACKER, Ransley Samuel Patrick
A/566, 29/4/11.

THACKRAH, Arthur Reginald
A/638, 9/5/12; dis. 2/5/14; Lan. Fus., 1/9/14, Army Cyc. Corps; G,F,E; Capt.; M(1). 31 Becmead Avenue, Streatham, S.W. 16.

THALLON, Norman Hector
6/5/7812, 24/11/15; No. 8 O.C.B., 4/8/16; Suff. R., 27/11/16, Lab. Corps; Lieut.

THATCHER, Hubert Dozell
6/4/6315, 18/9/15, L/C.; R.W. Surr. R., 4/8/16; F; 2/Lieut.; w.
133 Ingleheart Road, Catford, S.E. 6.

THEAKSTON, Andrew
D/12128, 15/10/17; R.A.F., C/S, 21/5/18; General List, 5/3/19; 2/Lieut.

THEIS, Frank Albert
12354, 31/12/17; No. 15 O.C.B., 7/6/18; R.W. Kent R., 4/2/19; 2/Lieut. Ormehurst, Whitworth Road, South Norwood, S.E. 25.

✠ THEOBALD, Arnold
6/1/6802, 13/10/15; No. 9 O.C.B., 8/3/16; R. Scots, 23/7/16; F; Lieut.; w; M.C. Died 29/6/18.

THEOBALD, John Campbell
D/13938, 2/9/18; trfr. K.R. Rif. C., 25/4/19.
Brookvale, Shaldon, Teignmouth, Devonshire.

THOM, Andrew
B/10652, 2/2/17, L/C.; No. 14 O.C.B., 7/6/17; York. & Lanc. R., 25/9/17, Indian Army; I,S; Lieut.
The Villa, New Road, Shepperton-on-Thames.

THOM, Frederic Robert
6/5/C/9015, 19/1/16; No. 7 O.C.B., 4/11/16; Ches. R., 28/2/17, D. of Corn. L.I.; P; Lieut.
Reynella, Killucan, Co. Westmeath, Ireland.

THOMAS, Alan Ernest Wentworth
6/3/5804, 23/8/15; R.W. Kent R., 9/1/16; F; Capt.; w(4); D.S.O., M.C., M(1). New University Club, St. James Street, S.W. 1.

THOMAS, Alwyne Bell Wyndham
A/12174, 29/10/17; demob. 29/1/19.
Old Court, Cranleigh, Surrey.

THOMAS, Aubrey Ralph
A/64, 8/4/08; dis. 7/4/10.
30 Narbourne Avenue, Clapham, S.W. 4.

THOMAS, Bert
C/11758, 26/7/17; No. 14 O.C.B., 4/1/17; R.W. Fus., 25/6/18, att. R. Suss. R.; F; 2/Lieut.; w.
Beech House, Chirk, North Wales.

THOMAS, Cecil Edwin
C/B/13335, 19/6/18; demob. 22/1/19.
30 Windsor Terrace, Beckton, E. 16.

THOMAS, Cecil James
A/13104, 22/5/18, L/C.; trfr. K.R. Rif. C., 7/4/19.
Lodge Croft, Fradley, Nr. Lichfield, Staffordshire.

THOMAS, Charles George
C/10170, 11/12/16, L/C.; R.G.A., C/S, 15/8/17; R.G.A., 31/12/17; 2/Lieut. 28 Hill Lane, Southampton.

THOMAS, Charles Leslie
6/1/6596, 4/10/15, L/C.; M.G.C., C/S, 25/10/16; M.G.C., 24/2/17; F; Lieut.; w. 6 Dynevor Avenue, Neath, South Wales.

THOMAS, Charles Stanley
6/4/8399, 14/12/15, L/C.; No. 14 O.C.B., 27/9/16; Welch R., 18/12/16; 2/Lieut.; p.

THOMAS, Charles William
E/1560, 6/10/14, L/C.; D. of Corn. L.I., 27/11/14; Capt.
The Elm, Park Hill Road, Sidcup, Kent.

THOMAS, Christopher Joseph
E/2818, 29/1/15; R. Fus., 29/4/15.
12 Bedford Place, Russell Square, W.C. 1.

THOMAS, Daniel Martin
6/8446, 16/12/15; R.A., C/S, 24/1/16; R.F.A., 6/7/16; Lieut.
Banc y nos, Llanwrda, Camarthenshire.

THOMAS, David Arnold
6/8853, 11/1/16; R.F.A., C/S, 23/6/16; R.F.A., 19/1/17; F; Lieut.; w; Croix de Guerre (Belge).
Brynhill, Penylan, Cardiff.

THOMAS, Dennis
6/5/9416, 21/1/16; R.F.A., C/S, 1/9/16; R.F.A., 15/12/16; Lieut.
Lynden, New Road, Llanelly.

THOMAS, Douglas Lafayette
D/13005, 29/4/18; demob. 24/1/19.
Llewyn Onn, Porth, Rhondda, South Wales.

THOMAS, Douglas Walter
4/5/5216, 29/7/15, L/C.; R.W. Fus., 24/6/18, R.A.F.; F; Capt.; w; M.C.
460 Fulham Palace Road, Fulham, S.W. 6. (Now in Argentina.)

THOMAS, Edward Kenneth
4/1/5085, 26/7/15, Cpl.; dis. med. unfit, 13/11/16.
9 Turney Road, Streatham Hill, S.W. 2.

THOMAS, Edward Miall
6/2/8319, 11/12/15; No. 14 O.C.B., 27/9/16; Mon. R., 27/3/17; Lieut. Gracswen, Cardiff.

THOMAS, Emrys Acron
6/5/5543, 11/8/15; 20th Lond. R., 28/1/16, secd. Tank Corps; Lieut.; w.

THOMAS, Frank Everett
C/D/12057, 27/9/17; Indian Army, 8/10/18, Welch R.; 2/Lieut.
Glen Usk, Mantle Street, Wellington, Somerset.

THOMAS, Frederick James
A/10730, 12/2/17; No. 1 Cav. C/S, 5/7/17; Derby. Yeo., 26/2/18; 2/Lieut.
Abergweli Vicarage, Abergweli, Nr. Carmarthen, Wales.

THOMAS, George Canton
4/3/4431, 24/6/15; R. War. R., 29/11/15; F; 2/Lieut.; w.
25 Starbuck Road, Milford Haven, Pembrokeshire.

THOMAS, Harvey Albert
A/1706, 13/10/14; dis. 27/10/14

THOMAS, Henry Munro
K/H/2521, 31/12/14, L/C.; Welch R., 26/8/15; F; Lieut.
Walton Pines, Clevedon, Somerset.

THOMAS, Herbert James
C/186, 1/5/08; dis. 30/4/09.

THOMAS, Herbert William
6/8320, 11/12/15; R.E., 10/5/16; Lieut.
24 Trafalgar Terrace, Swansea.

THOMAS, Hubert Oglesby
C/12583, 6/2/18; No. 16 O.C.B., 5/7/18; demob. 14/1/19.
6 St David's Avenue, Carmarthen, South Wales.

THOMAS, Ithel
6/1/6153, 9/9/15; dis. med. unfit, 21/7/16.
Ty Draw, Llanfair Road, Penygraig, Glamorganshire.

THOMAS, John
A/B/D/12175, 29/10/17; No. 17 O.C.B., 10/5/18; Ches. R., 3/2/19; 2/Lieut. 23 Beaufort Drive, Wallasey, Cheshire.

THOMAS, John Arthur Marlow
A/Sq/D/13065, 13/5/18; trfr. K.R. Rif. C., 25/4/19.
Woodlands, Hadley Road, Middlesex.

THOMAS, Kempson Frederick Welman
4/6/5/3908, 31/5/15; Welch R., 22/1/16, Indian Army; P,M,I; Capt. c/o Cox & Coy., Bombay, India.

✠ THOMAS, Kenneth
D/1412, 29/9/14, Cpl.; K.R. Rif. C., 27/11/14; F; Capt.
Killed in action 3/6/16.

THOMAS, Lechmere Cay
4/5/4703, 8/7/15; E. Surr. R., 29/11/15; Lieut.; M.C. and Bar, M(1). Dynevor Avenue, Neath, South Wales.

APPENDIX II.—RECORDS OF RANK AND FILE.

THOMAS, Leonard Rhys
C/210, 8/5/08; Lond. Univ. O.T.C., 1/7/09, R.A.S.C.; G,M,Persia; Lt. Col.; D.S.O., M(2).
Services Club, Stratford Place, W.

THOMAS, Leslie Clason
6/4/7851, 25/11/15; No. 14 O.C.B., 26/11/16; Welch R., 28/2/17; Lieut.
Pencacran, Neath, South Wales.

THOMAS, Lewis Rosser
6/5/8863, 12/1/16; No. 8 O.C.B., 4/8/16; K.R. Rif. C., 21/11/16; F; Lieut.; w.
59 Bateman Street, Cambridge.

THOMAS, Meredith Dillon
D/1445, 29/9/14; 14th Lond. R., 13/11/14; p.
Box Grove, Guildford, Surrey.

✠ THOMAS, Reginald Ernest
6/1/Sq/5670, 16/8/15; R.A., C/S, 12/1/17; R.G.A., 8/4/17; 2/Lieut.
Killed in action 13/9/18.

THOMAS, Reginald James
4/2/4315, 17/6/15; Bedf. R., 6/11/15, Leic. R.; F; Lieut.; w(2).
150 Maldon Road, Colchester, Essex.

THOMAS, Reginald Lloyd
A/14001, 13/9/18; demob. 30/1/19.
29 Broomfield Road, Heaton Moor, Stockport.

✠ THOMAS, Reginald Spenser Dudley
6/1/8400, 14/12/15; No. 13 O.C.B., 4/11/16; R.W. Fus., 28/2/17; F; 2/Lieut.
Killed in action, 18/9/18.

THOMAS, Ronald Llewellyn
A/1724, 15/10/14; Welch R., 24/12/14, R.A.F.; G,E,I; Capt.
Maescynrig, Merthyr Tydfil.

THOMAS, Rowland William
C/D/12255, 26/11/17; No. 16 O.C.B., 7/6/18; trfr. 28th Lond. R., 13/9/18.
Plas Morfa, Greenfield, Holywell, Flintshire.

THOMAS, Samuel Joyce
6/8497, 20/12/15; A.S.C., C/S, 5/6/16; R.A.S.C., 9/7/16; F,It; Lieut.
Lamb Building, Temple, E.C.4. (Now in British West Indies).

✠ THOMAS, Stanley Meredith. See MEREDITH-THOMAS, S.

THOMAS, Stephen Kerr
1/3567, 10/5/15; Dorset R., 28/7/15, att. Som. L.I.; Lieut.; w.
40 Hampstead Way, N.W.11.

THOMAS, Sydney Herbert
A/10483, 12/1/17; R.A., C/S. 27/4/17; R.G.A., 1/9/17; F; Lieut.
63 Old Lodge Lane, Purley, Surrey.

THOMAS, Thomas Emlyn
6/5/C/8041, 30/11/15; trfr. R.W. Fus., 9/11/16; F; Cpl.
Groes Farm, Nr. Bridgend, Glamorgan, South Wales.

THOMAS, Trevor Frederick Felix
6/2/Sq/6784, 11/10/15; R.A., C/S, 9/2/17; R.G.A., 31/5/17, att. R.A.F.; F; Major; g; M(1).
Ki Orah, 61 Redlands Road, Penarth, Glamorganshire.

THOMAS, Thomas John
4/4163, 10/6/15; R.E., 17/8/15; F; Lieut.
Stradey Road, Furnace, Llanelly, South Wales.

THOMAS, Tudor Mansel
C/10166, 11/12/16; trfr. Class W. Res., 31/5/17.
18 Penylan Place, Cardiff.

THOMAS, Walter Percy
4/1/4057, 7/6/15; 1st Lond. R., 28/10/15; Lieut.

THOMAS, William
C/10360, 5/1/17; No. 21 O.C.B., 5/5/17; S. Lan. R., 28/8/17, att. Som. L.I. and R.E.; P; Lieut.
46 High Street, Cymmer Porth, Rhondda.

THOMAS, William Arthur
6/3/5423, 5/8/15, L/C.; Bedf. R., 22/11/15, secd. K. Af. Rif.; F,EA; Lieut.; w(2).
38 Loraine Road, N.7.

THOMAS, William Gethin
4/1/5055, 22/7/15; R.F.A., 16/11/15; F; Capt.; w.
Emporium, Brynamman, Carmarthen, South Wales.

THOMAS, William Henry
D/E/13909, 26/8/18; demob. 10/1/19.
Linton, 185 Bacup Road, Clough End, Manchester.

THOMAS, William Vivian
C/11529, 18/6/17; R.F.C., C/S, 2/8/17; R.F.C 8/9/17, R.A.F.; 2/Lieut.
Pentilla, Fitzalan Road, Church End, Finchley, N.3.

THOMAS, Wynn ap Howel
C/44, 6/4/08; dis. 5/4/10; rej. C/1353, 26/9/14; R.A.S.C., 6/10/14; F; Major; M(2).
40 Goldhurst Terrace, Hampstead, N.W.6.

THOM-POSTLETHWAITE, Andrew Cecil Scott
D/1479, 29/9/14; Bedf. R., 10/3/15; F; 2/Lieut.; resigned and rejoined R.G.A., Bdr.
2 Rodway Road, Bromley, Kent.

THOMPSON, Alfred Augustus
A/B/C/D/12149, 22/10/17; No. 1 O.C.B., 10/5/18; R. Lanc. R., 29/10/18; 2/Lieut.
Kay Green Lane, Birdwell, Nr. Barnsley.

THOMPSON, Alfred Irwin
6/3/9300, 3/2/16; No. 7 O.C.B., 4/11/16; trfr. 18th Lond. R., 2/2/17.
Brookmount, Londonderry, Ireland.

THOMPSON, Arthur Clement
4/1/5047, 22/7/15; Midd'x. R., 16/12/15; F; Capt.; w(3); M.C.
Horsted, Talton Road, Forest Town, Johannesburg, South Africa.

THOMPSON, Arthur Cyril
4/2/4102, 7/6/15; E. Surr. R., 10/9/15, Leic. Yeo.; F; Lieut.
c/o The London and River Plate Bank, Valparaiso, Chile, South America.

THOMPSON, Arthur Thomas Fraser
B/3075, 18/3/15; R.F.C., 12/8/15, North'n. R.; Lieut.

THOMPSON, Austen Gilchrist
C/1002, 5/8/14; S. Lan. R., 19/9/14; S; Capt.; w; M.C., Greek Military Cross.
Hayes Rectory, Kent. (Now in India).

THOMPSON, Brian Trail
B/13585, 22/7/18; demob. 29/1/19.
3 Finchley Avenue, Hendon Lane, Finchley, N.3.

THOMPSON, Cyprian Edmund
B/11068, 16/4/17; R.F.C., C/S, 2/8/17; R.F.C., 8/9/17, R.A.F.; E,F; Lieut.
12 Long Street, Cape Town, South Africa.

THOMPSON, Edgar Pullein
6/8945, 17/1/16; dis. med. unfit, 31/5/16.
Newnham Rectory, Baldock, Hertfordshire.

THOMPSON, Edward Leslie
4/2/4386, 22/6/15, L/C.; R.A.S.C., 29/11/15; F,M; Lieut.
Sunny Bank, The Norcholme, Gainsborough, Lincolnshire.

✠ THOMPSON, Francis Clement
H/2514, 7/1/15; R.F.A., 28/4/15; G,E,F; Lieut.
Died of wounds 3/10/17.

✠ THOMPSON, Frederic George
6/1/7703, 22/11/15; No. 8 O.C.B., 4/8/16; Bedf. R., 24/10/16; F; 2/Lieut.
Killed in action 11/4/17.

THOMPSON, Frederick George
A/10826, 1/3/17; R.F.A., C/S, 24/8/17; R.F.A., 4/2/18; F; 2/Lieut.
24 Greenway, Bromley Common, Kent.

THOMPSON, Geoffrey John
A/915, 5/8/14; Essex R., 12/9/14; F; Capt.; M.C., M(1).
69 Belsize Park Gardens, Hampstead, N.W.3.

✠ THOMPSON, George Eric
6/5/5274, 31/7/15; L'pool. R., 6/12/15; F; 2/Lieut.
Killed in action 3/9/16.

✠ THOMPSON, Harold
C/928, 5/8/14; North'n. R., 15/8/14; F; Lieut.
Killed in action 9/5/15.

THOMPSON, Harold Francis
F/1859, 16/10/14; S. Staff. R., 17/3/15; Lieut.
17 Mount Pleasant Road, Saffron Walden.

THOMPSON, Harral
6/4/9075, 21/1/16; No. 5 O.C.B., 14/8/16; Manch. R., 18/12/16; F; Lieut.
51 Chestnut Grove, Bootle, Liverpool.

THOMPSON, Herbert Darbyshire
A/B/D/12498, 28/1/18, L/C.; R.A.F., C/S, 21/5/18; demob. 30/5/19.
Hampsthwaite, Harrogate, Yorkshire.

THOMPSON, Hugh Richard
A/14091, 21/9/18; demob. 29/1/19.
1 Rus-in-Urbe, Kingstown, Ireland.

THOMPSON, James
6/2/7704, 22/11/15; No. 14 O.C.B., 28/8/16; R. Lanc. R., 18/12/16, R.G.A.; F; Staff Capt.; w.
The Stockwell Brewery, Stockwell, S.W.

THOMPSON, James Douglas
6/5/9412, 9/2/16; R.F.A., C/S, 4/8/16; Interpreter, 29/11/16; S,SR; Capt.; M.B.E., Order of S. Stanislaus (Russia).
11 Pierremont Crescent, Darlington, Co. Durham.

APPENDIX II.—RECORDS OF RANK AND FILE.

THOMPSON, John Daniel
C/13342, 14/6/18; demob. 24/1/19.
97 Lower Beechwood Avenue, Co. Dublin.

THOMPSON, John Foster
Sq/3020, 8/3/15; 3rd Drag. Gds., 22/4/15. att. Tank Corps; F,SR; Capt.; O.B.E., Order of S. Anne (Russia). M(1).
Hannington, Nr. Basingstoke, Hampshire.

THOMPSON, Maurice Fielding
6/8227, 10/12/15; dis. med. unfit, 23/6/16.
Thurnley, Strawberry Hill, Twickenham.

THOMPSON, Maurice Scott
A/873, 4/8/14; Durh. L.I., 19/9/14, Intelligence; F,S; Capt.; O.B.E., Serbian White Eagle, M(4).
College Cottage, Reigate Heath.

THOMPSON, Miles Atkinson
Sq/3001, 3/3/15; Linc. Yeo., 24/8/15; Capt.
Willington Club, Grosvenor Place, S.W.

THOMPSON, Percy Thirlwall
A/11895, 20/8/17; A.S.C., C/S, 4/3/18; R.A.S.C., 12/5/18; S; Lieut.
Hathaway, Cressington Park, Liverpool.

THOMPSON, Peter Benjamin
D/Sq/11845, 9/8/17, L/C.; No. 1 Cav. C/S, 28/2/18; R. Regt. of Cav., 28/8/18; 2/Lieut.
c/o Standard Bank of South Africa, 10 Clements Lane, E.C.

THOMPSON, Raymond Percival
4/1/4373, 21/6/15, Cpl.; Worc. R., 23/12/15, emp. M. of Munitions; Lieut.; w.

✠ THOMPSON, Reginald
D/1407, 29/9/14; E. Lan. R., 7/11/14; Lieut.
Killed in action 23/10/16.

THOMPSON, Reginald Campbell
C/173, 20/4/08; dis. 19/4/13; General List, 2/1/15, Intelligence; M; Capt.; M(3).
Milburn Lodge, Boars Hill, Oxford.

✠ THOMPSON, Richard Henry Vaughan
A/1046, 31/8/14; R. Fus., 12/9/14; Capt.; M(1).
Killed in action 26/9/16.

THOMPSON, Richard Lowe
A/11658, 12/7/17, L/C.; No. 14 O.C.B., 7/12/17; 7th Lond. R., 28/5/18; F; 2/Lieut.
Westbrook House, Boxford, Newbury, Berkshire.

✠ THOMPSON, Roger Eykyn
Sq/1293, 24/9/14, Cpl.; Hamps. Yeo., 11/11/14, Hamps. R.; F; Capt.
Killed in action 12/4/18.

THOMPSON, Rupert Spens
C/12645, 22/2/18; trfr. R.A.F., 4/5/18.
Garthlands, Reigate Heath, Surrey.

THOMPSON, Thomas Anthony William
6/D/6508, 30/9/15, C.Q.M.S.; R.A.O.C., 16/10/16; Major, D.A.D.O.S.
15 Romer Road, Fairfield, Liverpool.

THOMPSON, William Eccles
D/11149, 24/4/17; No. 14 O.C.B., 10/8/17; Oxf. & Bucks. L.I., 27/11/17, att. Glouc. R.; S,E; Lieut.
Pontesbury, Robertson Road, Buxton, Derbyshire.

THOMPSON, William George
2/3330, 17/4/15; 20th Lond. R., 19/9/15, R.A.O.C.; F,S,P; Capt.; w.
17 Hillmorton Paddox, Rugby.

THOMPSON, William Outram
C/600, 22/1/12, L/C.; N. Lan. R., 11/9/14; w.
5a Streatham Place, Streatham Hill, S.W.2.

THOMPSON-BOLE, Charles William
C/A/11530, 18/6/17; dis. med. unfit, 15/4/18.
c/o Nat. Bank of South Africa, London Wall, E.C.

THOMSON, Albert
A/Sq/C/14099, 4/10/18; No. 11 O.C.B., 31/1/19; General List, 8/3/19; 2/Lieut.
Hotel Reina, Cristina, Gibraltar.

THOMSON, Alexander Ernest
D/10679, 5/2/17; No. 11 O.C.B., 5/7/17; Durh. L.I., 30/10/17; F; Lieut.; w.
Strathendrick, Falkirk, N.B.

THOMSON, Charles Dargavill
6/3/5395, 5/8/15, L/C.; No. 9 O.C.B., 5/6/16; High. L.I., 4/9/16; Lieut.; p.
The Studio, 22 West Kensington Gardens, W.14.

✠ THOMSON, Cyril Ground
K/Sq/2715, 18/1/15, L/C.; W. Som. Yeo., 10/4/15; G,E,P,F; Capt.; w-g; M.C.
Killed 22/9/18.

THOMSON, Douglas
B/207, 6/5/08; dis. 5/5/12.
21 Eaton Rise, Ealing, W.5.

THOMSON, Edwin Victor Coats
D/12113, 11/10/17; A.S.C., C/S, 10/12/17; R.A.S.C., 3/2/18; F; 2/Lieut.
c/o Messrs. Evatt & Coy., 2 Wedd Quay, Penang, Straits Settlements.

THOMSON, Ian Kenneth
A/2934, 15/2/15, L/C.; York. R., 5/6/15, att. R. Lanc. R.; F,S; Lieut.; w. M(2).
Burgie House, Forres Morayshire, Scotland

✠ THOMSON, James
4/5/4767, 12/7/15; Bord. R., 20/11/15; Capt.
Killed in action 31/8/17.

THOMSON, James Scott
A/13952, 4/9/18; demob. 31/1/19.
1 Broomhill Avenue, Paistick, Glasgow.

THOMSON, John Leslie Leopold
6/1/7122, 1/11/15; M.G.C., C/S, 1/2/17, No. 12 O.C.B.; R. Berks. R., 25/9/17, att. R.A.F.; F; 2/Lieut.
43 Anson Road, Tufnell Park, N.7.

THOMSON, John Sydney
6/2/8097, 1/12/15, Cpl.; R.F.C., C/S, 1/2/17; R.F.C., 4/4/17.
Bohemia, Finchley.

THOMSON, John Wallace
B/11406, 30/5/17; R.F.C., C/S, 2/8/17; R.F.C., 8/9/17, R.A.F.; Lieut.
114 Lantwich Road, Crewe.

THOMSON, Leonard
4/6/2/4986, 19/7/15; 22nd Lond. R., 14/12/15; Lieut.
88 Victoria Avenue, Southend-on-Sea.

THOMSON, Ralph Paul
B/13618, 24/7/18; No. 11 O.C.B., 24/1/19; demob. 3/2/19.
152 Marylebone Road, N.W.1.

THOMSON, Robert
4/1/4836, 15/7/15; Gord. Highrs., 22/11/15, att. High. L.I.; S; Lieut.
1 Church Street, Buckhaven, Fife, N.B.

✠ THOMSON, Robert
6/8512, 29/12/15; No. 9 O.C.B., 8/3/16; R. Scots, 23/7/16; F; Lieut.; w.
Died of wounds 20/9/19.

✠ THOMSON, Spencer
E/1581, 6/10/14; R. Fus., 8/10/14; Capt.; M.C.
Killed in action 24/4/17

✠ THOMSON, Walter Halton
F/2639, 11/1/15; High. L.I., 22/4/15; F; 2/Lieut.
Killed in action 3/7/16.

THOMSON, William Barr
D/E/13940, 2/9/18; demob. 11/1/19.
Rosendene, Woodland Avenue, Toller Road, Stoneygate, Leicester.

THOMSON, William Frederick John
A/10277, 1/1/17; No. 20 O.C.B., 7/6/17; W. Rid. R., 25/9/17; It; 2/Lieut.; M.C., Croce di Guerra.
230 Strand, W.C.2.

THORLEY, Francis Leonard
C/11531, 18/6/17, L/C.; No. 14 O.C.B., 9/11/17; York. & Lanc. R., 30/4/18; 2/Lieut.
Church House, Leigh, Stoke-on-Trent.

✠ THORN, George Frederick
6/Sq/5639, 16/8/15, L/C.; R.F.A., C/S, 4/8/16; R.F.A., 15/12/16; Capt.; M.C. and Bar.
Killed 1919.

THORNBER, Cyril
A/9837, 3/11/16, L/C.; R.A., C/S, 4/4/17; R.G.A., 1/10/17; Lieut.

THORNE, Arnold
6/3/8888, 13/1/16; R.A., C/S, 4/8/16; R.G.A., 12/11/16; F; Lieut.
St. Andries, 10 Cranes Park Avenue, Surbiton, Surrey.

THORNE, Ralph Gerard Athol
A/1181, 14/9/14; S. Lan. R., 15/8/14, att. N. Lan. R.; Capt.
23 Lowndes Square, S.W.1.

THORNE, Reginald Frederic
6/5/7963, 29/11/15; No. 14 O.C.B., 27/9/16; R.A.S.C., 9/1/17; F; Lieut.
112 Abbey Road, N.W.6.

THORNELOE, Joseph Eric
1/3611, 13/5/15; Worc. R., 21/8/15; F; Capt.; M.C. and Bar.
White Lodge, Knighton Road, Leicester.

APPENDIX II.—RECORDS OF RANK AND FILE.

THORNELOE, Thomas Bernard Callis
6/Sq/7280, 8/11/15; R.F.A., C/S, 4/8/16; trfr. Class W. Res., 29/9/16.
White Lodge, Knighton Road, Leicester.

THORNEYCROFT, Gerald Hamo
C/14242, 28/10/18; demob. 29/1/19. Penn, Wolverhampton.

THORNHILL, Clement
6/3/7123, 1/11/15; R.E., C/S, 5/8/16; R.E., 20/10/16.
15 Tantallon Road, Balham, S.W.12.

✠ THORNS, Francis Joseph
1/3207, 8/4/15; R. Berks. R., 21/8/15; F; 2/Lieut.
Killed in action 31/5/16.

THORNTON, Arthur Yule Smith
6/1/6957, 21/10/15; E Kent Yeo., 4/9/16, att. E. Kent R.; Lieut.
Arcadia, 56 Herongate Road, Wanstead, E.12.

✠ THORNTON, Douglas Saville
6/3/5487, 9/8/15, L/C.; Notts. & Derby. R., 21/4/16; 2/Lieut.
Killed in action 1/10/16.

THORNTON, Nigel Heber
A/1274, 23/9/14; R.E., 15/8/14; F; Staff Major; w; Croix de Guerre (French).
Birkin Lodge, Camden Park, Tunbridge Wells, Kent.

THORNTON, William George
B/11713, 19/7/17; No. 14 O.C.B., 4/1/18; E. Kent R., 25/6/18; 2/Lieut.
56 Northwick Road, Evesham, Worcestershire.

✠ THORNTON-SMITH, Arthur Donald
6/3/8042, 30/11/15, L/C.; K.R. Rif. C., 4/9/16; F; Capt.; D.S.O., M(1).
Killed in action 16/8/17.

THOROGOOD, John William
4/2/4242, 14/6/15; Midd'x. R., 22/8/15; Lieut.; w.
2 Kerrison Lodge, Ealing. W.5.

THORP, Gerald Dixon
6/1/8976, 17/1/16; No. 14 O.C.B., 26/11/16; Lan. Fus., 27/3/17; F; Lieut.
Waldershaigh, Bolsterstone, Nr. Sheffield.

THORP, Robert Gordon
D/11024, 4/4/17; No. 14 O.C.B., 10/8/17; Hunt. Cyc. Bn., 27/11/17, att. Bedf. R.; 2/Lieut.
50 Sutton Court, Chiswick, W.4.

THORP, Sam
4/5/4820, 12/7/15; Manch. R., 6/12/15; secd. R.E.; F; Capt.
12 Gladstone Road, Chesterfield.

THORP, Tom Evans
A/10081, 1/12/16; No. 14 O.C.B., 5/3/17; L'pool. R., 26/6/17; F; Lieut.
Belmont, Norman Road, Stalybridge, Cheshire.

THORPE, Alfred John
B/9909, 13/11/16, L/C.; No. 14 O.C.B., 6/4/17; R. Lanc. R., 31/7/17; F; Capt.; w.
c/o The Leopoldina Rly Coy., Ltd., Caixa 291, Rio de Janeiro, Brazil

THORPE, Charles
4/3/4243, 14/6/15; R. Lanc. R., 3/1/16; Lieut.
15 Trafalgar Road, Pendleton, Manchester.

THORPE, Colin Reynell
6/4/8847, 10/1/16; No. 14 O.C.B., 28/8/16; Manch. R., 18/12/16; Lieut.
St. George's Vicarage, Stockport.

THORPE, Francis Cedric Alexander
6/3/6705, 7/10/15, Cpl.; R.F.C., C/S, 1/2/17; R.F.C., 9/5/17, R.A.F.; Lieut.
131 South End, Croydon, Surrey.

THORPE, Frederic John
K/F/2428, 21/12/14; Leic. R., 22/4/15; M,P; Staff Capt.; w; M(1).
The Technical Institute, Wellingborough.

✠ THORPE, Norman John
6/2/6494, 27/9/15; No. 7 O.C.B., 6/4/16; Hamps. R., 17/7/16, att. M.G.C.; 2/Lieut.
Killed in action 12/5/17.

THORPE, Walter Langford
D/10921, 20/3/17; R.F.A., C/S, 24/8/17; R.F.A., 4/2/18; F; Lieut.
Knockroe House, New Ross, Co. Wexford.

THRALE, Richard Alwen
4/Sq/5048, 22/7/15, L/C.; No. 2 Cav. C/S, 31/3/16; Bedf. Yeo., 11/8/16, att. York. Drag. Yeo.; Lieut.; w.
Shirley Lodge, Shirley, Croydon.

THRAVES, Frank Haworth
6/5/5960, 1/9/15; L'pool. R., 1/6/16; Lieut.; w.
113 Ullet Road, Sefton Park, Liverpool.

THRELFALL, Charles Herbert
6/5/D/9367, 7/2/16, L/C.; Garr. O.C.B., 23/5/17; Suff. R., 18/8/17; Lieut.
Kenwood, 50 Anerley Road, Anerley, S.E.20.

THRELFALL, Henry Charles
C/13257, 10/6/18, L/C.; demob. 14/2/19.
Elm Road North, Prenton, Birkenhead.

✠ THRELFALL, John Alexander
6/5/7423, 12/11/15; L'pool. R., 4/8/16; 2/Lieut.
Died of wounds 10/5/18.

THRELFALL, Walter
A/D/11964, 3/9/17; R.F.A., C/S, 15/3/18; R.F.A.; 2/Lieut.
3 Northcote Road, Preston, Lancashire.

THRELKELD, Thomas Percy
6/Sq/7124, 1/11/15; R.A., C/S, 31/3/16; R.G.A., 6/7/16; Capt.; w.
31 Leinster Gardens, Lancaster Gate, W.2.

✠ THRING, Ashton Edward
6/Sq/5687, 16/8/15; R.F.A., 25/11/15; 2/Lieut. Died 9/2/17.

THROCKMORTON, Geoffrey William Barclay
Sq/319, 15/7/08; dis. 14/7/12; rej. Sq/885, 5/8/14; Berks. Yeo., 26/8/14; E,G,P; Staff Capt.; w(2); M(1).
18 Milner Street, Lennox Gardens, S.W.1.

THRUPP, Anthony Robert
4/3988, 3/6/15; Manch. R., 2/1/16; F; Lieut.; w.
60a Church Road, Hove, Sussex.

THRUSSELL, Henry Charles Murray
4/3/4142, 10/6/15; trfr. 13th Lond. R., 2/5/16.

THURBURN, Cecil Augustus Boyd
6/1/9389, 8/2/16; No. 8 O.C.B., 27/5/16; Notts. & Derby. R., 21/11/16; Lieut.; w.
Effra, Bedwordine Road, Norwood, S.E.19.

THURGOOD, Cyril Franklin
B/13494, 8/7/18; trfr. 14th Lond. R., 6/12/18.
Crumps, Sawbridgeworth, Hertfordshire.

THURGOOD, Cyril James
F/2643, 11/1/15; Notts. & Derby. R., 3/6/15, R.G.A.; F; Lieut.; w.
Noel Cottage, Much Hadham, Hertfordshire.

THURLOW, Jack
B/12428, 17/1/18, L/C.; No. 7 O.C.B., 9/8/18; R.W. Kent R.; 2/Lieut.
The Durdans, Stowmarket, Suffolk.

THURSFIELD, Alfred Henry Grosvenor
6/Sq/8375, 13/12/15; No. 1 Cav. C/S, 2/8/16; Worc. Yeo., 27/11/16; E; Lieut.
Lea House, Kidderminster, Worcestershire.

THWAITE, Frank
B/10110, 4/12/16; No. 14 O.C.B., 6/4/17; R. War. R., 31/7/17, M.G.C.; F,It; Lieut.
9 Harvard Court, West Hampstead, N.W.6.

✠ THWAITES, Charles Bertram
6/4/5865, 26/8/15; trfr. Fife & Forfar Yeo., 9/3/16, R. Highrs.; F; Pte.
Killed in action 29/9/16.

THYNNE, Richard Granville
Sq/1226, 16/9/14; 1st Life Gds., 1/10/14, Scots Gds.; F; Lieut.
c/o Messrs. Drummond, 49 Charing Cross, S.W.1.

TIBBETTS, Joseph Lister
6/1/7813, 24/11/15; R.F.C., 2/6/16, R.A.F.; F; Lieut.; p.
Blythswood, Barnsley, Yorkshire.

TIBBETTS, Walter Philip
6/3/Sq/9019, 20/1/16; R.A., C/S, 26/10/16; R.G.A., 19/2/17; F; Lieut.; w; M(1).
Bank of England, E.C.

TIBBITT, Eric Montague
E/1495, 1/10/14, L/C.; General List, 17/3/15, Midd'x. R., M.G.C.; F; Major; M(1).
18 Carleton Road, Tufnell Park, N.7. (Now in Honduras).

TIBBITT, Walter Tracey
6/D/7371, 10/11/15; Garr. O.C.B., 23/5/17; Suff. R., 18/8/17, att. S. Staff. R.; I; Lieut. 18 Carleton Road, Tufnell Park, N.7.

TICE, Alan Benjamin Lucas
C/13215, 5/6/18; trfr. 14th Lond. R., 6/12/18.
4 Granville Road, Littlehampton, Sussex.

✠ TICKLE, Andrew Brown
6/4/5783, 23/8/15; L'pool. R., 16/12/15; Lieut.
Killed in action 14/7/17.

TICKLE, Frank Charles
A/11264, 11/5/17; No. 14 O.C.B., 5/10/17; Midd'x. R., 26/2/18; 2/Lieut.
Oldbury, Wealdstone, Harrow.

TIDD, Geoffrey Maurice
6/A/8667, 3/1/16, Cpl.; H. Bde. O.C.B., 6/3/17; Dorset R., 29/5/17, att. 25th Lond. R.; I; Lieut.
Enfield, College Road, Dulwich, S.E.21. (Now in F.M.S.).

340

APPENDIX II.—RECORDS OF RANK AND FILE.

✠ TIDDY, *Claude Julian*
6/2/6928, 19/10/15, L/C.; No. 14 O.C.B., 29/8/16; dis. to R. Mil. Coll., 23/1/17; Dorset R., 21/12/17; F; Lieut.; w.
Killed in action 11/8/18.

TIDDY, *Edwin Healy*
6/2/6215, 13/9/15, L/C.; 21st Lond. R., 6/6/16; Lieut.; w(2).
14 Church Road, Forest Hill, S.E. 23.

TIDMAN, *Sydney Thomas*
6/4/9081, 24/1/16; R.A., C/S, 4/8/16; R.G.A., 3/11/16; F; Lieut.
27 Maple Road, Leytonstone, Essex.

TILEY, *Alfred George*
2/3889, 31/5/15; dis. med. unfit, 29/10/15; re-enlisted, Lab. Corps; Pte.
44 Albion Road, Dalston, E. 8.

✠ TILEY, *George Charles*
2/3800, 27/5/15; N. Lan. R., 10/9/15; F; 2/Lieut.
Killed in action 21/10/16.

TILL, *Stanley James*
4/1/4328, 19/6/15, L/C.; R.F.A., 30/9/15; F; Capt.; w; M.C., M(2).
52 Queen Victoria Street, E.C. 4.

TILLETT, *Frederick Reginald*
A/13961, 6/9/18; dis. med. unfit, 5/4/19.
Glenale, 234 Romford Road, Forest Gate, E. 7.

✠ TILLETT, *Reginald Alfred William*
6/Sq/6867, 18/10/15; Glouc. Huss., 17/1/16, att. R.F.C.; 2/Lieut.
Killed in action 24/3/17.

✠ TILLEY, *Alan Herbert*
6/2/7238, 5/11/15; No. 14 O.C.B.; Oxf. & Bucks. L.I., 22/11/16; F; 2/Lieut.
Died of wounds 10/4/17.

TILLEY, *Denis Claude*
B/11426, 29/5/17; trfr. 28th Lond. R., 3/9/17.
Greenhill, Christchurch, Hampshire.

TILLEY, *Thomas Henry*
13910, 26/8/18; demob. 10/1/19.
29 Moreton Road, Exmouth, South Devonshire.

TILLIE, *William Arthur*
C/327, 4/11/08; dis. 2/3/11.
Elmslead Lodge, Chistlehurst, Kent.

✠ TILLOTSON, *John Launcelot*
6/3/8256, 8/12/15, L/C.; No. 14 O.C.B., 28/8/16; Dorset R., 22/11/16; F; 2/Lieut.; M(1).
Killed in action 23/4/17.

TILLY, *Arthur*
6/1/5640, 16/8/15; Oxf. Huss., 25/1/16; Staff Capt.
154 Bedford Hill, S.W. 12.

TIMBERLAKE, *William Harold*
A/11279, 14/5/17; No. 14 O.C.B., 7/9/17; Glouc. R., 17/12/17; Lieut.; M.C.
c/o Messrs. J. Dickenson & Coy., 65 Old Bailey, E.C.

TIMBRELL, *Edward Richard Laing*
D/B/12870, 26/3/18, L/C.; trfr. D. of Corn. L.I., 10/5/19.
12a Primrose Mansions, Battersea Park, S.W. 4.

TIMLIN, *Albert Edward*
B/Sq/A/12376, 4/1/18; No. 21 O.C.B., 7/6/18; Lein. R., 4/2/19; 2/Lieut.
109 North Strand, Dublin.

TIMMIS, *Laurence Barnett*
B/9878, 8/11/16; R.A., C/S, 23/2/17; R.G.A., 1/9/17; F; Lieut.
50 Claremont Road, Moss Side, Manchester.

TIMMIS, *Thomas Henry*
D/10238, 29/12/16; R.F.C., C/S, 16/4/17; R.F.C., 16/5/17, R.A.F.; It; Lieut.
Shenstone House, Kidderminster, Worcestershire.

TIMMONS, *Terence*
6/3/8741, 6/1/16; No. 14 O.C.B., 26/11/16; L'pool. R., 28/2/17; 2/Lieut.
Fordstown, Kells, Co. Meath, Ireland.

TIMSON, *Rowland Clunbury*
D/11181, 3/5/17, L/C.; Garr. O.C.B., 5/10/17; Lab. Corps, 15/12/17, Glouc. R.; 2/Lieut.
The Kraal, Berkhamsted, Hertfordshire.

TINDAL, *Albert Roxburgh*
C/13258, 10/6/18; trfr. 14th Lond. R., 6/12/18, Gord. Highrs.
Hiawatha, Burnside, Rutherglen, Nr. Glasgow, N.B.

TINDAL, *John Johnston*
6/2/6958, 21/10/15; No. 9 O B.C., 8/3/16; R.F.C., 6/7/16, Gord. Highrs., Tank Corps; Capt.; w.

✠ TINDAL, *Louis Nicolas Lindsay*
4/5/4813, 12/7/15; Devon. R., 4/10/15; F; Lieut.; M.C.
Killed in action 27/5/18.

TINDALL, *Charles Godfrey*
F/1783, 16/10/14; R.W. Kent R., 13/11/14; Capt.; w; M.C.
Bidborough Grange, Tunbridge.

✠ TINDALL, *Howard Simson*
F/2869, 5/2/15; R. Berks. R., 3/6/15; Lieut.
Killed in action 31/7/17.

TINKER, *John Elderbert Buchanan*
4/3144, 30/3/15, L/C.; R.E., 7/7/15; F,NR; Capt.; M.C.
Secretary's Office, General Post Office, E.C.

TINKER, *Joseph J.*
6/5/6052, 3/9/15; N. Lan. R., 22/1/16; Lieut.
30 Wolsley Road, St. Helens.

TINKLER, *George de Lisle B.*
6/Sq/8911, 13/1/16; No. 2 Cav. C/S, 5/1/17; R. Regt. of Cav., 7/7/17; 2/Lieut.
Cossington, Leicester.

✠ TINKLER, *George Henry*
6/2/7705, 22/11/15; No. 8 O.C.B., 4/8/16; S. Staff. R., 21/11/16; 2/Lieut.
Killed in action 25/4/17.

TINNISWOOD, *Robert Westgarth*
6/Sq/7784, 23/11/15; A.S.C., C/S, 27/10/16; R.A.S.C., 20/12/16; S; Lieut.
Greenside, Thursby, Nr. Carlisle, Cumberland.

TINSLEY, *George Laming*
D/11021, 11/4/17; R.G.A., C/S, 29/6/17; R.G.A., 25/11/17; F; 2/Lieut.; M.C.
110 West Parade, Lincoln.

TIPPING, *Ernest Baumer*
A/10716, 8/2/17; R.F.C., C/S, 16/4/17; R.F.C., 16/5/17; 2/Lieut.
Ardmore, 24 Burcott Road, Purley, Surrey.

✠ TISDALL, *Michael Henry*
Sq/1521, 2/10/14; N. Som. Yeo., 7/1/15, R.A.F.; F; Capt.; w.
Killed 23/12/19.

TISDALL, *Walter Brian*
Sq/1520, 2/10/14, L/C.; R.A.S.C., 21/1/15, R.F.C., R.A.F.; E,F; Capt.; Croix de Guerre (Belge).
12 Funchar Road, Oxford. (Now in Argentina).

TITLEY, *Edward Addison*
A/D/13041, 3/5/18; trfr. K.R. Rif. C., 11/6/19.
Manor Cottage, Cornwall Road, Harrogate.

TOBITT, *Cyril Richmond*
6/4/7484, 15/11/15, Cpl.; K.R. Rif. C., 4/9/16, R.E.; F; Capt.; w.
Pebmarsh, Burrs, Essex.

TOD, *Alex Stewart*
6/5/9498, 15/2/16; No. 2 O.C.B., 14/8/16; High. L.I., 18/12/16.
White House, Wemyss Castle, Fife.

TODD, *Francis Edward Thornton*
4/2/4409, 24/6/15, L/C.; R.A.S.C., 24/1/16; Lieut.
Dane End, Northwood, Middlesex.

TODD, *Frederick Ernest*
C/10787, 19/2/17; trfr. 18th Lond. R., 20/4/17, R.E.; F,S; g.
Woodlands, Upper Ballinderry, Lisburn, Ireland.

TOFTS, *Vincent Glenton*
4/2/4351, 21/6/15; Manch. R., 6/1/16, att. M.G.C.; F; Lieut.
Lynton House, The Park, Upper Norwood, S.E. 19.

TOLCHARD, *William Reginald*
4/3/4410, 24/6/15, Sgt.; R.G.A., 8/10/15; Capt.; M.C.
Fore Street, Buckfastleigh, Devonshire.

TOLL, *Charles Bryan Limbrey*
A/14059, 25/9/18; demob. 30/1/19.
Strete Manor House, Nr. Dartmouth, South Devonshire.

TOLLER, *Geoffrey Ernest*
6/2/7224, 4/11/15; M.G.C., 4/8/16, cmp. M. of Labour; Lieut.; w.
13 Auriol Road, West Kensington, W. 14.

✠ TOLLER, *George Reginald*
K/E/2408, 21/12/14; Linc. R., 8/7/15; Lieut. *Died* 27/7/17.

TOLLEY, *Claude Edmund*
6/1/5290, 31/7/15, L/C.; R.E., 22/12/15; Lieut.
6 Elyne Road, Stroud Green, N. 4.

TOLLEY, *Cyril James Hastings*
6/3/7814, 24/11/15; No. 8 O.C.B., 4/8/16, M.G.C., C/S; M.G.C., 23/11/16, Tank Corps; F; Lieut.; p; M.C.
Wollacombe, East Dean Road, Eastbourne, Sussex.

TOLLEY, *Richard George*
B/12816, 20/3/18; No. 13 O.C.B., 9/8/18; trfr. 5th Lond. R., 4/2/19.
26 Liverpool Road, Thornton Heath, Surrey.

APPENDIX II.—RECORDS OF RANK AND FILE.

TOLSON, Roger Ward
C/12661, 27/2/18; H. Bde. O.C.B., 7/6/18; Scots. Gds., 4/2/19;
2/Lieut. *Ebor House, Poppleton, York.*

TOMES, Gerald Forster
B/10634, 31/1/17, Sgt.; R.A., C/S, 16/11/17; R.G.A., 13/5/18;
2/Lieut. *8 Warren Road, Prestatyn, North Wales.*

✠ TOMKINS, Frank Savell
E/1567, 6/10/14; Glouc. R., 27/11/14; Lieut.
 Killed in action 8/8/15.

TOMKINS, Robert Henry
A/14092, 2/10/18; trfr. K.R. Rif. C., 7/4/19.
 Woodstock, Cedar Road, Sutton, Surrey.

TOMKINS, Walter Graeme
1/3242, 12/4/15; York. R., 28/7/15; 2/Lieut.
 14 Blackwellgate, Darlington.

TOMLINSON, Clifford Gibaud
4/2/4058, 7/6/15; Notts. & Derby R., 17/9/15; F; Capt.; M(1).
 P.O. Box 119, Port Elizabeth, South Africa.

TOMLINSON, Lawrence Digby
6/3/6216, 13/9/15, L/C.; R.E., C/S, 2/7/16; R.E., 15/9/16; F;
Lieut. *25 Grosvenor Crescent, Scarborough, Yorkshire.*

TOMPKINS, Robert Henry
4/6/5217, 29/7/15; E. Surr. R., 29/12/15; I; Lieut.
 13 Arundel Road, Brighton.

TOMPSON, Bertram Edward
1/9651, 28/9/16; No. 14 O.C.B., 26/11/16; Worc. R., 27/3/17;
S; Lieut. *58 Regent Road, Southfields, Leicester.*

✠ TOMS, Horace James Henry
F/2981, 27/2/15; Notts. & Derby R., 21/6/15; F; 2/Lieut.; M(1).
 Killed in action 9/4/17.

✠ TOMSON, James Wyndham
H/2025, 2/11/14; Leic. R., 11/3/15; Capt.
 Killed in action 24/9/18.

TONGE, William
B/13529, 15/7/18; trfr. K.R. Rif. C., 7/4/19.
 49 Moreton Street, Chadderton, Oldham, Lancashire.

TONGUE, Alfred Norman
6/2/8681, 4/1/16; No. 14 O.C.B., 30/10/16; Manch. R., 25/4/17;
F; Lieut.; p-w.
 2 Victoria Avenue, Ellesmere Park, Eccles, Lancashire.

✠ TONGUE, Claude Leslie
B/11407, 30/5/17; Garr. O.C.B., 28/12/17; Worc. R., 22/6/18;
2/Lieut. *Died 26/10/18.*

TONKIN, Oswald Powell
6/Sq/7706, 22/11/15, L/G.; Sco. Horse, 11/5/16; Lieut.; M.C.
 21 Howard Gardens, Cardiff.

TOOLE, Howard John Laurence
4/3/4432, 24/6/15; 19th Lond. R., 1/11/15; Capt.

TOOLEY, John Cecil
6/5/5314, 2/8/15; 20th Lond. R., 4/9/16, att. T.M. Bty.; F;
Capt.; w. *60 Alderbrook Road, Nightingale Lane, S.W. 12.*

TOOSEY, Robert Brewster
6/8257, 8/12/15; dis. med. unfit, 6/5/16.
 44 Grosvenor Road, Claughton, Birkenhead.

TOOTELL, George Derek Leigh
D/12957, 19/4/18; H. Bde. O.C.B., 4/10/18; Gds. M.G.R.,
10/3/19; 2/Lieut. *Nordan Hall, Leominster, Herefordshire.*

TOOTH, Ernest Anthony
B/1842, 16/10/14; D. of Corn. L.I., 20/10/14; Capt.

TOOTH, Gerald Edward Guy
B/1829, 16/10/14; Leic. R., 28/11/14; F; Capt.; M.C. and Bar,
Croix de Guerre (French).
 Havenholme, Hadley Wood, Middlesex.

TOOVEY, Cecil Wotton
A/519, 18/11/10; Midd'x. R., 10/5/13, secd. Indian Army;
I,M,Afghan; Major; w; M.C., M(1).
 c/o Messrs. Cox & Coy., Bombay, India.

TOPHAM, Denis Bevan
B/1064, 2/9/14; Midd'x. R., 30/9/14, Gren. Gds.; G,F; Lieut.
 Guards Club, Brook Street, W. 1.

TOPHAM, Sidney
6/2/6568, 30/9/15; Gren. Gds., 23/8/16, Indian Army; M,I; Capt.
 42 Hadlow Road, Tonbridge.

✠ TORIN, Richard Maynard
Sq/2980, 25/2/15; R.E., 13/4/15; Lieut.
 Killed in action 24/4/15.

TORRENS, Arthur Stanley Dormer
A/14134, 8/10/18; demob. 29/1/19.
 11 Bridge Avenue Mansions, Hammersmith, W. 6.

TORRY, George Claude
Sq/2549, 4/1/15; R.F.A., 18/2/15; Lieut.
 Elm Lodge, Sheen Road, Richmond.

TORY, Robert Newton
C/Sq/11070, 16/4/17; trfr. 28th Lond. R., 29/8/17.
 Anderson Manor, Blandford, Dorset.

TOTTENHAM, Harry Leslie William
B/Sq/11996, 10/9/17; trfr. R.H.A., 1/1/18; F; Gnr.
 The Grange, Moy, Co. Tyrone, Ireland.

TOTTENHAM, Reginald
B/Sq/11997, 10/9/17; Tank Corps C/S, 4/1/18; Tank Corps,
4/3/19; 2/Lieut. *The Grange, Moy, Co. Tyrone, Ireland.*

TOTTON, Jurin
Sq/626, 29/3/12, L/C.; R.F.A., 23/9/14; Lieut.
 St. Ambrose, Wallington, Surrey.

TOVEY, Harry Wakelam
C/10147, 8/12/16, L/C.; No. 14 O.C.B., 5/3/17; R.N.V.R.,
26/6/17; F; Sub. Lieut.
 27 Nursery Road, Hockley, Birmingham.

TOWERS, John
A/12466, 24/1/18; R.E., C/S, 12/5/18; R.E., 6/11/18; 2/Lieut.
 289 Byres Road, Hillhead, Glasgow.

✠ TOWGOOD, Arthur Cecil Carden
6/3/6165, 11/9/15; Midd'x. R., 20/1/16; 2/Lieut.
 Killed in action 13/5/17.

TOWLE, Ernest
6/1/6298, 16/9/15; Bord. R., 21/1/16, att. L'pool. R.; F; Lieut.;
w. *Tullybeg, White Road, Blackburn, Lancashire.*

TOWLER, Frank
A/238, 22/5/08; dis. 21/5/13; R.E., 23/3/16; F.
 11 Briston Grove, Crouch Hill, N. 8.

TOWNDROW, Frederic Edward
6/3/5424, 5/8/15; K.R. Rif. C., 4/9/16; F,I,Afghan; Lieut.
 c/o Messrs. Grindlay & Coy., 54 Parliament Street, S.W. 1.

TOWNLEY, Claude Frank
C/10441, 10/1/17; No. 20 O.C.B., 7/6/17; Indian Army, 15/10/17.

TOWNSEND, Albert Victor
6/4/7372, 10/11/15; R. Ir. Fus., 4/8/16, secd. K. Af. Rif.; EA;
Lieut. *259 Essex Road, Canonbury, N. 1.*

TOWNSEND, Donald Lavaff
4/1/4476, 28/6/15; S. Staff. R., 2/10/15; 2/Lieut.

TOWNSEND, Ernest George
C/10146, 8/12/16, L/C.; No. 14 O.C.B., 5/3/17; Glouc. R.,
26/6/17, att. M.G.C.; Lieut. *Fordham Grange, Somerset.*

TOWNSEND, Frederick Cooling
A/10975, 29/3/17; R.E., C/S, 16/9/17; R.E., 14/12/17; F; Lieut.
 Lindum House, Metheringham, Lincoln.

TOWNSEND, Kenneth Arthur
4/Sq/4244, 14/6/15; R.H.A., 28/8/15; Lieut.
 c/o Townsend Bros., 101 Leadenhall Street, E.C.

TOWNSEND, Samuel
6/3/5488, 9/8/15; R.G.A., 23/12/15; F; Capt.
 39 Willow Way, Didsbury, Manchester.

✠ TOZER, Horace Gordon
K/A/2249, 7/12/14; York. R., 17/2/15; F; 2/Lieut.
 Killed in action 1/10/15.

TOZER, James Clifford
K/A/2105, 16/11/14; R.A.O.C., 22/1/15; Major; m.
 1 Belmont Villas, Devonport.

TRACEY, Arthur George
6/3/5840, 26/8/15; R.G.A., 29/12/15, R.A.O.C.; Lieut.
 38 Radley Road, Bruce Grove, N 17.

TRAFFORD, Philip George
B/12780, 15/3/18; No. 14 O.C.B., 23/8/18; demob. 19/12/18.
 Lusdum House, High Street, Scunthorpe, Lincolnshire.

TRAFFORD, Walter Egerton
K/2951, 18/2/15; R.F.A., 12/2/15; I; Lieut.; p.
 27 Avondale Road, South Croydon, Surrey.

✠ TRAILL, Kenneth Robert
C/1044, 26/8/14; R. Berks. R., 12/9/14; Lieut.; w.
 Killed in action 1/7/16.

APPENDIX II.—RECORDS OF RANK AND FILE.

TRANMER, Joe Hamerton
5/5232, 30/7/15; Manch. R., 6/1/16; 2/Lieut.
    8 Cromer Road, Aigburth, Liverpool.

✠ TRASK, Charles William Trevor
D/10861, 12/3/17; No. 12 O.C.B., 10/8/17; Som. L.I., 27/11/17, att. Welch R.; 2/Lieut.   Killed in action 18/8/18.

TRATMAN, Edgar Kingsley
A/12785, 31/1/18; No. 19 O.C.B., 10/5/18; Glouc. R., 2/2/19; 2/Lieut.   Airdrie House, Cotham Grove, Bristol.

TRAVERS, Charles Tindal
6/7625, 19/11/15; dis. to R. Mil. Coll., 28/1/16; Wilts. R., 16/8/16, att. R.F.C., R.A.F.; F; Lieut.; w; A.F.C.
    Bredegar House, Bredegar, Kent.

TRAVERS, Frederick Dudley
4/Sq/4031, 7/6/15, L/C.; Herts. Yeo., 1/1/16, R.F.C., R.A.F.; M,E,S; Lieut.; D.F.C., Croix de Guerre, M(1).
    11 Minster Road, West Hampstead, N.W.2.

TRAVERS, Joseph James
6/5/7063, 2/10/15; dis. med. unfit, 23/7/16.
    121 Chapel Street, Dublin, Ireland.

TRAVERS, Sidney Joe
6/1/9532, 17/2/16; No. 14 O.C.B., 30/10/16; R. Suss. R., 24/1/17, att. Glouc. R.; F,It; Lieut.; M.B.E.
    Hill Top, Kingsdown, Deal.

TRAVIS, Harry
D/10395, 8/1/17, L/C.; No. 14 O.C.B., 5/5/17; S. Lan. R., 28/8/17; F; Lieut.
    5 Evesham Avenue, Monkseaton, Northumberland.

TRAYNOR, Peter
6/1/6259, 16/9/15; 7th Lond. R., 13/7/16; Lieut.

✠ TREADWELL, Robert Naylor
A/2068, 12/11/14; R. Berks. R., 2/12/14, R.F.C.; Lieut.; w; M.C.   Died of wounds 9/9/17.

TREASURE, Adolphus
6/5/7158, 2/11/15; dis. med. unfit, 8/8/16.
    Sydney House, Treorchy, Glamorganshire.

TREBLE, Ralph John
4/3/5182, 29/7/15, Cpl.; No. 3 O.C.B., 25/2/16; Hamps. R., 20/7/16; F; Lieut.
    The School House, Awbridge, Nr. Romsey, Hampshire.

TREDCROFT, John Lennox
K/2260, 7/12/14; R.A.S.C., 31/12/14; F; Major.
    Claymore, Edgborough Road, Guildford, Surrey.

TREDINNICK, Francis Septimus
4/Sq/4323, 21/6/15, Cpl.; R.F.A., C/S, 4/8/16; R.F.A., 10/11/16; F; Lieut.   223 Burntwood Lane, Tooting, S.W.17.

TREDINNICK, Nicholas William
6/6299, 16/9/15; R.F.A., 13/10/15; Lieut.; M.C., M(1).
    c/o Messrs. Cox & Coy., Bombay, India.

TREE, Wilfred Charles
C/10145, 8/12/16; No. 20 O.C.B., 5/5/17; 7th Lond. R., 28/8/17, att. M.G.C.; F; 2/Lieut.
    13 Coldershaw Road, West Ealing, W.13.

✠ TREGARTHEN, Ernest William
6/1/7315, 8/11/15; No. 7 O.C.B., 6/4/16; R.W. Fus., 17/7/16, R.A.F.; Lieut.   Killed -/3/18.

TREGASKIS, Oswald
6/2/8258, 8/12/15, L/C.; No. 14 O.C.B., 27/9/16; Devon. R., 18/12/16; Lieut.   357 London Road, Thornton Heath, Surrey.

TREGENZA, Walter Archibald
B/11724, 19/7/17; No. 11 O.C.B., 9/11/17; Lond. R., 26/3/18.
    Kent College, Canterbury, Kent.

TREGLOWN, Gordon Bernard
6/1/5641, 16/8/15; No. 11 O.C.B., 16/5/16; D. of Corn. L.I., 4/9/16; S; Lieut.   Deopham Vicarage, Wymondham, Norfolk.

✠ TRELEAVEN, Noel Houghton
6/2/6495, 27/9/15; No. 7 O.C.B., 5/4/16; W. York. R., 4/8/16; 2/Lieut.   Killed in action 23/11/16.

TREMLETT, Frederic Clifford
A/11237, 2/5/17; dis. med. unfit, 27/7/17.
    53 Oxford Street, Weston-super-Mare.

TRENCH, Clive Newcome
D/13905, 26/8/18; demob. 25/1/19.
    Sopwell Hall, Cloughjordan, Ireland.

TRENCH, Ivor Chenevix
F/1836, 16/10/14; General List, 17/3/15, Wilts. R.; G,F; Lieut.; w.   Meadowlands, Alderley Edge, Cheshire.

TRENCH, Thomas Percival
6/4/8074, 1/12/15; No. 7 O.C.B., 11/8/16; trfr. R.G.A., 2/2/17; F; Gnr.   Glenmalyre, Ballybrettas, Queens Co., Ireland.

TRENCH, William Langton
2/3568, 10/5/15, L/C.; Worc. R., 21/8/15, W. York. R.; F; Lt. Col.; M.C.   Oxford and Cambridge Club, Pall Mall, S.W.1.

TRENERRY, Edgar Harold
4/6/5/4768, 12/7/15; dis. 22/5/16.

TRENERRY, Edgar Williams
A/10031, 29/11/16; No. 14 O.C.B., 30/1/17; trfr. 16th Lond. R., 18/4/17.   Glenview, Perranporth, Cornwall.

TRERY, Charles Herbert
Sq/3472, 3/5/15, L/C.; R.F.A., 13/8/15; Lieut.
    84 Woodside, Wimbledon, S.W.19.

TRESIDDER, William Douglas
6/5/6914, 18/10/15; R.F.A., C/S, 4/8/16; R.F.A., 24/11/16; F; Lieut.; w.   Scrofield House, Horncastle, Lincolnshire.

TRETHEWEY, Frank Lince
C/12058, 27/9/17; dis. med. unfit, 13/2/19.
    Holmsted Place, Cuckfield, Sussex.

TREVOR, Caleb Henry
6/5/9428, 10/2/16; R.A., C/S, 7/8/16; R.G.A., 19/12/16; Lieut.
    43 Stratfield Road, Oxford.

TREVOR, Charles Reginald Heber
6/2/9271, 2/2/16; R.F.C., 14/8/16, R.A.F.; F; Lieut.
    Brynhenlog, Abcraman, Aberdare, South Wales.

TRIGG, Austin Amos
7426, 15/11/15, L/C.; 4th Lond. R., 13/7/16, K.R. Rif. C., M.G.C.; F,S; Capt.; w.
    Heathlands, Slough, Buckinghamshire.

TRIGG, Herbert William
4/1/5049, 22/7/15; R.F.A., 16/11/15; Lieut.; w(2).
    Connaught Club, Marble Arch, W.1.

TRIGGS, Harold Thomas
4/3665, 17/5/15; R. Suss. R., 2/10/15; F; Lieut.; w, p.
    6 Bedford Square, W.C.1.

TRIM, Frank Ernest
4/4588, 1/7/15; E. Surr. R., 15/10/15; F; Lieut.
    Burford, Malcolm Road, Wimbledon, S.W.19.

TRISTRAM, Ralph
6/1/9150, 25/1/16; No. 8 O.C.B., 4/8/16; North'd. Fus., 21/11/16; F; Lieut.   121 Ridgway, Wimbledon, S.W.19.

TRITTON, Frederick William
4/3/4620, 5/7/15; R.E., 29/11/15; Lieut.

TROTMAN, Cyril George
B/13450, 3/7/18; trfr. K.R. Rif. C., 7/4/19.
    53 Hurst Street, Cowley Road, Oxford.

TROTTER, Wilfrid Pym
6/3/7964, 29/11/15; R. Fus., 4/9/16; F; Lieut.; g; M.C. and Bar, M(1).   1 Sydney Place, Onslow Square, S.W.7.

TROTTER, William
K/E/2758, 21/1/15; North'd. Fus., 3/6/15; E,M,F; Lieut.
    338 West 56th Street, New York City.

TROUGHTON, Ernest Robert
F/2731, 18/1/15, L/C.; Durh. L.I., 18/5/15; Capt.

TROUGHTON, Sidney Joseph
3/3473, 3/5/15; Wilts. R., 28/7/15, secd. Nigeria Regt.; F,Germ.EA; Lieut.; w.
    c/o J. R. Troughton Esq., Waterloo Bridge Wharf, S.E. (Now in Madrid).

✠ TROUNCE, Sydney Abel
6/3/8376, 13/12/15; No. 14 O.C.B., 29/9/16; Suff. R., 18/12/16; 2/Lieut.   Killed in action 5/5/17.

TROUP, Francis Gordon
A/732, 11/11/13, L/C.; 10th Lond. R., 20/9/14; Capt.
    5 Bedford Row, W.C.2.

✠ TROWBRIDGE, Charles James
C/12608, 13/2/18.   Died 26/3/18.

✠ TROWER, Alfred Bence
C/11499, 14/6/17, L/C.; H. Bde. O.C.B., 5/10/17; Sco. Gds., 26/2/18; F; 2/Lieut.   Killed in action 29/5/18.

APPENDIX II.—RECORDS OF RANK AND FILE.

TROWER, *Eric Lawford*
Sq/3058, 15/3/15; R.N.A.S., 20/5/15, R.A.F.; Lieut.
    Papeet, Tahiti, South Sea Islands.

TROWER, *Ralph Frank*
6/3/D/Sq/6706, 7/10/15; R.A., C/S, 12/1/17; R.F.A., 5/6/17; F; Lieut.; w-p.   *Bayham, Alexandra Road, Epsom.*

✠ TRUBSHAWE, *Eric James Vyvyan*
3/3358, 22/4/15, L/C.; R.E., 22/9/15; F; 2/Lieut.
    Died of wounds 2/2/17.

✠ TRUBY, *George Edward*
6/1/8887, 13/1/16, L/C.; No. 14 O.C.B., 30/10/16; Linc. R., 24/1/17; F; 2/Lieut.   *Killed in action 31/7/17.*

TRUEMAN, *Jack Kelson Wentworth*
H/1689, 12/10/14; Wilts. R., 23/10/14; F; Lieut.; w; M.C., M(2).

TRUMAN, *Douglas Ernest John*
4/5/6/Sq/4897, 15/7/15, L/C.; R.A., C/S, 26/10/16; R.G.A., 17/3/17; F; Lieut.; w.   *118 Westbourne Terrace, W. 2.*

TRUMAN, *Ralph Duvergier*
C/D/13243, 7/6/18; trfr. K.R. Rif. C., 30/5/19, R.A.O.C.; Cpl.
    Corbar, Torrington Road, North Finchley, N. 12.

✠ TRUMAN, *Thomas Archibald*
B/11408, 28/5/17; A.S.C., C/S, 1/9/17; R.A.S.C., 27/10/17; 2/Lieut.   *Died 17/9/18.*

TRUSCOTT, *Claude*
B/13619, 24/7/18; demob. 19/2/19.
    Rilla Mill, Callington, Cornwall

TRUSCOTT, *Ernest Palmer*
D/10421, 10/1/17; No. 20 O.C.B., 7/6/17; trfr. 28th Lond. R., 3/8/17.   *57 Station Road, Winchmore Hill, N. 21.*

TRUSCOTT, *Hubert Lewis Alfred*
6/2/8504, 20/12/15; No. 14 O.C.B., 26/11/16; Shrop. Yeo., 27/3/17; Lieut.   *Rilla Mill, Callington, Cornwall.*

TRUSCOTT, *James Ralph*
A/2033, 9/11/14; R.A.S.C., 16/12/14; F; Lt. Col.; M(1).
    Amblecote, Cobham, Surrey.

TRUSCOTT, *Roy Francis*
K/A/2096, 16/11/14, L/C.; General List, 11/5/15; F; Lt. Col.; O.B.E., M(2).   *3 Elm Court, Temple, E.C. 4.*

TRUTCH, *Charles Joseph Hyde*
6/1/6166, 11/9/15; R.N.V.R., 23/12/15, R.N.A.S., R.A.F.; Capt.
    The Hut, Newbold-on-Avon, Rugby.

TUCK, *Francis Harold*
6/3/9258, 2/2/16; trfr. R.F.A., 10/11/16; R.F.A., 12/8/17; F; Lieut.   *Dorincourt, Sandown, Isle of Wight. (Now in France).*

TUCKER, *Charles Joseph*
6/1/6947, 20/10/15, L/C.; No. 7 O.C.B., 11/8/16, No. 14 O.C.B.; trfr. 18th Lond. R., 8/6/17.
    National Bank House, Westland Row, Dublin, Ireland.

TUCKER, *Claud Henry*
A/B/D/12164, 25/10/17; No. 6 O.C.B., 10/5/18; Midd'x. R., 3/2/19; F; Capt.   *13 St. Leonards Road, Ealing, W. 13.*

TUCKER, *Douglas Herbert*
C/D/12059, 27/9/17; No. 8 O.C.B., 5/4/18; M.G.C., 8/10/18; 2/Lieut.   *Church Farm, Steeple Ashton, Trowbridge, Wilts.*

TUCKER, *Ernest Vivian*
6/3/9096, 24/1/16; R.F.C., C/S, 3/2/17; R.F.C., 6/6/17, R.A.F.; 2/Lieut.   *84 Cathedral Road, Cardiff.*

TUCKER, *Francis Edwin*
B/11685, 17/7/17; trfr. R.F.C., 13/12/17, R.A.F.; Cpl.
    69 Alexandra Road, Hendon, N.W. 4.

TUCKER, *Frederick Charles*
6/5/7707, 22/11/15; No. 14 O.C.B., 30/10/16; Notts. & Derby. R., 25/4/17; F; Lieut.; w.   *64 Middle Street, Yeovil.*

TUCKER, *Sydney Ewart*
4/1/4657, 5/7/15, L/C.; Manch. R., 6/1/16; Lieut.

TUCKER, *Thomas Carter*
4/1/5085, 26/7/15; R.F.A., 13/12/15; F; Lieut.
    21 Woodlands Gardens, Muswell Hill, N. 10.

TUCKER, *Valentine*
E/1850, 16/10/14, L/C.; 6th Lond. R., 24/3/15; Lieut.
    4 Thicket Wood, Anerley, S.E. 20.

TUCKER, *William Francis Courtenay*
B/12757, 13/3/18; No. 18 O.C.B., 9/8/18; North'n. R., 6/3/19; 2/Lieut.   *84 Stanhope Avenue, Finchley, N. 3.*

TUDOR, *William Joseph*
C/14281, 8/11/18; No. 11 O.C.B., 24/1/19; General List, 8/3/19; 2/Lieut.   *299 Bartolome Mitre, Buenos Aires, South America.*

TUDOR-HART, *Owen*
E/1506, 1/10/14; North'd. Fus., 16/12/14, R.F.C.; F; Lieut.; w-p; M.C.   *Bank of Montreal, 47 Threadneedle Street, E.C.*

TUDOR-JONES, *Robert Glynne*
H/2594, 24/12/14; R.W. Fus., 18/3/15, R.A.F.; F; Capt.; w.
    c/o Messrs. Townsend, Wood & Calderwood, Swindon, Wiltshire.

TUGHAN, *Harold Stanley*
6/2/7627, 19/11/15; No. 14 O.C.B., 28/8/16; 18th Lond. R., 18/12/16; F; Lieut.   *Ivydene, Muswell Hill, N. 10.*

TUGHAN, *Norman Charles*
C/12288, 3/12/17; No. 15 O.C.B., 7/6/18; 18th Lond. R., 4/2/19; 2/Lieut.   *Ivydene, Muswell Hill, N. 10.*

TUKE, *Harry Gordon*
C/11085, 19/4/17; trfr. 16th Lond. R., 30/5/17.
    Thames View, Chiswick Mall, W.4.

✠ TULLEY, *John Rudrum*
6/D/8228, 7/12/15; R.N.A.S., 9/12/16; F; Flt. Sub. Lieut.
    Killed 29/6/17.

TULLEY, *Percy Charles*
D/6/5841, 26/8/15, Sgt.; No. 14 O.C.B., 5/3/17; E. Kent R., 26/6/17; F; Lieut.   *Glebe House, Hurstpierpoint, Sussex.*

✠ TULLY, *Henry Robson*
A/10472, 12/1/17, Cpl.; No. 14 O.C.B., 5/7/17; North'd. Fus., 30/10/17; 2/Lieut.   *Died of wounds 27/5/18.*

TULLY, *Terence Bernard*
6/Sq/8204, 1/12/15, Cpl.; R.F.C., 23/8/16; G,E; Capt.; w; A.F.C., M(1).   *81 Oxford Terrace, Hyde Park, W. 2.*

TUMMELL, *Albert Henry*
4/Sq/4256, 14/6/15, L/C.; Notts. & Derby. Yeo., 9/10/15, att. Lab. Corps; Lieut.
    c/o H. Burtsal, 116 Hamilton House, Bishopgate, E.C.

TUNBRIDGE, *Alexander Richard Trearsly*
A/2779, 19/1/15; L'pool. R., 13/4/15; Lieut.

TUNBRIDGE, *Graham*
A/11917, 27/8/17; No. 14 O.C.B., 4/1/18; Welch R., 25/6/18; 2/Lieut.   *8 Northampton Place, Swansea.*

TUNMER, *William Hayman*
F/1716, 15/10/14; E. Surr. R., 27/11/14, M.G.C.; Lieut.
    8 Fulham Park Road, S.W. 6.

TUNWELL, *John William*
3/3323, 19/4/15, Sgt.; E. Surr. R., 2/9/15, General List; F; Capt.; M(1).   *141 Finchley Road, N.W. 3.*

TUPPER, *Geoffrey William Henry*
Sq/166, 18/4/08; Midd'x R., 24/3/09; I,M; Major; M(1).
    6 Holmbush Road, Putney, S.W. 15.

TUPPER, *Henry*
6/2/8533, 24/12/15, L/C.; No. 14 O.C.B., 29/9/16; E. Kent R., 18/12/16; F; Capt.; M.C. and Bar.
    Bignor, Pulborough, Sussex.

TURBERVILLE, *Giles Francis*
6/2/5716, 19/8/15; R.F.C., 6/7/16, R.A.F.; F; Lieut.
    15 Artillery Street, S.E. 1.

TURING, *John Leslie*
6/2/9468, 14/2/16; No. 8 O.C.B., 4/8/16; Sea. Highrs., 18/12/16; F; Lieut.; w; M.C.   *Crocker Hill House, Chichester, Sussex.*

TURK, *Jack*
6/1/6217, 13/9/15; E. Kent R., 1/6/16; F; Capt.; w; M.C.
    27 Victoria Road, Deal, Kent.

TURNBULL, *Charles Lockwood*
B/10751, 21/2/17; R.F.C., C/S, 13/3/17; R.F.C., 15/5/17, M.G.C.; F; Lieut.
    The Vicarage, Drighlington, Bradford, Yorkshire.

✠ TURNBULL, *Gerald Illtyd*
6/1/7281, 8/11/15; Welch R., 4/9/16; Lieut.
    Died of wounds 9/4/18 as Prisoner of War.

TURNBULL, *John Bruce*
6/2/9469, 14/2/16, Cpl.; No. 14 O.C.B., 26/11/16; Shrop. Yeo., 28/2/17; Lieut.; w.
    c/o Hoare, Millert & Coy., 5 Fairlie Place, Calcutta.

APPENDIX II.—RECORDS OF RANK AND FILE.

TURNBULL, *Joseph*
C/13375, 21/6/18; trfr, 14th Lond. R., 6/12/18.
4 Curzon Street, Maryport, Cumberland.

TURNBULL, *Paul Stanislas*
6/1/7316, 8/11/15; Welch R., 4/9/16; F; Lieut.; w.
The Heath, Cardiff.

TURNBULL, *Thomas*
B/12718, 8/3/18, Sgt.; No. 16 O.C.B., 18/10/18; N. Lan. R., 17/3/19; 2/Lieut.
Braeton, West Park Road, Blackburn, Lancashire. (Now in Singapore).

TURNER, *Alexander Wakefield*
A/10085, 4/12/16, Sgt.; R.G.A., C/S, 7/11/17; R.G.A., 29/4/18; 2/Lieut.
Highfield House, Guildford, Surrey.

TURNER, *Allison*
6/5/7006, 23/10/15; R. Lanc. R., 12/6/16; F; Lieut.; w.
158 Great Norbury Street, Hyde, Cheshire.

TURNER, *Arthur Wallace*
6/4/8848, 10/1/16; No. 14 O.C.B., 30/10/16; 9th Lond. R., 24/1/17, Indian Army; F; Capt.
192 Botanic Gardens Road, Durban, Natal, South Africa.

TURNER, *Charles Edward Gordon*
A/11221, 5/5/17; M.G.C., C/S, 7/9/17; Tank Corps, 27/3/18; 2/Lieut.

TURNER, *Charles Kenneth*
6/3/6372, 20/9/15; Worc. R., 16/1/16; F; Lieut.; g
Ringstead, 26 Milton Road, Bournemouth.

TURNER, *Christopher Edward*
B/10092, 4/12/16; No. 14 O.C.B., 6/4/17; Devon. R., 31/7/17, att. Hamps. R.; F; Lieut.
Fern Villa, Star Road, Peterborough.

TURNER, *Christopher Rede*
Sq/584, 20/11/11; dis. 2/8/12.

TURNER, *Clarence Edward Henry*
C/14182, 16/10/18; demob. 16/1/19.
Pyon House, Bodenham Road, Hereford.

✠ TURNER, *Crosby Russell Swanson*
H/2906, 11/2/15; Dorset R., 2/6/15, K.R. Rif. C.; 2/Lieut.; M(1).
Killed in action 27/7/16.

✠ TURNER, *Cuthbert*
4/1/4621, 5/7/15; No. 11 O.C.B., 16/5/16; Bord. R., 4/9/16; F; 2/Lieut.
Killed in action 23/4/17.

TURNER, *Denys Sharman*
B/12405, 17/1/18; No. 1 O.C.B., 8/2/18; North'n. R., 30/7/18; F; 2/Lieut.
Fremeaux, Kingsthorpe, Northampton. (Now in Ceylon)

TURNER, *Edward Thomas*
4/1/4264, 16/6/15, C.Q.M.S.; No. 15 O.C.B., 7/6/18; Wilts. R., 5/2/19; 2/Lieut.
Oakville, Devonshire Road, Honor Oak Park, S.E. 23.

TURNER, *Emil Donald*
B/12781, 15/3/18; No. 1 O.C.B., 6/9/18; Lan. Fus., 16/3/19; 2/Lieut.
Ingleside, 29 Alexandra Road, Crosley, Nr. Liverpool.

TURNER, *Ernest Lancelot*
A/10939, 28/3/17, Sgt.; R.E., C/S, 13/1/18; R.E., 26/4/18; 2/Lieut.
c/o Mr. John Turner, Park Road, Great Barr, Walsall.

TURNER, *Frederick Bentley*
D/10177, 11/12/16, Sgt.; Garr. O.C.B., 5/10/17; Lab. Corps, 15/12/17; F; 2/Lieut.
Caroline House, Heath Street, Hampstead, N.W. 3.

TURNER, *George Frederick*
Sq/920, 5/8/14; 5th Drag. Gds., 15/8/14; F; Lieut.; M(1).
Bucks Club, 18 Clifford Street, W. 1.

✠ TURNER, *George Perrior*
H/1978, 26/10/14; Hamps. R., 10/3/15, att. T.M. Bty.; 2/Lieut.
Killed in action 30/6/16.

TURNER, *George Reynolds Newsum Darnley*
D/10862, 12/3/17; Garr. O.C.B., 30/11/17; dis. med. unfit, 8/2/18.
Dunstead, Langley Mill, Nr. Nottingham.

TURNER, *Harold Neale*
D/11809, 9/8/17; A.S.C., C/S, 1/11/17; R.A.S.C., 25/1/18; 2/Lieut.
Elm Grove Cocoa Works, Wallington, Surrey.

TURNER, *Harold Percival*
6/1/7534, 16/11/15; No. 14 O.C.B., 28/8/16; Essex R., 24/10/16; F; Lieut.; w-p.
49 Lexden Road, Colchester.

TURNER, *Harry*
4/6/2/5000, 19/7/15; Linc. R., 29/11/15, att. 4th Drag. Gds.; F; Lieut.; w.
Yew Tree House, Hanchurch, Nr. Newcastle, Staffordshire.

TURNER, *Edgar Henry Breen*
B/11316, 16/5/17; dis. med. unfit, 2/10/17.
Taleymevan, Pwllheli, North Wales.

TURNER, *Horace Frederick*
4/14324, 30/12/18; dis. med. unfit, 3/4/19.

TURNER, *Hugh Henry Whichcote*
C/10157, 11/12/16; No. 14 O.C.B., 5/3/17; E. Kent R., 26/6/17; F; Lieut.
Avenue House, Brighton Road, Horley, Surrey.

TURNER, *James Clifford*
D/13906, 26/8/18; trfr. K.R. Rif. C., 7/4/19.
39 Hindes Road, Harrow, Middlesex.

TURNER, *James William Cecil*
6/9069, 21/1/16; R.F.A., C/S, 9/6/16; R.F.A., 9/9/16; Lieut.; M.C.
7 Lyttleton Road, Steckford, Birmingham.

TURNER, *John Harry*
4/5/4685, 8/7/15; E. York. R., 18/10/15; F; Lieut.; g.
Mundy Street, Heanor, Derbyshire.

TURNER, *John Hastings*
B/1703, 13/10/14; Midd'x. R., 16/11/14.

TURNER, *Lyon Viccars*
6/8890, 13/1/16; R.A., C/S, 31/5/16; R.F.A., 6/7/16, R.G.A.; S; Lieut.
41 Berkeley Road, Westbury Park, Bristol.

TURNER, *Percy Lewis John*
A/13197, 3/6/18; No. 22 O.C.B., 5/7/18; R. Berks. R., 12/2/19; 2/Lieut.
The Cottage, Wallingford, Berkshire.

TURNER, *Percy Snelling*
6/1/7485, 15/11/15, L/C.; No. 14 O.C.B., 1/8/16; Hamps. R., 24/10/16; F; Lieut.; w(2); M(1).
Craig-y-don, Caterham Valley, Surrey.

✠ TURNER, *Robert Henry*
4/3/5183, 29/7/15; No. 4 O.C.B., 7/3/16; Linc. R., 13/7/16; Lieut.; w.
Died of wounds 22-23/3/18.

TURNER, *Robert Lloyd*
E/2802, 26/1/15; R.E., 20/4/15; F; Lieut.; M(1).
Chesterton, Seaford, Sussex.

TURNER, *Stanley Albert*
H/1999, 2/11/14; R. Fus., 17/2/15; F,S; Capt.
The Homestead, Marsh Farm, Twickenham.

TURNER, *Victor Fosbery*
6/5/8591, 3/1/16, Sgt.; No. 14 O.C.B., 29/9/16; K.R. Rif. C., 24/1/17; F; Capt.; w; M(1).
82 Mark Lane, E.C. 3.

TURNER, *William Anthony*
D/12890, 5/4/18; demob. 23/1/19.
36 Via G. Filangieri, Naples, Italy.

TURNER, *William Thomas*
D/13878, 21/8/18; demob. 4/2/19.
26 Wincanton Road, Southfields, S.W. 18.

TURNEY, *George Alec*
4/1/4637, 5/7/15; trfr. R.F.A., 3/11/16; R.F.A., 12/8/17; F; Major; w; M.C.
Sherfield, Royston, Hertfordshire.

TURNILL, *Leslie Gordon*
D/13912, 26/8/18; demob. 23/1/19.
Little Casterton, Stamford, Rutland.

TURPIN, *Arthur Roynon*
6/2/8469, 21/12/15, Cpl.; R.F.C., C/S, 1/2/17; R.F.C., 9/5/17; F; Lieut.
Orford Cottage, Western Road, Bath.

TURVILL, *John*
6/2/9477, 14/2/16; Intelligence Corps, 25/10/16; F,It; Lieut.; Croix de Guerre.
25 Birchin Lane, Cornhill, E.C. 3.

TUSON, *Cyril Barnett*
Sq/668, 26/11/12; R.F.A., 23/9/14; F; Lieut.
2 Camomile Street, Bishopsgate, E.C. 3.

TUSTAIN, *John Alexander*
B/D/A/12197, 5/11/17; demob. 22/2/19.
9 Chandos Road, Heaton Chapel, Nr. Stockport.

TUSTIN, *Charles Victor*
4/5/4686, 8/7/15; Camb. R., 5/10/15, att. E. Surr. R. and E. Kent R.; Lieut.; w.
10 Devonshire Road, Greenwich, S.E. 10.

APPENDIX II.—RECORDS OF RANK AND FILE.

TUTE, Stanley Harries
B/11681, 16/7/17; A.S.C., C/S, 1/11/17; R.A.S.C., 25/1/18; E;
2/Lieut.   c/o Nat. Prov. Bank of England Ltd., Doncaster.

TUTT, Bertram George Howard
4/1/3989, 10/6/15; Hamps. R., 28/8/15; Capt.

TUTT, Henry Reginald
4/4687, 8/7/15, dis. med. unfit, 8/8/16.
                           School House, Hudleigh, Southend-on-Sea.

TWEEDALE, Norman
6/3/9014, 19/1/16; R.A., C/S, 24/11/16; R.F.A., 7/4/17; F;
Lieut.; M.C.   Brooklands. Bary Road, Rochdale.

TWEEDIE, Gilbert
4/3/4010, 5/6/15; 20th Lond. R., 27/8/15, secd. M.G.C.; Lieut.; w.

TWEEDIE, Harley Alec
Sq/1298, 24/9/14; 11th R. Regt. of Cav., 29/9/14, att. 10th Huss. and R.A.F.; F,I; Major; O.B.E., A.F.C.
                           2 Whitehall Court, S.W.1.

✠ TWEEDY, William Wildman
6/1/6597, 4/10/15; North'd. Fus., 4/8/16, R.E.; 2/Lieut.
                           Killed in action 27/5/18.

TWIGG, Reginald Stanley
6/2/6408, 23/9/15, L/C.; No. 11 O.C.B., 7/5/16; R.F.C., 4/9/16, R.A.F.; Lieut.

TWINCH, Herbert
11618, 5/7/17; A.S.C., C/S, 1/11/17; R.A.S.C., 25/1/18; It; 2/Lieut.   Cippenham Lodge, Slough.

TWITCHIN, Arthur Frere
D/E/13836, 13/8/18; R.G.A., C/S, 2/10/18; R.G.A., 11/4/19; 2/Lieut.   3 Grange Road, Clifton, Bristol.

✠ TWYNAM, Geoffrey Raistrick
D/12858, 19/8/18.   Died 16/11/18.

TYACK, George Henry
C/D/12309, 13/12/17; No. 18 O.C.B., 10/5/18; trfr. 28th Lond. R., 14/10/18.   11 Queens Road, Sketty, Swansea.

TYCE, Clifford George
A/4122, 8/6/15, Sgt.; Norf. R., 6/12/15, secd. M.G.C.; F; Lieut.; M.C.   Mancroft, Claremont Road, Eaton, Norwich.

TYDD, Benjamin Samuel
B/10047, 29/11/16, L/C.; R.A.F., C/S, 3/5/18; R.A.F., 13/6/18; 2/Lieut.   Hawthornden, Englefield Green, Surrey.

TYLER, Eric Hutchinson
C/12646, 22/2/18; No. 13 O.C.B., 9/8/18; R. Suss. R., 5/3/19; 2/Lieut.   Grange Meade, Furness Road, Eastbourne, Sussex.

✠ TYLER, Gilbert Edward
2/3474, 3/5/15, L/C.; 19th Lond. R., 8/8/15; 2/Lieut.; M.C.
                           Died of wounds 18/9/16.

TYLOR, Cyril Edward
4/3/4436, 24/6/15; trfr. R.G.A., 7/7/16; R.F.C., -/6/17; F; Lieut.; w, p.
       Knockmore, Highcliff Drive, Leigh-on-Sea, Essex.

TYLOR, Vivian Alfred
K/2369, 17/12/14; Welch R., 1/1/15, M.G.C.; F; Major; w; M.C., M(1).   Court Royal, Tunbridge Wells.

TYMMS, Douglas James
6/3/6835, 14/10/15; No. 9 O.C.B.; K.O. Sco. Bord., 23/7/16, att. M.G.C.; F; Lieut.   62 Marina, St. Leonards, Sussex.

✠ TYRER, John Rawsthorne
1/3801, 27/5/15; Manch. R., 2/1/16, R.F.C.; F; Lieut.
                           Killed in action 9/10/17.

TYRER, Oliver
K/E/2382, 17/12/14; R.F.A., 18/1/15; F,S; 2/Lieut.; w.
                           Plas Newton, Chester.

TYSER, Hugh
D/2545, 4/1/15; S. Lan. R., 12/4/15; F,S; Capt.
                           3 Rutland Court, S.W.7.

TYSON, Donovan Henry
B/12868, 27/3/18; R.F.A., C/S, 26/7/18; R.F.A., 5/4/19; 2/Lieut.
                       222 Abbey Road, Barrow-in-Furness.

✠ TYSON, William Noel Dawson
6/2/7239, 5/11/15; No. 14 O.C.B.; Ches. R., 21/11/16; Lieut.; w.
                           Killed in action 29/9/18.

TYTLER, George Edward Bruce
4/1/4300, 17/6/15; R.G.A., 12/10/15; S; Lieut.
     Hong Kong & Shanghai Bank, Nagaski, Japan.

UDALL, Thomas Clement Beauchamp
2/3324, 19/4/15, Sgt.; No. 14 O.C.B.; M.G.C., 25/9/16; F; Capt.; M(1).   Oakdale, Southborough, Kent.

✠ ULLYOTT, Cecil
6/3/8770, 6/1/16; No. 14 O.C.B., 28/8/16; E. York. R., 22/11/16; 2/Lieut.   Killed in action 23/8/18.

✠ ULOTH, Arthur Curtis Wilmot
6/4/6236, 14/9/15, L/C.; R. Suss. R., 6/7/16; F; Lieut.; w; M.C.   Died of wounds 19/9/18.

UMBERS, Edwin Harry
6/3/6542, 30/9/15; No. 7 O.C.B., 6/4/16; W. York. R., 17/7/16, R.A.F.; F; Lieut.   Mount Osborne, Barnsley, Yorkshire.

UNDERHAY, Cyril Thomas
6/2/6714, 9/10/15; 11th Lond. R., 10/1/16; Lieut.; w(2); M.C.
            11 Harlech Road, Palmers Green, N.13.

UNDERHILL, William Russell
1/Sq/9750, 18/10/16, L/C.; R.G.A., C/S, 22/6/17; R.G.A., 25/11/17; 2/Lieut.
       Chilthorne, Woodcote Grange Road, Coulsdon, Surrey.

✠ UNDERWOOD, George Milne
6/8977, 17/1/16; No. 9 O.C.B., 8/3/16; R.F.C., 6/7/16; F; 2/Lieut.
                           Killed in action 6/3/17.

UNDERWOOD, John Maurice
B/13451, 3/7/18; demob. 29/1/19.   185 Windsor Road, Oldham.

UNDERWOOD, William Francis Cridlan
B/D/12204, 8/11/17, Cpl.; demob. 20/3/19.
                           54 Rainbow Hill, Worcester.

✠ UNWIN, Francis John
4/5/4726, 9/7/15; Shrop. L.I., 4/11/15, R.A.F.; F,S,E; Lieut.
                           Missing 17/9/19.

UNWIN, Frederick Ralph
K/F/2473, 28/12/14; R.E., 10/4/15; Lieut.

UPCOTT, John William
6/3/8194, 6/12/15, L/C.; No. 14 O.C.B., 28/8/16; Mon. R., 18/2/16, att. R.F.C.; Lieut.
                    9 Herbert Grove, Southend-on-Sea.

UPHAM, Gilbert Alfred
6/1/6137, 9/9/15; trfr. 15th Lond. R., 23/8/16.
                     Glennays, Dexons Green, Dudley.

UPHAM, Samuel Victor
A/10083, 1/12/16, Cpl.; R.A., C/S, 14/7/17; R.F.A., 8/12/17; F; Lieut.; w.
   Emscote, Fortescue Road, Preston, Paignton, South Devonshire.

✠ UPJOHN, William Moon
6/8377, 13/12/15; Welch Gds., 10/12/15; Lieut.
                           Killed in action 24/8/18.

UPSON, John Randolph
D/Sq/13000, 29/4/18, Sgt.; demob. 4/1/19.
            9 Great Dover Street, Borough, S.E.1.

UPTON, Edmund Robert Bruce
6/3/5530, 9/8/15; North'n. R., 20/10/15, secd. Indian Army; F,SA,P; Capt.; w.
        20th D.C.O. Infantry, Loralai, Baluchistan.

UPTON, James Baskerville
A/14106, 7/10/18; demob. 31/1/19.
                 Berry Hall, Solihull, Warwickshire.

UPTON, Ralph Eldridge Roebuck
6/1/6138, 9/9/15; Hamps. R., 14/7/16; F; Lieut.; w; M.C.
c/o W. Willing Jones Esq., Granville House, Arundel Street, W.C.1.

UPTON, Sidney Henry Fowler
D/Sq/11095, 23/4/17; trfr. 28th Lond. R., 28/8/17.
          Rosendene, 97 Hune Road, Worthing, Sussex.

✠ URBAN, Oscar Arthur
4/3890, 31/5/15; E. Surr. R., 7/10/15; F; 2/Lieut.; w.
                           Killed in action 3/9/16.

UREN, Arthur Stanley
6/3/7887, 26/11/15; dis. med. unfit, 26/9/16.
       10 St. Hilda's Road, Old Trafford, Manchester.

UREN, Harold John
B/10668, 5/2/17, Sgt.; R.F.A., C/S, 17/12/17, No. 5 O.C.B.; Devon. R., 3/2/19; 2/Lieut.
         6 Victoria Drive, West Kirby, Cheshire.

UREN, Percy David
6/5/5275, 31/7/15, L/C.; Manch. R., 2/12/15, Lan. Fus., emp. M. of Labour; F; Lieut.
        36 Central Road, West Didsbury, Manchester.

APPENDIX II.—RECORDS OF RANK AND FILE.

✠ URIDGE, Edgar John Gibbins
6/7708, 22/11/15; R.F.A., C/S, 9/6/16; R.F.A., 9/10/16; F; 2/Lieut. *Killed in action 26/6/17.*

✠ URQUHART, Francis Clement
6/4/6028, 2/9/15; R.A., C/S, 29/1/16, No. 9 O.C.B.; Gord. Highrs., 6/7/16, Lab. Corps, att. R. Scots; Lieut. *Died of wounds 13/4/18.*

URQUHART, Robert Charles Duff
B/13624, 24/7/18; demob. 29/1/19.
Tavistock Hotel, Covent Garden, W.C. 2.

URQUHART, William
6/4/5911, 30/8/15; 7th Lond. R., 19/11/15; Lieut.; M.C.
75 Bearfield Avenue, Finchley, N.

USHER, Frank Edward
D/E/13811, 9/8/18; No. 22 O.C.B., 20/9/18; R. War. R., 14/2/19; 2/Lieut.
The Firs, Penns Lane, Erdington, Birmingham.

USHER, Lawry Bradley
6/7965, 29/11/15; No. 14 O.C.B., 29/9/16; E. Kent R., 24/1/17; F; Capt. *39 St. Marys Mansions, Maida Hill, W.*

UTLEY, Henry James Dominic
D/A/11875, 16/8/17; R.F.C., C/S, 18/1/18; R.F.C., 6/3/18; 2/Lieut. *Emsworth, Hampshire.*

UTTERTON, Frank LeCouteur
1/3891, 31/5/15; York. & Lanc. R., 27/8/15; F; Lieut.; w.
28 Halons Road, Eltham, S.E. 9.

UTTING, Reginald James
6/1/7966, 29/11/15; M.G.C., C/S, 25/11/16; M.G.C., 24/3/17; F; 2/Lieut.; w. *59 Croftdown Road, N.W. 5.*

UTTLEY, James Arthur
6/2/9259, 2/2/16; R.E., C/S, 2/9/16; R.E., 18/11/16; F; Lieut.
Southborne, Albert Square, Bowdon, Cheshire.

UZIELLI, Clive Frederick
6/3/7599, 18/11/15; R. Lanc. R., 6/7/16; F; Lieut.; w(2); M.C.
Bath Club, Dover Street, W. 1.

VALLANCE, Roper Guy Aymer
C/12584, 6/2/18; trfr. R.A.F., 21/5/19.
Macknade, Faversham, Kent.

✠ VALLANCE, Lancelot William
6/2/7282, 8/11/15; R.F.A., C/S, 31/3/16; R.F.A., 21/8/16; 2/Lieut. *Killed in action 31/10/16.*

VALLANCE, Leonard Gerald
1/9758, 16/10/16; No. 14 O.C.B., 5/3/17; trfr. 16th Lond. R., 11/7/17. *61 Kennington Park Road, S.E. 11.*

VALLIS, Eric Walter Harvey
6/3/5717, 19/8/15; Som. L.I., 15/1/16; M; Lieut.
Surveyors Office, Dulverton, Somerset.

VALON, Jean Paul Melville
E/2856, 4/2/15; L/C.; R. Suss. R., 31/3/15, Tank Corps; F; Capt.; M(1). *c/o W. A. Valon & Son, 5 Victoria Street, S.W. 1.*

VANDELEUR, Cecil Ronald Pakenham
F/3/1856, 16/10/14; dis. med. unfit, 6/10/16.
St. Andrews, Lustleigh, South Devonshire.

VANDELEUR, Crofton Talbot Bayly
Sq/1901, 16/10/14, L/C.; N. Som. Yeo., 20/2/15; F; Lieut.
Wardenstown, Killucan, Co. Westmeath, Ireland.

VAN DER HORST, Alexander
A/B/12177, 29/10/17, L/C.; No. 11 O.C.B., 10/5/18; 7th Lond. R., 3/2/19; 2/Lieut. *14 Grosvenor Road, Finchley Church End, N. 3.*

VAN DER STEEN, Cecil Jack Percival
D/11093, 13/4/17; Garr. O.C.B., 5/10/17; Lab. Corps, 25/1/18; F; Lieut. *25 Phœnix Lodge Mansions, Brook Green, W. 6.*

VAN DRUTEN, Henry John
3/3119, 25/3/15; Midd'x. R., 21/6/15, R. Suss. R.; F; Capt.; w.
80 Greencroft Gardens, Hampstead, N.W. 6.

VANDYK, Edward
4/3892, 31/5/15; Linc. R., 26/10/15; F,P; Capt.
Hotel Rubens, Buckingham Palace Road, S.W. 1.

VAN EEGHEN, Leslie Vivian Frederick
B/10128, 6/12/16, L/C.; R.G.A., C/S, 22/6/17; R.G.A., 25/11/17; E,P; Capt. *(Now in Holland).*

VANN, Alfred George Thomas Simpson
C/13289, 14/6/18, Sgt.; General List, 28/4/19; 2/Lieut.
Coates Rectory, Cirencester, Gloucestershire.

VANNECK, Richard Grant
K/2115, 16/11/14; R. Fus., 23/11/14; Capt.; M.C.
43 Westbourne Gardens, W. 2.

VANOS, Herbert Augustus
B/Sq/10988, 2/4/17, L/C.; No. 1 Cav. C/S, 28/2/18; 6th Drag., 14/2/19; 2/Lieut. *59 Edith Road, West Kensington, W.14.*

✠ VAN PRAAGH, Ralph Bertram
A/1284, 23/9/14; K.R. Rif. C., 14/11/14; 2/Lieut.; w.
Killed in action 9/4/17.

✠ VANSITTART, Arnold Bexley
Sq/576, 13/11/11; 11th Huss. 14/8/14; 2/Lieut.
Died of wounds 12/5/15.

VAN SOMEREN, Henry Arnold Avenel
Sq/877, 4/8/14, L/C.; R.F.A., 5/12/14; F; Capt.; w.
29 Strand Road, Rangoon.

VAN SOMEREN, Walter Noel
C/12060, 27/9/17; R.F.C., C/S, 30/11/17; R.F.C., 17/12/17, R.A.F.; F; Flying Off.; w.
Hillside, Arnewood Road, Stourfield Park, Bournemouth.

VAN SOMEREN, William Vernon Logan
E/1503, 1/10/14, Cpl.; R. Fus., 27/11/14; F; Lt. Col.; D.S.O., M.C., Croix de Guerre (Belge), M(2).
Hillside, Arnewood Road, Stourfield Park, Bournemouth. (Now in Straits Settlements).

VARCOE, William Stuart
C/12628, 18/2/18; No. 21 O.C.B., 5/7/18; trfr. 28th Lond. R., 22/8/18, K.R. Rif. C., R.A.O.C.
Parkgwyn, St. Stephens, Grampound Road, Cornwall.

VARDY, Reginald Guy. See WEIDEMANN, Reginald Guy

VARDY, William Andrew Shakespeare
C/13217, 5/6/18; trfr. 14th Lond. R., 6/12/18.
Winksley Vicarage, Ripon.

✠ VARLEY, Ernest
B/9896, 10/11/16; L'pool. R., 3/4/17, Lab. Corps; 2/Lieut.; w. *Died 2/3/18.*

VARLEY, John
6/2/5575, 12/8/15; trfr. R.G.A., 7/7/16; R.G.A., 24/6/17; 2/Lieut.
c/o Bank of Adelaide, 11 Leadenhall Street, E.C.

VARLEY, Richard Stanley
E/1558, 6/10/14, L/C.; N. Staff. R., 6/3/15; Lieut.; w.
11 Stanley Gardens, Kensington Park, W. 11.

✠ VARLEY, William
6/3/5866, 26/8/15; R.A., C/S, 24/1/16; R.G.A., 2/7/16; 2/Lieut. *Killed in action 24/3/18.*

VARNON, Cecil Archibald
C/11052, 12/4/17; dis. med. unfit, 9/1/18.
58 Clapton Common, E. 5.

VAUGHAN, Alfred Robert Leslie
D/11846, 9/8/17; No. 3 O.C.B., 8/2/18; Ches. R., 27/8/18; 2/Lieut. *Heath Side, Barony, Nantwich.*

VAUGHAN, Charles Griffith
C/Sq/10348, 5/1/17, L/C.; R.A., C/S, 9/6/17; R.F.A., 10/11/17; F; Lieut.; g. *Garforth, Nr. Leeds. (Now in Rio de Janeiro).*

VAUGHAN, Charles Stuart
C/948, 5/8/14; R.A.O.C., 22/1/15; F; Capt.
Addiscombe Lodge, Teignmouth, South Devonshire.

VAUGHAN, Francis Gerald
E/3037, 11/3/15; Oxf. & Bucks. L.I., 17/7/15; Lieut.
Haberfield Hall, Easton-in-Gordons, Nr. Bristol.

✠ VAUGHAN, John
4/5/4704, 8/7/15; L'pool. R., 7/8/15; F; 2/Lieut.
Killed in action 30/7/16.

✠ VAUGHAN, John David
6/6915, 18/10/15; Welch R., 29/10/15; 2/Lieut.; M.C.
Died of wounds 18/3/17.

VAUGHAN, Joseph Royston
C/13216, 5/6/18; trfr. K.R. Rif. C., 7/4/19.
538 Kensington Hill, Brislington, Bristol.

VAUGHAN, Philip Beaumont
C/14302, 20/11/18; No. 3 O.C.B., 10/2/19; E. Kent R., 20/3/19; 2/Lieut. *20 East Cliff, Dover.*

VAUGHAN-CLARK, Donald Aubrey
6/Sq/7390, 11/11/15, L/C.; R.A., C/S, 18/8/16; R.F.A., 9/12/16; F; Lieut.; w. *Chinyika, P.O. Arcturus, Southern Rhodesia.*

VAUGHAN-CLARK, Ralph Tanner
12562, 6/2/18; R.F.A., C/S, 15/1/18; demob.
Chinyika, P.O. Arcturus, Southern Rhodesia.

APPENDIX II.—RECORDS OF RANK AND FILE.

VAUGHAN-JONES, Alan
B/85, 13/4/08; dis. 12/4/13; trfr. 25th Lond. R., 31/8/14; R.A.F.; F; Lieut. Myrtlebury, West End Avenue, Pinner, Middlesex.

✠ VAUGHAN-JONES, Edward
B/3076, 18/3/15, Cpl.; R.W. Fus., 11/6/15; F,S; 2/Lieut.; w(2).
Killed in action 11/5/18.

✠ VAUGHAN-JONES, Gerald
B/573, 8/11/11; trfr. 25th Lond. R., 31/8/14; R.E., -/10/14, R.F.C.; F; Lieut. Killed in action 26/2/17.

VAUGHAN-JONES, Vivian
B/84, 13/4/08; dis. 12/4/09; rej. B/10765, 19/2/17, Sgt.; demob. 31/1/19. 26 Clifton Villas, Maida Hill, W. 9.

VAUGHAN-WILLIAMS, Arthur Clayton
6/5/C/8122, 2/12/15; No. 13 O.C.B., 4/11/16; R.W. Fus., 28/2/17; P; Lieut.; w. Manor Lodge, Old Windsor, Berkshire.

✠ VAUGHTON, Guy Eglington
6/4/6929, 19/10/15, L/C.; Essex R., 14/7/16; 2/Lieut.
Killed in action 20/11/17.

VAUGHTON, Sidney James Johnson
D/10886, 19/3/17; M.G.C., C/S, 6/7/17; Tank Corps, 28/11/17; Lieut. 29 Mary's Road, Stechford, Birmingham.

VAUS, Eric Lankester
4/3612, 13/5/15, Sgt.; 7th Lond. R., 15/11/15; F; Capt.; w(2).
12a Catherine Road, Surbiton, Surrey.

✠ VAUSE, Thomas Christopher
4/2/5134, 26/7/15; W. York. R., 18/10/15; F; 2/Lieut.
Killed in action 3/9/16.

VEALE, Alfred Pocock
6/8195, 6/12/15; R.E., 31/3/16; F; Capt.; g.
The Uplands, Saltford, Bristol.

VEITCH, Charles Clemett
6/2/C/5642, 16/8/15, Sgt.; No. 19 O.C.B., 9/11/17; 7th Lond. R., 1/5/18; F; Lieut.
c/o British East African Corporation Ltd., Box 12, Mombasa, British East Africa.

VEITCH, George Douglas
F/2613, 7/1/15; W. Rid. R., 11/5/15.
Fishwick, Kingsteignton, Newton Abbot, South Devonshire.

VENDY, Ernest Frederick
C/14295, 11/11/18; trfr. K.R. Rif. C., 7/4/19.
Church Langton, Market Harborough, Leicestershire.

VENN, John Widdicombe
1/3475, 3/5/15; North'd. Fus., 28/7/15; Lieut.; w.
65 Emys Road, Eastbourne.

VENNING, John
C/845, 4/8/14, L/C.; 1st Lond. R., 28/9/14, 6th and 8th Lond. R.; F; Major; w; M.C., M(1).
12 Cadogan Mansions, Sloane Square, S.W. 1.

VEREKER, George Gordon Medlicott
S/506, 4/11/10; Interpreter, 10/10/14, Gren. Gds.; F; Capt.; M.C., M(2). Sharpitor, Salcombe, South Devonshire.

VERNON, Vincent Charles
B/12817, 20/3/18; No. 3 O.C.B., 6/9/18; trfr. Gord. Highrs., 27/1/19. Northfield, 27 Brighton Grove, Rusholme, Manchester.

✠ VERNON, William Henry Lovell
K/2233, 3/12/14, L/C.; Oxf. Yeo., 10/4/15; 2/Lieut.
Killed in action 7/10/16.

VERRALL, William James Egerton
D/11121, 28/4/17, L/C.; Garr. O.C.B., 5/10/17; Worc. R., 15/12/17. Southdown Lodge, Salvington, Nr. Worthing.

VERRY, Reginald Tyrrell
A/11214, 7/5/17; A.S.C., C/S, 1/10/17; R.A.S.C., 30/11/17; F; 2/Lieut. Bowden House, Seaford, Sussex.

✠ VESEY-FITZGERALD, William Herbert Leslie. See FITZGERALD, W. H. L. V.

VESPER, Philip Edgar
1/3656, 17/5/15; E. Surr. R., 21/8/15, M.G.C., F,E,P; Lieut.
20 St. Mary's Road, South Norwood, S.E. 25.

VESTEY, Percy Charles
D/1478, 29/9/14; Suff. R., 12/12/14; Lieut.
Shirley, South Croydon, Surrey.

VEYSEY, Geoffrey Charles
6/4/8889, 13/1/16; R.A., C/S, 4/8/16; R.G.A., 1/11/16; F; Lieut.; p. 81 Hamlet Gardens, Ravenscourt Park, W. 6.

VIALS, George Edward Turner
4/3576, 10/5/15; W. Rid. R., 28/5/15; Lieut.
53 Billing Road, Northampton.

VICK, Donald William
6/3/5744, 20/8/15; Durh. L.I., 21/12/15; w,p.

VICK, Richard Iles
F/1780, 16/10/14; R. Fus., 4/1/15, Hamps. R., att. S. Wales Bord.; F,I; Lieut.; w. Newlands, Horsham, Sussex.

✠ VICKERS, Noel Muschamp
4/3/3991, 3/6/15; Notts. & Derby. R., 10/9/15, York. R.; Lieut.
Killed in action 3/8/16.

✠ VICKERS, Thomas Bernard
6/2/9541, 18/2/16, L/C.; R.E., C/S, 13/1/17; R.E., 31/3/17, secd. Indian Army; I,EA; Lieut. Killed in action 16/7/21.

VIDAL, William Espeut
6/7709, 22/11/15; R.E., 10/2/16; Lieut.; w.
34 Park Road, Chiswick, W. 4.

VIDLER, John George Holbrook
C/14156, 14/10/18; demob. 29/1/19.
Tyla Gwyn, Pontllan Fraith, Monmouthshire.

VIDLER, Stuart Mason
6/1/8978, 17/1/16, L/C.; No. 14 O.C.B., 26/11/16, No. 2 O.C.B.; Special List, 27/3/17, S. Persia Rifles; Persia; Capt.
Brook Cottage, Stanwell, Nr. Staines, Middlesex.

VIGERS-HARRIS, A. D. See HARRIS, A. D. V.

VIGNE, Frederick
6/Sq/7967, 29/11/15; No. 1 Cav. C/S, 24/4/16; North'd. Huss., 28/7/16, att. M.G.C.; Lieut.

VIGNOLES, Edwin Herbert
4/3/6/4321, 17/6/15, L/C.; Sigs. C/S, 30/4/17; R.E., 4/11/17; F; 2/Lieut. San Martin 1184, Mendoza, Argentina, South America.

VIGOR, Harold Charles Paul
6/1/5260, 16/9/15; R.G.A., 7/7/16; R.G.A., 24/6/17; Lieut.
c/o Standard Oil Coy. of New York, Shanghai, China.

✠ VIGOR, William Petter
1/3803, 27/5/15; R. War. R., 5/9/15; 2/Lieut.
Killed in action 13/8/16.

VILLIERS, Thomas Vernon
6/2/6749, 11/10/15; R.F.C., 4/8/16, R.A.F.; Lieut.
7 Northwick House, St. John's Wood, N.W. 8.

✠ VINCENT, Alfred Copplestone Waldon. See WALDON-VINCENT, A. C.

✠ VINCENT, Charles
D/11552, 21/6/17; No. 3 O.C.B., 8/2/18; E. Kent R., 30/7/18; 2/Lieut. Killed in action 17/10/18.

✠ VINCENT, Charles Tunnadine Matson
B/10330, 4/1/17; trfr. 16th Lond. R., 9/5/17, att. 12th Lond. R. and M.G.C.; F; L/C. Died 11/7/21.

VINCENT, Clarence James
K/E/2381, 17/12/14, L/C.; E. York. R., 17/3/15, att. Manch. R.; E,P,S; Lieut. The College, Chester.

VINCENT, Henry Edward
6/4/7815, 24/11/15; No. 14 O.C.B.; Ches. R., 24/10/16; F; Capt.; M.C., M(1). 41 St. Annes Street, Salisbury.

VINCENT, Hilary Madden Godfrey
A/10511, 15/1/17; No. 20 O.C.B., 7/6/17; Devon. R., 25/9/17, att. T.M. Bty.; F,It; Lieut.
Nat. Prov. & Union Bank, Prudential Buildings, Plymouth.

VINCENT, James Sydney
C/13200, 3/6/18; R.E., C/S, 25/8/18.
22 Canon Street, Aberdare, Glamorganshire.

✠ VINCENT, William Morris
E/1565, 6/10/14; Suff. R., 12/12/14, att. Essex R.; 2/Lieut.
Killed in action 26/3/17.

✠ VINCENT-JACKSON, Montagu John
F/1754, 16/10/14; Notts. & Derby. R., 13/11/14; Lieut.
Killed in action 4/2/16.

VINE, Leslie Edward
6/3/7857, 26/11/15; R.F.C., 7/8/16, R.A.F.; F; Lieut.
54 Ashleigh Avenue, Bridgwater, Somerset.

VINEN, Lawrence Northcote
Sq/3186, 6/4/15, L/C.; R.F.A., 9/7/15; F; Capt.; M.C.
P.O. Shannon, Bloemfontein, South Africa.

APPENDIX II.—RECORDS OF RANK AND FILE.

'oel
5: No. 8 O.C.B., 4/8/16; Midd'x. R., 21/11/16;
Killed in action 12/10/18.

VINER, Horace
6/5/6106, 6/9/15; R.E., 13/10/15; Lieut.

VINES, Hubert George
C/12075, 1/10/17, Sgt.; demob. 23/1/19.
10 Grove Avenue, Muswell Hill, N. 10.

VINT, Edward John Cyril
4/3/3990, 3/6/15; 20th Lond. R., 19/9/15, att. T.M. Bty.; F,S;
Capt.   Drakes Broughton, Pershore, Worcestershire.

✠ VINT, William Percival
2/3278, 15/4/15; R. Ir. Rif., 20/6/15, M.G.C.; F; Major.
Killed in action 5/8/18.

VINTER, Eustace Arthur Fitzgerald
6/3/8196, 6/12/15, L/C.; R.E., C/S, 2/9/16; R.E., 18/11/16; F;
Lieut.   27 Charleville Road, West Kensington, W. 14.

VINTER, Percival Jackson
K/2518, 31/12/14; Devon. R., 13/3/15; Lieut.
The Hannings, Framlingham, Suffolk

VIPOND, Alfred Edward
4/1/5050, 22/7/15, Sgt.; demob 2/2/19.
Cadogan Villa, Stanwix, Carlisle.

VITALI, Francesco Remo
C/Sq/10143, 8/12/16, L/C.; No. 1 Cav. C/S, 5/7/17; Yeo.,
23/11/17; Lieut.   Stoneleigh, Epsom.

VIZARD, Lewis Newton
6/3/7317, 8/11/15, L/C.; No. 11 O.C.B., 7/5/16; M.G.C.,
4/9/16; F,It; Lieut.; M.C., Italian Silver Medal for Valour.
2 Clarence Parade, Cheltenham.

VIZARD, William Gervass
F/1808, 16/10/14; Dorset R., 14/3/15; I,M; Major; M(1).
Whitepost House, Redhill, Surrey.

VOLLMER, Percy
4/5/4832, 13/7/15, L/C.; Manch. R., 20/11/15; F; Capt.
41 Spear Street, Manchester.

VON DER HEYDE, John Leslie
6/5/6978, 23/10/15; R. Suss. R., 6/6/16; S; Staff Capt.; M.C.,
M(1).   1st R. Suss. R., British Army of the Rhine.

✠ VON HEYDER, Harold
2/3243, 12/4/15, L/C.; Suff. R., 8/7/15, L'pool. R.; F; 2/Lieut.
Killed in action 13/8/16.

VORLEY, John Stuart
4/5/4769, 12/7/15; R. Ir. Fus., 20/11/15, secd. Nigeria Regt.;
Lieut.

VOS, Simon
4/3/4299, 17/6/15; Devon. R., 29/6/16; Lieut.
22 West Bank, Amhurst Park, N. 16.

VOSPER, Frank Permain
A/13042, 6/5/18; demob. 29/1/19.
70 Regents Park Road, N.W. 1.

VOSPER, Roy Atherley
A/10263, 29/12/16; R.F.C., C/S, 16/4/17; R.F.C., 16/5/17,
R.A.F.; F; Lieut.   1 Casthorpe Road, Edgbaston, Birmingham.

VOSPER, William
C/10810, 28/2/17; trfr. 16th Lond. R., 18/5/17, att. R.A.S.C.;
R.S.M.; m.   Claremont, Launceston, Cornwall.

VOSS, Fergus
6/9168, 26/1/16; R.E., 9/5/16; Lieut.
Ardenza, Sprugfield Road, Belfast, Ireland.

VOSS, Walter James
6/8043, 30/11/15; R.F.A., C/S, 29/1/16; R.F.A., 6/7/16; 2/Lieut.;
w; M(1).

VOST, Henry
D/11586, 2/7/17; R.F.C., C/S, 23/10/17; R.F.C., 12/12/17,
R.A.F.; F; 2/Lieut.; Inj.
110 Slade Lane, Levenshulme, Manchester.

VOWLER, John Creed Guillim
B/12198, 5/11/17; R.E., C/S, 13/1/18; R.E., 26/4/18; F; Lieut.
Roseneath, Launceston, Cornwall.

VOWLES, Alfred Charles
C/9969, 20/11/16; No. 14 O.C.B., 30/1/17; Dorset R., 29/5/17,
Wilts. R.; M; Lieut.
Dunyat Cottage, Compton Bishop, Axbridge, Somerset.

VOWLES, Charles Ernest
6/2/6409, 23/9/15; No. 11 O.C.B., 7/5/16; D. of Corn. L.I.,
4/9/16; F; Lieut.; w.   Caer-Brito, 12 Ashley Hill, Bristol.

VOWLES, Robert Douglas
D/10237, 29/12/16; No. 14 O.C.B., 7/6/17; S. Lan. R., 25/10/17;
Lieut.   2 Ashley Park, Chesterfield Road, Bristol.

VOYLE, Stanley George
4/1/4658, 5/7/15; R. Lanc. R., 27/12/15, Indian Army; F,I,E;
Capt.   18 Ladbroke Gardens, Kensington, W. 11.

WADDELL, Laurence William
2/3253, 13/4/15; Essex R., 20/10/15, R.A.F.; S,E; Lieut.
Warwick Bridge, Carlisle.

WADDINGTON, Joseph
A/2755, 21/1/15; L'pool. R., 13/4/15; F,It; Capt.
Dobson Hall, Chipping, Nr. Preston, Lancashire.

✠ WADE, Albert Luvian
K/H/2123, 14/11/14, L/C.; Midd'x. R., 17/4/15, att. T.M. Bty.;
F; Lieut.   Killed in action 28/4/17.

WADE, Gerald Darnton
B/D/11998, 10/9/17; No. 20 O.C.B., 5/4/18; Yorks. L.I., 8/10/18;
2/Lieut.   Lane Head, Rawdan, Nr. Leeds, Yorkshire.

✠ WADE, Oliver John
3/3142, 29/3/15; R.W. Kent R., 21/6/15, R.F.C.; E,F; 2/Lieut.
Killed in action 22/10/16.

WADE, Victor Fleming
B/11311, 17/5/17; No. 16 O.C.B., 5/10/17; Ches. R., 12/3/18;
2/Lieut.   19 Church Road, Tranmere, Birkenhead.

WADE-BROWN, Laurence Frank
A/11659, 12/7/17; Tank Corps C/S, 21/12/17; Tank Corps,
8/10/18; 2/Lieut.
Comb Martin, Oakdale Road, Weybridge, Surrey.

WADMORE, Alfred Mervyn
6/B/6836, 14/10/15; dis. med. unfit.
Elmhurst, Albert Road, Clevedon, Somerset.

WADNER, Erik Gustaf Christopher
6/1/9390, 8/2/16; No. 14 O.C.B., 28/8/16; 7th Lond. R., 24/10/16,
emp. M. of Munitions; F; Lieut.; w.
44 Park Lane, Clissold Park, N. 16.

WADSWORTH, William Reade
B/10315, 4/1/17; No. 20 O.C.B., 5/5/17; R.W. Fus., 28/8/17; S;
Staff Capt.   Changing House, Congleton Road, Macclesfield.

WAGG, Frederick John
6/3/8704, 4/1/16; No. 13 O.C.B., 4/11/16; Sea. Highrs., 28/2/17;
F; Lieut.   Meade House, Biggleswade, Bedfordshire.

WAGGETT, John Leslie
Sq/137, 18/4/08; 1st R. Regt. of Cav., 16/9/14; F,I,M; Lieut.;
M.C.   8L Hyde Park Mansions, W.

WAGHORN, Henry Webb
F/2682, 14/1/15; R.W. Kent R., 14/4/15, att. R. Dub. Fus.;
Capt.; w.

WAGHORN, Horace Charles Franklin
C/10374, 8/1/17, L/C.; R.G.A., C/S, 12/9/17; R.G.A., 4/2/18;
F; 2/Lieut.
Fernhurst, 58 Grosvenor Avenue, Wallington, Surrey.

✠ WAGHORN, Leonard Pengelly
Sq/579, 13/11/11; R.W. Kent R., 14/8/14, R. Berks. R.; 2/Lieut.
Killed in action 6/10/14.

WAGHORNE, George Ernest
6/3/6440, 25/9/15; No. 7 O.C.B., 7/4/16; 9th Lond. R., 17/7/16;
2/Lieut.; w.
Holmecroft, Sandford Mill Road, Cheltenham.

WAGSTAFFE, William Warwick
A/522, 18/11/10; R.A.M.C., 23/4/13, att. 11th Huss.; F; Major;
O.B.E., M(1).   Purleigh, Sevenoaks, Kent.

WAINWRIGHT, Eric Herbert
F/1781, 16/10/14, Sgt.; R.E., 10/4/15; F; Capt.
Oatlands Wood, Oatlands Avenue, Weybridge.

WAINWRIGHT, Tom Archibald
B/10558, 19/1/17; No. 14 O.C.B., 5/7/18; Hunt. Cyc. Bn.,
30/10/17; 2/Lieut. 40 Topsfield Parade, Crouch End, N. 8.

WAITE, Archibald Harvey
6/3/9247, 2/2/16; R.A., C/S, 18/8/16; R.G.A., 3/12/16; F;
Lieut.   St. Kelvin, Aldermans Hill, Palmers Green, N. 13.

APPENDIX II.—RECORDS OF RANK AND FILE.

WAITE, *Wilfred Fabian*
H/1828, 16/10/14, Sgt.; Lan. Fus., 25/2/15; F; Lieut.; w;, M(1).
    8 New Court, Carey Street, W.C. 2.

✠ WAITHMAN, *Victor de Vipont*
1/3143, 29/3/15; trfr. 2nd Cty. of Lond. Yeo., 19/10/15, R. Lanc. R.
    Died of wounds 21/4/18.

✠ WAKEFIELD, *Frank Mahon*
6/Sq/5643, 16/8/15; Dorset Yeo., 28/10/15, att. M.G.C.; Lieut.
    Died 2/1/19.

WAKEFIELD, *Harold Brougham*
6/7816, 24/11/15; R.F.C., 17/3/16, R.A.F.; Lieut.
    Sedgwick House, Kendal.

WAKEFIELD, *Roy Frampton*
C/Sq/10183, 13/12/16, Cpl.; No. 2 Cav. C/S, 11/1/18; 6th R. Regt. of Cav., 18/10/18.
    Langford Downs, Lechlade, Gloucestershire.

WAKEFORD, *Cecil Austin*
12451, 22/1/18; H. Bde. O.C.B.; Welch Gds., 22/2/19; 2/Lieut.
    55 Peterborough Road, Hurlingham, S.W. 6.

WAKEFORD, *Laurence*
B/11427, 1/6/17; R.E., C/S, 30/9/17; R.E., 9/11/17; Lieut.; w.
    Personal Attendance Committee, 39 Grosvenor Place, S.W. 1.

WAKELIN, *Robert Wilfred*
6/4/9100, 24/1/16; A.S.C., C/S, 26/6/16; R.A.S.C., 30/7/16; F; Lieut.
    Freebownes, Witham, Essex.

✠ WAKELY, *William Norman*
6/5644, 16/8/15; L'pool. R., 20/8/15, att. M.G.C.; 2/Lieut.
    Killed in action 8/5/17.

WALCOTT, *Edward Patrick McLeod*
6/1/9368, 7/2/16; No. 8 O.C.B., 4/8/16; R. Highrs., 21/11/16; Lieut.; w.
    32 Goldington Avenue, Bedford.

WALDEN, *Percy Walter George*
6/2/5574, 12/8/15; Hamps. R., 25/3/16; I.
    Quay Hill, Lymington, Hampshire.

✠ WALDIE, *Charles Percival*
H/2018, 5/11/14; R.W. Surr. R., 8/2/15; 2/Lieut.
    Killed in action 26/9/15.

✠ WALDON-VINCENT, *Alfred Copplestone*
B/912, 5/8/14; Dorset R., 1/9/14; Capt.; w.
    Killed in action 26/9/16.

WALDRON, *Basil Cuthbert A.*
4/3430, 29/4/15; Durh. L.I., 28/7/15; 2/Lieut.; w.
    71 Selby Hill Road, Brumbrook, Birmingham.

WALDRON, *Cecil Frank*
6/1/7892, 27/11/15; trfr. 16th Lond. R., 2/5/16.
    Trevelgue, The Mount, New Malden.

WALE, *Eric Harry*
B/753, 23/1/13; S. Staff. R., 11/9/14, R.E.; F; Capt.; M.C., M(1).
    73 Coton Hill, Shrewsbury.

✠ WALEY, *Aubrey John*
C/1033, 24/8/14; R. Fus., 12/9/14; Lieut.; w.
    Killed in action 31/7/17.

WALEY, *Frank Raphael*
C/958, 5/8/14; K.R. Rif. C., 12/9/14, S. Lan. R.; F; Capt.; M.C.
    32 Gloucester Square, W. 2.

WALFORD, *George Augustus*
C/11061, 16/4/17; No. 14 O.C.B., 10/8/17; R. Suss. R., 27/11/17; F; 2/Lieut.; w.
    c/o A. Perlo, Domodossola, Italy.

✠ WALFORD, *Leonard Nithsdale*
Sq/743, 18/11/13; 12th Lond. R., 8/7/14; Lieut.
    Killed in action 8/5/15.

✠ WALFORD, *Percy Frederic*
6/2/7318, 8/11/15, Sgt.; K.R. Rif. C., 4/9/16; 2/Lieut.
    Killed in action 11/4/17.

WALKER, *Alfred James Norman*
4/2/4440, 27/6/15; York. & Lanc. R., 29/10/15, att. M.G.C.; Lieut.
    32 Cambrian Road, Queens Road, Richmond.

WALKER, *Cecil Hirst*
6/3/6640, 4/10/15; No. 11 O.C.B., 7/5/16; 8th Lond. R., 4/9/16, Rif. Brig., att. T.M. Bty.; F,E; Lieut.
    6 Carlton Vale, Maida Vale, N.W. 6.

WALKER, *Charles Nigel Gordon*
A/392, 31/3/09; dis. 11/2/10.

WALKER, *Clarence Godfrey*
6/4/7373, 10/11/15, Cpl.; No. 14 O.C.B., 27/10/16, M.G.C., C/S; M.G.C., 30/1/17; Lieut.; M.C.
    c/o Cleghorn & Harris, 88 Old Street, E.C.

✠ WALKER, *Clarence Howard*
4/3893, 31/5/15; Essex R., 7/10/15; 2/Lieut.
    Died of wounds 28/9/16.

WALKER, *David Easson*
4/9718, 11/10/16; No. 14 O.C.B., 27/12/16; Sco. Rif., 27/3/17; S; Lieut.
    Silvermere, Woodside Avenue, Woodside Park, N.12.

WALKER, *Edward*
A/10710, 12/2/17, L/C.; No. 14 O.C.B., 7/9/17; 7th Lond. R., 17/12/17; F; Lieut.; w.
    The Gables, Deganwy, North Wales. (Now in Switzerland).

WALKER, *Edward Louis Haviland*
6/1/7081, 29/10/15, L/C.; R.A., C/S, 4/8/16; R.G.A., 24/11/16; F; Lieut.; w, g.
    2 Onslow Gardens, Wallington, Surrey.

WALKER, *Garth Hamilton*
C/14232, 25/10/18; trfr. K.R. Rif. C., 7/4/19.
    The Grange, West Drayton, Middlesex.

WALKER, *Geoffrey*
C/9938, 17/11/16, Cpl.; R.F.C., C/S, 13/3/17; R.F.C., 19/4/17, R.A.F.; F; Lieut.; w.
    29 Granville Park, Blackheath, S.E. 13.

WALKER, *Gerald Gladstone*
4/3/4688, 8/7/15; dis. to R. Mil. Coll., 29/8/16; N. Lan. R., 1/5/17, att. R.F.C., R.A.F.; Lieut.; M.C., M(1).
    Glenferry, Regent Road, Altrincham.

WALKER, *Gordon*
3/3359, 22/4/15; Norf. R., 8/7/15; F; Lieut.
    Richmond Hill Hotel, Richmond, Surrey.

WALKER, *Harry*
A/2756, 21/1/15, L/C.; General List, 11/5/15, R. Muns. Fus., Bedf. R.; S; 2/Lieut.
    White Lodge, Seething, Brooke, Norwich.

WALKER, *Henry*
6/1/6466, 27/9/15; trfr. R.G.A., 15/11/16.
    Alverscote, Oxford.

WALKER, *Herbert Dutton*
A/12452, 22/1/18; No. 21 O.C.B., 7/6/18; Notts. & Derby. R., 4/2/19; 2/Lieut.
    11 Argyll Road, Blackpool.

WALKER, *James McDonald*
D/10948, 30/3/17; R.F.C., C/S, 4/5/17; R.F.C., 14/6/17, R.A.F.; F; Capt.; w; D.F.C.
    20 Granby Road, Newington, Edinburgh, Scotland.

WALKER, *James Rowantree*
4/Sq/5056, 22/7/15, L/C.; R.A., C/S, 13/10/16; R.F.A., 11/3/17; F; Lieut.; p.
    75 Park Avenue, Hull, East Yorkshire.

WALKER, *Lamplough*
A/14331, 30/12/18; No. 11 O.C.B., 24/1/19; General List, 8/3/19; EA; 2/Lieut.
    17 Walker Street, Morecombe, Lancashire.

WALKER, *Leonard*
2/3244, 12/4/15; York. R., 8/7/15; F,It; Lieut.; w.
    Creig-y-don, York Road, Woking, Surrey.

WALKER, *Leonard Charles*
C/11083, 18/4/17; R.F.C., C/S, 1/6/17; R.F.C., 4/7/17, R.A.F.; F; Lieut.
    13 Gourock Road, Eltham, S.E. 9. (Now in Kenya Colony).

WALKER, *Leonard Joseph*
B/13620, 24/7/18; trfr. K.R. Rif. C., 7/4/19.
    North Lodge, Abberley, Worcester.

WALKER, *Malcolm Ure*
B/12746, 11/3/18; No. 8 O.C.B., 20/9/18; demob.
    10 Queen Street, Alloa, Scotland.

✠ WALKER, *Oscar Robert*
B/1212, 14/9/14, L/C.; Worc. R., 24/11/14, att. R. Fus.; Capt.
    Killed in action 4/6/15

WALKER, *Patrick Spink*
1/3802, 27/5/15; R Fus., 8/9/15, R.F.A.; F; Lieut.; w.
    c/o Nat. Bank of India, 26 Bishopsgate, E.C

WALKER, *Ralph Cuthbert*
D/11848, 9/8/17; No. 3 O.C.B., 8/2/18; R. War. R., 30/7/; 2/Lieut.

WALKER, *Reginald Charles*
C/10595, 19/1/17; No. 20 O.C.B., 7/6/17; 7th Lond. R., 25/9/; P,E; 2/Lieut.
    Oberon House, 2 Buckland Avenue, Dove

WALKER, *Robert John*
A/10493, 12/1/17; R.F.A., C/S, 18/5/17; R.F.A., 17/11/17; Lieut.
    3 The Quadrant, Redlands, Brist

WALKER, *Robert Palfreeman*
C/11803, 2/8/17; A.S.C., C/S, 1/11/17; R.A.S.C., 25/1/18; Lieut.
    21 Silver Hill Road, Ecclesall, Sheffie

APPENDIX II.—RECORDS OF RANK AND FILE.

WALKER, Sidney Frederick
6/5/5752, 31/7/15; L/C.; R. Lanc. R., 27/12/15; F; Capt.; w(3).
Lynton, Victoria Park, Bangor, North Wales.

WALKER, Sidney Walls
C/11500, 14/6/17; R.F.C., C/S, 2/8/17; R.F.C., 2/10/17, R.A.F.; Lieut.
Tragnair, Stormont Road, Highgate, N. 6.

WALKER, Theodore Herbert
6/1/6707, 7/10/15; No. 11 O.C.B., 7/5/16; D. of Corn. L.I., 4/9/16; S,F; Capt.; w.
c/o H. E. King Esq., 8 Broughton Drive, Grassendale, Liverpool. (Now in Java).

WALKER, William
6/3/5805, 23/8/15; trfr. 13th Lond. R., 9/6/16.

WALKER, William
A/11215, 7/5/17; R.A., C/S, 8/2/18; R.G.A., 1/10/18; 2/Lieut.
71 King Street, Manchester.

WALKERLEY, George Bourke
C/D/12037, 24/9/17, L/C.; No. 19 O.C.B., 5/4/18; E. Kent R., 24/9/18, att. R. Suss. R.; F; Lieut.
Langleybury, Harpenden, Hertfordshire.

WALL, Geoffrey Cresswell
A/1175, 14/9/14; K.R. Rif. C., 3/10/14, R.A.F.; F,E; Capt.
17a Alexandra Road, St. Johns Wood, N.W. 8.

WALL, Gerald Robin P.
E/2631, 7/1/15; Linc. R., 11/4/15, att. R.F.C., R.A.F.; Lieut.; w.
32 Lancaster Gate, W. 2.

WALL, Harry
6/1/8804, 10/1/16; No. 14 O.C.B., 26/11/16; Worc. R., 28/2/17; F; Lieut.
Laurel Crescent, Keighley, Yorkshire.

WALL, William Arthur
6/3/6930, 19/10/15; trfr. R.G.A., 25/9/16; F.
248 Trinity Road, Wandsworth Common, S.W.

WALLACE, Gerald William
6/1/6168, 11/9/15, L/C.; Midd'x. R., 21/4/16, M.G.C.; F,P; Lieut.
10 Lawn Crescent, Kew Gardens, Surrey.

✠ WALLACE, Harry Herbert
6/2/6678, 7/10/15, L/C.; North'd. Fus., 4/9/16; 2/Lieut.
Died of wounds 21/1/17.

✠ WALLACE, James Hope. See HOPE-WALLACE, J.

WALLACE, John Boyd
6/8705, 4/1/16; R.A., C/S, 7/8/16; R.G.A., 19/12/16.
41 St. Vincent Place, Glasgow.

WALLACE, John Selby Burrell
C/13263, 10/6/18; No. 22 O.C.B., 23/8/18; demob. 16/1/19.
c/o R. Blake Esq., Old Mill House, Cobham, Surrey.

WALLACE, Thomas Harold
B/12719, 8/3/18; No. 2 O.C.B., 20/9/18; demob.
Eaglemont, Joubert Park, Johannesburg, South Africa.

WALLACE, William
D/12933, 15/4/18; No. 8 O.C.B., 18/10/18; Linc. R., 17/3/19; 2/Lieut.
Stanhope House, Stanhope, Co. Durham.

WALLBRIDGE, Arthur Charles
A/11210, 7/5/17, L/C.; R.E., C/S, 7/10/17; R.E., 11/1/18; F; 2/Lieut.
c/o Messrs. King & Sons, Durban, Natal, South Africa.

WALLER, Eric de Warrenne
D/13809, 6/8/18; trfr. K.R. Rif. C., 30/5/19.
The Limes, Worting, Basingstoke, Hampshire. (Now in U.S.A.).

WALLER, Herbert Onslow
B/9873, 7/11/16; No. 14 O.C.B., 30/1/17; Sea. Highrs., 29/5/17; P; Lieut.; M.C.
c/o William Cooper and Nephews, Berkhamsted, Hertfordshire.

WALLER, John Herbert
1/9675, 2/10/16; dis. med. unfit.

WALLER, Kenneth
D/12958, 10/4/18; No. 5 O.C.B., 8/11/18; R. Dub. Fus., 17/3/19; 2/Lieut.
50 Upper Beechwood Avenue, Ranelagh, Dublin, Ireland.

WALLER, Leslie
K/2975, 25/2/15; Notts. & Derby. R., 19/5/15.

WALLER, Leslie Reginald
6/4/6723, 9/10/15, Sgt.; E. Kent R., 25/9/16, att. Devon. R.; Lieut.
8 Great Eastern Avenue, Southend.

WALLER, Robert Monsel
4/5/4770, 12/7/15; dis. med. unfit, 8/8/16.
48 Albany Street, Regents Park, N.W. 1.

WALLER-STEVENS, James Leslie
K/Sq/2311, 10/12/14, Cpl.; R.F.A., 2/4/15; F,S,E,P; Lieut.
Loxwood, Sussex.

WALLICH, Maurice George Leonard
F/3039, 11/3/15; R.W. Surr. R., 10/7/15; Lieut.; w, p; M(1).
1625 St. Andrews Place, Los Angelos, California.

✠ WALLINGTON, Charles Harold
D/9992, 23/11/16; No. 14 O.C.B., 5/3/17; Devon. R., 26/6/17, att. L'pool. R.; F; 2/Lieut.
Killed in action 20/9/17.

WALLIS, Frederick John
D/12100, 8/10/17, Cpl.; demob. 23/1/19.
Delgany, Stanley Park Road, Sutton, Surrey.

WALLIS, Harold Frank
6/B/8075, 1/12/15; L/C.; R.A., C/S, 6/7/18; R.F.A., 3/4/19; 2/Lieut.
43 Shacklewell Lane, E. 8.

WALLIS, Henry James
6/D/9016, 19/1/16; R.F.C., C/S, 8/10/16; trfr. North'n. R., 23/3/17.

WALLIS, Herbert John
B/10296, 1/1/17, Cpl.; demob. 23/1/19.
2 Walrond Street, Streatham, S.W. 16.

WALLIS, Owen Brian Symonds
C/13244, 7/6/18; trfr. 14th Lond. R., 6/12/18, Gord. Highrs.; Pte.
26 Overstrand Mansions, Battersea Park, S.W. 11.

WALLIS, Reginald
6/1/7391, 11/11/15; 11th Lond. R., 4/8/16; F; Lieut.; w.
London House, Hook, Hampshire.

WALLIS, Robert George
4/6/3819, 21/5/15, Sgt.; R.A.O.C., 24/9/16; F; Capt.
43 Shacklewell Lane, E. 8.

WALLIS, Timothy Charles
6/5/7374, 10/11/15; No. 7 O.C.B., 3/7/16; Conn. Rang., 21/11/16, att. R. Ir. Rif.; F; Lieut.; M.C.
Maryville, Charleville, Co. Cork, Ireland.

WALLS, Frederick Bell
B/13452, 27/6/18, L/C.; trfr. K.R. Rif. C., 7/4/19.
c/o The Limes, Lurgan, Co. Armagh, Ireland.

WALMSLEY, Arthur Mainprize
4/5/5184, 29/7/15; R.G.A., 27/11/15; F; Capt.; M(1).
58 Carlton Road, Boston.

WALMSLEY, Nigel Williams
1/3208, 8/4/15; N. Lan. R., 8/7/15, R.A.F.; S,E; Lieut.; w; M.C., M(1).
The Oaks, Epping, Essex.

WALMSLEY, Thomas Wesley
D/13804, 9/8/18; demob. 21/1/19.
The Oaks, Epping, Essex.

✠ WALPOLE, Horatio Spencer
2/8706, 4/1/16; Cold Gds., 24/3/16; F; Lieut.; w.
Killed in action 9/4/18.

WALSH, Aubrey Edwin Bethune
D/E/13837, 14/8/18; dis. med. unfit, 8/10/18.
Garah Lodge, Kings Kerswell, South Devonshire.

✠ WALSH, Chester Cecil
D/10024, 27/11/16; trfr. 18th Lond. R., 2/2/17; M(1).
Missing -/8/18.

WALSH, Frank Tempest
C/10345, 5/1/17; No. 14 O.C.B., 7/6/17; E. Lan. R., 25/9/17, att. D. of Corn. L.I.; I; Lieut.
Woodcroft, Oxford Road, Guiseley, Nr. Leeds.

✠ WALSH, John
B/1085, 2/9/14; dis. 10/10/14; R. Fus.; Major; M(1).
Died of wounds 19/2/17.

WALSH, Michael
6/D/8668, 3/1/16; R.A.O.C., 22/11/16; M; Major, D.A.D.O.S.; M(1).
St. Pancras House, N.W.

WALSH, Percy George
4/1/3914, 24/5/15; Shrop. L.I., 10/9/15, att. Lan. Fus.; F; Lieut.
c/o Messrs. Cox & Coy., 16 Charing Cross, S.W. 1.

WALSH, Walter Graham
C/10574, 19/1/17; M.G.C., C/S, 8/6/17; M.G.C., 19/12/17; F; Lieut.
3 The Sanctuary, Westminster, S.W. 1.

WALSHAM, Ernest Frederick
B/1359, 26/9/14; W. York. R., 14/12/14; Lieut.

APPENDIX II.—RECORDS OF RANK AND FILE.

✠ WALSHAM, Harold
K/H/2235, 3/12/14; K.R. Rif. C., 8/4/15; 2/Lieut.
Died of wounds 18/9/15.

WALSHE, Douglas Hunter
6/3/8334, 11/12/15; R.E., C/S, 2/9/16; R.E., 18/11/16; F; Lieut.; M(1). 67 Chester Road, Southport, Lancashire.

WALTER, Elwyn Henry
K/2203, 30/11/14; General List, 23/12/14, R.A.F.; F; Capt.
Bethune, Brackenfel, Cape Province, South Africa.

WALTER, Frederick Whitmell
D/13892, 23/8/18; trfr. 14th Lond. R., 6/12/18, Gord. Highrs; Cpl. 5 St. Mary Road, Walthamstow, E. 17.

✠ WALTER, Joseph Stanley
D/1406, 29/9/14; R.W. Surr. R., 27/11/14; Capt.; w; M.C., M(1). Killed 21/5/18.

WALTERS, Anthony Melmoth
Sq/994, 5/8/14; 14th R. Regt. of Cav., 12/9/14, R.F.C.; Lieut.
The Charterhouse, E.C.

WALTERS, Arthur Owen
6/1/8802, 10/1/16; R.A., C/S, 4/8/16; R.G.A., 3/11/16; F; Major; w(3); M(2).
6 Velindre Place, Whitchurch, Glamorganshire.

✠ WALTERS, Ernest Henry
4/5/4724, 9/7/15; Manch. R., 21/12/15; 2/Lieut.
Killed in action 26/9/16.

WALTERS, Harold Stephen
6/1/6598, 4/10/15; Suff. R., 4/8/16; F; Lieut.; w.
Marlow, Chatsworth Road, Willesden Green, N.W. 2.

WALTERS, Hubert Melmoth
A/13160, 29/5/18; H. Bde. O.C.B., 14/9/18; Gds. M.G.R., 10/3/19; 2/Lieut. The Charterhouse, E.C.

WALTERS, Leonard Austin
6/5/8378, 13/12/15; R.A., C/S, 4/8/16; R.G.A., 3/11/16; F; Lieut. 61 Westow Hill, Upper Norwood, S.E. 19.

WALTERS, Leslie Allan
4/5/4771, 12/7/15; Dorset R., 20/11/15, att. R.A.F.; M,I,E; Lieut.
c/o Messrs. Cox & Coy., F. Dept., 16 Charing Cross, S.W. 1.

WALTERS, Leslie Charles
6/5/7159, 2/11/15, L/C.; R.F.A., C/S, 4/8/16; R.F.A., 10/11/16, R.G.A.; F; Lieut. 61 Westow Hill, Upper Norwood, S.E. 19.

✠ WALTERS, Leslie Hadfield
6/1/6496, 27/9/15; No. 7 O.C.B., 5/4/16; Suff. R., 17/7/16; 2/Lieut. Died of wounds 17/2/17.

WALTERS, Walters Ward
1/3360, 22/4/15; Shrop. L.I., 18/6/15; F; Lieut.; w.
Rolleston, Umberleigh, North Devonshire. (Now in Australia).

WALTON, Allan Roger
H/1710, 14/10/14; Ches. R., 28/10/14; F; Capt.; w(2); M.C.
Netherlea, Bramhall, Cheshire.

WALTON, Ian Erskine Lawson
118, 18/4/08; dis. 31/12/09.

WALTON, James Arthur
D/11847, 9/8/17, Sgt.; demob. 29/1/19.
Firwood, Lime Grove, Thornton-le-Fylde, Lancashire.

WALTON, Robert Gabbett Dundonald
D/12926, 4/4/18; No. 21 O.C.B., 4/10/18; Conn. Rang., 17/3/19; 2/Lieut. The Ferneries, Kilhee, Co. Clare, Ireland.

✠ WANKLYN, William Hibbert
K/2206, 30/11/14; E. Kent Yeo., 27/1/15; 2/Lieut.
Killed in action 11/5/17.

WANSTALL, Cotterill Forster
6/1/5733, 19/8/15; R.A.S.C., 27/11/15; F,S,I; Capt.
Hazeldene, Thorougood Road, Clacton-on-Sea.

WANSTALL, Geoffrey Harry Torrens
6/2/5595, 12/8/15; Dorset R., 20/11/15; F; Lieut.; w(2).
Wollaston Vicarage, Stourbridge. (Now in Canada).

✠ WARBURTON, Henry Heap
4/1/5018, 22/7/15; Lan. Fus., 16/12/15, M.G.C.; F; 2/Lieut.
Killed in action 9/9/16.

✠ WARD, Allan Dudley Walter
D/1404, 29/9/14; R.W. Surr. R., 17/3/15; 2/Lieut.
Died 23/7/17.

WARD, Basil Charles Maurice
B/9883, 8/11/16; No. 14 O.C.B., 30/1/17; E. Surr. R., 25/4/17, R.A.F.; F; Lieut.; w. 32 Kew Road, Richmond, Surrey.

WARD, Cecil Gordon
6/1/7160, 2/11/15; Glouc. R., 4/8/16, att. N. Lan. R.; M; Staff Capt. 44 Headland Park, Plymouth, Devonshire.

✠ WARD, Cecil Wellesley
6/7852, 25/11/15; R.F.A., C/S, 4/8/16; R.F.A., 1/12/16; 2/Lieut.
Killed in action 11/9/17.

WARD, Charles Edward
6/7968, 29/11/15; R.F.C., 2/6/16, R.A.F.; F; Capt.; w.
R.A.F. Club, 13 Bruton Street, W.

WARD, Charles Frederic
6/1/6599, 4/10/15, L/C.; R.W. Kent R., 4/8/16; Lieut.
40 Hillcourt Road, East Dulwich, S.E. 22.

✠ WARD, Cyril Bertram
6/3/7407, 13/11/15; 21st Lond. R., 6/6/16; F; 2/Lieut.; w.
Died of wounds 1/11/16.

✠ WARD, Dacre Stanley
4/5/4689, 8/7/15; 12th Lond. R., 27/11/15; 2/Lieut.
Killed in action 1/7/16.

WARD, Douglas John
K/B/2374, 17/12/14, L/C.; R. Berks. R., 9/3/15; Lt. Col.; M.C.
Singapore Club, Singapore.

WARD, Francis Aislabie
C/10364, 5/1/17; trfr. R.G.A., 25/4/17.

✠ WARD, Harold Arthur
D/10454, 11/1/17, L/C.; No. 20 O.C.B., 7/6/17; Worc. R., 25/9/17; 2/Lieut. Killed in action 20/4/18.

WARD, Henry James
D/2884, 8/2/15; R. Dub. Fus., 22/4/15; Lieut.
Danebury, Upper Tooting Park, Balham, S.W. 17.

WARD, Henry Payne
D/E/13911, 26/8/16; No. 22 O.C.B., 22/11/18; R.W. Surr. R, 15/2/19; 2/Lieut. Burleigh, Reigate Road, Redhill, Surrey.

WARD, Kenneth Glen
A/11634, 9/7/17; trfr. W. Rid. R., 18/5/18.

✠ WARD, Noel Loftus Moore
2/3818, 27/5/15, L/C.; Essex R., 18/12/15; F; 2/Lieut.
Killed in action 15/10/16.

✠ WARD, Norman Hartley
6/3/8149, 3/12/15, L/C.; Midd'x. R., 4/9/16, att. N. Lan. R.; 2/Lieut. Died of wounds 8/3/17.

✠ WARD, Percy Duncan
C/755, 23/1/14; trfr. H.A.C., 31/8/14; rej. K/2142, 19/11/14; Lan. Fus., 9/1/15; Capt.; w. Died of wounds 11/10/16.

✠ WARD, Percy Harry Bavister
6/3/6979, 23/10/15, L/C.; R.F.C., 4/9/16; F; 2/Lieut.; w(2).
Killed in action 19/5/17.

WARD, Richard
6/1/5688, 16/8/15; W. York. R., 15/11/15; F; Lieut.
16 Norfolk Road, Harrogate.

WARD, Stephen Barron
D/12934, 15/4/18; No. 5 O.C.B., 8/11/18, No. 20 O.C.B.; W. Rid. R., 17/3/19; 2/Lieut. Sidney House, Wellington, Salop.

WARD, Vincent Aubrey
4/4898, 15/7/15; dis. 26/7/15.

WARD, William Alexander
4/Sq/4260, 15/6/15, L/C.; Worc. Yeo., 5/8/15, att. R.E. Sigs; Lieut. 83 Edburton Avenue, Brighton.

✠ WARD, William Leigh
A/10033, 29/11/16; No. 14 O.C.B., 30/1/17; Som. L.I., 29/5/17; F; 2/Lieut. Killed in action 21/12/17.

WARDLE, George Benjamin
6/2/5596, 12/8/15; R.W. Kent R., 1/6/16, N. Lan. R.; WA,F; Lieut. 48 Mayfield Avenue, Dover, Kent.

WARDROPER, John Baptist
6/1/D/6261, 16/9/15; R.Q.M.S.; demob. 25/7/19.
40 Egerton Gardens, West Ealing, W. 13.

WARE, Alfred James
2/9775, 24/10/16; No. 14 O.C.B., 30/1/17; Rif. Brig., 29/5/17; 2/Lieut.; w. 10 Riversleigh Avenue, Lytham, Lancashire.

WARHURST, William Henry
6/2/9076, 22/1/16; No. 5 O.C.B., 14/8/16; R.N.V.R., 21/11/16; F; Sub. Lieut. Inversnaid, Lyme Grove, Marple, Cheshire.

APPENDIX II.—RECORDS OF RANK AND FILE.

WARMINGTON, Guy Wilson
D/13682, 26/7/18; demob. 5/2/19.
    The Hut, West Ewell, Surrey.

WARNER, Edward Pashley
3/3400, 26/4/15; R.E., 7/7/15; F; Lieut.; w.
    10 Place Madou, Brussels.

WARNER, George
A/293, 24/6/08; dis. 30/9/08.
    7 Kings Bench Walk, Temple, E.C. 4.

WARNER, John
B/11682, 16/7/17; A.S.C., C/S, 1/11/17; R.A.S.C., 25/1/18; 2/Lieut.
    Ronceval, West Mersea.

WARNER, Leonard Conway
6/1/6300, 16/9/15; trfr. R.G.A., 7/7/16.
    Yealmpton Vicarage, Plymouth.

WARNER, Noel Scott
D/A/11849, 9/8/17; R.E., C/S, 1/2/18; R.E., 2/8/18; 2/Lieut.
    58 Lichfield Street, Walsall. (Now in Mexico).

✠ WARNER, Robert
4/3/4164, 10/6/15, L/C.; York. & Lanc. R., 15/11/15; 2/Lieut.
    Killed in action 6/3/17.

WARNFORD-DAVIS, Roy Dennis
F/1773, 16/10/14, Sgt.; Dorset R., 21/2/15; I,M; Capt.
    Wantage House, 14 Ladbroke Road, W. 11.

WARR, Arthur Hedley
D/11106, 23/4/17; No 12 O.C.B., 10/8/17; N. Cyc. Bn., 27/11/17, Glouc. R., North'd Fus.; F; 2/Lieut.; w.
    56 Cromwell Grove, Levenshulme, Manchester.

WARRAN, William Simeon Edmund
6/4/6679, 7/10/15; Indian Army, 18/6/17; Lieut.
    Lyndhurst, 40 Langham Road, West Green, N.15.

WARRE, Edmond Lancelot
H/1972, 26/10/14; K.R. Rif. C., 2/11/14, R.A.F.; F; Capt.
    Colenorton, Eton, Windsor.

WARRE, Felix Walter
K/2167, 23/11/14; K.R. Rif. C., 27/11/14; F; Major; w; C.B.E., M.C., M(3).
    34 New Bond Street, W. 1.

✠ WARRELL-BOWRING, Walter John
D/3059, 15/3/15, L/C.; R.W. Surr. R., 18/6/15; 2/Lieut.
    Killed in action 30/7/16.

WARREN, Charles Robert
6/4/9248, 2/2/16; No. 8 O.C.B., 4/8/16; Devon. R., 27/11/16, Lab. Corps; Lieut.

WARREN, Denis Franklin
C/A/12076, 1/10/17, L/C.; dis. med. unfit, 28/1/19.
    10 Holly Walk, Leamington.

WARREN, Desmond Cecil Robert
Sq/3065, 18/3/15; R.A.S.C., 5/7/15; F,NR; Capt.; M.B.E.
    Derrintovey, Carrickmines, Co. Dublin.

WARREN, Frank Denis
6/Sq/8849, 10/1/16; R.A., C/S, 7/8/16; R.F.A., 17/11/16; Lieut.; w; M.C. and Bar, M(1).
    452, Seven Sisters Road, Finsbury Park, N. (Now in Africa).

WARREN, George Sydney
K/A/2533, 31/12/14; R. Fus., 25/3/15; F; Capt.
    5 Airlie Gardens, Campden Hill Road, W. 8.

WARREN, John Fone
D/11169, 1/5/17; R.E., C/S, 4/11/17; R.E., 1/2/18; F,M; Lieut.
    38 Southside Road, Plymouth, Devonshire.

WARREN, John Howard
C/237, 20/5/08; dis. 19/5/10.
    Yvetot, Overton Road, Sutton, Surrey.

WARREN, John Robert Hoare
C/A/D/12090, 4/10/17; No. 1 O.C.B., 10/5/18; R. Lanc. R., 29/10/18; 2/Lieut.
    Fore Street, Buckfastleigh, South Devonshire.

WARREN, John William Ernest
C/8943, 17/11/16; M.G.C., C/S, 1/3/17; M.G.C., 25/6/17; F; Lieut.
    Eastcroft, Rayleigh, Essex.

WARREN, Justus Tom
C/14190, 18/10/18; demob. 22/4/19.
    Fox, Fowler & Coy., Bankers, Exeter.

✠ WARREN, Theodore Stewart Wolton
4/3/4316, 17/6/15; Durh. L.I., 5/11/15; F; 2/Lieut.
    Killed in action 17/7/16.

✠ WARREN, William Stanley
6/4/6680, 7/10/15; No. 14 O.C.B., 26/11/16; Bord. R., 27/3/17; F; 2/Lieut.; w.
    Died 10/10/17.

WARRILOW, Oswald Joseph
2/9687, 2/10/16; No. 14 O.C.B., 27/12/16; Ches. R., 25/4/17; F; Lieut.
    8 Gainsborough Road, Crewe, Cheshire.

WARRY, Richard Arthur
Sq/575, 13/11/11; dis. 3/12/13; rej. A/829, 4/8/14; K.R. Rif. C., 31/8/14; F; Capt.
    Wellington Club, 1 Grosvenor Place, S.W. 1. (Now in Switzerland).

WARWICK, Francis
6/6218, 13/9/15; dis. 22/9/15.

✠ WASE, John Edgelow
6/4/6715, 9/10/15; No. 9 O.C.B., 6/3/16; L'pool. R., 6/7/16, R.A.F.; F; Lieut.; w.
    Killed 19/8/18.

WASHINGTON, Godfrey Francis Eaton
A/13181, 31/5/18; No. 22 O.C.B., 23/8/18; K.R. Rif. C., 13/2/19; 2/Lieut.
    28 Alexandra Court, Queens Gate, S.W.

WASON, Rigby
273, 15/6/08; dis. 14/6/09.
    91 Onslow Square, S.W. 7.

WATCHORN, Richard William Ambler
A/11943, 30/8/17; R.F.C., C/S, 26/11/17; R.F.C., 23/1/18, R.A.F.; 2/Lieut.
    Ponthafren, Newtown, Montgomeryshire.

WATERFIELD, Aubrey William
Sq/2885, 8/2/15; North'n. Yeo., 28/3/15; F,It; Major.
    Heronden House, Eastry, Kent.

WATERFIELD, William Edwin Percival
K/A/2266, 7/12/14; York. R., 17/2/15; F; Capt.; g.
    33 Leyland Arcade, Southport, Lancashire.

WATERHOUSE, Michael Theodore
Sq/653, 1/11/12; Nott. Yeo., 8/8/14; Capt.; M.C., M(1).
    Staple Inn Place, W.C.

WATERS, Harold Sutherland
6/3/7005, 25/10/15, L/C.; K.R. Rif. C., 5/5/16; 2/Lieut.

WATERS, Harry George
D/10900, 16/3/17, L/C.; No. 14 O.C.B., 7/9/17; S. Staff. R., 17/12/17; F; 2/Lieut.
    Wheatsheaf Hotel, Horsell, Woking, Surrey.

WATERS, John Dallas
C/934, 5/8/14; R. Fus., 12/9/14; F; Lt. Col.; w(2); D.S.O., M(4).
    7 Fig Tree Court, Temple, E.C. 4.

WATERS, Vincent Percival
B/D/11999, 10/9/17, L/C.; No. 9 O.C.B., 22/3/18; M.G.C., 29/10/18; 2/Lieut.
    Lake Road, Windermere.

WATERS, William Haviland
4/3/4301, 17/6/17; R. Ir. Fus., 7/10/15. R. Innis. Fus., Indian Army; F,I; Capt.; w(2); M.C.
    c/o Messrs. Cox & Coy., Hornby Road, Bombay, India.

WATERS, William Joseph Frank
A/Sq/10049, 29/11/16; No. 1 Cav. C/S, 31/7/17; R. Regt. of Cav., 22/2/18, att. 6th Drag. Gds.; 2/Lieut.
    Thorn's Farm, Lymington, Hampshire.

WATERSON, John Malcolm
C/11476, 11/6/17; R.F.C., C/S, 2/8/17; R.F.C., 8/9/17.
    25 Wood Vale, Forest Hill, S.E. 23.

WATHERSTON, Christopher Fell
6/1/8994, 19/1/16; No. 14 O.C.B., 29/9/16, M.G.C., C/S; M.G.C., 25/1/17; w.
    Cheslan, Rotherhill Avenue, Streatham, S.W. 16.

WATKIN, Arthur John
C/11731, 23/7/17; No. 14 O.C.B., 7/12/17; Notts. & Derby. R., 20/5/18; F; 2/Lieut.
    24 Guilford Street, W.C. 1.

WATKIN, Charles Cuthbert
C/13312, 17/6/18; R.E., C/S, 18/10/18; demob. 24/1/19.
    Holly House, Darfield, Nr. Barnsley, Yorkshire.

WATKINS, George Dare
K/B/2552, 4/1/15; R. Dub. Fus., 22/4/15, att. Conn. Rang.; Capt.
    Collingsbourne, Liverpool Road, Kingston Hill.

WATKINSON, Frank Stephen
C/13245, 7/6/18; No. 22 O.C.B., 23/8/18; Midd'x. R., 13/2/19; 2/Lieut.
    41 Fairfax Road, Bedford Park, W. 1.

WATKINS-PITCHFORD, Henry Otley
D/13810, 9/8/18; demob. 29/1/19.
    1 Oatlands Drive, Weybridge, Surrey.

APPENDIX II.—RECORDS OF RANK AND FILE.

WATNEY, James Henry
6/9369, 7/2/16; dis. med. unfit, 19/5/16.
c/o S. Worsey, Brine Baths Hotel, Nantwich, Cheshire.

☩ WATNEY, Valentine Howell
C/375, 23/3/09; dis. 23/3/13; rej. E/1670, 12/10/14; R. Berks. R., 28/12/14, M.G.C.; F; Lieut.; w. Died of wounds 3/2/17.

☩ WATNEY, William Herbert
C/1158, 14/9/14; Rif. Brig., 5/10/14; F; Lieut.
Killed in action 10/5/15.

WATSON, Arthur
4/3/4099, 7/6/15; S. Lan. R., 7/9/15.
Elm Lodge, St. Helens, Lancashier.

WATSON, Arthur Ernest
6/8597, 3/1/16; R.F.A., C/S, 21/7/16; R.F.A., 13/10/16; F; Major. Briar Dene, Church Lane, Merton Park, S.W. 19.

WATSON, Arthur Frederick
D/10233, 29/12/16, L/C.; R.A., C/S, 27/4/17; R.G.A., 1/9/17; F; Capt. Roundhay, Kingston Road, Leatherhead.

WATSON, Arthur Geoffrey
4/3/3992, 3/6/15; Leic. R., 20/8/15; F; Lieut.; w(2).
53 Beaufort Road, Edgbaston, Birmingham.

☩ WATSON, Arthur Paton
6/5/5962, 1/9/15; L'pool. R., 21/4/16; 2/Lieut.
Died of wounds 13/10/16.

WATSON, Donald
6/5/5963, 1/9/15, L/C.; L'pool. R., 1/6/16; F; Lieut.; w; M.C.
District Bank House, Keswick, Cumberland.

WATSON, Edward Alexander
6/3/9509, 15/2/16; No. 2 O.C.B., 14/8/16; W. Rid. R., 18/12/16.

WATSON, Frank Bernard
K/E/2406, 21/12/14; 1st Lond. R., 21/3/15, R.A.S.C.; G,E,F; Capt.; w. Wykeham House, Sandgate, Kent.

WATSON, Geoffrey Caiger
4/5/4775, 12/7/15; R. Ir. Fus., 18/9/15; Lieut.; M.C.

WATSON, Gilbert
D/E/13773, 7/8/18; R.A., C/S, 2/10/18.
Pembroke Villa, Newmarket, Cambridgeshire.

WATSON, Harold Arthur
B/12694, 6/3/18; R.F.C., C/S, 1/7/18; demob. 27/3/19.
Cremona, Bush Street, Pembroke Dock, South Wales.

☩ WATSON, John Eben
F/1812, 16/10/14, Sgt.; R. Sco. Fus., 18/11/14; 2/Lieut.
Killed in action 26/9/15.

WATSON, John Russell
C/14282, 8/11/18; No. 11 O.C.B., 24/1/19; General List, 8/3/19; 2/Lieut. Boka de Comerico, Buenos Aires, South America.

WATSON, Keith Fenwick Clennell
A/9841, 3/11/16; No. 14 O.C.B., 30/1/17; Rif. Brig., 29/5/17; 2/Lieut. Greencroft, Annan, Scotland. (Now in China).

☩ WATSON, Laurence Charles
K/F/2761, 21/1/15; Hamps. R., 15/5/15; 2/Lieut.
Killed in action 12/8/15.

WATSON, Lawrence Cecil
6/4/9572, 18/4/16, L/C.; No. 14 O.C.B., 30/10/16; Durh. L.I., 28/2/17; F; Lieut.; w. 11 Uplands Road, Darlington.

WATSON, Leonard Roy
4/3/4477, 28/6/15; Notts. & Derby. R., 8/11/15; Lieut.; w; M.C., M(1). 18 Hamilton Road, Harrow.

WATSON, Leslie Albert
A/Sq/13159, 29/5/18; demob. 8/1/19.
Relwot, Millway Road, Andover, Hampshire.

WATSON, Lionel Kenneth
6/1/9413, 9/2/16; No. 8 O.C.B., 4/8/16; North'd. Fus., 21/11/16; 2/Lieut.; M(1).

WATSON, Malcolm John
4/1/4245, 14/6/15; dis. 9/3/16.
Carsia 34, Rio de Janeiro, Brazil.

WATSON, Maurice Murray
B/2034, 9/11/14; S. Staff. R., 17/3/15; Lieut.
62 Marney Road, Clapham Common, S.W. 11.

WATSON, Robert Johnston
6/5/C/8882, 12/1/16; No 7 O.C.B., 4/11/16; R. Ir. Rif., 28/2/17; F; Lieut.; w. Arranmore, Monkstown, Co. Dublin, Ireland.

WATSON, Robert Stanley
6/8322, 11/12/15; dis. to re-enlist, R.N.A.S., 9/6/15.
5 Osborne Terrace, Newcastle.

WATSON, Sidney Bernard
6/1/7060, 28/10/15; 9th Lond. R., 4/9/16; Lieut.; w.
Roslin, Grove Park, Lee, S.E. 12.

WATSON, Walter Ernest
C/11732, 23/7/17, L/C.; Dental Surgeon, 28/2/18, att. R.A.M.C.; E; Lieut. 12 De Parys Avenue, Bedford.

WATSON, William Frank
K/2316, 10/12/14; R.A.S.C., 20/2/15; G,P,F; Capt.; w(2); O.B.E., M(4).
Hurst House, Broomhill Walk, Woodford Green, Essex. (Now in West Indies).

WATSON, William Henry Alder
6/6428, 23/9/15; dis. med. unfit, 4/4/16.
Hendre, Overton Park, Cheltenham.

WATSON, William Scott
1/3209, 8/4/15; Sea. Highrs., 2/6/15; I,M; Lieut.
Highgate Farm, Scridington, Sleaford, Lincolnshire.

WATSON-WILLIAMS, Eric. See WILLIAMS, E. W.

☩ WATT, Basil Harry
F/2912, 10/2/15, L/C.; Cam'n. Highrs., 7/5/15; 2/Lieut.
Killed in action 25/9/15.

WATT, Donald Edward
C/Sq/10845, 6/3/17; No. 14 O.C.B., 4/1/18; R. Fus., 25/6/18; F; 2/Lieut. 19 Alleyn Park, West Dulwich, S.E. 21.

WATT, Geoffrey
6/5/C/9486, 15/2/16; No. 14 O.C.B., 30/10/16; E. York. R., 28/2/17; F; Lieut.; w. Oundle, North Ferriby, East Yorkshire.

☩ WATT, Kenneth Murray
1/9668, 30/9/16; No. 14 O.C.B., 27/12/16; Bedf. R., 27/3/17; E,P; 2/Lieut. Killed in action 1/10/17.

WATT, Thomas Hanson
B/12688, 4/3/18; No. 3 O.C.B., 6/9/18; R. Suss. R., 17/3/19; 2/Lieut. 15 Carlisle Road, Eastbourne, Sussex.

WATTERS, John Leed
A/13182, 31/5/18; No. 22 O.C.B., 5/7/18; R. Scots, 5/2/19; 2/Lieut. Carrick, Market Street, Altrincham, Cheshire.

WATTS, Alan Kingsford
K/F/2506, 31/12/14; dis. 9/7/15; joined 28th Lond. R.; E. Surr. R., 26/4/17; F,It; Lieut.; g; Italian Service Medal.
69 Cheriton Road, Folkestone.

WATTS, Alfred Gordon
6/2/7969, 29/11/15; R.A., C/S, 7/8/16; R.G.A., 8/11/16; F; Capt. 13 Park Crescent, Brighton, Sussex.

WATTS, Ansley Douglas
D/11860, 13/8/17; R.A., C/S, 15/3/18; General List, 8/3/19; 2/Lieut. Box 162, Windhuk, South West Africa.

☩ WATTS, Dudley Haldane
B/1329, 26/9/14; R.W. Kent R., 9/11/14; 2/Lieut.
Killed in action 26/9/15.

WATTS, Edward George Stewart
A/10040, 29/11/16; R.W. Surr. R., 9/3/17, att. Suff. R. and York. R.; 2/Lieut. Barkby, Cottenham Park Road, S.W. 19.

WATTS, Frederick James
1/3438, 1/5/15; Essex R., 18/7/15, att. R.A.F.; F,I; Capt.; M(2).
17 Tennyson Avenue, Wanstead, Essex.

WATTS, Harold George
6/2/5315, 2/8/15; Bedf. R., att. Herts. R.; F; Lieut.; w.
Westfield, Cranbrook, Kent.

WATTS, Leslie Hamilton
C/11532, 18/6/17; No. 10 O.C.B., 5/10/17; Welch R., 26/2/18; F; Lieut. Cobham Cottage, Marlow, Buckinghamshire.

WATTS, Percy George Purnell
6/2/5531, 9/8/15; 12th Lond. R., 19/12/15, att. 29th Lond. R.; Lieut. 14 Deodar Road, Putney, S.W. 15.

WATTS, Percy Martin
6/4/8575, 31/12/15; R.A., C/S, 4/8/16; R.G.A., 1/11/16; Lieut.; w. Roselea, Macclesfield, Cheshire.

WATTS, Philip Sydney
6/4/9260, 2/2/16; No. 14 O.C.B., 28/8/16; R. Marines, 21/11/16; Lieut.; w. 313 Oxford Road, Macclesfield.

WATTS-RUSSELL, John Charles
C/47, 7/4/08; trfr. 28th Lond R., 20/4/10; R. Muns. Fus., 6/1/15; Capt.; w. H. Cooke & Coy., 21 Bury Street, S.W. 1.

WAUD, Christopher William Henry Pierre
A/1697, 13/10/14; R.W. Surr. R., 14/12/14; Capt.; p.
Sutherland House, London Street, Hyde Park, W. 2.

APPENDIX II.—RECORDS OF RANK AND FILE.

WAUGH, Alexander Rabon
6/2/6139, 9/9/15; dis. to R. Mil. Coll., 29/8/16; Dorset R., 1/5/17, att. M.G.C.; Lieut.; p.
Underhill, North End Road, Hampstead, N.W. 3.

WAUGH, Charles Sahler
A/9822, 31/10/16; No. 14 O.C.B., 27/12/16; Yorks. L.I., 25/4/17; F; Lieut.; w. Feidberg, Westfield Road, Rathgar, Dublin.

WAUGH, Tom Cecil
B/13530, 15/7/18; No. 22 O.C.B., 23/8/18; R. War. R., 13/2/19; 2/Lieut. 25 Tuddenham Road, Ipswich.

WAVELL, Claude William Fuglar
A/14332, 30/12/18; No. 11 O.C.B., 24/1/19; General List, 8/3/19; 2/Lieut.
Leindenhurst, Gurnard, Isle of Wight. (Now in Ceylon).

WAY, Horatio Lewis
4/2/4550, 1/7/15; N. Staff. R., 7/10/15; F; Capt.; w(2); M.C.
37 Leppoc Road, Clapham Park, S.W. 4.

WAY, John Chudleigh
B/12000, 10/9/17; dis. to R. Mil. Coll., 27/9/17.
c/o Mrs. Young, The Trowlock, Broom Road, Teddington.

WAYLAND, Edward James
A/11903, 23/8/17; R.E., C/S, 30/9/17; R.E., 9/11/17; 2/Lieut.

WAYMAN, Lewis John
6/1/6262, 16/9/15; E. Ang. Div. Cyc. Coy., 1/12/15, att. Shrop. Yeo.; E,M; Lieut.; M(1).
12a Holmes Road, Kentish Town, N.W. 5.

✠ WAYTE, Samuel Wilfrid
1/Sq/9757, 18/10/16; R.A., C/S, 1/2/17; R.F.A., 5/6/17; F; 2/Lieut.; w(2); M.C. Died of wounds 7/10/17.

✠ WEARNE, Kenneth Martin
6/2/5671, 16/8/15; R.W. Surr. R., 7/7/16; 2/Lieut.
Killed in action 20/9/17.

WEATHERELL, Robert Kingsley
A/1932, 22/10/14; Suff. R., 18/11/14, att. Lein. R. and Essex R.; F,G,E,P; Capt.; w.
Normanby, Nr. Scunthorpe, Lincolnshire.

WEATHERLY, Cecil Octavius
E/14121, 9/10/18; demob. 10/1/19.
Hollycot, Runfold, Nr. Farnham, Surrey.

WEAVER, Christopher Charles
6/3/D/6467, 27/9/15; R.F.C., C/S, 28/12/16; R.F.C., 4/4/17, York. R.; 2/Lieut.
Sunnyside, Grasmere Road, Gledholt, Huddersfield.

WEAVER, Henry Edward
4/3/4478, 28/6/15; R.N.V.R., 9/8/15.

WEBB, Albert Victor
A/13985, 10/9/18; No. 11 O.C.B., 24/1/19; General List, 8/3/19; 2/Lieut.
78 Bungsar Road, Kuala Lumpur, Federated Malay States.

WEBB, Alexander Thomas
3/3325, 19/4/15, Cpl.; Som. L.I., 24/10/15; F,I,M; Lieut.; w.
12 Manor Road, Wallington, Surrey.

WEBB, Arthur
9/9984, 22/11/16; No. 21 O.C.B., 5/5/17; Oxf. & Bucks. L.I., 28/8/17; Lieut.

WEBB, Arthur Herbert Guy
4/4551, 1/7/15, L/C.; R.A.S.C., 27/11/15; F; Capt.
Woodside, Park Hill Road, Chingford, Essex.

✠ WEBB, Athelstan Sylvester Kenshole
4/1/4827, 13/7/15; North'd. Fus., 11/10/15; Lieut.; w.
Killed in action 21/3/18.

WEBB, James Daglass
C/11058, 13/4/17; No. 14 O.C.B., 7/9/17; S. Staff. R., 17/12/17; 2/Lieut. The Hollies, Whitehall Lane, Buckhurst Hill, Essex.

WEBB, John Leslie
4/3894, 31/5/15; Norf. R., 18/9/15, R.E.; F,I; Major.
23 Prospect Road, Southborough, Tunbridge Wells, Kent. (Now in India).

WEBB, Kenneth Percy
K/D/2152, 23/11/14; R.A.O.C., 8/2/15; P,E; Major, D.A.D.O.S.; M(1). 22 Westbourne Gardens, W. 2.

WEBB, Robert Duncan
6/5/C/7486, 15/11/15; No. 14 O.C.B., 26/11/16; E. Kent R., 27/3/17, att. Bedf. R.; Lieut.
121 Bearwood Road, Smethwick, Staffordshire.

WEBB, Robert Frederick
4/Sq/5150, 29/7/15; R.F.A., 15/10/15; Lieut.

WEBBER, Joseph Edward
6/3/7600, 18/11/15; No. 14 O.C.B.; R.N.V.R., 21/11/16.
27 Gordon Road, Cardiff.

WEBER, Albert Francis
Sq/3521, 6/5/15, Sgt.; R.A., C/S, 13/10/16; Special List, 15/5/17, att. Notts. & Derby. R. and R.F.C.; F; Lieut.
Blythwood, Bromley, Kent.

WEBER, Leo Theodore
6/4/9301, 3/2/16; R.F.A., C/S, 4/8/16; R.F.A., 15/12/16; F; Lieut. 59 Narrow Bridge Street, Peterborough.

WEBER, Reginald John Craig
6/3/6076, 6/9/15; Hamps. R., 21/12/15; E,P; Capt.
70 Thornton Avenue, Bedford Park, W. 4.

WEBSTER, Derek
6/Sq/6077, 6/9/15, Sgt.; R.A., C/S, 15/3/17; R.F.A., 8/9/17; F; Lieut. 8 Lanark Mansions, W. 9.

WEBSTER, Frank Poole
6/5/5672, 16/8/15; R.E., 21/9/15; Lieut.

✠ WEBSTER, George Thomas
6/1/7970, 29/11/15; No. 2 O.C.B., 14/8/16; M.G.C.; 2/Lieut.; w.
Died of wounds 7/12/17.

WEBSTER, George William
4/6/5/4950, 19/7/15; W. York. R., 18/10/15; F,I; Capt.
c/o G. E. Webster Esq., 14 Westfield Road, Wakefield.

WEBSTER, George William
C/10598, 20/1/17; Garr. O.C.B., 23/5/17; Suff. R., 14/7/17, att. M. of Munitions; Lieut.
Dorney Cottage, Wittering Lane, Heswall, Cheshire.

WEBSTER, Gerald Frederick
A/13018, 1/5/18; trfr. 14th Lond. R., 6/12/18, Gord. Highrs.; Sgt.
Torville, Bodmin, Cornwall.

✠ WEBSTER, Harold Wolstan
H/1982, 29/10/14, L/C.; R.E., 23/11/14; Major.
Died of wounds 12/4/18.

WEBSTER, Herbert Stanley
6/8850, 10/1/16; R.E., 2/2/17; F; Capt.
Lathkill House, Renals Street, Derby.

WEBSTER, Robert
6/1/7082, 29/10/15; trfr. 8th Lond. R., 9/3/17.
75 Fairlop Road, Leytonstone, E.11.

WEBSTER, Thomas Herbert
B/11428, 1/6/17; No. 14 O.C.B., 9/11/17; Leic. R., 30/4/18; F; 2/Lieut. 33 The Fosse, Leicester.

✠ WEBSTER, Thomas William
6/2/5396, 5/8/15; No. 1 O.C.B., 25/2/16; 11th Lond. R., 8/7/16; 2/Lieut. Killed in action 1/10/16.

WEBSTER, William Scott
A/12499, 28/1/18; R.F.A., C/S, 28/6/18.
Drago, Summerfield Road, Bridlington.

✠ WEEKES, Reginald Penkivil Olive
6/2/6468, 27/9/15, L/C.; No. 11 O.C.B., 7/5/16; R.F.C., 4/9/16; F; 2/Lieut. Killed in action 7/5/17.

WEEKS, Alfred Edward Norman
C/14157, 14/10/18; trfr. K.R. Rif. C., 25/4/19.
87 St. Dunstans Road, Barons Court, W. 6.

✠ WEGG-PROSSER, Cecil Francis
C/1354, 26/9/14; General List, 1/4/15, R. Suss. R., Rif. Brig.; F; 2/Lieut. Killed in action 3/9/16.

WEIDEMANN, Reginald Guy. Now VARDY, R. G.
A/551, 24/2/11; W. York. R., 18/9/14; F; Staff Capt.; w.
Bank of England, E.C.

WEIGALL, Gerald John Villiers
K/2190, 26/11/14; Kent Cyc. Bn., 28/12/14; Capt.

WEIL, Rene George
6/3/6301, 16/9/15, L/C.; D. of Corn. L.I., 14/7/16; I; Lieut.; w.
89 High Street, Wimbledon, S.W. 19.

WEILY, John Henry
6/4/9414, 9/2/16; No. 7 O.C.B., 11/8/16, Garr. O.C.B.; Lab. Corps, 14/7/17; E,P; Lieut.
Glenmore, Ballysaggartmore, Lismore, Co. Waterford.

WEINMAN, Alfred St. Maud Carruthers
A/B/C/12150, 22/10/17; trfr. R.G.A., 1/3/18; R.A.F., 19/10/18; 2/Lieut. 22 Woburn Place, Russell Square, W.C. 1.

355

APPENDIX II.—RECORDS OF RANK AND FILE.

✠ WEIR, George
6/5/9492, 15/2/16; R.A., C/S, 14/9/16; R.F.A., 22/1/17; F; Lieut.; g.
Died 5/10/18.

✠ WEISS, Edward Stanley
6/Sq/8197, 6/12/15; R.F.C., C/S, 10/10/16; R.F.C., 26/2/17; 2/Lieut.
Killed in action 22/11/17.

WELBOURN, William
C/12272, 29/11/17, L/C.; No. 22 O.C.B., 7/6/18; Linc. R., 12/2/19; 2/Lieut. 20 Coniston Road, Addiscombe, Croydon.

WELCH, Donald Hubbard
A/10508, 15/1/17; R.G.A., C/S, 25/4/17; R.G.A., 1/2/18; 2/Lieut. Openwood, Worplesdon, Surrey.

WELCH, Geoffrey Hulme
C/14296, 11/11/18; demob. 4/3/19. 50 Warwick Road, Ipswich.

WELCH, James Johnson
6/8669, 3/1/16; R.A., C/S, 9/6/16; R.G.A., 13/9/16; Lieut.
3 Gildridge Road, Eastbourne.

WELDON, Edward Vernon
6/2/9525, 16/2/16; dis. med. unfit, 26/9/16.

WELLER, John Adrian
A/11904, 23/8/17; R.F.C., C/S, 30/11/17; R.F.C., 17/12/17, R.A.F.; 2/Lieut.
45 St. Johns Road, Watford, Hertfordshire.

WELLER, William Herbert
4/2/4033, 7/6/15; R.W. Surr. R., 22/11/15, att. Lan. Fus. and Glouc. R.; F,S; Lieut.; w.
Languedoc, Grange Road, Egham, Surrey.

WELLINGS, Francis Ernest
A/12508, 29/1/18, L/C.; No. 2 O.C.B., 7/6/18; R.W. Fus., 6/2/19; 2/Lieut. Stottesdon, Clesburg Mortimer, Salop.

WELLS, Cyril Joseph
6/5/5291, 2/8/15; Notts. & Derby. R., 17/12/15, att. M.G.C.; Lieut. Elmwood, Mosbrough, Sheffield.

WELLS, George Stanley
A/11217, 30/4/17; R.E., 31/7/17; Lieut.; M.C.
The Cottage, Little Brickhill, Bletchley, Buckinghamshire.

✠ WELLS, Henry Maurice Watkin
F/1787, 16/10/14, L/C.; R. Berks. R., 9/3/15, R.F.C.; Lieut.
Killed in action, 15/9/16.

WELLS, Percy Edward
K/F/2286, 8/12/14; Oxf. & Bucks. L.I., 9/6/15; Lieut.
The Berries, Chingford, Essex.

WEMYSS, Macduff Erskine
D/11850, 9/8/17; R.E., C/S, 7/10/17; R.E., 11/1/18; F; 2/Lieut. 28 Stodman Street, Newark, Nottinghamshire.

WENDEN, Clerihew Gordon
4/2/4246, 14/6/15; trfr. 5th Lond. R., 31/3/16, K.R. Rif. C., M.G.C.; F; Pte.; w(2). c/o Grindlay & Coy., Bombay, India.

WENHAM, Charles Hugh
A/2023, 2/11/14; Rif. Brig., 23/2/15; F; Capt.; M(1).
Witley Manor, Godalming.

WENN, Harold Jackson
6/2/7558, 17/11/15, L/C.; No. 14 O.C.B.; S. Lan. R., 24/10/16; F; Lieut.; w. 240 Iffley Road, Oxford.

✠ WENTWORTH, Cyril John
6/2/7161, 2/11/15; No. 14 O.C.B.; R. Suss. R., 21/11/16; 2/Lieut.
Died of wounds 3/2/17.

WERTHEIM, Bruno William
C/D/12038, 22/9/17; No. 22 O.C.B., 14/10/18; trfr. 14th Lond. R., 6/12/18.
Messrs. Hammond Richards, 26 Lincolns Inn Fields, W.C. 2.

WESSON, Percy Edmund
A/13183, 29/5/18; No. 22 O.C.B., 5/7/18; R. War. R., 2/2/19; 2/Lieut. 2 Broad Street, Warwick.

WEST, Arthur Augustus
6/3/6853, 16/10/15; Notts. & Derby. R., 1/6/16, Leic. R.; F; Lieut.; w. 4 Elm Tree Road, St. John's Wood, N.W. 8.

WEST, Douglas Arthur
6/4/5450, 6/8/15; R.G.A., 15/10/15; F; Lieut.; M.C., M(1).
245 Barry Road, East Dulwich, S.E. 22.

WEST, Frank Leslie
D/9987, 22/11/16, L/C.; No. 14 O.C.B., 6/4/17; Bedf. R., 31/7/17, att. Leic. R.; Lieut. The Woodlands, Penylan, Cardiff.

WEST, Frederick Victor
4/3/3745, 24/5/15, L/C.; W. Rid. R., 5/10/15; F; Lieut.; g.
Beaumont Chambers, 6 Pocklington Walk, Leicester.

WEST, George
C/1239, 23/9/14; Suff. R., 7/10/14, att. Norf. R.; F,S; Lt. Col.; w. 105 Adelaide Road, Hampstead, N.W. 3. (Now in Burma).

WEST, Gilbert Lewis
E/14150, 11/10/18; demob. 30/1/19.
The White House, Mettingham, Bungay, Suffolk.

✠ WEST, Harold Douglas
6/5/8586, 3/1/16, Sgt.; No. 14 O.C.B., 29/9/16; K.R. Rif. C., 18/12/16; 2/Lieut.
Died of wounds 25/3/18.

WEST, Harold Francis
B/10529, 17/1/17; R.G.A., C/S, 25/4/17; R.G.A., 1/10/17; F; Lieut. 1 Ravenslea Road, Wandsworth Common, S.W. 12.

WEST, Herbert Martin
C/12280, 3/12/17; R.E., C/S, 10/3/18; R.E., 12/7/18; F; 2/Lieut.
P.O. Box 6514, Johannesburg, South Africa.

WEST, James Edward
C/12609, 13/2/18; No. 17 O.C.B., 9/8/18; Oxf. & Bucks. L.I., 5/3/19; 2/Lieut. 7 Mallory Flats, St. John Street, E.C. 1.

WEST, John Henry
D/12130, 15/10/17; No. 6 O.C.B., 16/5/18; R.W. Surr. R., 3/2/19; 2/Lieut.
Melrose, 43 Overhill Road, East Dulwich, S.E. 22.

WEST, Leslie Arthur
D/E/13839, 14/8/18; No. 22 O.C.B., 22/11/18; R. Berks. R., 15/2/19; 2/Lieut. 7 Tavistock Road, Westbourne Park, W. 11.

WEST, Norman Barsby
6/3/6854, 16/10/15; No. 7 O.C.B., 6/4/16; Lan. Fus., 17/7/16; F; Capt.; w.
Durley Dean, 208 Victoria Avenue, Southend-on-Sea.

WEST, Oswald Lionel
D/11172, 30/4/17, L/C.; No. 14 O.C.B., 5/10/17; Manch. R., 26/2/18, secd. Durh. L.I.; F; 2/Lieut.
Lodone, Alderley Edge, Cheshire.

WEST, Rawdon Henry Pith
3/3401, 26/4/15; R. Marines, 28/5/15; Capt.; M.C.
Clumber House, Bridlington.

WEST, Reginald William
4/3/4552, 1/7/15; Manch. R., 18/10/15; F; Staff Capt.; w, g.
127 Mount View Road, Stroud Green, N. 4.

WEST, Walter Henry Thomas
6/2/6645, 7/10/15; dis. med. unfit, 8/8/16.
Granville House, 68 Deodar Road, Putney, S.W. 15.

WESTALL, Arthur
6/5/5276, 31/7/15, L/C.; Manch. R., 2/12/15, att. R.A.F.; F; Lieut. 368 Stretford Road, Manchester.

WESTBURY, Frederick Seymour
6/4/9302, 3/2/16; No. 14 O.C.B., 30/10/16; Notts. & Derby. R., 24/1/17; F; Lieut. 85 North Main Street, Youghal, Co. Cork.

✠ WESTBY, Thomas
6/2/5397, 5/8/15; R. Marines, 10/11/15; Lieut.; M.C.
Killed in action 30/12/17.

WESTCOTT, Patrick Alfred
B/10526, 15/1/17, L/C.; I.W.T., 14/6/17, R.E.; Lieut.
20 Bedford Place, W.C. 1.

WESTERMAN, Charles Edward Drummond
D/9983, 22/11/16, L/C.; No. 14 O.C.B., 5/5/17; Manch. R., 28/8/17; Lieut. East Hyde, Luton, Bedfordshire.

WESTERN, Frederick Harold
4/5/4814, 12/7/15; Camb. R., 20/10/15, att. E. Kent R.; Lieut.; w. 10 Devonshire Road, Greenwich, S.E. 10.

✠ WESTHORP, William Hast
6/1/9435, 11/2/16, L/C.; No. 13 O.C.B., 4/11/16; North'd. Fus., 28/2/17; 2/Lieut.
Killed in action 28/4/17.

WESTINGTON, Reginald Hugh
6/3/5784, 23/8/15; Som. L.I., 12/1/16; M,I; Capt.; w(2); M(3).
5 Anson Place, St. Judes, Plymouth, Devonshire.

WESTLAKE, Bernard Ashby
D/Sq/12959, 19/4/18; demob. 21/1/19.
Little Oak Hall, Bassett, Southampton.

✠ WESTLAKE, John Howard
6/5/7284, 8/11/15; No. 11 O.C.B., 8/5/16; R.F.C., 4/9/16; 2/Lieut.
Died of wounds 7/5/17.

WESTMACOTT, Charles Rendel
E/14085, 30/9/18; demob. 10/1/19.
Chelmavich, Saffrons Road, Eastbourne.

APPENDIX II.—RECORDS OF RANK AND FILE.

WESTMACOTT, Oscar
A/14051, 23/9/18; demob. 23/1/19.
The Sanctuary, Probus, Cornwall.

WESTRON, Henry
E/14177, 16/10/18; demob. 10/1/19.
Anrothe, South Canterbury Road, Canterbury.

WESTROPE, Charles Hall
B/13453, 3/7/18; dis. med. unfit, 12/5/19.
High Street, Ashwell, Hertfordshire.

WESTRUP, George Vere
6/3/5603, 15/8/15; Hamps. R., 17/12/15; S,E; Lieut.
32 Charlwood Road, Putney, S.W. 15.

WESTWELL, William Walter
D/10232, 29/12/16; No. 14 O.C.B., 6/4/17; trfr. Manch. R., 20/6/17.
103 Lovely Lane, Warrington.

WETHERALL, Charles Ridley
K/2575, 4/1/15; Devon. R., 13/3/15; E,M; Capt.; w.
Wellesley House, Broadstairs.

✠ WETHERALL, Francis Gyrth Johnston
F/2895, 9/2/15; R. Muns. Fus., 18/6/15; P; Lieut.; w.
Killed 19/9/18.

WETHERALL, Frederick William
6/4/7535, 16/11/15; dis. to re-enlist in M.G.C., 5/4/16.
Severus Mount, Worcester.

WETTON, Charles Douglas
K/B/2304, 14/12/14, L/C.; S. Lan. R., 3/4/15, secd. M.G.C.; F; Major.
34 Hillfield Park, Muswell Hill, N.10.

WEYMOUTH, William Robert Francis
F/1810, 16/10/14; R. Fus., 13/3/15; 2/Lieut.

WHADCOAT, Clarence Campbell
Sq/830, 4/8/14, Cpl.; 10th R. Regt. of Cav., 12/11/14, 14th Huss.; M; Lieut.
The Bungalow, Cher Magna, Bristol.

WHALE, James
6/1/6681, 7/10/15; No. 3 O.C.B., 25/2/16; Worc. R., 20/7/16; Lieut.; w.
4 Parkhill Street, Dudley, Worcestershire.

WHALEY, Reginald John
6/2/8680, 4/1/16; No. 14 O.C.B., 30/10/16, M.G.C., C/S; M.G.C., 30/1/17; Lieut.
3 Moorland Avenue, Baildon, Nr. Bradford, Yorkshire.

WHALLEY, Alfred Herbert
6/4/9474, 14/2/16, L/C.; No. 14 O.C.B., 30/10/16; W. Rid. R., 24/1/17; Lieut.; w; M.C.
57 Sholebroke Avenue, Leeds.

WHARTON, Carl Ernest
A/11009, 3/4/17; R.F.C., C/S, 1/6/17; R.F.C., 4/7/17, R.A.F.; F; Lieut.; p.
St. Colum, Cedar Road, Sutton, Surrey.

✠ WHEATCROFT, Ronald Duncan
B/738, 11/11/13; Notts. & Derby. R., 16/8/14; Lieut.
Died of wounds 2/7/16.

✠ WHEATLEY, Frank Rees
2/3667, 17/5/15; Essex R., 21/8/15; 2/Lieut.
Killed in action 11/8/16.

WHEATLEY, William Vernon
2052, 9/11/14; E. Surr. R., 13/3/15, secd. M.G.C., emp. M. of Labour; Lieut.; w.

WHEELDON, Percy John
A/11619, 5/7/17; R.G.A., C/S, 23/1/18; R.G.A., 22/7/18; F; 2/Lieut.
57 The Chine, Muswell Hill, N. 10.

WHEELDON, Thomas
4/6/4/4987, 19/7/15; R.W. Surr. R., 22/11/15, att. R. War. R.; F,It; Capt.
45 Nithsdale Avenue, Market Harborough, Leicestershire.

WHEELER, Arnold
6/2/7971, 29/11/15; R.W. Surr. R., 9/3/17; Lieut.

WHEELER, George
4/2/5135, 26/7/15; Essex R., 4/12/15; E,P; 2/Lieut.
10 High Street, Colchester.

WHEELER, Harold Edward Kenneth
D/13805, 9/8/18; trfr. K.R. Rif. C., 7/4/19.
3 Minard Road, Catford, S.E. 6.

WHEELER, Hugh
B/11714, 19/7/17; No. 14 O.C.B., 4/1/18; Dorset R., 25/6/18; 2/Lieut.
40 St. James Avenue, Elmers End, Beckenham.

WHEELER, Leopold Frederick
6/1/6154, 9/9/15; No. 1 O.C.B., 6/9/16; R.F.C., 25/1/17, R.A.F.; Lieut.; w-p.
South View House, Midsomer Norton, Bath.

WHEELER, Ronald
6/Sq/9155, 26/1/16, Sgt.; No. 2 Cav. C/S, 22/2/17; 1st R. Regt of Cav., 7/7/17; F; Lieut.
52 High Street, Eton, Buckinghamshire. (Now in U.S.A.)

✠ WHEELER-O'BRYEN, Myles
D/Sq/1485, 29/9/14, L/C.; R. War. R., 25/2/15; F; Lieut.
Killed in action 2/10/16.

WHEELER-O'BRYEN, Wilfrid James
6/3/5532, 9/8/15; R. War. R., 4/11/15, att. Lan. Fus.; F; Capt.; w(2); M.C. and Two Bars, M(1). *Burghill, Sydenham, S.W. 26.*

WHEEN, Alan Frith
B/11319, 19/5/17, L/C.; No. 14 O.C.B., 5/10/17; Ches. R., 26/3/18; 2/Lieut.
Edward Wheen & Sons, 80 Princess Street, Manchester.

WHELAN, Eric Edward
B/9910, 13/11/16; dis. 18/7/17.

WHELAN, Frank Joseph
C/10571, 17/1/17, L/C.; R.G.A., C/S, 26/9/17, No. 3 O.C.B.; Midd'x. R., 25/9/18; Lieut.
7 Fenchurch Street, E.C. 3.

WHELDON, Wynn Powell
B/1714, 15/10/14; R.W. Fus., 7/12/14; F; Major; w; D.S.O., M(1).
University College of North Wales, Bangor.

WHELLER, Edward William
6/1/9179, 27/1/16; R.A., C/S, 4/8/16; R.G.A., 9/12/16; F,M; Lieut.
41 Aldridge Road Villas, Notting Hill, W. 11.

WHELPTON, John Snow
6/1/8379, 13/12/15; No. 14 O.C.B., 29/9/16; E. York. R., 24/1/17; F; Lieut.
52 Victoria Avenue, Hull.

✠ WHICKER, Frederick Paul
6/1/6373, 20/9/15; No. 1 O.C.B., 25/2/16; 22nd Lond. R., 8/7/16; F; Lieut.
Died of wounds 12/4/18 as Prisoner of War.

✠ WHILLIER, Leonard Alfred
A/733, 11/11/13; Bedf. R., 27/9/14, Suff. R.; F; Lieut.
Killed in action 15/9/16.

WHINGATES, Guy
Sq/494, 11/5/10; dis. 3/4/11.

WHIPP, William Alltoft Summers
A/11197, 7/5/17, L/C.; No. 14 O.C.B., 5/10/17; Linc. Yeo., 26/2/18, Linc. R.; F; Lieut.
c/o General Steam, 22 Place du Dock, Ghent, Belgium.

WHISKARD, Geoffrey Granville
A/571, 2/11/11, Sgt.; dis. 1/11/15.
66 Warwick Gardens, West Kensington, W. 14.

WHITAKER, Cyril Horace
C/13377, 21/6/18; trfr. 14th Lond. R., 6/12/18, Gord. Highrs.; Pte.
51 Penn Road, Holloway, N. 7.

WHITAKER, Frank Gordon
6/2/7569, 17/11/15, L/C.; No. 14 O.C.B., 30/9/16; Hamps. R., 24/10/16; I; Lieut.
c/o B. Gritt Esq., Regeringsgaten, Stockholm.

✠ WHITAKER, Hubert Joseph Ingham
D/1413, 29/9/14; R.N. Div., 7/10/14; G; Sub. Lieut.
Killed in action 3/5/15.

WHITAKER, Thomas Dudley
4/Sq/4517, 28/6/15, L/C.; E. Rid. Yeo., 5/10/15, att. E. York. R.; S; Lieut.; w.
Lalang Rorpat Kiri Estate, Yoh Perak, Federated Malay States.

WHITBY, Edwin Guy
C/B/12585, 6/2/18; No. 20 O.C.B., 20/9/18, No. 18 O.C.B.; R. Suss. R., 18/3/19; 2/Lieut.
Nat. Prov. Bank Ltd., Coulsdon, Surrey.

WHITBY, Geoffrey Graham
4/4165, 10/6/15; R Mar Art., 30/8/15; F; Lieut.; w.
Bursay, St. David's Hill, Exeter.

WHITBY, Lyndall Theodore
6/1/6573, 2/10/15; Dorset R., 4/9/16, D. of Corn. L.I.; F; Capt.; w; M.C. and Bar.
Stoke St. Gregory, Nr. Taunton.

WHITBY, Ralph Edward
6/2/5718, 19/8/15, Sgt.; W. York. R., 21/4/16; F; Capt.; w.
North Road, Hatfield, Hertfordshire.

WHITBY, Thomas Frederick
6/4/8380, 13/12/15; No. 8 O.C.B., 4/8/16; R.W. Fus. 21/11/16; F; 2/Lieut.; g.
93 Bristol Road, Edgbaston, Birmingham.

WHITE, Bernard Kerr
C/1243, 23/9/14; High. L.I., 27/9/14, R.A.F.; F; Capt.; w.
85 Gloucester Road, S.W. 7.

APPENDIX II.—RECORDS OF RANK AND FILE.

WHITE, *Cyril Francis Douglas*
B/45, 6/4/08; dis. 5/4/10.

WHITE, *Cyril Warren*
B/D/12199, 5/11/17; R.A., C/S, 29/3/18; demob.
    Ivor House, Durdham Park, Bristol.

WHITE, *Edward Aldhelm*
6/9040, 20/1/16; dis. med. unfit, 23/6/16.
    Firbank, Weybridge, Surrey.

WHITE, *Frank Henry*
4/1/4109, 7/6/15.   *60 Overcliff Road, Lewisham, S.E. 13.*

WHITE, *Frank Leslie*
K/E/2281, 7/12/14; 17th Lond. R., 12/2/15; Lieut.; *w.*
    76 East India Dock Road, Poplar, E. 14.

WHITE, *Frederic George*
4/5/5136, 26/7/15; 12th Lond. R., 19/12/15; Lieut.; *w*(2).
    Sweet Briar, 36 Woodhouse Grove, Manor Park, E. 12.

WHITE, *Frederick William*
D/10456, 11/1/17; R.A., C/S, 29/6/17; R.G.A., 25/11/17; F; 2/Lieut.   *Bryansburn, Bangor, Co. Down, Ireland.*

WHITE, *George Campbell*
C/Sq/13168, 4/6/18; R.E., C/S, 25/8/18.
    Beechbank, Harrow-on-the-Hill, Middlesex.

WHITE, *George Wingrove*
C/14210, 18/10/18; demob. 30/1/19.
    Little Sutton Farm, Langley, Buckinghamshire.

WHITE, *Harold David*
C/10440, 10/1/17; R.F.C., C/S, 23/10/17; R.F.C., 12/12/17, att. K.R. Rif. C.; 2/Lieut.
    Sunningdale, Purley Park Road, Purley, Surrey.

✠ WHITE, *Harold Wickham*
6/3/5533, 9/8/15; dis. med. unfit, 24/6/16.   Died 1916.

WHITE, *Helenus Martin A.*
C/14312, 30/11/18; demob. 29/1/19.
    Wood Lodge, Kill Avenue, Monkstown, Ireland.

WHITE, *Henry Cracroft*
C/12234, 15/11/17; R.A., C/S, 15/3/18; R.G.A., 12/2/19; 2/Lieut.
    Bloxham Hall, Lincoln.

WHITE, *Henry Melville*
Sq/3522, 6/5/15, L/C.; R.F.A., 18/8/15; Lieut.
    Old Basford Mills, Old Basford, Nottinghamshire.

WHITE, *John*
6/5/7392, 11/11/15; No. 11 O.C.B., 7/5/16; R. War. R., 4/9/16, R.E.; F; Major; O.B.E., M(2).
    San Remo, Solihull, Warwickshire.

✠ WHITE, *John Stephen Grantham*
3/3668, 17/5/15; R.W. Fus., 21/8/15; Lieut.; *w.*
    Died of wounds 31/7/17.

WHITE, *Joris MacDonald*
C/12648, 23/2/18; R.E., C/S, 16/6/18; R.E., 1/11/18; 2/Lieut.

✠ WHITE, *Leslie James Hansford*
B/1328, 26/9/14; Som. L.I., 14/12/14; F,P,E,I; Capt.; *w.*
    Died 2/5/21.

WHITE, *Percy*
1/Sq/9667, 30/9/16; R.A., C/S, 23/1/17; R.G.A., 19/4/17; F; Lieut.   *2 Reedville, Oxton, Birkenhead.*

WHITE, *Reginald Lewis*
4/5/4772, 12/7/15; No. 11 O.C.B., 7/5/16; Norf. Yeo., 5/9/16, att. Devon. R.; E,P,F; Lieut.
    54 Warrington Crescent, Maida Vale, W. 1.

✠ WHITE, *Robert Christian*
6/3/6543, 30/9/15; No. 7 O.C.B., 6/4/16; Bord. R., 17/7/16; Lieut.; *w.*   Died of wounds 18/9/18.

✠ WHITE, *Stafford Charles*
4/3286, 15/4/15, L/C.; L'pool. R., 30/10/15; Lieut.
    Killed in action 31/7/17.

WHITE, *Stephen Sherwill Prescott*
D/12137, 18/10/17; R.E., C/S, 25/11/17; R.E., 22/2/18; 2/Lieut.
    Luversall, Cobham, Surrey.

WHITE, *Sydney John*
6/4/8150, 3/12/15, L/C.; No. 11 O.C.B., 7/5/16; R.E., 22/8/16; F; Capt.; *M.C., M*(1).
    44 Bassett Road, North Kensington, W. 10.

WHITE, *Taliesyn Gwyn*
6/2/8202, 6/12/15; No. 14 O.C.B., 30/1/17; Welch R., 25/4/17; F; Capt.; *w,p; M.C.*   *Caecerrig, Pontardulais, South Wales.*

WHITE, *Theodore Francis Hansford*
B/1321, 26/9/14; Som. L.I., 14/12/14, D. of Corn. L.I., R.E.; F; Lieut.; *g.*   *1 Acacia Road, St. Johns Wood, N.W. 8.*

✠ WHITE, *Thomas*
1/3246, 12/4/15; N. Lan. R., 21/8/15; 2/Lieut.
    Died of wounds 8/7/16.

WHITE, *Thomas Mutlow*
6/D/9596, 4/7/16; No. 14 O.C.B., 27/12/16; trfr. 16th Lond. R., 11/4/17.   *Cambridge House School, Margate.*

WHITE, *Thomas Wilfred*
D/11118, 23/4/17; No. 14 O.C.B., 7/9/17; R. Ir. Fus., 17/12/17; 2/Lieut.   *22 Clarence Avenue, Londonderry.*

WHITE, *Walter Newton*
6/Sq/7754, 22/11/15; trfr. Bedf. Yeo., 9/5/16.
    86 Larkhall Rise, Clapham, S.W. 4.

WHITEBROOK, *John Cudworth*
6/3/5605, 14/8/15; Mon. R., 27/12/15, att. Manch. R.; F; Lieut.; *w, g.*   *24 Old Square, Lincoln's Inn, W.C. 2.*

WHITEHEAD, *Gerard*
C/11533, 18/6/17; No. 16 O.C.B., 5/10/17; Manch. R., 12/3/18; 2/Lieut.   *The Rectory, Bootle, Cumberland.*

WHITEHEAD, *Hugh Christopher*
Sq/1224, 16/9/14; Dorset Yeo., 19/12/14; Capt.
    6 Bolton Street, Piccadilly, W.

WHITEHEAD, *James Buckley*
B/10091, 4/12/16; No. 14 O.C.B., 6/4/17; Manch. R., 31/7/17; F; Lieut.; *w; M.C.*   *403 Park Road, Oldham, Lancashire.*

WHITEHEAD, *James Whiley*
B/11014, 31/3/17; R.F.C., C/S, 2/8/17; R.F.C., 3/9/17, R.A.F.; 2/Lieut.   *Victoria House, Foxrock, Co. Dublin.*

WHITEHEAD, *Leonard Charles*
B/C/D/12205, 8/11/17; No. 5 O.C.B., 10/5/18; trfr. 28th Lond. R., 16/8/18.   *Sulby Hall, Rugby.*

✠ WHITEHEAD, *Mark*
6/5/5316, 2/8/15; L'pool. R., 7/1/16; F; 2/Lieut.
    Missing believed Killed 12/8/16.

WHITEHORN, *Roger Herbert*
D/Sq/12981, 24/4/18, L/C.; No. 2 Cav. C/S, 7/11/18, No. 11 O.C.B.; General List, 8/3/19; 2/Lieut.
    30 Chesterford Gardens, Hampstead, N.W. 3.

WHITEHOUSE, *Francis Reginald Beaman*
6/2/9391, 8/2/16; R.E., C/S, 2/9/16; R.E., 18/11/16; F; 2/Lieut.; *w-g.*
    The Rosery, 87 Greenfield Road, Harborne, Birmingham.

✠ WHITEHURST, *Albert Percival*
6/2/7972, 29/11/15, L/C.; No. 14 O.C.B., 30/10/16; Worc. R., 24/1/17; F; 2/Lieut.; *M*(1).   Killed in action 25/3/18.

✠ WHITELAM, *Lewis*
4437, 24/6/15; W. Rid. R., 15/11/15; F; 2/Lieut.
    Killed in action 3/9/16.

WHITELAW, *Norman James*
A/14100, 4/10/18; No. 11 O.C.B., 24/1/19; General List, 8/3/19; 2/Lieut.   *c/o Nat. Bank of South Africa, London Wall, E.C.*

WHITELEY, *Clifford Tracey*
6/3/5970, 27/8/15; R.F.A., 29/11/15; F; Lieut.
    Wavercrest, Beaconsfield Road, Clacton-on-Sea.

WHITELOCK, *William Percival*
4/5/Sq/4690, 8/7/15, Cpl.; No. 2 Cav. C/S, 1/9/16; 7th R. Regt of Cav., 20/12/16, att. Linc. Yeo.; E,P; Lieut.
    Hampden Club, N.W. 1.

✠ WHITEMAN, *Harold Ernest*
6/2/8381, 13/12/15; Hamps. R., 20/4/16, R.F.C.; Lieut.
    Killed 23/10/16.

WHITEMAN, *William Alexander*
C/12586, 6/2/18; No. 13 O.C.B., 9/8/18.

WHITFIELD, *Allan Bertrand*
B/1268, 23/9/14, L/C.; R. War. R., 19/10/14; Capt.; *M*(1).
    21 Bennetts Hill, Birmingham.

✠ WHITFIELD, *Francis Albert Alexander*
6/2/3431, 29/4/15, Sgt.; A.S.C., C/S, 27/10/16; R.A.S.C., 26/2/17; Lieut.   Died -/11/20.

WHITFIELD, *George Arthur*
D/13001, 29/4/18; No. 22 O.C.B., 7/6/18; E. Surr. R., 11/2/19; 2/Lieut.   *97 Worple Road, Wimbledon, S.W. 19.*

APPENDIX II.—RECORDS OF RANK AND FILE.

WHITGREAVE, John Lockley
A/3523, 6/5/15; dis. 6/5/15.

WHITHAM, Albert
C/10167, 11/12/16; R.W. Surr. R., 9/3/17.
The Grange, Beckett Park, Leeds.

WHITHAM, Gilbert Shaw
K/2886, 8/2/15; York & Lanc. R., 10/2/15, emp. M. of Munitions; Lieut.
19 Alexandra Road, Ulverston, Lancashire.

WHITING, Henry Joseph
A/2896, 9/2/15, L/C.; York. R., 5/6/15; F; Lieut.
Australian Club, Melbourne, Australia.

✠ WHITING, John Robert Bethune
B/11072, 14/4/17; trfr. 14th Lond. R., 27/7/17; F; Pte.
Died of wounds 2/4/18.

WHITING, Walter Fowler
A/10069, 1/12/16; No. 14 O.C.B., 30/1/17; Suff. R., 29/5/17, att. R.W. Fus.; F; Lieut.
The Woodlands, Stowmarket.

WHITING, William Arthur
A/13996, 11/9/18; trfr. 14th Lond. R., 6/12/18.
150 Lower Richmond Road, Putney, S.W. 15.

WHITLAW, Charles Francis
2/2857, 4/2/15; dis. med. unfit, 30/7/15; Devon. R., 7/4/18, att. Wilts. R.; F; Lieut.
Amerden, Taplow, Buckinghamshire.

WHITLOCK, William Harrison
6/2/5489, 9/8/15; Devon. R., 8/6/16, R.A.F.; M,E,F; Lieut.
Instow, The Gardens, West Harrow.

WHITMAN, Herbert Francis Spencer
6/Sq/8259, 8/12/15; R.A., C/S, 4/8/16, Garr. O.C.B.; Lab. Corps, 14/4/17.
25 Gledhow Gardens, Kensington, S.W. 5.

✠ WHITMARSH, Alec
B/11409, 29/5/17; No. 14 O.C.B., 9/11/17; 8th Lond. R., 30/4/18, att. 23rd Lond. R.; F; 2/Lieut.
Died of wounds 1/9/18.

WHITTALL, Arthur James
K/2116, 16/11/14; R.W. Surr. R., 15/12/14, secd. Intelligence Corps; F; Lieut.
Lloyds, E.C. 3.

WHITTAM, Lionel Cuthbert Lewis
A/14026, 18/9/18; demob. 25/1/19.
Rosedale, Manor Place, Paignton, South Devonshire.

WHITTEMORE, Charles Lawrence
C/12594, 12/2/18; R.E., C/S, 12/5/18; R.E., 27/9/18; 2/Lieut.
c/o H. L. Whittemore Esq., 115 Edgewood Road, Ardmore, Pennsylvania, U.S.A.

✠ WHITTINGHAM, Leonard Burton
C/10821, 1/3/17; No. 14 O.C.B., 10/8/17; Worc. R., 27/11/17; 2/Lieut.
Died of wounds 26/4/18.

✠ WHITTINGHAM, Lewis Stuart
6/3/7283, 8/11/15; R.W. Fus., 4/9/16, att. R. Innis. Fus.; F; 2/Lieut.
Killed in action 28/2/17.

WHITTLE, Desmond William Maxwell
4/3993, 3/6/15; R.F.A., 3/9/15; 2/Lieut.

WHITTLE, Frank
C/11782, 30/7/17; No. 2 O.C.B., 4/1/18; Lab. Corps, 14/5/18; F; 2/Lieut.; Legion of Honour.
War Office, S.W. 1.

WHITTLE, Horace Edwin
4/6/3/4988, 19/7/15; trfr. 25th Lond. R., 4/3/16; E. Surr. R., 30/5/17, Indian Army; F,I; Capt.
3 Bexhill Terrace, Merton Road, Wandsworth, S.W. 18.

WHITTLE, Walter Kenneth
6/5/6029, 2/9/15; W. York. R., 7/7/16, att. R.F.C. and York. Huss.; F; Lieut.
Standard Bank of South Africa, Adderley Street, Capetown, South Africa.

WHITTUCK, Francis Gerald
11851, 9/8/17; No. 22 O.C.B., 19/4/18, No. 12 O.C.B.; Som. L.I., 4/2/19; 2/Lieut.
Roseneath, Willsbridge, Gloucestershire.

WHITWAM, James
D/13783, 7/8/18; trfr. K.R. Rif. C., 7/4/19.
Ashfield, Golcar, Nr. Huddersfield.

WHITWORTH, John William
A/12461, 21/1/18; No. 23 O.C.B., 7/6/18; N. Staff. R., 4/2/19; 2/Lieut.
Glencoe, 70 Beeches Road, West Bromwich.

WHYATT, Gilbert Henderson
4/9712, 10/10/16; R.A., C/S, 20/2/17; R.G.A., 29/6/17; F; Lieut.; w.
Ellesmere, Welholme Avenue, Grimsby.

✠ WHYATT, Raymond Selwyn
4/9727, 13/10/16; No. 18 O.C.B., 3/1/17; Notts. & Derby. R., 25/4/17; F; 2/Lieut.; M.C.
Killed in action 17/10/18.

WHYMARK, Eric John
C/11781, 30/7/17; No. 14 O.C.B., 7/12/17; L'pool. R., 25/6/18; F; 2/Lieut.
3 Elm Vale, Fairfield, Liverpool.

✠ WHYTE, Alan Hill
6/9549, 18/3/16; No. 9 O.C.B.; Arg. & Suth'd. Highrs., 4/9/16; F; 2/Lieut.
Killed in action 9/4/17.

WHYTE, David Spence
6/4/6972, 22/10/15; No. 11 O.C.B., 7/5/16; 18th Lond. R., 4/9/16; Lieut.; w.
125 East Dulwich Grove, S.E. 22.

✠ WHYTE, George Herbert
4/2/3994, 3/6/15; 18th Lond. R., 10/8/15; F,S,E; Capt.; M.C.
Killed in action 23/12/17.

WHYTE, John
6/5/5969, 1/9/15, L/C.; No. 9 O.C.B., 6/3/16; R.F.C., 6/7/16, R.A.F.; 2/Lieut.
43 Lygon Road, Edinburgh.

WHYTE, John Harold
6/Sq/9041, 20/1/16; No. 2 Cav. C/S, 22/2/17; trfr. 2nd Lond. Yeo., 27/7/17.
3 Marlborough Road, Dublin.

WHYTE, Lancelot Law
6/Sq/7285, 8/11/15; R.A., C/S, 24/1/16; R.F.A., 6/7/16; F; Lieut.; w; M.C., M(1).
7 Charlotte Square, Edinburgh.

WICKHAM, Cedric Humphrey
1/3081, 13/3/15, L/C.; R.W. Kent R., 21/6/15, att. Midd'x. R.; F,It; Capt.; w, Inv.
c/o Standard Bank of South Africa, Nairobi, Kenya Colony, East Africa.

WICKHAM, Denis Henry
A/1183, 14/9/14; Conn. Rang., 5/10/14; Lieut.; w; M(1).
Seapoint Lodge, Broadstairs.

WICKHAM, Henry Gilbert Latham
C/Sq/14301, 12/11/18; demob. 12/1/19.
Lavender Mead, Wonston, Sutton Scotney, Hampshire.

WICKHAM, Joseph Bazalgette
Sq/463, 23/2/10; dis. 22/2/14; rej. Sq/884, 5/8/14; 4th Drag. Gds., 15/8/14; F; Capt.; Croix de Guerre.
New University Club, St. James Street, S.W. 1.

✠ WICKHAM, Lister Durell
B/773, 2/3/14; Linc. R., 31/8/14; G,F; Capt.; Inv.
Killed in action 3/7/16.

✠ WICKHAM, Neigel John Latham
A/918, 5/8/14; Conn. Rang., 19/9/14; Capt.
Killed in action 19/4/16.

✠ WICKINGS-SMITH, Basil Guildford
A/5, 1/4/08; dis. 31/3/11.
Drowned in the Lusitania.

WICKINGS-SMITH, Claude Trebeck
A/428, 15/6/09; dis. 14/6/13; rej. C/12262, 29/11/17, L/C.; No 4 O.C.B., 10/5/18; Res. of Off., 4/2/19; 2/Lieut.
Grovelly, Winchester Road, Walton-on-Thames.

WICKINGS-SMITH, Cyril
A/270, 3/6/08; dis. 30/11/10; rej. A/D/11206, 5/5/17; demob. 14/10/19.
125 Tavistock Street, Bedford.

WICKINS, Frederick William
6/4/9085, 24/1/16, L/C.; No. 2 O.C.B., 14/8/16; Manch. R., 24/1/17; F,It,S; Staff Capt.
191 Kingston Road, Teddington-on-Thames.

WICKS, Albert Tom
6/8670, 3/1/16; R.A., C/S, 31/5/16; R.G.A., 18/8/16; Lieut.
Newlyn, New Street, Wells, Somerset.

WIDDICOMBE, Claud
A/10269, 1/1/17; Cpl.; demob. 7/2/19.
Rozel, Brixham, South Devonshire.

WIFFEN, Alfred Kemp
6/5/7487, 15/11/15, L/C.; Notts. & Derby. R., 4/9/16, att. Leic. R., secd. M.G.C.; F; Lieut.; w.
Lamcote Field Farm, Ratcliffe-on-Trent, Nottinghamshire.

WIGAN, Sir Roderick Grey
A/11965, 3/9/17; A.S.C., C/S, 12/4/17; R.A.S.C., 6/1/18; F; 2/Lieut.; Croix de Guerre.
Harehope Hall, Alnwick, Northumberland.

APPENDIX II.—RECORDS OF RANK AND FILE.

WIGG, Frank Samuel
A/10298, 1/1/17; No. 14 O.C.B., 5/5/17; Norf. R., 28/8/17, att. Suff. R.; F; Lieut.
Marnehurst, Gladstone Road, Fakenham, Norfolk.

WIGG, Vivian
4/3895, 31/5/15; 11th Lond. R., 14/12/15, att. R.F.C., R.A.F.; Lieut.

WIGGINS, Robert Victor Neville
B/11715, 19/7/17; No. 14 O.C.B., 9/11/17; Shrop L.I., 30/4/18; F; 2/Lieut.; w.
Hill House, Watlington, Oxon.

WIGHT, Stewart Athol
B/12720, 8/3/18; No. 2 O.C.B., 20/9/18, No. 13 O.C.B.; dis. med. unfit, 26/3/19.
239 Hills Road, Cambridge.

☩ WIGHTMAN, Arthur Bennett
6/5/5367, 3/8/15, Sgt.; Manch. R., 6/12/15; F; Capt.; w(2), g; M.C.
Died 2/5/21.

WIGHTMAN, William Osborne
6/3/8527, 29/12/15; R.A., C/S, 4/8/16; R.G.A., 24/11/16; F; Lieut.
The Croft, Somers Road, Reigate.

WIGRAM, Charles Knox
4/4059, 7/6/15; dis. 7/6/15.

WIGRAM, Robert
Sq/1024, 10/8/14; 7th R. Regt. of Cav., K.R. Rif. C.; F; 2/Lieut.
Gonder Lodge, Penn, Buckinghamshire.

WILBORE, Charles Eric Bradfield
A/Sq/C/12472, 24/1/18; No. 11 O.C.B., 7/1/18; Res. of Off., 6/2/19; 2/Lieut.
The Haylands, Clugwell, Essex.

WILCOCK, Percy John Colman
12355, 31/12/17, L/C.; H. Bde. O.C.B., 8/4/18; Welch Gds., 24/9/18; 2/Lieut.
Downside Lodge, Fitzgerald Avenue, East Sheen, Surrey.

WILD, Arnold Henry
6/Sq/9195, 29/1/16; A.S.C., C/S, 1/9/16; R.A.S.C., 25/10/16; Lieut.; M(1).
3 Middle Temple Lane, E.C. 4.

WILD, Ovid Frederick
D/11876, 16/8/17; Sigs. C/S, 14/12/17; R.E., 24/5/18; F; 2/Lieut.
12 Queen Anne's Grove, Bedford Park, W. 4.

WILDBLOOD, Fred William Rhead
B/13547, 17/7/18; demob. 28/2/19.
Argyle House, Blythe Bridge, Staffordshire.

WILDBLOOD, Horace Barrs
6/Sq/6219, 13/9/15; No. 1 Cav. C/S, 24/4/16; Worc. Yeo., 27/9/16; E.P; Lieut.
9 Park View, Wigan.

☩ WILDBLOOD, William Arthur
Sq/2675, 12/1/15, L/C.; R.A.S.C., 13/5/15; Lieut.
Killed in action 16/6/17.

WILDE, Bertram Harcourt
B/13625, 24/7/18; No. 11 O.C.B., 24/1/19; General List, 8/3/19; 2/Lieut.
Northwood, Blackpool, Lancashire.

WILDE, Horace Morley
6/5/5738, 21/8/15; L'pool. R., 2/1/16, att. Lab. Corps; Lieut.
Northwood, Blackpool, Lancashire.

WILDE, John Austen
6/1/7853, 25/11/15; R.F.A., C/S, 4/8/16; R.F.A., 10/11/16; F; Lieut.; w.
18 Clifton Terrace, Brighton. (Now in Hong Kong).

WILDE, Reginald Coleridge
6/5/5737, 21/8/15; L'pool. R., 2/1/16; F,P; Capt.; w; D.S.O., M.C., M(1).
Northwood, Blackpool, Lancashire.

WILDEY, Cecil Eldon
A/12552, 4/2/18; No. 5 O.C.B., 5/7/18; R.W. Surr. R., 3/3/19; 2/Lieut.
46 Endlesham Road, Balham, S.W. 12.

☩ WILDGOOSE, Ernest Henry
6/3/8430, 15/12/15; R.E., C/S, 5/8/16; R.E., 20/10/16; F; 2/Lieut.
Killed in action 22/3/18.

WILDGOOSE, Horace Edmund
C/10854, 5/3/17; No. 12 O.C.B., 10/8/17; Notts. & Derby. R., 27/11/17; 2/Lieut.
Industrial House, Matlock, Derbyshire.

WILDING, Harold Waudby
6/5/8076, 1/12/15; No. 8 O.C.B., 4/8/16; Yorks. L.I., 21/11/16, R.E.; F; Lieut.; w.
11 Rigby Street, Liverpool.

WILDSMITH, Alfred Bernard
6/2/5368, 1/8/15; R.F.A., 21/10/15; F; Capt.; Inv.
31 Lynton Road, Acton, W. 3.

☩ WILDSMITH, Raymond Charles
6/2/6931, 19/10/15; 25th Lond. R., 4/8/16; 2/Lieut.
Killed in action 7/6/17.

WILDY, Cyril William
6/5/6682, 7/10/15; 25th Lond. R., 25/12/15, att. W. Rid. R. and R.E. Sigs.; F,It; Lieut.; M(1).
Sunfield, Pangbourne, Berkshire

WILES, Alfred
6/4/5964, 1/9/15; L'pool. R., 1/6/16; F; Lieut.; w; M(1).
The Hollies, Half Edge Lane, Eccles, Nr. Manchester.

WILEY, Eustace
6/4/9043, 20/1/16; dis. to re-enlist in K.R. Rif. C., 19/5/16.

WILFORD, Harry Norman
2/3247, 12/4/15, L/C.; R.F.A., 20/9/15; E,S; Lieut.
The Knoll, Rothwell, Northamptonshire.

WILKES, John Findlater
6/5/7821, 24/11/15; No. 7 O.C.B., 11/8/16; R. Dub. Fus., 18/12/16; Lieut.; w.
2 Grosvenor Terrace, Dalkey, Co. Dublin.

☩ WILKES, Norman Bayley
6/4/9042, 20/1/16; No. 14 O.C.B., 30/10/16; S. Staff. R., 28/2/17; F; 2/Lieut.
Killed in action 29/4/18.

WILKEY, Leslie Sutton
C/D/12250, 22/11/17; No. 4 O.C.B., 10/5/18; R.W. Kent R., 4/2/19; 2/Lieut.
42 Fox Lane, Palmers Green, N. 13.

WILKIE, Alfred
K/E/2431, 21/12/14; R.E., 8/2/15; Capt.
21 Ayresome Avenue, Roundhay, Leeds.

WILKIE, Harry Spence
6/5/9184, 28/1/16; R.F.A., C/S, 4/8/16; R.F.A., 24/11/16; F; Lieut.; M.C.
Platten, Kirriemuir, Scotland.

WILKIE, Jack Ferguson McLachlan
6/8123, 2/12/15; No. 9 O.C.B., 8/3/16; R. Highrs., 6/8/16; Lieut.; w.
Stanley Villas, Monifieth, Forfar.

WILKIE, James
6/5/5576, 12/8/15; R.E., 21/11/15; F; Lieut.; M.C.
17 Courtenay Road, Waterloo, Liverpool.

WILKINGS, Sidney Arthur
C/D/14233, 25/10/18; trfr. K.R. Rif. C., 13/5/19.
15 Park Street, Plymouth.

WILKINS, Alan Edward
3/9608, 4/9/16, L/C.; No. 14 O.C.B., 27/12/16; Dorset R., 27/3/17, F; Lieut.
60 Friern Road, East Dulwich, S.E. 22.

WILKINS, Frank James
2/3711, 20/5/15, L/C.; York. & Lanc. R., 2/9/15, att. M.G.C.; F; Capt.
19 Rydal Road, Streatham, S.W. 16.

WILKINS, Frank Leonard
4/1/4352, 21/6/15; R.A.S.C., 9/10/15; G,E,P; Capt.; M(1).
19 Fordhook Avenue, Ealing, W. 5.

WILKINS, George Frederic
6/7973, 29/11/15; A.S.C., C/S, 6/3/16; R.A.S.C., 7/5/16; S; Lieut.
Pinelands, Weybridge.

WILKINS, Harold Leslie
4/1/4198, 14/6/15; Manch. R., 18/10/15; F; Capt.; w(2); M(1).
66 Brownlow Road, New Southgate, N. 11.

☩ WILKINS, John Christopher Martin
5/5233, 30/7/15; Devon. R., 4/12/15, D. of Corn. L.I.; Lieut.; w.
Killed in action 24/3/18.

WILKINSON, Alexander Geoffrey
K/Sq/2564, 4/1/15; E. Rid. Yeo., 2/3/15; E,P; Lieut.
Neasham Abbey, Darlington, Co. Durham.

WILKINSON, Alfred Hughes
6/3/8576, 31/12/15; No. 14 O.C.B., 8/9/16; General List, 27/2/17; Lieut.
Sand Hall, North Cove, East Yorkshire.

WILKINSON, Arthur
A/9838, 3/11/16; No. 14 O.C.B., 27/12/16; Durh. L.I., 27/3/17; F; 2/Lieut.
32 First Avenue, Acton Park, W. 3.

☩ WILKINSON, Bernard Jocelyn
1/3613, 13/5/15; York. R., 26/8/15; 2/Lieut.
Killed in action 8/7/16.

WILKINSON, Clifford Keene
4/3896, 31/5/15; R.F.A., C/S, 17/7/16; R.F.A., 7/8/16; Lieut.
4 St. Philips Road, Surbiton.

WILKINSON, Evelyn Miles
C/D/12091, 27/9/17; Tank Corps C/S, 8/3/18; Tank Corps, 3/3/19; 2/Lieut.
Lyndhurst, Glenageary, Co. Dublin, Ireland.

APPENDIX II.—RECORDS OF RANK AND FILE.

WILKINSON, Francis Henry Juxon
6/2/5534, 9/8/15; R.F.A., 30/11/15; F; Capt.; w(2).
27 Marlborough Hill, N.W. 8.

WILKINSON, Francis Willie
4/3187, 6/4/15, L/C.; R.W. Kent R., 21/6/15, R.G.A.; F; Lieut.
10 Essex Grove, Upper Norwood, S.E. 19.

☩ WILKINSON, Frederick James
6/5/7424, 12/11/15; No. 8 O.C.B., 4/8/16; R. Lanc. R., 21/11/16; 2/Lieut.
Killed in action 9-12/4/17.

WILKINSON, Geoffrey Herbert
6/D/9594, 26/6/16, Sgt.; R.A., C/S, 3/4/17; R.G.A., 25/6/17; F; Lieut.; g.
10 Orme Square, W. 2.

WILKINSON, Harold Ascensus
6/5/5317, 2/8/15, L/C.; North'd. Fus., 6/7/16, att. M. of Munitions; F; Lieut.
68 Bury Road, Noel Park, Wood Green, N. 22.

WILKINSON, Herbert Augustus
6/Sq/6220, 13/9/15; Dorset Yeo., 25/1/16, att. R.A.F.; E,P; Lieut.
The Elms, Sidcup, Kent.

☩ WILKINSON, Horace
3/3569, 10/5/15, L/C.; N. Lan. R., 2/11/15; Capt.
Died of wounds 31/10/18.

WILKINSON, James William
6/3/8771, 6/1/16; No. 14 O.C.B., 26/11/16; N. Lan. R., 27/3/17; F; Lieut.
Highgate Terrace, 31 Garstang Road, Fulwood, Preston, Lancashire.

WILKINSON, John Bartle Probert
C/12587, 6/2/18; No 17 O.C.B., 5/7/18; demob. 19/1/19.
Master, Poor Law Institution, Crosland Moor, Huddersfield.

☩ WILKINSON, John Graham
C/1169, 14/9/14; Hamps. R., 11/12/14; I,M; Capt.; w.
Killed in action 20/7/18.

WILKINSON, John Harry
B/11367, 25/5/17; R.F.C., C/S, 2/8/17; R.F.C., 8/9/17, R.A.F.; Lieut.
2 Cross Street, Gainsborough, Lincolnshire.

WILKINSON, John Percy
C/11804, 2/8/17; North'd. Fus., 25/6/18; 2/Lieut.
Limes Cottage, Henry Street, Cockermouth, Cumberland.

☩ WILKINSON, Marcus Leonard
6/3/9129, 24/1/16; No. 2 O.C.B., 14/8/16; North'd. Fus., 18/12/16; 2/Lieut.
Died of wounds 8/7/17.

WILKINSON, Noel William Grieves
6/4/5645, 16/8/15, Sgt.; Manch. R., 9/1/16, att. R.A.F.; G,F; Lieut.; w.
4 Cromer Road, Aigburth, Liverpool.

WILKINSON, Percy
E/14163, 11/10/18; No. 22 O.C.B., 22/11/18; Manch. R., 15/2/19; 2/Lieut.
Brookside, Prestbury, Nr. Macclesfield.

WILKINSON, Reginald Felix
A/14052, 20/9/18; demob. 23/1/19.
Drayton, New Road, Bromsgrove, Worcestershire.

☩ WILKINSON, Robert Bruce
A/10297, 1/1/17; No. 14 O.C.B., 6/4/17; N. Lan. R., 31/7/17; 2/Lieut.
Died of wounds 12/12/17.

WILKINSON, Sidney Herbert
4/2/4032, 7/6/15; W. Rid. R., 23/10/15, emp. M. of Labour; Lieut.

WILKINSON, Sydney John
4/3476, 3/5/15; R.A.S.C., 24/5/15; Capt.; M(1).
102 Adelaide Road, Hampstead, N.W. 3.

WILKINSON, Thornton
C/823, 4/8/14; W. Rid. R., 18/9/14.

☩ WILKINSON, Walter Lightowler
6/1/6140, 9/9/15, L/C.; Arg. & Suth'd. Highrs., 21/6/16; F; Capt.
Killed in action 9/4/17.

WILKS, Philip Eardley
C/10823, 28/2/17, L/C.; R.G.A., C/S, 1/8/17; R.G.A., 17/12/17; 2/Lieut.
St. Mary's Hall, Coventry.

☩ WILKS, Walter Charles
K/2242, 3/12/14; Army Chaplain, 19/12/14, att. S. Staff. R.; w; M.C.
Killed in action 4/10/17.

WILLAN, Harold Curwen
6/8674, 4/1/16; R.A., C/S, 26/5/16; R.G.A., 30/8/16; F,I; Lieut.; M.C.
6 Castle Garth, Kendal, Westmorland. (Now in F.M.S.)

WILLBOURN, Cyril
4/1/4317, 17/6/15; E. York. R., 20/12/15, Army Cyc. Bn.; F; Capt.
22 St. Johns Avenue, Bridlington, East Yorkshire. (Now in East Africa).

WILLBOURN, Eric Stuart
A/11966, 3/9/17; Sigs. C/S, 16/11/17; R.E., 19/4/18; F; 2/Lieut.
22 St. Johns Avenue, Bridlington, East Yorkshire. (Now in F.M.S.)

WILLCOCK, Percy Douglas
6/2/8327, 10/12/15; No. 14 O.C.B., 30/10/16; N. Lan. R., 25/4/17, att. R.A.F.; F; Lieut.; g.
81 Liverpool Road, Birkdale, Southport, Lancashire.

WILLCOCKS, Roger Escombe
E/1/1507, 1/10/14; R.A.O.C., 10/1/18; Capt.
Byworth, Roehampton, S.W. 15.

WILLCOX, Walter Tyrrell
4/3/4322, 17/6/15; W. York. R., 5/9/15, att. R.F.C., R.A.F.; F; Lieut.; p.
c/o E. B. Vignoles, Little Orchard, Streatley-on-Thames.

WILLETT, Lewis Howard
A/688, 31/1/13, Cpl.; R. Highrs., 14/8/14; F,M; Major; w(2); O.B.E.
The Fleetway House, Farringdon Street, E.C. 4.

☩ WILLETT, Richard
4/5/4899, 15/7/15; Lan. Fus., 27/12/15; 2/Lieut.; w.
Killed in action 31/7/17.

WILLETT, Samuel Walter
5/6/7893, 20/11/15; R.A., C/S, 7/8/16; R.F.A., 17/11/16; F,NR; Lieut.; w.
3 Hensingham Road, Whitehaven.

WILLETTS, John Bradley
C/12303, 10/12/17, L/C.; No. 21 O.C.B., 7/6/18; W. Rid. R., 5/2/19; 2/Lieut.
29 Sandford Road, Moseley, Birmingham.

WILLIAMS, Albert Godfrey Roy
2/9610, 6/9/16, L/C.; R.A., C/S, 28/12/16; R.F.A., 19/5/17; F,It; Lieut.; M.C.
11 Cumberland Road, Kew Gardens, Surrey.

WILLIAMS, Albert Ogwen
6/5/5965, 1/9/15; L'pool. R., 1/6/16; 2/Lieut.; w.
32 Clifton Road, Newsham Park, Liverpool.

WILLIAMS, Arthur
6/5/8124, 2/12/15; No. 8 O.C.B., 4/8/16; Yorks. L.I., 21/11/16; F,It; Lieut.
Oakfield, Aberdare Road, Mountain Ash, South Wales.

WILLIAMS, Arthur David
K/2110, 16/11/14; R.W. Fus., 3/12/14; Lieut.
92 Clifton Hill, St. Johns Wood, N.W. 8.

WILLIAMS, Arthur Horsford
A/11219, 4/5/17; No. 14 O.C.B., 5/10/17; Devon. R., 26/2/18, att. M.G.C.; F; 2/Lieut.
13 Teilo Street, Cardiff.

☩ WILLIAMS, Arthur Trevor
6/5/8125, 2/12/15; No. 8 O.C.B., 4/8/16; R.W. Fus., 21/11/16, att. R.A.F.; F; 2/Lieut.
Killed in action 4/9/17.

WILLIAMS, Ashley Charles
4/3/6/4324, 19/6/15; dis. med. unfit, 24/3/16.
38 Great Ormond Street, W.C. 1.

WILLIAMS, Basil Conrad Leader. See LEADER-WILLIAMS, B. C.

WILLIAMS, Basil Winstanley Michael
5/3/645, 18/6/12, C.S.M.; R.A.O.C., 11/10/16, R.F.C., R.A.F.; Major; M(1).
c/o Air Ministry, Aircraft Depot, Karachi, India.

WILLIAMS, Bennett Montgomerie
K/E/2372, 17/12/14; Durh. L.I., 24/3/15, att. Som. L.I.; F; Capt.; w; M.E., Croix de Guerre.
Smelting Syke, Hexham, Northumberland.

WILLIAMS, Bernard Acton
A/Sq/9835, 3/11/16, L/C.; No. 1 Cav. C/S, 28/2/18; R. Regt. of Cav., 28/8/18; 2/Lieut.
Arnold House, Long Eaton.

☩ WILLIAMS, Bernard Hallett
6/5/6053, 3/9/15; No. 4 O.C.B., 7/3/16; N. Lan. R., 21/7/16; F; 2/Lieut.
Killed in action 31/7/17.

WILLIAMS, Charles Bernard
6/4/7974, 29/11/15; No. 14 O.C.B., 20/9/16; R.W. Fus., 24/10/16; 2/Lieut.
Salop House, Oswestry.

APPENDIX II.—RECORDS OF RANK AND FILE.

✠ WILLIAMS, *Charles James*
C/887, 5/8/14; Bedf. R., 19/9/14; F; Capt.; g.
　　　　　　　　　　　　Died of wounds 19/12/15.

WILLIAMS, *Charles Reginald McGregor*
6/4/7536, 16/11/15; R.F.A., C/S, 31/3/16; R.F.A., 5/8/16, emp. M. of Labour; Lieut.
　　10 Rothesay Road, Newport, Monmouthshire.

WILLIAMS, *David Benjamin Sproule*
C/9972, 20/11/16; Garr. O.C.B., 23/4/17; Worc. R., 16/6/17.

WILLIAMS, *David Emrys*
B/12782, 15/3/18; No. 17 O.C.B., 9/8/18; R.W. Fus.; 2/Lieut.
　　Bryn Awel, Bryn, Nr. Corwen, North Wales.

✠ WILLIAMS, *David Jenkins*
6/5/8077, 1/12/15; No. 14 O.C.B., 28/8/16; Mon. R., 22/11/16; 2/Lieut.
　　　　　　　　　　　　Died of wounds 20/9/17.

WILLIAMS, *Edgar Alan*
6/5/8671, 3/1/16; No. 8 O.C.B., 4/8/16; M.G.C., 24/10/16; F; Capt.; M(1).
　　13 Glanyrafon Terrace, Blaina, Monmouthshire.

WILLIAMS, *Edward Glyn*
6/2/8044, 30/11/15; No. 8 O.C.B., 4/8/16; R.W. Fus., 21/11/16, att. R. Muns. Fus.; F,It; 2/Lieut.; w(2); M(1), Italian Decoration for Valour.
　　Gellywion, Radyr, Nr. Cardiff.

WILLIAMS, *Egbert Rowland*
A/B/D/12176, 29/10/17; No. 5 O.C.B., 8/2/18; Yorks. L.I., 28/5/18; 2/Lieut.

WILLIAMS, *Eric Alfred Bransby*
A/13090, 20/5/18; No. 24 O.C.B., 15/11/18; Tank Corps, 22/3/19; 2/Lieut.
　　31 George Street, Hanover Square, W. 1.

WILLIAMS, *Eric Hugh*
E/1592, 6/10/14; R.W. Surr. R., 29/10/14; G; Capt.
　　33 Lexham Gardens, W. 8.

WILLIAMS, *Eric Morgan*
6/3/5734, 19/8/15; R.W. Kent R., 27/12/15, att. R.A.F.; F; Lieut.
　　Marling, Evans & Coy., 29 Mincing Lane, E.C. 3.

WILLIAMS, *Eric Watson*
B/720, 23/6/13, Cpl.; R.A.M.C., 7/9/14; F; Major; M.C.
　　12 Victoria Square, Clifton, Bristol.

WILLIAMS, *Ernest Rhys*
B/E/13428, 1/7/18; No. 22 O.C.B., 23/8/18; trfr. 29th Lond. R., 13/12/18.
　　45 Vardre Road, Clydash on Tawe, Glamorganshire.

WILLIAMS, *Erroll Holdsworth*
C/10383, 8/1/17; R.F.C., C/S, 16/4/17; R.F.C., 16/5/17; F; Lieut.; D.F.C.
　　202 Kings Road, Reading.

WILLIAMS, *Evan Howard*
6/2/9480, 14/2/16, L/C.; No. 14 O.C.B., 26/11/16; Shrop. Yeo., 28/2/17.

WILLIAMS, *Evan Ivor*
K/E/2238, 3/12/14; Welch R., 7/1/15.
　　Great House, Pendoglan, Glamorganshire.

WILLIAMS, *Francis Victor Watkin*
1/3288, 15/4/15; Rif. Brig., 16/7/15; F; Lieut.
　　Osmotherley Vicarage, Northallerton, Yorkshire.

WILLIAMS, *Frederick Charles*
C/10584, 22/1/17, L/C.; M.G.C., C/S, 6/7/17; M.G.C., 19/12/17, Tank Corps; F; 2/Lieut.
　　6 Brooklands, Victoria Street, Hereford.

WILLIAMS, *Frederick Harold*
A/11905, 23/8/17; No. 5 O.C.B., 5/10/17; R.E., 29/1/18; 2/Lieut.
　　20 Bedford Place, W.C. 1.

WILLIAMS, *Geoffrey Bridgewater*
A/420, 21/5/09; dis. 2/8/12; Leic. R., 21/8/16; Lieut.; w(2), p; M.C. and Bar.
　　12 Lincolns Inn Fields, W.C. 2.

WILLIAMS, *Geoffrey Hyde*
H/1958, 26/10/14; York. & Lanc. R., 10/2/15; F,It; Capt.; w; M.C.
　　The Homestead, Datchet, Buckinghamshire.

WILLIAMS, *George*
B/E/13574, 19/7/18; No. 22 O.C.B., 20/9/18; Midd'x. R., 5/2/19; 2/Lieut.
　　15/16 Aldermanbury, E.C. 2.

WILLIAMS, *George Arthur*
Sq/514, 4/11/10; 1st City of Lond. Yeo., 11/11/13, S. Lan. R.; E,G,M; Staff Capt.; M(3).
　　c/o E. G. Williams Esq., 4 Stanford Road, Kensington, W. 8.
　　(Now in India).

✠ WILLIAMS, *George Stewart Louis Stanislaus Stevens*
6/2/8498, 20/12/15, L/C.; No. 14 O.C.B., 30/10/16; R.W. Fus., 24/1/17; F,E; Lieut.; w.
　　　　　　　　　　　　Killed in action 8/9/18.

✠ WILLIAMS, *George Trevor*
Sq/1087, 3/9/14; R.F.A., 13/10/14; F,G,E,M,I; Capt.
　　　　　　　　　　　　Died 19/4/18.

WILLIAMS, *Geraint Lloyd*
D/10285, 1/1/17; No. 17 O.C.B., 3/1/17; R.W. Fus., 25/4/17; 2/Lieut.
　　Llwyn Gwern, Caradoc Road, Aberystwyth.

WILLIAMS, *Gomer Oscar*
B/12356, 31/12/17; No. 17 O.C.B., 10/5/18; trfr. 28th Lond. R., 11/7/18; F.
　　18 St. Pauls Road, West Hartlepool.

WILLIAMS, *Harold*
6/3/6932, 19/10/15; R.A., C/S, 24/1/16; R.G.A., 13/9/16; China; Lieut.
　　Greenbank House, Chester.

WILLIAMS, *Harold Beck*
6/1/7083, 29/10/15, Sgt.; No. 14 O.C.B.; Hamps. R., 24/10/16; F; Lieut.; w.
　　112a Bensham Manor Road, Thornton Heath, Surrey.

WILLIAMS, *Harold Erskine*
4/Sq/D/3804, 27/5/15; No. 14 O.C.B., 30/10/16; Norf. Yeo., 28/2/17, att. Norf. R.; F; Lieut.
　　c/o Edward Rodham Esq., Marlborough House, Bexhill-on-Sea.

WILLIAMS, *Harold Newall*
6/5/7518, 15/11/15; R.W. Fus., 4/8/16, att. 4th Lond. R.; F; Capt.; M.C., M(1).
　　c/o Collins & Coy., 6 Stanley Street, Liverpool.

WILLIAMS, *Harold Patton*
6/5/5673, 16/8/15; Manch. R., 18/1/16.
　　The Willows, Northland Road, Londonderry.

WILLIAMS, *Harold William*
6/1/7570, 17/11/15; No. 11 O.C.B., 7/5/16; E. Kent R., 4/9/16; w.
　　59 Strand, W.C. 2.

✠ WILLIAMS, *Harry Ben*
2/3248, 12/4/15, Sgt.; No. 14 O.C.B., 28/8/16; L'pool. R., 24/10/16; F; 2/Lieut.; M.C.
　　　　　　　　　　　　Killed in action 3/5/17.

WILLIAMS, *Hector Redvers*
A/13123, 24/5/18, L/C.; trfr. K.R. Rif. C., 7/4/19; L/C.
　　169 Primrose Villas, Heywood, Lancashire.

WILLIAMS, *Henry Lewis Ellis*
6/2/8045, 30/11/15; No. 8 O.C.B., 4/8/16; S. Wales Bord., 21/11/16.
　　87a Severn Road, Canton, Cardiff.

WILLIAMS, *Herbert David*
D/2998, 1/3/15, L/C.; Lan. Fus., 26/8/15, emp. M. of Labour; Lieut.

WILLIAMS, *Herbert Samuel*
D/E/13774, 7/8/18; No. 22 O.C.B., 20/9/18; R. War. R., 5/2/19; 2/Lieut.
　　20 Salisbury Road, Moseley, Birmingham.

✠ WILLIAMS, *James*
F/1768, 16/10/14; Lan. Fus., 5/4/15; Capt.
　　　　　　　　　　　　Died of wounds 22/7/16.

WILLIAMS, *James Edwin Gresham*
E/1674, 12/10/14; dis. med. unfit, 2/11/14.
　　Skelton Manor House, York.

WILLIAMS, *James Hamlett*
A/9905, 13/11/16, L/C; trfr. R.F.C., 13/12/17.
　　Grosvenor House, Winsford, Cheshire.

WILLIAMS, *John*
C/10137, 7/12/16; No. 14 O.C.B., 5/3/17; R.N.V.R., 26/6/17.

WILLIAMS, *John Clwyd*
C/Sq/10781, 19/2/17, L/C.; No. 2 Cav. C/S, 11/1/18; 3rd R. Regt. of Cav., 22/6/18; F; Lieut.; w.
　　Five Wents, Swanley, Kent.

WILLIAMS, *John Fortescue Hugh*
1/3326, 19/4/15; Wilts. R., 10/7/15; M,I, Persia; Capt.; w.
　　c/o Cox & Coy., Bombay, India.

WILLIAMS, *John George*
5/3/6222, 13/9/15; No. 5 O.C.B., 14/4/16; Hamps. R., 4/9/16; F; Lieut.
　　6 Market Street, Weymouth, Dorset.

✠ WILLIAMS, *John Herschell*
6/4/6641, 4/10/15; R.F.A., C/S, 31/3/16; R.F.A., 21/8/16; F; 2/Lieut.
　　　　　　　　　　　　Killed in action 17/6/17.

WILLIAMS, *John Lias Cecil*
B/2093, 16/11/14; R.W. Fus., 6/1/15; F; Capt.; w.
　　33 Cambridge Street, Hyde Park, W. 2.

APPENDIX II.—RECORDS OF RANK AND FILE.

WILLIAMS, John Morley Pedr
6/5/6792, 13/10/15; R. Fus., 4/8/16.
30 Temple Road, South Croydon, Surrey.

WILLIAMS, John Oswald
6/1/6973, 22/10/15; R.W. Fus., 6/7/16, Lab. Corps; S; Capt.
H.M. Treasury, Lagos, Nigeria, West Africa.

WILLIAMS, John Stanley
C/12629, 18/2/18; No. 1 O.C.B., 9/8/18; S. Wales Bord., 4/3/19; 2/Lieut.
Lancaster House, Tenby, Pembrokeshire.

WILLIAMS, John Tarbuck
6/9558, 1/3/16; dis. med. unfit, 18/8/16.
38 Streathbourne Road, Tooting Common, S.W. 17.

WILLIAMS, John Trevor
1/9644, 27/9/16; No. 14 O.C.B., 7/6/17; Indian Army, 25/9/17.
106 Woodville Road, Cardiff.

✠ WILLIAMS, Leslie Caradoc
4/5089, 26/7/15; R.F.A., 12/10/15; F; Lieut.
Killed in action 27/8/17.

WILLIAMS, Leslie Charles
3/6/578, 13/11/11, Sgt.; No. 14 O.C.B., 29/9/16; Suff. R., 18/12/16; E; Lieut.; w; M.C.
41 Sternhold Avenue, Streatham, S.W. 2.

✠ WILLIAMS, Meredyth Robert Owen
6/3/6263, 16/9/15; North'd. Fus., 1/6/16; 2/Lieut.
Killed in action 14/3/17.

WILLIAMS, Milbourne Bransby
K/D/2778, 25/1/15; Welch R., 20/2/15; F; Major; w.
Killay House, Sketty, Glamorganshire.

WILLIAMS, Montagu
4/3805, 27/5/15; dis. med. unfit, 22/5/16.

WILLIAMS, Nigel Oldham
6/4/7162, 2/11/15, L/C.; 7th Lond. R., 4/9/16; Capt.; M.C.
c/o Baron, Hartley Ltd., 8 Shaftesbury Avenue, W. 1.

✠ WILLIAMS, Norman Ernest
4/2/4443, 26/6/15, Sgt.; 10th Lond. R., 18/12/15, R.F.C.; 2/Lieut.
Killed in action 9/11/17.

WILLIAMS, Norman Hooper
C/12662, 27/2/18; Sigs. C/S, 14/6/18; R.E., 24/3/19; 2/Lieut.
Alison Lodge, Court Road, Eltham, S.E. 9.

WILLIAMS, Orlando Cyprian
A/423, 21/5/09; dis. 1/11/11; General List, -/3/15; G,E,P; Major; M.C., Italian Silver Medal for Military Valour, Legion of Honour, M(4).
4 Campden Hill Gardens, W. 8.

WILLIAMS, Owen Lockhart Rees
6/Sq/8490, 20/12/15; No. 1 Cav. C/S, 24/4/16; N. Som. Yeo., 16/9/16, secd. Tank Corps; Lieut.

✠ WILLIAMS, Percy John
4/3/4411, 24/6/15; trfr. 5th Lond. R., 13/3/16; E. Surr. R., 25/10/16; 2/Lieut.
Died of wounds 17/5/17.

WILLIAMS, Percy Thomas
B/D/A/12020, 17/9/17; R.E., C/S, 10/2/18; R.E., 31/5/18; 2/Lieut.
220 Battery Street, San Francisco, U.S.A.

WILLIAMS, Ralph
D/12897, 9/4/18; R.E., C/S, 23/8/18; R.E., 18/1/19; 2/Lieut.

WILLIAMS, Rees John
6/4/7163, 2/11/15; Welch R., 6/7/16; F; Capt.; w; D.S.O., M(1).
Oakdene, Taffs Well, Cardiff.

WILLIAMS, Reginald Firmston
6/2/5689, 16/8/15, Sgt.; North'd. Fus., 21/4/16; F; Capt.; w.
Ardmillan, Bramhall, Cheshire.

WILLIAMS, Richard
6/1/5719, 19/8/15; R.A., C/S, 31/3/16; R.G.A., 19/8/16; F; Lieut.; M.C.
Grammar School, Cowbridge, Glamorganshire.

✠ WILLIAMS, Richard James
6/4/9171, 27/1/16; No. 14 O.C.B., 29/9/16; 9th Lond. R., 18/12/16; F; 2/Lieut.
Died of wounds 29/4/18.

WILLIAMS, Robert
6/1/7020, 26/10/15; R.W. Fus., 4/8/16, Welch R.; F; Capt.; w; M.C., M(1).
16 Mexfield Road, East Putney, S.W. 15.

WILLIAMS, Robert John
4/4318, 17/6/15; trfr. Welch Horse Yeo., 30/1/16; Welch Horse Yeo., 22/11/16, att. M.G.C.; F; Lieut.
Bank House, Builth Wells, Breconshire.

WILLIAMS, Ronald Gus
3/3575, 10/5/15; Welch R., 5/11/15.
Richmond House, Clytha Square, Newport, Monmouthshire.

WILLIAMS, Sidney Charles
4/2/4060, 7/6/15, L/C.; R.W. Surr. R., 23/10/15, att. Suff. R.; F; Lieut.; w.
Andersea, Baskerville Road, Wandsworth Common, S W. 18.

WILLIAMS, Stanley
B/11683, 16/7/17; No. 14 O.C.B., 7/12/17; N. Staff. R., 28/5/18; F; 2/Lieut.; w.
St. Godwalds, Bromsgrove, Worcestershire.

✠ WILLIAMS, Theodore Cecil Ormond
F/1864, 16/10/14; Notts. & Derby. R.; Capt.; M.C.
Died of wounds 24/3/18.

WILLIAMS, Thomas
A/13161, 29/5/18; No. 22 O.C.B., 23/8/18; Education Officer, 8/12/18; F; Capt.
St. Pauls Vicarage, Burnley.

WILLIAMS, Tom Henry
C/14303, 21/11/18; demob. 24/1/19.
Bryncelyn, Gwilym Road, Cwmllynfell.

WILLIAMS, Tom Stuart
B/11716, 19/7/17; No. 11 O.C.B., 9/11/17; Wilts. R., 26/3/18; F; 2/Lieut.
Fairholme, Tollesbury, Essex.

WILLIAMS, Vaughan Edwardes Garth
4/1/4319, 17/6/15; York. R., 12/1/16; F; Lieut.
Frenchgate, Richmond, Yorkshire.

WILLIAMS, Victor Erle Nash
4/2/5137, 26/7/15; N. Staff. R., 29/11/15, R. Berks. R., R.W. Surr. R., Lab. Corps; F; Capt.; g.
Fleur-de-lis House, Fleur-de-lis, Via Cardiff.

✠ WILLIAMS, Vivian Pedr
6/5/8883, 12/1/16; No. 8 O.C.B., 4/8/16; R.W. Fus., 21/11/16; 2/Lieut.
Killed in action 22/4/18.

WILLIAMS, Walter Henry
4/1/5185, 29/7/15, L/C.; R.G.A., 1/12/15; Lieut.
Lloyds Bank, Paignton, Devonshire.

WILLIAMS, Walter Oliver Hugh
6/2/5646, 16/8/15; Worc. R., 4/1/16; F; Lieut.
1 Stanwell Road, Penarth, Glamorganshire.

WILLIAMS, William Albert Thomas
6/4/5536, 9/8/15; trfr. Mon. R., 23/2/16.
1 Gilfach Street, Bargoed, South Wales.

WILLIAMS, William Arthur
3/3361, 22/4/15; 19th Lond. R., 17/8/15; w.
5 Newton Villas, Porthcawl.

WILLIAMS, William Charles
D/13741, 2/8/18; trfr. K.R. Rif. C., 7/4/19.
Elmhurst, Blackheath, Staffordshire.

WILLIAMS, William Edward
6/3/7866, 26/11/15, L/C.; No. 14 O.C.B., 26/11/16; Mon. R., 27/3/17; F; Lieut.
54 St. Georges Road, Wallasey, Cheshire.

WILLIAMS, William Edward Miller
C/12667, 27/2/18; demob. 25/1/19.
10 Manor Gardens, Holloway, N. 7.

WILLIAMS, William Emyr
6/4/8676, 4/1/16; No. 13 O.C.B., 4/11/16; R.W. Fus., 28/2/17; P,E; Lieut.; w.
Islwyn, Wrexham.

✠ WILLIAMS, William Harold Trant
2/9770, 23/10/16, Cpl.; R.F.C., C/S, 13/3/17; R.F.C., 19/4/17; 2/Lieut.
Died of wounds 22/8/17 as Prisoner of War.

WILLIAMS, William Henry
6/3/7488, 15/11/15; No. 8 O.C.B., 4/8/16; trfr. M.G.C., 19/1/17.
24 High Street, Aberdare, Glamorganshire.

✠ WILLIAMS, William Henry
6/3/8229, 7/12/15; No. 14 O.C.B., 26/11/16; Mon. R., 28/2/17; Capt.
Killed in action 30/5/18.

WILLIAMS, William Hubert
2/3279, 15/4/15, Cpl.; N. Lan. R., 24/8/15, att. M.G.C.; S; Lieut.
19 Kitchener Drive, Orrell Park, Liverpool.

WILLIAMS, William Reed
A/D/11967, 3/9/17, L/C.; No. 6 O.C.B., 5/4/18; Welch R., 12/11/18; 2/Lieut.
324, Cowbridge Road, Canton, Cardiff.

WILLIAMS-IDRIS, John Hugh. See IDRIS, J. H. W.

APPENDIX II.—RECORDS OF RANK AND FILE.

WILLIAMSON, *Edgar Hugh*
6/8263, 8/12/15; A.S.C., C/S, 26/6/16; R.A.S.C., 30/7/16; F; Lieut.   *Services Club, Stratford Place, W.*

WILLIAMSON, *Heigham*
2/3432, 29/4/15; Essex R., 28/7/15.
55 Manchuria Road, West Side, Clapham Common, S.W. 4.

WILLIAMSON, *Howard Baker*
6/1/8382, 13/12/15; No. 11 O.C.B., 7/5/16; Worc. R., 4/9/16; F; Capt.; M.C.
c/o W. B. Wakes Esq., Bellair, Natal, South Africa.

✠ WILLIAMSON, *Hugh Henshall Clifford*
C/1167, 14/9/14; R. Highrs., 26/9/14, Cold. Gds.; Lieut.
Killed in action 15/9/16.

WILLIAMSON, *John Ernest*
3/3362, 22/4/15; Notts. & Derby. R., 19/9/15, att. Durh. L.I.; F; Capt.   *Chellaston, Derby.*

WILLIAMSON, *John Martin*
6/2/6429, 23/9/15, L/C.; North'd. Fus., 24/10/16; F; Capt.; w; M.C.   *31 Frances Road, Windsor, Berkshire.*

WILLIAMSON, *Lawrence*
6/5/D/9151, 25/1/16; No. 13 O.C.B., 4/11/16; trfr. 16th Lond. R., 2/2/17, M.G.C., Lab. Corps; F; w; M(1).
Burgh House, Well Walk, Hampstead, N.W. 3.

WILLIAMSON, *Leslie Alfred*
4/2/5219, 29/7/15; R.F.A., C/S, 31/3/16; 8th Lond. R., 25/9/16; F; Lieut.; w.
25 Wetherby Mansions, Earls Court Square, S.W. 5.

WILLIAMSON, *Robert James*
4/5218, 29/7/15; trfr. 18th Lond. R., 17/10/16; W. Rid. R., 1/5/18; F; Lieut.
39 Grove Park, Rathmines, Co. Dublin, Ireland. (Now in India).

WILLIAMSON, *Thomas Wesley*
A/10735, 8/2/17; R.F.C., C/S, 4/5/17; R.F.C., 5/8/17, R.A.F.; F; Lieut.; cr. s.d.
8 Kellyville Park, Maryborough, Queens Co., Ireland.

WILLINK, *John Humphrey Wakefield*
A/9831, 1/11/16; M.G.C., C/S, 1/2/17; Cold. Gds., 25/5/17; F; Lieut.; g.
c/o J. W. Willink Esq., Dean of Norwich, The Deanery, Norwich.

WILLIS, *Eric Constant*
D/11112, 25/4/17; R.F.C., C/S, 1/6/17; R.F.C., 4/7/17, R.A.F.; F; Lieut.; D.F.C., M(1).   *6 Greenbank Road, Birkenhead.*

WILLIS, *Frederick Arthur William*
E/1546, 6/10/14; R. War. R., 10/2/15, R.F.C.; E; Lieut.; *Inv.*
55 Belsize Avenue, Hampstead, N.W. 3. (Now in Assam).

WILLIS, *Harold Woodland*
C/14262, 1/11/18; trfr. K.R. Rif. C., 7/4/19.
Lyndon, 2 Lysia Street, Fulham, S.W. 6.

WILLIS, *Hector Vivian*
D/13002, 29/4/18; No. 5 O.C.B., 8/11/18; Essex R., 17/3/19; 2/Lieut.   *Pratt Street, Soham, Cambridgeshire.*

WILLIS, *John Robert*
6/4/8859, 11/1/16; No. 14 O.C.B., 29/9/16; Worc. R., 18/12/16, att. R.A.F.; F,It; Lieut.; M.C.
Rylstone, 327 Upper Richmond Road, Putney, S.W. 15.

✠ WILLIS, *Thomas Ambrose*
4/1/3995, 3/6/15, L/C.; 18th Lond. R., 17/9/15; Lieut.
Killed in action 8/12/17.

WILLIS-FLEMING, *Edward*
6/Sq/8199, 6/12/15; No. 1 Cav. C/S, 20/10/16; Leic. Yeo., 28/6/17, att. 11th Huss.; F; Lieut.
Westcroft, Cleveland Walk, Bath.

WILLMAN, *John Henry Hilary*
6/5/8198, 6/12/15; No. 8 O.C.B., 4/8/16; Devon. R., 21/11/16, att. Hamps. R.; F; Lieut.   *65 Greenway Avenue, Taunton.*

✠ WILLMER, *Arthur Franklin*
H/1971, 26/10/14, Sgt.; Rif. Brig., 24/12/14; F; Major; w(2).
Died of wounds 20/9/16.

WILLMOT, *Alexander John*
6/1/8260, 8/12/15; R.E., 14/7/16; NR; Lieut.; Order of S. Stanislaus, M(1).   *210 Camden Road, N.W. 1.*

WILLMOTT, *Francis William Ambrose*
2/3402, 26/4/15; Dorset R., 28/7/15, att. D. of Corn. L.I.; S; Lieut.; w.   *Park House, Park Hill, Ealing, W. 5.*

WILLMOT, *Frank Dudley Kenneth*
6/4/9225, 31/1/16; No. 14 O.C.B., 26/11/16; Notts. & Derby. R., 27/3/17.   *2 Curzon Street, Burton-on-Trent.*

WILLMOT, *Harold Francis*
6/4/5842, 26/8/15; R.F.A., 12/1/16; F; Major; M(1).
c/o Nat. Prov. & Union Bank, 15 Bishopsgate, E.C. 2.

WILLMOTT, *Maurice Gordon*
4/3/4199, 14/6/15, L/C.; K.R. Rif. C., 24/12/15; F; Capt.; w; M.C., M(1).   *52 Bedford Row, W.C. 1.*

WILLOUGHBY, *Rowland James*
D/10922, 24/3/17; No. 11 O.C.B., 5/7/17; Devon. R., 30/10/17; P.F; Lieut.   *Erleigh Court, The Mount, Shrewsbury, Salop.*

WILLOUGHBY, *Thomas Howard*
4/3/4433, 24/6/15, L/C.; D. of Corn. L.I., 21/4/16, Hamps. R.; F,S,R; Lieut.   *Lloyds Bank, Crawley, Sussex.*

WILLS, *Gerald Berkeley*
K/B/2119, 16/11/14; 23rd Lond. R., 24/4/15; F,S,P; Major; w; M.C.   *7 Stone Buildings, Lincoln's Inn, W.C. 2.*

✠ WILLS, *John Scott*
A/10695, 12/2/17; No. 11 O.C.B., 5/7/17; Durh. L.I., 30/10/17; F; Lieut.   *Killed in action 4/9/18.*

WILLS, *Thomas Edwin*
B/A/D/12001, 10/9/17; Dental Surgeon, 14/5/18, att. R.A.M.C.; Capt.   *Belgrave House, Torquay.*

WILLSON, *Charles Cyril Wagstaffe*
C/13259, 10/6/18; trfr. 14th Lond. R., 6/12/18, Gord. Highrs., att. R.F.A.; Sgt.   *Cynallie, 61 Bargery Road, Catford, S.E. 6.*

✠ WILLSON, *Edgar Brian*
K/2641, 11/1/15; York. & Lanc. R., 11/2/15, M.G.C.; Lieut.
Killed in action 27/5/18.

WILLSON, *Frederick James*
C/A/11456, 4/6/17; R.G.A., C/S, 23/1/18; R.A.S.C., 26/8/18; 2/Lieut.   *6 St. Margarets Road, Wanstead Park, Essex.*

✠ WILLSON, *Harold Hitton*
6/2/7711, 22/11/15; Suff. R., 4/9/16; 2/Lieut.   Died 10/1/17.

WILLSON, *Reginald Thomas*
D/9958, 24/11/16, L/C.; demob. 29/1/19.
Croft House, Lichfield Street, Burton-on-Trent.

WILMER, *Douglas Horsford*
B/594, 27/11/11; dis. 18/1/13.
Grasmere, St. Albans Crescent, Woodford Green, N.

WILMOT, *Francis*
6/3/8526, 29/12/15, L/C.; No. 14 O.C.B.; Shrop. L.I., 24/10/16; F; Lieut.; w.   *93 Tierney Road, Streatham Hill, S.W. 2.*

WILMOT-JOHNSON, *Lewis*
B/796, 25/5/14; Suff. R., 18/9/14; Capt.; w; M(1).

WILMOTT, *Hubert Edwin*
D/12129, 15/10/17, Cpl.; demob. 23/1/19.
12 Hillside Gardens South, Wallington, Surrey.

WILMSHURST, *Reginald Arthur*
B/12397, 14/1/18; trfr 28th Lond. R., 5/6/18.
5 Moreton Road, South Croydon.

WILMSHURST, *Thomas Vincent Buckham*
C/11501, 14/6/17; No. 10 O.C.B., 5/10/17; Shrop. L.I., 26/2/18; 2/Lieut.   *Ashleigh, St. Julian's Avenue, Ludlow, Salop.*

WILSHER, *Horace Stanley*
6/4/5535, 9/8/15; trfr. 6th Lond. R., 31/7/16.
The Gables, Pulton Broad, Lowestoft.

WILSHERE, *Frank Edgar*
4/3/3996, 3/6/15, L/C.; Rif. Brig., 21/10/15, R.F.C., R.A.F.; F; Capt.   *Leighcliff Lodge, Leighcliff Road, Leigh-on-Sea, Essex.*

✠ WILSHIN, *John Howell*
B/9918, 15/11/16; No. 14 O.C.B., 30/5/17; R. Fus., 29/5/17; F; 2/Lieut.; w.   *Died of wounds 21/4/18.*

WILSON, *Alfred*
D/10878, 9/3/17; R.F.A., C/S, 24/8/17; R.F.A., 23/2/18; F; 2/Lieut.   *Wayside, St. Martin's Hill, Canterbury.*

WILSON, *Alfred Allan*
4/3/4257, 14/6/15; York. & Lanc. R., 21/8/15, R.E.; Lieut.
c/o Nat. Prov. Bank, 15 Bishopsgate, E.C. 2.

APPENDIX II.—RECORDS OF RANK AND FILE.

WILSON, Anthony Fawcett
6/5/6866, 15/10/15, L/C.; dis. med. unfit, 26/9/16.
Outhwaite, Renwick, Kirkoswald R.O.O., Cumberland.

WILSON, Bassett Fitzgerald
A/1182, 14/9/14; K.R. Rif. C., 5/10/14; Capt.; M.C.
Breckenbrough Hall, Thirsk.

WILSON, Bernard Henry
B/11/84, 16/7/17; R.F.C., C/S, 23/10/17; R.F.C., 12/12/17, R.A.F.; lt; Lieut.
Stoneycroft, Anderton Park Road, Moseley, Birmingham.

WILSON, Bertrand Timmins
B/11031, 11/4/17; No. 14 O.C.B., 7/9/17; N. Staff. R., 17/12/17; F; Lieut.; w.
Glenthorn, Exmouth Street, Swindon, Wiltshire.

WILSON, Cecil Frederick Charles
B/9866, 6/11/16; R.F.C., C/S, 2/8/17; R.F.C., 8/9/17, R.A.F.; Lieut.
Haverford West, Pembrokeshire.

WILSON, Charles Ernest
B/9888, 9/11/16; No. 20 O.C.B., 7/6/17; War. Yeo., 25/9/17; F; Lieut.
Twincham, Haywards Heath, Sussex.

WILSON, Charles Henry
A/14110, 30/9/18; demob. 30/1/19.
237 London Road, Sheffield.

WILSON, Cyril Noel
A/408, 28/4/09; Res. of Off., 4/2/13.

WILSON, David Hood
6/9044, 20/1/16; No. 9 O.C.B., 8/3/16; R. Highrs., 6/7/16; S; Capt.; w.
54 David Street, Kirkcaldy, Fifeshire.

WILSON, Edwin Harold
6/4/6708, 7/10/15; R.F.A., C/S, 4/8/16; R.F.A., 10/11/16; F; 2/Lieut.
Redcliffe, 22 Pathfield Road, Streatham, S.W. 16.

WILSON, Eric
E/14178, 16/10/18; demob. 10/1/19.
6 Princes Square, Plymouth.

✠ WILSON, Eric Crawcour
K/H/2500, 31/12/14; R.W. Kent R., 29/4/15; Lieut.
Killed in action 28/10/18.

WILSON, Ernest Edward
6/1/8261, 8/12/15; dis. med. unfit, 14/9/16.
10 The Shrubberies, South Woodford, Essex.

WILSON, Frederick Rushworth
B/13652, 26/7/18; demob. 18/2/19.
7 Bromley Avenue, Sefton Park, Liverpool.

WILSON, Geoffrey Cecil
B/1203, 14/9/14; R.G.A., 10/10/14; F; Lieut.; w, Inj.
6 Brent Villas, Hendon, N.W. 4.

WILSON, George
6/5/8907, 13/1/16; No. 8 O.C.B., 4/8/16; trfr. 9th Lond. R., 8/6/17.
32 Elm Park Avenue, Ranelagh, Co. Dublin.

WILSON, George Alexander
6/5/5966, 1/9/15, L/C.; L'pool. R., 6/7/16; Lieut.

WILSON, George Buchanan
4/3/4100, 7/6/15; D. of Corn. L.I., 20/8/15; Capt.

WILSON, George Cedric
6/Sq/6569, 30/9/15; 2nd Life Gds., 22/3/16; Lieut.
Heath Cottage, Wickham Buildings, Nr. Witham, Essex.

WILSON, George Stewart
D/10013, 27/11/16, Sgt.; R.E., C/S, 5/5/17; R.E., 27/7/17; Lieut.; M(1).
31 Manchester Road, Knutsford, Cheshire.

WILSON, Gillead
6/5/5370, 5/8/15, L/C.; L'pool. R., 3/1/16; F; Lieut.
8 Royal Street, Liverpool.

WILSON, Harold
6/2/D/5674, 16/8/15; No. 14 O.C.B., 26/11/16; E. Lan. R., 28/2/17; F; Lieut.
10 Turncroft Villas, Darwen, Lancashire.

WILSON, Harold Alfred
6/5/C/7571, 17/11/15; No. 7 O.C.B., 3/7/16; trfr. M.G.C., 29/12/16.
45 Ednenvale Road, Ranelagh, Dublin, Ireland.

WILSON, Harold Ward
4/5/5051, 22/7/15, L/C.; 20th Lond. R., 31/12/15; F,P,E; Capt.; w(2); M.C.
Millbrook Cottage, Millfield Lane, Highgate, N.

WILSON, Harry
A/9812, 30/10/16; R.A., C/S, 1/2/17; R.F.A., 5/6/17; F; Lieut.; w(2); M.C.
The Chestnuts, Sevenoaks Road, Orpington, Kent.

WILSON, Harry
D/13708, 29/7/18; trfr. K.R. Rif. C., 7/4/19.
Mossgate, Great Corby, Nr. Carlisle.

✠ WILSON, Henry
1/3746, 24/5/15; Midd'x. R., 21/8/15; 2/Lieut.
Killed in action 15/9/16.

WILSON, Henry
6/2/6499, 27/9/15, L/C.; No. 11 O.C.B., 7/5/16; M.G.C., 4/9/16; Lieut.; w(2), p; M.C.

WILSON, Henry Noel
6/5/9491, 15/2/16; No. 14 O.C.B., 26/11/16; Sco. Rif., 27/3/17, R.E.; 2/Lieut.
5 St. James Terrace, Glasgow, W.

WILSON, Herbert Stewart
E/1571, 6/10/14; Som. L.I., 13/1/15, Yorks. L.I.; F; Staff Capt.
Travellers Club, Pall Mall, S.W. 1.

WILSON, Hubert
6/D/7710, 22/11/15, Cpl.; R.A.O.C., 15/10/16; Lieut.
35 Balham Park Road, S.W. 12.

WILSON, John Blenken
B/D/13553, 26/7/18; demob. 5/3/19.   16 Bedford Place, London.

WILSON, John Erskine
D/10628, 25/1/17; R.A., C/S, 29/6/17.
Garfield, Billinge Avenue, Blackburn, Lancashire.

WILSON, John Ronald
4/3669, 17/5/15, Sgt.; R.F.C., 4/9/16, R.A.F.; F; Lieut.; w.
119 Willifield Way, Hendon, N.W. 11.

WILSON, John Rupert
6/2/5537, 9/8/15; R. Suss. R., 1/6/16, att. Midd'x. R.; F,S; Lieut.; w.
Woodcroft, Bromsgrove, Worcestershire.

WILSON, John Seaver
6/4/8003, 29/11/15, L/C.; No. 14 O.C.B.; M.G.C., 24/10/16; Capt.

WILSON, John William Wilson
6/1/8383, 13/12/15; R.A.O.C., 14/5/16; Lieut.
Cety-Venn, Leatherhead.

WILSON, Joseph Lupton
B/12335, 31/12/17; Sigs. C/S, 31/5/18; R.E., 25/10/18; 2/Lieut.
Westfield, Armley, Leeds.

WILSON, Kenneth John
6/5/7086, 30/10/15, L/C.; No. 7 O.C.B., 18/5/16; E. Ang. Div. Cyc. Coy., 4/8/16; F,It; Capt.; M(1).
30 Morton Gardens, Wallington, Surrey.

WILSON, Kenneth Valentine Fox
A/11918, 27/8/17; No. 14 O.C.B., 7/12/17; R. War. R., 28/5/18; 2/Lieut.
Ivy House, Coton Road, Nuneaton, Warwickshire.

✠ WILSON, Marshall Meredith
4/5138, 26/7/15; Bord. R., 7/12/15, R.F.C.; Lieut.
Killed 29/1/18.

WILSON, Michael Dover
B/422, 21/5/09; R.W. Surr. R., 15/8/14, Linc. R.; F; Capt.; w; M.C., M(1).
Colts Hill, Capel, Tonbridge.

✠ WILSON, Neville Inchbold
K/B/2232, 3/12/14, L/C.; R.W. Fus., 13/3/15; Lieut.; M.C.
Killed in action 6/4/18.

WILSON, Robert Percy
A/930, 5/8/14; R.W. Kent R., 14/10/14; I; Capt.
The White House, Sundridge, Kent.

WILSON, Sholto Douglas Major
F/1811, 16/10/14; Hamps. R., 16/10/14; G,E,P; Staff Capt.; M.B.E.
Cedars Cottage, Sneywell, Winchfield, Hampshire.

WILSON, Sidney Irvin
6/5/C/9017, 19/1/16; No. 14 O.C.B., 30/10/16; 21st Lond. R., 28/2/17, 23rd Lond. R., att. 5th Lond. R.; F; Lieut.; w.
52 Hollybank Avenue, Clonskeagh, Dublin, Ireland.

WILSON, Stanley Reginald
6/5/6878, 18/10/15; No. 11 O.C.B., 7/5/16; W. Rid. R., 4/9/16; F,It; Lieut.; M(1).   47 Ommaney Road, New Cross, S.E. 14.

WILSON, Theodore Goodman
D/10870, 12/3/17, L/C.; R.G.A., C/S, 15/8/17; R.G.A., 31/12/17; F; 2/Lieut.; w(2).
Cliffside, Kendall, Westmoreland.

✠ WILSON, Wesley Holford
B/A/12008, 13/9/17; R.F.C., C/S, 18/1/18; R.F.C., 6/3/18; 2/Lieut.
Killed 23/9/18.

APPENDIX II.—RECORDS OF RANK AND FILE.

WILSON, William Shelmerdine
B/13454, 3/7/18; trfr. K.R. Rif. C., 7/4/19.
Overdale, Upper Woodcote, Purley, Surrey.

WILSON, William Smith
4/1/4247, 14/6/15, L/C.; High. L.I., 19/10/15; F; Lieut.
Glenwhask, Kenmuir Avenue, Bishopsbriggs, Glasgow.

WILSON-HILL, Frank W. See HILL, F. W.

WILTON, Ernest Wesley
4/1/3280, 15/4/15; E. Surr. R., 1/6/16; Lieut.; w.
84 Shakespeare Avenue, Alexandra Park, Bath.

WILTON, Vincent Raine
6/1/7712, 22/11/15; W. York. R., 4/9/16; F,I; Lieut.
37 Aberdeen Walk, Scarborough, Yorkshire.

✠ WILTSHIRE, Charles Reginald
4/Sq/4258, 14/6/15, L/C.; Bedf. Yeo., 17/9/15; 2/Lieut.
Died of wounds 13/7/16.

WIMSHURST, Arthur Leslie
6/5/6141, 9/9/15; N. Staff. R., 24/1/16, att. York. & Lanc. R. and R.A.F.; F; Lieut.
12 Balfan Road, Acton, W. 3.

✠ WINCH, Harry Wilson
6/2/7319, 8/11/15, L/C.; Lond. Div. Cyc. Coy., 5/8/16; 2/Lieut.
Killed in action 2/4/17.

WINCH, Hubert Edward
4/Sq/4374, 21/6/15; R.F.A., C/S, 31/3/16; R.F.A., 5/8/16, att. R.F.C., R.A.F.; 2/Lieut.
Trinley, Suffolk.

✠ WINCHLEY, Charles Reginald
4/2/4320, 17/6/15; Notts. & Derby. R., 7/10/15; F; 2/Lieut.
Killed in action 20/7/16.

WINCKLEY, Frederick William
A/10253, 29/12/16, Cpl.; R.G.A., C/S, 25/4/17; R.G.A., 19/8/17; F; Lieut.; w-g.
Emsdale, Lillington, Leamington.

WINDER, Henry Edward
6/3/6233, 13/9/15; E. Surr. R., 4/8/16; F; Lieut.; w.
Langton, 29 Nicosia Road, Wandsworth Common, S.W. 18. (Now in South Africa).

WINDROW, William
C/13396, 24/6/18; trfr. 14th Lond. R., 6/12/18, Gord. Highrs.; Sgt.
72 Adelaide Road, Leyton, Essex.

WINDSOR, Harry Lovibond
4/6/5186, 29/7/15; 11th Lond. R., 29/9/15, 9th Lond. R., Hamps. R.; S,E,P,F; Capt.
P.O. Box 16, Kokstad, East Griqualand, Cape Province, South Africa.

WINDSOR, Washington Reginald
A/10477, 12/1/17; trfr. R.G.A., 2/5/17.
Green End, Boxmoor, Hertfordshire.

WINFREY, Richard Finch
6/1/8908, 13/1/16; No. 13 O.C.B., 4/11/16; K.R. Rif. C., 28/2/17; Lieut.; M(1).
The Links, Kirby Muxloe, Leicester.

✠ WINGFIELD, Granville Harry
A/2603, 7/1/15; K.R. Rif. C., 5/6/15; 2/Lieut.
Killed in action 12/7/16.

WINGFIELD, Laurence Arthur
4/2/4518, 28/6/15; R. Fus., 26/8/15, att. R.F.C. and R.A.F.; F; Lieut.; p and escaped; M.C., D.F.C.
74 Cheapside, E.C. 2.

WINGFIELD, Richard William Digby
3/3170, 1/4/15, L/C.; Midd'x. R., 21/6/15, Indian Army; Lieut.
8 Polworth Road, Streatham, S.W. 16.

WINGRAVE, James Septimus
6/4/6724, 9/10/15, L/C.; No. 14 O.C.B.; trfr. R.G.A., 8/12/16.
418 Camden Road, N. 7.

✠ WINKLEY, Stanley Hugh
7975, 29/11/15; R.F.C., R.A.F.; F; 2/Lieut.
Killed in action 1/4/18.

WINKWORTH, Donovan William
6/3/7572, 17/11/15; Yorks. L.I., 4/9/16; F; Lieut.; w.
The School House, Plumpton, Sussex.

WINKWORTH, Henry Stephen
Sq/2168, 11/9/14; 2nd Drag. Gds., 21/11/14, att. R.A.F.; F; Lieut.
22 Hill Street, Knightsbridge, S.W. 7.

WINN, Harold
6/1/6030, 2/9/15; Devon. R., 7/7/16; I,M; Capt.
Droveway, St. Margarets Bay, Dover, Kent.

WINN-JONES, William Hugh
B/K/2/2150, 19/11/14 Sgt.; Mon. R., 27/12/15; F; Capt.
82 Westbourne Road, Penarth, Glamorganshire.

WINNY, John Stanley
B/10341, 4/1/17, L/C.; R.G.A., C/S, 22/6/17; R.G.A., 25/11/17; F; 2/Lieut.
33 New Street, Uttoxeter, Staffordshire.

WINSLAND, Darrell Frank
A/1095, 7/9/14; R.A.S.C., 10/10/14; Capt.
Timber Lodge, Ashtead, Surrey.

WINSTANLEY, William
E/14032, 18/9/18; R.G.A., C/S, 1/11/18.
Central Boys School, Mexborough, Nr. Rotherham.

✠ WINTER, Edward John Desmond
B/12691, 28/2/18; No. 7 O.C.B., 9/8/18; R. Muns. Fus., 6/3/19; 2/Lieut.
Died 30/3/20.

WINTER, Harold Knight
4/5/4821, 12/7/15; Ches. R., 8/12/15; Lieut.
14 Merton Place, Birkenhead.

WINTER, Horace James
K/A/2104, 16/11/14; Worc. R., 13/3/15; F; Capt.
4 Eton Avenue, Hampstead, N.W. 3.

WINTER, John Edwin
D/13817, 12/8/18; demob. 29/1/19.
140 Tong Road, Armley, Leeds.

WINTER, Sydney Samuel
6/4/9045, 20/1/16; R.A., C/S, 7/8/16; R.G.A., 8/11/16; F; Lieut.; w.
28 Park Lane, Norwich.

WINTERBOTTOM, John Robert
6/Sq/8581, 1/1/16, L/C.; R.F.A., C/S, 4/8/16; R.F.A., 1/12/16; F; Lieut.; w.
Westholme, 6 Warbreck Hill Road, Blackpool.

WINTLE, John Edwin
C/10597, 22/1/17, L/C.; No. 14 O.C.B., 7/6/17; Linc. R., 25/9/17; 2/Lieut.
7 Powderham Road, Newton Abbot, South Devonshire.

WIPPELL, Donald Hugh
A/1116, 7/9/14; York. R., 19/9/14; Lieut.; w.

WISDOM, Augustus Henry
6/4/3188, 6/4/15; dis. med. unfit, 14/8/16.
59 Lavenham Road, Southfields, S.W. 8.

WISE, Claude William
6/7817, 24/11/15; R.A.S.C., 30/4/16; F; Capt.
38 Ennismore Gardens, South Kensington, S.W. 7.

✠ WISEMAN, Stanley
4/4302, 17/6/15; Essex R., 15/11/15, att. Oxf. & Bucks. L.I.; F; 2/Lieut.
Killed in action 10/3/17.

✠ WISEMAN, Vincent Harvey
6/3/6570, 30/9/15; No. 11 O.C.B., 7/5/16; Yorks. L.I., 4/9/16; 2/Lieut.
Killed in action 9/4/17.

WISHART, Alan Clunie
D/12881, 3/4/18, Sgt.; trfr. K.R. Rif. C., 13/5/19.
5 Arundel Avenue, Liverpool.

WITHERS, Alfred Edward
6/2/6683, 7/10/15; R.F.C., C/S, 1/2/17; R.F.C., 12/4/17, R.A.F.; F; Lieut.
92 Holden Road, Finchley, N. 12.

✠ WITHEY, Charles Ernest
6/2/5675, 16/8/15; R. Lanc. R., 31/12/15; Capt.; w(2).
Killed in action 20/9/17.

WITT, Harold Tansley
Sq/112, 18/4/08; dis. 17/4/09; rej. Sq/1222, 15/9/14, S.S.M; M. of Munitions.
5 Chancery Lane, W.C. 2.

WITTER, Preston Hammond
D/E/13941, 2/9/18; demob. 10/1/19.
Riverslea, Dee Banks, Chester.

WITTHAUS, Frederick Percy
B/11364, 28/5/17, Sgt.; demob. 23/1/19.
Hayton, East End Road, Church End, Finchley, N. 3.

WITTS, Cecil Arthur
6/2/6544, 30/9/15; E. Kent R., 9/6/16, Indian Army; Lieut.

WITTS, John Travell
Sq/905, 5/8/14; Glouc. R., 15/8/14; Major. D.A.A.G.; w; M.B.E., M(1).

WITTS, Leslie John
1/Sq/9763, 20/10/16, L/C.; R.F.A., C/S, 10/8/17; R.F.A., 6/1/18; F; Lieut.; w.
110 Wilderspool Road, Warrington, Lancashire.

WOLFE, Clarence Albert Edward
A/B/12189, 1/11/17, L/C.; A.S.C., C/S, 19/8/18; R.A.S.C., 13/10/18; 2/Lieut.

APPENDIX II.—RECORDS OF RANK AND FILE.

WOLFE, Robert Samuel
A/14325, 30/12/18; demob. 30/1/19.
Ballydehob, Co. Cork, Ireland.

WOLFF, Algernon Montague
K/D/4/2354, 15/12/14; dis. 9/6/15.

WOLFF, Henry Samson
A/10739, 15/2/17; R.F.C., C/S, 13/3/17; R.F.C., 19/4/17; F; Lieut. The Lodge, Hoop Lane, Golders Green, N.W.11.

WOLF-MILNER, Basil Spencer
C/14243, 28/10/18; dis. 26/3/19.
Longstone, Lindop Road, Hale, Cheshire.

WOLLASTON, Hugo John Buchanan
Sq/684, 24/1/13; R.A.F.

☥ WOLLASTON, John Dudley
D/11115, 27/4/17; R.F.C., C/S, 23/10/17; R.F.C., 12/12/17, R.A.F.; 2/Lieut.
Killed 3/4/18.

☥ WOLLEN, Douglas Charles
4/2/4375, 21/6/15, L/C.; High. L.I., 1/6/16, R.F.C.; 2/Lieut.
Killed in action 13/4/17.

☥ WOLSTENHOLME, George Mellor
6/9180, 28/1/16; No. 8 O.C.B., 4/8/16; York. R., 21/11/16; Lieut.; M.C.
Killed in action 5/10/18.

WOLSTENHOLME, Robert Angus
6/5/C/6933, 19/10/15, Sgt.; demob. 23/1/19.
16 Erskine Hill, Hendon, N.W.4.

WOMERSLEY, Leonard Dale
F/1851, 16/10/14; Essex R., 2/11/14; G,P,E; Capt.; w(2).
The Grange, Crowborough, Sussex.

WOMERSLEY, Thomas Allen
Sq/161, 18/4/08; dis. 17/4/11; R.E., 25/10/16; Lieut.; w; M.C.
9 Jasper Road, Upper Norwood, S.E.19.

☥ WONNACOTT, Thomas Henry
4/2/4587, 1/7/15; Devon. R., 20/11/15; 2/Lieut.
Killed in action 9/5/17.

WOOD, Alexander
A/977, 5/8/14; Suff. R., 30/9/14, R.A.S.C.; F; Lieut.; w.
Redroof, Pyrford, Surrey.

WOOD, Alexander Reginald
D/A/11852, 9/8/17; demob. 13/12/18.
93 Victoria Mansions, Stockwell, S.W.

WOOD, Ben Hanvey
A/11944, 30/8/17; R.E., C/S, 25/11/17; R.E., 22/2/18; 2/Lieut.
Lulworth, Chorley New Road, Bolton, Lancashire.

WOOD, Benjamin
6/4/5597, 12/8/15; York. R., 1/6/16; I,M; Lieut.
116 Victoria Grove, Shipley.

WOOD, Bromley Dawson
B/372, 22/3/09; dis.

WOOD, Charles Baker
C/D/Sq/12061, 27/9/17, Cpl.; No. 2 Cav. C/S, 11/4/18; 5th R. Regt. of Cav., 24/2/19; 2/Lieut.
11 Victoria Street, Liverpool.

WOOD, Edgar James
C/13313, 17/6/18; trfr. 14th Lond. R., 6/12/18.
55 Evering Road, Stamford Hill, N.16.

WOOD, Edward Reginald
Sq/3806, 27/5/15; W. Kent Yeo., 8/7/15, att. Intelligence; P; Capt.
Bidborough Grange, Nr. Tunbridge Wells, Kent.

WOOD, Frank
C/10186, 13/12/16; Devon. R., 15/3/17, R.E.; F; 2/Lieut.
40 Aston Street, Iffley Road, Oxford.

WOOD, Frank Featherstone
6/1/6155, 9/9/15; N. Lan. R., 1/6/16; Lieut.; w(2); M.C.
21 Westbourne Road, Birkdale.

WOOD, Frederick
C/10617, 22/1/17; No. 20 O.C.B., 7/6/17; R. Lanc. R., 25/9/17; Lieut.
Belvedere, St. Johns Park, Menston in Wharfdale, Yorkshire.

WOOD, Frederick Lee
6/8200, 6/12/15; dis. med. unfit, 8/8/16.
50 Harold Road, Upper Norwood, S.E.27.

WOOD, George Frederic Algernon de Burley
K/H/2191, 26/11/14; E. Kent R., 23/3/15; F; Lieut.
Latimer House, Chiswick Mall, W.4.

WOOD, Gordon Jack Sharland
6/2/7225, 4/11/15; A.S.C., C/S, 10/4/16; R.A.S.C., 14/5/16; Lieut.
69 Alleyn Park, Dulwich, S.E.21.

WOOD, Henry Stanley
6/4/8979, 18/1/16; No. 14 O.C.B., 30/10/16; W. Rid. R., 24/1/17; Lieut.
Oak Villa, Allerton, Bradford.

☥ WOOD, Herbert
4/6/4989, 19/7/15; 20th Lond. R., 28/11/15; F; Lieut.; w.
Killed in action 1/9/18.

WOOD, Howard Gilmour
6/2/6410, 23/9/15; No. 11 O.C.B., 7/5/16; R.F.C., 4/9/16, R.A.F.; F; Capt.; w.
Union Terrace, Enville Street, Stourbridge.

WOOD, Hubert Leopold
D/11877, 16/8/17; R.F.C., C/S, 26/11/17; R.F.C., 23/1/18, R.A.F.; F; 2/Lieut.
Hazeldene, Swanley Junction, Kent.

WOOD, Hugh McKinnon
Sq/679, 24/1/13; dis. med. unfit, 24/4/14; rej. C/13389, 24/6/18; trfr. Class W. Res., 13/12/18.
16 Portland Place, W.1.

WOOD, James Conrad Peter
B/1679, 12/10/14; R.N.A.S., 10/11/14, R.A.F.; SWA,F; Major; White Rose of Finland.
St. Nicolas, 108a Upper Tulse Hill, S.W.

WOOD, James Gordon
6/2/6190, 13/9/15, Sgt.; No. 14 O.C.B.; Essex R., 24/10/16; F; Lieut.; w(2); M.C., M(1).
Brackendale, Tewitwell Road, Harrogate, Yorkshire.

WOOD, James Smith
6/1/D/6004, 2/9/15, L/C.; No. 14 O.C.B., 27/12/16; York. R., 25/4/17, att. North'd. Fus.; F,It; Lieut.; M.C.
Westleigh, Trinity Street, Huddersfield.

WOOD, John
6/3/5812, 21/8/15; Garr. O.C.B., 12/12/16; R.W. Surr. R., 10/2/17; Lieut.
Nyewood, Nr. Petersfield, Hampshire.

WOOD, John Gillespie
E/1612, 6/10/14; Ches. R., 17/10/14; F; Capt.; w(2).
c/o Messrs. Wood & Mackenzie, 14 Young Street, Edinburgh.
(Now in F.M.S.)

WOOD, John Talfourd
Sq/415, 8/5/09; dis. 31/7/11; rej. Sq/1939, 22/10/14, Cpl.; Dorset Yeo., 16/12/14, R.A.S.C.; F,It; Capt.
Kingswood, Boyn Hill Avenue, Maidenhead.

WOOD, Keith Priestley
6/3/9372, 8/2/16; No. 14 O.C.B., 30/10/16, M.G.C., C/S; M.G.C., 30/1/17, Tank Corps; F; Capt.; w.
Penang, Summerhill Road, Dartford, Kent.

WOOD, Leonard Francis
6/Sq/6789, 12/10/15; A.S.C., C/S, 17/4/16; R.A.S.C., 21/5/16, att. R.A.F.; F; Lieut.
Villa Felicie Helene, Heide, Calmpthout, Belgium.

WOOD, Leonard Stanley
4/1/4098, 7/6/15; R.A.S.C., 25/8/15; M; Major; M.B.E., M(2).
170 Erlanger Road, New Cross, S.E.14.

☥ WOOD, Mathew Rodney
E/2686, 14/1/15; Lan. Fus., 1/5/15; Capt.; w; M.C.
Killed in action 22/10/17.

WOOD, Maurice
4/2/5087, 26/7/15, L/C.; Bord. R., 4/12/15; Lieut.
67a Longridge Road, Earls Court, S.W.5.

WOOD, Paul Butterworth
1/9748, 17/10/16; No. 14 O.C.B., 27/12/16; Ches. R., 25/4/17, att. T.M.Bty.; F; Lieut.
4 Seventh Avenue, Broadway, Blackpool.

☥ WOOD, Peter Norris
4/2/4479, 26/6/15; R. Lanc. R., 29/11/15; M; 2/Lieut.
Died of wounds 17/1/17.

☥ WOOD, Ralph
Sq/220, 12/5/08; dis. 31/12/09. W. Rid. R. and R.A.F.
Died of wounds 18/10/18.

WOOD, Reginald Bishop
A/E/13968, 6/9/18; No. 22 O.C.B., 22/11/18; S. Staff. R., 5/2/19; 2/Lieut.
213 Wimbledon Park Road, S.W.18.

WOOD, Reginald Townsend
C/953, 5/8/14, L/C.; Lan. Fus., 29/2/15; R. Ir. Rif.; Capt.

WOOD, Robert
3/3363, 22/4/15, Sgt.; Bedf. R., 25/8/15; 2/Lieut.; M(1).
Royal Gardens, Windsor.

APPENDIX II.—RECORDS OF RANK AND FILE.

WOOD, Robert
A/11945, 30/8/17, Sgt.; dis. 11/8/19.
24 Grove Road, Windsor.

WOOD, Stanley Hargreaves
6/Sq/8942, 17/1/16; R.A., C/S, 22/9/16; R.F.A., 22/1/17; E.P;
Lieut. 116 Victoria Grove, Shipley, Yorkshire.

✠ WOOD, Thomas Anthony
6/2/7854, 25/11/15, Sgt.; K.R. Rif. C., 4/8/16; Capt.
Died 16/7/18.

WOOD, Wilfrid Jules Cloquet
6/5/C/8098, 1/12/15; No. 13 O.C.B., 4/11/16; Shrop. L.I., 28/2/17; F; Lieut.; g. Inv.
Grammar School, Kingsbridge, South Devonshire.

WOOD, William Herbert
6/1/7192, 3/11/15; M.G.C., C/S, 31/10/16; M.G.C., 28/12/16.
Carlton Bank, Shepley, Nr. Huddersfield.

WOOD, William Lyon
K/D/2365, 17/12/14; R.E., 9/1/15; F; Major; w; O.B.E., M(3).
2 Magdala Crescent, Edinburgh. (Now in Argentina).

WOODBRIDGE, Edgar Thomas
B/E/13544, 17/7/18; R.A., C/S, 2/10/18; demob.
Elm Lawn, Uxbridge.

WOODBRIDGE, Robert
A/902, 5/8/14; dis. 8/8/14.

✠ WOODBRIDGE, Stephen Anthony Ruston
E/1553, 6/10/14, L/C.; R. War. R., 27/11/14; 2/Lieut.
Died of wounds 15/9/16.

WOODCOCK, Arthur Wedgwood
C/1112, 7/9/14; Lan. Fus., 20/10/14; Lieut.
Engadine, The Park, Sidcup.

WOODCOCK, Francis Henry
4/2/4508, 28/6/15; Suff. R., 17/10/15; F; Lieut.
45 Princes Street, Ipswich.

WOODCOCK, Henry Hubert Walter Winter
6/8556, 30/12/15; R.A., C/S, 9/6/16; R.G.A., 13/9/16; Lieut.
8 Netherall Gardens, Hampstead, N.W.3.

✠ WOODCOCK, Leonard Albert
6/2/6411, 23/9/15, L/C.; North'd. Fus., 1/6/16; 2/Lieut.
Died of wounds 10/4/17.

WOODCOCK, Victor Harry
C/9959, 20/11/16; No. 14 O.C.B., 6/4/17; Manch. R., 31/7/17, R.E.; 2/Lieut.

WOODFORDE, Lionel Ffooks
B/1097, 7/9/14, L/C.; R. Fus., 5/10/14; Capt.; M.C., M(1).
99 Church Street, Kensington, W.8.

WOOD-GREAVES, Marcus
6/5/C/8126, 2/12/15; No. 14 O.C.B., 26/11/16, 2nd Cty. of Lond. Yeo., 27/3/17.
Fernside, Pake field, Lowestoft.

WOODHALL, Percival Claude
B/13471, 5/7/18; demob. 29/1/19.
Hollybank, Uttoxeter, Staffordshire.

WOODHAMS, Denys Herbert Osmond
A/B/D/12151, 22/10/17; No. 1 O.C.B., 16/5/18; R. Lanc. R., 29/10/18; 2/Lieut. 141 Copers Cope Road, Beckenham, Kent.

✠ WOODHAMS, Eric William
Sq/2976, 25/2/15, L/C.; Bedf. Yeo., 4/6/15; F; Lieut.
Died of wounds 11/12/17.

WOOD-HILL, Bernard
6/1/8921, 14/1/16; No. 8 O.C.B., 4/8/16; K.R. Rif. C., 21/11/16, F; Lieut.; w.
Kings College, Junior School, Wimbledon Common, S.W.19.

WOODHILL, Harry
6/2/7818, 24/11/15; R.F.A., C/S, 18/8/16; R.G.A., 26/11/16; Lieut. 26 Cavendish Road, Chorlton-cum-Hardy, Manchester.

WOODHOUSE, Eric Henry Joseph
6/4/9262, 3/2/16; No. 14 O.C.B., 30/10/16; Midd'x. R., 24/1/17; F; 2/Lieut.; w. 3/4 Clements Inn, W.C.2.

WOODHOUSE, Kenneth Leighton
C/11534, 18/6/17; No. 19 O.C.B., 9/11/17; Norf. R., 28/5/18; 2/Lieut. 89 Hereford Road, Bayswater, W.2.

WOODLEY, John Middleton
6/5/6221, 13/9/15; No. 4 O.C.B., 7/3/16; trfr. L'pool. R., 26/5/16; F. 10 Chetwynd Road, Birkenhead, Cheshire.

✠ WOODLEY, Stanley William
4/3670, 17/5/15, Sgt.; R.A.S.C., 27/11/15, R.F.C.; 2/Lieut.
Killed in action 22/1/17.

✠ WOODMAN, Douglas
6/4/3/7193, 3/11/15, Sgt.; R.F.C., C/S, 1/2/17; R.F.C., 12/4/17; F; 2/Lieut. Killed in action 11/3/18.

WOODMAN, Dudley Ernest
B/13455, 3/7/18; demob. 29/1/19.
4 Royston Road, Penge, S.E.20.

WOODROFFE, Brian
B/12799, 15/3/18; No. 7 O.C.B., 9/8/18; Lan. Fus., 6/3/19; 2/Lieut. 36 Avon Street, Walney, Barrow-in-Furness.

WOODROFFE, Norman Frederic
A/339, 17/12/08; dis. 16/12/12; 9th Lond. R., 6/9/14; Capt.; w; O.B.E.

WOODROFFE, Percy Stanbrook
6/1/8201, 6/12/15; R.A., C/S, 24/1/16; E. Kent R., 4/9/16, R.A.F.; Lieut.

WOODROW, Benjamin
B/Sq/9881, 8/11/16; No. 1 Cav. C/S, 31/7/17; R. Regt. of Cav., 22/2/18, att. Bedf. Yeo.; F; 2/Lieut.
Meath House, Buxton, Derbyshire.

WOODS, Frank Unsworth
6/4/9132, 25/1/16; No. 8 O.C.B., 4/8/16; N. Lan. R., 21/11/16; F; Lieut.; w. Abbotshaw, Kiln Lane, St. Helens, Lancashire.

WOODS, Gerald West
C/10818, 27/2/17; Tank Corps C/S, 18/5/17; Tank Corps, 3/11/17; F; Lieut. 5 Claremont Road, Luton, Bedfordshire.

WOODS, Henry James
B/12840, 22/3/18; No. 2 O.C.B., 20/9/18; Oxf. & Bucks. L.I., 16/3/19; 2/Lieut. 34 Midland Road, Olney, Buckinghamshire.

WOODS, John Gerard
6/5/5967, 1/9/15; L'pool. R., 20/1/16; Lieut.
Gerard Hall, Aughton, Ormskirk, Lancashire.

WOODS, Robert
D/10430, 10/1/17; No. 14 O.C.B., 5/7/17; trfr. E. Surr. R., 26/10/17. 88 Oxford Road, Waterloo, Liverpool.

WOODS, Robert Francis
6/5/8262, 8/12/15; No. 7 O.C.B., 11/8/16; R. Dub. Fus., 18/12/16; 2/Lieut.
Nohant, Avoca Avenue, Blackrock, Dublin.

WOODS, Roy
1/3747, 24/5/15; Midd'x. R., 21/8/15; Lieut.

WOODS, Thomas
6/5/6430, 23/9/15; No. 3 O.C.B., 25/2/16; Manch. R., 21/7/16, att. 15th Lond. R.; Lieut.; w.
Allandale, Kiln Lane, St. Helens, Lancashire.

WOODWARD, Athelstane Isherwood
6/3/7752, 22/11/15; No. 8 O.C.B., 4/8/16; trfr. R.E., 29/12/16; R.N.V.R., 18/12/17; Sub. Lieut.
The Vicarage, Herne Bay, Kent.

WOODWARD, Charles Forman
6/3/5319, 4/8/15; Notts. & Derby. R., 4/11/15; F; Lieut.
Upton Hall, Southwell, Nottinghamshire.

WOODWARD, Ernest George
6/1/7240, 5/11/15, L/C; No. 11 O.C.B., 7/5/16; Manch. R., 4/9/16; Lieut.; p; M(1).

WOODWARD, Henry Phipps John
C/Sq/13358, 26/6/18; trfr. 6th R. Regt. of Cav., 11/6/19.
Church Farm, East Brent, Somerset.

WOOF, Thomas Newton
6/3/6579, 4/10/15; S. Staff. R., 1/6/16; Lieut.; M.C. and Bar.
Acacias, Sutton, Surrey.

WOOLDRIDGE, Charles Stanley
B/10533, 17/1/17; No. 14 O.C.B., 5/7/17; Devon. R., 30/10/17; F,It; Capt.; w; M.C.
Westlands, West Park Street, Dewsbury.

WOOLDRIDGE, Walter Reginald
D/13828, 12/8/18; demob. 29/1/19.
Carlton Lodge, Norwood Road, S.E.24.

WOOLEY, Henry Arnold
A/306, 29/6/08; dis. 28/6/10. High Lea, Wembley, Middlesex.

✠ WOOLF, Cecil Nathan Sidney
Sq/736, 11/11/13; 13th R. Regt. of Cav., 8/9/14, 20th Huss.; 2/Lieut. Died of wounds 30/11/17.

WOOLF, Philip Sidney
Sq/735, 11/11/13; 13th R. Regt. of Cav., 8/9/14, 20th Huss.; Lieut.; w; M(1). 15 Grosvenor Road, Westminster, S.W.1.

368

APPENDIX II.—RECORDS OF RANK AND FILE.

WOOLFE, John Harry
B/11429, 1/6/17; A.S.C., C/S, 1/9/17; R.A.S.C., 27/10/17; F; 2/Lieut.
Coniston, Studland Road, Bournemouth, W.

WOOLLACOTT, Redvers
D/13748, 2/8/18; No. 11 O/C/B., 24/1/19; General List, 8/3/19; 2/Lieut.

WOOLLAND, John
D/2952, 18/2/15, L/C.; R.G.A., 20/8/15; Lieut.; w.
Mount Drake, Plymouth.

WOOLLARD, Frederic Stanley
6/2/5490, 9/8/15; R.A., C/S, 24/1/16; R. War. R., 15/4/16; F; Lieut.
Stony Stratford, Buckinghamshire.

✠ WOOLLATT, Claud Humpston
C/1115, 7/9/14; R.W. Surr. R., 13/11/14; Capt.
Killed in action 21/8/16.

WOOLLATT, Randal
C/10587, 22/1/17, Sgt.; R.A., C/S, 12/4/18; R.G.A., 24/2/19; 2/Lieut.
Roughwood, The Avenue, Claygate, Surrey.

WOOLLETT, Francis Hutton Egerton
6/3/5814, 25/8/15; 7th Lond. R., 14/12/15; att. R.A.F.; E,F; Lieut.
The Elms, Bredgar, Sittingbourne, Kent.

WOOLLEY, Alfred Russell
C/12304, 10/12/17; No. 6 O.C.B., 7/6/18; R. War. R., 4/2/19; 2/Lieut.
Blenheim Gate, School Road, Moseley, Birmingham.

WOOLLEY, Charles Leonard
A/1280, 23/9/14; R.F.A., 14/10/14; Capt.; p.
Royal Societies Club, St. James Street, S.W. 1.

WOOLLEY, Ernest John
A/37, 3/4/08; 22nd Lond. R., 31/10/10, 8th and 15th Lond. R.; F; Major; w; M.C., M(2).
Pinners Hall, Austin Friars, E.C. 2.

WOOLLEY, Harry
A/13105, 22/5/18; trfr. 14th Lond. R., 6/12/18.
41 Lower Redland Road, Redland, Bristol.

WOOLLISCROFT, Harold Claude
12357, 1/1/18; No. 20 O.C.B., 10/5/18; L'pool. R., 4/2/19; 2/Lieut. Shanklin, Grosvenor Avenue, Great Crosby, Liverpool.

WOOLLS, George Harman
D/3063, 16/3/15; dis. 28/4/15.

✠ WOOLMAN, John Gray
B/10338, 4/1/17, Cpl.; No. 14 O.C.B., 7/6/17; York. & Lanc. R., 25/9/17; F; 2/Lieut.; w.
Killed in action 2/11/18.

✠ WOOLMER, Stanley Herbert France
6/3/6338, 20/9/15; K.R. Rif. C., 1/6/16; 2/Lieut.
Killed in action 3/9/16.

WOOTTON, Charles Eric
A/12453, 21/1/18; No. 23 O.C.B., 7/6/18; Worc. R., 5/2/19; 2/Lieut.
432 Bearwood Road, Smethwick, Staffordshire.

WOOTTON, Harold Ernest
B/10340, 4/1/17, L/C.; No. 14 O.C.B., 7/6/17; Welch R., 25/9/17, att. S. Wales Bord. and S. Lan. R.; I; Lieut.
432 Bearwood Road, Smethwick, Staffordshire.

WOOTTON, Herbert Lloyd
6/4/5806, 23/8/15; R.E., 26/2/16; Lieut.
35 Clarendon Road, Putney, S.W.

WORDEN, Alan Fletcher
6/5/6378, 18/9/15; No. 3 O.C.B., 25/2/16; Lan. Fus., 19/7/16; F; Lieut.; w.
9 Farnborough Road, Birkdale, Southport, Lancashire.

WORDEN, Geoffrey Mawdsley
6/1/6470, 27/9/15, Cpl.; No. 14 O.C.B., 28/8/16; Dorset R., 21/11/16; F,M; Lieut.; w.
50 Ramsford Road, Chelmsford, Essex.

WORDHAM, Charles William
6/3/8737, 10/12/15; R.A., C/S., 23/3/16; R.G.A., 27/9/16; Lieut.
c/o Marryat & Coy., 28 Hatton Gardens, E.C. 1.

WORLEY, Kenneth James Macdonald
A/D/13184, 31/5/18, L/C.; trfr. 6th R. Regt. of Cav., 11/6/19, 4th Drag. Gds.
The Meads, Woodcote Valley Road, Purley, Surrey.

WORMALD, Charles Ralph
6/3/6167, 11/9/15; trfr. Lond. Elec. Eng., 16/6/16.
26 Emerson Road, Ilford.

✠ WORMALD, Guy
B/7, 1/4/08; dis. 31/3/12; rej. B/1063, 2/9/14; Lan. Fus., 12/9/14; Capt.
Killed in action 14/9/16.

WORMELL, Eric
D/10903, 19/3/17; R.F.C., C/S, 4/5/17; R.F.C., 14/6/17, R.A.F.; F; Lieut.
Lammermore, Eaton Road, Coventry.

WORNUM, Austin Porter
C/Sq/1631, 9/10/14; R.A.S.C., 28/11/14, R.A.F.; F; Capt.
58 Belsize Park, South Hampstead, N.W.

WORRALL, Charles Arthur
C/12663, 27/2/18; trfr. R.A.F., 21/5/18; R.A.F.; E; 2/Lieut.
46 Eastbourne Street, Oldham, Lancashire.

WORRALL, Gilbert
A/14348, 6/1/19; demob. 29/1/19.
Tower House, 6 St. Georges Square, Barrow-in-Furness.

WORSLEY, Herbert Henry Knight
6/5/5425, 5/8/15; L/C.; dis. 21/10/15; Nigeria R.; SWA; Lieut.
Ballywalton Park, Co. Down, Ireland.

WORSLEY, James Harrison
6/5/5277, 31/7/15; L'pool. R., 6/2/15; F; Lieut.; w(2); M.C., M(1).
Aughton, Nr. Ormskirk, Lancashire.

✠ WORSLEY, John Fortescue
C/509, 4/11/10; dis. 8/12/13; Gren. Gds.; Lieut.; w; M.C.
Killed in action 27/11/17.

WORSLEY, Ralph Edward
F/1900, 16/10/14; Dorset R., 12/12/14; P; Lieut.
c/o Messrs. Turner, Morrison & Coy., 6 Lyons Range, Calcutta, India.

WORSLEY, Richard Robert le Geyt
C/Sq/13167, 4/6/18; R.E., C/S, 10/11/18; demob.
20 Northcote Avenue, W. 5.

WORSWICK, Christopher Francis Worsley-
D/2633, 7/1/15; R. Dub. Fus., 22/4/15, Leic. R.; Lieut.

WORTHINGTON, Frederick Henry
4/3/4101, 7/6/15; L/C.; North'd. Fus., 21/4/16; F; Capt.; w.
Fife Lodge, Hale Road, Hale, Cheshire.

WORTHINGTON, John Ramsay
6/5/5968, 1/9/15, L/C.; L'pool. R., 21/4/16, emp. R. Lanc. R.; Lieut.; M.B.E.
Monaville, Chapman Road, Preston, Lancashire.

WORTHINGTON, Thomas Shirley Scott
A/13162, 29/5/18; demob. 30/1/19.
Grove House, Mobberley, Cheshire.

WORTLEY, Harold
6/3/7164, 2/11/15; Yorks. L.I., 4/8/16; F; Lieut.; g.
4 Riversdale Road, Egremont, Cheshire.

WOTTON, Walter Reginald
A/10074, 1/12/16; trfr. R.A.M.C., 10/4/17.

✠ WOULFE, Gerald Lascelles
B/1200, 14/9/14; North'n. R., 27/11/14; 2/Lieut.
Killed in action 14/7/16.

WRAIGHT, George Frederick Harold
6/5/8528, 29/12/15, Sgt.; No. 14 O.C.B., 28/8/16; 18th Lond. R., 18/12/16; F; Capt.; w; M.C.
Carson House, Regents Park Road, Church End, Finchley, N. 3.

✠ WRATHALL, Reginald John
6/2/8447, 16/12/15.
Died 30/10/18.

WRAY, Charles Bowers
6/5/5746, 21/8/15; N. Lan. R., 27/12/15; F; Capt.; w, p.
39 Bath Street, Southport, Lancashire.

WRAY, Charles Napoleon Osterfield
4/3/4553, 1/7/15, Sgt.; R.A.S.C., 27/11/15; F,NR; Lieut.
Station Road, Harpenden, Hertfordshire.

✠ WRAY, Cormac Patrick James
6/5676, 16/8/15; R. Innis. Fus., 25/8/15; F; 2/Lieut.
Killed in action 16/7/16.

WRAY, Herbert Hans
C/11502, 14/6/17; No. 19 O.C.B., 9/11/17; E. Lan. R., 30/4/18; F; 2/Lieut.
Carrick, Limavady, Co. Derry, Ireland.

WREFORD, Reynell John Raymond George
B/10689, 7/2/17; R.G.A., C/S, 16/5/17; R.G.A., 2/9/17; 2/Lieut.
18 Maberley Road, Upper Norwood, S.E. 19.

APPENDIX II.—RECORDS OF RANK AND FILE.

WREFORD-GLANVILLE, *Heyman Wreford*
H/2591, 4/1/15; R.A.S.C., 27/3/15; F; Capt.; French Silver Medal of Honour, M(1).
Grays Inn, W.C.2.

WREN, *George Lawrence*
A/13124, 24/5/18; trfr. 14th Lond. R., 6/12/18, att. Gord. Highrs.
73 Braxted Park, Streatham, S.W.16.

WRENN, *Frederick Herbert*
6/5/7125, 1/11/15; R.M.L.I., 15/1/16; Lieut.
Donard, Thames Ditton, Surrey.

WRIGHT, *Albert*
C/Sq/12236, 15/11/17, L/C.; No. 23 O.C.B., 9/8/18; North'n. R., 5/3/19; 2/Lieut.
Belle Vue, Broadway, Kettering.

WRIGHT, *Bernard Norman*
4/3/4171, 12/6/15; Essex R., 11/9/15, att. R.F.C.; F; Lieut.
Southdowns, Arlington Road, Eastbourne.

WRIGHT, *Bruce Haken*
B/12191, 5/11/17, R.E., C/S, 13/1/18; R.E., 26/4/18; 2/Lieut.
c/o Lond. City & Mid. Bank, Threadneedle Street, E.C.

✠ **WRIGHT**, *Charles James Stewart*
B/835, 4/8/14; Leic. R., 11/9/14; Capt.
Killed in action 14/7/16.

WRIGHT, *Charles Milbourne*
4/3751, 25/5/15; *dis.* to re-enlist, Leic. R., 30/9/15; R.W. Surr. R., 15/4/17; Lieut.; *w*; M.C.

WRIGHT, *Edgar Dunstan*
6/4/7489, 15/11/15; No. 11 O.C.B., 7/5/16; R.W. Fus., 4/10/16, att. R.A.F.; F; Lieut.; *Inj.*
21 Lynmouth Road, Fortis Green, N.2.

✠ **WRIGHT**, *Edmund Lancelot*
K/H/2097, 16/11/14, Cpl.; Shrop. L.I., 18/6/15; 2/Lieut.
Died of wounds 16/7/16.

WRIGHT, *Edward*
D/10442, 10/1/17, Sgt.; demob. 23/1/19.
17 Caddington Road, Cricklewood, N.W.2.

WRIGHT, *Edwin Ernest Stanley*
6/4/9226, 31/1/16, Sgt.; No. 22 O.C.B., 23/8/18; R. Suss. R., 13/2/19; 2/Lieut.
112 Gresham House, E.C.

WRIGHT, *Eric John*
6/4/9476, 14/2/16; No. 8 O.C.B., 4/8/16, M.G.C., C/S; M.G.C., 23/11/16, Tank Corps; Lieut.
1 Saltburn Place, Fosser Lane, Bradford.

WRIGHT, *Ernest*
A/10958, 30/3/17, L/C.; R.F.A., C/S, 24/8/17; trfr. R.F.A., 24/9/18.
6 The Headlands, Kettering.

WRIGHT, *Ernest Wigginton*
A/11946, 30/8/17; No. 14 O.C.B., 7/12/17; trfr. 28th Lond. R., 6/3/18.

WRIGHT, *Francis Alexander Pickford*
B/340, 13/1/09; *dis.* 13/1/13.

WRIGHT, *Fred Ashmead*
D/11853, 9/8/17; No. 5 O.C.B., 5/4/18; Notts. & Derby. R., 29/10/18; 2/Lieut.
Radburne, Derby.

WRIGHT, *George Edward*
E/1550, 6/10/14, Cpl.; R.A.S.C., 8/10/15.
St. Davids, Thurleigh Road, Balham, S.W.12.

WRIGHT, *George Eustace Dempster*
6/1/9319, 4/2/16; R.A., C/S, 7/8/16; R.G.A., 18/10/16.

WRIGHT, *George Thomas*
4/5139, 26/7/15; R.G.A., 1/12/15; E,P,F; Capt.
146 High Street, Colchester, Essex.

WRIGHT, *Henry Adrian*
C/Sq/12242, 22/11/17, Cpl.; No. 1 Cav. C/S, 16/5/18; General List, 7/3/19; 2/Lieut.
Royal Colonial Institute, Northumberland Avenue, W.C.2.

WRIGHT, *Henry Bridges*
A/B/12178, 29/10/17; H. Bde. O.C.B., 6/9/18; Gren. Gds., 10/3/19; 2/Lieut.
Butterley Hall, Ripley, Derbyshire.

✠ **WRIGHT**, *Herbert Melville*
6/2/6431, 23/9/15, L/C.; No. 14 O.C.B.; York. R., 24/10/16; 2/Lieut.
Killed in action 2/4/17.

WRIGHT, *Ian Syme*
B/11410, 26/5/17, L/C.; R.A., C/S, 4/1/18; R.F.A., 1/4/18; F; 2/Lieut.
4 Athole Gardens, Uddington.

WRIGHT, *Irwin Clayton*
B/12316, 20/12/17; No. 16 O.C.B., 7/6/18; W. York. R., 6/2/19; 2/Lieut.
28 Sunny Bank, Oakworth, Nr. Keighley, Yorkshire.

WRIGHT, *James Albert*
6/1/7573, 17/11/15, L/C.; No. 11 O.C.B., 7/5/16; E. Kent R., 19/12/16; 2/Lieut.; *w.*
9 Hilldrop Crescent, Hampstead, N.7.

WRIGHT, *John Ireland Edward Somerville*
D/11161, 24/4/17; No. 14 O.C.B., 7/9/17; 7th Lond. R., 17/12/17, att. R.F.C.; 2/Lieut.

WRIGHT, *Maxwell Campbell*
6/4/6321, 20/9/15, L/C.; No. 2 O.C.B., 25/2/16; Gord. Highrs., 6/7/16; F; Capt.; M.C. and Bar, M(1).
123 Hamilton Place, Aberdeen.

WRIGHT, *Miles Brown*
6/4/5/4874, 15/7/15; trfr. 13th Lond. R., 2/5/16, 29th Lond. R.; F; NR; L/C.
c/o W. P. Nesbitt Esq., Broken Scar, Darlington, Durham.

WRIGHT, *Norman Charles*
D/12882, 3/4/18; No. 16 O.C.B., 18/10/18; R. Berks. R., 17/3/19; 2/Lieut.
7 Addington Road, Reading.

WRIGHT, *Norman Farquhar*
4/3/4773, 12/7/15; trfr. 15th Lond. R., 19/5/16.
12 Woodland Gardens, Muswell Hill, N.10.

WRIGHT, *Oliver Reginald*
A/11242, 11/5/17; R.F.A., C/S, 28/12/17; R.F.A., 2/9/18; Germ. SWA; 2/Lieut.
71 Greyling Street, Pietermaritzburg, Natal, South Africa.

WRIGHT, *Percy Elwin*
4/4143, 10/6/15; R.G.A., 11/11/15; F; Capt.
31 Princethorpe Road, Sydenham, S.E.26.

✠ **WRIGHT**, *Peter*
B/1206, 14/9/14; R.F.A., 31/10/14; Major.
Killed in action 11/1/18.

WRIGHT, *Philip Lowndes*
K/B/2230, 3/12/14; Oxf. & Bucks. L.I., 4/2/15; F,It; Major; D.S.O., M.C., M(2).
80 Gloucester Place, Portman Square, W.1.

WRIGHT, *Ralph Fletcher*
C/1232, 23/9/14; W. Rid. R., 17/10/14, Army Cyc. Corps; Lieut.

WRIGHT, *Robert*
C/14274, 6/11/18; trfr. K.R. Rif. C., 25/4/19, M.G.C.
Brynartro, Llanbedr, Merioneth, North Wales.

WRIGHT, *Robert Henry Russell*
C/D/12078, 1/10/17, Cpl.; demob. 23/1/19.
61 Old Road, Lee, Kent.

✠ **WRIGHT**, *Samuel King*
E/1545, 6/10/14; W. Rid. R., 17/10/14; G; Lieut.
Killed in action 7-11/8/15.

WRIGHT, *Vernon Clifford*
6/4/6374, 20/9/15; R.A.S.C., 27/11/15, R.F.A.; SWA,F; Lieut.
17 Rothesay Avenue, Nottingham.

WRIGHT, *William Edgar*
6/3/8384, 13/12/15; R.F.C., C/S, 18/8/16; R.F.C., 8/9/16, R.A.F.; Lieut.
33 Cobden Road, Chesterfield.

WRIGHT, *William Roland Henry*
F/2538, 4/1/15; R.W. Surr. R., 21/4/15, att. R.F.C. and R.A.F.; F; Lieut.
Boundary House, Scarisbrick New Road, Southport.

WRIGLEY, *Herbert*
B/10918, 22/3/17; trfr. R.A.F., 9/4/18; Cpl.
Highfield, College Road, Oldham.

WRIGLEY, *Kenneth Atkinson*
D/14013, 12/9/18; No. 18 O.C.B., 10/2/19; Notts. & Derby. R., 18/3/19; 2/Lieut.
Durdant House, Kedleston Road, Derby.

✠ **WRONG**, *Colin Bassett*
C/1166, 14/9/14; *dis.* 12/12/14; R. Muns. Fus.; P; Capt.; M.C.
Killed in action 28/12/17.

WROTH, *Edward Charles*
K/A/2124, 14/11/14; R. War. R., 5/3/15; F,It; Lieut.; *w.*
51 Beauchamp Avenue, Leamington Spa.

WYATT, *Charles Dumella*
6/4/6497, 27/9/15, Sgt.; R.A., C/S, 7/7/16; R.G.A., 13/9/16; F,P,E; Capt.; *g.*
The Hutch, West Moors, Dorset.

WYATT, *George Alfred*
6/4/5577, 12/8/15; R.A., C/S, 24/1/16; *dis.* med. unfit, 26/9/16.
Tremayne, The Greenway, Uxbridge, Middlesex.

APPENDIX II.—RECORDS OF RANK AND FILE.

WYATT, Gwynne Olliver
6/2/6234, 13/9/15; No. 7 O.C.B., 7/4/16; 12th Lond. R., 21/7/16; F; Lieut.; w. 10 West Pallant, Chichester, Sussex.

WYATT, Louis
A/13944, 2/9/18; trfr. K.R. Rif. C., 7/4/19. Brunswick Place, Pocklington, Yorkshire.

WYBOURN, David William
C/11759, 26/7/17; No. 14 O.C.B., 7/12/17; R.W. Fus., 28/5/18, S. Wales Bord., Lab. Corps; F; Lieut. Black Prince Hotel, Ynysddu, Monmouthshire, South Wales.

WYCHERLEY, Sydney Mahon
4/3/4509, 28/6/15; R.F.A., 1/10/15; F; Lieut. Ormsby, St. Johns, Lewes, Sussex.

WYKEHAM-MARTIN, Charles Cornwallis
1876, 16/10/14; K.R. Rif. C., 5/12/14, Oxf. & Bucks. L.I.; F,S; Capt.; M(1). c/o Cox & Coy., 16 Charing Cross, S.W. 1.

WYLIE, Robert
6/Sq/5318, 2/8/15; R.F.A., 10/12/15; F; Lieut.; w; M.C. 124 College Road, Bromley, Kent.

WYLIE, Samuel
C/D/12092, 4/10/17; No. 11 O.C.B., 16/5/18; Res. of Off., 3/2/19; 2/Lieut.

WYLLIE, John Wilson
6/3/9334, 7/2/16; R.A., C/S, 17/11/16; R.G.A., 1/5/17; Lieut. Newfield, Ayr.

WYNNE, Arthur David
C/12273, 29/11/17; R.F.A., C/S, 15/3/18; R.G.A., 8/2/19; 2/Lieut. North Road House, Clapham Park, S.W. 4.

WYNNE, Richard Nicholas
C/13260, 10/6/18; trfr. 14th Lond. R., 6/12/18. 157 Aldborough Road, Seven Kings, Essex.

WYNNE, Sydney Michael
B/12002, 10/9/17; H. Bde. O.C.B., 4/1/18; Ir. Gds., 25/6/18; 2/Lieut. Clogeravagh, Sligo, Ireland.

WYNN-EVANS, James Leslie
6/4/6264, 16/9/15; 11th Lond. R., 18/1/16; Lieut. Thornycroft, Queens Park, Chester.

WYNYARD, Henry Buckley William
Sq/214, 8/5/08; dis. 31/12/09.

YARNOLD, Arthur Douglas
A/13139, 27/5/18; trfr. 14th Lond. R., 13/11/18; L/C. Oaklands, Pensax, Abberley, Nr. Worcester.

✠ YARROW, Henry Edwin Goodwin
B/2977, 25/2/15; K.O. Sco. Bord., 18/6/15; 2/Lieut. Killed in action 30/7/16.

YARROW, Kenneth Guthrie
K/C/2164, 23/11/14; R. Highrs., 5/3/15, R.A.S.C.; Lieut. 18 Abbey Road, N.W.

YARWOOD, Ernest Sydney
D/11165, 2/5/17; No. 16 O.C.B., 5/10/17; Linc. R., 12/3/18; 2/Lieut. Dodleston, Chester.

YARWORTH, Thomas Harry
6/2/8557, 30/12/15, L/C.; No. 14 O.C.B., 29/9/16; Suff. R., 18/12/16, att. Essex R., Camb. R. and R. Berks. R.; F; Lieut. New House Farm, St. Briavels, Gloucestershire.

YATES, Arthur Lowndes
C/429, 15/6/09; R.A.M.C., 3/4/12; Capt.; M.C., M(1).

✠ YATES, Charles Cecil
K/B/2165, 23/11/14; N. Lan. R., 9/1/15; Lieut. Killed in action 15/5/16.

YATES, Herbert Leslie
B/12819, 20/3/18; No. 2 O.C.B., 20/9/18; Norf. R., 16/3/19; 2/Lieut. Leverington House, Wisbech, Cambridgeshire.

YATES, Robert
4/4691, 8/7/15; R.E., 21/7/15; F; Major; D.S.O., M.C., M(3). Hill Crest, Blurton Road, Fenton, North Staffordshire.

YATES, Robert Ernest
E/14122, 9/10/18; R.A., C/S, 1/11/18; R.G.A., 13/4/19; 2/Lieut. Grammar School, Amersham, Buckinghamshire.

YEADON, William Cecil
6/5545, 8/8/15; R.A.S.C., 8/1/16; F; Lieut. Prospect House, Yeadon, Yorkshire.

YEATES, Victor Maslin
C/10792, 24/2/17; R.F.C., C/S, 4/5/17; R.F.C., 14/6/17, R.A.F.; F; Lieut. 48 Boyne Road, Lewisham, S.E. 13.

YEATMAN, Francis Dyson
B/856, 4/8/14; Midd'x. R., 15/8/14; F; Lieut.; w. 2 Paper Buildings, Temple, E.C. 4.

✠ YEATMAN, Harry Farr
Sq/205, 6/5/08; Dorset Yeo., 9/10/14; Capt. Killed in action 21/11/17.

YEO, Henry Reginald
C/13390, 24/6/18; No. 22 O.C.B., 23/8/18; Suff. R., 5/3/19; 2/Lieut. Rougham Rectory, Bury St. Edmunds.

YEO, Percival Douglas
B/9907, 13/11/16; M.G.C., C/S, 1/3/17; M.G.C., 26/6/17, Tank Corps; F; 2/Lieut.; w. 6 Cranmore Way, Muswell Hill, N.10.

✠ YEOMANS, Cecil George
6/2/6642, 4/10/15; dis. med. unfit, 8/8/16. Died.

YERBURY, Francis Harold Bevan
A/11620, 5/7/17; R.E., C/S, 13/1/18; R.E., 31/5/18; 2/Lieut. 24 Lancashire Road, St. Andrews Park, Bristol.

YORK, Richard Ernest
A/11236, 8/5/17; R.F.C., C/S, 1/6/17; R.F.C., 4/7/17, R.A.F.; 2/Lieut. 55 George Street, Lozells Aston, Birmingham.

YOULL, Geoffrey Blenkinsopp
6/1/8672, 4/1/16; No. 14 O.C.B., 30/10/16; North'd. Fus., 28/2/17; F; 2/Lieut.; w. 18 Grainger Street West, Newcastle-on-Tyne.

YOULL, William Chartres
6/1/8230, 7/12/15; No. 14 O.C.B., 29/9/16; North'd. Fus., 24/1/17; Lieut. 18 Grainger Street West, Newcastle-on-Tyne.

YOUNG, Arthur
4/1/3909, 31/5/15; R.F.A., 5/10/15; F; Lieut. 76 Derwent Road, Palmers Green, N. 13.

✠ YOUNG, Arthur Conway
4/3807, 27/5/15; R. Ir. Fus., 7/10/15; F; 2/Lieut.; w. Killed in action 16/8/17.

YOUNG, Charles Edwin
D/11135, 26/4/17; trfr. K.R. Rif. C., 27/5/19. The Ford, Dunmow, Essex.

YOUNG, Charles Greenwood
A/10254, 29/12/16; No. 14 O.C.B., 5/3/17; Rif. Brig., 26/6/17; F; Lieut. 59 Wilbury Avenue, Hove, Sussex.

YOUNG, Charles Owen
4/2/4434, 24/6/15, L/C.; R.A.S.C., 4/12/15; Lieut.

YOUNG, Charles Walter
2/3614, 13/5/15; K.R. Rif. C., 10/8/15; Lieut.; w(2).

YOUNG, Clement Leslie
6/5/6684, 7/10/15; R. Suss. R., 14/7/16; 2/Lieut. 4 Grove House, Stamford Grove, N. 16.

✠ YOUNG, Colin Gurner
B/336, 7/12/08; W. Rid. R., 14/8/14, att. Welch R.; Capt.; w. Killed in action 24/4/17.

YOUNG, Cyril
6/1/5720, 19/8/15; No. 4 O.C.B., 7/3/16; dis. med. unfit, 3/8/16. Blore Rectory, Ashbourne.

YOUNG, Dallas Hales Wilkie
116, 18/4/08; dis. 17/1/10.

YOUNG, David
A/10290, 1/1/17; No. 14 O.C.B., 6/4/17; N. Lan. R., 31/7/17; 2/Lieut. Erskine Manse, Burntisland, Scotland.

YOUNG, Douglas Alec Radford
D/11087, 23/4/17; Garr. O.C.B., 5/10/17; Lab. Corps, 15/12/17; F; 2/Lieut. Kimcote Rectory, Lutterworth.

YOUNG, Francis Theophilus
2/3249, 12/4/15; E Kent R., 15/9/15; F; Lieut. c/o Mrs. R. Young, The Ladies Club, Marine Mansions, Bexhill-on-Sea.

YOUNG, George
6/5/5278, 31/7/15, Sgt.; dis. to re-enlist, 29/11/15, att. 34th Lond. R.; F; R S M.; M(1). 21 Broxton Road, Wallasey, Cheshire.

371

APPENDIX II.—RECORDS OF RANK AND FILE.

YOUNG, George Davis
A/10709, 10/2/17; No. 14 O.C.B., 5/7/17; North'd. Fus., 30/10/17; F; 2/Lieut.; w.
3 Rosebery Avenue, Blyth, Northumberland.

YOUNG, George Staven
6/1/5890, 30/8/15; Arg. & Suth'd. Highrs., 18/12/15, secd. K. Af. Rif.; F,EA; Lieut.
31 Throgmorton Street, E.C. 2.

YOUNG, George Young
6/D/8385, 13/12/15; trfr. R.G.A., 5/2/17.
52 Osmond Road, Hove.

✠ YOUNG, Harold Victor
6/D/4990, 19/7/15, Sgt.; No. 6 O.C.B., 15/2/17; R.F.C., 25/4/17; F; 2/Lieut.; w.
Died of wounds 8/12/17.

YOUNG, Harvey Brassington
B/13430, 1/7/18; demob. 25/1/19.
47 Brodrick Road, Wandsworth Common, S.W. 17.

YOUNG, Horace Norman
A/10999, 31/3/17; R.F.C., C/S, 4/5/17; R.F.C., 14/6/17, R.A.F.; Lieut.; D.F.C.
Fairview, Precs, Salop.

YOUNG, James
A/11906, 23/8/17; R.E., C/S, 30/9/17; R.E., 9/11/17; 2/Lieut.
3 Abbotsford Park, Edinburgh.

YOUNG, James Allan Baillie
D/10667, 5/2/17; R.F.C., C/S, 2/8/17; R.F.C., 3/9/17, R.A.F.; 2/Lieut.
8 Woodlands Crescent, Muswell Hill, N. 10.

YOUNG, James Homer Hamilton
C/11462, 4/6/17, L/C.; R.F.C., C/S, 4/1/18; R.F.A., 1/7/18; F; 2/Lieut.
14 St. Leonards Terrace, Chelsea, S.W. 3.

✠ YOUNG, John Arthur
A/2887, 8/2/15; York. & Lanc. R., 8/4/15, Notts. & Derby. R.; Capt.
Killed in action 4/10/17.

YOUNG, Leonard Henry Hockley
D/10647, 2/2/17, L/C.; No. 1 Cav. C/S, 5/7/17; R. Regt. of Cav., 22/2/18; 2/Lieut.
14 Frognal Avenue, Harrow, Middlesex.

YOUNG, Sidney Michael
B/13586, 22/7/18, L/C.; trfr. K.R. Rif. C., 25/4/19, M.G.C.; L/C.
51 Gayton Road, Harrow.

YOUNG, Thomas James
6/4/6412, 23/9/15; 11th Lond. R., 30/12/15; 2/Lieut.

YOUNG, Walter
2/3748, 24/5/15, L/C.; R.E., 20/9/15; F; Lieut.; M.C.
Croydon Lodge, Pakefield, Lowestoft, Suffolk.

YOUNG, William
B/12747, 11/3/18, L/C.; H. Bde. O.C.B., 9/8/18; N. Lan. R., 3/3/19; 2/Lieut.
50 Cornhill Terrace, Leith, Scotland.

YOUNG, William Lawrence
C/13749, 3/8/18; trfr. Class W. Res., 27/9/18.
Craigton, St. Andrews Drive, Pollokshields, Glasgow.

ZACHARIAS-JESSEL, Victor Albert Villiers. See JESSEL, V. A. V.

ZEEDERBERG, Frederick Coventry
Sq/5019, 22/7/15; Dorset Yeo., 4/11/15, att. Dorset R.; F; Lieut.; g.
Hill Park, Mowbray, Nr. Cape Town, South Africa.

ZEITLYN, Elsley
B/366, 18/3/09; trfr. 10th Lond. R., 26/7/09.

ZINK, Frederick Charles
6/1/7165, 2/11/15; dis. to re-enlist, 24/4/16.
1 Randolph Gardens, Maida Vale, W. 9.

ZOHRAB, Reginald Herbert Travers
3/3477, 3/5/15, L/C.; W. Rid. R., 21/4/16, secd. M.G.C.; Lieut.

ZUCCO, George Desylla
6/1/5647, 16/8/15, L/C.; W. York. R., 16/1/16; F; Lieut.; w
44 Springfield Road, N.W. 8.

Corps Staff.

Clerical. Orderly Room and Quartermaster Stores.

O.R.C.S	BROCK, L. R.	Sgt.	MONTEATH, C. O.	Cpl.	CURL, J. W.
Sgt.	ARDEN, F. C.	L/Sgt.	BOUNDEN, A. G.	L/Cpl.	BURNS, F. C.
Sgt.	FRENCH, L.	L/Sgt.	HALE, J. B.	L/Cpl.	DOWDEN, P. R.
Sgt.	HOLBOURN, S. V.	L/Sgt.	SEABROOK, C. W.	L/Cpl.	LANE, H. J.
Sgt.	KIMBER, F. W.	Cpl.	ELAM, H.	Pte.	BROCK, F. C.
Sgt.	MILLER, F. J.	Cpl.	KENDALL, A. W.		

Instructors.

Sgt.	KIMPTON, J. E.
Sgt.	McKELROY, J.
Sgt.	PETHERICK, J. T.

Shoeing-smiths.

Cpl.	ELSWORTH, E. J.
Pte.	KEMPSTER, E. J.
Pte.	PAGE, F. D.

Armourer.

✠ Armr. Sgt. BURNS, T.

Saddler.

Pte. COX, W. C.

Grooms.

Trpt. Sgt.	BLIGHT, W. R.
Pte.	ALLEN, A. J.
Pte.	EVERITT, R.
Pte.	JONES, P.
✠ Pte.	KERR, J.
Pte.	LYNHAM, T.
Pte.	NORWOOD, W.

Batmen.

Pte.	BRACKENBURY, C.
Pte.	DAVIS, F.
Pte.	GASK, G.
Pte.	GRAHAM, J.
Pte.	NORTH, G. A.
Pte.	REID, A.
Pte.	STAMMERS, G. H.
Pte.	WORTH, S.

Band.

Band Sgt.	AVERY, W.	Pte.	FITTON, J.	Pte.	LAYZELL, F. R.
Band Sgt.	LEGGETT, A. W.	Pte.	FREER, W. E.	Pte.	MARSHALL, C. W.
Cpl.	WOOD, W.	Pte.	GOLBOURN, A. W.	Pte.	MAYNARD, H. W.
L/Cpl.	BATEMAN, P. H.	Pte.	GOODALL, W. J.	Pte.	OSBORNE, P. H.
L/Cpl.	STAFFORD, W. T.	Pte.	GOURVITCH, L.	Pte.	PARKINSON, H. J.
L/Cpl.	WRATTING, W.	Pte.	HARDY, A. H.	Pte.	SPAYNE, H. A.
Pte.	BAYLIS, J. A. G.	Pte.	HEWITT, H. F.	Pte.	WHITING, W. G.
Pte.	CARNEY, S. T.	Pte.	HIBBINS, R. W.	Pte.	WHITTRED, H. G.
Pte.	CARTER, W. J.	Pte.	HINKINS, H.	Pte.	WILKINGS, C.
Pte.	CHILD, W. G. A.	Pte.	HOLMES, H. R.	Pte.	WILLIAMS, H.
Pte.	COLLINS, C. J.	Pte.	HOLMES, A. E.	Pte.	WILLIAMS, T. B.
Pte.	COPUS, J. C.	Pte.	HOLT, R. S.	Pte.	YOUNG, F. W.

Trumpeters.

L/Cpl.	KAY, P.
Pte.	GREGORY, W.
Pte.	HINCHCLIFFE, G.
Pte.	HOPKINS, J. A. W.

Buglers.

Sgt.	ARDEN, W.
L/Cpl.	SALLIS, W. J.
Pte.	MURRAY, T.
Pte.	ROMER, N. A. V.
Pte.	SMITH, W. G. E.

Tailors.

Sgt.	WHITLEY, E. G.
Pte.	BROOME, J. W.

Barbers.

Pte.	FLOWERS, R.
Pte.	WYATT, A. E

Mess Waiters.

L/Sgt.	BOOTH, F.	Pte.	HARRIS, H. G.	Pte.	NEWELL, H. G.
L/Cpl.	BASHFORD, J. H.	Pte.	HOLLAND, C.	Pte.	PERRY, W.
Pte.	ALLEN, A.	Pte.	HOLLINSHEAD, E.	Pte.	SEABROOK, J.
Pte.	BASHFORD, G. F.	Pte.	JOHNSON, W. C.	Pte.	SEARLE, E. E.
Pte.	COOPER, A. E.	Pte.	JURGENS, F.	Pte.	SLADE, A. M. S.
Pte.	COOPER, E. S.	Pte.	KERRIDGE, C.	Pte.	STONEHOUSE, W. J.
Pte.	COOPER, H. A.	Pte.	LAKE, W. E.	Pte.	VINCENT, F. T.
Pte.	DELDERFIELD, J.	Pte.	LYNN, T.	Pte.	WADE, C.
Pte.	GREEN, C. F.	Pte.	MAYER, A.	Pte.	WALTON, R.
Pte.	GROVES, C.	Pte.	MAYER, F. F.	Pte.	WRIGHT, W.
		Pte.	MAYER, J. B.		

Cooks.

Sgt. Cook	BASHFORD, J. E.		Pte.	WALLER, C. R.
Sgt. Cook	BICKERSTAFF, E.		Pte.	WILLMORE, H.
Sgt. Cook	PYMM, F.		Pte.	BENNETT, S.
Pte.	STRETTON, A. J		Pte.	COULSON, C. E.

Attached Staff.

Instructors.

R.S.M.	BURNS, A.	L/Sgt.	CRONE, M.	Sgt.	PLUMLEY, P. J.
R.S.M.	CANDY	Sgt.	DUNN, H. T.	Sgt.	SANDIFORD, W.
R.S.M.	JOHNSTONE, W.	Sgt.	EVANS, J. M.	Sgt.	SCOGGINS, A. R.
R.S.M.	VASSILA, S. C.	L/Sgt.	FRASER, R.	Sgt.	SLADE, J. W.
C.S.M.	BECKETT, W.	Sgt.	FULLER, R. T.	L/Sgt.	STEWART, H. E.
C.S.M.	BEDDOES, J.	Sgt.	GILMORE, C.	L/Sgt.	STITCHER, P.
C.S.M.	BRISTOW, R.	Sgt.	GLADMAN, P. G. A. G.	Sgt.	VINCENT, F. I.
C.S.M.	CURTIS, W. H.	Sgt.	GODSELL, F. W.	R.R.Sgt.	WASH, C.
S.S.M.R.R.	DARBY, J.	Sgt.	HAMPTON, T. S.	L/Sgt.	WATKINS, C. H.
C.S.M.	FORDHAM, H.	Sgt.	HARBOD, B. W., M.M.	Sgt.	WILLIAMS, C.
C.S.M.I.	FRANKLIN, H., M.C.	Sgt.	HODKINSON, W. D.	Sgt.	WILLIAMS, W. W.
C.S.M.	HARRIS, W. J.	Sgt.	JENKINS, B.	Sgt.	WOOD, A. S.
C.S.M.	LEE, R. E.	✠ Sgt.	KAY, A.	Sgt.	YATES, A. J.
C.S.M.	MONAGHAN, J.	Sgt.	KEMP, H. C.	Sgt.	YOUNG, W. H.
S.Q.M.S.	O'CONNELL, A.	Sgt.	KIRKPATRICK, H. D.	Cpl.	BROWN, G. E.
S.Q.M.S.	WHITTINGHAM, A. H.	Sgt.	LEWIS, J. E.	Cpl.	CONNON, G.
S.F.S.	REDDING	Sgt.	McADAMS, J.	Cpl.	HAMMOND, J.
S.F.S.	THORNTON, J.	Sgt.	MEIKLE, A. F. T.	Cpl.	MATHER
Sgt.	ALDRIDGE, T.	Sgt.	MORTLOCK, H. R.	Cpl.	MUSLIN, R.
Sgt.	BENDALL, W. J.	R.R.Sgt.	MOSELEY, T. S.	Cpl.	SHIELDS, J. A.
L/Sgt.	BUCKLAND, L. F.	Sgt.	MURRAY	Cpl.	STANLEY, F.
Sgt.	COKER, A. H.	Sgt.	MURRAY, T. J.	Cpl.	SULLIVAN, W.
Sgt.	COUBROUGH, D.	Sgt.	OVENDEN, B.	L/Cpl.	COLLINGS, E.
Sgt.	CRESSEY, R.	L/Sgt.	PARKER, A. W.	L/Cpl.	McKENZIE, H.

Provost Staff.

Sgt.	CHRISTIE, C. A.
Cpl.	COLEY, A.

Shoeing-smiths.

Pte.	COPEMAN, C.
Pte.	HILLMAN
Pte.	FOSTER, J.
✠ Pte.	ANDERSON, C.
Pte.	RIGLEY

Pioneers.

Pnr. Sgt.	COOK, J. A.
L/Cpl.	DEMPSEY, J. J.
L/Cpl.	JORDAN, C. D.
Pte.	BERRY, A. J.
Pte.	BRADLEY, W. H.
Pte.	BRIDGER, A.
Pte.	DRING, H.
Pte	DUFF, J.
Pte.	DYMOCK, H. F.
Pte.	GOLDSPINK, E.
Pte.	GOODENOUGH, W.
Pte.	HALL, S.

H.Q. Orderlies.

Pte.	HODGSON, G. R.
Pte.	TATTERSALL, J. R.
Pte.	WOODWARD, F.

Cooks.

Pte.	ALBON, J. A.
Pte.	CAREY, F. E.
Pte.	MAUGHAN, J.
Pte.	MAY, W.
Pte.	RULE, H. S.
Pte.	WALTHER, W. H.
Pte.	WHATMAN, A. W.
Pte.	WILTON, T. H.

Mess Waiters.

Pte.	GILL, T.
Pte.	LETTON, R. C.
Pte.	MOYES, M. E.
Pte.	STAVELEY
Pte.	WEST, C. M.
Pte.	WITHERS, G.

Pte.	HIDE, F.
Pte.	LEE, D. F.
Pte.	LOVELL, I. T.
Pte.	NEWDICK, H.
Pte.	PAGE, R. A. C.
Pte.	PHILLIPS, W. H.

Medical Orderly.

Cpl.	WHITE, J.

Grooms.

Pte.	BALFOUR, G.
Pte.	CLARK, G.
Pte.	COURT, T.
Pte.	DOBBS, S.
Pte.	GRAHAM, J.
Pte.	HARPER, A.
Pte.	PHILLIPS, F. C.
Pte.	SMITH, M.
Pte.	HOLMWOOD, W. T.
Pte.	KEMPSTER, J. M.
Pte.	LOVELL, C.
Pte.	PEACEY, B.
Pte.	PRIOR, G.
Pte.	SELL, J.
Pte.	SHEEHAN, J.
Pte.	TAYLOR, J.
Pte.	TUPPEN, H. J.
Pte.	WELLS, S.
Pte.	WHITE, H. T.
Pte.	WINTER, T.

Batmen.

Pte.	BAKER, J. E.
Pte.	ELLIS, G. S.
Pte.	HICKS, S. J.
Pte.	MITCHELL, H. R.
Pte.	POWELL, W.
Pte.	PRIOR, W. J.
Pte.	ROBILLIARD, G.
Pte.	STANMORE, S.
Pte.	THORNE, A. E.
Pte.	WALKER, H. A.
Pte.	WALKER, J. H.
Pte.	WHITE, W. J.
Pte.	YARROW, A. J.

Clerk.

Pte.	CONNOR, C. McN.

Storeman.

Pte.	SUMMARSCALES, G.

Saddler.

Pte.	GREEN, F. A.

Pte.	ROSS, A.
Pte.	SMITH, C. W.
Pte.	VICKERY, A. J.
Pte.	WEBB, W. F.
Pte.	WHITE, C.
Pte.	WILSON, E. W.

Appendix III.

Hospitals.

Lady Brownlow's Hospital at Ashridge used by the Corps from October 1914 to March 1915.
- Commandant .... Miss Minna Blount
- Quartermaster .... Mrs. Dorrien Smith.

V.A.D. Hospitals.

Barncroft and The Beeches (March 1915 to July 1919).
- Commandant (March 1915 to March 1917) ...... Miss Blount.
- Matron (do.) ...... Mrs. Porter.
- Commandant (March 1917 to October 1918) ...... Mrs. Porter.
- Matron (do.) ...... Mrs. Haygarth Brown.

Nurses.

Mrs. ALLEN	Mrs. FERGUSON	Miss H. PARSONS
Miss ASHTON	Mrs. FENNING	Miss PERRY
Mrs. AYLWIN	Miss FRERE	Miss RAM
Miss H. BALD	Mrs. FULLER	Mrs. RAWES
Miss M. BALD	Miss FERGUSON	Mrs. ROBINSON
Miss E. BLOUNT	Mrs. GOMPERTZ	Miss ROBINSON
Mrs. P. BLOUNT	Miss HARKER	Mrs. ROSS
Mrs. R. BLOUNT	Miss HARRAGON	Miss SIMPSON
Miss BONWENS	Miss HORSEMAN	Mrs. SLADE
Mrs. HAYGARTH BROWN	Mrs. JANION	Mrs. BRUCE SMITH
Miss BYHAM	Mrs. JOHNSON	Mrs. LEBLANC SMITH
Miss CAMBRIDGE	Miss LEGH	Miss M. SPRUNT
Miss CHANDLEY	Mrs. LEWIS	Miss STUBPNAGEL
Mrs. CHUBB	Miss F. LING	Mrs. TAIT
Miss CHUBB	Miss MACGREGOR	Mrs. THOMPSON
Mrs. COATES	Mrs. MERRIMAN	Miss A. WHEATLEY
Mrs. COBBLEY	Mrs. MILLS	Miss A. WHITFIELD
Miss CRAWFORD	Miss MONKHOUSE	Miss J. WILLIAMS
Miss DALLAS	Miss G. NORTH	Miss Y. WILLIAMS
Miss FAWCETT	Miss PAINE	Miss V. WILLIAMS
Miss F. FAWCETT	Miss PARKINTON	

Members of Selection Boards.

Headquarters Selection Board.

Sir Duncan Baillie, K.C.S.I.
Sir W. O. Clark
Sir A. L. Goodson
A. E. Holt Esq.
G. Ogilvy Jackson Esq.
A. C. Kent Esq.
H. Marsh Esq.
Major D. M. Robertson-Macdonald
Sir John Miller, K.C.S.I.
R. Montague Scott Esq.

B. Whitehead Esq.
Capt. W. A. G. Woods
C. F. Martelli Esq.
Col. E. F. Gastrell
Capt. Sir W. A. Eastwood
Maj. Gen. F. W. P. Angelo
Maj. Gen. H. M. Duperier, R.E.
Capt. G. Pemberton-Leach
Major C. W. Mead, T.D.

Major J. A. Hay, T.D., O.C. Depot ⎫
Capt. A. G. Mathews   ⎟ Serving
Capt. W. R. Field   ⎬ in the
Capt. Hugh K. Ryan   ⎟ Corps.
Lieut. S. Brett   ⎟
Lieut. C. Terrall   ⎭
H. C. Hawkins Esq.
D. C. Cree Esq.
G. Godfrey Esq.
S. W. W. Jones Esq.
H. C. Fanshaw Esq.

Irish Selection Board.

The Rt. Hon. Mr. Justice Ross, P.C.
Sir Edward O'Farrell, C.B.
Dr. Dennis J. Coffey, M.A., M.B.
Rt. Hon. Wm. F. Bailey, C.B.

Surgeon John McArdle
Maurice Headlam Esq.
Col. J. McDonnell, C.B.
J. D. A. Johnson Esq., Ll.D.
James Sealy Esq.

Brig. Gen. F. Waldron
W. Dick Esq.
Charles St. G. Orpen Esq.
R. W. Brown Esq. Hon Secretary.

Scottish Selection Board.

His Grace the Duke of Montrose
The Rt. Hon. Lord Kinnaird, K.T.
The Rt. Hon. Lord Scott Dickson
The Hon. Lord Salvesen
Sir Wm. Bilsland, Bart.
Sir John M. Clark, Bart.
Maj. Gen. Sir Hamilton Bower, C.B.
Sir Edward Parrott
Maj. Gen. J. A. H. Pollock, C.B.
The Rt. Revd. Bishop Campbell, D.D.
The Revd. Prof. A. R. McEwen, D.D.

The Very Revd. J. C. Russell, D.D.
Professor Medley
Col. Lyell
Col. R. L. McEwen, D.L.
Col. John A. Roxburgh
Col. Seton
Maj. R. E. Findlay
Dr. J. Carswell
Provost Malcolm Smith
Provost Gilchrist
A. L. Brown Esq., J.P.

H. S. Murray Esq., J.P.
Chas. J. Cleland Esq., M.V.O., D.L.
A. G. Cogman Esq.
Cyril N. Dunderdale Esq.
Robert Macintosh Esq.
Chas. W. Somerville Esq.
Wm. Leonard Tod Esq.
J. McHutchen Dobbie Esq.
J. W. Arthur Esq.
L. MacQueen Douglas Esq.
Hon. Secretary.

Welch Selection Board.

Maj. Gen. H. H. Lee (Chairman)
The Rt. Hon. the Earl of Plymouth
Col. A. Hepburn
Capt. J. Reynolds McLean
Maj. Gen. Sir Ivor J. C. Herbert, Bart., M.P.
Lynn Thomas Esq., C.B.
Col. E. M. Bruce Vaughan, J.P.
The Lord Mayor of Cardiff
Alderman C. H. Bird
J. A. Jones Esq.

Sir J. W. Curtis, J.P.
L. Llenfer Thomas Esq., M.A.
Col. Henry Lewis, D.L., J.P.
His Honour Judge Kelly
Col. C. S. Denniss, J.P.
The Rt. Hon. Lord Aberdare
H. M. Thompson Esq., M.A.
T. D. Watson Esq.
J. Herbert Cory Esq., M.P.
The Lord Bishop of Llandaff

Principal E. H. Griffiths, F.R.S.
The Rt. Hon. Lord Pontypridd
Col. J. Gaskell
Sir James Hills-Johnes, V.C., G.C.B.
Godfrey L. Clark Esq.
Oliver H. Jones Esq.
Dan Radcliffe Esq.
W. North Lewis Esq.
Trefor S. Jones Esq.
R. Silyn Roberts Esq. Hon. Secretary.

Exeter Selection Board.

T. Baker Esq., J.P. Mayor of Plymouth
Col. B. W. Blake
Revd. Predy. Buckingham, J.P.
Lt. Col. Cardew
Vice Admiral C. H. Coke
W. A. Cunningham Esq.

Lt. Col. H. Davy, R.A.M.C.
General Fagan
W. B. Heberden Esq.
Sir Robert Newman, Bart.
James G. Owen Esq., J.P. Mayor of Exeter.
C. T. K. Roberts Esq.

The Rt. Hon. Sir E. Satow
Sebastian Snow Esq.
Col. Walcott
Vice Admiral R. W. White
The Revd. Edward Reid. Hon. Secretary.